D1375075

AA

The Restaurant Guide 2001

AA Lifestyle Guides

Produced by AA Publishing
Maps prepared by the Cartographic Department of
The Automobile Association
Maps © The Automobile Association 2000
Cover illustration by Sue Climpson, Whitchurch,
England
Design by Nautilus Design UK Ltd, Basingstoke,
Hampshire

Cover photo by The Stockmarket Photo Agency Inc.

Advertisement Sales Telephone 01256 491545

Typeset/Repro Anton Graphics, Andover, Hampshire

Printed and bound in Italy by Rotolito, Lombarda

Restaurant assessments and rosette awards are
based on reports of visits carried out anonymously
by the AA's Hotel and Restaurant Inspectors.
Although our Inspectors are a highly trained and
very experienced team of professional men and
women, it must be stressed that the opinions
expressed are only opinions, based on the
experience of one or more particular occasions,
and assessments are therefore to some extent
necessarily subjective and may not reflect or
dictate a reader's own opinion on another
occasion. See page 6 for a clear explanation of
how, based on our Inspectors' inspection
experiences, establishments are graded. If the meal
or meals experienced by an Inspector or Inspectors
during an inspection or inspections fall between
award levels the restaurant concerned may be
awarded the lower of any award levels considered
applicable.

Restaurant descriptions have been contributed
by the following team of writers:
Jon Boden, Andrew Campbell, David Hancock,
Robert Hayward, Clarissa Hyman, Julia Hynard,
Denise Laing, Mark Manson, Hugh Morgan, Allen
Stidwell
Features by Simon Wright and Jo Sturges

A CIP catalogue record for this book is available
from the British Library

Published by AA Publishing, which is a trading
name of Automobile Association Developments
Limited whose registered office is Norfolk House,
Priestley Road, Basingstoke, Hampshire RG24 9NY
Registered number 1878835.

ISBN 0 7495 25339

AA Photo Library
With contributions from Robert Mort p17

Photographs in the gazetteer provided by
establishments.
Special thanks to:
Rookery Hall, Nantwich (p4, p17)
Percy's Country Hotel, Virginstow (p20)
Beeches Farmhouse, Doveridge (p3)
Longueville Manor, St Saviour (p21)
Nuthurst Grange, Hockley Heath (p21)
Mallory Court, Leamington Spa (p20)
Cringeltie House, Peebles (p5)

Contents

How to Use *this Guide*

Rookery Hall, Nantwich

4. ❀ the AA Rosette Award for cooking quality. Every restaurant included has been awarded one or more rosettes, up to a maximum of five. See page 6 for a clear explanation of how they are graded.

5. Directions are given wherever they have been supplied by the proprietor.

1. The Guide's entries are divided into sections. London restaurants are listed alphabetically by name. There is also a London postcode index on page 764. In the rest of Britain, establishments are listed in country and county order, by town, and then alphabetically within that town. There is also an index by establishment name.

2. 쳃 indicates an entry new to the Guide this year

3. ⬳ indicates an establishment which responded '50% or more' when asked what percentage of their ingredients are organically sourced.

6. The establishment's address and postcode

7. The map number. In the London section, each restaurant has a map reference number to help locate its approximate position on the Central or Greater London maps on pages XX. In the remainder of the Guide, the map references refer to the 16 page atlas starting on page XX First is the map page number, followed by the National Grid Reference. To find the location, read the first figure across and the second figure vertically within the lettered square.

8. E-mail addresses may be subject to change during the currency of the guide.

Sample entry

❶— *ANY TOWN,*

Any Restaurant ❀ ❀   **❷**   쳃

Converted 16th-century farmhouse with a pleasant, relaxed style and friendly youn g staff. Local produce is an important part of menus here, and a spring meal began with oak-smoked salmon (they have their own smoke house), followed by Welsh Black beef. Desserts are straightfoward, allowing flavours to shine through, the inspector was enthusiastic about an assiette of chocolate which included a 'meltingly delicious' fondant. The wine list has a good selection of wines by the glass, and the New World is a particular strength.

❶❻— **Accommodation:** 24 en suite ★ ★
❺— **Directions:** 1.5 miles from Any town

High Street SX0 2QQ ————**❻**
Map 4: SU97————**❼** ⬳—**❸**
Tel: 02228 5557833
Fax: 02228 5557834
E-mail: test@btnet.co.uk———**❽**
Chef: The Chef ————**❾**
Owners: The Owners
Cost: *Alc* £42.50, set-price ——**❿**
L £21.50. H/wine £14.50
Times: Noon-2pm (Sun till 2.30)/7-9.30pm. Closed D ——**⓫**
Sun, all Mon
Additional: Children 12+ ——**⓬**
Seats: 50 ————**⓭**
Style: Classic/country house ——**⓮**
Civil licence: 100 ————**⓯**

9. The names of the chef(s) and owner(s) (entries of two rosettes and above only). These are as up-to-date as we could make them at the time of going to press, but changes in personnel often occur, and may affect both the style and the quality of the restaurant.

10. Alc is the cost of a meal for one person, including coffee and service but not wine. Set-price lunch and dinner menus come next. If these meals have more or less than three courses we have indicated this. The cost of the house wine or one of the cheaper wines on the list follows. Prices quoted are a guide only, and are subject to change without notice. ☺ indicates where restaurants have told us they offer dinner for under £25 a head (excluding wine).

11. The opening and closing times of the restaurant, and the days of the week the restaurant is closed, together with seasonal closures. Note that opening times are liable to change without notice. It is always a good idea to telephone any establishment which you are intending to visit to avoid disappointment.

12. In addition to meals in the restaurant, bar meals are served at lunch and/or dinner; Sunday lunch is served; Children are welcome, any age limitations are specified; Vegetarian - as most places have a vegetarian choice we have only indicated where we have been told that this is not available, or only by prior

Cringeltie House Hotel, Peebles

arrangement. However, it is always a good idea to check with the establishment to ensure that no one is disappointed.

13. The number of seats in the restaurant. Not all restaurants will take private parties, the number given is for the maximum number of people in a party. Jacket and tie are compulsory in a few restaurants, and this is specified.

14. We asked places to pick two words from a selection, or come up with their own, in order to indicate the style of the establishment

15. Establishments that do not allow smoking in the dining room may allow it elsewhere, in a lounge or bar, for instance. If you are a smoker, it is worth checking beforehand.

16. Civil Wedding Licence - establishments which are licensed for civil weddings have told us the maximum number of guests they can accommodate for the ceremony. Please note, in Scotland a licence is not required for religious ceremonies at any location.

17. Accommodation is shown if an establishment belongs to either the AA Guest Accommodation Scheme or the AA Hotel Scheme. The star rating refers to hotels.

18. All establishments take major credit cards, except where we specify otherwise.

'Telephone for further details' appears where an establishment has not supplied us with current details.

AA Rosette Awards

How the AA assesses restaurants for Rosette Awards

The AA's rosette award scheme was the first nation-wide scheme for assessing the quality of food served by restaurants and hotels. The rosette scheme is an award scheme, not a classification scheme and although there is necessarily an element of subjectivity when it comes to assessing taste, we aim for a consistent approach to our awards throughout the UK. It is important, however, to remember that many places serve enjoyable food but do not qualify for an AA award.

Our awards are made solely on the basis of a meal visit or visits by one or more of our hotel and restaurant inspectors who have an unrivalled breadth and depth of experience in assessing quality. They award rosettes annually on a rising scale of one to five.

So what makes a restaurant worthy of a Rosette Award?

For our inspectors the top and bottom line is the food. The taste of the food is what counts for them, and whether the dish successfully delivers to the diner what the menu promises. A restaurant is only as good as its worst meal. Although presentation and competent service should be appropriate to the style of the restaurant and the quality of the food, they cannot affect the rosette assessment as such, either up or down.

The following summaries attempt to explain what our inspectors look for, but are intended only as guidelines. The AA is constantly reviewing its award criteria and competition usually results in an all-round improvement in standards, so it becomes increasingly difficult for restaurants to reach award level.

One rosette
At the simplest level, one rosette, the chef should display a mastery of basic techniques and be able to produce dishes of sound quality and clarity of flavours, using good, fresh ingredients

Two rosettes
To gain two rosettes, the chef must show greater technical skill, more consistency and judgement in combining and balancing ingredients and a clear ambition to achieve high standards. Inspectors will look for evidence of innovation to test the dedication of the kitchen brigade, and the use of seasonal ingredients sourced from quality suppliers.

Three rosettes
This award takes a restaurant into the big league, and, in a typical year, fewer than 10 per cent of restaurants in our scheme achieve this distinction. Expectations of the kitchen are high, and inspectors find little room for inconsistencies. Exact technique, flair and imagination will come through in every dish, and balance and depth of flavour are all-important.

Four rosettes
This is an exciting award because, at this level, not only should all technical skills be exemplary, but there should also be daring ideas, and they must work. There is no room for disappointment. Flavours should be accurate and vibrant.

Five rosettes
This award is the ultimate awarded only when the cooking is at the pinnacle of achievement. Technique should be of such perfection that flavours, combinations and textures show a faultless sense of balance, giving each dish an extra dimension. The sort of cooking that never falters and always strives to give diners a truly memorable taste experience.

ROSETTE AWARD

AA

2000

AA Rosette Award for
Culinary Excellence

Villeroy & Boch

AA Star Classification

Quality standards you can expect from an AA recognised hotel

All hotels recognised by the AA should have the highest standards of cleanliness, proper records of booking, give prompt and professional service to guests, assist with luggage on request, accept and deliver messages, provide a designated area for breakfast and dinner with drinks available in a bar or lounge, provide an early morning call on request, good quality furniture and fittings, adequate heating and lighting and proper maintenance. A guide to some of the general expectations for each star classification is as follows:

What you can expect from a one star hotel ★

Polite, courteous staff providing a relatively informal yet competent style of service, available during the day and evening to receive guests. At least one designated eating area open to residents for breakfast and dinner. Last orders for dinner no earlier than 6.30pm, a reasonable choice of hot and cold dishes and a short range of wines available. Television in lounge or bedroom. Majority of rooms en suite, bath or shower room available at all times.

What you can expect from a two star hotel ★★

Smartly and professionally presented management and staff providing competent, often informal service, available throughout the day and evening to greet guests. At least one restaurant or dining room open to residents for breakfast and dinner. Last orders for dinner no earlier than 7pm, a choice of substantial hot and cold dishes and a short range of wines available. Television in bedrooms. En suite or private bath or shower and WC.

What you can expect from a three star hotel ★★★

Management and staff smartly and professionally presented and usually uniformed. Technical and social skills of a good standard in responding to requests. A dedicated receptionist on duty, clear direction to rooms and some explanation of hotel facilities. At least one restaurant or dining room open to residents and non-residents for breakfast and dinner whenever the hotel is open. A wide selection of drinks served in a bar or lounge, available to residents and their guest throughout the day and evening. Last orders for dinner no earlier than 8pm, full dinner service provided. Remote control television, direct dial telephone. En suite bath or shower and WC.

What you can expect from a four star hotel ★★★★

A formal, professional staffing structure with smartly presented, uniformed staff, anticipating and responding to your needs or requests. Usually spacious, well appointed public areas. Bedrooms offering superior quality and comfort than at three star. A strong emphasis on food and beverages and a serious approach to cuisine. Reception staffed 24 hours per day by well-trained staff. Express checkout facilities where appropriate. Porterage available on request and readily provided by uniformed staff. Night porter available. Newspapers can be ordered and delivered to your room, additional services and concierge as appropriate to the style and location of the hotel. At least one restaurant open to residents and non-residents for all meals seven days per week. Drinks available to residents and their guests throughout the day and evening, table service available. Last orders for dinner no earlier than 9pm, an extensive choice of hot and cold dishes and comprehensive list of wines. Remote control television, direct dial telephone, a range of high quality toiletries. En suite bath with fixed overhead shower, WC.

What you can expect from a five star hotel ★★★★★

Flawless guest services, professional, attentive staff, technical and social skills of the highest order. Spacious and luxurious accommodation and public areas with a range of extra facilities. As a minimum, first-time guests shown to their bedroom. Multilingual service consistent with the needs of the hotelís normal clientele. Guest accounts well explained and presented. Porterage offered and provided by uniformed staff. Luggage handling on arrival and departure. Doorman or means of greeting guests at the hotel entrance, full concierge service. At least one restaurant open to residents and non-residents for all meals seven days per week. Staff showing knowledge of food and wine. A wide selection of drinks, including cocktails, available in a bar or lounge, table service provided. Last orders for dinner no earlier than 10pm. High quality menu and wine list properly reflecting and complementing the style of cooking and providing exceptional quality. Evening turn-down service. Remote control television, direct dial telephone at bedside and desk, a range of luxury toiletries, bath sheets and robes. En suite bath with fixed overhead shower, WC.

AA Hotel Booking Service

Now you have a free, simple way to book a place to stay for a week, weekend, or a one-night stopover – The AA Hotel Booking Service

From farmhouse charm to five star luxury, we have just the place for you. Whether you wish to stay in a rustic farm cottage, a smart city centre hotel, a family lodge; or if you just want a cosy weekend for two – we can accommodate you.

If you are touring around Britain or Ireland and need accommodation, then just give the AA Hotel Booking Service a call. Provide us with your location and overnight requirements and we'll do the rest!

Why not try booking on-line. Full entries of AA recognised accommodation can be found and booked through the AA Hotel Booking Service via the AA Web Site

Telephone 0870 5050505

Office hours
Monday - Friday 9am - 6pm   Saturday 9am - 1pm
The service is not available Sundays or Bank Holidays
Book on-line: www.theaa.com

AA

The Premier Collection

Basket

Restaurants awarded three, four or five AA Rosettes represent the top ten percent of the AA Restaurant Guide. Their achievement is highlighted in The Premier Collection list which follows.

Villeroy & Boch

250 Years of Excellence

Fuse two quality brand names together such as Villeroy & Boch and the AA and you have an enviable partnership indeed. Villeroy & Boch is proud to be associated with the AA in promoting food excellence. For some time now we at Villeroy & Boch have used our expertise in the production of ceramics to manufacture specially commissioned plates which are given to all of the AA Rosette winning restaurants.

Twist Alea

There are few companies who can boast a heritage that spans three centuries. The company has endured political turmoil, wars and revolutions, but since our inception in 1748, the Villeroy & Boch name has endured to become a brand that is synonymous with quality and design innovation. It is Villeroy & Boch's use of quality materials and decoration that gives our products excellent durability. Our products are fully dishwasher safe and can therefore withstand years of constant use, keeping their patterns as bright as the day they were bought.

Chefs and consumers alike will be well versed in the art of lifting a plate, turning an item of cutlery or scrutinising a glass to reveal its origin. And few could fail to have come across the Villeroy & Boch name whether it be in a friend's home, in a number of leading restaurants or hotels, in many quality stores or in Villeroy & Boch's own retail outlet in Bluewater, Kent.

The Villeroy & Boch products shown in these pages are just a snapshot of our extensive tableware, glassware and giftware portfolio which can boast something for every consumer whether traditional or contemporary.

Beach House

Switch Beach House

Switch Coffee House

If you would like a brochure and stockist list, telephone 020 8875 6060 (24 hrs)

❀ ❀ ❀ ❀ ❀ .

LONDON

Le Gavroche Restaurant,
43 Upper Brook Street W1,
020 7408 0881

Restaurant Gordon Ramsay,
68 Royal Hospital Road SW3
020 7352 4441

La Tante Claire at The Berkeley,
Wilton Place, SW15
020 7235 6000

ENGLAND

DEVON
Gidleigh Park, CHAGFORD,
TQ13 8HH
01647 432367

OXFORDSHIRE
Le Manoir Aux Quat' Saisons,
GREAT MILTON, OX44 7PD
01844 278881

SCOTLAND

HIGHLAND
Altnaharrie Inn, ULLAPOOL
IV26 2SS
01854 633230

❀ ❀ ❀ ❀

LONDON

Mandarin Oriental Hyde Park,
66 Knightsbridge SW1
020 7235 2000

Petrus, 33 St James Street SW1
020 7930 4272

Putney Bridge,
The Embankment SW15
020 8780 1811

ENGLAND

BERKSHIRE
The Fat Duck, High Street, BRAY
SL6 2AQ
01628 580333

Waterside Inn, Ferry Road
BRAY, SL6 2AT
01628 620691

CUMBRIA
Michael's Nook , GRASMERE
LA22 9RP
015394 35496

GLOUCESTERSHIRE
Le Champignon Sauvage
Restaurant, 24 Suffolk Road
CHELTENHAM, GL50 2AQ
01242 573449

Lords of the Manor,
UPPER SLAUGHTER, GL54 2JD
01451 820243

HEREFORDSHIRE
Castle House, Castle Street
HEREFORD, HR1 2NW
01432 356321

LINCOLNSHIRE
Winteringham Fields,
WINTERINGHAM
DN15 9PF, 01724 733096,

RUTLAND
Hambleton Hall, Hambleton
OAKHAM, LE15 8TH
01572 756991

SOMERSET
Restaurant Lettonie,
35 Kelston Road, BATH, BA1 3QH
01225 446676

REPUBLIC OF IRELAND

DUBLIN
The Merrion Hotel,
Upper Merrion Street, DUBLIN 21
01 6030600

❀ ❀ ❀

LONDON

EC1
Gaudi Restaurante,
63 Clerkenwell Road
020 7608 3220

EC4
City Rhodes Restaurant,
1 New Street Square
020 7583 1313

SW1
Le Caprice Restaurant,
Arlington House, Arlington Street
020 7629 2239

The Halkin Hotel, Halkin Street
Belgravia
020 7333 1000

The Lanesborough,
Hyde Park Corner
020 7259 5599

Roussillon, 16 St Barnabas Street
020 7730 5550

Sheraton Park Tower,
101 Knightsbridge
020 7235 8050

The Square, 6-10 Bruton Street
020 7495 7100

Zafferano,
15 Lowndes Street
020 7235 5800

Azurea

SW3
Bibendum Restaurant,
Michelin House, 81 Fulham Road
020 7581 5817

The Capital, Basil Street
Knightsbridge
020 7589 5171

Floriana, 15 Beauchamp Place
020 7838 1500

Zaika,
257-259 Fulham Road
020 7351 7823

SW7
Hilaire, 68 Old Brompton Road
020 7584 8993 5312

SW10
Aubergine, 11 Park Walk
020 7352 3449

SW17
Chez Bruce, 2 Bellevue Road
Wandsworth Common
020 8672 0114

W1
cheznico, 90 Park Lane
020 7409 1290

The Dorchester, The Oriental,
Park Lane
020 7629 8888

Lindsay House Restaurant,
21 Romilly Street
020 7439 0450

Le Meridien Piccadilly, The Oak Room
21 Piccadilly
0870 400 8400

Mirabelle, 56 Curzon Street
020 7499 4636

Nobu, Old Park Lane
020 7447 4747

L'Odeon, 65 Regent Street
020 7287 1400

Orrery, 55-57 Marylebone High Street
020 7616 8000

Pied a Terre, 34 Charlotte Street
020 7636 1178

Quo Vadis, 26-29 Dean Street
020 7437 9585

W6
River Cafe, Thames Wharf Studios
Rainville Road
020 7381 8824

W8
Royal Garden Hotel,
2-24 Kensington High Street
020 7937 8000

W11
Halcyon Hotel, 81 Holland Park
020 7727 7288

W14
Chinon Restaurant,
23 Richmond Way
020 7602 5968

WC2
The Savoy, River Restaurant,
Strand
020 7836 4343

ENGLAND

BERKSHIRE
Fredrick's Hotel,
Shoppenhangers Road
MAIDENHEAD , SL6 2PZ
01628 581000

The Vineyard at Stockcross,
Stockcross,, NEWBURY, RG20 8JU
01635 528770

BRISTOL
Harveys Restaurant,
12 Denmark Street, BRISTOL
BS1 5DQ
0117 927 5034

BUCKINGHAMSHIRE
Hartwell House, Oxford Road
AYLESBURY, HP17 8NL
01296 747444

Cliveden Hotel, Waldo's, TAPLOW
SL6 0JF
01628 668561

CAMBRIDGESHIRE
The Pink Geranium, Station Road
MELBOURN, SG8 6DX,
01763 260215

CHESHIRE
The Chester Grosvenor Hotel,
Eastgate, CHESTER, CH1 1LT
01244 324024

CORNWALL & ISLES OF SCILLY
Well House Hotel, St Keyne
LISKEARD, PL14 4RN
01579 342001

Seafood Restaurant, PADSTOW
PL28 8BY
01841 532700

St Martin's on the Isle, Lower
Town
ST MARTIN'S, TR25 0QW
01720 422090

ST MAWES, Hotel Tresanton
Lower Castle Road, TR2 5DR
01326 270055

CUMBRIA
Sharrow Bay Country House Hotel
Sharrow Bay, HOWTOWN, CA10 2LZ
017684 86301

Rampsbeck Country House Hotel,
WATERMILLOCK, CA11 0LP
017684 86442

Gilpin Lodge Country House Hotel
Crook Road, WINDERMERE
LA23 3NE
015394 88818

Holbeck Ghyll Country House
Hotel, Holbeck Lane, WINDERMERE
LA23 1LU
015394 32375

DERBYSHIRE
Fischer's Baslow Hall, Calver Road
BASLOW, DE45 1RR
01246 583259

The Old Vicarage, Ridgeway Moor
RIDGEWAY, S12 3XW
0114 2475814

DEVON
Holne Chase Hotel,
Two Bridges Road, ASHBURTON
TQ13 7NS
01364 631471

Michael Caines at The Royal
Clarence, Cathedral Yard
EXETER, EX1 1HD
01392 319955

The Horn of Plenty, GULWORTHY
PL19 8JD
01822 832528

Arundell Arms, LIFTON, PL16 0AA
01566 784666

Chez Nous Restaurant,
13 Frankfort Gate, PLYMOUTH
PL1 1QA
01752 266793

Pophams, Castle Street, WINKLEIGH
EX19 8HQ
01837 83767

DORSET
Summer Lodge, EVERSHOT
DT2 0JR
01935 83424

GLOUCESTERSHIRE
Buckland Manor, BUCKLAND
WR12 7LY
01386 852626

Hotel On The Park,
38 Evesham Road, CHELTENHAM
GL52 2AH
01242 518898

The Greenway, Shurdington
CHELTENHAM, GL51 5UG
01242 862352

Lower Slaughter Manor,
LOWER SLAUGHTER, GL54 2HP
01451 820456

The Close Hotel, 8 Long Street
TETBURY, GL8 8AQ
01666 502272

GREATER MANCHESTER
Juniper, 21 The Downs
ALTRINCHAM, WA14 2QD3
0161 929 4008

Crowne Plaza Manchester-The
Midland, Peter Street
MANCHESTER, M60 2DS
0161 236 3333

HAMPSHIRE
36 On The Quay, 47 South Street
EMSWORTH, PO10 7EG
01243 375592

The Three Lions, Stuckton
FORDINGBRIDGE, SP6 2HF
01425 652489

Le Poussin at Parkhill,
Beaulieu Road, LYNDHURST
SO43 7FZ
023 8028 2944

Chewton Glen Hotel,
Christchurch Road, NEW MILTON
BH25 6QS
01425 275341

Old Manor House Restaurant,
21 Palmerston Street, ROMSEY
SO51 8GF
01794 517353

ISLE OF WIGHT
George Hotel, Quay Street
YARMOUTH, PO41 0PE
01983 760331

KENT
Eastwell Manor, Eastwell Park
Boughton Lees, ASHFORD
TN25 4HR
01233 213000

Read's Restaurant, Mummery Court
Painters Forstal, FAVERSHAM
ME13 0EE
01795 535344

Sandgate Hotel et Restaurant La
Terrasse, The Esplanade, Sandgate
FOLKESTONE, CT20 3DY
01303 220444

LANCASHIRE
Northcote Manor, Northcote Road
LANGHO, BB6 8BE
01254 240555

Paul Heathcotes Restaurant,
104-106 Higher Road
LONGRIDGE, PR3 3SY
01772 784969

LINCOLNSHIRE
Harry's Place, 17 High Street
Great Gonerby, GRANTHAM
NG31 8JS
01476 561780

NORFOLK
Morston Hall, Morston, BLAKENEY
NR25 7AA
01263 741041

Adlard's Restaurant,
79 Upper St Giles Street, NORWICH
NR2 1AB
01603 633522

French Garden

NOTTINGHAMSHIRE
Hart's Restaurant,
1 Standard Court, Park Row
NOTTINGHAM, NG1 6GN
0115 9110666

OXFORDSHIRE
Chavignol, 7 Horsefair
CHIPPING NORTON, OX7 5AL
01608 644490

Feathers Hotel, Market Street
WOODSTOCK
OX20 1SX
01993 812291

SHROPSHIRE
Merchant House,
62 Lower Corve Street, LUDLOW
SY8 1DU
01584 875438

Mr Underhills Restaurant,
LUDLOW, SY8 1EH
01584 874431

Overton Grange Hotel,
Hereford Road, LUDLOW, SY8 4AD
01584 873500

Sol Restaurant, 82 Wyle Cop
SHREWSBURY, SY1 1UT
01743 340560

Old Vicarage Hotel, WORFIELD
WV15 5JZ
01746 716497

SOMERSET
Bath Priory, Weston Road
BATH, BA1 2XT
01225 331922

The Royal Crescent Hotel,
16 Royal Crescent, BATH
BA1 2LS
01225 823333

Homewood Park Hotel,
HINTON CHARTERHOUSE, BA3 6BB
01225 723731

Hunstrete House Hotel
HUNSTRETE, BS39 4NS
01761 490490

Andrews on the Weir, Porlock Weir
PORLOCK, TA24 8PB
01643 863300

Charlton House, Charlton Road
SHEPTON MALLET, BA4 4PR
01749 342008

Castle Hotel, Castle Green
TAUNTON, TA1 1NF
01823 272671

Little Barwick House,
Barwick Village, YEOVIL
BA22 9TD
01935 423902

STAFFORDSHIRE
Old Beams Restaurant with Rooms,
Leek Road, WATERHOUSES
ST10 3HW
01538 308254

SUFFOLK
Hintlesham Hall Hotel,
HINTLESHAM, IP8 3NS
01473 652334

SURREY
Pennyhill Park Hotel & Country Club, London Road, BAGSHOT
GU19 5EU
01276 471774

SURREY
Michels' Restaurant, 13 High Street
RIPLEY, GU23 6AQ
01483 224777

SUSSEX, EAST
One Paston Place, 1 Paston Place
BRIGHTON, BN2 1HA
01273 606933

Röser's Restaurant,
64 Eversfield Place, HASTINGS
TN37 6DB
01424 712218

SUSSEX, WEST
Gravetye Manor Hotel,
EAST GRINSTEAD, RH19 4LJ
01342 810567

South Lodge Hotel, Brighton Road
LOWER BEEDING, RH13 6PS
01403 891711

Alexander House, East Street
TURNERS HILL, RH10 4QD
01342 714914

TYNE & WEAR
21 Queen Street, Quayside
NEWCASTLE UPON TYNE
NE1 3UG
0191 222 0755

WARWICKSHIRE
Mallory Court Hotel, Harbury Lane
Bishop's Tachbrook
ROYAL LEAMINGTON SPA
CV33 9QB
01926 330214

WEST MIDLANDS
Birmingham Marriott,
12 Hagley Road, Five Ways
BIRMINGHAM, B16 8SJ
0121 452 1144

WILTSHIRE
Manor House Hotel,
CASTLE COMBE, SN14 7HR
01249 782206

WILTSHIRE
Howard's House Hotel,
Teffont Evias, SALISBURY, SP3 5RJ
01722 716392

WORCESTERSHIRE
Brockencote Hall Country House Hotel, CHADDESLEY CORBETT
DY10 4PY
01562 777876

Croque-en-Bouche Restaurant,
221 Wells Road, Malvern Wells
MALVERN, WR14 4HF
01684 565612

Epicurean, 76 High Street
PERSHORE, WR10 1DU
01386 555576

YORKSHIRE, NORTH
Middlethorpe Hall Hotel,
Bishopthorpe Road, Middlethorpe
YORK, YO23 2GB
01904 641241

YORKSHIRE, SOUTH
Smith's of Sheffield,
34 Sandygate Road, SHEFFIELD
S10 5RY
01142 266 6096

YORKSHIRE, WEST
Box Tree Restaurant,
35-37 Church Street, ILKLEY
LS29 9DR
01943 608484

Pool Court at 42,
44 The Calls
LEEDS, LS2 7EW
0113 244 4242

CHANNEL ISLANDS

JERSEY
Longueville Manor Hotel,
St Saviour, JE2 7WF
01534 725501

SCOTLAND

ABERDEENSHIRE
Darroch Learg Hotel, Braemar Road
BALLATER, AB35 5UX
013397 55443

ARGYLL & BUTE
Isle of Eriska, Eriska, Ledaig,
ERISKA
PA37 1SD
01631 720371

Airds Hotel, PORT APPIN,
PA38 4DF
01631 730236

AYRSHIRE, NORTH
Braidwoods, Drumastle Mill
Cottage
DALRY, KA24 4LN
01294 833544

AYRSHIRE, SOUTH
Lochgreen House,
Monktonhill Road
Southwood, TROON, KA10 7EN
01292 313343

DUMFRIES & GALLOWAY
Kirroughtree House, Minnigaff
NEWTON STEWART, DG8 6AN
01671 402141

Knockinaam Lodge Hotel,
PORTPATRICK, DG9 9AD
01776 810471

EDINBURGH, CITY OF
Atrium, 10 Cambridge Street,
EH1 2ED
0131 228 8882

The Sheraton Grand Hotel,
1 Festival Square, EH3 9SR
0131 229 9131

FIFE
Cellar Restaurant, 24 East Green
ANSTRUTHER, KY10 3AA
01333 310378

Ostlers Close Restaurant,
Bonnygate, CUPAR, KY15 4BU
01334 655574

The Peat Inn, PEAT INN, KY15 5LH
01334 840206

West Port, 170-172 South Street
ST ANDREWS, 01334 473186

GLASGOW, CITY OF
One Devonshire Gardens Hotel,
1 Devonshire Gardens, G12 0UX
0141 339 2001

HIGHLAND
Arisaig House, Beasdale, ARISAIG
PH39 4NR
01687 450622

Three Chimneys Restaurant,
COLBOST, IV55 8ZT
01470 511258

Inverlochy Castle Hotel, Torlundy
FORT WILLIAM, PH33 6SN
01397 702177

The Cross, Tweed Mill Brae
Ardbroilach Road, KINGUSSIE
PH21 1TC
01540 661166

LOTHIAN, EAST
La Potiniere, Main Street
GULLANE, EH31 2AA
01620 843214

PERTH & KINROSS
Kinloch House Hotel,
BLAIRGOWRIE
PH10 6SG
01250 884237

Kinnaird, Kinnaird Estate
DUNKELD, PH8 0LB
01796 482440

STIRLING
Roman Camp Country House
Hotel,
CALLANDER, FK17 8BG
01877 330003

DUNBARTONSHIRE, WEST
Cameron House Hotel, BALLOCH
G83 8QZ
01389 755565

WALES

CARDIFF
The St David's Hotel & Spa,
Havannah Street, Cardiff Bay
CF10 5SD
029 2045 4045

CEREDIGION
Ynyshir Hall, EGLWYSFACH
SY20 8TA
01654 781209

CONWY
Tan-y-Foel Country House Hotel,
Capel Garmon, BETWS-Y-COED
LL26 0RE
01690 710507

The Old Rectory Country House,
Llanrwst Road,
Llansanffraid Glan Conwy, CONWY
LL28 5LF
01492 580611

Bodysgallen Hall Hotel,
LLANDUDNO, LL30 1RS
01492 584466

St Tudno Hotel, Promenade
LLANDUDNO, LL30 2LP
01492 874411

GWYNEDD
Plas Bodegroes, Nefyn Road
PWLLHELI, LL53 5TH
01758 612363

Hotel Maes y Neuadd, TALSARNAU
LL47 6YA
01766 780200

MONMOUTHSHIRE
Walnut Tree Inn, ABERGAVENNY
NP7 8AW
01873 852797

POWYS
Carlton House Hotel,
Dolycoed Road, LLANWRTYD
WELLS
LD5 4RA
01591 610248

SWANSEA
Fairyhill, REYNOLDSTON, SA3 1BS
01792 390139

NORTHERN IRELAND

BELFAST
Deanes, 38/40 Howard Street
BELFAST, BT1 6PD
028 90560000

DOWN
Shanks, The Blackwood
Crawfordsburn Road, BANGOR
BT19 1GB
028 91853313

REPUBLIC OF IRELAND

CORK
Longueville House Hotel,
MALLOW
022 47156

DONEGAL
Harvey's Point Country Hotel,
Lough Eske, DONEGAL
073 22208

DUBLIN
The Clarence, 6-8 Wellington Quay
DUBLIN
01 4070800

The Hibernian Hotel,
Eastmoreland Place, Ballsbridge
DUBLIN
01 6687666

KERRY
Park Hotel Kenmare, KENMARE
064 41200

Aghadoe Heights Hotel,
KILLARNEY
064 31766

KILDARE
The Kildare Hotel & Country Club,
STRAFFAN
01 6017200

LIMERICK
Dunraven Arms Hotel, ADARE
061 396633

Descriptions • Prices • Location maps
Hundreds of colour photographs

Available from all good booksellers
via our internet site: www.theaa.com
or by calling 01206 255800

Britain's
Largest
Travel
Publisher

Chefs' Chef
of the decade

No honour is quite as great as that bestowed by one's peers. Ask a professional footballer which award means most to them and they will invariably reply the PFA Player of the Year - the one the players themselves vote for. AA Chefs' Chef of the Year is the one the chefs themselves vote for, and this goes a long way in explaining the status the award has achieved in its relatively short existence. The calibre of previous winners - Gordon Ramsey, Jean-Christophe Novelli, Kevin Viner, Rick Stein - serves only to emphasise the impeccable pedigree that Chefs' Chef has rapidly established.

This year's award is a special one. On the 10th anniversary of the AA Rosette Awards we asked chefs to take a look back at the remarkable culinary decade that has just passed, to select the most influential and important chef of the 1990s - the AA Chefs' Chef of the Decade.

All the chefs featured in the 2000 edition of the guide were asked to choose an overall winner from a list comprising the winners and runners-up of previous years. These were:

> Raymond Blanc
> John Burton-Race
> Michael Caines
> Pierre Koffman
> Nico Ladenis
> Jean-Christophe Novelli
> Gordon Ramsay
> Rick Stein
> Kevin Viner
> Marco Pierre White

The contest solicited by far the greatest number of responses in any year so far and the winner will be announced at the AA Hotel and Restaurant Awards in October. At this stage we can disclose the top three, none of whom, interestingly, are previous winners of AA Chefs' Chef of the Year.

Raymond Blanc

When the family tree of the great chefs is compiled, Raymond Blanc will have a whole branch to himself. Whereas most other giants of the kitchen have emerged from the great culinary stud-farms (what a debt is owed to the brothers Roux!) M. Blanc has no such antecedents. Self-taught and fiercely motivated, he rose to prominence some 25 years ago, achieving one AA Rosette (when there was a maximum of three) at The Rose Revived on the banks of the Thames. The first Quat' Saisons then followed in an unassuming Oxford premises, squeezed between a

lingerie shop and a branch of Oxfam. In 1983 he took possession of Great Milton Manor, a rambling 15th century Cotswold house, which of course became the now legendary Le Manoir Aux Quat' Saisons. The Blanc empire now extends to three Petit Blanc offshoots in Birmingham, Cheltenham and Oxford, but the hub of the empire remains the kitchen at Le Manoir. A kitchen, ironically enough, which has proved the breeding ground for a new generation of star chefs.

Pierre Koffman

Whilst the 1990s were unquestionably the decade of the celebrity chef, Pierre Koffman provided a sharp contrast as the absolute model of discretion. Culinary trends came and went, chefs shot to fame and faded from view. Pierre Koffman's place at the top echelon of his profession remained unchallenged.

An apprenticeship in France and Switzerland was followed by time spent at Le Gavroche and then the newly opened Waterside Inn, where he stayed as chef de cuisine until 1977. A short period back in France gave way to the launch of La Tante Claire, where the combination of the honest Gascon cooking of his youth and the tradition of the grande cuisine, earned him five AA Rosettes. His latest move has been to take his talents to the Berkeley Hotel, doubling the covers and providing the great professional with a fresh challenge.

Marco Pierre White

Where would the 90s restaurant scene have been without Marco Pierre White?

He began the decade as the explosive young talent, an almost frighteningly powerful combination of charisma, single-mindedness and raw talent. He ended it by saying goodbye to a personal presence at the stove, while remaining at the helm of a string of London's most impressive restaurants, ranging from the ultra-contemporary Quo Vadis to the venerable grandeur of The Criterion and The Oak Room. Along the way he collected enough Rosette plates to start a china shop, including the ultimate five Rosettes at both The Hyde Park Hotel and The Oak Room. Let us not forget, at the root of all this industry there remains an extraordinary chef, at once classical and revolutionary. An absolute master of his craft.

The AA·
wine awards

The third year of the AA Wine Award and the entries poured in like never before. From the short and irreverent to the weighty and studious, lists of all shapes and sizes winged their way to the AA offices. After hours of deliberation the judging panel (including Nick Tarayan of last year's winner Leith's Restaurant and Trevor Hughes of T&W Wines) finally separated the First Growths from the Vins de Table and this year's shortlist emerged. Featuring some familiar names and some exciting newcomers, the finalists are as eclectic a bunch as ever. They all have one thing in common though - in every case, an exceptional enthusiasm for wine shines through.

Trevor Hughes, Managing Director, T&W Wines, with last year's winner, Nick Tarayan, and Roy Gardner, Cheif Executive of Centrica

A Vintage Year

Just as the quantity is up this year, so is the quality. In fact the sheer number of outstanding lists prompted a new innovation for this year's guide. Scattered throughout the book you will find a number of special awards recognising lists that are remarkable in a particular respect. Be it the coverage of a specific region or simply the excellence of the presentation, these are all lists that deserve special recognition.

Matchmaking

For the second round of judging, we once again turned to the thorny subject of matching wine with food. Something of an art, the panel agreed that the secret is to look at the meal as a whole rather than tackling each dish in isolation. Although there can be no hard and fast rule for such a subjective task some useful guidelines are applicable.

- -Light wines before heavy
- -Young wines before old
- -White before red
- -Simplicity before complexity
- -Match the wine to the sauce

Anton Mosimann, legendary chef-patron of Mosimann's in Belgravia, provided us with a challenging menu that succeeded in provoking combinations that ranged from the inspired to the outrageous.

Anton Mosimann's
Menu

With wines suggested by Edoardo Amadi of the Vineyard at Stockcross

Terrine of Maize-Fed Chicken with Woodland Mushrooms
Riesling Muenchberg, Domaine Ostertag 1992

Seared Salmon with Roast Scallops and Cappuccino of Peas
Sauvignon Blanc, Líapres Midi, Peter Michael Winery, Napa 1997

Fillet of Beef with Celeriac and Red Wine Jus
Vino Nobile di Montepulciano, Casa Vinicola Carpentino, Riserva, Tuscany 1990

Chocolate Tart with White Coffee Ice Cream
Tokaji, Aszu, 5 Puttonyos, Chateau Megyer, Hungary 1988

Petits Fours
Quinta do Noval, Portugal 1985

The Top Twenty Five

The Fat Duck, Bray, Berkshire
Hotel du Vin & Bistro, Bristol
The Old Bridge, Huntingdon, Cambridgeshire
Marygreen Manor, Brentwood, Essex
Belmore Hotel, Sale, Greater Manchester
Le Poussin at Parkhill, Lyndhurst, Hampshire
Chewton Glen, New Milton, Hampshire
The George of Stamford, Stamford, Lincolnshire
The Capital, London SW3
L'Escargot - Ground Floor Restaurant, London W1
Mirabelle, London W1
Orrery, London W1
Putney Bridge, London SW1
Restaurant Gordon Ramsay, London SW3
Rousillon, London SW3
Le Manoir Aux Quat' Saisons, Great Milton, Oxfordshire
Hambleton Hall, Hambleton, Rutland
Hintlesham Hall, Hintlesham, Suffolk
Gravetye Manor, East Grinstead, West Sussex
The Cottage in the Wood, Malvern, Worcestershire
Kinnaird, Dunkeld, Perth & Kinross
The Peat Inn, Peat Inn, Fife
Hotel Maes y Neuadd, Talsarnau, Gwynedd
Fairyhill, Reynoldston, Swansea
Llangoed Hall, Llyswen, Powys
Ynyshir Hall, Egwysfach, Ceredigion

AA Wine Award for England and Overall Winner

The Vineyard at Stockcross

Newbury, Berkshire

Confronted with a wine list this enormous (two volumes), the obvious question to ask is why so big? In the case of wine lists, bigger is certainly not always better and many large lists are so unwieldy and inaccessible as to be a real deterrent to customer choice. Not in this instance. The Vineyard offers an 'International List' of astonishing depth that comprehensively covers both the classic wine growing regions of the old world and the well-established regions of the new. California, is treated to a separate tome, reflecting the enthusiasm and investments of Sir Peter Michael whose wines from his own Sonoma Valley winery preface what must be one of the greatest collections of Californian wines outside of the state itself. Given the extent of the list, the attention to detail is impressive with obvious care and intelligence having been applied to some beautifully balanced selections, particularly from Bordeaux and Burgundy. An astonishing achievement.

AA Wine Award for Scotland

The Witchery by The Castle

Edinburgh

Another doorstopper of a list, but once again impeccably selected and carefully balanced. The Witchery's offering also boasts the additional virtue of meticulous annotation, a user-friendly approach that the panel felt was missing from too many lists. There is depth from across the world with good vintages from the classic regions and a similar respect applied to the new world with, for instance, no less than five vintages of Penfolds Grange Hermitage.

AA Wine Award for Wales

St Tudno Hotel & Restaurant

Llandudno, Conwy

Present on the shortlist last year, the wine list at St Tudno has not stood still in the intervening months. Janette and Martin Bland have continued to add to an already impressive selection, filling a few gaps and strengthening some of the weaker areas. Another list that benefits from extensive and informative descriptions, there is a palpable enthusiasm apparent throughout the selections and a consistent favouring of wines of real character as opposed to purely commercial appeal.

Trevor Hughes, Managing Director, T&W Wines

 Wine Awards   Sponsored by **T&W Wines**

The AA Wine Awards
Sponsored by T&W Wines of Thetford

The Glory of *the Garden*

Tina Bricknell-Webb, Percy's Country Hotel

Mallory Court, Leamington Spa

Among life's real pleasures is dining alfresco in a beautiful setting. Unfortunately, in Britain, an experience only for special occasions due to the vagaries of our infamous 'weather'. However, it is the very weather that helps create our exquisite countryside, which can then, alternatively, be enjoyed as a vista from within a cosy dining room. More and more frequently, British restaurateurs are creating beautiful gardens either as a backdrop to dining, an environment for eating out of doors or last, but by no means least, as a source of fresh vegetables and herbs to enhance their dishes.

Some of these gardens are newly created, either by professional landscape artists or the enthusiastic amateur; while others, attached to large houses and part of a 'grand concept', have fallen into neglect. Some were created hundreds of years ago, while others were established more recently when people had the wherewithal to devote much time and effort to creating garden plans. Now these gardens are being rescued from their decline.

A labour of love

A fine example of the former is Holne Chase Hotel, near Ashburton in Devon. Only four years ago Philippa and Sebastian Hughes took on the mammoth task of returning the 300 acres of grounds to their former glory - all the more daunting as their experience of gardening consisted mostly of tending window boxes! The two acres of walled kitchen garden, once full of ivy, weeds and broken greenhouses and cold frames, is currently the Hughes' pride and joy. The undergrowth has been cleared to reveal the original box hedging and the walls, stripped of ivy, now boast fig and pear trees once again. Aubergines, peppers, courgettes and a flourishing grapevine now adorn the greenhouses.

A grand project

By far the grandest and most expensive of the garden projects is that at Raymond Blanc's Le Manoir aux Quat' Saisons at Great Milton in Oxfordshire. This has been a fourteen year project, the brainchild of the celebrated chef who was keen that his clientele should have 'an understanding of food and where it came from. The gardens are just as important to us as the restaurant, bedrooms

and the interior design.' The two-acre herb and vegetable garden, once a shoulder-high forest of weeds, now supplies Le Manoir's kitchens throughout the summer months, producing 70 varieties of herb from all over the world and 90 types of vegetables, all organically grown.

A film star

One of the most famous walled gardens is that at Kinloch House Hotel at Blairgowrie in Perth & Kinross, set among 25 acres of parkland and woods overlooking Loch Maree and the Sidlaw Hills. Since its restoration began in 1996, the attractive walled garden, set out in the shape of a Celtic Cross, has been filmed extensively. In spite of its northerly situation, the garden produces all the fruit and vegetables for the hotel within its one acre. The two gardeners grow everything organically, maintaining the rebuilt hot and cold houses and a large polytunnel which extends the season to provide potted plants, cut flowers, fresh herbs, salads and other vegetables throughout the year. The gardens are hugely popular with guests and are open to non-residents.

Strawberry fields

Even further north, but on the west coast of Scotland and washed by the warm waters of the Gulf Stream, is Loch Torridon. On the shores of the loch at the foot of the Torridon Mountains, is Loch Torridon House Hotel where the garden had been neglected for a number of years until David Gregory began restoration work. The two-acre garden now provides, on average and weather permitting, about 75% of the produce used in the restaurant at the height of the season.

Across the sea

Far to the south, on the island of Jersey, famous for its garden produce, the kitchen garden of Longueville Manor at St Saviour was given a serious makeover at the beginning of the 1990s. Although the hotel stands in 17 acres of well-kept grounds with specimen trees and a lake, the granite-walled kitchen garden had fallen upon hard times. This neglected potato patch has once again burst into life and the hotel is now virtually self-sufficient in produce. The Victorian glasshouses have been restored and provide 'out of season' vegetables as well as exotic houseplants, orchids and home-grown lemons and peaches.

The herb garden

Most restaurants with even a small patch of garden will grow their own herbs and even those who can only muster a window-box or a tub in a small backyard will often plant a few of the basic herbs. However, there are restaurants where the herb garden is the centrepiece of the grounds and of which they are justifiably proud.

At Nuthurst Grange at Hockley Heath in the West Midlands, a symmetrical layout of box hedges divides the herbs into separate groups. Mallory Court, near Leamington Spa, also has a large and beautiful herb garden laid out within neat box hedges, but here the design is on a slightly larger scale and the appearance is more relaxed. The owners of the Four Seasons Restaurant at Nantgaredig, Carmarthenshire have only recently created their herb garden but it still provides an abundance of fresh herbs including sorrel and different varieties of thyme. The herb garden provides a feature point in their garden and is further enhanced by an elegant iron pergola.

Nuthurst Grange, Hockley Heath

Back to the soil

Most restaurateurs who grow their own vegetables do so because they appreciate the extra flavour and quality they can obtain. Nowadays most of them realise that all this hard work should not be defeated by adding copious amounts of chemicals. Among these are Nigel and Heather Chapman, the owners of Woolley Grange at Bradford-on-Avon, Wiltshire. To this end they have brought in Lucy Scott who has been tackling the overgrown plot with a vengeance. The land had not been touched for a long time, but the chefs are able to use some self-sown plants that were already growing, such as Jeruslam artichokes, horseradish, land cress and rhubarb. Lucy's aim is 'that there will always be something on the menu which has come fresh from the Woolley garden'.

At Percy's Country Hotel, Virginstow, near Okehampton in Devon, the garden is in the process of conversion to organic. Chef Tina Bricknell-Webb and husband Tony are supervising the extensive, beautifully tended kitchen garden's change-over from modern gardening methods but this is a slow process. It takes a full two years from registering the plot with the Soil Association before you can plant what will be your first truly organic crop. This crop may be slow maturing, such as asparagus, so it could be several years before the land has its seal of approval.

Modesty becomes her

Although most of the gardens featured in this article have been rather grand, or at least running to an acre or so, many places with much more modest circumstances are achieving excellent results. Swan House at Beccles in Suffolk has access to fruit, vegetables and herbs grown organically by one of the partners while, in the East End of London, tucked behind Heather's Vegetarian Restaurant is a tiny but delightful courtyard garden entirely filled with organically grown edible plants and herbs. One of London's hidden surprises, this secluded south-facing arbour supplies the restaurant with lovage, angelica, lavender (for biscuits), bay, fig, honeysuckle, kiwi, sage, rosemary and chives.

Longueville Manor, St Saviour

THE GLORY OF THE GARDEN

Restaurant
of the *year*

What makes a Restaurant of the Year? Take a look at this year's winners and you'll be hard pressed to find a common thread, or even a single adjective, that could legitimately be applied to all three. In many ways, it would be difficult to imagine two more contrasting approaches than Heston Blumenthal's electric alchemy at The Fat Duck and Franco Taruschio's warm-hearted craft at The Walnut Tree. Somewhere in the middle you could reasonably place Deanes, but it would be hard to argue that Michael Deane's cosmopolitan, Asian-tinged style is particularly closely related to either of the other two winners. In contrast to last year, none of the restaurants are even new to the guide and all could now be described as established (especially true of course of The Walnut Tree with nearly 40 years under its belt!). Yes, all have achieved the coveted Three Rosette level or better but you only have to look back to last year to find the three mainland winners all at the Two Rosette level.

The truth is, there is no blueprint for a Restaurant of the Year, no set criteria. These are all places that have especially impressed our team of inspectors and after much passionate debate, come out at the top of the pile. There is, of course, one virtue that all three have in common – they are all exceptionally good places to eat and thus deserved winners, one and all.

England

The Fat Duck at Bray

'Currently the most exciting food in the UK' - commented an inspector after a lunch at Heston Blumenthal's groundbreaking restaurant. This is not however, the place to provide an example for aspiring young chefs. The menu here is shot through with bizarre sounding combinations and wild flights of imagination. It's the kind of complexity that often spells disaster in kitchens where the basics of depth of flavour, quality of ingredients and balanced combinations fall victim to extravagant pretension on the part of the chef. No such charges can be legitimately made of Heston Blumenthal. Dishes such as cuttlefish canelloni of duck with maple syrup and white turnip or roast spiced cod with braised cockscombs, lentils and a sweet wine jus are as intelligent as they are inspired. Make no mistake though, whilst the inspiration is apparent, it's the perspiration behind the scenes that makes it all work. Some dishes spend months in the design stage, being honed and chiselled (and no doubt sometimes abandoned) before they're let out of the lab. It's an extraordinary approach. In the UK at least, The Fat Duck is simply unique.
Tel. 01628 580333

2001

Scotland & Northern Ireland

Deanes, Belfast

Michael Deane's contribution to eating out in Northern Ireland is considerable. First at Helen's Bay and then in central Belfast, he has been a pioneer of good eating in the north of the island. He's done it in some style too; three-foot gilded cherubs hang from the ceiling in the downstairs brasserie, with deep red velvet upholstery adding to an almost bordello-like feel. Upstairs, in the fine-dining restaurant, the decor is more restrained and more appropriate, perhaps to Michael Deane's food. Tinged though it is with spiky oriental influences, the cooking is at heart, understated and classical. It's precise too, with the frequent use of spice being immaculately judged, especially with fish. The brasserie offers a scaled-down version of the repertoire and like the restaurant, is often packed. Success, born of enterprise, hard work and a special talent.

Tel. 028 905 60000

Wales

The Walnut Tree, Abergavenny

When Franco and Ann Taruschio opened their country inn in the mid-1960s, the Italian influence on Welsh cuisine extended little further than the high street cafés still to be found in many South Wales towns. In every one of the past four decades, the Walnut Tree would have been on any list of the best places to eat - not just in Wales, but in the whole of the UK. In essence the building is a simple country pub and all the better for it. The complete absence of pretension is a breath of fresh air and the honesty of the approach is nowhere better represented than on the plate. Many dishes are striking in their simplicity, spaghetti with cockle sauce for instance, had one of our inspectors in raptures. This is cooking that comes from the heart as much as the head and surely there can be no better recommendation than that.

Tel. 01873 852797

RESTAURANT OF THE YEAR

LONDON

aka ❀

Happening venue in 19th-century post office vaults with industrial chic decor and opulent accessories. Mezzanine restaurant, overlooking the Manhattenesque cocktail-bar, serving accurately cooked and simply presented dishes with sensational flavours.

Directions: Telephone for directions

18 West Central Street WC1A 1JJ
Map: E4
Tel: 020 7836 0110
Fax: 020 7836 1771

Telephone for further details

Alastair Little
W11 ❀❀

Alastair Little's W11 outpost is a modern, simply-decorated room with a high ceiling and a skylight, the decor a bit frayed around the edges, according to a reporter. To it he has brought his laudable philosophy of top-rate ingredients cooked simply and accurately. The easy-reading, daily-changing menu centres on the Mediterranean, Italy in particular, so you have antipasto, pasta in the shape of perhaps spaghetti with braised octopus, and pistachio ice cream with *baci di dama*. Winter-warming soups – white bean and *cavolo nero*, say – or perhaps bourride, the latter with 'excellent depth of flavour', might show up among starters, and roasting is a favoured treatment for main courses: haunch of venison with crispy pancetta, stuffed leg of rabbit, or exemplary cod with lentil and spinach sauce ('three principal ingredients which delivered the equivalent of more'). Puddings are well-reported, too, not least precisely poached pear with 'deep, rich' chocolate sauce and vanilla ice cream.

Directions: ⊖ Ladbrook Grove, from tube turn R, Lancaster Rd is 1st R

136a Lancaster Road
W11 1QU
Map: C2
Tel: 020 7734 5783
Fax: 020 7229 2991
Chef: Tony Abarno
Owners: Alastair Little,
Kirsten Tormod Pedersen,
Mercedes André-Vega
Cost: *Alc* £23, set-price D £27.50. ☺
H/wine £14
Times: Noon-2.30pm (3pm Sat)/6.30-11pm. Closed Sun, Bhs
Additional: Children welcome
Seats: 40
Style: modern
Smoking: Air conditioning

Alastair Little
Soho ❀❀

Alastair Little's original Soho restaurant is showing some signs of wear and tear. On an inspection visit, the buzz and thrill of previous meals seemed rather lacking. Breads are delicious, but there was little inspiration in the Caesar salad or roast breast of chicken with potato gratin and wild mushroom sauce, or a bourride of sliced fish, prawns and mussels. Other dishes, perhaps more typical of the Little stamp, include grilled sardines with salsa verde, six native oysters with spicy sausages and shallot relish, and skate wing with rocket and herb dressed potatoes. From the dessert list, Venetian rice pudding with blood orange salad still conjures up the simple, sunny flavours with which his name is associated.

Directions: ⊖ Leicester Square, Tottenham Court Road.

49 Frith Street W1V 5TE
Map: D4
Tel: 020 7734 5183
Fax: 020 7734 5206
Chef: James Rix
Owners: Alastair Little,
Kirsten Tormod Pederson
Cost: *Alc* £35, set-price L £25/D £33.
H/wine £14
Times: Noon-3pm/6-11pm.
Closed L Sat, all Sun, Bhs
Additional: Children welcome
Seats: 47 & 18. Private dining room 25
Style: Minimalist
Smoking: No pipes & cigars, Air conditioning

Alba Restaurant

Italian restaurant with a cool modern interior just a stone's throw from the Barbican. Cooking focuses on dishes from Piedmont and northern Italy, and the cheeseboard includes rare Piedmont cheeses.

Additional: Bar food L; Children welcome
Style: Modern
Smoking: No-smoking area; Air conditioning

Directions: ⊖ Barbican

107 Whitecross Street EC1Y 8JD
Map: F4
Tel: 020 7588 1798
Fax: 020 7638 5793
Cost: Set-price D £11.90. ☺
H/wine £11.50
Times: Noon-3pm/6-11pm.
Closed Sat, Sun, Bhs

Al Duca

Given its location just off Jermyn Street, this modern Italian restaurant is surprisingly user-friendly: simple, plain, unadorned tables, a clean-cut pale look with big etched-glass windows, immaculately clad staff, and reasonable prices, with both lunch and dinner working around a set-price menu of up to four courses. Dishes are simple in concept, and the quality of the ingredients, sound cooking techniques and little messing around in the kitchen mean that flavours are direct, from starters of aubergine and buffalo Mozzarella salad, or fillet of wild boar with wild mushrooms and baby spinach to a main course of rabbit leg wrapped in Parma ham served with organic polenta and endive. Pasta takes in reginette with peas and Italian bacon, and macaroni with broccoli, garlic, anchovies and Pecorino. Fish is a strong point – smoked tuna is thinly sliced in a salad of aromatic leaves, and roast cod makes a fine main course with white beans and spring onions and chargrilling is a favoured medium, from swordfish with tapenade and tomato and rocket salad, to ribeye steak with ratatouille. Tiramisu heads up the desserts, and the all-Italian wine list offers enough at below £20 a bottle to make the final bill seem a bargain.

Directions: Telephone for directions

4/5 Duke of York Street SW1Y 6LA
Map: D4
Tel: 020 7839 3090
Fax: 020 7839 4050
Chef: Michele Franzolin
Owner: Cuisine Collection
Cost: Set-price L £18/D £21. ☺
H/wine £11
Times: Noon-2.45pm/6-11pm.
Closed Sun, Xmas & Etr
Additional: Children welcome
Seats: 56
Style: Modern
Smoking: Air conditioning

Alfred

Utilitarian but stylish eatery. The decor is simple, the service straightforward and friendly, and the food does not disappoint. Try roast cod with potato pancake, pea purée and a light chicken jus.

Additional: Sunday L; Children welcome
Style: Chic/Minimalist
Smoking: No pipes & cigars; Air conditioning

Directions: Close to Shaftesbury Theatre. ⊖ Tottenham Court Road

245 Shaftesbury Avenue WC2 8EH
Map: D3
Tel: 020 7240 2566
Fax: 020 7497 0672
Cost: Alc £23, set-price L & D £13.90
& £17. ☺ H/wine £12.50
Times: Noon-3.30pm/6-11.30pm.
Closed L Sat, D Sun, 25 Dec, Bhs

Anglesea Arms

Corner pub in a residential area with an interesting menu chalked up for each service. Options include whole roast Cornish mackerel, warm salad of pigeon breast, and chocolate truffle cake.

Directions: Off Goldhawk Road. ⊖ Goldhawk Road, Ravenscourt Park

35 Wingate Road W6 0UR
Map Gtl: C3
Tel: 020 8749 1291
Fax: 020 8749 1254
E-mail: fievans@aol.com

Telephone for further details

Anna's Place ❀

Small, homely Swedish restaurant of long-standing. Anna has retired, but still puts in an appearance (and makes her presence felt). The menu continues Anna's original Swedish theme (gravad lax, Swedish meatballs) but now incorporates more global dishes such as chicken wun-tun.

Times: Noon-2.15pm/7-11pm. Closed L Mon-Fri, all Sun, Xmas, New Year
Additional: Children welcome
Style: Traditional
Credit cards: None

Directions: Left off Balls Pond Road into Mildmay Park. On the corner of Newington Green. Bus 73, 171, 141 to Newington Green

90 Mildmay Park N1 4PR
Map GtL: D3
Tel: 0171 249 9379
Cost: *Alc* £22. Set price D £10. ☺
H/wine £9.95.

Apprentice Restaurant ❀

Enjoy the modern interior of a restaurant housed in a converted spice warehouse and try tagine of lamb with apricot and coriander or celeriac, leek and smoked cheese crumble, prepared by Butler's Wharf Chef School.

Times: Noon-3pm/6-11pm. Closed Sat, Sun, Bhs
Additional: Children welcome
Style: Modern
Smoking: No-smoking area; No pipes & cigars

Directions: On S side of river, 2 minutes from Tower Bridge. ⊖ Tower Hill, London Bridge

Cardamon Building
31 Shad Thames SE1 2YR
Map: G3
Tel: 020 7234 0254
Fax: 020 7403 2638
E-mail: enquiries@chef-school.co.uk
Cost: *Alc* £20, set-price L £13.50/D £15.50 & £18.50. ☺

Armandier ❀❀   NEW

Following on from the success of his first restaurant, La Ciboulette, in the King's Road, French-born chef Daniel Gobet moved to the heart of Lancaster Gate in 1998 to establish Armandier and Bistro Daniel. The latter is an informal basement bistro while the smaller, more elegant restaurant is on the ground floor, but both feature competent French cooking with a distinct Provençal bias. Simply decorated in pastel green and cream, with plush banquette seating and an intimate, relaxed, atmosphere, Amandier offers a well-balanced choice of dishes on a set-price menu. A starter of goats' cheese soufflé with globe artichoke and chive beurre blanc was a model of lightness and subtle flavour. For main course, moist, well-cooked sea bass was accompanied by a 'tian' of provençale vegetables and drizzled with delicious saffron olive oil, while the successful banana tarte Tatin for dessert came with a rich caramel sauce. Less expensive and more rustic dishes on the more extensive bistro *carte*.

Directions: ⊖ Paddington

26 Sussex Place W2 2TH
Map: A3
Tel: 020 7262 6073
Fax: 020 7723 8395
Chef: Daniel Gobet
Owners: Azziz Ahmed, Daniel Gobet
Cost: *Alc* £32.50, set-price L £18. ☺
H/wine £12.95
Times: Noon-2.30pm/7-10.45pm. Closed 24-25 Dec, Bhs
Additional: Children welcome
Style: Classic/chic
Seats: 25. Private dining room 70
Smoking: No pipes & cigars; Air conditioning

Aroma II ❀

Award-winning Oriental restaurant. Either watch the chef preparing your food or admire the large fish tank from the comfort of your

118 Shaftesbury Avenue W1V 7DJ
Tel/Fax: 020 7437 0377
Cost: *Alc* fr £15, set-price L/D fr £4. ☺ H/wine £8.50

Aroma II

Times: Noon-11.30pm
Additional: Sunday L; Children welcome
Style: Classic/Relaxed
Smoking: No-smoking area; Air conditioning

chair. The sizeable menu includes stir-fried chicken with green pepper in black bean sauce.

Directions: ⊖ Leicester Square. North along Charing Cross Road, then left into Shaftesbury Avenue at Cambridge Circus. ⊖ Piccadilly Station, East along Shaftesbury Avenue

Assaggi ❀

Located above a pub, this is a little piece of Sardinia with ever-changing menus and great hospitality. Fresh fish features – turbot with capers and spinach was 'expertly cooked and delicious'.

Additional: Children welcome
Style: Informal/modern
Smoking: No pipes & cigars; Air conditioning

Directions: ⊖ Westbourne Grove

39 Chepstow Place W2 4TS
Map GtL: C3
Tel: 020 7792 5501
Cost: *Alc* £35. H/wine £11.50
Times: 12.30-2.30pm/7.30-11pm. Closed Sun, 2 wks Xmas-New Year, Bhs

Athanaeum Hotel ❀

116 Piccadilly W1V 0BJ
Map: C3
Tel: 020 7499 3464
Fax: 020 7493 1860
E-mail: info@athenaeumhotel.com
Cost: *Alc* £35. H/wine £13.95
Times: 12.30-2.30pm/6-11pm. Closed L Sat & Sun
Additional: Children welcome
Style: Classic/informal
Smoking: No pipes & cigars; Air conditioning
Accommodation: 157 en suite
★ ★ ★ ★

There's a Mediterranean feel to both the menu and the restaurant at this stylish Piccadilly hotel. Char-grilling is a favourite method, and desserts, such as banana Tatin, are skilfully created.

Directions: ⊖ Hyde Park Corner, Green Park

Atlantic Bar and Grill

A lot of fun at night, when it's noisy, smoky and awash with fashion victims, the Atlantic is more sedate at lunchtimes, allowing people actually to see the Art Deco-ish surroundings of ornate ceilings and marble pillars. Bar staff make up exotic cocktails, there are plenty of wines by the glass, and service is young, informal and enthusiastic. Not everyone might be here for the food, but the kitchen certainly delivers the business, using top-quality produce – Newlyn cod, Aberdeen Angus beef, Orkney scallops – and working to a globally-inspired menu. Bresaola, sashimi, and Sauternes-steeped foie gras are all among starters, alongside perhaps applewood-smoked chicken salad or an attractive-looking dish of scallops and salmon wrapped in Parma ham with celeriac remoulade and pomegranate. Well-timed fillet of beef comes as a main course topped with pea purée and a perfectly-fried quail's egg along with four fat, crisp chips, while salmon, tuna and crab go into a fishcake served with langoustine sauce and honey-roast tomatoes and basil. Finish with something fruity like fresh-tasting strawberry parfait, or caramelised lemons and oranges with satsuma-infused chocolate custard.

20 Glasshouse Street W1R 5RQ
Map: D3
Tel: 020 7734 4888
Fax: 020 7734 3609
Chef: Richard Sawyer
Owner: Oliver Peyton
Cost: *Alc* £35, set-price L £14.50/D £14.50 (pre-theatre) & £16.50. ☺ H/wine £13.50
Times: Noon-3pm/6-11pm (from 7pm Sun). Closed L Sat & Sun, Bhs
Additional: Bar food; Children welcome (L only)
Seats: 180. Private dining room 70
Style: Chic
Smoking: Air conditioning

Directions: Just off Piccadilly Circus.
⊖ Piccadilly Circus

Aubergine

11 Park Walk SW10 0AJ
Map: A1
Tel: 020 7352 3449
Fax: 020 7351 1770
Chef: William Drabble
Owners: A to Z Restaurants Ltd
Cost: *Alc* £45, set-price L £16 & £19.50/D £59.50 (6 course, menu gourmand) . H/wine fr £13
Times: Noon-2.30pm/7-10.30pm(11pm Fri & sat). Closed L Sat, all Sun, 2 wks end Aug, 1 wk Xmas
Additional: Children 10+
Seats: 50-55
Style: Chic/French
Smoking: No pipes & cigars; Air conditioning

Directions: From Fulham Road, heading west, 2nd road L after MGM cinema

This is a stylish, relaxing dining room that provides trend-setting cooking, unfussy service and cognitive post-meal thoughts about the ever-upwards progress of William Drabble. Although the menu remains little changed since last year, Drabble is maturing, consolidating and perfecting complex dishes presented with an understated innocence on the plate, and driving home his own brand of cooking. He has a great eye for the seasons, there is scope and variety to the menu and his slide-rule approach to seasoning, timing and freshness of ingredients is exemplary. Even the bread is better than almost any other to be had in London. A boudin of pigeon with foie gras, caramelisd turnips and truffle jus was full of earthy, robust flavours, but perhaps needed the counterpoint of some lighter elements. By contrast, veal sweetbreads wrapped in ventrèche with braised peas, onions and lettuce was not just beautifully fresh and aromatic, but a dish that worked the full range of the palate. The weakest part of the inspection meal was, as so often happens, the dessert, a chocolate fondant with clementine sorbet that simply lacked the panache of the previous courses. The extensive wine list needs care, especially when trawling the wines by vintage, but willing staff are happy to help.

The Avenue ⊛

Large modern restaurant with a grand piano in the tall window, a tiled floor and an exceptionally long bar. The menu is brasserie style delivering simple, bright and colourful dishes.

Directions: ⊖ Green Park. R past The Ritz, R into St James's Street

7-9 St James's Street SW1A 1EE
Map: C3
Tel: 020 7321 2111
Fax: 020 7321 2500

Telephone for further details

Babur Brasserie ⊛⊛

119 Brockley Rise Forest Hill SE23 1JP
Map GtL: D2
Tel: 020 8291 2400
Fax: 020 8291 4881
E-mail: babur-brasserie@ compuserve.com
Chef: Enam Rahman
Cost: *Alc* £18. ☺ H/wine £7.95
Times: Noon-2.30pm/6-11.30pm. Closed L Fri, 25 & 26 Dec
Additional: Sunday L; Children welcome
Seats: 56
Style: Informal/Modern
Smoking: No-smoking area; Air conditioning

A life-sized model of a Bengal tiger leaps out of the wall above the whitearched frontage heralding your arrival at this renowned south London Indian. Inside, the decor is less remarkable than the brilliantly coloured menu – the tigers' head motif denoting the strength of heat in various dishes (one means hot, two roaring) – and places the emphasis on regional specialities. The great strength here is the freshness of herbs and spices, which give clear and individual flavours to the inventive and evolving cuisine. A well-reported meal included 'keenan boti' – lamb chops marinated in fennel and mustard seeds and cooked in a tandoori oven; 'mausami murgh' – Thai style dish, a broth made of chicken bone stock with sweet carrots and tomatoes poached in it, together with white chicken meat, tempered with coconut milk and topped with rice. French influenced, but Indian flavoured puddings include a soufflé, brioche and truffles, as well as delicious lassi and many ices. The small list of fruity wines is bolstered by a more select list on request. Service is polite, helpful and polished.

Directions: 5 mins walk from Honor Oak BR Station, where parking is available

Bank Restaurant ⊛

Huge, design-led, fast-paced restaurant with a lot to offer. Open for breakfast at 7am, and heaving from 5pm with well-heeled drinkers in the bar. Sample the likes of smoked haddock and Ricotta tart, and braised beef with parsnip mash.

Additional: Bar food; Sunday L; Children welcome
Style: Modern   **Smoking:** Air conditioning

Directions: ⊖ Holborn. On corner of Kingsway and Aldwych opposite Bush House

1 Kingsway WC2B 6XF
Map: E4
Tel: 020 7234 3344
Fax: 020 7234 3343
E-mail: reservations@bgr.plc.uk
Cost: *Alc* £45, set-price L & (pre-theatre) D £13.90-£17.50. ☺ H/wine £12.50
Times: Noon-2.45pm (Sat & Sun 11.30-3pm)/5.30-11pm . Closed Bhs

Base Restaurant ❀❀

Set amidst the bustle of trendy Hampstead High Street, this small restaurant is fairly inconspicuous. It is divided into two separate businesses – one a small, informal coffee bar with counter and high stools; the other the long and narrow restaurant. Pierre Khodja brings the Mediterranean and North Africa to his menu, dishes such as lobster tagine, or pan-fried red mullet with provençale risotto and rosemary. Also, he has a strong understanding of the concept of simplicity and execution is spot-on, as we found at a winter meal: pan-fried prawns, large and succulent, served on a rustic-style white bean ragout flavoured with pesto; tender, crisp-skinned roast quail with mushroom risotto; roast veal cutlet with celeriac purée and well-made Madeira jus; and baked sea bass served on sliced potatoes roasted with chilli and red peppers. Service is relaxed and informal.

Directions: ⊖ Hampstead. Next to Waterstone's

71 Hampstead High Street NW3 1QP
Map GTL: C4
Tel: 020 7431 2224
Fax: 020 7433 1262
E-mail: martinjacobs@compuserve.com
Chef: Pierre Khodja
Owners: M Boni, P Khodja, D Zilkha, E Gatt, M Jacobs,
Cost: *Alc* £35, set -price L £12.99. H/wine £12
Times: Noon-3pm/6.30-10.30pm. Closed D Sun, 25 Dec,1 Jan
Additional: Sunday L; Children welcome
Seats: 60. Private dining room 25
Style: Modern/urban/living room
Smoking: No-smoking area; Air conditioning

Beak Street ❀❀

This place used to be Leith's Soho, but has now been taken over by new owners, however, Alex Floyd has stayed on as head chef. The restaurant is not large, and is quite buzzy and cosy. Plain walls, light wooden floors and simple furniture add to the minimalist effect which is lightened by pictures, a theme of beaks (noses!). There's a longer, larger selection on the longer evening carte now, but the food is awesome: starters like seared scallop risotto of vegetables, chorizo and white beans, and salad of marinated duck breast with roast pears and aged balsamic; and main dishes such as linguine with clams, basil, ratatouille oil and parmesan, and black leg chicken with ventreche ham, cauliflower timbale and sage. Wild mushroom, artichoke and sweet garlic risotto was a great success recently, as was fillet of cod in a herb crust with basil sauce. Passion fruit ice cream definitely had the 'wow!' factor, lifting the delicate white chocolate tart to unimagined heights. Staff are pleasant and chatty, uniformed and relaxed.

CLOSED

41 Beak Street W1R 3LE
Map: D4
Tel: 020 7287 2057
Fax: 020 7287 1767
E-mail: beakstreet@firmdale.com
Chef: Alex Floyd
Owners: Firmdale Hotels plc
Cost: *Alc* £32.50, set-price L/D (pre-theatre) £19.50. ☺ H/wine £11.75
Times: Noon-2.30pm/6-11.15pm. Closed L Sat, all Sun, Xmas, Bhs
Additional: Children welcome
Seats: 45. Private dining room 20
Style: Chic/Modern
Smoking: No-smoking area; Air conditioning

Directions: ⊖ Piccadilly Circus, Oxford Circus

Belair House ❀

This striking Palliadian-style mansion is in a great setting – a small park in a leafy residential area close to Dulwich College – and offers a comfortable, bold (predominantly sunshine yellow and navy blue), light-filled interior . The modern menu is particularly good value for lunch.

Gallery Road SE21 7AB
Map GtL: D2
Tel: 020 8299 9788
Fax: 020 8299 6793
Cost: *Alc* £28, set-price L £17.50/D £24.95. ☺ H/wine £15
Times: Noon-2.30pm/7-10.30pm (Mon – Sat). Closed Sun D in winter
Additional: Bar food Mon-Fri; Sunday L; Children welcome
Style: classic
Smoking: No pipes & cigars

Directions: From Brixton: Gallery Road is the 1st turning off the South Circular after passing West Dulwich train station. From Catford: 1st turning off South Circular after Dulwich College.

Belvedere ❀❀

Restaurant in a magnificent tiered orangery in Holland Park. No expense is spared in the creation of the opulent surrounding and the extravagance of the dishes, including three foie gras starters out of the nine offered. Good service is provided by friendly French staff and the extensive wine list is top drawer. Cooking is supposed to be modern British but the menu descriptions are distinctly franglais. A starter of endive tart was light and well risen with caramelised foie gras balancing the bitterness of the vegetable. Rump of tender, sweet lamb was full of flavour, pink and juicy with crisp fat, served pot-au-feu-style in a lovely clear broth with ceps, embryo root vegetables and fresh herbs. Pudding was a perfectly executed biscuit glacé aux noisettes set on a raspberry sauce.

Directions: On Kensington High Street side of Holland Park.
⊖ Holland Park

Abbotsbury Road Holland Park
W8 6LU
Map GtL: C3
Tel: 020 7602 1238
Fax: 020 7610 4382
Chef: Jeremy Hollingsworth
Owner: Jimmy Lahoud
Cost: Alc £25-30, set-price L £14.95 & £17.95. H/wine £14.50
Times: Noon-2.30pm/6-11pm
Additional: Sunday L; Children welcome
Seats: 90
Smoking: Air conditioning
Civil licence: 150

Bengal Clipper ❀

Indian restaurant in listed building situated on Butler's Wharf serving everything from stuffed chicked masala, one of the most popular dishes, to lamb pasanda, cooked with cream, cashew nuts and freshly ground ginger.

Butlers Wharf SE1 2YE
Map GtL: D3
Tel: 020 7357 9001
Fax: 020 7357 9002
E-mail:
clipper@bengalrestaurants.co.uk
Cost: Alc £20, set-price L/D £10.☺ H/wine £9.95
Times: Noon-3pm/6-11.30pm.
Closed 26 Dec
Additional: Sunday L; Children welcome
Style: Modern
Smoking: Air conditioning

Directions: By Tower Bridge.
⊖ Tower Hill

Bentley's ❀❀

Fish and seafood are the business at Bentley's, as they have been since 1916. The upstairs restaurant has a traditionally English feel, with its banquettes and booths, pictures on the walls, white-clothed tables and quality crockery. And while angels-on-horseback, Dover sole meunière and cod and chips with tartare sauce are as traditional as the surroundings, the kitchen moves with the times too. Tiger prawns are grilled with garlic and chilli, seared scallops are partnered by white beans, chorizo and red peppers, and crayfish goes into gnocchi along with wild mushrooms and basil oil. Generally a restraining hand is behind the mixing and matching of flavours, and timing and the quality of ingredients are never in doubt. Mussel soup is gently spiked with coriander, while a summer main course of herb-roasted bream with herbed asparagus and Jersey Royals, followed by summer fruit soup with fromage frais ice cream were felt to be perfect examples of seasonality at its best. Meat-eaters are not entirely ignored, and the set-price menu is good value. The wine list is an interesting assortment, with the ten sold by the glass or bottle a good bet.

11-15 Swallow Street W1R 7HD
Map: C3
Tel: 020 7734 4756
Fax: 020 7287 2972
Chef: Jamie Kimm
Owner: Giuseppe F Dewilde
Cost: Alc £30, set-price L £14.75/D £19.50. H/wine £17.85
Times: Noon-3pm/6-11.30pm.
Closed 25 Dec, 1 Jan
Additional: Vegetarian dishes not always available
Seats: 70. Private dining room 16. Jacket & tie preferred
Style: Classic/Traditional
Smoking: No-smoking area

Directions: ⊖ Piccadilly Circus. Swallow Street links Regent St & Piccadilly and is opposite St James's Church on Piccadilly

Bibendum 🏵🏵🏵

Michelin House 81 Fulham Road
SW3 6RD
Map: A1
Tel: 020 7581 5817
Fax: 020 7823 7925
E-mail: manager@bibendum.co.uk
Chef: Matthew Harris
Owners: Sir Terence Conran,
Lord Hamlyn, Simon Hopkinson,
Graham Williams
Cost: H/wine £11.95·
Times: 12.30-3pm/7-11.30pm.
Closed Xmas
Additional: Sunday L; Children
welcome
Seats: 72
Style: Classic/Formal

The roly-poly figure on the front of the building is one of the
area's most distinctive landmarks. The comfortable, first-floor
dining room (above the oyster bar) is always a fun place to eat,
although the wall tables for two are perhaps set a little too close
together. Good, enthusiastic staff and a recherché wine list all
add to the experience. There are few gimmicks in the kitchen,
just the intent to produce excellent brasserie food, albeit at
'gastronomic' prices. The choice is extensive, anything from
endives au gratin to veal chop with béarnaise sauce or deep-
fried fillet of plaice with chips and tartare sauce – plus a couple
of convivial main course dishes for two. Good olives and bread
set the right tone, followed, on our inspection visit, by a Parma
ham and sage salad with a punchy sauce. A touch heavy on the
sage, it was nothing compared to the 'high as a kite' roast
grouse with bread sauce. Perhaps a better choice would have
been the calves' sweetbreads with garlic parsley and ceps or the
grilled lobster 'en persillade'. Chocolate fondant with prunes in
Armagnac was well conceived.

Directions: ⊖ South Kensington

Bice 🏵🏵

13 Albemarle Street W1X 3HA
Map: C3
Tel: 020 7409 1011
Fax: 020 7493 0081

Telephone for further details.

The first Bice opened in Milan in 1926, now there are twenty in
places like Beverly Hills, Paris and Tokyo; this fashionable
Italian is in the basement of DKNY, almost opposite Brown's
Hotel in exclusive Mayfair. The decor has a restrained 1920s
feel, with pale wood panelling (matching chair backs have a
simple, elegant curve), banquettes line the walls and there's a
bevelled mirror frieze above. At lunchtime the place is
dominated by regulars – there's a weekly changing menu in
addition to the *carte* to keep them happy. Service is quietly
attentive and watchful. The menu – in Italian with English
translations – is full of familiar favourites: Parma ham with
melon, linguine alle vongole (mussels), risotto al tartufo nero
(black truffles), zuppa di verdra (minestrone), veal cutlet
Milanese style, pannacotta with caramelised pear in red wine,
tiramisu, along with dishes offering a more modern slant.
Cooking is very sound and reliable. An all Italian wine list
(apart from champagne) is arranged by region with a wide
price range and a reasonable choice by the glass. Good breads,
coffee and espresso.

Directions: Off Piccadilly, near Old Bond Street. ⊖ Green Park

Birdcage of Fitzrovia ✿✿

110 Whitfield Street
W1P 5RU
Map: C3
Tel: 020 7323 9655
Fax: 020 7323 9616
Chef: Michael Von Hruschka
Owners: Michael Von Hruschka &
Caroline Faulkner
Cost: Set-price L £26.50/D £38.50.
H/wine £20
Times: Noon-2.30pm/6-11.30pm.
Closed L Sat, all Sun
Additional: Children welcome
Seats: 32
Style: Eclectic
Smoking: No-smoking area

Unquestionably one of the most unusual restaurants in
London – or anywhere else for that matter. The interior is a
knick-knack packed cross between Chinese palace, Arabic
souk, bedouin tent and Japanese tea house, an ensemble that
works strangely well. The food is equally idiosyncratic – fusion
taken to an extreme with elements of Thai, Japanese, French
and Indian and a weird and wonderful list of ingredients that
make it virtually impossible to categorise. A 'Tryptich of squid'
sounded ironic verging on silly, but the title actually worked
with a trio of intense squid ink soup, buckwheat noodles with
baby calamari, and squid and shiso leaf maki rolls with
wakame seaweed. From a choice of dishes labelled variously as
'ackee whitefish in paperbark with lavender drenched potato'
or 'seaweed porcini and hemp risotto with coriander
mascarpone', the inspector went for broke with the night's
special, the 'Jabberwocky Surprise'. He who dares wins – and
the reward was a superb Thai green chicken curry with lime
rice, despite being a little heavy-handed on the fish sauce and
limes. Pudding, a 'naughty sherry-laced biscotti and ginger
trifle' was less Mrs than Signora Beeton and none the worse
for that. *Most eccentric wine list (see page 18).*

Directions: ⊖ Goodge Street

Bistro 190 ✿
Fish Restaurant at 190 ✿✿

Two very different restaurants under one roof. The
immensely popular Bistro 190 is on the ground floor of the
Gore Hotel. The light, high-ceilinged room has huge windows
overlooking Queensgate, walls are strewn with old prints and
large mirrors while the atmosphere is comfortably relaxed.
Main courses might include veal shank braised with tomato,
coriander and a lemon, parsley and garlic gremolata,
alternatively red mullet saltimbucca with green onion mash
and beurre noire. Summer pudding is a simple option for
dessert. To reach Fish 190 you need to go through the
clamorous bar opposite the bistro, and head downstairs
where the atmosphere is more subdued. The decor is
reminiscent of a gentleman's club with spotlit tables and wall
panelling. The menu naturally features mainly fish dishes with
langoustine, lobster, scallops and sea bass for example. The
wine list offers a global choice.

190 Queen's Gate SW7 5EU
Map: A1
Tel: 020 7581 5666
Fax: 020 7581 8172

Telephone for further details

Directions: Next to Gore Hotel on
Queensgate. ⊖ South Kensington

The Black Truffle ❀❀

40 Chalcot Road NW1 8LS
Map GtL: C4
Tel: 020 7483 0077

Telephone for further details

The latest among a popular little group of Italian
neighbourhood restaurants, including the Red Pepper and the
Purple Sage. This one is aptly named, with its cool black
laminated tables, black walls, black silk venetian blinds, and
suited staff – there was even one truffled dish on the menu.
Olive-studded ciabatta and fresh, soft focaccia with extra virgin
green olive oil and buffalo Mozzarella came with a variety of
cold grilled vegetables – great ingredients and big flavours.
From the pasta and rice selection, pan-fried ravioli filled with
pheasant mince was glazed with Parmesan and topped with
wonderful black truffle. Other options included saffron and
marrowbone risotto, and sea bream with olive paste. The
highlight was a lovely chocolate fondant with a deep chocolate
filling and some sharp fresh berries.

Directions: Telephone for directions

Bluebird ❀❀

350 King's Road SW3 5UU
Map: B1
Tel: 020 7559 1000
Fax: 020 7559 1111
Chef: Andrew Sargent
Owner: Conran Restaurants
Cost: Alc £32, set-price L & D £12.75
& £15.75. ☺ H/wine £12.75
Times: Noon-3.30pm (Sat & Sun
brunch, 11-4pm)/6-11pm (10.30pm
Sun)
Additional: Sunday brunch; Children
welcome
Seats: 240.
Private dining rooms 20-42
Style: Modern/contemporary
Smoking: Air conditioning

Bluebird is part of a complex including a flower shop, café,
kitchen shop and exclusive supermarket housed in a listed
building dating from 1923. The 240-seater restaurant, on the
first floor, is suspended from the steel roof structure, with
giant bluebird kites soaring overhead. A cathedral-like nave
runs down the centre of the room and a continuous roof light
the length of the restaurant. A starter of pan-fried foie gras
was quickly seared to give a succulent centre and a hint of
crispiness to the outside. Rump of lamb, pink and tender,
was set on a creamy sauce soubise with good boulangère
potatoes and additional vegetables taken as side orders.
Pudding was a classic crème brûlée; classics get a good
showing here, including chicken Kiev, entrecote steak with
sauce béarnaise, and Chateaubriand with matchstick
fries.

Directions: ⊖ Sloane Square

Blue Print Café ❀

The Design Museum Shad Thames
Street SE1 2YD
Map: G3
Tel: 020 7378 7031
Fax: 020 7357 8810
Cost: Alc £28.50. ☺ H/wine £14.50

*Treat yourself to lunch in this stylish Conran Restaurant set in the
Design Museum with unrivalled views of the Thames. The menu
changes twice a day, but you can expect modern British and
Mediterranean food.*

Times: Noon-3pm/6-11pm. Closed D Sun, 25 Dec
Additional: Sunday L; Children welcome
Style: Bistro-style/Modern
Smoking: Air conditioning

Directions: SE of Tower Bridge, on mezzanine of the Design
Museum

Blues Bistro & Bar ❀

42-43 Dean Street
W1V 5AP
Map:
Tel: 020 7494 1966
Fax: 020 7494 0717
E-mail: info@bluesbistro.com

*Set in the heart of Soho, Blues is a friendly and efficient New York
style restaurant offering good quality modern global cuisine. The
seared fillet of tuna with Asian greens and wasabi comes well
recommended.*

Directions: From Shaftesbury Ave into Dean St, past Old Compton St, 20yds on L

Blues Bistro & Bar

Cost: *Alc* £25, set-price L £15. ☺
H/wine £11
Times: Noon-3.30pm/5.30-11.30pm.
Closed L Sat & Sun, Bhs
Additional: Bar food; Children
welcome
Style: Chic/Modern
Smoking: No pipes & cigars; Air
conditioning

Boisdale ✿

Victorian establishment with mahogany panelling, Corinthian columns, tartan upholstery and Scottish cooking. Features include live trad jazz, over 200 single malts and a huge selection of Cuban cigars.

Additional: Bar food; Sunday L
Style: Classic/traditional
Smoking: Air conditioning

Directions: ⊖ Victoria

15 Eccleston Street SW1W 9LX
Map: C2
Tel: 020 7730 6922
Fax: 020 7730 0548
E-mail: info@boisdale.co.uk
Cost: *Alc* £30, set-price L/D £12.90 &
£17.45. ☺ H/wine £15
Times: Noon-2.30pm/7-11pm.
Closed L Sat, all Sun, Bhs

Bombay Bicycle Club ✿

Appealing Indian restaurant with wall murals, bentwood chairs, flowers and palms. Pasanda khybari comprised thin slices of lamb in a creamy sauce, while a Madras fish curry packed quite a punch.

Directions: ⊖ Clapham South

95 Nightingale Lane SW12 8NX
Map: G3
Tel: 020 8673 6217
Fax: 020 8673 9100

Telephone for further details

The Brackenbury ✿

Local restaurant in Brackenbury Village serving honest and robust cooking – duck soup, sea bass with Jerusalem artichoke purée, and sticky toffee pudding and custard.

Additional: Bar food; Sunday L; Children welcome
Style: Informal/Rustic
Smoking: No pipes & cigars

Directions: Off Goldhawk Road. ⊖ Hammersmith & Goldhawk Road

129-131 Brackenbury Road W6 0BQ
Map Gtl: C3
Tel: 020 8748 0107
Fax: 020 8741 0905
Cost: *Alc* £25, set-price L £10.50 &
£12.50. ☺ H/wine £10.50
Times: Noon-2.45pm/7-10.45pm.
Closed L Sat, D Sun

Brown's Hotel, 1837 ✿✿

Brown's is the oldest hotel in London, and the first to have a dining room. It retains its traditional style and quality appointments, though the menu is modern and imaginative, supported by an incredible wine list. The inspector chose one of the four grazing menus, which offer the opportunity to

Albemarle Street Mayfair
W1X 4BP
Map: C3
Tel: 020 7408 1837
Fax: 020 7408 1838
Chef: Andrew Turner
Owner: Raffles International

Brown's Hotel, 1837

Cost: *Alc* £36-£45, set-price L £19 &
£24/D £36. ☺ H/wine £20
Times: 12.30-2pm/7-10.30pm.
Closed L Sat, all Sun, Bhs
Additional: Bar food L; Children
welcome
Seats: 60. Private dining room 12
Style: Classic/traditional
Smoking: No-smoking area; Air
conditioning
Civil licence: 60
Accommodation: 118 en suite
★ ★ ★ ★

sample more of what is offered on the *carte* in smaller portions.
In this case it was the nine-course option kicking off with
ravioli of bluefin tuna, with basil purée and tomato and tuna
consommé. A theatrical dish, with the ravioli served in a
cocktail glass and the consommé in a cafetière, which is then
plunged and poured over the pasta. Other highlights were a
seared Landes foie gras with mango and essence of truffle, and
soufflé Suissesse served as a savoury at the end of the meal.

Directions: Main entrance in
Albemarle Street, off Piccadilly.
⊖ Piccadilly Circus, Green Park

Buchan's ❀

62-64 Battersea
Bridge Road
SW11 3AG
Map GtL: C2
Tel: 020 7228 0888
Fax: 020 7924 1718
Cost: *Alc* £25, set-price L £9.50 ☺
H/wine £10.50
Times: Noon-2.45pm/7-10.45pm.
Closed 25 & 26 Dec, 1 Jan, Good Fri,
Easter Mon
Additional: Bar food; Sunday L;
Children welcome
Style: Bistro-style/informal
Smoking: Air conditioning

*Traditional Scottish dishes (haggis, neeps and tatties) cohabit happily
with modern international cuisine such as chargrilled loin of tuna
with balsamic-dressed roquette salad. Wine bar conveniently
attached for pre/post prandial refreshment.*

Directions: 200yds S of Battersea
Bridge. ⊖ Sloane Square, South
Kensington

Butlers Wharf Chop House ❀

*Stylish all wood interior reminiscent of a pavilion or boathouse.
Cuisine is staunchly British in tone, with dishes such as poached
halibut and steak and kidney pudding setting a high standard. Best
Restaurant Group wine list (see page 18).*

Additional: Bar food; Sunday L; Children welcome
Style: Informal/Traditional
Smoking: Air conditioning

Directions: On river front, on SE side of Tower Bridge

The Butlers Wharf Building
36e Shad Thames SE1 2YE
Map: D3
Tel: 020 7403 3403
Fax: 020 7403 3414
Cost: *Alc* £30, set-price L £19.75 &
£23.75. ☺ H/wine £14.50
Times: Noon-3pm/6-11pm.
Closed L Sat (ex Bar), D Sun

Cadogan Hotel ❀❀

75 Sloane Street SW1X 9SG
Map: B2
Tel: 020 7235 7141
Fax: 020 7245 0994
E-mail: info@cadogan.com
Chef: Graham Thompson
Owner: Historic House Hotels Ltd
Cost: *Alc* £43, set-price L £18.90/D £27. ☺ H/wine £13.50
Times: Noon-2pm/5.30-10pm. Closed L Sat

Both Lillie Langtry and Oscar Wilde were regulars at the Cadogan, and the hotel's decor still catches the atmosphere of the late-Victorian/early-Edwardian era. The restaurant is a comfortable room, with upholstered chairs at well-spaced tables, leaded windows and plasterwork, and plates and paintings hanging on the walls. The kitchen moves with the times, offering mille-feuille of red mullet, aubergine and langoustine, rack of lamb in tarragon jus with polenta and aubergine confit, and grilled sea bass with chorizo and basil oil. Even luxury ingredients are given modish treatments – lobster goes into ravioli with flat beans, seared scallops are dressed with orange and cardamom – while among puddings lemon soufflé comes with lime and basil sorbet, and figs are roasted with rosemary and served with Mascarpone ice cream. The wine list is wide-ranging, with a decent showing of half-bottles.

Additional: Bar food; Sunday L; Children 8+
Seats: 40. Private dining room 36.
Style: Traditional
Smoking: No pipes & cigars; Air conditioning
Civil licence: 30
Accommodation: 65 en suite ★★★★

Directions: ⊖ Sloane Square, Knightsbridge

Le Café du Marché ❀

Popular friendly rustic French restaurant with exposed ceiling rafters, wooden floor and red brick walls. Expect delicacies such as tarte Tatin de foie de canard au raisin, and filet de boeuf sauce au poivre.

Charterhouse Mews
Charterhouse Square
EC1M 6AH
Map: E5
Tel: 020 7608 1609
Fax: 020 7336 7459

Cost: *Alc* £26, set-price L/D £24.45. H/wine £9
Times: Noon-2.30pm/6-10pm. Closed L Sat, all Sun, 24 Dec-1 Jan
Additional: Children welcome
Style: Rustic
Smoking: Air conditioning

Directions: ⊖ Barbican

Cambio de Tercio

163 Old Brompton Road SW5 0LJ
Map: A1
Tel: 020 7244 8970
Fax: 020 7373 8817

Telephone for further details

Bullring colours, accessories and photographs provide the decorative theme for this modern Spanish restaurant. A particular feature of the menu is a special ham from rare-breed, acorn-fed black pigs.

Directions: Close to junction with Drayton Gardens.
⊖ Gloucester Road

Cannizaro House ❀❀

West Side Wimbledon Common
SW19 4UE
Map GtL: C2
Tel: 020 8879 1464
Fax: 020 8879 7338
E-mail: cannizaro.house@thistle.co.uk
Chef: Pascal Vallée
Owner: Thistle Hotels plc
Cost: *Alc* £51, set-price L/D £29.75.
☺ H/wine £16.95
Times: Noon-2.30pm/7-11.30pm
Additional: Sunday L; Children 12+
Seats: 50. Private dining room 100.
Jacket & tie preferred
Style: Country house/formal
Smoking: No-smoking area; No pipes
& cigars
Civil licence: 60
Accommodation: 45 en suite ★★★★

Impressive house a few miles from the centre of London set in mature landscaped grounds. The elegant restaurant with its massive crystal chandelier leads out onto the terrace, where pre-dinner drinks are served in summer. Tables are dressed with crisp white linen adorned with floral arrangements, and piano music drifts in from the adjoining drawing room, where a log fire burns in the cooler months. Traditional service with trolleys and cloches is provided by attentive young staff, and there is a detailed wine list which tends to concentrate on classics. A starter of guinea fowl in a light puff pastry was served with glazed artichoke and turned vegetables lifted by a lovely balsamic and juniper dressing. Baked loin of lamb was correctly cooked, moist and tender, and a beautifully presented pistachio crème brûlée proved a stunning dessert set off by a slice of deep-fried pineapple.

Directions: From A3 (London Rd) Tibbets Corner, take A219 (Parkside) R into Cannizaro Rd, then R into West Side

Cantina del Ponte

Simply styled Mediterranean-themed restaurant with wooden tables, terracotta tiled floors and views onto Tower Bridge and the Thames. Linguini clams, beef fillet tagliata, and pannacotta and mixed berry compote were all fresh, accurately cooked and highly enjoyable.

Additional: Sunday L; Children welcome
Style: Informal/Modern
Smoking: Air conditioning

Directions: SE side of Tower Bridge, by riverfront

The Butlers Wharf Building
36c Shad Thames SE1 2YE
Map GtL: G3
Tel: 020 7403 5403
Fax: 020 7403 0267
Cost: Alc £20. ☺ H/wine £11.95
Times: Noon-3pm/6-11pm.
Closed D Sun, 25 Dec

Cantina Vinopolis

A huge modern glass building houses the Vinopolis Gallery and the Cantina restaurant. Inside, bare brick walls arch across the huge vaulted roof above terracotta floor tiles and burgundy seating. A shelf filled with wine bottles runs the entire way around the vast two-roomed restaurant, and staff wear white T-shirts or shirts to denote rank, and long green aprons. The quality of the cooking is immediately obvious, as is the freshness of the ingredients. Chargrilled asparagus and artichoke hearts with rocket and lemon mayonnaise perfectly fitted the bill at a recent lunch, with everything bursting with flavour. Seared blue fin tuna was simply served on sliced warm new potatoes with a tomato confit and chorizo salad, and this combination also drew praise for its excellent quality and timing. Vanilla bean pannacotta with summer fruit minestrone was superb in texture and execution, the fruit en poached peaches and raspberries in a red fruit coulis. The brasserie-style menu offers some dishes, notably salads and pastas, which can double as starter or main course, and the prices are sensible.

Directions: ⊖ London Bridge

1 Bankside SE1
Map: F3
Tel: 020 7940 8333
Fax: 020 7940 8334
Chef: Jason Whitelock
Owners: Trevor Gulliver,
Claudio Pulze
Cost: Alc £35. ☺ H/wine £12
Times: Noon-3pm/6-10.30pm.
Closed D Sun
Additional: Children welcome
Seats: 180
Style: Classic

The Capital

Basil Street Knightsbridge SW3 1AT
Map: B2
Tel: 020 7589 5171
Fax: 020 7225 0011
E-mail:
reservations@capitalhotel.co.uk
Chef: Eric Chavot
Owner: David Levin
Cost: Alc £54, set-price L £24.50/D
£60. H/wine £14.50

A façade by Viscount Linley of hand-made casements enclosing engraved windows designed by a French master craftsman says a lot about the thought that has gone into everything at this luxury hotel behind Harrods. The restaurant, decorated in natural shades, is of understated elegance, with two large gilded mirrors at either end with displays of turned wooden bowls and other artefacts. Chef Eric Chavot applies his own style and ingenuity to the classic French repertoire, mixing and matching to produce some happy marriages. A lightly textured boudin of foie gras is successfully partnered with pearl barley risotto, and another starter, of slivers of tuna carpaccio stacked on leaves with blobs of intense beetroot purée with 'wonderful' scallop beignets, all sitting on sweet, spicy and hot shredded white radish, has been described as 'a delightful dish'. Skill with top-rate produce shines out of main courses too. Breasts and legs of pan-fried pigeon, tender and flavoursome, have been 'cooked to perfection'; in this case they were accompanied by a pool of petits pois and baby broad beans with an intense meat jus. Monkfish is modishly roasted with Serrano ham, and gigot of rabbit is cooked with calamari, but Chavot is equally at home turning out retro-sounding beef bourguignon, or shepherd's pie made with fillet of lamb. Puddings are 'wonderful', as in a chocolate bombe with spicy apricot purée and banana ice cream, or layers of coffee ice cream, caramel mousse and coffee cream. Praise is piled on appetisers – a 'magnificent' fat, hot oyster on scrambled egg – and breads, and service is professional, with a friendly and helpful sommelier.

Directions: Between Harrods and Sloane Street.
⊖ Knightsbridge

Times: Noon-2.30pm/7-11pm (10.30pm Sun)
Additional: Bar food; Sunday L; Children 6+
Seats: 35. Private dining room 10-24
Style: Chic/formal
Smoking: No pipes & cigars; Air conditioning
Accommodation: 48 en suite ★ ★ ★ ★

AA Wine Shortlisted for *Award–see page* 18

Le Caprice ❀❀❀

Tucked away between The Ritz and the NCP, Le Caprice is not so much a restaurant as an institution. Its continued success, attracting stars and star-struck alike, is maintained by a versatile menu, the quality and modernity of its cooking, plus great service and atmosphere. Decor is plain white, punctuated by black and white stills of the famous. The counter is comfortable and equally popular with diners as the mirror facing means you can watch the world go by unobserved. Mix and match as you please. There are no rules or table etiquette – if you want three starters or two puddings, well, go ahead and order them. Our inspector, however, kept to a conventional approach, starting with dressed Cornish crab with land cress spiced with mustard and some oiled green leaves, a fabulous combination of freshness and flavour combinations. Tender, grilled baby squid was served Maghreb-style with cumin and coriander flavoured braised chickpeas and tiny, spicy chorizo sausages. Other dishes range from eggs Benedict to honey-baked ham hock with colcannon and mustard sauce. Finish with a suitably theatrical experience – baked Alaska over which Kirsch is poured at the table, then set alight. Applause all round.

Directions: ⊖ Green Park. Arlington St runs beside the Ritz, Le Caprice is at the end

Arlington House Arlington Street
SW1A 1RT
Map: C3
Tel: 020 7629 2239
Fax: 020 7493 9040
Chefs: Mark Hix, Elliot Ketley
Owners: Jeremy King, Christopher Corbin, Belgo Group plc
Cost: Alc £30-£35. H/wine £11.50
Additional: Children welcome
Seats: 80
Style: Classic/Modern
Smoking: No pipes; Air conditioning

Caraffini ❀❀

Attractive Italian restaurant where pale yellow walls are hung with blue-framed photographs and prints, and blue fabrics and white linen set off matching flower arrangements. The recently installed acoustic ceiling has dramatically reduced the noise level, which has been the cause of criticism in the past. Kick off with antipasti or salads, maybe tiny squid tossed with petit pois, chilli, tomato and polenta, or chargrilled vegetables flavoured

61-63 Lower Sloane Street
SW1W 8DH
Map: B2
Tel: 020 7259 0235
Fax: 020 7259 0236
Chefs: John Patino, Serafino Ramalhoto
Owners: Frank di Rienzo, Paolo Caraffini

with truffle oil. Among the pasta and rice options you'll find linguine in clam sauce, ravioli of ricotta and spinach with rocket and asparagus, and a risotto alla marinara with fresh seafood. A good choice of fish and meat dishes includes chargrilled monkfish with green parsley sauce, and fillet of veal pan-fried with wild mushrooms.

Directions: Sloane Square

Catch

The name indicates a fishy theme to this newcomer, but meat dishes are also well represented. Whole roasted sea bass went down well, as did a rich and gooey chocolate fondant.

Directions: Gloucester Road

The Cavendish St James's

Cost: Alc £25. ☺ H/wine £9.95
Times: 12.15-2.30pm/6.30-11.30pm. Closed Sun, Bhs
Additional: Children welcome
Seats: 70
Style: Informal/chic
Smoking: Air conditioning

158 Old Brompton Road SW5
Map: A1
Tel: 020 7370 3300

Telephone for further details

81 Jermyn Street
SW1Y 6JF
Map: D3
Tel: 020 7930 2111
Fax: 020 7839 2125
Cost: Alc £25, set-price L & D £25.
☺ H/wine £12.95
Times: Noon-2.30pm/6-10.30pm. Closed L Sat & Sun
Additional: Bar food; Children welcome
Style: Informal/Modern
Smoking: No-smoking area; No pipes & cigars; Air conditioning
Accommodation: 251 en suite
★ ★ ★ ★

Hotel restaurant where consistent European menu with significant Spanish influence produces dishes such as cutlet of wild boar on a chive and leek mash with a port sauce. Decor is modern and service informal and friendly.

Directions: Green Park, Piccadilly Circus

Caviar House

Just down the road from the Ritz, this is an unashamedly expensive restaurant for the celebration of caviar. Pass through the small shop, perhaps, to the diminutive restaurant with its modern decor, light colours, mirrors and windows looking out onto Piccadilly. Come here in the mood to splash out; seven different kinds of caviar are offered by the spoon (starting around £8 and climbing fast), served with blinis, sour cream and new potatoes. Luxuries abound: first-rate foie gras terrine with a Sauternes jelly and toasted brioche; steamed sea bass with confit of leeks, champagne sauce and sevruga (just a coffee spoon full). Somewhat uninspiring desserts feature the likes of raspberry tart with vanilla ice cream, so why not try a caviar course instead. There's a two course set menu that helps keep the bill to a gasp rather than a heart attack. Surprisingly, the short but well-chosen wine list offers a number of imaginative bottles under the £20 mark, as well as famous names and a smattering of halves and by-the-glass.

161 Piccadilly W1V 9DF
Map: C3
Tel: 020 7409 0445
Fax: 020 7493 1667

Telephone for further details

Directions: Green Park

Chapter Two ❀❀

43-45 Montpelier Vale Blackheath
Village SE3 0TJ
Map GtL: E3
Tel: 020 8333 2666
Fax: 020 8355 8399
Chef: Adrian Jones
Owner: Selective Restaurants Group
Cost: Set-price L £18.50/D
£19.50(£22.50 Fri & Sat). ☺
H/wine £13.50
Times: Noon-2.30pm/6.30-10.30pm.
Closed 1-4 Jan
Additional: Sunday L; Children 1+
Seats: 70
Style: Chic
Smoking: No-smoking area; No pipes
& cigars; Air conditioning

Bright, modern and convivial – this enthusiastic venture hits all
the right marks with atmosphere. The culinary approach is
equally successful with the menu offering sound modern British
style cuisine that takes in venison sausage, basil mash, truffle
sauce, grilled salmon and even mushy peas. Dishes are simple
and direct but well composed. For example trio of pork with a
warm new potato salad and roast spring onions, or red mullet
with basil risotto and baby spinach. The dessert menu might
feature the likes of raspberry trifle with passion fruit cream, or
champagne sorbet with a caramel orange. The strength of the
main dishes is fully complemented by quality in the details: the
bread is some of the finest our inspector had eaten, the wine list
short and modern and the coffee rich and luxuriant.

Directions: In centre of Blackheath village

Chelsea Village Hotel ❀

Although there is an abundance of eateries within this palatial
complex, it was the Kings Brasserie that caught our eye as providing
especially cosmopolitan, modern and skilfully cooked food, such as
an evenly balanced wild mushroom risotto.

Smoking: No-smoking area; Air conditioning
Civil licence: 50
Accommodation: 300 en suite ★★★★

Directions: From ⊖ Fulham Broadway, turn L, 300yds on L

Stamford Bridge
Fulham Road SW6 1HS
Map: A1
Tel: 020 7565 1435
E-mail:
reservation@chelseavillage.co.uk
Cost: Alc £25, set-price L £12.75/D
£15.75. ☺ H/wine £12.95
Times: Noon-2.30pm/6-10.30pm
Additional: Bar food; Sunday L;
Children welcome
Style: Bistro-style/Modern

Chesterfield Hotel ❀

A comfortable and inviting restaurant in a luxurious and
sophisticated hotel. The 'pre-theatre' menu offers duck tortelloni
with kumquat, borlotti beans and fennel. The more comprehensive
standard carte includes escalopes of monkfish and lobster on a
champagne sabayon.

Smoking: No-smoking area; No pipes & cigars; Air conditioning
Civil licence: 100
Accommodation: 110 en suite ★★★★

Directions: ⊖ Green Park. Bottom of Berkeley Square, on
corner of Charles Street & Queen Street

35 Charles Street Mayfair W1X 8LX
Map: C3
Tel: 020 7491 2622
Fax: 020 7491 4793
E-mail: reservations@
chesterfield.redcarnationhotels.com
Cost: Alc £25, set-price L £12.50/(pre
theatre) D £15.50. ☺ H/wine £16
Times: Noon-2.30pm/5.30-11pm.
Closed L Sat
Additional: Bar food L; Sunday L
Style: Classic/Traditional

Chez Bruce ❀❀❀

There is a deceptive simplicity to Bruce Poole's cooking. He knows just how to combine top quality produce with spot-on, big flavours, always delivering exactly what is promised. Dishes are immediate appetite-sharpeners: stuffed saddle of rabbit and pig's trotter with endive and mustard; assiette of lamb with minted new potatoes and baby carrots; or prune and almond tart with Jersey cream. There are also bistro classics such as filet de boeuf with frites and sauce béarnaise. Deep-fried squid with tartare sauce was as crisp and fresh as you can get. Artichokes and sage combined unusually well to give another layer of interest to tender, pot roast shin of veal with perfectly timed saffron risotto milanese. It was a tough call between the Valrhona chocolate tart and the warm and creamy, vanilla-rich rice pudding with poached pears. The restaurant itself is modern in style with wooden flooring, a light colour scheme and contemporary prints. Tables are smartly appointed with crisp linen and small potted plants. Service, from a predominantly French waiting staff, is both friendly and attentive. A high quality, user-friendly wine list is divided into red and white types, helpfully sorted by price.

Directions: 2 mins walk from Wandsworth Common (BR). ⊖ Balham (5 mins)

2 Bellevue Road Wandsworth
Common SW17 7EG
Map GtL: C2
Tel: 020 8672 0114
Fax: 020 8767 6648
Chef: Bruce Poole
Owners: Bruce Poole,
Nigel Plats-Martin
Cost: Set-price L £21.50/D £27.50.
H/wine £12.50
Times: Noon-2pm/7-10.30pm.
Closed D Sun, 23-30 Dec, Bh Mon
Additional: Sunday L; Children
welcome at L only
Seats: 75. Private dining room 18
Style: Informal/Modern
Smoking: No pipes & cigars; Air
conditioning

Chez Max ❀❀

Discreetly situated in a quiet residential area, this basement neighbourhood local offers a bistro-style experience with attentive, friendly and knowledgeable service. The French cooking is imaginative, and the attention to detail apparent in home-marinated olives, baked olive bread and super Charentais butter. The menu is written, uncompromisingly, totally in French but staff are at hand and are happy to explain in detail. Risotto aux champignons sauvages et roquette translates in the mouth as an enjoyable risotto first course, with pronounced mushroom flavours, the rocket giving a pleasant peppery addition. Gigot de mer farcie au foie gras, orange et anchois, sauce Brouilly épicé (monkfish tail battened-out and stuffed with a rough mix of anchovies, orange and foie gras and served on a spiced, light red wine sauce), our main course on a May menu, proved over ambitious, the stuffing too overpowering and bulky for the delicate fish. A soufflé à la pistache dessert was spot on though, proving a highlight with its near perfect texture and intense pistachio flavour.

Directions: Turn of Fulham Road into Ifield Road, restaurant 500yds on L. ⊖ Earls Court

168 Ifield Road
SW10 9AF
Map: C2
Tel: 020 7835 0874
Fax: 020 7244 0618
E-mail: chezmax1@aol.com
Chef: Nick Reeves
Owners: Graham Thomson,
Steven Smith
Cost: Set-price D £29.50. H/wine £12
Times: Noon-2.30pm/7-10.30pm.
Closed Sun, Xmas, Bhs
Additional: Bar food L; Children
welcome
Style: Informal/French
Seats: 50
Smoking: No-smoking area;
Air conditoning

Chez Moi ❀❀

Perhaps it is the 'chez' in the name that makes Colin Smith and Richard Walton's long-standing restaurant sound bistro-ish, but it is certainly not that. Romantic? Yes. Deep red walls, gilt-framed mirrors, little lamps on some of the tables (lighting is well judged), it has an intimate appeal. Originally, it offered a very French menu, but about ten years ago Richard Walton started looking further afield for inspiration. However, one does not get dishes with exotic ingredients, but rather whole dishes from around the world: Indian chicken dosa, Polish

1 Addison Avenue
W11 4QS
Map GtL: C3
Tel: 020 7603 8267
Fax: 020 7603 3898
Chef: Richard Walton
Owners: Richard Walton, Colin Smith
Cost: Alc £30, set-price L £15.
H/wine £10.75
Times: 12.30-2pm/7-11pm.
Closed L Sat, all Sun, Bhs

borsch, and an authentic, successful Moroccan lamb tagine, alongside veal kidneys in mustard sauce and rack of lamb à la diable. Desserts are more familiar with petit pot au chocolat à l'orange (on the menu since opening in 1967), lemon tart (an excellent one, too), and a traditional crème brûlée. The menu does not change very much over time (the regulars complain if it does). The wine list is mainly French, with only a limited choice outside Bordeaux and Burgundy, but there's a good choice of digestifs and dessert wines by the glass.

Additional: Children welcome (no small babies)
Seats: 45
Style: Chic
Smoking: No pipes & cigars; Air conditioning

Directions: N side of Holland Park Avenue, opposite Kensington Hilton. ⊖ Holland Park

cheznico

90 Park Lane W1A 3AA
Map: B3
Tel: 020 7409 1290
Fax: 020 7355 4877

Telephone for further details

Although dishes have been simplified, standards have in no way slipped; in many ways, as chef Paul Rhodes acknowledges, this pared-down new style is harder to deliver, with no place to hide behind superflous but impressive garnishes and fripperies. Nothing will surprise but everything is excellent of its kind. Prices are remarkable for food of this quality – the dearest dish on the *carte* is a fillet of beef for £18.00. An exemplary tortellini of sweet-tasting langoustines were wrapped in the finest, most ethereally light, yellow egg pasta, served with a handsome lobster sauce. Classic osso bucco with superb Parmesan risotto was immaculate, made with melting, tender shin of veal, garnished with gremolata and served with a great, marrow-filled shin bone. Puddings are classic – lemon tart, crème brûlée, nougat glace and so on – but they can do the classics here as well as anywhere, and a chocolate tart could not have been bettered. The dining room, however, has a kind of grand, French formality which is perhaps now showing its age. The same heavyweight wine list is available with prices to match – not trimmed down as yet to match the scale of the food.

Directions: Part of Grosvenor House Hotel

Chinon Restaurant

23 Richmond Way W14 0AS
Map GtL: C3
Tel: 020 7602 5968
Fax: 020 7602 4082

Telephone for further details

Tucked away in a small row of shops at the back of Shepherds Bush, with no parking for miles, is not exactly location, location, location as the famous dictum would have it. Still, it is worth the battle with the urban elements to reach the haven that is Chinon. Subtle lighting and carefully chosen music calm the nerves, fruity red house wine and large boules of crusty bread tend to the immediate needs of the inner man or woman. The cooking is on the ball, although the kitchen seems to make life deliberately difficult for itself by offering two-in-one dishes when one would do just fine – excellent crab ravioli teamed with a pot of spicy crab bisque, for example. Other starters might include smoked salmon with fresh crab and salmon caviar or foie gras and chicken liver terrine. Dishes are described with a certain understatement but it is worth knowing that lamb with sweet and sour aubergine, harissa and potato purée is cooked French-style, almost too bloody but fatless so when served with something as powerful as harissa, taste can suffer. Pastry skills are a strength – a trembling, warm chocolate tart was served with an intense chocolate truffle and vanilla ice.

Directions: ⊖ Shepherd's Bush. Off Blythe Road which is off Shepherd's Bush Road

The Chiswick ❀

Modern, impeccably tasteful restaurant where the mixture of English and continental influenced dishes provides plenty of variety. Starters such as oysters or foie gras might give way to a main of grilled chicken breast with wild mushroom gnocchi.

Additional: Sunday L (noon-3pm); Children welcome
Style: Informal/modern
Smoking: No-smoking area; No pipes & cigars; Air conditioning

Directions: On Chiswick High Road close to junction with Turnham Green Terrace. ⊖ Turnham Green (3 mins)

131-133 Chiswick High Road
W4 2ED
Map: B3
Tel: 020 8994 6887
Fax: 020 8994 5504
E-mail: thechiswick@talk21.com
Cost: *Alc* £26, set-price L/D £9.50 & £12.95. ☺ H/wine £10.50
Times: 12.30-2.45pm/7-11pm. Closed L Sat, D Sun, 1 wk Xmas-New Year

Chor Bizarre ❀

6 Albemarle Street W1X 3HA
Map: C2
Tel: 020 7629 9802
Fax: 020 7493 7756
E-mail: cblondon@aol.com

Telephone for further details

Chor Bizarre means thieves' market – perfectly appropriate for this riot of colour, abundance of artefacts and eclectic furniture – a great setting for Indian cooking exploding with flavours.

Directions: ⊖ Green Park

Christopher's ❀

Reputedly London's first gaming house, this building now houses a three-floor American eatery. Try one of their good quality tender steaks, or alternatively grilled marinated chicken caesar salad with Parmesan and corn croutons. Best list of wines by the glass (see page 18).

Style: Classic/Italianate
Smoking: Air conditioning

Directions: 100 yds from the Royal Opera House. ⊖ Covent Garden

18 Wellington Street WC2E 7DD
Map: E3
Tel: 020 7240 4222
Fax: 020 7836 3506
E-mail: enquiries@christophers.uk.net
Cost: *Alc* £35, set-price D £14.50. ☺ H/wine £13
Times: Noon-3.30pm/5pm-midnight. Closed D Sun, Xmas/New Year
Additional: Bar food; Sunday L; Children welcome

Churchill Inter-Continental ❀❀

A big, modern room with polished wooden floors and large bar to one side, Clementine's Restaurant offers a Mediterranean-inspired selection of dishes. Sunday brunch-cum-lunch is a popular institution where eggs Benedict meets roasted Scottish beef from the Buccleuch Estate and Yorkshire pud. The dinner *carte* tempts but does not intimidate with dishes such as pumpkin and chestnut soup; pigeon and foie gras terrine; fillets

30 Portman Square W1A 4ZX
Map: B4
Tel: 020 7299 2033
Fax: 020 7299 2200
Chef: Justin Higgens
Cost: *Alc* £35, set-price L £19 & £24/D £25. ☺ H/wine £15
Times: 12.30-3pm/6-11pm (10.30pm Sun). Closed L Sat

of Dover sole wrapped in smoked bacon with watercress sauce; noisette of lamb with a butter bean and garlic purée. Vegetables are pedestrian – steamed broccoli, mange-tout and the like. A short selection of desserts includes light vanilla cheesecake with mixed berry compote. Family-friendly, there are fish fingers and chips and banana split on the good Children's Menu. Only for the under-12s, mind.

Directions: Close to Marble Arch, just off Oxford Street

Additional: Sunday L;
Children welcome
Seats: 100
Style: Mediterranean
Smoking: No-smoking area;
Air conditioning
Accommodation: 440 en suite
★ ★ ★ ★ ★

Chutney Mary
Restaurant ❀

535 Kings Road Chelsea SW10 0SZ
Map GtL: C2
Tel: 020 7351 3113
Fax: 020 7351 7694
E-mail: action@realindianfood.com
Cost: *Alc* £35-£38, set-price
L/D£12.50 & £15. ☺ H/wine £11.50
Times: 12.30-2.30pm /7-11pm.
Closed D 25 Dec
Additional: Sunday L;
Children welcome
Style: Anglo-Indian
Smoking: No-smoking area;
No pipes & cigars; Air conditioning

Smart and bright with polished gilt and copious greenery, the split level dining room and garden conservatory make for an excellent venue for high quality Indian cuisine. Lentil dumplings in a crisp pastry set a high standard.

Directions: On corner of King's Road and Lots Road; 2 mins from Chelsea Harbour. ⊖ Fulham Broadway

Cibo ❀❀

3 Russell Gardens W14 8EZ
Map GtL: C3
Tel: 020 7371 6271
Fax: 020 7602 1371
Chef: Roberto Federici
Owner: Gino Taddei
Cost: *Alc* £27.50, set-price L £12.50.
H/wine £11
Times: 12.15-2.30pm/7-11pm. Closed
L Sat, D Sun, 1 wk Xmas
Additional: Sunday L; Children
welcome; Vegetarian choice not
always available
Seats: 60. Private dining room 10 or
16
Style: Modern

Dried flower arrangements, big oil paintings and pictures with their canvases pushed out so they resemble sculptures dominate this bright, busy restaurant. The seats are comfortable, and in summer the windows are folded back so dining is almost alfresco. Menus are in Italian with English subtitles, and fish and shellfish prevail, although carnivores could choose something like bresaola with goats' cheese and then braised rabbit with polenta and mushrooms. But who needs meat when presented with a menu that takes in baby squid stuffed with lobster, breadcrumbs and herbs in a light tomato sauce, then baked monkfish with asparagus and saffron? Grilling is applied to lobster, stewing (in wine, garlic and tomatoes) to mixed shellfish (a large portion of mussels, clams, langoustines, prawns and squid), baking to whole sea bass with fresh herbs, and marinating to swordfish, served as carpaccio. Dishes are fresh-tasting and well-timed, pastas are commended, and puddings provide a 'great finish' in the shape of perhaps bouncy pannacotta with berries. The wine list, assembled by an enthusiast, is entirely Italian.

Directions: Russell Gardens is a residential area off Holland Road. ⊖ Kensington (Olympia), Shepherd's Bush

City Rhodes Restaurant ✿✿✿

1 New Street Square EC4A 3JB
Map: E4
Tel: 020 7583 1313
Fax: 020 7353 1662
Chefs: Gary Rhodes, Michael Bedford
Owners: Sodexho
Cost: A/c £65. H/wine £17.50
Times: Noon-2.30pm/6-9pm.
Closed Sat & Sun, Xmas-New Year
Additional: Children 8+
Seats: 90. Private dining room 12
Style: Chic/modern
Smoking: No pipes & cigars;
Air conditioning

Directions: Off Shoe Lane, behind
International Press Centre

Enter the ground-floor lobby, with its reminders of what a celebrity chef looks like – or this particular one anyway – and take the stairs up to the spacious first-floor restaurant, a predominantly blue space comfortably furnished in modern style. Gary Rhodes may have reinvented British cooking and made the faggot chic, but the menu here seems nowadays to be nearer mainland Europe, and the staff are largely French. That faggot is still on the menu, flavoured with foie gras and served as a starter with buttery fondant potatoes, but then so too are seared scallops bordelaise, fresh buttered noodles with Périgord truffles, and moules marinière accompanying steamed baby turbot on spinach. Euro-sceptics could stick to creamy smoked haddock kedgeree followed by braised oxtail with creamed Savoy cabbage; others might try foie gras layered with apple, then roasted 'gigot de lotte' with casseroled minestrone vegetables. Either way, there's no denying the skill at work in the kitchen using top-notch ingredients and good judgement in seasoning. Lamb shank with kidneys on a croûton was impressively tender and flavoursome, and praise has been heaped on red wine lasagne with a creamy wild mushroom sauce. Rhubarb tart with rhubarb and vanilla sorbet, and bread-and-butter pudding will warm the cockles of someone's heart, while an inspector was struck by the simplicity and precision of an open caramelised pineapple tart with matching sorbet.

Claridge's ✿✿

The restaurant at this grandest of grand hotels is a large pink-toned room with original Art Deco mirrored murals and lighting, plus bronzed and gilded doors. Polished, old-world service, and plenty of it, ensures that guests feel as pampered as they deserve – given the prices. Tournedos of beef renaissance and Grand Marnier soufflé with orange sorbet have appeared on the menus since the hotel was founded over a century ago. At lunchtime, a roast – perhaps rack of lamb – is still carved from a trolley, but the *carte* is less dyed-in-the-wool than might be expected. Truffled lobster is served with polenta and rocket, for example, and black pudding, braised shallots and crushed parsnips are the accompaniments for tournedos of Aberdeen Angus, while puddings might stretch to passion fruit pannacotta. The kitchen is equally at home, however, with classics of lobster bisque with Armagnac, Dover sole meunière and Chateaubriand with béarnaise.

Directions: At the corner of Brook & Davies Street

Brook Street W1A 2JQ
Map: C3
Tel: 020 7629 8860
Fax: 020 7499 2210
E-mail: info@claridges.co.uk
Chef: John Williams
Cost: A/c £39.50, set-price L
£29.50/D £39.50. H/wine £16.50
Times: 12.30-2.45pm/7-10.45pm
Additional: Bar food; Sunday L:
Children welcome
Seats: 100. Private dining room.
Jacket & tie preferred
Style: classic/art deco
Smoking: No-smoking area;
Air conditioning
Civil licence: 200
Accommodation: 197 en suite
★ ★ ★ ★

Clarke's

A meal at Sally Clarke's is always a model of clarity and sparkling tastes from impeccably-sourced ingredients, many grown or produced specially for the restaurant. The format remains unchanged – a set, no-choice dinner menu and a lunch menu offering the choice of one, two or three courses at set prices. The setting still retains its trademark green and cream colour scheme. The big bread basket circulates regularly, offering rye, Parmesan, apricot, olive and so on. The menu of carefully-constructed, accurately-balanced and perfectly-cooked dishes featured, on the night of our inspection, a typically vibrant salad of poached haddock, rocket, purple potato crisps, chive and horseradish dressing, followed by breast of corn-fed chicken with corn and tarragon relish, thyme polenta and young greens. Two tip-top cheeses were served with oat biscuits. For pudding, our inspector enjoyed a plum and blackberry trifle with pistachios and vanilla cream, arranged in concentric circles.

Directions: ⊖ Notting Hill Gate

124 Kensington Church Street
W8 4BH
Map GtL: C3
Tel: 020 7221 9225
Fax: 020 7229 4564
E-mail: restaurant@sallyclarke.com
Chefs: Sally Clarke, Elizabeth Payne
Owner: Sally Clarke
Cost: Set-price L £8.50-£30/D £44
Times: 12.30-2pm/7-10pm.
Closed Sat L, all Sun, 10 days Xmas,
Aug 2wks
Additional: Children welcome;
Vegetarian dishes by arrangement
Seats: 90
Style: Informal/Chic
Smoking: No-smoking area;
No pipes & cigars; Air conditioning

Club Gascon

Old Lyons tea house with marble walls, wooden floors and leather panelling. Rather than three stodgy courses, you are guided to choose a little something from each of six savoury courses. From the La Route du Sel section of cold starters, our inspector chose a superb pot au feu of duck, lavender and asparagus, then crisp fat chips with fleur de sel from Le Potager. The cuisine has a particular focus on the South-West of France, so the foie gras selection (the biggest on the menu) is no surprise, and a duck foie gras mi-cuit with piquillo pepper was good, followed by a plancha of hot baby squids, tomato and fried herbs from L'Ocean. The best dish of the day, though, came from Les Paturages – slow cooked dishes so typical of Gascony – in this case braised lamb cooked for seven hours and served with orange and crystallised garlic. The inspector flagged at the final savoury section (Le Marché), but enjoyed a superb almond pie for dessert.

Directions: ⊖ Barbican or Farringdon. Opposite Smithfield Market

57 West Smithfield EC1A 9DS
Map: F4
Tel: 020 7796 0600
Fax: 020 7796 0601
Chef: Pascal Aussignac
Owners: Pascal Aussignac,
Vincent Labeyrie
Cost: Alc £25, set-price L & D £30.
☺ H/wine £11
Times: Noon-2pm/7-10pm.
Closed L Sat, all Sun, Bhs
Additional: Children welcome
Seats: 50
Style: Stylish/contemporary
Smoking: Air conditioning

Coast Restaurant ✿✿

The large glass front on the ground floor is testament to the fact that Coast was once a car showroom. An oak parquet floor and predominantly green decor are the backdrop to an innovative, cosmopolitan approach to cooking. Caramelised pineapple crops up alongside Norfolk smoked eel with pancetta and red wine sauce – that's just for starters – and cannelloni of wild mushrooms and Swiss chard accompanies roast breast of black-leg chicken as a main course. Pasta and risotto leap off the menu, a notable dish at inspection being quail ravioli, the savoury meat counterbalanced by a light, buttery broth of peas, broad beans, pancetta and herbs: 'simply lovely'. Roasting is a favoured medium for main courses – fillet of cod with sautéed ceps and mashed potatoes, or cannon of Welsh lamb with aubergine caviar and goats' cheese – although the same skill applies to other treatments,

26b Albemarle Street W1X 3FA
Map: C3
Tel: 020 7495 5999
Fax: 020 7495 2999
Chef: Stephen Terry
Owner: Oliver Peyton
Cost: Alc £40. H/wine £13.50
Times: Noon-3pm/6pm-midnight.
Closed Sun, Bhs
Additional: Children welcome
Seats: 120. Private dining room 30
Style: Modern
Smoking: Air conditioning

as in properly-seared yellow-fin tuna, grilled medium to rare, with a lemon and thyme risotto. The sweet-of-tooth could go for something like wild strawberry trifle, a confection of fruit, whipped cream, compote and jelly. Lottery winners can choose something in four figures from the wine list, although there's a decent choice by the glass.

Directions: ✆ Green Park

The Collection ✿

264 Brompton Road SW3 2AS
Map: B1
Tel: 020 7225 1212
Fax: 020 7225 1050
Cost: *Alc* £30, set-price D £35.
H/wine £12.95
Times: Noon-3,30pm/7-12.30am.
Closed Sun L, 25, 26 Dec & 1-3 Jan
Additional: Bar food; Children welcome
Style: Eclectic/innovative
Smoking: Air conditioning

Split-level fashion warehouse renovation with a stylish interior. Beef carpaccio, roast aubergine, crispy duck, and crab cakes with seared scallops are among dishes from around the globe.

Directions: ✆ South Kensington

The Connaught ✿✿

Carlos Place W1Y 6AL
Map: C3
Tel: 020 7499 7070
Fax: 020 7495 3262
E-mail: info@the-connaught.co.uk
Chef: Michel Bourdin
Owner: The Savoy Group
Cost: *Alc* £45, set-price L £28.50/D £55. H/wine £22

If it's Monday, it must be steak, kidney and mushroom pie... The Connaught remains a bastion of unchanging, old-style luxury and quiet comfort. The Restaurant and the Grill Room, under the direction of the highly-esteemed Michel Bourdin, share the same impeccable service and exhaustive menu that combines classical French cuisine with traditional British cooking. The *carte*, written in French, is not the easiest or clearest to read, but you will find everything from caviar and oysters to 'Pâté de turbot froid au homard' and 'Filet de boeuf en croûte légère Strasbourgeoise'. A lobster, crab and langoustine cocktail with a Marie Rose sauce transformed an old dish into a memorable experience thanks to the texture, freshness and succulence of the ingredients. A huge portion of perfect, fluffy 'Crêpe soufflée Belle Epoque' rounds a meal off in suitable style. Take your time to wade through a wine list knee-deep in Premiers Crus.

Times: 12.30-2.30pm /6.30-10.45pm. (Grill Room closed L Sat)
Additional: Sunday L; Children welcome
Seats: 70 (Grill Room 35). Private dining rooms 12 & 22.
Jacket & tie preferred
Style: Traditional/Country-house
Smoking: Air conditioning
Accommodation: 90 en suite ★ ★ ★ ★ ★

Directions: On corner of Mount Street and Carlos Place.
✆ Bond Street/Green Park

Conrad International London

Completely refurbished restaurant and bar serving Mediterranean and Asian food. Renamed Aquasia, it has marine themes, water features, unimpaired views over the marina, and an open terrace in summer.

Chelsea Harbour SW10 0XG
Map GtL: C2
Tel: 020 7823 3000
Fax: 020 7351 6525
Cost: Alc £33, set-price L £17. ☺
H/wine £19.50
Times: 12.30-2.30pm/7-10.30pm
Additional: Bar food; Sunday L;
Children welcome
Style: Chic/Modern
Smoking: No-smoking area;
Air conditioning
Civil licence: 180
Accommodation: 160 en suite
★ ★ ★ ★ ★

Directions: ⊖ Fulham Broadway,
Earls Court

The Cook House

A tiny restaurant with a short four-course menu hand-painted onto the window. Excellent salmon and leek tart was followed by roast partridge with sweet chestnuts and lovely fat chips.

Directions: ⊖ Putney Bridge

56 Lower Richmond Road Putney
SW15 1JT
Map GtL: C2
Tel: 020 8785 2300

Telephone for further details

Coulsdon Manor

This sympathetically restored Victorian manor house – one-time home of Lord Byron – is set in 140 acres of attractive parkland. There's a comfortable Terrace Bar with lighter fare, though the formal Manor House Restaurant is the place for serious diners. The main carte features upmarket, country house cooking with a modern slant and showcases a wine recommendation with each dish. The repertoire could feature a pressed terrine of guinea fowl with rosemary jus to start, or hot sushi of rare seared tuna with green horseradish vinaigrette and sweet pickled vegetables. Optional middle courses may include a vegetable consommé with fresh black linguini pasta or poached egg Benedictine. Sweet potato mash, Parisenne apple, confit of vegetables and a red wine jus provide the accompaniment for pork fillet marinated in star anise, while oven-baked monkfish filled with a sun-dried tomato mousse, wrapped in cured bacon is delivered with a herb and tomato beurre blanc sauce among main course offerings. Hot chocolate fondue or coffee soufflé with a Tia Maria sabayon to finish.

Directions: M23 N until road becomes A23. After 2.5 miles, R after Coulsdon S Railway Station onto B2030 (Purley). Follow uphill 1 mile, L past pond, 0.5 mile, and turn R into Coulsdon Court Rd.

Coulsdon Court Road Croydon
CR5 2LL
Map GtL: D1
Tel: 020 8668 0414
Fax: 020 8668 3118
E-mail:
coulsdonmanor@marstonhotels.co.uk
Chef: Neil Bradshaw
Owner: Marston Hotels
Cost: Alc fr £35, set-price L £18/D
£26. ☺ H/wine £13
Times: 12.30-2pm/7-9.30pm (10pm
Fri & Sat). Closed L Sat
Additional: Bar food; Sunday L;
Children welcome
Seats: 100. Private dining room 48-
120
Style: Classic/Traditional
Smoking: No smoking in dining room
Civil licence: 130
Accommodation: 35 en suite ★ ★ ★ ★

The Criterion

Designed in 1873 by Thomas Verity, the building features London's only neo-Byzantine restaurant. The grand entrance, flanked by potted palms, leads into a vast bar topped with

224 Piccadilly W1V 9LB
Map: C3
Tel: 020 7930 0488
Fax: 020 7930 8380
Chefs: Tim Payne, Darren Bunn

great drum lamps. In the restaurant, ornate marble walls and a glittering gold mosaic arched ceiling combine to evoke images of Arabian Nights. Tarte Tatin of endive with excellent grilled scallops and balsamico made a favourable start to the meal, and a main course of guinea fowl en cocotte had perfect colour, taste and texture. Desserts were a triumph, including lemon tart with a trembling custard and tangy flavour, and a dish of red fruits in a blackberry jelly – classic Marco Pierre White – served with a lovely vanilla sabayon.

Directions: Piccadilly Circus

Owners: Marco Pierre White & Forte
Cost: *Alc* £45, set-price L & D £14.95
& £17.95. ☺ H/wine £15
Times: 12.30-2.30pm/5.30-11.30pm.
Closed L Sun, 25 Dec, 1 Jan
Additional: Children welcome
Seats: 170
Style: Classic/chic
Smoking: Air conditioning

Crowne Plaza London – Heathrow ✵

A bright, modern setting with lemon-yellow walls and well-placed modern art prints. The hotel restaurant maintains high-flying credentials – our inspector enjoyed an excellent piece of baked cod as the centrepiece of a classy meal.

Style: Informal/Modern
Smoking: No-smoking area; Air conditioning
Accommodation: 458 en suite ★ ★ ★ ★

Directions: From M25 J15 take M4. At J4 take A408. Straight on at traffic lights. Hotel on slip road on L

West Drayton Stockley Road
UB7 9NA
Map Glt: A2
Tel: 01895 445555
Fax: 01895 445122
E-mail: cplhr@netscapeon line.co.uk
Cost: *Alc* fr £21.50, set-price L/D
£20.50. ☺ H/wine £13.95
Times: 11-11pm
Additional: Bar food; Sunday L;
Children welcome

Crowthers Restaurant ✵

Intimate, refined, well cared for establishment. Dishes are well thought out and carefully executed, as demonstrated by a dish of best end of lamb in a provençale herb crust with a garlic and rosemary sauce.

Style: Classic/Traditional
Smoking: No pipes & cigars; Air conditioning

Directions: Train to Mortlake; train or tube to Richmond. Between junction of Sheen Lane & Clifford Ave

481 Upper Richmond Road West
East Sheen SW14 7PU
Map GtL: B2
Tel/Fax: 020 8876 6372
Cost: Set-price D £23.75.
H/wine £11.50
Times: D only, from 7pm. Closed L
Sat, all Sun & Mon, 1 wk Xmas, 2
wks Aug, (L by arrangement)
Additional: Children welcome

Cucina ✵✵

The warm glow of the Mediterranean is captured in the simple bright decor and the tastes and smells of the Pacific Rim by the direct, astute menu. Starters might include Turkish aubergine, coriander lavoche and crème fraîche; or deep fried beer battered sardines with tomato, fennel and caper chutney. The first two courses form a happy marriage with mains such as chargrilled salmon with saffron, tomato and parsley linguine; or polenta crusted chicken with grilled artichokes, Trevisse and Mascarpone sauce keeping the taste buds interested. Puddings continue in the theme of interesting and lively combinations. Expect baked ricotta terrine with rhubarb compote and polenta cookies or bitter chocolate tart with espresso ice cream. The wine list is extensive and informative and the cheese board includes Exmoor Blue, Waterloo and Swaledale.

Directions: Opposite Hampstead BR station. Belsize Park, Hampstead

45a South End Road NW3 2QB
Map GtL: C4
Tel: 020 7435 7814
Fax: 020 7435 7815
E-mail: cucinarestaurant@tbtmail.com
Chefs: Andrew Poole
Owners: Vernon Mascarenhas &
Andrew Poole
Cost: *Alc* £30, set-price L fr £7.95. ☺
H/wine £10.95
Times: Noon-2.30pm/7-10.30pm.
Closed D Sun, 3 days Xmas
Additional: Sunday L; Children
welcome
Seats: 60. Pivate dining room 26-30
Style: Modern
Smoking: No pipes & cigars;
Air conditioning

Dakota ❀❀

Decor-wise, less is more at this large corner restaurant: apart
from a couple of areas of timbers bound with leather thongs, all
is plain, light and smart, with banquette seating and large
square-paned windows. South-west America is the focus, with
some influences imported across the Mexican border, and the
menu, partly because it tends to name all the components of a
dish, some unfamiliar, might put off the more conservative – a
pity, as what arrives on the plate is well-conceived, coherent and
well-executed. Plump griddled scallops are well matched by
their avocado cream and citrus salsa, and roasted pasilla- and
honey-glazed best end of lamb, tender and pink, is arranged
around couscous-like quinoa salad and finished with a silky
reduced sauce of papaya, habanero and mint. Ingredients are
first-rate: rosemary-marinated monkfish, 'a beautiful bit of fish',
is perfectly cooked and accompanied by white bean and
artichoke stew. The theme continues into puddings of, say,
pineapple and rum chimichanga – 'a delicious dessert' of a
pancake-like parcel filled with purée – with orange and
poppyseed ice cream. Service is attentive and helpful, and the
wine list, arranged by style, has around a dozen sold by the glass.

Directions: ⊖ Notting Hill Gate. From tube take Pembridge Rd
then L into Chepstow Crescent. Over crossroads into Ledbury
Rd. Dakota on junction with Talbot Rd

127 Ledbury Road W11 2AQ
Map GtL: C3
Tel: 020 7792 9191
Fax: 020 7792 9090
E-mail: mail@dakotafood.co.uk
Chef: Jamie Osman
Owner: Hartford Group Plc
Cost: Alc £35, set-price L £17. ☺
H/wine £12
Times: Noon-3.30pm/7-11pm
Additional: Children welcome
Seats: 80. Private dining room 25
Style: Chic/contemporary
Smoking: Air conditioning

Dans Restaurant ❀❀ .

A long-established restaurant with many well-heeled locals as
regular customers. Several interconnecting rooms make up the
dining rooms, with a conservatory and mature gardens at the
end. The floors are bare, the decor cream and green, and old
farm animal prints adorn the walls. Owner Dan Whitehouse is
always present, and service under him is friendly and skilful.
Eclectic influences are evident from the frequently changing
menu, such as grilled chicken biryani with poppadum and chilli
dip; king prawn tempura with mirin and soy dip; spinach, feta
cheese, red onion and wild mushroom salad; pappardelle pasta
with asparagus, pepper and fresh basil. From this interesting
array a cream of mushroom and tarragon soup was enjoyed for
its lovely flavour, while roasted spring vegetable brochette with
parmesan and two sauces was pronounced 'excellent'. Pan-
fried monkfish fillet with nutmeg spinach, and grilled lamb
cutlets both maintained the high standard of the starters with
their freshness and accurate cooking. After such enjoyable
dishes there were no unpleasant surprises from the dessert, a
classic lemon tart, lightly caramelised and tangy.

Directions: At Kings Road end of Sydney Street.
⊖ South Kensington

119 Sydney Street SW3 6NR
Map: B1
Tel: 020 7352 2718
Fax: 020 7352 3265
Chef: Frankie Mordie
Owner: David Whitehead
Cost: Set-price L £15.50/D £25.50. ☺
H/wine £12.50
Times: 12.15-2.30pm/7.15-10.30pm.
Closed L Sat, all Sun, Xmas, Etr, Bhs
Additional: Children 4+
Seats: 50. Private dining rooms 12 &
32
Style: Informal/Chic

The Depot
Waterfront Brasserie ❀❀

A room with a view on the banks of the Thames, enjoy the
relaxed atmosphere and admire the clean, simple decor with
parquet flooring. Queen scallops served with coriander butter
and tomato dressing make a tasty starter. Fishcakes are often
on the menu in different guises, try them with smoked haddock

Tideway Yard Mortlake High Street
SW14 8SN
Map GtL: C2
Tel: 020 8878 9462
Fax: 020 8392 1361

Telephone for further details

and avocado salad, other main courses might include char-grilled calves liver with crispy pancetta champ. For dessert peach melba crème brûlée with shortbread proves an excellent combination. There is an impressive selection of reasonably priced wines including many by the glass.

Directions: Between Barnes Bridge and Mortlake train stations

The Dorchester, Grill Room

Park Lane W1A 2HJ
Map: C3
Tel: 020 7629 8888
Fax: 020 7317 6363
E-mail:
foodandbeverage@dorchesterhotel.com
Chef: Henry Brosi
Owner: Dorchester Hotel Group Ltd
Cost: A/c £40.20, set price L £29.50/D £39.50. H/wine £22
Times: 12.30-2.30pm/6-11pm
Additional: Sunday L; Children welcome
Seats: 81
Style: Classic/Traditional
Smoking: Air conditioning
Civil licence: 500
Accommodation: 248 en suite
★★★★★

This grand, world-renowned Mayfair hotel exudes style and impeccable service. The Grill's opulent Hispanic decor – reminiscent of a baroque palace – gleams; from the magnificent gilded ceiling to the candles reflecting off the polished oak tables, the red leather chairs, mini-sofas, heavy maroon curtains or beautiful tapestries – it's rich, decadent and comfortable. The Grill is a bastion of traditional British cooking, but even here times change. Since taking on the top job in the kitchen, new executive chef Henry Brosi is eager to make his mark and bring a fresh identity. New menus will have a seasonal approach and showcase truly Classic dishes along with a new selection of lighter ones. However, at our mid-May visit the new menus, though imminent, hadn't been introduced. We began with a warm bacon and onion tart with crispy aubergines, followed with escalope of sea bass served on oven roasted aubergine purée with baby fennel and a rosemary jus, and finished with home-made rice pudding with fresh raspberries – served from the trolley. Appetisers, petits fours and good coffee are all hallmarks.

Directions: Two-thirds of the way down Park Lane, fronting a small island garden. ⊖ Hyde Park Corner

The Dorchester, The Oriental

Park Lane W1A 2HJ
Map: C3
Tel: 020 7629 8888
Fax: 020 7317 6363
E-mail:
foodandbeverage@dorchesterhotel.com
Chefs: Henry Brosi, Kenneth Poon
Owner: The Dorchester Group Ltd
Cost: A/c £60, set-price L £29/D £42-£88. ☺ H/wine £22

Though those used to eating Chinese food in Hong Kong will be no strangers to grand settings, the whole experience of eating great Chinese food served impeccably by tail-coated waiters in first-class surroundings is confined to the Dorchester in Britain. That alone would make it worthy of note, but this is also food of considerable stature, and it is worth taking time to discuss with the head waiter which dishes to choose and how best to construct a balanced meal. The absence of MSG comes

The Dorchester – The Oriental

Times: Noon-2.30pm/7pm-11pm.
Closed L Sat, all Sun, Aug, Xmas &
31 Dec, Bhs
Additional: Children welcome
Seats: 81. Private dining rooms 6 – 16
Style: Modern/French
Smoking: Air conditioning
Civil licence: 500
Accommodation: 248 en suite
★ ★ ★ ★ ★

Directions: See Dorchester Grill
Room (previous entry)

as a surprise at first, but ultimately benefits the experience,
allowing flavours to ring true more effectively. A hot starter
dish of honey-cured barbecue pork was all it implied,
garnished with some exquisitely sculptured carrot. As a
contrast, cold shredded duck and chicken with fresh apricot
and onions in a peanut sauce was akin to bang-bang chicken
but given extra spin and depth. Hot-and-sour soup was
sublime, neither dimension being allowed to dominate and
both muted when compared to the typical, clumsy handling of
this dish. Fragrant stir-fried beef with lemongrass and black
pepper had the edge over an intriguing dish of braised minced
pork with silky tofu and a sea-spiced sauce. Even the rice is of
imperial grade. Excellent vegetarian choice.

English Garden Restaurant ❀❀

10 Lincoln Street SW3 2TS
Map: B1
Tel: 020 7584 7272
Fax: 020 7581 2848
Chef: Malcolm Starmer
Owner: Searcy's Corrigan Restaurant
Cost: A/c £28.50, set-price L £19.50.
☺ H/wine £12.50
Times: Noon-3pm/6-11pm
Additional: Sunday L; Children
welcome
Seats: 45. Private dining room 25-30
Style: Modern
Smoking: Air conditioning

Stylish two room restaurant in a quiet street off the King's
Road. The front room has been recently redecorated with
cream walls, dark ceiling and downlighters whilst the back
room remains unchanged with white-painted brick walls and a
large domed sky-light creating a pleasing conservatory style
atmosphere. The seasonally changing menus offer high quality
modern cuisine including starters such as cannelloni of crab
and lobster with shellfish juices, and boudin of Guinea fowl
with buttered beans and pancetta. These might reasonably be
followed by fillet of sea bass, leeks and shrimp butter; or roast
chicken with Jerusalem artichoke, taleggio and red wine.
Desserts are a particular strong point. At inspection an
individually baked gooseberry and elderflower tart
demonstrated real skill in the pastry department and good
judgement in the balancing of the filling.

Directions: ⊖ Sloane Square

L'Escargot –
The Ground Floor Restaurant ❀❀

48 Greek Street W1V 5LQ
Map: D4
Tel: 020 7439 7474
Fax: 020 7437 0790
Chef: Andrew Thompson
Owner: Jimmy Lahoud
Cost: A/c £28.15, set-price L / D (set-
price D pre-theatre only) £14.95 &
£17.95. ☺ H/wine £14

Established in 1927, The Ground Floor Restaurant exhibits
1920s original artwork from a list of Tate Modern names. The
atmosphere is animated and staff are mostly French, and
attentive if sometimes a little distant. Black banquettes and
crisp white linen are broken up by coloured glass vases filled
with bright, modern flower arrangements. Roasted scallops
were sweet and well-timed, with small and tender langoustines,

but rather mysteriously served on curried lentils with coriander salad. More successful was a deliciously succulent dish of richly flavoured braised pork cheeks and a small square of crispy belly pork. Celeriac fondant was a clever alternative to potatoes. Desserts include caramelised pineapple tart with coconut and lime sorbet. Coffee is served with snail-shaped chocolates. The lengthy wine list is well balanced and whilst it includes a good range under £25, there are a fair few at over £1,000.

Directions: ⊖ Tottenham Court Rd, Leicester Sq

L'Escargot – The Picasso Room ❀❀

If, like restaurateur Jimmy Lahoud, you happen to own a few Picassos, you might as well show them off. The intimate, discreet setting for this remarkable collection has a clubby atmosphere with smart leather tub chairs and crisp linen. An extensive wine list, the choice takes in many Burgundy and Bordeaux heavyweights, somewhat overwhelms the weekly menu du jour (if that's not a contradiction in terms), although the *carte* tries to match the gravity of the wine list. Tartlet of escargots (but of course) with wild mushrooms is made with fine pastry and given a flavour lift by a red wine poached egg. The cooking is firmly French in style: John Dory is served with wilted gem lettuce, frogs' legs and langoustine velouté, and roast mallard with a savoury Tatin of mulled shallots, wilted greens, Ratte potatoes and red wine jus. A savarin of red fruit compote made a lovely spring dessert.

The Ground Floor Restaurant

Times: 12.15-2.15pm/6-11.30pm. Closed L Sat, all Sun, 25 & 26 Dec, 1 Jan
Additional: Children welcome
Seats: 80. Private dining rooms 26-60
Style: Classic/Chic
Smoking: No pipes & cigars; Air conditioning

AA Shortlisted for Wine Award-see page 18

48 Greek Street W1V 5LQ
Map: D4
Tel: 020 7439 7474
Fax: 020 7437 0790
Chef: Dean Bouvet
Owner: Jimmy Lahoud
Cost: Set-price L £27.50/D £42. H/wine £14
Times: 12.15-2.15pm/7-11pm. Closed L Sat, all Sun & Mon, 25 & 26 Dec, 1 Jan, Aug
Seats: 30
Style: Formal
Smoking: Air conditioning

Directions: ⊖ Tottenham Court Rd, Leicester Sq

Fifth Floor Restaurant ❀❀

Harvey Nichols Knightsbridge
SW1X 7RJ
Map: B2
Tel: 020 7235 5250
Fax: 020 7823 2207
Chef: Henry Harris
Owner: Harvey Nichols Ltd
Cost: *Alc* £37.50, set-price L £23.50.
H/wine £12.50
Times: Noon-3pm (3.30pm Sat,
Sun)/6.30-11.30pm. Closed D Sun,
25 & 26 Dec
Additional: Bar food L; Sunday L;
Children welcome
Seats: 110
Style: Chic/Modern
Smoking: No-smoking area; No pipes;
Air conditioning

Ironically, as the crowds no longer queue to get in to Harvey Nicks' flagship restaurant, the food is both served in a more orderly fashion and is of better quality. Venetian blinds and glass separate diners from the lively goings-on in the food court, sushi bar and terrace café, but avoid the bar area, however, unless you're making an important fashion statement. Henry Harris has put together an attractive selection of dishes: salt cod fishcakes, pepper and lemon aïoli; tripe with black beans and chilli; pot-roasted rabbit with a Black Sheep ale gravy and herb dumplings. Flavour is to the fore in dishes such as warm salad of guinea fowl, and fegato alla veneziana. Top-class, carefully-sourced ingredients define dishes such as saffron, cockle and clam risotto, and Lincolnshire duck with smoked eel and dandelion salad. A fine selection of desserts might include pannacotta with confit of kumquats and the intriguing Guinness 'petit pot' au chocolat, although a Mejdool date custard tart would have been better served warm than straight from the fridge.

Directions: ⊖ Knightsbridge. Entrance on Sloane Street

Fire Station ❀

150 Waterloo Road SE1 8SB
Map: E2
Tel: 020 7620 2226

Former fire station by Waterloo Station, very much a pub in the outer section and a diner in the inner area. The honest cooking reflects Eastern and Mediterranean influences.

Telephone for further details

Directions: ⊖ Waterloo

Floriana ❀❀❀

15 Beauchamp Place
SW3 1NQ
Map: C3
Tel: 020 7838 1500
Fax: 020 7584 1464
Chef: Fabio Trabocchi
Owners: Riccardo Mazzucchelli,
Sami Hawa
Cost: *Alc* £45, set-price L £15
Times: Noon-4pm/6.30pm-1.30am
Additional: Bar food; Sunday L;
Children welcome
Seats: 100. Private dining room 30
Style: Modern/Italian

A serious approach to dining is evident from the moment you arrive at this smart modern Italian restaurant. Staff are immaculately dressed and silent as they work. The interior, by Emily Tod Hunter, is chic and modern with light sandstone walls, marble effects and mirrors plus shafts of daylight from the atrium roof. Banquette seating is covered with chocolate coloured hide and taupe velvet cusions. The cooking is a delight: light, flavourful and skilful. Floriana 'Classics', depending on the day of the week, include gold and saffron risotto Milanese style, and spider crab salad with fried aubergine and tomato. Other specialities, identified with an 'f' on the menu, are minestrone with 'frutti di mare', steamed sea

Floriana

Smoking: Air conditioning

bass with fresh sea urchins and steam-roasted Landais chicken with Cremonese mustard and green sauce, the mustard, sauce and accompanying consommé served in separate bowls to make a great combination and concept dish. Desserts tend more to the pan-European than the strictly Italian – the gourmet assiette was made up of chocolate fondant and lemon tart as well as pannacotta and pistachio ice cream embellished with tuile 'sails'.

Directions: ⊖ Knightsbridge

Foundation ❀❀

Just the place in which to recover after a hard morning's shopping in the emporium on the floors above, Foundation offers sleek, modern surroundings of wooden floors, polished concrete and dark blue abstract canvases. Gone is the wall of water, but the 30-foot bar remains, along with surprisingly comfortable chrome-framed dining chairs and unclothed tables with paper napkins. 'Modern Mediterranean' is how the restaurant describes its style, but the menu can jump from classics of galantine of duck ('skilfully made and as good to look at as it was to eat'), to chargrilled sirloin steak with a confit of shallots and red wine sauce. Fish is well-reported, as in 'beautifully fresh, accurately cooked' roast cod with wilted spinach, ceps and button onions served with exemplary mashed potato. Puddings might take in a light raspberry ripple cheesecake or prune and vanilla tart. Those who can't wait to get back upstairs could go for the one-course selection of salads and pastas, and wash it down with one of a dozen or so wines sold by the glass.

Directions: ⊖ Knightsbridge. Entrance off Seville Street opposite The Sheraton Hotel

Harvey Nichols Seville Street
Knightsbridge SW1X 7RJ
Map C3
Tel: 020 7201 8000
Fax: 020 7201 8080
Chef: Mark Guillain
Owners: Harvey Nichols Ltd
Cost: *Alc* £25.30. H/wine £12.50
Times: Noon-4pm. Closed D
Additional: Sunday L; Children welcome
Seats: 75
Style: Modern/chic
Smoking: No-smoking area; air conditioning

Four Seasons Hotel ❀❀

Stained glass, marbling and wood panelling in rich blue, bottle green and deep cranberry colours gives Lanes Restaurant its own distinctive look. This is enhanced by the restaurant's collection of interesting glassware and modern ice sculpture. The hotel and restaurant are famous for the wonderful views over Hyde Park and their own private garden. A selection of six breads are offered with unsalted butter. Maintaining standards in large hotels can be a problem and unfortunately

Hamilton Place
Park Lane
W1A 1AZ
Map : C3
Tel: 020 7499 0888
Fax: 020 7493 1895
Chefs: Eric Deblonde,
Shaun Whatling
Cost: *Alc* £45, set-price L £32/D £30.50. ☺ H/wine £16

two of the courses were served cold on the last visit of our inspector on a Sunday night. On the positive side a main course of beef was excellent, rare, very tender, full of flavour and the demi glace was spot on. Service is attentive and the wine list includes a large selection by the glass.

Accommodation: 220 en suite ★ ★ ★ ★ ★

Directions: ⊖ Hyde Park Corner, Green Park. Set back from Park Lane in Hamilton Place

Four Seasons Hotel Canary Wharf

Contemporary-style restaurant with a theatre kitchen set behind heat and soundproofed windows. The menu provides an imaginative choice of northern Italian dishes, supported by an Italian wine list.

Additional: bar food; Sunday L; Children welcome
Style: Chic
Smoking: No-smoking area; Air conditioning
Accommodation: 142 en suite ★ ★ ★ ★ ★

Directions: Leave A13 and follow signs for Canary Wharf/Isle of Dogs/Westferry Circus. Hotel off 3rd exit of Westferry Circus rdbt

Westferry Circus
Canary Wharf E14 8RS
Map GtL: E3
Tel: 020 7510 1999
Fax: 020 7510 1998
Cost: *Alc* £30, set-price L £24/D £28. ☺ H/wine £15
Times: Noon-3pm, 6-10.30pm

The Fox Reformed

Wine bar and something of a local institution, with a charming walled garden (heated). Chalkboard menus might offer crab cakes with sauce tartare, and bresaola with artichoke hearts.

Additional: Bar food D; Sunday L
Style: Informal
Smoking: Air conditioning

Directions: Opposite the junction with Woodlea Road

176 Stoke Newington Church Street
N16 0JL
Map GtL: D4
Tel/Fax: 020 7254 5975
Cost: *Alc* £20. ☺ H/wine £8.95
Times: 6.30-11.30pm.
Closed L Mon-Fri, 25 & 26 Dec

Frederick's Restaurant

Modern art, recently installed, gives a brighter feel to this long established restaurant in busy Camden Passage. The interiors are light and stylish with flashes of Mediterranean colour, iron-framed chairs, evenly spaced tables and polished floorboards. The garden is always popular in the summer months, a secluded area with neatly kept lawn and trees. The menu offers classical favourites with some imaginative twists. Marinated butter beans were served instead of the usual olives, and the starter comprised a crispy filo parcel of goats' cheese with roast red peppers, rocket and basil. Griddled guinea fowl glazed with Parmesan was served with simple clean-tasting risotto accompanied by humble field mushrooms. A well-executed lemon tart had rich, intensely flavoured filling and came with fresh, sharp blackberry compote.

Directions: ⊖ Angel – 2 mins walk to Camden Passage. Restaurant amongst the antique shops

Camden Passage Islington N1 8EG
Map GtL: D3
Tel: 020 7359 2888
Fax: 0202 7359 5173
Chef: Andrew Jeffs
Owner: Louis Segal
Cost: *Alc* £30, set-price L/D £12.50. ☺ H/wine £10.95
Times: Noon-2.30pm/6-11.30pm. Closed Sun, Bhs
Additional: Bar food; Children welcome
Seats: 150. Private dining rooms 20 & 32
Style: Modern/formal
Smoking: No-smoking area; Air conditioning
Civil licence: 40

Times: Noon-2.30pm/6-11pm (6.30-10.30pm Sun)
Additional: Bar food; Sunday L; Children welcome
Seats: 90. Private dining rooms 4-400
Style: Chic/Modern
Smoking: No-smoking area; Air conditioning
Civil licence: 300

French House Dining Room

Casual friendly restaurant with a rustic eclectic menu that features enjoyable food such as chicken, broad bean and rocket salad with a garlic mayonnaise, and mackerel with pickled courgette. All simple food, very well executed.

Additional: Bar food
Style: Traditional/Intimate

Directions: Above the French House pub. ⊖ Leicester Square, Piccadilly Circus

49 Dean Street W1V 5HL
Tel: 020 7437 2477
Fax: 020 7287 9109
Cost: *Alc* £25. ☺ H/wine £11
Times: Noon-3.15pm/6-11.15pm.
Closed Sun, Xmas-New Year, Bhs

Friends Restaurant

Traditional-style restaurant set in a four hundred-year-old oak-beamed building with open fireplaces and a truly welcoming atmosphere. A passion fruit vinaigrette in a dish of smoked halibut on green salad was excellent.

Directions: Follow A404 from Harrow. In the centre of Pinner.
⊖ Pinner (2 min walk)

11 High Street Pinner
HA5 5PJ
Map GtL: A4
Tel: 020 8866 0286
Cost: *Alc* £30, set-price L £16.50/D £25. H/wine £11
Times: Noon-3pm/6.30-midnight.
Closed D Sun, all Mon, 15-29 Aug
Additional: Sunday L; Children welcome
Style: Classic/Traditional
Smoking: No-smoking area; No pipes & cigars

Fung Shing Restaurant

Friendly Cantonese restaurant located in a converted Victorian warehouse in Chinatown. Enjoyable options included steamed scallops with garlic and soy, and stewed duck with plum sauce.

Additional: Sunday L; Children welcome
Style: Classic/Modern
Smoking: Air conditioning

Directions: ⊖ Leicester Square. Behind Empire Cinema

15 Lisle Street WC2H 7BE
Map : D3
Tel: 020 7437 1539
Fax: 020 7734 0284
Cost: *Alc* £14.65, set-price L /D£16.
☺ H/wine £12
Times: Noon-11.30pm.
Closed 24-26 Dec, Bh (evening only)

The Gate ✸✸

A beautiful wrought-iron gate leads to the concealed courtyard of the former artist's studio. Simple yellow decor is broken up by huge black and white photos of Picasso and Monroe. Tables are close and chairs barely comfortable; white paper tablecloths cover unadorned tables. The vast North-facing window adds light if not always warmth. The short vegetarian menu is inventive and dishes are cooked with skill and precision. Mediterranean tart was served with mixed leaves

51 Queen Caroline Street W6 9QL
Map GtL: C3
Tel: 020 8748 6932
Fax: 020 8563 1719
E-mail: mailroom@gateveg.co.uk
Chef: Richard Whiting
Owners: Michael & Adrian Daniel
Cost: *Alc* £19.50. ☺
Times: Noon-3pm/6-11pm.
Closed Sun

dressed with rocket oil, a good foil to the creamy tart. Delicious, warm and slippery polenta with a wonderful variety of wild mushrooms came with crisp chard, roasted young fennel and tomato. Vegetarians can be evangelical about dishes such as warm purple potato salad with chargrilled baby corn and cherry tomatoes finished with a chilli crème fraîche dressing, and an African platter of spicy, sweet potatoes in a groundnut sauce with beans and okra in tomato sauce. There's no need to dress up to come here, but every need to book.

Additional: Children welcome
Seats: 50
Style: Chic/Minimalist
Smoking: No pipes & cigars

Directions: Telephone for directions

Gaudi Restaurante

63 Clerkenwell Road EC1M 5PT
Map: E4
Tel: 020 7608 3220
Fax: 020 7250 1057
Style: gaudi@turnmills.co.uk
Chef: Nacho Martinez
Owner: John Newman
Cost: *Alc* £30-£35, set-price L £15.
H/wine £12.50
Times: Noon-4pm/7pm-1am.
Closed Sat, all Sun, Xmas, Etr
Additional: Children welcome
Seats: 60. Private dining room 35
Style: Chic/Spanish
Smoking: No-smoking area;
Air conditioning

In homage to the great Catalan architect of the same name, the restaurant explodes in a sensual riot of wrought ironwork, tiles, stained windows, fantastic shaped pillars and a pastiche art collection. More practically, there are well-spaced tables, an open plan kitchen, and a tapas bar and nightclub attached. Nacho Martinez was one of the best modern Spanish cooks in Madrid before he was lured to London where he's taken instant root and is offering the capital an eye-opening, exciting selection of the sort of light and vivid Spanish food rarely found outside of the country. Roasted Spanish pepper is stuffed with cod mousse, served on a leek and courgette nest, accompanied by squid ink sauce – all traditional ingredients, but lined up in an untraditional way. Empanadillas, a Spanish staple, is lifted out of the ordinary by the filling of scallops, cabbage and carrots and the chickpea sauce. Exemplary grilled lobster comes with seasonal vegetable ragout, Jabugo ham and Idiazabal cheese. Baked sea bream in coarse salt with red cabbage and aïoli, pine nuts and sultanas is a brilliant reworking of a classic Catalan dish. No less outstanding was a dessert of Manchego cheese mousse with quince, walnuts and honey. The all-Spanish wine list is remarkably well-priced.

Directions: ⊖ Farringdon. 1st L into Turnmill St. Situated on corner with Clerkenwell Road

Le Gavroche
Restaurant ❁❁❁❁❁

43 Upper Brook Street
W1Y 1PF
Map: B3
Tel: 020 7408 0881
Fax: 020 7491 4387
Chef: Michel A Roux

Booking is as essential today as it was thirty years ago, a relevant point given that many diners have been regulars ever since Le Gavroche opened. Staff are predominantly French and although service can be a little starchy, you want for nothing and the buzz of the place helps pass the time with a real sense of relaxed enjoyment. Much of the cooking on the classically-styled *carte* still shows an endearing respect for tradition (including the hallowed presence of dishes such as the legendary Soufflé Suissesse), but the most recent inspection visit began with a rather uninspiring starter of ravioli of langoustines with basil and tomato, a lovely modern idea let down by flagging execution. The meal improved with a main course of crispy veal sweetbreads with a dominating sweet and sour jus on lightly creamed spinach, with an unusual garnish of dried pigs' trotter. A garnish of creamed foie gras set between sauté potatoes added extra depth and aroma, although overall, this might be a dish more notable for spectacle value than for refinement or flawless precision. Bitter chocolate and praline indulgence was impressively constructed, the crushed praline layered with fine leaves of bitter chocolate, topped off with a light chocolate ganache and enough gold leaf to have you checking your fillings... The wine list remains an odyssey of French flair and decadence.

Directions: From Park Lane, into Upper Brook Street (one way), restaurant is on R. ⊖ Marble Arch

Cost: *Alc* £100, set-price L £38.50. H/wine £30
Times: Noon-2pm/7pm-11pm. Closed Sat & Sun, Xmas, New Year, Bhs
Additional: Children welcome; vegetarian dishes not always available
Seats: 60. Private dining room 8-20
Style: Classic/French
Smoking: Air conditioning

Gilbey's ✿✿

77 The Grove Ealing W5 5LL
Map GtL: B3
Tel: 020 8840 7568
Fax: 020 8840 1905
Chef: Ian Penn
Owners: Michael, Lin, Bill & Caroline Gilbey
Cost: *Alc* £18, set-price L & D £10.50. ☺ H/wine £6.70
Times: Noon-3pm/7-10pm. Closed 5 days at Xmas & New Year
Additional: Sunday L; Children welcome
Seats: 50. Private dining room 30
Style: Informal/chic
Smoking: No pipes & cigars

This is the sort of neighbourhood restaurant where you feel the chef actually gives the customers dishes they want to eat, rather than those he or she feels they should have. At the end of a little parade of shops in a peaceful side street, the sunny decor features a pale stripped wooden floor, yellow walls that sport colourful Mediterranean-style pictures and rather uncomfortable wicker chairs. There is a verdant garden patio to the rear, plus pavement tables for alfresco eating. The short but well-constructed menu feels modern but not intimidating: pumpkin and rosemary risotto with Parmesan shavings and crispy vegetables; roast duck breast with fondant potato and cabbage braised in mulled wine. The cooking remains of a remarkably even standard, from the mosaic of chicken and leeks with tarragon emulsion to the brioche-and-butter pudding with Devonshire clotted cream. Wines are imported direct from France and the Gilbey family also have their own vineyard, Pheasants Ridge, near Henley-on-Thames.

Directions: ⊖ Ealing Broadway (3 mins)

The Glasshouse ⊛⊛

Pleasant neighbourhood restaurant – and neighbourhoods don't get much prettier than this part of Kew. It has certainly struck a chord with the locals, a combination of favourable reviews, an upbeat menu and good cooking has ensured that this place is packed, so do book ahead. The modern set-price menu changes daily, some dishes such as roast foie gras with fig and port Tatin, and pan-fried fillet of beef attracting a supplement to the menu price. Mainstream options include spaghetti of oysters, clams and squid with crème fraîche and gremolata, and rump of lamb with tomatoes, black olives and garlic crushed potatoes. Desserts range from iced pistachio and chocolate parfait to steamed prune, date and ginger pudding with crème anglaise.

Directions: 20 yards from ⊖ Kew Gardens

14 Station Road Kew TW9 3PZ
Map GtL: B2
Tel: 020 8940 6777
Fax: 020 8940 3833
Chef: Anthony Boyd
Owners: Larkbrace Ltd
Cost: Set-price L £22/D £27.50. ☺
H/wine £13.50
Times: Noon-2.30pm/7-10.30pm.
Closed D Sun
Additional: Children 10+
Seats: 60
Style: Informal/modern
Smoking: No pipes & cigars;
Air conditioning

The Good Cook ⊛

Enjoy the good food served in this recently-opened modern-style restaurant, in an old bank conversion. The choice might include salt cod cakes with roast plantain, beetroot risotto or pork tenderloin with mash and spring vegetables.

Style: Informal/Modern
Smoking: No pipes & cigars; Air conditioning

Directions: ⊖ Kensington High St. Opp Kensington Palace entrance

1 Kensington High Street W8
Map GtL: C3
Tel: 020 7795 6533
Fax: 020 7937 8854
E-mail: book@good-cook.com
Cost: *Alc* £20, set-price L £8/D £14.50(pre theatre). ☺
H/wine £12.95
Times: Noon-3pm/6-10.30pm.
Closed D Sun
Additional: Sunday L; Children welcome

Goring Hotel ⊛⊛

Beeston Place Grosvenor Gardens SW1W 0JW
Map: C2
Tel: 020 7396 9000
Fax: 020 7834 4393
E-mail: reception@goringhotel.co.uk
Chef: Derek Quelch
Owner: George Goring
Cost: Set-price L £24/D £35.
H/wine £18.50
Times: 12.30-2.30pm/6-10pm.
Closed L Sat
Additional: Bar food; Sunday L;
Children welcome
Seats: 70. Private dining rooms 4-50

Recently refurbished restaurant in gentle creams, yellows and gold leaf, with light streaming in through huge windows. The look is classical, and the pomp and ceremony provided by the formal service have probably changed little since the hotel opened. The menu is typically British with many dishes crafted from fine UK produce, but in recent times there has been a drift to more contemporary dishes. The wine list is extensive and relates particularly well to the menu. A high level of skill was apparent in a starter of rillette of rabbit with vegetable vinaigrette, which was served at just the right temperature (not too cold). Main courses comprise a good choice of fish, vegetarian and meat dishes, perhaps fillet of sea bass with

Provençale vegetables, glazed wild mushroom and leek tart, and noisettes of lamb with coriander polenta.

Directions: ✚ Victoria – onto Victoria Street, turn L into Grosvenor Gdns, cross Buckingham Palace Road, 75 yds turn L into Beeston Place

Style: Classic/traditional
Smoking: No pipes & cigars; Air conditioning
Civil licence: 50
Accommodation: 74 en suite ★ ★ ★ ★

Granita

The interior is unapologetically 90s minimalist, light blue walls, steel bar counter, plain wooden floor and modern wooden tables decorated only by the cutlery and white linen napkins. Menus are short, breads are of good quality and so are the basic ingredients used by the kitchen. The simple dishes are the best where the kitchen serves them untouched or simply grills them. Lamb chargrilled on skewers (in origin a Lebanese dish) was perfect, served tender and pink with squash and butter beans in a light lemon gravy. Also recommended are both a bowl of mussels with corn cucumber and lime leaves, and Lebanese pizza. A dessert of pear and almond tart had excellent crispy pastry, 'not too sweet' and came served with plenty of pear and almonds.

Directions: ✚ Highbury & Islington, Angel. Opposite St Mary's Church.

127 Upper Street Islington N1 1QP
Map GtL: D3
Tel/Fax: 020 7226 3222
Chef: Ahmed Kharshoum
Owners: Vikki Leffman & Ahmed Kharshoum
Cost: Alc £25, set-price L £11.95 & £13.95. ☺ H/wine £10.50
Times: 12.30-2.30pm(Sun 3pm)/6.30-10.30pm(Sun 10pm). Closed L Tue, all Mon, 10 days Xmas, 5 days Etr, 2 wks Aug
Additional: Sunday L; Children welcome at L
Seats: 72
Style: Informal/Minimalist
Smoking: No pipes & cigars; Air conditioning

Great Eastern Hotel, Aurora NEW

There is something of an inside out feeling to the rejuvenated Great Eastern. A stroll around the streetside curtilage of the hotel will take you past entrances to Aurora (serious fine dining), Terminus (bustling modern brasserie), Miyabi (micro Japanese), The George (John Bullish pub food) and finally Fishmarket (Conran-style crustacea). The heavyweight among the restaurants is undoubtedly Aurora, which offers formal surroundings (classical pillars and marbled floors), and professional service, though there is nothing stiff about the place, and the menu is bright and punchy. In true City style the restaurant can be packed at lunchtime and there are some lighter dishes, such as a delicate tartare of tuna that began one inspection meal. No shortage of more robust options though, including an authentic tournedos Rossini, or partridge served with a Gewurztraminer jus. Finish with chocolate Aurora – a glass plate of three darkly flavoured offerings accompanied by a jug of hot chocolate sauce.

Liverpool Street EC2M 7QN
Map GtL: D3
Tel: 020 7618 5000
Fax: 020 7618 5001
E-mail: sales@great-eastern-hotel.co.uk

Telephone for further details

Directions: ✚ Liverpool Street

Greenhouse Restaurant

Natural light streams through the picture windows at this attractive restaurant, where the walls are hung with prints of vegetables, and fine plants are scattered about the room. Overhead there are decorative ceiling fans, outside a pretty terraced garden, and an exceptionally friendly staff provides professional service. Impressive dishes from the new chef include a lobster ravioli with ginger – fine pasta and great flavours – set on a shallot, fennel and carrot fricassée with a Sauternes and orange sauce. Perfectly roasted sea trout with a crisp skin and tender pink flesh was served with a delightful

27a Hay's Mews W1X 7RJ
Map: C3
Tel: 020 7499 3331
Fax: 020 7499 5368
Chef: Paul Merreck
Owner: David Levin
Cost: Alc £31, set-price L £18.50. H/wine £12.50
Times: 12.30-2.30pm/6.30-11.15pm. Closed L Sat, 26 Dec-New Year, Bhs
Additional: Sunday L; Children welcome

Greenhouse Restaurant

Seats: 95
Smoking: Air conditioning

Directions: Behind Dorchester Hotel just off Hill St. ⊖ Green Park or Hyde Park

green pea purée on a fluffy Parmentier crêpe. The dessert was a moist, light whole orange cake, using every aspect of the fruit, set off with rich white chocolate cream and candied fennel.

Green Olive ❀❀

Inviting neighbourhood-style restaurant, down a side street near Little Venice, on ground floor and basement levels with stripped wooden floors and exposed brick walls. The menu is modern Italian supported by an exclusively Italian wine list with some reasonable prices. Warm salad of prosciutto, artichokes, broad beans and glazed sweetbreads topped with freshly grated black truffle was an honest, simple and beautifully cooked starter with excellent flavours. Another winner was a main course of roasted fillet of tuna served pink in good thick slices, full of meaty flavour, served with a timbal of broad beans and peas and olive dressing. Among the desserts sampled a light citrus cheesecake was a perfectly balanced dish, and a chocolate marble brownie was almost like a chocolate fondant, with delicious dark rich hot melting chocolate.

5 Warwick Place W9 2PX
Map GtL: C3
Tel/Fax: 020 7289 2469
Chef: Stefano Savio
Owner: Bejan Bezhadi
Cost: *Alc* £26.50, set-price D £22 & £28. ☺ H/wine £12
Times: D only, 7-10.30pm.
Additional: Sunday L (12.30-2.30pm)
Seats: 60. Private dining room 18
Style: Rustic
Smoking: No pipes & cigars; Air conditioning

Directions: ⊖ Warwick Avenue

Green's Restaurant and Oyster Bar ❀❀

36 Duke Street SW1Y 6DF
Map: C3
Tel: 020 7930 4566
Fax: 020 7491 7463
Chef: Eddie Bleakly
Owner: Simon Parker-Bowles
Cost: *Alc* £40. ☺ H/wine £12
Times: Noon-3pm/6-11pm.
Closed Sun 1 May-1 Sep, Xmas, Etr
Additional: Bar food; Sunday L; Children 2+
Seats: 54. Private dining room 36
Style: Classic/Traditional
Smoking: No pipes; Air conditioning

There is a lot to like about this very reliable establishment in the club-land area of the West-End. The two main rooms both offer bar counter and stools and both follow a club-based model. However, an obliging contrast is created in the atmosphere of the two rooms – the one traditional with wood-panelled walls and green leather upholstery, the other light with yellow walls, framed prints and modern downlighters. The menu majors on the simple and straight forward (oysters, smoked salmon with soda bread, cold baked Suffolk ham with home-made chutney) whilst offering some interesting combinations such as deep-fried Burgundy snails with chick pea mousse, and fillet of venison with black pudding and parsnip purée. Desserts might include warm chocolate pudding with Amaretti ice cream, winter fruit compote or bread-and-butter pudding.

Directions: Opposite the Cavendish Hotel

Gresslin's NEW

13 Heath Street Hampstead NW3 6TP
Map GtL: C4
Tel: 020 7794 8386
Fax: 020 7433 3282
E-mail: restaurant@gresslins.co.uk
Cost: Alc £26, set-price L £15/D £16.95(Mon-Thu). ☺ H/wine £10.50
Times: Noon-2.30pm/7-10.30pm. Closed D Sun, L Mon, last 2 wks Aug, Bhs
Additional: Sunday L; Children welcome
Style: Chic/Modern
Smoking: No smoking in dining room; Air conditioning

Main street restaurant decorated simply and with modern taste. Expect European cuisine, sometimes with an Oriental influence. The menu might include baked sea bass, confit of sweet potato, cucumber and sour cream. Good fresh ingredients.

Directions: ⊖ Hampstead. 1 minute walk from station.

Grosvenor House, La Terrazza ✿ NEW

Park Lane W1A 3AA
Map: B3
Tel: 020 7495 2275
Fax: 020 7629 9337

Brasserie-style operation (a revolution away from the formal hotel dining of yesteryear) offering contemporary Italian dishes alongside established favourites – great risotto, succulent halibut and quivering pannacotta among the highlights.

Telephone for further details

Directions: ⊖ Marble Arch. Halfway down Park Lane

Halcyon Hotel

81 Holland Park
W11 3RZ
Map GtL: C3
Tel: 020 7727 7288
Fax: 020 7229 8516
E-mail:
information.halcyon@virgin.net
Cost: Alc £39, set-price L £18 & £23/D £35. H/wine £16

We learned of changes in the kitchen here after the Guide went to press. Nigel Davis has taken over from Toby Hill. 'The Room' has a curiously half-finished look – there are pale eau de nil walls, fake wooden panelling and a marble tiled floor and that's about it – at least for some, others rather enjoy the airy lightness of the place. The menu reads well and has an elegant simplicity. Mosaic of foie gras and smoked ham hock

Halcyon Hotel

Times: Noon-2.30pm/7-10.30pm.
Closed L Sat, D 25 Dec, Bhs
Additional: Bar food; Sunday L;
Children welcome (ex 14+ in bar)
Seats: 50. Private dining room 12
Style: Modern
Smoking: No pipes & cigars; Air
conditioning
Accommodation: 42 en suite ★★★★

with toasted brioche was as good as it sounded; venison with braised cabbage, rösti and bitter chocolate sauce was beautifully accomplished. Langoustine ravioli with shellfish sauce boasted paper-thin pasta and plentiful, full-flavoured filling. Garnishing is intelligently restrained, at the most dribbles of tasty high-coloured liquids, but mostly the kitchen works with excellent ingredients which need no embellishment.

Directions: 200 metres up Holland Park Ave from Shepherds Bush roundabout. ⊖ Holland Park (2 mins)

The Halkin Hotel, Stefano Cavallini at The Halkin ✿✿✿

Halkin Street Belgravia SW1X 7DJ
Map GtL: C2
Tel: 020 7333 1000
Fax: 020 7333 1100
E-mail: res@halkin.co.uk
Chef: Stefano Cavallini
Owner: Como Holdings
Cost: *Alc* £55. Set-price L £23/D £55.
H/wine £17.50
Times: 12.30-2.30pm/7.30-11pm (Sun 7-10pm). Closed L Sat & Sun
Additional: Bar food; Children 6+
Seats: 45. Private dining room 30
Style: Chic/modern
Smoking: No pipes & cigars; Air
conditioning
Accommodation: 41 en suite ★★★★

The Halkin's restaurant even looks Italian, with its sweep of marble floor, tall, round-topped windows looking on to greenery, interesting glass screen and staff wearing designer-label clothes. But as if to prove that this is Belgravia, steamed lobster, foie gras terrine and truffle-stuffed Bresse chicken jump off the menu. Other dishes are inspired by more rustic traditions: a bed of lentils, white beans and pearl barley for roast langoustines, for instance, gnocchi for tufted duck with wild mushrooms; even sweetbreads and osso buco make an appearance, while on the menu degustazione rarely-seen hare pops up in a salad dressed with balsamic vinegar. Some unusual but successful pairings have seen chocolate stracci pasta with a good sauce of pigeon and potatoes, lamb cutlet stuffed with pork meat served with roast potatoes, and 'great' celeriac sauce with roast mallard of excellent flavour. Some concepts are simple – a salad of partridge and apple, or deep-fried mixed fish with rocket salad – while desserts are a pleasure to behold, be they pumpkin and date tart or pannacotta with sautéed berries and rum sauce. Italy, naturally enough, features on the serious wine list.

Directions: Between Belgrave Square & Grosvenor Place. Access via Chapel St into Headfort Place and L into Halkin St

Heather's ✿

74 Macmillan Street SE8 3HA
Map GtL: D3
Tel: 020 8691 6665
Fax: 020 8692 3263
Cost: Set-price D £13. ☺
H/wine £8.50
Times: D only 7-11.30pm. Closed Mon, 2 wks Sep
Additional: Sunday L (12.30-3.30pm); Children welcome
Style: Bistro-style/informal
Smoking: No smoking in the dining room

Vegan and vegetarian restaurant with a beautiful walled garden. Everything except the ice cream is made on the premises, and it boasts the largest organic wine list in the country.

Directions: 400 mtrs from Deptford railway station on the Thames Path Walk opposite St Nicholas' Church.

Hilaire ✿✿✿

68 Old Brompton Road SW7 3LQ
Map: A1
Tel: 020 7584 8993
Fax: 020 7581 2949
Chef/Owner: Bryan Webb
Cost: Set-price L £21.50/D £37.50. ☺
H/wine £14
Times: 12.15-2.30pm/6.30-11pm. Closed L Sat, all Sun, 2 wks Aug, 2wks Xmas
Additional: Children welcome; vegetarian dishes on request
Seats: 55. Private dining room 20

Small but stylish South Ken restaurant decorated in yellow, with a busy lunchtime trade. A good selection of wines includes a better than average choice by the glass. Bryan Webb's cooking places the emphasis on freshness, clear taste and first-class ingredients and has the confidence to keep things simple and uncluttered. Buffalo Mozzarella with Piedmontese pepper and rocket is as simple as you can get, but it is a dish transformed when the components are of this quality. Superbly fresh wild salmon was chargrilled to perfection, on a May menu served with baby Jersey Royals,

fresh asparagus and the welcome absence of complicating
sauces. The tenderest piece of spring lamb, cooked pink, was
beautifully set off by roasted augergine coated with pesto and
herbs, and served with a dish of Dauphinoise potatoes.
Techniques, too, are straightforward – goujons of cod are
lightly breaded, served with dressed mixed leaves and a spicy,
aromatic Thai dip. Desserts might include rhubarb ripple ice-
cream or the sharp, intense flavours of a blood orange and
grapefruit champagne jelly with passionfruit. Cheeses from
Neal's Yard.

Directions: On N side of Old Brompton Rd. ⊖ South
Kensington, half way between tube and junction with
Queensgate

Style: Informal/Chic
Smoking: No pipes & cigars; Air
conditioning

The Hogarth ❀

*A bright and upmarket terrace-style brasserie in a smart, purpose-
built hotel. Main courses might include roasted lamb fillet in a truffle
sauce. Desserts along the lines of millefeuille of soft red fruit with a
champagne sabayon.*

Additional: Bar food; Sunday L; Children welcome
Style: Bistro-style/Informal
Smoking: No-smoking area; Air conditioning
Accommodation: 85 en suite ★ ★ ★

Directions: ⊖ Earl's Court

33 Hogarth Road Kensington
SW5 0QQ
Map GtL: C3
Tel: 020 7370 6831
Fax: 020 7373 6179
E-mail: hogarth@marstonhotels.co.uk
Cost: *Alc* £18. ☺ H/wine £12.95
Times: 10am-10pm

Hotel Inter-Continental
London – Le Soufflé ❀❀

The jewel in the crown of this large modern hotel. Le Soufflé
offers modern French cuisine of depth and quality. The *carte* is
exhaustive and features dishes along the lines of fillet of
monkfish wrapped in salmon mousse and leek, poached in a
bouquet garni of organic vegetables and herbs; roast breast
and confit leg of cardamom-spiced duck with latkas, creamed
spinach and a rich cherry jus; and trio of lamb with a tian of
ratatouille and basil. A separate set-price menu offers a
selection of seasonal organic dishes which might result in a
starter of Dover sole soufflé, a main of roast scallops and
lobster tortellini and a light lemon tart with clotted cream ice
cream for dessert. This could be accompanied by one of five
organic wines or a selection from the extensive main wine list.

Seats: 80
Style: Traditional/Formal
Smoking: Air conditioning
Accommodation: 460 en suite ★ ★ ★ ★ ★

Directions: On Hyde Park Corner. ⊖ Hyde Park Corner

1 Hamilton Place Hyde Park Corner
W1V 0QY
Map: C2
Tel: 020 7409 3131
Fax: 020 7491 0926
E-mail: london@interconti.com
Chef: Peter Kromberg
Owner: Bass Hotels &
Resorts/InterContinental
Cost: *Alc* £45, set-price L £29.50/D
£46. H/wine £16
Times: 12.30-3pm/7-10.30pm
(11.15pm Sat). Closed L Sat, D Sun,
all Mon, 2 wks Jan
Additional: Bar food; Sunday L;
Children 5+

The House ❀❀

In a quiet backwater, The House is domestic in scale, with two
opened-up ground-floor rooms and an alcove forming the
main dining room, with three small private rooms on the
upper floors. There's something very English about the decor,

3 Milner Street SW3 2QA
Map: B1
Tel: 020 7584 3002
Fax: 020 7581 2848
Chef: Graham Garrett
Owner: Searcy Corrigan Restaurants

The House

Cost: Set-price L £14.50/D £21. ☺
H/wine £13
Times: Noon-2.30pm/6-11pm.
Closed L Sat, all Sun, 26 Dec-2 Jan,
2 wks Aug
Seats: 26. Private dining room 6-14
Style: Country-house
Smoking: No pipes and cigars

with floral fabric on the walls, an original fireplace and period furnishings. A change of ownership and a new chef in late 1999 brought a new focus to the menu. Respect is paid to some time-honoured combinations: cold poached skate is flaked and accompanied by potato terrine layered with parsley and capers and finished with caper dressing, main-course ham hock comes with split peas and parsley broth, and venison pie with pickled red cabbage. On the other hand, a spirit of adventure is at work behind other dishes. Crispy boneless chicken wings give some oomph to deeply flavoured curried parsnip soup, and roast scallops are married to confit of belly pork and served with garlic purée and fennel. The same approach is brought to puddings that range from perhaps coconut pannacotta, through baked apple dumpling to 'excellent' banana and toffee crumble topped with rich chocolate sorbet. The short but varied wine list offers just a handful by the glass.

Directions: ⊖ South Kensington, Sloane Square

Hyatt Carlton Tower Hotel, Grissini ❀❀

A sleek, modern interior design, with large windows looking down on Cadogan Gardens, friendly Italian staff, an all-Italian wine list of quality and, of course, the restaurant's name leave no doubt as to the provenance of the food on offer here. But the kitchen applies its own interpretation to the tried and tested and shows a fine appreciation of flavours. Bresaola with rocket and Parmesan sounds familiar enough among the antipasti, but a more imaginative approach produces ravioli with salt cod and sun-dried tomato sauce, linguine with lobster, spring onions and tomato sauce, and trofiette with a ragout of baby rabbit, aubergines, marjoram and Pecorino. Main courses, split between meat and fish, might turn up simply-roasted lamb with roast potatoes and stuffed aubergine, and no less successful honey-glazed duck breast with a white mustard sauce and glazed beetroot, or grilled swordfish and queen scallops in a lemon and mint sauce with caponata. Puddings are the real McCoy too: semifreddo al cappuccino, tiramisu, or pannacotta with chocolate sauce, and cheeses are exclusively Italian.

Directions: ⊖ Knightsbridge, Sloane Sq. From Knightsbridge station down Sloane St. Hotel entrance is 2nd L

Cadogan Place SW1X 9PY
Map : B2
Tel: 020 7858 7172
Fax: 020 7235 9129
E-mail: ctower@hytlondon.co.uk
Chef: Giuseppe Lavarra
Cost: Alc £30, set-price L £16/D £25.
☺ H/wine £20
Times: 12.30-2.45pm/6.30-10.45pm.
Closed L Sat, D Sun, Etr
Additional: Sunday L; Children welcome
Seats: 80. Private dining room 50
Style: Modern/Italian
Smoking: No-smoking area; Air conditioning
Accommodation: 220 en suite
★★★★★

Ikkyu

The atmosphere is completely authentic at what is essentially a Japanese drinking place where food is also served. Yakitori (grilled food) is a speciality, and there is some great sashimi.

Directions: Goodge Street

67a Tottenham Court Road W1P 9PA
Map: C3
Tel: 020 7636 9286

Telephone for further details

Il Forno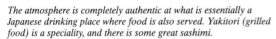

Italian restaurant serving a wide range of modern, light dishes as well as pasta and pizza. Try French bean salad with cured bacon and shallot sauce, then soft organic polenta with chicken livers, and roasted cod with white beans. Telephone for further details.

Directions: Tottenham Court Road

63-64 Frith Street W1V 5TA
Map: D4
Tel: 020 7734 4545
Fax: 020 7287 1027

Telephone for further details

Isola

One of the last hyped restaurants of the 90s to open at considerable expense in a chic Knightsbridge location. The design is retro-American diner with a street-level-to-ceiling glass front, and knowledgeable service is provided by staff buttoned up the midriff in grey waistcoats. The menu and wine list are all-Italian: home-made grissini are offered followed by a basket of Italian breads and a shallow pool of olive oil. There is a main menu, set lunch and a taster menu for the evening. From the first came a subdued Fontina mousse with white onions and slivers of black truffle, followed by a rustic saddle of rabbit with garlic confit, charged cherry tomatoes, sun-dried tomatoes and parsley, in which the flavours were not shy. To finish a quince Tatin was served with a thrilling verbena ice cream.

Directions: Telephone for directions

145 Knightsbridge SW1X 7PA
Map: E2
Tel: 020 7838 1044

Telephone for further details

The Ivy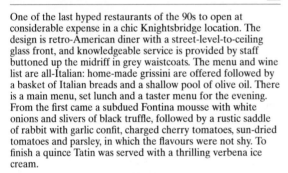

Glamorous celebrity haunt in a quiet street just two minutes' walk from Cambridge Circus. Formally attired doormen greet/vet diners as they enter into the ambient sophistication of the simply decorated dining room. The decor of wooden floors, stained glass windows, green leather banquettes and unobtrusive modern art hits the right mark of stylish prestige without being intimidating. Similarly the modern European menu tends to feature dishes with a familiar, comforting aspect whilst maintaining high fine-dining standards. For example a lunch menu might well include rib of beef with Yorkshire pudding, roast potatoes, mashed carrots and winter greens, or shepherd's pie with honeyed parsnips and bubble-and-squeak. Those of less traditional tastes will find happy contentment in starters such as seared scallops with creamed salt cod and spiced tomato, or mains such as bluefin tuna with spiced lentils and wild rocket. Desserts might include baked ruby plums with almond creamed polenta.

Directions: Leicester Square, Covent Garden

1 West Street Covent Garden WC2H 9NE
Map: D3
Tel: 020 7836 4751
Fax: 020 7240 9333
Chefs: Des McDonald, Alan Bird
Owners: Jeremy King, Christopher Corbin & Belgo Group plc
Cost: *Alc* £30-£35, set-price L £15.50(Sat & Sun). ☺ H/wine £11.50
Times: Noon-3pm(3.30pm Sun)/5.30-midnight. Closed D 24 Dec, 25 & 26 Dec, 1 Jan, Aug Bh
Additional: Sunday L; Children welcome
Seats: 100. Private dining room 25-60
Style: Classic/Traditional
Smoking: No pipes; Air conditioning

Jak's ＠＠

NEW

Another 'Chapter' has opened for partners Michael Mann and chef Adrian Jones in the restaurant world. Formerly at Chapter Two in Blackheath (see entry) they have moved into town to fashionable Chelsea to develop Jak's, a former private members club. Downstairs, in the basement, low ceilings, white walls dotted with modern paintings and eclectic piped music set the informal scene in which to enjoy the excellent-value set-price dinner menu on offer. The menu is intentionally kept short – five choices at each course – dishes are cooked with flair and feature carefully sourced ingredients. A typically robust meal may begin with saffron risotto with Parma ham, or pasta with roast rabbit and truffle oil, with main course options like a perfectly-cooked fillet of beef topped with fresh salsa verde, served on layers of wok-fried foie gras, crisp green beans, savoy cabbage and salt beef. Finish with Bakewell tart with vanilla custard, or a satisfying rice pudding topped with caramelised pineapple. Short list of wines with a fair range of New World bottles under £20.

77 Lower Sloane Street SW1W 8DA
Tel: 020 7730 9476
Fax: 020 7823 5040
E-mail: info@jaksclub.com
Chef: Adrian Jones
Owner: Justin Wheeler
Cost: Set-price L £15/D £20 ☺
H/wine £13.50
Times: Noon-2.15pm/6.30-10pm.
Closed Fri, Sat, D Sun
Additional: Bar food; Sunday L;
Children welcome
Seats: 56. Private dining room 12
Style: Informal/Minimalist
Smoking: No-smoking area; Air conditioning

Directions: ↔ Sloane Square

J. Sheekey ＠＠

A slick, professional fish restaurant that marries traditional dishes with modern presentation. Simplicity is a keynote with fish and seafood served fresh and prepared with due respect. On a recent visit a dressed crab was served out of the shell with a cayenne and dark crabmeat mayonnaise to give a distinctive and contrasting zesty flavour. This was followed by a main of peppered bluefin tuna on a bed of Italian barley and herb salsa. Other fish mains include Cornish fish stew with fennel and potato, and smoked haddock fillet with fried egg and crispy bacon. Meat dishes are also available on request and the set-price lunch menu will normally offer a non-fish dish along the lines of Barbary duck breast with caramelised orange sauce and Pont-Neuf potatoes. The rooms are cosy with closely spaced tables, panelled walls and black and white photos of acting stars.

28-32 St Martin's Court WC2N 4AL
Map: D3
Tel: 020 7240 2565
Fax: 020 7240 8114
Chef: Tim Hughes
Owners: Jeremy King, Christopher Corbin & Belgo Group plc
Cost: Alc £35, set-price L £9.75 & £13.50. ☺ H/wine £11.50
Times: Noon-3pm/5.30pm-midnight. Closed D 24 Dec, 25 &26 Dec, 1 Jan, Aug Bh
Additional: Sunday L; Children welcome
Seats: 112
Style: Classic/Traditional
Smoking: No pipes; Air conditioning

Directions: ↔ Leicester Square

Kai Mayfair ＠

65 South Audley Street W1Y 5FD
Map: C3
Tel: 020 7493 8988
Fax: 020 7493 1456
E-mail: kai@kaimayfair.co.uk
Cost: Alc £40. H/wine £19
Times: Noon-2.30pm/6.30-11.30pm. Closed Xmas
Additional: Children welcome
Style: Modern
Smoking: Air conditioning

Directions: ↔ Marble Arch. On to Park Lane, situated behind The Dorchester

Opulent restaurant with oriental overtones in the rich golds and deep reds of the decor. Dishes include 'enrichment of the surprised piglet' and 'goat on the great wall'.

Kastoori ❀

Reliable, tasteful, family-run vegetarian restaurant offering enticing flavours of the sub-continent. Sample freshness with aubergine, potato and bean curries with a range of accompaniments, topped off with a quenching (and very moreish) sweet lassi.

Additional: Sunday L; Children welcome
Style: Informal/Modern
Smoking: Air conditioning

Directions: ⊖ Tooting Bec, Tooting Broadway (between the two)

188 Upper Tooting Road SW17 7EJ
Map GtL: C2
Tel/Fax: 020 8767 7027
Cost: ☺ H/wine £7.50
Times: 12.30-2.30pm/6-10.30pm.
Closed L Mon & Tue, 1 wk mid Jan

Kensington Place ❀❀

201/205 Kensington Church Street
W8 7LX
Map GtL: C3
Tel: 020 7727 3184
Fax: 020 7229 2025
E-mail: kpr@placerestaurants.com
Chef: Rowley Leigh
Owners: Moving Image Restaurants
Cost: Alc £27, set-price L £14.50.
H/wine £10.50
Times: Noon-3pm (3.30pm Sat & Sun)/6.30-11.45pm (10.15pm Sun).
Closed 4 days Xmas
Additional: Sunday L; Children welcome
Seats: 140. Private dining room 40
Style: Modern
Smoking: Air conditioning

A timeless property with a well-earned strong reputation. The restaurant stubbornly rejects the vagaries of culinary fadism, choosing instead to plough its own straight furrow. Starters include cream of fennel soup and fried squid crème fraîche and chilli jam, but our choice of chicken and goats' cheese mousse was beyond reproach and well set-off by a sweet, berry sauce. Venison noisettes with a sauce of sweet pineapple, pine nuts and sour capers demonstrated the strength of the adventurous main courses, although the meat was a little overcooked. A warm chestnut tart with chocolate sauce did not quite make the most of its own advantages, but the chocolate sauce was suitably light and the pear nicely understated. The decor is somewhat eclectic with the emphasis more on a sense of fun (complementing the friendly, unaffected manner of the staff) than on spacious luxury. The wine list is extensive and includes a choice of six dessert wines.

Directions: 150yds before junction of Kensington Church St & Notting Hill Gate

Laicram Thai ❀❀

Small well-established restaurant with wood carvings and Thai prints. Good cooking, a light hand with the chilli, and freshly sourced ingredients. Starters might feature minced pork dumplings in garlic and soya sauce, deep-fried prawns with sweet chilli sauce, mini crab and coriander cakes, beef and chicken satay or deep fried vegetables. Roast duck curry is the house speciality main course, with good use of sauces. Other

1 Blackheath Grove Blackheath
SE3 0AT
Map GtL: E2
Tel: 020 8852 4710

Telephone for further details

possibilities are Goong Tod whole prawns fried with garlic, pepper and spring onions and Phat Pak stir fried mixed vegetables in a Thai sauce including broccoli, young corn, chinese cabbage and bean shoots, all accompanied by freshly steamed fragrant rice. Desserts are a highlight with mango mousse, or a delightful mini selection of sticky rice, coconut milk pudding and sweet baked cake wrapped in vine leaves.

Directions: Off the main shopping street, in a side road near the Post Office. Opposite the station

The Landmark

222 Marylebone Road NW1 6JQ
Map: E4
Tel: 020 7631 8230

As we went to press, AA five rosetted chef John Burton-Race had moved from Berkshire to take over the kitchen here at the Landmark. One to watch. Check our website (www.theaa.com/hotels) for the latest details.

Directions: Marylebone – directly opposite

The Lanesborough ❀❀❀

Hyde Park Corner SW1X 7TA
Map: C3
Tel: 020 7259 5599
Fax: 020 7259 5606
E-mail:
reservations@lanesborough.co.uk
Chef: Paul Gayler
Cost: *Alc* £31-£57.20, set-price L £15-£26.50/D £32-£44. ☺
H/wine £19
Additional: Bar food L; Sunday L; Children welcome
Seats: Private dining rooms; Jacket & tie preferred
Style: Chic/Formal
Smoking: Air conditioning
Accommodation: 95 en suite
★ ★ ★ ★

The glass-roofed Conservatory with its exotic mix of fountains, plants and a pianist is an unusual setting for this style of food, but the atmosphere is relaxed, perhaps because it is open 7 days a week from 7am to last orders at 11pm. Staff are young and attentive but need a little more supervision as well as language skills. The menu is a good balance of the sort of caviar and oyster dishes every smart Knightsbridge restaurant 'must have', alongside more imaginative ones. An excellent salsa lobster ceviche was made with good meaty chunks marinated in lemon and served with a dressing flavoured with lemongrass, coriander and ginger. Baby turbot with artichoke and mushrooms in a light beurre blanc was disappointingly overcooked – served whole, and when removed from the bone it ended up looking disconcertingly like kedgeree. Tender sticks of rhubarb cleverly replaced the conventional sponge fingers in a light rhubarb charlotte served with rhubarb sauce and mixed berries. Lovely petits fours and good espresso.

Directions: On Hyde Park Corner. Hyde Park Corner

Launceston Place Restaurant

1a Launceston Place W8 5RL
Map: A2
Tel: 020 7937 6912
Fax: 020 7938 2412
Chef: Philip Reed
Owners: Moving Image plc
Cost: Alc £32, set-price L/D £18.50.
☺ H/wine £10
Times: 12.30-2.30pm/7-11.30pm.
Closed L Sat, D Sun, Easter, Xmas,
New Year, Bhs
Additional: Sunday L; Children
welcome
Seats: 85. Private dining room 14
Style: Country house
Smoking: No pipes; Air conditioning

An oasis of calm in the midst of Kensington shopping fever, Launceston Place remains consistently one of the best of its kind. Perfect for both lady lunchers and discerning diners, the food is classic yet imaginative, prepared with considerable effort and technical skill. Dishes rarely disappoint. A Caesar salad included fresh anchovies and achieved a good balance between the Parmesan and croûtons; super risotto with pancetta and sage would have made a fine supper dish in its own right. A main course of salmon fishcakes with tomato beurre blanc was served with a simple, well-dressed green salad, and excellent pork with spinach came with sharp apple sauce and really crisp crackling. Desserts might include lemon curd roulade with raspberries or roast pineapple with fried vanilla cream. Service is professional.

Directions: Just south of Kensington Palace. ⊖ Gloucester Road, High Street Kensington

Lawn

1 Lawn Terrace SE3 9LJ
Map GtL: D3
Tel: 020 7379 0724
Fax: 020 7234 3343
E-mail: reservations@bgr.plc.uk

Converted printworks with a suspended second floor, complete with ducting, steel girders and wires. Dishes sampled were a creamy spinach soup and a beautifully fresh pan-fried fillet of plaice.

Cost: Alc £35, set-price L/D £11.95 & £15.50.☺ H/wine £13.50
Times: Telephone for opening times
Additional: Sunday L; Children welcome
Style: Modern
Smoking: Air condtioning

Directions: Turn R out of Blackheath BR station, up the hill, 1st road on R

Leith's Restaurant

92 Kensington Park Road W11 2PN
Map GtL: C3
Tel: 020 7229 4481

As we went to press we learned of changes (including a change of name) afoot at this three AA rosetted restaurant. Check our website (www.theaa.com/hotels) for the latest details.

Directions: ⊖ Notting Hill Gate. 550yds north of station

Lemonia

Large, bustling, airy place with a very good range of Greek/Greek-Cypriot dishes. Lemonia means lemon, which explains why you get lemon with just about everything, but the cooking is sound, with kleftico, a braised shank of lamb, coming in for particular praise at inspection.

Additional: Children welcome
Style: Bistro-style/rustic
Smoking: No cigars & pipes; Air conditioning

Directions: ⊖ Chalk Farm. 200 metres from Primrose Hill Park

89 Regent's Park Road NW1 8UY
Map GtL: C3
Tel: 020 7586 7454
Fax: 020 7483 2630
Cost: *Alc* £20-25, set-price L £7.95/D £13.50. ☺ H/wine £11
Times: Noon-3pm/6-11.30pm.
Closed L Sat, D Sun, 25 & 26 Dec

Lindsay House Restaurant

21 Romilly Street
W1V 5TG
Map: D3
Tel: 020 7439 0450
Fax: 020 7437 7349
Chef: Richard Corrigan
Owners: Searceys-Corrigan Ltd
Cost: *Alc* £30, set-price L £23/D £42.
☺ H/wine £16
Times: Noon-2.15pm/6-11pm. Closed L Sat, all Sun, 2 wks Aug, 1 wk Xmas
Seats: 48. Private dining rooms 6-8, 16-30
Style: Chic
Smoking: No-smoking area; Air conditioning

Richard Corrigan's individual and uncompromising style of cooking always packs the house out. The Georgian building might be chic, clubby and stylish but this is Soho after all and the cooking suits the address. Robust and gutsy but with a studied veneer of sophistication, this is the place to pig out, literally, on numbers such as ravioli of suckling pig with braised celery and tarragon or cutlet of organic farmed pork with crubeen, apricots and turnips. Great butchery skills are on display in dishes such as ballotine of foie gras with toasted pain de campagne. Seafood dishes include baked snapper with merguez sausage and marjoram, and native scallops with ceps, artichoke, pancetta and red wine jus. There is an exciting use of vegetables here – Jerusalem artichoke mousse, fennel bavarois, salsify, and pumpkin all appeared on a February menu. Desserts have a clarity of concept and an understanding of flavour combinations that is invigorating: white chocolate parfait, griottine cherries, chocolate sorbet; poached pear with quince and Sauternes jelly, blue cheese bavarois; pecan tart, maple syrup ice cream. Neal's Yard cheeses are served with brown soda bread.

Directions: ⊖ Leicester Square

Lola's

Mediterranean-influenced restaurant on the upper floor of an old tram shed in the hustle and bustle of Camden passage. The decor features light pastel shades of cream with isolated flashes of colour, imaginative art and an overall feeling of airiness. A

359 Upper Street Islington N1 2UD
Map GtL: D3
Tel: 020 7359 1932
Fax: 020 7359 2209
E-mail: lolasrest.uk@btinternet.com
Chef: Gary Lee

Lola's

Owners: Carol George, Morfudd Richards
Cost: *Alc* £25, set-price L £10 & £15/D £10 & £15. ☺ H/wine £10.50
Times: Noon-2.30pm (3pm Sat & Sun)/6-11pm. Closed D Sun, 25 & 26 Dec, 1 Jan
Additional: Sunday L; Children welcome
Seats: 80
Style: Rustic/Eclectic
Smoking: Air conditioning

pressed chicken, apple and black pudding terrine proved a 'simple and brilliant' starter with the flavours fresh and clean, the textures nicely varied and an accompanying salad crisp and vibrant. For mains a fillet of fresh and tasty salmon was evenly seasoned and accurately roasted with a simple accompaniment of spinach and Jersey Royals. Vin Santo syllabub made an ideal conclusion to a robust meal – light, bright and vibrant with hints of refreshing citrus. A final touch of a drop of Italian wine poured on top of the dessert added a whole new dimension to the dish and typified the kitchen's careful attention to detail.

Directions: ⊖ Angel

London Heathrow Marriott Hotel ❀❀

NEW

Bath Road UB3 5AN
Map 4: TQ07
Tel/Fax: 020 8990 1100

Telephone for further details.

This modern hotel restaurant benefits from a freshness of concept. The room is smart, light and airy with an open kitchen and live piano music drifting through from the central atrium. Quality ingredients are accurately cooked and simply presented. On a recent visit precise baby gnocchi was combined with al dente spinach, freshly shaved Parmesan and a rosemary and tomato sauce to produce an excellent starter. Monkfish followed and proved a real delight – simple, accurately cooked and superbly fresh. A good home-made lemon tart with decent pastry and clear, precise lemon flavour rounded things off nicely. Good levels of service are maintained by attentive and friendly staff.

Directions: Telephone for directions

London Marriott County Hall ❀❀

The County Hall SE1 7PB
Tel: 020 7902 8000
Fax: 020 7928 5300
Chef: David Ali
Cost: ☺ H/wine £13.50
Times: Noon-2.30pm/5.30pm-11pm
Additional: Bar food; Sunday L; Children welcome
Seats: 90
Style: Informal/Traditional

A curved dining room reminiscent of a ship's dining room offers wonderful views across the river towards the houses of parliament. The decor is light, bright and well proportioned. A contemporary European approach to cuisine results in starters such as seared scallops, smoked bacon salad and caramelised pineapple, or onion tart Tatin with chorizo and artichoke salad. Main courses such as Dover sole; roast curried haddock with smoked salmon bubble-and-squeak; or pot roasted rabbit,

London Marriott County hall

Smoking: No-smoking area; No pipes; Air conditioning
Accommodation: 200 en suite
★ ★ ★ ★ ★

sweetbreads and taglioni with morel cream feature on both the dinner *carte* option and the lunch and pre-theatre set price menu. Desserts such as banana and caramel crème brûlée, and fig tart Tatin with cinnamon ice cream may be enjoyed with a choice from the substantial selection of pudding wines.

Directions: ⊖ Westminster, Waterloo

London Marriott Grosvenor Square ❀❀

The hotel is superbly located in Grosvenor Square. The panelled (clubby but not the least bit stuffy) mezzanine-floor restaurant provides a comfortable setting for cooking that's backed up by crisp linen and posh china. Hospitality and well-practised service remain strengths. The kitchen owes allegiance to the Mediterranean mostly, but ventures fashionably further afield with the occasional ravioli of Thai-spiced duck, chilli and sweet soy dressing. Our meal featured Cornish crab cake with scallop tempura and roasted garlic salad, tender, sweet Herdwick lamb, roast potato and onion galette, tomato jam and balsamic sauce, with a lemon and raspberry tart for dessert.

Directions: ⊖ Bond Street. Hotel entrance is on Duke St, off Oxford St

Grosvenor Square W1A 4AW
Map: C3
Tel: 020 7493 1232
Fax: 020 7491 3201
E-mail: businesscentre@londonmarriott.co.uk
Chef: Nick Hawkes
Owners: Marriott International
Cost: *Alc* £25, set-price L £20.50/D £12.95. ☺ H/wine £13
Times: Noon-3pm/5-10.30pm. Closed L Sat
Additional: Bar food; Sunday L; Children welcome
Seats: 80. Private dining room 34
Style: classic
Smoking: No-smoking area; Air conditioning
Accommodation: 221 en suite
★ ★ ★ ★

The Lowndes Hyatt Hotel ❀

21 Lowndes Street SW1X 9ES
Map: B2
Tel: 020 7823 1234
Fax: 020 7235 1154
E-mail: lowndes@hyattintl.com
Cost: ☺ H/wine £13.50
Times: 11.30-11pm. Closed 25 Dec
Additional: Bar food L; Sunday L;
Children welcome
Style: Informal/modern
Smoking: No pipes & cigars; Air
conditioning
Accommodation: 78 en suite ★ ★ ★ ★

*Smart new brasserie serving a mix of light meals as well as more
elaborate dishes. There's an al fresco eating area for warmer weather,
and dishes might include seafood tempura, duck breast with lentils
and crème brûlée.*

Directions: ⊖ Knightsbridge. From
Sloane Street take first L into Lowndes
Square, located on the bottom right
hand corner

Luca ❀

*Minimalist, classic, chic restaurant. The menu offers some interesting
vegetarian options. You might expect cuisine along the lines of roast
corn fed chicken wrapped in parma ham with braised arrocina
beans, garlic butter and watercress.*

Style: Modern/Minimalist
Smoking: No-smoking area; Air conditioning

Directions: Telephone for directions

85 Maple Road KT6 4AW
Map GtL: B1
Tel: 020 8399 2365
Fax: 020 8390 5353
Cost: *Alc* £25. ☺ H/wine £11
Times: D only 6.30-10.30pm.
Closed Mon, 25 & 26 Dec
Additional: Sunday L (12.30-2.30pm);
Children welcome

Maison Novelli ❀❀

A recently enlarged restaurant where stylish blue/purple decor
with large mirrors and wooden floors complement similarly
sophisticated cuisine. Jean-Christophe Novelli is now able to
concentrate all his energy here, and this is evident in dishes
such as a succeful first course of steamed wild mushrooms in a
poppy seed pancake, or pan-fried potato and foie gras terrine
with hazlenut dressing. A recent meal included smoked
haddock fish cake, and finished with the hot and cold chocolate
signature dessert – 'superb' chocolate fondant with white
chocolate ice cream, spun sugar spring and tuille sail – a 'first
class pud' enthused the inspector. Espresso and petits fours
brought things to a close.

Directions: ⊖ Farringdon

29 Clerkenwell Green EC1R 0DU
Map GtL: D3
Tel: 020 7251 6606
Fax: 020 7490 1083
Chef/Owner: Jean-Christophe Novelli
Cost: *Alc* £26.95-£47.20.
H/wine £14.95
Times: Noon-3pm/6-11pm.
Closed L Sat, all Sun
Additional: Children welcome
Style: Rustic/French
Seats: 80-110; Private dining rooms
30 & 80
Smoking: Air conditioning

Mandarin Oriental
Hyde Park ❀❀❀❀

David Nicholls, together with Hywel Jones, is responsible for
the subtle sophistication of the cooking at the Foliage
Restaurant, which at its best can only be described as stunning.
Dishes are simple in concept but subtle in treatment, fresh and
full of flavour. The style is modern French: poached Scottish

66 Knightsbridge SW1X 7LA
Map: B2
Tel: 020 7235 2000
Fax: 020 7235 4552
Chefs: David Nicholls, Hywel Jones
Cost: *Alc* £32.50, set-price L £19/D
£32.50. H/wine £18

lobster, vinaigrette of crab, confit tomatoes and caviar dressing; pan-fried sea bream, Jerusalem artichoke brandade, grilled clams, warm cucumber and oyster vinaigrette; baked apple and Calvados soufflé, pain epicé ice cream. There are some beguiling takes on contemporary trends, as in a hot Cuban chocolate fondant with whisky ice cream and chocolate caramel craquelin or a rolled rabbit terrine, vinaigrette of girolles, fondant potato and pan-fried foie gras. Seasonality is important – an early summer menu included broth of new season peas, jambonette of duck and pearl barley, as well as grilled fillets of red mullet, provençale vegetables, confit of Ratte potatoes and new season asparagus. Another twist on a modern classic is a signature pot-roast pork with stuffed trotter, leaf spinach, tomatoes and basil. The lunch menu is remarkably good value for cooking of this order – perhaps 'Salad of grilled scallops and roast melon, coconut cream and curry oil' followed by 'Foie gras duck', savoy cabbage mille-feuille, creamed potatoes, jus gras' and 'Bergamot flavoured crème brûlée, almond Financier and poached raspberries'.

Directions: ⊖ Knightsbridge

Times: Noon-2.30pm/7-10.30pm. Closed L Sat, all Sun, Xmas, New Year
Additional: Bar food; Children welcome
Seats: 45-50. Private dining room 20-200
Style: Chic/Modern
Smoking: Air conditioning
Civil licence: 200
Accommodation: 200 en suite
★ ★ ★ ★ ★

Manna

Gourmet vegetarian restaurant in Primrose Hill, the large dining room divided from the conservatory front by etched windows. Manna meze is a good option for sampling a range of dishes.

Additional: Sunday L; Children welcome
Style: Informal/Chic
Smoking: No smoking in dining room; Air conditioning

Directions: ⊖ Chalk Farm. Telephone for further directions

4 Erskine Road Primrose Hill NW3 3AJ
Map GtL: C3
Tel/Fax: 020 7772 8028
Cost: *Alc* £19.50, set-price L £15/D £11.50. ☺ H/wine £9.50
Times: 12.30-3pm/6.30-11pm. Closed L Mon-Fri

Mash ❀

Fun, bright, modern and deftly fashionable, this restaurant/deli/brewery/installation art gallery is not afraid to be different. A char grilled rump of beef and a chocolate and rice crispies fondant testified to a good combination of quality and novelty.

Additional: Bar food; Sunday brunch; Children welcome
Style: Modern/Funky
Smoking: Air conditioning

Directions: ⊖ Oxford Circus. At the Oxford Street end of Great Portland Street

19-20 Great Portland Street W1 5DB
Map: C3
Tel: 020 7637 5555
Fax: 020 7637 7333
Cost: Set-price L £10. ☺ H/wine £13

Matsuri

Stylish St James's teppan-yaki and sushi restaurant with comparatively accessible menus and unintimidating atmosphere. Staff are relaxed and friendly, and comfortable guiding diners through the menu, something that helps set this place apart. Matsuri means festival in Japanese and lots of touches around the dining room reflect this theme; though classically Japanese minimalist in appearance, its blond wood lends a softer ambience. Diners are seated around large hotplates where chefs are suitably flamboyant with the

15 Bury Street SW1Y 6AL
Map: D3
Tel: 020 7839 1101
Fax: 020 7930 7010
E-mail: matsuri@japanglobe.net
Chef: Kanehiro Takase
Owner: JRK (UK) Ltd
Cost: *Alc* £40, set-price L £40/D £35. ☺ H/wine £18.50
Times: Noon-2.30pm/6-10.30pm. Closed Sun, Bhs

economy and precision of movement that is a hallmark of this Japanese theatre of cuisine. Teppan-yaki such as lobster, salmon, tuna, turbot, sea bass and other assorted seafood, excellent beef, pork, chicken and duck, or teppan-grilled vegetables and mushrooms are all on offer. Cracking sashimi, great tempura, good steamed rice and miso soup. Choose from various set-menu options or select piece by piece. Fresh fruit is the thing for dessert, and there is a selection of sake and cocktails amongst the rounded wine list. Small sushi bar with top-notch food prepared to order.

Additional: Children welcome
Seats: 133. Private dining room 18
Style: Modern/Traditional
Smoking: Air conditioning

Directions: ⊖ Green Park. Towards Piccadilly Circus, R into St James', 1st L into Jermyn St, 1st R

Mayfair Inter-Continental, Opus 70 ✺

Stratton Street W1A 2AN
Map: C3
Tel: 020 7344 7070
Fax: 020 7344 7071
E-mail: mayfair@interconti.com
Cost: *Alc* £35, set-price L/D £16.50 & £20. ☺ H/wine £12
Times: Noon-2.30pm/6-11pm. Closed L Sat, Bhs L
Additional: Sunday brunch; Children welcome
Style: Informal/modern
Smoking: No-smoking area; Air conditioning
Civil licence: 400
Accommodation: 290 en suite
★ ★ ★ ★ ★

Stand alone hotel restaurant with a chatty style and modern cooking. The scallop and mussel broth worked really well, as did the venison with redcurrant demi-glace.

Directions: From Hyde Park Corner, turn L off Piccadilly, just below Green Park tube station

Meliá White House Regents Park ✺✺

Albany Street NW1 0PD
Map: D4
Tel: 020 7387 1200
Fax: 020 7388 0091
Chef: Colin Norman
Cost: *Alc* £25-£30, set-price L £18.75 & £22.75/D £23.50. ☺ H/wine £13.50
Times: 12.30-2.30pm/6.30-11pm. Closed L Sat, all Sun
Additional: Children welcome
Seats: 100
Style: Classic/Traditional
Smoking: No-smoking area; Air conditioning
Accommodation: 582 en suite
★ ★ ★ ★

Well run hotel in a 1930s apartment building under new management. Continuity in the kitchen has ensured the maintenance of a high quality set-price lunch and dinner menu. A three course lunch might begin with open game lasagne incorporating rich confit game and braised baby fennel. A main dish of chargrilled provençale vegetables in chilli, garlic and herbs with asparagus ravioli and a tomato vinaigrette ensures that vegetarians are well catered for, whilst pot-roast lamb shank will mollify the most ravenous of carnivores. The dinner menu follows similar lines and a typical meal might open with an assiette of fish featuring a creamed roulade of haddock, hickory smoked salmon with horseradish and a tartare of tuna. Braised duck legs with rosemary, thyme and juniper might follow and apple and prune sponge could complete the picture.

Directions: ⊖ Great Portland Street

Memories of China Restaurant ❀❀

This smart, upmarket and long-established Chinese is situated on the ground floor of a modern building in Ebury Street. There is a comfortable bar with wicker armchairs, while the restaurant has a cool, clean-cut feel with its red calligraphic Chinese designs painted on white walls. Screens act as partitions to help divide up the room, while Bauhaus chairs surround well-clothed tables set against a dark tiled floor. Service is efficient, the management are much in evidence and are welcoming. Asterisks alongside items on the menu indicate recommended specialities, and there are various set meals (none for one person), plus a lengthy *carte*. At a May visit we sampled two specialities, starting with moreish quick fried courgettes stuffed with minced prawns, followed by Mongolian barbecue lamb in lettuce puffs (the ingredients are wrapped in crisp lettuce leaves). We finished with an agreeable spicy beancurd casserole; desserts are mostly ices and fruit. The wine list encompasses some six-dozen wines, half French, the others from around the world – just the house red and white are offered by the glass.

67 Ebury Street SW1W 0NZ
Map: C2
Tel: 020 7730 7734
Fax: 020 7730 2992

Telephone for further details

Directions: At the junction of Ebury Street & Eccleston Street.
⊖ Sloane Square, Victoria

Le Meridien Piccadilly, The Oak Room ❀❀❀

One of the grandest dining rooms in London, with plenty of pillars and chandeliers, luxury and 'outright glitz'. Marco Pierre White's announcement of his retreat from the hurly burly of the kitchen was of course a major event of last year, but the cooking here is still clearly focussed. A May inspection meal took in an *amuse bouche* of roasted scallop on a sauce verte, followed by a well balanced ballotine of salmon with herbs, salad of crayfish with wild sorrel and caviar. A main course of braised ox tail en crepinette with fumet of red wine consisted of the ox tail rendered almost to rillette consistency inside pigs' cauls. Intensely flavoured but not overpowering, the richness of the dish was lifted by delicate seasoning. The 'fabulous' jus had bags of flavour, and the panache of crisp spring vegetables was accurately cooked. The meal finished with a cadau of chocolate - a straightforward multi-layered chocolate torte wrapped in tempered sheet chocolate. The wide range of skilfully made petits fours include tuiles, fruit tarts, madelaines and truffles. Service is excellent.

21 Piccadilly W1V 0BH
Map: D3
Tel: 020 7473 0202
Fax: 020 7437 3574
Chef: Robert Reid
Cost: *Alc* £80, set-price L £37.50/D £55. H/wine £18
Times: Noon-2.30pm/7-11.15pm. Closed 2 wks Xmas & New Year, 2 wks Aug
Additional: Children welcome
Style: Classic/formal
Seats: 70. Private dining room 70
Smoking: No pipes & cigars; air conditioning
Accommodation: 266 en suite
★ ★ ★ ★ ★

Le Meridien Piccadilly –
The Terrace ❀❀

21 Piccadilly W1V 0BH
Map: D3
Tel: 0870 400 8400
Fax: 020 7465 1616

Telephone for further details

Michel Rostang acts as the consultant to the airy, split-level restaurant, and his influence is evident in the characteristically French menu. Dishes have a light, simple feel, ingredients are of high quality and the menu is flexible enough to offer many starters as main courses if preferred. A smoked and fresh salmon terrine with celery and a wafer of walnut bread was a well judged starter, followed by a technically accomplished main course of superb roast saddle of rabbit with green olives and fresh tagliarini. Cooked to order, a soft pistachio and rhubarb cake with raspberry coulis needed a little longer in the oven and the defining flavours needed more clarity. It was, however, beautifully presented with a compote of rhubarb, crushed pistachio and raspberry coulis. The large glass frontage of the restaurant, simply but elegantly furnished in reds and greens, adds to the spacious feel high above the comings and goings of busy Piccadilly down below.

Directions: ⊖ Piccadilly Circus

Le Meridien
Waldorf ❀❀

Aldwych WC2B 4DD
Map: E4
Tel: 0870 400 8484
Fax: 020 7836 7244

Telephone for further details

This historic hotel with its special atmosphere and famous Palm Court, offers one of the most romantic settings in town for dinner. The cool, leafy Palm Court Lounge remains an institution – something from a bygone age – with its huge glass ceiling brushed by Kentia palm trees, gold leaf, natural light, columns, and harpist who plays in the afternoons and three-piece jazz band in the evenings (there's a hugely successful jazz brunch on Sundays too). Oh-so-stylish, it's one of London's most fashionable places for tea – good value and unstuffy – with a wonderful ambience. Service from a smartly presented team is friendly and polished. The menu revolves around a bistro-style theme, and there's an informal all-day brasserie. Our test dinner took in a simple but accurately cooked risotto of asparagus with Parmesan, fine fresh turbot served with spinach in a citrus butter sauce, and a beautiful banana parfait.

Directions: ⊖ Covent Garden

Mezzo ❀❀

100 Wardour Street W1V 3LE
Map: D3
Tel: 020 7314 4000
Fax: 020 7314 4040
Chef: David Laris
Owner: Conran Restaurants
Cost: *Alc* £33, set-price L/D £12.50 & £15.50. ☺ H/wine £12.75
Times: Noon-3pm/6-12am (6-7.15pm pre-theatre). Closed L Sat, 25 Dec
Additional: Sunday L; Children welcome
Seats: 350. Private dining room 44
Style: Chic/modern
Smoking: Air conditioning

In top gear, Mezzo really buzzes; it may be crammed to the gills with staff rushing hither and thither, the chefs a blur of activity beyond the sheer glass wall and a constant flow of people up and down the sweeping staircase, but it works. The classic Conran menu and cooking style is ingredient-led, relying primarily on quality but it delivers the goods. Seared tuna with wasabi and soy, and bocconcini and roast aubergine ravioli were both light and constructed with the minimum of fuss. Roast sea scallops with leek and rock oyster sauce was outstanding, outclassing a rather pedestrian roast salmon, bok choy and spiced lentils. Much praise for a dessert of pain perdu, poached pear and chocolate ice-cream. Upstairs Mezzonine is more Asian-orientated, with chicken satay,

Vietnamese rare beef noodle soup and Thai red pork curry with fragrant rice as well as 'ordinaries' such as minute steak, fries and garlic butter. A special seven-piece tasting menu for two is a clever idea.

Directions: ⊖ Piccadilly Circus

Milestone Hotel ❀   NEW

Hotel restaurant in restored Victorian building. Menu includes roast breast of guinea fowl with puy lentils, butternut, coriander and orange, which might be followed by lime and lemon sherbet with a plum and sultana compote.

1 Kensington Court W8 5DL
Map: A2
Tel: 020 7917 1200
Fax: 020 7917 1010

Cost: *Alc* £30, set-price L £15.50. H/wine £18.50
Times: 12.30-2.30pm/5.30-11pm
Additional: Bar food; Sunday L; Children 1+
Style: Classic/Country-house
Smoking: Air conditioning; Jacket & tie preferred
Accommodation: 57 en suite, 6 apartments ★ ★ ★ ★ ★

Directions: ⊖ Kensington High St. 400yds from station

Millennium Baileys Hotel ❀

Contemporary-style restaurant in a revitalised 19th-century building. Modern British dishes include fishcakes with mustard seed and coriander butter sauce, and calves' liver with swede and potato mash.

140 Gloucester Road SW7 4QH
Map: A2
Tel: 020 7373 6000
Fax: 020 7370 3760
E-mail: baileys@mill-cop.com

Telephone for further details

Directions: ⊖ Gloucester Road. Opposite Tube station

Millennium Britannia Mayfair ❀❀

The Shogun Japanese restaurant on the side of this hotel serves 'some of the best Japanese food in London'. At a recent inspection meal most of the diners were Japanese, a sure endorsement of the authenticity of the cooking, and the appropriateness of the surroundings. There is none of the minimalism of other similar restaurants, but instead the room is divided up by 'kyudo – archery arrows – very warlike decorations' and there's also a statue of a samurai warrior. An inspection meal started with long-cooked pork belly which was 'meltingly good', and served with a flavourful broth. Tongue was another fine choice, though the wafer-thin slices were slightly chewy, and dobun mushi soup was also enjoyable. Tempura of prawns and vegetables were as crisp and dry as they should be, and sushi was pristinely fresh. The service is friendly and attentive as always at this professionally managed Mayfair hotel.

Grosvenor Square W1A 3AN
Map: C3
Tel: 020 7629 9400
Fax: 020 7629 7736
E-mail: britanniarestaurant@mill-cop.com
Chef: Neil Gray
Cost: *Alc* £30, set-price L fr £18. ☺ H/wine £17.50
Times: Noon-3pm/6-10pm.
Closed L Sat
Additional: Bar food; Sunday Brunch; Children welcome
Seats: 90. Private dining room 72
Style: Classic/Traditional
Smoking: No-smoking area; Air conditioning
Accommodation: 341 en suite ★ ★ ★ ★

Directions: ⊖ Bond Street, Green Park

Millennium Gloucester

4-18 Harrington Gardens SW7 4LJ
Map: A1
Tel: 020 7373 6030
Fax: 020 7373 0409
E-mail: gloucester@mill-cop.com

Telephone for further details

Dinner is served in the showcase South West 7 restaurant. The menu is Italian with options like traditional osso bucco and roasted stuffed monkfish alongside the pasta and pizzas.

Directions: ⊖ Gloucester Road

Millennium Knightsbridge

17 Sloane Street Knightsbridge
SW1X 9NU
Map: B2
Tel: 020 7235 4377
Fax: 020 7235 3705

Telephone for further details

A modern, stylish and chic Sloane Square hotel close to Harvey Nichols and Harrods, and surrounded by exclusive designer houses. The smart open-plan, first-floor restaurant is decked out in stainless steel, acres of plate mirrors and contemporary 'groovy' seating. Staff are friendly and service is attentive without being intrusive. The menu is a continental mix of European, Asian and North American with some dishes reflecting touches of all three. On a May menu, good breads - ciabatta, cottage bloomer and thick slices off a crusty loaf (?) preceded a layered terrine of duck, foie gras and artichoke with a well-balanced fig compote that proved the star turn. Main course sea bass with prawn and ginger chow mein and rice fritter came across less successfully for our palate, its multiple flavours overpowering the subtle fish (its skin not crisp). A well-presented ice banana parfait with chocolate marquee and caramelised banana saw things back on track. Good full-flavoured double espresso to finish.

Directions: ⊖ Knightsbridge

Mims ❀❀

A really nice, unpretentious restaurant about as far North as you can go and still be inside the M25 and as far from the glitz and glamour of the West End as vinegar is from wine. Decor is a little unconventional with a black-painted frontage, tiled floors, granite-topped tables and a couple of modern foody prints; the menu is a photocopied, hand-written affair but the food speaks for itself. The cooking is clever and noteworthy, confident enough to confound expectations that guinea fowl stuffed with mushrooms and cheese would be anything but palatable. In fact, the Mozzarella worked to subdue the mushroom flavour and added an interesting 'sub' taste of its own, and the stuffing allowed the flavour of the meat to come through. Like Cape Canaveral on a plate, everything was served pointing skywards. Fish dishes are popular, perhaps a well-judged mackerel baked with tomato, lemon and curry oil, or grilled black bream with grilled courgette salad. Raspberry cheesecake comes with crêpe cigars stuffed with poached raspberries.

Directions: On East Barnet Road, next to garage and almost opposite Sainsbury's

63 East Barnet Road EN4 8RN
Map GtL: C4
Tel/Fax: 020 8449 2974
Chef/Owner: Ali Alsersy
Cost: Set-price L £10.50/D £14. ☺
H/wine £9.50
Times: 12.30-2.30pm/6.30-10.30pm.
Closed Mon
Additional: Bar food; Sunday L; Children 7+; Vegetarian dishes on request
Seats: 45
Style: Informal/Minimalist
Smoking: No-smoking area; No pipes & cigars

Mirabelle ❀❀❀

One of the great pluses of the Mayfair restaurant is the hugely stylish bar – a great place to spend a couple of hours with a bottle or two of Champagne. Four large stone-coloured vases, full to bursting with flowers, are the main colour fixes; the floor is old parquet and the banquettes made of brown leather. Martin Caws has transferred from Marco Pierre White's flagship Oak Room, and keeps the Mirabelle's style and standard up to the mark. The *carte* has something for all; lemon sole grilled on the bone and served with Jersey royals may be at the simple end of the scale, whilst a tarte Tatin of endive and caramelised sea scallops or ballotine of wild salmon with herbs and salmon caviar put the kitchen through its paces. There are classics such as a refined-but-gutsy soupe de poisson, eggs Benedict with hollandaise and escalope of calves' liver and bacon with sauce diable, as well as slow-cooked comfort food such as braised oxtail 'Mirabelle' and tender pot-roast pork with spices and ginger. The wine list also has plenty to choose from world-wide, with some cheapies thrown in plus a good selection by the glass. An astonishing selection of 50 Chateau d'Yquems are the undoubted highlight of the dessert wine section.

Directions: ⊖ Green Park

56 Curzon Street W1Y 8DL
Map: C3
Tel: 020 7499 4636
Fax: 020 7499 5449
Chef: Martin Caws
Owner: Marco Pierre White
Cost: *Alc* £35, set-price L £14.95 & £17.95. ☺ H/wine £16
Times: Noon-2.30pm /6-11.30pm
Additional: Sunday L; Children welcome
Seats: 110. Private dining rooms 36, 48
Style: Affordable glamour
Smoking: Air conditioning

AA Wine Shortlisted for Award-see page 18

Mitsukoshi ·❀❀

The lower Regent Street location of this department store basement restaurant means the Japanese embassy staff round the corner in Piccadilly are regular customers. Decorated in traditional minimalist style Mitsukoshi offers guests an

Dorland House, 14-20 Lower Regent Street SW1Y 4PH
Map:
Tel: 020 7930 0317
Fax: 020 7839 1167
Chef: Mr Motohashi

authentic 'straight out of Tokyo' experience. Prices are steep but for the quality of ingredients used, and in all Japanese cuisine ingredients are the point, that is to be expected. Hushed tones are common at lunch but the subdued atmosphere heats up in the evenings. Staff here are exceptionally well informed and are happy to guide diners through the maze that Japanese cuisine can be. Set meals are worthwhile for the amateur but the real quality shines through on the *carte*. Superb sushi and sashimi highlight the excellent buying and all the usual staples are available.

Cost: *Alc* £25.30, set-price L £12/D £20. ☺ H/wine £18
Times: 12-3pm, 6-10.30pm. Closed Sun, Easter & Christmas
Additional: Children welcome
Style: Classic/traditional
Seats: 56. Private dining rooms 12 & 24
Smoking: No pipes & cigars; Air conditioning

Directions: ⊖ Piccadilly Circus

Momo ✿

Unpretentious simple modern decor announces a serious, fresh approach to Japanese cuisine that's big on value and authenticity. Salmon and swordfish sushi and a warm mixed aubergine and minced pork dish were particularly enjoyed.

14 Queens Parade W5 3HU
Map GtL: B3
Tel/Fax: 020 8997 0206
Cost: *Alc* £25, set-price L £16/D£25. ☺ H/wine £9.50
Times: Noon-3pm/6-10.30pm. Closed Sun, 1 wk after Xmas, 1 wk Aug

Additional: Children welcome
Style: Modern/minimalist

Directions: ⊖ North Ealing (opposite)

Monkey's ✿✿

A very popular neighbourhood restaurant with monkey-themed decor and attentive service. The two set-price menus offer a good variety of dishes, advance booking is highly recommended.

1 Cale Street Chelsea Green SW3 3QT
Map: B1
Tel: 020 7352 4711

Telephone for further details

Directions: Corner of Cale St & Markhay St. ⊖ Sloane Sq (5 mins)

Mon Plaisir ✿✿

Founded in the 1940s, Mon Plaisir is now something of an institution and can be not only busy but, noted an inspector one lunchtime, packed with regulars, not a tourist in sight, and that included a man who's lunched here every day for the past 20 years. The series of rooms still conveys the image of a French bistro, accentuated by a smart but casual style, all-French staff and a menu of 'les classiques', all exemplarily cooked, of the likes of gratinée à l'oignon, coquilles St-Jacques meunière, and coq au vin. The more fashion-conscious could opt for escabèche of red mullet with mesclun and tapenade, followed by roast duck breast in Szechuan pepper with Armagnac jus, served with beetroot and onion marmalade and parsnip purée, or moist, flavourful rabbit salad layered with red onion confit, then perfectly grilled lobster in garlic butter. Chips are said to be excellent, and crème brûlée or tarte Tatin make an appropriate finale.

21 Monmouth Street WC2H 9DD
Map: D4
Tel: 020 7836 7243
Fax: 020 7240 4774
Chef: Richard Sawyer
Owner: Mr A Lhermitte
Cost: *Alc* £28, set-price L £14.95/D £23.50. ☺ H/wine £10.50
Times: Noon-2.15pm/5.50-11.15pm. Closed L Sat, all Sun, Bhs
Additional: Children welcome
Seats: 96. Private dining room 28
Style: Informal/French
Smoking: Air conditioning

Directions: ⊖ Leicester Square. Off Seven Dials

Monsieur Max ❀❀

Bare floorboards, magnolia-coloured walls, attractive floral displays and a large window fronting the High Street, set the scene at this popular, if slightly pretentious, neighbourhood restaurant. Decor befits the substantial French bourgeois cuisine of Max Renzland, while quietly efficient French staff add to the friendly, hospitable ambience. Warm, sliced French bread, served without side plates, arrives as soon as you are seated. Then cholesterol challenging rillettes of pork and duck with toasted poilane bread, followed by grilled dorade served on a bed of spinach, aubergine and lemon confit, coco haricots blanc stewed with cherry tomatoes and spiced balsamic vinaigrette, finished off with a cold chocolate fondant served with mint chocolate chip ice cream, our choice from a spring lunch menu. Must try dishes here include breast of chargrilled Domes quail or pithiviers of Burgundian snails to start, pot roasted Anjou squab pigeon or fillet of south coast sea bass the mains, old-fashioned rice pudding with Madagascan vanilla for dessert. The revamped wine list showcases predominantly French wines; look out for some less frequently featured Bordeaux vineyards.

133 High Street Hampton Hill
TW12 1NJ
Map: C2
Tel: 020 8979 5546
Fax: 020 8979 3747

Telephone for further details

Directions: On W side of Bushy Park

Montcalm-Hotel Nikko London ❀❀

The refurbished restaurant at the Japanese-owned hotel still offers remarkably good value for money with two courses, a half-bottle of house wine, coffee and petits fours for £20. Although the hotel boasts 'the best Japanese breakfast outside Japan', the cooking is eclectic, ranging from marinated swordfish with sauce vierge to scallop ravioli with rosemary tomato butter and wilted rocket. A wide choice of main courses includes Barbary duck cooked three styles with artichokes and aubergine, and calves' liver with mountain Gorgonzola, polenta, fried shallots and 8-year old balsamic vinegar. Some dishes, such as lobster lasagne with lobster bisque, perfumed with Marc de Bourgogne, carry a supplement. Puddings such as chocolate fondant might be a little clichéd, but we doubt they are short of takers for the steamed treacle pudding with Glenfiddich ice-cream.

Directions: From Marble Arch ⊖ turn L then 1st L (Great Cumberland Place). After traffic lights hotel is a crescent on R

Great Cumberland Place W1A 2LF
Map: B4
Tel: 020 7402 4288
Fax: 020 7724 9180
E-mail: reservations@montcalm.co.uk
Chef: Stephen Whitney
Cost: Set-price L/D £25. ☺
H/wine £15
Times: 12.30-2.30pm/6.30-10.30pm.
Closed L Sat & Sun
Additional: Bar food; Children welcome
Seats: 70. Private dining room 60
Style: Modern/informal
Smoking: No-smoking area; No pipes; Air conditioning
Accommodation: 120 en suite
★★★★

Moro

*Robust and flavoursome Spanish and North African cuisine,
enhanced by an informal, bustling atmosphere and nice features
such as an open kitchen with wood burning stove. Wood roasted
skate with fennel tabbouleh recommended.*

Additional: Bar food; Children welcome
Style: Informal
Smoking: Air conditioning

Directions: Exmouth Market is on the corner of Rosebery
Avenue and Farringdon Road.

34-36 Exmouth Market EC1R 4QE
Map: E5
Tel: 020 7833 8336
Fax: 020 7833 8339
Cost: *Alc* £30. ☺ H/wine £9.50
Times: 12.30-2.30pm/7-10.30pm.
Closed Sat, Sun, Xmas, New Year,
Bhs

Mortons

This elegant dining room on the first floor of a fashionable
private Mayfair club, offers lovely views over Berkeley Square
for those fortunate enough to secure a window table. Since
Mark Broadbent's (formerly of The Chiswick) arrival at the
helm, menus read much less ambitiously with a distinct change
in philosophy toward good, honest local restaurant than a
'destination'. The repertoire reads straight-down-the-line
modern European with the occasional Oriental tilt: salad
imam bayildi with tsatsiki and griddled flat bread; tataki of
yellowfin tuna, Japanese pickles and wasabi; tranche of
halibut, Jasson's Temptation and fennel fondant are typical of
style. Other dishes that vie for selection might include a
potato pancake, wood pigeon, onion marmalade and truffle oil
starter, or roasted cod, choucroute and Gewürztraminer or
steamed sea bass, Thai spices, coconut and pak choi main
courses. For dessert, pithivier of caramelised apples and
clotted cream or chocolate nemesis with blood orange ice
cream show the format.

Directions: ⊖ Bond Street. On northern side of Berkeley Sq

28 Berkeley Square W1X 5HA
Map: C3
Tel: 020 7493 7171
Fax: 020 7495 3160
Chef: Mark Broadbent
Owners: Simon Lowe, Howard Malin,
Andrew Leeman
Cost: *Alc* £36, set-price L £19.50.
H/wine £15
Times: Noon-2.30pm/7-10.45pm.
Closed L Sat, all Sun, Bhs
Additional: Children welcome
Seats: 60
Style: Chic/Modern art deco

Neal Street Restaurant ⊛⊛

Baskets of fresh produce grace the entrance enticing dinners
with visually stunning displays of mushrooms, asparagus and
breads that signal proprietor Antonio Carluccio's passion.
Times change, but inside Conran's 70s design trademarks are
still evident; white-painted brick walls, quarry tiles, chrome and
marble all feature to create a simple, bright, contemporary and
relaxed ambience – the charming menu graphic, designed by
David Hockney, lives on too. Carluccio is famous for his love
of mushrooms, and they feature prominently on the Italian
repertoire – wild mushroom soup, mixed sauté funghi of the
day, warm mushrooms and pancetta salad, pappardelle with
mixed funghi are examples. On a May menu we resisted the
fungal temptations and started with asparagus – served cold
(but not described so) – with a balsamic dressing, and an
agreeable nettle gnocchi with pesto, followed by main course
offerings of sea bream (on the bone) in sea water with a
seaweed and samphire garnish which won out over the calves'
liver Veneziana served with sautéed spinach. Chocolate is the
inspired way to finish, a semifreddo of Sicilian almonds having
less impact.

Directions: ⊖ Covent Garden (2 mins)

26 Neal Street WC2H 9PS
Map: D4
Tel: 020 7836 8368
Fax: 020 7836 2790

Telephone for further details

the new end

Taste good honest wholesome food, simply-cooked with great flavours in a popular modern restaurant. The baked fillet of cod is excellent, served with a good artichoke ragout. Follow that with chocolate fondant with ice cream.

102 Heath Street Hampstead
NW3 1DR
Map GtL: C4
Tel: 020 7431 4423
Fax: 020 7794 7508
E-mail: info@thenewend.co.uk

Cost: *Alc* £31, set-price L/D £17.80 (pre & post theatre). H/wine £13.95
Times: Noon-3pm/6-11pm. Closed L Tue, all Mon
Additional: Sunday L; Children welcome
Style: Modern
Smoking: No pipes & cigars

Directions: ⊖ Hampstead. 400yds from station

New World

This enormous 700-seater Hong Kong-style restaurant in Chinatown draws the crowds, and is a favourite haunt for the Sunday dim sum ritual. Set on several floors, New world is flamboyantly decorated in the traditional 'lucky' colours of red and gold, though its vastness perhaps lends a slightly soulless, dining hall feel. Dim sum is the thing here, and an informative menu offers photos and short descriptions of the fifty or so dim sum available, while, on the reverse, there are another ten rice and some twenty noodle dishes. Dim sum is served daily from 11am until 6pm from circulating trolleys wheeled by cheery, helpful staff. The myriad of delights include all the usual offerings; shu mai (minced prawn and pork dumplings), har gua (prawn dumplings), fung jau (chicken's feet in chilli and black bean sauce), as well as the more esoteric row shui mug yee (assorted bits of octopus), law pak go (fried turnip paste cake) and lin yung bau (a steamed bun with lotus seed paste), all worth checking out.

1 Gerrard Place W1V 7LL
Map: D3
Tel: 020 7434 2508
Fax: 020 7287 3994

Telephone for further details.

Directions: In Chinatown, just S of Shaftesbury Avenue

Nico Central

The sunny yellow walls remain but the Picasso prints have gone to be replaced by a more frequently changing selection of art works. The service remains slick and swift, geared to the needs of business lunching. The repertoire is mainstream modern French: boudin blanc with apple galette and grain mustard sauce; seared scallops with grilled peppers salsa; confit of duck with braised cabbage and date sauce; pan-fried sea bream with garlic and pesto mash. The cooking is careful and accurate – seared salmon with spinach and pine kernels and a vanilla beurre blanc was typically well-made and a coherent combination of elements. Daily specials might include pavé steak with french beans, polenta and mushroom sauce. There is a strong French showing amongst the 60-bin wine list, including a fair choice of half-bottles and wines by the glass.

35 Great Portland Street W1N 5DD
Map: C4
Tel: 020 7436 8846
Fax: 020 7436 3455
Chef: Thierry Leyer
Owner: The Restaurant Partnership
Cost: *Alc* £30. ☺ H/wine £13
Times: Noon-2pm/6.30-11pm. Closed L Sat, all Sun, Xmas, Etr, Bhs
Additional: Children 6+
Seats: 50. Private dining room 10-12
Style: Chic
Smoking: No pipes & cigars; Air conditioning

Directions: Oxford St end of Portland St. ⊖ Oxford Circus

Nicole's ❀

Choose between mirrors and stainless steel or leather chairs and wooden floors in this split level bar and restaurant. Dishes such as smoked haddock chowder were of a very high standard, although almost overshadowed by the quite exceptional house speciality bread.

Smoking: No-smoking area; No pipes & cigars; Air conditioning

Directions: ⊖ Green Park, Bond St

158 New Bond Street W1 9PA
Map: D4
Tel: 020 7499 8408
Fax: 020 7409 0381
Cost: Alc £35. H/wine £11.50
Additional: Bar food L ; Children welcome
Style: Modern

Noble Rot ❀   NEW

French-influenced dishes like salade de gesiers Perigourdine with summer truffles and foie gras, or even foie gras and piquillo pepper terrine with chilli salt, and a glass of Miranda Golden Botrytis from the carte.

Directions: ⊖ Oxford Circus. Follow Regent St 3rd right into Maddox St, 1st left is Mill St

W1R 9TS
Tel: 020 7629 8877
Fax: 020 7629 8878
E-mail: noblerot@noblerot.com

Telephone for further details

Nobu ❀❀❀

One of London's trendiest dining rooms, this Mayfair branch of the ground-breaking New York restaurant is a fashion statement in itself. Situated on the first floor of the starkly minimalist and hip Metropolitan Hotel, Nobu – with its own Park Lane pavement entrance – woos the crowds with some of the most imaginative and astonishing cuisine in town. 'There's a special buzz, almost as though diners are aware of something quite extraordinary happening on the plate.' Tables in the large dining room are turned-around at night, an indication of Nobu's popularity and enduring appeal – after some four years it's been around far too long to be just the fad of the fickle trend-followers. The cosmopolitan clientele are predictably well-heeled, and out for fun. Service is swanky, brisk and efficient, delivered by an army of well-informed staff. The menu is clearly Japanese in style but is enlivened by South American flourishes – with noted references to some Chilean and Peruvian influences. There's a humility about the food too, simple presentation but the palate is taken by surprise at every course. We sampled the set 'omakase' (chef's choice) on our test visit, which eases the burden of decision making, and delivered seven distinct experiences. Restraint, balance, variety and texture all play their part, along with impeccable ingredients, to produce a unique experience: light pan-fried veal fillets, barely cooked with a fruit sauce; salmon tartare with wasabi and caviar; sea bass ceviche; sushi; seared tuna with a sesame hot sauce are all fine examples. 'What an experience,' the closing comment from one inspector. Two wine lists complement the food, one starting at around £50, the other more reasonable.

Metropolitan Hotel
19 Old Park Lane W1Y 4LB
Map: C3
Tel: 020 7447 4747
Fax: 020 7447 4749

Telephone for further details.

Directions: ⊖ Hyde Park, Green park

Noho ❀

Minimalist restaurant in the heart of ad-land serving Thai-inspired food. Dishes sampled on this occasion were pork and prawn steamed wontons, Thai fishcakes, and a chicken green curry.

Directions: Telephone for directions

32 Charlotte Street W1P 1HP
Map: C4
Tel: 020 7636 4445

Telephone for further details

L'Odeon ❀❀❀

65 Regent Street W1R 7HH
Map: C3
Tel: 020 7287 1400
Fax: 020 7287 1300
Chef: Colin Layfield
Owners: Pierre & Kathleen Condou
Cost: *Alc* £30, set-price L £19.50. ☺
H/wine £16
Times: Noon-2.45pm/5.30-11.30pm.
Closed Sun, Bhs
Additional: Bar food; Children
welcome
Seats: 250. Private dining room 20
Style: Chic/Modern
Smoking: No-smoking area; No pipes
& cigars; Air conditioning

The views over Regent Street are commanding. Decor is mainstream modern with bare floors, blue banquette seating and buttermilk coloured walls. Staff are young, predominantly French, and wear light blue Oxford shirts and white aprons. Large modern flower arrangements make a statement on the bar. The standard of cooking under Colin Layfield is high, and the restaurant continues to be a popular, well-patronised spot. The *carte* takes its cue from a wide variety of influences – typical dishes include sweet pea risotto, crispy Parma ham, poached egg; pan-fried liver, chorizo and sweet potato mash, braised red cabbage; roast tuna, sesame crust, niçoise salad. Fish soup had excellent flavours of anise and shellfish, smooth in texture and lifted by a spicy, garlicky rouille. The aroma of deliciously enjoyable breast of duck, celeriac purée and foie gras ravioli simply wafted over the table. This is a kitchen that takes considerable care in preparation, not least in desserts such as chocolate fondant with ginger ice cream. A serious vintage list complements more contemporary choices.

Directions: Piccadilly Circus, entrance in Air Street, opposite Café Royal

Odettes ❀❀

130 Regents Park Road NW1 8XL
Map : C4
Tel: 020 7586 5486
Fax: 020 7586 2575
Chef: Simon Bradley
Owner: Simone Green
Cost: *Alc* £25, set-price L £10. ☺
H/wine £11.95
Times: 12.30-2.30pm/7-11pm.
Closed L Sat , D Sun, 10 days Xmas &
New Year
Additional: Sunday L; Children
welcome
Seats: 65
Style: Classic/Informal
Smoking: No pipes & cigars

Hanging baskets brighten up the front of this Primrose Hill landmark in summer, when the front wall is opened up for a feeling of open-air dining. Dozens of mirrors are the decor, with a conservatory at the back down some steps and a separate wine bar downstairs. If the setting is reassuringly familiar, the kitchen's style has evolved over the years. Crab and chive sushi with tuna sashimi may crop up alongside ballotine of foie gras with toasted brioche; a dish of marinated quail, roast tiger prawns, green masala chicken and chilli-crusted mackerel may precede simply grilled fillet of halibut with stir-fried greens, or veal chop with herb polenta and a confit of baby onions and tomatoes. Some dishes have a full-blooded ring to them – an assiette of duck (warm smoked breast, confit sausage, pan-fried liver and heart), or pig's head with Dijon mustard and a poached egg – but things normally come together well: pink slices of Szechuan-spiced Gressingham duck breast, for example, arranged around nicely caramelised endive and young Chinese leaf in a reduced gravy with a roasted peach and smooth creamed potatoes. Desserts can outnumber the main courses, running from perhaps saffron and Grand Marnier potted custard to a trifle of stewed rhubarb layered with Mascarpone on a syrup-saturated sponge base. The set lunch (no choice) is considered a bargain, and quality is the byword of the masterly wine list, with over 30, including sweet wines, sold by the glass.

Directions: By Primrose Hill. ⊖ Chalk Farm

One Aldwych –
Axis ⊛⊛

For once, cutting-edge decor is well served by a menu that gets its priorities right and puts flavour above frippery. The striking entrance of One Aldwych leads to a triumphal flight of stairs down to the soaring Axis bar and restaurant; the style is ultra-chic in its use of wood, muted colours and black leather chairs. The menu has a pleasing simplicity which excites because of its very lack of complication. A smoked haddock and cheese soufflé tart was buttery and fresh, and a hay-baked leg of lamb, served with clapshot potatoes, carrots and home-made mint sauce, was wonderful in its pink tenderness and excellence of flavour. Other dishes include roast partridge with sauce Colbert, game chips and Savoy cabbage, and elderflower jelly with Champagne sorbet. Stylish ingredients and techniques, however, are not neglected – viz seared zander on cashew nut, raisin and tamarind confit, and warm lightly-spiced soft-shelled crab with grilled lime and green mango salsa.

Directions: ⊖ Charing Cross. On corner of Aldwych & Wellington St, opp Lyceum Theatre

1 Aldwych WC2B 4BZ
Map: E3
Tel: 020 7300 0300
Fax: 020 7300 0301
E-mail: sales@onealdwych.co.uk
Chef: Mark Gregory
Cost: Alc £35, set-price L/pre-theatre D £15.75 & £19.75. ☺ H/wine £19
Times: Noon-2.45pm/5.45-11.30pm. Closed L Sat, all Sun, Xmas/New Year
Additional: Children welcome
Seats: 116. Private dining room 48
Style: Chic/Modern
Smoking: Air conditioning
Civil licence: 60
Accommodation: 105 en suite
★★★★★

One Aldwych –
Indigo ⊛⊛

Indigo is on the first floor of this magnificent building, positioned to take advantage of views across Waterloo Bridge. The decor is neutral, the colours reflect the atmosphere of the restaurant: relaxed and informal.The food is billed as creative and healthy, and the menu is divided into starters, pasta and risotto, salads, main courses, and desserts, supplemented by 'specials' which change weekly at lunch and dinner. Carpaccio of beef was served with truffle oil, and arrived with big curls of parmesan and an oiled rocket salad. Confit of Aylesbury duck was served with a polenta, topped with brown lentils. Puddings are very good, particularly the crunchy chocolate tart.

Directions: See previous entry (One Aldwych – Axis)

1 Aldwych WC2B 4BZ
Tel: 020 7300 0400
Fax: 020 7300 0401
E-mail: sales@onealdwych.co.uk
Chef: Julian Jenkins
Cost: Alc £35, set-price D £15.50 & £19.50 (pre-theatre). ☺ H/wine £19
Times: Noon-3pm/6-11.15pm
Additional: Bar food; Children welcome
Seats: 62. Private dining room 48
Style: Informal/Chic
Smoking: No pipes & cigars; Air conditioning
Civil licence: 60
Accommodation: 105 en suite
★★★★★

1 Lombard Street –
The Brasserie ⊛⊛

Modern premises with plain decor enlivened by uplighting and some ornate plasterwork. With tiled floors underfoot and an impressive glass domed roof above the circular bar, the elegance of what was once a banking hall sets a high standard for the cuisine. With very few exceptions the cooking is equal to the task with the lengthy, seasonally changing menu offering

1 Lombard Street
EC3V 9AA
Map GtL: G3
Tel: 020 7929 6611
Fax: 020 7929 6622
E-mail: ja@1lombardstreet.com
Chef: Herbert Berger
Owners: Soren Jessen, Jessens & Co

often elaborate and decorative, but always quality dishes such as fresh and crisp Caesar salad with fresh pancetta and anchovies. On a recent visit a main of smoked haddock fishcake was a little on the heavy side but nevertheless offered a good distinct flavour and the vegetables of the day showed imagination and were of good, fresh quality. A lemon tart was definitely a highlight of the meal with excellent pastry and a really intense flavour complemented by a delightful passionfruit and orange coulis, and passionfruit sorbet.

Cost: *Alc* £25-£30, set-price D £15 & £19.80. ☺
Times: 11.30-3pm/6-10pm.
Closed Sat, Sun, 1 wk Xmas
Additional: Bar food; Children welcome
Seats: 150. Private dining room 40
Style: Classic/Informal
Smoking: No pipes; Air conditioning

Directions: ⊖ Bank. Opposite Bank of England

L'Oranger ❀❀

5 St James's Street SW1A 1EF
Map: C3
Tel: 020 7839 3774
Fax: 020 7839 4330
Chef: Kamel Benamar
Owner: A-Z Restaurant Ltd
Cost: Set-price L £20-£24.50/D £37. H/wine £16
Times: Noon-2.30pm/6-10.45pm.
Closed L Sat, all Sun, Xmas, Bhs
Additional: Children 6+
Seats: 55. Private dining room 20
Style: French
Smoking: No pipes & cigars; Air conditioning

From the desperate hubbub of St James's Street the serene hush that greets diners is almost soporific and the legions of thoughtful staff have you seated and smiling distantly before you have time to wonder where your hat and coat are. A recent meal succeeded in bringing out the poet in our inspector who described a starter of red mullet and salt cod terrine as 'a wonderful kaleidoscope of subtle textures and flavours that had me thinking of seaweed, attractive mermaids and crashing waves at the base of mountainous cliffs.' This perhaps says more about our inspector than the dish, but nobody could argue with the precision of the composition, or the freshness and quality of the ingredients. By the time a main of skirt of beef bordelaise and a dessert of warm chocolate fondant had been attended to, our inspector's extensive vocabulary of superlatives had been almost exhausted. A truly excellent meal.

Directions: ⊖ Green Park. St James's Street is accessible by car via Pall Mall

Organic Café ❀ NEW

25 Lonsdale Road NW6 6RA
Map GtL: C3
Tel: 020 7372 1232

First organic restaurant to be accredited by the Soil Association. It has an honest approach; ingredients are respectfully treated and skilfully cooked to deliver flavours. No credit or debit cards.

Telephone for further details

Directions: Telephone for directions

The Orient ❀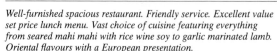

Well-furnished spacious restaurant. Friendly service. Excellent value set price lunch menu. Vast choice of cuisine featuring everything from seared mahi mahi with rice wine soy to garlic marinated lamb. Oriental flavours with a European presentation.

Additional: Children welcome **Style:** Chic/Modern
Smoking: No-smoking area; Air conditioning

Directions: ⊖ Green Park. Next to The Ritz Hotel

160 Piccadilly W1V 9DF
Map: C3
Tel: 020 7499 6888
Fax: 020 7659 9300
E-mail:
chinahouse@chinahouse.co.uk
Cost: *Alc* £40, set-price D (pre-theatre) £19.50. ☺ H/wine £14
Times: Noon-3pm/6pm-midnight. Closed L Sat, all Sun

Orrery ❀❀❀

The restaurant, all cool white and clean lines, is located above the shop – the Conran shop, of course. The long thin room overlooks Marylebone Church gardens and the High Street through floor to ceiling arched windows. There is also a terrace bar for light meals and drinks in summer. Chris Galvin knows how to cook and how to keep the French-accented dishes essentially simple and full of flavour – seared fillet of red mullet with pesto and aubergine caviar was all it should be, as was a roast breast of duck with excellent crisp and golden pommes sarladaise, turnips, bok choy and spot-on sherry vinegar jus. There are enough fashionable ingredients and ideas to satisfy the switched-on local clientele but they are kept in check by an understanding of combinations – caramelised calves' sweetbreads, salsify, corn salad and truffle vinaigrette; swiss chard and goats' cheese croustillant, buttered leeks, vine tomatoes and pumpkin oil; roast leg of Pyrénées lamb, baked in hay, haricots blancs, herbes de Provence. Pudding was 'fantastic' – an original Agen prune and Armagnac ice-cream with Granny Smith rösti. Staff are notably chatty and friendly and the British sommelier deserves a special mention.

55-57 Marylebone High Street W1M 3AE
Map: B4
Tel: 020 7616 8000
Fax: 020 7616 8080
E-mail: patrickf@conran-restaurants.co.uk
Chef: Chris Galvin
Owner: Conran Restaurants
Cost: *Alc* £50, set-price L £23.50/D £45. H/wine £13
Times: Noon-3pm/7-11pm. Closed 25 & 26 Dec, Good Fri
Additional: Bar food; Sunday L; Children welcome
Seats: 80
Style: Modern/Elegant
Smoking: No pipes

Directions: ⊖ Baker Street. At very northern end of Marylebone High Street

AA *Shortlisted for* Wine Award-see page 18

Orsino ❀

Unassuming, buzzing Italian eatery, bright and spacious. Menu might include risotto with spinach, roast butternut squash and fontina, or grilled calf's liver with roast celeriac, onions and thyme. Fruit and cheese available alongside dessert.

Smoking: No-smoking area; No pipes & cigars; Air conditioning

Directions: ⊖ Holland Park

119 Portland Road W11 4LN
Map GtL: C3
Tel: 020 7221 3299
Fax: 020 7229 9414
Cost: ☺ H/wine £12
Times: Noon-midnight. Closed 25 Dec
Additional: Children welcome
Style: Modern/Italian

Orso Restaurant

A long-established Italian restaurant in the heart of Covent Garden. Indeed the basement dining room was originally the flower section of the market and it features original white tiling on walls and pillars. Honest hearty food matches the jovial, welcoming atmosphere. A bilingual menu invites you to sample the delights of pizza with rock shrimp, hot pepper, parsley, arugula and tomato. The more classically minded diner might prefer to start with an appetiser of buffalo Mozzarella, tomato and basil salad; followed by a first course of flat pasta with pot-roast lamb, white bean and bitter broccoli; and an entrée of slow-roast crispy duck with roast apricots and herb potatoes. The lightness of the desserts calls to mind the Mediterranean summer – lemon cake with mascarpone, and warm poached pear with passion fruit for example. The wine list is 100% Italian and the bread is, of course, a strong point.

Directions: ⊖ Covent Garden. 1 block in from The Strand, 2 blocks down from Royal Opera House

27 Wellington Street WC2E 7DA
Map: D3
Tel: 020 7240 5269
Fax: 020 7497 2148
E-mail: joeallen.ldn@btinternet.com
Chef: Martin Wilson
Cost: Alc £28.50, set-price D £15(early evening only). ☺
H/wine £12
Times: Noon-midnight. Closed Xmas
Additional: Sunday L; Children welcome
Seats: 100
Style: Modern
Smoking: No-smoking area; No pipes & cigars; Air conditioning

Osteria Antica Bologna

Rustic Italian restaurant with wooden floors, tables and chairs and lots of wrought ironwork. Good menu descriptions reveal some more unusual dishes – authentic family fare – and vegetarians are well catered for.

Directions: Off Battersea Rise, between Wandsworth & Clapham Commons

23 Northcote Road SW11 1NG
Map GtL: C2
Tel/Fax: 020 7978 4771

Telephone for further details

Osteria d'Isola

Those wanting a fine dining experience can take the stairs up to the raised ground floor and head for the elegant surroundings of Isola, while downstairs is Osteria d'Isola, a larger, comfortable room done out in shades of stone and creamy beige with pockets of colour – the bar a strong square of bright green. Down here, a window at ceiling height allows passers-by the chance to gawp in, while the open-plan kitchen at the back offers diners another diversion. The idiom is seriously Italian, with classics of osso buco milanese or vitello tonnato mingling with modern reworkings: ravioli stuffed with roasted beetroot, sage and horseradish, or grilled quail with polenta and red onion salsa. A chickpea pancake piled with rocket and ricotta mixed with honey makes a good fresh-tasting starter, and the kitchen pulls out all the stops for main courses of rump of lamb, slow-roasted Roman-style with anchovies and olives, or Livornese fish stew. Desserts – tiramisu, pannacotta, panettone pudding – are as Italian as the long, thoroughbred wine list, with masses sold by the glass and themed 'tasters' giving punters the chance of trying five different glasses.

Directions: ⊖ Knightsbridge. Opposite Household Cavalry Barracks and Bowater House

NEW

145 Knightsbridge SW1X 7PA
Map: B2
Tel: 020 7838 1055
Fax: 020 7838 1099
Chef: Bruno Loubet
Owner: Oliver Peyton
Cost: Alc £25, set-price L £15. ☺
H/wine £13
Times: Noon-3pm/6-10.30pm. Closed Bhs
Additional: Bar food; Sunday L; Children welcome
Seats: 106
Style: Modern
Smoking: No-smoking area; Air conditioning

Oxo Tower Restaurant

8th Floor Oxo Tower Wharf Barge House Street SE1 9PH
Map: E3
Tel: 020 7803 3888
Fax: 020 7803 3838
E-mail: marc.whitley@harveynichols.co.uk
Chef: Simon Arkless
Owner: Harvey Nichols Restaurants Ltd
Cost: Set-price L £27.50/D £60.65. H/wine £12.50
Times: Noon-3pm/6-11.30pm). Closed L Sat, 25 & 26 Dec, 1 Jan
Additional: Sunday L; Children welcome
Seats: 130. Plus seating for 80 outside
Style: Chic/modern
Smoking: No pipes; Air-conditioning

The wide view of the Thames, with a terrace for good weather, seems more important than a decor of industrial minimalism, despite loads of style details and a revolving ceiling, at this eighth-floor restaurant on the South Bank, and window seats are clearly fought over. The kitchen takes a modish approach, pairing grilled scallops with spicy Thai cabbage, or pan-fried duck foie gras with poached gingered figs. Some main courses receive similar treatment – roast fillet of sea bass comes with cannellini beans, chorizo and meat juices – while others show a regard for tradition and seasonality: a well-balanced main course of a cut from the leg of smoked Tamworth bacon with stuffed cabbage, caramelised apples and mustard sauce, say, or crepinettes of oxtail with sauce bourguignonne and mashed potato. The pudding list might see vanilla pannacotta with Muscat-poached fruit rubbing shoulders with chocolate and banana bread pudding with banana ice cream. Alternatively, eat in the brasserie, which offers similarly stylish dishes, and a good value set menu.

Directions: ⊖ Blackfriars. In between Blackfriars Bridge and Waterloo Bridge

Ozer ⊛⊛
NEW

Ozer is easy to walk past. The screen-like windows give little away; the door is a heavy, almost medieval affair. Within, the look is vaguely oriental with one wall of blood red marble, another of streaky white. Scatter cushions in crimson and gold add a sumptuous note to the bar area. The setting suits the 'Modern Ottoman' cooking in which basic Turkish ideas are rethought and adapted for contemporary tastes through the prism of French technique. Sea bass, for example, may be bathed in fish stock and Turkish tea, and served with mussel jus and shredded cabbage. Both saffron seafood pilaf with dill oil, and shoulder of lamb, gently roasted and basted and served with a marmalade of kumquats and limequats, showed the cooking at its best – accomplished skills, good ingredients and the awareness of simplicity as a virtue. A run-of-the-mill pain perdu was considerably improved by delicious rose ice cream. Other desserts explore a sweet-savoury dimension – for example, roasted pear with fresh coriander and pistachio.

5 Langham Place W1N 7DD
Map: C4
Tel: 020 7323 0505
Fax: 020 7323 0111
E-mail: res@ozer.co.uk
Chef: Jerome Tauvron
Owner: Huseyin Ozer
Cost: *Alc* £35, set-price L /D (until 7.30pm) £17.95. ☺ H/wine £13.50
Times: Noon-2.30pm/6-11pm. Closed L Sat, all Sun
Additional: Bar food; Children 2+
Seats: 85
Style: Chic/Modern
Smoking: No pipes & cigars; Air conditioning

Directions: From Oxford Circus, N up Regent Street which becomes Langham Place. Restaurant opp The Langham Hilton

Parade

A welcome addition to the neighbourhood, with a simple interior, clean lines, smooth black leather chairs and plain white walls hung with large modern art works. Ravioli is presented in the modern style, one large piece of pasta stuffed with aubergine and feta cheese, red onions and pesto; other first courses display an equally upbeat style – tuna tataki, soy, ginger, cucumber and spring onions, for example, or cep and field mushroom risotto cakes, Mozzarella and rocket. Stuffed leg of rabbit with black pudding, cannellini and Savoy cabbage was, overall, a satisfying, well-balanced dish for a winter's day. Vegetables are suited to the season – stuffed breast of pheasant may come with turnip dauphinoise and red cabbage, or celeriac purée, onion Tatin, parsnips and thyme with haunch of venison. The pace is sustained with a tempting list of desserts; our inspector especially enjoyed a hot chocolate pudding with orange sorbet, a fine rendition of this increasingly popular combination. Dinners are priced either per individual course (with all dishes the same price) or as a set two or three-course meal; the clever part is that there is no difference in terms of choice between the two.

Directions: ⊖ Ealing Broadway. Turn L from tube station along High Street, turn L into The Mall. Restaurant on L

18-19 The Mall Ealing W5 2PJ
Map GtL: B3
Tel: 020 8810 0202
Fax: 020 8810 0303
Chef: Robert Jones
Owners: Rebecca Mascarenhas, James Harris
Cost: Set-price L £12 & £15/D £18.50 & £22.50. H/wine £9.50
Times: 12.30-2.30pm/7-11pm. Closed Bhs
Additional: Bar food; Sunday L; Children welcome
Seats: 100. Private dining room 40
Style: Modern/Minimalist
Smoking: No pipes & cigars; Air conditioning

The Peasant

Ornate corner pub with a traditional feel downstairs and a funky restaurant upstairs. The Mediterranean menu offers semolina fried calamari, baked sea bass with roasted courgettes, and pannacotta and amaretto caramel.

Additional: Bar food; Children welcome

Directions: ⊖ Farringdon, Angel

24 St John Street EC1 4PH
Map: E4
Tel: 020 7336 7726
Fax: 020 7241 5576
E-mail: eat@thepeasant.co.uk
Cost: Alc £20. ☺ H/wine £10
Times: 12.30-3pm/6.30-11pm. Closed L Sat, all Sun, Bhs

The People's Palace

Spacious high-ceilinged restaurant, well positioned for an extensive view over the Thames. Wide selection of modern European dishes ranging from seared scallops, lemon fennel and curry cream to honey roast Magret of duck.

Additional: Bar food; Sunday L; Children welcome
Smoking: No-smoking area; Air conditioning

Directions: Level 3 of the Royal Festival Hall

Royal Festival Hall Belvedere Road SE1 8XX
Map: E3
Tel: 020 7928 9999
Fax: 020 7928 2355
Cost: Alc £25, set-price L £12.50/D £15.50. ☺ H/wine £11.50
Times: Noon-3pm/5.30-11pm. Closed Bhs

Pescatori

Pleasant fish and seafood restaurant on Charlotte Street spanning the ground and first floors. Bright and airy, the cleverly themed decor gives the impression of a Mediterranean fishing village, while an impressive display of fresh fish and seafood, packed in ice, provides a splendid central feature. There are a few concessions to non fish eaters, otherwise it's wall-to-wall fish and shellfish on the reasonably lengthy menu – its Italian influence apparent in the likes of two risottos, five types of pasta, bruschetta, and prosciutto. One might choose

57 Charlotte Street Fitzrovia W1P 1LA
Map: C4-D3
Tel: 020 7580 3289
Chef: Michele Espenica
Owner: Lavarini Olivelli Fraquelli
Cost: Alc £35, set-price L £17.95. ☺ H/wine £11.75
Times: Noon-3pm/6-11.30pm. Closed L Sat, all Sun, Xmas, Etr, Bhs
Additional: Children welcome

coral scallops tossed in a shellfish sauce on roquette, or roasted asparagus, olive oil, rock salt and Parmesan to start. Main course crab and salmon fishcakes are served with a guacamole and coriander salsa, seared sword fish with pesto and marinated grilled vegetables, and sea bass with fennel and flat parsley – a large bowl of French fries comes with entrées. Good choice of home-made desserts, where an apple and raspberry nut crumble could tempt. Decent espresso with agreeable petits fours, and predominantly Italian wine list with a number by the glass.

Seats: 50 & 80
Style: Informal/Mediterranean
Smoking: No-smoking area;
Air conditioning

Directions: Telephone for directions

Pétrus

The setting takes second place to the food on the plate despite the spacious tables and large still-life food paintings. Perhaps it is the high ceiling, the bland beige colouring and the lack of division between tables at the front of the room and the bar area that makes it feel rather like a converted car showroom. The front of house, in fact, runs as smoothly as a tycoon's limo. Marcus Wareing cooks with great precision, technical and visual skills plus an attention to detail that stretches up to the zenith, although there were odd, unseasonal notes on a freezing winter's night in dishes such as fish carpaccio, a gazpacho amuse-gueule and summer fruit sorbets. The six-course tasting menu gives an indication of Wareing's ambitions: marinated foie gras, apple and artichoke salad, creamed vinaigrette; braised halibut with cos lettuce, peas and a velouté of horseradish; pigeon of Bresse with truffled lentils and confit new potatoes, Madeira jus; Valhrona chocolate fondant with a feuilletine biscuit and white chocolate sorbet. When he relaxes a little and adds perhaps a dash more passion to his intellectual commitment and undoubted talent, he will be reaching for the stars indeed.

Directions: Green Park

33 St James's Street SW1 1HD
Map: D3
Tel: 020 7930 4272
Fax: 020 7930 9702
Chef: Marcus Wareing
Owner: Gordon Ramsay, Marcus Wareing
Cost: Set-price L £22/D £35. H/wine £15
Times: Noon-3pm/6.45-11pm. Closed L Sat, all Sun, Xmas, Bhs
Additional: Children 5+
Seats: 50
Style: French/chic
Smoking: No pipes & cigars; Air conditioning

Pharmacy Restaurant

Exciting and chic concept restaurant with a design installation on a medical theme. It's all very tasteful with nothing to put you off the high quality dishes on offer, such as smoked haddock kedgeree or sweet potato capelletti.

Additional: Bar food D; Sunday L; Children welcome
Style: Chic/Modern
Smoking: Air conditioning

Directions: Notting Hill Gate

150 Notting Hill Gate W11 3QG
Map Gtl: C3
Tel: 020 7221 2442
Fax: 020 7243 2345
E-mail: mail@pharmacylondon.com
Cost: Alc £55, set-price L £15.50 & £17.50. ☺ H/wine £14
Times: Noon-4.30pm/6.45-12am. Closed 25 Dec, 1 Jan, Bhs

Phoenix Bar & Grill

Boldness and simplicity characterise both the decor and menu in this chic, modern restaurant. The set menu may include grilled salmon with red pepper and caperberry salad, with rhubarb compote and marmalade ice cream for dessert.

Style: Chic/modern
Smoking: No-smoking area; Air conditioning

Directions: Telephone for directions

162 Pentlow Street SW15 1LY
Map Gtl: C2
Tel: 020 8780 3131
Fax: 020 8780 1114
Cost: Set-price L/D £12. ☺ H/wine £9.75
Times: 12.30-2.30pm/7-11pm. Closed L Sat in winter, Bhs

Pied à Terre ❀❀❀

34 Charlotte Street W1P 1HJ
Map: C4
Tel: 020 7636 1178
Fax: 020 7916 1171
E-mail: p-a-t@dircon.co.uk
Chef: Shane Osborn
Owner: David Moore
Cost: Set-price L £23. H/wine £18
Times: 12.15-2.15pm/7.15-10.30pm.
Closed L Sat, all Sun, last wk Aug,
2 wks Xmas/New Year
Additional: Children welcome
Seats: 38. Private dining room 12-14
Style: Informal/Chic
Smoking: Air conditioning

Shane Osborn has taken over the most notorious pressure cooker of a kitchen in London, and rises well to the challenge, but although the food is still very good, it lacks some degree of previous precision. One of the best dishes sampled was a fine combination of roasted langoustine tails with tomato mille-feuille, tomato vinaigrette and garlic cream. This showed real class, as did a 'canellon' of baby squid with saffron sauce and red pepper purée. Cleverly constructed but ultimately more two dimensional was a foie gras compilation of seared and poached liver with fresh pasta sheets layered with foie gras, a Sauternes consommé and fresh peas. Homage to Richard Neat was paid in a pig on a platter dish of braised pork cheek, roasted belly pork, steamed trotter and roasted fillet with celeriac puree. Although pretty on the plate, there were too many clashing flavours in a dessert of banana Tatin with banana and passionfruit sorbet and passionfruit parfait. Despite the flamboyant floral arrangements, the dining room retains a minimalist feel; the Warhol pop art has vanished, replaced by interesting, almost tribal abstracts.

Directions: ⊖ Goodge Street. S of BT Tower

Le Pont de la Tour ❀❀

The Butlers Wharf Building
36d Shad Thames SE1 2NQ
Map: G3
Tel: 020 7403 8403
Fax: 020 7403 0267
Chef: David Burke
Owner: Conran Restaurants Ltd
Cost: Alc £38, set-price L £28.50.
H/wine £11.95
Times: Noon-3pm/6-11.30pm.
Closed L Sat, 28 Dec
Additional: Bar food; Sunday L;
Children welcome
Seats: 105. Private dining room 20
Style: Formal/Elegant
Smoking: Air conditioning

When the sun shines to make the water of the Thames look almost tropical there can be few more desirable venues for enjoying quality modern European cuisine. The bankside location is stunning and diners are constantly attracted to the superb views of Tower Bridge and the myriad boats that patrol the river. The cooking is simple and effective with a significant degree of skill complementing the high quality produce. The menu keeps a firm eye on the seasons and seafood is a speciality, as was testified to by a recent starter of tartare of tuna with crab and coriander. Consistency was demonstrated in the quality of a fresh lobster in a simple main incorporating an accurately dressed green salad. Quality was also the dominant theme in a milk and white chocolate parfait that concluded the meal with succinctness and vibrancy.

Directions: SE side of Tower Bridge

La Porte des Indes ❀❀

32 Bryanston Street W1H 7AE
Map: D4
Tel: 020 7224 0055
Fax: 020 7224 1144
E-mail: pilondon@aol.com
Chef: Mehernosh Moay
Owner: Blue Elephant Group
Cost: *Alc* £40, set-price L £16.75/D
£31. ☺ H/wine £10.50.
Times: Noon-2.30pm (3pm Sun)/7-
midnight (Sun 6-10.30pm).
Closed L Sat, Xmas
Additional: Sunday brunch;
Children welcome
Seats: 300. Private dining rooms
10 & 12
Style: Classic
Smoking: Air conditioning

Tucked away behind Oxford Street near Marble Arch, La Porte des Indes is typical of the Blue Elephant Group in having spectacular decor. The sheer size of the restaurant, 300 covers plus, is belied by its modest entrance. However the layout and decor, coupled with judicious placing of tables, can afford an intimate experience. Beyond the entrance, the main restaurant is on two floors with a glass cupola above the stairs which lead down through a large galleried opening to the floor below where there is a comfortable bar area. In the stairwell there is a marble waterfall extending to the height of two floors and the floor areas are littered with potted palms. The *carte* is extensive, with an emphasis on the French Creole cuisine of Pondicherry. The cooking is competent and subtle Crab Malabar (flakes of crab and corn), battered aubergine filled with cheese and herb pâté and chicken tikka all fell in to this category but not the fillet of sole with mint and coriander chutney in banana leaves. The buffets at lunchtimes, particularly Sundays, have proved popular with smaller groups, as you can easily experiment with new dishes. The wine list includes French, New Zealand, South African, Australian and even Indian wines along with a selection of beers.

Directions: ⊖ Marble Arch. Behind Cumberland Hotel

The Purple Sage

92 Wigmore Street W1H 9DR
Map: C3
Tel: 020 7486 1912
Fax: 020 7486 1913

Smart, modern but informal Italian restaurant whose strength lies in simplicity, freshness and accuracy of flavour. Pasta dishes include ravioloni: hand-made pasta circles filled with a crumb and prawn mix and dotted with mussels.

Cost: *Alc* £19. ☺ H/wine £9.50
Times: Noon-4pm/6-midnight. Closed L Sat, all Sun
Additional: Children welcome
Style: Informal/Rustic
Smoking: Air conditioning

Directions: ⊖ Bond Street

Putney Bridge ❀❀❀❀

The Embankment SW15 1LB
Map GtL: C2
Tel: 020 8780 1811
Fax: 020 8780 1211
Chef: Anthony Demetre
Owner: Gerald Davidson
Cost: *Alc* £39.50, set-price L & D
£19.50. H/wine £13.50
Times: Noon-2pm/7-10.30pm. Closed
D Sun, all Mon, Xmas
Additional: Sunday L;
Children welcome
Seats: 100
Smoking: Air conditioning

Putney Bridge is a fantastic building, one of the coolest hot spots by the river. The bar and deck are soon filled with drinkers, and the upstairs restaurant packed out with discerning diners. Anthony Demetre's exciting style of modern French cooking is not just technically good, but full of extra dimensions and always exceeding expectations. Dishes are visually outstanding, but never short of depth in a sensibly sized menu that does not overstretch the kitchen. Dinners include the full-works complement of two pre-starters as well as two pre-desserts plus petits fours. A textured fennel jelly with fennel cream and a crisp strand of seaweed really set the standards, as did a rich, chic velouté flavoured with lemongrass. Starters proper include succulent red mullet fillets with cauliflower, nasturtium, courgette and tomato salad and a heavenly marriage of foie gras with hazelnuts and cherries. More inspiration with a well-timed and flavoured guinea fowl on great braised cabbage, and a simply magical lobster in the shell, the claw meat stuffed in a piquillo pepper with a phenomenal herby pesto, squid ink polenta, roast pumpkin and julienne of haricots verts all drawn together by a powder of sweet spices slashed across the plate. Great desserts include a signature Warm Valrhona chocolate moelleux with almond milk sorbet. Service is warm and pleasant, and the sommelier is impressively knowledgeable.

AA Wine Shortlisted for Award-see page 18

Directions: ✆ Putney Bridge. Walk out of station and across bridge. Restaurant is the first building on R, facing onto river

Quaglino's ❀

Buzz and glamour are the keywords at this spectacular restaurant approached down a sweeping staircase, with an 'altar' of crustacea and a menu concentrating on brasserie fare like duck confit with black pudding and apple, and fish and chips with tartare sauce.

Additional: Bar food; Sunday L; Children welcome
Style: Buzzing/glamorous
Smoking: Air conditioning

Directions: Bury St is off Jermyn St, ✆ Green Park

16 Bury Street St James's
SW1Y 6AL
Map: C3
Tel: 020 7930 6767
Fax: 020 7839 2866
Cost: Alc £25, set-price L/D £12.50 & £15 ☺ H/wine £12.75
Times: Noon-3pm/5.30pm-1am.
Closed 25 Dec

Quality Chop House ❀

Perhaps the only place around to offer 'Eggs, Bacon and Chips' and 'Sevruga Caviar with Blinis' on the same menu. 'Progressive working class catering' is the name of the game in this quality establishment dating back to the nineteenth century.

Additional: Sunday L; Children welcome
Style: Informal/traditional
Smoking: No-smoking area; Air conditioning

Directions: On the south side of Farringdon Road, from its junction with Rosebery Avenue. ✆ Farringdon

94 Farringdon Road EC1 3EA
Map: E4
Tel: 020 7837 5093
Fax: 020 7833 8748
Cost: Alc £27. ☺ H/wine £11
Times: Noon-3pm/6.30-11.30pm.
Closed L Sat, 24 Dec-3 Jan

Quincy's Restaurant ❀

Victorian townhouse converted into a small family-run restaurant. Daily soup and fresh fish supplement the monthly menu of options such as medallions of veal and lamb noisettes.

Additional: Children 14+
Style: Classic/traditional
Smoking: No pipes & cigars; Air conditioning

Directions: Situated between Hendon Way & Cricklewood Lane

675 Finchley Road NW2 2JP
Map GtL: C4
Tel: 020 7794 8499
Cost: Set price D £27. H/wine £10
Times: D only, 7-11.30pm.
Closed Mon

Quo Vadis ❀❀❀

Conversation-stopping and thought-provoking art – reptile skeletons on the ceiling, chicken skulls, paintings made from butterflies, original Warhol paintings and Marco Pierre White's DIY canvases – make a change from your average bare walls and brickwork interior. Add to this a dessert of crystal jelly

26-29 Dean St W1V 6LL
Map: D4
Tel: 020 7437 9585
Fax: 020 7434 9972
Chef: Spencer Patrick
Owners: M Pierre White, J Lahoud, F J Peire

with gleaming raspberry, orange and banana jewels which could have been made for a photo-shoot and you get a sense of the impact both off and on the plate. The menu divides into sections such as 'soups and salads' and 'roasts and grills', with a wide choice from grilled tuna with aubergine caviar, tomato and basil to superb roast chicken 'properly garnished' with sauces in silver boats, watercress and wholesome vegetables. We started with an hors d'oeuvre of warm quiche of Gruyère and leeks which was simply the epitome of all that a dream quiche should be, golden buttery pastry and a good layer of flavourful filling, not too dry and not too runny. Chef Spencer Patrick is not just a whizz of a quiche-maker, he also knows how to deliver a superbly tender roast rump of lamb with herbs, velvety pommes purées and green salad. Diners tend to dress in dark suits and be unnaturally attached to their mobile phones.

Cost: *Alc* £33, set-price L & pre-theatre D £20. H/wine £14
Seats: 90
Style: Informal/Chic
Smoking: No pipes; Air conditioning

Directions: ⊖ Leicester Square

Radisson Edwardian Berkshire Hotel 🏵🏵

Oxford Street W1N 0BY
Map: C3
Tel: 020 7629 7474
Fax: 020 7495 1686

Telephone for further details

Sandwiched between Oxford Street's popular department stores, this is the ideal base from which to shop on a grand scale. An intimate, warm and friendly hotel – and the atmosphere extends to the cosy first-floor restaurant with its wooden floors and contemporary design. The mixed business and shopping clientele enjoy the modern British menu, which has much to recommend it. A starter of pan-fried foie gras on a toasted brioche was marginally spoilt by the addition of too much fig confit and white truffle oil at a recent test meal, but steamed sea bass with broth of lemon grass, bok choy and oyster mushrooms was a balanced, well-flavoured main dish. Apple and rhubarb crumble was crunchy, and past successes have included banana pizza with honey and ginger ice cream, and praline parfait with griottine cherries.

Directions: ⊖ Bond Street (opposite)

Radisson Edwardian Hampshire Hotel 🏵

Leicester Square WC2H 7LH
Map: C3
Tel: 020 7839 9399
Fax: 020 7930 8122
E-mail: reshamp@radisson.com

Typical dishes in the stylish Apex Restaurant are a good confit duck leg, and grilled red mullet with roasted peppers. The new chef will introduce changes in the months to come.

Telephone for further details

Directions: The S side of Leicester Square on the corner with St Martin's Street

Radisson Edwardian Mountbatten Hotel 🏵🏵

Monmouth Street Seven Dials Covent Garden WC2H 9HD
Map: E3
Tel: 020 7836 4300
Fax: 020 7240 3540
E-mail: resmoun@radisson.com
Chef: Aziz Joudar

Recently refurbished hotel restaurant now boasting wooden floors, smart furnishings and a smart, cool, sophisticated environment. Service at 'The Dial' (as it is now called) is, in keeping with the rest of the hotel, unfailingly friendly and helpful and its excellent position within Covent Garden makes it a popular choice with theatre-goers. An inspection meal opened with a capuccion of artichoke with truffle oil that was quite simply delicious. After such a promising start the asparagus terrine with tomato salsa and a herb confit did seem a little muted but a deliciously fresh and well-timed roast fillet of sea bass with aubergine caviar and oyster beignets put the meal right back on course. A lemon crème brûlée with a compote of blueberries demonstrated a devoted approach to desserts. The restaurant's wine list is small but well balanced and good value for London. It also includes a good selection of wines by the glass.

Directions: ⊖ Leicester Square

Rain ✻

Pretty, underwater-themed fusion restaurant on the outer edge of the Notting Hill trustafarian beat. There's a value-led weekend lunch/brunch menu, but more complex evening dishes really sum up the philosophy of the place: Hunanese roast rack of lamb with aromatic spices, Vietnamese glazed pumpkin and okra tempura.

Additional: Bar food; Sunday L; Children welcome
Style: chic/rustic
Smoking: Air conditioning

Directions: ⊖ Ladbroke Grove. N end of Portobello Road

Rani ✻

Comfortably furnished vegetarian Indian restaurant, adorned with photographs of rural India. Gujarati dishes feature and bhakervelli is a recommended starter. There is also a separate pizza menu.

Directions: Five minutes' walk from Finchley Central Station

Ransome's Dock ✻✻

The decor might not be the fanciest in town – vivid electric blue with American ash tables and a selection of abstract art – but this old dockside ice factory is still one of the most enjoyable places to eat in town. The food, too, might not be the most refined, but it's hard to beat for honest, simple dishes done with real taste and understanding. The overall style is modern European – winter salad of chicory, pears, Roquefort and walnuts, perhaps, or pheasant supreme wrapped in Spanish bacon with Pardina lentils and baby turnips – but, arguably it is Martin Lam's modern British dishes that really hit the spot with their clever combination of great regional ingredients and updated traditional techniques. Smoked Trelough duck breast with fresh mango relish, Guernsey veal fillet paired with polenta and aubergine, and steak, mushroom and Guinness pie served with Brussels sprout tops and mashed potato. Caramelised rice puddings are a mouth-watering favourite, perhaps with berry compote or poached quinces.

Directions: Between Albert and Battersea Bridges

Cost: *Alc* £30, set-price L £22.50/D £27.50. ☺ H/wine £15.75
Times: 12.30-2.30pm/5.30-11pm. Closed L Sat & Sun
Additional: Bar food; Children welcome
Seats: 100. Private dining rooms 10-100
Style: Classic
Smoking: No-smoking area; Air conditioning
Accommodation: 127 en suite
★ ★ ★ ★

303 Portobello Road W10 5TD
Map GtL: C3
Tel: 020 8968 2001
Fax: 020 7449 6961
Times: Noon-3pm/7pm-1am. Closed L Mon-Thu

7 Long Lane Finchley N3 2PR
Map GtL: C4
Tel/Fax: 020 8349 4386
E-mail: ranivegetarian@aol.com

Telephone for further details

35-37 Parkgate Road Battersea SW11 4NP
Map GtL: C2
Tel: 020 7223 1611
Fax: 020 7924 2614
E-mail: martinlam@compuserve.com
Chef: Martin Lam
Owners: Martin & Vanessa Lam
Cost: *Alc* £30, set-price L £12.50. ☺ H/wine £13-£20
Times: Noon-4.30pm/6-11pm. Closed D Sun, Xmas
Additional: Sunday L; Children welcome
Seats: 55
Style: Modern/dockside
Smoking: No pipes; Air conditioning

Rasa Sumudra

Charlotte Street has long been famous for its restaurants, and the site at Number 5 has seen innumerable restaurants come and go. This latest establishment belongs to the new generation of Indian restaurants, the interior is modern and deceptively large. Owned by the growing Rasa Group, a chain of mainly vegetarian restaurants, though this one serves predIominatly fish-based cooking and, unlike most Indian restaurants, which are based on a Northern Indian cuisine, it features food from the Southern state of Kerala, whose speciality is seafood. The *carte* is divided into seafood and vegetarian starters and main courses but there are also lunch and Kerala feast set-price menus. There are fantastic flavours to be had: Samudra Rasan was an outstanding shellfish soup which included prawns (marinated in a spicy paste of chillies and onions), crabs, mussels and squid. Regional specialities include Cheemen Theeyal: prawns cooked with shallots, coriander seeds and Padugngi Charu: a lemon sole with fish tamarind and red chilli based Masala all served with 'zingy' lemon rice. Desserts are delicious and the Pal Payasam, essentially a rice pudding cooked in coconut milk, was a lovely way to finish the meal.

Directions: ⊖ Tottenham Court Road, Goodge Street

5 Charlotte Street W1P 1HD
Map : C4
Tel: 020 7637 0222
Fax: 020 7637 0224
Chef: Anil Narayanan
Owner: Das Shreedharan
Cost: *Alc* £25, set-price L £10/D £30. ☺ H/wine £10.50
Times: Noon-3pm/6-10.45pm. Closed L Sun, 2 wks Dec
Additional: Sunday L; Children welcome
Seats: 100. Private dining room
Style: Traditional
Smoking: No-smoking area; Air conditioning
Civil licence: 200

Rasa W1

The pink colour scheme and the shrine to Krishna are the trademarks of this splendid Indian group. Rasa in Stoke Newington and Rasa W1 share the same vegetarian menus. The Rasa W1 location is a boon for shoppers in Bond Street/Oxford Street – the price and quality of the Keralan regional cooking is incredible for the area and the pace is gentle. Open with pre-meal snacks – basically substantial variations on the poppadom theme – served with superb pickles and chutneys. Starters take in koonu samosa (filled with vegetable Masala), and a recommended fresh bhel mix of chickpeas, bhel, sev, peanut and onions blended with tamarind juice and fresh coriander. A sweet-and-sour dish of sweet mangoes and green bananas cooked in yogurt with green chillies and ginger, served with lemon rice, is a must-try main course, but dosas and curries are also on offer with imaginative combinations and the emphasis on fresh ingredients. Pal payasam is a good finish – spiced rice pudding with cashew nuts and raisins. The address of the Stoke Newington branch is 55 Stoke Newington, Church Street, London N16 0AR. Tel: 020 7249 0344.

Directions: ⊖ Bond Street

6 Dering Street
W1R 9AB
Map: C4
Tel: 020 7629 1346
Fax: 020 7491 9540
E-mail: dasrasa@hotmail.com
Chef: R S Binuraj
Owner: Das Sreedharan
Cost: *Alc* £25. ☺ H/wine £9.95
Times: Noon-3pm/6-11pm. Closed L Sun, Xmas & New Year
Additional: Children welcome
Seats: 75
Style: informal/traditional
Smoking: Air conditioning

The Real Greek NEW

The Real Greek is exciting enough to make you want to throw a few plates. But that happens to be the antithesis of everything Theodore Kyriakou is trying to do. His aim is to educate our retsina-abused palates about the glorious realities of regional Greek cooking. Located in a former pub at the pioneering end of trendy Shoreditch, the interior has been subtly gentrified with an open-to-view kitchen. The ambitious cooking offers startling combinations and flavours from a

15 Hoxton Market N1
Map: G5
Tel: 020 7739 8212
Fax: 020 7739 4910
E-mail: the.realgreek@talk21.com
Chef: Theodore Kyriakou
Owners: Paloma Campbell, Theodore Kyriakou
Cost: *Alc* £28, set-price L £10. ☺ H/wine £10.50

menu that's divided into three – mezedes, small and main dishes. Best go in a group to make the most of preserved chicken with walnuts and olive oil, dolmades – stuffed vine leaves (that are a revelation), barbecued squid with olive oil and lemon, home-salted fillet of cod, and potato and garlic aïoli with roast beets. Dishes to order again and again are wild boar sausages with Macedonian-style stuffed prunes and apricots, Athenian-style roast loin of pork and honeyed quince with endive fricassé, an astonishing hot-pot of partridge stuffed with walnuts, garlic and herbs with ewe's milk pasta and Mizithra cheese, and an even more sensational Kakavia saffron fish stew that included brill and conger eel. Best dessert was a rose petal meringue roulade filled with a blackberry scented soft cheese. The all-Greek wine list is arranged in groups to go with certain foods, with a fair few available by the glass.

Directions: Behind Holiday Inn in Old Street. Take exit 2 from Old Street ⊖ Walk up Old Street towards Shoreditch. Turn L into Pitfield Street, R into Boot Street, 1st L into Hoxton Market.

Times: Noon-3pm/5.30-10.30pm. Closed Sun, Bhs
Additional: Children welcome
Seats: 65. Private dining room 8-10
Style: Informal/chic
Smoking: No pipes & cigars

Redmond's

Unprepossessingly set among a parade of suburban shops, Redmond's is light and spacious, with a polished wood-strip floor, yellow walls sporting large, colourful abstracts, stylish designer chairs and good cutlery on crisp white-clothed tables. The whole effect is pleasingly fresh, modern and well thought out – exactly like the menus. The kitchen deals in the likes of fettucine with pheasant, leeks and ginger, roast cod with a risotto of saffron, spinach and mussels, and roast rump of lamb with aubergine caviar and wild mushroom sauce. Ballotine of ham hock, black pudding and foie gras made a fine starter at inspection, given a lift by an excellent dressing of balsamic vinegar and grain mustard, while 'beautifully tender' braised oxtail in a rich sauce with prunes with bubble-and-squeak was a well-conceived, hearty dish in winter. Desserts tend towards variations on the familiar, from banana tarte Tatin or crème brûlée to classic lemon tart, its pastry exemplary, perhaps with blood-orange sorbet and strawberry sauce. The wine list is well-chosen, with a good spread of prices, although more by the glass would be appreciated.

Directions: Located half-way between Putney and Richmond on the South Circular Road at the Barnes end of Sheen

170 Upper Richmond Road West SW14 8AW
Map GtL: B2
Tel: 020 8878 1922
Fax: 020 8878 1133
Chef: Redmond Hayward
Owners: Redmond & Pippa Hayward
Cost: Set-price L £12.50/D £22. ☺
H/wine £13
Times: Noon-2pm (2.30pm Sun)/7-10pm. Closed L Sat, D Sun, 4 days Xmas
Additional: Sunday L; Children welcome
Seats: 54
Style: Informal/modern
Smoking: No-smoking area; No pipes & cigars; Air conditioning

The Red Pepper ❀

One of a group of very popular Italian neighbourhood restaurants characterised by strong service and friendliness. The menu specialises in pizza and pasta, simply constructed dishes big on flavour and freshness.

Directions: ⊖ Warwick Avenue

8 Formosa Street W9 1EE
Map: C4
Tel: 020 7266 2708
Fax: 020 7266 5522

Telephone for further details

The Red Room

203-206 Piccadilly
W1V 9LE
Map: C3
Tel: 020 7851 2464
Fax: 020 7851 2469
Cost: *Alc* £25, set-price L/D
£14.50/£17.50. ☺ H/wine £11.50
Times: Noon-3pm/5.30-10.45pm.
Closed D Sun, Xmas
Additional: Bar food L; Sunday L;
Children welcome
Style: informal/modern
Smoking: No-smoking area; Air
conditioning

Posh eating area of Waterstone's in Piccadilly – the largest bookshop in Europe, The Red Room features a modern British menu with a strong Med flavour. Willing staff, a well-priced two-course lunch menu and a nice quiet setting make it a reasonable choice for the area.

Directions: ⊖ Piccadilly Circus

Restaurant Gordon Ramsay ✿✿✿✿✿

66 Royal Hospital Road SW3 4HP
Map: B1
Tel: 020 7352 4441
Fax: 020 7352 3334
Chef/Owner: Gordon Ramsay
Times: Noon-2.45pm/6.45-11pm.
Closed Sat, Sun, 2 wks at Xmas, Bhs
Additional: Children welcome
Seats: 44
Style: Chic/Modern
Smoking: No pipes & cigars; Air
conditioning

For all the bad boy reputation and somewhat unsavoury publicity, Ramsay's 'attitude' does not extend to the customer, and unlike many others he graces the stove with his presence at virtually every service. This ultimately pays the highest dividends, and Ramsay is now approaching the very pinnacle of gastronomic achievement. The frothy sauces have been left behind, and his style has become increasingly classical, conservative in the best of senses, with remarkable consistency of execution to match. Even the bread rolls seem better than ever before. His pasta-making skills, for example, are now so perfected that a tortellini of crab with coriander on shellfish sauce with asparagus and spinach becomes a benchmark for all other pasta dishes. Ramsey has the courage to take a slightly unfashionable tack with his use of rich sauces, as in an oven-roasted Challandaise duck with carrots and celeriac with endive tarte and sauce Saint Emilion. Lighter dressings are given intensity by key seasonings – truffle vinaigrette enhances a panaché of roasted sea scallops with sautéed foie gras in a ceps consommé. Pot-au-feu of pigeon is served with sautéed foie gras in a ceps consommé. Pre-desserts, a light orange water jelly and a sublime dried fruit pannacotta, come with the trademark painter's palette of cornets. Tarte Tatin is as good as it gets – perfect pastry with toffeed edges, smooth caramel, just the right amount of acidity to the apple and a side dish of first-class vanilla ice. Restaurant service is exemplary, well-managed and executed with much good humour, spot-on timing and knowledge.

AA Wine Shortlisted for Wine Award-see page 18

Directions: ⊖ Sloane Square. Situated a few yards from National Army museum

Restaurant Twentyfour ❊

Modern minimalist restaurant located in what used to be the NatWest tower. Enjoy views of the Dome and Tower Bridge over a breast of cannette duck, red onion Tatin, spring greens, fondant potato and redcurrant jus.

Additional: Children welcome
Style: Modern/Minimalist
Smoking: No pipes & cigars; Air conditioning; Jacket & tie preferred

Directions: ⊖ Bank, Liverpool St

Tower 42 Old Broad Street EC2
Map: G4
Tel: 020 7877 7703/2424
Fax: 020 7877 7742
Cost: Alc £35, set-price L £26.50. H/wine £12.50
Times: 11.45-2.30pm/6-9.30pm. Closed Sat & Sun

Rhodes in the Square ❊❊

Modern decor with oblong blocks of colour glowing from rich blue walls. Comfort is the guiding principle with armchair style seating encouraging relaxed comportment; and sturdy, unfussy cuisine an invitation to jovial dining. Starters from the set-price menu include seared tuna fish with poached egg Benedict, pan-fried white pudding sausage with cabbage and crispy bacon, and lobster omelette Thermidor. Main courses include interesting takes on old friends such as red wine beef lasagne with a chestnut mushroom cream sauce and roast loin of lamb flavoured with bone marrow and anchovy and served with an artichoke and mushroom duxelle. Puddings tend towards the tried and tested such as bread-and-butter pudding and sticky toffee pudding, although a frozen espresso mousse with bitter sweet oranges caters to the more adventurous sweet tooth. The wine selection is good and service is friendly and attentive.

Directions: ⊖ Pimlico

Dolphin Square Chichester Street SW1V 3LX
Map: D1
Tel: 020 7798 6767
Fax: 020 7798 5685
E-mail: rhodesinthesquare@sodexho-uk.com
Chef: Michael James
Owner: Gary Rhodes, Sodexho Partnership
Cost: Set-price L £16.50 & £19.50/D £31
Times: fr Noon/fr 7pm. Closed L Sat, all Sun & Mon, Bhs
Additional: Children welcome
Seats: 70
Style: Chic/Art Deco
Smoking: No pipes & cigars; Air conditioning
Civil licence: 100

Riso Restaurant ❊❊

Sunny yellow walls with large modern canvases, a terracotta floor, windows on to the street and quite likely crowds of customers are what you'll find at this neighbourhood Italian in a residential area. The short menu might not offer too many surprises – although courgette and Swiss chard soup, and saffron gnocchi with rabbit and chestnuts are not found every day – but what distinguishes the kitchen's output is simplicity and clean, fresh flavours. Starters of, say, marinated anchovies

76 South Parade W4 5LF
Map: A1
Tel/Fax: 020 8742 2121
Chef: Sandro Medda
Owners: Mauro Santoliquido, Maurizio Rimerici
Cost: Alc £20. ☺ H/wine £11.50
Times: D only, 7-10.30. Closed Xmas
Additional: Sunday L (noon-3pm); Children welcome

and courgettes, and pan-fried polenta with Parmesan and rocket are followed by a tranche of pastas, all of which can be taken as a main course: black tagliolini with mussels, clams and tomato sauce, or 'excellent' gnocchi with Mascarpone, courgettes and ricotta. The handful of mains, split evenly between fish and meat, seems almost an afterthought, but they might include chargrilled calves' liver, or hake in a vinegar, garlic and chilli sauce. Puddings wave the flag in the form of pannacotta with chocolate sauce, and 'brilliant' poached pears, as do cheeses, olive oil and the decent wine list.

Seats: 55
Style: Informal/modern

Directions: ⊖ Chiswick Park. Turn L, restaurant 400m on L

Ristorante L'Incontro ❀❀

A very classy restaurant with new understated decor that exudes quality. Large, highly polished grey tiles furnish the floor and suede loose covers in peach or pale olive dress the tub chairs. Service is equally stylish in a restrained discreet way with an abundance of waiters and waitresses in long white aprons and white collarless dress shirts. The heart of the cuisine is in Venice with cooking that is essentially simple but based on first-rate raw materials that are carefully handled to preserve their full natural flavours. Sea scallops lightly seared with chopped herbs and served around a pile of frisée opened a recent meal in a very pleasing fashion. A beautifully tender duck breast followed. This was cooked till slightly pink and sliced around a mound of soft potato purée with whole, fully cooked cherry tomatoes. Tiramisu, lemon tart or bonet conclude in true classic style.

87 Pimlico Road SW1W 8PH
Map: C1
Tel: 020 7730 3663/6327
Fax: 020 7730 5062
Chef: Simone Rettore
Owner: Santin Group Ltd
Cost: *Alc* £38.50, set-price L £14.50 & £18.50. H/wine £15.75
Times: 12.30-2.30pm/7-11.30pm (10.30pm Sun). Closed L Sat & Sun, Xmas, 1 Jan, Etr
Additional: Children welcome
Seats: 60. Private dining room 30-35
Style: Chic/Modern
Smoking: No pipes; Air conditioning

Directions: From Lower Sloane Street, left into Pimlico Road, restaurant is on R. ⊖ Sloane Square

The Ritz ❀❀

150 Piccadilly W1V 9DG
Map: C3
Tel: 020 7493 8181
Fax: 020 7493 2687
E-mail: enquire@theritzhotel.co.uk
Chef: Giles Thompson
Cost: *Alc* £39, set-price L £35/D £51. H/wine £22
Times: 12.30-2.15pm/6-11.15pm
Additional: Bar meals L; Sunday L; Children welcome
Style: Classic/traditional

An absolutely stunning setting, with Versailles inspired gilding and trompe l'oeil, and immaculate service to match from tail-coated staff. There are trolleys for bread (of which there is a huge variety) and the roast of the day - beef Wellington on a February visit. The inspector began with a 'nice little salad' of spiced leaves with three excellent seared scallops and a tomato dressing. A main course of two noisettes of lamb topped with slivers of foie gras was straightforward and accurately cooked. Dessert was a chocolate moelleux with chestnut and coffee ice cream. Petits fours were good - pastry is definitely a strength here.

Directions: Green Park. Ten minutes walk from Piccadilly Circus

Riva Restaurant 🏵🏵

Muted, neutral colours create a soothing influence. This is just as well since the popularity of the restaurant often outstrips its capacity creating a bustling, sociable atmosphere. The kitchen takes its cue from the culinary traditions of Northern Italy producing starters along the lines of Culatello ham and dried figs on piadina accompanied by smoked goose prosciutto and burrata tartufata with chicory and nuts. To follow, the simplicity of dishes such as linguine with mussels, clams and bottarga; and grilled squid with wild herbs compete for your attention with more outlandish combinations such as breaded veal cutlet with fried zucchini and matchstick potatoes. The kitchen is also industrious in trying out unusual ingredients such as fillets of sturgeon combined with estuary-grown seaweed. The success of the desserts hinges on accurate and respectful manifestations of Italian classics such as zabaglione and pannacotta.

Directions: Junction of Church Rd with Castelnau Rd. Hammersmith

169 Church Road Barnes SW13 9HR
Map GtL: C3
Tel: 020 8748 0434
Chef: Francesco Zanchetta
Owner: Andrea Riva
Cost: Alc £30. H/wine £10.50
Times: Noon-2.30pm/7-11pm. Closed L Sat, Xmas, Etr, last 2 wks Aug
Additional: Sunday L; Children welcome
Seats: 50
Style: Bistro-style/Rustic
Smoking: No pipes & cigars; Air conditioning

River Café 🏵🏵🏵

A makeover has jazzed up the interior of this temple to Italian rustic cooking: a colour scheme of white and cobalt blue, frosted-glass windows, the clock still ticking away, and a long counter of shiny stainless steel with the famous wood-fired oven glowing away at the end. Tubular chairs, paper-covered tables and casual staff dumb down the image almost to the point where newcomers might think they were in for some bargain dining, especially as it's possible to have a civilised conversation with strangers at adjacent tables. But not so: top-notch ingredients, some rarely found outside Italy, show remarkable purchasing power, and are treated simply and strikingly, and although herbs, spices and vegetables – borlotti beans, salsa rossa, sea kale, green radicchio, for instance – are integral to most dishes, 'natural flavour is king here' seems to be a unanimous comment. Good use is made of that oven, producing perfectly timed whole Dover sole, with a faint fragrance of smoke and the sea, roasted with capers and marjoram and simply garnished with braised spinach, or pot-roast leg of organic pork, succulent and tasting of itself, wrapped in Parma ham and sliced on a bed of garlicky Swiss chard. Sauces, when they are used, enhance the main component of a dish rather than damp it down: one of anchovy and rosemary for pink leg of lamb, or chilli and mint for chargrilled wild salmon with deep-fried artichokes. Starters hit all the right notes too, from risotto with bresaola full of the flavours of chicken stock, parsley and Parmesan, to buffalo Mozzarella with marinated black olives and mixed leaves dressed with herb vinegar. Cheeses, always in their prime, are a must-have, which may leave little room for puddings of perhaps chestnut torta with 'loads of flavour' topped with chocolate and served with 'super' velvety, winy ice cream. The

Thames Wharf Studios
Rainville Road W6 9HA
Map Gtl: C3
Tel: 020 7381 8824
Fax: 020 7381 6217
E-mail: admin.rc@btinternet.com
Chefs: Rose Gray, Ruth Rogers & Theo Randall
Owners: Rose Gray, Ruth Rogers
Cost: Alc £50. H/wine £9.50
Times: 12.30-2.45pm/7-9pm. Closed D Sun, Xmas, New Year, Etr
Additional: Bar food; Children welcome
Seats: 108
Style: Modern
Smoking: No pipes & cigars

Seats: 130. Private dining room 50
Smoking: Air conditioning
Civil licence: 50

all-Italian wine list has a good choice by the glass, and staff, well versed in the list, can make sensible recommendations.

Directions: Off Fulham Palace Rd. Junction of Rainville Road and Bowfell Road. ⊖ Hammersmith

R.K. Stanleys

Up-market diner with open booth and counter seating. Home-made breads with leek and onion soup were followed by sausages scented with rosemary and thyme served with parsnip mash.

Additional: Children welcome
Style: Traditional
Smoking: No pipes & cigars; Air conditioning

Directions: ⊖ Oxford Circus

6 Little Portland Street
W1N 5AG
Map: B3
Tel: 020 7462 0099
Fax: 020 7462 0088
E-mail: fred@rkstanleys.co.uk
Cost: *Alc* £17.50. ☺ H/wine £11.95
Times: Noon-3.30pm/5.30-midnight. Closed all Sun, L Sat, Xmas, New Year, Bhs

Rosmarino

NEW

'All very Heals' remarked an inspector of this new kid on the block. Approached under a big canopy covering the front terrace, within is a split-level area dominated by a large wooden bar with a huge flower display. A wooden floor, pale walls and closely set tables complete the picture. Pastas and salady dishes make up the bulk of the starters, some less familiar than others: linguine al vongole, through barley soup with king prawns and peas, or warm salad of scallops in tomato sauce, to 'perfect', creamy-textured black truffle risotto. Simple treatments of prime materials are the hallmarks of main courses. 'First-class' chargrilled tuna is accompanied by rocket and tomato salad, pan-fried calves' liver comes with polenta and onions, and roast rack of lamb with grilled asparagus and lamb's lettuce. Tiramisu is a good example of the breed, and there might be lightly caramelised, spicy fresh fruit salad with yogurt ice cream. A handful of French bottles are heavily outnumbered by the Italians on the wine list, where around a half-dozen are sold by the glass.

Directions: ⊖ St John's Wood. Off Abbey Road

1 Blenheim Terrace NW8 0EH
Map: A1
Tel: 020 7328 5014
Fax: 020 7625 2639
E-mail: rosemarinonw8@hotmail.com
Chef: Mario Zacchi
Owner: A to Z Restaurant Ltd
Times: Noon-2.30pm/7-10.45pm. Closed Etr
Additional: Children welcome
Style: Classic/Informal
Smoking: Air conditioning

Roussillon

This is a menu worthy of serious study: as well as two tasting menus (Garden and Seasonal), the *carte* is divided into sections entitled 'The Sea', 'The Land', 'Chocolate' and so on. There is an emphasis on seasonal, quality ingredients, often organic, even biodynamically-reared Dorset lamb. Sources may be credited – Red Torfrey Farm chicken, for example, which comes in three services, the breast cooked with salsify and shallots, the leg slow-cooked and served with mixed Kentish leaves, with a crop and toe consommé. Combinations push back the wilder shores of the imagination but the cooking is precise and elements come together on the plate. Grilled Gloucestershire purple potatoes, scallops with winter leaves and crustacean and brown butter vinaigrette was a wonderous combination, followed by grilled lamb fillet with leeks and girolles and herb potato purée. Other dishes typical of Alexis Gauthier's individual approach might include sautéed Scottish langoustines with tender caramelized carrots, bitter Kentish

16 St Barnabas Street
SW1W 8PB
Map: C1
Tel: 020 7730 5550
Fax: 020 7824 8617
E-mail: alexis@roussillon.co.uk
Chef: Alexis Gauthier
Owners: James & Andrew Palmer, Alexis Gauthier
Cost: *Alc* £26, set-price L £13 & £16/D £26. ☺ H/wine £13.50
Times: Noon-2.30pm/7-10.45pm. Closed all Sun, L Sat, 24 Dec-5 Jan
Additional: Children 6+
Style: Classic/Traditional
Seats: 46. Private dining room 28
Smoking: No-smoking area; No pipes & cigars; Air conditioning

dandelion and pickled ginger, as well as pan-fried sea bream with beetroot and blood orange. A dessert of roasted pineapple with pineapple and lemongrass sorbet was surprisingly subdued, however. All this takes place in a smart, modern setting decorated in light green with herb and plant prints on the wall.

Directions: ⊖ Sloane Square. Off Pimlico Road

AA Wine Shortlisted for *Award-see page 18*

Royal China ✿

Book a seat at this very popular and enjoyable Hong Kong restaurant and marvel at the very quick and efficient service. Lobster and snow peas is a house speciality and is full of flavour.

Directions: ⊖ Queensway, Bayswater

13 Queensway
W2 4QJ
Map: A3
Tel/Fax: 020 7221 2535

Telephone for further details

Royal Garden Hotel, Tenth Floor Restaurant ✿✿✿

Wonderful views over Hyde Park are to be had from the Royal Garden's restaurant, a bright, modern and comfortable space. Recent meals have shown that the kitchen is working in overdrive, with straightforward-sounding chicken liver parfait with apricot bread, or roast rack of lamb with ratatouille and cardamom jus illustrating not only supreme technical confidence but artistry too. A strong Eastern element is behind some dishes, from starters of sautéed tiger prawns with a coconut and galangal broth, described as 'a brilliant dish', or Thai monkfish with coriander dressing, to a main course of oriental-style duck confit with braised choy sum. Some classic combinations are used to good effect, as in grilled beef fillet atop horseradish purée potatoes with morel sauce. Carefully considered partnerships lift dishes out of the ordinary and into another realm: a sauce of gravad lax for baked cod under a soft herb crust, and caramelised onion risotto for roast breast of pigeon. A fondness for tropical fruits is behind some of the attractively presented puddings – passion fruit cream with an orange sablé, or pineapple and coconut mille-feuille – while the sweeter-toothed could go for mosaic of banana and toffee, or chocolate pudding with marbled chocolate ice cream.

2-24 Kensington High Street W8 4PT
Map Gtl: C3
Tel: 020 7937 8000
Fax: 020 7361 1991
E-mail: guest@royalgdn.co.uk
Chef: Derek Baker
Cost: *Alc* £40, set-price L £24. H/wine £14.25
Times: Noon-2.30pm/5.30-11pm. Closed L Sat, all Sun, 2 wks Jan, 2 wks Aug
Seats: 100
Style: Chic/Modern
Smoking: No-smoking area; Air conditioning
Civil licence: 100
Accommodation: 398 en suite
★ ★ ★ ★ ★

France heads up the wine list, where half a dozen bottles are also sold by the glass and where, under the circumstances, prices are not unreasonable.

Directions: Next door to Kensington Palace. ⊖ High Street Kensington

Royal Horseguards ❀

Whitehall Court SW1A 2EJ
Map: D3
Tel: 020 7839 3400
Fax: 020 7925 2263
Cost: *Alc* £28, set-price L £20/D £23.
☺ H/wine £14.75
Times: Noon-2.30pm/6-10.30pm.
Closed L Sat, Sun Bh

Housed in a listed building the hotel restaurant has recently been smartly refurbished in vibrant colours. On a recent visit a succulent, well flavoured cod wrapped in Alsace bacon won glowing approval from our inspector.

Additional: Children welcome
Style: Chic/Modern
Smoking: No-smoking area; Air conditioning
Accommodation: 280 en suite ★ ★ ★ ★

Directions: ⊖ Embankment

Royal Lancaster Hotel, Park Restaurant ❀❀

Lancaster Terrace W2 2TY
Map GtL: C3
Tel: 020 7551 6037
Fax: 020 7724 3191
E-mail: fanb@royallancaster.com
Chef: John Robinson
Owner: The Lancaster Landmark Hotel Co Ltd
Cost: Set-price L/D £19.50 & £23.50.
☺ H/wine £17
Times: 12.30-2.30pm/6.30-10.30pm.
Closed L Sat, all Sun
Additional: Children welcome
Seats: 60. Private dining room 6.
Jacket & tie preferred
Style: Classic/Elegant
Smoking: Air conditioning
Accommodation: 416 en suite
★ ★ ★ ★

The tree-lined avenues of Hyde Park and the fountains of the Italian Gardens form the perfect backdrop for high quality modern-European cuisine. The set-price options are bold and striking. Starters such as air-dried ham and fig salad with peach and shallot dressing, or stir-fried monkfish with strips of vegetables and Chinese leaf and a spicy vinaigrette are sure to kick-start the taste buds. Follow with seared Venison fillet accompanied by creamed celeriac and blueberry game jus, or with roast fillet of salmon on crushed potatoes with spinach, baby asparagus and shellfish cream sauce. All this adventure is contrasted with a 'classics' menu which offers accomplished manifestations of reliable favourites such as grilled fillet steak with a béarnaise, red wine or peppercorn sauce. A dessert of nougat parfait with peach and raspberry compote or chocolate fondant with blood orange sauce rounds things off nicely.

Directions: Opposite Hyde Park on the Bayswater Road. On 1st

RSJ, The Restaurant on the South Bank 🏵

The restaurant occupies three floors of this converted stable with yellow painted walls and exposed timber beams. Modern British food is served predominantly. The raviolone of lobster with smoked chicken jus can certainly be recommended.

Smoking: No pipes & cigars; Air conditioning

Directions: On the corner of Coin St and Stamford St; near National Theatre and LWT studios

13a Coin Street SE1 8YQ
Map: E3
Tel: 020 7928 4554
Fax: 020 7401 2455
E-mail: sally.webber@rsj.uk.com
Cost: Set-price L/D £16.95. ☺
H/wine £10.95
Times: Noon-2.30pm/5.30-11pm.
Closed L Sat, all Sun, 4 days Xmas
Additional: Children welcome
Style: Informal/Modern

Sabras Restaurant 🏵🏵

This immaculate, small family-run restaurant has been in business for well over a quarter of a century and serves some of London's best Indian vegetarian food. Sabras is an unpretentious place with a strong local following. Tables are Formica-topped and functional but with comfortable seating. The wholly vegetarian menu is full of interest, covering Mumbai specialities (from Bombay), south Indian pancakes, north Indian dal-subji dishes, plus Gujarati offerings (the owners' home area). Everything is freshly prepared, with well-balanced spicing ensuring flavours show clearly. Farsaan (starters) are served with good chutneys, but the best way to explore is to order a plate of assorted starters; our favourite was the range of dhosas (Indian pancakes). A main dish highlight, panch kuti dahl (mix of five or six varieties of lentils raita – 'the best we've had'), contained not just cucumber and carrot but also home-made curd and spices. There are wines and beers on offer, but try one of the many lassi – mango is best.

263 High Road Willesden Green
NW10 2RX
Map GtL: C3
Tel: 020 8459 0340

Telephone for further details.

Directions: ⊖ Willesden Green

St John 🏵

Former smokehouse provides the location for an unpretentious restaurant. The service is friendly, so relax and enjoy the straightforward cookery: roast bone marrow and parsley salad, or pot roast Gloucester old spot and butter beans.

Style: Modern/Minimalist
Smoking: Air conditioning

Directions: ⊖ Farringdon. 100 metres from Smithfield Market on N side

26 St John Street
EC1M 4AY
Map: F5
Tel: 020 7251 0848
Fax: 020 7251 4090
E-mail: tg@stjohnrestaurant.co.uk
Cost: Alc £29.75. H/wine £11
Times: Noon-3pm/6-11pm. Closed L
Sat, all Sun, Xmas & New Year
Additional: Bar food; Children
welcome

St Quentin Brasserie 🏵🏵

A warm welcome and professional service await at this quintessential French brasserie offering a slice of Paris in Knightsbridge. Inside, upholstered brass-rail topped banquettes line the sides of the room, 1920's mirrors hang above, and a crystal chandelier together with matching wall lights completes the scene – and, in true brasserie fashion, tables almost touch. The main carte changes seasonally but with a number of dishes, such as filet de boeuf Rossini for example, being fixtures. Written in French with straightforward English translations, the emphasis is on traditional French offerings: frogs legs with

243 Brompton Road SW3 2EP
Map: B2
Tel: 020 7589 8005
Fax: 020 7584 6064

Telephone for further details

garlic and parsley butter; ballotine of foie gras; chicken and leek terrine; seared scallops with fennel and orange salsa; skate with capers; magret of duck with pickled red cabbage and juniper sauce; chocolate mousse and tarte au citron. Ingredients are first rate and the kitchen shows sound skills. The shortish, exclusively French wine list concentrates on the middle ranks along with vin du pay, and offers a good choice by the glass. French crusty baguettes left in baskets at the table accompany, while strong espresso provides the finish.

Directions: ⊖ South Kensington. Opposite Brompton Oratory

Salloos Restaurant

Hidden away in a charming Knightsbridge mews, a classic, timeless interior houses generations' worth of experience and reputation. Tandoori chops continue to be a speciality as does an unusual 'Haleem Akbari' shredded lamb dish.

Style: Classic/Formal
Smoking: No pipes & cigars; Air conditioning

Directions: Nr. Hyde Park Corner – take 1st L into Wilton Place, 1st R opposite Berkeley Hotel. ⊖ Knightsbridge

62-64 Kinnerton Street SW1X 8ER
Map: B2
Tel: 020 7235 4444
Fax: 020 7259 5703
Cost: *Alc* £35, set-price L £16. ☺
H/wine £12.50
Times: Noon-2.30pm/7-11.15pm.
Closed Sun, Xmas, Bhs
Additional: Children 6+

The Salt House ⊛   NEW

Pared down informal pub with a relaxed atmosphere and a straightforward, consistently good value menu. Expect seasonal ingredients put together with controlled abandon, for example pappardelle with braised mustard sauce or deep fried sweetbreads with aïoli.

Smoking: No pipes & cigars; Air conditioning

Directions: Telephone for directions

63 Abbey Road NW8 0AE
Map Gtl: C3
Tel: 020 7328 6626
Fax: 020 7625 9168
Cost: *Alc* £25, set-price L £12.50. ☺
H/wine £10
Times: Noon-3pm/6.30-10.30pm(7pm
Sat, Sun). Closed L Mon
Additional: Bar food; Sunday L;
Children welcome
Style: Informal/modern

Santini ⊛⊛

A cool, elegant restaurant in a modern uncluttered style – marble floors, floor to ceiling windows with Venetian blinds, and tables decorated with small posies in elegant vases. The service is excellent with plenty of waiters in long white aprons and smartly-suited head waiters. The menu offers five or six choices in each of the four sections; antipasti, pasta, fish and meat. Menu descriptions are brief, but staff are happy to explain dishes, and in addition to the menu there are interesting chef's recommendations. Pasta Misa consisted of three different pastas, all perfectly cooked; pappardelle with artichoke sauce, ravioli filled with ricotta and spinach with fresh thyme and gnocchi served with a rich tomato and basil sauce. A John Dory dish from the chef's recommendations was 'excellent', thin slices of fish on a bed of new potatoes and artichoke quarters glazed with a 'beautiful' champagne sauce. A warm apple tart was as 'good to eat as it was to look at' and the espresso was everything it should be. The wine list is predominantly Italian but there are one or two French wines.

Directions: On corner of Ebury Street and Lower Belgrave Street. ⊖ Victoria

29 Ebury Street SW1W 0NZ
Map: C1
Tel: 020 7730 4094
Fax: 020 7730 5062
Chefs: Giuseppe Rosselli &
Giuliano Vilardo
Owner: Gino Santin
Cost: *Alc* £38.50, set-price L £17 &
£19.75. H/wine £15.75
Times: 12.30-2.30pm/7-11.30pm.
Closed L Sat & Sun, Xmas, 1 Jan, Etr
Sun
Additional: Children welcome
Seats: 65. Private dining room 30.
Jacket & tie preferred
Style: Chic/Modern
Smoking: No pipes; Air conditioning

Sartoria ❀❀

The Conran take on Italian classic cooking is showcased in a bespoke interior that pays homage to its location in the form of tailors' bastes around the walls, but this is far from being a rag trade concept restaurant. The sophisticated interior incorporates sofas, Eames chairs and cherry tables, and the screens that separate the private dining area give it an almost Japanese feel. Two starters of insalata of wood pigeon with artichokes and polenta, and roasted friggittelli peppers with tuna and gremolata showed an emphasis on quality ingredients and were well executed with clear flavours. The pace was sustained with first-rate roasted monkfish with wild mushrooms and organic cavolo nero, and grilled leg of lamb with roasted onion squash, olives and herbs. Desserts are imaginative – blood orange polenta cake, or roast quince with crema di Mascarpone. There are also some unusual Italian cheeses. The impressive wine list focuses on Italian wines and a notable list of grappas.

20 Savile Row
W1X 1AE
Map: D3
Tel: 020 7534 7000
Fax: 020 7534 7070
Chef: Lee Purcell
Owner: Conran Restaurants Ltd
Cost: *Alc* £30, set-price L (Sat only) £16.50. H/wine £14
Times: Noon-3pm/6.30-11.30pm.
Closed L Sun, 25 Dec
Additional: Bar food L; Children welcome
Seats: 120. Private dining rooms 16
Style: Classic/Chic
Smoking: Air conditioning

Directions: ⊖ Piccadilly Circus, Oxford Circus. Corner of New Burlington Street & Saville Row, off Regent Street

Sauce ❀

Basement cafe/diner operation registered with the Soil Association serving 95% organic produce. The informal modern decor creates a relaxed and friendly atmosphere. Satisfying cuisine: rib-eye steak with braised shallots and fat fries for example.

214 Camden High Street
NW1 8QR
Map GtL: C3
Tel: 020 7482 0777
Fax: 020 7284 2484
E-mail: dining@sauce.prestel.co.uk

Cost: *Alc* £15, set-price L £6.95. ☺ H/wine £9.95
Additional: Bar food; Sunday L; Children welcome
Style: Informal/Modern
Smoking: No pipes & cigars; Air conditioning

Directions: ⊖ Camden Town, turn right, approx 150 yards on right. Just before traffic lights

Savoy Grill ❀❀

An institution of great class and a unique style that has stood the test of time. The cooking offers a selection of the modern and the traditional, in both cases handled with great aplomb by chef Simon Scott and his team. During a recent meal our inspector opted for a starter of foie gras terrine. Although a little more solid in texture than had been expected the clarity of flavour in this dish was superb, as was the accurate accompaniment of crisp dressed salad leaves, toasted brioche and thinly sliced truffle. For mains a centrepiece fish cake avoided the normal pitfalls of excessive potato usage and instead offered an honest, beautifully flavoured salmon filling. This was served on a bed of tomato and black olives and accompanied by a delicate spinach cream sauce. A well-stocked dessert trolley offers simple classics such as crème brûlée and pecan pie.

Strand WC2R 0EU
Map: E3
Tel: 020 7836 4343
Fax: 020 7240 6040
Chef: Simon Scott
Owner: The Savoy Group plc
Cost: *Alc* £45, set-price L £45.
H/wine £19.50
Times: 12.30-2.30pm/6-11.15pm.
Closed L Sat, all Sun, Aug
Additional: Children 14+
Seats: 90. Jacket & tie preferred
Style: Traditional
Smoking: No pipes; Air conditioning
Accommodation: 207 en suite
★ ★ ★ ★ ★

Directions: ⊖ Embankment. Walk east through the riverside gardens to the hotel

The Savoy –
River Restaurant

Strand WC2R 0EU
Map: E3
Tel: 020 7420 2698
Fax: 020 7240 6040
E-mail: info@the-savoy.co.uk
Chef: Anton Edelmann
Cost: *Alc* £50, set-price L £29.75/D
£39.50 (£44.50 Fri & Sat).
H/wine £19
Times: 12.30-2.30pm/6-11.30pm,
(Sun 7-10.30pm)
Additional: Sunday L;
Children welcome
Seats: 150. Private dining rooms.
Jacket & tie preferred
Style: Formal
Smoking: No-smoking area;
Air conditioning
Accommodation: 207 en suite
★ ★ ★ ★ ★

One of the THE places to be seen, The River Room retains all the style befitting a great room that can trace its culinary heritage back to Escoffier himself. Positioning is everything, not all tables are that well located, so securing one of the coveted window tables can make it a really memorable experience. The menu highlights a few of Anton Edelmann's signature dishes alongside the traditional roasts served from silver-domed trolleys and carved at the table. Ingredients are of the highest quality – Iberian ham with roast pepper and tomato salad with basil; tournedos of Buccleuch beef Rossini; organic fillet of Welsh lamb on braised fennel. Although there are plenty of classics such as fillet of sole and lobster Walewska, and goose liver pâté with wild mushrooms and haricot vert salad, the inclusion of dishes such as sashimi with green horseradish or pineapple tarte Tatin infused with spices and served with vanilla ice cream show an awareness of contemporary trends. A brioche cobbler with caramelised apple, pear and cinnamon ice cream belied its name and turned out to be a very superior bread-and-butter pudding.

Directions: ⊖ Embankment. Walk east through the riverside gardens to the hotel

Schnecke NEW

58-59 Poland Street W1V 3DF
Map: C4
Tel: 020 7287 6666
Fax: 020 7287 3636
E-mail: soho@schnecke-restaurants.com
Cost: *Alc* £20, set-price L £14.99/D
£17.99. ☺ H/wine £13
Times: Noon-midnight (Sun
10.30pm). Closed 25 Dec

An authentic Alsation-themed restaurant with an easygoing air and an intimate, homely atmosphere. The menu is built upon the basics of tartes, flambées (sweet and savoury), choucroute, snails and beer. A schnecke aux epinards was a highlight.

Additional: Bar food; Sunday L; Children welcome
Style: Bistro-style/Chic
Smoking: No pipes & cigars; Air conditioning

Directions: Telephone for directions

Scotts ❀

20 Mount Street W1Y 6HE
Map: C3
Tel: 020 7629 5248
Fax: 020 7499 8248
Cost: *Alc* £40, set-price L £26.50.
H/wine £17.50
Times: Noon-3pm/6-11pm.
Closed 25 & 26 Dec
Additional: Bar food; Sunday L;
Children welcome
Style: Chic/Formal
Smoking: No-smoking area; No pipes;
Air conditioning

Rich purples and golds dominate in this exclusive, stylish restaurant. Approach to cuisine is as traditional and accurate as the meticulously correct service. Seafood is a particular strength, as demonstrated by an excellent shellfish platter.

Directions: Mount St runs between
Park Lane and Berkeley Sq.
⊖ Green Park

Selsdon Park Hotel ❀❀

The imposing Jacobean mansion lies in extensive grounds that also include a professional, 18-hole golf course. The grand restaurant offers an extensive choice, normally not the best of signs, but the enthusiasm behind the scenes is evident and one can only applaud a kitchen making such an effort to provide a real 'meal experience' for a numerous and diverse clientele. Adventurous, visually-striking Chef-recommended dishes include Thai crab cakes, apricot and pickled ginger jam, and crispy breast of lamb, sauerkraut and chorizo sausage, although we presume that non-Chef-recommended dishes are an equally good option. These might include clams with white wine, cream and tarragon, and grilled lobster with mango and vanilla butter. Rather bland orange tart, however, was ill-matched with milk chocolate ice-cream a bit. The wine list is geared to high-rollers, and also includes excellent vintage port by the glass.

Directions: 3m SE of Croydon off A2022

Addington Road
Sanderstead
Croydon CR2 8YA
Map 4: TQ36
Tel: 020 8657 8811
Fax: 020 8651 6171
Chef: Alan White
Owner: Principal Hotels
Cost: Alc £24.95, set-price L £19.95/D £24.95. ☺ H/wine £12.50
Times: Noon-2pm/7-10pm
Additional: Bar food; Sunday L; Children welcome
Seats: 250. Private dining rooms 120
Style: Classic/formal
Smoking: No smoking in dining room; Air conditioning
Civil licence: 80
Accommodation: 204 en suite
★★★★

755 Fulham Road

As we went to press Alan & Georgina Thompson of AA three-rosetted restaurant 755 Fulham Road, were moving to Gloucestershire. The Royalist is due to open in the summer – check our website for the latest details (www.theaa.com/hotels).

Digbeth Street Stow-on-the-Wold
GL54 1BN
Tel: 01451 830670
Fax: 01451 870048

Shepherds ❀

Tradition reigns supreme at this long-established restaurant close to the Tate Gallery. Expect good old-fashioned service and classic English dishes – chicken liver pâté with Cumberland sauce, braised oxtail with turnips, and 'nursery' puddings like bread-and-butter pudding and spotted dick.

Additional: Bar food; Children welcome
Style: Traditional
Smoking: No-smoking area; Air conditioning

Directions: Near Tate Gallery and Westminster Hospital.
⊖ Pimlico

Marsham Court Marsham Street
SW1P 4LA
Map: D2
Tel: 020 7834 9552
Fax: 020 7233 6047
Cost: Set-price L £23.50/D £25.50. H/wine £12.50
Times: 12.30-2.45pm/6.30-11pm. Closed Sat, Sun, Bhs

Sheraton Park Tower, Restaurant One-O-One ❀❀❀

Classically-trained Pascal Proyart does not restrict himself just to the great standards of the fish restaurant repertoire – grilled lobster with garlic butter; seafood pot-au-feu with lemon and chervil; sole meunière, ratte potato, shallot confit and sautéed spinach – but allows his creative instincts to take wing in voguish dishes such as pan-seared salmon fillet with szechuan pepper and lime, sautéed pak choy, black pasta and lemongrass coconut. A 'signature' dish of black truffle risotto with warm king crab royal legs, the rice folded inside a little egg pancake with a modish truffly froth was a really clever little number, stylish and impressive. Precisely-cooked roast sea bass with truffle herb mash, Brussels sprout chiffonade and girolle jus

101 Knightsbridge SW1X 7RN
Map: B2
Tel: 020 7290 7101
Fax: 020 7235 6196
Chef: Pascal Proyart
E-mail: andrew.morgan@sheraton.com
Owner: Starwood Hotels and Resorts
Cost: Alc £47, set-price L £21 & £25/D £45 & £55 (4 courses). H/wine £20
Times: Noon-2.30pm/7-10.30pm
Additional: Children 12+
Seats: 65

was also creamy and foamy but lacked a certain *je ne sais quoi.* For carnivores, there is Scottish fillet of beef roasted in mustard and parsley with shallot confit, wild mushrooms and red Burgundy sauce. Desserts might include 'moelleux au chocolat Monjari' with pineapple sorbet and a piña colada emulsion. The restaurant itself, in marine sea greens and blues with a giant stained-glass and chrome fish sculpture, is cutting-edge cool, with a view of Knightsbridge to match.

Style: Modern
Smoking: No pipes; Air conditioning
Accommodation: 289 en suite
★ ★ ★ ★ ★

Directions: ⊖ Knightsbridge. E, just after Harvey Nichols

Sheraton Skyline ❀

With easy access to the Heathrow terminals this classy hotel restaurant offers an antidote to airline food for the jetsetters, or just a good night out for the earth-bound. Cassoulet of prawns and scallops, and five-spice loin of venison recommended.

Style: Classic/traditional
Smoking: No-smoking area; Air conditioning
Civil licence: 400
Accommodation: 351 en suite ★ ★ ★ ★

Directions: Telephone for directions

Bath Road Hayes UB3 5BP
Map 4: TQ08
Tel: 020 8564 3000
Fax: 020 8750 9150
E-mail: salvatore-calabrese@sheraton.com
Cost: *Alc* £35, set-price D £27.50.
H/wine £16
Times: D only 6-11.30pm. Closed Bhs
Additional: Children 10+

Simply Nico ❀❀

Although long-divorced from the eponymous founder-chef, the cooking at the cheerful, yellow-painted restaurant sticks to familiar French bourgeois territory. There's little difference between the lunch and evening menus, except for a modest hike in price, and service is always slick and efficient. Ever-popular dishes include confit of duck with Sarladaise potatoes and cep mushrooms, and roast cod with bacon and Savoy cabbage. Another favourite, roast maize-fed chicken breast with creamy morel sauce, was nicely browned and succulent, but the accompanying peeled, young broad beans were on the verge of being undercooked. The SN chain's version of pommes purée remains amongst London's best. Classic desserts usually include a fruity crème brûlée, perhaps made with blackcurrants or raspberries. Clafoutis with grape and vanilla ice-cream is another good choice.

48a Rochester Row SW1P 1JU
Map: D2
Tel: 020 7630 8061
Fax: 020 7828 8541
Chef: Paul Taylor
Owner: The Restaurant Partnership
Cost: Set-price L £ 20.50 & £23.50/D £25.50. H/wine £13
Times: Noon-2pm/7-10.30pm.
Closed L Sat, all Sun, Xmas, Bhs
Additional: Children 5+
Seats: 45
Style: Bistro-style/Rustic
Smoking: No pipes & cigars; Air conditioning

Directions: ⊖ Victoria. From Victoria Station take Vauxhall Bridge Road – 2nd on L at 2nd set of lights

Singapore Garden Restaurant ❀

A smart Chinese restaurant offering Singaporean and Malaysian specialities. Staff are elegantly dressed in national costume and service is attentive and professional. A fiery hot squid Blachan was ideal for blowing the cobwebs away.

Additional: Sunday L; Children welcome
Style: Informal/Modern
Smoking: No pipes & cigars; Air conditioning

83/83a Fairfax Road NW6 4DY
Map GtL: C4
Tel: 020 7328 5314
Fax: 020 7624 0656
Cost: *Alc* £25, set-price L £8/D fr £17.50. ☺ H/wine £11.50
Times: Noon-2.45pm/6-10.45pm (11.15pm Fri & Sat). Closed 1 wk Xmas

Directions: Off Finchley Road, on R before Belsize Park roundabout. ⊖ Swiss Cottage, Finchley Road. No parking restrictions

Sonny's Restaurant ⚜⚜

Rebecca Mascarenhas's restaurant empire has grown since she opened Sonny's fourteen years ago, but this remains the quintessential neighbourhood restaurant. A café at the front serves daytime dishes (eggs Benedict, croque monsieur, smoked salmon and scrambled eggs), and there is a small deli with its own distinctive frontage and separate entrance. The restaurant proper extends a long way back with a slight split level, and the overall decor is clean-cut modern with white walls sporting a variety of contemporary pictures/prints. The menu is very much in the modern style, too, with Mediterranean influences and the occasional ingredient from further afield like lemon grass in the pumpkin seed broth served with a red mullet starter. Pan-fried pig's trotter with crab, chorizo, tomato and basil, and roasted sea bass with grilled potatoes, baby carrots and cumin oil are typical of the style. Quince Bakewell tart with quince ice cream is a highly recommended dessert.

Directions: From Castlenau end of Church Road, on left by shops. ⊖ Hammersmith

94 Church Road Barnes SW13 0DQ
Map: C3
Tel: 020 8748 0393
Fax: 020 8748 2698
Chef: Leigh Diggins
Owners: Rebecca Mascarenhas, James Harris
Cost: Alc £34, set-price L £12 & £15 ☺ H/wine £9.50
Times: 12.30-2.30pm/7.30-11pm. Closed D Sun, Bhs
Additional: Bar food L; Sunday L; Children welcome
Seats: 100. Private dining room 20
Style: chic/modern
Smoking: No pipes & cigars; Air conditioning

Sotheby's, The Café ⚜

Restaurant spreading from an alcove into the main entrance hall of Sotheby's auctioneers. In between breakfast and afternoon tea (try the Champagne tea), a short lunchtime menu is offered.

Additional: Children welcome
Style: Chic/Modern
Smoking: No smoking in dining room; Air conditioning

Directions: ⊖ Bond Street

34 Bond Street W1A 2AA
Map: D4
Tel: 020 7293 5077
Fax: 020 7295 5920
Cost: Alc £22. ☺ H/wine £11.50
Times: L only, noon-3pm. Closed Sat, Sun, Xmas, 2 wks mid Aug

Spiga ⚜

Busy Italian restaurant with simple contemporary decor and wood-burning pizza ovens. Good staff and a good vibrant atmosphere. Pasta dishes include homemade tagliolini with rock shrimps, garlic, chilli, fresh tomato sauce and rocket salad.

Cost: Alc £23. ☺ H/wine £11.50
Times: Noon-3pm/6-midnight
Additional: Bar food; Sunday L; Children welcome
Style: Modern
Smoking: No pipes & cigars; Air conditioning

Directions: At the Shaftesbury

84-86 Wardour Street W1V 3LF
Map: D4
Tel: 020 7734 3444
Fax: 020 7734 3332

La Spighetta ⚜

Simply appointed Italian restaurant with tiled floors and white walls adorned with volcanic rock. Thinnest, crispest pizza bufala, duck parcels, and an excellent tiramisu were highlights.

Directions: Halfway down Baker Street towards Oxford Street, turn L into Blandford Street. ⊖ Baker Street

43 Blandford Street W1H 3AE
Map: B4
Tel/Fax: 020 7486 7340

Telephone for further details

The Square ❀❀❀

Almost a decade on, and The Square remains one of the top-rated restaurants in London. It's a hard act to sustain at this level, and although some inconsistencies were evident over the last year, Philip Howard can still deliver the goods. A ravioli of partridge on a pool of creamy partridge-flavoured sauce with some finely-shredded cabbage was top-drawer Mayfair, as were desserts such as pear clafoutis with prune and Armagnac, and an orange assiette comprising tart, bavarois, soufflé and madeleine. Less successful dishes at inspection have included an under-performing haunch of venison with celeriac purée. It's not for lack of care in the sourcing of ingredients though, with the listing of such fabulous esoterica as late-picked Muscat grapes with roast foie gras and caramelized endive or risotto of calves' tail with fillet of veal and butternut squash. Non-PC carnivores can let rip with flamboyant dishes such as parsley soup with snails, foie gras, sweetbreads and fleurons, or tournedos Rossini (welcome back!), but those who don't eat meat are advised to confess in advance – a sample menu of 18 dishes included nothing suitable for vegetarians. All the action takes place in a smart dining room, hung with colourful oil abstracts. An obviously well-heeled clientele gives the place a buzz as they work through an extremely good wine list.

6 Bruton Street W1X 7AG
Map: C3
Tel: 020 7495 7100
Fax: 020 7495 7150
Chef: Philip Howard
Owners: Philip Howard &
Nigel Platts-Martin
Cost: Alc £48, set-price D £45.
H/wine £18.50
Times: Noon-2.45pm/7-11pm.
Closed L Sat & Sun, 25-26 Dec, 1 Jan
Additional: Children 10+
Seats: 70. Private dining room 18
Smoking: No pipes & cigars;
Air conditioning

Directions: ⊖ Bond Street

The Stafford ❀❀

Friendly formality and understated luxury are the trademarks of the quietly located St James's hotel. The American Bar is well frequented and famous for its collection of celeb photos, caps and ties, and, in the restaurant, menus balance traditional grills with more creative dishes. Large tables are set with fine china, a ceiling mural and false window give a trompe l'oeil effect and Grecian statues add a country house feel. Lighting is subdued but not so dim you cannot read or see the food. A starter of a pyramid-shaped crabcake with spring onion, coriander and sweet pepper coulis was remarkable for freshness of flavour; fillet of venison with buttered cabbage, fondant potatoes, wild mushrooms and red wine sauce was tender and well prepared. Desserts might include quince tart with dried apricot ice-cream. A long, serious wine list offers some amazing vintages from the 350-year-old cellars.

16-18 St James's Place SW1A 1NJ
Map: D4
Tel: 020 7493 0111
Fax: 020 7493 7121
E-mail: info@thestaffordhotel.co.uk
Chef: Chris Oakes
Owner: Shire Inns
Cost: Alc £46, set-price L £29/D £33.
H/wine £18.50
Times: 12.30-2.30pm/6-10.30pm.
Closed L Sat
Additional: Bar food; Sunday L;
Children 8+
Seats: 55. Private dining rooms 44.
Jacket & tie preferred
Style: Traditional
Smoking: No-smoking area; No pipes
& cigars; Air conditioning
Civil Licence: 45
Accommodation: 81 en suite ★ ★ ★ ★

Directions: ⊖ Green Park. 5 mins St James's Palace

Stephen Bull Restaurant ❀❀

Stephen Bull's premier restaurant – just off Marylebone High Street – hasn't changed much over the years, its interior showcasing modern yet undramatic styling. The simple decor features mirrored or pastel-coloured walls with several original paintings, stripped-wood floor, and stylish black leather chairs around white-clothed, paper-square topped tables. Service, from white-shirted waiters, is rather functional and prosaic. The set-price menu is modern and full of interest: seared tuna with coriander, black and white bean salad; pan-fried sea bass, pesto risotto, grilled fennel and chorizo; and

5-7 Blandford Street W1H 3AA
Map: B4
Tel: 020 7486 9696
Fax: 020 7224 0324

Telephone for further details

roasted rabbit with red onion marmalade, butter beans and black pudding show the style. On a May menu the truffled vichyssoise with mustard seed croutons proved a sound choice, as was the escalope of salmon, glazed vegetables, potted prawns and red wine sauce that followed. The rice pudding brûlée with plums in red wine was well judged. The good length, varied wine list from around the world is presented by style, with ten wines by the glass. Little rounded cheese straws to nibble, freshly sliced breads and good espresso.

Directions: Off Marylebone High St, 75 yards down on L. ⊖ Bond Street

Stephen Bull Smithfield ❀❀

Handy for the Barbican and popular with city types, this is Stephen Bull in informal mode. A discreet entrance leads into a spacious angular room – more New York loft-style than Clerkenwell – with large expanses of plain-coloured walls in various shades ranging from ochre to pale mauve, interspersed with large pieces of modern art. Closely arranged, black unclothed tables and not-so-comfortable modern chairs adorn wooden floors. The menu affords a small vegetarian selection, is nicely varied and offers light, modern dishes with a Mediterranean twist that are not over complicated and allow flavours to show to advantage. Starters could feature a sound fish soup with rouille, or perhaps a carpaccio of venison with Caesar dressing. A lamb and salad niçoise main course was judged 'a real treat with near perfect niçoise' on a February visit, while a 'well-prepared' red pepper and olive risotto with saffron provided an agreeable alternative. Grilled pears with walnut and honey ice cream provided the finish. Pleasant, attentive service, good coffees, and wines listed by style offer quality by the glass.

Directions: Halfway between Clerkenwell Rd & Smithfield Market

71 St John Street EC1 4AN
Map: E5
Tel: 020 7490 1750
Fax: 020 7490 3128

Telephone for further details

The Stepping Stone ❀❀

A great little local restaurant with a chic, minimalist look, lively atmosphere and the sort of clientele who appreciate rare-grilled tuna with cracked wheat, mango and chilli salsa, or roast stuffed loin of rabbit, celeriac mash and green beans. A consistent quality of ingredients and cooking standards ensure that dishes always succeed. The formula is an admirable one – a daily changing choice of dishes, a number of which are available on an 'early bird' basis. Starters are assembly jobs, and none the worse for that – warm duck salad and orange dressing; seared home-smoked salmon, potato salad; roasted marinated quail, chilli and lemongrass dressing. Main courses might include roast skate with crushed potatoes, parsley and capers, or roast rump of lamb, polenta, courgette and aubergine. Finish with apple fritters and apricot sauce, or banana cream pie with brown sugar parfait. Irish cheeses are served with home-made grape chutney.

Directions: ⊖ Clapham Common. From Lavender Hill/Wandsworth Road crossroads, head up Queenstown Road towards Chelsea Bridge. Restaurant on L after 0.5 mile

123 Queenstown Road SW8 3RH
Map GtL: C2
Tel: 020 7622 0555
Fax: 020 7622 4230
Chef: Matthew Owsley-Brown
Owners: Gary & Emer Levy
Cost: Alc £23, set-price L £11.75/early D £10. ☺ H/wine £11
Times: Noon-2.30pm/7-11pm. Closed L Sat, D Sun, 5 days Xmas, Bh Mon
Additional: Sunday L; Children welcome
Seats: 65
Style: Informal/Modern
Smoking: No-smoking area; No pipes & cigars; Air conditioning

Stratfords

7 Stratford Road W8 6RF
Map Gtl: C3
Tel: 020 7937 6388
Fax: 020 7938 3435
E-mail: stratfords@stratfords-restaurant.com
Cost; Alc £30, set-price L /D£10.50 & £12.50. ☺ H/wine £10.80
Times: Noon-3pm/6-11pm
Additional: Sunday L; Children welcome
Style: Traditional
Smoking: No pipes

French fish restaurant freshly decked out in crisp white and seaside blue. A simple menu of daily fish in a variety of sauces is offered, with some meat options available.

Directions: ⊖ High Street Kensington

The Sugar Club ❀❀

Adventurous menu with a leaning towards the Orient tinged with New Zealand influence. Some unusual combinations and esoteric ingredients result in intriguing dishes such as spicy kangaroo salad with coriander, mint, peanuts and lime-chilli dressing. On a recent visit our inspector's choices were rather more conservative – marsupial novelty losing out to a quite simple starter of grilled scallops. The top quality scallops were sweet and fresh and a topping of sweet chilli sauce was not so powerful as to dominate. This was followed by spring lamb on a cassava fritter topped with sour aubergine pickle. A mango and white chocolate crème brûlée for dessert was praised by our inspector as 'really one of the best I have ever taken.' The décor is light and fresh with a polished wood block floor and modern pictures on plain walls. The wine list is well written and informative.

21 Warwick Street W1R 5RB
Map Gtl: C3
Tel: 020 7437 7776
Fax: 020 7437 7778
Chef: David Selex
Owners: Ashley Sumner, Vivienne Hayman
Cost: Alc £28. ☺ H/wine £10.50
Times: Noon-3pm/6-11pm. Closed Xmas Eve & 25 Dec, Bh L
Additional: Children 7+
Seats: 140. Private dining room 50
Style: Modern/Minimalist
Smoking: No-smoking area; No pipes & cigars; Air conditioning

Directions: ⊖ Oxford Circus

Suntory Restaurant ❀❀

Part of a world-wide chain and London's oldest Japanese restaurant, the Suntory offers typical Japanese cooking at surprisingly reasonable prices at lunchtime, but the sky can also be the limit here, especially at dinner. This veteran has built up quite a following over the years, especially among those on expense accounts, diplomatic expat Japanese (the embassy is just around the corner in Piccadilly) and affluent westerners. There are two dining rooms, the Shabu Shabu room and Teppanyaki grill room. The menu also offers the familiar sashimi, tempura, teriyaki, sushi. It's all hushed tones, the usual minimalism and lacks real buzz, even in the evening. The Sake is worth ordering.

72 St James's Street SW1A 1PH
Map: C3
Tel: 020 7409 0201
Fax: 020 7499 0208

Telephone for further details

Directions: At the bottom of St James's Street. ⊖ Green Park

Swag & Tails

Pretty flower-adorned Victorian pub (with swagged and tailed curtains). Great for a steak sandwich and a pint or a decent three-course meal. The constantly changing blackboard menu reflects seasonally available produce.

Directions: ➜ Knightsbridge

10-11 Fairholt Street SW7 1EG
Map: B2
Tel: 020 7584 6926

Telephone for further details

Swallow International Hotel

Classy hotel restaurant with adjoining piano cocktail bar. Relaxed service and a soothing atmosphere make an ideal setting for modern, sophisticated cuisine. Thai-spiced monkfish and mussels on a potato, cucumber and red onion salad is a tempting option.

Style: Informal/Modern
Smoking: No-smoking area; No pipes; Air conditioning
Accommodation: 421 en suite ★ ★ ★ ★

Directions: ➜ Gloucester Road, Earls Court

Cromwell Road SW5 0TH
Map: A2
Tel: 020 7973 1000
Fax: 020 7244 8194
E-mail: international@swallow-hotels.co.uk
Cost: *Alc* £32, set-price D £27. ☺
H/wine £15
Times: D only, 6-11pm. Closed Sun, 25 & 26 Dec
Additional: Children welcome

Tajine

This warm-hearted Moroccan restaurant just off Baker Street, now in its third year, has established itself as a popular local. Inside, the small room is packed with tables set against a backdrop of the warm colours of Marrakech, hot and heady with aromatic scents that waft from its steaming tagine pots. Homely and generous North African food is the style, where must-haves include the likes of merguez, couscous and tagines, of course. Harissa is not served unless requested, though does add an extra layer of flavour to the melded creations. The Moroccan rosé makes a suitable accompaniment to the meal, and the mint tea is especially refreshing. Bread (fresh and moist) is encrusted with sesame seeds and shows a Turkish influence. Service is very friendly, bustling and solicitous.

7a Dorset Street W1
Map: B4
Tel/Fax: 020 7935 1545
Chef: Gonul Ozturk
Owner: Meholi Barraoli
Cost: *Alc* £17, set-price L £7.50. ☺
H/wine £10.50
Times: Noon-3pm/D until 10.30pm. Closed L Sat, all Sun, Xmas, Bhs
Additional: Children 5+
Seats: 36
Style: Informal/Traditional
Smoking: No pipes & cigars; Air conditioning

Directions: ➜ Baker St

Tamarind

20 Queen Street W1X 7PJ
Map: C3
Tel: 020 7629 3561
Fax: 020 7499 5034
E-mail: tamarind@btclick.com
Chef: Atul Kochhar
Owner: Indian Cuisine Ltd
Cost: *Alc* £28, set-price L £14.95/D £25. ☺ H/wine £14.50
Times: Noon-3pm/6pm-midnight. Closed L Sat, 25 & 26 Dec, 1 Jan
Additional: Children welcome
Seats: 98
Style: Classic/Modern
Smoking: Air conditioning

The cooking might be Northern Frontier, but the address is pure Mayfair. The designer basement restaurant with its gold-coloured pillars, copper place settings and comfortable wrought-iron and tan leather chairs make a stylish setting for urbane Indian cooking. The lighting cleverly changes as the day progresses. Fish dishes are particularly interesting – one of their signatures is John Dory with crispy spinach. Familiar items, such as sheesh kebab and rogan josh are listed alongside unusual guinea fowl in fenugreek sauce or lamb shanks cooked with five spice mix and leafy spinach. Vegetarian choice includes broccoli and cauliflower marinaded in cumin and yoghurt and cooked in the tandoor oven, visible through a window at the end of the room. Malpua or semolina pancakes with fresh fruits and vanilla ice cream made an unusual dessert. The selection of Champagne on the very Western wine list includes a sparkler from India. Staff are numerous and attentive. *Best Indian Restaurant wine list (see page 18).*

Directions: ⊖ Green Park. Head for Hyde Park, and turn 4th R into Half Moon St and walk to end (Curzon St). Turn L, and Queen St is 1st R

La Tante Claire ❀❀❀❀❀

When it comes to classical French cooking, Pierre Koffman's Tante Claire remains the benchmark restaurant. It cannot be described as cutting edge, but it is highly consistent, exacting and utterly pleasurable, and one must credit the sheer professionalism of the team who still remain friendly and approachable. The big, serious wine list features heavyweight names at heavyweight prices, but having said that, there is plenty around the £20 to £35 mark and a whole section of fairly priced French regional wines. The menu, written in French, includes Koffmann trademarks such as pigs' trotter and salmon cooked in goose confit (one of the inspector's all-time memorable dishes). A meal starts here with bread that is amongst the best in the country, eight irresistibly moreish varieties. Appetisers live up to their name – duck rillette in pastry with mâche salad and a slither of duck confit with heavenly depth of flavour, for example. Ravioli of langoustine with spring vegetables and beurre blanc was constructed from exquisitely fine pasta, then filled with top quality, succulent shellfish and poached in a lovely, light and frothy chicken stock finished with basil purée and some wild mushrooms. Main-course cutlet of veal with cèps was very simple but exact, of superb tenderness and an awesome depth of flavour. The jus made from the cooking juices was faultless and the dish was served with a simple fondant potato which again had been timed to perfection. It is nearly impossible to resist the cheeseboard, so enticing is the selection from Jacques Vernier and so superb the condition. An assiette of chocolate was a masterly variation on a theme with soufflé, mousse, sorbet and tart. Leave room for petits fours that include a chocolate tray and a really oozy, boozy rum baba.

Berkeley Hotel Wilton Place
Knightsbridge SW1X 7RL
Map: B2
Tel: 020 7823 2003
Fax: 020 7823 2001
Chef/owner: Pierre Koffmann
Cost: *Alc* £70, set-price L £28.
H/wine £20
Times: 12.30-2pm/7-11pm. Closed L
Sat, all Sun, 2 wks fr 23 Dec, Bhs
Additional: Children 12+
Seats: 60. Private dining room 14.
Jacket & tie preferred
Style: Chic/Formal
Smoking: No pipes & cigars; Air
conditioning

Directions: 300 metres along
Knightsbridge from Hyde Park Corner.
⊖ Hyde Park Corner

Tatsuso Restaurant ❀❀

At lunchtime this Japanese restaurant is humming with conversation and city pinstripes, but in the evening it is quieter. Choose to sit at the traditional tables, or on the floor Japanese style at a series of low tables in the private rooms. Or if your bank balance is healthy, make for the sushi bar and eat food that's worth its weight in gold. A selection of typical dishes was the choice at a recent meal: teppan beef and prawns with two

32 Broadgate Circle
EC1M 6BT
Map: G4
Tel: 020 7638 5863
Fax: 020 7638 5864
Chef: Nobuyuki Yamanaka
Owner: Terutoshi Fujii
Cost: *Alc* £40, set-price L £38/D £58.
H/wine £14

sauces – a creamy tart one for the beef and a thin dashi with tempura-style grated daikon thickening. Good sushimi was expensive despite being quite standard, and a thin soup, pickles and rice were all enjoyable.

Directions: Ground floor of Broadgate Circle. ⊖ Liverpool St

Times: 11.30am-2.30pm/6-9.45pm.
Closed Sat & Sun
Seats: 120. Private dining rooms 6 & 8
Style: Traditional/Formal
Smoking: No pipes & cigars; Air conditioning

Teatro

Teatro has the look of the moment: opaque glass, banquettes and bare wooden floors plus a menu that mixes old and new. There are well-executed dishes such as fishcakes with lime and coriander mayonnaise, and osso buco with polenta and gremolata, as well as a wide choice from 'foie gras du jour' to fresh tagliatelle of Scottish langoustines and pesto, and roasted veal cutlet with orange braised endive, celery and pine nuts. Before the curtain goes up, you can fortify yourself with a good pre-theatre menu – perhaps Teatro salad niçoise, then seared salmon with spiced lentils and gaufrette chips followed by English cheese with pecan and raisin bread, or passion fruit parfait with fresh fruits. At the time of writing, another branch of Teatro was due to open in Leeds in summer 2000.

Directions: ⊖ Leicester Square, Piccadilly Circus

93-107 Shaftesbury Avenue
W1V 8BT
Map: C3
Tel: 020 7494 3040
Fax: 020 7494 3050
Chef: Stuart Gillies
Owners: Lee Chapman, Leslie Ash
Cost: Alc £38, set-price L & D £15 & £18. ☺ H/wine £12.50
Times: Noon-4.30pm/6-11.45pm.
Closed Sat L, all Sun, 24-31 Dec, Easter Day
Additional: Bar food; Children welcome
Seats: 100
Style: Minimalist/Chic
Smoking: No pipes; Air conditioning

Teca

Modern Italian dining in a crisp and formal environment. The decor and furnishings are modern but not overly minimalist and an open plan wine cellar makes a charming feature. The menu is short and to-the-point offering pasta dishes such as home-made tagliatelle with mussels and courgettes, alongside fish and meat dishes such as pan-fried salmon served with broccoli cream and truffle oil, and roasted pork fillet with gratinated fennels. A robust, almost peasant-style dish of lamb shank with spinach and mixed vegetables stood up well at inspection with the lamb tender and falling off the bone. Desserts such as puff pastry parcels with mixed berry compote and chantilly cream, or ricotta and raisin cake with chocolate sauce round the meal off with satisfying vivacity. The level of service is very good with a fair degree of flair shown by the Italian managers.

Directions: ⊖ Bond Street

54 Brook Mews W1Y 2NY
Map: C3
Tel: 020 7495 4774
Fax: 020 7491 3545
Chef: Marco Torri
Owner: A-Z Restaurant Group
Cost: Set-price L £16 & £19/D £19-£27. H/wine £13
Times: Noon-2.30pm/7-10.30pm.
Closed L Sat, all Sun
Additional: Bar food; Children welcome
Seats: 65
Style: Modern
Smoking: Air conditioning

The Thai Garden

Modest informal restaurant with loyal local following, serving Thai vegetarian and seafood dishes. You could opt for fried mushrooms with gingers, onions and spring onions for example, or fried fish topped with mushrooms and vegetables.

Style: Informal/Minimalist
Smoking: No-smoking area

Directions: 2nd left off Roman Road (1-way street); ⊖ Bethnal Green

249 Globe Road
E2 0JD
Map GtL: D3
Tel: 020 8981 5748
Cost: Alc £15, set-price L £7.50/D £16-£21. ☺ H/wine £7.50
Times: Noon-3pm/6-11pm.
Closed L Sat & Sun, Bhs
Additional: Children welcome

3 Monkeys Restaurant

White-painted minimalism, an entry bridge over the downstairs bar area, and an open-to-view kitchen gives a modern edge to this super Indian. Lunch has a restricted meal choice, dinner brings more unusual regional offerings such as yetti ajadina – semi-dry prawns with curry leaves.

136-140 Herne Hill
SE24 9QH
Map GtL: D2
Tel: 020 7738 5500
Fax: 020 7738 5505
E-mail: jpeacock@monkeys3.demon.co.uk
Cost: *Alc* £24, set-price £20 ☺ H/wine £12.95
Times: D only, 6pm-12.30am.
Closed 25 Dec, 1 Jan.
Additional: Bar food D, Sunday L; Children welcome
Style: minimalist
Smoking: No-smoking area; air conditioning

Directions: adjacent to Herne Hill Station

Titanic

Trendy venue with loud music and subdued lighting creating a subterranean effect. Food has a contemporary simplicity – potato blini with smoked salmon, tender hickory-smoked pork and dark chocolate bread pudding.

81 Brewer Street W1R 3FH
Map: D3
Tel: 020 7437 1912
Fax: 020 7439 4747

Telephone for further details

Directions: Nearest ⊖ Piccadilly Circus

Turners Restaurant ⊛

A cosy restaurant in fashionable Walton Street owned and hosted by celebrity chef Brian Turner who puts in occasional shifts in the kitchen. Yellow rag-rolled walls and a through theme of blues and yellows creates a calm and slightly Mediterranean atmosphere. The approach is modern French with skilful realisations of dishes such as brill braised with fennel served with tomato confit, and prime rib of grilled beef with a garlic sauce. At inspection a starter of artichoke heart filled with smoked haddock brandade and a tarragon butter sauce did seem to lack backbone but a main of roasted tournedos of monkfish with a pepper and coriander compote was fresh and lively. Dessert options might include caramelised pear tart with a dark chocolate ice cream, blueberry and fromage frais mousse, or mille-feuille of pancakes and roasted strawberries. The French-dominated wine list is extensive and reasonably priced.

87-89 Walton Street SW3 2HP
Map: A1
Tel: 020 7584 6711
Fax: 020 7584 4441
E-mail: pmturners@aol.com
Chef: Jon Lucas
Owner: Brian J Turner
Cost: *Alc* £45.20, set-price L £17/D £29.50. H/wine £15.50
Times: 12.30-2.15pm/7.30-11.15pm.
Closed Sun, Bhs
Additional: Children welcome
Seats: 54
Style: Traditional
Smoking: Air conditioning

Directions: ⊖ South Kensington, Knightsbridge. Behind Harrods

Vama ⊛

The fossil flagstone floor, old oil paintings in heavy wooden antique frames and handmade crockery all come from India, and dishes might include meat and seafood platter - marinated chicken, butterfly prawn and a moist, succulent piece of salmon.

438 King's Road SW10 0LJ
Map: C3
Tel: 020 7351 4118
Fax: 020 7565 8501
E-mail: andyv@aol.com
Cost: *Alc* £30, set-price L £5.95. H/wine £10.50

Vama

Times: 12.30-3pm/ 6.30-11.30pm.
Closed Xmas
Additional: Sunday L; Children welcome
Style: Classic/chic
Smoking: Air conditioning

Directions: Sloane Square, approx 20 mins walk down the King's Road or take 11 or 22 bus

Vasco & Piero's Pavillion

This long-established and ever-popular Soho Italian – much-loved by politicians and music types – offers a friendly welcome to diners. The cooking has its roots in Umbria, is uncomplicated yet refined and offers simple but elegant presentation. Starters could include spinach and ricotta tortelloni with butter and sage, or perhaps tagliatelle with black Umbrian truffles.

Style: Chic/Modern
Smoking: No pipes; Air conditioning

Directions: On corner of Great Marlborough Street & Noel Street. Oxford Circus

15 Poland Street W1V 3DE
Map GtL: D4
Tel: 020 7437 8774
Cost: Alc £32, set-price D £19.50. ☺ H/wine £9.95
Times: Noon-3pm/6-11pm.
Closed L Sat, all Sun, Bhs
Additional: Children 5+

Veeraswamy Restaurant

Although proudly proclaiming itself as 'the oldest Indian restaurant in Britain', decor and influences are uncompromisingly modern. The result is fresh, flavoursome dishes such as Mysore chilli chicken.

99-101 Regent Street W1R 8RS
Map: C3
Tel: 020 7734 1401
Fax: 020 7439 8434
E-mail: action@realindianfood.com
Cost: Alc £35, set-price L/D(post theatre) £11. ☺ H/wine £11.50
Times: Noon-2.30pm/5.30-10.30pm.
Closed D 25 Dec
Additional: Sunday L; Children welcome
Style: Chic/Modern
Smoking: No pipes & cigars; Air conditioning

Directions: Entrance near junction of Swallow St & Regent St, located in Victory House. Entrance in Swallow Street.

La Ventura Restaurant

Relaxed, friendly and informal restaurant, where impressive lunchtime fare included celery and blue cheese risotto, and roast breast of chicken with Savoy cabbage and sautéed pumpkin.

Directions: Finsbury Park. At junction of Crouch Hill and Japan Crescent

28 Crouch Hill N4 4AU
Map GtL: D4
Tel: 020 7281 5811

Telephone for further details

Veronica's

3 Hereford Road Bayswater W2 4AB
Map GtL: C3
Tel: 020 7229 5079
Fax: 020 7229 1210
Cost: Alc £28, set-price L & D £12.50
& £16.50. ☺ H/wine £10.50
Times: Noon-3pm/6pm-12.30am.
Closed L Sat, all Sun, Xmas, Bhs
Additional: Children welcome
Style: chic/rustic

Directions: ⊖ Bayswater,
Queensway. Hereford Rd runs
parallel to Queensway in between
Bayswater Rd and Westbourne Grove.

Part of a little parade of shops on the ground floor of a Victorian building. The menu features British traditional cooking culled from recipes dating back centuries. Finnan haddock pie, roast lamb and caper sauce, and Richmond maids of honour feature alongside fish'n'chips, and steak, kidney and mushroom pie.

Viet-Hoa

NEW

Vietnamese restaurant with a relaxed, low-key café feel. The kitchen offers a strong representation of Vietnamese cuisine – clear Chinese and Thai overtones but generally lighter in style. Try stir-fried beef with pickled greens.

Style: Informal
Smoking: Air conditioning

Directions: ⊖ Old Street or Liverpool Street Station

70-72 Kingsland Road E2
Map GtL: D4
Tel/Fax: 020 7729 8293
Chef/Owner: Quzen Ly
Cost: Set-price L £5/D £8. ☺
H/wine £7.90
Times: Noon-3.30pm/5.30-11.50.
Closed Xmas Eve, 1 Jan
Additional: Children welcome
Seats: 150

Villandry

Sharing floor space with an excellent food store, there are temptations galore for food lovers in this informal, stylish venue. The restaurant makes a strong pitch with dishes such as mackerel salad and wild sea trout.

Style: Informal
Smoking: No smoking in dining room; Air conditioning

Directions: ⊖ Great Portland Street. Restaurant entrance at 91 Bolsover St

170 Great Portland Street W1N 5TB
Map: C4
Tel: 020 7631 3131
Fax: 020 7631 3030
Cost: Alc £25, set-price D £15. ☺
H/wine £11
Times: Noon-4pm (Sun 11am)/6-
11pm. Closed D Mon & Sun
Additional: Bar food; Sunday L;
Children welcome

Vong

Designer restaurant where the classics of the West meet the mystique of the East. Aromas are intriguing, combinations generate immediate interest and the simple and uncluttered furnishings add to the experience. To open a recent meal a very fresh piece of tuna was evenly seared, carefully seasoned and combined with a pleasantly contrasting soy, ginger and mustard sauce. The result was simple, light and punchy. A divine piece of squid seduced our inspector's taste buds in the main course and Valrhona chocolate cake with coconut ice cream ended the meal off with a well executed blast of

The Berkeley Hotel Wilton Place
Knightsbridge SW1X 7RL
Map: B2
Tel: 020 7235 1010
Fax: 020 7235 1011
Chef: Jean Georges Vongerichten
Cost: Alc £55, set-price L £16/D
£16.50. ☺
Times: Noon-3pm/6-midnight
Additional: Sunday L; Children
welcome
Seats: 140

flavour. Other signature dishes include chicken and foie gras dumpling with truffle sauce, raw tuna and vegetables wrapped in rice paper, and duck broth with egg noodles. The wine list is serious and extensive including a good choice of half bottles.

Directions: ⊖ Hyde Park Corner, Knightsbridge

Style: French/Thai
Smoking: No-smoking area; No pipes & cigars; Air conditioning
Accommodation: 168 en suite
★ ★ ★ ★ ★

Westbury Hotel ❀❀

New Bond Street W1A 4UH
Map: C3
Tel: 020 7629 7755
Fax: 020 7495 1163
Chef: Jon McCann
Owner: Cola Holdings
Cost: Set-price L £19.50/D £21.50. ☺ H/wine £16
Times: Noon-2.30pm/6-10pm
Additional: Bar food; Sunday L; Children welcome
Seats: 46. Private dining rooms 15
Style: Classic/modern
Smoking: No pipes & cigars; Air conditioning
Accommodation: 255 en suite
★ ★ ★ ★

Once inside the Westbury's relaxing, unhurried restaurant it's easy to forget that the throng of Bond Street and Oxford Street is nearby. The room is an airy, comfortable setting for a menu that should please the most discerning of the hotel's international clientele. Those wanting something simple could opt for plainly-grilled fillet steak with a green salad, or Scottish lobster cooked as they like it, but the thrust of the operation is more modish in approach: lobster and crab salad with mango and lime, or goats' cheese ravioli with peppers and basil, followed by something like veal cutlet with borlotti beans, sun-dried tomatoes, rocket and rosemary. Timing is flawless – witness an inspector's 'wonderful, succulent' pigeon breast oozing with moisture atop well-matched cep and red wine risotto – while a judicious hand with flavours shone out of a main course of crisp-skinned, flaky roast cod with confit of aubergine and cumin, the last 'just where it should be, lurking in the background'. Puddings can be indulgent, among them perhaps white chocolate tart with bitter chocolate sorbet, or 'lusciously smooth', sweet banana crème brûlée with rum and raisin ice cream, while good coffee and petits fours bring a meal to a climax.

Directions: ⊖ Oxford Circus, Piccadilly Circus, Bond Street

White Onion ❀❀

Fashionable split level restaurant – very much a part of the Islington scene. Simple, understated decor and a 'happening' atmosphere complement the honest modern French cuisine. To start expect green split pea soup with a nutmeg froth or perhaps marinated chicken with balsamic vinegar on a light red pepper mousse. Main courses range from deep-fried goujonettes of cod with parsley sauce to beef fillet with black-peppercorn sauce and black peppercorn sorbet. The interest is

297 Upper Street
N1 2TU
Map GtL: D3
Tel/Fax: 020 7359 3533
Chef: Eric Guignard
Owner: Bijan Behzadi
Cost: Set-price D £24.50. ☺ H/wine £16
Times: fr Noon/6.30-11pm. Closed L Mon-Fri

fully maintained with desserts along the lines of roasted nectarines with nutty toffee sauce and apricot sorbet, or lemon mousse with a citrus salad perfumed with mint tea. The wine list is largely French dominated although Italy and the New World do make an appearance.

Directions: ⊖ Angel/Highbury & Islington (midway between two). Close to Almeida St

Additional: Sunday brunch; Children welcome
Seats: 62
Style: Modern/Minimalist
Smoking: No pipes & cigars; Air conditioning

Wilson's

The decor has changed since last year. The shop windows now give a clear view onto the road, the tartan curtains have gone and the walls have been painted a light blue and egg yellow above the dado rail. The owners have been running this restaurant for twenty years and it has an idiosyncratic Scottish charm. The menu, while not exclusively Scottish includes Scottish smoked salmon and Finnan haddock, and Aberdeen Angus beef. The kitchen obviously uses first class ingredients and the general standard of cooking is really very good. Finnan haddock comes with a spinach and bacon salad which was 'beautifully dressed'. A pan-fried pheasant on Savoy cabbage with chorizo sausage and red wine sauce was moist, full of flavour and the combination of the sausage was inspired. Desserts are well considered: Athol Brose with strawberries and framboise was particularly good, and the wine list is short but well chosen.

Directions: ⊖ Hammersmith

236 Blythe Road W14 0HJ
Map GtL: C3
Tel: 020 7603 7267
Fax: 020 7602 9018
E-mail: bob@wilsons-restaurant.co.uk
Chef: R Hilton
Owners: R Hilton, R Wilson
Cost: ☺ H/wine £10.50
Times: D only, 7-10pm. Closed Sun, Bhs
Seats: 44
Style: Informal/Traditional
Smoking: Air conditioning

Wiltons

55 Jermyn Street SW1Y 6LX
Map: C3
Tel: 020 7629 9955
Fax: 020 7495 6233

Telephone for further details.

As much a part of Jermyn Street as the bespoke shirt makers, this most English and traditional of restaurants is something of an institution, where pillars of establishment are known by name to discreet, long-serving staff. Interconnecting rooms feature green-plush seating, a mixture of secluded booths and tables, and panelled walls covered with prints, pictures and photographs – it's all rather clubby but comfortable. The menu remains resolutely traditional British and would not have looked out of place in a grand hotel of the 1930s or 40s: Beluga caviar, paté de foie gras, lobster bisque, whitebait, standard grills and fish dishes (lobster Thermidor, Dover sole meunière) and desserts the like of sherry trifle or savoury alternatives. However, it also offers some more modish dishes such as chargrilled tuna or sea bass with ginger, spring onion, wild mushrooms and soy dressing. The quality of raw materials is of the best and cooking is generally very sound. The wine list majors on France and familiar names, most notably white Burgundies and famous clarets. There is also an impressive cigar list and excellent espresso.

Directions: Opposite Turnbull & Asser (shirtmakers), near Piccadilly Circus. ⊖ Green park

YMing ❀❀

35-36 Greek Street W1V 5LN
Map: D4
Tel: 020 7734 2721
Fax: 020 7437 0292
E-mail: cyming2000@aol.com
Chef: Hung Lim
Owner: Christine Yau
Cost: A/c £15, set-price L/D £15. ☺ H/wine £9.50
Times: Noon-11.45pm. Closed Sun, 25-26 Dec
Additional: Bar food; Children welcome
Seats: 60. Private dining room 30
Style: chic
Smoking: No-smoking area; Air conditioning

Directions: Off Shaftesbury Ave, behind Palace Theatre

Aquamarine walls, comfortable soft furnishings, reasonably well-spaced tables and a relaxed atmosphere are hallmarks of this Chinese restaurant. The menu, offering plenty of choice without being overlong, brings together dishes from Beijing, Hunan, Szechuan, Mongolia and even Tibet, with four set meals for the less adventurous. Prawns in chilli and spiced salt make a good, light opener, with marinated smoked chicken and Ming-style cauliflower among other choices. As well as Peking duck and sizzling dishes, main courses include empress beef-flank slowly cooked with herbs and spices – fresh, light and 'utterly delicious' 'treasure case' (scallops, squid and prawns with fresh herbs steamed in a lotus leaf), and some specials of the day: perhaps strips of sweet and tender lamb cooked with contrasting lemon zest. Accompaniments extend to hot and spicy ma po tofu and crispy noodles, and desserts are predictable. Stick with lychees and drink tea.

Yumi Restaurant ❀❀

Consistently one of London's best Japanese restaurants, run by Yumi herself, with Mama San the absolute star, cosseting guests in authentic style. Downstairs, the formal restaurant serves a good range of dishes including specialities such as cooked belly pork in sake and soy sauce, fried tofu with beef and vegetable topping, and home-made minced sardine balls and rice cakes cooked in broth. The chef at the ground-floor sushi bar originates from the Shizuoka prefecture to the south of Tokyo, an area renowed for its cuisine, in particular its sushi. Not only is his deft preparation a joy to watch, but you'll also get a great sushi experience.

Directions: A few yards east of the junction of George Street and Gloucester Place. ⊖ Marble Arch

110 George Street W1H 5RL
Map: B4
Tel: 020 7935 8320
Fax: 020 7224 0917
E-mail: t.osumi@talk21.com
Chef: M Sato
Owners: Y Fujii & T Osumi
Cost: A/c £30, set-price D £39. ☺ H/wine £13.90
Times: D only, 5.30-11pm
Additional: Children welcome
Seats: 73. Private dining room 16
Style: Traditional
Smoking: No pipes & cigars; Air conditioning

Zafferano 🍃🍃🍃

If rustic/chic is not a contradiction in terms, then Zafferano is a perfect example of the genre. It is also one of the best Italian restaurants around, owned by Giorgio Locatelli whose many gifts include an ingrained understanding of the idea of good ingredients married to simple preparation. That is not to say the cooking lacks extra levels of techniques, but you can eat quite simply here – bresaola or carpaccio, for example, followed by tortellini in brodo or chicken breast with spinach – or choose dishes with an added degree of refinement such as pheasant and black truffle ravioli with rosemary. Ingredients sing of wild and ancient Mediterrranean shores – bottarga, turnip tops, chickpeas, rocket, cavolo nero, spelt and smoked swordfish. A main course of cod with lentils and parsley sauce lost its way slightly, but an orange pine nut tart with Cointreau ice-cream was fresh and precise. Look out for uninhibited dishes such as calves' sweetbreads in a sweet and sour sauce, and roast monkfish with walnuts and capers. Staff are friendly and courteous, and the all-Italian wine list is not too prohibitively priced, especially given the enviable Belgravia location. Little wonder this small restaurant remains so hugely popular.

Directions: Off Knightsbridge – around corner from The Sheraton Park Tower Hotel. ⊖ Knightsbridge

15 Lowndes Street
SW1X 9EY
Map: B2
Tel: 020 7235 5800
Fax: 020 7235 1971
Chef/Owner: Giorgio Locatelli
Cost: Set-price L £21.50/D £35.50.
H/wine £12.50
Times: Noon-2.30pm/7-11pm.
Closed Xmas, Easter
Additional: Sunday L; Children welcome
Seats: 55
Style: Chic/Rustic
Smoking: No pipes & cigars; Air conditioning

Zaika 🍃🍃🍃

Vineet Bhatia's inventive, assured take on the vastness of the subcontinent's cuisine continues to impress diners at this swish Fulham Road address. The decor is a long way from the flock wallpaper school of Indian restaurant design. Rich colour highlights combine with earth tones and ethnic touches to reinvent the genre for the new millennium. The cuisine is worlds apart from the neighbourhood tandoori also. Vineet borrows ideas and inspiration from across the whole country, from his South Indian duck with coconut milk and curry leaves to Northern inspired classics like tandoori saffron prawns, but all are informed by his own eclectic and educated palate. The inspector waxed lyrical about his nariyal jhinga; sweet succulent prawns in coconut masala tempered with lime leaves and served with a carom seed naan. The tandoori smoked salmon with dill, mustard and spices eaten on a cold December lunchtime had the inspector's tastebuds 'doing back flips'.

Directions: ⊖ South Kensington

257-259 Fulham Road SW3 6HY
Map: A1
Tel: 020 7351 7823
Fax: 020 7376 4971
Chef: Vineet Bhatia
Owners: Cuisine's Collection
Cost: Alc £28, set-price L
£12.95/£14.95/D £22. ☺ H/wine £13
Times: Noon-2.30pm, 6.30-10.45pm.
Closed L Sat, Bhs
Additional: Sunday L; Children welcome
Style: Modern/contemporary
Seats: 70. Private dining room 14
Smoking: No pipes & cigars; Air conditioning

Zander 🍃   NEW

Restaurant with a contemporary feel offering a large brasserie-style menu. The 'zander of the day' was accurately timed and succulent, served with crispy potatoes, avocado and apple salsa, and wild asparagus.

Telephone for further details

Directions: Telephone for directions

Crowne Plaza London St James
Buckingham Gate SW1E 6AF
Map: C2
Tel: 020 7834 6655
Fax: 020 7630 7587
E-mail: sales@cplonsj.co.uk

ENGLAND
BEDFORDSHIRE

BEDFORD, **Knife & Cleaver** ✿

Opposite the medieval church, this 17th-century inn has an elegant conservatory restaurant. A summer meal began with a warm salad of scallops with lardons of bacon, Parmesan and orange vinaigrette, followed by oak smoked duck breast on an apple and ginger galette.

The Grove Houghton Conquest
MK45 3LA
Map 5: TL04
Tel: 01234 740387
Fax: 01234 740900

Telephone for further details

Directions: M1 J12/13, between A6 & B530. 2m N of Ampthill, 5m S of Bedford

BEDFORD, **Woodlands Manor Hotel** ✿

Set in wooded grounds and gardens on the village outskirts, the elegant restaurant offers imaginative cooking, mainly British but also with a French influence. Why not have the double sirloin steak carved at your table?

Green Lane Clapham MK41 6EP
Map 5: TL04
Tel: 01234 363281
Fax: 01234 272390
E-mail:
woodlands.manor@pageant.co.uk
Cost: Alc £31.45, set-price D £25.
H/wine £13.95
Times: 12.30-2.30pm/7.30-9.45pm.
Closed L Sat
Additional: Bar Food; Sunday L;
Children welcome
Style: Classic/Formal
Smoking: No smoking in dining room;
Jacket & tie preferred
Civil licence: 50
Accommodation: 33 en suite ★ ★ ★

Directions: 2 miles N of Bedford,
towards Kettering on A6

DUNSTABLE, **Old Palace Lodge Hotel** ✿

Ivy clad Victorian family residence transformed into a fine hotel and an elegant restaurant. Start with an assiette of salmon and crab followed perhaps by fillet of beef with bacon and chicken livers.

Civil licence: 40 **Accommodation:** 68 en suite ★ ★ ★

Directions: From M1 J11 take Dunstable exit at roundabout. After 2 miles road passes under bridge. Hotel on R opposite church.

Church Street LU5 4RT
Map 4: TL02
Tel: 01582 662201
Fax: 01582 696422
Cost: Alc £24.95, set-price L
£16.95/D £19.95. ☺ H/wine £12.50
Times: 12.30-1.45pm/7-9.45pm
Additional: Bar food L; Sunday L;
Children welcome
Style: Modern/Traditional
Smoking: Air conditioning

FLITWICK,
Menzies Flitwick Manor ✸✸

Delightful country house restaurant with long windows
overlooking the garden, pretty fabrics and well spaced tables.
Friendly and efficient service is provided by a charming and
well-established staff. Guests can ponder the menus in the
drawing room with a drink and canapés before dinner. A
starter of asparagus and truffle risotto was creamy and well
timed, served with shaved Parmesan. It was followed by a
beautifully presented paillard of salmon on a delicate pistachio
beurre blanc. Other options could be a mille-feuille of roasted
vine cherry tomatoes surrounded by pan-fried sea scallops on a
tomato and red onion salsa, and roast haunch of venison on a
purée of celeriac with a Burgundy five-hour sauce. Desserts
range from a symphony of Agen prunes to hot espresso soufflé
with rich chocolate sauce.

Church Road MK45 1AE
Map 4: TL03
Tel: 01525 712242
Fax: 01525 718753
Chef: Richard Salt
Cost: *Alc* £40, set-price D £29.50.
H/wine £18
Times: Noon-1.30pm/7-9.30pm
Additional: Sunday L; Children 12+
Seats: 55. Private dining rooms 8 &
14
Style: Traditional/Country-house
Smoking: No smoking in dining room
Civil licence: 55
Accommodation: 17 en suite ★★★

Directions: M1 J12, through
Westoning. On approaching Flitwick
take 1st left into Church Road. Manor
200yds on left.

WOBURN,
Paris House Restaurant ✸✸

A tranquil deer park surrounds the pricey, mock-Tudor
restaurant where the atmosphere is, nonetheless, warm,
attentive and pleasingly informal. The classical French cuisine
is well tried and tested and descriptions come straight to the
point: Mediterranean fish soup; smoked chicken and bacon
salad; fillet of beef in red wine and shallot sauce; salmon in
Champagne sauce. Comfort food in the form of honey-glazed

Woburn Park MK17 9QP
Map 4: SP93
Tel: 01525 290692
Fax: 01525 290471
E-mail: gailbaker@parishouse.co.uk
Chef/Owner: Peter Chandler
Cost: *Alc* £46.50, set-price L £25/D
£50. H/wine £13
Times: Noon-2pm/7-10pm.
Closed D Sun, all Mon, Feb
Additional: Sunday L; Children
welcome
Seats: 48. Private dining room 16
Style: French country house
Smoking: No pipes & cigars

Directions: On A4012, 1.5 miles out
of Woburn towards Hockcliffe,
through huge archway

belly of pork with braised cabbage and mashed potatoes was tender and well-flavoured, although the skin could perhaps have been crisper. Alongside old favourites, such as breaded lemon chicken and hot raspberry soufflé, there are some more novel listings including deep-fried squid on a bed of salad in chilli and liquorice sauce, and a wittily conceived 'upside down Millennium Dome with blackcurrant mousse'. The lengthy wine list is well written and has some good bottles, but mark-ups are high.

BERKSHIRE

ASCOT,

Royal Berkshire Hotel NEW

London Road Sunninghill SL5 0PP
Map 4: SU96
Tel: 01344 623322
Fax: 01344 627100

The smart restaurant at the Royal Berkshire offers a wide choice from an extensive menu. Impressive extras include home-made bread, a complimentary appetiser, and good petits fours.

Telephone for further details

Directions: From A30 towards Bagshot turn R opposite Wentworth Club onto A329, 2m, Hotel entrance on R

BRACKNELL, Coppid Beech

The chalet-style complex includes a ski slope, adjacent ice-rink and bier keller but that's as far as the Alpine theming goes. At Rowans Restaurant, however, you're less likely to find bratwurst than sausage composed of chicken, prawn and leek with sautéed spring onions and sauce indienne. Other modern, eclectic dishes include bouillabaisse that packs a real punch, or breast of duck with pineapple and cracked pepper, bok choi and rosti. Sea bass is given an upmarket treatment with aubergine caviar, tempura oyster and sauce vierge. There's a welcome sighting of veal sweetbreads, here roasted with winter vegetables, parsnip purée and thyme Madeira gravy or used as a stuffing of raviolini along with lobster, served in a Bercy sauce with mussels and tarragon.

John Nike Way RG12 8TF
Map 4: SU86
Tel: 01344 303333
Fax: 01344 301200
E-mail: sales@coppid-beech-hotel.co.uk
Chef: Neil Thrift
Cost: Set-price L £17.95/D £24.95.
Times: Noon-2.30pm/7-10.30pm (10pm Sun)
Additional: Sunday L (12.30-2.30pm); Children welcome
Seats: 100. Private dining room 200
Style: Classic/formal
Smoking: No-smoking area; Air conditioning
Accommodation: 205 en suite ★ ★ ★ ★
Civil Licence: 150

Directions: From M4 J10, follow A329(M) to 1st exit. At roundabout take 1st exit to Binfield; hotel 300 metres on R

BRACKNELL,
Stirrups Country House Hotel

Maidens Green RG42 6LD
Map 4: SU86
Tel: 01344 882284
Fax: 01344 882300
E-mail: reception@stirrupshotel.co.uk
Cost: *Alc* £25, set-price L /D £20. ☺
H/wine £9.75
Times: Noon-2pm(3pm Sun)/7-10pm
(9pm Sun)
Additional: Bar food; Sunday L;
Children welcome
Style: Traditional/Country -house
Smoking: No smoking in dining room
Accommodation: 28 en suite ★★★

*A popular venue where both the restaurant and bar serve
contemporary-style dishes. Rack of lamb is a favourite, and lemon
sole with garlic, basil and chive mustard is recommended.*

Directions: 3m N of Bracknell on B3022 towards Windsor

BRAY, # Chauntry House Hotel

SL6 2AB
Map 4: SU97
Tel: 01628 673991
Fax: 01628 773089
E-mail: res@chauntryhouse.com
Chef: Jean de la Ronziere
Owners: Carmox Management
Cost: *Alc* £35, set-price L £20.50. ☺
H/wine £12.50
Times: Noon-2.30pm/7-9.30pm.
Closed Xmas & New Year
Additional: Sunday L; Children
welcome
Seats: 40. Private dining rooms 12 &
20
Style: Informal/Country-house
Smoking: No smoking in dining room
Civil licence: 55
Accommodation: 15 en suite ★★★

A fine example of an 18th-century country house, in a
charming, prosperous village with a remarkable amount of fine
restaurants. Chauntry House offers views over the Victorian
walled garden and local cricket field and its interior is bright
and airy with well-spaced tables. The cooking is assured and
dishes from the set-price menus (which change every few
weeks) are in the main English or European in origin. A first
course of crab and ginger ravioli had fresh crab in a perfect
parcel, served with a julienne of vegetables and spicy coriander
sauce. Saddle of rabbit was 'lovely – moist and tender' and
came with a further helping of rabbit in cabbage. The saucing
was good with a smooth tangy mustard sauce. Desserts are
excellent – baked pear in puff pastry was 'just right, not too
sweet in perfect pastry'.

Directions: From M4 J8/9 take A308M, then A308 (Windsor). L
on B3028. Into Bray & hotel 100yds on R

BRAY,

The Fat Duck ✿✿✿✿

High Street Maidenhead
SL6 2AQ
Map 4: SU97
Tel: 01628 580333
Fax: 01628 776188
Chef: Heston Blumenthal
Owners: Heston & Zanna Blumenthal
Cost: *Alc* £50, set-price L £23.
H/wine £16
Times: Noon-2pm(2.30pm Sun)/7-
9.30pm(10pm Fri & Sat). Closed D
Sun, all Mon, 2 wks at Xmas
Additional: Sunday L; Children
welcome
Seats: 45
Style: Chic/Minimalist
Smoking: No-smoking area; No pipes
& cigars

Heston Blumenthal's challenging cooking is not easy to
categorise – it is in a class of its own. To call it innovative
modern French seems inadequate when confronted with 'veal
sweetbread roast in salt crust with hay and pollen, confit
parsnips, cockles a la plancha, lettuce and truffle cream', or
'mille feuille of pain d'epices ice cream, pineapple and chilli
jelly, Fleur de Sel'. All the gutsy, earthy roast pigs' ears,
trotters, cheeks, andouille, kidneys, pork hock, chorizo,
botifarra, cockscombs and more are not for the faint-hearted.
Other ingredients take you through the markets of the
Mediterranean: piquillo peppers, olive oil from Maussane,
truffled brandade, borlotti beans. These all fire the
imagination, and Blumenthal has the technical abilities to
translate these fantasies onto the plate. Strong, harmonious
flavours defined an immaculate 'risotto of crab and rocket,
chlorophyll and cassonnade of red pepper, crab ice cream and
passion fruit seeds'. There was also a wow factor with the
'pastilla of Anjou pigeon with cherries, roast breast with
spiced nuts and Manjari chocolate, watercress veloute'. A less
convincing combination of flavours, however, in this high-wire
act was 'roast scallop, caramelised cauliflower purée,
marinated cep and jelly of oloroso sherry'. Explorations of a
savoury-sweet kind are presented in pre-desserts of bacon-
flavoured caramel crisp, basil-flavoured blancmange and the
like. But the bottom line is that Blumenthal can cook –
'chocolate fondant, rice pudding with orange flower water,
apricot purée and coconut sorbet' was the composition of a
masterchef. *Best Sherry List (see pages 18-19).*

AA Wine Shortlisted for
Award-see page 18

Directions: M4 J8/9 (Maidenhead), take A308 towards Windsor.
turn L into Bray. Restaurant in centre of village on L

BRAY-ON-THAMES,
Monkey Island Hotel ❀

A truly idyllic riverside setting with lush willows, wandering peacocks and a sociable rabbit population. The menu is elaborate with a hint of imperial grandeur: roast loin of venison with a bitter chocolate sauce for example.

Old Mill Lane SL6 2EE
Map 4: SU97
Tel: 01628 623400
Fax: 01628 784732
E-mail: monkeyisland@btconnect.com
Cost: Alc £38.
Times: 12.30-2.30pm (Sun 3.30pm)/7.30-9.30pm. Closed D Sun
Additional: Sunday L; Children welcome
Style: Classic/Country-house
Smoking: No smoking in dining room
Civil licence: 80
Accommodation: 26 en suite ★★★★

Directions: M4 J8/9, A308 towards Windsor, before flyover turn L towards Bray Village, then follow signs

BRAY, **Waterside Inn** ❀❀❀❀

The Waterside is an institution, and as such suffers the fate of great institutions. As time and fashion roll ever onwards, what once was the benchmark experience can come to seem stuffy, formal and heavy-going. Even the decor now seems a bit old-hat, although arguably it matters less when there is a Thames-side setting as stunning as this. But it still feels like a long-running although enjoyable performance rather than an exciting, innovative experience in tune with the needs of the 21st century. The shame is that the attempts to bring a contemporary edge to the cooking, on our visit, seemed doomed to failure - although failure here would seem remarkable in many other establishments. The 'menu exceptionnel' promises samples of dishes from the *carte* and is probably the best choice. Terrine of foie gras flavoured with Sauternes and gooseberry paired lovely liver with shockingly sharp gooseberries. All the elements in a pan-fried scallop lightly seasoned with curry powder on a bed of Brussel sprouts with an orange nage were surprisingly below par. A flash of brilliance appeared in essence of chicken and lemongrass consommé, but roasted best end and leg of milk-fed lamb with seasonal vegetables and minted hollandaise sauce lacked flavour and impact. The selection of chocolate desserts was impressive in presentation as always.

Ferry Road SL6 2AT
Map 4: SU97
Tel: 01628 620691
Fax: 01628 784710
E-mail: waterinn@aol.com
Chefs: Michel Roux, Mark Dodson
Owner: Michel Roux
Cost: Alc £95, set-price L £32 (£48 Sun)/D £71.50. H/wine fr £25
Times: Noon-1.30pm (2.30pm Sun)/7-9.30pm. Closed Mon & Tue (ex for D Tue Jun-Aug), 26 Dec-1 Feb
Additional: Sunday L; Children 12+
Seats: 75. Private dining room 8
Style: Classic
Smoking: No pipes & cigars
Civil licence: 70

Directions: M4 J8/9. On A308 towards Windsor, turn L before M/way overpass for Bray (B3028). Restaurant clearly signposted.

BURCHETT'S GREEN, **The Crown** ❀

The rustic intimacy of this pleasing pub-restaurant, located in the centre of a conservation area, is well matched by the simple, well-composed cuisine on offer – notably a tantalisingly rich coq au vin served with mash.

Style: Bistro-style/Rustic **Smoking:** No pipes & cigars

Directions: From M4 J8/9 take A404(M) take exit signposted Henley & Burchett's Green

SL6 6QZ
Map 4: SU88
Tel: 01628 822844
Cost: Alc £25. ☺ H/wine £10.95
Times: Noon-3pm/7-midnight. Closed L Sat
Additional: Bar food; Sunday L; Children welcome

COOKHAM DEAN,
Inn on the Green

The Old Cricket Common SL6 9NZ
Map 4: SU88
Tel: 01628 482638
Fax: 01628 487474
E-mail:
enquiries@theinnonthegreen.com
Cost: Alc £25, set-price L £12.95/D
£15.95. ☺ H/wine £10.50
Times: Noon-3pm/7-midnight
Additional: Bar food; Sunday L;
Children welcome
Style: Rustic/Traditional
Smoking: No-smoking area
Civil licence: 40
Accommodation: 8 en suite

*Former pub idyllically located on the village green, opposite the
cricket pitch. Anglo-French cooking is served in the beamed,
candlelit dining room or the conservatory overlooking the courtyard.*

Directions: From Marlow or Maidenhead follow Cookham
Dean signs. In Cookham Dean turn into Hills Lane; into
National Trust road by War Memorial

HURST,
Castle Restaurant & Bar NEW

Impressive, 500-year-old building, formerly a run-down pub,
located next to the village bowling green and opposite the
parish church. Carefully restored back to its former glory, with
wood-panelled walls, exposed fireplaces, and a section of
original Saxon wattle and daub, it now houses an intimate bar
and restaurant. Visitors will find that the standard pub menu
has been replaced by an exciting, often ambitious, modern
menu featuring imaginative, well-constructed British dishes.
Young chef, Damian Broom, successfully combines unusual
flavours in such dishes as cannon of venison with bitter
chocolate and cherry sauces and, for pudding, Napoleon of
beetroot and rhubarb with a goats' cheese sabayon. The
highlight of our early summer inspection was a 'tar tar' of
kingfish with roquette and watercress sauce, but a perfectly
cooked fillet of lamb, served on wilted spinach and tip-top baby
vegetables with a lamb consommé also impressed. For dessert,
choose the warm fondant of bitter chocolate and ginger, the
intriguingly named 'a study of herbs' (a selection of three herb
mousses), or opt for the excellent cheese board, perhaps
including Stinking Bishop and Bath Triple Cream. Good coffee
and hand-made petits fours. Friendly, efficient service.

Church Hill Nr Twyford
RG10 0SJ
Map 4: SU77
Tel: 0118 934 0034
Fax: 0118 934 0334
E-mail: info@castlerestaurant.co.uk
Chef: Damion Broom
Owners: Anthony Edwards,
Amanda Hill

Cost: Alc £33, set-price L £12.95 & £17.95/D £33.
H/wine £10.35
Times: Noon-2.30pm/7-10pm. Closed 26 Dec
Additional: Sunday L; Children 12+
Seats: 70. Private dining rooms 11 & 36
Style: Rustic
Smoking: No-smoking area

Directions: 10 minutes from M4 J10

MAIDENHEAD,
Fredrick's Hotel ❀❀❀

Shoppenhangers Road
SL6 2PZ
Map 4: SU88
Tel: 01628 581000
Fax: 01628 771054
E-mail: reservations@fredricks-hotel.co.uk
Chef: Brian Cutler
Owner: Fredrick W Lösel
Cost: *Alc* £50, set-price L £25.50/D £35.50. H/wine £16
Times: Noon-2pm/7-9.45pm.
Closed L Sat, 24 Dec-3 Jan
Additional: Bar food; Sunday L; Children welcome
Seats: 60. Private dining room 130
Style: Classic/Traditional
Smoking: No cigars & pipes; Air conditioning
Civil licence: 120
Accommodation: 37 en suite ★★★★

Directions: From M4 J8/9 take A404(M), then turning for Cox Green/White Waltham. L into Shoppenhangers Lane. Restaurant on R

The restaurant at this rather glitzy hotel in a quiet location is a bright and attractive room of panels, chandeliers and fresh flowers overlooking a patio (drinks and meals served here in summer) and gardens. A classic French streak runs through the menu – moules marinière, tournedos of Aberdeen Angus with wild mushrooms – and some commendably simple treatments work well, as in asparagus with hollandaise, grilled Dover sole, or duckling roasted with Bramley apples. But the kitchen shows the same confidence with some fresh ideas. Langoustines, for instance, are accurately wrapped in potato for extra texture and accompanied by a tomato and chilli salsa of good balance, and sweetbreads are partnered by scallops and Sauternes sauce. Some main courses receive similar treatments – turbot is poached in coconut and coriander sauce and served with crab ravioli – and judicious use is made of luxury items, foie gras with partridge *en cocotte*, for example, or with pig's trotter and sweetbreads in truffle dressing. Everything is well handled and accurately timed – lamb, with a compote of baby artichokes and garlic and Madeira sauce, appearing pink and tender – and vegetables are said to be 'well-executed'. End with something like chocolate and passion fruit mousse or bread-and-butter pudding and enjoy the petits fours with coffee. The four-page wine list sticks mainly to France, and there are five house wines.

MAIDENHEAD,
Ye Olde Bell Hotel ❀

The restaurant is situated in the main oak-beamed building, which dates from 1135. Expect traditional Chateaubriand, and breast of chicken with grilled polenta, pickled samphire and creamy aniseed sauce.

Additional: Bar food; Sunday L; Children welcome
Style: Traditional/Country-house
Smoking: No smoking in dining room
Civil licence: 90
Accommodation: 46 en suite ★★★

Directions: From M40 J4 take A404, then A4130. Turn R at East Arms pub in Hurley

Hurley SL6 5LX
Map 4: SU88
Tel: 01628 825881
Fax: 01628 825939
Cost: *Alc* £30, set-price L £17.95/D £23.95. ☺ H/wine £12.95
Times: Noon-3.30pm/7.30-midnight.

MARSH BENHAM, Red House ❀❀

Former 16th-century coaching inn, totally refurbished with a new kitchen and a country house-style restaurant. The warm red brick walls and wooden floors give a smart but informal feel. The rooms are decorated with etchings, oils and bookcases full of books. Homemade breads are 'warm and tasty', and the food can be elaborate and ambitious – tortellini of goats' cheese resting on ratatouille with fresh tomato coulis and extra virgin oil infused with basil, for example. Oxtail braised in red wine and filled with a mushroom mousse served with mashed potatoes and roasted root vegetables was well cooked. Pasta is obviously a skill here – deemed 'excellent' when served with a poached fillet of brill. Desserts are delicious and might include apple tart with calvados butter and vanilla ice cream, or a chocolate tart soufflé. There is a good house Chardonnay from Gascony and the wine list covers the medium price range well, but there are few choices by the glass.

Directions: 400yds off A4, 5 miles from Hungerford; 3 miles from Newbury

Nr Newbury RG20 8LY
Map 4: SU46
Tel: 01635 582017
Fax: 01635 581621
Chef: Rupert Rowley
Owner: Mr Gwyn-Jones
Cost: Alc £21. ☺ H/wine £11.95
Times: Noon-2.30pm/7-10.30pm. Closed D Sun, all Mon
Additional: Bar food; Sunday L; Children 3+
Seats: 60
Style: Bistro-style/Informal
Smoking: No-smoking area; No pipes & cigars

NEWBURY,
Donnington Valley Hotel ❀❀

The restaurant at this modern hotel is a light and airy galleried room overlooking an outdoor water feature, gardens and golf course. The kitchen has evolved its own style, turning out luxury items like foie gras with truffle, honey-roast tamarillos and Sauternes jelly, or whole lobster pan-fried with garlic, through Torbay sole glazed with a lemon and herb butter, to good old fillet steak and chips. More mainstream to the operation are perhaps roasted breast of pigeon with parsnip and apple tarte Tatin, and roasted pork fillet with sweet-and-sour red cabbage, apple and potato rösti and grain mustard jus. Vegetarians get a handful of main courses to choose from; cheeses are predominantly French, and desserts are of the hot sticky date pudding and white chocolate and cherry torte variety. California is a strong point of the wine list: owner Sir Peter Michael has a vineyard there.

Directions: Exit M4 J13, take A34 S/bound and exit at Donnington Castle sign. Turn R then L at next junction. Hotel 1m on R

Old Oxford Road Donnington RG14 3AG
Map 4: SU46
Tel: 01635 551199
Fax: 01635 551123
E-mail: general@donningtonvalley.co.uk
Chef: Kelvin Johnson
Owner: Sir Peter Michael
Cost: Alc £32, set-price L £18/D £23. ☺ H/wine £12.50
Times: Noon-2pm/7-10pm
Additional: Bar food; Sunday L; Children welcome
Seats: 120. Private dining rooms 50, 60
Style: Informal/modern
Smoking: No smoking in dining room; Air conditioning
Civil licence: 85
Accommodation: 58 en suite ★★★★

NEWBURY, **Regency Park Hotel**

Bowling Green Road Thatcham
RG18 3RP
Map 4: SU46
Tel: 01635 871555
Fax: 01635 871571
Chef: Paul Green
Owner: Pedersen Caterers
Cost: *Alc* £34.45, set-price L /D
£15.50 & £19.50. ☺ H/wine £12.25
Times: Noon-2pm(12.30pm Sun)/7-
10pm(9.30pm Sun)
Additional: Bar food; Sunday L;
Children welcome
Seats: 100. Private dining room 140
Style: Contemporary
Smoking: No smoking in dining room
Accommodation: 82 en suite ★ ★ ★ ★

Fine dining in the stylish and modern Watermark restaurant. Cool pastel shades and designer Italian furniture set a chic tone for the interior. The backdrop of a landscaped sloping garden with a charming waterfall feature as focal point creates an overall ambience of luxurious tranquillity. The food is best described as contemporary but unfussy. A starter of roast boneless quail with herbed mushroom duxelle and warm tomato vinaigette was succulent and well executed. An unfamiliar Canadian dish from the specials board offered well timed white fish served simply with a chervil and potato salad. For dessert a rhubarb and ginger crème brûlée was accurately prepared, although the ginger was surprisingly subdued. Vegetarian dishes might include spinach and ricotta ravioli with sweet shallot butter sauce. The wine list is extensive but not daunting, with a good range of wines offered by the glass.

Directions: From Thatcham A4, towards Newbury, turn R into Northfield Road, then L at mini roundabout. Hotel is on R

NEWBURY,
Vineyard at Stockcross

Stockcross RG20 8JU
Map 4: SU46
Tel: 01635 528770
Fax: 01635 528398
E-mail: general@the-vineyard.co.uk
Chef: Billy Reid
Owner: Sir Peter Michael

It could be argued this is a wine list with a restaurant attached, except that Billy Reid's cooking has the confidence and style to match the stunning range of wines. Prize-winning Peter Michael Californian wines are naturally showcased, but the extensive list also includes an excellent selection for £20 and

under and there's plenty of sensible, friendly and down-to-earth advice available to help you choose. The range of dishes on offer is also lengthy, so more credit goes to a kitchen that copes so well. Beautifully made terrine of guinea fowl, Agen prunes and sherry vinaigrette started an inspection meal on a positive note, lifted to even higher levels by a main course of sea bass, cep cream sauce, leaf beets and boulangère potatoes, accurately cooked and harmonious as a whole. A pure refreshing quality was added by a coconut sorbet with an excellent pineapple Tatin and mango coulis. The two-tier setting for all this gastro-pleasure has been as carefully planned as everything else. Modern sculptures, including the 'dancing flames' on the outside pool, beautifully set and well-spaced tables, and huge tall glass vases of lilies all add up to a sense of crisp, contemporary comfort. Staff are friendly but discreet, service is polished. All in all, it's a little bit of London in the Home Counties, mixed with a dash of California. *Best Americas List (see pages 18-19)*. Wine Award National Winner.

Smoking: No-smoking area; Air conditioning
Civil licence: 70
Accommodation: 33 en suite ★ ★ ★ ★

Directions: Take A34 Newbury by-pass to A4 Bath Road interchange, then take B4000 to Stockcross, hotel on R

Cost: *Alc* fr £39.75, set-price L £16-£22/D £42-£75. H/wine £12
Times: Noon-2pm/7-10pm. Closed Xmas
Additional: Sunday L; Children welcome
Seats: 74. Private dining room 50-55
Style: Classic/Country house

AA Wine Award-see page 18
Shortlisted for

PANGBOURNE, Copper Inn ❀❀

The Copper Inn's light and airy restaurant is an easy place to relax in: comfortable seats at well-set tables, pictures and tapestries on the walls, and, outside, a terrace for alfresco eating in summer. The wide-ranging menu has more than a hint of the Mediterranean to it, with penne tossed with mussels, prawns and cockles in a spicy tomato sauce followed by poached chicken breast with truffle risotto, or Serrano ham with marinated artichoke heart and then crispy duck leg with cannellini and black bean sauce. Roasting is put to good effect: rack of Welsh salt-marsh lamb with ratatouille sauce and minty couscous, or loin of venison with a sauce of crushed green peppercorns and a fried polenta cake. Crème brûlée, or dark chocolate and Grand Marnier mousse bring things to a happy conclusion, and eight wines are offered by the glass on the France-dominated list.

Directions: 5 miles from M4 J12, at junction of A329 Reading/Oxford and A340; next to parish church.

Church Road RG8 7AR
Map 4: SU67
Tel: 0118 9842244
Fax: 0118 9845542
E-mail: michel@copper-inn.co.uk
Chef: Stuart Shepherd
Owner: Michel Rosso
Cost: *Alc* £27.50, set-price L £13.50. ☺ H/wine £12.95
Times: Noon-2.30pm/7-9.30pm
Additional: Bar food; Sunday L; Children welcome
Seats: 60. Private dining rooms 10
Style: Informal/Modern
Smoking: No-smoking area
Civil licence: 80
Accommodation: 22 en suite ★ ★ ★

SHINFIELD, L'Ortolan

Five AA Rosetted chef John Burton-Race has moved to The Landmark Hotel, London (see entry)

Tel: 020 7631 8000
Fax: 020 7631 8080
E-mail:
reservations@thelandmark.co.uk

SONNING-ON-THAMES,
The French Horn ❀❀

Delightful riverside setting with sweeping, lazy views of the infant Thames with its abundance of wildfowl and weeping willows. If that's not enough to give your soul a lift then any number of carefully composed dishes from the three dinner menus may rise to the task. Certainly a plate of freshly seared foie gras with caramelised pears left the inspector nodding approvingly. A main dish of boned pigeon in its own juices provoked slightly less enthusiasm, although the jus was accurate and the presentation succinct. Presentation was also to the fore in a super chocolate fondant with vanilla ice cream. The wine list plants its root firmly in France although a New World selection has been introduced. In particular there is a stunning list of burgundies including a bottle priced at £7000 for those noble souls determined to part with their money in the cause of decadence.

RG4 6TN
Map 4: SU77
Tel: 0118 9692204
Fax: 0118 9442210
E-mail:
thefrenchhorn@compuserve.com
Chef: Gille Company
Owners: The Emmanuel Family
Cost: *Alc* £50, set-price L £21/D £33.
H/wine £12.50
Times: Noon-2pm/7-9.30pm.
Closed 1 Jan, Good Fri
Additional: Sunday L; Children 3+
Seats: 60. Private dining room 24
Style: Classic/Formal
Smoking: No pipes & cigars
Accommodation: 20 en suite ★ ★ ★

Directions: M4 J8/9 & A4, village centre, on the river

STREATLEY,
Swan Diplomat Hotel ❀❀

High Street RG8 9HR
Map 4: SU58
Tel: 01491 878800
Fax: 01491 872554
E-mail: sales@swan-diplomat.co.uk
Chef: Matthew Smith
Owner: Diplomat Hotels
Cost: *Alc* fr £35, set-price D fr £32.
H/wine £14
Times: D only, 7.30-10pm
Additional: Bar food; Sunday L
(12.30-2pm); Children welcome
Seats: 60. Private dining rooms 18 & 32
Style: Traditional/Country-house
Smoking: No pipes & cigars
Civil licence: 100
Accommodation: 46 en suite ★ ★ ★ ★

The Swan has been a Thames-side landmark for over a century and little wonder when the setting is quite so chocolate box. The view may well be Jerome K Jerome but, recently promoted from the ranks, chef Matthew Smith's food is much more up to date. Classics like bouillabaisse and chicken liver and foie gras parfait sit comfortably aside more modish ideas like grilled loin of veal with morel mash, peppered beans and roast shallot. An inspector described the veal loin as 'an accomplished dish and certainly the highlight of the meal'. Matthew Smith shows his restraint and respect for classical methods in such assured dishes as pan-fried scallops and langoustines with cauliflower purée and red lentils. Puddings tend towards the tried and tested but a carefully executed chocolate tart was impressively filled and only slightly let down by less than crisp pastry.

Directions: Follow A329 from Pangbourne, on entering Streatley turn R at traffic lights. The hotel is on L before bridge

WINDSOR,

Aurora Garden Hotel ❀

A conservatory-style dining room ensures a light and airy atmosphere during the day, and comprehensive views of the attractive illuminated water gardens at night. A grilled tuna steak was a worthy centrepiece for an enjoyable meal.

Bolton Avenue SL4 3JF
Map 4: SU97
Tel: 01753 868686
Fax: 01753 831394
E-mail: aurora@auroragarden.co.uk
Cost: *Alc* £21, set-price D £15.95. ☺
H/wine £10.50
Times: Noon-2pm/7-9.30pm.
Closed L Sat
Additional: Bar food; Sunday L;
Children welcome
Style: Traditional/Country-house
Smoking: No smoking in dining room
Civil licence: 60
Accommodation: 19 en suite ★ ★

Directions: From M4 take A308
(Staines); at 3rd roundabout take
3rd exit (Bolton Ave). Hotel is 500yds
on R

WINDSOR,

Castle Hotel ❀

Watch the world go by from the restaurant. A recent meal began with Thai fishcakes and 'zingy' chilli jam, breast of guinea fowl with Calvados and mustard cream, and vanilla and yoghurt bavarois with poached pear.

Additional: Bar food; Sunday L: Children welcome
Style: Informal/traditional
Smoking: No smoking in dining room
Accommodation: 111 en suite ★ ★ ★

Directions: In town centre opposite Guildhall

High Street SL4 1LJ
Map 4: SU97
Tel: 0870 4008300
Fax: 01753 830224
E-mail:
heritagehotels_windsor.castle@forte-hotels.com
Cost: *Alc* £35, set-price L £9.95/D
£22.95. ☺ H/wine £13.50
Times: Noon-2pm, 7-10pm

WINDSOR,

Sir Christopher Wren Hotel ❀❀

The impressive hotel dining room offers fine views over the Thames, and the ease and grace of the service ensures an enjoyable experience for every diner. An excellent *amuse-bouche* – tian of foie gras with creamed leeks on toasted brioche – got the meal off to a good start. The first course, cannelloni of smoked haddock with Cajun scallops was served with a pea chutney, Thai spiced apple and bitter leaf salad. Unusual combinations are a feature of the menu, and the main course teamed lobster with lamb, flavoured with ginger. Other unusual partnerships include roast halibut set on a mussel and Parmesan polenta with a crab velouté, and wild boar, Burgundy snails and vegetable couscous. The chef displays admirable skill in combining such unlikely ingredients into a harmonious whole. The wine list is traditional in style, with French classics well represented.

Directions: Telephone for directions

Thames Street SL4 1PX
Map 4: SU97
Tel: 01753 861354
Fax: 01753 860172

Telephone for further details

WINKFIELD,
Rose and Crown

A two hundred year-old beamed pub with delicious food, good wine and informal, relaxed surroundings. Fillet of salmon with spinach and tarragon butter sauce amongst the top quality main course dishes.

Additional: Bar food; Sunday L; Children 7+
Style: Traditional/Country-house
Smoking: No pipes & cigars

Directions: M3 J3 from Ascot racecourse on A332, take 2nd exit from Heatherwood Hospital rdbt, then 2nd L

Woodside Windsor Forest SL4 2DP
Map 4: SU97
Tel: 01344 882051
Fax: 01344 885346
Cost: *Alc* £25. ☺ H/wine £8.75
Times: Noon-2.30pm/7-9.30pm.
Closed D Sun & Mon

YATTENDON,
Royal Oak Hotel

This quintessential English country inn has welcomed guests for 300 years. The imaginative brasserie-style menu includes risotto of smoked haddock with leek, tomato and a pea purée, grilled calves' liver and bacon, with warm pear tart to finish.

Additional: Vegetarian dishes by request
Style: Classic/chic
Smoking: No smoking in dining room
Accommodation: 5 en suite ★ ★
Directions: M4 J12, follow signs for Pangbourne turn L for Yattendon; in village centre

The Square RG18 0UG
Map 4: SU57
Tel: 01635 201325
Fax: 01635 201926
Cost: Set-price D £32.50.
H/wine £9.95
Times: D only, 7-9pm (10pm Fri & Sat). Closed Sun

BRISTOL

BRISTOL, Aztec Hotel

Attractive split level dining room, serving a good choice of dishes. An autumn menu took in roasted plum tomato with goats' cheese, followed by seared scallops with tomato and thyme risotto, and lemon tart, crème fraiche and raspberry sauce.

Directions: On Aztec West Business Park, at interchange of M4/M5

Aztec West Business Park
Almondsbury BS12 4TS
Map 3: ST57
Tel: 01454 201090
Fax: 01454 201593
E-mail: aztec@shireinns.co.uk

Telephone for further details

BRISTOL, **Bells Diner**

1 York Road Montpellier BS6 5QB
Map 3: ST57
Tel: 0117 9240357
Fax: 0117 9244280
Cost: Alc £20, set-price L £16.50. ☺
H/wine £10
Times: Noon-2.30pm/7-10.30pm.
Closed D Sun, L Mon
Style: Informal/Rustic
Smoking: No-smoking area; No pipes
& cigars

Casual dining in a relaxed environment. Fish soup, tomato tarte Tatin or goats' cheese soufflé are typical starters, followed by chargrilled turkey breast marinated in molasses, roast pheasant, or some interesting vegetarian options.

Directions: Corner premises in York Road, Montpellier

BRISTOL,
Berkeley Square Hotel

Well balanced wine list and innovative menu at this smart Georgian hotel. Try duck liver paté, served in puff pastry cases, followed by calves' liver with caramelised onion and port sauce. Finish with honey and fruit jelly with pistachio ice cream.

Directions: Top of Park Street turn L at traffic lights into Berkeley Square, hotel on R

15 Berkeley Square Clifton BS8 1HB
Map 3: ST57
Tel: 0117 9254000
Fax: 0117 9252970
E-mail:
berkeleysquare@bestwestern.co.uk

Telephone for further details

BRISTOL,
Blue Goose Restaurant

344 Gloucester Road Horfield
BS7 8UR
Map 3: ST57
Tel: 0117 9420940
Fax: 0117 9444033
Cost: Set-price D £16.95. ☺
H/wine £10.25
Times: D only, 6.30-midnight.
Closed Sun, Bhs
Additional: Children welcome
Style: Informal/Modern
Smoking: No-smoking area;
Air conditioning

Modern restaurant with vibrant blue walls and an open kitchen. An interesting menu includes moussaka of wild boar – a successful dish, though the hot chocolate pudding was the highlight.

Directions: From city centre, A38 N (Stokes Croft) approx 2 miles to Horfield. On L, corner of Ash & Gloucester Roads

BRISTOL,
Bristol Marriott City Centre

Lower Castle Street Old Market
BS1 3AD
Map 3: ST57
Tel: 0117 9294281
Fax: 0117 9276377

Telephone for further details

A modern hotel, and a modern British menu to match. Start with prawns in garlic butter with herb crostini, followed by roast duck breast, or fillet of lobster with parsley whipped potato, buttered asparagus and lemongrass.

Directions: Close to Bristol city centre, opposite castle ruins

BRISTOL,
Bristol Marriot Royal Hotel

College Green BS1 5TA
Map 3: ST57
Tel: 0117 9255100
Fax: 0117 9251515
E-mail: bristol@swallow-hotels.co.uk
Chef: Giles Stonehouse
Cost: Alc £37.50, set-price D £37.50.
H/wine £13.75
Times: D only, 7.30-10.15pm. Closed
Sun, Bhs
Additional: Children welcome
Seats: 72
Style: Classic/Traditional
Smoking: No-smoking area; Air
conditioning
Civil licence: 72
Accommodation: 242 en suite
★ ★ ★ ★

The stunning Palm Court restaurant, built in the heyday of Victorian architectural achievement, rises four floors to a spectacular stained glass ceiling, an awesome setting for any meal. The harpist who plays in this exalted atmosphere three evenings a week would seem to be an inspired choice, and the consistently impressive cooking of Giles Stonehouse is equally fitting for these formal surroundings. Attentive restaurant staff unfold napkins, brush down tables and keep an eye on wine glasses with due ceremony, and tasty breads freshly made with cheese, or olives, onions or courgettes, are sliced to order. The extensive menus are geared to all tastes, and might include chicken liver parfait with a red onion marmalade to whet the appetite, followed perhaps by pan-fried hake fillet with intensely-flavoured Morecambe Bay shrimps and a beurre blanc sauce, served on a mound of olive mash. Vacherin filled with mango and papaya sorbet came with tiny diced strawberries marinated in Grand Marnier, not quite the classic dish but a pleasing variation on the theme nevertheless.

Directions: Close to Bristol city centre, at the Old Market, opposite castle ruins

BRISTOL, Budokan

31 Colston Street BS1 5AP
Map 3: ST57
Tel: 0117 914 1488
Fax: 0117 914 1489
E-mail: budokan@dircon.co.uk
Cost: Alc £18, set-price L £6. ☺
H/wine £10
Times: Noon-2pm/6-midnight. Closed
Sun, Bhs
Additional: Bar food; Children
welcome

Experience an innovative approach to dining at this informal eatery. Fresh, healthy ingredients and authentic Oriental flavours abound with dishes along the lines of skewered baby squid with coconut, tamarind and peanut dip or poached salmon ramen.

Style: Modern/minimalist
Smoking: No smoking in dining room; Air conditioning

Directions: Telephone for directions

BRISTOL, Glass Boat Restaurant

Welsh Back BS1 4SB
Map 3: ST57
Tel: 0117 9290704
Fax: 0117 9297338
E-mail: ellie@glassboat.co.uk
Cost: *Alc* £26, set-price D £17.50. ☺
H/wine £11
Times: Noon-2pm/6-11pm. Closed L
Sat, all Sun
Additional: Children welcome
Seats: 130. Private dining room 20-40
Style: Classic/Elegant
Smoking: No-smoking area; No pipes
& cigars; Air conditioning
Civil licence: 130

*Delightful surroundings on a quiet part of the river, brightly
coloured modern decor with wooden floors and subtle lighting.
Mainly mediterannean-style cuisine, dessert a highlight, rich, dark
chocolate tart with a warm velvety texture.*

Directions: By Bristol Bridge in the old centre of Bristol

BRISTOL,
Harveys Restaurant

12 Denmark Street BS1 5DQ
Map 3: ST57
Tel: 0117 9275034
Fax: 0117 9275001
Chef: Daniel Galmiche
Owners: John Harvey & Sons
Cost: *Alc* £39.95, set-price L £21.95.
H/wine £14
Times: Noon-2pm/ fr 7pm. Closed L
Sat, all Sun, 3rd wk Feb, 2 wks Aug,
Bhs
Additional: Children 5+
Seats: 60. Private dining room 40
Style: Relaxed
Smoking: Air conditioning

Set in original 13th century wine cellars, converted by Sir
Terence Conran, so no trace of cobwebs here. The cooking
style is modern French, and a summer inspection meal began
with two goats' cheese mousse canapés, followed by an *amuse
bouche* of a demi tasse of hot vichysoisse topped with truffle
cream. In a starter of mille feuille of langoustines with
caramelised cauliflower purée and essence of crab, the crab
sauce was definitely the highlight, and the langoustines 'sweet
and succulent'. Main course fillet of beef was 'excellent', and
dessert 'a sculpture on the plate' – a pyramid, point down-
wards, filled with bitter chocolate mousse and griottines –
'superb'. The wine list is comprehensive and cleverly chosen,
the claret section particularly noteworthy.

Directions: City centre off Unity Street at bottom of Park Street,
opposite City Hall and Cathedral; follow signs for Harveys Wine
Museum

BRISTOL,

Hotel du Vin & Bistro

*A beautifully restored warehouse is the setting for this new addition
to the small hotel group. The Bistro offers a Mediterranean-based
menu with updated British dishes – perhaps roast tomato soup with
pesto, or deep-fried cod with minted pea purée.*

E-mail: admin@bristol.hotelduvin.co.ltd
Cost: Alc £32. H/wine £11.50
Times: Noon-2pm/6-10pm
Additional: Sunday L; Children welcome
Style: Bistro-style
Smoking: No pipes & cigars
Accommodation: 40 en suite ★ ★ ★ ★

Directions: From M4 J19, M32 into Bristol. With 'Bentalls' on L
take R lane at next lights. Turn R onto opposite side of
carriageway. Hotel easily visible, 200yds in side road.

Narrow Lewins Mead BS1 2NU
Map 3: ST57
Tel: 0117 925 5577
Fax: 0117 925 1199

AA Shortlisted for Wine Award-see page 18

BRISTOL,

Howards Restaurant ⊛⊛

1a-2a Avon Crescent Hotwells
BS1 6XQ
Map 3: ST57
Tel: 0117 9262921
Fax: 0117 9255585
Chef: David Short
Owner: Christopher Howard
Cost: Alc £25, set-price L £15/D
£16.50. ☺ H/wine £8.95
Times: Noon-2pm/7-11pm.
Closed L Sat, all Sun, Bhs
Additional: Children welcome
Seats: 60. Private dining room 27
Smoking: No-smoking area

This restaurant has received much praise over the years and
deservedly so. There are two dining rooms, one seating around
20 with the upstairs slightly larger. The seating is a little
crowded but pleasantly laid out with white linen and fresh
flowers. The restaurant has a fine dockside position which
offers views of the Clifton Suspension bridge. The seasonal
carte and set-price menus – (including special menus for those
ubiquitous mother's days, etc.) contain many bistro classics –
home-made game terrine, warm chicken liver and smoked
bacon salad, green-lipped New Zealand mussels grilled with
garlic butter and bread-crumbs, and roast breast of duck with
an orange and green peppercorn sauce. Fillet of salmon topped
with a crab and herb mousse and wrapped in a puff pastry
lattice came with an excellent dauphinoise. Desserts may
include raspberry crème brûlée and coffee profiteroles.

Directions: 5 minutes. from city centre following signs for
M5/Avonmouth. On the dockside over small bridge, close to SS
Great Britain

BRISTOL,

Markwicks ❀❀

'Provence meets modern Britain in an Art Deco setting' was how an inspector described this coolly elegant restaurant in a former bank vault. The short and pacy menus deliver the goods in the form of classic fish soup with aïoli and rouille, lamb tournedos with ratatouille and a garlic and rosemary sauce, and breast of Trelough duck with sage and onion purée and glazed apples. 'Flavours were all there' in an Italian-inspired starter of tender pan-fried scallops with sun-dried tomato and pesto. A fish main course, depending on what's available at the market, might be a selection of simply presented sea trout, monkfish, sea bass and halibut on a bed of spinach with a light balsamic dressing. Offal crops up – perhaps calves' sweetbreads with wild mushroom sauce – and vegetables, now grown organically especially for the restaurant, are said to be 'an exciting selection'. Puddings maintain the momentum, from two light, wafer-thin pancakes each tied like parcels around a scoop of mint and coffee ice creams, to 'perfectly executed' apricot and Mascarpone tart. The policy is to keep the price of wines 'as low as possible' so customers can experiment, and the generous house selection alone should keep most people happy.

43 Corn Street BS1 1HT
Map 3: ST57
Tel/Fax: 0117 9262658
Chef: Stephen Markwick
Owners: Stephen & Judy Markwick
Cost: Alc £31, set-price L £14.50 & £17.50/D £25. H/wine £11.50
Times: Noon-2pm/7-10pm. Closed L Sat, all Sun, 1 wk Xmas, 1 wk Etr, 2 wks Aug, Bhs
Additional: Children welcome
Seats: 24. Private dining rooms 4-20
Style: Classic/Chic
Smoking: No pipes & cigars

Directions: Top end of Corn Street beneath Commercial Rooms

BRISTOL,

Red Snapper Restaurant ❀

1 Chandos Road BS6 6PG
Map 3: ST57
Tel: 0117 9737999
Fax: 0117 9247316
E-mail: redsnapper@cix.co.uk
Cost: Alc £22.50, set-price L £10.50 & £14. ☺ H/wine £9.50
Times: Noon-2pm/7-10pm. Closed L Mon, D Sun, 25 Dec for 1.5 wks
Additional: Sunday L; Children welcome
Style: Informal/stylish
Smoking: No pipes & cigars

Simple and stylish, Red Snapper has a warm jazzy atmosphere with brightly painted but unadorned walls. Cooking is contemporary with an emphasis on fish – like chargrilled tuna with salsa verde.

Directions: Telephone for directions

BRISTOL, Riverstation

Avant-garde glass and steel building with a light and airy minimalist interior, converted from an old dock-side river police station. The upbeat first-floor restaurant has a balcony, while the more informal deli/café/bistro downstairs has decking, both allowing alfresco dining overlooking the harbour. The interior is characterised by clean lines and quality materials; glass, marble, steel, zinc and wood all have their place. The modern menu has a strong Mediterranean influence with innovative combinations and a simplicity of style that places the emphasis on quality, freshness and flavours. This translates on the plate as hot smoked salmon on a soft potato pancake with crème fraîche and dill, or goats cheese and marjoram soufflé with aubergine confit. Pan-fried fillets of red mullet, olive oil mash, fennel and tapenade, or griddled scallops on a bed of watercress with sweet chilli sauce and crème fraîche illustrate main course offerings. Desserts show their style in a chocolate and raspberry torte, and vanilla custard with paw paw salsa. Good espresso and wine selection, including a welcome choice by the glass.

Directions: Telephone for directions

The Grove BS1 4RB
Map 3: ST57
Tel: 0117 9144434
Fax: 0117 9349990
Chef: Peter Taylor
Owners: Peter Taylor, S A Bell, J S Payne, M Hall
Cost: *Alc* £21, set-price L £13.50. ☺ H/wine £9.50
Times: Noon-2.30pm/6-10.30pm(11pm Sat). Closed L Sat, 24-30 Dec
Additional: Bar food; Sunday L; Children welcome
Seats: 120
Style: Informal/Modern
Smoking: No-smoking area

BRISTOL, Severnshed NEW

The building was designed by Isambard Kingdom Brunel, and the food is described as 'modern Middle Eastern organic'. Sourdough bread was delicious, followed by 'wonderfully fresh' grilled squid marinated in harissa. Fig, almond and rum tart finished things nicely.

Additional: Bar food: Sunday L; Children welcome
Style: Informal/chic
Smoking: No smoking in dining room

Directions: Telephone for directions

The Grove Harbourside
BS1 4RB
Map 3: ST57
Tel: 0117 9251212
Fax: 0117 9251214
E-mail: info@severnshed.co.uk
Cost: *Alc* £21.50, set-price L. 10.50 & £12.50. ☺ H/wine £8.95
Times: 12.30-2.30pm, 7-10.30pm

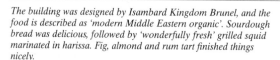

BUCKINGHAMSHIRE

AYLESBURY, Hartwell House

Louis XVIII spent five years in exile at Hartwell from 1809, and the decor can hardly have changed since he left. 'Magnificent' is the word that springs to mind to describe both the exterior of the property, set in 90 acres of parkland that includes a lake spanned by a stone bridge, and the interior decor. This includes the dramatic staircase with its Jacobean carved figures and the ornately-carved plaster ceilings, fireplaces, paintings and period furnishings. If a visit is like moving into a stately home, staff are friendly and unpretentious and keep their feet firmly on the ground. Luxuries there may be – Sevruga caviar accompanies confit of salmon with blinis in an oyster dressing, truffle is added to celeriac purée for pot-roast fillet of beef – but attention to detail rather than over-refinement is the hallmark. Langoustine and tomato timbale, for instance, provide a good sweet contrast to robustly-flavoured, velvet-textured fish soup, and

Oxford Road HP17 8NL
Map 4: SP81
Tel: 01296 747444
Fax: 01296 747450
E-mail: info@hartwell-house.com
Chef: Daniel Richardson
Owner: Historic House Hotel Ltd
Cost: Set-price L £29/D £45. H/wine £13.90
Times: 12.30-1.45pm/7.30-9.30pm
Additional: Sunday L; Children 8+
Seats: 56. Private dining rooms 18 & 30. Jacket & tie preferred
Smoking: No smoking in dining room
Accommodation: 46 en suite ★ ★ ★ ★

creamed sweet potatoes flavoured with sage and mulled wine are a good foil to another starter of smoked pheasant and wild mushroom sausage. A sure judge is behind what makes dishes work, with well-hung venison sliced on leeks and boulangère potatoes in a juniper sauce with chestnut purée and – a novel touch – roasted marinated cauliflower making a well-balanced main course, while simple things are effective too, as in pan-fried Dover sole with a potato and artichoke gâteau and buttered young vegetables. Desserts are a picture, among them maybe passion fruit and lime tart on diced tropical fruit, with passion fruit coulis drizzled around the plate, all topped with dollops of lime sorbet. Extras like petits fours meet high expectations, as do complimentary pre-starters of perhaps a big fat scallop in a lemony sauce.

Directions: 2 miles from Aylesbury on A418 (Oxford) on R

BUCKINGHAM, **Villiers Hotel**

3 Castle Street MK18 1BS
Map 4: SP63
Tel: 01280 822444
Fax: 01280 822119
E-mail: villiers@villiers-hotels.demon.co.uk
Chef: Paul Stopps
Cost: Alc £26, set-price D £23.25. ☺
H/wine £11.90
Times: D only, 7-10pm. Closed D Sun, 26 Dec
Additional: Bar food; Sunday L(12.30-2pm); Children welcome
Seats: 50. Private dining room 250
Style: Traditional/Country-house
Smoking: Air conditioning
Civil licence: 250
Accommodation: 46 en suite ★ ★ ★

Bright lemon coloured walls are adorned with an interesting collection of old local photographs. Henry's Restaurant offers a daily-changing set priced menu and a more adventurous *carte*. The chef makes interesting use of spices, a starter of warm crab and ginger strudel on a light avocado salsa, drizzled with chilli oil producing a good combination of flavours. Main dishes might include calves' livers topped with lardons of pancetta, served on two mustard potato cakes. Pear tarte Tatin might tempt you for dessert, scented with cardamom seeds and topped with sweetened crème fraîche.

Directions: Town centre – Castle Street is to R of Town Hall near main square.

BURNHAM, **Burnham Beeches** ❀

Hotel restaurant in an extended Georgian manor house nestling on the fringes of woodland. The highlight of an inspection meal was a perfectly executed vanilla and strawberry parfait, although the salmon with olive and herb crust was also very good.

Civil licence: 140
Accommodation: 82 en suite ★ ★ ★

Directions: Off A355 via Farnham Royal roundabout

Grove Road SL1 8DP
Map 4: SU98
Tel: 01628 429955
Fax: 01628 603994
Cost: Alc £32, set-price L £17.50/D £22.50. ☺ H/wine £14.95
Times: 12.30-2pm/7-9.30pm. Closed L Sat
Additional: Bar food L ; Sunday L; Children welcome
Style: Country-house
Smoking: No pipes & cigars

BURNHAM,

Grovefield Hotel ❀

Picture windows containing views of seven acres of lawns and surrounding woodland make for a relaxing dining location. Cuisine is ambitious within a largely classic remit. Try tea-spiced calves liver or the wild boar grill.

Additional: Bar food; Sunday L; Children welcome
Style: Traditional/Country-house
Smoking: No smoking in dining room
Accommodation: 40 en suite ★ ★ ★

Directions: Telephone for details

Taplow Common Road SL1 8LP
Tel: 01628 603131
Fax: 01628 668078
E-mail: info@grovefield.macdonald-hotels.co.uk
Cost: Alc £25, set-price L £12.95/D £18.50 & £25. ☺ H/wine £14.50
Times: Noon-2.30pm/7-10pm.
Closed L Sat

DINTON,

La Chouette ❀❀

La Chouette translates as owl, which gives away Frédéric Desmette's passion for ornithology – the white-washed walls of the restaurant are decorated with prints and photos of birds of prey. He also runs the whole operation single handedly – bar, restaurant, and the cooking – and as M Desmette is quite a character, a meal here is a little different, described by himself as 'Belgian atmosphere'. The food is, of course, excellent. On our last visit we tried the four-course set menu. Bread came hot on a cutting board, our first course was a salad of marinated Scottish salmon, then grilled fillet of sea bass, 'delicious fresh fish', served with beurre blanc, followed by a tender leg of lamb with heaps of vegetables and an interesting variation on pommes dauphinoise. Dessert, billed as a surprise, was a light sabayon made with oranges and Cointreau. Best to book.

Directions: On A418 at Dinton

Westlington Green
Nr Aylesbury
HP17 8UW
Map 4: SP71
Tel/Fax: 01296 747422
Chef/Owner: Frédéric Desmette
Cost: Alc £35, set-price L £11/D £27.50. H/wine £11
Times: Noon-2pm/7-9pm.
Closed L Sat, all Sun
Additional: Children welcome
Seats: 35
Style: Country-house
Smoking: No pipes & cigars

HADDENHAM, # Green Dragon ❀

8 Churchway HP17 8AA
Map 4: SP70
Tel: 01844 291403
E-mail: paul.berry@virgin.net
Cost: Alc £24. ☺ H/wine £10.95
Times: Noon-2pm/7-9.30pm.
Closed D Sun
Additional: Bar food L; Sunday L; Children welcome
Smoking: No-smoking area

Cheerful pub restaurant, with yellow and blue decor. Pan-fried witch sole, and terrine of chocolate and rum-soaked brownies – a chocoholic's dream – followed duo of chicken.

Directions: From M40 take A329 towards Thame, then A418. Turn 1st R after entering Haddenham

IVINGHOE, **The King's Head**

LU7 9EB
Map 4: SP91
Tel: 01296 668388
Fax: 01296 668107
Cost: *Alc* £45, set-price L £14.50 (wk days only)/D £28.25. H/wine £17.25
Times: 12.15-1.45pm/7.15-9pm. Closed D Sun
Additional: Sunday L; Children welcome
Style: Traditional/Elegant
Smoking: No smoking in dining room; Air conditioning

Elegant 17th-century coaching inn with a traditional feel complemented by consistently good food and service. Try homemade steak, mushroom and kidney pie, or tartlets of fresh vegetable served on a mushroom and cream sauce.

Directions: From M25 J20. Take A41(M) towards Tring. Turn R, B488 (Ivinghoe). Hotel on R at the junction with B489

LONG CRENDON, **The Angel** NEW

Original wattle and daub walls possibly date this attractive old coaching inn, set in the heart of the village, as pre 16th-century. In decor and gastronomic terms The Angel is right up-to-date, serving a broad range of modern dishes with a distinct Mediterranean influence throughout the neatly furnished dining areas and air conditioned conservatory. Chesterfields front the inglenook fireplace and daily-changing specials board in the bar. Emphasis here is on excellent fresh fish, with roasted Spanish sardines in garlic butter preceding crispy-fried sea bass on provençale vegetables with sweet Thai chilli dressing, or chargrilled tuna with red onion and asparagus piperade, herb mayonnaise and balsamic dressing. Alternative choices run from crispy duck and bacon salad with hoi sin dressing to beef fillet on wild mushroom polenta with confit of red onion, truffle oil and Parmesan crackling, and sticky toffee banana tart with caramel ice cream to finish. Extensive wine list; good showing of half-bottles and New World wines.

47 Bicester Road Aylesbury HP18 9EE
Tel: 01844 208268
Fax: 01844 202497
Chef: Trevor Bosch
Owner: Angela Good
Cost: *Alc* £30, set-price L £12.50 & £14.50. ☺ H/wine £12.50
Times: Noon-3pm/7-10pm. Closed D Sun
Additional: Bar food L; Sunday L; Children welcome
Seats: 75. Private dining rooms 6 & 15
Style: Chic/Modern
Smoking: No-smoking area; air conditioning

Directions: Beside B4011, 2m north west of Thame

MARLOW,
The Compleat Angler

Superb panelled restaurant overlooking the Thames and Marlow Weir, with a clubby, comfortable atmosphere. Tables are positioned to take advantage of the view through the partly-stained glass windows. Service is polished and attentive. A summer inspection meal began with a well-flavoured appetiser of cappuchino of leek and potato soup, followed by a starter of pigeon and foie gras terrine with wild mushroom salad, presented as a pyramid, with flavours full and clear – and the foie gras 'spot on'. Next up, seared fillet of sea bass on potato and Jerusalem artichoke mash – good fresh fish, on a

Marlow Bridge
SL7 1RG
Map 4: SU88
Tel: 0870 400 8100
Fax: 01628 486388
Chef: Alan Swinson
Owners: Granada
Cost: *Alc* £34.50, set-price L £21.50/D £34.50. ☺ H/wine £15
Times: 12.30-2.30pm/7-10pm
Additional: Bar food L; Children welcome

The Compleat Angler

Seats: 90. Private dining room 120
Style: Classic/Formal
Smoking: No-smoking area; No pipes
Civil licence: 120
Accommodation: 65 en suite ★ ★ ★ ★

Directions: From M4 J8/9 or M40 J4
take A404; hotel is on S bank of river
by bridge

bed of deliciously nutty spinach. For dessert, hot chocolate
fondant with home made vanilla ice cream, which provided a
good contrast to the flavour and texture of the chocolate.

MARLOW,

Danesfield House ❀❀

Henley Road SL7 2EY
Map 4: SU88
Tel: 01628 891010
Fax: 01628 890408
E-mail: sales@danesfieldhouse.co.uk
Chef: Michael Macdonald
Cost: *Alc* £45, set-price L £25.50/D
£36.50. ☺ H/wine £19.50
Times: Noon-2.30pm/7-10pm
Additional: Sunday L; Children 4+
Seats: 45. Private dining rooms up to
120; Jacket & tie preferred
Style: Classic/Country-house
Smoking: No smoking in dining room
Civil licence: 120
Accommodation: 87 en suite ★ ★ ★ ★

Oak panelling, large tables dressed in white linen, silver cutlery
and seamless service all contribute to the fine dining
experience here. The wine list is of epic proportions with an
emphasis on the French. Quality ingredients and finely-tuned
execution contribute to impressive cuisine – roasted monkfish
is served on a bed of orange candied endive, a surprisingly
successful combination. Pistachio soufflé was a highlight worth
waiting for, with a lovely flavour, and lightness.

Directions: M40 J4, A404 to Marlow, then A4155 to Henley.
Hotel 2 miles on L

TAPLOW,

Cliveden Hotel, Waldo's ❀❀❀

Maidenhead SL6 0JF
Map 4: SU98
Tel: 01628 668561
Fax: 01628 661837
E-mail:
stephen.carter@clivedenhouse.co.uk

The initial impact of this great house is awesome. It stands at
the top of a wide, gravelled boulevard and visitors are treated
as house guests, recapturing the Astor country house tradition
of fine hospitality and service. John Wood has arrived to take

Cliveden Hotel, Waldo's

Chef: John Wood
Cost: Alc £58, set-price L £84.
H/wine £19
Times: D only, 7-10pm. Closed Sun,
Mon, Xmas
Seats: 25. Jacket & tie preferred
Style: Classic/Formal
Smoking: No smoking in dining room;
Air conditioning
Accommodation: 38 en suite
★ ★ ★ ★ ★

Directions: On B476, 2 miles N of
Taplow

charge of both restaurants (see entry below for The Terrace),
and is ensuring the standard of cuisine is now equal to the
setting. Waldo's is the place for serious night-time dining in
discreet, well-upholstered luxury, where a historically
fascinating collection of paintings provides a good talking
point. Dishes which really show off Wood's style include
lasagne of shellfish, mullet and basil nage; pan-fried fillet of sea
bass, curried scallop brandade, parsley and coriander infusion;
terrine of roast black leg chicken with a warm salad of
sweetbreads. Top quality produce is matched by spot-on timing
in a starter of vanilla roasted monkfish with lobster risotto and
Barolo reduction. A clever dish of Trelough duck cooked three
ways with lentils and spring greens was pulled together by an
accurate, well-balanced red wine balsamic jus. Super pre-
dessert of a mini rhubarb trifle with a sliver of ginger cake
paved the way for a top drawer chocolate assiette – five perfect
little desserts, from a fondant of moist sponge filled with a
velvety, oozing ganache, to white chocolate and orange sorbet
where the fruit provided just the right amount of contrast. The
Cliveden wine list is comprehensive, but choice per glass is
limited.

TAPLOW, Cliveden Hotel, The Terrace ❀❀

The Terrace dining room is a magnificent room with floor to
ceiling windows overlooking the gardens and river, two large
marble fireplaces, huge chandeliers and a high ceiling painted
like a skyscape. The carte offers good choices at each stage and
the set-price lunch (two choices at each course) is good value
at £26. Typical dishes include salad of pot-roast Bresse pigeon,
beetroot remoulade and Burgundy jus dressing, and roast
skate, saffron potato, brown shrimp, cucumber and caper nut
brown butter. A winter meal took in a chicken, sweetbread
and foie gras terrine, beautifully presented and served with
excellent brioche. Next up was skate with brown shrimp and
capers, which was cooked well but might have benefited from
de-boning. Of three chocolate desserts, two were stunning – a
thick, dense yet light chocolate tart, which had a 'fabulous
intensity of flavour'. A chocolate bombe, filled with light pale
mousse surrounded by ganache, was also excellent. The third, a
'beautifully decorated' mini gateau was less vibrant but still
enjoyable.

Maidenhead SL6 0JF
Map 4: SU98
Tel: 01628 668561
Fax: 01628 661837
E-mail:
stephen.carter@clivedenhouse.co.uk
Chef: John Wood
Cost: Alc £60, set-price L £26.
H/wine £25
Times: 12.30-2pm/7.30-10pm.
Additional: Children welcome
Seats: 80. Private dining room 60;
Jacket & tie preferred
Style: Country house/traditional
Smoking: No smoking in dining room
Civil Licence: 170
Accommodation: 38 en suite ★ ★ ★ ★

Directions: On B476, 2 miles N of
Taplow

CAMBRIDGESHIRE

BYTHORN, Bennett's Restaurant

A delightful inn with a choice of seating areas. The floor is a mixture of stone and wood contributing to a warmly antiquated ambience. Start with chicken and spinach pancakes followed perhaps by pan-fried calves liver.

Style: Bistro/Traditional **Smoking:** No smoking in dining room

Directions: Between Kettering & Huntingdon on A14/A1-M1 link road

The White Hart Huntingdon
PE18 0QN
Map 4: TL07
Tel/Fax: 01832 710226
Cost: H/wine £9.95
Times: 11.30-3pm/6-11.30pm.
Closed D Sun, L Mon
Additional: Bar food; Sunday L;
Children welcome

CAMBRIDGE,
Midsummer House

Midsummer Common CB4 1HA
Map 5: TL45
Tel: 01223 369299
Fax: 01223 302672
Chef: Daniel Clifford
Cost: Alc £43.50, set-price L
£19.50/D £25(Tue-Thu).
H/wine £12.95
Times: Noon-2pm/7-10pm. Closed L
Sat, D Sun, all Mon, 26 Dec-5 Jan
Additional: Sunday L; Children 1+
Seats: 65. Private dining room 18
Style: Modern/French
Smoking: No smoking in dining room

Backing onto the river, the restaurant overlooks a pretty, walled courtyard garden. Brightly coloured decor and paintings set off the white table linen, service is formal and efficient. Perfectly timed seared scallops are complemented by celeriac purée with a light truffle vinaigrette, and topped with slices of truffle. Tender paupiette of partridge, topped with duxelle and foie gras, comes neatly wrapped in savoy cabbage and pancetta as a pleasing and well-balanced combination. Lemon tart had a fine crisp brûlée topping.

Directions: Park in Pretoria Road, off Chesterton Road, then walk across footbridge to restaurant

CAMBRIDGE, 22 Chesterton Road

Converted Victorian house with an intimate, comfortable dining room. The highlight of our visit was a carefully-sliced and perfectly seared main course of lambs' liver with enjoyable mustard mash and a good robust shallot jus.

Additional: Children 10+
Style: Classic/Traditional
Smoking: No pipes & cigars; Air conditioning

Directions: Telephone for directions

22 Chesterton Road CB4 3AX
Map 5: TL45
Tel: 01223 351880
Fax: 01223 323814
Cost: Set-price D £23.50. ☺
H/wine £9.75
Times: D only, 7-9.45pm. Closed
Sun, Mon, 1 wk Xmas-New Year

DUXFORD,
Duxford Lodge Hotel ❀❀

Ickleton Road CB2 4RU
Map 5: TL44
Tel: 01223 836444
Fax: 01223 832271
E-mail: duxford@btclick.com
Chef: Antonello Carta
Owners: Ronald & Suzanne Craddock
Cost: Alc £32.75, set-price L £9.99 &
£13.99/D £22.50. ☺ H/wine £10
Times: Noon-2.30pm/7-9.30pm.
Closed L Sat, 26-30 Dec
Additional: Bar food; Sunday L;
Children welcome
Seats: 44. Private dining room 24
Style: Country-house
Smoking: No-smoking area; No pipes
& cigars; Air conditioning
Accommodation: 15 en suite ★ ★ ★

Situated in a quite residential setting in the heart of Duxford
Village the hotel's 'Le Paradis Restaurant' – so called to reflect
the bird of paradise prints which adorn the walls – overlooks
the gardens on two sides. The restaurant offers both *carte* and
set-price menus. The food is billed as modern English and
French but the menus sound more 1980's than 2000. Starters
include a salad of smoked salmon with lime dressing, pearls of
honeydew melon in Cointreau syrup and a pâté served with a
Cumberland sauce. Perhaps followed by a main course of roast
guinea fowl with white beans served on a bed of spinach with
fondant potatoes. The desserts include a white and dark
chocolate mousse served with a raspberry coulis which was
good. The wine list is divided up into grape varieties, and is
reasonably priced.

Directions: M11 J10, take A505 E then 1st R to Duxford; take R
fork at T-junction, entrance 70 yards on L

ELY, Lamb Hotel ❀

2 Lynn Road CB7 4EJ
Map 5: TL58
Tel: 01353 663574
Fax: 01353 662023
Cost: Alc £20, set-price L £11.50/D
£16.95. ☺ H/wine £8.95
Times: Noon-2.30pm/7-9.30pm
Additional: Children welcome
Style: Traditional/Formal

*Fourteenth-century coaching inn restaurant in the shadow of Ely
Cathedral. Try stir-fried pork with oyster cream sauce, or supreme of
chicken with an oatmeal crust, chive rösti and a red wine jus.*

Smoking: No smoking in dining room
Accommodation: 32 en suite ★ ★ ★

Directions: Follow A10 to Ely, then city centre signs. Hotel on
corner of High St adjacent cathedral

ELY, Old Fire Engine House ❀

25 St Mary's Street CB7 4ER
Map 5: TL58
Tel: 01353 662582
Fax: 01353 668364
Cost: Alc £26. ☺ H/wine £9
Times: 12.30-2pm/7.15-9pm. Closed
D Sun, 2 wks fr 24 Dec, Bhs
Additional: Sunday L; Children
welcome

*An honest eatery housed in an 18th-century brick building with a
genuine and consistent approach to fresh cooking. Look out for
traditional British cooking – the changing menu might offer pork
chops in Suffolk cider, for example.*

Style: Informal/Country-house
Smoking: No smoking in dining room.

Directions: Facing St Mary's Church in town centre

FOWLMERE,
The Chequers Inn Restaurant

Royston SG8 7SR
Map 5: TL44
Tel: 01763 208369
Fax: 01763 208944
Cost: *Alc* £19.30. ☺ H/wine £9.30
Times: Noon-2pm/7-10pm.
Closed 25 Dec
Additional: Bar food; Sunday L;
Children welcome
Style: Rustic

Directions: Between Royston &
Cambridge, B1368 turn off A10

*Three seating area options (traditional bar, conservatory and more
upmarket gallery restaurant) meet most preferences as do the
innovative, Mediterranean influenced dishes along the lines of
sautéed pheasant breast with wild forest mushroom sauce.*

HUNTINGDON, **Old Bridge Hotel**

Built in the 18th century, on the Ouse, the Old Bridge
nowadays is a mixture of the old and the modern. The same
menu applies throughout, so choose between the relaxed
Terrace or the more formal, non-smoking restaurant or go
outside; whichever, get here early as the place can be buzzing.
'Please eat as much or as little as you like' exhorts the menu,
contributing to the relaxed atmosphere, helped along by eager
and attentive service. Starters take in Thai crab cakes (three
tasty crisp balls; 'loved them', noted an inspector), jambon
persillé, Caesar salad and smoked salmon blinis. The term
'eclectic' can also be used to describe main courses: fillet of
beef with boulangère potatoes and béarnaise sauce, steamed
steak and kidney pudding with mash, and chargilled pork chop
with black pudding and sage and onion sauce. Fillet of cod
might be pan-fried and served with a poached egg and tartare
butter sauce, and desserts could run to summer pudding with
thick Jersey cream. The wine list is a notable collection of
bottles, with a decent number offered by the glass.

Smoking: No smoking in dining room
Civil licence: 80
Accommodation: 24 en suite ★ ★ ★

Directions: Off A1 near junction with A1-M1 link and
A604/M11

1 High Street PE18 6TQ
Map 4: TL27
Tel: 01480 424300
Fax: 01480 411017
E-mail: oldbridge@huntsbridge.co.uk
Chef: Martin Lee
Owner: John Hoskins
Cost: *Alc* £23. ☺ H/wine £9.95
Times: Noon-3pm/6.30-10pm
Additional: Bar food; Sunday L;
Children welcome
Seats: 40 & 70
Style: Smart/Relaxed

AA Shortlisted for
Wine Award-see page 18

KEYSTON, **Pheasant Inn**

Picture postcard village inn with white walls and a thatched roof.
The interior is no less idyllic, with open fires, oak beams, pictures,
farm memorabilia and stuffed animals. Sitting areas range from
those with scrubbed tables to others with tablecloths and
carpeting, but the same menu is offered throughout and diners
are invited to order as much or as little as they like. Dishes roam
the globe with starters from a spring menu including fish soup

Huntingdon PE18 0RE
Map 4: TL07
Tel: 01832 710241
Fax: 01832 710340
Owner: John Hoskins
Times: Noon-2pm/6-10pm
Additional: Bar food; Sunday L;
Children welcome
Style: Informal/rustic

with rouille, Gruyère cheese and toasted sippets, and terrine of roast chicken with butter beans and pancetta. Among the mains are roast cod with parsley mash, roast carrots, braised lettuce and red wine sauce, and slow-roasted pork belly on Thai-spiced barley risotto with pak choi and tiger prawns.

Seats: 100. Private dining room 30
Smoking: No-smoking area

Directions: In the village centre, clearly signposted off A14

MADINGLEY,
Three Horseshoes Restaurant ❀

High Street CB3 8AB
Map 5: TL36
Tel: 01954 210221
Fax: 01954 212276

Both interior and exterior conducive to a special dining experience, with friendly, attentive service. Sushi might be followed by 'riceless' risotto, and caramelised lemon tart is a highlight, with a creamy, sharp filling. Extensive wine list.

Cost: Alc £20. ☺ H/wine £9.95
Times: Noon-2pm/6.30-10pm
Additional: Sunday L; Children welcome
Seats: 60
Style: Informal
Smoking: No smoking in dining room

Directions: 1.5 m from M11 J13, 2 miles W of Cambridge

MELBOURN, Pink Geranium ❀❀❀

Station Road SG8 6DX
Map 5: TL34
Tel: 01763 260215
Fax: 01763 262110
Chef: Mark Jordan
Owner: Lawrence Champion
Cost: Alc £40, set-price L £12 & £16/D £30
Times: Noon-2pm/7-9.30pm. Closed D Sun, all Mon
Additional: Sunday L; Children welcome
Seats: 60. Private dining room 14
Style: Traditional/Cottage
Smoking: No smoking in dining room
Civil licence: 28

There's a been a change of ownership at the chintzy, 16th-century restaurant, but chef Mark Jordan remains along with his brigade, although the style of cooking seems simpler. Starters might include velouté of haricot blanc with white truffle and chives, or ballantine of ham hock, confit potato and tarragon and tomato jus. Seared tuna with niçoise salad was garnished with fresh anchovy fillets, pesto sauce, warm new potatoes and hard-boiled egg. Carefully-roasted chump of lamb came out nice and pink, served with large circles of aubergine confit and fondant potato plus a well-flavoured tarragon and tomato jus. Tranche of codling is given a makeover with bok choy, thyme rösti and cep froth, but there's enough sense backstage to leave seared calves' liver, onion mash and balsamic jus well enough alone. From a choice which included pineapple tarte Tatin and orange crème brûlée, our inspector went for the chocolate fondant with toffee ice cream, followed by strong cafetière coffee and home-made petits fours.

Directions: On A10 between Royston and Cambridge. In centre of village, opposite church

---

MELBOURN,
Sheene Mill ❀❀

Station Road
SG8 6DX
Map 5: TL34
Tel: 01763 261393
Fax: 01763 261376
E-mail: mail@stevensaunders.co.uk
Chefs: Steven Saunders,
Craig Rowland
Owners: Steven & Sally Saunders

A former mill totally transformed, with an elegant well spaced restaurant, bar and patio, complete with mill pond and ducks. Service is well supervised and professional, contributing to an enjoyable dining experience. A good value set-price menu complements the medium sized, imaginative *carte*. There is a strong oriental influence to starters, which include spicy duck pancakes and plum dip or king prawn tempura with sushi dip.

The Thai scallop salad is particularly successful and well presented. Main courses include a French influenced fish selection and modern British meat, fowl and game. Calves' liver, pink and delicious, is served with crispy bacon, braised onion, champ and a light but robust red wine jus.

Sheene Mill

Cost: *Alc* £28, set-price L £10. ☺ H/wine fr £10
Times: Noon-2.30pm/6.30-10pm. Closed D Sun, 26 Dec
Additional: Bar food; Sunday L; Children welcome
Seats: 120
Style: Modern
Smoking: No-smoking area; No pipes & cigars; Air conditioning
Civil licence: 100
Accommodation: 9 en suite

Directions: Take 2nd exit from A10 Melbourn by-pass signed Melbourn. Sheene Mill is 300yds down Station Road on R

PETERBOROUGH,
Orton Hall Hotel

Impressive country house with original oak panelling in its spacious restaurant. Interesting dishes such as braised lamb shank or homecooked pasta with roast garlic and coriander sauce are delivered with attentive and smiling service.

Orton Longueville PE2 7DN
Map 4: TL19
Tel: 01733 391111
Fax: 01733 231912
Cost: *Alc* £28, set-price L £15.95/D £21.50. ☺ H/wine £11.50
Times: Noon-2pm/7-9.30pm
Additional: Sunday L; Children 12+
Style: Country-house
Smoking: No smoking in dining room
Civil licence: 100
Accommodation: 65 en suite ★★★

Directions: Telephone for directions

SIX MILE BOTTOM,
Swynford Paddocks   NEW

This elegant mansion was once home to Lord Byron's half-sister. An excellent choice of dishes might include succulent roast fillet of pork with poached pear, with perhaps steamed syrup sponge and custard for pudding.

Style: Country-house
Smoking: No smoking in dining room
Civil Licence: 60
Accommodation: 15 en suite ★★★

Directions: On A1304 6miles SW of Newmarket

Newmarket CB8 0UE
Map 5: TL55
Tel: 01638 570234
Fax: 01638 570284
E-mail: sales@swynfordpaddocks.com
Cost: Set-price L/D £24.50. H/wine £14.50
Times: 12.30-2pm, 7-9.30pm. Closed L Sat
Additional: Sunday L

STILTON, Bell Inn Hotel ❀❀

Great North Road PE7 3RA
Map 5: TL18
Tel: 01733 241066
Fax: 01733 245173
E-mail: reception@thebellinn.co.uk
Chefs: James Trevor, Gavin Sansom
Owner: Liam McGivern
Cost: Set-price L&D £21.50. ☺
H/wine £9.95
Times: Noon-2pm/7-9.30pm. Closed
L Sat, 25 Dec
Additional: Sunday L
Seats: 60. Private dining room 12
Style: Rustic/Traditional
Smoking: No-smoking area
Civil licence: 80
Accommodation: 19 en suite ★★★

In a pleasant village, the Bell Inn was built in the 16th century as a coaching inn when the nearby A1 was known as the Great North Road. Dick Turpin is said to have holed up here, and the village gave its name to the famous cheese. The bar still has stone floors, a beamed ceiling and a log fire, and an enterprising menu along the lines of smoked haddock fishcakes followed by traditional faggots with marrowfat peas. But the kitchen's energies are concentrated in the galleried restaurant, with its raftered ceiling and comfortable surroundings. This is where you can expect starters of sautéed veal sweetbreads on chargrilled polenta with rosemary sauce, chicken liver parfait, or mussel and smoked bacon risotto. Combinations work well – spicy black pudding on creamy mash with fresh, tender scallops – while flavoured butters are a favoured accompaniment for main-course fish: one of herbs for pan-fried sea bass, lemon for fillet of turbot. A mini-tower of confit and marinated prunes gives added oomph to pink roasted Gressingham duck breast sliced on fondant potatoes with a delicate orange sauce, while pastry skills are evident in puddings of treacle tart, or lemon tart with refreshing raspberry sorbet.

Directions: From A1(M) J16 follow signs to Stilton. Hotel on High Street in centre of village

STOW CUM QUY,
Cambridge Quy Mill Hotel ❀ NEW

Rustic-style restaurant converted from the dining room, parlour, kitchen and buttery of the old miller's house. Salmon and sole trellis with hollandaise sauce proved an enjoyable main course.

Newmarket Road CB5 9AG
Map 5: TL56
Tel: 01223 293383
Fax: 01223 293770
E-mail:
cambridgequay@bestwestern.co.uk
Cost: *Alc* £17.15. ☺ H/wine £9.95
Times: Noon-2.30pm/7-9.45pm.
Closed 27-31 Dec
Additional: Bar food; Sunday L;
Children welcome
Style: Informal/Rustic
Smoking: No smoking in dining room
Civil licence: 80
Accommodation: 22 en suite ★★★

Directions: Turn off A14 at junction E of Cambridge onto B1102 for 50yds, hotel entrance opposite church

WANSFORD, Haycock Hotel

PE8 6JA
Map 4: TL09
Tel: 01780 782223
Fax: 01780 783031
Cost: Alc £16, set-price L £9.95/D
£15.95. ☺ H/wine £12
Times: Noon-2.30pm, 6.15-9.45pm
Additional: Bar food L; Sun L;
Children welcome
Style: Bistro
Civil Licence: 100
Accommodation: 50 en suite ★★★

*Fifteenth-century country hotel and inn with conservatory in a
riverside location. A recent meal took in leek and potato soup with
chive cream, roast loin of pork stuffed with black pudding, and
pannacotta peach melba.*

Directions: In village centre between A1 and A47

WISBECH,
Crown Lodge Hotel ⊛

*Popular hotel restaurant with a loyal following. An inspection meal
began with a good range of homemade rolls and a starter of 'crystal
clear' chicken consommé. Banana fritter and ice cream was preceded
by succulent rack of lamb.*

Downham Road Outwell PE14 8SE
Map 5: TF40
Tel: 01945 773391
Fax: 01945 772668
Cost: Alc £20.50 ☺ £8.25
Times: 12.30-2pm. 6.30-9.30pm.
Closed 25-26 Dec, 1 Jan

Additional: Bar food; Sunday L; Children welcome
Style: Informal/Modern
Accommodation: 10 en suite ★★

Directions: 5miles SE of Wisbech on A1122 close to junction
with A1101

CHESHIRE

ALDERLEY EDGE,
Alderley Edge Hotel ⊛⊛

Set in charming grounds, the hotel was built around the middle
of the 19th century for one of Manchester's cotton kings.
Within, all is comfortable and smartly appointed, with a
welcoming bar and adjacent lounge leading into the split-level
conservatory-style restaurant, with its countryside views. A
serious wine list and serious prices on a busy menu are what to
expect. Seared foie gras with braised oxtail quinoa, roast
shallot fondu and a sherry reduction is typical of starters, with
roast fillet of beef with pappardelle bolognese and wood-baked
porcini, or steamed 'leaves' of cod with caponata and fennel
confit among main courses. An inspector fared well with

Macclesfield Road SK9 7BJ
Map 7: SJ87
Tel: 01625 583033
Fax: 01625 586343
E-mail: sales@alderley-edge-
hotel.co.uk
Chef: Duncan Poyser
Owner: J W Lees (Brewers) Ltd
Cost: Alc £40, set-price L £14.50/D
£25.50. H/wine £12.95
Times: Noon-2pm/7-10pm
Additional: Bar food L; Sunday L;
Children welcome

Alderley Edge Hotel

Seats: 80. Private dining rooms 18, 25. Jacket & tie preferred
Style: Classic/Country-house
Smoking: No pipes; Air conditioning
Civil licence: 100
Accommodation: 46 en suite ★ ★ ★

Parmesan soufflé then flavoursome best end of lamb on a gratin of aubergine and potato. 'Variation on a Theme of Lemon', melting Valrhona chocolate pudding with vin santo ice cream and espresso sauce, or gingerbread soufflé with raisin and rum ice cream might bring a meal to a close.

Directions: A538 to Alderley Edge, then B5087 Macclesfield road

ALSAGER,

Manor House Hotel ❀❀

Audley Road ST7 2QQ
Map 7: SJ75
Tel: 01270 884000
Fax: 01270 882483
E-mail: mhres@compasshotels.co.uk
Chef: Ian Turner
Owners: Compass Hotels Ltd
Cost: Alc £26.50, set-price L £13.95/D £21. ☺ H/wine £10.50
Times: Noon-2pm/7-9.30pm. Closed L Sat, D Sun, Bhs
Additional: Sunday L; Children welcome
Seats: 90. Private dining room 30
Style: Country-house
Smoking: No smoking in the dining room
Civil licence: 50
Accommodtion: 57 en suite ★ ★ ★

The Manor House is a modern hotel developed around an old farmhouse, the original oak beams of which are a feature of the restaurant and bars. A good range of dishes is offered from a choice of menus. Starters range from a trio of smoked seafood (halibut, trout and wild salmon) with sweet pepper coulis and crisp potato wafers to Thai chicken satay. There is a choice of flambé dishes, steaks, or scampi and king prawns flamed with brandy and finished with a shellfish sauce. Other main course options include roast sea bass served on roast fennel with a saffron and chive sauce, or roast honey-glazed duck breast with a cassoulet of duck leg meat and a sweet cranberry and claret jus. Finish with a classic crème brûlée, or warm apple feuillette with walnut ice cream and Calvados sauce.

Directions: M6 J16, then A500 towards Stoke-on-Trent. After 0.5m take 1st slip road, Alsager, L at top, 2m, hotel on L before village

BOLLINGTON,

Mauro's Restaurant ❀❀

Ever-popular family Italian restaurant serving a traditional range of dishes from Parma ham with artichokes and Mozzarella cheese, to bean soup with home-made Italian sausage and home-made gnocchi with mixed vegetable sauce. The fish of the day might be red snapper with fresh herbs, or else the choice is along the comfortingly familiar lines of chicken cacciatore and vitello alla milanese. Italians don't need to be taught the virtues of good ingredients – the freshest of scallops were simply cooked in brown garlic butter, a simplicity that brought out their full juicy sweetness. Beautifully flavoured calves' liver, cooked in butter and sage, was served with sautéed potatoes, onions, green beans and creamy spinach. Tiramisu is spongy and rich. Real Italian coffee comes with almond biscuits.

88 Palmerston Street SK10 5PW
Map 7: SJ97
Tel: 01625 573898
Chef/Owner: Vincenzo Mauro
Cost: *Alc* £25, set-price L £8.90 & £11.30/D £12.50. ☺ H/wine £10.50
Times: Noon-1.45pm/7-10pm. Closed Sun & Mon, L Sat

Additional: Bar food L; Children welcome
Seats: 50
Style: Classic/Traditional
Smoking: No pipes & cigars in dining room

Directions: Situated on the main street of the village, at the Pott Shrigley end

CHESTER,

Chester Grosvenor Hotel ❀❀❀

Eastgate CH1 1LT
Map 7: SJ46
Tel: 01244 324024
Fax: 01244 313246
E-mail: chesgrov@chestergrosvenor.co.uk
Chef: Simon Radley
Cost: *Alc* £52.50, set-price L £25/D £45. H/wine £12.75
Times: Noon-2.30pm/7-9.30pm. Closed all Sun & Mon, 25 Dec-25 Jan ex 31 Dec
Additional: Children welcome
Seats: 45. Jacket & tie preferred
Style: Classic/Formal
Smoking: No smoking in dining room; Air conditioning
Civil licence: 150

The Arkle restaurant is in the classic style, with highly-polished mahogany tables, silk drapes and a small glass atrium. The stone-effect walls are hung with portraits of race horses. The front-of-house team are enthusiastic and expert; behind the scenes, Simon Radley puts on a fine display of sophisticated techniques and gets maximum impact out of luxury ingredients. It's all quite a show, starting with the extensive selection of loaves, presented on a board and sliced at the table. Grilled Scottish lobster comes with a cassoulet of cannellini beans and fish saveloy; steamed pastry of duck with spices and sugared apples. But there is also an underlying simplicity of conception in a pavé of foie gras with 'pain de campagne' or Bresse chicken steamed with Périgord truffle and vegetables. A dish of organic pork is an absolute pig-fest – fillet in pancetta, braised cheek, trotter, black pudding plus a

French onion sauce. Another variation on a theme, chilled mandarin curd with orange granita and hot orange soufflé, was successful in uniting different depths and textures of a single flavour. The superb wine list goes up to £1100 for a Haut Brion, and the 'Opus 1 Collection' is a collector's dream.

Directions: City centre adjacent to the Eastgate Clock and Roman Walls

CHESTER,
Crabwall Manor ❀❀

Accommodation: 85 en suite
★★★★★

Parkgate Road Mollington CH1 6NE
Map 7: SJ46
Tel: 01244 851666
Fax: 01244 851400
E-mail: sales@crabwall.com

The conservatory restaurant overlooking the garden and grounds, offers an imaginative menu. Tender, tasty slices of lobster with a celeriac remoulade made a great start to a spring inspection meal here. Good fresh sea bass with red pepper purée was another highlight. The wine list includes a range of half bottles and vintage wines to choose from. Service is friendly and efficient.

Chefs: Kate Cook, Kevin Woods
Owners: Carl Lewis, Michael Truelove
Cost: Alc £35-£40. ☺ H/wine £13.50
Times: Noon-2pm/7-9.30pm.
Closed L Mon
Additional: Sunday L; Children welcome
Style: Country-house
Smoking: No smoking in dining room; Air conditioning
Accommodation: 48 en suite ★★★★

Directions: From A56 take A5117 then A540. Set back from the A540 north of Chester

CHESTER,
Craxton Wood ❀❀

See Puddington, Cheshire

CHESTER, **Curzon Hotel** ❀

52-54 Hough Green CH4 8JQ
Map 7: SJ46
Tel: 01244 678581
Fax: 01244 680866
E-mail: curzon.chester@virgin.net
Cost: *Alc* £20, set-price D £16.50. ☺
H/wine £9.90
Times: D only, 7-9pm.
Closed 2 wks Xmas
Additional; Children welcome
Style: Traditional/Country-house
Smoking: No smoking in dining room
Accommodation: 16 en suite ★ ★

Traditionally-furnished restaurant, with open fires, candlelight and beautiful English rose drapes, overlooking the rose garden. The menu is modern international with some Swiss specialities.

Directions: From M53 take A483 Wrexham/Chester, turning R towards Chester. At 3rd roundabout take 2nd L onto A5104 (Saltney). Hotel 500yds on R.

CHESTER,
Mollington Banastre Hotel ❀

Parkgate Road CH1 6NN
Map 7: SJ46
Tel: 01244 851471
Fax: 01244 851165
Cost: *Alc* £35, set-price L £18.95/D
£23.95. ☺ H/wine £11.50
Times: 12.30-2pm/7-9.45pm.
Closed L Sat & Sun
Additional: Bar food; Children
welcome
Style: Chic
Smoking: No smoking in dining room;
Air conditioning
Civil licence: 200
Accommodation: 63 en suite ★ ★ ★ ★

Attractive Garden Room restaurant with distinctive hand-painted wall decorations. Typical dishes are roast breast of Barbary duckling on blueberry blinis, and baked hake with caper cream.

Directions: Bear L at end of M56 onto A5117, L at roundabout onto A540, the hotel is 2 miles on R

CREWE, **Crewe Hall** ❀❀   NEW

Standing in 500 acres of grounds and dating back to the 17th century, Crewe Hall is a stately home with all the expected grandeur. Inside it's elaborate and comfortable, and quality modern cooking is served in the elegant restaurant. An early summer meal beagn with home made canapés in the bar, and then a choice of excellent home made breads, fresh and well-textured. An enjoyable starter of sweet and fresh scallops was served with a curried apple won ton and very fresh mixed leaf

Weston Road
CW1 6UZ
Map 7: SJ75
Tel: 01270 253333
Fax: 01270 253322
E-mail: restaurant@crewehall.com
Chef: Jonathan File
Cost: Set-price L £12.95 & £16.50,
set-price D £33. H/wine £12.95
Times: Noon-2pm, 7-9.30pm

salad. Top quality calves' liver followed, correctly cooked to retain its juices and served on shallot mash with an apple Tatin. Smoked bacon, morels and raisins added interest, and the presentation was 'super'. Pudding was a tart and tangy lemon and lime egg custard on passion fruit coulis and raspberry sorbet. The wine list is interesting and the staff are friendly and caring.

Directions: From M6 J16 take A500 towards Crewe. At rdbt take A5020. At next rdbt take 1st exit to hotel

Additional: Sunday L: Children welcome
Style: Country-house
Seats: 60. Private dining room 4-200
Smoking: No smoking in dining room
Civil Licence: 200
Accommodation: 25 en suite ★ ★ ★ ★

HANDFORTH, Belfry House Hotel

Stanley Road SK9 3LD
Map 7: SJ88
Tel: 0161 4370511
Fax: 0161 4990597
E-mail: office@belfryhousehotel
Cost: Alc £32, set-price L £12-£19.95/D £19.95. ☺ H/wine£14.50
Times: 12.30pm-2pm/7-10pm.
Closed D 25th Dec, 26 Dec, 1 Jan
Additional: Bar food; Sunday L;
Children welcome;
Style: Classic
Smoking: No-smoking area; Jacket & tie preferred
Civil licence: 150
Accommodation: 75 en suite ★ ★ ★ ★

A classic Art Deco setting is matched by the sophisticated nature of this long established hotel and restaurant. Begin with quenelles of duck and chicken liver parfait followed perhaps by poached lemon sole in dry vermouth and lobster sauce.

Directions: A34 to Handforth, at end of village

KNUTSFORD, Cottons Hotel

Busy hotel restaurant, offering well-presented dishes. Well made terrine of tomatoes with goats' cheese was followed by deliciously fresh, accurately cooked roast cod. Red pepper meringue ('very good') came with raspberries, strawberries and whipped cream.

Directions: From M6 J19/A556 (Stockport). Turn R at lights (A50 to Knutsford). Hotel 1.5miles on R.

Manchester Road WA16 0SU
Map 7: SJ77
Tel: 01565 650333
Fax: 01565 755351
E-mail: cottons@shireinns.co.uk

Telephone for further details

KNUTSFORD, Mere Court Hotel ❀ NEW

Take a window seat to view the lake and gardens and select from an intelligent modern British menu. Good quality produce is used in bright combinations like squab pigeon in a marjoram scented broth with young vegetables.

Additional: Bar food; Sunday L; Children welcome
Style: Traditional/Country-house
Smoking: No smoking in dining room
Civil licence: 70
Accommodation: 37 en suite

Directions: Telephone for directions

Warrington Road Mere WA16 0RW
Map 7: SJ77
Tel: 01565 831000
Fax: 01565 831001
E-mail: sales@merecourt.co.uk
Cost: Alc fr £25, set-price L £14.95/D £22.50. ☺ H/wine £14
Times: Noon-2pm/7-10pm.
Closed L Sat

NANTWICH, Rookery Hall ❀❀

Worleston CW5 6DQ
Map 7: SJ65
Tel: 01270 610016
Fax: 01270 626027
E-mail: rookery@aol.com
Chef: Craig Grant
Cost: *Alc* £25, set-price D £39.50.
H/wine £16
Times: Noon-2pm/7-9.30pm. Closed
L Sat
Additional: Bar food; Sunday L;
Children welcome
Seats: 35. Private dining room 66
Style: Classic/Country-house
Smoking: No smoking in dining room
Civil licence: 66
Accommodation: 45 en suite ★ ★ ★

Although Rookery Hall has its antecedents in the early years of the 19th century, a Victorian makeover gave it the appearance of a small château that it carries today. Views over the back lawns and fountain are had from the restaurant, a panelled, candlelit room with an ornate plaster ceiling and decently spaced tables. The kitchen brings a spirited approach to fine ingredients, marrying marinated king scallops to horseradish potatoes in a starter, and main-course roast cannon of pork to vanilla with cider and apple sauce. Both meat and fish are handled with confidence, as in an interesting starter of smoked cod ravioli with crisp deep-fried rocket and gazpacho sauce, and a main course of 'good, tender' roasted rump of veal on well-flavoured Sarladaise potatoes with minted broad beans and honeyed baby carrots, or bamboo-steamed grey mullet with garlic, spring onions and pak choi on lemongrass essence. 'Coulibiac' might turn up among puddings – actually creamy rice pudding studded with winter fruits encased in pastry accompanied by a brandy snap of blackberry ice cream garnished with raspberries – while the wine list, short and to the point, offers around a dozen by the glass.

Directions: On the B5074 north of Nantwich; situated 1.5 miles on right towards Worleston village

PRESTBURY,
White House Restaurant ❀❀

SK10 4DG
Map 7: SJ87
Tel: 01625 829376
Fax: 01625 828627
E-mail: stay@chesire-white-house.com
Chefs: Ryland Wakeham,
Mark Cunniffe
Owners: Ryland & Judith Wakeham
Cost: *Alc* £26.50, set-price L
£13.95/D £18.50. ☺ H/wine £13.50
Times: Noon-2pm/7-10pm. Closed D
Sun, L Mon, 25 Dec

Historic old building in the village centre, with a modern style interior enhanced by coloured glass, contemporary lighting and pictures. Service is laid back yet professional and friendly. The inspector started with a twice-baked Cornish crab soufflé, complemented nicely by a light mushroom and ginger cream. Distinctive, bold flavours and a good combination made this dish a highlight. The crisp half duckling was also very flavoursome, with a strong port and orange sauce. A neatly presented fresh peach tart tatin with a lovely texture was among the offerings for dessert. The well-balanced wine list is chosen with care, especially the house wines.

Additional: Bar food L; Sunday L;
Children welcome
Seats: 70. Private dining room 40
Style: Modern
Smoking: No-smoking area

Directions: Village centre on A538 N of Macclesfield

PUDDINGTON,
Craxton Wood ❀❀

Parkgate Road Ledsham CH66 9PB
Map 7: SJ37
Tel: 0151 3474000
Fax: 0151 3474040
E-mail: info@craxton.macdonald-
hotels.co.uk
Chef: Ian Cobham
Owner: Macdonald Hotels plc
Cost: A/c £32, set-price L £16.50/D
£25. ☺ H/wine £15.50
Times: 12.30-2pm/7-9.45pm. Closed
L Sat
Additional: Bar food; Sunday L;
Children welcome
Seats: 104. Private dining room 40.
Jacket & tie preferred
Style: Chic/Formal
Smoking: No smoking in dining room;
Air conditioning
Civil licence: 300
Accommodation: 73 en suite ★★★

Extensions and upgrading have brought changes to the original house, built over 100 years ago, and the conservatory part of the large restaurant overlooks the garden. This is a room of soft colours, rich fabrics, crisp white napery and bone china, with a kitchen that personalises classics of Mediterranean fish soup (with tapenade crostini) and Chateaubriand (in a stout and mushroom sauce). It can also turn its hands to grilled shark steak with tomatoes, shallots and chilli oil, or 'delicious' boned poussin stuffed with barley and mixed fruit with a good gravy of pan juices flavoured with sage. Seared red mullet comes on five spice couscous with a Thai-style coriander broth, and no less a successful starter has been a terrine of pork, leek and apricot well-matched by pear and date chutney. 'Really delicious' crêpes Suzette are theatrically flamed at the table, with perhaps Dutch apple pie with vanilla ice cream, or fresh fruit crème brûlée among alternatives.

Directions: From end of M56 (direction N Wales) take A5117 (Queensferry). R at 1st roundabout onto A540 (Hoylake). Hotel 200yds after next traffic lights

SANDIWAY, **Nunsmere Hall** ❀❀

Tarporley Road CW8 2ES
Map 7: SJ67
Tel: 01606 889100
Fax: 01606 889055
E-mail: reservations@nunsmere.co.uk
Owners: Mr & Mrs McHardy
Cost: A/c £35, set-price L £22.50.
H/wine £17
Times: Noon-2pm/7-10pm
Additional: Bar food; Sunday L;
Children 12+
Seats: 60. Private dining room 45.
Jacket & tie preferred
Style: Traditional/Formal
Smoking: No smoking in dining room
Accommodation: 36 en suite ★★★

The quintessential country-house hotel, Nunsmere Hall has a stunning location, set in extensive grounds surrounded by a 60-acre lake. The building dates from 1900 and the Crystal

Restaurant is classically elegant. However, the style of food from the newly installed chef is more cosmopolitan in style with modern influences and Mediterranean flavours much in evidence. You might expect to start with tuna carpaccio with confit tomatoes and deep fried anchovies, moving on to chargrilled beef fillet with mustard mash and lardons, before arriving at vanilla pannacotta with liquor-poached fruits. Some imaginative vegetarian options include balsamic beetroot and roasted vegetable terrine, and Caerphilly and spring onion sausage. The wine list offers significant depth and plenty of character too.

Directions: From M6 J19 take A56 for 9 miles. Turn L onto A49 towards Tarporley, hotel 1 mile on L

WARRINGTON,
Daresbury Park Hotel ❀❀

Chester Road Daresbury WA4 4BB
Map 7: SJ68
Tel: 01925 267331
Fax: 01925 265615
E-mail: richard.grey@devere-hotels.com
Chef: David Chapman
Owner: De Vere plc
Cost: Alc £40, set-price D £30. H/wine £14
Times: D only, 7-10pm. Closed Sun, Bhs
Additional: Bar food; Sunday L; Children welcome
Seats: 60. Private dining room 2-300
Style: Modern
Smoking: No-smoking area; Air conditioning
Civil licence: 200
Accommodation: 181 en suite
★ ★ ★ ★

A £10.5 million redevelopment has recently been completed at Daresbury Park, to include a magnificent glass rotunda and two new restaurants: the bistro-style Looking Glass Restaurant and the more formal Cheshire Room. The latter, which earns our two rosette award, is split-level, cool and contemporary in appearance, with sumptuous fabrics and carpeting. Service is friendly, polished and attentive without being in the least bit stuffy. Menus are presented to diners in the smart bar area, where drinks are served to the table. The meal taken on this occasion, only 48 hours after the restaurant's opening, began with tomato and basil risotto with grilled goats' cheese, followed by pan-fried sea bass. This was very fresh, accurately cooked and served with scallops, pesto mash and vinaigrette.

Directions: M56 J11 onto A56 to Warrington. Just on L off roundabout

WARRINGTON,
Park Royal International ❀

An ideal location – village tranquillity alongside easy access from the motorway network – enhances the not inconsiderable appeal of the hotel restaurant. Braised Lakeland lamb steaks with winter vegetables are a good reason to break your journey.

Stretton Road Stretton WA4 4NS
Map 7: SJ68
Tel: 01925 730706
Fax: 01925 730740
E-mail: hotel@park-royal-int.co.uk
Cost: Alc £25, set-price L £13.25/D £18.45. ☺ H/wine £9.95

Park Royal International

Times: Noon-2.30pm(1.30pm Sat)/7-10pm
Additional: Bar Food; Sunday L; Children welcome
Style: Traditional
Smoking: No-smoking area; No pipes & cigars; Air conditioning
Civil licence: 100
Accommodation: 140 en suite
★ ★ ★ ★

Directions: M56 J10, follow A49 signed Warrington, R towards Appleton Thorn at 1st lights; hotel 200yds on R

WARRINGTON, **Rockfield Hotel**

Hotel restaurant serving Anglo-Swiss cuisine. Fondues feature, and a delicious chicken fillet Tessin – moist chicken breast filled with cream cheese, wrapped in smoked bacon and served with fresh asparagus sauce.

Smoking: No smoking in dining room
Civil licence: 50
Accommodation: 12 en suite ★ ★

Directions: From M6 J20 take A50 (Warrington) to fork with A56 (1.5 miles). Turn L into Victoria Rd. Alexandra Rd is 60 yds on R.

Alexandra Road Grappenhall WA4 2EL
Map 7: SJ68
Tel: 01925 262898
Fax: 01925 263343
Cost: Set-price L £11.95/D £16.95. ☺ H/wine £9.95
Times: Noon-3pm/7-midnight.
Closed D Sun, Etr
Additional: Sunday L
Style: Classic/Country-house

WILMSLOW,
Mottram Hall Hotel NEW

Named after Nathaniel Booth, who built the Hall in 1650, the restaurant here serves an interesting, contemporary menu. A summer meal started with salmon and haddock fishcakes, and moved on to casserole of chicken with woodland and wild mushrooms and leek mash.

Style: Classic/Contemporary
Smoking: No smoking in dining room
Civil Licence: 180
Accommodation: 132 en suite ★ ★ ★ ★

Directions: Telephone for directions

Wilmslow Road Mottram St Andrew SK10 4QT
Map 7: SJ88
Tel: 01625 828135
Fax: 01625 829284
E-mail: dmh.sales@devere-hotels.com
Cost: Set-price L £19, D £26. H/wine
Times: 12.30pm-2pm, 7-9.45pm.
Closed L Sat
Additional: Sunday L; Children welcome

WILMSLOW, **Stanneylands Hotel**

Converted from a farmhouse at the turn of the century into the substantial residence of a Manchester tycoon, Stanneylands has been a family-run hotel for over 20 years. Set in delightful gardens, it's a comfortable and relaxing place with some style. The panelled dining room, with its collection of Dendy Sadler lithographs, offers a choice of traditional and more contemporary fare, from fillet of beef with béarnaise sauce to loin of venison baked under crushed aniseed and juniper.

Stanneylands Road SK9 4EY
Map 7: SJ88
Tel: 01625 525225
Fax: 01625 537282
Chef: Martin Swindley
Owners: The Beech family
Cost: Alc £35, set-price L £13.50/D £32. H/wine £12
Times: 12.30-2pm/7-10pm.
Closed D Sun, 1 Jan

Stanneylands Hotel

Additional: Sunday L; Children welcome
Seats: 60. Private dining room 50-80
Style: Traditional/Country-house
Smoking: No-smoking area; Air conditioning
Civil licence: 90
Accommodation: 31 en suite ★ ★ ★

Directions: From M5 J5 follow Wilmslow/Moss Nook. At traffic lights R, through Styal, L at Handforth sign – follow into Stanneylands Rd

Some ideas are culled from around the world, as in a starter of Szechuan-style tuna with a coriander and mango salad, while good timing was laudable in an inspector's meal of plump, sweet sautéed scallops with velvety artichoke purée and a drizzle of sauce vierge, followed by nicely-pink duck breast roasted in honey and black pepper served with confit potatoes and pak choi. Puddings, which tend to be fruity, hit the spot too, among them iced banana parfait, and tarte Tatin with clotted cream.

CORNWALL & ISLES OF SCILLY

BRYHER,

Hell Bay Hotel ❀

Unassuming dining room featuring original art work. Quality fresh ingredients form a good basis for enjoyable home cooked dishes such as roast topside of English beef served with a Yorkshire pudding and a natural pan gravy.

Additional: Bar food L; Children 6+
Style: Modern
Smoking: No smoking in dining room
Accommodation: 17 en suite ★ ★ ★

Directions: By boat from main island of St Mary's

Isles of Scilly TR23 0PR
Map 2: SW17
Tel: 01720 422947
Fax: 01720 423004
E-mail: hellbay@aol.com
Cost: Set-price D £21.50. ☺ H/wine £7.50
Times: D only, 7.15-9pm. Closed 28 Oct-10 Mar

BUDE, Atlantic House Hotel ❀

Personally run hotel in a quiet area overlooking the beach, a few minutes walk from the town centre. The fixed-price dinner menu offers sound country house-style cooking – poached pear with a mint sauce and robust Stilton mousse, for example.

Additional: Bar food L; Children welcome
Style: Traditional
Smoking: No smoking in dining room
Accommodation: 13 en suite ★ ★

Directions: From M5 J31, follow A30 past Okehampton. Then A386 (Bude) to join A3072 (Holsworthy & Bude)

17-18 Summerleaze Crescent
EX23 8HJ
Map 2: SS20
Tel: 01288 352451
Fax: 01288 356666
E-mail: ahbude@aol.com
Cost: Set-price D £15. ☺ H/wine £6.95
Times: D only, 7-8pm.

CALLINGTON,
Thyme & Plaice ❀❀

Double-fronted former baker's shop, opposite the church. The comfortable, relaxed seating area with wood flooring and a large open fire leads to a welcoming and cosy dining area with large tables, giving a feeling of space and luxury. Modern British cuisine is served at lunch and dinner.

Additional: Children 9+
Seats: 20
Style: Informal/Modern
Smoking: No smoking in dining room

Directions: Follow signs to Callington. Turn L at traffic lights and R into Church St

3 Church Street PL17 7RE
Map 2: SX36
Tel/Fax: 01579 384933
E-mail: dine@thymeandplaice.com
Chef: Matthew Dixon
Owners: Matthew Dixon & Alison Britchford
Cost: *Alc* £25, set-price D £19.95. ☺
H/wine £8.25
Times: D only, 7-9.30pm.
Closed Sun-Wed, 3 wks Jan

CONSTANTINE,
Trengilly Wartha Inn ❀❀

The popular, user-friendly country inn is located in an Area of Outstanding Natural Beauty. Whether you choose to eat in the semi-formal but unfussy restaurant or in the busy bar, the emphasis is on fresh Cornish produce. 'Openers' take in Helford oysters as well as caramelised scallops with mushrooms and spinach, followed by anything from Thai green chicken curry to cassoulet or smoked duck stir-fry. Fish dishes include steamed salmon with herb butter and grilled lemon sole with fries. Desserts are impressive, and it was worth the wait for molten chocolate fondant with bitter orange sauce, presented with art school designs lovingly crafted onto the plate. The bar menu includes own-blend sausages and excellent pasties. The cracking wine list, which has been put together by a real enthusiast, has now been developed into a secondary business.

Directions: In Constantine village turn L at top of hill, follow signs for Gweek, one mile out of village turn L, follow signposts to hotel.

Nancenoy TR11 5RP
Map 2: SW87
Tel/Fax: 01326 340332
E-mail: trengilly@compuserve.com
Chef: Mike Maguire
Owners: Mike & Helen Maguire, Nigel & Isabel Logan
Cost: Set-price D £25. ☺
Times: D only, 7.30-9.30pm.
Closed 25 Dec
Additional: Bar food; Sunday L; Children welcome
Seats: 28
Style: Modern/Semi-formal
Accommodation: 8 (7 en suite) ★★

CONSTANTINE BAY, # Treglos Hotel ❀

The professionalism and high standards of this long established hotel extend to the well-appointed restaurant. An imaginative, creative mind is evident in dishes such as sea bass with sautéed fennel and yellow capsicums.

Additional: Bar food L; Sunday L; Children 7+
Style: Traditional/Country-house
Smoking: No smoking in dining room; Air conditioning; Jacket & tie preferred
Accommodation: 44 en suite ★★★

Directions: Take B3276 (Constantine Bay). At village stores turn R, hotel is 50 yards on L

Padstow PL28 8JH
Map 2: SW87
Tel: 01841 520727
Fax: 01841 521163
E-mail: enquiries@treglos-hotel.demon.co.uk
Cost: *Alc* £26, set-price L £10/D £24. ☺ H/wine £11
Times: Noon-2.15pm/7.30-9pm

FALMOUTH,
Royal Duchy Hotel ❀❀

Cliff Road TR11 4NX
Map 2: SW83
Tel: 01326 313042
Fax: 01326 319420
E-mail: info@royalduchy.co.uk
Chef: Dez Turlan
Cost: *Alc* fr £27.90, set-price L
£9.95/D £22. ☺ H/wine £8.95
Times: Noon-2pm/7-9pm
Additional: Bar food L; Sunday L;
Children welcome
Seats: 100. Private dining room 22.
Jacket & tie preferred
Style: Classic/Formal
Civil licence: 100
Accommodation: 43 en suite ★ ★ ★ ★

A short walk from the centre, this welcoming hotel is right on the seafront, with good views across the bay from lounges and restaurant. Dinner is off a set-price menu supplemented by a number of chef's suggestions: poached chicken breast with lobster mousse and fennel-infused sauce from the Healthy Options, chargrilled cutlets of West Country lamb with minty hollandaise and boulangère potatoes from the Grills. Otherwise the kitchen deals in such mainstream main courses as roast cod under a herb crust with prawn butter, or honey-roasted duck breast, cooked just so, fanned on the plate with a sticky Madeira sauce. Caesar salad is everything it should be, and starters might stretch to pan-fried mussels with a saffron jus, or smooth smoked chicken and almond soup hinting of coriander. Puddings can be dramatically flamed at the table – caramelised pineapple and peaches flambéed with schnapps and topped with peach ice cream – with 'exceedingly rich' chocolate and cappuccino mousse among alternatives. Tasting notes make the wine list an interesting read, with most of the world's wine-producing countries represented.

Directions: Hotel is at Castle end of Promenade

FOWEY, Food for Thought ❀❀

The Quay PL23 1AT
Map 2: SX15
Tel: 01726 832221
Fax: 01726 832077

Telephone for further details

Beamed restaurant, beautifully located right on the quayside overlooking the water. As might be expected, local fish figures strongly on the *carte*, which offers a choice of nine or more dishes at each of three courses. From the main menu expect the likes of chargrill of local fish (monkfish, scallops, sea bass, red mullet, John Dory and sole) dressed with olive oil and served with aïoli and sauce rouille, or a wigwam of lamb, garlic mash and rosemary-scented sauce. An additional choice of specialities from the Fowey River might include oysters set on a bed of ice with shallot vinegar; mussels steamed with white wine, cream, shallots and garlic, and whole local lobster from the live tank, served simply grilled with garlic or plain butter. Desserts encompass sticky date pudding with toffee sauce and vanilla ice cream, and white chocolate and Amaretto crème brûlée.

Directions: Walk down to Quay from town centre car park

FOWEY, Fowey Hall 🏵🏵

Hanson Drive PL23 1ET
Map 2: SX15
Tel: 01726 833866
Fax: 01726 834100
Chef: Anthony Duce
Cost: Set-price D £29.50. ☺
H/wine £14
Times: D only, 7.30-9.30pm
Additional: Bar food; Children 12+
Seats: 40. Private dining room 14
Style: Country-house/Formal
Smoking: No smoking in dining room
Civil licence: 30
Accommodation: 25 en suite ★★★

Directions: Into town centre, pass
school on R, 400mtrs turn R into
Hanson Drive

Fowey Hall was built by a former Lord Mayor of London, and
the Hanson family completed the mansion in 1899. The dining
room is stunning, candlelit at night, with wood-panelling, lofty
ceilings, plasterwork and pillars. An enjoyable dinner
demonstrated close attention to detail, accurate cooking and
careful presentation. A pressed rabbit and duck terrine was
wonderfully gutsy, with a nice contrast between the relatively
loose texture of the duck and the firmness of the rabbit.
It was accompanied by good date chutney – not too sweet.
The main course comprised three chunky squares of seared
salmon set on wilted spinach topped with asparagus spears
and baby carrots, along with crab dumplings complemented by
a herb butter sauce. To finish, toasted raspberry marshmallow
came with an excellent vanilla ice cream and drizzled
raspberry coulis.

FOWEY, Fowey Hotel 🏵🏵

A classic late-Victorian grand hotel in a superb setting
overlooking the River Fowey. The dining room has a strong
traditional feel (all plush and burgundies) but the windows are
full of river views, giving lots of water-borne activity to watch
while awaiting the next course. The short, to-the-point menu
backs up the kitchen's understanding of the power of
simplicity. Thus, at inspection, a starter of perfectly-seared
lemon scallops sitting atop a garlic-infused croûton came with
a clean, fresh, crisp lime salsa that provided a perfect cutting
edge. Then a wonderful balancing act between sweet and
savoury came through in an oven-roasted duck breast served
with a ginger and pimento couscous and mango sauce. Tangy
glazed lemon tart lived up to its name.

Directions: From A390 take B3269 for approx 5m, follow signs
for Fowey continue along Pavillion Road for 0.75m. 2nd R

The Esplanade PL23 1HX
Map 2: SX15
Tel: 01726 832551
Fax: 01726 832125
E-mail:
fowey@richardsonhotels.co.uk
Chef: Ben Pearson
Owner: Mr E K Richardson
Cost: Set-price D £23.95. ☺
H/wine £13
Times: 12.30-2.30pm/7-9pm (Sun –
Buffet)
Additional: Bar food L; Sunday L;
Children 5+
Seats: 70
Style: Classic/Country-house
Smoking: No smoking in dining room
Accommodation: 30 en suite ★★★

GILLAN, Tregildry Hotel 🏵🏵

The restaurant at this small, family-run hotel is an airy room,
decorated in warm colours and featuring unusual Indonesian-
style furniture, with stunning sea views; the grounds have
direct access to the beach and the coast path. The menu
follows a format of three choices at each course, the first two
taking in fish, meat and something vegetarian: a salad of

TR12 6HG
Map 2: SW52
Tel: 01326 231378
Fax: 01326 231561
E-mail: trgildry@globalnet.co.uk
Chef: Huw Phillips
Owners: Huw & Lynne Phillips
Cost: Set-price D £23.50 . ☺

roasted goats' cheese with hazelnut dressing, say, or lentil and red wine soup. Other successful starters have been grilled scallops on batons of kohlrabi and courgettes with Gruyère and a delicate lime sauce, and warm chicken liver and bacon salad. Main courses deliver all their promised flavours too, as in pink rack of local lamb on braised red cabbage with a wild mushroom and Madeira sauce, or grilled halibut with mint and peppercorn butter. Vegetables are given an interesting twist – broccoli with hollandaise, braised potatoes topped with breadcrumbs, and leeks with mushrooms and traditional-type puddings of perhaps sticky toffee, with a 'deliciously syrupy' sauce and clotted cream, passion fruit cheesecake, or trifle precede a selection of West Country cheeses. The wine list is a carefully assembled collection, and the house white comes recommended.

Directions: A3083 from Helston (Lizard Road), take 1st L for St Keverne. Follow signs for Manaccan and Gillan

H/wine £10.75
Times: D only, 7-8.45pm. Closed Nov-Feb
Additional: Children welcome
Seats: 20
Style: Informal/Chic
Smoking: No smoking in dining room
Accommodation: 10 en suite ★★

HELSTON,
Nansloe Manor ❀❀

Meneage Road TR13 0SB
Map 2: SW62
Tel: 01326 574691
Fax: 01326 564680
E-mail: info@nansloe-manor.co.uk
Chef: Howard Ridden
Owners: The Ridden Family
Cost: Set-price L £12.95/D £22.50. ☺ H/wine £10.95
Times: D only, 7-8.30pm
Additional: Sunday L (noon-2.30pm); Children 10+
Seats: 40. Jacket & tie preferred
Style: Traditional/Country-house
Smoking: No smoking in dining room
Accommodation: 7 en suite ★★

Grade II listed Georgian hotel with an air of understated elegance. A spring meal began with a moist and tender rillette of duck confit, with sun dried tomatoes, Parmesan crackling, pesto and balsamic reduction. This was followed by roasted cod fillet on a casserole of Thai spices, ginger wine and honey roasted sweet potato. A good, thick, succulent piece of fish, nicely crusted on the top, and the balance of spices was just right. Puddings might include steamed spiced chocolate sponge pudding, served with chocolate ice cream and rum poached fresh dates.

Directions: 300yds from junction of A394 and A3083 down a well-signed drive

LISKEARD, **Well House Hotel** ❀❀❀

A charming setting, peacefully tucked away between Liskeard and Looe, for this small, welcoming hotel. Canapés make for an impressive start to things, and on an inspection visit included a delicate chicken liver parfait and tempura of squid and scallop. Breads, too, are excellent. An interesting starter of tortellini of smoked eel roast asparagus, scallops and

St Keyne
PL14 4RN
Map 2: SX26
Tel: 01579 342001
Fax: 01579 343891
E-mail: wellhse@aol.com
Chef: Mathew Corner
Owners: Nick Wainford, Ione Nurdin

hollandaise was rather a complicated combination of flavours – two fresh, fleshy scallops, and homemade tortellini with a very rich stuffing of smoked eel and spinach. The roast asparagus was wrapped in bacon and the whole dish surrounded by a rich hollandaise. The main course was also quite complex, pig's trotter stuffed with Toulousian cassoulet, served with garlic tarte Tatin. For dessert, trio of pineapple, ravioli, brûlée and Tatin, the brûlée was particularly good, and the presentation of all three excellent .

Cost: Set-price L £21.95/D £26.95.
H/wine £9.95
Times: 12.30-1.30pm/7.15-8.45pm
Additional: Sunday L; Children 8+ at D
Seats: 32
Smoking: No smoking in dining room
Accommodation: 9 en suite ★ ★

Directions: At St Keyne Church follow signs to St Keyne Well, the restaurant is 0.5 miles further

MARAZION,

Mount Haven Hotel ❁

A stone walled baronial-hall-style hotel dining room. Service is friendly and the cuisine modern, varied and accurately prepared. Fortunate diners may discover sole with fennel and Pernod sauce, nicely rounded off with a a superb Sacher Torte.

Turnpike Road TR17 0DQ
Map 2: SW53
Tel: 01736 710249
Fax: 01736 711658
E-mail:
mounthaven@compuserve.com
Cost: Alc £24.95, set-price D £19.95.
☺ H/wine £10.25
Times: D only, 7-9pm (8.30pm Oct-Apr). Closed Dec-Jan
Additional: Bar food D; Sunday L (noon-2pm); Children welcome
Style: Informal/Traditional
Smoking: No smoking in dining room
Accommodation: 17 en suite ★ ★

Directions: Through village to end of built-up area

MAWNAN SMITH, **Budock Vean –**
The Hotel on the River ❁❁

The high-ceilinged restaurant features a minstrels' gallery and portraits of famous Cornishmen, as well as views over the golf course and gardens. Locally sourced ingredients, especially seafood, are a strength, and a spring menu incuded dishes such as flash-grilled Scottish salmon with lime and tarragon hollandaise, or a warm poached egg salad with bacon, spring onion and croutons to start, followed perhaps by best end of Cornish lamb, grilled fillet of local lemon sole, or roast fillet of cod with prawns and capers. Cheeses are local, and come with biscuits and celery.

Style: Country-house
Smoking: No smoking in dining room; Air conditioning
Civil licence: 120
Accommodation: 58 en suite ★ ★ ★ ★

Falmouth TR11 5LG
Map 2: SW72
Tel: 01326 252100
Fax: 01326 250892
E-mail: relax@budockvean.co.uk
Chef: Darren Kelly
Owners: The Barlow Family
Cost: Alc £25, set-price L £12/D £24.50. ☺ H/wine £9.95
Times: D only 7.30-9.45pm
Additional: Bar food L; Sunday L (noon-2.30pm); Children 7+
Seats: 100. Private dining room 30.
Jacket & tie preferred

Directions: Three miles S of Falmouth. Straight on at Mawnan Smith for 1.5 miles. Hotel on L

MAWNAN SMITH,

Meudon Hotel 🏵

Dine beneath a fruiting vine in the conservatory restaurant overlooking sub-tropical gardens sweeping down to the beach. Try éclair of Newlyn crabmeat and roasted breast fillet of free-range guinea fowl.

Additional: Bar food L; Sunday L; Children welcome
Style: Traditional/Country-house
Smoking: No smoking in dining room; No pipes & cigars; Air conditioning; Jacket & tie preferred
Accommodation: 29 en suite ★ ★ ★

Directions: From Truro take A39 towards Falmouth. At 'Hillhead' roundabout turn R. Hotel 4m on L

Falmouth TR11 5HT
Map 2: SW72
Tel: 01326 250541
Fax: 01326 250543
E-mail: info@meudon.co.uk
Cost: *Alc* £19, set-price L £12.50/D £25. ☺ H/wine £11.50
Times: 12.30-2pm/7.30-9pm.
Closed 3 Jan-9 Feb

MAWNAN SMITH,

Trelawne Hotel 🏵🏵

TR11 5HS
Map 2: SW72
Tel: 01326 250226
Fax: 01326 250909

Telephone for further details

The Trelawne is a privately-owned hotel in a stunning location. The attractive restaurant, Hutches, faces out towards the gardens and the sea, with views over to Falmouth and St Mawes. The regular menu is supplemented by daily specials – the soup or sorbet served between courses, the 'harvest from land or sea', and a special dessert. A typical meal might begin with a timbale of Cornish smoked salmon with crème fraîche, cucumber, and dill-infused vinaigrette, followed perhaps by confit of guinea fowl breast on a celeriac rösti with a prune and Armagnac sauce. To finish, there is a choice of tempting desserts (ranging from chocolate marquise to Bramley apple tart) and a selection of West Country cheeses.

Directions: From Truro, take A39 towards Falmouth. R at Hillhead rdbt, take exit signed Maenporth. After 3m, past Maenporth Beach, hotel on top of hill on L

MOUSEHOLE,
Cornish Range

6 Chapel Street TR19 6SB
Map 2: SW42
Tel: 01736 731488
Fax: 01736 732173
E-mail: ryfox@compuserve.com
Cost: *Alc* £20-£23. ☺ H/wine £9.95
Times: D only, 7-9.30pm (Sun Apr-May, Oct-Nov)
Additional: Sunday L (Nov-Apr); Children welcome
Style: Informal/Stylish
Smoking: No-smoking area; No pipes & cigars

Great atmosphere, smiling service, and contemporary artwork on the walls. Expect sea-fresh fish from Newlyn, perhaps with a Mediterranean or Asian tweak, typified by griddled tuna with Thai curry and coconut milk.

Directions: Mousehole is 3 miles from Penzance, via Newlyn

MOUSEHOLE,
Old Coastguard Inn ❀❀

The Parade TR19 6PR
Map 2: SW42
Tel: 01736 731222
Fax: 01736 731720
E-mail: bookings@oldcoastguardhotel.co.uk
Chefs: A Wood, Keith Terry, Mary Kitchen, Steven Coyne
Owners: P Wood, W Treloar
Cost: *Alc* £24.95, set-price D £24.95. ☺ H/wine £9.25
Times: Noon-3pm/6-11pm
Additional: Bar food; Sunday L; Children welcome
Seats: 50
Style: Informal/Modern
Smoking: No smoking in dining room
Accommodation: 22 en suite ★★

This bright, informal modern restaurant has superb views across Mounts Bay – unsurprisingly as this was once the coastguard station and look out. The atmosphere is relaxed and friendly, and the restaurant is popular with locals and visitors alike. Fresh fish naturally plays an important role here, in dishes like pan-fried scallops with Puy lentils and grape dressing, crab soup with Parmesan, rouille and croutons, whole roasted lemon sole, or pan fried monkfish with coconut and chilli sauce. Meat eaters are not ignored, however, pan-fried duck breast with port sauce, for example, or fillet steak. Leave room for dessert – maybe fresh fruit Pavlova, or stem ginger and orange pudding.

Directions: From Penzance take coast road through Newlyn. Inn 1st large building on L as you enter the village, just after public car park

NEWQUAY,

Corisande Manor Hotel

Riverside Avenue Pentire TR7 1PL
Map: 2: SW86
Tel: 01637 872042
Fax: 01637 874557
E-mail: relax@corisande.com
Cost: Set-price D £21.50. ☺ H/wine £10
Times: D only at 8pm
Additional: Children welcome; Vegetarian by arrangement only

Built by a German about 100 years ago, the house looks like a Schloss on the Rhein. The set dinner might offer a choice of venison medallions or baked turbot.

Style: Traditional/Country-house
Smoking: No smoking in dining room
Accommodation: 9 en suite ★ ★

Directions: Off the main road down the Pentire headland, left at Newquay Nursing Home into Pentire Crescent, then R into Riverside Avenue

NEWQUAY,

Porth Veor Manor Hotel ❀

Porth Way TR7 3LW
Map 2: SW86
Tel: 01637 873274
Fax: 01637 851690
E-mail: booking@porthveor.co.uk
Cost: Alc £19.95, set-price D £13.95. ☺ H/wine £8.45
Times: D only, 6.30-8-45pm. (L by reservation only). Closed D Sun & Mon

Views across the extensive gardens and grounds out to the beach complement the relaxed atmosphere of the restaurant. Expect interesting combinations such as chicken with a fig and bay sauce or cod with sweet and sour onions.

Additional: Bar food L; Sunday L (12.30-2pm); Children welcome
Smoking: No smoking in dining room
Accommodation: 22 rooms ★ ★

Directions: Leave Newquay on A3058. After 1 mile turn L onto B3276 (Padstow Coast Rd). Hotel is on L at bottom of hill

PADSTOW, **Brocks** ❀❀

The Strand PL28 8AJ
Map 2: SW97
Tel: 01841 532565
Fax: 01841 533991
E-mail: brockx@compuserve.com
Chef: Carl Hamilton
Owners: Tim & Hazel Brocklebank
Cost: Alc L £15, D £30, set-price D £19.50 & £23.50. ☺ H/wine £11.95
Times: 12.30-2pm/7-9.30pm (10pm Fri & Sat). Closed Sun, 5 Jan-5 Feb
Additional: Children welcome
Seats: 40. Private dining room 20
Style: Rustic/Modern
Smoking: No smoking in dining room

Just off the harbour, Brocks is a bright and airy first-floor restaurant with yellow walls under its pitched, beamed ceiling and ladderback chairs at white-clothed tables. You could start with something like cauliflower and cumin soup with goats' cheese dumplings, or bresaola with mustardy leeks, and progress to rump of Cornish lamb with niçoise sauce, although fish, as fresh as it gets, dominates the short, zappy menu. Oysters from Fowey with shallot vinegar, or seared scallops with spinach, ginger and soy shine out among starters, and lobster, landed at the quay, comes as a straightforward main course with lemon mayonnaise and mixed-leaf salad. Brill is roasted and served atop saffron mash with red pepper salsa. Smoked haddock in grain mustard sauce made a vibrant winter dish for an inspector. Banana tarte Tatin has been commended for its 'melt-in-the-mouth pastry', and cheeses are all West Country farmhouse. The wine list is a short assembly of fewer than twenty bottles, with four sold in three sizes of glass, including a 'monster'.

Directions: Follow one way around harbour. Just past bandstand on L

PADSTOW, **Margot's** ❀

11 Duke Street PL28 8AB
Map 2: SW97
Tel: 01841 533441
E-mail: oliveradrian@hotmail.com

Intimate bistro-style restaurant with regularly changing art display and simple decoration. A sea trout starter with salmon and spinach

tartlet led nicely into pot roast guinea fowl. The sticky toffee pudding is 'simply heavenly'.

Style: Bistro/Informal
Smoking: No smoking in dining room

Directions: Telephone for directions

PADSTOW, The Old Custom House Inn, Pescadou Restaurant ✿

Bistro-style restaurant in a harbour-side hotel. Mussels steamed in white wine might be followed by pan-fried supreme of salmon, or confit of duck with buttered spinach and parsnip mash, with lemon tart to finish.

Directions: From Wadebridge take A389 (Padstow). Take 2nd R after Padstow School, round sharp bend at bottom of hill. inn is opposite entrance to harbour car park

Cost: Set-price D £22.95. ☺ H/wine £9.95
Times: Noon-2pm/7-9.30pm. Closed Mon, Tue, Jan & Nov, restricted opening hours in Dec
Additional: Children welcome

South Quay PL28 8ED
Map 2: SW97
Tel: 01841 532359
Fax: 01841 533372

Telephone for further details

PADSTOW, St Petroc's House ✿

A delightful period property just a short walk up the hill from the harbour. A charmingly informal atmosphere and enjoyable, simple food ensures bustling popularity. Enjoy a generous tranche of roast cod with an interesting onion confit.

Smoking: No smoking in restaurant; Air conditioning
Accommodation: 13 en suite

Directions: Follow one-way around harbour, take 1st L, situated on the R

4 New Street PL28 8EA
Map 2: SW97
Tel: 01841 532700
Fax: 01841 532942
E-mail: seafoodpadstow@cs.com
Cost: Alc £23.75. ☺ H/wine £14.95
Times: Noon-2pm/7-9.30pm. Closed Mon, 1 wk Xmas, 1st May
Additional: Sunday L; Children welcome
Style: Bistro/Informal

PADSTOW, The Seafood Restaurant ✿✿✿

Even on a Monday night, you're likely to find the place packed, appropriately, to the gills. Price, seemingly, does not deter the crowds, but everyone is treated equally courteously whether they're in jeans or suits. The white-walled interior is open and urban with Lloyd Loom black wicker chairs, sharp white linen and modern paintings by Phil Kelly. The cooking remains true to its aims and lets the quality of the seafood take centre stage. Well-made fish and shellfish soup with rouille and Parmesan is a favourite, but the European tradition now competes for space with oriental and Asian concepts such as stir-fried mussels with black beans, coriander and spring onions. Simplicity ruled with a lovely char-grilled Dover sole with sea salt and lime, while spinach and coriander stir-fried in olive oil allowed the full flavour of pristine fresh brill fillets to shine through. For dessert, try the pannacotta with stewed rhubarb or vanilla ice cream with a dribble of unctious Pedro Ximenez Viejo Solera. The excellent wine list has been chosen with a careful eye on the menu.

Directions: Take A389 towards Padstow, after 3m turn R at T-junction. At signs for 'Padstow town centre' turn R to centre. Restaurant on Riverside

Riverside PL28 8BY
Map 2: SW97
Tel: 01841 532700
Fax: 01841 533574
E-mail: seafoodpadstow@cs.com
Chef: Rick Stein
Owners: Rick & Jill Stein
Cost: Alc £41.45, set-price L £30.50/D £36. H/wine £14.95
Times: Noon-1.30pm/7-10pm. Closed Xmas wk, May Day
Additional: Children 3+
Seats: 104
Style: Modern
Smoking: Air conditioning
Accommodation: 13 en suite ★★

PENZANCE, Harris' Restaurant ✿

Miniature hide-away restaurant with a pleasing atmosphere and an unusual but rather charming pink colour scheme. Expect modern British and French cuisine such as crab florentine on a bed of spinach or poached Newlyn lobster.

Additional: Children welcome; Vegetarian dishes not always available
Smoking: No smoking in dining room

Directions: Telephone for directions

46 New Street TR18 2LZ
Map 2: SW43
Tel: 01736 364408
Fax: 01736 333273
Cost: Alc £28-£50. H/wine fr £11.95
Times: fr noon/fr 7pm. Closed L Sun, D Sun (in summer), all Mon, 3 wks in winter

POLPERRO, The Kitchen ✿

Cosy pine-furnished restaurant where international influences are reflected in the extensive menu – sea bass with roasted tomato and basil sauce, Moroccan-style salmon with coriander and garlic, and Goan lamb xacuti.

Additional: Children 12+
Style: Bistro-style, informal
Smoking: No smoking in the dining room

Directions: Between the hotel and the car park

The Coombes PL13 2RQ
Map 2: SX25
Tel: 01503 272780
Cost: Alc £22. ☺ H/wine £9.50
Times: D only, 7-9.30pm.
Closed Oct-Etr

PORT GAVERNE,
Port Gaverne Hotel ✿

A 17th-century coastal inn with an intimate dining room, where sautéed scallops on buttered samphire were followed by pan-fried goujons of monkfish with rice pilaff and orange and ginger sauce.

Directions: Signposted from B3314, 2 miles from Delabole

Port Isaac PL29 3SQ
Map 2: SX08
Tel: 01208 880244
Fax: 01208 880151

Telephone for further details

PORT ISAAC,
The Castle Rock Hotel ✿

Works by local artists adorn the walls, and the menu is imaginative and ambitious – hot pastry of goats' cheese with roasted aubergine, cumin and mint delivered all the promised flavours. Good selection of New World wines.

Additional: Bar food; Children welcome
Style: Modern
Smoking: No smoking in dining room
Accommodation: 17 en suite ★★

Directions: From A39 take B3314, then B3267 to top of Port Isaac

4 New Road PL29 3SB
Map 2: SW98
Tel: 01208 880995
Cost: Alc £24.95, set-price D £24.95. ☺ H/wine £9.25
Times: Noon-2.30pm, 7-9.30pm. Closed D Sun & Mon

PORTHLEVEN,
Critchards Seafood Restaurant ✿

Three-hundred year old converted mill offering a relaxed Mediterranean ambience and multi-national cuisine. Fighting-fresh

The Harbour Head TR13 9JA
Map 2: SW62
Tel: 01326 562407
Fax: 01326 564444

fish from Newlyn forms the basis of some interesting dishes with a Pacific Rim twist.

Additional: Children 5+
Style: Rustic/Meditteranean-style
Smoking: No smoking in dining room

Directions: Overlooking the harbour

Cost: *Alc* £25. ☺ H/wine £11.95
Times: D only 6.30-9.30pm. Closed Sun, Jan

PORTREATH, Tabb's Restaurant

A summer meal began with excellent bread, followed by pan-fried chicken livers in a cream, onion and sherry sauce, with a main course of seared tuna with harissa mushrooms and red pepper sauce. Iced pistachio bavarois to finish.

Cost: *Alc* £23, set-price D £15. ☺ H/wine £9.95
Times: D only, 7-9pm. Closed Tue, 2 wks Jan, 2 wks Nov
Additional: Sunday L (12.15-1.45pm); Children welcome
Seats: 30
Style: Informal/Rustic
Smoking: No smoking in dining room

Directions: At the centre of the village, under the viaduct

Railway Terrace TR16 4LD
Map 2: SW64
Tel/Fax: 01209 842488
Chef: Nigel Tabb
Owners: Melanie & Nigel Tabb

PORTSCATHO, Rosevine Hotel ❀❀

Porthcurnick Beach St Mawes TR2 5EW
Map 2: SW83
Tel: 01872 580206
Fax: 01872 580230
E-mail: info@makepeacehotels.co.uk
Chef: Keith A Makepeace
Owners: The Makepeace Family
Cost: Set-price D £27. H.wine £11
Times: Noon-2.30pm/7.15-9.30pm
Additional: Bar food L; Sunday L; Children 5+ at D
Seats: 50
Style: Classic/Formal
Smoking: No smoking in dining room
Accommodation: 17 en suite ★★★

A Georgian country house with palm filled gardens and views across the bay to Portscatho. The spacious dining room is formal but not stuffy, with young, friendly staff. Locally sourced ingredients play a vital role on the set price menu, which offers a good choice at each course. An early summer menu included sautéed duck and chicken livers, flamed in brandy and finished with cream, or Cornish Yarg soufflé, followed by whole grilled local plaice, or loin of pork steak, marinated in honey, garlic and cider and served with caramelised apples in a Calvados sauce. Finish with desserts from the trolley or selected cheeses.

Directions: Off A3078, hotel signed on R, 2 miles after Ruan High Lanes

RUAN HIGH LANES,

The Hundred House Hotel

TR2 5JR
Map 2: SW93
Tel: 01872 501336
Fax: 01872 501151
Cost: Set-price D £25. H/wine £9
Times: D only at 7.30pm.
Closed Nov-Feb
Additional: Vegetarian dishes not always available
Style: Informal/Country-house
Smoking: No smoking in dining room
Accommodation: 10 en suite ★★

Directions: On A3078 4 miles after Tregony on R

Traditional country house with a spacious candlelit dining room. The daily dinner menu offers the best of Cornish produce, including local fish. Desserts are a speciality and should not be missed.

ST AUSTELL,

Boscundle Manor Hotel

Listed manor house with an attractive dining room where a new chef is preparing the likes of Dover sole with rosemary white butter sauce, and sirloin steak with grain mustard bèarnaise.

Smoking: No smoking in dining room
Accommodation: 10 en suite ★★

Directions: 2 miles E of St Austell, off A390 on road signposted Tregrehan

Tregrehan PL25 3RL
Map 2: SX05
Tel: 01726 813557
Fax: 01726 814997
E-mail: stay@boscundlemanor.co.uk
Cost: Set-price D £22.50. ☺
H/wine £10.50
Times: D only, 7.30-8.30pm.
Closed Sun, Nov-Mar
Additional: Children welcome
Style: Classic/Country-house

ST AUSTELL, Carlyon Bay Hotel

Sea Road Carlyon Bay PL25 3RD
Map 2: SX05
Tel: 01726 812304
Fax: 01726 814938
E-mail: info@carlyonbay.co.uk
Cost: Set-price L £12.50/D £24. ☺
H/wine £9.50
Times: 12.30-2pm/7-9pm
Additional: Bar food; Children welcome
Style: Classic/Traditional
Smoking: Air conditioning; Jacket & tie preferred
Civil licence: 150
Accommodation: 73 en suite ★★★★

Admire spectacular sea views from this well-staffed clifftop hotel. Traditional and modern English cuisine is offered, or try more exotic fare, such as Thai crab broth scented with coriander and lime.

Directions: A390 towards St Austell; from town follow Charlestown then Carlyon Bay/Crinnis. Hotel at end of Sea Road near Cornwall Coliseum

ST IVES, Carbis Bay Hotel

Friendly hotel with a traditional dining room. Cornet of smoked salmon with prawns and blue stilton paté might be followed by tournedos of beef fillet in puff pastry. For dessert – mixed berry compôte with shortbread.

Directions: Telephone for directions

Carbis Bay TR26 2NP
Map 2: SW54
Tel: 01736 795311
Fax: 01736 797677
E-mail: carbisbayhotel@talk21.com

Telephone for further details

ST IVES, Chy-an-Dour Hotel

Uninterrupted views over St Ives, the harbour and Porthminster Beach complement good home cooking in this delightful family-run restaurant. Continental influence is evident in dishes such as slices of barbary duck breast with a plum coulis.

Additional: Bar food; Children 5+
Style: Classic/Modern
Smoking: No smoking in dining room
Accommodation: 23 en suite

Directions: Hotel on main road into St Ives, A3074

Trelyon Avenue TR26 2AD
Map 2: SW54
Tel: 01736 796436
Fax: 01736 795772
E-mail: chyndour@aol.com
Cost: Set-price D £18. ☺ H/wine £6.30
Times: D only, 7-8pm. Closed Jan-mid Feb

ST IVES,
Garrack Hotel & Restaurant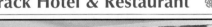

Burthallan Lane Higher Ayr
TR26 3AA
Map 2: SW54
Tel: 01736 796199
Fax: 01736 798955
E-mail: garrack@accuk.co.uk
Chef: Ben Reeve
Owners: Frances, Michael & Stephen Kilby
Cost: Set-price D £23.50. ☺
Times: D only, 7-9pm
Additional: Bar food; Children welcome
Seats: 48
Style: Classic/Informal
Smoking: No smoking in dining room
Accommodation: 18 en suite ★ ★ ★

This family owned and managed hotel and restaurant stands in two acres of grounds overlooking Porthmeor beach, the St Ives Tate Gallery and the old town of St Ives. The restaurant is a great supporter of local suppliers and the vegetables are from their own garden. The chef is a fervent supporter/member of the Food in Cornwall Association and the beef comes highly recommended as does the fish/seafood (four styles of lobster are offered). The modern English menu incorporates some Mediterranean and Asian influences. A main course of organic fillet of beef is served with aubergine glazed with lavender honey, crushed black peppercorns and ginger jus. The beef is succulent and the sauce admirable. The dish is served with Savoy cabbage and cumin seeds, noisette and new potatoes and steamed cauliflower. Desserts might include honey roast figs with banana and poppy seed parfait, and an almond and kirsch cheesecake served with a raspberry coulis. The wine list is well-considered and includes a number of halves, glasses and Cornish wines.

Directions: Follow signs for 'Porthmeor Beach and Car Parks'

ST IVES,

Mermaid Seafood Restaurant

21 Fish Street TR26 1LT
Map 2: SW54
Tel: 01736 796816
Fax: 01736 799099
E-mail:
mermaidtrevor@btinternet.com
Cost: *Alc* £25, set-price L /D £9.95.
☺ H/wine £7.95
Times: Noon-2pm/6.30-10pm (times
may vary out of peak season).
Closed Jan
Additional: Sunday L;
Children welcome
Style: Bistro/Rustic
Smoking: No smoking in dining room;
Air conditioning

Just a short walk from the harbour, this family run restaurant is as popular as ever. Wonderful seafood features prominently – plump and juicy scallops enlivened by a burst of lime and ginger were the highlight of an inspection meal.

Directions: Along Harbour Street towards the Sloop Inn, turn L. Restaurant is at top of street on R.

ST IVES, **Pedn-Olva Hotel**

West Porthminster Beach TR26 2EA
Map 2: SW54
Tel: 01736 796222
Fax: 01736 797710

Water's edge hotel with glorious views of the bay. A summer visit took in a puff pastry case of peppers, mushrooms and tomatoes, well flavoured saddle of lamb on red onion confit, and finished with tiramisu.

Telephone for further details

Directions: Take A30 to Hayle, then A3074 to St Ives. Sharp R at bus station, into railway station car park, down steps to hotel

ST IVES, **Porthminster Beach Restaurant**

Porthminster TA26 2EB
Map 2: SW54
Tel/Fax: 01736 795352
Cost: *Alc* £20. ☺ H/wine £8.95
Times: Noon-5pm, 7-midnight

Great location. Watch the waves and enjoy the vibrant food – local fish given a twist – wok-fried calamari or pan-fried salmon steak on wasabi mash. For meat-eaters – Morrocan nut crusted lamb or confit of duck.

Additional: Childen welcome
Style: Modern

Directions: Telephone for directions

ST KEYNE, **The Old Rectory**

Liskeard
PL14 4RL
Map 2: SX26
Tel: 01579 342617
Fax: 01579 342293
Chef: Glen Gatland
Owners: Mrs B Saville, Mr M Lyons
Cost: *Alc* £25, set-price D £21.50.
H/wine £8.50

Delightful hotel dating from the early 19th century, and set in lovely secluded gardens. Glen Gatland continues to consolidate his repuataion as an imaginative and interesting chef. A spring menu took in peppered chicken livers set on a watercress croute, blackened supreme of salmon with squid ink linguine, and warm roasted tomato and garlic tartlette amongst the starters. Main courses ranged from local skate wing, pan

The Old Rectory

Times: D only, 7.30-9pm.
Closed Xmas & New Year
Additional: Children 15+
Seats: 16. Jacket & tie preferred
Style: Classic/Country-house
Smoking: No smoking in dining room
Accommodation: 6 en suite ★★

fried with beurre noir and garden herbs, to roast tenderloin of pork with a wild mushroom and Masala sauce, or roast Barbary duck breast. For dessert, hot banana soufflé or caramelised tangy lemon tart should do the trick.

Directions: 3 miles from Liskeard on B3254

ST MARTIN'S,
St Martin's on the Isle ❀❀❀

Isles of Scilly TR25 0QW
Map 2: SW28
Tel: 01720 422092
Fax: 01720 422298
Chef: Patrick Pierre Tweedie
Owner: Peter Sykes
Cost: Set-price D £25. H/wine £14
Times: D only, 7-9.30pm.
Closed Nov-Feb
Additional: Bar food L;
Children welcome
Seats: 60
Smoking: No smoking in dining room
Civil licence: 60
Accommodation: 30 en suite ★★★

Scallop and Dublin Bay prawn chowder; poached 'epigramme of sole and salmon' with creamed lobster sauce; pot-roasted guinea fowl with rosemary-roasted potatoes and onion gravy; mango and pineapple mille-feuille with rum sauce – not just your average seaside bill of fare, but also proof that isolation and physical separation from the mainland need be no bar to excellence. The sophisticated menu at this island hideaway, designed in the 1980s from a cluster of cottages nestling in the hillside, is served in the light, bright first-floor Tean Restaurant overlooking the sea, with walls hung with artwork from local artists. The set menu (dinner only) is sensibly short, but changes daily. The wine list has some interesting options but could be better laid out and there are only a couple of choices by the glass. Coffee and liqueurs are served in the Round Island Bar. Simple bar lunches.

Directions: 28 miles from Penzance via helicopter, steamship or aircraft, then 20-minute launch boat ride to Isles of Scilly

ST MARYS, Star Castle Hotel

Panoramic views can be enjoyed from this lovely hotel, uniquely set in a star-shaped fortress which dates back to the 16th century. A spring menu might include smoked chicken and walnut salad, pan-fried mackerel with a vegetable nage, or avocado mousse with gazpacho sauce to begin, followed perhaps by pan-fried calves' liver with balsamic vinegar and wholegrain mustard mash, grilled lemon sole, or baked cod with a crab meat crust and coriander cream sauce. The selection of local cheeses is excellent.

Style: Traditional/Country-house
Smoking: No smoking in dining room
Accommodation: 33 en suite ★ ★ ★

Directions: Flights available from Lands End, Plymouth, Exeter, Bristol & Southampton. Helicopter or ferry from Penzance. Hotel taxi meets all guests from airport or quay

The Garrison,
Isles of Scilly TR21 0JA
Map 2: SW28
Tel: 01720 423342
Fax: 01720 422343
E-mail: reception@
starcastlescilly.demon.co.uk
Chef: Christopher Evans
Owners: John & Mary Nicholls
Cost: Set-price D £25. ☺
H/wine £9.95
Times: D only, 6.30-10pm.
Closed end Oct-Feb
Additional: Bar food L; Children 5+
Seats: 40 & 50

ST MAWES, Hotel Tresanton

On the edge of the village, towards the tip of the unspoiled Roseland Peninsula, the Tresanton is made up of a clutch of old houses on different levels. Olga Polizzi bought the property in 1997 and spent two years converting it into what is now an attractively designed mixture of the old and the modern. The restaurant has tongue-and-groove walls and a mosaic floor, with a terrace over the sea looking across Carrick Roads to Falmouth in the distance. The menus have an Italian slant, and fish and crustacea are the stars of the show, the short lunch menu including, say, tomato and basil soup with Mozzarella, then grilled tuna with lentil salsa and rocket salad. Dinner involves around half a dozen choices per course: scallops modishly accompanied by black pudding, chorizo and apple, or saffron-marinated salmon with shaved fennel and orange salad, followed by monkfish saltimbocca – a good chunk of 'stunning' fish, cooked to perfection, wrapped in wafer-thin ham, served on risotto and topped off with a caper and onion salsa – or roast brill with sauce vierge. Meat, from an organic butcher, is not overlooked, from a salad of roast quail, ricotta, sage, pine nuts and sultanas on lightly dressed leaves, to fillet of beef with wild mushrooms and artichokes. Pannacotta, and almond and lemon polenta cake might be joined on the list of desserts by pear tarte Tatin with nutmeg ice cream, and sticky toffee pudding with a dollop of apricot sorbet. The wine list is a global collection of some quality, with four of both white and red offered by the glass.

Lower Castle Road
TR2 5DR
Map 2: SW83
Tel: 01326 270055
Fax: 01326 270053
E-mail: info@tresanton.com
Chef: Peter Robinson
Owner: Olga Polizzi
Cost: *Alc* £30, set-price L £15 & £20/D £24.50. ☺ H/wine £11
Times: Noon-2.30pm/7-9.30pm.
Closed Jan-mid Feb
Additional: Bar food L; Sunday L; Children welcome
Seats: 48. Private dining room 60
Style: Classic/Chic
Smoking: No smoking in dining room
Civil licence: 70

Directions: Telephone for directions

ST MAWES, Rising Sun Hotel

Wonderful views and a relaxed atmosphere accompany the polished cuisine at this ever-popular harbour-side hotel restaurant. Local seafood features prominently alongside offerings such as char-grilled fillet of beef on a pumpkin and rosemary mash.

Style: Classic
Smoking: No smoking in dining room. Jacket & tie preferred
Accommodation: 8 en suite ★ ★

Directions: On harbour front

Truro TR2 5DJ
Map 2: SW83
Tel: 01326 270233
Cost: *Alc* £23, set-price L £10. ☺
H/wine £9.50
Times: Noon-2.30pm/7-9.30pm
Additional: Bar food; Sunday L; Children welcome

ST MELLION,
St Mellion International Hotel

Relaxed, recently-refurbished restaurant in purpose-built hotel with excellent views of the golf course. Settle down to duck breast and asparagus salad followed by mignons of beef fillet with tiger prawns and red cabbage.

Additional: Sunday L (noon-2pm); Children welcome
Style: Rustic/Country-house
Smoking: No smoking in dining room; Air conditioning
Civil licence: 120
Accommodation: 24 en suite ★ ★ ★

Directions: On A388 about 4 miles N of Saltash

Saltash PL12 6SD
Map 2: SX36
Tel: 01579 351351
E-mail: stay@st-mellion.co.uk
Cost: *Alc* £25-£30(summer), set-price D £17.95(winter). ☺ H/wine £10.95
Times: D only, 7-9pm

ST WENN, **Wenn Manor**

Straightforward dishes, accurately cooked. Start, perhaps, with rustic Stilton and courgette soup, followed by a 'generous country portion' of rack of lamb, and to finish, brown sugar meringues with banana – 'superb flavour and crispiness and yet retaining a hint of gooeyness' enthused the inspector.

Directions: Halfway between A30/A39, next to church in village

Bodmin PL30 5PS
Map 2: SW96
Tel: 01726 890240
Fax: 01726 890680

Telephone for further details

TALLAND BAY,
Talland Bay Hotel

A 16th-century country house with an oak-panelled restaurant and open log fires. Seafood is a speciality, including crab and lobster from Looe bought in to order for perfect freshness.

Additional: Bar food L; Sunday L; Children 5+
Style: Traditional/Country-house
Smoking: No smoking in dining room
Accommodation: 19 en suite ★ ★ ★

Directions: From Plymouth take A38 to Looe, then towards Polperro. 1m ignoring 1st sign for Talland Bay, a further mile to crossroads, follow sign for hotel

Nr Looe PL13 2JB
Map 2: SX25
Tel: 01503 272667
Fax: 01503 272940
E-mail: tallandbay@aol.com
Cost: *Alc* £31, set-price L £12/D £22. ☺ H/wine £10.75
Times: 12.30-2pm/7.30-9pm.
Closed Jan

TINTAGEL, **Trebea Lodge** ❀

A sympathetically decorated 18th-century manor house with an oak panelled, candlelit dining room. Dishes such as pan-fried sea trout with herb hollandaise are a popular choice.

Additional: Children 12+
Style: Traditional/Country-house
Smoking: No smoking in dining room
Accommodation: 7 en suite ★ ★

Directions: From centre of Tintagel take B3263 towards Bocastle. Turn R at RC church and R at top of Trenale Lane

Trenale PL34 0HR
Map: 2: SX08
Tel: 01840 770410
Fax: 01840 770092
Cost: Set-price D £23. ☺ H/wine £9.75
Times: D only, 8-10pm

TRESCO, Island Hotel

A stately and dignified hotel restaurant, strong on sea views, attentive service and good fresh ingredients. Dishes such as seafood panache in a citrus nage testify to a hard-working, dedicated approach.

Additional: Bar food L; Sunday L; Children welcome
Style: Informal/Modern
Smoking: No smoking in dining room; No pipes & cigars
Accommodation: 48 en suite ★★★

Directions: Situated on north-eastern tip of island

Isles of Scilly TR24 0PU
Map 2: SW17
Tel: 01720 422883
Fax: 01720 423008
E-mail: islandhotel@tresco.co.uk
Cost: Alc £33.50, set-price L £22/D £33.50. H/wine £11.65

TRESCO, New Inn ⊛

A gastronomic centre-piece of this idyllic island, the hotel restaurant is not afraid of strong flavours (pot roasted breast of guinea fowl with aubergine and juniper berry caviar) but is equally at home with fresh simplicity (seabass on samphire).

Additional: Bar food; Children welcome
Style: Bistro/Informal
Smoking: No smoking in dining room
Accommodation: 14 en suite ★★

Directions: 250yds from the harbour (private island, contact hotel for details)

Isles of Scilly TR24 0QQ
Map 2: SW17
Tel: 01720 422844
Fax: 01720 423200
E-mail: newinn@tresco.co.uk
Cost: Set-price D £21.50. ☺
H/wine £9.65
Times: D only, 7-9pm

TRURO, Alverton Manor ⊛⊛

Tregolls Road TR1 1ZQ
Map 2: SW84
Tel: 01872 276633
Fax: 01872 222989
E-mail: alverton@connexions.co.uk
Chefs: Robert Brandreth, Mark Oldham
Owners: Mr M Sagin, Mr Helsby
Cost: Alc £25, set-price L £17/D £21.50. ☺ H/wine £9.95
Times: Noon-2pm/7-9.30pm
Additional: Bar food; Sunday L; Children welcome
Seats: 50. Private dining room 60
Style: Country-house
Smoking: No smoking in dining room
Civil licence: 150
Accommodation: 34 en suite ★★★

Built as a family home and at one time a convent, this gracious sandstone house stands in six acres of grounds. The elegant restaurant has mullioned windows and the unobtrusive staff are polite and formal. A winter meal might begin with potted pheasant and foie gras with blackberry and pear chutney, served with sage bread. Ragout of monkfish comes with king scallops, king prawns, and a timbale of wild rice, or perhaps share a one and a half pound fillet of roast beef, wrapped in Parma ham and served with a traditional bèarnaise sauce and vegetables.

Directions: From the Truro by-pass, take A39 to St Austell. Just past the church on L.

VERYAN, **Nare Hotel** 🏵🏵

A beautifully situated hotel, with stunning sea views. Add to this a hard-working team in the kitchen and the excellent quality of local produce and you have a winning combination. A winter menu included dishes such as salad of Portloe lobster with herb dressing, duck and raisin terrine with fruit chutney, or stir fried lemon chicken with honey and chilli dressing to start, which might be followed by baked guinea fowl breast with orange and cranberry sauce, grilled Dover sole, or calf's liver with bacon. Puddings include homemade ice creams and sorbets and 'flambé of the day'.

Style: Country-house/Formal
Smoking: No pipes & cigars
Accommodation: 36 en suite ★★★★

Directions: Through village passing New Inn on L, continue 1 mile to sea

Carne Beach TR2 5PF
Map 2: SW93
Tel: 01872 501111
Fax: 01872 501856
E-mail: office@narehotel.co.uk
Chef: Malcolm Sparks
Owner: Bettye Gray
Cost: *Alc* £35, set-price L £15/D £32. H/wine £11.50
Times: 12.30-2.30pm/7.15-9.30pm
Additional: Bar food L; Sunday L; Children 7+
Seats: 80. Jacket & tie preferred

CUMBRIA

ALSTON,
Lovelady Shield House 🏵🏵

CA9 3LF
Map 12: NY74
Tel: 01434 381203
Fax: 01434 381515
E-mail: enquiries@lovelady.co.uk
Chef: Barrie Garton
Owners: Peter & Marie Haynes
Cost: Set-price D £29.50. H/wine £11.50
Times: Noon-2pm/ 7.30-9pm. Closed Jan
Additional: Sunday L; Children 7+
Seats: 30. Private dining room 12; Jacket & tie preferred
Style: Classic/Country-house
Smoking: No smoking in dining room
Civil licence: 100
Accommodation: 10 en suite ★★

An attractive country house with classically styled restaurant, sumptuous lounge and inviting bar. Local and regional produce forms the basis of the daily-changing dinner menu, which offers around three of each starters and main courses, an intermediate soup course, plus a selection of desserts or local cheeses. To start there might be a soft chicken and vegetable terrine with a salad of fresh and sun-dried tomatoes, or a little pot of gently spiced baked crab topped with feta cheese and served with oatcakes. Typical main courses include slices from a freshly roasted loin of Mansergh Hall lamb, cooked rosy pink and served with a sauce of pan juices, whole redcurrants and garden mint, or a brace of young quail, briefly casseroled with chestnuts, bacon and white wine, scented with thyme and finished with cream.

Directions: Off A689, 2.5 miles from Alston; signposted at the end of drive

AMBLESIDE, Drunken Duck Inn

Barngates LA22 0NG
Map 7: NY30
Tel: 015394 36347
Fax: 015394 36781
E-mail: info@drunkenduckinn.co.uk
Cost: Alc £20. ☺ H/wine £9.80
Times: Noon-2.30pm/6-9pm.
Closed 25 Dec
Additional: Bar food; Sunday L:
Children welcome
Style: Informal/Traditional
Smoking: No smoking in dining room
Accommodation: 11 en suite

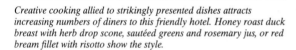

With beamed ceilings and open fires this inn is packed with character and charm. Dishes such as monkfish tails in bacon and pan-fried beef fillet await you. Real ales from the in-house brewery available.

Directions: Take A592 from Kendal, follow signs for Hawkshead, in 2.5m sign for inn on R. 1m up hill

AMBLESIDE,
Fisherbeck Hotel

Lake Road LA22 0DH
Map 7: NY30
Tel: 015394 33215
Fax: 015394 33600
Cost: Set-price D £18.95. ☺
H/wine £8.95
Times: D only, 7-8.30pm.
Closed for 4 wks from 26 Dec

Creative cooking allied to strikingly presented dishes attracts increasing numbers of diners to this friendly hotel. Honey roast duck breast with herb drop scone, sautéed greens and rosemary jus, or red bream fillet with risotto show the style.

Additional: Bar food; Children 5+
Style: Modern/Traditional
Smoking: No smoking in dining room
Accommodation: 18 en suite ★★

Directions: Telephone for directions

AMBLESIDE,
Nanny Brow Country House ❀❀

Clappersgate LA22 9NF
Map 7: NY30
Tel: 015394 32036
Fax: 015394 32450
E-mail: reservation@nannybrow.co.uk
Chef: Darren Prideaux
Owners: Michael & Carol Fletcher
Cost: Alc £25, set-price D £30. ☺
H/wine £16.99
Times: D only, 7.30-9pm
Additional: Sunday L; Children
welcome
Seats: 60. Private dining room 30
Style: Classic
Smoking: No smoking in dining room
Civil licence: 70
Accommodation: 18 en suite ★★★

Idyllically located country house, built in 1902 of white-rendered stone under a local slate roof with great views of the River Brathey and the Langdale Valley beyond. The cosiness of the hotel's name belies the robust modern style of the cooking. Start with a tian of crab and tomato, langoustine carpaccio and caviar chantilly, followed perhaps by a hearty main course of braised pig's trotter, ham hock and foie gras with a pea purée and morel fumet. Local produce is strongly featured, none more so than lamb from the proprietor's own flock of Romney sheep. Roast cannon of lamb comes with fondant potato, caramelised shallots and a tomato and basil jus. A vegetarian alternative might be tomato tarte fine, with tapénade, herb salad and basil oil. For something sweet, there could be a toasted pistachio and white chocolate timbale served with strawberry sorbet.

Directions: One mile from Ambleside on A593 to Coniston

AMBLESIDE,
Regent Hotel ❀

Waterhead Bay LA22 0ES
Map 7: NY30
Tel: 015394 32254
Fax: 015394 31474
Cost: *Alc* £20.50, set-price L £10/
D £24. ☺ H/wine £10.95
Times: Noon-2pm/7-8.30pm

*An elegant split level hotel restaurant overlooking an attractive
courtyard provides a convivial, civilised setting for some excellent
food. Amongst the dishes on offer Whitley Bay crab cake and rack
of local Fell lamb met with particular approval.*

Additional: Bar food L; Children 8+
Style: Classic/Chic
Smoking: No smoking in dining room
Accommodation: 30 en suite ★ ★ ★

Directions: 1 mile S of Ambleside at Waterhead Bay

AMBLESIDE,
Wateredge Hotel ❀

Borrans Road Waterhead LA22 0EP
Map 7: NY30
Tel: 015394 32332
Fax: 015394 31878
E-mail:
contact@wateredgehotel.co.uk
Cost: Set-price D £29.50
Times: D only, 7-8.30pm. Closed mid
Dec-early Jan
Additional: Bar food L; Children 7+

*Carefully refined antiquity in a converted 17th-century fisherman's
cottage. The restaurant retains slate floor, oak beams and log fire
whilst offering modern comfort and cuisine. Look forward to breast
of guinea fowl on apricot confit.*

Style: Modern/Country-house
Smoking: No smoking in dining room
Accommodation: 23 en suite ★ ★ ★

Directions: From A591 N to Ambleside, fork L at traffic lights
after Ambleside sign. Skirt lake for few hundred yards, hotel is
on L

APPLEBY-IN-WESTMORELAND,
Tufton Arms Hotel ⊛

Market Square CA16 6XA
Map 12: NY62
Tel: 017683 51593
Fax: 017683 52761
E-mail: info@fishing-shooting.co.uk
Cost: *Alc* £17, set-price D £23. ☺
H/wine £9.50
Times: Noon-2pm/7-9pm
Additional: Bar food; Sunday L;
Children welcome
Style: Classic
Smoking: No-smoking area
Civil licence: 100
Accommodation: 21 en suite ★ ★ ★

*Consistency, as well as imaginative combinations, remain the key
features at this brightly styled conservatory restaurant. At inspection,
baby hake in beer batter worked well with beurre blanc, and a well-
hung, tender partridge set on a crisp rösti was excellent.*

Directions: In centre of Appleby on B6260, 12 miles from
M6 J38

BASSENTHWAITE,
Armathwaite Hall ⊛⊛

Keswick CA12 4RE
Map 11: NY23
Tel: 017687 76551
Fax: 017687 76220
E-mail: information@armathwaite-
hall.com
Chef: Kevin Dowling
Owners: Graves Family
Cost: *Alc* £40, set-price L £16/D £35.
H/wine £13.50
Times: 12.30-1.45pm/7.30-9.30pm
Additional: Bar food L; Sunday L;
Children 5+ at D
Seats: 100. Jacket & tie preferred
Style: Traditional/Country-house
Smoking: No smoking in dining room
Civil licence: 100
Accommodation: 42 en suite ★ ★ ★ ★

Hugh Walpole once described Armathwaite Hall as having
'perfect and irresistible atmosphere', and nothing in the
intervening years has affected his hymn of praise. On the
contrary, this archetypal country house hotel on the shores of
Bassenthwaite remains timeless in its appeal, and nothing less
than sumptuous in its style. Such a centre of lavish hospitality
requires an equally impressive gastronomic standard, and chef
Kevin Dowling provides all of the necessary ingredients. His
six-course dinner menu, or a choice from the *carte*, is presented
formally in the imposing panelled dining room, and is a gift for
lovers of good food. The emphasis is on fresh seasonal cooking
with both classical and modern influences, with lunches tending
to be lighter than dinner. A recent meal included succulent
tiger prawns flashed with sesame seeds, followed by delicious
chicken and leek sausages, onion jus and fluffy creamed

potatoes. Leave room for the creative home-made desserts, and the complimentary platter of chocolate truffles which accompanies coffee.

Directions: From M6 J40 take A66 to Keswick then A591 towards Carlisle. Turn L by Castle Inn, 8m to hotel

BASSENTHWAITE,
Overwater Hall Hotel ⚜

Intimate restaurant in a dignified 18th-century mansion boasting eighteen acres of gardens and a resident ghost – and who could blame him for sticking around with dishes like caramelised pork fillet served with spiced African couscous on offer.

Additional: Sunday L (12.30-1.30pm); Children 5+
Style: Traditional/Country-house
Smoking: No smoking in dining room
Accommodation: 13 en suite ★★

Ireby CA5 1HH
Map 11: NY23
Tel/Fax: 017687 76566
E-mail:
welcome@overwaterhall.demon.co.uk
Cost: Set-price D £24. ☺
H/wine £9.75
Times: D only, 7-8.30pm

Directions: Take A591 from Keswick to Carlisle, after 6 miles, turn R at the Castle Inn. Hotel is signposted after 2 miles.

BORROWDALE, Borrowdale Gates
House Hotel ⚜⚜

The house was built in 1860 as a private residence and enjoys a sedate woodland setting and stunning views of the towering fells that form the Borrowdale Valley. The hotel is family run and while the style of the restaurant is formal, the service is friendly. The kitchen uses local ingredients at their freshest, as in a wood pigeon and chanterelle salad, drizzled with truffle oil or Kyle of Lochalsh scallops delicately pan fried and set on a bed of wilted spinach, with crisp pancetta and a citrus butter sauce. The fish is wonderfully fresh at Borrowdale and main courses of whole lemon sole and fillet of brill, gently steamed and served with a pesto dressing, were excellent. Equally well cooked was a roast Dalemain pheasant: a breast of pheasant served with a pork and leek sausage, chestnut and potato purée, cranberry confit and a thyme jus. The desserts are executed with a twist, such as apple and almond tart and a banana and toffee crème brûlée.

Grange-in-Borrowdale
Keswick CA12 5UQ
Map 11: NY21
Tel: 017687 77204
Fax: 017687 77254
E-mail: hotel@borrowdale-gates.com
Chef: Micheal D Heathcote
Owners: Terry & Christine Parkinson
Cost: A/c £37.50, set-price D £29.
H/wine £12.75
Times: 12.15-1.30pm/7-8.45pm.
Closed Jan
Additional: Bar food L; Sunday L;
Children 7+ at D
Seats: 60. Jacket & tie preferred
Style: Traditional/Country-house
Smoking: No smoking in dining room
Accommodation: 29 en suite ★★★

Directions: B5289 from Keswick.
After 4 miles turn R over double
humpback bridge to Grange village.
Hotel 400yds through village on R

BRAMPTON, Farlam Hall Hotel

Hallbankgate CA8 2NG
Map 12: NY56
Tel: 016977 46234
Fax: 016977 46683
E-mail: farlamhall@dial.pipex.com
Chef: Barry Quinion
Owners: Quinion & Stevenson families
Cost: Set-price D £32. H/wine £13.50
Times: D only, 8 for 8.30pm.
Closed 25-30 Dec
Additional: Children 5+
Seats: 40. Private dining room 20. Jacket & tie preferred
Style: Country-house
Smoking: No pipes & cigars
Accommodation: 12 en suite ★ ★ ★

Family owned, the delightful 16th-century house sits in extensive landscaped grounds. The spacious dining-room has massive windows overlooking the gardens and ornamental lake, and caters mostly for hotel guests, but non-residents are equally welcome at dinner. The menu is short and concisely described, traditional in style with a few modern influences. Broccoli and hazelnut soup with crunchy croûtons made a good start to a meal which continued with sea-fresh steamed halibut on a bed of leeks and white sauce. Other alternatives might be hot chicken livers with salad leaves and crispy bacon, followed by breast of local pheasant with red cabbage braised with ginger and apple, served with a light game sauce. After English cheeses, there may be shortbread with poached pears and vividly flavoured blackcurrant ice-cream and coulis. Smart dress preferred.

Directions: On the A689 Brampton to Alston road. Not in Farlam Village

CARLISLE,
Crosby Lodge Hotel ⚶

High Crosby Crosby-on-Eden CA6 4QZ
Map 11: NY35
Tel: 01228 573618
Fax: 01228 573428
E-mail: crosbylodge@crosby-eden.demon.co.uk
Cost: Alc £35, set-price L £17/D £30. ☺ H/wine £12.50
Times: 12.15-1.45pm/7-9pm.
Closed Xmas & New Year
Additional: Bar food L; Sunday L; Children welcome
Style: Traditional/Country-house
Smoking: No smoking in dining room
Accommodation: 11 en suite ★ ★ ★

Grade II listed building dating from 1802, with a lavish restaurant overlooking parkland and the River Eden. Food and service are traditional in style and there's an excellent wine list.

Directions: 3 miles from M6 J44 on A689 towards Carlisle Airport/Brampton. R at Low/High Crosby sign, 1 mile on R

CARLISLE, Magenta's ⊛⊛

Modish minimalism is the keynote here. This remarkably light and airy cellar restaurant with its whitewashed brick walls and bright modern artworks is comfortable and informal. Ambition and a weather eye on current trends are clearly guiding principles. Chris and Paul Taylor offer a contemporary, eclectic menu which sensibly matches carefully-sourced ingredients. An inspector's spring meal started with an assiette of salmon featuring grilled salmon with celeriac and Pommery mustard, smoked salmon paupiette and salmon ceviche. Described as 'decadent and fragrant' the dish shows the level of aspiration here. Comforting classics such as smoked haddock with baby leeks, poached egg and a puff pastry case sit comfortably alongside inventive dishes like breast of duck with marinated beetroot, buttered spinach, fondant potato, confit root vegetables and redcurrant jus. Puddings continue in the same vein with an assiette of chocolate attracting praise for the 'accomplished' technical skills. The vogueish chocolate sorbet was particularly impressive.

Additional: Children welcome
Seats: 32
Style: Modern/Minimalist
Smoking: No smoking in dining room; No pipes & cigars

Directions: M6 J44 – Carlisle city centre roundabout take 3rd exit and 1st L. R at box junction. Follow road around onto Fisher St; restaurant is on L

18 Fisher Street CA3 8RH
Map 11: NY35
Tel/Fax: 01900 546363
Chefs: Chris & Paul Taylor
Owners: Chris & Paul Taylor, Alison Watkin
Cost: Alc £23, set-price D £18. ☺
H/wine £12.95
Times: D only, 7-9.30pm. Closed Sun

CARTMEL,
Aynsome Manor Hotel ⊛

A pleasant, small hotel whose smart restaurant offers a menu that changes daily and is built around local seasonal produce. Good value for money comes through in dishes such as guinea fowl with Marsala sauce. Desserts from the trolley or there's a selection of cheeses.

Style: Country-house/Georgian
Smoking: No smoking in dining room
Accommodation: 12 en suite ★ ★

Directions: Leave A590 signed Cartmel. Hotel is 0.5 mile N of Cartmel village on R

Grange-over-Sands LA11 6HH
Map 7: SD37
Tel: 015395 36653
Fax: 015395 36016
Cost: Set-price Sun L £13/D £17.50.
☺ H/wine £11
Times: D only, 7-8.30pm.
Closed D Sun, 2-28 Jan
Additional: Sunday L (12.30-1pm); Children 5+ at D

CARTMEL, Uplands Hotel ⊛⊛

In two acres of gardens a mile outside the village, Uplands looks over rolling fields to the Leven Estuary in the distance. The restaurant is a room of ivory-coloured walls bearing botanical prints and blue plates, pale yellow curtains at the windows, and a moss-green carpet. The menus, of three courses at lunch, four at dinner, with two or three choices of starter and main and around half a dozen desserts, take a straightforward approach, eschewing culinary fashions in favour of bringing together quality materials and making the most of them all. Dinner could start with as something as simple as langoustine tails – very fresh and succulent with a light and airy, but pungent, chive sauce, or a tartlet of onion

Haggs Lane
Grange-over-Sands
LA11 6HD
Map 7: SD37
Tel: 015395 36248
Fax: 015395 36848
E-mail: uplands@kencomp.net
Chef: Tom Peter
Owners: Tom & Diana Peter
Cost: Set-price L £15.50/D £28 .
H/wine £10.70
Times: 12.30 for 1pm/7.30 for 8pm.
Closed all Mon, L Tue & Wed, Jan, Feb

and blue cheese on a warm salad of tomatoes and basil. Simple treatments are given to main courses too: impeccably-timed baked fillet of turbot with champagne sauce, braised guinea fowl with port-based gravy, bread sauce and a prune and bacon roll, and tender, pink roast loin of lamb with caper jus. In between comes a tureen of soup and a small loaf of bread per table: perhaps Jerusalem artichoke, or broccoli and Stilton. And with as many as five vegetables served with the main course, from carrots and turnips mashed with horseradish to potatoes with cheese and onion, it's a wonder that guests make it to puddings along the lines of chocolate and Grand Marnier mousse, or pear soufflé. The forty-odd bottles on the wine list are fairly evenly split between Europe and the New World, and there are five house wines.

Additional: Sunday L; Children 8+;
Vegetarian dishes by request only
Seats: 28
Style: Informal/Country-house
Smoking: No smoking in dining room
Accommodation: 5 en suite

Directions: 1 mile up road signed Grange opposite the Pig & Whistle pub in Cartmel

CROOKLANDS, Crooklands Hotel ✿

nr Kendal LA7 7NW
Map 7: SD58
Tel: 015395 67432
Fax: 015395 67525
Cost: Alc £25. ☺ H/wine £9.95
Times: D only, 7-9pm.
Closed Sun & Mon, Xmas
Additional: Bar food;
Style: Rustic
Smoking: No-smoking area;
Air conditioning
Accommodation: 30 en suite ★ ★ ★

Directions: 1.5 miles from M6 J36;
4 miles from Kendal A65

The hotel building dates from 1750, and the Hayloft Restaurant has a rustic character. Baked cod, pheasant with wild mushroom sauce, and mixed grill are among the main course options.

CROSTHWAITE, The Punchbowl ✿✿

Kendal LA8 8HQ
Map 11: SD49
Tel: 015395 68237
Fax: 015395 68875
E-mail:
enquiries@punchbowl.fsnet.co.uk
Chef: Steven Doherty
Owners: Steven & Marjorie Doherty
Cost: Alc £18, set-price L £8. ☺
H/wine £10.25
Times: Noon-2pm/6-9pm. Closed
Mon, D Sun (Nov-Mar), 3 wks Nov
Additional: Bar food; Sunday L;
Children welcome
Seats: 60
Style: Rustic/Country-pub
Smoking: No smoking in dining room

Low ceilings, beams and three open fires are among original features that grace this 17th-century coaching inn. Much more a restaurant these days, this noted Lakeland gastropub has a serious approach to food, served in informal, yet smart surroundings with attentive and friendly service. The modern cooking style reflects chef patron Steven Doherty's pedigree. His rabbit and foie gras terrine, wrapped in bacon and served

Directions: M6 J36 (Kendal). L onto A540 (Barrow). R at Jaguar dealership and follow A5074 until Crosthwaite sign. Top of lane on L next to church

with a white truffle oil dressing, has a strong gamey flavour and makes for a sound start. Delicious, fresh oven-roasted cod fillet with delightfully crunchy prawn beignets and subtle Thai dipping sauce, served with good rice noodles and vegetables or salad, makes for a more adventurous choice from the main course offerings. Save room for desserts, like a tarte Tatin of caramelised apple served with crème fraîche, while chocolate lovers might dither over a choice of warm chocolate brownie with butterscotch sauce and crème fraîche or warm chocolate nemesis with home-made praline ice cream, not to mention the wrapped chocolates that come with good filter coffee to finish. Great value lunches.

DALTON-IN-FURNESS, Clarence House Country Hotel

Hidden in the sleepy village of Dalton this stylish, smart restaurant is a real find. The conservatory is bright and fresh with greenery and idyllic views. Simplicity and purity permeate the menu, which might include pan-seared Oban scallops.

Additional: Bar food L; Sunday L; Children welcome
Style: Classic/Country-house
Accommodation: 17 en suite ★ ★ ★

Directions: From A590 in Lindal take Dalton-in-Furness rd signed Barrow. At 2nd rdbt take 1st exit into Dalton. Hotel on R at top of hill

LA15 8BQ
Map 7: SD27
Tel: 01229 462508
Fax: 01229 467177
Cost: Set-price L £6.50/D £20.95. ☺
H/wine £8.75
Times: Noon-6pm/7-9pm. Closed D Sun, 25 & 26 Dec

GRANGE-OVER-SANDS, Clare House

A traditional Lakeland dining room in an elegant Victorian country house hotel. The scenery is breathtaking and the cuisine a pleasing mix of traditional dishes and interesting specialities. Expect baked salmon stuffed with ginger and currants.

Style: Traditional/Country-house
Smoking: No smoking in dining room
Accommodation: 17 rooms (16 en suite) ★
Credit cards: None

Directions: From M6 take A590 then B5277 to Grange-over-Sands. Park Road follows the shore line. Hotel on L

Park Road LA11 7HQ
Map 7: SD47
Tel: 015395 33026/34253
Cost: Set-price D £23. ☺ H/wine £9
Times: D only, 6.45-7.15pm. Closed Dec-Apr
Additional: Children welcome

GRASMERE,
Gold Rill Hotel ✸

The spacious dining room has wonderful views over Grasmere Lake. Cutlets of Lakeland lamb are served with honey and mustard mash, and fillets of plaice wrapped around a prawn mousseline.

Additional: Bar food L; Children 5+
Style: Country-house
Smoking: No smoking in dining room; Air conditioning
Accommodation: 25 en suite ★ ★ ★

Directions: M6 J36 then A590/A591: Red Bank Road in centre of village opposite St Oswalds Church. Hotel 200yds on L

Red Bank Road LA22 9PU
Map 11: NY30
Tel/Fax: 015394 35486
E-mail: enquiries@gold-rill.com
Cost: *Alc* £25, set-price D £20. ☺
H/wine £11.80
Times: D only, 7.30-8.30pm

GRASMERE, Grasmere Hotel ❀

Broadgate LA22 9TA
Map 11: NY30
Tel/Fax: 015394 35277
E-mail:
enquiries@grasmerehotel.co.uk
Cost: Set-price D £18.50. ☺
H/wine £10
Times: D only, 6.30-8.30pm.
Closed Jan
Style: Traditional/Country-house
Smoking: No smoking in dining room;
Air conditioning
Accommodation: 12 en suite ★ ★

Directions: Off A591, a short distance
from the village centre, by the river

Victorian country house with secluded gardens backing onto the
River Rothey. Good quality ingredients speak for themselves in the
straightforward dishes; desserts include speciality trifles.

GRASMERE, Michael's Nook
Country House Hotel ❀❀❀❀

Ambleside LA22 9RP
Map 11: NY30
Tel: 015394 35496
Fax: 015394 35645
E-mail: m-nook@wordsworth-
grasmere.co.uk
Chef: Michael Wignall
Owner: Reg Gifford
Cost: Set-price L £37.50/D fr £47.50.
H/wine £12.50
Times: 12.30-1.30pm/7.30-8.30pm
Additional: Children 7+; Vegetarian
menu by arrangement
Seats: 50. Private dining room 35.
Jacket & tie preferred
Style: Classic/Country-house
Smoking: No smoking in dining room
Civil licence: 30
Accommodation: 14 en suite ★ ★ ★

Directions: On N side of Grasmere.
From A591, turn uphill at The Swan,
bear L for 400yds.

A country house that truly feels like a country house, with
many personal items around, including various awards earned
by Reg Gifford's dogs at Crufts and other events. There are two
dining rooms, one has an elegant simplicity, the other is richly
furnished with gilt and fine oak panelling, but there is nothing
stuffy about the place, and the formal and knowledgeable
service comes with a human touch. The wine list is another of
Mr Gifford's passions, along with dogs and antiques, and majors
on France, although the layout is in a slightly idiosyncratic style
with a familiar cru nestling alongside a £995.00 Petrus. Michael
Wignall's cooking is ambitious but delivered with abundant
technical skill and considerable assurance. There were truly
magical flavours from a main course assiette of rabbit with
shallot purée and cabbage farce, balancing earthy tastes with
tender meat. Sea bass with crisp pasta and bouillabaisse sauce
was meaty, moist and bathed in a perfumed fish stock with
peppers, diced tomato and plump mussels. A choice of two
soups are offered as part of the four-course set menu – we
sampled a sparkling consommé of guinea fowl with an accent of
white truffle oil. A fine British and Irish cheese menu includes
an award-winning Lancashire Crumbly. Bramley apple mousse

with roast apple and crumble sorbet remains a winner – smooth mousse topped with vivid green, nicely-tart sorbet, layers of lightly spiced roasted apple and a good chunky crumble surrounded by a vanilla foam that just explodes in the mouth.

GRASMERE,

Rothay Garden Hotel ❀❀

Broadgate LA22 9RJ
Map 7: NY30
Tel: 015394 35334
Fax: 015394 35723
E-mail: rothay@grasmere.com
Cost: Set-price L £9.95/D £24. ☺
H/wine £12.95
Times: Noon-1.45pm/7.30-9pm
Additional: Sunday L; Children 5+
Seats: 65
Style: Country-house
Smoking: No smoking in dining room
Accommodation: 25 en suite ★★★

Directions: Turn off A591, opp Swan Hotel, into Grasmere, 300yds on L

Built in the mid-19th century of traditional Lakeland stone, Rothay Garden is everything you would expect of a country-house hotel in this part of the world: comfortable, relaxing lounges, a cosy bar and a smart conservatory restaurant overlooking two acres of floodlit riverside gardens. Typical of the area, too, is a daily-changing set-price menu, a handful of choices at each course, that sticks largely to locally-sourced materials. Westmorland lamb goes into a terrine along with pheasant and broccoli as a starter, and main courses might run to fillet of Cumberland pork, cooked in a creamy sun-dried tomato sauce and accompanied by tagliatelle and stuffed aubergine, and Windermere char, pan-fried and sauced with white wine and cream. A soup, subtly-flavoured spinach and almond, say, follows a starter, which in the local tradition could be as luxurious as foie gras terrine, before the main business: perhaps tender roasted breast of pheasant (from Grizedale) with wild mushroom sauce and dauphinoise potatoes. A hot chocolate muffin with white chocolate sauce, or sticky toffee pudding may round things off. As long as at least two glasses are ordered, over sixty bottles of wine are sold by the glass.

GRASMERE, White Moss House ❀❀

There's an air of intimacy at this country house at the northern end of Rydal Water. With no bar as such, pre-dinner drinks are served in the lounge, and guests take their seats together at eight o'clock in the chintzy, cottagey dining room, with its bare wooden tables and scenic place mats. Guests have no choice either, until pudding, when there are likely to be three, all hinging on often long-forgotten recipes: Eton mess, cabinet pudding, or a good rendition of plum duff with an accomplished Malmsey sauce and pouring cream. Meals start with a soup – broccoli and basil, perhaps, or baby fennel, apple and asparagus – and the intermediate course is likely to be a soufflé, say, of naturally smoked Fleetwood haddock with chives and Westmorland smoked cheese, or something fishy: a duo of

Rydal Water Ambleside LA22 9SE
Map 11: NY30
Tel: 015394 35295
Fax: 015394 35516
E-mail: sue@whitemoss.com
Chef: Peter Dixon
Owners: Sue & Peter Dixon
Cost: Set-price D £29. H/wine £10.95
Times: D only, at 8pm. Closed Sun
Additional: Children welcome;
Vegetarian dishes by request only
Seats: 18
Style: Traditional/Country-house
Smoking: No smoking in dining room
Accommodation: 8 en suite ★

salmon composed of fish from Shetland poached with chervil and champagne married to River Eden fish smoked in oak and bracken accompanied by a salad of unusual leaves. Organic and local meats show to good effect in main courses of free-range, maize-fed guinea fowl on Puy lentils, or Mansergh Hall spring lamb roasted just pink in a herb crust. Interesting things are done to as many as five vegetables, and after pudding comes a selection of British cheeses. The wine list is impressive, with over 300 bottles, and at least 10 are served by the glass.

Directions: On A591 between Grasmere and Ambleside opposite Rydal Water

GRASMERE, Wordsworth Hotel ❀❀

Nr Ambleside LA22 9SW
Map 11: NY30
Tel: 015394 35592
Fax: 015394 35765
E-mail: enquiry@wordworth-grasmere.co.uk
Chef: Bernard Warne
Cost: Alc £30, set-price L £19.50/D £30 & £32.50. H/wine £13
Times: 12.30-2pm/7-9pm (Fri, Sat 9.30pm)
Additional: Children welcome
Seats: 65. Private dining rooms 26-100.
Style: Classic/Traditional
Smoking: No smoking in dining room; Air conditioning

With the fells rising in the background, garishly-outfitted 'crag rats' (hikers) thronging the streets and the WW tourist trade lapping round its doors, this is a busy hotel in the heart of the poet's picturesque village. The decor is all swags and glazed cotton but the tables are a little cramped. Service is attentive. An attempt to add a touch of fusion to a stylishly-layered foie gras and duck confit terrine with apple chutney and a chinese-style soy-based sauce was interesting, prawn and mussel chowder was made on a good bisque-style base, and gamey venison collops sandwiched a piece of foie gras on top of fondant potatoes. Raspberry soufflé with Drambuie custard was 'light and fluffy'.

Civil licence: 110 **Accommodation:** 37 en suite ★ ★ ★ ★

Directions: In the village centre next to the church

HAWKSHEAD, Highfield House Country Hotel ❀

Bright and cheerful dining room, well positioned for splendid mountain views through the large windows. A simple, honest approach to cooking is manifest in dishes such as roasted loin of bacon with sautéed black pudding and caramelised shallots.

Hawkshead Hill LA22 0PN
Map 7: SD39
Tel: 015394 36344
Fax: 015394 36793
E-mail: highfield.hawkshead@btinternet.com
Cost: Set-price D £20. ☺ H/wine £10
Times: D only, 6.30-9.30pm
Additional: Bar food L (noon-2pm); Children welcome

Style: Informal/Country-house
Smoking: No smoking in dining room
Accommodation: 11 en suite ★ ★

Directions: From Ambleside take A593 south and turn L at Clappersgate onto B5286 to Hawkshead. Turn R onto B5285, hotel up hill on L

HOWTOWN, Sharrow Bay ❀❀❀

Sharrow Bay Penrith CA10 2LZ
Map 12: NY41
Tel: 017684 86301
Fax: 017684 863949
E-mail: enquires@sharrow-bay.com
Chefs: Juan Martin, Colin Akrigg
Owners: Brian G Sack,
Nigel Lightburn
Cost: Set-price L £36.25/D £47.25.
H/wine £14.75
Times: 1-1.30pm/8-8.30pm. Closed
Dec-Feb
Additional: Sunday L; Children 13+;
Vegetarian dishes not always
available
Seats: 62. Jacket and tie preferred
Style: Classic/Country-house
Smoking: No smoking in dining room;
Air conditioning
Civil licence: 35
Accommodation: 26 rooms (24 en
suite) ★ ★ ★

Reputedly the first country-house hotel in Britain, Sharrow Bay opened its doors in 1948. It might have set the pattern for many others, with antiques, stylish decorations and comfortable soft furnishings filling the lounges, but its position is unique: right on the shore of Ullswater, with lovely views over the lake to the fells beyond. The kitchen's output is prodigious, with a colossus of a dinner menu and a lunch menu almost as long; add to this breakfast and afternoon tea, and what amazes is that standards never falter. Portions are generous, but a lighter feel to the cooking has gradually been introduced, a thin fennel purée and a muted ginger sauce for 'superbly seared' scallops, for instance, so people feel they might actually make it to the sixth course of British cheeses. Starters vary from a soup, or terrines – perhaps guinea fowl and caramelised apple wrapped in local ham – to soufflé suissesse or a simple salad of lobster, potatoes, asparagus and avocado with tarragon dressing. Fish is the next course, the only one, along with the sorbet that follows it, with no choice: maybe fillet of sea bass on softly fried aubergine with red pepper coulis. Good sourcing results in pink, tender, flavourful lamb fillet in a herby crust with ratatouille and a light tomato and rosemary jus, or full-blooded tournedos of Scottish fillet steak with all the works: a croquette of oxtail, roasted shallots, pease pudding, horseradish mash and Burgundy sauce. Sticky toffee pudding is said to have originated here, and other desserts range from traditional apple charlotte with vanilla sauce to warm chocolate gâteau with matching sauce and white chocolate sorbet. The broad church of a wine list runs from vins de pays to pedigree clarets, all at fair prices, and over 20 bottles are sold by the glass.

Directions: Turn off A592 through Pooley Bridge, turn R (signed to Howtown), hotel 2 miles

KENDAL, The Castle Green Hotel in Kendal ❀

The Greenhouse Restaurant offers views of Kendal Castle and the Lakeland fells in its new promenade extension. Cooking remains vibrant and imaginative – book at weekends.

Smoking: No smoking in dining room
Civil licence: 300
Accommodation: 65 en suite ★ ★ ★

Directions: From M6 J37 to Kendal (5 miles). Hotel 1st on R approaching Kendal.

LA9 6BH
Map 7: SD59
Tel: 01539 734000
Fax: 01539 735522
E-mail: reception@castlegreen.co.uk
Cost: *Alc* £21.95, set-price L £12/D
£21.95. ☺ H/wine £9.95
Times: Noon-2pm/7-10pm (11pm Sat)
Additional: Bar food; Children
welcome
Style: Chic/Modern

KENDAL, Crooklands

See Crooklands, Cumbria

KENDAL, Georgian House

9 Highgate LA9 4EN
Map 7: SD59
Tel: 01539 722123
Fax: 01539 721223
E-mail: thegeorgianhouse@email.com
Cost: Alc £20. ☺ H/wine £10
Times: Noon-2pm/6-11pm.
Closed Mon, 25 Dec, 1 Jan
Additional: Bar food D; Sunday L;
Children welcome
Style: Chic/Modern
Smoking: No smoking in dining room

The eclectic menu and innovative interior design of this smart restaurant would be comfortably at home in the heart of London. Try seared lobster and crab mousse with bouillabaisse jus, followed by steaming hot chocolate fritters with an understated anglais. Booking advised.

Directions: M6 J36, A591 to Kendal. Restaurant is 100yds on R, after 1st pedestrian crossing

KESWICK, Dale Head Hall

Expect peace and tranquillity at this pleasant hotel a stone's throw away from Lake Thirlmere. Dine in an intimate room with a low-beamed ceiling, and enjoy a set meal of carrot soup, symphony of seafoods, and lemon tart.

Additional: Children 12+
Style: Traditional/Country-house
Smoking: No smoking in dining room
Accommodation: 12 en suite ★ ★

Lake Thirlmere CA12 4TN
Map 11: NY22
Tel: 017687 72478
Fax: 017687 71070
E-mail: enquiry@dale-head-hall.co.uk
Cost: Set-price D £27.50
Times: D only, 7.30-8pm

Directions: 12 miles from M6 J40, half way between Keswick and Grasmere.

KESWICK, Highfield Hotel

Small restaurant in a quiet residential setting, enjoying idyllic views of parkland and mountains. A recent meal took in twice-baked Stilton soufflé, baked halibut with crab and tomato mousse, and warm chocolate sponge to finish.

Additional: Sunday L; Children 8+; Vegetarian dishes not always available
Style: Informal/Traditional
Smoking: No smoking in dining room
Accommodation: 18 en suite ★ ★

The Heads CA12 5ER
Map 11: NY22
Tel: 017687 72508
Cost: Set-price L £12/D £18. ☺
H/wine £12
Times: Noon-2pm, 6-8.30pm.
Closed Dec & Jan (ex Xmas & New Year)

Directions: From M6 J40 follow A66 towards Keswick

KESWICK,

Horse and Farrier Inn NEW

Threlkeld CA12 4SQ
Map 11: NY22
Tel: 017687 79688
Fax: 017687 79824
Cost: *Alc* £17. ☺ H/wine £9.95
Times: Noon-2pm/6.30-9.30pm

*Huddled underneath the dramatic Blencathra Mountain, this
beautifully restored 17th-century inn and restaurant offers top
quality food in a relaxed atmosphere. Grilled scallops marinated in
saffron and coriander show the style.*

Additional: Bar food; Sunday L; Children welcome
Style: Bistro/Informal
Smoking: No-smoking area; No pipes & cigars
Accommodation: 9 en suite ★ ★

Directions: Telephone for directions

KESWICK,

Underscar Manor

Applethwaite CA12 4PH
Map 11: NY22
Tel: 017687 75000
Fax: 017687 74904
Chef: Robert Thornton
Owners: Pauline & Derek Harrison,
Gordon Evans
Cost: *Alc* £38, set-price L £25/D £30.
H/wine £14.50
Times: Noon-1pm/D at 8.30pm
Additional: Children 12+
Seats: 50. Jacket & tie preferred
Style: Country-house
Smoking: No smoking in dining room

Approached up a long drive, Underscar Manor is a mid-
Victorian mansion built in the Italianate style, with arched
windows and a campanile. Set on a hillside in 40 acres of fine
grounds in the foothills of Skiddaw, it has lovely views over
Derwent Water. The conservatory-style restaurant, its windows
hung with soft drapes, is an elegant setting for Robert
Thornton's cooking. He works along fashionable lines, merging
often unexpected elements. King prawns, for instance, are
given the tandoori treatment and served with tabouleh,
Parmesan shavings, arrabbiata sauce and deep-fried vegetables
– and that's just a starter. Top-quality ingredients are used to
good effect, as in pan-fried foie gras with brandied grapes and
a well-defined Sauternes sauce, and roast Barbary duck with a
juniper and orange sauce and caramelised oranges. Rice
pudding comes in a copper pan alongside a compote of exotic
fruits, light puff pastry encloses traditional apple tart with
cinnamon ice cream, and the assiette of sweet tastings is a
delightful array of skilfully prepared desserts: fresh strawberry
sablé, a light lemon tart with crisp pastry, passion fruit sponge,
and coffee ice cream.

Directions: From M6 J40, A66 Keswick/Workington for 17m. At
large roundabout take 3rd exit. Turn immediate R at signpost for
Underscar; hotel 0.75m on R

MUNGRISDALE, The Mill Hotel

CA11 0XR
Map 11: NY33
Tel: 017687 79659
Fax: 017687 79155
Cost: Set-price D £27. H/wine £5.95
Times: D only, 7-8pm. Closed Nov-Feb
Additional: Children welcome
Style: Country-house
Smoking: No smoking in dining room
Accommodation: 7 en suite ★
Credit cards: None

Directions: Mungrisdale is signed on A66, mid way between Penrith and Keswick. Hotel 2 miles N of A66

Set in the Lake District National Park this former mill cottage dates back to the mid-17th-century. A collection of Victorian paintings adorn the walls, and the short five course menu offers a good choice of fresh local dishes.

NEAR SAWREY, Sawrey House Country Hotel ❀❀

NEW

Ambleside LA22 0LF
Map 7: SD39
Tel: 015394 36387
Fax: 015394 36010
E-mail: enquiries@sawrey-house.com
Chef: Nigel Skinkis
Owners: Colin & Shirley Whiteside
Cost: Set-price D £27.50. H/wine £9.95
Times: D only, 7.30-8pm. Closed Jan
Additional: Children 10+
Seats: 30
Style: Informal/Country-house
Smoking: No smoking in dining room
Accommodation: 11 en suite

Stylish Victorian mansion set high on a hill overlooking Grizedale Forest and Esthwaite Water in the heart of Beatrix Potter country. The main draw here, however, is a kitchen that's driven by ambition. Our inspector's initial worry on reading the 'imaginative creations' on the menu was 'would they work?' On the whole they did. From the opening confit of duck with foie gras terrine, wild mushrooms and creamed truffle vinaigrette (rich depth, top drawer seasoning), to a white chocolate mousse with citrus sauce, the promise was there. In between came sweet potato soup with coriander, chilli and yogurt, pan-fried sea bass with brandade of cod, sesame carrots, coriander and ginger butter sauce, good own-baked bread, coffee and petits fours. The wine list offers a good choice.

Directions: From Ambleside take A593 S. L at Clappersgate onto B5286 towards Hawkshead then take B5285 towards Sawrey/Ferry. Hotel 1.5m on R

NETHER WASDALE,

Low Wood Hall Hotel ❀❀

The introduction of an elegantly furnished fine dining room has provided a boost to the food at Low Wood Hall. The new dining room reflects the original Victorian style of the property, and the Mediterranean-themed restaurant is now used more for breakfast. Pre-dinner drinks are served in the lounge, where diners, disappearing into sumptuous sofas, are presented with menus and a little something to whet this appetite. The food is modern English but, from a basket of warm buns, a luscious treacle bread evoked childhood memories. A terrine of corn-fed chicken, guinea fowl, rabbit and wild mushrooms was skilfully made, but the main course was the highlight – grilled noisettes of lamb with a clean, light jus packed with rosemary and lamb goodness, served on a refined ratatouille with just enough garlic to work with the lamb.

CA20 1ET
Map 6: NY10
Tel/Fax: 019467 26111
E-mail:
lowwoodhallhotel@bt.internet.com
Chef: Alan Skivington
Owner: Geraldine Turner
Cost: Set-price D fr £25. H/wine fr £14.95
Times: D only at 8pm. Closed Sun, early Jan
Additional: Children 10+
Seats: 30. Private dining room 12
Style: Country-house
Smoking: No smoking in dining room
Accommodation: 12 en suite ★★

Directions: Exit A595 at Gosforth & bear L for Wasdale, after 3 miles turn R for Nether Wasdale

NEWBY BRIDGE,

Lakeside Hotel ❀❀

Hotel in the grand style with a delightful setting on the shores of Lake Windermere, next to the steamers and steam railway. The restaurant is richly furnished and elegant, with knowledgeable staff on hand to assist with your selection from the menu and comprehensive wine list. Pre-dinner drinks are taken in the conservatory overlooking the gardens, which run down to the lake. The menu places emphasis on freshly cooked, quality local ingredients, although the style of cooking has more cosmopolitan influences, and guests are wowed by the stunning presentation of the dishes. Great flavour flooded through a main course of roasted breast of wood pigeon with a light truffle and rocket salad, and a dessert of chocolate mousse with griottine cherries was particularly eye-catching.

LA12 8AT
Map 7: SD38
Tel: 015395 31207
Fax: 015395 31699
E-mail: sales@lakesidehotel.co.uk

Telephone for further details

Directions: M6 J36 follow A590 to Newby Bridge, R over bridge, follow Hawkshead road for 1m

PENRITH,

A Bit on the Side ❀

Tucked away down a side street in the town centre, this trendy little eatery offers modern, succinctly presented food. A fragrant tomato and basil soup was 'refreshing' whilst a baked chocolate tart to finish was faultless.

Brunswick Square CA11 7LG
Map 12: NY53
Tel: 01768 892526
Cost: Alc £21, set-price L £10.95. ☺
H/wine £8.95

Times: Noon-3pm/6.30-11.45pm.
Closed L Tue, Sat & Sun, all Mon
Additional: Children 7+ **Style:** Informal/Rustic
Smoking: No-smoking area

Directions: Follow town centre signs from M6 J40. Brunswick Sq is opposite Bluebell Lane car park

RAVENSTONEDALE,

Black Swan Hotel ❀❀

The M6 is only ten minutes away, but the picturesque village feels like another world. Imaginative dinners are served either in the hotel's cosy bar or dining room filled with polished antique furniture. Ingredients are carefully sourced: roasted loin of Mansergh Hall lamb, for example, is served on mushy peas and saffron potatoes with a red wine and garden mint reduction. Although the cooking can be stunning in terms of clarity of flavour, it would perhaps benefit from a simpler, less complex approach; garnishing and saucing can seem intrusive. However, our Inspector enjoyed a very fresh, crisp-skinned grilled seabass accompanied by garden pea mousse, sautéed lobster tail and a froth of vanilla. A dessert of chocolate torte with peppermint mousse rounded off the four-course dinner menu – a steal at £25.00, although there is a good value *carte* as well.

Directions: M6 J38/A685 (Brough). Through Kirkby Stephen, then to Ravenstonedale

Nr Kirkby Stephen CA17 4NG
Map 12: NY70
Tel: 015396 23204
Fax: 015396 23604
E-mail: reservations@blackswanhotel.com
Chef: Norma Stuart
Owners: Norma & Gordon Stuart
Cost: Set-price L £12/D £25. ☺
H/wine £6
Times: Noon-2pm/6.30-9.15pm
Additional: Bar food; Sunday L; Children welcome
Seats: 36. Private dining room 12.
Jacket & tie preferred
Style: Traditional/Formal
Smoking: No smoking in dining room.
Accommodation: 20 en suite ★★

TEBAY, Westmorland Hotel ❀

Orton CA10 3SB
Map 12: NY53
Tel: 015396 24351
Fax: 015396 24354
Cost: Set-price D £21. ☺
H/wine £10.50
Times: D only, 7-9pm
Additional: Bar food; Children welcome
Style: Modern/Traditional
Smoking: No smoking in dining room; Air conditioning
Civil licence: 120
Accommodation: 53 en suite ★★★

As refreshing as the stunning moorland views from the restaurant, the menu blends both traditional and modern approaches resulting in well-composed dishes such as Dutch calves' liver with a robust mustard jus.

Directions: Next to Westmorland's Tebay Services on M6, easily reached from S-bound carriageway by using road linking the 2 service areas

---

TEMPLE SOWERBY,

Temple Sowerby House Hotel ❀

This intimate, candlelit restaurant is an ideal venue for those seeking unpretentious, simply cooked food with great clarity. Local game and fresh fish feature on the menu along with modern interpretations of classic desserts. Attentive service and a varied wine list add to the dining experience.

Additional: Bar food L; Children welcome
Style: Country-house
Smoking: No smoking in dining room
Accommodation: 13 en suite ★★★

Directions: On A66 5 miles E of Penrith in village centre

Nr Penrith CA10 1RZ
Map 12: NY62
Tel: 0800 146157
Fax: 017683 61958
E-mail: stay@temple-sowerby.com
Cost: Alc £28.50. ☺ H/wine £14.75
Times: 11-6pm/7-10.30pm

THIRLSPOT,

Kings Head Hotel and Inn

Thirlmere Keswick CA12 4TN
Map 11: NY31
Tel: 017687 72393
Fax: 017687 72309

Dramatic lakeland views from this informal but elegant restaurant await the discerning diner. Go traditional with roast sirloin of beef with Yorkshire pudding, or maybe opt for chargrilled swordfish with flash fried vegetables.

E-mail: kings@lakelandsheart.demon.co.uk
Cost: Set-price D £20. ☺ H/wine £9.95
Times: D only 7-9pm
Additional: Bar food; Children welcome
Style: Classic/Country-house
Smoking: No smoking in dining room
Accommodation: 17 en suite ★ ★ ★

Directions: From M6 J40 take A66 towards Keswick. From Keswick take A591 towards Grasmere. Hotel 4m on L

TROUTBECK,

Broadoaks Country House

Bridge Lane Nr Windermere
LA23 1LA
Map 7: NX40
Tel: 015394 45566
Fax: 015394 88766

Lakeland stone-constructed Victorian country house hotel overlooking the Troutbeck valley and wooded hillsides. The restaurant menu is extensive and successful. A Gressingham duck with a port and blackcurrant sauce was particularly enjoyed.

E-mail: broadoaks.com@virgin.net
Cost: Set-price L £15.95/D £35. ☺ H/wine £10.50
Times: Noon-2pm (reservation only)/7-8.30pm
Additional: Sunday L; Children 10+
Style: Country-house/Victorian
Smoking: No smoking in dining room
Civil licence: 100
Accommodation: 12 en suite ★ ★ ★

Directions: From M6 J36 take A591 towards Ambleside, then R on A592 to Troutbeck

TROUTBECK,

Queens Head Hotel ❀

Town Head Nr Windermere
LA23 1PW
Map 7: SD49
Tel: 015394 32174
Fax: 015394 31938

A 17th-century coaching inn with a unique four-poster bar; log fires, slate floors and oak beams add extra atmosphere. Cooking is simple and direct: steak, ale and mushroom cobbler or home-cured salmon with fresh mango, lime and herb salsa.

Cost: Alc £17.50, set-price L /D £15.50. ☺ H/wine £9.95
Times: Noon-2pm/6.30-9pm. Closed 25 Dec
Additional: Bar food; Sunday L; Children welcome
Style: Informal/Traditional
Smoking: No-smoking area
Accommodation: 9 en suite

Directions: On A592, approx 2 miles from Windermere

ULLSWATER,
Leeming House

Watermillock Penrith CA11 0JJ
Map 12: NY42
Tel: 0870 400 8131
Fax: 017684 86443
Cost: Set-price D £27.50. H/wine £15
Times: Noon-2pm/7-9pm
Additional: Sunday L; Children welcome
Style: Classic/Country-house
Smoking: No smoking in dining room
Civil licence: 30
Accommodation: 40 en suite ★★★

Directions: 8 miles from M6 J40; 8 miles from Penrith

Set back from the shores of Ullswater, the restaurant enjoys beautiful views of the garden, lake and distant fells. A varied menu should suit all tastes, with dishes such as chicken in a red bean sauce with cashew nuts and rice.

WATERMILLOCK,
Brackenrigg Inn ❁   NEW

Penrith CA11 0LP
Map 12: NY42
Tel: 01768 486206
Fax: 01768 486945
E-mail: enquiries@brackenrigginn.co.uk
Cost: Alc £20. ☺ H/wine £9.95
Times: Noon-2.30pm(2pm Mon-Fri in winter)/6.30-9pm.
Additional: Bar food; Sunday L; Children 14+ at D
Style: Informal/Traditional
Smoking: No smoking in dining room
Accommodation: 11 en suite

Stunning views over Ullswater and distant peaks complement the quality modern British cuisine at this charming 18th-century coaching inn. Try mussel and leek tart infused with saffron and served with a lemon butter sauce.

Directions: From M6 J40 take A66 towards Keswick. At 1st rdbt take A592 for 6m to Watermillock. Inn on R

WATERMILLOCK,
Old Church Hotel ❁

A Lakeland setting, friendly staff and an emphasis on fresh, local ingredients. A spring meal took in salad of baked goats' cheese with walnuts, breast of duck with sweet and sour sauce, and sticky toffee pudding.

Directions: M6 J40, A592, 2.5miles SW of Pooley Bridge

Old Church Bay CA11 0JN
Map 12: NY42
Tel: 017684 86204
Fax: 017684 86368
E-mail: info@oldchurch.co.uk

Telephone for further details

WATERMILLOCK,

Rampsbeck Hotel ❀❀❀

Nr Penrith CA11 0LP
Map 12: NY42
Tel: 017684 86442
Fax: 017684 86688
E-mail:
enquiries@rampsbeck.fsnet.co.uk
Chef: Andrew McGeorge
Owners: T I & M M Gibb, Mrs M J
MacDowall
Cost: *Alc* £39.50, set-price L £25/D
£29. H/wine £11.25
Times: Noon-1pm/7-8.30pm. Closed
8 Jan-9 Feb
Additional: Bar food L; Sunday L;
Children 7+
Seats: 40. Private dining room 15
Style: Traditional/Country-house
Smoking: No smoking in dining room
Accommodation: 20 en suite ★★★

Acres of parkland and gardens surround this fine country
house, dating from the 18th century, on the shore of Ullswater.
Traditionally furnished, with a comfortable, relaxing
atmosphere, it has an elegant restaurant with stunning views
over the lake. Lunch is taken seriously here – tian of crab with
lemon mayonnaise may be followed by roast breast of Barbary
duck in Madeira sauce with glazed baby vegetables and potato
purée – but dinner is inevitably the centre of attention.
Andrew McGeorge's techniques might have their roots in fine
French traditions, but to them he adds his own style. Mussels
and scallops are popped into a first-course cassoulet along with
noodles and saffron, and main-course roast breast of guinea
fowl is accompanied by a matching boudin and a cep-flavoured
jus. Bold flavours sing out of some dishes – roasted calves'
sweetbreads and seared foie gras with roast fillet of veal and
Madeira sauce, say, or lobster and a sauce of the same
crustacean with steamed fillet of Dover sole – while sometimes
the finest produce speaks for itself, as in a simple but effective
starter of baked fillet of cod, flaking at the touch of a fork,
given a slight oomph with pesto dressing. Timing is
immaculate, with three circular slices of pork fillet roasted just
pink, 'tender, succulent, first-class', plated on top of a tower of
spinach, fondant potatoes and wild mushrooms, with a
perfectly-pitched port jus. An inspector found eating pudding
an 'orgasmic' experience, cutting through crusty almond pastry
to reach a perfectly poached whole pear and scooping up
mouthfuls along with prune and Armagnac ice cream, a poire
William sabayon and prune purée. Service is commendable,
and the broad-ranging wine list is grouped according to the
characteristics of the wines.

Directions: M6 J40, follow signs to Ullswater on A592, turn R at
lake's edge. Hotel 1.25 miles along lake shore

WINDERMERE,
Beech Hill Hotel ❀

Newby Bridge Road Cartmel Fell
LA23 3LR
Map 7: SD49
Tel: 015394 42137
Fax: 015394 43745
E-mail:
beechhill@richardsonhotels.co.uk
Cost: Set-price D £27.50. H/wine
£12.95
Times: Noon-2pm/7-9.30pm
Additional: Bar food; Sunday L;
Children welcome
Style: Classic/Traditional
Smoking: No smoking in dining room;
Air conditioning
Accommodation: 58 en suite

Few establishments can boast such stunning views as those afforded by this relaxed hotel restaurant. Imaginative cooking blends fashionable trends with more traditional dishes, with mains such as chargrilled beef fillet on puréed yam.

Directions: On A592, Newby Bridge 4 miles from Windermere

WINDERMERE,
Fayrer Garden House ❀❀

Built in 1904 in a prime spot high above the lake, Fayrer Garden House is surrounded by five acres of mature grounds. The panelled hall leads into the richly-furnished conservatory restaurant, which has lovely views over the lake and fells. Dinner is off a daily-changing four-course menu with five choices of starters and main courses, interspersed with a sorbet or soup: cream of mushroom with sage, say. Local produce includes Morecambe Bay shrimps, served as a starter bound with cauliflower and new potatoes with boiled egg, and Cartmel Valley pheasant, pan-fried and accompanied by wilted cabbage and a lightly meaty jus with apricots; crab is from Cornwall and salmon from Scotland. The centrepiece of dinner might be baked fillet of North Sea cod under a herb crust with a buttery chive sauce and a warm salad of spinach, lobster and asparagus, preceded by an innovative starter of peppered Cumberland beef in a black bean sauce with stir-fried vegetables in filo and sweet potato wafers. Puddings tend towards the temptingly decadent, as in a tart of white and dark chocolate truffle drizzled with white chocolate sauce garnished with summer berries. Service is formal and attentive, and the long wine list should have something for all tastes.

Lyth Valley Road Bowness-on-
Windermere LA23 3JP
Map 7: SD49
Tel: 015394 88195
Fax: 015394 45986
E-mail: lakescene@fayrergarden.com

Chef: Edward Wilkinson
Owners: Iain & Jackie Garside
Cost: Set-price D £27.50. ☺ H/wine £11.95
Times: D only, 7-8.30pm
Additional: Bar food L; Children 5+
Style: Country-house
Smoking: No smoking in dining room; Air conditioning
Accommodation: 18 en suite ★★

Directions: On A5074 1 mile from town centre

WINDERMERE,
Gilpin Lodge Hotel ❀❀❀

Crook Road LA23 3NE
Map 7: SD49
Tel: 015394 88818
Fax: 015394 88058
E-mail: hotel@gilpin-lodge.co.uk
Chef: Grant Tomkins
Owners: John & Christine Cunliffe
Cost: *Alc* L £20 (Mon-Sat), set-price
D £35. H/wine £12.50
Times: Noon-2.30pm/7-9pm
Additional: Bar food L; Sunday L;
Children 7+
Seats: 60. Private dining room 12
Style: Country-house/Elegant
Smoking: No smoking in dining room
Accommodation: 14 en suite ★ ★ ★

Directions: M6 J36 & A590/(Kendal),
then B5284 for 5 miles

This turn-of-the-century white house in a scenic and tranquil spot is charmingly and stylishly decorated, comfort very much in mind, with antiques dotted about, pictures on the walls and lots of fresh flowers. The restaurant – actually three rooms, each with its own individual decor – though elegant, has a homely feel to it; tables are large, linen crisp, and silver and glassware highly polished. Lunch can run to pan-fried calves' liver with bacon and bubble-and-squeak, or seared fillet of smoked haddock on spinach with a brandade of the same fish and spring onions, while dinner is a four-course business, typically something like pan-fried breast of wood pigeon with horseradish and rosemary rösti and Puy lentil jus, then tomato and celery soup, followed by roast monkfish with keta caviar and chive velouté. The kitchen's labours pay dividends, as witnessed by an inspector's starter of an assiette of calves' liver comprising a thin sliver resting on mash, a postage-stamp portion of liver and celeriac ravioli, and, the show-stopper of the trio, a terrine of thin strips of meat layered with mousse all wrapped in bacon – overall, 'stunning and imaginative'. Another mousse, of light, delicately flavoured salmon and sole, served warm with a chive beurre blanc, is equally impressive, and even a main course of straightforward-sounding, pan-fried, corn-fed chicken breast with Parmesan polenta has been enlivened by impeccably timed, chargrilled provençale vegetables 'tasting of the sun' and a zingy, sweet tomato sauce. All the stops are pulled out for desserts: there might be lemon tartlet with berries and raspberry sorbet, soft fruit and port crème brûlée, and light yet rich and moist sticky toffee pudding with maple toffee sauce and walnut ice cream (like everything else, made in the kitchen). The long wine list, expertly assembled with an eye for quality, opens with seven house bottles.

WINDERMERE,
Holbeck Ghyll ❀❀❀

Holbeck Lane LA23 1LU
Map 7: SD49
Tel: 015394 32375
Fax: 015394 34743
E-mail: accommodation@holbeck-ghyll.co.uk
Chef: Stephen Smith
Owners: David & Patricia Nicholson

In an area not short of dramatic views, Holbeck Ghyll still manages to stand out. Panoramic vistas stretch across the lake to the magnificent Langdale Fells beyond. Aged 26, Stephen Smith in the kitchen of the former 19th-century hunting lodge displays a confidence and array of skills that might take others years longer to accumulate. The style is economical and precise

Holbeck Ghyll

Cost: Set-price L £19.50/D £39.50. H/wine £14.50
Times: 12.15-2pm/6.45-9.30pm
Additional: Sunday L; Children 8+
Seats: 40. Private dining room 16
Style: Country-house/Relaxed
Smoking: No smoking in dining room
Civil licence: 65
Accommodation: 20 en suite ★ ★ ★

with top-notch ingredients given the room to express themselves. An *amuse-bouche* of artichoke cappuccino with girolles likely to set the pace and tone, followed by technically excellent mosaic of spring rabbit benefiting from the judicious use of truffle. Sea bass fillet has been brilliantly and vividly paired with red pepper consommé and confit cherry tomatoes. Saddle of roe deer is unusually pot-roasted, served with fondant potato and red wine sauce. Desserts are often on classical lines; a cherry clafoutis was typically well-honed and accomplished. The wine list offers character and depth with prices that show some welcome restraint. Mr Smith is a young chef whose progress we will watch with interest.

Directions: 3 miles N of Windermere on A591. Turn R into Holbeck Lane. Hotel is 0.5 mile on L

WINDERMERE, Jerichos ❀❀

162 Birch Street LA23 1EG
Map 7: SD49
Tel/Fax: 015394 42522
E-mail: enquiries@jerichos.co.uk
Chefs: Chris Blaydes, Sarah Connolly
Owners: Chris & Joanne Blaydes
Cost: Alc £20-£30. ☺ H/wine £11.75
Times: D only, 6.45-9.30pm. Closed Mon, 25 & 26 Dec, 1 Jan, last wk Feb, 1st wk Mar
Additional: Children 12+
Seats: 36. Private dining room 24
Style: Modern
Smoking: No smoking in dining room

Broad green slate steps and a patio lead up to the entrance of this relatively small, restaurant. Jerichos is modern in design, with clean lines, low voltage lighting and an open plan kitchen. Seasonal produce inspires the weekly menus. Chef/proprietor Chris Blaydes continues to keep a sharp and imaginative thrust to his cooking. The homemade bread rolls are delicious and a starter of tomato and cumin soup with crème fraîche and toasted pine kernels was 'intriguing'. Pan fried marinated veal cutlet on Dijon mashed celeriac and parsnip, with caramelised onion marmalade and confit of garlic and reduced white jus, made use of good quality ingredients. Desserts are impressive and included a vanilla and rosemary brûlee. The wine list does not match the menu in imagination but there are many served by the glass.

Directions: In town centre

WINDERMERE,
Langdale Chase Hotel ❀❀

Langdale Chase
LA23 1LW
Map 7: SD49
Tel: 015394 32201
Fax: 015394 32603
E-mail: sales@langdalechase.co.uk
Chef: Wendy Lindars
Owner: Thomas G Noblett

Few restaurants enjoy such stunning views as this one. From its elevated position overlooking Lake Windermere and the distant Langdale Pikes there is much to be seen and enjoyed, but the cooking is more than a match for any potential distractions. In stark contrast to the grandeur and historic atmosphere of the house, the food is modern and cosmopolitan with an emphasis on simple combinations of very fresh produce. A short eclectic set menu is supplemented with dishes from the *carte*, and be eaten in the restaurant or formal bar. Pan-fried scallops topped with parma ham crisps set on buttered spinach with a light chive beurre blanc pleased the inspector, as did roast Gressingham duckling with a confit of roasted vegetables and jus flavoured with five spices. The grande assiette of desserts, a home-made selection including light lemon cheesecake, crème brulee, apricot compote and caramelised banana, was very highly rated. Freshly-baked brown soda bread with apricots and sundried tomato bread infused with Italian herbs demonstrate the overall quality.

Directions: 2 miles S of Ambleside and 3 miles N of Windermere

Cost: *A/c* £25, set-price L £14.50/D £25.50. ☺ H/wine £11.50
Times: 12.15-2.15pm/7-9pm
Additional: Bar food; Sunday L; Children welcome
Seats: 80. Private dining rooms 12, 28
Style: Country-house
Smoking: No smoking in dining room; Air conditioning
Civil licence: 130
Accommodation: 27 en suite ★★★

WINDERMERE, Lindeth Fell Hotel

The recently built restaurants look over the gardens to Lake Windermere. Typical dishes are roast guinea fowl with parsnip and parsley mash, and grilled halibut with prawns and Muscat sauce.

Directions: 1 mile S of Bowness on A5074 Lyth Valley Road

Lyth Valley Road Bowness LA23 3JP
Map 7: SD49
Tel: 015394 43286
Fax: 015394 47455
E-mail: kennedy@lindethfell.co.uk
Cost: Set-price D £21. ☺ H/wine £8.50
Times: D only, 7.30-8.30pm
Additional: Sunday L (12.30-2pm); Children 7+
Style: Modern/Country-house
Smoking: No smoking in dining room
Accommodation: 14 en suite ★★

WINDERMERE,
Linthwaite House Hotel ❀❀

Linthwaite House, built as a private residence in Edwardian times, gives the full Lakeland experience: attractive grounds to

Crook Road Bowness LA23 3JA
Map 7: SD49
Tel: 015394 88600
Fax: 015394 88601
E-mail: admin@linthwaite.com
Chef: Ian Bravey
Owner: Mike Bevans
Cost: Set-price D £39. H/wine £17
Times: 12.30-1.30pm/7.15-9pm
Additional: Bar food L; Sunday L; Children 7+
Seats: 60. Private dining room
Style: Country-house
Smoking: No smoking in dining room
Civil licence: 55
Accommodation: 26 en suite ★★★

wander round, deep armchairs and open fires, and a conservatory, bar and terrace overlooking the lake and fells. Dinner in the recently extended restaurant – banquette seating, mirrors of all shapes and sizes in the extension, bric-à-brac in the original room – kicks off with a *bonne bouche*, perhaps ragout of wild mushrooms liberally sprinkled with truffle oil. The broad-ranging menus are full of appeal, taking in the likes of oven-baked monkfish tail wrapped in air-dried ham with red wine sauce, an interesting vegetarian choice, like a filo parcel of goats' cheese and spinach with spicy tomato coulis, and roasted saddle of fell lamb nicely flavoured with garlic and rosemary and complemented by a light mint and redcurrant jus. Meals could start with Caesar salad, leek and potato soup, or 'excellent quality' seared scallops subtly flavoured with paprika, with classic tarte Tatin and Calvados custard, or a trio of sorbets – plum, elderflower and orange – drawing things to a conclusion. Canapés and petits fours are well spoken of, and amusing and interesting observations on the wine list add to the overall welcoming feel of the place.

Directions: Take 1st L off A591 at roundabout NW of Kendal (B5284). Follow for 6 miles, hotel is 1 mile after Windermere Golf Club on L

WINDERMERE, Low Wood Hotel

LA23 1LP
Map 7: SD49
Tel: 015394 33338
Fax: 015394 34072

Telephone for further details

Accomplished cooking in the Windermere Restaurant – try roasted red pepper and courgette soup to begin, followed perhaps by pan-seared salmon with salsa verdi and roasted fennel. Desserts might include sticky toffee pudding to their own recipe.

Directions: M6 J36, A590 then A591 to Ambleside. Hotel on R

WINDERMERE,
Miller Howe Hotel

Rayrigg Road LA23 1EY
Map 7: SD49
Tel: 015394 42536
Fax: 015394 45664
E-mail: lakeview@millerhowe.com
Chef: Susan Elliott
Owner: Charles Garside
Cost: Set-price L £15 (Sun £18.50)/D £35 . H/wine £18.50
Times: 1-1.30pm/D at 8pm.
Additional: Sunday L; Children 8+
Seats: 64. Jacket & tie preferred
Style: Country-house
Smoking: No smoking in dining room; Air conditioning
Civil licence: 64
Accommodation: 12 en suite ★ ★

One of the Lake District's most popular hotels, the stunning views over Windermere through the large glass windows are reflected on a mirrored wall. The decor remains Italianate in style with a honey-coloured limestone floor, verdigris wrought iron, golden ceilings and magnificent trompe l'oeil. In addition to the famous, orchestrated set dinner, lights dimmed and everyone served simultaneously, guests now have extra choice that also caters for vegetarians and special diets. Dinner might begin with seared foie gras on oven-baked black pudding with spiced apple chutney, sherry vinegar Puy lentil sauce and deep-fried sage, followed by poached fillet of salmon on a lime, chilli, ginger and red chard stirfry with honey soy sesame jus and pickled pink ginger. The dessert menu usually includes sticky toffee pudding à la John Tovey. Bucks Fizz for breakfast.

Directions: On A592 between Windermere and Bowness

WINDERMERE, Storrs Hall Hotel

Cooking with an accent on flavour at this elegant Georgian mansion overlooking Windermere. Wonderfully gamey pigeon breast was followed by pot-roasted chicken and a chocolate-almond tart.

Additional: Bar food L; Sunday L; Children 12 +
Style: Classic/Country-house
Smoking: No smoking in dining room; Jacket & tie preferred
Accommodation: 18 en suite ★ ★ ★

Directions: On A592, 2 miles S of Bowness on the Newby Bridge Road

Bowness-on-Windermere LA23 3LG
Map 7: SD49
Tel: 015394 47111
Fax: 015394 47555
E-mail: reception@storrshall.co.uk
Cost: Set-price L £15/D £32.
H/wine £12
Times: Noon-2pm/7-9pm.
Closed Jan

WINDERMERE, Wild Boar Hotel

Plush, comfortable restaurant in a traditional coaching inn. The carte shows focus and skill, and dishes might include roast fillet of lamb, fricasée of asparagus, button mushrooms and artichokes, or pan-fried Dover sole.

Directions: 2.5m S of Windermere. Take B5284 towards Crook. Hotel on R after 3.5m

Crook LA23 3NF
Map 7: SD49
Tel: 015394 45225
Fax: 015394 42498
E-mail: wildboar@ehl.co.uk

Telephone for further details

WITHERSLACK,
Old Vicarage Hotel

Church Road Grange-Over-Sands
LA11 6RS
Map 7: SD48
Tel: 015395 52381
Fax: 015395 52373
E-mail: hotel@oldvicarage.com
Cost: *Alc* £28, set-price L £12.50 & £15.50/D £12.50. ☺ H/wine £11.50
Times: D only, 6-9pm.
Additional: Sun L (12.30-2pm); Children 10+
Style: Country-house
Smoking: No smoking in dining room
Accommodation: 13 en suite ★ ★

A Georgian country house hotel set in a peaceful, unspoiled Lakeland valley. A recent inspection meal took in cream of artichoke and sea salad, grilled breast of Gressingham duck, and crème brûlée with damsons.

Directions: From M6 J36 take A590 to Barrow. Sign for Witherslack on R. 1st L after phone box

DERBYSHIRE

ASHBOURNE, Callow Hall ❀❀

Mappleton Road DE6 2AA
Map 7: SK14
Tel: 01335 300900
Fax: 01335 300512
E-mail: enquiries@callowhall.co.uk
Chefs: David & Anthony Spencer
Owners: David, Dorothy &
Anthony Spencer
Cost: *Alc* £39.50, set-price L
£20.50/D £38. H/wine £11.75
Times: D only, 7.30-9.15pm.
Closed D Sun, 25 & 26 Dec
Additional: Sunday L (12.30-1.45pm);
Children welcome
Seats: 60. Private dining room 24;
Jacket & tie preferred
Style: Country-house
Smoking: No smoking in dining room
Accommodation: 16 en suite ★ ★ ★

Anthony Spencer is certainly stamping his own personality on the menu at Callow Hall but this guide stalwart has never faltered in its consistency and style. During the Spencer family's 18 years at Callow they have transformed this outwardly stern, grey stone Victorian hall into an oasis of warmth and welcome. The romantic dining room with its traditional country house feel sees diners clamouring to sample assured dishes such as asparagus spears with a confit of peppers and tomato, Parmesan and balsamic dressing. Meaty confits also make an appearance and the duck leg paired with caramelised apple and redcurrant jelly showed an awareness of the few occasions when it is sensible to combine meat with fruit. Home dried tomatoes are also a frequent partner for fish; served with tapenade and either halibut or cod which has been gently baked to produce succulent, moist fish. Puddings also impress; an inspector praised the 'unusual twist on bread and butter pudding' that was warm bread and almond pudding with an Amaretto creme Anglaise.

Directions: 0.75 mile from Ashbourne; A515 (Buxton), sharp L by Bowling Green Pub, 1st R Mappleton Road

ASHFORD-IN-THE-WATER,
Riverside House Hotel ❀❀

'Updated classics' perhaps best describes the dishes on offer at this lovely country house retreat. Standing beside the river Wye in its own lovingly cared for mature gardens, Riverside House dates back to 1630. The oak panelled dining room is the setting for a cuisine that continues to develop and improve. John Whelan's inventive yet restrained food brings lots of classic influences firmly into the 21st century. Squab pigeon came cooked 'perfectly pink' with wilted spinach and 'an unusual yet clever' vanilla scented potato galette. That modern classic smoked haddock with welsh rarebit was reworked as a terrine and showed 'a lovely balance of texture and subtle flavours'. Pan-fried loin of veal comes with time tested partners parsnips and risotto but the spin here was rather more modish. The risotto was of pearl barley and the parsnips were sliced into crisps. Puddings too range from the classic (witness hot coffee

Fennel Street Bakewell
DE45 1QF
Map 7: SK17
Tel: 01629 814275
Fax: 01629 812873
E-mail: riversidehouse@enta.net
Chef: John Whelan
Owner: Penelope Thornton Hotels Ltd
Cost: *Alc* £35, set-price L £16.95/D
£26. ☺ H/wine £16
Times: Noon-2pm/7-9.30pm
Additional: Bar food; Sunday L;
Children 12+
Seats: 40. Private dining room 24
Style: Classic/Country-house
Smoking: No smoking in dining room
Civil licence: 300

Riverside House Hotel

Accommodation: 15 en suite ★★★

Directions: 2 miles from centre of Bakewell on A6 (Buxton). In Ashford village next to Sheepwash Bridge

souffle with amaretti biscuits and almond Anglaise) to the slavishly current: apple crumble mousse with green apple sorbet, apple sauce and dried apple crisps.

BAKEWELL,
Croft Country House Hotel

Relax in this delightfully intimate country house in the heart of the Peak District. Balanced set menu boasts chicken with mushroom and thyme sauce or tomato tarte Tatin, all made from fresh ingredients.

Directions: A6 from Bakewell towards Buxton, 1.7 miles turn R (A6020). After 0.75 mile turn L signed Great Longstone. Hotel on R in village.

Great Longstone DE45 1TF
Map 8: SK26
Tel: 01629 640278
Cost: Set-price D £26.50 .
H/wine £8.75
Times: D only, at 7.30pm.
Closed New Year
Style: Country-house
Smoking: No smoking in dining room
Accommodation: 9 en suite ★★

BAKEWELL,
Renaissance Restaurant

A tasteful barn conversion that really comes into its own in the summer months with its delightful walled garden, but serves top quality cuisine all year round such as a well-sourced, perfectly cooked cut of venison.

Style: Classic/Traditional
Smoking: No smoking in dining room

Directions: From Bakewell roundabout in town centre take A6 Buxton exit. 1st R into Bath Street (one-way)

Bath Street DE45 1BX
Map 8: SK26
Tel: 01629 812687
Cost: Alc £21.55, set-price D £12.95.
☺ H/wine £10.99
Times: Noon-2pm/7-10pm. Closed D Sun, all Mon, 1st 2 wks Jan & Aug
Additional: Bar food L; Sunday L; Children welcome

BAKEWELL, Rutland Arms Hotel

Historic hotel in the heart of Bakewell offering an interesting menu; dishes might include pan-fried medallions of venison loin with peppered fresh berries, and roast quail stuffed with duck.

Style: Chic/Elegant
Smoking: No smoking in dining room
Accommodation: 35 en suite ★★★

Directions: In the town centre opposite war memorial. Parking opposite side entrance

The Square DE45 1BT
Map 8: SK26
Tel: 01629 812812
Fax: 01629 812309
E-mail: rutland@bakewell.demon.co.uk
Cost: Set-price D £19.50. ☺
H/wine £9.50
Times: Noon-2.15pm/7-9pm
Additional: Bar food; Sunday L; Children welcome

BASLOW,
Cavendish Hotel ❀

Country house hotel on the edge of the Chatsworth estate. Try fresh asparagus strudel, or perhaps marinated sea bass, followed by sirloin of Castlegate beef stuffed with foie gras. Finish with hot fig Tatin and cardamom ice cream.

Bakewell DE45 1SP
Map 8: SK27
Tel: 01246 582311
Fax: 01246 582312
Email: info:@cavendish-hotel.net

Cost: Set-price L £30.50/D £38.75. H/wine £17.50
Times: 12.30-2pm/7-10pm
Additional: Sunday L; Children welcome
Style: Classic/Formal
Smoking: No smoking in dining room
Accommodation: 24 en suite ★ ★ ★

Directions: In the centre of Baslow village

BASLOW,
Fischer's Baslow Hall ❀❀❀

Calver Road DE45 1RR
Map 8: SK27
Tel: 01246 583259
Fax: 01246 583818
Chef: Max Fischer
Owners: Max & Susan Fischer
Cost: Set-price L £20 & £24/D £45.
H/wine £13
Times: Noon-2pm/7-9.30pm.
Closed L Sat, D Sun, 25-26 Dec
Additional: Sunday L; Children 12+
after 7pm
Seats: 40. Private dining rooms 12 &
24. Jacket & tie preferred
Style: Country-house/Formal
Smoking: No smoking in dining room
Civil licence: 70
Accommodation: 6 en suite ★ ★

The Derbyshire manor house stands in five acres of gardens, including a wonderful potager. Inside, the lavish use of fabrics reflects Max Fischer's individual style, and the public rooms are also home to his personal collection of paintings and antiques. His individual style of cooking is rooted in the classics but given wing by the use of seasonal elements and garden flavours, and by skilled saucing. Rabbit saddle wrapped in Parma ham is served on pea purée with girolles; veal loin with Madeira jus has a farce of pistachio and morel mushrooms; roast breast of duckling is simply paired by fresh spring cabbage. Duck sausage – a light mousse studded with pieces of rich confit – on perfectly seared foie gras with cannellini bean panaché was 'absolutely delicious'. Fish of the day, perfectly timed and of top-top quality roast sea bass, came with leaf spinach, baby artichokes and lovely, buttery crushed potatoes. Poached Yorkshire forced rhubarb is layered with lemon nougat glace and served with strawberry sorbet. Service is friendly and attentive, professional but unpretentious. Café-Max offers more bistro-style food such as risotto with fresh peas and mint, Derbyshire Dales bronze chicken breast with roast vegetables and slow-braised belly of pork with honey glaze on celeriac purée.

Directions: From Baslow on A623 towards Calver. Hotel on R

BELPER,

Makeney Hall Hotel

Conservatory restaurant overlooking landscaped gardens to the
Derwent Valley. Main courses range from creamy artichoke and
truffle risotto to haunch of venison with orange and juniper crumb.

Smoking: No smoking in dining room; Air conditioning
Civil licence: 120 **Accommodation:** 45 en suite ★ ★ ★

Directions: Join A6 N of Derby & turn R into Milford. Hotel is
0.25 mile, just past Garden Centre

Makeney Milford DE56 0RS
Map 8: SK34
Tel: 01332 842999
Fax: 01332 842777
Cost: Alc £24, set-price L £11.50/
D £18.50. H/wine £11.50
Times: Noon-2pm/7-10pm.
Closed L Sat, D Sat (ex residents)
Additional: Bar food; Sunday L;
Children welcome
Style: Country-house

BUXTON, **Best Western**
Lee Wood Hotel

Dinner is served either in the large conservatory or the more
traditional dining-room, with tasty canapés fresh from the oven
offered over drinks in the bar beforehand. The menu is
extremely lengthy, sometimes a worrying sign, but our
inspection visit revealed a proficient kitchen that was working
well. Tortellini with salmon and dill was well-flavoured, lacking
only sufficient sauce to do it justice; a correctly made smoked
chicken and leek consommé was rich and savoury; and to
follow, a top quality pork fillet was served with excellent sage,
cider and cream sauce plus an unusual, savoury apricot and
ginger crumble. To finish, we enjoyed an ultra light passion
fruit mousse with seasonal fruit sauce. The speciality menu
includes lobster Thermidor and Scotch steaks, and we remain
intrigued by a novel starter dish on the main *carte* – hot
Derbyshire oatcake folded over bacon and scrambled egg,
edged with a HP sauce gravy. Well, he who dares, wins!

Directions: Follow A5004 Long Hill to Whaley Bridge. Hotel
approx 200 metres beyond the Devonshire Royal Hospital on L

The Park SK17 6TQ
Map 7: SK07
Tel: 01298 23002
Fax: 01298 23228
E-mail: leewoodhotel@btinternet.com
Chef: Chris Bates
Owner: John Millican
Cost: Alc £27, set-price D £24.50. ☺
H/wine £11.50
Times: 12.15pm-2pm/7.15-9.30pm
Additional: Bar food; Sunday L;
Children welcome
Seats: 80. Private dining room 12/24
Style: Conservatory
Smoking: No-smoking area; No pipes
& cigars
Civil Licence: 120
Accommodation: 40 en suite ★ ★ ★

DARLEY ABBEY,
Darleys Restaurant

The River Derwent in full spate is a sight to inspire awe and
the inspector who visited Darleys recalls his visit was
unforgettable for that backdrop alone. Ian Wilson's

Darley Abbey Mill DE22 1DZ
Map 8: SK33
Tel/Fax: 01332 364987
E-mail: davidpinchbeck@hotmail.com
Chef: Ian Wilson
Owner: David Pinchbeck
Cost: Alc £35, set-price L £14.50/D
£22. ☺ H/wine £14
Times: Noon-2.30pm/7-10pm.
Closed D Sun, Bhs
Additional: Sunday L; Children
welcome
Seats: 70
Style: Modern/Stylish
Smoking: No-smoking area ; Air
conditioning

accomplished food is the cause of many happy memories too. Fresh, sunny flavours like salad niçoise with char grilled aubergine, yoghurt and parmesan dressing jostle for position with comforting traditional British combinations such as lamb and rosemary sausage with pease pudding and shallot gravy. Technical skills are tested with such dishes as an 'earthy and fragrant' wild mushroom risotto with fried quail egg, truffle oil and crisp leeks. Puddings too attract much praise but tend to be a little less involved than the hot food. Chilled chocolate terrine with Amaretto cappuccino reads intriguingly and caramelised rhubarb brûlée with ginger biscuits proved hard to resist.

Directions: From Derby take A6 N. Darley Abbey is signed on R. Restaurant is adjacent to river over a single lane bridge

Darleys Restaurant

DERBY, Menzies
Mickleover Court Hotel ❀

Brasserie restaurant in an impressive modern hotel. Saffron and wild mushroom risoto and delice of salmon with parsley mash jostle for attention amongst a varied, high quality range of dishes.

Etwall Road Mickleover DE3 5XX
Map 8: SK33
Tel: 01332 521234
Fax: 01332 521238
E-mail: info@menzies-hotels.co.uk

Cost: Alc £23. ☺ H/wine £12
Times: 12.30-2.30pm/7-10pm
Additional: Bar food; Sunday L; Children welcome
Style: Bistro/Modern
Smoking: No-smoking area; Air conditioning
Civil licence: 140
Accommodation: 100 en suite ★★★★

Directions: From Mickleover take A516 (Uttoxeter) hotel is L of 1st roundabout

DOVERIDGE, The Beeches
Farmhouse Hotel ❀❀

Doveridge DE6 5LR
Map 7: SK13
Tel: 01889 590288
Fax: 01889 590559
E-mail: beechesfa@aol.com
Chef: Barbara Tunnicliffe
Owners: Barbara & Paul Tunnicliffe
Cost: Alc £34. H/wine £10.50

Barbara Tunnicliffe's accomplished cooking has been rightly getting a lot of press attention recently. Inspectors have been impressed by the daring and precision of such dishes as fillets of John Dory with a praline top described as 'quirky but really successful adding an intriguing bitter sweetness'. The fish came with fondant potato, spiced savoy cabbage and a 'superb' spinach mousse. Impressive starters have included an 'succulent' duck breast filled with wild mushrooms and a fricassée of root vegetables. Puddings took in a well constructed assiette of lemon and raspberry.

Directions: From A50 take exit sighposted Doveridge and follow signs for Waldley. At grass triangle turn R; hotel is 1st L

Times: Noon-2pm/7-9pm.
Closed 24-26 Dec
Additional: Sunday L;
Children welcome
Seats: 65. Private dining room
Style: Traditional/Country-house
Smoking: No smoking in dining room
Accommodation: 10 en suite

HATHERSAGE,
The George at Hathersage ❀

The interior of this restaurant is a blend of Old English and Mediterranean styles which provide a warm informal atmosphere. Contemporary menu includes everything from smoked chicken salad to ham knuckle and foie gras terrine.

Style: Informal/Innovative
Smoking: No smoking in dining room
Accommodation: 19 en suite ★ ★ ★

Directions: In village centre on A625

Main Road S32 1BB
Map 8: SK28
Tel: 01433 650436
Fax: 01433 650099
E-mail: info@george-hotel.net
Cost: Alc £25-£30, set-price L £19.50/D £22. ☺ H/wine £13.75
Times: 12.30-2.30pm/7-10pm
Additional: Bar food L; Sunday L; Children welcome

HATHERSAGE,
Hathersage Inn Hotel ❀

Stone-built inn, with friendly staff and an interesting menu. Begin perhaps with a Parmesan basket filled with Brie and tomato salad, followed by fillet of plaice stuffed with crab mousse. Finish with citrus and almond pudding.

Directions: In centre of village on A625

Main Road S32 1BB
Map 8: SK28
Tel: 01433 650259
Fax: 01433 651199

Telephone for further details

MATLOCK, Riber Hall ❀❀

Tansley DE4 5JU
Map 8: SK35
Tel: 01629 582795
Fax: 01629 580475
E-mail: info@riber-hall.co.uk
Chef: John Bradshaw
Owner: Alex Biggin
Cost: Set-price L £13 & £16/D £25-£34. ☺ H/wine £14.75
Times: Noon-1.30pm/7-9.30pm

This lovely Elizabethan manor house sits at the base of the Pennines in a carefully tended walled garden. Period style is the thing here, but the food is far more up to date, although both British and French classical traditions are shown the respect they deserve. The fresh sunny flavours of dishes like terrine of leek, potato and red mullet with a tomato and herb dressing contrast nicely with more comfortingly traditional notes of breast of pheasant with sauté cabbage, glazed chestnuts and a brandy sauce. Puddings show ambition too, the ubiquitous assiette of chocolate this time including a glorious milk chocolate sorbet and also a rich marquise and white chocolate sauce.

Directions: One mile up Alders Lane and Carr Lane off A615 at Tansley

Additional: Bar food L; Sunday L; Children welcome
Seats: 60. Private dining rooms; Jacket & tie preferred
Style: Country-house
Smoking: No smoking in dining room
Civil licence: 50
Accommodation: 14 en suite ★ ★ ★

MELBOURNE, The Bay Tree ❀

Former 17th-century coaching inn. Interesting dishes might include beef carpaccio with quails' egg salad, followed by Dover sole wrapped around homemade crab meat sausage, or calves' liver with pancetta and onion rings.

Directions: Town centre

4 Potter Street DE73 1DW
Map 8: SK32
Tel: 01332 863358
Fax: 01332 865545

Telephone for further details

RIDGEWAY, The Old Vicarage ❀❀❀

The dining-room has a new look, painted in toning shades of butter yellow which acts as a backdrop for the large, vibrant wildflower paintings. The floor is stripped oak and the beautiful large sash windows with their original internal shutters have been left unadorned to offer maximum light. Tessa Bramley's clever, seasonal menus display a gentle touch and a subtlety of flavouring. Wok-cooked king scallops with ginger and lime chinese greens and caramelised pecans was a balanced combination of sweet and sour flavours. Beautifully seared foie gras topped a thin slice of top quality calves' liver, which in turn was set on a bed of divinely delicious champ. Tender braised red cabbage and shredded Savoy made a clever interplay of textures, colours and flavours, and the saucing was richly flavoured but not overpowering. An incredibly light and delicately flavoured rhubarb and ginger soufflé had a kick in the tail – a hidden purée which socked the senses. This was served with a small tangerine-flavoured cream and a brandy snap of rhubarb sorbet, all perfectly judged and harmonious. There is also an impressive selection of British and Irish cheeses. The comprehensive wine list includes about 20 interesting halves. Look out for some competitively priced bin end selections. Service, as ever, is slick and attentive.

Ridgeway Moor S12 3XW
Map 8: SK48
Tel: 01142 475814
Fax: 01142 477079
E-mail: eat@theoldvicarage.co.uk
Chefs: Tessa Bramley, Nathan Smith, Andrew Gilbert
Owner: Tessa Bramley
Cost: Set-price L/D £30 & £43. H/wine £16.50
Times: 12.30-2.30pm/7-10.30pm. Closed L Sat, D Sun, all Mon, 26 Dec, 31 Dec, 1 Jan
Additional: Sunday L; Children welcome
Seats: 50. Private dining room 24
Style: Chic/Modern
Smoking: No smoking in dining room
Civil licence: 65

Directions: SE of Sheffield off A616 on B6054; follow signs for Ridgeway Cottage Industries. Restaurant is 300yds on L

RISLEY, Risley Hall Hotel ❀❀

A series of small dining rooms ensures intimacy whatever the level of business. All rooms are country house in style and feature white linen, good glassware and attractive crockery. On a recent inspection simple but pleasing canapés such as stuffed cherry tomato and a mini beef kebab began the evening nicely. A starter of fresh asparagus on rocket with Jersey royals and Parmesan demonstrated careful execution of good quality fresh ingredients. A gold head sea bream was perfectly fresh and well timed and, when set on wide strips of steamed carrots and new pots, constituted an excellent main dish. A dessert of lemon tart combined good zesty cream with enjoyable pastry. An accompaniment of well flavoured mandarin sorbet worked well. Overall an excellent meal in an appealing establishment.

Derby Road DE72 3SS
Map 8: SK43
Tel: 01159 399000
Fax: 01159 397766

Telephone for further details.

Directions: From M1 J25 take Sandiacre exit, L at T-junct, 0.5 miles on L

ROWSLEY, East Lodge Hotel

A Victorian lodge standing in ten acres of attractive grounds. A generally traditional approach and an eye for quality results in dishes such as wild berry brûlée and honey roasted duckling with a black cherry sauce.

Additional: Bar food L; Sunday L; Children 5+
Style: Country-house
Smoking: No smoking in dining room; Air conditioning
Civil licence: 70
Accommodation: 15 en suite ★★★

Directions: Hotel drive access on A6, 5 miles from Matlock and 3 miles from Bakewell

DE4 2EF
Map 8: SK26
Tel: 01629 734474
Fax: 01629 733949
E-mail: info@eastlodge.com
Cost: Set-price L £12.95/D £22.95. ☺
H/wine £9.95
Times: Noon-2pm/7-9.30pm

SOUTH NORMANTON,
Swallow Hotel ✦

Modern hotel where the heptagonal Pavilion restaurant offers contemporary-style cooking, including a robust fish soup with rouille, and a well textured fillet of beef.

Additional: Sunday L; Children welcome
Style: Classic/formal
Smoking: Air conditioning
Civil licence: 80
Accommodation: 160 en suite

Directions: From M1 J28 – A38 (signed Mansfield). After 100 yds 1st L into car park

Carter Lane East DE55 2EH
Map 8: SK45
Tel: 01773 812000
Fax: 01773 580032
Cost: Alc fr £24.95. ☺ H/wine £12
Times: 12.30-2pm/7-9.45pm.
Closed L Mon-Sat

THORPE,
Izaak Walton Hotel ✦

Ashbourne DE6 2AY
Map 7: SK15
Tel: 01335 350555
Fax: 01335 350539
E-mail: reception@izaakwalton-hotel.com
Cost: Set-price L £15/D £24. ☺
H/wine £11.25
Times: D only, 7.30-9.30pm.
Additional: Bar food; Sunday L (12.30-2pm); Children welcome
Style: Classic/Country-house
Smoking: No smoking in dining room
Civil licence: 70
Accommodation: 30 en suite ★★★

17th-century hotel, with breathtaking views of the Dovedale Valley from the Haddon Restaurant. Typical dishes are scallops Selina, char-grilled beef Belinda, and Swiss lemon cheesecake.

Directions: One mile W of Thorpe on the Ilam road

DEVON

ASHBURTON,
Holne Chase Hotel ❀❀❀

Two Bridges Road, Newton Abbot
TQ13 7NS
Map 3: SX77
Tel: 01364 631471
Fax: 01364 631453
E-mail: info@holne-chase.co.uk
Chefs: Ross Hadley, Philippa Hughes
Owners: Sebastian & Philippa Hughes
Cost: Set-price L £20-£25/D £32.50.
H/wine £11.50
Times: Noon-2pm/7.15-8.45pm
Additional: Bar food L; Sunday L;
Children 10+ at D
Seats: 40. Private dining room 12
Style: Country-house
Smoking: No smoking in dining room
Accommodation: 17 en suite ★★★

Idyllic setting in the Dart Valley for this former hunting lodge,
where the formal dining room overlooks the extensive
grounds. The atmosphere is relaxed and service friendly and
efficient. An early summer meal began with duck ravioli with
vanilla oil and stir fry – two portions of ravioli with 'deliciously
flavoured' confit of duck, served on oriental vegetables. This
was followed by a duo of Devon beef with roasted root
vegetables and red wine sauce. The beef was excellent, and
offered a good contrast of textures – one succulent rarer side
of medium fillet, together with a piece of braised shoulder.
Passion fruit cheescake to finish was delightfully presented,
with a full-flavoured filling and served with a clear vanilla
syrup. Petits fours included truffles, fudge and macaroons.

Directions: Travelling N & E, take 2nd Ashburton turn off A38.
2 miles to Holne Bridge, hotel is 0.25 miles on R. From
Plymouth take 1st Ashburton turn

AXMINSTER,
Fairwater Head Hotel ❀

Hawkchurch EX13 5TX
Map 3: SY29
Tel: 01297 678349
Fax: 01297 678459

Telephone for further details

Views over the Axe Valley distinguish this friendly country house
hotel. The daily set menu based on local ingredients offers winning
choices like duck with orange and cointreau sauce, and worthwhile
desserts.

Directions: Turn off B3165 (Crewkerne to Lyme Regis Road)
hotel signposted to Hawkchurch

AXMINSTER,

Lea Hill Hotel

The 14th-century Devon long-house has all the right period trimmings – beams, stone floors – plus a peaceful rural location. The food, however, is a fresh blast of modern ideas. James Hubbard's cooking shows tremendous composure, aesthetic precision and deftness – and there are no superfluous additions, an admirable trait. Our autumn inspection meal produced an impressive starter of seared scallops served with a sweet pepper couscous and pesto, a dish that was all about flavour and balance. Fresh monkfish, baked with rosemary and garlic, was made by the close attention to detail that produced a silky smooth mash and beautifully judged vinaigrette, which provided a cutting top note. Assiette of Lea Hill desserts showed the same dedication: sensibly delicate portions of melt-in-your-mouth pastry work that included bread-and-butter pudding, pecan tart, and mixed berries ice cream in a brandy snap basket. The level of commitment and dexterity shows through in small details: good flavoured breads, memorable canapés, and excellent petits fours.

Directions: From Axminster follow A358 towards Chard. After 2 miles turn L to Smallridge and follow signs to Membury. 0.5m on R after village.

Membury EX13 7AQ
Map 3: SY29
Tel: 01404 881881
Fax: 01404 881890
E-mail: leahillhotel.co.uk
Chef: James Hubbard
Owners: Mr & Mrs C Hubbard
Cost: Set-price D £27. H/wine £11.50
Times: D only, 7-9pm.
Closed D Sun, Jan-Feb
Additional: Bar food L; Children 12+
Seats: 30. Private dining room 12
Style: Traditional/Country-house
Smoking: No smoking in dining room
Accommodation: 11 en suite ★ ★

BAMPTON,

Bark House Hotel

The beautiful Exe Valley provides a suitable backdrop for this cottage-style hotel set in a delightful tiered garden. Inside the beamed restaurant the atmosphere is understated and simple, with tasteful white linen, polished glassware and leather chairs suggesting a traditional attitude to dining. A short set menu offers little choice, but dishes are designed around the very best of fresh ingredients, and flavours are generally accurate and enjoyable. Imaginative starters might include pear and watercress soup served with light and soft milk rolls, or courgette terrine with a sweet pepper and onion confit, to be followed perhaps by a moist steamed pudding of lamb and kidney, a dish packed with tender meat and a decent gravy. Fish often features on the menu, and fillet of turbot was obviously fresh, and served with a well-made dill sauce. Basil ice cream scored top marks with the inspector for its creamy consistency and perfect herb flavour, while a meringue nest with cream, fresh raspberries and strawberry coulis came a close second.

Directions: 9 miles N of Tiverton on A396

Oakford Bridge Tiverton EX16 9HZ
Map 3: SS92
Tel: 01398 351236
Chef/Owner: Alastair Kameen
Cost: Set-price L £15.75 by arrangement only /D £21.50. ☺
H/wine £8.75
Times: 12.30-1.30pm/7.15-9pm.
Closed D Mon-Wed, restricted in winter
Additional: Children 7+
Seats: 14
Style: Traditional/Country-house
Smoking: No smoking in dining room
Accommodation: 5 rooms (4 en suite)
★ ★
Credit cards: None

BARNSTAPLE,

Halmpstone Manor

This historical manor, now a country-house hotel, is set in its own gardens off a country lane amid rolling farmland. Dinner in the panelled and candlelit restaurant is a five-course affair with no choice until dessert, which follows a selection of cheeses. A soup might start things off – carrot and coriander,

Bishop's Tawton
EX32 0EA
Map 2: SS53
Tel: 01271 830321
Fax: 01271 830826
Chef: Jane Stanbury
Owners: Mr & Mrs C Stanbury

say, or, in season, asparagus – followed by something fishy such as Clovelly scallops with a cream and white wine sauce, or sea bass with herbs. Lamb or beef might figure as main courses; otherwise there could be chicken breast with duxelle, or guinea fowl roasted with lime, accompanied by as many as five vegetables. We finished our meal with apple crumble and local clotted cream, before rounding things off with coffee and mints.

Directions: From Barnstaple take A377 to Bishop's Tawton. At end of village turn L for Cobbaton; sign on R

Cost: Set-price D £32.50.
H/wine £9.80
Times: D only, 7-9pm.
Closed Nov-Jan
Seats: 24. Jacket & tie preferred
Style: Classic/Country-house
Smoking: No smoking in dining room
Accommodation: 5 en suite ★ ★

BARNSTAPLE, Royal & Fortesque Hotel, The Bank

Former bank with ornate plasterwork ceilings and oak-panelled walls. It offers a brasserie-style menu with choices ranging from baguettes to special fish, pasta and Mexican dishes.

Additional: Children welcome
Style: Bistro/Informal
Accommodation: 50 en suite ★ ★ ★

Directions: A361 into Barnstaple, along Barbican Rd signposted town centre; turn R into Queen St & L (one way) Boutport St. Hotel on L

Boutport Street EX31 1HG
Map: 2: SS53
Tel: 01271 324446
Fax: 01271 342289
Cost: Alc £16. ☺ H/wine £9.75
Times: 11-10.30pm.
Closed Sun, 25 & 26 Dec, 1 Jan

BEER, Old Steam Bakery Restaurant

Sarah and Michael Stride bring flavours of the Pacific Rim to their easygoing restaurant. This former bakery retains a sense of history with its mullioned windows but the cuisine is right up to date. Michael is not afraid to mix up his influences and the results of these cocktails are very successful indeed. Classics such as roast rack of lamb with spinach, rösti potato, black truffle and port jus sit comfortably aside more avant-garde offerings. Chicken with ginger, coriander and lemongrass comes with Thai broth and rice noodles. Locally landed seafood is a favourite here and is shown to great advantage in such assured dishes as a warm sushi of scallops with nori, mousseline of fish and a wasabi beurre blanc. Desserts are kept fairly straightforward and tend to be more classical in style but who can resist a perfect soufflé or lemon tart?

Directions: Turn off A3052 (Exeter to Lyme Regis). Beer is 2 miles from Seaton.

Fore Street EX12 3JJ
Map 3: SY28
Tel: 01297 22040
Fax: 01297 625886
Chef: Michael Stride
Owners: Michael Stride & Sarah Doak-Stride
Cost: Set-price L £18.50/D £27.50. ☺
H/wine £10.50
Times: Noon-2.30pm/7-10.30pm(10pm in winter).
Closed L Mon,Wed & Sat, all Tue.
Opening times differ in winter
Additional: Children welcome
Seats: 38-40
Style: Informal/Rustic
Smoking: No-smoking area; No pipes & cigars

BIDEFORD, Yeoldon Country House Hotel

Victorian manor house hotel offering an imaginative choice of dishes based on fresh local produce. The highlight was supreme of chicken with cream cheese, spinach and wild mushroom sauce.

Directions: From Barnstaple take A39 towards Bideford. Take 3rd R into Durrant Lane. Hotel 0.25m

Durrant Lane Northam EX39 2RL
Map 2: SS42
Tel: 01237 474400
Fax: 01237 476618

Telephone for further details

BOVEY TRACEY,

Edgemoor Hotel ❀❀

Haytor Road
Lowerdown Cross
TQ13 9LE
Map 3: SX87
Tel: 01626 832466
Fax: 01626 834760
E-mail: edgemoor@btinternet.com
Chef: Edward Elliott
Owners: Pat & Rod Day
Cost: Set-price L £16.95/D £24.50. ☺
H/wine £8.45.
Times: 12.15-1.45pm/7pm-9pm.
Closed 1 wk at New Year

The Edgemoor, in a previous existence, was once the Bovey Tracey Grammar School, but school meals were never like this. The menu changes monthly; January, for example, included pan-fried pigeon breast dressed with blackberry sauce topped with toasted pinenuts, and fillet of pork rolled in honey and mustard with a caramelised apple and cider and mustard sauce. Raw ingredients are carefully chosen. There is a daily changing fish selection and, sometimes, more unusual items such as a ragout of local venison, ostrich and wild boar in a rich red wine sauce served in a puff pastry diamond. Desserts are not for the faint-hearted; a raspberry and cream eclair with a warm chocolate sauce was at least a foot in length.

Additional: Sunday L; Children 10+
Seats: 30. Private dining room 8
Style: Country-house
Smoking: No smoking in dining room
Accommodation: 17 en suite ★ ★ ★

Directions: From A38 take A382 (Drumbridges). Cross first mini roundabout & turn L at 2nd roundabout. Bear L towards Haytor. Hotel 0.25 mile on R

BRANSCOMBE,

The Masons Arms ❀

EX12 3DJ
Map 3: SY18
Tel: 01297 680300
Fax: 01297 680500
E-mail: reception@masonsarms.co.uk
Cost: Set-price D £24. H/wine £11
Times: D only, 7-8.45pm

Charming 14th-century village inn with character and characters. Nooks and crannies provide an atmospheric setting for honest cooking that draws heavily upon excellent local seafood. Good wine list.

Additional: Bar food; Sunday L; Children 10+
Style: Traditional/Rustic
Smoking: No smoking in dining room
Accommodation: 22 rooms (most en suite) ★ ★

Directions: Turn off A3052 (Exeter to Lyme Regis) and follow road through Branscombe

BRIXHAM, **Maypool Park** ⊛

Galmpton TQ5 0ET
Map 3: SX95
Tel: 01803 842442
Fax: 01803 845782
E-mail: peacock@maypoolpark.co.uk
Cost: Alc £24, Set-price D £19.50. ☺
H/wine £8.25
Times: D only 7-9pm
Additional: Bar food L; Sunday L
(noon-2pm); Children 12+
Style: Country-house
Smoking: No smoking in dining room
Accommodation: 10 en suite ★ ★

Pleasant country hotel with great views and a nice balance of relaxed formality in the dining room. Crab en cocotte, chicken with crab and vermouth, and San Diego ice pie revealed good combinations of fresh ingredients and sound cooking skills.

Directions: Turn off A3022 at Churston into Manor Vale Road for Maypool, pedestrian ferry and Greenway Quay and continue for 2 miles

BRIXHAM, **Quayside Hotel** ⊛

41-49 King Street TQ5 9TJ
Map 3: SX95
Tel: 01803 855751
Fax: 01803 882733
E-mail: quayside.hotel@virgin.net
Cost: Alc £25, set-price D £18. ☺
H/wine £10
Times: D only, 7-9.30pm
Additional: Bar food; Children 14+
Style: Classic/Chic
Smoking: No smoking in dining room
Accommodation: 29 en suite ★ ★ ★

Directions: From Exeter take the
A380 towards Torquay, then A3022
to Brixham. Hotel overlooks harbour

Hotel created from six period fisherman's cottages with views over the harbour. In the intimate restaurant local seafood is a speciality, including lobster and Dover sole, alongside South Devon lamb.

BROADHEMBURY, **Drewe Arms** ⊛

Simplicity is the keynote at this ever-popular 15th-century cob and thatch inn. An enjoyable winter meal took in scallops with hollandaise and excellent, 'wonderfully fresh' bass with orange and chilli, followed by a silky toffee apple brûlée.

Additional: Bar food; Sunday L; Children welcome
Style: Informal
Smoking: No smoking in dining room
Credit cards: None

Directions: From M5 J28, 5 miles on A373 Cullompton to
Honiton. Pub 1 mile NE of Broadhembury turning

EX14 0NF
Map 3: ST10
Tel: 01404 841267
Fax: 01404 841765
E-mail: drewe.arms@btinternet.com
Chefs: Kerstin Burge, Andrew Burge
Owners: Nigel, Kerstin, &
Andrew Burge
Cost: Alc £25, set-price L/D £25. ☺
H/wine £10.50
Times: Noon-2pm/6-10pm. Closed D
Sun, 25 Dec

BURRINGTON, Northcote Manor

An idyllic setting, impressive grounds and the warmth and natural friendliness of the staff make this lovely gabled manor house a delightful place to stay. An innovative and interesting menu is offered in the Manor House restaurant, taking in dishes such as Tatin of endive topped with John Dory, pithivier of pheasant and terrine of ham hock with sauce gribiche. A summer starter of duck with sesame crackers and oriental stir-fry was followed by turbot with broad beans and morels – a 'very fresh', accurately cooked and enjoyable piece of fish. The simpler dishes stood out, where concentration on top quality produce resulted in consistent, successful flavour combinations. Apple tarte Tatin with clotted cream, for example, was 'great – spot on'. Excellent wine list.

Directions: Do not enter Burrington Village. Follow A377 (Barnstaple-Crediton road). Entrance opposite Portsmouth Arms railway station and pub

Umberleigh EX37 9LZ
Map 3: SS61
Tel: 01769 560501
Fax: 01769 560770
E-mail: rest@northcotemanor.co.uk
Chef: Chris Dawson
Owner: David Boddy
Cost: Set-price L £18.50/D £32.50. H/wine £12.50
Times: L until 2pm (booking essential), 7-9.30pm. Closed D Mon
Additional: Bar food L; Sunday L; Children 10+
Style: Country-house
Seats: 34. Private dining room 12; Jacket & tie preferred
Smoking: No smoking in dining room
Civil Licence: 50
Accommodation: 11 en suite ★★★

CHAGFORD, Gidleigh Park

Michael Caines might be branching out (see entry for The Royal Clarence, Exeter), but it's clear his roots are still firmly planted in Gidleigh Park. Anyone fearing a slip in standards as the chef spreads his considerable talent a little thinner can be reassured; there is no complacency evident from the Gidleigh kitchen. The legendary country house commands deep loyalty and affection, and indeed there is nowhere else quite like it. Similarly the cooking. There is little revolutionary here, and a glance at the menu reveals plenty of classical leanings. But, sometimes, it is not what is done but the way in which it is done that counts, and thus it is the depth of flavour, accuracy and deftness of touch that separate Caines from the crowd. A raviolo of langoustine with courgette tagliatelle, white wine sauce and basil oil may not sound earth-shattering as a concept, but our inspector was taken aback by the purity and balance of a dish which allowed the sweetest of shellfish to take centre stage. In the same vein, roast pigeon with a potato galette, pan-fried foie gras and a Madeira sauce that far outstripped its relatively low-key billing. If there is a supernova amongst these stars it is likely to come with the desserts which are masterpieces of balance and contrast. All this is allied to a wine list shot through with the enthusiasm of Paul Henderson. There's much to choose from and our advice is to take advantage of the articulate and knowledgeable staff.

Newton Abbot TQ13 8HH
Map 3: SX78
Tel: 01647 432367
Fax: 01647 432574
E-mail: gidleighpark@gidleigh.co.uk
Chef: Michael Caines
Owners: Paul & Kay Henderson
Cost: Set-price L £32/D £62.50. H/wine £22
Times: 12.30pm-2pm/7pm-9pm
Additional: Bar food L; Sunday L; Children 7+
Seats: 35. Private dining room 28
Style: Classic/Country-house
Smoking: No smoking in dining room
Accommodation: 15 en suite ★★★

Directions: Chagford Square turn R at Lloyds Bank into Mill Street, after 150 yd R fork, straight across crossroads into Holy Street. Restaurant is 1.5 miles

CHAGFORD, Mill End Hotel ❀❀

You don't have to worry about reserving a table with a view; every one in the 18th-century watermill restaurant has a splendid one, either looking out over the river or over the walled garden. The decor may be traditional, with linen napery and silver cutlery, but the cooking is modern British. A good play on the theme of duck and orange was enjoyed in a starter of duck terrine with spicy chutney, savoury citrus coulis and toasted brioche. Thoughtful ideas include salmon tart with salmon mousse finished with leeks and creamed saffron sauce, or a medallion of wild boar loin with parsnip mash and Calvados and apple sauce. The wine list has plenty of choice, including a good selection of half-bottles and a page of bin ends.

Directions: From A382 (Moretonhampstead) – don't turn into Chagford at Sandy Park

Sandy Park TQ13 8JN
Map 3: SX78
Tel: 01647 432282
Fax: 01647 433106
E-mail: millendhotel@talk21.com
Chef: Alan Lane
Owner: Keith A Green
Cost: Alc £27.50. H/wine £11
Times: 12.30-2pm/7.30-9pm.
Closed Jan
Additional: Bar food L; Sunday L;
Children 5+
Seats: 40. Jacket & tie at D
Style: Classic Country-house
Smoking: No smoking in dining room
Accommodation: 17 en suite ★★★

CHAGFORD, 22 Mill Street ❀❀

Amanda Leaman and Duncan Walker enjoy a lively trade at this shop-front restaurant. The unfussy two or three course set-price lunch menu offers choices such as warm globe artichoke heart with mushroom duxelle and hollandaise, followed by ragout of lambs liver, kidneys and loin with roast vegetables, then a hot raspberry souffle. The six course set menu is excellent value with dishes such as seared scallops in shellfish and pickled ginger consomme, asparagus hollandaise, grilled fillet of dartmoor beef with sauteed foie gras and madeira, three sorbets and bitter chocolate mousse with warm cherries and banana ice cream. The set two or three course dinner menu might feature seared fillet of tuna with salad of green beans, anchovies and quails eggs, or roast squab pigeon with shallot puree and port sauce.

22 Mill Street TQ13 8AW
Map 3: SX78
Tel: 01647 432244
Fax: 01647 433101

Telephone for further details

Directions: 200yds on L after turning R out of Chagford Square

CHITTLEHAMHOLT, Highbullen Hotel ❀

Imaginative country-house style food using fresh local ingredients – rustic textured game and pork terrine, seafood au gratin served with proper vegetables, and a good selection of home-made puddings.

Directions: From M5 J27 take A361 to South Molton, then B3226 (Crediton rd); after 5.2m turn R to Chittlehamholt. Hotel 0.5 mile beyond village

Umberleigh EX37 9HD
Map 3: SS62
Tel: 01769 540561
Fax: 01769 540492

Telephone for further details

CLOVELLY, Red Lion Hotel ❀

Eighteenth-century inn serving good local/regional produce – gateau of prawn and local crab, Cornish lamb with celeriac and rosemary mash, classic bouillabaisse of local fish, plus west country cheeses and, of course, clotted cream.

Smoking: No smoking in dining room
Accommodation: 11 en suite ★★

Directions: M5 J27. Leave A39 at Clovelly Cross onto B3237. At bottom of hill take 1st L by white railings to harbour

The Quay EX39 5TF
Map 2: SS32
Tel: 01237 431237
Fax: 01237 431044
Cost: Set-price D £20. ☺
H/wine £8.60
Times: D only, 7-10pm
Additional: Bar food; Sunday L (noon-3pm); Children welcome
Style: Informal/Traditional

COLYFORD,
Swallows Eaves ❀

A 1930s wisteria-cloaked village hotel with an elegant dining room. Expect lovingly prepared dishes such as strips of chicken breast sautéed with honey and mustard, pillows of salmon with lemon parsley butter or char-grilled strawberries with Sabayon.

Additional: Children 14+; Vegetarian on request
Style: Traditional
Smoking: No smoking in dining room; Jacket & tie preferred
Accommodation: 8 en suite ★★

Directions: In the centre of the village on A3082

Swan Hill Road EX13 6QJ
Map 3: SY29
Tel: 01297 553184
Fax: 01297 553574
E-mail: swallows-eaves@talk21.com
Cost: Set-price D £22.50. ☺
H/wine £10.85
Times: D only, 7- 8pm.
Closed Dec-Feb

CREDITON, **Coombe House**
Country Hotel ❀❀

Real commitment and enthusiasm show through in the menu here, where contemporary trends are tempered by simplicity and judicious balancing of flavours. Deft chicken mousse and smoked turbot canapés were served warm, successfully releasing their flavours. Pan fried scallops with mango, lime, chilli and tahini, although ambitious, came across well. Roast ballotine of rabbit was spot on, with the moist outer layer of rabbit encasing a delightful herby farce, accompaniments, including the sauce, were carefully chosen and well executed. Dark valhrona chocolate tart was a masterpiece of powerful flavour combined with pastry so light it literally melted in the mouth.

Directions: Signed L from A377, 1.5 miles NW of Crediton

Coleford EX17 5BY
Map 3: SS80
Tel: 01363 84487
Fax: 01363 84722
E-mail: relax@coombehouse.com
Cost: Set-price L £16.50/D £25. ☺
H/wine £9.50
Times: Noon-2pm/7-9.30pm
Additional: Bar food; Sunday L;
Children welcome
Style: Traditional/ Country-house
Smoking: No smoking in dining room
Civil licence: 80
Accommodation: 15 en suite ★★★

DARTMOUTH,
Carved Angel Restaurant ❀❀

New owners Paul and Andie Roston, and Peter Gorton from the acclaimed Horn of Plenty in Gulworthy (see entry) have allowed Joyce Molyneux to finally retire. The chef stays the same, however, and David Jones' confident, assured cooking goes from strength to strength. Ingredients are the thing here and Devon's abundant natural larder is showcased to great

2 South Embankment TQ6 9BH
Map 3: SX85
Tel: 01803 832465
Fax: 01803 835141
Chef: David Jones
Owners: Paul & Andie Roston,
Peter Gorton
Cost: Set-price L £21.50 & £29.50/D
£39.50. H/wine £15
Times: 12.30-2.30pm/7-9.30pm.
Closed D Sun, L Mon, 2wks Jan
Additional: Sunday L; Children at L
only; Vegetarian dishes only available
at L
Seats: 55. Private dining room 20
Style: Informal/Modern
Smoking: No smoking in dining room

effect in well-constructed dishes which perhaps still owe a debt to Joyce's love for the Mediterranean. Colder climes and a fondness for slow cooking produce dishes like braised lamb shank with colcannon and caper gravy, a welcome warmer on a February menu. Seafood is always a good bet at a restaurant this close to the ocean, and an inspector's spring visit brought praise for the admirably restrained starter of seared scallops with split pea purée and crisp pancetta. Puddings range from French classics, poached pear with pistachio sablé and poire William sorbet, to more eclectic offerings like a coconut parfait with banana beignets and pineapple coulis.

Directions: Dartmouth centre, on the water's edge

DARTMOUTH,

Hooked

5 Higher Street TQ6 9RB
Map 3: SX85
Tel/Fax: 01803 832022
Owners: Mark & Lyn Coxon
Cost: *Alc* £28, set-price L £12. ☺
H/wine £10
Times: Noon-2.30pm/7-9.30pm.
Closed L Mon, all Sun, Xmas, Jan
Additional: Children welcome
Seats: 50. Private dining room 20
Smoking: No pipes & cigars; Air
conditioning

Five Higher Street has seen some changes since it was built for the mayor of Dartmouth in the 14th century, its latest incarnation being this restaurant exclusively dedicated to fish and seafood. Two ground-floor dining rooms and an upstairs room of oak panelling purportedly salvaged from the wreck of a Spanish galleon provide the relaxed, unpretentious environment for some imaginative, accomplished cooking: from cappuccino fish soup with smoked crevettes and harissa croûtons, to roulade of lemon sole with lobster tortellini, baby leeks and lobster emulsion. Oyster parfait, 'as clean as a breaking wave' and of quivering texture, contrastingly partnered by a julienne of pickled vegetables, shows an original approach to the mollusc, and translucent, juicily sweet seared scallops with crispy Parma ham and yellow pepper sauce is no less successful a starter. Freshness and accurate timing can be taken as read, while puddings encompass tiramisu as well as the bold: fennel broth with an ice cream of rosemary, thyme and star anise, perhaps.

Directions: From A38, through Totnes, to Dartmouth. Past Naval College towards town centre. Take 3rd R to T-jnct, then R, 1st L, 1st L again. Restaurant on L

EXETER, Barton Cross Hotel

Huxham Stoke Canon EX5 4EJ
Map 3: SX99
Tel: 01392 841245
Fax: 01392 841942

Telephone for further details.

The enthusiasm and dedication of the kitchen here is undiminished. Making the most of fresh local produce such as pheasant, mussels, salmon and crab the kitchen demonstrates a genuine common sense approach with accurate cooking and well thought out combinations. For a starter you might try a smooth and intense duck liver parfait, studded with orange and surrounded with lardons and mushroom. Main courses might include fillet of sea bass roasted with shallots and served in a lobster bouillon and desserts along the lines of white and dark chocolate marquise with prune and Armagnac ice-cream. The building itself is quite delightful - a 17th-century thatched country house set deep in the mid-Devon countryside. Deep cob walls, stately beams and a popular galleried upper level all help in creating an intimate rustic atmosphere.

Directions: 0.5 mile off A396 at Stoke Canon, 3m N of Exeter

EXETER, Buckerell Lodge Hotel

Topsham Road EX2 4SQ
Map 3: SX99
Tel: 01392 221111
Fax: 01392 491111

A choice of menus is offered in Raffles Restaurant, a typical meal comprising seared scallops with chilli marmalade, succulent brill on tomato couscous, and a wicked chocolate marquise.

Telephone for further details

Directions: 5 minutes from M5 J30, follow signs for Exeter city centre. Aiport 5 miles, station 2 miles

EXETER, Michael Caines at The Royal Clarence

NEW

Cathedral Yard EX1 1HD
Map 3: SX99
Tel: 01392 319955
Fax: 01392 439423

What a transformation! The historic building now houses Michael Caines' first diffusion outlet (see Gidleigh Park), and the public areas have been completely refurbished. As well as a stylish café-bar, there is now a stunningly smart and colourful dining room with large abstract canvasses and bay windows fronting on to the Cathedral. The atmosphere is buzzy without being too noisy, intimate without feeling confined. Staff are casually dressed, the emphasis is on friendly, relaxed and informal service. The cooking, as might be expected given Caines' pedigree, is inspiring, accurate and enjoyable. A terrine of chicken liver and foie gras parfait with green bean salad was near-perfection; equally, the simplicity of a tartlette of poached free-range egg with onion confit, smoked bacon, wild

Telephone for further details

Directions: Opposite Cathedral

mushrooms and a light chicken jus succeeded thanks to exemplary ingredients beautifully cooked. Main courses were a touch less successful – roasted cod with leek fondue and chive butter sauce, and grilled tuna with grain mustard sauce and spiced spinach both lacked some degree of flavour. Desserts might include chocolate tart with coffee ice cream, or banana parfait dipped in chocolate with lime coulis. Coffee, served in perfectly sized, warmed cups, was singled out for particular praise.

EXETER,

St Olaves Court Hotel ❀❀

Mary Arches Street EX4 3AZ
Map 3: SX99
Tel: 01392 217736
Fax: 01392 413054
E-mail: info@olaves.co.uk
Chef: Graham Beal
Owners: Mr & Mrs Hughes
Cost: *Alc* £30, set-price L & D £15.50. ☺ H/wine £11.50
Times: Noon-2pm/6.30-9.30pm. Closed L Sat & Sun
Additional: Children welcome
Seats: 45. Private dining rooms 12-14
Style: Classic/Chic
Smoking: No smoking in dining room
Accommodation: 15 en suite ★ ★ ★

The intimate Golsworthy's Restaurant is a magnet for everyone from holidaymakers to business people, all attracted by the promise of reliably high standards of cuisine. Just a few minutes' walk away from the cathedral, this attractive Georgian hotel stands in its own walled garden, and offers an unexpected oasis in the city centre. New chef Graham Beal has been running the kitchen for just a short time, but has already made his mark. His fixed-price lunch menu offers great value, with starters like confit of duck terrine, two full-flavoured and very meaty tranches served with nicely dressed leaves and thin ham. A recent delicious rack of lamb was served gently pinkish, suitably complemented by artichokes, shallots and garlic, and a good jus. Desserts are an art in themselves, with each one an inspiration of spun sugar which reaches impossible heights, and demonstrates impeccable flair. A glazed lemon tart was piquant, and a lemon and lime ice cream-filled brandy snap basket did not disappoint.

Directions: Follow signs to city centre, then 'Mary Arches P'; hotel is opposite car park entrance

GULWORTHY,

Horn of Plenty ❀❀❀

Tavistock PL19 8JD
Map 2: SX47
Tel/Fax: 01822 832528
E-mail: enquiries@thehornofplenty.co.uk
Chef: Peter Gorton
Owners: Paul & Andie Roston, Peter Gorton

Monday night's Pot Luck night, as they are never sure what will be delivered in this part of West Devon; there's more choice at other times but, even restricted to three dishes, the quality of Peter Gorton's cooking more than compensates. Lamb features regularly, the rack roasted with port and rosemary sauce or the leg braised with Madeira jus. Scallops

Horn of Plenty

Cost: Set-price L fr £14.50/D £35.
H/wine £15.50
Times: Noon-2pm/7-9pm. Closed L
Mon, 3 days over Xmas

are served on salad leaves with a slice of salmon and a beurre
blanc sauce with chives, or may be sautéed with shiitake
noodles and light curry-flavoured sauce. Wood pigeon is
another favourite – as a first course on potato rösti with
caramelised apple and balsamic vinaigrette, or roasted as a
main course with glazed baby onions and port sauce. Hot rice
pudding fritters were nice and crispy, set off by a sharpish plum
sauce and vanilla ice cream. Details – petits fours and
imaginative canapés – are all carefully considered, and a
special mention must be made of the malty, nutty brown bread
made by an Okehampton bakery to a recipe given to them by
previous chef-patron, Sonia Stevenson. It's so popular with
guests there would probably be a riot were it to disappear from
the menu.

Additional: Sunday L; Children
welcome
Seats: 60
Style: Informal/Country-house
Smoking: No smoking in dining room
Civil licence: 150
Accommodation: 10 en suite ★★★

Directions: 3 miles from Tavistock on A390. Turn R at
Gulworthy Cross, then signed

HAYTOR, Bel Alp House ❀

*Window tables offer glorious views of rolling countryside. Enjoy
roast quail with a cherry and rice stuffing or oven baked loin of cod
with a red pepper sauce followed perhaps by chocolate sponge
pudding.*

Style: Country-house
Smoking: No smoking in dining room
Accommodation: 8 en suite ★★★

TQ13 9XX
Map 3: SX77
Tel: 01364 661217
Fax: 01364 661292
Cost: Set-price D fr £22.50. ☺
H/wine £9
Times: D only, 7-8.30pm

Directions: 1.5 miles W of Bovey Tracey off B3387 to Haytor

HAYTOR VALE, Rock Inn ❀

*Set in a pretty hamlet on the edge of Dartmoor the Rock Inn has
been a coaching inn since around 1750. The restaurant offers open
fires, historic charm and hearty cuisine such as Dartmoor rabbit in
mustard sauce.*

Additional: Bar food; Sunday L; Children welcome
Style: Traditional/Country-house
Smoking: No smoking in dining room
Accommodation: 9 en suite ★★

Newton Abbot TQ13 9XP
Map 3: SX77
Tel: 01364 661305
Fax: 01364 661242
E-mail: inn@rock-inn.co.uk
Cost: Alc £25. ☺ H/wine £8.95
Times: Noon-2pm/7-9.30pm

Directions: In Haytor on A3387, 3 miles from A382

HEDDON'S MOUTH,

Heddon's Gate Hotel ✹

Set in exceptionally beautiful surroundings overlooking the Heddon Valley, this Victorian hunting lodge offers top quality ingredients, carefully sourced and cooked for 8 o'clock sharp. Look out for the cheese selection.

Additional: Children welcome. Vegetarian dishes not always available
Style: Traditional/Country-house
Smoking: No smoking in dining room
Accommodation: 14 en suite ★ ★

Directions: A39 from Lynton. After 4miles, R towards Martinhoe/Woody Bay. First L after 0.5 mile, follow signs to Hunters inn/Heddon's Mouth. Hotel on R

Martinhoe Barnstaple EX31 4PZ
Map 3: SS64
Tel: 01598 763313
Fax: 01598 763363
E-mail: info@hgate.co.uk
Cost: Set-price d £26. H/wine £10
Times: D only, 8-9pm. Closed Nov-Mar

HONITON,

Combe House at Gittisham ✹✹

EX14 3AD
Map 3: SY19
Tel: 01404 540400
Fax: 01404 46004
E-mail: stay@combe-house.co.uk
Chef: Phillip Leach
Owners: Ruth & Ken Hunt
Cost: *Alc* £30. Set-price D £30. H/wine £15.50
Times: Noon-2pm/7-9.30pm
Additional: Bar food L; Sunday L; Children welcome
Seats: 60. Private dining room 40
Style: Traditional/Country-house
Smoking: No smoking in dining room
Civil licence: 100
Accommodation: 15 en suite ★ ★ ★

Reached via a long driveway, Combe House is a magnificent Elizabethan manor in 3,500 acres of woodland and pastures. Carved oak panelling, a log fire, antiques, lots of flowers and family portraits dating from the 18th century are what you will find inside, with wines (the list is strong in the Antipodes) brought up from the ancient cellars. The dining room, comfortable and elegant but surprisingly compact, has lovely countryside views and a menu that shows the kitchen fusing ideas from around the world. A starter of grilled mackerel fillet comes with sweet-and-sour leeks and remoulade sauce, and main-course braised oxtail with pan-fried foie gras, Puy lentils and a red wine reduction. Wild mushrooms picked from the estate form the centre of a timbale of partridge mousse with a wonderfully complex port sauce to create a good balance of flavours and textures. This might be followed by orange-marinated salmon, the fruit giving a gentle undercurrent of flavour, with a delicate crab sauce, all atop a mixture of spinach, noodles and broccoli florets. Puddings have their roots firmly in Europe, with mocha pannacotta, profiteroles with butterscotch sauce, and Swiss apple flan among them.

Directions: In Gittisham village off A30 & A303 south of Honiton

ILSINGTON,
Ilsington Country Hotel

Nr Newton Abbot TQ13 9RR
Map 3: SX77
Tel: 01364 661452
Fax: 01364 661307
E-mail: hotel@ilsington.co.uk
Cost: Set-price L £12.95/D £23.95. ☺
H/wine £8.95
Times: Noon-2pm/6.30pm-9pm
Additional: Bar food; Sunday L;
Children welcome
Style: Classic/Country-house
Smoking: No smoking in dining room
Accommodation: 25 en suite ★★★

Peaceful hotel on the southern slopes of Dartmoor. An innovative menu offers Devon beef with stir-fried red cabbage and pear with Marsala sauce, and seared monkfish with risotto.

Directions: From A38 take exit to Newton Abbot/Bovey Tracey. At Drum Bridges Roundabout take 3rd exit (Ilsington/Liverton). 1st R after 400yds. Continue 3 miles.

IVYBRIDGE,
Glazebrook House Hotel

South Brent TQ10 9JE
Map 3: SX66
Tel: 01364 73322
Fax: 01364 72350

Telephone for further details

An uncomplicated approach to quality seasonal produce results in enjoyable dishes, such as wild mushroom soup, filo vegetable parcel, and warm pear tart with chocolate sauce.

Directions: From A38, between Ivybridge and Buckfastleigh, follow 'Hotel' signs to South Brent

KINGSBRIDGE,
Buckland-Tout-Saints

For most of the last millennium the manor house at Buckland-Tout-Saints opened its doors to royalty, the nobility and members of Government. It is hardly surprising, therefore, that the present beautifully-proportioned property, rebuilt in

Goveton TQ7 2DS
Map 3: SX74
Tel: 01548 853055
Fax: 01548 856261
E-mail: buckland@tout-saints.co.uk
Chef: Jean-Philippe Bidart

Queen Anne's time, is the epitome of high living and lavish hospitality. The grand country house restaurant is a charming room with its very high ceilings and light oak-panelled walls. The mainly French cooking, the creation of new chef Jean-Philippe Bidart, is unobtrusively served by staff dressed in traditional black and white. A starter of seared scallops, onion mâche, and chickory and saffron sabayon was highly praised for its strong and contrasting flavours, while the vegetarian main choice of courgette and tomato gâteau on a bed of home-made tagliatelle was also thoroughly enjoyed. Vibrant vegetables add lots of colour and flavour to the meal, and the pear mille-feuille with shortbread biscuits and a thick crème anglaise was a satisfying dessert. A careful balance between fish and meat is struck on the dinner *carte* and the fixed-price lunch menus. Coffee can be taken in the stylish lounge.

Owners: Captain & Mrs Mark Trumble
Cost: *Alc* £30-£35, set-price L £18. ☺ H/wine £9.75
Times: Noon-1.45pm/7-9pm
Additional: Bar food L; Sunday L; Children welcome
Seats: 40. Private dining room 18
Style: Country-house
Smoking: No smoking in dining room
Civil licence: 100
Accommodation: 10 en suite ★ ★ ★

Directions: 2 miles N of Kingsbridge on A381. Through village of Goveton, 500 yds past church

KINGSKERSWELL,

Pitt House Restaurant

Picture-postcard 15th-century thatched cottage. Excellent local meat and fish are well-handled: roast breast of guinea fowl was moist and tender, and old friends like crème brûlée and Bakewell tart with clotted cream round off a meal.

Additional: Sunday L; Children 10+
Smoking: No smoking in dining room

Directions: Torquay road from Newton Abbot, 1st R, follow road to junction & turn L, parish church on R. Take 1st R, restaurant 50yds on L

2 Church End Road
Nr Newton Abbot
TQ12 5DS
Map 3: SX86
Tel: 01803 873374
Cost: Set-price L £12.50 & £14.50/D £21 & £25. ☺ H/wine £10.70
Times: Noon-2pm/7-11pm. Closed L Sat, Sun (ex 1st Sun in month) & Tue, D Sun, all Mon, 2 wks Jan, 2 wks summer

LEWDOWN,

Lewtrenchard Manor

In an elevated position amid beautifully kept gardens surrounded by lovely countryside, this Jacobean manor exudes understated charm and elegance. Oak panelling, ornate ceilings, leaded windows and large fireplaces, with period furnishings and warm colours, characterise the public rooms, while the panelled dining room is relatively intimate. If menu descriptions often make dishes sound complicated – 'roast pheasant with sweetcorn and foie gras pancakes with Muscat grapes accompanied by a warm salad of black pudding and apples' – what arrives on the plate is generally a good balance of flavours and textures. A starter of lambs' liver and smoked bacon terrine with lentil dressing has been described as 'accomplished and well-conceived', and loin of venison with creamed celeriac, roasted shallots and thyme jus is a well-thought-out main course. Fish might run to fillet of sea bass dusted with star anise with courgette fettucine and tomato and basil compote, and the most avid chocoholics would find enough of the stuff in chocolate fondant with matching sauce and ice cream.

Okehampton EX20 4PN
Map 2: SX48
Tel: 01566 783256
Fax: 01566 783332
E-mail: s&j@lewtrenchard.co.uk
Chef: David Swade
Owners: James & Sue Murray
Cost: Set-price L £19.50/D £32. H/wine £11
Times: Noon-1.30pm/7-9pm (booking essential)
Additional: Bar food; Sunday L; Children 8+ at D
Seats: 35. Private dining room 16. Jacket & tie preferred
Style: Country-house
Smoking: No smoking in dining room
Civil licence: 60
Accommodation: 9 en suite ★ ★ ★

Directions: Take A30 for Lewdown, after 6 miles turn L at signpost for Lewtrenchard. Follow signs for 0.75 mile

LIFTON, Arundell Arms ❀❀❀

PL16 0AA
Map 2: SX38
Tel: 01566 784666
Fax: 01566 784494
E-mail: arundellarms@btinternet.com
Chefs: Philip Burgess, Nick Shopland
Owner: Anne Voss-Bark
Cost: Alc £33.50, set-price L £17 &
£21/D £29.50. H/wine fr £11
Times: 12.30-2pm/7.30-9.30pm.
Closed 3 days Xmas
Additional: Bar food; Sunday L;
Children welcome
Seats: 70. Private dining room 24
Style: Classic/Modern
Smoking: No smoking in dining room
Accommodation: 28 en suite ★★★

Practice long ago made perfect. The delightful 18th-century former coaching inn has been under the personal direction of Anne Voss-Bark for 40 years, and is renowned for its 20 miles of salmon and trout fishing. The restaurant has been recently restyled, adding modern overtones to the classical styling. Great pride is taken in using, where possible, local suppliers who are credited in the menu. As well as a menu of the day, there are two *cartes*, with a choice of dishes in each. The complexity of the cooking goes up a notch in the latter, but the cooking in both is fresh and vibrant. An inspection meal of deep-fried fritters of sole in a light saffron batter with green mayonnaise, followed by fillet of grilled free-range chicken with thyme, limes and herb butter was precisely executed and full of super, natural flavours. Caramelised baked custard tart on clementines and orange and passion fruit sauce, under a trellis of spun sugar, transformed this humble little pie into a star turn. The comprehensive wine list includes a really good selection of half-bottles.

Directions: Just off A30 in village of Lifton

LYDFORD,
Castle Inn Hotel ❀

Settles, flagstone floors, beams and log fires create real atmosphere at this restaurant. Expect the likes of salmon noisettes with creamy roquette sauce, and venison steak with raspberry and port.

Additional: Bar food; Sunday L; Children welcome
Style: Rustic/Traditional
Smoking: No-smoking area; No pipes & cigars; Air conditioning

Directions: From A30 take A386 towards Tavistock. Lydford signposted to R after 5 miles

Okehampton EX20 4BH
Map 2: SX58
Tel: 01822 820241/2
Fax: 01822 820454
Cost: Alc £16.95, set-price D £16.95.
☺ H/wine £8.45
Times: Noon-2.30pm/7-9.15pm

LYDFORD, Dartmoor Inn ❀❀   NEW

This 16th-century coaching inn has been lovingly restored to provide intimate spaces for both dining and relaxing. The rustic, informal ambience has been created using Shaker style colours, handmade quilts and pieces of folk art. Described as 'modern British', the food falls somewhere between Parisian brasserie and honest pub grub, with brasserie style offerings including a classic liver and bacon dish with onions and a port

EX20 4AY
Map 2: SX58
Tel: 01822 820221
Fax: 01822 820494
Chefs: Philip Burgess, Ian Brown
Owners: Karen Burgess,
Philip Burgess, Anne Voss-Bark
Cost: Set-price L £9.75/D £18.50. ☺
H/wine £9.50

Dartmoor Inn

Times: Noon-2.15pm/6.30-10pm.
Closed D Sun, all Mon
Additional: Bar food: Sunday L;
Children welcome, (5+ D Fri & Sat)
Seats: 65
Style: Informal/Rustic
Smoking: No smoking in dining room

Directions: On A386, Tavistock to
Okehampton road

wine sauce, or a warm salad of lightly poached egg with crisp
bacon lardons, leeks vinaigrette and a saffron dressing. More
pubby in style were the farmhouse sausages with onion gravy
and mash. The 'wonderful, homemade, real potato chips'
deserve a special mention. Puddings range from the exotic
delights of baked tamarillos with vanilla ice cream to the more
traditional pleasures of a carefully prepared rhubarb pudding
with a compote of the fruit and saffron custard.

LYMPSTONE,

River House Restaurant

The Strand EX8 5EY
Map 3: SX98
Tel: 01395 265147
Chef: Shirley Wilkes
Owner: Michael Wilkes
Cost: Alc £19, set-price L/D £37.
H/wine £10.75
Times: Noon-1.30pm/7-9.30pm.
Closed Sun & Mon, 25-27 Dec, 1 Jan,
Bhs Mon
Additional: Children 6+
Seats: 34. Private dining room 14
Style: French
Smoking: No smoking in dining room

Directions: In Lower Lympstone,
approx 2 miles off A376 Exeter-
Exmouth road

More like a private house than a restaurant, it is no wonder that
visitors feel immediately at home amongst the fine antique
furniture. Stunning views out over the Exe estuary compete with
the food for interest, and the sunsets can be so glorious that a
deliberately calm colour scheme has been chosen as a foil. Shirley
Wilkes' cooking is rarely overwhelmed by the vivid images across
the water, and her flair is evident from the *cartes* and the various
fixed-price lunch menus which offer attractive alternatives for
those economising or watching their weight. Choices for dinner
might be roast duck with a damson sauce, or rack of lamb with
rosemary, oregano and madeira sauce, following on such starters
as lemon-flavoured linguini with asparagus, smoked salmon
and herbs, or red onion and red pepper marmalade tarts with
melted Somerset brie. A much-raved about 'Best and Booziest
Bread-and-Butter Pudding' might not be to everyone's taste,
but the home-made ice creams should please most palates.
Several wines are available by the glass.

LYNMOUTH, Rising Sun Hotel ⚜⚜

Harbourside EX35 6EQ
Map 3: SS74
Tel: 01598 753223
Fax: 01598 753480
E-mail:
risingsunlynmouth@easynet.co.uk
Chef: Steven Batchelor
Owner: Hugo Jeune
Cost: *Alc* £34, set-price D £27.50.
H/wine £9.95
Times: Noon-2pm/7-9pm
Additional: Bar food L; Sunday L;
Children 7+
Style: Chic/Traditional
Seat: 32
Smoking: No smoking in dining room
Accommodation: 16 en suite ★ ★

The oak panelled, candlelit dining room provides an atmospheric canvas for some excellent gastronomic creations by the talented and attentive chef, Steven Batchelor. To begin, a selection of superbly cooked Brixham scallops were nicely contrasted in texture and flavour by a pesto risotto and a tomato and black olive relish. A stunningly presented tenderloin of pork wrapped in bacon set on a round of mash topped with wild mushrooms and crisply fried julienne of leek with an intense prune jus continued the high standards. Lemon tart was well flavoured and piquant. The strong wine list has some good house wines.

Directions: M5 J23 (Minehead). Take A39 to Lynmouth. Opposite the harbour

MARTINHOE, Old Rectory Hotel ⚜

An 18th-century rectory near the North Devon Coastal Path. Good use is made of fresh ingredients, including home-grown produce from the kitchen garden, with all the promised flavours delivered.

Smoking: No smoking in dining room
Accommodation: 9 en suite ★ ★

Directions: M5 J27 onto A361, R onto A399 Blackmore Gate, R onto A39 Parracombe. At Martinhoe Cross, 3rd road on L to Woody Bay/Martinhoe

Parracombe Barnstaple EX31 4QT
Map 3: SS64
Tel: 01598 763368
Fax: 01598 763567
E-mail:
reception@oldrectoryhotel.co.uk
Cost: Set-price D £25. H/wine £8.50
Times: D only at 7.15pm. Closed D
Mon-Thu (Mar & Nov), Dec-Feb
Style: Classic/Country-house

MORETONHAMPSTEAD,
Blackaller Hotel ⚜

Named after the black alder trees which grow along the riverbanks beside this 17th-century woollen mill. The comfortable restaurant, with its inglenook fireplace and carefully chosen old pine tables and chairs, serves modern British cuisine.

Accommodation: 6 en suite
Credit cards: None

Directions: From M5 take A30 Okehampton road. Then follow Marsh Barton sign onto B3212 (Moretonhampstead). Take North Bovey road from there

North Bovey TQ13 8QY
Map 3: SX78
Tel: 01647 440322
Fax: 01647 41137
Cost: Set-price D £23. ☺
H/wine £9.50
Times: D only, (prior booking only)
7.30-8.30pm
Style: Informal/Rustic
Smoking: No smoking in dining room

MORETONHAMPSTEAD,
Manor House Hotel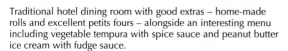

Traditional hotel dining room with good extras – home-made rolls and excellent petits fours – alongside an interesting menu including vegetable tempura with spice sauce and peanut butter ice cream with fudge sauce.

Directions: 2m from Moretonhampstead towards Princetown on B3212

TQ13 8RE
Map 3: SX78
Tel: 01647 440355
Fax: 01647 440961

Telephone for further details

PARKHAM,
Penhaven Country Hotel

Orangery restaurant with views to the gardens and Exmoor in the distance. The braised shoulder of lamb was full of flavour, and the choice of vegetables rather impressive.

Additional: Sunday L (12.15 – 1.30); Children 10+
Style: Country-house
Smoking: No smoking in dining room
Accommodation: 12 en suite ★ ★ ★

Directions: From A39 at Horns Cross, follow signs to Parkham and turn L after church

Bideford EX39 5PL
Map 2: SS32
Tel: 01237 451711
Fax: 01237 451878
E-mail: reception@penhaven.co.uk
Cost: *Alc* £26, set-price L £11.50/D £16.50. ☺ H/wine £11.95
Times: D only 7.15-9pm

PLYMOUTH, **Boringdon Hall** ❀

Set in a medieval galleried hall, this popular hotel dining room specialises in locally caught fish. An inspector's meal took in white fish with prawns and salmon, pork with spiced cabbage, and chocolate fudge cake.

Directions: From A38 to Marsh Mills rdbt, follow signs for Plympton, dual carriageway to small island. L over bridge, follow brown tourist signs

Colebrook Plympton PL7 4DP
Map 2 SX45
Tel: 01752 344455
Fax: 01752 346578

Telephone for further details.

PLYMOUTH, **Chez Nous** ❀❀❀

13 Frankfort Gate
PL1 1QA
Map 2: SX45
Tel/Fax: 01752 266793
Chef: Jacques Marchal
Owners: Jacques & Suzanne Marchal

Well-established French restaurant, where the cooking demonstrates a clear approach and a sense of continuity, without the distraction of passing trends and current styles.

Quality local produce is a strong feature, requiring no unnecessary embellishment (even the main ingredients in the snail casserole are home-grown). The blackboard menu is written in French, charmingly interpreted by Madame Marchal, and the surroundings are engagingly comfortable and refreshingly free of designer chic. The choice of starters includes the aforementioned snails, and scallops with ginger, while main courses take in pork, venison, cod, chicken and beef, all delivered with uncomplicated saucing. Dishes sampled were a starter of pigeon and foie gras bound in a Madeira jelly and served with a complimentary glass of wine, and a main course of brill with a sweet pepper sauce. The wine list is, appropriately, Gallic through and through.

Cost: Set-price L/D £34. H/wine £10.50
Times: 12.30-2pm (reservation only)/7-10.30pm. Closed L Sat, all Sun & Mon, 3 wks Feb, 3 wks Sep, Bhs
Additional: Children 10+; 24hrs notice for vegetarian dishes
Seats: 28
Style: Informal/French
Smoking: No pipes & cigars

Directions: Frankfort Gate is a pedestrianised street between Western Approach & Market Avenue

PLYMOUTH,
Duke of Cornwall Hotel

Millbay Road PL1 3LG
Map 2: SX45
Tel: 01752 275850
Fax: 01752 275854
E-mail: duke@heritagehotels.co.uk
Chef: Tim Bailey
Owner: Mr C Chapman

This Plymouth landmark specialises in elegant dining in a room whose rich, warm decor is enhanced by a magnificent Victorian chandelier. The food however is thoroughly up to date and Tim Bailey's overseas experience has brought many fusion ideas to his classically based cuisine. Traditional favourites such as roast loin of West Country pork with a sage apple and pear stuffing compete for attention with more contemporary styled dishes. An inspector's wok-cooked loin of lamb with tempura vegetables and a balsamic reduction was 'accurately cooked' and showed off some impressive technique in the kitchen. Puddings see the net of inspiration cast rather closer to home with treacle tart and custard and lemon meringue pie with a compote of soft berries flying the flag for modern British cuisine.

Cost: A/c fr £19.95, set-price D fr £19.95. ☺ H/wine £12.95
Times: D only, 7-10pm
Additional: Bar food; Children welcome
Seats: 65. Private dining rooms 50
Style: Classic/Modern
Smoking: No smoking in dining room
Accommodation: 72 en suite ★★★

Directions: City centre, follow signs 'Pavilions', hotel road is opposite

PLYMOUTH, Kitley House Hotel ⊛

Yealmpton PL8 2NW
Map 2: SX45
Tel: 01752 881555
Fax: 01752 881667
E-mail: reservations@kitleyhousehotel.com
Cost: Set-price L £12.50/D £24.50. ☺
Times: Noon-2.30pm/7-9.30pm
Additional: Bar food L; Sunday L; Children 1+
Style: Country-house/Historic
Smoking: No smoking in dining room
Civil licence: 70
Accommodation: 20 en suite ★★★

A million miles away from city centre dining, this Victorian dining room harks back to a more genteel style of life. Typical main dishes include locally caught sea bass fillets on a warm tomato salad.

Directions: From Plymouth take A379 (Kingsbridge). Entrance between villages of Brixton & Yealmpton on R (10 mins)

PLYMOUTH,

Langdon Court Hotel

Down Thomas PL9 0DY
Map 2: SX45
Tel: 01752 862358
Fax: 01752 863428

Telephone for further details

Fish comes straight from the Barbican market to the kitchen at this Tudor hotel. Start with pan-fried Bantry Bay mussels, and follow them with fresh fish-filled crêpes. Save some room for the speciality ice creams.

Directions: From A379 at Elburton, follow brown tourist signs

PLYMOUTH,

Tanners Restaurant

NEW

Prysten House Finewell Street
PL1 2AE
Map 2: SX45
Tel: 01752 252001
Fax: 01752 252105
Chefs/Owners: Christopher &
James Tanner
Cost: Set-price L £10 & £12.50/D
£16.95 & £18.95. ☺ H/wine £10.50

Housed in Plymouth's oldest building complete with simple interior, stone floors and water well, the restaurant offers superb-value contemporary dishes. Roast quail with caramel vinaigrette and potato-crusted salmon with champagne sauce come highly recommended.

Times: Noon-2.30pm/7-9.30pm. Closed Sun & Mon, 1st wk Jan
Additional: Children 12+
Style: Medieval
Seats: 45
Smoking: No-smoking area; No pipes & cigars

Directions: Town centre. Behind St Andrews Church on Royal Parade

ROCKBEARE,

The Jack in the Green ❀

Exeter EX5 2EE
Map 3: SY09
Tel: 01404 822240
Fax: 01404 823445
E-mail: jackinthegreen@virgin.net
Cost: Set-price L/D £17.95. ☺
H/wine £9.50

Popular roadside pub with plenty of beams, brasses and old plates. Staff are notably willing and confident, serving dishes like seared calves' liver, and lamb steak with bubble and squeak.

Times: Noon-2pm/6-9.30pm. Closed Xmas
Additional: Bar food; Sunday L; Children welcome
Style: Rustic/Traditional
Smoking: No-smoking area; Air conditioning

Directions: 5 miles E of Exeter on A30

SALCOMBE, **Bolt Head Hotel** ❀

Well known locally for its seafood and fish specialties this brightly furnished restaurant enjoys magnificent views of the Salcombe estuary and surrounding countryside. Treat yourself to a Dover sole Almondine or Lobster Thermidor.

South Sands TQ8 8LL
Map 3: SX73
Tel: 01548 843751
Fax: 01548 843061
E-mail: info@bolthead-salcombe.co.uk
Cost: Set-price L £16/D £27.50.
H/wine £9
Times: Noon-2.15pm/7-9pm.
Closed Nov-Mar
Additional: Bar food L; Sunday L;
Children welcome
Style: Modern/Traditional
Smoking: No smoking in dining room
Accommodation: 28 en suite ★ ★ ★

Directions: At Malborough follow
National Trust signs for Sharpitor; the
hotel is above the beach at South
Sands

SALCOMBE,
Soar Mill Cove Hotel ❀❀

Soar Mill Cove Malborough TQ7 3DS
Map 3: SX73
Tel: 01548 561566
Fax: 01548 561223
E-mail: info@makepeacehotels.co.uk
Chefs: Keith Makepeace,
Andrew Cannon, Ian MacDonald
Owners: The Makepeace Family
Cost: Alc L £20-£25, set-price D £34.
H/wine £13.50
Times: Noon-3pm/7.15-9.30pm.
Closed from 2 Jan – Feb
Additional: Bar food L; Sunday L:
Children welcome
Seats: 50. Private dining room 24
Style: Chic/Country-house
Smoking: No smoking in dining room
Accommodation: 21 en suite ★ ★ ★

In an Area of Outstanding Natural Beauty surrounded by miles of National Trust coastline, this one-storey modern hotel faces the rocks, sand and sea of Soar Mill Cove. The restaurant, which shares the view, is opened up on warm evenings, and at night the flashes of the Eddystone Lighthouse can be seen from here. Menus are generous in scope, encompassing shellfish (from the bay) chowder, roast breast of Gressingham duck carved on crispy bubble-and-squeak with a piquant Madeira and wild mushroom sauce, and braised steak of local boar in a caramelised apple and Luscombe cider sauce. Fish, as might be expected, is a strong suit, from appetisers of plaice goujons ('lovely, tiny, crisp') or prawns in pastry, through a simple starter of a salad of white crabmeat and avocado, to steamed sea bass on a bed of baby spinach. Well-timed soufflés show up as a starter with Cornish Yarg or a main course with another cheese and vegetables, and puddings end things on a high: bananas flamed at the table and served with coconut ice cream, or a zingy lemon trio of tart, soufflé and sorbet.

Directions: A381 to Salcombe, through village follow signs to sea

SALCOMBE,

Tides Reach Hotel

The tide doesn't quite reach but comes close at this delightfully situated waterfront hotel on South Sands. Meals are served in the pleasant, aptly-named Garden Room, though the sights and sounds of the sea are ever present and reflected on a menu that draws inspiration from its surroundings. A starter of succulent chargrilled Salcombe Estuary scallops with roasted leeks, beurre blanc sauce and puff pastry lid was well constructed. Fresh ingredients, good texture and balance also distinguished a main-course grilled blue-fin tuna accompanied by a simple potato and roasted shallot salad, which served to enhance rather than overpower. A rich dessert of chocolate tuiles layered with white chocolate mousse on a good depth mocha sauce was the ultimate indulgent choice on a February dinner menu. An appetiser filo pastry tartlet filled with prawns and avocado with a tomato concasse commenced proceedings, good home-made breads and rolls provided worthy accompaniment, while strong filter coffee and agreeable petits fours rounded things off. The solid wine list has a strong francophile leaning and a generous selection of half bottles.

Directions: Take cliff road towards sea and Bolt Head

South Sands TQ8 8LJ
Map 3: SX73
Tel: 01548 843466
Fax: 01548 843954
E-mail: enquire@tidesreach.com
Chef: Finn Ibsen
Owners: Edwards Family
Cost: Set-price D £30. H/wine £13.75
Times: D only 7-9pm
Additional: Bar food L; Children 8+
Seats: 80; Jacket & tie preferred
Style: Stylish/Traditional
Smoking: No smoking in dining room
Accommodation: 35 en suite ★ ★ ★

SAUNTON,

Preston House Hotel

Intertesting combinations and quality ingredients reflect the serious approach to food here. Start with rillettes of Devon pork, or crab and Gruyère tartlet, and move on to rack of Welsh salt marsh lamb, or seared spiced sea trout.

Additional: Children 15+
Style: Classic/Country-house
Smoking: No smoking in dining room
Accommodation: 12 ensuite ★ ★

Directions: From Barnstaple on A361, follow signs to Braunton. In Braunton turn L at lights. Signed Saunton/Croyde. Hotel 4miles on L

Braunton EX33 1LG
Map 2: SS43
Tel: 01271 890472
Fax: 01271 890555
E-mail: prestonhouse-
saunton@zoom.co.uk
Cost: Set-price D £27.95.
H/wine 10.95

SIDMOUTH,

Brownlands Hotel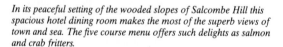

In its peaceful setting of the wooded slopes of Salcombe Hill this spacious hotel dining room makes the most of the superb views of town and sea. The five course menu offers such delights as salmon and crab fritters.

Additional: Bar food L; Sunday L; Children 8+
Style: Classic
Smoking: No smoking in dining room
Accommodation: 14 en suite ★ ★
Credit cards: None

Directions: Take A3052 (Exeter – Sidford), turn R at crossroads past Blue Bull Inn onto Fortescue Rd. Hotel in 1 mile

Sid Road EX10 9AG
Map 3: SY18
Tel: 01395 513053
E-mail: brownlands.hotel@virgin.net
Cost: Set-price D £19.95. ☺
H/wine £9.75
Times: Noon-1.15pm/7-8pm.
Closed Nov-Mar

SIDMOUTH, Riviera Hotel ⊛

The Esplanade EX10 8AY
Map 3: SY18
Tel: 01395 515201
Fax: 01395 577775
E-mail: enquiries@hotelriviera.co.uk
Cost: *Alc* £28.50, set-price L £17/D
£27. H/wine £11.90
Times: 12.30-2pm/7-9pm
Additional: Bar food L; Sunday L;
Children welcome
Style: Classic/Formal
Smoking: No smoking in dining room;
No pipes & cigars; Air conditioning
Accommodation: 27 en suite ★ ★ ★ ★

A fine Regency hotel in a prime location. The restaurant impresses with the likes of an imaginative roulade of marinated salmon. A main course of noisettes of English lamb was delicious and full of flavour.

Directions: From M5 J30, take A3052 to Sidmouth. In the centre of The Esplanade, overlooking Lyme Bay

SIDMOUTH, Victoria Hotel ⊛

Highlights of a six-course meal included an artistic mille feuille of crisp Parma ham with goats' cheese, onion confit and pesto, and roast saddle of lamb with a full-flavoured jus.

Directions: At the western end of the esplanade

Esplanade EX10 8RY
Map 3: SY18
Tel: 01395 512651
Fax: 01395 579154

Telephone for further details

SOUTH MOLTON,
Marsh Hall Hotel ⊛

An 18th-century property set in large grounds amid rolling countryside. The straightforward menu features Devon lamb, Exmoor venison and home-grown fruit, vegetables and herbs.

Additional: Bar food D **Style:** Country-house
Smoking: No smoking in dining room
Accommodation: 7 en suite ★ ★

Directions: Off A361 signed North Molton; first R, then R again

EX36 3HQ
Map 3: SS72
Tel: 01769 572666
Cost: Set-price D £21. ☺ H/wine
£9.50
Times: D only, 7-8.30pm

STAVERTON, Sea Trout Inn ⊛⊛

A charming 15th-century white-painted inn set high up in the lush Dart Valley. Once called the Church House Inn, it was renamed by a jubilant previous landlord after landing a large sea trout in the River Dart nearby. There are two traditional bars with oak beams and log fires; the Lounge Bar features old copper, horse-brasses and fish in showcases, while the Village Bar is frequented by locals. The more formal conservatory-style restaurant overlooks the pretty gardens and is decorated with further fishing antiques. Its modish, daily-changing menu features fresh local produce, and typical offerings might include a fan of avocado served with crab meat and accompanied by a

TQ9 6PA
Map 3: SX76
Tel: 01803 762274
Fax: 01803 762506
Chef: Kim Olson
Owner: Nick Brookland
Cost: *Alc* £18.95, set-price D £18.95.
☺ H/wine £7.45
Times: D only, 7-8.30pm. Closed D
Sun, 25 & 26 Dec
Additional: Bar food; Sunday L;
Children welcome
Seats: 35. Private dining room 18-25

Sea Trout Inn

Style: Rustic/Country-house
Smoking: No smoking in dining room
Accommodation: 10 en suite ★ ★

lime and lemon dressing, or perhaps bruschetta topped with chargrilled vegetables and drizzled with a tapanade and basil pesto sauce to start. Roasted brill with wild mushrooms and shallots in a brown fish jus, or chargrilled fillet steak set on a bed of spinach and sautéed with crushed black peppercorns demonstrate main course style. The wine list affords good-value drinking with a number of inexpensive house offerings.

Directions: From A38 follow A384 at Buckfastleigh (Dart Bridge) and proceed to Staverton

TAVISTOCK, Bedford Hotel ❀❀   NEW

Impressive castellated property built in 1820 on the site of an earlier Benedictine abbey in the centre of town. An innovative menu is offered in the Woburn Restaurant, where good technical skills are evident in dishes featuring imaginative combinations of fresh, quality produce. Home-made rolls and an appetiser of seared tuna on fine french beans provided a promise of things to come. Wonderfully fresh scallops were served lightly seared with citrus and red pepper beurre blanc, making a beautifully presented first course. To follow, chicken breast wrapped in Parma ham came with a fricassée of wild mushrooms on a square of dauphinoise potatoes accompanied by a selection of perfectly cooked spring vegetables. To complete the meal, a piquant lemon mousse was served with mixed fruits and a couple of quenelle-shaped portions of clotted cream.

1 Plymouth Road PL19 8BB
Map 2: SX47
Tel: 01822 613221
Fax: 01822 618034
Chef: Peter Roberts
Owner: Warm Welcome Hotels
Cost: Alc £25, set-price D £22.50. ☺
H/wine £10
Times: Noon-2.30pm/7-9.30pm
Additional: Bar food; Sunday L;
Children 3+
Seats: 50. Private dining room 25
Style: Classic/Traditional
Smoking: No smoking in dining room
Accommodation: 29 en suite ★ ★ ★

Directions: Leave M5 J31 - take (Okehampton) A30. Take A386 - Tavistock. On entering Tavistock follow signs for town centre. Hotel opposite church

THURLESTONE,
Heron House Hotel ❀

Friendly staff and wonderful views at this family-run hotel. An autumn meal took in gravad lax with honey and mustard dressing, followed by halibut with lemon caper sauce, with white chocolate mousse in a tuille basket to finish.

Thurlestone Sands Nr Salcombe
TQ7 3JY
Map 3: SX64
Tel: 01548 561308/561600
Fax: 01548 560180

Telephone for further details

Directions: Take A385 to Totnes. Then A381, through Kingsbridge towards Salcombe. Take L turn signed Hope Cove. 50yds beyond Galmpton sign take R to Thurlestone Sands

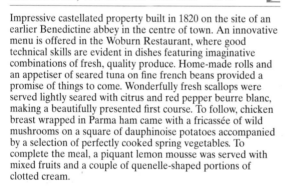

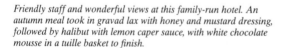

THURLESTONE, **Thurlestone Hotel**

Kingsbridge TQ7 3NN
Map 3: SX76
Tel: 01548 560382
Fax: 01548 561069
E-mail: enquires@thurlestone.co.uk
Cost: Alc £14, set-price L £14/D £28.
☺ H/wine £9.75
Times: 12.30-2.30pm/7.30-9pm
Additional: Bar food L; Sunday L;
Children welcome
Style: Classic/Modern
Smoking: No smoking in dining room;
Air conditioning
Accommodation: 67 en suite ★ ★ ★ ★

*A stylish, beautifully furnished hotel dining room with views over
twenty acres of sub-tropical gardens out to the bay beyond. A
delicate piece of smoked trout was well balanced by cream cheese,
cauliflower soup and bacon snippets.*

Directions: A381 (Kingsbridge), then A379 (Churchstow), turn
onto B3197, then turn into lane signposted Thurlestone

TORQUAY, **Corbyn Head Hotel, Orchid Restaurant** NEW

Torquay Road Sea Front TQ2 6RH
Map 3: SX96
Tel: 01803 213611

Telephone for further details

Directions: Follow signs to Torquay
seafront, turn R, hotel on R

A candlelit restaurant with stunning views over the bay, and
professional, attentive service. White linen tablecloths and a
fresh orchid on each table add to the smart, formal
atmosphere. An early summer meal kicked off with good
canapés, a quail's egg on tomato concasse in a filo tartlet, and a
peppered beef kebab. 'Wonderfully fresh' well textured bread
rolls of various flavours came next, followed by a starter of
mille feuille of seared scallops and cherry tomato compote.
The scallops were 'fresh, sweet and juicy', placed between
layers of thin disks of filo style pastry. A main course of fillet of
Scotch beef with tarragon mash and caramelised shallots was
next up, the beef 'full of flavour' and perfectly cooked, the
shallots 'delicious'. Lemon tart for dessert came with a
blackcurrant coulis and intense cassis sorbet. The tart was
'wonderfully lemony and suitably tangy', and flavours were
'sharp, zesty and intense' all round. Strong cafetière coffee
came with petits fours.

TORQUAY, **Grand Hotel** ❀

Edwardian hotel with an elegant restaurant – carved cornices and crystal chandeliers – overlooking the terrace, swimming pool and sea. Highlights were lamb with Madeira and thyme followed by vibrant fruit parfait.

Additional: Bar food L; Sunday L; Children welcome
Style: Informal/Chic
Smoking: No smoking in dining room
Accommodation: 110 en suite ★★★★

Directions: From M5 take A380 to Torquay. At seafront turn 1st R. Hotel on corner 1st on L

Sea Front TQ2 6NT
Map 3: SX96
Tel: 01803 296677
Fax: 01803 213462
E-mail: grandhotel@netsite.co.uk
Cost: Alc fr £36.65, set-price L fr £15.95/D £24.95. ☺ H/wine £12.50
Times: 12.15-2.30pm/7-10.30pm

TORQUAY, **The Grosvenor Hotel, Mima's Restaurant** ❀❀

Belgrave Road TQ2 5HG
Map 3: SX96
Tel: 01803 215515
Chef: Richard Hunt
Cost: Alc £35. ☺ H/wine £8.50
Times: 12-2.30pm/7-10pm.
Closed 25 Dec-1 Jan
Style: Traditional Country-house
Smoking: No-smoking area; No pipes & cigars; Air conditioning

Although physically connected to The Grosvenor Hotel, the restaurant is managed separately by head chef Richard Hunt. The atmosphere is welcoming and intimate, with rather cottagey style decor. The food, however, lifts the place above the local norm with a short, well-constructed dinner *carte*, bistro-style lunch menu and a wide range of produce made on the premises. A starter of tiger prawn and monkfish brochette with tomato and coriander salad was simple, fresh and delicious, the accompanying swirl of spicy marinade full of clearly defined flavours. Medallions of beef fillet marinated in red wine and garlic with a wild mushroom tartlet and Madeira glaze were rich and tender. Desserts are a high-spot – chocolate and pistachio terrine with a cool crème anglaise sauce had perfect texture, but home-made honey and lemon ice-cream won the day. If you're driving, avoid the potent Grand Marnier truffles, two of which would probably put you over the limit.

Directions: Just off main beach/seafront road

TORQUAY, **Imperial Hotel** ❀

Unrivalled views over Torbay and a carefully considered mix of traditional and contemporary dishes, drawing heavily on the excellence of local fish and seafood. Fillet of brill with thyme and orange in foie gras sauce comes recommended.

Park Hill Road TQ1 1DG
Map 3: SX96
Tel: 01803 294301
Fax: 01803 298293
Cost: Alc £35, set-price L £12.95 & £15.95/D £25. H/wine £12.95

Imperial Hotel

Times: D only, 7-9.30pm
Additional: Bar food; Sunday L
(12.30-2pm); Children welcome
Smoking: No smoking in dining room;
Air conditioning; Jacket & tie
preferred
Civil licence: 60
Accommodation: 154 en suite
★ ★ ★ ★ ★

Directions: M5 to Exeter, A380 then A3022 to Torquay. Park Hill Road is off Torwood Street/Babbacombe Road, just N of new harbour

TORQUAY, Mulberry House Hotel

Light, airy and spacious restaurant decorated in rose and white set off by classic furnishings and country flower arrangements. The chef-proprietor offers carefully prepared dishes using the freshest of ingredients.

Style: Classic/Country-house
Smoking: No smoking in dining room; Jacket & tie preferred
Accommodation: 3 rooms

1 Scarborough Road TQ2 5UJ
Map 3: SX96
Tel: 01803 213639
Cost: Alc £17.50. ☺ H/wine £10
Times: Noon-2pm/7.30-9.30pm.
Closed L Mon-Thu
Additional: Children welcome

Directions: From seafront turn up Belgrave Rd, then 1st L into Scarborough Rd.

TORQUAY, Osborne Hotel ✤

Hesketh Crescent Meadfoot TQ1 2LL
Map 3: SX96
Tel: 01803 213311
Fax: 01803 296788
E-mail: enq@osborne-torquay.co.uk
Cost: Alc £27.50, set-price D £20. ☺
H/wine £11.50
Times: D only, 7-9.45pm
Additional: Bar food; Sunday L;
Children welcome
Style: Classic/Country-house
Smoking: No smoking in dining room;
Air conditioning

Forming the centrepiece of an elegant Regency terrace, The Osborne commands superb views over the nearby beach and Torbay itself. A pressed duck terrine with a roasted tomato dressing was particularly enjoyable.

Accommodation: 29 en suite ★ ★ ★

Directions: Follow A3022 to seafront, turn L towards Harbour. At Clock Tower turn L; at next junction/traffic lights turn R. Over brow of hill and gates of Hesketh Crescent and hotel are opposite.

TORQUAY, Toorak Hotel

Hotel restaurant offering both traditional and more innovative dishes – start with citrus fruit terrine, and move on to steamed fillet of cod, or honey glazed pork with sausage and bacon toad in the hole.

Directions: Opposite Riviera Conference Centre

Chestnut Avenue TQ2 5JS
Map 3: SX96
Tel: 01803 400400
Fax: 01803 400140

Telephone for further details

TOTNES, Durant Arms Restaurant

Ashprington TQ9 7UP
Map 3: SX86
Tel: 01803 732240
Fax: 01803 732471
Cost: *Alc* £20, set-price L £5.95. ☺
H/wine £9.45
Times: 11.30-2.30pm/7-9.15pm.
Closed D 25 & 26 Dec
Additional: Bar food; Sunday L;
Children welcome
Style: Classic/Country-house
Smoking: No-smoking area
Accommodation: 6 en suite

Directions: Telephone for directions

Attractive 18th-century pub in the heart of Ashprington, with friendly proprietors and a good atmosphere. Fish is featured strongly with other options of steak, venison and ostrich.

TWO BRIDGES, Prince Hall Hotel

Arthur Conan Doyle's Hound of the Baskervilles was supposedly set in this old stone house in the heart of Dartmoor, but there is nothing menacing to be found within the solid granite walls nowadays. On the contrary, the mellow house and its friendly, welcoming owners offer a haven from worldly stresses, and the small and intimate restaurant is a very good place to unwind. The traditional country-house dining room, with its fresh flowers and iced water on each table, is a comfortable setting for the short set menu which changes every day. Consider starters like home-made venison and game soup with a dash of port, or Devon seafood mornay served in a scallop shell. Move on to fillets of John Dory on a bed of kale with basil and tomato sauce, or try roasted breast of guinea fowl with caramelised onions, and a port wine and waterberry jus. Desserts are equally tantalising, like the irresistible Eton Mess – crushed meringue tossed with fresh strawberries, whipped cream and fruit coulis, or apple and fruits of the forest crumble and clotted cream.

PL20 6SA
Map 2: SX67
Tel: 01822 890403
Fax: 01822 890676
E-mail: info@princehall.co.uk
Chefs: Adam Southwell, Les Pratt
Owners: Adam & Carrie Southwell
Cost: Set-price D £29. ☺
H/wine £9.15
Times: D only, 7-8.30pm.
Closed mid Dec-mid Feb
Additional: Children 12+
Seats: 24
Style: Traditional/Country-house
Smoking: No smoking in dining room
Accommodation: 9 en suite ★★

Directions: From Two Bridges take B3357 Dartmeet Road; hotel is hidden 1 mile on R

TWO BRIDGES,
Two Bridges Hotel

Riverside gardens for summer, crackling log fires in winter, the splendours of Dartmoor all year – add to these a collection of ephemera, an abundance of easy chairs, and an engaging lived-in atmosphere and you come up with the Two Bridges. The restaurant menu here deals in bold flavours, from a terrine of

Dartmoor
PL20 6SW
Map 2: SX67
Tel: 01822 890581
Fax: 01822 890575
Chef: Andrew Shortman
Owners: Philip & Lesley Davies

Two Bridges Hotel

Cost: Alc £24.95, set-price D £19.95.
☺ H/wine £9.95
Times: D only, 7-9.30pm
Additional: Bar food; Sunday L (noon-2.30pm); Children welcome
Seats: 85. Private dining room 22
Style: Classic/Traditional
Smoking: No smoking in dining room
Accommodation: 29 en suite ★ ★

Directions: From Tavistock take B3357, hotel at junction with B3312

duck confit, guinea fowl, wild mushrooms and black pudding with spiced pear chutney ('wonderful, potent flavours, beautifully moist') to a main course of steamed fillet of brill on roasted fennel with crisped basil and a sharp lime and ginger velouté. Equally, you might find a puff pastry casket of wild mushrooms with spinach to start, followed by best end of local lamb sliced over leek and mint couscous accompanied by root vegetables and rosemary sauce, or pan-fried fillet of Brixham plaice with saffron risotto.

VIRGINSTOWE,

Percy's Country Hotel ❀❀

Coombeshead Estate,
Nr Okehampton EX21 5EA
Map 2: SX38
Tel: 01409 211236
Fax: 01409 211275
E-mail: info@percys.co.uk
Chef: Christina Bricknell-Webb
Owners: Christina &
Tony Bricknell-Webb
Cost: Alc £28.50, set-price L £16.50.
H/wine £9.95
Times: 12.30-2pm/7-9pm
Additional: Bar food L; Sunday L;
Children 12+
Seats: 36. Private dining room 12 & 24
Smoking: No smoking in dining room
Accommodation: 8 en suite

Restored 16th-century Devon longhouse, with a 130 acre estate including extensive vegetable and herb gardens. Home-grown vegetables, herbs and salad leaves are complemented by seasonal fresh local produce. Typical dishes include starters of pan-fried soft smoked roes on herbed tagliatelle with beurre noisette, or duck liver and wild mushroom parfait on sage toast. Main courses of roast home-reared lamb with lavender, honey and garlic jus, or grilled turbot with bearnaise sauce might be followed by caramelised apple tart with clotted cream, or cardamom and lime crème brûlée.

Directions: Follow signs to restaurant from Gridley Corner A388 (St Giles on the Heath) or at Metherell Cross, B3218 (Okehampton-Bude)

WHIMPLE, Woodhhayes ✿

Charming Georgian house set in four acres of grounds. A summer dinner might include goats' cheese soufflé on dressed salad leaves, followed by peppered salmon with juniper and vermouth sauce, and orange and mint mousse for dessert.

EX5 2TD
Map 3: SY09
Tel: 01404 822237
Fax: 01404 822337

Telephone for further details

Directions: Leave new A30 at Daisymount junction. Follow signs for Whimple. L at T junction.).25m, R into Church Road, hotel 0.5m on R

WINKLEIGH, Pophams ✿✿✿

The best way to get a table is to phone on the morning in case of any cancellations, as the tiny three-table kitchen-restaurant tends to be booked solidly for months in advance. It's lunch only (and then only on three days a week), but Melvin Popham and Dennis Hawkes really provide an afternoon of entertainment; most guests arrive around noon and leave around 4pm. Freshness, quality and simplicity are the keynotes, and the choice from the chalked board might include butternut squash soup with Parmesan shavings, followed by breast of Barbary duck with sage, apple and onion purée and Madeira sauce, then fresh lemon tart with vanilla ice cream. Our inspector's first course, roast cod with tomato, ginger and garlic was a perfect piece of the freshest cod, bright white and melt-in-the-mouth fresh placed on a vibrant, piquant sauce. Simplicity again defined the roast fillet of local beef with Madeira sauce and shiitake mushrooms. Succulent, tender and full of flavour it was accurately cooked to medium rare, and served with a Madeira sauce of notable depth. A sticky stem ginger pudding with brandy and ginger wine sauce served with clotted cream was, to quote, 'as close to the perfect pudding as I have tasted for some time.'

Castle Street EX19 8HQ
Map 3: SS60
Tel: 01837 83767
Chef: Melvyn Popham
Owners: Melvyn Popham, Dennis Hawkes
Cost: Alc £27.50. Unlicenced (BYO)
Times: L only, 11.45-2.30pm. Closed Sat -Tue, Feb
Additional: Vegetarian dishes not always available
Seats: 10
Style: Bistro/Informal
Smoking: No smoking in the dining room; Air conditioning

Directions: In village centre, about 9 miles from Okehampton

WOOLACOMBE, Watersmeet Hotel ✿

Mortehoe EX34 7EB
Map 2: SS44
Tel: 01271 870333
Fax: 01271 870890
E-mail: watersmeethotel@compuserve.com
Cost: Alc £23.50, set-price D £26.50 . ☺ H/wine £10.45
Times: Noon-2.30pm/7-8.30pm. Closed Dec, Jan
Additional: Bar lunch L; Children 8+
Style: Country-house/Formal
Smoking: No smoking in dining room; Jacket & tie preferred
Accommodation: 25 en suite ★ ★ ★

With magnificent views over the bay, this popular hotel restaurant provides professional and attentive service and an innovative range of dishes. A tian of fresh Devon crab and coriander on a gazpacho coulis was flavoursome and well textured.

Directions: M5 J27. Follow A361 to Woolacombe, R at beach car park, 300yds on R

YELVERTON,
Moorland Links Hotel

With panoramic views over well-kept lawns to the Tamor valley beyond, this spacious hotel restaurant offers a classy setting for high quality cuisine. A well-balanced prawn and scampi tartlet was particularly noteworthy in an enjoyable visit.

PL20 6DA
Map 2: SX56
Tel: 01822 852245
Fax: 01822 855004
Cost: Set-price L /D £21. ☺
H/wine £8.95
Times: 12.30-2pm/7.30-10pm.
Closed Sat L & Bh L, 24-26 & 30-31
Dec,1 Jan 30
Additional: Bar food; Sunday L;
Children welcome
Style: Modern/Traditional
Smoking: No smoking in dining room
Civil licence: 160
Accommodation: 45 en suite ★ ★ ★

Directions: On A386, within
Dartmoor National Park

DORSET

BEAMINSTER,
Bridge House Hotel ❀❀

Traditional British favourites are given a modern twist at this country-house hotel, the origins of which lie in the 13th century. Diners can choose to eat in the airy conservatory, which overlooks the lovingly-tended garden, or in the impressive Georgian panelled dining room. Despite the antiquity of the building the atmosphere is informal and relaxed and staff are praised for their attentive, friendly and pretension-free service. Comforting dishes like a mushroom and leek risotto vie for attention with more contemporary offerings. A spicy, warm chorizo and black pudding salad showed both ambition and a healthy disrespect for the vagaries of fashion. The fairly conservative clientele appreciate the unfussiness of many of the dishes available and who can doubt the pleasures of a simply-grilled whole lemon sole. Puddings tend to be well-loved favourites; the inspector thoroughly enjoyed his warm pear and apple tart.

3 Prout Bridge DT8 3AY
Map 3: ST40
Tel: 01308 862200
Fax: 01308 863700
E-mail: enquiries@bridge-house.co.uk
Chef: Linda Paget
Owner: Peter Pinkster
Cost: Set-price L £9.50 & £13.50/D
£23.25 & £27.75. ☺ H/wine £9.95
Times: Noon-2pm/7-9pm
Additional: Bar food L; Sunday L
Seats: 36. Private dining room 16
Style: Country-house/Comfortable
Smoking: No smoking in dining room
Accommodation: 14 en suite ★ ★ ★

Directions: On A3066, 200mtrs down hill from town centre

BLANDFORD FORUM,
Castleman Hotel ❀❀

The hotel has been in the same family for over 150 years and has a character all of its own. The building dates from the 16th-century and for a small hotel has extensive public areas (two large lounges in addition to the bar). The evening *carte* offers some seven choices at each course and the cooking has a

Chettle DT11 8DB
Map 3: ST80
Tel: 01258 830096
Fax: 01258 830051
E-mail: chettle@globalnet.co.uk
Chefs: Barbara Garnsworthy,
Richard Morris

comfortable country feel with enough modern interpretation to retain interest. The dishes, all freshly cooked, might include venison and pigeon breast terrine with toast, crab apple jelly and salad, followed by seared Scottish scallops on roast vegetables in warm basil dressing. Finish with one of the tempting desserts, perhaps pecan nut and treacle tart with clotted cream, or cheese – Stilton, Denhay Cheddar and unpasteurised French Brie.

Directions: 1 mile from A354. Hotel is signposted in village

Owners: Barbara Garnsworthy, Edward Bourke
Cost: Alc £25, set-price L £15. ☺
H/wine £9
Times: D only, 7-10pm. Closed Feb
Additional: Sunday L (noon-2pm); Children welcome
Seats: 50
Style: Classic/Country-house
Smoking: No smoking in dining room

BOURNEMOUTH,
Bistro on the Beach

Lively, informal bistro where the waterside setting makes up for a less than glamourous building. A very popular venue where early booking is rewarded by the likes of grilled salmon with a tabouleh salad.

Times: D only, 7-11.30pm.
Closed Sun-Tue, 19 Mar-3 Apr, 29 Oct-20 Nov
Additional: Sunday L; Children welcome
Style: Bistro/Informal
Smoking: No pipes & cigars; Air conditioning

Directions: Telephone for directions

Solent Promenade Southbourne
BH6 4BE
Map 4: SZ09
Tel: 01202 431473
Fax: 01202 252091
E-mail:
bistro@ryancatering.fsnet.co.uk
Cost: Alc £22.50, set-price D £14.95.
☺ H/wine £8.95

BOURNEMOUTH, Chine Hotel

Boscombe Spa Road BH5 1AX
Map 4: SZ09
Tel: 01202 396234
Fax: 01202 391737
E-mail: reservations@chinehotel.co.uk
Cost: Set-price L £14.50/D £18.50. ☺
H/wine £10.50
Times: 12.30-8.30pm. Closed L Sat
Additional: Bar food L; Sunday L; Children 4+
Style: Classic/Traditional
Smoking: No smoking in dining room
Civil licence: 130
Accommodation: 92 en suite ★ ★ ★

Large, well run hotel restaurant with superb views and attentive service. First courses may include good home-made soups or chicken and wild mushroom terrine. Main courses offer a good range of fresh fish and roasts.

Directions: From M27, A31 and A338 follow signs to Boscombe Pier, Boscombe Spa Road is off Christchurch Road near Boscombe Gardens

BOURNEMOUTH, Farthings

Formal service in this town centre restaurant, where it's clear the kitchen is hungry for success. A summer meal got off to an excellent start with seared fresh hand picked Lulworth Cove scallops – 'these had to be the tenderest and sweetest scallops

5/7 Grove Road BH1 3AS
Map 4: SZ09
Tel: 01202 558660
Fax: 01202 293766

Telephone for further details

that I have ever tasted' enthused the inspector. Noisette of lamb with cep mousseline was enjoyable and attractively presented, with good flavours. To finish, warm apple crumble and pear ice cream, the crumble in a small round pastry case with well flavoured apples and crunchy crumble. A nice touch was the tall curled tuille basket which kept the heat of the plate from melting the ice cream. Petits fours included a small Welsh cake and a crouton of pastry topped with cream and fresh fruits. Well balanced wine list.

Directions: On rdbt top of hill on Bath Road going from Pier to Lansdowne

BOURNEMOUTH,
Langtry Manor Hotel ✿

A stately Edwardian atmosphere permeates the decor and service in this impressive hotel restaurant. Home-made asparagus and salmon soup followed perhaps by prime English sirloin steak offers a taste of aristocratic dining.

Additional: Bar food L
Style: Country-house
Smoking: No smoking in dining room; Jacket & tie preferred
Civil licence: 120
Accommodation: 26 en suite ★ ★ ★

Directions: On the East Cliff, at corner of Derby and Knyveton Roads

26 Derby Road East Cliff BH1 3QB
Map 4: SZ09
Tel: 01202 553887
Fax: 01202 290115
E-mail: lillie@langtrymanor.com
Cost: Set-price D £21.75. ☺
H/wine £11.95
Times: D only, 7-9pm

BOURNEMOUTH,
Menzies Carlton Hotel ✿

Hotel restaurant overlooking the outdoor pool, gardens and coast, and offering a choice of menus. A main course of well timed, perfectly pink roast rump of lamb was particularly enjoyable.

Directions: M3/M27, follow A338 (Bournemouth). Follow signs to town centre and East Overcliff. Hotel is on seafront

East Overcliff BH1 3DN
Map 4: SZ09
Tel: 01202 552011
Fax: 01202 299573

Telephone for further details

BOURNEMOUTH,
Queens Hotel ✿

Large open-plan restaurant with a water fountain feature. The fixed price menu might include grilled whole Poole plaice or pan-fried escalope of pork fillet topped with Serrano ham and Gruyère cheese.

Additional: Bar food; Sunday L; Children welcome
Style: Modern/Traditional
Smoking: No smoking in dining room; Air conditioning; Jacket & tie preferred
Accommodation: 114 en suite ★ ★ ★

Directions: Follow signs to East Cliff, hotel is one road back from seafront

Meyrick Road East Cliff BH1 3DL
Map 4: SZ09
Tel: 01202 554415
Fax: 01202 294810
E-mail: hotels@arthuryoung.co.uk
Cost: Set-price L £8.50/D £17.95. ☺
H/wine £10.50
Times: 12.30-1.30pm/7-8.30pm

BOURNEMOUTH,

Royal Bath Hotel

Oscar's is the fine dining option at this popular hotel; an elegant panelled room providing the setting for local specialities such as sauté of Poole Bay seabass. A spring meal took in scallops with butternut squash risotto and spring lamb with braised root vegetables, finishing with a glazed chocolate bombe and strawberry purée.

Additional: Sunday L
Seats: 48. Private dining room 10-400
Style: Classic/Traditional
Smoking: No-smoking area; No pipes & cigars before 10pm; Air conditioning; Jacket & tie preferred
Accommodation: 140 en suite ★★★★★

Directions: Follow signs for Bournemouth Pier and beaches

Bath Road BH1 2EW
Map 4: SZ09
Tel: 01202 555555
Fax: 01202 554158
E-mail: royal.bath@devere-hotels.com
Chef: Peter Leyland-Jones
Owner: De Vere Group
Cost: Alc £38, set-price L £17.50/D £30. H/wine £14.50
Times: 12.30-2pm/7.30-10pm

BOURNEMOUTH,

Saint Michel

NEW

Swallow Highcliff Hotel, Saint Michaels Road BH2 5DU
Map 4: SZ09
Tel/Fax: 01202 315716
Cost: Alc £25, set-price L £12.50. ☺ H/wine £11.50
Times: Noon-2pm/7-9.30pm. Closed L Sat, D Sun
Additional: Bar food L; Children welcome
Style: Classic/Brasserie
Smoking: No-smoking area; No pipes & cigars; Air conditioning

Brasserie-style restaurant and bar, with jade walls and marble floors and tables. The cooking is Anglo-French – twice baked Finnan haddock soufflé followed by grilled calves' liver with bacon.

Directions: Follow signs for Bournemouth International Centre; along Exeter Rd to mini-rdbt, up hill onto Priory Rd. 3rd L into St Michaels Road. 50metres on L.

BOURNEMOUTH,

Swallow Highcliff Hotel

A splendid cliff-top hotel, with sought-after window tables in the popular restaurant. Traditional dishes have a modern twist, like glazed breast of barbary duck and pink peppercorn sauce, and a superb chocolate tart.

Directions: Take A338 dual carriageway through Bournemouth, then follow signs for Bournemouth International Centre to West Cliff Rd, then 2nd turning right

St Michael's Road West Cliff BH2 5DU
Map 4: SZ09
Tel: 01202 557702
Fax: 01202 292734

Telephone for further details

BRIDPORT, Riverside Restaurant ❀❀

West Bay DT6 4EZ
Map 3: SY49
Tel: 01308 422011
Chefs: Paul Morey, Nic Larcombe
Owners: Arthur & Janet Watson
Cost: *Alc* £23, set-price L £10.50 &
£13.50 (Mar, Apr & Oct, Nov). ☺
H/wine £12.50
Times: 11.30-2.30pm/6.30-9pm.
Closed D Sun & all Mon (ex Bhs), 1
Dec-mid Feb
Additional: Children welcome
Seats: 80. Private dining room 10-18
Style: Informal
Smoking: No pipes & cigars

Directions: In the centre of West Bay
by the river

Take the walkway over the river to reach this waterside
restaurant with outstanding views of the village and harbour.
Within is a relaxing, buzzy atmosphere, a decor of
predominantly blue and yellow, with wooden floors and tables
and glass on three sides allowing everyone to enjoy the setting.
Seafood – 'absolutely fresh, cooked very well' – is the
speciality, with a handful of meat and a fair choice of
vegetarian offerings. Simplicity works well, as in langoustines
with mayonnaise, or fillet of brill with samphire and butter
sauce, but more complicated treatments get the thumbs up too:
mussels are steamed with a spicy sauce of tomatoes, onions,
garlic and coriander without getting overpowered, and a main
course of roasted cod fillet comes with a ragout of Swiss chard,
chorizo, chickpeas and tomatoes. Those pushing the boat out
could start with sevruga caviar and follow it with local lobster
grilled with garlic butter, but more modest fish are also given
due consideration, as in crispy-skinned pan-fried red mullet,
'lovely and moist', paired with fluffy couscous enhanced with
pesto, peppers and Parmesan. Knickerbocker glory will keep
the kids happy, and sweet-lovers could go for treacle tart. As
you'd expect, white wines dominate the wine list, and there's
even a bottle from Greece.

CHARMOUTH,
Thatch Lodge Hotel ❀❀

Once a monk's retreat for nearby Forde Abbey, the building of
pink-washed cobb walls under a thatched roof dates from 1320
and is set in an Area of Outstanding Natural Beauty. The
restaurant, featuring an oak-beamed ceiling and fine inglenook
fireplace, offers a set, four-course dinner menu based around
fresh produce supplied daily, including local smoked salmon and
Denhay ham. The meal is preceded by canapés, and some choice
is offered at the starter and dessert stage. Dishes might include
creamy wild mushroom risotto, roasted leg of local lamb with
mustard and herb crust served on a bed of braised red cabbage
with a rich red wine sauce and garden mint sauce. For pudding,
hot vanilla soufflé with raspberry and Cointreau filling is tipped
(not to be missed). Finish with Stilton cheese and home-grown
grapes in season. Dinner is available only by prior reservation.

The Street DT6 6PQ
Map 3: SY39
Tel/Fax: 01297 560407
Chef: Andria Ashton-Worsfold
Owners: Andria Ashton-Worsfold,
Chris Worsfold
Cost: Set-price D £27.50. H/wine £11
Times: D only at 8pm. Closed Sun &
Mon, Jan/Feb
Additional: Vegetarian dishes not
always available
Seats: 12
Style: Classic/Country-house
Smoking: No smoking in the dining
room
Accommodation: 6 en suite ★★

Directions: Charmouth, off A35, 2 miles E of Lyme Regis.
Hotel on R half way up High Street

CHIDEOCK,
Chideock House Hotel ✿

Main Street DT6 6JN
Map 3: SY49
Tel: 01297 489242
Fax: 01297 489184
Cost: *Alc* £25. ☺ H/wine £10
Times: D only, 7-9pm.
Closed D Sun, Mon, Jan
Additional: Sunday L; Children welcome; Vegetarian dishes not always available
Style: Informal/Country-house
Smoking: No smoking in dining room
Accommodation: 9 en suite ★ ★

Cosy candlelit restaurant with oak beams and an open fire. Expect the likes of pan-fried organic salmon with ginger and sultanas, or fillet of Angus beef with red wine sauce.

Directions: 3 miles W of Bridport, on A35 in centre of village

CHRISTCHURCH, Splinters ✿✿

12 Church Street BH23 1BW
Map 4: SZ19
Tel: 01202 483454
Fax: 01202 480180
E-mail: eating@splinters.uk.com
Chef: Jason Davenport
Owners: Timothy Lloyd, Robert Wilson
Cost: *Alc* £34.95, set-price L £16/D £22.50. ☺ H/wine £12.95
Times: Noon-2.30/7-10pm.
Closed Sun, Mon, 26 Dec
Additional: Bar food L; Children welcome
Seats: 45. Private dining room 8-24
Style: Informal/Intimate
Smoking: No smoking in dining room

On a cobbled street leading to the priory church, Splinters is made up of a series of dining areas, a mixture of the modern and the old, with, upstairs, a lounge for pre-dinner drinks and after-dinner coffee. The menu picks up ideas from here and there -Thai-spiced chicken soup with coconut, say, followed by fillet of Aberdeen Angus topped with rocket pesto and served with red wine and balsamic dressing – and generally fuses the components into tasty, attractive dishes. 'First-class, carefully cooked' scallops come with monkfish sausage and chilli jam, and saddle of rabbit with crisp pancetta and a sauce of garlic and thyme. Fish has also been handled well in a main course of sautéed fillets of brill, 'cooked to perfection', in a herby butter sauce along with asparagus and tomatoes. Strawberry soufflé with mango sorbet makes an indulgent pudding, or there might be something along the lines of iced apple parfait with vanilla cream.

Directions: Splinters is directly in front of Priory gates

CHRISTCHURCH,

Waterford Lodge Hotel

Mock Tudor, 19th-century property with a traditionally-styled restaurant. Main course options include cassoulet of steamed lobster or wild Wiltshire rabbit in Armagnac, each with a recommended wine.

Additional: Bar food; Sunday L; Children 5+ D only
Style: Classic/Traditional
Smoking: No smoking in dining room
Accommodation: 18 en suite ★ ★ ★

Directions: From A35 Somerford roundabout take A337 towards Highcliffe, at next roundabout turn R to Mudeford, hotel on L

87 Bure Lane Friars Cliff Mudeford
BH23 4DN
Map 4: SZ19
Tel: 01425 272948
Fax: 01425 279130
E-mail: waterford@bestern.co.uk
Cost: Set-price L £14.50/D £25.50.
H/wine £10.20
Times: Noon-1.30pm/7-9.30pm

CORFE CASTLE,

Mortons House Hotel

A stand alone restaurant within a stone-walled, oak-panelled hotel, offering robust cuisine along the lines of griddled scotch fillet steak with sautéed oyster mushroom. Desserts might include Dorset apple cake with caramelised clotted cream.

Additional: Bar food L; Sunday L; Children welcome
Style: Traditional/Country-house
Smoking: No smoking in dining room
Accommodation: 17 en suite ★ ★ ★

Directions: In centre of village on A351

East Street BH20 5EE
Map 3: SY98
Tel: 01929 480988
Fax: 01929 480820
Cost: Alc fr £23, set-price L £16/D £24. ☺ H/wine £12
Times: Noon-2pm/7-8.30pm

CRANBORNE,

La Fosse at Cranborne ⊛

London House The Square BH21 5PR
Map 4: SU01
Tel: 01725 517604
Fax: 01725 517778
Cost: Alc £25, set-price L £6.95/D £11.95 ☺ H/wine £9.95
Times: Noon-2pm/7-10pm.
Closed L Sat, D Sun, all Mon
Additional: Sunday L; Children welcome
Style: Country-house
Smoking: No smoking in dining room

A charming village restaurant. Lunch is particularly good value but dinner is also reasonably priced, and dishes such as fresh crab on a tower of avocado mousse with coriander and lime are of excellent quality.

Directions: M27 – W onto A31 to Ringwood, then to Verwood, then Cranborne

DORCHESTER, The Mock Turtle

Fish is a real strength at this tastefully decorated, relaxed but professional town house restaurant. Ragout of sole, salmon, squid and prawn with home-made chips taken next to the open fire is a real treat.

Smoking: No smoking in dining room

Directions: Town centre, top of High West Street

34 High West Street DT1 1UP
Map 3: SY69
Tel: 01305 264011
Cost: Alc £23.75, set-price L/D fr £5.
☺ H/wine £9.50
Times: Noon-2pm/6.30-9.30pm.
Closed L Sat & Mon, all Sun
Additional: Children welcome
Style: Informal/Traditional

DORCHESTER Yalbury Cottage

This is a 17th-century thatched cottage with inglenook fireplaces and oak beams in both the lounge and restaurant. The three course set-price menu includes goats' cheese ravioli, local diver-caught scallops, pan-seared and served with tomato confit and sherry vinaigrette. Canapés included a delicious tiny asparagus tartlet served warm and 'brimming with freshness'. Breast of Gressingham duck cooked pink was served with a filo parcel of confit of duck set on a thyme flavoured jus with shallots, all of which went well together. Other main courses include medallions of monkfish with wilted spinach and a red pepper and spring onion sauce and roast rack of lamb with pommes Anna. The coffee crème brûlée, served in a demi-tasse, had intense flavour, evenly caramelised and very good. The dessert menu also includes seasonal variations. The wine list is comprehensive from around the world.

Directions: Two miles east of Dorchester, off A35

Lower Bockhampton DT2 8PZ
Map 3: SY69
Tel: 01305 262382
Fax: 01305 266412
E-mail: yalbury.cottage@virgin.net
Chef: Russell Brown
Owners: Derek & Heather Furminger
Cost: Set-price D £26. H/wine £11
Times: D only, 7-10.30pm. Closed Jan
Additional: Children welcome
Seats: 26-30
Style: Traditional
Smoking: No smoking in dining room
Accommodation: 8 en suite

EVERSHOT, Summer Lodge

Literary gourmets will appreciate the fact that the dining-room of this delightful hotel was designed by a 19th-century architect called Thomas Hardy who also dabbled a bit in writing novels. The old dower house is a true hideaway, the atmosphere is peaceful and comfortable, full of charming flower arrangements and watercolours. The set menu changes daily, and features a daily special, perhaps home-cured gravad lax with a caperberry, shallot and wild parsley salad or classic lobster Thermidor. The cooking draws extensively on local produce – Dorset ham is used in a terrine with smoked sausages and braised vegetables, served with home-made piccalilli and granary loaf; cod from Lyme Regis is served on

DT2 0JR
Map 3: ST50
Tel: 01935 83424
Fax: 01935 83005
E-mail: reception@summerlodgehotel.com
Chef: Gregory Nicholson
Owners: Nigel & Margaret Corbett
Cost: Alc £45, set-price L £12.50/D £42. H/wine £12.50
Times: Noon-2.30pm/7-9.30pm
Additional: Bar food L; Sunday L; Children 7+
Seats: 42. Private dining room 24; Jacket & tie preferred
Style: Country-house/Formal
Smoking: No smoking in dining room
Civil licence: 60
Accommodation: 19 en suite ★ ★ ★

Directions: 1 mile W off A37, between Dorchester and Yeovil. Entrance in Summer Lane

smoked cabbage with artichokes and a shallot and tarragon sauce. Interesting ideas include a bitter-sweet orange and coriander sauce to give edge to crisp breast of Gressingham duck, roast foie gras and fondant potatoes.

FERNDOWN, The Dormy ❀❀

Hennessy's is the new fine dining restaurant at the well-established Dormy Hotel, which is set in extensive grounds adjacent to the Ferndown Golf Club. Completely refurbished in rich colours, the restaurant has large, well-spaced tables set with fine china, and smartly uniformed staff providing professional service. Starters sampled include risotto al salto, pan-fried into a cake, with a perfectly poached egg and rocket salad, and a carefully timed salmon roulade with fresh herbs, chive cream and quenelle of caviar. Quality produce and immaculate timing were also evident in main courses of calves' liver with celeriac and chive purée, and fillet of pork with garlic mash and smoked mushrooms, and the supporting ingredients were well matched to complement both of the meats.

Directions: Off A347 from Bournemouth

New Road BH22 8ES
Map 4: SU00
Tel: 01202 864100
Fax: 01202 895388
E-mail: sergio.nova@devere-hotels.com
Chef: Robert Bird
Owner: De Vere Hotels
Cost: Alc £35.50, set-price L £17.50/D £22.50 (£30 Fri & Sat). ☺ H/wine £14
Times: Noon-2pm/7-10pm. Closed L Mon & Sat, all Sun
Additional: Children welcome
Seats: 50. Private dining room 16 & 20
Style: Classic/Traditional
Smoking: No smoking in dining room; Air conditioning
Accommodation: 120 en suite ★★★

HIGHCLIFFE,
The Lord Bute Restaurant ❀❀

A sweeping curved window looking out over pretty gardens adds a very light dimension to this pleasant restaurant. The modern building is tucked away behind one of the original lodges to Highcliffe Castle, and it retains the classic style both inside and out. In this formal setting the *carte* (at dinner only) and set menus offer a good choice of both the familiar and the slightly unexpected, and a steady local trade proves that the mixture is popular. To begin with there might be St Mark's mushrooms – grilled cup mushrooms filled with French Brie and Stilton, with fresh orange segments and black cherry sauce; or spiced crab and halibut fishcakes with a Mexican salsa. Main choices could include Castle duck – grilled Barbary duck breast served with a crisp noodle basket filled with oriental vegetable stirfry, and sweet and sour plum sauce. Grilled steaks, and fish dishes like Dorset coast sea bass with a black bean sauce infused with coriander and saffron cream, give a hint of this restaurant's flavour. Various coffees and mint chocolates provide an upbeat ending.

Lymington Road BH23 4JS
Map 4: SZ29
Tel: 01425 278884
Fax: 01425 279258
E-mail: mail@lordbute.co.uk
Chefs: Christopher Denley & Kevin Brown
Owners: Simon & Christopher Denley, Stephen Caunter
Cost: Alc £25, set-price L £13.95/D £22.50. ☺ H/wine £11.25
Times: Noon-2pm/7-9.45pm. Closed L Sat, D Sun, all Mon
Additional: Sunday L; Children 10+
Seats: 80
Style: Classic
Smoking: No-smoking area; Air conditioning

Directions: Follow the A337 to Lymington, situated opposite St Mark's churchyard in Highcliffe

MAIDEN NEWTON,
Le Petit Canard ⊛⊛

Relaxing pastel shades provide the background for this simply decorated restaurant, part of a coaching inn dating back to the 17th century. The room is lit by candles and tiny white lights, the tables are well spaced and jazz plays in the background. The style of cooking is a mix of modern British and French producing an interesting choice of dishes. To start, perhaps pan-fried fillets of skate on caper risotto with balsamic black butter. The eponymous canard might appear, among the main-course options, in the form of ginger, honey and garlic marinated breast of Gressingham duck with a sauce from the marinade juices. For something sweet try the glazed lemon tart with blueberry compote, or black pepper ice cream with mango sorbet and kiwi salsa.

Directions: In the centre of Maiden Newton 8 miles from Dorchester

Dorchester Road DT2 0BE
Map 3: SY59
Tel: 01300 320536
Fax: 01300 321286
E-mail: craigs@le-petit-canard.freeserve.co.uk
Chef: Gerry Craig
Owners: Gerry & Cathy Craig
Cost: Set-price D 25. H/wine £12
Times: D only, 7-9pm. Closed Sun & Mon, 2 wks Oct, 2 wks Jan
Additional: Children 12+
Seats: 28
Style: Classic/Informal
Smoking: No smoking in dining room

POOLE,
Haven Hotel ⊛⊛

La Roche restaurant, as its name suggests, has been built out over the rocks of Poole Harbour so it appears to be almost floating on the sea. Part of a covered terrace that runs the length of the building, it's a bit barn-like, long and thin with high ceilings, but its position on the sea is the attraction. Fish is the business, although there might also be foie gras with a potato pancake and Sauternes sauce, followed by roast guinea fowl with wild mushroom risotto and Madeira sauce. Lobster makes an appearance as a starter – topped with tarragon jelly – and as a main course – grilled whole, accompanied by snail butter and prosaically served with chips and salad, or you could start with cockle and parsley soup, or grilled sardine fillets with bacon and herb salad, and go on to well-timed roasted fillet of halibut in a chicken jus, chargrilled Dover sole with chilli, mint and lemon butter, or perhaps fillet of turbot, nicely cooked but rather overwhelmed by boulangère potatoes and red wine sauce. Finish with something like tropical fruit crumble, or Grand Marnier soufflé with orange sauce, and stick to white wines.

Directions: Follow signs to Sandbanks Peninsula; hotel next to Swanage ferry departure point

Banks Road Sandbanks BH13 7QL
Map 4: SZ09
Tel: 01202 707333
Fax: 01202 708796/708281
E-mail: reservations@havenhotel.co.uk
Chef: Karl Heinz Nagler
Cost: Alc £30 (La Roche), set-price L £15/D £24.50. ☺ H/wine £10.50
Times: 12.30-2pm/7-9.30pm (La Roche D only, Tue-Sat)
Additional: Sunday L; Children 4+
Seats: 59 (La Roche), 164. Private dining room 48
Style: Modern/Minimalist
Smoking: No smoking in dining room; Air conditioning
Civil licence: 60
Accommodation: 94 en suite ★★★★

POOLE, **Mansion House Hotel** ✸✸

Thames Street BH15 1JN
Map 4: SZ09
Tel: 01202 685666
Fax: 01202 665709
E-mail:
enquiries@themansionhouse.co.uk
Chef: Gerry Godden
Owners: Robert Leonard,
Jackie & Gerry Godden
Cost: Set-price L £16.50/D £19.50 &
£24. ☺ H/wine £12.50
Times: Noon-2pm/7-9.30pm.
Closed L Sat, D Sun, L Bh Mon
Additional: Sunday L; Children 5+
Seats: 85. Private dining rooms 14 &
30
Style: Classic
Smoking: No-smoking area;
Air conditioning
Civil licence: 30
Accommodation: 32 en suite ★ ★ ★

The 'Roast of the Day' carved from a silver trolley makes a welcome appearance, lunchtimes and Saturday nights, amongst the modern British repertoire of pan-fried risotto and Gorgonzola cake with red pepper essence and pesto, or seared salmon and scallops with courgette and tomato chutney and lemongrass sauce. Tucked away off the Old Quay, the sophisticated, Georgian hotel-restaurant, with its grand piano and wood-panelled walls, has a pleasant if rather formal atmosphere but the welcoming staff make it anything but stuffy. We enjoyed a nicely-risen twice-baked cheese soufflé in a cheese and chive sauce, and an excellent trio of home-made sorbets which provided a pleasant contrast to a slightly greasy main course of breast of duck with a spring roll of confit duck leg served with an oriental sauce. Bread comes from Sally Clarke's bakery in London.

Directions: Follow signs to Channel Ferry/Poole Quay, L at bridge, 1st L is Thames Street

POOLE, **Salterns Hotel** ✸✸

38 Salterns Way Lilliput
BH14 8JR
Map 4: SZ09
Tel: 01202 707321
Fax: 01202 707488
Chef: Nigel Popperwell
Owners: John & Beverley Smith
Cost: Alc £25, set-price L £15.50/D
£19.50. ☺ H/wine £12.50
Times: 12.30-2pm/7-9.30pm

Chef Nigel Popperwell has 12 years at the stove under his belt at this perennial favourite but his cuisine continues to move forward and to keep up with the times. With an outlook over Poole's natural harbour towards Brownsea Island the airy waterside restaurant is elegant and refined. Contemporary tastes influence a menu well grounded in classical technique. Hand-dived Kimmeridge Bay scallops come with a honey roasted parsnip purée and a zesty spring onion and ginger vinaigrette; a super combination of old world and new world flavours. Good use is made of local ingredients throughout the *carte* with Dorset lamb and Bridport bacon making a strong showing. A modish main course of roasted veal cutlet with marjoram and a confit of apricots, lemon and apple demonstrates a willingness to look beyond British shores for inspiration.

Additional: Bar food; Sunday L; Children welcome
Seats: 50. Private dining room 50
Style: Chic/Elegant
Smoking: No-smoking area; Air conditioning
Civil licence: 120
Accommodation: 20 en suite ★★★

Directions: From Poole take B3369 for Sandbanks; after 1.5 miles in Lilliput turn R (Salterns Way). Hotel on R at end

POOLE, **Sandbanks Hotel**

15 Banks Road Sandbanks BH13 7PS
Map 4: SZ09
Tel: 01202 707377
Fax: 01202 708885
E-mail: reservations@sandbankshotel.co.uk
Cost: *Alc* £32, set-price L £14.50/D £18.50. ☺ H/wine £11.95
Times: 12.30-2pm/7-9pm. Closed L Sat
Additional: Bar food; Sunday L; Children welcome
Style: Traditional/Formal
Smoking: No smoking in dining room; Air conditioning; Tie required at D
Accommodation: 116 en suite ★★★

Enjoy panoramic views from the restaurant terrace while you feed on poppy-seed pancake filled with a ragout of wild mushrooms in a horseradish cream. Why not follow that with a white chocolate and raspberry marquise?

Directions: From Poole or Bournemouth, follow signs to Sandbanks Peninsula. Hotel on L

POWERSTOCK, **Horseshoes** ❀

Country pub where the wood-panelled bar and dining room offer a regularly changing menu featuring plenty of fish – perhaps poached salmon with dill sauce or sea bass with roasted peppers.

Powerstock DT6 3TF
Map 3: SY49
Tel/Fax: 01308 485328

Telephone for further details

Directions: In the village of Powerstock, 5 miles NE of Bridport, signposted off A3066 Beaminster Road.

SHAFTESBURY, **La Fleur de Lys** ❀❀

Get good directions; this friendly, intimate former coaching inn restaurant can be a little difficult to find but perseverance is rewarded. David Shepherd offers a French-inspired menu that makes good use of carefully sourced local produce. Restrained garnishing and careful marrying of complementary flavours are paramount here. Interesting experiments can pay off too – a scallop and langoustine starter is served in herb jelly with a spiced pepper cream. More conventional but equally successful was roast saddle of lamb served with baked garlic, flageolet beans, tomato and mint, in a light rosemary sauce. Classic flavours continue at pudding with chocolate soufflé with chocolate sauce and tuile biscuits, but the odd exotic surprise,

25 Salisbury Street SP7 8EL
Map 3: ST82
Tel/Fax: 01747 853717
E-mail: lafleurdelys@fsbdial.co.uk
Chefs: D Shepherd, M Preston
Owners: D Shepherd, D M Griffin, M Preston
Cost: *Alc* £30, set-price D £21.50 & £25.50. ☺ H/wine £12
Times: 12.30-2.30pm/7-10pm. Closed D Sun, L Mon, 2 wks Jan
Additional: Sunday L; Children welcome
Seats: 40

La Fleur de Lys

Style: Informal/Intimate
Smoking: No smoking before 10pm

tulip of Mexican anise liqueur ice cream with pineapple, mango and oranges, say, can just as easily turn up.

Directions: Town centre, near the Post Office, on the main road

SHAFTESBURY,

Royal Chase Hotel 🏵🏵

Royal Chase Roundabout SP7 8DB
Map 3: ST82
Tel: 01747 853358
Fax: 01747 851969
E-mail:
royalchasehotel@btinternet.com
Chef: Andrew Wheatcroft
Owner: Graham Roper
Cost: Alc £21. ☺ H/wine £12
Times: Noon-2pm/6.30-9.30pm.
Closed L Wed
Additional: Bar food D; Sunday L;
Children welcome
Seats: 65. Private dining room 130
Style: Traditional
Smoking: No smoking in dining room
Civil licence: 78
Accommodation: 33 en suite ★★★

Set in its own pleasant grounds on the fringes of Shaftesbury, this former monastery continues to provide an appealing respite from worldly affairs. Inside the Byzant restaurant – so called after an effigy which was carried during an ancient water rite – the tables are uncrowded, the chairs comfortable, and the friendly staff discreet and co-operative. There is plenty of choice on the *carte*, too, with fresh fish always available, a couple of dishes for non-meat-eaters, and a few grills in addition to four or five other main choices. Try a starter like filo basket filled with a warm wild mushroom fondue, or chicken terrine layered with saffron and prawns, served with a tomato and basil concasse. The day's catch might include red mullet, brill or sole, or the menu might offer medallions of beef fillet on Irish champ potato with a red onion gravy, pork fillet with a chicken and smoked bacon farce on an apricot sauce, or noisette of lamb roasted with a red currant and red wine jus. Puddings include the chef's daily special, and coffee and mints are extra.

Directions: On roundabout where A350 crosses A30 (avoid town centre)

SHAFTESBURY,
Wayfarers Restaurant

Sherborne Causeway SP7 9PX
Map 3: ST82
Tel/Fax: 01747 852821
Chef: Mark Newton
Owners: Mark & Clare Newton
Cost: *Alc* £30, set-price L & D
£15.95. ☺ H/wine £9.75
Times: Noon-1.30pm(bookings
only)/7-9.15pm. Closed L Sat, D Sun,
all Mon, 2 wks after 25 Dec
Additional: Sunday L; Children 8+
Seats: 35
Style: Informal/Country-house

Directions: 2 miles W of Shaftesbury
on main A30 heading towards
Sherborne and Yeovil

In an 18th-century cottage bordering farmland, with beamed
ceilings, a selection of prints on the stone walls, and a large
inglenook, recent upgrading has given Wayfarers a green
carpet, chartreuse and gold Queen Anne chairs and primrose
top cloths on white linen. The kitchen takes a modern,
Continental approach to its work, producing a starter of
tortellini of crab with sweetcorn in shellfish sauce, and main
courses of chicken mousse studded with morels and lightly
smoked chicken, all wrapped in Parma ham, served on glazed
apple risotto, or sautéed fillet of sea bream with pommes
parisienne and pesto. If roast fillet of venison stuffed with
chestnuts, herbs and apples, accompanied by quince purée,
sounds like something out of Old England, you could precede
it with langoustine tails deep-fried in tempura with garlic and
chilli mayonnaise. Mille-feuille of butter sablés with coconut
ice cream, pineapple sorbet and tropical fruit salad ends things
on an exotic note. The wine list has been assembled with care,
and all five house wines are particularly good value.

SHERBORNE,
Eastbury Hotel

Long Street DT9 3BY
Map 3: ST61
Tel: 01935 813131
Fax: 01935 817296
Cost: *Alc* £25, set- price L £18.95/D
£12.95. ☺ H/wine £8.95
Times: Noon-2pm/7-9.30pm

*Leading off the intimate stone-walled bar the hotel restaurant offers
a light, conservatory style atmosphere overlooking a charming
walled garden. Main course dishes might include lobster ravioli with
a shellfish vinaigrette.*

Additional: Bar food; Sunday L; Children welcome
Style: Colonial
Smoking: No smoking in dining room
Civil licence: 120
Accommodation: 15 en suite ★ ★ ★

Directions: From bottom of Cheap Street turn R. Hotel 800yds
on R

SHERBORNE, **Grange Hotel** **NEW**

Oborne DT9 4LA
Map 3: ST61
Tel: 01935 813463
Fax: 01935 817464

*Superb views over perfectly manicured gardens from a two-hundred
year old country house hotel restaurant. Food style pivots on quality*

ingredients prepared in a traditional fashion, such as venison with a cranberry jus, or summer pudding.

Additional: Sunday L (noon-2pm); Children 10+
Style: Traditional/Country-house
Smoking: No smoking in dining room
Accommodation: 10 en suite ★★

Directions: Situated just off A30, 1m E of Sherborne. Clearly signposted.

Cost: *Alc* £25. ☺ H/wine £10.90
Times: D only, 7-9.30pm. Closed D Sun, 10 days after Xmas, 10 days in Aug

SHERBORNE,

Pheasants Restaurant ❀❀

In a Grade II listed building, Pheasants is at the top of the high street in a town notable for having two castles. Inside are antiques and a decor of apricot, with stone walls, pictures in the bar and classical music playing in the background. The contemporary British idiom used in the kitchen translates into such dishes as sautéed Cornish scallops and poached asparagus with a dressing of orange, dill and capsicum, and half a local duckling basted with honey and ginger and served with a Cognac sauce. Skill with fish shines through steamed plaice and mussels with a well-balanced citrus butter sauce, and vegetables have been praised for both freshness and flavour. Jam roly-poly may bring tears to the eyes of nostalgia-lovers, here served with raspberries and orange-flavoured custard, and there might also be chocolate truffle tartlet. Sunday lunch sees traditional roast beef with all the trimmings and perhaps fillet of wild salmon with an oriental treatment and stir-fried vegetables.

Directions: At the top of the High Street, A30 (Salisbury/Yeovil)

24 Greenhill DT9 4EW
Map 3: ST61
Tel/Fax: 01935 815252
Chefs: Neil Cadle, Chris Wicks
Owner: Andrew Overhill
Cost: Set-price L £16/D £25. ☺ H/wine £9.90
Times: Noon-2pm/6.30-10pm. Closed D Sun, all Mon, L Tue-Fri, 2 wks mid Jan
Additional: Sunday L; Children welcome
Seats: 40. Private dining room 10
Style: Traditional
Smoking: No pipes & cigars
Accommodation: 6 en suite

STURMINSTER NEWTON,

Plumber Manor ❀❀

Hazelbury Bryan Road DT10 2AF
Map 3: ST71
Tel: 01258 472507
Fax: 01258 473370
E-mail: book@plumbermanor.com
Chef: Brian Prideaux-Brune
Owner: Richard Prideaux-Brune
Cost: *Alc* £23, set-price D £23.29. ☺ H/wine £10
Times: D only 7.30-9pm. Closed Feb
Additional: Sunday L (12.30-2pm); Children welcome
Seats: 65. Private dining rooms 12-25
Style: Country-house
Smoking: No smoking in dining room
Accommodation: 16 en suite ★★★

Plumber Manor is a lovely old family house, and if the formula holds few surprises it's because that's what their loyal customers have come to expect. That's not to damn with faint praise, only to acknowledge that good, unaffected cooking using quality ingredients is often to be preferred to high risk experimentation under the guise of innovation. Stuffed and boned quail in filo had good pastry and great flavour, the game well matched by the wild rice. A light mustard sauce was a good background for some peppered monkfish. Other main courses might include pheasant with red wine and mushrooms or roast leg of lamb Shrewsbury. Chocolate and amaretto torte and strawberry mille-feuille are amongst the list of popular Plumber Manor puddings. The Prideaux-Brunes are a model of hospitality, making every guest feel at home and part of the family.

Directions: In Sturminster Newton cross the packhorse bridge, R to Stalbridge (A537). 1st L to Hazelbury Bryan. 2 miles on L opposite Red Lion

SWANAGE, Grand Hotel

Enjoy wonderful views while you peruse the menu – try oriental sliced duck breast with sweet red onion salad, and move on to pan-fried escalope of veal, or red mullet fillet with lemon, tomato and bacon.

Directions: From North Beach end of town into Ulwell Road, 2nd on R

Burlington Road BH19 1LU
Map 4: SZ07
Tel: 01929 423353
Fax: 01929 427068
E-mail: grandhotel@bournemouth-net.co.uk

Telephone for further details

WAREHAM,
Kemps Country House Hotel

Victorian rectory with views over the Purbeck Hills and a conservatory extension to the dining room. The daily menu might offer roast cod, supreme of guinea fowl, or rib-eye steak.

Additional: Bar food L; Sunday L; Children welcome
Style: Victorian
Smoking: No smoking in dining room
Accommodation: 14 en suite ★ ★

Directions: On A352 midway between Wareham and Wool

East Stoke BH20 6AL
Map: 3: SY98
Tel: 01929 462563
Fax: 01929 405287
E-mail: kemps.hotel@euphony.net
Cost: *Alc* £21.95, set-price L £9.95/D £20.95. ☺ H/wine £9.95
Times: Noon-1.30pm/7-9.30pm. Closed Sat L

WAREHAM, Priory Hotel

Set amidst four acres of well-tended gardens on the banks of the River Frome, the historic former priory balances true professionalism with friendliness. Dinners are served in the vaulted cellar restaurant; weekdays, lunch is taken in the Garden Room. The cooking is skilfull but sometimes perhaps a little more complicated than needs be – a terrine of salmon, lobster and baby leeks with spicy prawns and shellfish dressing contained simply too many ingredients, with a resultant muddle of flavours. Fillet of beef with wild mushroom risotto and rich truffle jus worked better, with the meat cooked just as ordered. Other main courses might include baked halibut with asparagus and baby vegetables on a tarragon and champagne butter sauce or pan-fried calves' liver with crispy pancetta and shallots on a raisin and brandy sauce. As well as home-made desserts there are good English farm cheeses. Jolly fine afternoon teas.

Directions: Town centre between the church and the River Frome

Church Green BH20 4ND
Map 3: SY98
Tel: 01929 551666
Fax: 01929 554519
E-mail: reception@theprioryhotel.co.uk
Chef: Stephen Astley
Owners: Stuart & John Turner
Cost: *Alc* £40.80, set-price D £26.50 (Sat £31.50). H/wine £12.50
Times: 12.30-2pm/7.30-10pm
Additional: Sunday L; Children 8+
Seats: 45. Private dining room 25
Style: Country-house
Smoking: No smoking in dining room
Accommodation: 19 en suite ★ ★

WEYMOUTH, Moonfleet Manor

Fleet DT3 4ED
Map 3: SY67
Tel: 01305 786948
Fax: 01305 774395
E-mail:
moonfleetlfh@netscapeonline.co.uk

Telephone for further details

Directions: A354 from Dorchester. R into Weymouth at Manor rdbt. R at next rdbt, L at next rdbt, up hill (B3157) then L, 2miles toward sea

Hidden away at the end of a winding lane, and enjoying fabulous sea views from the restaurant, Moonfleet Manor is a real find. The menu offers plenty of fish and local meat – crab cake with an orange and saffron cream sauce could start things off nicely, before moving on to fillet of beef, roasted with garlic shallots, finished with a brioche and herb crust and parmentier potatoes, say, or roast cod with wilted rocket, new potatoes and chorizo with balsamic jus. For dessert – sweet champagne and strawberry soup with blood orange sorbet on a nest of angel hair noodles is the finishing touch.

WEYMOUTH, Perry's Restaurant

A Georgian terrace house on the old harbour, Perry's has a good feel to it, rather like going into someone's house. Decor is understated, with half-panelled walls and tables with wrought iron legs and marble tops (clothed in white linen at dinner). Staff wear black trousers and shirts and white aprons to match the black and white pictures, or maybe it's the other way round. A good, modern British menu is strong on fresh seafood dishes such as earthy, well-seasoned shellfish soup with Parmesan and French bread, and a fillet of grey mullet so fresh it was almost swimming, served with chilli and spring onion dressing and home-made chips. Other choices include twice-baked Blue Vinny cheese soufflé with apple and celeriac, and confit of crispy duck leg on braised red cabbage with Cassis sauce. There are good chocolatey desserts such as dark chocolate mousse with coffee sauce.

4 Trinity Road The Old Harbour DT4 8TJ
Map 3: SY67
Tel/Fax: 01305 785799
Chef: Andy Pike
Owners: Alan & Vivien Hodder
Cost: Alc £23, set-price L £17.50. ☺ H/wine £9.50
Times: Noon-2pm/7-9.30pm. Closed L Sat & Mon, D Sun (except Easter-Sep), 25-26 Dec, 1 Jan
Additional: Sunday L
Seats: 60. Private dining room 40
Style: Informal/Traditional
Smoking: No-smoking area; No pipes & cigars

Directions: On western side of old harbour – follow signs for Brewers Quay

WEYMOUTH, The Sea Cow

A spacious welcoming restaurant with bistro-style furnishings set out beneath an old beamed ceiling. Honest, well-balanced cooking was demonstrated by local John Dory simply prepared with spinach and garlic.

Smoking: No smoking in dining room

Directions: On the quay – park in large car parks near town bridge, 5 mins walk to restaurant

7 Custom House Quay DT4 8BE
Map 3: SY67
Tel: 01305 783524
Fax: 01305 767730
E-mail:seacowweymouth@aol.com
Cost: Alc £23. ☺ H/wine £11.45
Times: Noon-2pm/7-10.15pm. Closed D Sun, L Mon, 1 Jan
Additional: Sunday L; Children welcome
Style: Informal/Rustic

WIMBORNE MINSTER,
Beechleas Restaurant

17 Poole Road BH21 1QA
Map 4: SZ09
Tel: 01202 841684
Fax: 01202 849344
Cost: Set-price D £15.75 & £22.75.
☺ H/wine £11.75
Times: L by arrangement only; D
6.30-9pm. Closed Xmas-mid Jan
Additional: Children welcome
Style: Country-house
Smoking: No smoking in dining room
Accommodation: 9 en suite ★★

Directions: On A349 at Wimborne

Listed Georgian house with a conservatory restaurant. The set price dinner menu offers honest food, including naturally reared produce from a local organic farm.

WIMBORNE MINSTER,
Les Bouviers

Oakley Hill Merley BH21 1RJ
Map 4: SZ09
Tel/Fax: 01202 889555
E-mail: info@lesbouviers.co.uk
Chef: James Coward
Owners: James Howard,
Kate Howard
Cost: *Alc* £28.95, set-price L £9.95 &
£13.75/D £24.95. ☺ fr H/wine
£11.95
Times: Noon-2.15pm/7-10pm.
Closed L Sat, D Sun
Additional: Sunday L; Children
welcome
Seats: 30. Private dining room 12
Style: Country-house
Smoking: No-smoking area

Calming shades of green and purple dominate in this warm, intimate and somewhat eccentric French influenced restaurant. The seating is distributed between various areas including a plant filled conservatory and the atmosphere is relaxed and comfortable. For the adventurous, the 'menu surprise' offers a mystery seven-course meal selected by the chef from the best of the day's market accompanied by four wines selected by the sommelier and served by the glass - a tempting prospect given the quality of the conventional menu which offers a progression of five courses. One combination might be: 'to approach' an assiette of smoked salmon with a potato salad, lime and a poached quails egg; 'to refresh' a homemade sorbet; 'to pursue' pan-fried whole Dover sole with a Vermouth wine sauce, 'to carry through' calves liver on braised lentils with smoked bacon and onion; and 'to foreclose' a tangy lemon tart with clotted cream.

Directions: 0.5 miles south of A31 Wimborne by-pass on A349

DURHAM, COUNTY

BEAMISH, Beamish Park Hotel

Smart, classic dining room serving modern British food. A summer meal took in sautéed chicken livers on a savoury drop scone, with balsamic jus, a successful dish, followed by roast breast of duckling with bean brandade and 'lovely' fruit tea sauce. Other main courses might include seared wild salmon on broad bean and home cured pancetta risotto. For dessert, the inspector enjoyed pannacotta with roast apricots and home dried raisin syrup – 'delightful pannacotta, perfect texture, melt in the mouth', with the syrup and apricots harmonising well, making this an 'ideal summer dessert.'

Additional: Sunday L; Children welcome
Seats: 70. Private dining room 70
Style: Bistro-style/Informal   **Accommodation:** 47 en suite ★ ★ ★

Directions: Just off A6076 Newcastle to Stanley road

Beamish Burn Road Marley Hill
NE16 5EG
Map 12: NZ25
Tel: 01207 230666
Fax: 01207 281260
E-mail: beamishparkhotel@bt.click
Chefs: Martin Charlton, Alan Russell
Owner: William Walker
Cost: Alc £16.65, set-price L £12.95.
☺ H/wine £9.95
Times: Noon-2pm/7-10.15pm

CHESTER LE STREET,
Austin's Bar & Bistro

Durham County Cricket Club County
Ground Riverside DH3 3QR
Map 12: NZ25
Tel: 0191 3883335
Cost: Alc £21. ☺ H/wine £9.50
Times: Noon-9.30pm. Closed D Sun,
25 & 26 Dec, 1 Jan
Additional: Bar food L; Sunday L;
Children welcome
Style: Chic/Modern
Smoking: No smoking in dining room;
Air conditioning

Directions: From A1M J63 follow
Riverside sign

Set in the bright modern surroundings of the social and sporting premises of Durham County Cricket Ground, this bistro bar presents contemporary cooking bound to bowl you over.

DARLINGTON, Hall Garth Hotel

Set in 67 acres, this 16th century country house has an elegant, candlelit dining room, serving modern English cuisine. A spring menu might include black pudding and caramelised red onion tart with lemon chutney, or confit of duck leg in filo pastry with a beetroot and honey sauce. Follow that with, perhaps, roast rump of lamb, or roulade of salmon with asparagus, smoked salmon and dill, poached in white wine. For dessert, try white chocolate truffle with mango coulis, or hot bread-and-butter pudding flavoured with cinnamon.

Directions: A1(M) exit 59 (A167) (Darlington), top of hill turn L signed Brafferton, hotel 200 yds on R

Coatham Mundeville DL1 3LU
Map 8: NZ21
Tel: 01325 300400
Fax: 01325 310083
Chef: Kirk Alderson
Owner: Regal Hotel Group
Cost: Alc £25 (Mon-Thu), set-price D
£22.95(Fri & Sun). ☺ H/wine £11.50
Additional: Sunday L; Children
welcome
Seats: 34. Private dining room 12
Style: Country-house/Stylish
Smoking: No smoking in dining room
Civil licence: 150
Accommodation: 41 en suite ★ ★ ★

DARLINGTON,

Headlam Hall Hotel ✿

A Jacobean hall with a wide range of modern facilities, and a popular venue for weddings. A typical dinner menu includes roast best end of lamb, medallions of fillet steak, fricassée of fresh vegetables, and grilled fillet of salmon.

Additional: Sun L; Children welcome
Style: Country-house
Smoking: No-smoking area
Civil Licence: 150
Accommodation: 36 en suite ★ ★ ★

Directions: From Darlington take A67 W towards Barnard Castle, after 5 miles R signed Headlam Hall. 3 miles to hotel

Headlam Gainford DL2 3HA
Map 8: NZ21
Tel: 01325 730238
Fax: 01325 730790
E-mail: admin@headlamhall.co.uk
Cost: A/c £30, set-price L £14. ☺
H/wine £9.20
Times: Noon-2.30pm, 7-10pm.
Closed 25,26 Dec

DURHAM,

Bistro 21 ✿

Popular bistro in restored farmhouse with huge fireplaces and stone-lined cloisters. Grilled lamb cutlets with mint béarnaise and smoked bacon pâté served with truffle oil are both typical of the menu's European influences.

Directions: Off B6532 from Durham centre, pass County Hall on R and Dryburn Hospital on L; turn R at double roundabout into Aykley Heads

Aykley Heads House Aykley Heads
DH1 5TS
Map 12: NZ24
Tel: 0191 3844354
Fax: 0191 3841149
Cost: A/c £23.50, set-price L £12 &
£14.50. ☺ H/wine £10.50
Times: Noon-2pm/6-10.30pm.
Closed Sun, 25 Dec, Bhs
Additional: Children welcome
Style: Bistro/Rustic
Smoking: No smoking in dining room

DURHAM,

Swallow Royal County Hotel ✿✿

The County restaurant offers elegant fine dining with interesting dishes on both the set price and *carte* menus. Friendly and efficient service from smartly uniformed staff adds to the experience. Simple yet effective use of ingredients is the key here. The inspector enjoyed a fine example of a double-baked soufflé of cheddar cheese with grain mustard cream. Main courses such as a generous fillet of roast salmon might be accompanied by squares of mediterranean-style aubergine and peppers, with crushed potatoes. A classic tarte Tatin served with almond ice cream would round off a delightful culinary experience.

Old Elvet DH1 3JN
Map 12: NZ24
Tel: 0191 3866821
Fax: 0191 3860704
Chef: Ken Thompson
Owner: Whitbread (Marriott)
Cost: A/c fr £19.30, set-price L
£16.50/D £25.50. ☺ H/wine £13.50
Times: Last orders 10.15pm
Additional: Bar food L; Sunday L;
Children welcome
Seats: 90. Private dining room
Style: Classic/ Traditional

Swallow Royal County Hotel

Smoking: No-smoking area; No pipes
& cigars; Air conditioning
Accommodation: 151 en suite
★ ★ ★ ★

Directions: From A1(M) onto A690. Follow City Centre signs, straight ahead at 1st roundabout, L at 2nd, over bridge, L at lights, hotel on L

REDWORTH,

Redworth Hall Hotel ❀❀

Nr Newton Aycliffe DL5 6NL
Map 8: NZ22
Tel: 01388 770600
Fax: 01388 770654
E-mail: redworthhall@paramount-hotels.co.uk
Chef: Craig Nicholls
Owner: Paramount Hotels
Cost: Set-price D £37.50.
H/wine £11.95
Times: D only, 7-10pm.
Closed Sun, Bhs
Additional: Children 12+
Seats: 24. Private dining room 18
Style: Country-house
Smoking: No smoking in dining room
Civil licence: 220
Accommodation: 100 en suite
★ ★ ★ ★

The dining-room of the grand Elizabethan hotel has a stately air: mullioned windows, leaded glass and chandeliers add to the sense of grandeur. Housed in the original drawing-room, the room also has splendid stencilled and hand-painted walls by the Cornish artist Lyn Le Grice. The menu is bold, modern and ambitious. A panache of scallops and foie gras with lime brioche was superbly cooked, although faulty timing let down a corn-fed chicken supreme with a boudin blanc and morel ravioli with a light Madeira nage. The cooking overall, however, has much potential and there are some fine ideas here such as local venison with beetroot risotto, chorizo sausage braised cabbage and dry sherry sauce. There's little for vegetarians – only one starter and no main course on our sample menu – but the twice-baked Roquefort soufflé with celeriac and Granny Smith chutney does sound rather tempting.

Directions: From A1(M) take A68. Hotel is on A6072 (off A68) near Newton Aycliffe

ROMALDKIRK,

Rose & Crown Hotel ❀❀

Nr Barnard Castle DL12 9EB
Map 12: NY92
Tel: 01833 650213
Fax: 01833 650828
E-mail: hotel@rose-and-crown.co.uk
Chefs: Christopher Davy,
Dawn Stephenson
Owners: Christopher & Alison Davy
Cost: Set-price L £13.50/D £25.
H/wine £9.95
Times: D only, 7.30-9pm.
Closed D Sun, Xmas
Additional: Sunday L (noon-1.30pm);
Children 6+
Seats: 24
Style: Traditional
Smoking: No smoking in dining room
Accommodation: 12 en suite ★ ★

Simple effective cooking has provided the backbone of success at this welcoming, traditional inn. The dining room is an intimate, candlelit affair – ideal for sampling fresh game direct from the moors, or carefully prepared seafood. A spring meal took in creamed potato gnocchi with leaf spinach and roasted cherry tomatoes, followed by roast fillet of Teesdale lamb with potato, woodland mushroom and black pudding broth. The lamb was tender and succulent, cooked pink, and the cotemporary presentation of this dish added an extra dimension, the broth a rich, light jus with diced black pudding. Steamed syrup sponge with lemon curd ice cream finished things nicely – light sponge and zesty lemon flavours. The wine list offers a good global spread with France to the fore, and a good selection of half bottles and wines by the glass.

Directions: On B6277 in the centre of the village, near the church

RUSHYFORD,

Swallow Eden Arms Hotel ❀

DL17 0LL
Map 8: NZ22
Tel: 01388 720541
Fax: 01388 721871
Cost: *Alc* £18.95. ☺ H/wine £12.50
Times: D only, 7-9.30pm
Additional: Sunday L (noon-2pm);
Children welcome
Style: Classic/Traditional
Smoking: No smoking in dining room
Civil licence: 100
Accommodation: 45 en suite ★ ★ ★

Directions: From A1/M J60, follow A689 for 2 miles to Rushyford rdbt. Hotel opposite

South facing windows allow sunlight to set off the white, yellow and gold decor of this coaching inn restaurant. Dishes such as grilled fillet of salmon with parma ham testify to an imaginative and skilful approach to cuisine.

STOCKTON-ON-TEES,
Parkmore Hotel

636 Yarm Road Eaglescliffe
TS16 0DH
Map 8: NZ41
Tel: 01642 786815
Fax: 01642 790485
E-mail:
enquiries@parkmorehotel.co.uk
Cost: *Alc* £19. ☺
Times: Noon-2pm/6.45-9.30pm

Long established and popular hotel restaurant in an attractive Victorian mansion. An interesting and effective marsh reed theme dominates the decor. Dishes such as medley of fresh fish are well executed and enjoyable.

Additional: Bar food; Sunday L; Children 3+
Style: Classic/Traditional
Smoking: No smoking in dining room
Civil licence: 100
Accommodation: 56 en suite ★★★

Directions: On A135 between Yarm and Stockton-on-Tees, almost opposite Eaglescliffe Golf Course

WEST AUCKLAND, **Manor House** **NEW**

The Green DL14 9HW
Map 12: NZ12
Tel: 01388 834834
Fax: 01388 833566
Cost: H/wine £10.30
Times: Noon-2pm, 7-9.30pm.
Closed D Sun

Enjoy modern cooking artistically presented in the restaurant of this 14th-century manor. Try pan-fried medallions of monkfish, risotto milanese, mussels and bouillabaisse, or seared fillet of lamb, root vegetable, parsnip purée and Madeira sauce.

Additional: Bar food; Sunday L; Children welcome
Style: Country-house/F)ormal
Smoking: No-smoking area
Civil licence: 120
Accommodation: 36 en suite ★★★

Directions: On A68 in West Auckland. 8miles from A1(M) J58

ESSEX

BRENTWOOD, **Marygreen Manor** ❀❀

London Road CM14 4NR
Map 5: TQ59
Tel: 01277 225252
Fax: 01277 262809
E-mail: info@marygreenmanor.co.uk
Chef: Theresa Valentine
Owner: S P Pearson
Cost: *Alc* £32, set-price L £14.50 &

A 16th-century nobleman reputedly named this house the Manor of Mary Green in honour of his bride. Beamed ceilings and carved wood panelling are features of the public areas, and the grand baronial hall-style restaurant is a particularly impressive room, with its high timbered ceiling and heavy

crossbeams. The setting might suggest baron of beef and roast suckling pig, but instead the menu romps around modern, international ideas. A typical meal could range from king prawns stuffed with Mozzarella, wrapped in pancetta and served on a pinenut and basil dressing, take in duck breast with sautéed foie gras, Puy lentils and orange sauce accompanied by vegetable rösti and spaghetti of carrots, and finish with Florida Key lime pie with a base of Amaretti served with crème fraîche. Those craving something more simple can go for plainly grilled Dover sole or Scottish fillet steak with alumette potatoes. The wine list, notable for its helpful tasting notes, has a decent selection of house wines.

Smoking: No smoking in dining room; Air conditioning
Civil licence: 60
Accommodation: 43 en suite ★ ★ ★ ★

Directions: 1 mile from Brentwood town centre, 0.5 mile from M25 J28

£17.50/D £26. ☺ H/wine £16
Times: 12.30-2.30pm/7.15-10.15pm
Additional: Bar food; Sunday L
Seats: 80. Private dining room 50. Jacket & tie preferred
Style: Tudor

AA Wine *Shortlisted for* Award-see page 18

CHELMSFORD, **Pontlands Park**

Beautiful trompe l'oeil paintings adorn the restaurant, and the menu offers a diverse range of modern dishes. An autumn meal began with Thai fishcakes, followed by breast of duck and a chocolate brownie with caramel sauce.

Additional: Bar food L; Sunday; Children welcome
Style: Informal/modern
Smoking: No pipes & Cigars
Civil Licence: 100
Accommodation: 17 en suite ★ ★ ★

Directions: From M25 J28 take A12 then A130; leave by 1st sliproad (Great Baddow), take 1st L

West Hanningford Road
Great Baddow CM2 8HR
Map 5: TL70
Tel: 01245 476444
Fax: 01245 478393
E-mail:
sales@pontlandsparkhotel.co.uk
Cost: Alc £27, set-price L/D £15.50.
☺ H/wine £9.95
Times: Noon-2.30pm, 7-10pm.
Closed L Sat

COGGESHALL,
Baumann's Brasserie ❀

4-6 Stoneham Street CO6 1TT
Map 5: TL82
Tel: 01376 561453
Fax: 01376 563762
E-mail:
food@baumanns.fsbusiness.co.uk
Cost: Alc £25, set-price L £12.50/D £15.50. ☺ H/wine £9.95
Times: 12.30-2pm/7.30-10pm. Closed L Sat, D Sun, all Mon, 1st 2 wks Jan
Additional: Sunday L; Children welcome
Style: Classic/chic
Smoking: No-smoking area

An eclectic approach to décor complements an adventurous take on continental cuisine. Chef Mark Baumann offers dishes such as monkfish and tiger prawn brochette and caramelised banana pancakes.

Directions: In centre of Coggeshall opposite the clock tower

COGGESHALL, White Hart Hotel

Market End Colchester CO6 1NH
Map 5: TL82
Tel: 01376 561654
Fax: 01376 561789
E-mail: whathotel@ndirect.co.uk

Telephone for further details

Directions: From A12 towards Ipswich take A120, L towards Braintree; at B1024 crossroads turn L

An attractive beamed restaurant serving Italian dishes with a good vegetarian choice. A main course of tuna on a bed of rocket with a rich tomato and olive sauce showed the high quality of ingredients.

DEDHAM,
La Talbooth Restaurant

Colchester CO7 6HP
Map 5: TM03
Tel: 01206 323150
Fax: 01206 322309
E-mail: ltreception@talbooth.co.uk
Chefs: Terry Barber & Daniel Clarke
Owners: Gerald & Paul Milsom
Cost: Alc £35, set-price L £19.50/D £27. H/wine £12.50
Times: Noon-2pm/7-9.30pm. Closed D Sun in winter
Additional: Sunday L; Children welcome
Seats: 75. Private dining room 30
Style: Classic/chic
Smoking: No pipes & cigars
Civil licence: 50
Accommodation: 10 en suite (Maison Talbooth) ★ ★ ★

Le Talbooth is a local landmark, situated right on the river with beautiful views of the bridge, swans and other wildlife. The building is heavily beamed and has lattice windows; table appointments are traditional with pale pink linen, bud vases and large dried flower displays. Service is by a young and eager team. The cooking is imaginative, but those with more conservative tastes are encouraged to express their preferences. Thai fishcakes impressed with their evenly-balanced spicing of ginger, lemongrass and five spice. Accurately-timed scallops and langoustines added interest to a portion of saffron and Parmesan risotto. Technique was also to the fore in a well-flavoured loin of lamb served on a celeriac and goats' cheese galette, although red mullet and monkfish on a mille-feuille of Mediterranean vegetables with herby noodles seemed disjointed by comparison. A great wine list has an impressive South African section, as well as a good range by the glass.

Directions: 6 miles from Colchester: follow signs from A12 to Stratford St Mary, restaurant on L before village

GREAT DUNMOW,

Starr Restaurant ❀❀

Market Place CM6 1AX
Map 4: TL62
Tel: 01371 874321
Fax: 01371 876337
E-mail: terry@starrdunmow.co.uk
Chef: Mark Fisher
Owners: Brian & Vanessa Jones,
Terry & Louise George
Cost: Set-price L £22.50/D £21.80-
£35. ☺ H/wine £11.95
Times: Noon-2pm/7-9.30pm.
Closed D Sun

Popular local restaurant-with-rooms with a loyal following –
and deservedly so. The traditional beamed restaurant has been
extended into a sunny and bright conservatory dining area, and
the whole place is relaxed, attractive and comfortable. High
spot of our inspection meal was a superb mille-feuille of field
mushrooms topped with a lightly-poached egg and glazed with
a truffle hollandaise sauce, closely followed by pheasant served
two ways – the leg confit on a herby potato cake, and the
breast with apple and Calvados sauce. Each dish is served with
its own accompanying vegetables – steamed fillet of red
snapper comes with spring onion mash with creamed broad
beans and peas. The pudding menu packs a punch with dishes
such as lemon beignets rolled in cinnamon sugar served with
lemon curd, and all thoughts of school days are banished by
the boozy prunes with creamy rice pud.

Additional: Sunday L; Children welcome
Seats: 70. Private dining rooms 12 & 36
Style: Minimalist
Smoking: No smoking in dining room
Accommodation: 8 en suite

Directions: M11 J8, A120 7 miles E towards Colchester.
In town centre

GREAT YELDHAM,

White Hart ❀❀

Halstead CO9 4HJ
Map 5: TL73
Tel: 01787 237250
Fax: 01787 238044

Telephone for further details

'All country pubs should be like this' remarked the inspector of
this lovely old place. The atmosphere is welcoming, with
young, friendly staff, and its always pretty busy here. The beers
are good but the wine list is even better – and lots by the glass.
Kick off a meal with seared scallops, accompanied by stirfry
beansprouts and hoisin dressing, and follow that with roasted
salmon on baked aubergine and tomato compote with basil
pesto, say, or grilled chicken wrapped in pancetta on a buttered
spinach, potato and celariac rösti. Draw things to a close with
chocolate and pecan nut tart with crème fraîche.

Directions: On A1017 (old A604) midway between Braintree
and Haverhill

HARLOW,

Swallow Churchgate Hotel ❀

Churchgate Street Village Old Harlow
CM17 0JT
Map 5: TL73
Tel: 01279 420246
Fax: 01279 437720
E-mail: info@swallowhotels.com
Cost: Alc £27, set-price D £19.95. ☺
H/wine £12.50
Times: 12.30-2pm/7-10pm.
Closed L Sat
Additional: Bar food; Sunday L;
Children welcome
Style: Traditional/country-house
Smoking: No smoking in dining room
Civil licence: 150
Accommodation: 85 en suite ★ ★ ★

Inviting restaurant in a Jacobean chantry house. Expect the likes of grilled fillet of turbot with anchovies and watercress dressing, and baked canon of lamb with oriental vegetables in filo.

Directions: From M11 J7 take A414 towards Harlow. Take B183 at 4th roundabout, then L into village street; hotel past church, at bottom of hill

HARWICH, The Pier at Harwich ❀❀

The Quay CO12 3HH
Map 5: TM23
Tel: 01255 241212
Fax: 01255 551922
E-mail: leslie@thepieratharwich.co.uk
Chef: C E Oakley
Owner: Gerald Milsom
Cost: Alc £30, set-price L £15 &
£17.50/D £19.50. ☺ H/wine £12
Times: Noon-2pm/6-9.30pm
Additional: Sunday L;
Children welcome
Seats: 80. Private dining room 40
Style: Classic/informal
Smoking: No pipes & cigars
Accommodation: 6 en suite ★ ★ ★

Super views over the Estuary and busy harbour link in with the nautical-themed decor. Seafood is the thing here – and who can blame them when they are so close to the water's edge and also have their own saltwater lobster tanks. A flexible approach to the menu means that a number of dishes now have two prices depending on the portion size, so guests can have two starters if preferred or simply a big bowl of mussels and a glass of wine. Fish and chips are offered in large or extra large portions. Other piscine choices range from pan-fried skate wing with baby capers and lime in nutbrown butter to fillet of salmon with basil pesto crust on a rich tomato and chive sauce. Meat choice includes supreme of chicken stuffed with Suffolk ham and smoked cheddar cheese on a wild mushroom and white wine sauce. The downstairs Ha'penny Pier Bistro serves a simpler, family-friendly menu.

Directions: A12 to Colchester then A120 to Harwich town quay front

MANNINGTREE, Stour Bay Café ❁

It has the feel of an old cottage but sharply focussed and modern – old beams contrasting with a bright orange colour scheme and contemporary art. The menu changes constantly; house-cured mullet with Thai flavours was well-received.

Additional: Children welcome
Style: bistro-style/minimalist
Smoking: No-smoking area; No pipes & cigars

Directions: Town centre (A317 from Colchester to Ipswich) – large green building in High Street

39-43 High Street CO11 1AH
Map 5: TM13
Tel: 01206 396687
Fax: 01206 395462
Cost: Alc £25, set-price L £10. ☺
H/wine £9.25
Times: Noon-3.30pm/7-11.30pm.
Closed L Sat, all Sun & Mon, 3 wks
from 26 Dec

ROCHFORD, Hotel Renouf ❁

Attractive French restaurant overlooking the garden of this smart, red brick establishment. A choice of set price menus ensures variety, from salmon and monkfish in filo pastry with spinach sauce to pressed duck framboise.

Bradley Way SS4 1BU
Map 5: TQ89
Tel: 01702 541334
Fax: 01702 549563
E-mail: reception@hotelrenouf.fsnet.co.uk
Cost: Alc £25-£30, set-price L/D £17.50. ☺ H/wine £10.50
Times: Noon-1.45pm/7-9.45pm. Closed L Sat, D Sun (ex residents), 26 Dec-1 Jan
Additional: Children welcome
Style: Rustic
Smoking: No smoking in dining room; Air conditioning
Accommodation: 23 en suite ★★★

Directions: M25 J29, A127 into Rochford onto B1013

STANSTED, Whitehall Hotel ❁

Church End CM6 2BZ
Map 5: TL52
Tel: 01279 850603
Fax: 01279 850385
Cost: Alc £35, set-price L £17.50/D £22.50. ☺ H/wine £13.50
Times: 12.30-2pm/7.30-9.30pm.
Closed L Sat, D Sun, 26-30 Dec
Additional: Sunday L; Children welcome
Style: Country-house
Smoking: No pipes & cigars; Jacket & tie preferred
Civil licence: 80
Accommodation: 26 en suite ★★★

A 15th-century timber-vaulted dining hall hosting modern décor and cuisine. Good intentions in selecting a light steamed pancake of wild mushroom, courgette and garlic all too easily compromised by a delightful banana steamed pudding with fudge sauce.

Directions: From M11 J8 follow signs for Stansted Airport and then for Broxted

TOLLESHUNT KNIGHTS,
Five Lakes Hotel ✿

Spacious candlelit restaurant with opulent burgundy and gold decor. Dishes are based on local produce and include Blackwater rock oysters, and twice-baked wood pigeon soufflé.

Accommodation: 114 en suite ★ ★ ★ ★

Directions: Kelvedon exit A12 follow signs to Tiptree, over staggered crossroads past jam factory, take left fork, approx 2 miles turn R at T junction

Colchester Road Maldon CM9 8HX
Map 5: TL91
Tel: 01621 868888
Fax: 01621 869696
Cost: *Alc* £28.50, set-price D £23.50.
☺ H/wine £12.75
Times: D only, 7-10pm. Closed D Sun & Mon
Additional: Children welcome
Style: Modern/formal
Smoking: No smoking in dining room

WETHERSFIELD,
Dicken's Restaurant ✿✿

Polite restaurant consisting of two small dining rooms and a larger baronial dining room complete with minstrels' gallery. Decor is quite rustic with pale stripped wall paper and framed pictures of fruit and veg. Tables are adorned with white linen table cloths and napkins and attractive cut crystal vases with fresh flowers. Our first course consisted of a lovely meaty local venison terrine with a superb complement of home-made chutney. Grilled sea bass followed; a really fresh and well-cooked fish served on a bed of stir-fried Chinese vegetables. The meal was nicely rounded off by lime tart with caramel ice cream. The wine list is fairly comprehensive with a good range of prices and is categorised by style rather than region. Service is restrained and low key but helpful.

The Green CM7 4BS
Map 5: TL73
Tel/Fax: 01371 850723

Telephone for further details

Directions: From M11/Stansted Airport take A120, bypass Great Dunmow towards Barintree. Turn L to Great Saling, then R towards Shalford. Wethersfield is next village

GLOUCESTERSHIRE

BIBURY, Bibury Court ✿✿

Cirencester GL7 5NT
Map 4: SP10
Tel: 01285 740337
Fax: 01285 740660
E-mail:
reservations@biburycourt.co.uk
Chef: Tom Bridgeman
Owners: Jane Collier, Andrew & Anne Johnston
Cost: Set-price D £22.50 & £27.50.
☺ H/wine £11.50
Times: Noon-2pm/7-9pm
Additional: Bar food; Sunday L; Children welcome
Seats: 50. Private dining room 30
Style: Informal/Country-house
Smoking: No smoking in dining room
Accommodation: 18 en suite ★ ★ ★

Tucked away as it is behind the main village of Bibury, it's something of a shock to find this imposing Tudor mansion in its substantial grounds. The building has many historic links including a reputed visit by Charles II. Appropriate to its heritage the restaurant is resplendent with wood panelling and log fire, although the cuisine is thoroughly modern. Perusal of

Directions: On B4425 between Cirencester & Burford; hotel lies behind the church

the set-price menu introduces a choice of starters including home-smoked pigeon salad with avocado, black pudding and balsamic syrup. Amongst the main courses may be found pan-fried fillets of John Dory on horseradish mash with a shellfish bisque, while vegetarians can enjoy wild mushroom, spinach and feta basket with Tapenade dressing. A white, milk and bitter chocolate terrine with a Cointreau crème Anglaise would be an admirable end to your meal, but if you can wait an extra fifteen minutes a hot caramel soufflé with pistachio tuilles is calling for your attention.

BIBURY, Swan Hotel ❀❀

Cirencester GL7 5NW
Map 4: SP10
Tel: 01285 740695
Fax: 01285 740473
E-mail: swanhot1@swanhotel-cotswolds.co.uk
Chef: Shaun Naen
Owner: Elizabeth A Rose
Cost: Set-price D £28.50. ☺ H/wine £15.60
Times: D only, 7-9.30pm
Additional: Sunday L (noon-2.30pm); Children welcome
Seats: 60. Private dining room 12. No jeans or trainers
Style: Classic/Formal
Smoking: No smoking in dining room
Civil licence: 100
Accommodation: 18 en suite ★ ★ ★

17th-century coaching inn in beautifully peaceful surroundings. Covered in creepers with stunning private gardens adjacent, the building houses a brasserie and a fine and elegant dining room with rich fabrics and well-spaced tables. It is to the latter that this award applies. A recent meal started out very promisingly with a selection of excellent canapés including salmon and sesame seed toast, crab dumpling and a tiny croque monsieur. The combined flavours really got the taste buds going, further provoked by some tasty apricot flavoured bread, hot from the oven. A starter of creamy morel mushroom risotto with sautéed scallops and chives had great potential but was made slightly disappointing by the heaviness of the cooking. A minor trough however since the main course was certainly the best dish of the night: a beautifully cooked Barbary duck that yielded pink and tender flesh and subtle finish to the slightly crisp skin of honey and pepper.

Directions: On B4425 between Cirencester (7 miles) and Burford (9 miles). Beside bridge in centre of Bibury.

BLOCKLEY, Crown Inn & Hotel ❀

Built of mellow Cotswold stone, this 16th-century coaching inn is full of charm and character. A good choice of dishes can be enjoyed in either the bar or brasserie.

High Street GL56 9EX
Map 4: SP13
Tel: 01386 700245
Fax: 01386 700247
Cost: *Alc* £25. ☺ H/wine £10.95
Times: Noon-2.30pm/7-10pm

Additional: Bar food; Sunday L; Children welcome
Style: Bistro-style/Informal
Smoking: No smoking in dining room
Accommodation: 20 en suite ★ ★ ★

Directions: A44 W from Moreton-in-Marsh, right onto B4479

BOURTON-ON-THE-WATER,
Dial House Hotel ❀❀

The Chestnuts High Street GL54 2AN
Map 4: SP12
Tel: 01451 822244
Fax: 01451 810126
E-mail: info@dialhousehotel.com
Chef: Calum Williamson
Owners: Lynn & Peter Boxall
Cost: *Alc* £24.50. ☺ H/wine £9.95
Times: Noon-2pm/7-9.15pm
Additional: Bar food L; Sunday L;
Children 8+
Seats: 18. Private dining room 14
Style: Country-house
Smoking: No smoking in dining room;
Air conditioning
Accommodation: 14 en suite ★★

Beamed dining room with inglenook fireplace and original kitchen dating back to 1698. Starters might include a filo pastry horn filled with Scottish rope mussels in a saffron cream, or pan-fried pigeon breast with a beetroot and orange salad. From the main course menu our inspector enjoyed a roast tenderloin of pork with a tangy well judged prune and smoked bacon sauce, although the fish of the day option was very tempting. Puddings are traditional but well executed, including bread and butter pudding and vanilla mousse. The cheese board is rather eccentric but well worth investigating, particularly the aptly named 'Stinking Bishop.' The restaurant also offers a choice of over seventy wines, though only about eight are offered by the half bottle.

Directions: In village centre; A436 from Cheltenham, A40-A424 from Oxford

BUCKLAND, Buckland Manor ❀❀❀

Broadway WR12 7LY
Map 4: SP03
Tel: 01386 852626
Fax: 01386 853557
E-mail: buckland-manor-uk@msn.com
Chef: Ken Wilson
Owners: Roy & Daphne Vaughan
Cost: *Alc* £40.50, set-price L £28.50.
H/wine £15.50
Times: 12.30-1.45pm/7.30-8.45pm
Additional: Bar food L; Sunday L;
Children 8+
Seats: 40. Jacket & tie preferred
Style: Country-house/Formal
Smoking: No smoking in dining room
Accommodation: 13 en suite ★★★

On a hill next to a church, within peaceful grounds perfect for a stroll, the ancient manor of mellow stone creates a quintessentially English impression. Within, comfort rather than grandeur is the aim, with traditional furnishings, open fires, some antiques and large flower arrangements. Portraits in oil hang on the walls of the restaurant, a blue-carpeted room with well-spaced, polished wooden tables and upholstered chairs. The manor's own gardens or the Vale of Evesham are where most vegetables, fruit and herbs come from, with everything else impeccably sourced: Scottish venison, salmon and shellfish, Gressingham duck, and so on. A terrine of foie gras with potato and truffle, apple jelly and Madeira, and a main course of baked fillet of salmon with roasted langoustine with pasta, wild mushrooms and langoustine sauce make clear statements about the manor's style, and the menus generally seek to reassure rather than surprise. Timing is spot-on, and sauces a strong suit: witness one of Chartreuse and apple for roast breast of maize-fed chicken with glazed apples and Sarladaise potatoes, another of truffle for sautéed fillet of Aberdeen Angus with rösti, wild mushrooms and creamed spinach. Home-made sorbets and ice creams with fresh and poached fruits make a refreshing end to a meal, although most find the soufflés irresistible: perhaps coffee and Amaretto with chocolate sauce and coffee ice cream. The wine list is massive, so seek advice from the highly professional staff or stick to house wine.

Directions: 2 miles SW of Broadway. Take B4632 signposted Cheltenham, then take turn for Buckland. Hotel is through village on R

CHARINGWORTH,
Charingworth Manor ✿

Chipping Campden GL55 6NS
Map 4: SP13
Tel: 01386 593555
Fax: 01386 593353

Telephone for further details

Lovely 14th-century manor house with a wealth of original features and a beautiful setting. Warm cubed salmon with seared tuna might be followed by pan-fried monkfish stuffed with passion fruit, or chicken breast with Parma ham.

Directions: From A429 Fosse Way take B4035 towards Chipping Campden. Hotel 3miles on R

CHEDWORTH, Hare and Hounds ✿

Foss Cross GL54 4NN
Map 4: SP01
Tel: 01285 720288

An interesting menu of top quality pub food is on offer at this lovely old stone-built pub, where dishes might include chicken breast with haricot beans, saffron and chorizo, or John Dory with aubergine and spring onion ragout.

Telephone for further details

Directions: Telephone for directions

CHELTENHAM, The Bacchanalian at The Hotel on the Park ❀❀❀

An opulent and charming Regency town house; interiors are rich and warm with a great deal of attention to detail in terms of architectural features, soft furnishings and period furniture. The restaurant carries on the Regency theme with striking black and grey panels, and a mural of the nearby Pittville Pump Room. Two huge teddy bears enjoy a gourmet picnic every night at a table in the middle of the restaurant, and no wonder – Simon Hulstone's cooking is intelligent and thoughtful with great clarity of flavour. A starter of red mullet with Japonaise sauce and oyster tempura was described in almost Dickensian terms as 'humble, refined and honest', a good curtain-raiser to a main course of breast of guinea fowl with asparagus mousse and roast butternut squash. Tender and well seasoned, the meat rested upon a velvety smooth potato purée shot through with truffle, prompting the delightfully apt Wodehousian exclamation 'top banana!' Another, very different, main course, taken at lunch, was an excellent piece of seared sea bass with braised lentils in a rich, unctuous meaty sauce with sweet, slow-cooked, creamy garlic and gutsy chorizo sausage.

38 Evesham Road GL52 2AH
Map 3: SO92
Tel: 01242 227713
Fax: 01242 511526
E-mail: stay@hotelonthepark.co.uk
Chef: Simon Hulstone
Owner: Peter Dann
Cost: Alc £35, set-price L £15.95/D £21.50. ☺ H/wine £12.50
Times: Noon-2pm/7-9pm
Additional: Bar food; Sunday L; Children welcome
Seats: 40. Private dining room 18
Style: Classic/Regency
Smoking: No smoking in dining room
Accommodation: 12 en suite ★ ★ ★

Directions: A435 (Evesham) from Cheltenham centre, hotel at 3rd lights opposite Pittville Park

CHELTENHAM, The Beaujolais ❀

Set in the Montpellier area of town, this small, French-influenced bistro has a friendly feel. Good value-for-money food could include an excellent layered terrine of salmon and potato with dill-scented crème fraîche, and pot-roasted pheasant with red wine, shallot and wild mushroom jus.

Additional: Children welcome
Smoking: No pipes & cigars

Directions: Telephone for directions

15 Rotunda Terrace Montpellier GL50 1SW
Map 3: SO92
Tel: 01242 525230
Cost: Set-price L £12.95/D £15.95. ☺ H/wine £9.95
Times: 12.30-2pm/7-9.30pm (10pm Sat). Closed Sun, Mon, Xmas & Easter
Style: classic/traditional

CHELTENHAM,
Le Champignon Sauvage ❀❀❀❀

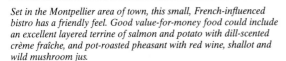

24 Suffolk Road GL50 2AQ
Map 3: SO92
Tel/Fax: 01242 573449
Chef: David Everitt-Matthias
Owners: David & Helen Everitt-Matthias

The pretty, but tiny, restaurant – no more than about 10 tables – is to be found on the south side of Cheltenham in a fairly nondescript street. The exterior is painted white with blue

paintwork and has a French look to it. Inside, the decor is sunny yellow, broken up by an eclectic display of artwork. There's a small lounge-bar with a couple of sofas and high bar stools and that's about it. But the food's the thing, and David Everitt-Matthias knows how to produce some truly delicious meals. This is *'cuisine terroir'* at its best – fresh, full flavours, original, even daring, combinations and impressive technical range. Braised beef cannelloni had a wonderful richness and confit-like intensity, wrapped in leek and matched with sauerkraut and caramelised carrots that in turn contrasted and complemented the flavour. Another first course, perfectly seared duck foie gras, was set atop roasted quince (for aromatic fruitiness) and walnuts (for crunchy contrast), drawn together by a rich Banyuls syrup. There were more savoury-sweet dimensions with pan-fried fillet of brill, pear, celeriac and an unusual caramel-rich, roasted barley jus, although the touch of vanilla was perhaps a flavour too many. The use of vegetables is inspired – roasted beetroot and beetroot purée with roasted roe deer flavoured with Szechuan peppercorns; 'dumpling' of cauliflower and macaroni with Cinderford lamb with cumin; wilted lettuce with gilt-head sea bream and bread jus flavoured with basil and garlic. The spice box is raided for desserts such as warm chocolate tart flavoured with coriander and served with lexia sultana ice-cream, or honey spice bread ice cream with hot fig tart. A tip-top cheeseboard is irresistible, especially when every item thereon is described in loving, precise detail by Helen Everitt-Matthias.

Cost: Set-price L £18.50/D £19.95 & £37.50. ☺ H/wine £10.50
Times: 12.30-1.30pm/7.30-9pm. Closed Sun & Mon, Etr, 2 wks Jun, 10 days Xmas/New Year
Additional: Children welcome; Vegetarian dishes not always available
Seats: 28
Style: Chic/Modern

Directions: South of town centre, near Boys' College on A40 (Oxford). Please phone for exact details

CHELTENHAM, **The Daffodil** ❀❀

Converted cinema now boasting a stylish art deco style restaurant. Many original features have been retained and in place of the cinema stage there now stands an open-plan kitchen where drama and art of the culinary fashion may be observed. The cooking is simple and accurate throughout a menu offering British cuisine with a French or Mediterranean slant. Start your meal with simple classics such as lightly peppered home-cured mackerel fillet, or feta cheese salad with Mediterranean vegetables, black olives and sundried tomatoes. Mains range from Thai vegetable strudel with wilted greens and black bean sauce to fillet steak on a potato and thyme rösti with béarnaise sauce. The dessert menu is so packed with temptation that the proprietors have generously included the option of a selection of bite size samples, which includes fresh raspberry crème brûlée and banana mousse with a light toffee sauce.

Directions: S of town centre, just off Suffolk Rd, nr Cheltenham Boys' College.

18-20 Suffolk Parade Montpellier GL50 2AE
Map 3: SO92
Tel: 01242 700055
Fax: 01242 700088
E-mail: daffodilrest@cs.com
Chef: Paul Wildish
Owner: Ken Bird
Cost: *Alc* £20, set-price L £12. ☺ H/wine £10.50
Times: Noon-2.30pm/6.30-10.30pm. Closed Sun, 25 & 26 Dec
Additional: Children welcome
Seats: 110
Style: Art-deco
Smoking: No-smoking area; Air conditioning

CHELTENHAM, **The Greenway** ❀❀❀

Although on the edge of suburban Cheltenham, the Greenway is in a tranquil Cotswolds setting. Built in the late 16th century, it offers a relaxed and gentle environment, with roomy, elegant lounges and a restaurant looking out over a sunken garden and lily pond, with the hills in the distance. Luxuries are used to good effect – lobster ravioli with sauce vierge, a topping of seared foie gras for pan-fried fillet of Scottish beef on port sauce – but the menus show a sense of balance, with a robust starter of squid ink risotto with battered Cornish squid sitting

Shurdington GL51 5UG
Map 3: SO92
Tel: 01242 862352
Fax: 01242 862780
E-mail: relax@greenwayhotel.demon.uk
Chef: Peter Fairclough
Cost: Set-price L fr £17.95/D £35. H/wine £14
Times: 12.30-2pm/7-9.30pm. Closed L Sat

Additional: Sunday L; Children 7+
Seats: 50. Private dining room 20
Style: Traditional/Country house
Smoking: No smoking in dining room
Civil licence: 45
Accommodation: 19 en suite ★ ★ ★

alongside a delicately composed risotto of goats' cheese with truffle dressing. Vegetarians are treated seriously – there might be colcannon topped with a poached egg and deep-fried leeks – and main courses are split evenly between meat and fish. Sage and onion, those time-honoured partners for roast pork, here go into mashed potato for roast medallion with pork dumplings on Calvados sauce, and fish might be grilled – fillets of red mullet with ratatouille dressing – or baked – halibut with crispy Parma ham with red onion marmalade on a morel cream sauce. 'I can't imagine anyone being disappointed by a meal here' noted an inspector, who finished with 'wonderfully sharp' lemon tart with noteworthy Grand Marnier ice cream, while chocoholics could go for warm fondant with caramel sauce and pistachio ice cream, and the savoury of tooth could opt for home-made crumpets glazed with farmhouse Cheddar topped with onion chutney and perhaps choose a glass of vintage port from the lengthy wine list.

Directions: 2.5 miles S of Cheltenham on A46 (Stroud)

CHELTENHAM,
Hotel Kandinsky, Café Paradiso ✿

Bayshill Road Montpellier
GL50 3AS
Map 3: SO92
Tel: 01242 527788
Fax: 01242 226412
E-mail: info@hotelkandinsky.com
Chef: Sarah Payton
Owner: LHM plc
Cost: *Alc* £35. ☺ H/wine £9.95
Times: Noon-2pm/7-10pm.
Closed D Sun(ex residents)
Additional: Bar food; Sunday L;
Children welcome
Seats: 40. Private dining room 10
Style: Informal/Chic
Smoking: No smoking in dining room
Accommodation: 48 rooms ★ ★ ★ ★

Situated in the hotel's old ballroom, the Café Paradiso is a lively Mediterranean restaurant with a real buzz about it. Sample fine cuisine or go for pizza, home made in the authentic imported Naples oven.

Directions: From M5 J11 follow A40 towards town centre. R at 2nd rdbt, 2nd exit at next rdbt into Bayshill Rd

CHELTENHAM,

Le Petit Blanc

A buzzing brasserie, part of a slowly expanding mini chain, located to the side of the imposing Queen's Hotel. Overall, there's a spacious, minimalist feel and a strong impression that this is where food and service are a priority. Influences are predominantly regional French with a few classics thrown in for good measure (naturally, when the owner is Raymond Blanc of Le Manoir aux Quat' Saisons, see entry). 'Blanc Vite' (fresh fast food on the plate), a children's menu and fixed-price menu are additional features. A gaggle of inspectors sampled starters that included smoked haddock and poached egg risotto; moules marinière; and deep-fried crabcake with green onion risotto and chilli oil dressing. Main courses produced an exemplary roast Barbary duck with albufera sauce; braised pig's cheeks with pommes mousseline and trompette noir; and braised shank of lamb with cassoulet. Floating island 'Maman Blanc', and a stunning pistachio ice cream were the stars of dessert.

Directions: To the side of the Queen's Hotel, town centre

The Queen's Hotel The Promenade
GL50 1NN
Map 3: SO92
Tel: 01242 266800
Fax: 01242 266801
E-mail: petit.chelt@virgin.net
Chef: Phillip Alcock
Owner: Raymond Blanc,
Sir Richard Branson
Cost: Alc £25, set-price L & D £ 12.50 & £15. ☺ H/wine £10
Times: Noon-3pm/6-10.30pm.
Closed 25 Dec
Additional: Bar food; Sunday L;
Children welcome
Seats: 150. Private dining room 80
Style: bistro-style/minimalist
Smoking: No-smoking area; Air conditioning

CHIPPING CAMPDEN,

Cotswold House

Overlooking the town square, the elegant 17th-century house, now under new management, has a lovely dining room that leads out onto a walled patio and garden. Meals start well, with canapés such as seared tuna on blinis. Dishes show an inventive mind at work – saffron risotto with crispy salmon roulade and parmesan crisps, for example. The impact of a fine loin of venison with herb crust, wild mushrooms and fondant potato was slightly undermined by an over-reduced truffle saucing, however. Other interesting dishes include ginger roasted squab pigeon with port a bella mushrooms, potato and carrot mille-feuille and foie gras sauce. Highlight of our inspection meal was a warm strawberry and almond tart, cooked to order and ideally partnered by a light Mascarpone ice cream.

Directions: 1 mile N of A44 between Moreton-in-Marsh and Broadway on B4081

The Square GL55 6AN
Map 4: SP13
Tel: 01386 840330
Fax: 01386 840310
E-mail:
reception@cotswoldhouse.com
Chef: Alan Dann
Owners: Ian & Christa Taylor
Cost: Alc £32. ☺ H/wine £12
Times: D only
Additional: Brasserie L & D; Sunday L; Children welcome
Seats: 40. Private dining room 22
Style: Classic/Traditional
Smoking: No smoking in dining room
Civil licence: 40
Accommodation: 15 en suite ★ ★ ★

CHIPPING CAMPDEN,

The Malt House

A classic Cotswolds cottage backing on to a formal garden with a croquet lawn, flanked by orchards and a kitchen garden is where you'll find this dining room with leaded windows, panelled walls and exposed beams. A wooden floor, opulent fabrics, oil paintings and fine china complete the picture, along with relaxed and informal service. The set menus, of three choices per course, are based on fine seasonal ingredients, with herbs and vegetables often from the garden. The style doesn't stray too far beyond the likes of grilled Welsh goats' cheese with grilled peppers and pesto, followed by seared duck breast with aubergine and red onion marmalade, or a rich and creamy

Broad Campden GL55 6UU
Map 4: SP13
Tel: 01386 840295
Fax: 01386 841334
Chef/Owner: Julian Brown
Cost: Set-price D £29.50. H/wine £17
Times: D only, 7.30-9pm.
Closed Tue, Wed
Additional: Children10+
Seats: 20. Jacket & tie preferred
Style: Classic/Country-house
Smoking: No smoking in dining room
Accommodation: 8 en suite

risotto with marinated artichokes drizzled with balsamic vinegar, then pan-fried fillet of Scottish salmon with gnocchi. Timing, seasoning and the composition of dishes are spot on. Take an inspector's main course of fillet of beef, cooked rare so it melted in the mouth, sitting on top of barely wilted spinach with finely diced sweated shallots, a rich and vibrant paste of chilli, garlic and nutmeg coating the meat, which was surrounded by golden-crisp potatoes roasted in goose fat with toasted pine nuts and sweet roasted cherry tomatoes: 'a taste explosion' of stunning appearance and textures. The same attention is given to puddings, as in a thin, nutty pastry tart enclosing light but rich chocolate fondant perfectly accompanied by home-made vanilla ice cream. France hardly gets a look in on the short but interesting wine list, where prices are on the high side.

Directions: Entering Chipping Campden on A44, turn R for Broad Campden, follow four sharp turns to Malt House

CHIPPING CAMPDEN,
Noel Arms Hotel ⊛⊛

High Street GL55 6AT
Map 4: SP13
Tel: 01386 840317
Fax: 01386 841136
Chef: Jason McNelly
Owners: Cotswold Inns & Hotels Ltd
Cost: H/wine £9.95
Times: D only, 7-9.30pm.
Additional: Bar food; Sunday L (noon-2pm); Children welcome
Seats: 50. Private dining room 12
Style: Traditional/country-house
Smoking: No smoking in dining room
Accommodation: 26 en suite ★ ★ ★

The Noel Arms was already hundreds of years old when Charles II rested here after his defeat at the 1651 Battle of Worcester. Things have changed since then, but this Cotswold-stone hotel retains much of its old-world charm. Refurbishment has brought rich fabrics and antiques to the stylish restaurant, where the largely traditional English style gives a nod to the rest of Europe and the East. Pan-fried breast of pigeon on a bed of chilli lentils, a terrine of game and wild mushrooms, and Cornish crab on a potato and mustard seed salad might be among the starters, with seared calves' liver with bacon and onion gravy, fillet of turbot braised in mushroom and soy stock, and roast rump of Cornish lamb in a tomato jus among main courses. Vegetarians get a good deal – buffalo Mozzarella with grilled aubergines in pesto dressing, followed by leek risotto with saffron cream and grilled asparagus, say – and the sweet-of-tooth could end a meal with rich chocolate tart with white chocolate ice cream, or crispy pineapple sorbet for those who prefer something sharper. Most major wine-producing countries are represented on a wine list that runs to around 50 bins.

Directions: Town centre

CHIPPING CAMPDEN,
Seymour House Hotel ❀❀

Focal and talking point of the 18th-century, wood-panelled dining room is a unique, ancient vine whose green leaves add an 'al fresco' feel. The cuisine is predominantly 'international', but a certain emphasis on pasta has led the hotel to become the home of the Pasta Club, regularly hosting meetings where their pasta skills are on display. The Italian connection also extends to dishes such as risotto nero and 'fiore della notte', a blend of mascarpone cheese and brandy sabayon topped with hot chocolate sauce. French-style dishes include sea bass with Champagne beurre blanc and wilted spinach, and Chateaubriand with béarnaise sauce; British influences show in a rack of Cornish lamb on beetroot fritters with a port and redcurrant sauce. Service is professional, crisp, but friendly.

Directions: Town centre

High Street GL55 6AH
Map 4: SP13
Tel: 01386 840429
Fax: 01386 840369
E-mail: enquiry@seymourhousehotel.com
Chef: Kevin Chatfield
Cost: Alc £25, set-price L £9.50. ☺
H/wine £13.50
Times: Noon-2pm/7-10pm
Additional: Bar food; Sunday L; Children welcome
Seats: 60. Private dining room 40
Style: informal
Smoking: No smoking in dining room
Civil licence: 65
Accommodation: 15 en suite ★ ★ ★

CHIPPING CAMPDEN,
Three Ways House ❀

With an evening restaurant plus brasserie/bar, there's an excellent choice from extensive menus, and the puddings are all one would expect from the home of the famous Pudding Club.

Mickleton GL55 6SB
Map 3: SO92
Tel: 01386 438429
Fax: 01386 438118
E-mail: threeways@puddingclub.com
Cost: Alc £32, set-price D £21. ☺
H/wine £10.50
Times: D only 7-9.30pm
Additional: Bar food; Sunday L (12.30-2.30pm); Children welcome
Style: Chic/Modern
Smoking: No smoking in dining room; Air conditioning
Civil licence: 40
Accommodation: 41 en suite ★ ★ ★

Directions: On B4632, in village centre

CIRENCESTER, **Crown of Crucis** ❀

A 16th-century coaching inn (now a classy hotel) with a bright, modern, pine-adorned restaurant. Trio of shellfish terrine proved a

Ampney Crucis GL7 5RS
Map 3: SP00
Tel: 01285 851806
Fax: 01285 851735
E-mail: info@thecrownofcrucis.co.uk
Cost: Alc £19, set-price D £17. ☺
H/wine £8.25
Times: Noon-2.30pm/7-10pm. Closed 25 Dec
Additional: Bar food; Sunday L; Children welcome
Style: Informal/Modern
Smoking: No smoking in dining room; Air conditioning
Accommodation: 25 en suite ★ ★ ★

light and subtle starter, duck breast in an orange and thyme infused jus an excellent main.

Directions: 3 miles E of Cirencester on A417 to Lechlade

CIRENCESTER, Polo Canteen

29 Sheep Street GL7 1QW
Map 4: SP00
Tel: 01285 650977
Fax: 01285 642777
Cost: *Alc* £25. ☺ H/wine £9.95
Times: Noon-2pm/7-10pm.
Closed Sun, 25-26 Dec
Additional: Children welcome
Style: Informal/Colonial
Smoking: Air conditioning

A bustling brasserie on the edge of town with breezy, brightly coloured polo themed decor. Menu style is simple and covers a wide range, from calves' liver to the house burger and chips.

Directions: Just off Cirencester ring road, opposite Waitrose

CIRENCESTER,
Stratton House Hotel

Gloucester Road GL7 2LE
Map 3: SP00
Tel: 01285 651761
Fax: 01285 640024
E-mail: shh/forestdale@forestdale.com
Cost: *Alc* £18.75, set-price D £18.75.
☺ H/wine £8.75
Times: D only, 7-10pm

Attractive 17th-century manor house with a traditional restaurant overlooking a pretty walled garden. A house speciality is braised hock of English lamb served with parsley mash and onion gravy.

Additional: Bar food; Sunday L (noon-2pm); Children welcome
Style: Country-house
Smoking: No smoking in dininmg room
Civil licence: 150
Accommodation: 41 en suite ★ ★ ★

Directions: M4 J15, A419 to Cirencester, hotel on L on A417. M5 J 11 to Cheltenham, follow B4070 to A417, hotel on R

CLEARWELL,
Tudor Farmhouse Hotel

Near Coleford GL16 8JS
Map 3: SO50
Tel: 01594 833046
Fax: 01594 837093
E-mail: reservations@tudorfarmhse.u-net.com
Cost: *Alc* £21.50, set-price D £20. ☺
H/wine £9.95
Times: D only, 7-9pm. Closed D Sun, 23-30 Dec

A converted 13th-century cottage adjacent to the main house contains this delightful hotel dining room. Features include wooden beams, exposed stone and open fireplaces. Dishes along the lines of lamb cutlets with a herb and black pepper crumb.

Additional: Children welcome
Smoking: No smoking in dining room
Accommodation: 21 en suite ★ ★

Directions: Leave Monmouth to Chepstow road at Redbrook, follow signs Clearwell, turn L at village cross, hotel on L

COLN ST ALDWYNS,
New Inn at Coln ❀❀

Cirencester GL7 5AN
Map 4: SP10
Tel: 01285 750651
Fax: 01285 750657
E-mail: stay@new-inn.co.uk
Chef: Stephen Morey
Owners: Mr & Mrs Brian Evans
Cost: Set-price L £22.50(Sun
£16.75)/D £26.50. ☺ H/wine £10.75
Times: Noon-2pm(Sun 2.30pm)/7-
9pm (9.30pm Fri & Sat)
Additional: Bar food; Sunday L;
Children 10+
Seats: 32. Private dining room 20
Style: Chic/Rustic
Smoking: No smoking in dining room
Accommodation: 14 en suite ★ ★

Genuine hospitality is a hallmark of this justifiably popular,
creeper-covered Cotswold stone inn, dating from the reign of
Elizabeth I. Flagstone floors, wooden beams and inglenook
fireplaces abound, and the hop-garlanded Courtyard Bar
serves a generous repertoire of three-course offerings. Stephen
Morey's British/Mediterranean influenced menus excite and
are based around quality ingredients, balance and simplicity.
Dinner in the cottagey restaurant, with its linen tableware,
fresh flowers and candlelight, begins with canapés – tartlet of
chicken liver parfait, chargrilled prawns and anchovy stick on a
memorable spring visit – while a starter featured confit of duck
with bamboo shoots, noodles and a plum and sweet chilli
sauce. Perfect rösti potatoes with red cabbage, confit of shallots
and a roasted garlic and cream sauce accompanied our main
course fillet of beef, while a mille-feuille of iced coffee parfait
with brandy snaps and bitter orange sauce continued an
impressively upbeat meal. Good coffee and delicate petits
fours – the lemon meringue pie was excellent, light and zesty –
to finish. 'I'd spend my own money here', enthused one
inspector.

Directions: 8 miles E of Cirencester between Bibury (B4425)
and Fairford (A417)

CORSE LAWN,
Corse Lawn House Hotel ❀❀

GL19 4LZ
Map 3: SO83
Tel: 01452 780771
Fax: 01452 780840
E-mail: hotel@corselawnhouse.u-
net.com
Chefs: Baba Hine, Andrew Poole
Owners: The Hine Family
Cost: *Alc* £30, set-price L £16.95/D
£25. H/wine £10.50
Times: Noon-2pm/7-9.30pm.
Closed 24-26 Dec
Additional: Bar food; Sunday L;
Children welcome
Seats: 50. Private dining rooms 16, 35
Style: Informal/Country-house

A cluster of Queen Anne buildings in a tranquil setting facing
a pond make up this friendly and comfortable hotel. The
interior, done out in Regency style, with some family antiques
and paintings, is in keeping with the building's age, and the
kitchen works around a broadly Anglo-French style, from
boudin blanc with mustard sauce and champ, to chargrilled
salmon with caper sauce. Choice is generous to a T, with a
carte and a set-price menu in tandem at both lunch and dinner,
so the range can extend from Mediterranean fish soup, or pork
terrine with apple chutney, to a successful version of cassoulet
involving seared tuna and seafood sausages in a tomato and
white bean broth, or stuffed saddle of rabbit with mustard
sauce and pasta. The highlight of one meal was a pudding of
vanilla cream with poached fruits, while those wanting

indulgence could opt for a trio of chocolate (parfait, bavarois and fudge cake). It's worth spending some time over the well-chosen wine list, although the house wines are sound enough.

Directions: Village centre, on B4211 5 miles south-west of Tewkesbury

EWEN, Wild Duck Inn ❀

Smoking: No smoking in dining room
Civil licence: 80
Accommodation: 19 en suite ★ ★ ★

Drakes Island GL7 6BY
Map 3: SU09
Tel: 01285 770310
Fax: 01285 770924
E-mail: wduckinn@aol.com

Telephone for further details

'An example to others of how good pub food can be' remarked an inspector of this charming 17th-century inn. A daily changing menu is punchy and ideally suited to the surroundings, and staff are easy-going and friendly.

Directions: Telephone for directions

FOSSEBRIDGE, Fossebridge Inn ❀

Tudor dining room with stone walls, beamed ceiling, flagstone floor and original fireplaces. Try Venison haunch steak with a turnip and swede dauphinoise or beer battered cod and chips.

Additional: Bar food L; Sunday L; Children welcome
Style: Informal/Traditional
Smoking: No smoking in dining room
Civil licence: 75
Accommodation: 10 en suite ★ ★

Cheltenham GL54 3JS
Map 4: SP01
Tel: 01285 720721
Fax: 01285 720793
E-mail:
fossebridgeinn@compuserve.com
Cost: Alc £20. ☺ H/wine £9.95
Times: 12-2.30pm/6.30-9.30pm

Directions: On A429 between Cirencester and Northleach

FRAMPTON-ON-SEVERN,
Restaurant on the Green ❀❀

A small, intimate country-house restaurant in a peaceful village next to purportedly the longest village green in England. The restaurant is crisp and clean and offers candle-lit dining and friendly, attentive service. On a recent inspection a chicken, pork and pistachio terrine opened the evening. The terrine was full flavoured and served with pickled walnut and a small mixed leaf salad. Well-cooked tender guinea fowl with crispy skin full of flavour formed the centrepiece of an excellent main dish. The fowl was nicely complemented by a rich but not overpowering cranberry and port jus and accompanying vegetables were all cooked to perfection - firm

The Green GL2 7DY
Map 3: SO70
Tel: 01452 740077
Chef/Owner: Gill Getvoldsen
Cost: Set-price L £10/D £23.95. ☺
H/wine £8.50
Times: Noon-2pm/7-midnight. Closed
D Sun, all Mon, L Tue & Wed
Additional: Sunday L(pre booked
only) ; Children 10+
Seats: 26
Style: Traditional/Country-house
Smoking: No smoking in dining room

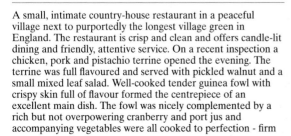

but far from raw. For dessert a dark chocolate, coffee and Mascarpone cheesecake on a ginger crunch base was very rich but rather lacking in precision. A list of approximately thirty wines includes Champagne, dessert wine and some half bottles.

Directions: From M5/J13 take A38 towards Bristol. Turn R at Frampton/Saul signpost, continue for 1 mile, L across village green, restaurant at end, on R

LOWER SLAUGHTER,

Lower Slaughter Manor ❀❀❀

The setting is quintessential English country house - a listed 17th-century manor house furnished with chintz and heavy drapes, white linen, shiny silver and cut glass. Thankfully, staff are less stuffy than the norm, happy to help and advise. An inspection meal started with a deceptively simple dish of scallops, simply roasted, nicely caramelised and just set in the middle, served with confit tomatoes, herb salad and a touch of creamy truffle dressing. Other first courses might include pressed terrine of chicken and guinea fowl with shallot and French bean salad, or *mi-cuit* foie gras with five spice relish. The kitchen is capable of intriguingly imaginative ideas: roast fillet of zander with a clam, bacon and parsley nage; honey roast breast of duck with apples and turnips and a lightly spiced sauce; crème caramel flavoured with lemongrass, ginger, coconut and roasted pineapple. Confit is a very abused word, but here it means slow-cooked cloves of garlic in goose fat served with seared fillet of sea bass and an intense lobster sauce.

Directions: Off A429, signposted 'The Slaughters'. 0.5 miles into village on R

GL54 2HP
Map 4: SP12
Tel: 01451 820456
Fax: 01451 822150

Telephone for further details

LOWER SLAUGHTER,

Washbourne Court Hotel ❀❀

Beamed ceilings, open log fires, flagstone floors and mullioned windows characterise this splendid 17th-century, honey-coloured Cotswold stone hotel set alongside the River Eye. There's a traditional English feel to the public rooms, especially in the formal dining room situated in the new part of the building, where tables are well spaced and enjoy views over the grounds and river. The style of cooking is modern, the menu innovative and extensive, and, on a spring visit, delivered a goats' cheese tart with sweet red onion confit and asparagus for appetiser, followed by pan-fried scallops with saffron risotto and a lime and ginger dressing. Sage mash and a Meaux mustard sauce accompanied the main dish of tenderloin of pork. Dessert – honey roasted apple on toasted brioche with vanilla ice cream and caramel sauce – was preceded by a pre-dessert chocolate marquise with crème anglaise, the highlight of the meal. The wine list offers an extensive, interesting and well-balanced selection with prices to match, and includes a good list of half-bottles.

Directions: Off A429 village centre by the river

GL54 2HS
Map 4: SP12
Tel: 01451 822143
Fax: 01451 821045
E-mail: washbourne@classic.msn.com
Chef: Sean Bollington
Owners: Mr & Mrs R Vaughan
Cost: Set-price L £19. H/wine £14.75
Times: 12.30-2pm/7.30-9pm
Additional: Bar food; Sunday L; Children 12+
Seats: 60. Private dining room 20. Jacket & tie preferred
Style: Classic/Country-house
Smoking: No smoking in dining room
Accommodation: 28 en suite ★ ★ ★

MORETON-IN-MARSH,
Manor House Hotel ❀❀

High Street GL56 0LJ
Map 4: SP23
Tel: 01608 650501
Fax: 01608 651481
E-mail: themanor2@aol.com

Telephone for further details

Directions: Off A429 at S end of town

Sixteenth-century coaching inn built in honey coloured Cotswold stone. The Mulberry restaurant has a brasserie feel to it, tied in with a relaxed and jovial atmosphere. On a recent visit the menu included a tomato tart with tapenade, red pepper coulis and basil; a roasted salmon with a haddock fishcake and saffron sauce and a simple lemon tart for dessert.

MORETON-IN-MARSH,
Marsh Goose Restaurant ❀❀

High Street GL56 0AX
Map 4: SP23
Tel: 01608 653500
Fax: 01608 653510
Chef: Sonya Kidney
Owners: Leo Brooke-Little & Sonya Kidney
Cost: Set-price L £17/D £30. H/wine £12.50
Times: 12.30-2.30pm/7.30-9.30pm. Closed all Mon, D Sun, L Tue
Additional: Sunday L; Children welcome
Seats: 45
Style: Informal/Modern
Smoking: No smoking in dining room

Directions: In the High Street opposite the war memorial

Although the 18th-century building is set in the High Street of the old market town, the re-styled interior is fresh and airy with modern artwork. Chef Sonya Kidney is back behind the stove and her modern British cooking, with some global influences, simply zips along, fuelled by keen intelligence, commitment and quality ingredients. Seasonal vegetables are important – in March, for example, you might find braised chicory with red mullet, or a jerusalem artichoke purée and butternut squash with rack of lamb. Combinations are colourful, both in flavour and visual effect – pigeon breast with beetroot tartare and globe artichoke purée; venison and veal terrine with pineapple chutney and bitter orange dressing; duck breast with braised bok choi, ginger, lime and sultanas. Not that the classics are neglected: for Sunday lunch there may be chicken, thyme and ox tongue terrine with apple and sultana chutney followed by roast loin of Gloucester Old Spot with braised red cabbage and mustard sauce, and sticky toffee pudding.

NAILSWORTH, Egypt Mill Hotel ❀

GL6 0AE
Map 3: ST89
Tel: 01453 833449
Fax: 01453 836098
Cost: Alc £25. ☺ H/wine £9.90
Times: D only, 7-9.45pm. Closed D Sun-Tue
Additional: Bar food; Sunday L(noon-2pm); Children welcome
Style: Traditional

Hotel restaurant in converted 16th-century mill. The menu caters for all tastes, from veal steaks served with a madeira sauce and garnished with galte potatoes and baby button mushrooms to roasted vegetable crumble.

Smoking: No smoking in dining room
Accommodation: 17 en suite ★ ★

Directions: On A46

NAILSWORTH, Waterman's ❀❀

Old Market GL6 0BX
Map 3: ST89
Tel: 01453 832808
Chef: Sarah Waterman
Owners: John & Sarah Waterman
Cost: Alc £23.50. ☺ H/wine £9.50
Times: D only 6-11pm. (Sat L 10-2pm). Closed all Sun & Mon, L Tue-Fri, 2 wks Jan
Additional: Bar food L Sat; Children welcome
Seats: 28. Private dining room 12
Smoking: No-smoking area; No pipes & cigars

Waterman's is housed in a small and cosy 16th-century Cotswold stone cottage and is easily found in the centre of the village of Nailsworth. Much of the vegetable produce comes from the owners' allotments. The herbs come from their charming courtyard where there is a herb garden and fountain – a delight for alfresco drinks and dining. The *carte* is supplemented by daily specials. Appetisers are provided on the house – fine cheese straws on the day our inspector was there. There are always two types of home-made bread (on this occasion sundried tomato and a heavy brown). The menu consists of six starters and main courses which generally are elaborate and well thought-out. The foie gras and bacon potato cakes topped with a poached egg were well-cooked and presented, containing 'fluffy' potato and a generous balance of foie gras to bacon. The prime English spring lamb noisettes roasted with lavender on a rough rosemary and olive oil mash were a great success – very tender noisettes, cooked pink as requested. The service is relaxed and friendly and the wine list is well-balanced.

Directions: Signposted off A46, in the centre of Nailsworth

PAINSWICK, **Painswick Hotel** ❀❀

Kemps Lane
GL6 6YB
Map 3: SO80
Tel: 01452 812160
Fax: 01452 814059
E-mail: reservations@painswick.com
Chef: Kevin Barron
Owners: Gareth & Helen Pugh

With the recent recruitment of chef Kevin Baron this professional and friendly hotel restaurant goes from strength to strength. The building dates from 1790 and began life as a rectory. The restaurant is decked out in good quality fabrics and pine panelling - the very image of simplicity and elegance.

The views of rolling countryside are stunning, though most will be too preoccupied with the truly excellent cuisine to notice. Take for example our starter of pan roasted scallops. Good quality, simply seared scallops were sweet, meaty and tender, The accompaniments of parcels of a nicely intense tomato confit, and clean tasting aubergine caviar with a hint of garlic set off the flavours nicely. A main of turbot, young leeks, crab tortellini and a wild mushroom broth attracted similar praise from our inspector who, having run out of traditional superlatives, concluded by describing the baked chocolate tart dessert as simply 'yummy.' Praise indeed.

Directions: From Painswick centre turn by the church, continue & turn R by the cross. Hotel 1st turn on R

Cost: Set-price L £13/D £26. ☺
H/wine fr £12.50
Times: 12.30-2pm/7-9.30pm
Additional: Bar food L; Sunday L; Children welcome
Seats: 32. Private dining room 18
Style: Classic/Country-house
Smoking: No smoking in dining room
Civil licence: 100
Accommodation: 19 en suite ★★★

PAXFORD,

Churchill Arms ❀❀

'A pub with food, not a restaurant with beer.' The catch phrase of this charming establishment is a reflection of its laid back, unpretentious attitude. Although features such as the fine inglenook fireplace, wood burning stove and the resident locals denote a charmingly traditional Cotswold pub the approach to service and cuisine is thoroughly modern and effortlessly professional. The often experimental menu is changed daily but might include dishes such as salad of duck with grapefruit segments and fennel salad, or ox tongue, crisp sweetbreads, diced beetroot and Cumberland sauce for the starters. A similarly eclectic approach may be found in the selection of main dishes, from brill, creamed leeks, beurre blanc with smoked salmon, to honey roast ham, egg and chips. With passion fruit mousse or sticky toffee pudding for dessert and a glass or two from the sizeable wine list or selection of real ales, diners are spoilt for choice and quality.

Directions: Situated 2m E of Chipping Campden

GL55 6XH
Map 4: SP13
Tel: 01386 594000
Fax: 01386 594005
E-mail: the-churchill-arms@hotmail.com
Chef: Ivan Ried
Owners: Sonya & Leo Brooke-Little
Cost: Alc £20. ☺ H/wine £9.50
Times: Noon-2pm/7-9pm
Additional: Bar food; Sunday L; Children welcome
Seats: 60
Style: Informal/Traditional
Smoking: Air conditioning

RANGEWORTHY,

Rangeworthy Court Hotel ❀

A historic country house sharing its extensive grounds with a church. Despite its country setting it is easily reached from the motorway system. Traditional English cuisine with interesting touches, and a separate vegetarian menu.

E-mail: hotel@rangeworthy.demon.co.uk
Cost: Alc £22.50, set-price L £12.50/D £15.50. ☺
H/wine £10.50
Times: Noon-2pm/7-9pm (9.30pm Sat)
Additional: Bar food; Sunday L; Children welcome
Style: Country-house
Smoking: No smoking in dining room
Civil licence: 60
Accommodation: 13 en suite ★★

Directions: Signposted off B4058, down Church Lane

Church Lane Wotton Road
BS37 7ND
Map 3: ST68
Tel: 01454 228347
Fax: 01454 228945

STONEHOUSE,

Stonehouse Court ⚜⚜

The original manor, built in 1601, is a Grade II listed building of great charm, with the John Henry Restaurant an attractive, panelled room with an open fireplace. The *carte* runs from grilled Dover sole with lemon butter, to slow-roast shank of lamb with glazed vegetables, with starters of a salad of salmon with asparagus and hollandaise, or twice-baked Stilton and walnut soufflé. Equally, those with a spirit of adventure could start with shallow-fried spring onion and cumin fishcake with beetroot crisps and dill and yogurt dressing, and go on to grilled salmon steak with crayfish mash and veal sauce, or chorizo sausage and pancetta pizza with roasted vegetables, rocket and truffle oil. Either way, end with a good choice of farmhouse cheeses, puddings of fresh fruit salad with lemongrass and peppercorn syrup, or apple and sultana strudel with five spice custard, and enjoy the wine.

Directions: M5 J13/A419 (Stroud. Straight on at 2 rdbts, under rail bridge. Hotel 100yds on R

Stroud GL10 3RA
Map 3: SO80
Tel: 01453 825155
Fax: 01453 824611
E-mail:
stonehouse.court@pageant.co.uk
Chef: Mohammed Ali Hussain
Owner: Pageant Hotels
Cost: *Alc* £25. ☺ H/wine £10.50
Times: Noon-2pm/7-9.30pm.
Closed L Sat
Additional: Bar food; Sunday L;
Children welcome
Seats: 60. Private dining room 40
Style: Traditional/Country-house
Smoking: No smoking in dining room
Civil licence: 120
Accommodation: 35 en suite ★★★

STOW-ON-THE-WOLD,

Fosse Manor ⚜

GL54 1JX
Map 4: SP12
Tel: 01451 830354
Fax: 01451 832486
E-mail:
fossemanor@bestwestern.co.uk
Cost: *Alc* £35, set-price L £15.50/D
£25. ☺ H/wine £11.95
Times: Noon-2pm/6.30-9.30pm.
Closed Xmas

Modern British cooking with some traditional and international influences in this informal, country-house style hotel restaurant. Dishes might include breast of pigeon with pepper and ham mash, or fillet of salmon with crab and herb crumb.

Additional: Bar food; Sunday L; Children welcome
Style: Country-house
Smoking: No smoking in dining room; Air conditioning
Civil licence: 40
Accommodation: 23 en suite ★★★

Directions: One mile S of Stow-on-the-Wold on the A429 (Cirencester)

STOW-ON-THE-WOLD,

Grapevine Hotel ❀

Sheep Street GL54 1AU
Map 4: SP12
Tel: 01451 830344
Fax: 01451 832278
E-mail: enquiries@vines.co.uk
Cost: Set-price L £10/D £26. ☺
H/wine £13.25
Times: Noon-2.30pm/7-9.15pm
Additional: Bar food; Sunday L;
Children welcome
Style: Informal/Conservatory
Smoking: No smoking in dining room
Civil licence: 60
Accommodation: 22 en suite ★★★

A delightful 17th-century hotel that takes its name from the knarled Hamburg vine which canopies the conservatory restaurant. A well cooked pigeon starter and lamb main followed by a chocolate fondant were all much enjoyed.

Directions: Take A436 towards Chipping Norton; 150yds on R facing green

STOW-ON-THE-WOLD,

The Royalist

Digbeth Street GL54 1BN
Tel: 01451 830670
Fax: 01451 870048

As we went to press Alan & Georgina Thompson of AA three-rosetted restaurant 755 Fulham Road, London, were moving to Gloucestershire. The Royalist is due to open in the summer – check our website for the latest details. (www.theaa.co.uk/hotels)

Telephone for further details

STOW-ON-THE-WOLD,

Wyck Hill House Hotel ❀❀

Burford Road GL54 1HY
Map 4: SP12
Tel: 01451 831936
Fax: 01451 832243
E-mail: wyckhill@wrensgroup.com
Chef: Ian Smith
Owner: Wren's Hotel Group
Cost: *Alc* £36.50, set-price L £13.50 & £19.95. H/wine £14.95
Times: 12.30-2pm/7-9.30pm(9pm Sun)
Additional: Bar food L; Sunday L; Children welcome
Seats: 60. Private dining room 40.
Jacket & tie preferred
Style: Traditional/Country-house
Smoking: No smoking in dining room; Air conditioning (in conservatory)
Civil licence: 80
Accommodation: 32 en suite ★★★★

Classical methods of preparation combined with a modern approach to presentation results in top quality English cuisine. All dishes are prepared entirely to order from fresh, often local ingredients. Any resulting delays in production are well worth enduring for dishes such as sauté of smoked duck with sun-dried tomatoes, caramelised onions and a small herb salad for starters. Main course dishes are generally simple but well executed such as supreme of fresh salmon, char grilled sirloin steak or sautéed breast of chicken, all served with fresh seasonal vegetables. Vegetarians are also well catered for with interesting combinations such as tarte Tatin of tomato, thyme and garlic with a walnut and shallot dressed salad, or warm pastry cup filled with creamed garlic mushrooms topped with a mille-feuille of crisp potatoes, leek and asparagus. For desserts expect blackberry and white chocolate mousse or a luxurious hot chocolate fondant pudding with white chocolate sauce.

Directions: A424 (Burford) 1.5 miles from Stow

STROUD, **Bear of Rodborough**

Rodborough Common GL5 5DE
Map 3: SO80
Tel: 01453 878522
Fax: 01453 872523
Cost: *Alc* £21.95, set-price L
£13.95/D £21.95. ☺ H/wine £9.75
Times: D only, 7-9.30pm
Additional: Sunday L (noon-2.30pm);
Children welcome
Style: Classic/Traditional
Smoking: No smoking in dining room
Civil licence: 80
Accommodation: 46 en suite ★ ★ ★

Directions: From M5 J13 follow signs
for Stonehouse then Rodborough

*Imposing 17th-century former coaching inn housing a charming
restaurant which sums up the building's traditional warmth. Both
tower of chicken breast, aubergine, tomato and mozzarella, and
lobster and brandy bisque are typical of the food served.*

STROUD, **Burleigh Court**

*An attractive manor house in a tranquil hillside location. An
adventurous, varied menu could feature steamed venison suet
pudding with sautéed pigeon and crusted root vegetables. Desserts
might include vanilla and Amaretto pannacotta.*

Additional: Bar food; Sunday L; Children welcome
Style: Classic/Country-house
Smoking: No smoking in dining room
Accommodation: 18 en suite ★ ★ ★

Directions: 0.75m off A419 E of Stroud

Minchinhampton GL5 2PF
Map 3: SO80
Tel: 01453 883804
Fax: 01453 886870
Cost: *Alc* £24.50, set-price L £17.50/
D £22.50. ☺ H/wine £12
Times: Noon-2pm/7-9pm.
Closed L Sat

TETBURY, **Calcot Manor** ⚛⚛

Calcot GL8 8YJ
Map 3: ST89
Tel: 01666 890391
Fax: 01666 890394
E-mail: reception@calcotmanor.co.uk
Chef: Michael Croft
Owner: Richard Ball
Cost: *Alc* £25, set-price L £13.50. ☺
H/wine £12.65
Times: Noon-2.30pm/7-9.30pm

This informal country house hotel was once a farmstead,
farmed by Cistercian monks. The manor house with 14th-
century tithe barn retains much of its original charm. The hotel
and dining room include elegant and relaxing sitting rooms and
the bright modish restaurant extends into a conservatory.
There are a choice of eating options and innovative well-
balanced menus. The conservatory *carte* menu offers two

prices – for 'ample' and 'generous' portions – on a number of the dishes. The dishes include many favourites, including chargrilled Mediterranean vegetables and grilled scallops served with a minted pea purée. There is a strong Mediterranean influence throughout; tomato tarte Tatin, Garganelli pasta, Osso Bucco etc. Desserts follow in the same vein: caramelised fig tarte Tatin, pannacotta with fresh strawberries and chocolate fondant served with pistachio ice cream.

Additional: Sunday L; Children welcome
Seats: 90. Private dining room 14
Style: Informal/Country-house
Smoking: No smoking in dining room
Civil licence: 90
Accommodation: 28 en suite ★ ★ ★

Directions: 4 miles W of Tetbury on A4135 close to intersection with A45

TETBURY, Close Hotel ✿✿✿

8 Long Street GL8 8AQ
Map: ST89
Tel: 01666 502272
Fax: 01666 504401
Chef: Daren Bale
Owner: Old English Inns
Cost: Alc £37.50, set-price L £16.50/D £29.50. H/wine £14.50
Times: Noon-2pm/ 7-9.30pm
Additional: Bar food; Sunday L; Children 12+
Seats: 36. Private dining room 24. Jacket & tie preferred

A genuine air of country house luxury can be found here, and the restaurant is delightful – small, cosy and pretty, with views over the garden and a welcome fire on a chilly May evening. Service is confident, relaxed and friendly, and the inspector enjoyed his 'excellent' foie gras appetiser, followed by field mushroom soup with truffle and cracked black pepper, which had great depth of flavour and yet was 'light and delicate'. A main course of roast monkfish tail with cucumber and vanilla risotto and a cappuccino of red wine and thyme was also good, the fish 'blindingly fresh'. Rhubarb soufflé to finish was perfectly timed and full of flavour, and the vanilla bean ice cream pronounced 'fab'.

Style: Classic/Country-house
Smoking: No smokingin dining room
Civil licence: 60
Accommodation: 15 en suite ★ ★ ★

Directions: From M4 J17 onto A429 to Malmesbury. From M5 J14 onto B4509

TETBURY, Snooty Fox ✿

Market Place GL8 8DD
Map 3: ST89
Tel: 01666 502436
Fax: 01666 503479
E-mail: res@snooty-fox.co.uk

Telephone for further details

'Good wholesome cooking' is what's served at this pretty 16th-century coaching inn. Try escabeche of red mullet fillet to start, and move on to medallions of pork tenderloin, say, or sea bass with sundried tomato risotto.

Directions: Town centre

THORNBURY, **Thornbury Castle**

Castle Street BS35 1HH
Map 3: ST69
Tel: 01454 281182
Fax: 01454 416188
E-mail:
thornburycastle@compuserve.com
Chef: Colin Woodward
Owner: The Baron of Portlethen
Cost: Set-price L £19.50/D £39.50.
H/wine £12
Times: Noon-2pm/7-10.30pm.
Closed 4 days Jan
Additional: Sunday L; Children
welcome
Seats: 60. Private dining room 30.
Jacket & tie preferred
Style: Tudor castle
Smoking: No smoking in dining room
Civil licence: 50
Accommodation: 20 en suite ★ ★ ★

Not many hotels can boast that 'Henry VIII slept here', but this castle does. Not only that, but he brought his wife, Anne Boleyn, and his daughter subsequently moved in. Nowadays, Thornbury is a luxuriously appointed country-house hotel, set in splendid grounds, with all the trappings of its age: panelling, tapestries, galleries and baronial dining rooms. If the surroundings are pretty ancient, the kitchen works around some modern ideas in the best Anglo-French traditions. Scallop and herb ravioli is accompanied by a timbale of white crab, fillet of Welsh beef comes with a juniper and broad bean sauce, a red wine and shallot tarte Tatin and parsley purée, and breast of Gressingham duck with crispy apple mille-feuille and Calvados sauce. Fish is well-reported, as in roast cod, given extra zing by bacon sauce, served with pea purée and rösti, and puddings range from classic crème brûlée, flavoured with brambles to give it an English slant, to traditional treacle tart (described as 'really good'). The wine list holds much of interest, but if price is a constraint stick to the page of 'everyday wines'.

Directions: At bottom of High Street turn left into Castle Street. The entrance is to left of St. Mary's Church

UPPER SLAUGHTER,
Lords of the Manor

GL54 2JD
Map 4: SP12
Tel: 01451 820243
Fax: 01451 820696
E-mail:
lordsofthemanor@btinternet.com
Chef: John Campbell
Owner: Empire Ventures Ltd
Cost: Alc £47, set-price L £14.95.
H/wine £14.95
Times: 12.30-2pm(2.30pm Sun)/7-
9.30pm
Additional: Bar food L; Sunday L
Seats: 50. Private dining room 50
Style: Traditional/Country-house
Smoking: No smoking in dining room
Civil licence: 50
Accommodation: 27 en suite ★ ★ ★

Built as a rectory in the 17th century, Lords of the Manor sits in eight acres of gardens and parkland, the mellow-stone house and lawns creating an idyllic pastoral scene. The dining room, overlooking the rear walled garden, is country house in style,

Directions: Follow sign towards The Slaughters off A429. The restaurant is in centre of Upper Slaughter

creating a smart but not pretentious environment, with solicitously polite but chatty staff helping things along. This is the setting for John Campbell's cuisine – combining modern British and classical French elements in some impressive, well-judged cooking, all backed up by an excellent wine list and an approachable, switched-on sommelier. If menu descriptions appear bald, that only helps to stimulate expectations about what will actually appear on the plate. A terrine of foie gras with pressed chicken, for instance, comes with chickpeas and fine cabbage wrapped in Serrano ham along with some wild mushrooms and deeply flavoured mushroom broth, all components 'fully expressing their flavours'. The same workmanship extends to other starters: 'cracklingly fresh' fillet of red mullet, timed to perfection, with langoustines and tapenade. That dishes are intelligently thought through is shown in a main course of 'fantastic' fillet of beef ('from a really good Scottish animal') with a raviolo, the pasta among the best, of 'wonderful', light foie gras and truffle, an intense sauce made from lamb and ox cheeks adding yet another dimension. Puddings don't falter either, with properly made pannacotta with a blob of Sauternes jelly, or a trio of 'great' chocolate tart, white chocolate sorbet, and fondant.

WINCHCOMBE, **Wesley House**

The half-timbered exterior of this 15th-century merchant's house holds a deceptively spacious restaurant. It's a comfortable room, too, with a wealth of beams, an inglenook and exposed stone; from the terrace (alfresco dining here in summer) is a view over the North Cotswold Edge. It's a popular place, with lunch taking in perhaps Parma ham and grilled goats' cheese with chilli dressing, grilled monkfish in a sun-dried tomato crust, then apple and plum crumble, and there's a good-value early-evening menu. Dinner is the main event, though, and dishes are well conceived and accurately cooked. Galantine of quail on buckwheat pancakes with grape chutney, a tian of smoked chicken and polenta with sweet pickled vegetables, or a salad of flaked smoked salmon with pancetta and a soft poached egg with citrus dressing may be among the starters, to be followed by fillet of Scottish beef with wild mushrooms and truffle sauce, baked halibut with braised leeks and saffron sauce, or chump of Cotswold lamb with onion confit and thyme sauce. Raspberry crème brûlée, or prune and Armagnac rice pudding are what to expect among desserts. South Africa is a speciality of the wine list, which kicks off with eight recommendations of the house.

High Street GL54 5LT
Map 4: SP02
Tel: 01242 602366
Fax: 01242 604096
E-mail:
reservations@wesleyhouse.co.uk
Chef: James Lovatt
Owner: Matthew Brown
Cost: *Alc* £28.50, set-price L
£12.50/D £18.50-£28.50. ☺
H/wine £11.50
Times: Noon-2pm/6.45-9pm.
Closed D Sun, 2 wks Jan
Additional: Bar food L; Sunday L;
Children welcome
Seats: 50
Style: Rustic/Formal
Smoking: No-smoking area; No pipes
& cigars
Accommodation: 6 en suite

Directions: In the centre of
Winchcombe on the main road

GREATER MANCHESTER

ALTRINCHAM, Juniper ✿✿✿

21 The Downs WA14 2QD
Map 7: SJ78
Tel: 0161 929 4008
Fax: 0161 929 4009
Chef: Paul Kitching
Owner: Mrs Nora & Mr Peter Miles
Cost: Alc £32. ☺ H/wine £18
Times: Noon-2pm/7pm-9.30pm
(10pm Sat). Closed L Sat & Mon,
all Sun
Additional: Children welcome;
Vegetarian dishes not always
available
Seats: 40
Style: Chic/Modern
Smoking: Air conditioning

Directions: A556 Chester-Manchester
Rd

Paul Kitching gets better and better, and has made Juniper into one of the region's foremost destination restaurants. The setting is simple but modern, with lots of greenery and a style that is a cross between Tuscan and art deco. Dishes, too, may appear simple but this is deceptive as behind the scenes there are intricate cooking procedures, followed by careful construction before completion. In other words, the food may sometimes be a little slow in arriving out of the tiny kitchen at peak times, but nothing is allowed to leave without Kitching's eagle-eyed scrutiny and approval. The cooking is French at heart – typically, smoked haddock with creamy crab bisque or roast breast of pheasant with pistachio nuts, leeks and barley. Exciting ideas show in dishes such as jellied terrine of sweet bacon with root vegetables, grilled Dover sole with swede purée and cardamom sauce, or grey-legged partridge with chocolate sauce. The eponymous berries may feature in a sauce to accompany roast wood pigeon with black pudding. Desserts are ravishing – but the signature soufflés, perhaps rice pudding soufflé with vanilla ice cream, are always hard to resist.

ALTRINCHAM,

Woodland Park Hotel ✿

Wellington Road Timperley
WA15 7RG
Map 7: SJ78
Tel: 0161 928 8631
Fax: 0161 941 2821
E-mail: info@woodlandpark.co.uk
Cost: Alc £20, set-price L £13.95/D
£15.95. ☺ H/wine £10.95
Times: Noon-2pm/7-10pm.
Closed L Sat & Sun
Additional: Bar Food L;
Children welcome
Style: Classic/Country-house
Smoking: No smoking in dining room;
Air conditioning
Civil licence: 60
Accommodation: 46 en suite ★★★

Conveniently-situated elegant restaurant with a conservatory bar,
offering modern British cuisine from a brasserie-style menu, ranging

*from marinated lamb stir fry with taboulah to chick peas braised in
Indian herbs and spices with basmati rice.*

Directions: 300 yds from Metro-Link Station – Navigation Road

MANCHESTER,

Copthorne Manchester

*Modern hotel restaurant overlooking the waterfront – sauté of
scallops on squid noodles was followed by steamed Gressingham
duck with five spices, balsamic vinegar and ginger infusion, and
rhubarb chutney.*

Directions: Close to M602

Clippers Quay Salford Quays M5 2XP
Map 7: SJ89
Tel: 0161 873 7321
Fax: 0161 873 7318

Telephone for further details

MANCHESTER,

Crowne Plaza Manchester – The Midland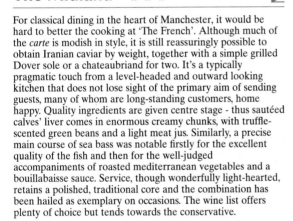

For classical dining in the heart of Manchester, it would be
hard to better the cooking at 'The French'. Although much of
the *carte* is modish in style, it is still reassuringly possible to
obtain Iranian caviar by weight, together with a simple grilled
Dover sole or a chateaubriand for two. It's a typically
pragmatic touch from a level-headed and outward looking
kitchen that does not lose sight of the primary aim of sending
guests, many of whom are long-standing customers, home
happy. Quality ingredients are given centre stage - thus sautéed
calves' liver comes in enormous creamy chunks, with truffle-
scented green beans and a light meat jus. Similarly, a precise
main course of sea bass was notable firstly for the excellent
quality of the fish and then for the well-judged
accompaniments of roasted mediterranean vegetables and a
bouillabaisse sauce. Service, though wonderfully light-hearted,
retains a polished, traditional core and the combination has
been hailed as exemplary on occasions. The wine list offers
plenty of choice but tends towards the conservative.

Directions: M62 J 12 towards liverpool, to M602 city centre,
follow Granada Studios signs, L into Water Street, past Studios,
Hotel on R

Peter Street M60 2DS
Map 7: SJ89
Tel: 0161 236 3333
Fax: 0161 932 4100
E-mail: sales@mhccl.demon.co.uk
Chef: Simon Holling
Owners: Bass Hotels & Resorts
Cost: *Alc* £45, set-price D £29.
H/wine £17.50
Times: D only, 7-11pm. Closed Bhs,
restricted opening Xmas
Additional: Children welcome
Style: Traditional/formal
Seats: 55; Jacket & tie preferred
Smoking: No pipes & cigars; Air
conditioning
Accommodation: 303 en suite
★ ★ ★ ★
Civil licence: 400

MANCHESTER,

The Lincoln

*A long, modern restaurant with full-length windows, a large semi-
circular bar and caricature prints. Highlights include swordfish with
wilted greens and burnt cream of lime and raspberry tartlet.*

Additional: Sunday L; Children welcome
Style: Chic/Modern
Smoking: Air conditioning

Directions: Telephone for directions

M2 3WS
Map 7: SJ89
Tel: 0161 834 9000
Tel: 0161 834 9555
Cost: *Alc* £40, set-price L/D £16.50.
☺ H/wine £11
Times: Noon-3pm/6-10.30pm.
Closed L Sat, D Sun

MANCHESTER, Little Yang Sing ✿

A light, bright lower-ground floor restaurant with lots of mirrors, offering an excellent choice of vegetarian dishes and dim sum. Try salt and pepper squid, or steamed duck with dried Chinese vegetables.

Additional: Children welcome
Style: Chinese/Traditional
Smoking: Air conditioning

Directions: Behind Piccadilly Plaza on the corner of George & Charlotte Street, on Metrolink route

17 George Street M1 4HE
Map 7: SJ89
Tel: 0161 228 7722
Fax: 0161 236 9257
Cost: *Alc* £18, set-price L £9.95/D £17. ☺ H/wine £10.95
Times: Noon-11.30pm.
Closed 25 Dec

MANCHESTER, Manchester Marriott Worsley Park Hotel ✿

Brindley's restaurant (named after a leading 18th-century canal engineer), offers an interesting and imaginative range of dishes. Seared salmon and scallops with polenta, or roast duck with celeriac and thyme mash show the style.

Additional: Sunday L; Children welcome
Style: Rustic/Country-house
Smoking: No-smoking area; Air conditioning
Civil licence: 250
Accommodation: 159 en suite ★★★★

Directions: From M60 J13 take A575. Hotel on L

Worsley Park Worsley M28 2QT
Map 7: SJ89
Tel: 0161 975 2000
Fax: 0161 799 6341
Cost: *Alc* £25-£30, set-price L £15/D £22.50. ☺ H/wine £12.75
Times: Noon-2pm/7-10pm.
Closed L Sat

MANCHESTER, Le Meridien Victoria and Albert ✿✿

A stone's throw from the Granada studios, it's not unusual to see actors enjoying the relaxed service at The Sherlock Holmes restaurant. Paul Patterson's influences are Mediterranean and oriental, but British classics also appear. On the menu simply grilled Dover Sole is distinguished by spot-on timing and the use of excellent fish. Classic French styles are also successful, with roast Bresse pigeon the highlight of one inspector's meal. Dessert might include crème brûlée with rhubarb sorbet.

Smoking: No-smoking area; No pipes & cigars; Air conditioning
Civil licence: 200 **Accommodation:** 156 en suite ★★★★

Directions: Head for city centre and follow signs for Granada Studio Tours. Hotel is opposite

Water Street M60 9EA
Map 7: SJ89
Tel: 0870 400 8585
Fax: 0161 834 2484
E-mail: lm14sz@forte-hotels.com
Chef: Paul Patterson
Owner: Granada
Cost: *Alc* £30, set-price D £20 & £25. ☺ H/wine £16.90
Times: D only, 7-10pm. Closed Sun, Mon & Bhs
Additional: Bar food; Children welcome
Seats: Private dining room 60
Style: Rustic/Modern

MANCHESTER, Moss Nook ✿✿

Moss Nook has been in the business for nearly 30 years and still pulls in the crowds. Part of the appeal must be the reassuring decor of predominantly dark red, with lace cloths on the tables, creating an atmosphere that seems miles away from the airport just down the road. The food is the other attraction, of course, based around a menu that doesn't stray too far from the classic repertoire, with Dover sole and fillet of beef topped with foie gras both making appearances. Turbot

Ringway Road M22 5WD
Map 7: SJ89
Tel: 0161 437 4778
Fax: 0161 498 8089
Chef: Kevin Lofthouse
Owners: Derek & Pauline Harrison
Cost: *Alc* £40, set-price L £18.50/D £31.50. H/wine £10
Times: Noon-2pm/7-9.30pm. Closed L Sat, all Sun & Mon, 2 wks Xmas

Moss Nook

Additional: Children 12+
Seats: 65. Jacket & tie preferred
Style: Classic
Smoking: No pipes

Directions: Close to Manchester
Airport – at junction of Ringway with
B5166

goes into a soufflé, served on vermouth sauce with pan-seared
asparagus, and a parcel of smoked salmon and crème fraîche is
added to lobster salad, while equally fine produce is used in
main courses: pink medallions of Welsh lamb arranged around
a mousse of chicken and tarragon, and slices of breast of
Lunesdale duckling with redcurrants and pommes Anna.
Other ideas, equally successful, might extend to grilled king
prawns with basmati rice and a sweet-and-sour sauce, or spicy
chicken breast and red onions with a coriander, chilli and lime
dressing.

MANCHESTER, The New Emperor ❀

52-56 George Street M1 4HF
Map 7: SJ88
Tel: 0161 228 2883
Fax: 0161 228 6620
E-mail: info@newemperor.co.uk
Cost: *Alc* £15, set-price L £12/D
£15.50. ☺ H/wine £9.50
Times: Noon-midnight
Additional: Children welcome
Style: Modern/traditional
Smoking: Air conditioning

Directions: Heart of Chinatown, near
Manchester Piccadilly

*Attracting a sizeable Chinese clientele, this is one of Manchester's
most popular Chinese restaurants. A good choice of dim sum is
complemented by casseroled bean curd with red cooked pork, and a
wide range of Cantonese dishes.*

MANCHESTER, Nico Central ❀

*Bright bistro-style interior with a touch of art deco, mirrored pillars
and a punchy pan-European menu. Part of the Restaurant
Partnership Group – see entries for Simply Nico and Nico Central in
London.*

Style: Modern/formal
Smoking: Air conditioning

Directions: Located in the Crowne Plaza Manchester – The
Midland

Mount Street M60 2DS
Map 7: SJ89
Tel: 0161 236 6488
Fax: 0161 236 8897
Cost: *Alc* £25, set-price L £14.95.☺
H/wone £12.50
Times: Noon-2.30pm, 6-10.30pm.
Closed L Sat & Sun, Bhs
Additional: Bar food; Children
welcome

MANCHESTER,
Rhodes & Co ❀❀

Waters Reach Trafford Park M17 1WS
Map 7: SJ89
Tel: 0161 868 1900
Fax: 0161 868 1901
E-mail: info@toptable.co.uk
Chef: Ian Morgan
Owners: Sodexho/Gary Rhodes
Cost: *Alc* £26, set-price L £11.50. ☺
H/wine £12.50
Times: Noon-2.30pm/6.30-9.45pm.
Closed L Sat & Sun
Additional: Bar food;
Children welcome
Seats: 85. Private dining room 70-80
Style: Informal/Modern
Smoking: Air conditioning

Designer setting with natural woods, aluminium surfaces, red
and cream paint work and an open kitchen. Cuisine is simple,
unfussy and direct. A choice of breads included sun dried
tomato and granary. A starter of layered mushroom pancake
impressed, 'really well executed' flat crêpes layered with well
seasoned duxelle farce and finished with frothy mushroom
butter. A well-thought out main course of chicken with petit
pois and a mint béarnaise sauce was a balanced dish which
delivered all the promised flavours. Iced pear parfait with
caramelised melba toast was another good combination.
Friendly staff and a good wine list all add to a pleasant, relaxed
experience.

Directions: Opposite Old Trafford Football Ground, off A5081

MANCHESTER,
Simply Heathcotes ❀❀

Jacksons Row Deansgate
M2 5WD
Map 7: SJ89
Tel: 0161 835 3536
Fax: 0161 835 3534
E-mail: simply@heathcotes.co.uk
Chef: Andrew Owen
Owner: Paul Heathcote
Cost: *Alc* £24.90, set-price L/D
£14.50. ☺ H/wine £11.50

Located in a former registery office, the Victorian redbrick
exterior contrasts with the light and airy restaurant,
predominantly white with splashes of canary yellow, bright
blue and red and with a mirrored wall to create a sense of
spaciousness. The *carte* includes some typical Heathcote dishes
such as roast Goosnargh duckling with cassoulet of baby
vegetables, and the *table d'hote* changes daily. Best dishes from

our inspection meal were ratatouille risotto with goats' cheese and an unusual but triumphant wonton stuffed with pesto sauce, as well as a main course of grilled calves' liver with caramelised red onion sauce, sage polenta and oyster mushrooms. The greatest surprise came with the desserts: goats' cheese, lemon and thyme ice cream made a subtle and unexpectedly good contrast to a baked pear tarte Tatin, and a perfectly executed cranberry and ginger soufflé convinced at least one cranberry and ginger hater to change her views, especially when paired with pecan nut ice cream.

Directions: M62 J17. Restaurant at the top end of Deansgate

Times: 11.45am-2.30pm/5.45-10pm (11 Sat, 6-9.30 Sun). Closed 25 & 26 Dec, 1 Jan, Bhs Mon
Additional: Bar food L; Sunday L; Children welcome
Seats: 170. Private dining room 10-60
Style: Informal/modern
Smoking: Air conditioning
Civil licence: 60

MANCHESTER, Stock NEW

4 Norfolk Street M60 1DW
Map 7: SJ89
Tel: 0161 839 6644
Fax: 0161 839 6655
Cost: Alc £25-30, set-price L/D £11.50-£13.50. ☺ H/wine £12
Times: Noon-10.30pm, Closed Sun, 25 & 26 Dec
Additional: Children welcome
Style: classic
Smoking: No pipes & cigars

Central, contemporary and chic, this mod Italian, located in the old Stock Exchange building is fast building a reputation. Asparagus risotto with Dolcelatte, linguine with crayfish tails and wild rocket, and a fabulous Amaretto cake all impressed. Related to Mauro's in Bollington (see entry, Cheshire). Best Italian Wine List (see page 18).

Directions: Telephone for directions

MANCHESTER,
Yang Sing ❀❀

Yang Sing has literally risen from the ashes of a disastrous fire that destroyed the premises in late 1997 and is now a comfortable blend of the traditional and the modern. Authentic Cantonese cooking is the attraction, and long opening hours, an enterprising wine list, and a lengthy menu, plus banquets and 60 to 70 daily specials not shown on the menu, all keep the customers packing in. Dim sum are served until late afternoon, so it's possible to pop in for a snack of crispy spring roll ('very meaty'), nicely spicy steamed beef balls with ginger and spring onion, and crab and prawn parcels. Otherwise, assemble a whole meal with spare ribs, squid with prawn sauce, spicy braised brisket or sweet-and-sour pork, and Chinese mushrooms with seasonal greens. A braised duck with mixed meats might do for the whole table, and the list of vegetarian options is extensive, from stir-fried diced vegetables in a bird's nest to bean curd casserole.

Directions: Off Town Hall Square

34 Princess Street M1 4JY
Map 7: SJ89
Tel: 0161 236 2200
Fax: 0161 236 5934
E-mail: info@yangsing.co.uk
Chef: Harry Yeung
Times: Noon- Closed 25 Dec
Additional: Sunday L; Children welcome
Seats: 140 & 100. Private dining rooms 36, 90, 240
Style: Modern/Cantonese
Smoking: Air conditioning

MANCHESTER AIRPORT,
Etrop Grange Hotel ❀

An elegant, popular hotel restaurant. Lunch offers a simple three-course carte, but dinner can be expanded to four or five courses. Rillettes of duck and green peppercorns, crab and cod rissoles, and pan-fried calves' liver, show the range.

Thorley Lane M90 4EG
Map 7: SJ88
Tel: 0161 499 0500
Fax: 0161 499 0790
Cost: Set-price D £31.45.
H/wine £12.95
Times: Noon-2pm/7-10pm.
Closed L Sat
Additional: Bar food; Sunday L;
Children welcome
Style: Traditional/country-house
Smoking: No smoking in dining room
Civil licence: 80
Accommodation: 64 en suite ★★★

Directions: Off M56/J5. At main airport roundabout, take 1st L (to Terminal 2), then 1st R (Thorley Lane), 200yds on R

MANCHESTER AIRPORT, **Radisson SAS Hotel Manchester Airport** ❀❀ NEW

Chicago Avenue M90 3RA
Map 7: SJ89
Tel: 0161 490 5000
Fax: 0161 490 5100
E-mail: sales@manzq.rdsas.com
Chef: Richard Williamson
Cost: *Alc* £28, set-price L £18/D £28.
☺ H/wine £17
Times: Noon-2.30pm/6-10.30pm
Additional: Bar food; Sunday L;
Children welcome
Seats: 140. Private dining room 2-300
Style: chic/modern
Smoking: No-smoking area; Air conditioning
Accommodation: 360 en suite

Directions: Leave M56 J5, follow signs for Terminal 2 and take 1st exit at roundabout for railway station, hotel is opposite the station

This strikingly designed, ultra-modern hotel, with a central atrium, is connected by an elevated passenger walkway to the airport's terminals and offers an excellent range of facilities for the international clientele that use it. The Phileas Fogg Restaurant is a long, curved area, with plenty of bare wood, halogen lights and striking fabrics; floor-to-ceiling windows look out over the runways. Imaginative starters take in roast tomato and sweet pepper soup with fried lamb and coriander yogurt, Welsh mussels done in cream and white wine with chives, and crisp-fried cod ('accurately cooked and deliciously fresh') on rocket with a lime and chilli dressing. Main courses have a more classical bent, among them sliced duckling breast with a sweet onion marmalade and pancetta, or seared chicken breast on grilled leeks with boulangère potatoes. But a quietly confident hand is at work, producing perfectly tender chargrilled rump of lamb in a well-matched tarragon jus partnered by an unusual but inspired warm niçoise salad. As much care and thought go into extras like breads and vegetables (sautéed greens have been described as 'superb'), while typical of desserts is accurately-timed baked chocolate pudding with a runny centre. The wine list, if pitched perhaps at the corporate slice of the market, is reasonably well-balanced.

OLDHAM, Hotel Smokies Park

Expect friendly service in the Italian restaurant of this modern hotel. Dishes might include chargrilled chicken with crispy pancetta, or salmon, whiting and spinach sausage with a white onion cream. Finish with pear and Mascarpone crumble.

Additional: Sunday L; Children welcome
Style: Modern
Smoking: Air conditioning
Accommodation: 73 en suite ★ ★ ★

Directions: On A627 between Oldham and Ashton-under-Lyme

Ashton Road Bardsley OL8 3HX
Map 7: SD90
Tel: 0161 785 5050
Fax: 0161 785 5010
E-mail: cosifantutti@smokies.co.uk
Cost: Alc £20, set-price L £5.95/D £16.95. ☺ H/wine £9.50
Times: Noon-2pm, 7-10pm.
Closed Sat L

OLDHAM, Menzies Avant Hotel

Relax in pleasant surroundings while the friendly restaurant staff treat you with excellent hospitality. Imaginative menu: filo pastry moneybag filled with sautéed leeks, almonds, spinach and mushrooms on a pool of cheddar cheese sauce.

Additional: Bar food; Sunday L; Children welcome
Style: Classic/Modern
Smoking: No-smoking area; Air conditioning
Accommodation: 103 en suite ★ ★ ★ ★

Directions: From M62 J20 take A627(M) towards Oldham, then A62 Manchester Street. Hotel on L

Windsor Road Manchester Street OL8 4AS
Map 7: SD90
Tel: 0161 627 5500
Fax: 0161 627 5896
E-mail: info@menzies-hotels.co.uk
Cost: Set-price L £9.50/D £17.50. ☺ H/wine £9.99
Times: Noon-3pm/7-10pm

OLDHAM, White Hart Inn ❀❀

51 Stockport Road Lydgate OL4 4JJ
Map 7: SD90
Tel: 01457 872566
Fax: 01457 875190
Chef: John Rudden
Owners: Charles Brierley, John Rudden
Cost: Alc £25, set price L £16-£18/D £30. ☺

The White Hart is a lovely old stone building on a hill overlooking the Pennines, combining the functions of bar, brasserie, restaurant, hotel and purveyor of sausages, and doing so successfully, judging by the bustle. A snug and lounge for drinkers, then the brasserie, with the recently added restaurant to the rear, with yellow walls, wooden floor, elegant lighting and high-backed wooden chairs. For the sausages ('great selection'), head for the brasserie, where you might also find light and 'perfectly executed' deep-fried cheese soufflés with a home-made tomato and chilli jam. Prime materials are used throughout, although the restaurant moves up a gear and adds a degree of sophistication to dishes, often using luxury ingredients. Starters might run to bouillabaisse with saffron mayonnaise, and main courses to roast Barbary duck breast studded with langoustine, served with wok-fried vegetables and tagliatelle, or pan-fried fillet of sea bass with lightly curried boulangère potatoes and spinach with nutmeg. To finish, chocolate tart with orange sorbet hits the spot, and English farmhouse cheeses are in good condition. An abbreviated version of the full wine list offers a good choice by the glass.

Directions: From Oldham take A669 Lees Road through Lees & Grotton. At top of steep hill turn R (A6050). Inn 50yds on L

Times: D only, 7-10pm.
Closed D Sun, Mon
Additional: Bar food; Sunday L (1-3.30pm); Children welcome
Seats: 40. Private dining room 16-20
Style: Classic/Informal
Smoking: No smoking in dining room; Air conditioning

ROCHDALE, Nutter's ❀❀

Edenfield Road Cheesden Norden OL12 7TY
Map 7: SD81
Tel/Fax: 01706 650167
E-mail: nutters@biteit.net
Chef: Andrew Nutter
Owners: Rodney, Jean & Andrew Nutter
Cost: *Alc* L £19.50 & D £29, set-price D £29.95. H/wine £10.80
Times: Noon-2pm (4.30pm Sun)/6.45-9.30pm (9pm Sun). Closed Tue, 1st 2 wks Aug
Additional: Sunday L; Children welcome
Seats: 52. Private dining room 40
Style: Chic
Smoking: No smoking in dining room

High on the moors is this ex-pub, a warm peach decor dominating the restaurant, with seating you can really relax into. Given the restraint of the surroundings, the fireworks on the menu can be a bit of a surprise: flash-seared salmon fillet with beetroot, lime and black pepper vinaigrette, for instance, followed perhaps by chicken breast accompanied by 'stir-fried breakfast' (actually diced bacon, black pudding and mushrooms) with a port and shallot sauce. But materials are not just thrown together for novelty's sake, and a grand plan for each dish means that things generally work well together. A chilled melon dressing gives a lift to a salad of asparagus and Parma ham, for example, and a mussel and Pernod chowder is a good match for roast cod with saffron mash. Technical skills are never in doubt, and materials are well sourced, from lemon sole fillets with rocket pesto and chive butter, to seared beef fillet with Brie and bacon fritters. The pace doesn't falter at pudding stage either, bringing on lemon curd cheesecake with baklava fritters, or apple, rum and raisin crème brûlée with apple sorbet.

Directions: On A680 between Rochdale and Edenfield

SALE, Belmore Hotel ❀❀ NEW

143 Brooklands Road M33 3QN
Map 7: SJ79
Tel: 0161 973 2538

With a balustraded terrace and mature Victorian gardens surrounding it, this tastefully furnished hotel restaurant reflects the luxurious ambience of bygone days. Although the cuisine is all of a very high standard the inspector was particularly impressed with the reasonably priced and intelligently compiled wine list, and with an extensive cheeseboard which ranks with the best in the country. As for the meal itself a pleasing lightness of touch was in evidence in dishes such as a delicate ravioli of lobster with truffle and artichoke velouté. Main courses offered a well-balanced selection with some robust offerings such as loin of lamb with broad beans and buttered spinach. An extensive vegetarian menu extended way beyond the merely token. To miss the cheese would be a sin, but if you can manage a dessert expect the likes of poached pear with praline and bitter chocolate sorbet.

Directions: From M6 J19/M60 J7 or M56 take A56 then A6144, turn R at lights (by Brooklands Stn) into Brooklands Rd, 0.5m turn L into Norris Rd for main entrance

Fax: 0161 973 2665
E-mail: belmore_hotel@hotmail.com
Chef: Wayne Hatenboer
Owner: Carol Deaville
Cost: Alc £30, set-price L £17.95/D £22.50. ☺
Times: Noon-2pm/6-9.30pm
Seats: 40. Private dining room 12
Additional: Bar food; Sunday L; Children welcome
Style: Classic/Formal
Smoking : No smoking in dining room
Civil licence: 60
Accommodation: 23 rooms ★ ★ ★ ★

WIGAN,
Kilhey Court Hotel ❀

The Laureate is a split-level conservatory restaurant overlooking the grounds and lakes. A choice of menus is offered, including a full vegetarian selection, and dishes are attractively presented.

Directions: On A5106 1.5m N of A49/A5106 junction

Chorley Road Standish WN1 2XN
Map 7: SD51
Tel: 01257 472100
Fax: 01257 422401

Telephone for further details

WIGAN, Wrightington Hotel ❀

See Wrightington, Lancashire

HAMPSHIRE

ALRESFORD, Hunters ❀

32 Broad Street SO24 9AQ
Map 4: SU53
Tel/Fax: 01962 732468
Cost: Alc £27, set-price D £12.50 & £15. ☺ H/wine £10.25
Times: Noon-2pm/7-9.30pm. Closed Sun, 1 wk Xmas
Additional: Sunday L; Children welcome
Style: Classic/Bistro-style
Smoking: No smoking in restaurant

Attractive restaurant of high reputation on the main street of this picturesque town. Nicely cooked calves' liver contrasted excellently with the sharpness of a shallot confit. A beautifully rich chocolate fondant rounded off a splendid meal.

Directions: Off A31 – in centre of Alresford

ALTON,

Alton Grange Hotel

Elegant restaurant with large specimen plants and over 60 Tiffany lamps. Well-executed dishes include terrine of venison with chestnuts, turbot with truffle and tarragon sauce, and hot chocolate pudding.

Additional: Bar food; Sunday L; Children 3+
Style: Stylish/intimate
Smoking: No smoking in dining room
Civil licence: 100
Accommodation: 30 en suite ★ ★ ★

Directions: Exit M3 J4 onto A331 towards Farnham. Then take A31 to roundabout signed B3004. Turn right, hotel 350 yards on L

London Road GU34 4EG
Map 4: SU73
Tel: 01420 86565
Fax: 01420 541346
E-mail: info@altongrange.co.uk
Cost: *Alc* £25, set-price D £19.50. ☺
H/wine £10.95
Times: Noon-2.30pm/7-9.30pm.
Closed 25-31 Dec

ANDOVER,

Esseborne Manor ✿✿

Hurstbourne Tarrant SP11 0ER
Map 4: SU34
Tel: 01264 736444
Fax: 01264 736725
E-mail: esseborne-manor@compuserve.com
Chef: Ben Tunnicliffe
Owner: Ian Hamilton
Cost: *Alc* £27, set-price L £15/D £18.
☺ H/wine £13
Times: Noon-2pm/7-9.30pm
Additional: Bar food L; Sunday L; Children welcome
Seats: 30. Private dining room 40
Style: Traditional/Country-house
Smoking: No smoking in dining room
Civil licence: 60
Accommodation: 15 en suite ★ ★ ★

An environment of 'deep comfort', as an inspector phrased it, is provided at this attractive manor surrounded by rolling countryside. Recent redecoration has brought fabric-covered walls to the stylish dining room, with its open fires and views, and engaging staff add to the enjoyment. The kitchen displays a natural understanding of ingredients and, using good-quality materials, produces finely balanced dishes within a pan-European framework. Seared scallops are partnered with creamed leeks and pancetta, and the flavours of another starter – confit of chicken leg on sage risotto – have been described as 'well-defined'. Fillet of beef might be chargrilled and served on olive rösti with tomato and coriander salsa, and haunch of venison might be roasted and accompanied by braised red cabbage and dauphinoise potatoes. Roasting might equally be applied to fish: monkfish with a mussel and crab broth, or 'delightful' crisp-skinned cod with wilted spinach and deep-flavoured sauce vierge. All the stops are pulled out for puddings of 'stunning' chocolate soufflé with coffee ice cream, and more homely quince and apple crumble tart with cinnamon-infused custard could also make an appearance.

Directions: Between Andover & Newbury on A343, just N of Hurstbourne Tarrant

BASINGSTOKE, Audleys Wood ❀

Alton Road RG25 2JT
Map 4: SU65
Tel: 01256 817555
Fax: 01256 817500
E-mail: audleys.wood@thistle.co.uk

Telephone for further details

Directions: M3 J6, then A339 (Alton).
Hotel 1.5m S of Basingstoke towards
Alton

*Impressive Gothic Renaissance-style residence with a stunning
vaulted ceiling in the restaurant. Set-price and carte menus offer
modern British dishes based on quality produce, alongside a decent
wine list.*

BASINGSTOKE,
Basingstoke Country Hotel ❀

*Once a country residence, the hotel now offers extensive conference
and leisure facilities, whilst the Winchester Restaurant offers smart,
intimate dining and efficient service. Braised shank of lamb on a
confit of haricot beans shows the style.*

Style: Country-house/Formal
Smoking: No smoking in dining room; Air conditioning
Civil licence: 80
Accommodation: 100 en suite ★ ★ ★

Directions: On A30 between Nately Scures and Hook

Nately Scures Hook RG27 9JS
Map 4: SU65
Tel: 01256 764161
Fax: 01256 768341
Cost: *Alc* £25, set-price L £12.50 &
£15.50. ☺ H/wine £12.75
Times: 12.30-2pm/7-9.45pm. Closed
L Sat, D Sun
Additional: Sunday L; Children 1+

BEAULIEU, Beaulieu Hotel ❀

*Hotel restaurant with lovely forest views. The menu leans towards
fish and game – home-made breads went down well as did the
guinea fowl breast with artichoke mousse and baby onions.*

Directions: On B3056 between Lyndhurst and Beaulieu,
opposite railway station

Beaulieu Road Lyndhurst SO42 7YQ
Map 4: SU30
Tel: 01703 293344
Fax: 01703 292729

Telephone for further details

BISHOP'S WALTHAM, Banks Bistro ❀

*Popular restaurant with a strong local following. A spring starter of
a 'light, flavoursome' crab cake was enjoyable, followed by a tender
fillet of beef with pepper and herb crust, and well-flavoured
chocolate and pecan pudding to finish.*

Additional: Bar food; Children welcome
Style: Bistro-style/Informal
Smoking: No-smoking area

Directions: M27 J7. Hedge End to Botley, follow signs to
Bishop's Waltham

Bank Street SO32 1AE
Map 4: SU51
Tel: 01489 896352
Fax: 01489 896288
Cost: *Alc* £18, set-price L £9.95/D
£11.95(Mon & Tue). ☺ H/wine £8.95
Times: Noon-2pm/7-10pm. Closed
Sun, Bhs

BISHOP'S WALTHAM,

BISHOP'S WALTHAM,
Cobblers Restaurant

The Square SO32 1AR
Map 4: SU51
Tel: 01489 891515
Chef: Nick Harman
Owner: Andy Cobb
Cost: *Alc* £21-£30, set-price L
£14.50/D £19.95. ☺ H/wine £9.95
Times: 11.45am-1.45pm/6.45-
9.30pm. Closed Sun & Mon
Additional: Children welcome
Seats: 60. Private dining room 16
Style: Chic
Smoking: No-smoking area;
No pipes & cigars

Directions: Bishop's Waltham is on
B2177, midway between Winchester
& Portsmouth/Southampton

Located in the centre of the village in an attractive Georgian townhouse. A smart restaurant with soft Mediterranean decor – light and airy at lunchtime, warm and cosy in the evening. *Carte* options include marinated white sardines with sun-blush tomatoes and black olive tapenade followed perhaps by rare-charred venison steak with black treacled onions and a juniper and red wine choucroute. The set-price menu follows a similarly modern British line including the likes of sugared beef fillet with mustard and garlic dauphinois potato and a four peppercorn and herb butter. Desserts range from crème brûlée with griottine cherries in kirsch to sticky ginger and orange pudding with marmalade and Cointreau ice-cream. The wine list covers a good range of countries and producers and offers useful descriptions.

BROCKENHURST,
Balmer Lawn Hotel

NEW

Lyndhurst Road SO42 7ZB
Map 04: SU30
Tel: 01590 623116
Fax: 01590 623864

Telephone for further details

Beautifully located hotel where dinner may start with drinks on the terrace overlooking the village green. A signature dish from the new chef is tea-smoked monkfish with cured ham.

Directions: Take A337 towards Lymington, hotel on L behind village cricket green

BROCKENHURST,
Carey's Manor Hotel

SO42 7RH
Map 4: SU30
Tel: 01590 623551
Fax: 01590 622799
Cost: *Alc* £27.50, set-price L
£15.95/D £27.50. H/wine £9.85
Times: 12.30-2pm/7-10pm.
Additional: Sunday L; Children 7+
Style: Classic/Traditional

A spacious hotel dining room with a subtle colour scheme and a tranquil ambience. Local ingredients are a welcome feature, particularly in a noteworthy fillet of John Dory with forest mushrooms.

Smoking: No smoking in dining room
Civil licence: 100
Accommodation: 79 en suite ★★★

Directions: M27 J1, follow signs for Lyndhurst and Lymington A337. Railway station 5 minutes from hotel

BROCKENHURST,
Forest Park Hotel

Converted 18th-century vicarage in a tranquil forest setting. Starters might include fresh crab or deep-fried Brie. Main courses along the lines of roast sirloin of beef with Yorkshire pudding or poached fresh salmon.

Rhinefield Road SO42 7ZG
Map 4: SU30
Tel: 01590 622844
Fax: 01590 623948
E-mail: ftp@forestdale.com

Cost: Set-price L £7.95 & £11.95/D £19.95. ☺ H/wine £8.95
Times: Noon-2pm/7-10pm
Additional: Bar food; Sunday L; Children welcome
Smoking: No smoking in dining room
Civil licence: 45
Accommodation: 38 en suite ★★★

Directions: From A337 to Brockenhurst turn into Meerut Road, follow road through Waters Green; at T junction turn R into Rhinefield Road

BROCKENHURST,
New Park Manor

Lyndhurst Road SO42 7QH
Map 4: SU30
Tel: 01590 623467
Fax: 01590 622268
E-mail:
enquiries@newparkmanorhotel.co.uk
Chef: Steve Hurst
Owners: Jon Essen Hotels
Cost: Alc £31, set-price L £11.95/D £27. ☺ H/wine £11.95
Times: Noon-2pm/7-10pm
Additional: Bar food L; Sunday L; Children 7+
Seats: 45. Private dining room 120
Style: Country-house
Smoking: No smoking in dining room
Civil licence: 50
Accommodation: 24 en suite ★★★

Once the favoured haunt of King Charles II and Nell Gwynne, the royal coat of arms hangs above the fireplace of this former hunting lodge. The panelled Stag Restaurant is intimate, seating only 20, with a log fire one end and a giant, ancient equestrian oil at the other. The cooking blends oriental and other contemporary elements with the basic French classical mix: boudin of sea bass and fresh salmon wrapped in sushi 'nori' with red ginger and lemongrass velouté; medallion of New Forest venison saddle with caramelised apples and liquorice-scented jus. The most memorable dish we sampled was breast of free-range chicken filled with foie gras, served with red rice and sunflower seed risotto – 'technically almost perfect, and tasted pretty good too', was our Inspector's reaction.

Directions: Turn off A337 between Lyndhurst and Brockenhurst and follow the hotel signs

BROCKENHURST, Rhinefield House ✿

Rhinefield Road SO42 7QB
Map 4: SU30
Tel: 01590 622922
Fax: 01590 622800
Cost: Alc £38, set-price L £16.95/D
£25.50. H/wine £13.50
Times: 12.30-2pm/7-10pm
Additional: Bar food; Sunday L;
Children welcome
Style: Rustic/Country-house
Smoking: No smoking in dining room
Civil licence: 80
Accommodation: 34 rooms ★ ★ ★

Built in 1890 on the site of a royal hunting lodge with a commanding view over the New Forest, the hotel offers rustic grandeur and high class cuisine. Try globe artichoke filled with celeriac mousse and wild mushrooms.

Directions: From M27 J1 follow signs to Lyndhurst, then take A35 to Christchurch. After 3 miles turn L to Rhinefield. Hotel approx 2 miles on R

BROCKENHURST, Simply Poussin ✿✿

The Courtyard Brookley Road
SO42 7RB
Map 4: SU30
Tel: 01590 623063
Fax: 01590 623144
Chef: Angus Hyne
Owner: Le Poussin Ltd
Cost: Alc £27.50, set-price L £10.50.
☺ H/wine £11.50
Times: Noon-2pm/7-10pm.
Closed Sun, Mon, 25 & 26 Dec
Additional: Children welcome
Seats: 30
Smoking: No smoking in dining room

Tucked away in a courtyard in what was originally a stable, Simply Poussin is plainly decorated, with classic Lloyd Loom furniture and lots of pictures on the walls. The starters here can vary from the simplicity of a salad of various dressed leaves tossed with slices of cured meats, through twice-baked cheese soufflé, to a tarte Tatin of beef tomatoes marinated in balsamic vinegar topped with pan-fried mackerel fillet in a herb dressing, all elements adding up to a cohesive whole. Free-range local pork is marinated in ale and pot-roast with honey and cloves and accompanied by roasted root vegetables to make an accomplished main course, or there might be 'tender and moist' haunch of rabbit, or herb-flecked seafood sausage on pearl barley risotto. Finish with something fruity, like strawberry and vanilla pannacotta with summer fruits, or blueberry frangipane tart.

Directions: Village centre through an archway between two shops

BROCKENHURST,
Thatched Cottage Hotel

Martin Matysik's love of the Orient combines with a classic training to produce innovative dishes with a traditional sensibility. This romantic restaurant with its feminine air and 16th-century architecture has the kitchen brigade on show and admirable restraint is shown by all in what can be a notoriously fiery environment. Not the best place to count calories, Martin's Swiss background produces heavyweight dishes of the order of sautéed duck foie gras with aubergine confit and sweet and sour veal jus, but these are balanced by the more delicate. Crab-stuffed courgette blossoms with tomato sorbet are a carefully constructed contrast. A commitment to sourcing the very best ingredients means everything brought into the kitchen is either organically produced or comes from the hotel's own kitchen garden. Ambitious main courses can include tenderloin of Aberdeen Angus beef with basil mash, onion rings and red wine sauce or a 'meticulously presented' lamb dish with spinach, walnuts and haricot bean tart. Soufflés are a speciality at dessert time. The inspector loved her meltingly rich chocolate pudding with fresh berry coulis.

16 Brookley Road
SO42 7RR
Map 4: SU30
Tel: 01590 623090
Fax: 01590 623479
E-mail:
thatchedcottagehotel@email.msn.com
Chef: Martin Matysik
Owners: The Matysik Family
Cost: Set-price D £35. H/wine £12.50
Times: 12.30-2.30pm/7-9.30pm.
Closed D Sun, all Mon, Jan
Additional: Children welcome at L only; Vegetarian dishes by request
Seats: 20. Private dining room 8
Style: Informal/Country-house
Smoking: No smoking in dining room
Accommodation: 5 en suite

Directions: On A337 in Brockenhurst, turning before level crossing

BROCKENHURST,
Whitley Ridge Hotel

The fine creeper-covered façade of Whitley Ridge is testament to the property's Georgian origins, when it was built as a hunting lodge. Within, classical period pieces and decor create a country-house atmosphere, and the comfortable lounges and lemon-coloured dining room all have lovely views over the New Forest. The kitchen goes in for curing, as in a starter of salmon given the dill and lime treatment and served on a herb pancake, and for marinating: pork fillet with fresh sage and honey, sauced with mustard cream, or chicken breast infused with Thai seasonings, then flame-grilled. Good-quality materials are handled well, as shown by an inspector's tasty starter of wild mushroom mousseline wrapped in a pancake, and a main course of tender and flavourful medallions of beef in a light, buttery sauce of anchovies and coriander. Vegetarians get a good deal, and puddings are of the familiar variety: crème brûlée, or lemon and lime tart, say.

Beaulieu Road SO42 7QL
Map 4: SU30
Tel: 01590 622354
Fax: 01590 622856
E-mail:
whitleyridge@brockenhurst.co.uk
Chef: Gary Moore
Owners: Mr & Mrs R Law
Cost: Alc £25, set-price D £23.50. ☺ H/wine £10.50
Times: D only, 6.30-9pm
Additional: Bar food L; Sunday L (Noon-2pm); Children welcome
Seats: 30. Private dining room 20
Style: Classic
Smoking: No smoking in dining room
Accommodation: 14 en suite ★★★

Directions: A337 (from Lyndhurst) turn L towards Beaulieu on B3055, approx 1 mile

BROOK, **Bell Inn** ❀

Recently refurbished restaurant in an 18th-century listed building. Elegant decor matches French style cuisine, for example flambéed steak diane or supreme of pheasant.

Style: Formal
Smoking: No smoking in dining room;
Accommodation: 25 en suite ★★★

Directions: M27 J1 (Cadnam) 3rd exit onto B3078, signed Brook, 0.5m

SO43 7HE
Map 4: SU21
Tel: 023 80812214
Fax: 023 80813958
E-mail: bell@bramshaw.co.uk
Cost: Alc £26.50, set-price L £14.50/D £26.50. ☺ H/wine £12
Times: 11.30-2.30pm/7.30-9.30pm
Additional: Bar food; Sunday L; Children welcome

BUCKLERS HARD,

Master Builder's House Hotel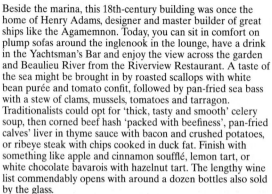

Beside the marina, this 18th-century building was once the home of Henry Adams, designer and master builder of great ships like the Agamemnon. Today, you can sit in comfort on plump sofas around the inglenook in the lounge, have a drink in the Yachtsman's Bar and enjoy the view across the garden and Beaulieu River from the Riverview Restaurant. A taste of the sea might be brought in by roasted scallops with white bean purée and tomato confit, followed by pan-fried sea bass with a stew of clams, mussels, tomatoes and tarragon. Traditionalists could opt for 'thick, tasty and smooth' celery soup, then corned beef hash 'packed with beefiness', pan-fried calves' liver in thyme sauce with bacon and crushed potatoes, or ribeye steak with chips cooked in duck fat. Finish with something like apple and cinnamon soufflé, lemon tart, or white chocolate bavarois with hazelnut tart. The lengthy wine list commendably opens with around a dozen bottles also sold by the glass.

Nr Beaulieu SO42 7XB
Map 4: SU40
Tel: 01590 616253
Fax: 01590 616297
E-mail: res@themasterbuilders.co.uk
Chef: Denis Rhoden
Owners: Jeremy Willcock, John Illsley
Cost: *Alc* £24.85, set-price L £13.95 & £16.95/D £22.50. ☺ H/wine £11.50
Times: Noon-3pm/7-10pm
Additional: Bar food; Children welcome
Seats: 80. Private dining room 40
Style: Chic/Sophisticated
Civil licence: 60
Accommodation: 25 en suite ★ ★ ★

Directions: Follow signs to Beaulieu off M27 J2. Turn L onto B3056. 1st L and hotel in 2 miles

CADNAM,

Bartley Lodge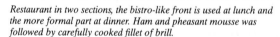

An 18th-century former hunting lodge near the New Forest. The hotel restaurant is centred around an impressive original chandelier and offers charming garden views and modern British cuisine such as woodland mushroom and shallot fricassé.

Lyndhurst Road SO40 2NR
Map 4: SU31
Tel: 023 8081 2248
E-mail: info@carehotels.co.uk
Cost: Set-price D £21.50. ☺ H/wine £10.95

Times: D only, 7-9pm
Additional: Bar food L; Sunday L (12.30-2pm); Children welcome
Style: Classic/Country-house
Smoking: No smoking in dining room
Civil licence: 80
Accommodation: 31 en suite ★ ★ ★

Directions: From M27 J1 follow signs for Lyndhurst – A337. Located just off roundabout on L

DENMEAD,

Barnard's Restaurant ❀

Restaurant in two sections, the bistro-like front is used at lunch and the more formal part at dinner. Ham and pheasant mousse was followed by carefully cooked fillet of brill.

Hambledon Road Nr Waterlooville PO7 6NU
Map 4: SU61
Tel/Fax: 02392 257788
Cost: *Alc* £27.50, set-price L £12.50. ☺ H/wine £10

Times: Noon-1.30pm/7-9.30pm. Closed L Sat, all Sun & Mon, 2 wks Aug
Additional: Bar food L; Children welcome
Style: Classic/traditional
Smoking: No-smoking area; No pipes & cigars

Directions: Opposite village church, from A3M J3 then B2150 (Waterlooville)

EAST TYTHERLEY, Star Inn

Enthusiastic new owners have brought a contemporary slant to the blackboard menu at this old coaching inn. Ravioli of pecorino and pumpkin with bok choi, or organic loin of pork with sage mash show the style.

Style: Informal/country inn
Smoking: No smoking in dining room
Accommodation: 3 en suite

Directions: From A3057 take Mottisfont Abbey turn, follow road through village, L at Bengers Lane, L into Dunbridge, R at Mill Arms, R at garage

SO51 0LW
Map 4: SU22
Tel: 01794 340225
Fax: 01264 810954
E-mail: bing@tinyworld.co.uk
Cost: Alc £21.☺ H/wine £9.50
Times: Noon-2.30pm, 7-9.30pm.
Closed D 25 Dec, 26 Dec
Additional: Bar food: Sun L: Children welcome

EMSWORTH, Spencers ❀❀

First-floor restaurant in an attractive Victorian building. The atmosphere is homely and bustling and the decor fresh and modern with gas lighting and cushioned bench seating. Denis Spencer offers an interesting menu that changes according to season. Fish is a particular speciality and diners may enjoy the delights of baked red mullet fillets wrapped in parma ham with nut brown sage butter, or stirfried squid with fresh ginger and green chillies. Those of a more carnivorous inclination may opt for sautéed lambs kidneys and artichokes with brandy and grain mustard cream whilst vegetarians will not feel left out with Mediterranean vegetables sautéed in olive oil, bound in tomato sauce and glazed with Mozzarella cheese. Alternatively a good range of salads available both as starter and main will cater to all tastes, scallop and bacon salad with paw paw, mango and chilli relish being one notable example. Desserts are simple in concept and gloriously precise in execution. Try Baked Alaska or fresh-fruit Pavlova.

Directions: Follow A259 to Emsworth roundabout, turn L into North Street, restaurant is 0.5 mile on L

36 North Street PO10 7DG
Map 4: SU70
Tel/Fax: 01243 372744
Chef: Denis Spencer
Owners: Denis & Lesley Spencer
Cost: Alc £22. ☺ H/wine £9.95
Times: D only, 7-10.30pm.
Closed Sun, Mon, 25 & 26 Dec
Additional: Children welcome
Seats: 34. Private dining room 10;
Jacket & tie preferred
Style: Modern
Smoking: No-smoking area; No pipes & cigars; Air conditioning

EMSWORTH, 36 On The Quay ❀❀❀

Located on the front of Emsworth Bay, Karen and Ramon Farthing run an exemplary husband and wife operation in the former 17th-century smugglers' inn. Ramon's cooking is sophisticated, complex and creative and depends, as the menu points out, on that essential ingredient 'Time'. Certainly, you need plenty of time to savour a meal here, not because service is slow but because it is well-judged and because food of this quality should not be carelessly consumed. Typical of the way he balances and pulls together contrasting elements was a warm salad of skate with lettuce, red onion, apple, cabbage, slivers of smoked salmon, balsamic vinegar and a light cream dressing, all topped with two plump tempura prawns. Another memorable dish was a Tatin of confit duck with foie gras and apples, an intriguingly original variation on a familiar theme, made with wafer-thin pastry. Some of his dishes are so photogenic they could come from the pages of a magazine – pannacotta of rhubarb, for instance, wrapped in a shard of rhubarb, was served with warm red fruit compote and set in a green glass dish. The special six-course Gourmet Menu allows diners the choice of having the meal described to them in advance, or having it served as a complete surprise.

47 South Street PO10 7EG
Map 4: SU70
Tel: 01243 375592/372257
Fax: 01243 375593
Chef: Ramon Farthing
Owners: Ramon & Karen Farthing
Cost: Set-price L £19.50/D £35.75.
H/wine £13.50
Times: Noon-2pm/7-10pm.
Closed L Sat & Mon, all Sun, 23-30 Oct, 1-22 Jan
Additional: Children welcome;
Vegetarian dishes not always available
Seats: 38. Private dining room 8-10
Style: Classic/Chic
Smoking: No smoking in dining room

Directions: Last building on R in South Street, which runs from the Square in the centre of Emsworth

EVERSLEY, New Mill ✿✿

New Mill Road Hook RG27 0RA
Map 4: SU76
Tel: 0118 9732277
Fax: 0118 9328780
E-mail: mark@thenewmill.co.uk
Chef: Simon Smith
Owners: Nick & Judy Scade
Cost: *Alc* £32, set-price L £14.50/D
£21.50. ☺ H/wine £10.75
Times: Noon-2pm/7-10pm.
Closed L Sat, 26 Dec, 1 Jan
Additional: Sunday L, Children
welcome
Seats: 80. Private dining rooms 2-40
Style: traditional/formal
Smoking: No pipes & cigars; Air
conditioning
Civil licence: 180

As the name suggests, the building comes complete with a mill wheel and all the trappings, low ceilings and view of Hampshire countryside; summer offers the opportunity to expand onto the terrace where heaters keep the chill away. It's a popular spot, with weddings, private dining rooms and a brasserie as extra lures, and it's all very professionally done. No surprises on the menu, which ranges from pan-fried Magret duck breast with chestnut and damson sauce to chargrilled sirloin steak with a warm smoked paprika and potato salad in main courses. A rather pedestrian warm pancakes of Peking duck with spring onions and cucumber on a plum and leek sauce opened our winter inspection meal. We were more impressed, however, by salmon en croûte with a lemon and sorrel mousse and a Muscat chive cream sauce that combined buttery flavours with a good piece of fish. Dessert was a chocolate mousse with a moreish hazelnut meringue.

Directions: From Eversley take A327 (Reading), cross river, turn L at cross roads into New Mill Road

FAREHAM, Lysses House Hotel ✿

A smart and stylish restaurant in an elegant listed Georgian house. Classic, bold cuisine includes charcoal grilled prime fillet steak with a Port wine sauce. Pecan nut and Jack Daniels tartlet typifies an adventurous dessert menu.

Smoking: No smoking in dining room
Civil licence: 90
Accommodation: 21 en suite ★★★

Directions: From M27 J11 follow signs to Fareham town centre; hotel is at top of High Street

51 High Street PO16 7BQ
Map 4: SU50
Tel: 01329 822622
Fax: 01329 822762
E-mail: lysses@lysses.co.uk
Cost: *Alc* £25, set-price L £13.95/D
£18.50. ☺ H/wine £9.95
Times: Noon-1.45pm/7.15-9.45pm.
Closed L Sat, all Sun
Additional: Bar food; Children
welcome
Style: Classic/Traditional

FAREHAM, Solent Hotel ✿

Smart hotel with a lively menu taking in honey-braised lamb shank on spicy apricot, sultana and pine nut risotto, and seared king scallops with red pepper and chilli jam.

Smoking: No smoking in dining room; Air conditioning
Civil licence: 100
Accommodation: 111 en suite ★★★★

Directions: From M27 J9, follow signs to Solent Business Park & Whiteley. At roundabout 1st L, then R at mini-roundabout

Rookery Avenue Whiteley PO15 7AJ
Map 4: SU50
Tel: 01489 880000
Fax: 01489 880007
E-mail: solent@shireinns.co.uk
Cost: *Alc* £28.50, set-price L
£16.95/D £28.50. ☺ H/wine £12
Times: 12.15-1.45pm/7.15-10.15pm.
Closed L Sat & Sun
Additional: Bar food; Children
welcome
Style: Traditional/Country-house

FLEET, The Gurkha Square

327 Fleet Road GU13 8BU
Map 4: SU85
Tel: 01252 811588
Fax: 01252 810101

Telephone for further details

Popular restaurant serving Nepalese food: tareko mis-mass (deep-fried veg in a lovely light batter) was served with mint sauce, followed by succulent barbecued lamb with a powerful chilli kick.

Directions: Telephone for directions

FORDINGBRIDGE, Ashburn Hotel

Station Road SP6 1JP
Map 4: SU11
Tel: 01425 652060
Fax: 01425 652150
E-mail: ashburn@mistral.co.uk
Cost: *Alc* £23, set-price D £17.50. ☺
H/wine £8.75
Times: D only 7-11pm. Closed 25 Dec

Traditional family-run hotel on the edge of Fordingbridge; the restaurant, overlooking beautifully landscaped gardens, offers a good choice of dishes from carte and set price menus.

Additional: Bar food D; Sunday L (noon-2pm); Children welcome
Style: Country-house/Elegant
Smoking: No smoking in dining room
Civil licence: 150
Accommodation: 20 en suite ★★

Directions: On B3078

FORDINGBRIDGE,
The Three Lions

Stuckton SP6 2HF
Map 4: SU11
Tel: 01425 652489
Fax: 01425 656144
Chef: J M Womersley
Owners: Mr & Mrs J M Womersley
Cost: *Alc* £26, set-price L £13.50. ☺
H/wine £13.50
Times: Noon-2.30pm/7-10pm. Closed D Sun, all Mon, mid Jan-mid Feb
Additional: Sunday L; Children welcome
Seats: 60. Private dining room 30
Style: Informal/Rustic
Smoking: No smoking in dining room
Accommodation: 3 en suite

Directions: 1m E of Fordingbridge, from either A338 or B3078. From Q8 garage follow Three Lions brown tourist signs

It is always a pleasure to return and eat at this unpretentious, converted 19th-century farmhouse, simply furnished with pine tables, where the central wood fireplace warms both bar and restaurant. Jane and Michael Womersley know what they do well and have the nous to stick to it. You won't find any over-ambitious combinations of ingredients or high towers on a plate here, just real food. The menu, chalked on the board, changes daily and features local ingredients such as venison and wild New Forest mushrooms. A good selection of wines by the glass gives lone diners and drivers a chance to enjoy more than one taste. A sample meal started with a super crab and prawn bisque, served in a tiny copper pan with prawns and crabmeat bursting above the well-flavoured, aromatic liquid. The quality of produce was highlighted in a main-course loin of new season lamb with 'crispy bits'. Wherever possible, organic vegetables are sourced – on this occasion, the inspector enjoyed a fine seasonal choice of celeriac purée, dauphinoise potatoes, carrots and red and green cabbage. There was no doubting the flavour of a tangy, creamy-smooth lime parfait with tropical fruit and passion fruit sauce. Coffee and chocolate truffles to finish.

LIPHOOK,

Nippon-Kan ❀❀

Old Thorns Hotel Griggs Green
GU30 7PE
Map 4: SU83
Tel: 01428 724555
Fax: 01428 725036
E-mail: reservations@
oldthorns.freeserve.co.uk
Chef: Takeo Suzuki
Owner: Kosaido Co Ltd
Cost: *Alc* £30, set-price L £16-£20/D £25-£40. ☺ H/wine £12
Times: Noon-2pm/6.30-9pm.
Closed Mon, 1 wk early Jan
Additional: Bar food; Sunday L; Children welcome
Seats: 40. Private dining room 80-90
Style: Japanese/Formal
Smoking: No pipes & cigars
Civil licence: 80
Accommodation: 32 en suite ★★★

Whilst the full range of classic Japanese cuisine is available at Old Thorns, people come here primarily for the theatre that is teppanyaki. A trained chef stands before his diners at a stainless steel hotplate and slices, prepares and sometimes even juggles prime beef, fish, vegetables and seafood which are quickly and healthily seared on the teppan. Choose one of the set menus which include salads, rice, clear soup pickles and appetisers, or from the *carte* which features the expected full range of Japanese dishes.

Directions: Approx 500yds from Griggs Green exit off A3, south of Liphook

LIPHOOK,

Old Thorns Hotel ❀

A warm intimate room with views over the hotel's extensive gardens. Modern European cuisine served by friendly staff, perhaps including pot roasted guinea fowl in a rich red wine sauce or seared tuna steak with sweet potato mash.

Griggs Green GU30 7PE
Map 4: SU83
Tel: 01428 724555
Fax: 01428 725036
E-mail: reservations@
oldthorns.freeserve.co.uk

Old Thorns Hotel

Cost: *Alc* £25, set-price L £15/D £20.
☺ H/wine £12
Times: Noon-2pm/7-9.30pm
Additional: Bar food; Sunday L;
Children welcome
Style: Country-house/Formal
Smoking: No smoking in dining room
Civil licence: 100
Accommodation: 32 en suite ★★★

Directions: Approx 500yds from Griggs Green exit off A3, south of Liphook

LYMINGTON, Stanwell House Hotel ✿

High Street SO41 9AA
Map 4: SZ39
Tel: 01590 677123
Fax: 01590 677756
Cost: *Alc* £28, set-price L £12.50/D
£22.50. ☺ H/wine £13.50
Times: Noon-2pm/7-9.30pm
Additional: Bar food; Sunday L;
Children welcome
Style: Bistro-style/Informal
Smoking: No smoking in dining room
Civil licence: 60
Accommodation: 30 en suite ★★★

Directions: 2 miles from M27 J1.
Take A337 through the New Forest
towards the coast

The bistro-style restaurant benefits from the hotel owners' gratifyingly individual style, making good use of quality fabrics and furnishings. Our meal included a pork and apple terrine which was well made with a good balance of flavours.

LYNDHURST, Crown Hotel ✿

High Street SO43 7NF
Map 4: SU30
Tel: 023 8028 2922
Fax: 023 8028 2751
E-mail: crown@marstonhotels.co.uk
Cost: *Alc* £30, set-price D £19.50. ☺
H/wine £12
Times: D only, 7-9.30pm
Additional: Bar food; Sunday L
(12.30-2pm); Children welcome
Style: Classic/Country-house
Smoking: No smoking in dining room
Accommodation: 39 en suite ★★★

Directions: Top end of Lyndhurst
High Street, opposite church

Newly refurbished restaurant with garden views in this historic hotel at the heart of the village. Cuisine ranges from modern continental influence to traditional country fayre, a Sunday lunch beef and ox kidney casserole for example.

LYNDHURST,

Le Poussin at Parkhill 🥕🥕🥕

Beaulieu Road
SO43 7FZ
Map 4: SU30
Tel: 02380 282944
Fax: 02380 283268
E-mail: lepoussin@parkhill.co.uk
Chef: Alexander Aitken
Cost: Set-price L £15.50/D £27.50.
H/wine £11.50
Times: Noon-2pm/7-9.30pm
Additional: Sunday L; Children
welcome
Seats: 70. Private dining room 40
Style: Classic/Traditional
Smoking: No smoking in dining room
Civil licence: 70
Accommodation: 20 en suite ★ ★ ★

Alex Aitken readily enthuses about the fine seasonal ingredients he is able to source – New Forest wild mushrooms, wood pigeon and venison from the unspoilt woodlands surrounding the Georgian house. He's even willing to take guests deer spotting. His restaurant, Le Poussin, has relocated but favourite dishes remain on the menu. Trio of meats, for example, includes rare fillet of beef with pink-cooked lamb and pork and lamb with a red wine and rosemary sauce and creamy dauphinoise potatoes. The eponymous bird comes in a pressed terrine with foie gras and fat prunes steeped in Earl Grey. A lightness of touch shows in fish dishes such as wing of skate with black pepper or pan-fried brill with creamed leeks. Classic dishes include twice-baked cheese soufflé and rich dark chocolate marquise served with a refreshing orange sorbet. The clearly explained menu is priced per number of courses and there is also a daily tasting menu of five courses available to the whole table. A passion for wine shines through the wine list; Bordeaux is listed by the area, and there is also a good selection of French half-bottles. Service is formal, precise and very French.

Directions: On entering Lyndhurst from M27 at Cadnam, take A35 towards Southampton. Immediately after turning for Lyndhurst Park Hotel take the next R towards Beaulieu, B3056. Hotel 1 mile on R.

AA Shortlisted for Wine Award-see page 18

MIDDLE WALLOP,

Fifehead Manor 🥕🥕

SO20 8EG
Map 4: SU23
Tel: 01264 781565
Fax: 01264 781400

Telephone for further details.

Traditional hotel dining room furnished and run with some flair. A recent visit opened with a starter of chilled beetroot soup with sour cream. The soup was a stunningly rich ruby colour and yielded a good clarity of flavour. A main course of fillet of turbot with parsley risotto, braised leeks and sautéed shiitake mushrooms was accurately cooked and nicely presented as a tower. A passion fruit feuille tante proved to be a lovely light passion fruit mousse with a delightfully muted flavour successfully spiked with triangles of crisp filo. A wide range of wines is on offer including a good selection supplied by the local English vineyard at Wickham.

Directions: From M3 J8 take A303 to Andover, then take A343 S six miles to Middle Wallop

MILFORD ON SEA,
The Rouille Restaurant

NEW

Replacing Rocher's, a restaurant of 10-years standing, new blood has brought city eclecticism to this village. Enthusiasm is evident in asparagus soup, seared salmon with sauce vierge and spiced aubergine, and crème brûlée with a strawberry, saffron ice cream and minted strawberries.

Additional: Sunday L; Children welcome
Style: classic/informal
Smoking: No-smoking area

Directions: A337 W from Lymington. In 3m take B3058 to Milford-on-Sea then road to Keyhaven; hotel on L

67-71 High Street SO41 0QG
Map 4: SZ29
Tel/Fax: 01590 642340
Cost: Alc £26.50, set-price L £9.95/D £9.95-£24.50. ☺ H/wine £12
Times: Noon-3pm/7-11.30pm.
Closed Mon & Tue, L Wed-Sat & D Sun, from Sep-Apr; 1st 2 wks Jan

MILFORD ON SEA,
South Lawn Hotel ✿

Lymington Road SO41 0RF
Map 4: SZ29
Tel: 01590 643911
Fax: 01590 644820
E-mail: enquiries@southlawn.co.uk
Cost: Set-price L £12.50/ D £22.50. H/wine £12
Times: Noon-1.45pm/7-8.45pm.
Closed L Mon, 20 Dec-19 Jan

A family owned former dower house where home cooking and fresh local produce are a strong feature. Starters might include home made carrot and coriander soup, followed perhaps by grilled fillets of locally caught plaice.

Additional: Bar food L; Sunday L; Children 7+
Style: Traditional/Country-house
Smoking: No smoking in dining room
Accommodation: 24 en suite ★ ★ ★

Directions: A337 from Lymington, L after 3 miles onto B3058; hotel 1 mile on R

MILFORD ON SEA, Westover Hall

Park Lane SO41 0PT
Map 4: SZ29
Tel: 01590 643044
Fax: 01590 644490
E-mail:
westoverhallhotel@barclays.net
Chef: Neil A Johnson
Owners: Nicola Musetti &
Stewart Mechem
Cost: Set-price L/D 27.50. ☺
H/wine £11.95
Times: Noon-2pm/7-9pm
Additional: Bar food L; Sunday L;
Children 7+
Seats: 40. Private dining room 10
Style: Modern/Country-house
Smoking: No smoking in dining room
Civil licence: 50
Accommodation: 14 en suite ★★★

Luxurious Victorian hotel dining room in a truly spectacular location overlooking the Needles. Jacobean ceiling moulds and pre-Raphaelite stained glass windows alongside simple modern dining decor create a feeling of timeless sophistication. A single lily on each table demonstrates a loving attention to detail on the part of the congenial owners. A straightforward set-price menu offers a good balance of dishes, all sourced locally. The inspector enjoyed a starter of confit of wild rabbit with a well-textured risotto. Nicely flavoured fresh pan-fried brill fillets formed the basis of a strong main course. These were agreeably complemented by a good dollop of aoili and plenty of garlic and saffron. A chocolate fondant demonstrating skill in texture and flavour finished the meal off nicely.

Directions: From M27/J1 take A337 then B3058. Hotel is situated just out of Milford centre, towards clifftop

NEW MILTON,
Chewton Glen Hotel

Christchurch Road
BH25 6QS
Map 4: SZ29
Tel: 01425 275341
Fax: 01425 272310
E-mail:
reservations@chewtonglen.com
Chef: Pierre Chevillard
Owners: Martin & Brigitte Skan

Over the last thirty years, Martin and Brigitte Skan have transformed Chewton Glen into a hotel of international status with levels of attentive service to match. The restaurant is split between a conservatory which leads onto the garden, and the adjacent, smartly-furnished dining-room. Pierre Chevillard continues to impress with his consistency, skill and imagination in the kitchen, and the extensive, well-presented wine list is a must for the enthusiast. Although a double-baked Emmental soufflé was deliciously light, delicately flavoured and sported a wonderful bronzed top, there was little sign of the Kirsch flavour as promised in the fondue sauce. A beautifully succulent fillet of lamb was cooked to perfection, perfectly offset by its crust of mustard, herbs and breadcrumbs and a well-flavoured thyme jus. Daily specials might include langoustines with paprika and tarragon mayonnaise or paupiette of roasted scallops and plaice. Mark Walter, head sommelier, has selected a dessert wine to accompany different puddings, for example, Brown Brothers liqueur Muscat with the sticky toffee pudding and vanilla ice-cream. The lunch menu has simpler offerings along the lines of home-cured gravad lax with mustard dressing and chargrilled rib-eye steak with parsley butter and pommes Pont-Neuf.

Style: Chic/Country-house
Smoking: No smoking in dining room; Air conditioning
Civil licence: 60
Accommodation: 55 en suite ★ ★ ★ ★ ★

Directions: On A35 (Lyndhurst) turn R through Walkford, then 2nd left into Chewton Farm Road

Cost: Alc L £23, set-price D £47.50. H/wine £17.25
Times: 12.30-1.45pm/7.30-9.45pm
Additional: Bar food L; Sunday L; Children 7+
Seats: 120. Private dining rooms 24 & 24. Jacket preferred at D

AA Wine Shortlisted for Award-see page 18

OLD BURGHCLERE, Dew Pond ❀❀

Set beside the dew pond from which it takes its name and housed within a pair of 16th-century drovers' cottages, this homely country restaurant enjoys peaceful rural views towards the Hampshire Downs. Relax on the terrace in summer, or in the cottagey lounge, with a pre-prandial drink and peruse the well-balanced set-price dinner menu. Traditional dishes are cooked in a modern style and presentation is unfussy and attractive. From home-made bread rolls, and crevettes marinated in coriander, chilli and lime with a good garlic mayonnaise for starters, move on to duck breast and a delicious crispy confit of leg with a shallot and cassis glaze, or saddle of roe deer with port wine sauce. Desserts take in apple tarte Tatin with vanilla pod ice cream and cinnamon crème anglaise and baked bananas with chocolate and caramel sauces. Global wine list arranged by taste.

Directions: Six miles S of Newbury. Take Burghclere turn off A34 (Winchester), follow signs for Old Burghclere

Nr Newbury RG20 9LH
Map 4: SU45
Tel: 01635 278408
Fax: 01635 278580
E-mail: dewpond@talk21.com

Telephone for further details

PETERSFIELD, Langrish House ❀ NEW

An idyllic setting of 17th-century architecture and rolling Hampshire countryside, the picture is completed by a menu offering interesting combinations of quality ingredients such as tian of crab and lobster with horseradish and lemongrass.

Additional: Sunday L; Children 11+
Style: Chic/country-house
Smoking: No smoking in the dining room
Civil licence: 60
Accommodation: 14 en suite ★ ★

Directions: From Petersfield take A272 towards Winchester and turn L in village with hotel sign

Langrish GU32 1RN
Map 4: SU72
Tel: 01730 266941
Fax: 01730 260543
Cost: Set-price L £17.50/D £24.95. ☺
H/wine £9.75
Times: 12.30-1.45pm/7-9.30pm.
Closed L Sat, D Sun

RINGWOOD,
Moortown Lodge Hotel

Expect a warm welcome from Jilly and Bob Burrows-Jones at their small Georgian hotel on the edge of the New Forest. Jilly's short dinner menu could include carrot and coriander soup, chicken breast stuffed with wild mushrooms and a marsala sauce, and prune and armagnac tart for dessert.

244 Christchurch Road BH24 3AS
Map 4: SU10
Tel: 01425 471404
Fax: 01425 476052
E-mail: hotel@burrows-jones.freeserve.co.uk
Cost: Set-price D £20.95. ☺
H/wine £9.95
Times: D only, 7-8.30pm. Closed Sun (ex residents), Xmas-mid Jan, 1 wk Jul
Additional: Children welcome
Style: French/Country-house
Smoking: No smoking in dining room
Accommodation: 6 rooms ★ ★

Directions: From Ringwood town centre take B3347 towards Christchurch for about 1.5 miles

---

ROMSEY, Bertie's

In the centre of the old market town, Bertie's is brightly decorated, with displays of fresh flowers, and has a friendly and relaxed atmosphere. Luxury sandwiches, and something like salade niçoise, or home-smoked haddock with new potatoes and spring onions are on offer at lunchtimes alongside a good-value set menu (also available weekday evenings) that might run from a salad of black pudding with bacon, to rissoles on carrot and parsnip mash. The dinner menu sees a kitchen judiciously combining textures and flavours: prawn salad with crispy onions and a creamy tomato sauce to start, followed by pan-seared chicken breast on cabbage and pancetta with a mustard sauce. Good timing is a hallmark of main courses of roasted rack of lamb on rösti with a mint jus, and seared duck breast with an orange and thyme sauce, and pastry skills show up in starters – perhaps a tartlet of melted onions and Stilton on a bed of leeks – as well as puddings: pineapple tarte Tatin with toffee sauce, say, or chocolate tart. A well-balanced wine list completes the rosy picture.

80 The Hundred SO51 8BX
Map 4: SU32
Tel: 01794 830708
Fax: 01794 507507
Chef: Michael Weir
Owner: David Birmingham
Cost: *Alc* £26, set-price L £11.95/D £14.95. ☺ H/wine £9.75
Times: Noon-2pm/6.30-10pm(10.30pm Sat). Closed Sun, Bhs
Additional: Bar food L; Children 1+
Seats: 50
Smoking: No-smoking area; No pipes & cigars

Directions: 200mtrs from Broadlands' gate in the centre of town

---

ROMSEY,
Old Manor House Restaurant

There are few restaurants, Italian or otherwise, where they smoke their own meat; even fewer where they use the giant fireplace of a lovely Tudor manor house. Mauro Bregoli is not only the chef/patron and smoker-in-chief, but a keen marksman and the collection of deer antlers bears witness to his skill. An old-fashioned master craftsman with the highest of standards, he home-produces and cures some of the meats and salumeria on the menu, such as cotechino (served hot with lentils) and neck of pork (with rocket salad). Eating here gives one an insight as to how things should really taste; there is no compromise on quality or on the traditional techniques of smoking, brining and cooking. Heavenly flavoured gnocchi are as light as feather pillows, served

21 Palmerston Street SO51 8GF
Map 4: SU32
Tel: 01794 517353
Chef: Mauro Bregoli
Owners: Mauro & Esther Bregoli
Cost: Set-price £17.50. H/wine £11.50
Times: Noon-2pm/7-9.30pm. Closed D Sun, all Mon, 1wk Xmas-New Year
Additional: Sunday L; Children welcome
Seats: 26
Style: Rustic/Italian
Smoking: No pipes & cigars

Old Manor House Restaurant

Directions: Opposite the entrance to Broadlands Estate

with a fresh-tasting tomato sauce with lots of fresh basil. Escalope of venison with cracked pepper filled the plate, and had great depth of flavour without undue gaminess. Unusual fish dishes include escalope of ling with a warm basil and caper vinaigrette and barbecued eel steak with salsa verde. All main courses are served with a simple selection of vegetables.

ROTHERWICK, Tylney Hall

Hook RG27 9AZ
Map 4: SU75
Tel: 01256 764881
Fax: 01256 745511
E-mail: sales@tylneyhall.com
Chef: Stephen Hine
Cost: Alc fr £50, set-price L £23/D £35. H/wine fr £15.50
Times: 12.30-2pm/7.30-9.30pm(10pm Fri & Sat)
Additional: Bar food ; Sunday L; Children welcome
Seats: 100. Private dining room 100; Jacket & tie preferred
Style: Traditional/Country-house
Smoking: No smoking in dining room
Civil licence: 100
Accommodation: 110 en suite
★ ★ ★ ★

Built in Victorian times in the Jacobean style, this mansion is set in 66 acres of parkland, including water gardens. Oak panelling, open fires and a sense of grandeur are what to expect inside, with a spacious dining room overlooking the outdoor pool with a vista of the countryside. Traditional dishes of honey-roast breast of Barbary duck, or a joint of the day carved from the trolley meet more modern ideas in the shape of starters of a tian of smoked salmon, lime and dill with gazpacho dressing, or chicken and chorizo terrine decorated with pesto. Fish is a strength, from brochette of tiger prawns and monkfish with red pepper coulis, to pan-fried fillet of sea bass with a watercress and lime cream, while rump of lamb might be given a garlic and rosemary jus. Up-to-the-minute desserts take in vanilla pannacotta with dried apricots and figs, coconut rice pudding with banana beignets and pineapple coulis, and a prune version of Bakewell tart. The globally inspired wine list is a lengthy tome, but professional staff are on hand to advise.

Directions: M3/J5 take A287 (Newnham). From M4/J11 take B3349 (Hook), at sharp bend L (Rotherwick), L again and L in village (Newnham), 1 mile on R

SILCHESTER,

Romans Hotel ✿

Stroll through the attractive grounds of this manor house before sitting down to grilled fillet of skate wing with tomato and coriander sauce or pan-fried rib eye steak with duck liver sauce and macaire potatoes.

Little London Road RG7 2PN
Map 4: SU66
Tel: 0118 9700421
Fax: 0118 9700691
E-mail: romanhotel@hotmail.com
Cost: *Alc* £25, set-price L £12/D £19.50. ☺ H/wine £13
Times: Noon-2pm/7-9.30pm. Closed L Sat
Additional: Bar food; Sunday L; Children welcome
Style: Traditional/Country-house
Smoking: No smoking in dining room
Civil licence: 65
Accommodation: 25 en suite ★ ★ ★

Directions: Signposted on A340 between Basingstoke and Tadley

SOUTHAMPTON,

Botleigh Grange Hotel ✿✿

This much-extended mansion set in extensive grounds, proves a popular venue for weddings and weekday conference delegates. The light and airy dining-room has a glass-domed ceiling and overlooks the gardens. Modern British cooking is the kitchen's style, and menus offer variety and a wide choice on *carte* and set-price repertoires. A starter of chargrilled asparagus with crab spring roll and chorizo, garnished with deep-fried herbs proved enjoyable. Ballontine of chicken with braised red cabbage, parsnips and shallots and a tarragon and redcurrant reduction made for a sound main course, though fish lovers might favour poached fillet of halibut with a Jerusalem artichoke cake and glazed beetroot and lobster sauce. A strong point on this spring visit proved to be a good textured passion fruit brûlée tarte with blackberry compote, while sticky toffee pudding with butterscotch sauce and vanilla ice cream offered a more traditional finalé.

Directions: On A334, 1.5 miles from M27 J 7

Hedge End SO30 2GA
Map 4: SU41
Tel: 01489 787700
Fax: 01489 788535
E-mail: enquiries@botleighgrangehotel.co.uk
Chef: Edward Denovan
Owner: David K Plumpton
Cost: *Alc* fr £25, set-price L/D £22. ☺ H/wine £11.95
Times: Noon-2pm/7-10pm. Closed L Sat
Additional: Bar food L; Sunday L; Children welcome
Seats: 150. Private dining room 500. Jacket & tie preferred
Style: Classic/Country-house
Smoking: No smoking in dining room
Civil licence: 200
Accommodation: 60 en suite ★ ★ ★

SOUTHAMPTON,
Woodlands Lodge Hotel ❀

Previously a royal hunting lodge, this 18th-century country house now hosts an ornately decorated dining room which, in turn, hosts sophisticated, classic cuisine. Sample coriander and sesame marinated best end of lamb.

Smoking: No smoking in dining room
Civil licence: 60
Accommodation: 16 en suite ★★★

Directions: Telephone for directions

Bartley Road Woodlands SO40 7GN
Map 4: SU41
Tel: 02380 292257
Fax: 02380 293090
E-mail: woodlands@nortels.ltd.uk
Cost: Alc £26.50-£30. ☺
H/wine £11.95
Times: D only, 7-9pm
Additional: Bar food L; Sunday L
(noon-2pm); Children welcome
Style: Classic/Country-house

WICKHAM, Old House Hotel ❀❀

The Square PO17 5JG
Map 4: SU51
Tel: 01329 833049
Fax: 01329 833672
E-mail: eng@theoldhousehotel.co.uk
Chef: Nicholas Ruthven-Stuart
Owners: John & Gloria Goodacre
Cost: Alc £30, set-price L £10 & £15.
☺ H/wine £10.95
Times: Noon-3pm/7-11pm.
Closed D Sun, L Mon, 10 days Xmas
Additional: Sunday L; Children
welcome
Seats: 36. Private dining room 12
Style: Classic/Traditional
Smoking: No smoking in dining room
Accommodation: 9 en suite ★★

Popular hotel restaurant in the charming Georgian village of Wickham, close to the M27. The building is 18th century and the decor follows a classic, traditional model. Ability is evident in the execution of the largely British and French dishes. The set price dinner menu offers starters along the lines of wild mushroom risotto with truffle oil and tian of white crab, herbs and crème fraîche. Main course options might include roast breast of Gressingham duck, sarlandaise potatoes and a sweet and sour blackcurrant sauce, or confit of Scottish salmon with piperade and sauce vierge. The dessert menu offers a taste of Arcadia with the likes of caramelised bread and butter pudding, tulip of fresh fruit sorbets and vanilla pannacotta with passion fruit sauce.

Directions: In the centre of Wickham, 3 miles N of Fareham at junction of A32/B2177

WINCHESTER,
Hotel du Vin & Bistro ❀❀

Robin Hutson's and Gerard Basset's elegant Georgian town house is stylish, unpretentious and popular – a formula now repeated in Tunbridge Wells, Bristol and soon Birmingham. Its modern bistro exudes charm and informality, with polished floorboards, and a bustling, vibrant atmosphere. Wine memorabilia, from pictures to hop garlands and bottles, crowd walls and fill every conceivable niche. The daily changing, contemporary menu, enlivened with a nod to the Mediterranean and beyond, offers an eclectic choice of simple, imaginative and well-presented dishes. Staff are plentiful,

14 Southgate Street
SO23 9EF
Map 4: SU42
Tel: 01962 841414
Fax: 01962 842458
E-mail:
admin@winchester.hotelduvin.co.uk
Chef: Andy Clark
Owner: The Alternative Hotel
Company
Cost: Alc £30. ☺ H/wine £11.95
Times: Noon-1.45pm/7-10pm

friendly and serve with fervour; French sticks are delivered with knife and breadboard no sooner than you are seated. A typical starter might feature caramelised onion tart with goats' cheese and tangy tomato chutney, while main courses of red snapper with spicy red lentils and a tamarind jus, or John Dory with caramelised salsify, trompette de mort and Sauterne jus, show the style. For dessert, try a feuilletine of raspberries with a Kirsch sabayon. The wine list, selected by a master hand, offers a great choice from worldwide vineyards, and coffee is noteworthy too. *Best Dessert Wine (see pages 18-19).*

Directions: M3 J11, follow signs for Winchester. Hotel on L just before town centre

Additional: Sunday L; Children welcome
Seats: 65. Private dining rooms 12 & 48
Style: Bistro-style/Informal
Smoking: No pipes & cigars
Accommodation: 23 en suite ★★★★

WINCHESTER, Hunters

Local artist Jenny Muncaster has been given a free rein to create wall paintings of wine and food throughout the restaurant, which reflect the modern international cuisine.

Style: Bistro-style/Modern
Smoking: No-smoking area

Directions: Towards top of the City just off High Street, 200 yards from Theatre Royal & Library car park

5 Jewry Street SO23 8RZ
Map 4: SU42
Tel: 01962 860006
Cost: Alc £25, set-price D £12.95. H/wine £9.95
Times: Telephone for opening times. Closed Sun, Xmas, New Year
Additional: Bar food L; Children welcome

WINCHESTER,
Lainston House Hotel

Sparsholt SO21 2LT
Map 4: SU42
Tel: 01962 863588
Fax: 01962 776672
E-mail: enquiries@lainstonhouse.com

Telephone for further details

Directions: 3m from Winchester off the B3049 to Stockbridge. Signposted

Charming country house hotel set in lovely grounds. The kitchen's distinctive style takes in imaginatively presented, skilfully prepared dishes such as terrine of smoked salmon and turbot wrapped in smoked salmon, roasted Scottish ribeye of beef with red wine and foie gras sauce, or saddle of lamb rolled in aromatic herbs and served with french beans, garlic fondant potatoes and a rosemary scented jus. Finish with baked pecan cheesecake.

WINCHESTER, Nine The Square

One of the oldest buildings in Winchester in prime position opposite the splendid cathedral. The decor combines the rustic with the modern and the atmosphere is relaxed and friendly

The Square
SO23 9HA
Map 4: SU42
Tel: 01962 864004
Fax: 01962 879586

both in the ground floor bistro and in the more formal first floor dining room. Oysters feature highly in the starter options either straight up or served with soda bread and a bottle of Guinness. Less dextrous diners may prefer the leek, rice and smoked salmon soup or perhaps the seared pigeon breast salad with mango salsa. A strongly Italian influence is evident in the main course options and pasta dishes such as rigatoni with salmon and pesto cream are sure to inspire Latin exuberance. Steamed lemon pudding with vanilla anglaise will finish the meal off with a zing, but if all that's too much for you can always sink into the furnishings with a hunk of stilton and a glass of port for company.

Chef: David Bennett
Owners: David & Debra Bennett
Cost: Alc £25, set price L £8.50. ☺
H/wine £ 11.50
Times: Noon-2pm, 7(6pm Fri & Sat)-10pm. Closed Sun, 25 & 26 Dec, some Bhs
Additional: Children welcome
Seats: 46. Private room 22
Style: Bistro-style/Modern
Smoking: No pipes & cigars; Air conditioning

Directions: In the main square, just outside the cathedral grounds and opposite the museum

WINCHESTER,
Old Chesil Rectory ❀❀

1 Chesil Street SO23 8HU
Map 4: SU42
Tel: 01962 851555
Fax: 01962 869704
Chef: Philip Storey
Owners: Philip & Catherine Storey
Cost: Set-price L £22.60/D £34.60.
H/wine £13.95
Times: Noon-3pm/7-midnight. Closed all Sun & Mon, 1wk Xmas-New Year, 1st wk Aug
Seats: 40. Private dining room 30
Style: Minimalist/formal
Smoking: No-smoking area

The Old Rectory has been little altered since it was built in 1459; the interior remains simple, with original beams and whitewashed panels. White linen, white candles and fresh white flowers plus a few simple prints are the only adornment. The up-to-date repertoire of modern British dishes is laid out in a series of short set menus; typically, the good value lunch menu might offer Jerusalem artichoke soup with smoked haddock, followed by fillet steak with rösti potatoes and Savoy cabbage. The evening *carte* goes up a notch with the likes of duck confit and foie gras terrine with onion marmalade or roasted brill with onion compote and wild mushrooms. And we are particularly tempted by the sound of a trio of pear desserts – sorbet, pie and poached pear with Roquefort.

Directions: From King Alfred's statue at the bottom of The Broadway, cross the small bridge and turn R; the restaurant is to the L, just off mini roundabout

WINCHESTER, **Royal Hotel** ❀

St Peter Street SO23 8BS
Map 4: SU42
Tel: 01962 840840
Fax: 01962 841582
E-mail: info@the-royal.com
Cost: Alc £24, set-price L £9.50. ☺
H/wine £12.95
Times: Noon-2.15pm/7-9.30pm
Additional: Bar Food L; Sunday L; Children welcome
Style: Traditional
Smoking: No smoking in dining room; Air conditioning
Civil licence: 120
Accommodation: 75 en suite ★★★

Air-conditioned conservatory restaurant attached to a 16th-century building, with a beautiful garden for summer dining. The menu of two or three courses always includes a fresh fish dish.

Directions: Take one-way system through Winchester, turn R off St George's Street into St Peter Street. Hotel on R

WINCHESTER, Wykeham Arms

75 Kingsgate Street SO23 9PE
Map 4: SU42
Tel: 01962 853834
Fax: 01962 854411
Cost: *Alc* £24. ☺ H/wine £10.95
Times: Noon-2.30pm/6.30-9pm.
Closed Sun, 25 Dec
Additional: Bar food L; Children 14+
Style: Informal/rustic
Smoking: No-smoking area; Air
conditioning

250-year-old inn sandwiched between the college and cathedral.
Rack of lamb was carefully cooked and carved, and the raspberry
and white chocolate trifle had a seriously boozy filling.

Directions: S out of city along Southgate Street. Take 3rd
turning L into Canon Street, inn on R at end

HEREFORDSHIRE

HEREFORD,
Ancient Camp Inn ⊛⊛

Ruckhall HR2 9QX
Map 3: SO53
Tel: 01981 250449
Fax: 01981 251581
Chef: Jason Eland
Owners: J Eland & L Eland
Cost: *Alc* £22.50, set-price D £19.95.
☺ H/wine £9.95
Times: Noon-2pm, 7-9pm. Closed D
Sun, all Mon, 2 wks Jan
Additional: Bar food L; Sunday L,
Children welcome at L only
Style: Traditional
Seats: 24. Private dining room 18
Smoking: No smoking in dining room
Accommodation: 5 en suite ★ ★

Country inn and restaurant built on the grounds of an old fort
high above the River Wye. The building has an interesting
history, originally intended to be a shop, it became a forge and
later a cider house. The restaurant still has the flagstone floor,
oak beams, open fires and old cider tables, and views from the
windows are stunning. The setting is relaxed, rustic and full of
unpretentious charm, and the menu reflects these virtues with
a direct and uncluttered cooking style that relies on quality
produce. Kick off with salad of duckling – confit of leg
wrapped in oak-smoked breast served with fresh fig and
beetroot purées – followed perhaps by fillet of cod baked with

a herb crust and served with a shellfish sauce scented with ginger. Desserts range from a traditional crumble of local apples and raspberries to a classic prune, Armagnac and vanilla tart.

Directions: Take A465 (Abergavenny road) from Hereford. Turn R to Ruckhall and Belmont Abbey. Inn is 2.5 miles

HEREFORD,
Castle House

NEW

Castle Street HR1 2NW
Map 3: SO53
Tel: 01432 356321
Fax: 01432 365909
E-mail: info@castlehse.co.uk
Chef: Stuart McCleod
Owners: Dr & Mrs A Heijn
Cost: Set-price L £16.95/D £27.95.
H/wine £14
Times: 12.30-2pm/7-10pm
Additional: Bar food; Sunday L;
Children welcome
Seats: 32
Style: Classic/Chic
Smoking: No pipes & cigars; Air
conditioning
Accommodation: 15 rooms ★ ★ ★ ★

Castle House, once the home of the Bishop of Hereford, is an elegant, substantial property, a balustrade running along at first-floor level. Opened as a hotel in 1999, it's been smartly, even luxuriously, converted, with the restaurant, where there is a wealth of objets d'art, a light, bright room with a view over the garden and moat. The set-price menus are sensibly restricted to three choices at each course at lunch, four at dinner, allowing the kitchen to direct its energies wisely. Descriptions are to the point, and 'keep it simple' might be pinned up on the kitchen wall, a philosophy that produced a 'dazzling' inspection meal, with attention to detail outstanding from canapés to petits fours. Lunch might open with medallions of codling with pak choi and saffron dressing and move on to breast of maize-fed chicken with puréed ceps and a lentil and bacon jus, while dinner might range from a simple salad of new season's asparagus with white truffle to potato-crusted halibut, a masterful dish 'reeking of springtime'. Raw materials are exemplary – Cornish scallops, local duckling – and the kitchen shows a confident grasp of flavours and a readiness to make some bold statements: sesame-crusted yellow fin tuna with daikon noodles and an oyster reduction, for instance, or pot-roast squab pigeon with a ravioli of the leg and an 'excellent' white pudding and citrus sauce, a dish of 'sparkling intensity'. A pre-dessert of 'brilliant' strawberry and champagne jelly leads the way to seriously praiseworthy puddings – an assiette of Valrhona chocolate concoctions, say, or variations on a theme of perhaps pineapple or citrus fruits. Four house wines kick off the list, which has been assembled with an eye to quality.

Directions: City centre, near cathedral

LEDBURY, Feathers Hotel ❀

High Street HR8 1DS
Map 3: SO73
Tel: 01531 635266
Fax: 01531 638955
Cost: *Alc* £21. ☺
Times: Noon-3pm/7-9.30pm
Additional: Bar food; Sunday L;
Children welcome
Style: Bistro-style/Rustic
Smoking: No-smoking area; No pipes
& cigars
Civil licence: 125
Accommodation: 19 en suite ★ ★ ★

Charming town centre coaching inn where the building's inherent charm and character is enhanced by exposed beams, wall timbers and log fires. The 'Fuggles' brasserie menu includes baked red sea bream fillet with tomato and basil sauce.

Directions: Ledbury is on A449/A438/A417, and the hotel is prominent on the main street

ROSS-ON-WYE, Chase Hotel ❀❀

Gloucester Road HR9 5LH
Map 3: SO52
Tel: 01989 763161
Fax: 01989 768330
E-mail: info@chasehotel.co.uk
Cost: *Alc* £23, set-price L & D £17.
☺ H/wine £9.50
Times: Noon-2pm/7-10pm. Closed 26
Dec
Additional: Bar food; Sunday L;
Children 5+
Seats: 50. Private dining room 100
Style: Classic/Country-house
Smoking: No smoking in dining room
Civil licence: 50
Accommodation: 38 en suite ★ ★ ★

Although within easy reach of the town centre, this Regency mansion is surrounded by extensive grounds and gardens. It's a comfortable place, with an elegant restaurant done out in warm, soft peachy tones; long, ornate mirrors provide decoration. The menus are traditional in style, taking in gravad lax with dill, or chicken and pork terrine with an apple and pear chutney, then main courses of chargrilled sirloin steak in wild mushroom sauce, or seared rainbow trout fillets with caper butter. Fine produce is used – rack of local lamb with a redcurrant, port and rosemary sauce, Bantry Bay mussels to garnish a mixed fish dish – and a more avant garde approach is often taken towards vegetarian dishes: sun-dried tomato and pesto capeletti with a spicy tomato sauce, say, or stir-fried vegetables with egg noodles and hoi sin sauce. Cheeses are English, and desserts might include bread-and-butter pudding with custard, or deep-fried banana fritters drizzled in syrup.

Directions: From town centre follow B4260 towards Gloucester, hotel 200yds on R

ROSS-ON-WYE,

Glewstone Court ✿

Georgian country house with an eclectic collection of antiques and artefacts. An interesting menu might take in kedgeree of asparagus, mi cuit tomatoes and wild mushrooms, sea bass with pistachio nut crust, or fillet of venison.

Style: Informal/Country-house
Smoking: No pipes & cigars
Accommodation: 8 en suite ★ ★

Directions: From Ross Market Place take A40/A49 (Monmouth/Hereford) over Wilton Bridge. At roundabout L onto A40 (Monmouth/S Wales), after 1 mile R for Glewstone

Glewstone HR9 6AW
Map 3: SO52
Tel: 01989 770367
Fax: 01989 770282
E-mail: glewstone@aol.com
Cost: Set-price D £26. H/wine £9
Times: Noon-2pm (Bistro)/7-9.30pm.
Closed L Sun, 25-27 Dec
Additional: Bar food; Sunday L;
Children welcome

ROSS-ON-WYE,

Hunsdon Manor Hotel ✿

A large dining room with a beechwood floor, Zoffany wallpapers and silk curtains. Dinner options might include fillet steak Diane, salmon with parsely aïoli, and Welsh leg of lamb.

Additional: Sunday L (bookings only); Children welcome
Style: Country-house
Accommodation: 25 en suite ★ ★ ★

Directions: On A40, 2 miles E of Ross-on-Wye

Gloucester Road Weston
under Penyard HR9 7PE
Map: 3: SO52
Tel: 01989 563376/562748
Fax: 01989 768348
Cost: Set-price L £16/D £24. ☺
H/wine £12
Times: Noon-2.30pm (bookings only)/7-9.30pm.

ROSS-ON-WYE,

Pencraig Court Hotel ✿

Good wholesome dishes prepared from fresh produce served in the attractive dining room of this large Georgian house. The daily-changing menu might include duck breast with gooseberry sauce or venison sausages on a bed of red cabbage.

Additional: Children welcome
Style: Classic/Country-house
Smoking: No smoking in dining room
Accommodation: 11 en suite ★ ★ ★

Directions: Approximately 3 miles S of Ross-on-Wye on A40

Pencraig HR9 6HR
Map 3: SO52
Tel: 01989 770306
Fax: 01989 770040
E-mail: mike@pencraig-court.co.uk
Cost: Set-price L £12.50/D £25. ☺
H/wine £9.50
Times: Noon-2.30pm/7.30-9.30pm.
Closed Sun, Feb

ROSS-ON-WYE,

Pengethley Manor ✿✿

A vineyard in the parkland around this elegant Georgian property produces Pengethley's own-label wine, one of around a dozen bottles of the house selection. The restaurant is a comfortable, well-proportioned room, with upholstered chairs at well-set tables, a gilt-framed mirror and drapes hanging at large windows giving rural views. Starters range from cappelletti Neapolitan to locally-smoked ham enclosing a parcel of diced apple, sauerkraut, bacon and asparagus, and main courses are of broad appeal too, from filet mignon to

Pengethley Park
HR9 6LL
Map 3: SO52
Tel: 01989 730211
Fax: 01989 730238
E-mail:
reservations@pengethleymanor.co.uk
Chef: Ferdinand van der Knaap
Owners: Patrick & Geraldine Wisker
Cost: Alc £25. ☺ H/wine £12.95
Times: Noon-2pm/7-9.30pm

Pengethley Manor

Additional: Bar food L; Sunday L; Children welcome
Seats: 50. Private dining room 25
Style: Classic/Country-house
Smoking: No smoking in dining room
Civil licence: 40
Accommodation: 25 en suite ★ ★ ★

Directions: 4m N on A49 Hereford road

Eastern-style duck breast on egg noodles and prawns, taking in perhaps oven-baked loin of salmon on a sauce of Dijon mustard and lemon cream on the way. A starter of chicken livers sautéed with currants, sherry and crème fraîche served with grilled chicory is a good combination of textures and flavours, and might be followed by grilled halibut layered with thin slices of potato with saffron butter vinaigrette. Finish with something like gooseberry brûlée, here served with warm custard.

ULLINGSWICK,
The Steppes Hotel

Nr Hereford HR1 3JG
Map 3: SO54
Tel: 01432 820424
Fax: 01432 820042
E-mail: bookings@ steppeshotel.fsbusiness.co.uk
Chef: Tricia Howland
Owners: Henry & Tricia Howland
Cost: Set-price D £26. H/wine £7.95
Times: D only at 7.30pm
Seats: 12. Jacket & tie preferred
Style: Country-house
Smoking: No smoking in dining room
Accommodation: 6 en suite ★ ★

Fourteenth-century dining room with inglenook fireplace, original red and black tiled floor and hefty oak beams. This is very much a hotel dining room with most emphasis being placed on a high quality, well conceived set dinner, although a *carte* option is available. A typical meal might open with watercress mousse with red pepper sauce followed by roast quail stuffed with chicken mousseline wrapped in bacon and served on a pool of blackcurrant sauce. Homemade ices may follow, or perhaps zabaglione with fresh strawberries. Cheeese enthusiasts will be well satisfied by a board including the likes of Tornegus, Llanboidy, Hereford Hop and Stinking Bishop. Tricia and Henry Howland play the hosts with enthusiasm and the overall style is formal but congenial.

Directions: Off A417 Gloucester to Leominster road

WEOBLEY, The Salutation Inn ✿✿

Market Pitch HR4 8SJ
Map 3: SO45
Tel: 01544 318443
Fax: 01544 318216
E-mail: info@salutationinn.com
Chef: Graham Leavsley
Owners: Mr C G & Mrs F T Anthony
Cost: *Alc* £26. ☺ H/wine £9.50
Times: Noon-2pm/7-9pm. Closed D Sun, all Mon, 25 Dec
Additional: Bar food; Sunday L
Seats: 38.
Style: Traditional
Smoking: No smoking in dining room
Accommodation: 4 en suite ★ ★

Combining a former Ale and Cider House and an adjoining cottage, the Salutation offers a traditional setting and friendly atmosphere in which to spend a pleasant lunchtime or evening out. The property is delightful; its timber-framed charm typifying the idyllic nature of the medieval village in which it stands. Cuisine is modern in approach but fairly traditional in content. Starters include an excellent duck terrine with duck livers wrapped in pastry and served with wholemeal toast and homemade onion marmalade. The seasonal fish of the day is always worth bearing in mind, though other options might include a rustic saddle of venison served with its own sausages and roasted shallots with a port and cranberry jus. With desserts decision making is, as ever, torturous but our inspector

The Salutation Inn

opted for apple crumble with Calvados ice cream - simple but delicious. Extensive vegetarian menu available.

Directions: Down hill into village, take 1st R, then 2nd R

HERTFORDSHIRE

HADLEY WOOD,

West Lodge Park Hotel ❀❀

It's hard to believe, when surrounded by parkland and gardens, that you are only 12 miles from the West End. The popular hotel restaurant (reservations recommended, even for residents), has a touch of the Alpine lodge about it – timbered ceilings, exposed brickwork and huge, heavily draped windows. Best dish sampled comprised translucent, perfectly-cooked diver scallops with fennel and red wine jus, an intriguing combo that worked rather well in practice. Equally well cooked was a baked fillet steak with guinea fowl and mushroom mousse in lamb crepinette. Simpler concepts include terrine of chicken and tarragon wrapped in bacon with Cumberland sauce, and grilled Dover sole with pommes Pont Neuf, plum tomato filled with pea purée and tartare cream sauce.

Directions: 1 mile S of M25 J24 on the A111; 1 mile from Cockfosters & Hadley Wood stations

Cockfosters Road EN4 0PY
Map GtL: C5
Tel: 020 8216 3900
Fax: 020 8216 3937
E-mail: beales_westlodgepark@ compuserve.com
Chef: Peter Leggat
Cost: Set-price L £23.95/D £38.25. H/wine £13.80
Times: 12.30-2pm/7.15-9.30pm
Additional: Bar food; Sunday L; Children welcome
Seats: 70. Private dining room 54; Jacket & tie preferred
Style: Country-house
Smoking: No smoking in dining room
Civil licence: 40
Accommodation: 55 en suite ★★★★

ST ALBANS, St Michael's Manor ❀

Blessed with a view of the beautiful 'secret gardens' the restaurant of this luxurious hotel lives up to its surroundings with an extensive, largely traditional menu. Try pan-fried fillet of Scotch beef followed by a speciality jam roly-poly.

Civil licence: 35
Accommodation: 23 en suite ★★★

Directions: At the Tudor Tavern in High Street turn into George Street. After Abbey & Boys' school on L, road continues into Fishpool Street. Hotel 1 mile on L

Fishpool Street AL3 4RY
Map 4: TL10
Tel: 01727 864444
E-mail: smmanor@globalnet.co.uk
Times: 12.30-2pm/7-9.30pm(10pm Sat/9pm Sun)
Additional: Bar food L; Sunday L; Children welcome
Style: Country-house
Smoking: No pipes & cigars

ST ALBANS, Sopwell House Hotel

Once owned by the Mountbatten family, Sopwell House is an extensive country-house hotel with leisure and health facilities and a conference centre. The Magnolia Conservatory Restaurant, a large, airy glass structure full of greenery, including the eponymous tree, is the hub, and despite the scale of the enterprise the kitchen delivers the goods, from steamed fillet of brill with clam chowder and saffron potatoes to chicken breast with onion tarte Tatin. That dishes are well conceived shines through starters of a roulade of duck confit and foie gras served with pickled walnuts, or chicken sausage well-balanced with sun-dried tomatoes and tarragon and a well-matched sweetcorn salsa. Fillet of beef (carved at the table) and grilled Dover sole are there for those who like their food plain, while an inspector tried roast haddock under a Welsh rarebit crust with rösti and cabbage in tomato sauce and found the fish 'cooked to perfection' and the whole dish a successful marriage of flavours. Puddings range from the fruity – pineapple upside-down cake – to the rich – chocolate and raspberry terrine with chocolate sauce – while the wine list helpfully has around a dozen bottles specially selected by the sommelier.

Cottonmill Lane Sopwell AL1 2HQ
Map 4: TL10
Tel: 01727 864477
Fax: 01727 844741
E-mail:
magnolia@sopwellhouse.co.uk
Chef: Warren Jones
Owner: Abraham Bejerano
Cost: *Alc* £35, set-price L £16/D
£24.95. ☺ H/wine £13.50
Times: 12.30-2pm/7.30-10pm. Closed
L Sat
Additional: Sunday L; Children
welcome
Seats: 110
Style: Traditional/Country-house
Smoking: No smoking in dining room;
Air conditioning
Civil licence: 150
Accommodation: 134 en suite
★ ★ ★ ★

Directions: On London Road from St Albans follow signs to Sopwell, over mini-roundabout, hotel on L

SAWBRIDGEWORTH,
Goose Fat & Garlic

Formerly operated as The Shoes this restaurant has been re-branded; it opened as Goose Fat & Garlic last January. The carpets have been replaced with polished wooden floors, the white walls have been painted in warm colours and the old wooden ceiling beams have been painted pale lime green. The style is far more informal and the menus cover a central European repertoire. The *carte* is augmented by lunchtime specials and a children's menu. The home-made bread is served with olive oil and balsamic vinegar. First courses include a house dish of rillette of goose, a pressed terrine which, in presentation and execution, was faultless. A main course of breast of chicken wrapped in parma ham and stuffed with morels, served on a bed of tagliatelle with truffle was followed by a light and tangy lemon tart with caramelised sugar on the top to give a little sweetness. The wine list is reasonably priced and covers the new and old worlds.

52 Bell Street CM21 9AN
Map 4: TL41
Tel: 01279 722554
Fax: 01279 600766
Chef: Ian Cawkwell
Owners: Lyndon Wootton,
Peter Gowan & Ian Cawkwell
Cost: *Alc* fr £21.50. ☺ H/wine
£11.95
Times: Noon-1.30pm/7-9.30pm(6.30-
10pm Fri & Sat). Closed L Sat & Mon,
all Sun, 2 wks after Xmas
Additional: Children welcome
Seats: 60
Style: Informal/Modern
Smoking: No-smoking area; Air
conditioning

Directions: From M11 J7 take A414 (Harlow); continue as road becomes A1186 (Bishop's Stortford). Sawbridgeworth is midway between Harlow and Bishop's Stortford

TRING, Pendley Manor ⚘

Originally built in 1872, this grand manor has many original features and impressive grounds. Main courses may include cannon of lamb, seared sea bass, roast butternut squash, or slow roasted belly of pork.

Cow Lane HP23 5QY
Map 4: SP91
Tel: 01442 891891
Fax: 01442 890687
E-mail: sales@pendley-manor.co.uk
Cost: Alc £28, set-price L £28/D £30. H/wine £13
Times: 12.30-2.30pm, 7-9.30pm
Additional: Bar food; Sunday L; Children welcome
Style: Country house
Smoking: No smoking in dining room
Civil Licence: 140
Accommodation: 74 en suite ★ ★ ★ ★

Directions: M25 J20. Take A41. Take Tring exit and follow signs for Berkhamsted. 1st L, R after rugby club

WARE, Marriott Hanbury Manor

No rosettes this year at this three AA Rosetted establishment – changes in the kitchen as we went to press made our current assessment invalid. Check our website (www.theaa.com/hotels) for the latest details.

Thundridge SG12 0SD
Map 5: TL31
Tel: 01920 487722
Fax: 01920 487692
Cost: Set-price L £27.50/D £35. H/wine £19.50
Times: 12.30-1.30pm(2pm Sun)/7.30-9.30pm(9pm Sun,7-10pm, Fri & Sat). Closed L Sat
Additional: Sunday L; Children 8+
Seats: 45. Private dining room 20
Smoking: No smoking in dining room; Air conditioning
Accommodation: 96 en suite ★ ★ ★ ★ ★

Directions: On A10, 12 miles N of M25 J25

WELWYN, Auberge du Lac ⚘⚘

At times the food here reaches sublime levels. On a recent visit a dessert of a perfectly light tiramisu soufflé combined with criminally good pistachio ice cream, amaretto cream and a vanilla pod was described by our inspector as 'heaven on a plate.' A first course of marinated red tuna in teriyaki and ginger vinaigrette with a crispy seaweed salad was comparable in concept and execution - Oriental influences performed with restraint and sophistication. The restaurant belongs to Brocket Hall, a charming lakeside 17th-century hunting lodge. The pace is relaxed and unhurried, the environment comfortable and calming.

Civil licence: 70

Directions: Telephone for directions

Brocket Hall AL8 7XG
Map 4: TL21
Tel: 01707 368888
Fax: 01707 368898
E-mail: auberge@brocket-hall.co.uk
Chef: Pascal Breant
Owner: Brocket Hall International
Cost: Alc £38, set-price L £25/D £38. H/wine £16
Times: Noon-2.30pm/7-10.30pm. Closed D Sun, all Mon
Additional: Sunday L; Children welcome
Seats: 70. Private dining room 16
Style: Traditional/Country-house
Smoking: No pipes & cigars; Air conditioning

KENT

ASHFORD, Eastwell Manor 🏵🏵🏵

Eastwell Park Boughton Lees
TN25 4HR
Map 5: TR04
Tel: 01233 213000
Fax: 01233 635530
E-mail: eastwell@btinternet.com
Chef: Steven Black
Owner: Mr T F Parrett
Cost: *Alc* £45, set-price L £16.50/D
£30. H/wine £15.50
Times: Noon-2.30pm/7-10pm
Additional: Bar food; Sunday L;
Children welcome
Seats: 80. Private dining room 2-120
Style: Traditional/Country-house
Smoking: No smoking in dining room
Civil licence: 200
Accommodation: 62 en suite ★★★★

Directions: M20 J9 follow A251
Faversham, hotel on L after
Kennington. From Canterbury, A28 to
Ashford L turn to Boughton Lees

Reached along a driveway through parkland, first impressions of the Jacobean-style manor are impressive: stone-mullioned leaded windows, turrets and tall chimneys. The dining room remains as grand as ever, with its dark wooden ceiling, chandeliers, open stone fireplace, big leather chairs and an abundance of silverware. Although luxuries are inevitable – seared foie gras with Sauternes syrup, caramelised orange, spinach and crispy parsnip, say, or a parcel of crab and smoked salmon with a soft-boiled quail's egg and sevruga caviar – the menus are generous in scope, from pan-fried calves' sweetbreads with champagne sauce, to fillet of beef with braised oxtail and Savoy cabbage with Madeira sauce, in between taking in seared scallops on tomato fondue with rösti and a dressing of lemongrass and tomato, or grilled Dover sole, filleted at the table. Materials are top-notch, and the kitchen knows what to do with them, turning out well-balanced dishes, as in a starter of herb-roasted quail, moist and tender, with ceps and braised lettuce in Gewürztraminer sauce, or a main course of suckling pig with apple compote, sage and onion mash and five spice sauce. Presentation is a forté, never more so than with puddings: perhaps 'delightfully smooth' chocolate mousse with a ginger and lime sorbet interlayered, mille-feuille-style, with thin wafers of chocolate. Service is professional and attentive by a predominantly French team, and France is also the focus of the long wine list.

BEARSTED,
Soufflé Restaurant 🏵🏵

31 The Green Maidstone ME14 4DN
Map 5: TQ85
Tel/Fax: 01622 737065
Chef: Nick Evenden
Owners: Nick & Karen Evenden
Cost: *Alc* £30, set-price L £13.50 &
£16.50/D (Mon-Fri) £22.50. ☺
H/wine £10.95
Times: Noon-2pm/7-9.30pm.
Closed L Sat, D Sun, all Mon
Additional: Sunday L; Children
welcome

Located in the centre of the village, the 16th-century building has a wonderful terrace and a beautiful view of Bearsted Green, and the cooking has lots to commend it. The menu takes its cue from Capital trends – a Caesar salad with prawns, Parmesan and chives pushed back the frontiers of definition with a generous amount of top-quality prawns. A main course of roast rump of lamb with sweetbreads, garlic and rosemary was more traditional in feel, with good, solid saucing that gave it real depth of flavour. Fondant potatoes made the perfect accompaniment. Dessert was strong on concept, but rather messily presented, a dish of winter fruits poached in mulled wine and served with pannacotta.

Directions: Telephone for directions

Seats: 40. Private dining room 25
Style: Classic/Chic
Smoking: No pipes & cigars

BIDDENDEN,
West House Restaurant

A labour of love for the owners and it shows in the devoted approach to preparation and uncompromising approach to service. Uncompromising in the sense that bookings are staggered as much as possible to ensure the quality of the food and service is often necessarily slow placed. But if you're going to wait for food it might as well be in a room as lovely as this one – beamed ceiling, bare floor boards and a centrepiece stove in the period inglenook. When the food arrives it fairly glows with the devotion, enthusiasm and respect for ingredients of the chef Susan Cunningham. A typical meal might include a starter of crab sausage with julienne of vegetables and a fish sauce, a main course of roast quail, barley risotto with bacon and sage and a dessert of warm chocolate mousse cake with a white chocolate sauce.

Directions: Junction of A2862 and A274. 14 miles S of Maidstone

28 High Street TN27 8AH
Map 5: TQ83
Tel/Fax: 01580 291341
E-mail:
westhouse.restaurant@virginnet.co.uk
Chef: Susan Cunningham
Owners: David & Susan Cunningham
Cost: Set-price D £27.50. ☺
H/wine £10.50
Times: D only, 7-9pm. Closed Sun-Tue, 25, 26 &31 Dec, 2 wks Jan, 1 wk Sep
Additional: Children welcome; request vegetarian dishes at time of booking
Seats: 20
Style: Traditional/Relaxed
Smoking: No pipes & cigars

CANTERBURY,
Augustine's Restaurant NEW

Delightful neighbourhood restaurant in a 17th-century building, nicely off the beaten track for tourists, with a growing local following. The focus is on a short menu and fresh ingredients.

Smoking: No-smoking area

Directions: Follow signs to St Augustines Abbey

1 & 2 Longport CT1 1PE
Map 5: TR15
Tel/Fax: 01227 453063
Cost: *Alc* £25, set-price L £8. ☺
H/wine £8.95
Times: Noon-2pm/6.30-11pm.
Closed all Mon, D Sun, Jan
Additional: Sunday L
Style: Informal/modern

CANTERBURY, Canterbury Hotel

71 New Dover Road CT1 3DZ
Map 5: TR15
Tel: 01227 450551
Fax: 01227 780145
E-mail:
canterbury.hotel@btinternet.com
Cost: *Alc* £25, set-price L £13.95/ D £16.95. ☺ H/wine £9.90
Times: Noon-2pm/7-10pm
Additional: Bar food; Children 6+
Style: classic
Smoking: No smoking in dining room
Accommodation: 23 en suite ★ ★

Directions: On A2, Dover road

Bright restaurant with a Continental feel (French staff/classic French menu), at the heart of a small Georgian-style hotel. The kitchen produces rich food, best summed up by lasagne of local lobster, and duo of duck with prunes, broccoli mousse and gratin dauphinoise.

CANTERBURY, **The Dove** ❀❀

Rustic establishment with local pub atmosphere and astonishingly good food. Owned by a disenchanted grand kitchen chef who brings his great accumulated skill to bear on local ingredients producing illustrious French and British creations in a relaxed, informal atmosphere. The menu is constantly changing with specials chalked up on the blackboard in true country pub style, but starters might include roulade of foie gras and confit duck served with a shallot and herb dressing. If the mackerel have been biting you might enjoy a whole grilled local fish flavoured with a shallot, garlic and tarragon dressing for a main course. Otherwise daube of beef braised in a provençale style may take your fancy. It is always pleasing to discover how good familiar classics can be and simple puddings such as lemon tart really benefit from the hand of an artist at this genuinely devoted and welcoming restaurant.

Plumpudding Lane ME13 9HB
Map 5: TR06
Tel: 01227 751360
Chef: Nigel Morris
Owners: Nigel & Bridget Morris
Cost: *Alc* £20-£25
Times: Noon-2pm/7-9pm. Closed D Sun, all Mon
Additional: Bar food; Sunday L; Children welcome
Seats: 20
Style: Rustic

Directions: Telephone for directions

CHATHAM,
Bridgewood Manor Hotel ❀❀

Bridgewood Manor is a modern hotel with a classic Gothic feel to its interior design. The elegant Squires Restaurant offers a good choice with a set-price menu of three courses, a seasonal *carte*, and a set gourmet menu with wines appropriate to each dish. A popular main course from the Spring Specialities *carte* was roast best end of English lamb with tarragon mousse and a thyme and capsicum sauce, while the gourmet menu offered Barbary duck leg with cherries on a bed of honeyed red cabbage. There is also a separate vegetarian repertoire, with the likes of asparagus bouchée with chive beurre blanc, and gnocchi romana scented with garden sage. Desserts are a particular strength here with options such as dark chocolate macaroon with clotted cream ice cream.

Civil licence: 150 **Accommodation:** 100 en suite ★★★★

Directions: From M2 J3 or M20 J6 follow A229 towards Chatham. At Bridgewood rdbt take 3rd exit (Walderslade). Hotel 50yds on L

Bridgewood Roundabout
Walderslade Woods ME5 9AX
Map 5: TQ76
Tel: 01634 201333
Fax: 01634 201330
E-mail: bridgewoodmanor@ marstonhotels.co.uk
Chef: Jean-Claude MacFarlane
Owner: Marston Hotels
Cost: *Alc* £30, set-price L fr £10/D fr £20. ☺ H/wine £12.25
Times: 12.30-2pm/7-10pm. Closed L Sat, 24-27 Dec (ex residents)
Additional: Bar food; Sunday L; Children welcome
Seats: 80. Private dining room 20-150
Style: Classic/Traditional
Smoking: No smoking in dining room; Air conditioning

CRANBROOK, **Kennel Holt Hotel** ❀❀

A delightful Elizabethan manor house with Edwardian additions set in five acres of gardens; and for garden

Goudhurst Road TN17 2PT
Map 5: TQ73
Tel: 01580 712032
Fax: 01580 715495
E-mail: hotel@kennelholt.demon.co.uk
Chefs: Neil Chalmers, Audrey Ratcliffe
Owners: Neil & Sally Chalmers
Cost: Set-price L £18.50/D £27.50. H/wine £12.50
Times: 12.30-3pm/ 7.30-11pm. Closed L Tue & Sat, all Sun & Mon, 2 wks Jan
Additional: Sunday L (Oct-Apr); Children 10+ at D
Seats: 25. Private dining room
Style: Country-house
Smoking: No smoking in dining room
Accommodation: 10 en suite ★★

enthusiasts Kennel Holt is only five minutes car drive away from Sissinghurst. The restaurant is decorated with a collection of Victorian tinsel prints and antique mirrors. The European menu is mainly French and might include onion soup, goats' cheese salad, and a confit of loin of pork. A surprising combination of roasted pheasant, green chilli and lime worked well, though the blanched vegetables and sweet potato crisps which accompanied it were perhaps less successful. The wine list here is the work of an enthusiast and its strength is in the clarets.

Directions: On A262 1 mile from A229 crossroads, 3 miles from Goudhurst towards Cranbrook

CRANBROOK, Soho South

23 Stone Street TN17 3HF
Map 5: TQ73
Tel: 01580 714666
Fax: 01580 715653
Chef: Nigel Tarr
Owners: Nigel & Linnea Tarr
Cost: Alc £24.50 ☺ H/wine £9.50
Times: 11am-2.30pm/6.30-9.30pm.
Closed Sun, Mon & Tue
Additional: Children 8+ at D
Seats: 30
Style: Informal/Rustic
Smoking: No pipes & cigars

Directions: In town centre, opposite Barclays Bank, 50 metres from tourist info centre & church

Clad in white painted weatherboard, the building dates to circa 1560 and was originally part of an Flemish weaving factory. The wooden tables, left bare at lunch time, are covered with white cloths in the evening, and the restaurant is decorated with bottled fruits and herbs. These are also put to good use in the menu of classic French bistro dishes, executed with care and showing an understanding of gutsy 'grandmère' flavours. Escargots Bourguignonne were served with a 'great' herby butter and good slices of baguette to soak up the melted butter. The cassoulet with chorizo was 'excellent', and the garlic sausage 'fabulous', the chorizo imported directly was equally good and the dish was served with a fine dressed herby salad. Puddings include crème brûlée, caramelised oranges and a delicious homemade meringue, chocolate sauce and quality ice cream. The staff are young and friendly, and the wine list offers interesting selections, including some English whites.

DARTFORD, Rowhill Grange NEW

Lovely restaurant, overlooking the gardens of this splendid country house hotel. A single marinated scallop made an excellent amuse bouche, and the highlight of the meal was vanilla rice pudding with a fig and red wine sauce.

Additional: Bar food; Sunday L; Children welcome
Style: Chic/country house
Smoking: No smoking in dining room; Jacket & tie preferred
Civil Licence: 120
Accommodation: 38 en suite ★★★★

Directions: M5 J3, take B2173 towards Swanley, then B258 towards Hextable. Straight on at 3 rdbts. Hotel 1.5m on L

Wilmington DA2 7QH
Map 5: TQ57
Tel: 01322 615136
Fax: 01322 615137
E-mail: admin@rowhillgrange.com
Cost: Alc £40, set-price L £19.95 & £24.95/D £29.95. H/wine £14.95
Times: Noon-2.30pm, 7-9.30pm.
Closed L Sat

DEAL, Dunkerley's Hotel ✿

19 Beach Street CT14 7AH
Map 5: TR35
Tel: 01304 375016
Fax: 01304 380187
E-mail:
dunkerleysofdeal@btinternet.com
Cost: *Alc* £25, set-price L £10. ☺
H/wine £9.50
Times: Noon-3pm/6-10pm.
Closed Mon
Additional: Bar food; Sunday L;
Children welcome
Style: Classic/Traditional
Smoking: No-smoking area; Air
conditioning
Accommodation: 16 en suite ★ ★ ★

Intimate Edwardian-style restaurant with interesting sketches of local maritime history. The hotel is almost opposite the pier, so not surprisingly the emphasis is on fresh seafood, treated with respect.

Directions: Turn off A2 onto A258 to Deal – 100yds before Deal Pier

DOVER,
Wallett's Court ✿✿

West Cliffe St Margarets-at-Cliffe
CT15 6EW
Map 5: TR34
Tel: 01304 852424
Fax: 01304 853430
E-mail: wc@wallettscourt.com
Chef: Steven Harvey
Owners: The Oakley Family
Cost: *Alc* £27.50, set-price L
£17.50/D £27.50. ☺ H/wine £14
Times: Noon-2pm/7-9pm
Additional: Sunday L; Children 8+
Seats: 60. Private dining room 40
Style: Traditional/Country-house
Smoking: No smoking in dining room
Accommodation: 16 en suite ★ ★ ★

Hotel dining room preserving many period features in keeping with the medieval barn complex in which it stands. The style is dominated by authentic country house decor such as white linen and old-fashioned silverware and benefits from the personal dedication of its family owners. The cuisine fuses traditional and modern approaches to largely British dishes utilising local and some organic produce with great aplomb. The inspector was very enthusiastic about a starter which took half a dozen rock oysters and combined them with hot chorizo pieces and a salad which was cleverly dressed using spicy drippings from the sausages. The main course was an excellent boullabaisse with excellent ingredients of crab, lobster, salmon and mussels to name only a few. Slight clumsiness in the presentation of a crème brûlée was made up for by its flavour and by an accompanying pot of rhubarb and ginger compote.

Directions: From A2 take A258 (Dover/Deal) 1st R to St Margarets, hotel on R

EDENBRIDGE, Haxted Mill & Riverside Brasserie ❀

Haxted Road TN8 6PU
Map 5: TQ44
Tel: 01732 862914
Fax: 01732 865705
E-mail: happymiller@talk21.com
Cost: *Alc* £35, set-price L £10. ☺
H/wine £10.95
Times: Noon-2pm(L Sat, May-Sep only)/6.30-10pm. Closed D Sun, all Mon, 23 Dec-6 Jan, 2 wks end Sep
Additional: Children welcome; Vegetarian dishes by request
Style: Classic/Rustic
Smoking: No smoking in dining room

Directions: Telephone for directions

Old stables have been converted to create a beamed dining room, and there's also a terrace for alfresco dining overlooking the 15th-century working watermill. The menu offers modern British dishes with some French influences.

EDENBRIDGE,
Honours Mill Restaurant ❀

Converted watermill with a rustic bar downstairs and formal restaurant upstairs. Sautéed escalope of salmon with sorrel and cream sauce might follow confit of duck with lardons, bacon and wilted spinach.

Additional: Sunday L; Children welcome; Vegetarian dishes by arrangement only **Style:** Rustic

Directions: Town centre, southern end of High Street, just N of the bridge

87 High Street TN8 5AU
Map 5: TQ44
Tel: 01732 866757
Cost: Set-price L £12.50 & £15.50/D £19.95. ☺ H/wine £10.15
Times: 12.15-2pm/7.15-9pm. Closed L Sat, D Sun, all Mon, 2 wks Xmas

FAVERSHAM, Read's Restaurant ❀❀❀

'Grub first, then ethics', according to Mr B Brecht, one of the many wits and wise men quoted on the menu, and who are we to argue with this fine philosophy? The treasury of quotations makes the *carte* even more enjoyable to contemplate, but the prospect of Whitstable oak-smoked haddock presented three different ways or fillet of Aberdeen Angus beef on a Shepherd & Neame Millennium Ale sauce with black pudding and melted onions needs no elaboration. David Pitchford cooks with all the confidence of one who has years of experience under his toque and dinners here are always of a consistently high level. Local produce is rightly celebrated – a first course of Hythe scallops served with caviar, sliced new potatoes and baby spinach was simply constructed from great ingredients. Another starter of terrine of foie gras marinated in cognac and white port with artichoke and mange tout salad and home-made toasted brioche was an equally fine feat of construction. Sufficient parsley in the mash really invigorated an excellent piece of Whitstable turbot, given a deeper note with red wine jus and topped with melted potted shrimps. Read's Chocoholics Anonymous is an extravaganza on a plate.

Mummery Court Painters Forstal ME13 0EE
Map 5: TR06
Tel: 01795 535344
Fax: 01795 591200
Chef: David Pitchford
Owners: Rona & David Pitchford
Cost: *Alc* £38.50, set-price L £18.50/D £24. ☺ H/wine £15
Times: Noon-2pm/7-9.30pm. Closed Sun & Mon
Additional: Children welcome
Seats: 40. Private dining room 20
Style: Classic/Modern
Smoking: No pipes & cigars
Civil licence: 60

Directions: M2 J6, turn L onto A2, then L into Brogdale Road, signposted Painters Forstal 1.5 miles S of Faversham

FOLKESTONE, Sandgate Hotel & Restaurant La Terrasse ❀❀❀

A mere pebble's throw away from the beach, the French-style hotel under the ownership of Zara and Samuel Gicqueau, goes from strength to strength. The tiered terrace which fronts the 19th-century building is lovely in warm weather for breakfast, teas and pre-dinner drinks. The charming yellow and blue restaurant, which features cast-iron fireplaces, is very much at the centre of operations. Silver and porcelain are French, and oil paintings of the the Loire Valley decorate the walls. The cooking is classical French cuisine with a modern interpretation. Foie gras is served three ways, including warm as an escalope on an unusual bed of 'pain d'épices' with pear and kumquat marmalade; pan-fried scallops nestle on sliced Charlotte potatoes with black truffles and their own jus. Fish predominates – fillet of sea bass was defined by wonderful freshness of flavour with truffle jus and endive, and turbot is roasted on the bone and served with girolle mushrooms, baby onions and 'Grenaille' potatoes in light poultry jus. French farmhouse cheeses are from 'Ma Normandie' in Wimereux. Desserts include hot pistachio soufflé with bitter chocolate sorbet. The wine lists features an unusually good choice of Champagne by the half-bottle.

Directions: On A259 coastal road in Sandgate, between Hythe and Folkestone

The Esplanade Sandgate CT20 3DY
Map 5: TR23
Tel: 01303 220444
Fax: 01303 220496
Chef: Samuel Gicqueau
Owners: Samuel & Zara Gicqueau
Cost: Alc £42, set-price L & D £22 (£31 weekends). H/wine £13.50
Times: 12.15-1.30pm/7.15-9.30pm. Closed D Sun, all Mon, L Tue, 4 wks Jan, 1st wk Oct
Additional: Sunday L; Children welcome; Vegetarian dishes not always available
Seats: 18-22
Style: Classic/French
Smoking: No smoking in dining room
Accommodation: 14 en suite ★★

HYTHE,
The Hythe Imperial Hotel ❀

A magnificent Victorian building with an opulent dining room which, like the hotel, is evocative of a bygone era. There is however some modern influence in the otherwise classical cuisine – a ribbon pasta Parpadelle was simple but highly effective.

Additional: Bar food L; Sunday L; Children welcome
Style: Classic/Traditional
Smoking: No smoking in dining room
Civil licence: 100
Accommodation: 100 en suite ★★★★

Directions: M20 J11/A261 to Hythe; follow signs to Folkestone, turn R into Twiss Rd opposite Bell Inn towards seafront

Princes Parade CT21 6AE
Map 5: TR13
Tel: 01303 267441
Fax: 01303 264610
E-mail: hytheimperial@marstonhotels.co.uk
Cost: Alc £37.50, set-price L £17.50/D £26. H/wine £13.50
Times: 12.30-2pm/7-9.30pm(10pm Fri & Sat). Closed L Sat

HYTHE, Stade Court ❀

Just a few steps away from the shingle strand and sparkling seas, this hotel features local seafood on its menus, with options of mixed fish terrine and whole roasted mackerel.

Additional: Bar food; Sunday L (noon-2.30pm); Children welcome
Style: Rustic/Traditional
Smoking: No smoking in dining room
Accommodation: 42 en suite ★★★

Directions: M20 J11 then A261 to Hythe

West Parade CT21 6DT
Map 5: TR13
Tel: 01303 268263
Fax: 01303 261803
E-mail: stadecourt@marstonhotels.co.uk
Cost: Alc £25, set-price L £13.95/D £20. ☺ H/wine £13
Times: D only, 7-9.30pm

LENHAM, **Chilston Park** ❀❀

Sandway ME17 2BE
Map 5: TQ85
Tel: 01622 859803
Fax: 01622 858588
Chef: Peter Malcher
Owners: Arcadian Hotels
Cost: Alc £35, set-price L £19.50/D
£29.95. H/wine £14.75
Times: Noon-2pm/7-10pm.
Closed L Sat
Additional: Bar food; Sunday L;
Children welcome
Seats: 35. Private dining rooms 2-110
Style: Traditional/Country-house
Smoking: No smoking in dining room
Civil licence: 90
Accommodation: 53 en suite ★ ★ ★ ★

An 'antique hunter's paradise' is the description given to this classically proportioned 17th-century red-brick mansion in acres of parkland. After dark, hundreds of candles are lit, giving the Marble Hall dining room, with its gilt-framed oil paintings and tapestries, a somewhat medieval feel. Menus are broadly European in scope, from ravioli of escargots with a grain mustard sauce, to rump of lamb with tapenade jus and a potato, tomato and basil galette. Prime materials are handled well, as in a truffley Mascarpone risotto with sautéed foie gras, all flavours merging well, or a 'really good dish' of whole baby lobster in a 'clever little' lobster vinaigrette, with asparagus and confit potatoes. The kitchen's on its mettle with humbler materials too, saddle of rabbit turning up with herb mousse and braised chicory, roasted skate wing with crushed potatoes and a red wine reduction, and puddings are no less impressive, from raspberry soufflé with a matching sorbet, to 'absolutely classic' densely flavoured chocolate tart with admirably thin pastry.

Directions: Telephone for directions

LENHAM, **The Lime Tree** ❀

Formal restaurant in family-run hotel, which still retains some 600-year-old features. The imaginative menu offers classic French cuisine, like wild boar steak with marinated prunes dressed with a stilton and port wine sauce.

Style: Classic/Formal
Smoking: No smoking in dining room; Jacket & tie preferred

Directions: Off A20. 8 miles from M20 J8

8-10 The Limes The Square ME17 2PL
Map 5: TQ85
Tel: 01622 859509
Fax: 01622 850096
Cost: Alc £35, set-price L £18.95/D
£23.50. ☺ H/wine £13.50
Times: Noon-2pm/6.30-9.30pm.
Closed L Mon & Sat, D Sun
Additional: Sunday L; Children
welcome

ROYAL TUNBRIDGE WELLS,
Hotel du Vin & Bistro ❀❀

Great concept, great feel, great hotel – and the food and drink is pretty good as well. All the bedrooms are sponsored by a well-known wine house, and the bistro, inevitably, is wine-themed with vinous ephemera and individual breadboards fashioned from the ends of wine crates. The kitchen sometimes goes one ingredient too far, but the cooking is generally sound. The repertoire is modern and the *carte* just large enough to make choice difficult. Fish is a strong point – we enjoyed both modish grilled squid with niçoise salad and comforting, classic

Crescent Road
TN1 2LY
Map 5: TQ53
Tel: 01892 526455
Fax: 01892 512044
E-mail:
reception@tunbridgewells.hotelduvin.
co.uk
Chef: Sam Mahoney
Owner: The Alternative Hotel
Company

Hotel du Vin & Bistro

Cost: *Alc* £25. ☺ H/wine £11.50
Times: Noon-1.30pm/7-9.30pm
Additional: Sunday L; Children welcome
Seats: 80. Private dining rooms 14-70
Style: Bistro-style/modern
Smoking: No pipes & cigars
Accommodation: 32 en suite ★★★★

Directions: Telephone for directions

smoked haddock on crushed potato with spinach, poached egg and caviar. Other dishes might include ballotine of guinea fowl and chorizo sausange, and roast duck breast with bok choy, rosti potato and wasabi jus. After dessert – hot chocolate fondant pudding or caramelised lemon tart with raspberry sorbet – repair to the Havana Room for a Cuban cigar and game of billiards.

ROYAL TUNBRIDGE WELLS,

Right on the Green ❀❀

Right on the green it is, an attractive, double-fronted building set back from the main road. The restaurant is on the ground floor, with wooden floorboards and orange-washed walls broken up by some colourful artwork and prints; upstairs, a light room with a soft blue decor is sometimes called into service but is normally used for private parties. The menus take Italy as their starting point. Risottos crop up as a starter – smoked haddock with saffron and spring onion, say – and in main courses: breast of chicken with one of leek and bacon, fillet of John Dory with another of clams and fennel. Pan-seared tuna on warm crushed potato with a poached egg makes a spot-on starter, and might be followed by sautéed rabbit with crisp pancetta, mustard sauce and braised endive, or well-timed baked red bream on cassoulet beans with marinated artichoke. Tarte Tatin is a favoured pudding: banana and peach with honey ice cream in summer, pear with cinnamon ice cream in winter. The annotated wine list makes interesting reading, and there are around a dozen in the house selection.

15 Church Road Southborough
TN4 0RX
Map 5: TQ53
Tel/Fax: 01892 513161
Chef: Steve Acton
Owner: Mr D Wright
Cost: Set-price L £12.95 & £15.95/D £27.50. ☺ H/wine £10.90
Times: Noon-2.30pm/7-9.30pm. Closed L Sat, D Sun, all Mon
Additional: Sunday L; Children welcome
Seats: 32. Private dining room 16
Style: Informal/Rustic

Directions: From A21 take A26 at South Borough turn. Restaurant 2 miles on R, next to antiques shop.

ROYAL TUNBRIDGE WELLS,

Royal Wells Inn ❀❀

The Royal Wells is a splendid white building overlooking the common, with the windows of the first-floor conservatory restaurant at the front making the most of the views. The menus wander near and far, offering starters as diverse as cannellini bean and barley soup, and a warm salad of squid and queen scallops in walnut oil, with main courses ranging from chicken Kiev with egg-fried rice to skate and mussels poached in white wine. An inspector started with oriental duck salad – 'loads of tender confit with crispy bits on a good mixed-leaf salad' – dressed with a sweetish Eastern-style sauce, and

Mount Ephraim
TN4 8BE
Map 5: TQ53
Tel: 01892 511188
Fax: 01892 511908
E-mail: info@royalwells.co.uk
Chef: Robert Sloan
Cost: *Alc* £21.25, set-price L £11.50. ☺ H/wine £9.95
Times: 12.30-2.15pm/7.30-10pm. Closed all Sun & Mon, 25 & 26 Dec, 1 Jan

Royal Wells Inn

Additional: Bar food;
Children welcome
Seats: 36. Private dining room 20-80
Style: Classic/Traditional
Civil licence: 60
Accommodation: 19 en suite ★ ★ ★

followed it, appropriately for November, with a 'great honest wintry comfort dish' of braised lamb shank with a ragout of tomatoes and flageolet beans and excellent buttery mashed potatoes. Orange fool makes a fresh and enjoyable end to a meal, with perhaps split-nationality American cheesecake with sweet-and-sour plum jam, or vanilla crème brûlée also on offer. House wines from France, Italy and Australia head up the wine list.

Directions: Situated 75 yards from the junction of A21 and A264

ROYAL TUNBRIDGE WELLS,
Signor Franco ❀

5a High Street TN1 1UL
Map 5: TQ53
Tel: 01892 549199
Fax: 01892 541378
E-mail: signor.franco@btinternet.com

The entrance to this first floor restaurant is discreetly tucked between two shops on the High Street. Start with Roman artichokes baked and dressed with olive oil and sundried tomatoes,say, followed by king prawns and scallops in white wine.

Telephone for further details

Directions: Near Tunbridge Wells railway station

ROYAL TUNBRIDGE WELLS,
The Spa Hotel ❀

Mount Ephraim TN4 8XJ
Map 5: TQ53
Tel: 01892 520331
Fax: 01892 510575
E-mail: info@spahotel.co.uk
Cost: Alc £30, set-price L £20/D £25.
☺ H/wine £11.75
Times: 12.30-2pm/7-9.30pm.
Closed L Sat
Additional: Bar food; Sunday L;
Children welcome
Style: Traditional
Smoking: No-smoking area; No pipes
& cigars; Jacket & tie preferred
Civil licence: 150
Accommodation: 71 en suite ★ ★ ★

Silver service hotel restaurant in an attractive Georgian country house. Seated under the impressive chandeliers guests can enjoy traditional cuisine along the lines of roast best end of lamb with an orange and basil sauce.

Directions: On A264 leaving
Tunbridge Wells towards East
Grinstead

ROYAL TUNBRIDGE WELLS,
The Tagore

Indian restaurant on two floors of a 17th-century listed building in the old market square. The ground floor features a fabric covered ceiling whilst the first floor includes original wooden beams. All dishes are individually cooked to order by the talented chef so a delicious if somewhat lengthy meal is assured. The menu is a veritable academic document of the eating habits of the sub-continent. It is for example nice to know that in enjoying a starter of Murg Malai Reshmi (boneless chicken fillet grilled in an earthen oven) one is keeping company with the aristocracy of Lucknow. Other starters include a lamb tikka kebab originating from the mountainous region of Kashmir. A main of Gosht Badami Pasanda was an accurately cooked lamb steak fillet in a rice sauce of saffron, yoghurt cream and almonds. All the variations of tone and flavour you would expect but executed with particular flair and precision.

4 Neville Street The Pantiles TN2 5SA
Map 5: TQ53
Tel: 01892 615100
Fax: 01892 549877
Chef: Rajendra Balmiki
Owner: Nur Monie
Cost: Alc £18. ☺ H/wine £10.95
Times: Noon-2.30pm/6-11pm. Closed 25 & 26 Dec
Additional: Children 6+
Seats: 85. Private dining room 40
Style: Minimalist/Formal
Smoking: No-smoking area; Air conditioning

Directions: Telephone for directions

ROYAL TUNBRIDGE WELLS, Thackeray's
House Restaurant

A generally conservative establishment in the lovely 17th-century house of the eponymous author. The decor strikes the right balance between classical and modern and much the same is true of the food. Typical dishes include a starter of basil risotto, a main course of marinated lamb rump with roast shallots and crushed chive potatoes. Both were enjoyed on a recent visit and demonstrated a very high quality of ingredients and a simple but effective approach to preparation. A rich chocolate, espresso and griottine cherry block with a well made if rather superfluous coffee sauce confirmed our inspector's high opinion of this place.

85 London Road TN1 1EA
Map 5: TQ53
Tel/Fax: 01892 511921

Telephone for further details.

Directions: At corner of London Road/Mount Ephraim Road overlooking Common, two minutes from Hospital

SEVENOAKS, Royal Oak Hotel ✿

Contemporary restaurant in a 17th-century coaching inn, with beech floors and Lloyd Loom furniture. The brasserie-style menu offers vegetable risotto, salmon fishcakes, and breast of pheasant with chestnut stuffing.

Style: Modern
Accommodation: 37 en suite ★ ★ ★

Directions: M25 J5; at far end of High Street, opposite Sevenoaks school, walking distance from the town centre

Upper High Street TN13 1HY
Map 5: TQ55
Tel: 01732 451109
Fax: 01732 740187
E-mail: info@brook-hotels.demon.co.uk
Cost: Alc £25, set-price L £12.95/D £19.95. ☺ H/wine £10.95
Times: Noon-3pm/6-10pm
Additional: Bar food; Sunday L; Children welcome; Vegetarian dishes not always available

SISSINGHURST, Rankins ✿✿

A timber-framed, weatherboarded building on the main road through Sissinghurst is the setting for the Rankins' rustic, cosy and warm restaurant, not dissimilar to a French bistro: simply decorated, with watercolours and prints on the walls, and, for such a small place, relatively well-spaced tables. Sunday lunch might see something like roast leg of English lamb with onion gravy and damson jelly among main courses, but otherwise the menus are an eclectic mix, taking in shallow-fried bites of

The Street
TN17 2JH
Map 5: TQ73
Tel: 01580 713964
Chef: Hugh Rankin
Owners: Hugh & Leonora Rankin
Cost: Set-price L £22/D £27. ☺ H/wine £9
Times: D only, 7.30-9pm.
Closed D Sun, all Mon & Tue, Bhs

halibut and cod with Thai spices and a tomato mayonnaise dip, curry-spiced leek, potato and apple soup, and pan-fried ribeye steak with creamy grain mustard sauce. Materials are well-sourced – salmon from Loch Fyne, for instance, is sliced, griddled and accompanied by caper butter – and proper puff pastry is used in a vegetarian main course for a basket of roast aubergines and mixed peppers, with apricots and mint, in a rich tomato sauce. Chocolate nemesis is a popular pudding, and there may also be vanilla and apricot ice creams, while the short, mainly French wine list manages to pack in quite a few styles.

Additional: Sunday L (12.30-2pm); Children welcome
Seats: 25
Style: Bistro-style/Rustic
Smoking: No smoking before 10pm

Directions: Village centre, on A262 (Ashford)

SITTINGBOURNE, Hempstead House Country Hotel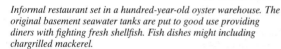

London Road Bapchild ME9 9PP
Map 5: TQ96
Tel: 01795 428020
Fax: 01795 436362
E-mail: info@hempsteadhouse.co.uk
Cost: Alc £25, set-price L £10 & £12.50. ☺ H/wine £10.95
Times: Noon-2pm/7-10pm. Closed Sun
Additional: Children welcome
Style: Traditional/Country-house

Classical furnishings enhance and blend with the more modern architecture producing an elegant and airy hotel dining room. Ambitious and sophisticated cuisine such as timbale of duck confit and foie gras served with toasted brioche.

Smoking: No smoking in dining room
Civil licence: 70
Accommodation: 14 en suite

Directions: On A2, 1.5 miles east of Sittingbourne

WHITSTABLE,
Whitstable Oyster Fisher Co

Horsebridge Beach CT5 1BU
Map 5: TR16
Tel: 01227 276856
Fax: 01227 770666
Cost: Alc £30-£60
Times: Noon-2pm/7-9pm. Closed D Sun, all Mon

Informal restaurant set in a hundred-year-old oyster warehouse. The original basement seawater tanks are put to good use providing diners with fighting fresh shellfish. Fish dishes might including chargrilled mackerel.

Additional: Children welcome
Style: Informal

Directions: On High Street, follow one-way then 1st L

WYE, Wife of Bath Restaurant

4 Upper Bridge Street TN25 5AW
Map 5: TR04
Tel: 01233 812540
Fax: 01233 813630
E-mail: john@w-o-b.demon.co.uk
Cost: Alc £20, set-price L £10/D £23.95. ☺ H/wine £12.75
Times: Noon-1.45pm/7-9.45pm. Closed Sun, Mon, 1 wk after Xmas, 1st wk Sep
Additional: Children welcome
Style: Traditional/Country-house
Smoking: No-smoking area; No pipes

Directions: Just off A28 Ashford to Canterbury Road

Lovely house in a village setting, serving an interesting menu featuring local produce. There's a daily fish option, Kent duckling with roast pear, and a house speciality – brown bread ice cream.

LANCASHIRE

ACCRINGTON, Dunkenhalgh Hotel ❀

Seven hundred-year-old manor house with period decor; an interesting menu takes in pan-fried supreme of Goosenagh chicken, and roasted saddle of Cornish monkfish.

Style: Traditional
Smoking: No smoking in dining room; Air conditioning; Jacket & tie preferred
Civil licence: 300
Accommodation: 121 en suite ★★★★

Directions: Adjacent to M65 J7

Blackburn Road Clayton-le-Moors BB5 5JP
Map 7: SD72
Tel: 01254 398021
Fax: 01254 872230
E-mail: info@dunkenhalgh.macdonald-hotels.co.uk
Cost: Set-price L £23.50, set-price L £14.95/D £23.50. ☺ H/wine £14.75
Times: Noon-2pm/7-9.45pm
Additional: Bar food; Sunday L; Children welcome

BLACKBURN, Clarion Hotel & Suites Foxfields ❀

Modern hotel in a rural location offering main courses of coriander crusted salmon with soy and ginger dressing, and rack of local lamb with a Dijon mustard and honey glaze.

Whalley Road Billington Clitheroe BB7 9HY
Map 7: SD62
Tel: 01254 822556
Fax: 01254 824613
Cost: Alc £21, set-price L £11.25/D £19.50. ☺ H/wine £11.80
Times: 12.30-2pm/7-9.45pm. Closed L Sat
Additional: Bar food; Sunday L; Children welcome
Style: Traditional/Formal
Smoking: No smoking in dining room; Air conditioning
Civil licence: 200
Accommodation: 44 en suite ★★★★

Directions: From A59 follow sign for Whalley, hotel is 0.5 mile on R

BLACKBURN, Millstone Hotel ❀

Stone-built coaching inn with a brasserie-style menu in the bars and an oak-panelled restaurant serving the likes of seared fillet of salmon, and roast breast of Oakamoor pheasant.

Church Lane Mellor BB2 7JR
Map 7: SD62
Tel: 01254 813333
Fax: 01254 812628
E-mail: millstone@shireinns.co.uk
Cost: Alc £22.65. ☺ H/wine £12.45
Times: Noon-2pm/6.30-9.45pm
Additional: Bar food; Sunday L; Children welcome
Style: Rustic/Traditional
Smoking: No smoking in dining room
Accommodation: 24 en suite ★★

Directions: M6 J31, follow A677 (Blackburn) for 2 miles. Turn L (Mellor), follow road to top of hill, hotel is on R

BLACKPOOL,

Kwizeen

47-49 Kings Street FY1 3EJ
Map 7: SD33
Tel: 01253 290045
Cost: *Alc* £19.25, set-price L £5.50/D
£10.50. ☺ H/wine £9.50
Times: Noon-2pm/6-10.30pm.
Closed Sun
Additional: Children welcome
Style: Bistro-style/Minimalist

*Honesty and passion permeate the whole atmosphere of this bright
modern restaurant. A relaxed, friendly approach to service
complements dishes such as salmon with a vanilla and lime sauce.*

Directions: Telephone for directions

CHIPPING,

Gibbon Bridge Hotel

*Attractive beamed restaurant with an adjoining conservatory
affording views of Longridge Fells; the hotel's award-winning
gardens keep the kitchen supplied with fresh vegetables, fruit and
herbs.*

Additional: Sunday L; Children welcome lunch only
Style: Traditional/Country-house
Smoking: No smoking in dining room
Civil licence: 150
Accommodation: 29 en suite ★★★★

Forest of Bowland Preston PR3 2TQ
Map 7: SD64
Tel: 01995 61456
Fax: 01995 61277
E-mail: reception@gibbon-
bridge.co.uk
Cost: *Alc* £30, set-price L £10/D
£23.50. ☺ H/wine £13.50
Times: Noon-1.30pm/7-9pm

Directions: In village turn R at T-junction for Clitheroe, hotel at
0.75 mile

CHORLEY,

Shaw Hill Hotel

*Country house-style restaurant; robust dishes include fillet of beef
with savoury Lancashire cake, mushrooms and caramelised endives,
and Goosnargh duck with apple and thyme compote.*

Additional: Bar food; Sunday L; Children welcome; Jacket & tie
preferred
Style: Traditional/Country-house
Civil licence: 200
Accommodation: 30 en suite ★★★

Preston Road Whittle-le-Woods
PR6 7PP
Map 7: SD51
Tel: 01257 269221
Fax: 01257 261223
Cost: *Alc* £27.95, set-price L £9.95/
D £19.95. ☺ H/wine £10.50
Times: Noon-1.45pm/7-9.45pm.
Closed L Sat, 26-31 Dec

Directions: From Chorley on A6, then A49. At lights turn L
past golf course, L to Dawson Lane. R at T-junct. Hotel 50yds
on R

LANGHO,

Northcote Manor ❀❀❀

Northcote Road
BB6 8BE
Map 7: SD73
Tel: 01254 240555
Fax: 01254 246568
E-mail:
admin@ncotemanor.demon.co.uk
Chef: Nigel Haworth
Owners: Nigel Haworth,
Craig Bancroft
Cost: *Alc* £42, set-price L £16/D £25
& £40. H/wine £14.50
Times: Noon-1.30pm/7-9.30pm .
Closed L Sat, 25 Dec
Additional: Bar food D; Sunday L;
Children welcome
Seats: 80. Private dining room 35;
Jacket & tie preferred
Style: Modern/Country-house
Smoking: No smoking in dining room

The vibrantly re-styled restaurant has given new edge to Nigel
Haworth's already exciting cooking at this delightful award-
winning country-house hotel set on the edge of the Ribble
Valley. The food is modern Lancastrian on a classic base.
Signature dishes remain his black pudding with pink trout and
corn-fed Goosnargh duckling, but newer additions to the
repertoire include soup of brown Flookborough shrimps, garlic
crisps, Parmesan rouille, as well as apple crumble soufflé,
Lancashire cheese ice cream and apple compote. The food,
however, is anything but parochial – there are few more stylish
or exquisitely presented combinations than braised fillet of
brill, scalded Orkney scallops on Jerusalem artichoke purée
and truffles, juices of wild garlic and celery, or roast breast of
woodpigeon on black pea purée, pan-roasted foie gras, bacon
cabbage, sherry vinegar jus. Most of the salad leaves, herbs and
vegetables are organically sourced or grown in the Northcote
gardens. For once the PR blurb is right, this really is 'the best
kept secret in the Ribble Valley.'

Civil licence: 40
Accommodation: 14 en suite ★ ★ ★

Directions: From M6 J31 take A59, follow signs for Clitheroe. At
first traffic lights L onto Skipton/Clitheroe Rd for 9 miles. L into
Northcote Rd. Hotel on R

LONGRIDGE, **Paul Heathcote's**

Restaurant ❀❀❀

104-106 Higher Road
PR3 3SY
Map 7: SD63
Tel: 01772 784969
Fax: 01772 785713
E-mail: longridge@heathcotes.co.uk
Chefs: Paul Heathcote,
Brendan Fyldes
Owner: Paul Heathcote
Cost: *Alc* £45, set-price L £16.50/D
£38. H/wine £13.50
Times: Noon-2pm/7-9.30pm.
Closed L Sat, all Mon & Tue,
1 Jan

Three menus are offered at Lancashire's most famous
restaurant: *carte*, gourmet five-course menu and a ten-course
dégustation menu. This is the essence of Modern British
cooking – regional ingredients and traditions combined with
classic French techniques. Terrine of veal tongue, sweetbreads
and braised cheek is served with gribiche dressing and ceps oil;
Lancashire cheese, saffron and white truffle flavour beignets to
enliven a velouté of Jerusalem artichokes. The cooking goes in
for big and bold flavours – grilled fillet of sea bass comes with
seared scallops, potato fondant, red wine and liquorice jus;
roasted squab pigeon with Puy lentils, foie gras and sweet
thyme sauce. Signature dishes include cinnamon scented

Paul Heathcote's Restaurant

Additional: Sunday L; Children welcome
Seats: 60. Private dining room 18

scallops, black pudding and bread-and-butter pudding. Service is very polished, but overall the cooking perhaps lacks the excitement once associated with the Heathcote name.

Style: Informal/Traditional
Smoking: No-smoking area

Directions: Follow signs for Golf Club & Jeffrey Hill. Higher Road is beside White Bull Pub in Longridge

LYTHAM ST ANNES,
Qbrasserie

A blend of stylish modern interior with an original Victorian building. Typical menu includes Lancashire sausage, corn-fed chicken with smoked Mozzarella, pan roasted haddock, and loin of pork on Bury black pudding.

Additional: Sunday L (in Spring); Children welcome
Style: Informal/Modern
Smoking: Air conditioning

Directions: Town Centre

5 Henry Street FY8 5LE
Map 7: SD32
Tel: 01253 733124
Fax: 01253 733326
E-mail: info@qbrasserie.co.uk
Cost: Alc £20.20, set-price L £6 & £8/D £6 & £8(6-7pm). ☺ H/wine £8.95
Times: Noon-2.30pm/6-11pm. Closed Sun (ex in Spring), 25 & 26 Dec, 1 Jan

PRESTON,
Simply Heathcotes ❀❀

A colourful mural breaks up the otherwise impeccably white decor. Minimalist modernity is the theme and an upcoming refurbishment promises to enhance this. The restaurant is split level with an informal bistro style area below and a more formal dining room upstairs. In a recent visit a starter of red pepper terrine was of a fresh sweet flavour and an excellently executed risotto of spiced chicken livers was a worthy alternative. Main courses sampled included a fillet of cod with mussel and caper butter employing fish of beautiful quality and a risotto of asparagus that made good use of lemon zest to lighten the richness of the Mascarpone. Desserts might include iced coffee and banana parfait with a mocha sauce, bread-and-butter pudding or lime crème brûlée.

Directions: Town centre

23 Winckley Square PR1 3JJ
Map 7: SD52
Tel: 01772 252732
Fax: 01772 203433
E-mail: brasserie@heathcotes.co.uk
Chef: Matt Nugent
Owner: Paul Heathcote
Cost: Alc £20-£23, set-price L/D £10.50 & £12.50. ☺ H/wine £11.50
Times: Noon-2.30pm/7-10pm (10.30pm wknds). Closed Bhs
Additional: Bar food L (D Thu-Sat); Sunday L; Children welcome
Seats: 70 & 50
Style: Informal/Modern
Smoking: No pipes & cigars; Air conditioning

SAWLEY,
Spread Eagle Inn ❀❀

Charting its history back to a mention in records of the 16th century, the Spread Eagle has a long and proud history of high quality. Hospitable service is now maintained by the dedicated owners Steven and Marjorie Doherty. Large picture windows facilitate sweeping views over the River Ribble and the Ribble Valley and the decor of the comfortable dining area is light and modern. The cuisine is best described as 'rich modern' although many of the combinations are traditional at core and an unashamed abundance of cream is just the thing to combat the brisk Lancashire climate. Pleasing starters such as carrot and coriander soup or smooth duck liver parfait infused with thyme might lead into a main of slices of baked ham with a creamy mushroom and white wine sauce or braised rolled shoulder of lamb with a split pea purée and a barley spiked sauce.

BB7 4NH
Map 7: SD74
Tel: 01200 441202
Fax: 01200 441973
Chef: Greig Barnes
Owners: Steven & Marjorie Doherty, Lionel Yates, Alan Bell
Cost: *Alc* £18, set-price L £8. ☺
H/wine £10.25
Times: Noon-2pm/6-9pm. Closed D Sun, all Mon, 25 Dec, 3 wks Nov
Additional: Bar food L; Sunday L; Children welcome
Seats: 60. Private dining room 30-80
Style: Rustic/Country pub
Smoking: No smoking in dining room

Directions: Telephone for details

WRIGHTINGTON,
High Moor Inn ❀

High Moor Lane WN6 9QA
Map 7: SD51
Tel: 01257 252364
Fax: 01257 255120
Cost: Set-price L & D £11 & £13. ☺
Times: Noon-2pm/5.30-10pm(set D 5.30-7pm, 8.30pm Sun).
Closed 26 Dec, 1 Jan
Additional: Bar Food L; Children welcome
Style: Rustic/Traditional

A 17th-century inn with masses of oak beams and a cosy atmosphere. Plenty of choice in the restaurant, including pot-roasted gammon with pease pudding and grain mustard sauce, and marinated salmon with spiced couscous and sour cream.

Directions: M6 J27, follow sign to Parbold, after hospital turn R into Robin Hood Lane, 1st L into High Moor Lane

WRIGHTINGTON,
Wrightington Hotel ❀

Moss Lane Standish WN6 9PB
Map 7: SD51
Tel: 01257 425803
Fax: 01257 425830

Telephone for further details

A modern hotel set in open countryside. From the June menu, roast rump of English lamb was carved onto Irish champ and served with a tartlet of baby vegetables and Madeira jus, while the market selection included Aberdeen Angus fillet steak.

Directions: From M6 J27, 0.25 mile towards Parbold. 200yds past church, fork R. Hotel is 100yds on R

LEICESTERSHIRE

CASTLE DONINGTON,

The Priest House on the River ❀

A historic hotel, now mostly contemporary in style, in a riverside setting. The kitchen follows the modern theme with a short carte that takes in wild pheasant galantine, slow braised shank of lamb with winter vegetables, and warm banana and toffee crumble.

Kings Mills DE74 2RR
Map 8: SK42
Tel: 01332 810649
Fax: 01332 811141
Cost: Alc £28.75, set-price L £13.50/D £24.50. ☺ H/wine £12.95
Times: Noon-2pm/7-9.30pm.
Closed L Sat
Additional: Bar food; Sunday L; Children welcome
Style: Classic/Country-house
Smoking: No smoking in dining room
Civil licence: 100
Accommodation: 45 en suite ★ ★ ★

Directions: In Castle Donington turn L at 1st traffic lights and follow to river.

HINKLEY,

Sketchley Grange Hotel ❀❀

Set among its own landscaped gardens on the edge of town, Sketchley Grange has been sympathetically extended from the original country house. Meals may be taken in Willows Restaurant or the more informal Terrace Bistro Bar. The highlight of a recent inspection was a dish of breast and confit leg of duck which combined tender flesh and crispy skin with a well chosen accompaniment of rösti, sweet and sour red cabbage and baby turnips. Other options might include fillet of beef on a ragout of cèps, baby turnips and roasted shallots, or Guinea fowl with Puy lentils and savoy cabbage. A substantial vegetarian menu offers such delights as duo of pancakes filled with stir-fry vegetables and sweet and sour sauce. A chocolate and praline tart with nice crisp pastry, solid ganache filling and a crunchy praline surface concluded the meal admirably.

Sketchley Lane Burbage LE10 3HU
Map 4: SP49
Tel: 01455 251133
Fax: 01455 631384
E-mail: sketchleygrange@btinternet.com
Chef: John Bacon
Cost: Alc £30, set-price L £13.95/D £21.95. ☺ H/wine £9.50
Times: Noon-2pm/7-10pm.
Closed D Sun
Additional: Sunday L; Children welcome
Seats: 80. Private dining room 40
Style: Traditional/Country-house
Smoking: No smoking in dining room; Air conditioning
Civil licence: 200
Accommodation: 55 en suite ★ ★ ★

Directions: From M69 J1 take B4109, at mini roundabout turn L, then 1st R

KEGWORTH, **Yew Lodge Hotel**

A fresh and informal hotel restaurant where contemporary French/British cooking prevails. Ballantine of chicken and prawn with lemon grass sauce might share the fixed price menu with parmesan, puy lentil and Mediterranean vegetables mille feuille.

Additional: bar food; Sunday L; Children welcome
Style: Informal/country house
Smoking: No smoking in dining room; Air conditionaing
Civil licence: 130
Accommodation: 63 rooms ★ ★ ★

Directions: Exit M1 J24, follow signs Loughborough & Kegworth on A6. At bottom of hill take 1st R into Packington Hill, Hotel 400yds on R

Packington Hill DE74 2DF
Map :
Tel: 01509 672518
Fax: 01509 674730
E-mail:
enquiries@yewlodgehotel.co.uk
Cost: *Alc* fr £20, set-price L £9.95/D £18.95. ☺ H/wine £10
Times: Noon-2.30pm/6.30-9.30pm

LEICESTER, **Belmont Hotel**

Elegant hotel restaurant with committed staff. Start with seared scallops and black pudding or ham hock terrine, followed perhaps by lambs' liver Lyonnaise, or pavé of beef.

Directions: From railway station, first R off A6 southbound

De Montfort Street LE1 7GR
Map 4: SK50
Tel: 0116 2544773
Fax: 0116 2470804
E-mail: info@belmonthotel.co.uk
Cost: Set-price L £12.95/D £19. ☺ H/wine £10
Times: 12.30-2pm/7-10pm. Closed L Sat, D Sun, Bh Mon
Additional: Sunday L; Children welcome
Style: Classic/Town House
Smoking: No-smoking area; No pipes & cigars
Civil licence: 60
Accommodation: 78 en suite ★ ★ ★

LEICESTER, **The Tiffin**

Impressive, up-market tandoori with a smartly-decorated conservatory, matched by similarly smart and professional staff. The menu offers a vast selection of north Indian dishes like chicken korma, delicious with pilau rice and naan bread.

1 De Montfort Street
LE1 7GE
Map 4: SK50
Tel: 0116 2470420
Fax: 0116 2625125
Cost: *Alc* £18, set-price D £18. ☺ H/wine £10.95
Times: Noon-2pm/6-11pm. Closed L Sat, all Sun, Xmas & New Year, L Bhs
Additional: Children welcome
Style: Informal/Modern
Smoking: No smoking in dining room; Air conditioning

Directions: Near railway station on the corner of De Montfort Street and London Road (A6)

MARKET HARBOROUGH,
Three Swans Hotel ❀

Formal hotel restaurant in this former coaching inn in the centre of town. The carte *is strong on classical dishes, while the fixed-price menu offers a more experimental approach. Ballotine of chicken and bacon was particularly enjoyed.*

Smoking: No-smoking area; No pipes & cigars; Air conditioning; Jacket & tie preferred
Civil licence: 150
Accommodation: 49 en suite ★ ★ ★

Directions: Follow High Street S through town centre; hotel is on R at traffic lights

21 High Street LE16 7NJ
Map 4: SP78
Tel: 01858 466644
Fax: 01858 434633
E-mail: sales@threeswans.co.uk
Cost: *Alc* £28, set-price L £13.95/D £21.95. ☺ H/wine £10.95
Times: Noon-2.15pm/7-10pm. Closed D Sun
Additional: Bar food; Sunday L; Children 2+
Style: Classic/formal

MELTON MOWBRAY,
Stapleford Park ❀❀

A landscape of woods and parkland, lake and gardens courtesy of Capability Brown awaits you. On a hazy summer afternoon you would be forgiven for thinking yourself an extra in a decadent period drama. It is somewhat surprising therefore to discover the fresh, vibrant statements of modern British cuisine with an unaffected, relaxed service style to boot in the opulence of the hotel dining room. The set-price menu changes daily offering starters along the lines of warm mussel and leek tart with a poached egg and saffron butter, or Guinea fowl and foie gras ballotine with lentil and truffle oil dressing and fig chutney. Main dishes might include caramelised loin of lamb or roast sea bass but the inclusion of an 'adult nursery dish' such as cottage pie or boiled beef and carrots with butter dumplings may prove a strong temptation to the more traditionally minded.

Directions: Follow Melton ring road A607 (Grantham) onto B676, 4 miles turn R signed Stapleford

Stapleford LE14 2EF
Map 8: SK71
Tel: 01572 787522
Fax: 01572 787651
Chef: Geoff Balharrie
Cost: *Alc* fr £25, set-price D £42. ☺ H/wine £18
Times: 11.30-2.30pm/7.30-9.30pm
Additional: Bar food L; Sunday L; Children 7+
Seats: 45. Private dining rooms 26; Jacket & tie preferred
Style: Country-house
Smoking: No smoking in dining room
Civil licence: 150
Accommodation: 51 en suite ★ ★ ★ ★

QUORN, Quorn Country Hotel ❀❀

Attractive hotel set in four acres of grounds leading down to the River Soar. There are two restaurants to choose from, the intimate Shires Restaurant, beamed and candlelit at dinner, or

Charnwood House
66 Leicester Road LE12 8BB
Map 8: SK51
Tel: 01509 415050
Fax: 01509 415557
E-mail: quorncountryhotel@fsnet.co.uk
Chef: David Wilkinson
Owner: Prima Hotels Ltd
Cost: *Alc* £29, set-price L £ 19/D £24. ☺ H/wine £12.95
Times: Noon-2.30pm/6.30-9.30pm
Additional: Bar food; Sunday L; Children welcome
Seats: 44 & 68. Private dining room 10-100
Style: Classic/Country-house
Smoking: Air conditioning (Orangery only)
Civil licence: 120
Accommodation: 23 en suite ★ ★ ★ ★

the conservatory-style Orangery. The choice of menus includes a weekly changing set-price luncheon and dinner menu, a vegetarian selection and an interesting *carte*. Fish dishes on the *carte* range from grilled Dover sole with lemon and herb butter to monkfish tail stuffed with sun-dried tomatoes, roast peppers and basil, wrapped in ham, garnished with stuffed red pepper and goats' cheese crumble and finished with a fresh herb and lemon jus. Main course options encompass medallions of ostrich, escalope of veal, steak tournedos and, a particular favourite with customers, roast Gressingham duck. Removing the bone before roasting ensures a crisp, tender, low fat duck (definitely not pink), served with plum and orange compote and finished with Grand Marnier sauce.

Directions: Off A6 in village centre

LINCOLNSHIRE

BELTON, Belton Woods Hotel

The Manor Restaurant offers a good choice of dishes with starters of mussels garnished with baby leeks and caviar, main courses of medallions of beef fillet or pan-fried monkfish and desserts including brioche bread-and-butter pudding.

Directions: 2 miles on A1 to Grantham, then A607 to Belton

Grantham NG32 2LN
Map 8: SK93
Tel: 01476 593200
Fax: 01476 574547
E-mail: devere.belton@airtime.co.uk

Telephone for further details

BOURNE, Black Horse Inn

Grimsthorpe
PE10 0LY
Map 8: TF02
Tel: 01778 591247
Fax: 01778 591373
E-mail: dine@blackhorseinn.co.uk
Chef: Brian Rey
Owners: Brian & Elaine Rey
Cost: *Alc* £19, set-price L £13.95. ☺
H/wine £10.95
Times: Noon-2pm/7-9.30pm
Additional: Bar food; Sunday L; Children welcome
Seats: 36. Private dining room 12
Style: Rustic/Traditional

The Black Horse Inn is in a small village almost on the doorstep of Grimsthorpe castle. It's an attractive place with a 'cosy feeling', a locals' bar, log fires and booths. Restaurant diners are ushered down a narrow corridor into a tiny lounge, with cottagey sofas and decor. The restaurant itself has wooden beams and original posts. *Amuse bouches* are served together with, in the case of the inspector's last visit, a consommé. The *carte* is supplemented by a number of reasonably priced daily specials. The smoked haddock with white truffle oil had good flavour and texture, a roast quail, wrapped in local ham, was nicely cooked, tender and served with a parsnip purée. Chocolate fondant to finish was richly flavoured. The wine list is well annotated and includes several wines by the glass, halves and some interesting pudding wines and port.

Smoking: No smoking in dining room
Accommodation: 6 en suite ★ ★

Directions: Follow A151 for 4 miles, west towards Grantham

CLEETHORPES, Kingsway Hotel

Gaze out over the Humber from your window seat in this traditionally-styled restaurant that serves good food like haddock risotto and roast best ends of lamb with mint sauce. The service is friendly and professional.

Additional: Bar food L; Sunday L; Children 5+
Style: Traditional/Formal
Accommodation: 50 en suite ★ ★ ★

Directions: At junction of A1098 and sea front

Kingsway DN35 0AE
Map 8: TA30
Tel: 01472 601122
Fax: 01472 601381
Cost: Alc £26, set-price L £12.75 & £14.75/D £18.75. ☺ H/wine £10.75
Times: 12.30-1.45pm/7-9pm. Closed 25 & 26 Dec

GRANTHAM, Harry's Place 🏵🏵🏵

Harry and Caroline Hallam's place is a Georgian house with a small and intimate ten-seater restaurant with deep rose-pink walls and antique furniture and china. The scale, plus a menu that involves only two choices per course, and a selection of cheeses, means, of course, that Harry is in total control: as an inspector noted when ordering a Bramley apple and Calvados soufflé it was 'literally cooked to order; I heard him whisking the egg whites'. The same soufflé, spot on, light and delicate with a rich apple flavour, was described as 'no frills or fancies', a phrase that could equally be applied to Harry Hallam's philosophy. Taking only top-notch ingredients, organic whenever possible, vegetables included, he unites them with a true understanding of the balance of flavours and textures, with the use of herbs a characteristic. Rouille of anchovies and saffron accompanies fish soup, a relish of mango, lime, ginger and basil comes with a salad of mussels, lobster and avocado, while a main course of fillet of turbot, lightly sautéed, is served with lentils and a sauce of red wine, coriander and basil. That saucing is a strong point is an understatement: a surprisingly 'subtle depth of flavour' in one of red wine, shallots, Madeira, tarragon, rosemary and thyme earned the accolade 'superb', while the fillet of Devon lamb it enhanced was 'cooked to perfection' to make it 'almost melt in the mouth'. Breads are freshly baked, puff pastry canapés are straight out of the oven, vegetables are said to be 'every mouthful a treat', and the wine list is restricted to around a dozen bottles, with just two, plus champagne and a dessert wine, sold by the glass.

17 High Street
Great Gonerby NG31 8JS
Map 8: SK93
Tel: 01476 561780
Chef: Harry Hallam
Owners: Harry & Caroline Hallam
Cost: Alc £41-£51.50. H/wine £20
Times: 12.30-2pm/7-9.30pm. Closed Sun & Mon, 25-26 Dec, Bhs
Additional: Children 5+; Vegetarian dishes on request at time of booking
Seats: 10
Style: Country-house/intimate
Smoking: No smoking in dining room

Directions: On the B1174 2 miles NW of Grantham

HORNCASTLE,
Magpies Restaurant 🏵🏵

'The warmth of welcome and unhurried, attentive service made me feel quite special' wrote an inspector, who was equally impressed by the cooking at this cottage-style restaurant. Good sourcing results in dishes full of natural flavour. Breast of Gressingham duck is roasted pink and

71-75 East Street LN9 6AA
Map 8: TF26
Tel: 01507 527004
Fax: 01507 524064
E-mail: magpies@fsbdial.co.uk
Chefs: Matthew Lee, Simon Lee
Owners: The Lee Family

accompanied by a well-matched sauce of honey and five spice, Lincoln Red fillet of beef comes in a red wine sauce with mushrooms and shallots, and roast loin of Gloucester Old Spot with apple sauce may turn up at Sunday lunch. Seafood is a strong point among starters, from smoked haddock risotto with Parmesan, or fish soup with saffron, to perfectly seared scallops hinting of garlic on a bed of finely sliced creamy leeks balanced with chive velouté. Vegetables are well-reported, and puddings, said to be 'very enjoyable', might run to chocolate marquise with creamy vanilla ice cream, pear and apple crumble, or crème brûlée.

Directions: 0.5 mile from Horncastle on A158 towards Skegness

Cost: Set-price L £10/D £20. ☺ H/wine £10
Times: D only, 7.15-9.45pm. Closed D Sun, Mon & Tue, 3 wks Aug
Additional: Sunday L (12.30-1.45pm); Children welcome
Seats: 40. Private dining room 8
Style: Informal/Traditional
Smoking: No smoking in dining room

LINCOLN, Castle Hotel ❀

Family-run hotel situated close to the city centre, castle and cathedral. A wide selection of interesting dishes is offered in the attractive open-plan restaurant, featuring quality seafood and local game.

Directions: Follow signs for 'Historic Lincoln' Hotel is at NE corner of castle

Westgate LN1 3AS
Map 8: SK97
Tel: 01522 538801
Fax: 01522 575457
E-mail: castlehotel@ukcomplete.co.uk

Telephone for further details

LINCOLN, Jew's House ❀

Unique stone building dating back to the 12th century. The set-up is somewhat formal but the service is friendly and attentive and the atmosphere intimate. Beef casserole proved to be a robust and earthy dish.

Style: Rustic/Intimate
Smoking: No smoking in dining room

Directions: Town centre. At the bottom of steep hill from the Cathedral

15 The Strait LN2 1JD
Map 8: SK97
Tel: 01522 524851
Fax: 01522 520084
Cost: Alc £29, set-price L £10/D £27.50. H/wine £10.50
Times: Noon-2pm/7-9pm. Closed Sun, Bhs
Additional: Children 5+

LINCOLN,
Washingborough Hall Hotel ❀❀

Church Hill Washingborough LN4 1BE
Map 8: SK97
Tel: 01522 790340
Fax: 01522 792936
E-mail: washingborough.hall@btinternet.com

A listed Georgian manor with a Victorian-style restaurant, complete with heavily embossed paper and grandfather clock in the corner. Tables are large and well-spaced, with white

linen cloths and lantern candles. House speciality is warm duck breast topped with slivers of foie gras on a bed of mixed leaves with warm morel mushrooms finished with a dressing of truffle oil and balsamic vinegar. Less de-luxe, but more than satisfying was a first-class pastry tart of caramelised tomatoes and herbs, served with creme fraiche and tapenade. Whole braised partridge was perched on a small mountain range of sweet and sour cabbage, camouflaged under a thicket of game chips. Caper, prawn and sun-dried tomato sauce gave interest to baked halibut on a bed of creamed potato with an accompaniment of fresh asparagus.

Directions: From B1188 onto B1190 Church Hill, after 2 miles turn R opposite Methodist church

Chef: David Hill
Owners: David Hill & Margaret Broddle
Cost: Alc £25, set-price L £11.25/D £22.50. ☺ H/wine £9.95
Times: 12.30-2pm/7-9.30pm. Closed L Sat
Additional: Sunday L; Children welcome
Seats: 40
Style: Traditional/country-house
Smoking: No smoking in dining room
Accommodation: 14 en suite ★ ★ ★

LINCOLN, Wig & Mitre ☺

The new premises provide a popular bar downstairs and smart restaurant and bar upstairs. Chargrilled lamb fillet on a purée of minted peas was an enjoyable main course.

Additional: Bar food; Sunday L; Children welcome
Smoking: No smoking in dining room

Directions: Close to cathedral, castle and car park at top of Steep Hill

30 Steep Hill LN2 1TL
Map 8: SK97
Tel: 01522 535190
Fax: 01522 532402
E-mail: reservations@wigandmitre.co.uk
Cost: Alc £22, set-price L £8.50 & £11. ☺ H/wine £10.45
Times: 8am-midnight

LOUTH, Beaumont Hotel ☺

Anglo-Italian cuisine in a smartly appointed Victorian hotel restaurant. Sturdy main courses such as gammon steak Hawaiian and sea bass portofino are offered alongside an Italian speciality pasta menu.

Additional: Bar food; Children welcome
Style: Chic/Country-house
Smoking: No pipes & cigars
Accommodation: 17 en suite ★ ★ ★

Directions: Telephone for directions

66 Victoria Road LN11 0BX
Map 8: TF38
Tel: 01507 605005
Fax: 01507 607768
Cost: Alc £16, set-price L/D £ 14.95. ☺ H/wine £9.95
Times: Noon-2pm/7-9.30pm. Closed Sun

LOUTH, Kenwick Park Hotel ☺☺

Traditional country-house hotel set in extensive grounds, where the Fairways Restaurant and conservatory bar overlook Kenwick Park Golf Course. Good quality ingredients are used in the comprehensive *carte*, which offers dishes such as marinated seafood nestling over lemon-scented prawns glazed with pink peppercorn vinaigrette, followed perhaps by corn-fed supreme of chicken served over fine strips of local carrots finished with wild mushroom and Madeira sauce. A tempting range of desserts includes a rum-soaked savarin layered with a warm compote of apricots and prunes, and a terrine of dark and white Belgian chocolate mousse set on crème anglaise.

Smoking: No smoking in dining room
Civil licence: 70 **Accommodation:** 24 en suite ★ ★ ★

Directions: From A571 follow signs for Mablethorpe & Manby. 2m from Louth

Kenwick Park LN11 8NR
Map 8: TF38
Tel: 01507 608806
Fax: 01507 608027
E-mail: enquiries@kenwick-park.co.uk
Chef: Mark Vines
Owner: S D Flynn
Cost: Set-price L £11.95 & £19.95/D £19.95. ☺ H/wine £13.45
Times: Noon-2.30pm/7-9.30pm
Additional: Bar food; Sunday L; Children welcome
Seats: 36. Private dining room 20; Jacket & tie preferred
Style: Country-house/Formal

SCUNTHORPE,
Forest Pines Hotel ❀

Ermine Street Broughton
DN20 0AQ
Map 8: SE81
Tel: 01652 650770
Fax: 01652 650495
E-mail: enquiries@forestpines.co.uk

Large hotel, formerly known as the Briggate Lodge Inn, where the elegant restaurant offers a wide choice of dishes with local produce much in evidence. (The crème brûlée is recommended.)

Cost: Alc £30, set-price L £17.25/D £19.50. ☺ H/wine £8.65
Times: Noon-2pm/7-10pm
Additional: Bar food; Sunday L; Children welcome
Style: Traditional/Formal
Smoking: No smoking in dining room
Civil licence: 180
Accommodation: 86 en suite ★★★★

Directions: From M180 J4, at rdbt take 1st exit towards Scunthorpe. Take 2nd exit at next rdbt. Hotel on L

SPALDING,
Cley Hall Hotel ❀   NEW

22 High Street PE11 1TX
Map 8: TF22
Tel: 01775 725157
Fax: 01775 710785
E-mail: cleyhall@enterprise.net

Georgian manor house with a café-bar as well as the restaurant located in the garden rooms and cellars. They offer a good range of dishes carefully prepared from quality ingredients.

Cost: Alc £25, set-price L & D £17. ☺ H/wine £8.75
Times: Noon-2.30pm/7-9.30pm (8pm Sun)
Additional: Bar food L; Sunday L; Children welcome
Style: Informal/country-house
Smoking: No smoking in dining room
Accommodation: 12 en suite ★★

Directions: At junction of A151 & A16 (Macdonald's roundabout) take turn for Spalding. Hotel is in 1.5m

STAMFORD,
The George of Stamford ❀

71 St Martins PE9 2LB
Map 8: TF00
Tel: 01780 750750
Fax: 01780 750701

Charming coaching inn with a formal, oak-panelled dining room. Local game terrine with pumpkin and ginger chutney might be followed by grilled Dover sole, or calves' liver with smoked bacon and sage and lime butter.

E-mail: reservations@ georgehotelofstamford.com
Cost: Alc £34, set-price L £14.50 & £16.50. H/wine £9.95
Times: Noon-2.30pm/7-10.30pm
Additional: Sunday L; Children 10+
Style: Traditional/Formal
Smoking: No pipes & cigars; Jacket & tie preferred
Civil licence: 50
Accommodation: 47 en suite ★★★

Directions: From A1 take B1081 to Stamford. Follow road to traffic lights, hotel on L

AA Wine Shortlisted for Award-see page 18

WINTERINGHAM,

Winteringham Fields ❀❀❀❀

DN15 9PF
Map 8: SE92
Tel: 01724 733096
Fax: 01724 733898
E-mail: wintfields@aol.com
Chef: Germain Schwab
Owners: Germain & Annie Schwab
Cost: *A/c* £58, set-price L £25/D £58.
H/wine £17.50
Times: Noon-1.30pm/7-9.30pm.
Closed Sun, Mon, 2 wks Xmas, last
wk Mar, 1st wk Aug
Additional: Children welcome
Seats: 42. Private dining room 10
Style: Classic
Smoking: No smoking in dining room
Accommodation: 10 en suite ★ ★

Although hidden away in a small village near the Humber, Winteringham Fields acts as a magnet not just for the local area but for people from around the entire country. Appetisers – perhaps aromatic game consommé, then pressed oxtail and foie gras – are served in the conservatory or the Victorian parlour-like sitting room, with a third offered at table in the 'discreetly elegant' marble-floored restaurant, where silk drapes hang at the windows, allowing diners, in the words of an inspector 'to concentrate on the food without being distracted by the surroundings'. A cowbell over the fireplace is from Germain Schwab's grandfather's farm in Switzerland; he loves to cook country dishes that 'remind me of my roots', and to do so he grows his own herbs and vegetables, buys meat from Lincolnshire farmers, including organic pork from the village, and takes daily deliveries of fish from Grimsby, while game comes from local shoots. All this makes him sound like a man in control as he ploughs his own furrow. A duo of pigeon breasts – milk-fed and woodsmoked – juicily tender, with a clear contrast of flavours, accompanied by soubise sauce just hinting of onions, and mille-feuille of lobster and polenta with a morel and lobster sauce are among successful starters, while an inspector enjoyed a lightly-smoked (in the kitchen, of course) skate wing wrapped around well-made pike mousse with a dry cider sauce. High ambition is not let down by main courses. Take a corn-fed chicken pot-roast with herbs and truffle in pig's bladder, the bird removed from the latter, skilfully carved, and served with a pot-au-feu of root vegetables: 'fantastic flavour'. A fondness for offal shows up in braised pig's cheeks with an apple and Calvados froth, or veal sweetbreads roasted in Parma ham and served with Puy lentils and foie gras mousseline, while a bold approach to some dishes pays dividends: bone-marrow scrambled eggs with braised fillet of brill bordelaise, for instance. If dishes are visually attractive, puddings are a delight to the eye, as in an assiette of espresso and cappuccino, a 'cup' of coffee and chocolate cream, with Mascarpone on a tuile 'saucer', and warm chocolate cake with coffee sauce, while cheeses alone – around 35, both British and European, all in peak condition – make a visit worthwhile.

Directions: Village centre, off A1077, 4 miles S of Humber Bridge

MERSEYSIDE

LIVERPOOL,
Becher's Brook Restaurant

There were changes in the kitchen just as we went to press at this popular cosy restaurant, which is popular with theatre-goers and provides classically-themed cuisine enhanced with imaginative, contemporary presentation. An inspection meal included roast cod with a vanilla broth and caviar sabayon and oyster beignet.

Additional: Children 7+
Style: Classic
Smoking: No smoking in dining room; Air conditioning

Directions: From M62 follow signs for City Centre and Catholic Cathedral. L into Mount Pleasant Rd, then L again into Hope St. Restaurant is 100yds on L

29a Hope Street L1 9BQ
Map 7: SJ39
Tel: 0151 707 0005
Fax: 0151 708 7011
Cost: Alc £32, set-price L £17.50. ☺
H/wine £11.50
Times: Noon-10pm.
Closed L Sat, all Sun, 31 Dec, Bhs

LIVERPOOL,
Liverpool Marriott City Centre

A classical elegant style greets you here, combining variety and imagination with excellent presentation to produce both modern English and European cuisine. The extensive carte menu includes galantine of guinea fowl and asparagus.

Additional: Sunday L; Children welcome
Style: Classic/Traditional
Smoking: No smoking in dining room; Air conditioning
Civil licence: 200
Accommodation: 146 en suite ★★★★

Directions: From City Centre follow signs for Queen Square Parking. Hotel adjacent

1 Queen Square L1 1RH
Map 7: SJ39
Tel: 0151 476 8000
Fax: 0151 474 5000
E-mail: liverpool@swallow-hotels.co.uk
Cost: Alc £30, set-price L £10.95/D £23. ☺ H/wine £12.50
Times: 12.30-2.30pm/6.30-11pm.
Closed L Sat

LIVERPOOL, ## 60 Hope Street

Trendy new place, welcome in the city, where you can expect to give a month's notice for Saturday night bookings. It's a listed Georgian building on three floors, including a basement café-bar, ground floor restaurant and first-floor private dining room. The restaurant is modern and airy with parquet floors and walls painted blue, white, cream and dark red. Spiral staircases lead up and down stairs, and a large oval reception table creates a feature at the centre of the room. Open ravioli of goats' cheese and red pepper was a great starter, with home-made pasta and delicious confit of red peppers. Pan-fried turbot – a lovely piece of fish – was served with lemongrass greens and sauce mouclarde, a slight curry flavour providing the perfect complement. Pudding was a sensational fried jam sandwich with Carnation milk ice cream; essentially a home-made brioche, filled with home-made jam and fresh strawberries and deep-fried to seal.

Directions: From M62 follow city centre signs, then brown tourist signs for Cathedral. Hope St near Cathedral

60 Hope Street L1 9BZ
Map 7: SJ39
Tel: 0151 7076060
Fax: 0151 7076016
E-mail: info@60hopestreet.com
Chef: Gary Manning
Owners: Colin Manning & Gary Manning
Cost: Alc £25. ☺ H/wine £11.95
Times: Noon-2.30pm/7-10.30pm.
Closed L Sat, D Sun, all Mon, 25 & 26 Dec
Additional: Bar food; Children welcome
Seats: 80. Private dining room 30; Jacket & tie preferred
Style: Modern/Contemporary
Smoking: No-smoking area; No pipes & cigars; Air conditioning

LIVERPOOL, **Ziba** ✿ NEW

15-19 Berry Street L1 9DF
Map 7: SJ39
Tel: 0151 708 8870

The minimalist ambience of this eatery is echoed in the precise cooking. The carte *includes dishes such as seared foie gras with sultanas, lobster terrine with baby leeks, or grilled sea bass with tapenade and braised fennel.*

Telephone for further details

THORNTON HOUGH,
Thornton Hall Hotel ✿✿

Neston Road CH63 1JF
Map 7: SJ38

Eighteenth-century country house, with original stained glass windows, and a very impressive leather and mother-of-pearl ceiling in the restaurant. Dishes on a summer menu might include black pudding and apple terrine with mustard seed jus, foie gras parfait with kumquat marmalade and sultana brioche, or roast king scallops in celariac velouté with truffle oil and chives. Main courses follow the same style – carpaccio of beef fillet with asparagus, guacamole and Parmesan wafers, or salmon coulibiac on a bisque sauce. Finish with warm raspberry savarin with pistachio and honey ice cream.

Tel: 0151 336 3938
Fax: 0151 336 7864
E-mail: thorntonhallhotel@
btinternet.com
Chef: Richard Birchall
Owners: The Thompson family
Cost: *Alc* £33, set-price L £11.50/
D £23 ☺ H/wine £11.75
Times: 12.30-1.45pm/7-9pm.
Closed L Sat, 27 Dec-3 Jan
Additional: Bar food; Sunday L;
Children welcome
Style: Traditional/Country-house
Seats: 45. Private dining room 24

Smoking: No pipes & cigars
Civil licence: 80
Accommodation: 63 ★ ★ ★

Directions: Telephone for directions

NORFOLK

BLAKENEY, **Morston Hall** ✿✿✿

Morston NR25 7AA
Map 9: TG04

In an Area of Outstanding Natural Beauty, two minutes' walk from the estuary, the hall dates from Jacobean times. A conservatory overlooks the three-acre garden, there are two comfortable lounges, and the elegant restaurant, blue-carpeted with matching upholstered chairs and first-class table appointments, is at the heart of the enterprise. Galton Blackiston devises well-balanced dinner menus of a set-price four-course formula with no choice until the end, when it's a toss-up between cheese and a dessert: perhaps 'superb' panettone crème brûlée with mango sorbet. Meals start in high style with canapés, maybe tiny pizzas with olives, anchovies and Mozzarella, with a starter of perhaps confit duck leg on purée potato, or wild mushrooms sandwiched between layers of pasta with flageolet bean purée. Technical skills shine out of the fish course, as in perfectly cooked, completely boned pan-fried skate wing with a delicate sauce of parsley, shrimps and capers. Pot-roasting is a favoured treatment of main-course meats: best end of lamb, perhaps, or pink duck breast fanned on fondant potatoes with an exemplary, rich, shiny jus accompanied by sautéed spinach and batons of roast parsnips. Breads and petits fours are both described as 'excellent', and those not wanting to bother with the wine list can take the easy option and choose one of the wines of the month.

Tel: 01263 741041
Fax: 01263 740419
E-mail: reception@morstonhall.co.uk
Chef: Galton Blackiston
Owners: Galton & Tracy Blackiston
Cost: Set-price D £34. H/wine £10
Times: D only, 7.30-8pm.
Closed 2 wks Jan
Additional: Sunday L (12.30-1pm);
Children welcome
Seats: 40
Style: Classic
Smoking: No smoking in dining room
Accommodation: 6 en suite ★ ★

Directions: On A149 (King's Lynn/Cromer) 2 miles W of Blakeney in the village of Morston

BURNHAM MARKET, Hoste Arms

The Green Nr King's Lynn PE31 8HD
Map 9: TF84
Tel: 01328 738777
Fax: 01328 730103
Chef: Andrew McPherson
Owner: Paul Whittome
Cost: Alc £25. ☺ H/wine £9.75
Times: Noon-2pm/7-9pm
Seats: 140
Smoking: No-smoking area; Air conditioning
Accommodation: 28 en suite ★ ★

Directions: In the centre of the village

Combine a stylish appearance with a down-to-earth atmosphere, add a mix of restaurant, hotel and traditional pub and you have an ideal place to visit. That's the Hoste Arms. There's a choice of areas in which to eat, ranging from bars and restaurants to a pleasant enclosed walled garden. Dishes such as Brancaster mussels steamed in white wine with cream, or roast breast of pheasant with red wine and black pudding risotto and sautéed mushrooms reflect the proximity of sea and rural pursuits, whereas tiger prawn stirfry with crispy noodles and soy shows a chef with more cosmopolitan interests. Our own test meal explored the chef's spin on traditional ideas with potted brown shrimps in cinnamon plus niçoise-style dressing and tapenade dressing, crisp-fried sea bass with leek and cherry tomato risotto, and chocolate brownie with chocolate sauce and clotted cream. The wine list is noted for its keenly-priced fine wines, believed to be amongst the lowest in the country.

COLTISHALL,
Norfolk Mead Hotel NEW

Lovely Georgian manor house providing the setting for well-executed dishes using quality local ingredients. Try potted Norfolk game with granary toast, or braised shank of lamb with perfectly cooked vegetables.

Directions: From Norwich take B1150. In Coltishall turn R after hump-backed bridge. Hotel 600yds on R just before church

Church Lane Norwich NR12 7DN
Map 9: TG21
Tel: 01603 737531
Fax: 01603 737521
E-mail: norfolkmead@aol.com

Telephone for further details

ERPINGHAM, Ark Restaurant

Very old flint and brick cottage in a village location, added to over the centuries and sympathetically restored by the owners. Inside there is a small lounge with a dispense bar where guests can enjoy a pre-dinner drink before entering the restaurant – a small space, seating just 26 diners, with simple country decor. The *carte* offers a choice of five dishes at each of three courses. Typical starters include a lasagne of wild mushrooms with their own herb pasta, or home-cured mackerel with tomato vinaigrette. More country cooking follows with Basque-style monkfish or loin of Gloucester Old Spot pork braised with Marsala and red wine. To finish there's a choice of British

The Street Norwich
NR11 7QB
Map 5: TG13
Tel/Fax: 01263 761535
Chef: Sheila Kidd
Owners: Sheila & Michael Kidd
Cost: Alc £26.75, set-price L £15.25/D £21.25. ☺
Times: D only, 7-9.30pm. Usually closed D Sun, all Mon, Tue in winter, part of Oct
Additional: Sunday L (12.30-2pm); Children welcome

cheeses from Neal's Yard Dairy or puddings along the lines of raspberry syllabub, or poached peach and apricots with Amaretto and home-made vanilla ice.

Smoking: No smoking in dining room
Credit cards: None

Directions: Off A140 4 miles N of Aylsham

GREAT YARMOUTH, Imperial Hotel ❀

Relaxed French-themed restaurant situated in the basement of the hotel. The menu follows suit with pleasantly unpretentious dishes. Try grilled Dover sole or pancake provençale with Mediterranean vegetables and real tomato sauce, topped with Mozzarella.

North Drive NR30 1EQ
Map 5: TG50
Tel: 01493 851113
Fax: 01493 852229
E-mail: imperial@scs-datacom.co.uk
Cost: Alc £22, set-price L £12.50/D £19.50. ☺ H/wine £12.50
Times: Noon-2pm/7-10pm. Closed L Sat, L Bhs
Additional: Bar food; Sunday L; Children welcome
Style: Classic/Informal
Smoking: No-smoking area; Air conditioning
Accommodation: 39 en suite ★ ★ ★

Seats: 26. Private dining room 8
Style: Informal/Traditional

Directions: On the seafront 100 yards N of Britannia Pier

GRIMSTON,
Congham Hall ❀❀

Thirty acres of attractive landscaped grounds, including parkland, orchard and a renowned herb garden, surround this quintessentially English country retreat. The Orangery Restaurant lends a summery feel with its warm terracotta decor, glass roof, plants and long windows overlooking the garden. James Parkinson and his team cook a modern British style with French and Mediterranean influences, making full use of the bountiful herbs and produce from the kitchen garden. Service is attentive, friendly and professional, delivering quality cuisine through a choice of interesting menus. On a memorable April visit an *amuse-bouche* of foie gras and lentil velouté followed a good assortment of canapés. Fresh red mullet with a pepper crust set on a galette of shellfish risotto with an essence of lobster sauce continued the 'extremely enjoyable experience', followed by honey-roasted duck sliced on a fig jus. Dessert proved a high point with a superb hot passion fruit soufflé, 'perfectly cooked, well risen with intense flavour', enthused our inspector, and came accompanied by an exotic sorbet. Quality home-made breads accompany, while good coffee and petits fours finish with a flurry.

Lynn Road King's Lynn PE32 1AH
Map 9: TF72
Tel: 01485 600250
Fax: 01485 601191
E-mail: reception@ conghamhallhotel.demon.co.uk
Chef: James Parkinson
Owners: Von Essen Hotels
Cost: Alc £34, set-price L £13.50/D £39.50. H/wine £13.50
Times: Noon-2.15pm/7-9.30pm
Additional: Bar food; Sunday L; Children 7+
Seats: 50. Private dining room 18
Style: Traditional/Country-house
Smoking: No smoking in dining room
Civil licence: 40
Accommodation: 14 en suite ★ ★ ★

Directions: 6 miles NE of King's Lynn on A14, turn R toward Grimston. Hotel is 2.5 miles on L; don't go to Longham

HETHERSETT, **Park Farm Hotel**

Part Georgian hotel and leisure complex with a spacious and comfortable air-conditioned restaurant. A fairly large and eclectic carte *is complemented by a daily changing set-price menu, including dishes such as chargrilled marlin.*

NR9 3DL
Map 5: TG10
Tel: 01603 810264
Fax: 01603 812104
E-mail: enq@parkfarm-hotel.co.uk
Cost: *Alc* £26, set-price L £13.25/D £19.50. ☺ H/wine £10.50
Times: Noon-2pm (2.30pm Sun)/7-9.30pm (9pm Sun)
Additional: Bar food; Sunday L; Children welcome
Style: Traditional
Smoking: No smoking in dining room; Air conditioning; Jacket & tie preferred
Accommodation: 48 en suite ★ ★ ★

Directions: 5 miles S of Norwich on B1172 (the old A11)

HOLT, **Yetman's**

Smallish restaurant converted from two cottages set in the bustling village of Holt. In season the exterior is awash with summer flowers and the interior continues in the theme of rural idyll with pastel colours, and open fire places. A glossy, nicely set out wine list guides you through a good range of styles and producers so that the right wine may be selected for the excellent examples of modern British cuisine on offer. A typical meal might open with a dish of local mussels, cockles, fresh Cornish squid and prawns with fennel, celery, shallots, lemon and fresh herbs. Grilled fillet of halibut might follow, complemented by spiced sweet potato mash and brown butter. Puddings are traditional but mesmerising – try fresh rhubarb fool, sticky toffee pudding or toasted cinnamon and apple pancakes.

Directions: Village centre

37 Norwich Road NR25 6SA
Map 9: TG03
Tel: 01263 713320
Chef: Alison Yetman
Owners: Peter & Alison Yetman
Times: D only, 7.30-9.30pm. Closed D Sun & Mon in winter,Tue, 3 wks Oct/Nov
Additional: Sunday L (12.30-2pm); Children welcome
Seats: 30. Private dining room 12
Style: Informal
Smoking: No-smoking area; No pipes & cigars

HORNING, **Taps** NEW

Light modern decor with wicker furniture in the reception room and pastel shades in the welcoming restaurant. A 'vibrant' hot crispy duck dish began an excellent meal, an oozing succulent hot chocolate soufflé concluded it.

Directions: From Norwich follow signs to 'The Broads' on A1151. Through Wroxham and turn R to Horning & Ludham (A1062) for 3 miles. Turn R into Horning, Lower Street 500yds on L

25 Lower Street NR12 8AA
Map 9: TG31
Tel: 01692 630219
Cost: *Alc* £20. ☺ H/wine £8.95
Times: Noon-2pm/7-9pm. Closed D Sun, all Mon
Additional: Sunday L; Children welcome
Style: Chic/modern
Smoking: No smoking in dining room

KING'S LYNN, **Rococo**

A 17th-century cottage in the heritage quarter of King's Lynn, this vibrant restaurant has yellow walls hung with mirrors and large modern canvases. The appealing modern menu makes for some difficult decisions, with starters like a crunchy pastry of Cromer crab and smoked salmon, or a warm salad of local

11 Saturday Market Place PE30 5DQ
Map 9: TF62
Tel/Fax: 01553 771483
E-mail: rococorest@aol.com
Chef: Nick Anderson
Owners: Nick & Anne Anderson
Cost: Set-price L £16.50/D £32. ☺

pigeon with quince crisps and chutney. Another local ingredient, Norfolk lamb, comes wrapped with couscous, cumin-scented jus and Jerusalem artichoke. Other main course options include roast monkfish with fondant potato, baby leeks and nero sauce, or a vegetarian Tatin of roasted vegetables with feta cheese. Desserts range from a light hazelnut mousse with brandy-soaked plums to warm date and orange sponge dripping with toffee and caramel sauce.

Directions: Follow signs to The Old Town, next to Tourist Information

H/wine £12.75
Times: Noon-2pm/6.30-10pm. Closed L Mon, all Sun, 24-31 Dec
Additional: Children welcome
Seats: 40
Style: Unique/Arty
Smoking: No-smoking area; No pipes & cigars

NORTH WALSHAM,
Beechwood Hotel ❀

Stylish country house hotel with links to Agatha Christie. The continued success of this pretty blue and white dining room is no mystery with dishes such as roast duckling with a baked Norfolk apple on offer.

Directions: From Norwich take B1150 to North Walsham (13 miles). Turn L at 1st traffic lights and R at next. Hotel 150mtrs on L

Cromer Road NR28 0HD
Map 9: TG23
Tel: 01692 403231
Fax: 01692 407284
Cost: Set-price L £12/D £23. ☺ H/wine £12.50
Times: Noon-2pm/7-9pm. Closed L Sat
Additional: Sunday L; Children 10+
Style: Traditional/Country-house
Smoking: No smoking in dining room
Accommodation: 10 en suite ★★

NORWICH,
Adlard's Restaurant ❀❀❀

The well-established, three-level restaurant has had a makeover – and emerges looking crisp, modern and elegant with unusual broad striped wallpaper, light wood floor and beautifully appointed tables. Staff are very professional and smartly turned out. An excellent wine list includes some very good bottles and some rare dessert wines by the glass or half bottle. Roger Hickman knows how to turn out a fine ballotine – of salmon with crème Chantilly and caviar, or of rabbit with shallot dressing. Combinations, such as sea bass with braised chicory, or loin of venison with red cabbage and roast parsnips are well judged. There is a fine choice of British and Irish cheeses or lovely desserts such as chocolate fondant with vanilla ice cream and prune and Armagnac soufflé. Good coffee is served with petits fours. Diners are requested not to smoke until after their main course.

Directions: City centre, 200 yards behind City Hall

79 Upper St Giles Street NR2 1AB
Map 5: TG20
Tel: 01603 633522
Fax: 01603 617733
E-mail: adlards@netcom.co.uk
Chef: Roger Hickman
Owner: David Adlard
Cost: Alc £32, set-price L £19/D £25. ☺ H/wine £12.50
Times: 12.30-1.45pm/7.30-10.30pm. Closed L Mon, all Sun, 1 wk after Xmas
Additional: Children welcome
Seats: 40
Style: Modern
Smoking: No pipes & cigars; Air conditioning

NORWICH, Annesley House Hotel

A smart conservatory restaurant overlooking attractive water gardens. Our inspector enjoyed a marinated chilli chicken starter, followed by a roast loin of pork, finished off with a good old fashioned syrup sponge pudding.

Additional: Bar food; Sunday L **Style:** Bistro-style
Smoking: No smoking in dining room
Accommodation: 26 en suite ★ ★

Directions: On A11 close to city centre

6 Newmarket Road NR2 2LA
Map 5: TG20
Tel: 01603 624553
Fax: 01603 621577
Cost: Alc £25. ☺ H/wine £9.50
Times: Noon-2pm/7-9pm.
Closed Xmas

NORWICH, Beeches Hotel & Victorian Gardens

Listed building with famous Victorian gardens. A choice of menus offers English dishes with Mediterranean influences – smoked chicken tart followed by seared salmon on roast tomatoes.

Times: D only 6.30-11pm. Closed Xmas

Directions: W of city on B1108, behind St John's RC Cathedral

2-6 Earlham Road NR2 3DB
Map 5: TG20
Tel: 01603 621167
Fax: 01603 620151
E-mail: reception@beeches.co.uk

Telephone for further details

NORWICH, Brummells Seafood Restaurant

Brummells has the easy-going air of a restaurant where you can feel at home in either a dinner jacket or casual clothes. The large seafood menu generally lives up to expectations, and our inspector was well pleased with a choice of mussels in cream and Muscadet with scallions, followed by expertly steamed monkfish with wild mushrooms and basil compote. The cooking roams the piscine globe for inspiration, from grilled sardines with chilli oil on a bed of marinated beansprouts to deep-fried breaded rock oysters served with Greek tzatziki, grilled fillets of zander with provençale sauce and Canadian lobster Thermidor. Sauces and preparations may be mixed and matched; there is demonstrable willingness to please. Vegetable selection is equally wide ranging, eight different ones on our visit. Don't miss out on dessert – the caramelised bananas in a warm orange and brandy syrup with vanilla ice cream is warmly recommend.

Directions: 40yds from Colegate, 5 minutes from Maids Head Hotel and Tombland

7 Magdalen Street NR3 1LE
Map 5: TG20
Tel: 01603 625555
Fax: 01603 766260
E-mail: brummell@brummells.co.uk
Chefs: Andrew Brummell,
John O'Sullivan
Owner: Andrew Brummell
Cost: £29.90. H/wine £11.95
Times: L from noon/D from 6pm
Additional: Sunday L; Children welcome
Seats: 30
Style: Rustic
Smoking: No-smoking area; Air conditioning

NORWICH, By Appointment

An Aladdin's Cave of an establishment with treasures both ornamental and culinary awaiting. A theatrical approach to the dining experience ties in well with rich exciting flavours such as panfried veal breaded in orange and lemon zest.

Smoking: No smoking in dining room

Directions: City centre, from St Andrews Hall, down St George's Street, into Colegate then 1st R into courtyard

27-29 St George's Street
NR3 1AB
Map 5: TG20
Tel/Fax: 01603 630730
Cost: Alc £25. ☺ H/wine £10.95
Times: D only, 7.30-9pm. Closed Sun
& Mon, 25 Dec
Additional: Children 12 +
Style: Classic/Traditional

NORWICH,

Cumberland Hotel

Vibrant restaurant themed around South Africa, with an abundance of pictures. Rich, chicken liver pâté was followed by char-grilled salmon fillet with tomato butter sauce, and deliciously gooey pecan pie.

Smoking: No smoking in dining room
Accommodation: 25 en suite ★ ★

Directions: 1 mile E of city centre on A47 to Yarmouth. Nr rail station & football ground

212-216 Thorpe Road NR1 1TJ
Map 5: TG20
Tel: 01603 434560
Fax: 01603 433355
E-mail: cumberland@paston.co.uk
Cost: ☺ H/wine £10.95
Times: D only, (L by arrangement)
6.30-9.30pm. Closed 26 Dec-2 Jan
Additional: Children 13+
Style: Informal/Rustic

NORWICH, **Femi's**

Pleasantly presented restaurant with fine paintings and an eclectic menu. Options include blinis, and roast mushroom and Roquefort tart, followed perhaps by roast rump of spiced lamb or grilled swordfish.

Additional: Children welcome
Style: Bistro-style/Modern
Smoking: No-smoking area; Air conditioning

Directions: City centre. 200yds from Castle and Cathedral. Behind Anglia Television

42 King Street NR1 1PD
Map 5: TG20
Tel/Fax: 01603 766010
Cost: *Alc* £22.50, set-price
L £9.50/D £17.50. ☺ H/wine £9
Times: Noon-2.30pm/6-10.30pm.
Closed Sun, 24 Dec-7 Jan

NORWICH,

Green's Seafood Restaurant

Main courses range from traditional shellfish platters to more sophisticated dishes such as roast sea bass with truffle oil and potato and celeriac rösti. Chocolate and amaretti biscuit torte might be too tempting to resist.

Directions: Near St John's RC Cathedral

82 Upper St Giles Street NR2 1LT
Map 5: TG20
Tel: 01603 623733
Fax: 01603 615268
E-mail:
greenseafood@tinyworld.co.uk

Telephone for further details

NORWICH, **Marco's Restaurant**

Small Italian restaurant in the heart of Norwich city centre. The setting is very elegant with Victorian panelled walls, plush carpets and framed drawings. The reasonably sized *carte* and the daily changing lunch menu are packed with Italian delights (with clear and detailed English descriptions) such as thin slices of specially cured fillet of wild boar served on a bed of salad leaves with Parmesan cheese and an olive oil and lemon juice dressing, or king prawns with olive oil, chillies, garlic and a fresh tomato sauce. Fish makes a welcome appearance with steamed fillets of sea bass served with a fresh ginger and garlic sauce. Discover Italian variations on an English classic with Marco's bread-and-butter pudding, or go for the lighter dessert option of a simple lemon sorbet.

Directions: City centre: from market place facing Guildhall, turn R then L into Pottergate

17 Pottergate NR2 1DS
Map 5: TG20
Tel: 01603 624044
Chef/Owner: Marco Vessalio
Cost: *Alc* £29, set-price L £15. ☺
H/wine £12.50
Times: Noon-2pm/7-10pm.
Closed Sun & Mon
Additional: Children welcome
Seats: 22
Style: Classic/Informal
Smoking: No smoking in dining room

NORWICH,
Marriott Sprowston Manor ❀

Surrounded by attractive parkland the elegant hotel restaurant offers modern cuisine with classical and regional influences. A nicely roasted loin of veal accompanied by glazed parsnips, sugar snaps and a piquant sauce was greatly enjoyed.

Times: 12.30-2pm/7-9.45pm. Closed Xmas/New Year (ex residents)
Additional: Bar food; Sunday L; Children welcome
Style: Country-house
Smoking: No smoking in dining room; Air conditioning
Civil licence: 100
Accommodation: 94 en suite ★ ★ ★ ★

Directions: Take A1151 (Wroxham), follow signs to Sprowston Park

Sprowston Park Wroxham Road
NR7 8RP
Map 5: TG20
Tel: 01603 410871
Fax: 01603 423911
Cost: *Alc* £35-£45.50, set-price L £13.50 & £16/D £22. ☺ H/wine £12.50

NORWICH,
Old Rectory ❀

Georgian dining room in Wedgwood blue overlooking the gardens, terrace and swimming pool. Perfectly cooked pan-fried salmon with tomato and coriander salsa was selected from the short daily menu.

Times: D only, 7-10pm. Closed Sun, 23 Dec-7 Jan
Additional: Vegetarian dishes by arrangement
Style: Classic
Smoking: No smoking in dining room
Accommodation: 8 en suite ★ ★

Directions: From A147 ring road take A1242 to Thorpe. Hotel on L after the church

103 Yarmouth Road Thorpe St Andrew NR7 0HF
Map 5: TG20
Tel: 01603 700772
Fax: 01603 300772
E-mail: rectoryh@aol.com
Cost: Set-price D £17. ☺ H/wine £9.75

NORWICH,
Pinocchio's Restaurant ❀

Smart city-centre bistro-style Italian restaurant, popular with local business folk. A recent meal included filo parcels stuffed with goats' cheese, followed by wild boar with bacon and mushroom, and tiramisu to finish.

Times: Noon-2pm/5.30-11pm. Closed L Mon, all Sun, 25-28 Dec
Additional: Children welcome
Style: Italian
Smoking: No-smoking area

Directions: From city centre follow Castle Meadow to traffic lights, 1st L into Bank Plain, leads to St Benedicts Street

11 St Benedicts Street NR2 4PE
Map 5: TG20
Tel/Fax: 01603 613318
E-mail: nigel@nraffies.freeserve.co.uk
Cost: *Alc* £20, set-price L £5. ☺

NORWICH,
St Benedicts Restaurant ❀

Enjoy casual surroundings and choose from a range of modern British cuisine or something with a Mediterranean inspiration. Menu

9 St Benedicts Street NR2 4PE
Map 5: TG20
Tel/Fax: 01603 765377
E-mail: nigel@nraffies.freeserve. co.uk

includes slow cooked crispy duck glazed with honey and served with spiced pears and mashed potato.

Style: Bistro-style
Smoking: No pipes & cigars

Directions: At city end of St Benedicts. Nearest car park Duke Street (day), on street (evening).

Cost: *Alc* £22, set-price L £5. ☺
H/wine £8.50
Times: Noon-2pm/7-10pm(10.30pm Fri & Sat). Closed Sun & Mon, 25-31 Dec
Additional: Children welcome

SWAFFHAM, Romford House

Friendly restaurant in a 400-year-old town house; dishes sampled include a rich French onion soup, and a seafood speciality of salmon, lemon sole and monkfish with lemon butter sauce.

Additional: Children welcome
Style: Classic/French
Smoking: No-smoking area; No pipes & cigars in restaurant

Directions: 16 miles from King's Lynn, in the main Market Place

5 London Street PE37 7DD
Map 9: TF80
Tel: 01760 722552
E-mail: peter.rose@ukgateway.net
Cost: *Alc* £22. ☺ H/wine £9.25
Times: 11-2pm/7-late. Closed L Mon, all Sun

THORNHAM, Lifeboat Inn NEW

Historic charm of a 16th-century smugglers' inn combined with modern-day comforts and service. Settle next to one of the open fireplaces and enjoy quality traditional and innovative dishes such as pan fried sea bass with coriander noodles.

Style: Country-house
Smoking: No smoking in dining room
Accommodation: 12 en suite ★★

Directions: From Hunstanton follow coast road, A149, for approx 6m, take first L after Thornham sign

Ship Lane PE36 6LT
Map 9: TF74
Tel: 01485 512236
Fax: 01485 512323
E-mail: reception@lifeboatinn.co.uk
Cost: *Alc* £21.50, set-price D £20. ☺
H/wine £8.50
Times: D only, 7-9.30pm
Additional: Bar food; Sunday L; Children welcome

THORPE MARKET,
Elderton Park Lodge Hotel

Gunton Park nr Cromer
NR11 8TZ
Map 9: TG23
Tel: 01263 833547
Fax: 01263 834673
E-mail:
enquiries@eldertonlodge.co.uk
Cost: *Alc* £26.50, set-price L £8.50/D £19.50. ☺ H/wine £10.50
Times: Noon-2pm/7-9pm
Additional: Sunday L; Children 10+
Style: Traditional/country-house
Smoking: No smoking in dining room
Accommodation: 11 en suite ★★

Listed building with a certain notoriety in connection with Lillie Langtry. It has a candlelit restaurant with classic decor serving modern British cooking, including an excellent rack of lamb.

Directions: On A149 (Cromer/North Walsham rd), 1 mile S of village

TITCHWELL,
Titchwell Manor Hotel 🏵

A charming hotel in an unspoilt coastal location. The restaurant makes the best use of the wealth of local produce, specialising in fish and shellfish, either in the elegant dining room or in the less formal seafood bar.

Brancaster PE31 8BB
Map 9: TF74
Tel: 01485 210221
Fax: 01485 210104
E-mail: margaret@titchwellmanor.co.uk
Cost: Set-price L £15/D £23. ☺
H/wine £10.50
Times: Noon-2pm/6.30-9.30pm.
Closed last 2 wks Jan
Additional: Bar Food; Sunday L;
Children welcome
Style: Country-house
Smoking: No smoking in dining room
Accommodation: 16 en suite ★★

Directions: On A149 coast road
between Brancaster and Thornham

WYMONDHAM,
Number Twenty Four 🏵

Grade II listed building, recently refurbished, with a spacious gold and cream interior. Dishes include pan-fried fillet of Lowestoft cod, and fillet of English beef with horseradish mash.

Additional: Children welcome
Style: Classic/French
Smoking: No-smoking area; No pipes & cigars

Directions: Town centre opposite war memorial

24 Middleton Street NR18 0BH
Map 5: TG10
Tel/Fax: 01953 607750
E-mail: numb24@msn.com
Cost: Alc £20, set-price L £10.95/ D
£18.95. ☺ H/wine £8.95
Times: Noon-2.30pm/7-9.30pm.
Closed Sun, Mon & Tue, 24-31 Dec

WYMONDHAM,
Wymondham Consort Hotel 🏵

Situated in the heart of a bustling market town, the intimate restaurant in this agreeable hotel offers warm and welcoming service and sophisticated cuisine. Tender pot roast beef and a rich crème brûlée come highly recommended

28 Market Street NR18 0BB
Map 5: TG10
Tel: 01953 606721
Fax: 01953 601361
Cost: Alc £20, set-price L £12.20/D
£18.20. ☺ H/wine £8.50
Times: Noon-2pm/7-10pm. Closed
Xmas & New Year
Additional: Bar food; Sunday L;
Children 10+
Smoking: No smoking in dining room
Accommodation: 20 en suite ★★

Directions: Town centre opposite
Barclays Bank

NORTHAMPTONSHIRE

CASTLE ASHBY, Falcon Hotel

Intimate hotel restaurant where an excellent passion fruit tart was the highlight of a meal, preceded by stuffed and rolled breast of quail, and succulent venison with crushed potatoes and scallions.

Directions: Follow signs for Castle Ashby, opposite War Memorial

NN7 1LF
Map 4: SP85
Tel: 01604 696200
Fax: 01604 696673
E-mail: falcan@castleashby.co.uk

Telephone for further details

DAVENTRY,

Fawsley Hall Hotel

A historic manor where Elizabeth I once stayed, the hotel restaurant is located in the old Tudor kitchen. No swan roast these days; instead our inspector had ravioli of wild mushrooms to begin, which had a good, deeply flavoured filling, and the tomato broth added a freshness and contrast. This was followed by roasted squab pigeon, fit to put before any queen – tender meat, topped with melting foie gras, served in crispy Savoy cabbage with perfectly smooth mashed potato and a texturally contrasting lentil sauce. The menu is short but nicely balanced – follow pan-fried foie gras, black pudding and mushy peas, for example, with fillet of brill, potato crust and courgette and tomato Champagne butter. The kitchen works hard but there are sometimes inconsistencies: a caramel and chocolate mousse in a chocolate cylindrical 'cigar' with home-made ice cream was rather let down by over-gelatined mousse.

Directions: From M40 J11 take A361, follow for 12 miles. Turn R towards Fawsley Hall

Fawsley NN11 3BA
Map 4: SP56
Tel: 01327 892000
Fax: 01327 892001
E-mail: fawsleyhall@compuserve.com
Chef: Jonathan Baron
Cost: *Alc* £40, set-price L £10/D £29.95. H/wine £17.50
Times: Noon-2pm/7-9.30pm
Additional: Bar food; Sunday L; Children welcome
Seats: 70. Private dining room 20
Style: Traditional/Country-house
Smoking: No-smoking area; No pipes & cigars
Civil licence: 100
Accommodation: 30 en suite ★★★★

FOTHERINGHAY, Falcon Inn

Attractive 18th-century stone pub set in a historic village close to the site of Fotheringhay Castle where Mary Queen of Scots was beheaded. The Falcon and chef/patron Ray Smikle are the latest additions to the select Huntsbridge Inns group of pubs that offer innovative food in a relaxing pub environment. Eat what you like, where you like and accompany your meal with excellent wines or a pint of ale. Sit in the unpretentious bar or head for the smart rear dining room or conservatory extension and order from the short, imaginative seasonally-changing menu. Dishes are robust and gutsy and the choice cosmopolitan with sound Mediterranean influences. Follow decent breads and quality olives with a hearty bowl of minestrone soup infused with fresh pesto, or chicken liver paté with red onion and apple chutney. For main course choose, perhaps, well presented roast cod with braised savoy cabbage, spiced lentils and a saffron, tomato and coriander sauce, or pork with fennel, onion and rosemary cake, fried polenta and balsamic and red pepper dressing. Finish with a zesty lemon tart or a plate of unpasteurised cheeses from Jeroboams. Good value set-price lunch menu.

Directions: Fotheringhay signed from A605 between Peterborough and Oundle

Nr Oundle PE8 5HZ
Map 4: TL09
Tel: 01832 226254
Fax: 01832 226046
Chef: Ray Smikle
Owners: John Hoskins, Ray Smikle
Cost: *Alc* £21, set-price L £9.50. H/wine £9.75
Times: Noon-2.15/6.30-9.30. Closed L Mon in winter
Additional: Bar food; Sunday L; Children welcome
Seats: 45. Private dining room 30
Smoking: No smoking in dining room

HELLIDON,

Hellidon Lakes Hotel ❀

Cherry wood-panelled restaurant with a superb outlook over the lake and golf course. The range of main courses might include grilled halibut with seared scallops, and lamb pavé with hazelnut crumble.

Smoking: No smoking in dining room; No pipes & cigars
Civil licence: 120
Accommodation: 71 en suite ★★★★

Directions: 1.5 miles off A361 at Charwelton, follow signs for Golf Club

Daventry NN11 6LN
Map 4: SP55
Tel: 01327 262550
Fax: 01327 262559
Cost: Set-price D £22.50. ☺ H/wine £10.75
Style: Traditional

HORTON, **The French Partridge** ❀❀

A long established and well-run restaurant with the style of an exclusive gentlemens' club, housed in a creeper-clad former coaching inn. Mary Partridge presides over the bar and restaurant area, assisted by a team of smartly presented and skilful staff. David Partridge's four-course dinner menu offers a good choice of dishes from the classical French repertoire peppered with modern eclectic options. Starters range from smooth pork and liver pâté in a brioche case to creamy fish chowder, and from coq au vin to lamb cutlets with Parmesan crumb crust and risotto. The intermediate course could be baked cod with lemon butter sauce or a tarte Tatin of roasted Mediterranean vegetables. Finish with a sweet or savoury course, perhaps Welsh rarebit or grilled panettone with pears poached in spiced red wine.

Directions: On B526, village centre, 6 miles from Northampton

NN7 2AP
Map 4: SP85
Tel: 01604 870033
E-mail: french@partridge.com
Chefs: David Partridge & Justin Partridge
Owners: D C & M Partridge
Cost: Set-price D £28-£29. H/wine £10
Times: D only, 7.30-9pm. Closed Sun & Mon, 2 wks Xmas, 2 wks Etr, 3wks end Jul/ early Aug
Additional: Children welcome
Seats: 40
Smoking: No smoking in dining room
Credit cards: None

KETTERING,

Kettering Park Hotel ❀

Popular mediterranean-style restaurant serving imaginative dishes. Typical starters include crispy Japanese chicken with honey and orange sauce. Fish comes fresh from Brixham each day, and why not try the 'Wine of the Week'.

Directions: A14 J9 - hotel on that roundabout

Kettering Parkway NN15 6XT
Map 4: SP87
Tel: 01536 416666
Fax: 01536 416171
E-mail: kpark@shireinns.co.uk

Telephone for further details

MARSTON TRUSSELL, **The Sun Inn** ❀

Smartly renovated hotel with elegant restaurant serving traditional country inn food. Expect melon cocktail or chicken liver parfait, then stir-fry chicken, vegetable lasagne, and roast rack of lamb, followed by bread and butter pudding and chocolate mousse.

Additional: Children welcome
Style: Traditional/Country-house
Smoking: No-smoking area
Accommodation: 20 en suite ★★

Directions: Off A4304, between the villages of Lubenham & Theddingworth

Main Street LE16 9TY
Map 4: SP68
Tel: 01858 465531
Fax: 01858 433155
E-mail: manager@suninn.com
Cost: Alc fr £15, set-price L fr £5.95. ☺ H/wine £10.95
Times: Noon-2pm/7-9.30pm

NORTHAMPTON,

Northampton Marriott

One dining room overlooks the lake and another has an authentic Italian feel. Choose grilled sirloin steak finished with a Diane sauce, or alternatively ravioli filled with asparagus and a mushroom and cream sauce.

Additional: Bar food; Sunday L (noon-2pm); Children welcome
Style: Classic/Formal
Smoking: No-smoking area; Air conditioning
Civil licence: 180
Accommodation: 120 en suite ★★★★

Directions: M1 J15, follow A508 then A45 (Wellingborough). L at roundabout signposted Delapre Golf Complex. Hotel on R

Eagle Drive NN4 7HW
Map 4: SP76
Tel: 01604 768700
Fax: 01604 769011
E-mail:
northampton@swallowhotels.co. uk
Cost: Alc £34, set-price L £15.25/D £22.75. ☺ H/wine £12.25
Times: D only, 7-9.30pm.
Closed Mon

ROADE,

Roade House Restaurant

'Heavingly busy' at an autumn inspection, but service was friendly and attentive nonetheless. A main course of cod with lentils and salsa verde impressed with the freshness of the fish and the 'lovely savoury stew' of the lentils.

Additional: Sunday L; Children welcome; Vegetarian dishes not always available
Style: Classic/Informal
Smoking: No smoking in dining room; Air conditioning

Directions: M1/J15 (A508 Milton Keynes) to Roade, L at mini-roundabout, 500yds on L

16 High Street NN7 2NW
Map 4: SP75
Tel: 01604 863372
Fax: 01604 862421
Cost: Alc £27, set-price L £17. ☺ H/wine £11
Times: 12.30-2pm/7-10pm.
Closed L Sat & Mon, D Sun

STOKE BRUERNE,

Bruerne's Lock Restaurant

Pretty red brick restaurant overlooking the canal. Start with tagliatelle with mussels, smoked bacon and thyme, followed perhaps by loin of monkfish in coconut milk, lime and ginger bouillon. Leave room for the sticky toffee pudding.

Directions: On A508 between Northampton & Milton Keynes

The Canalside Towcester NN12 7SB
Map 4: SP74
Tel: 01604 863654
Fax: 01604 863330
E-mail: bruernes_lock@msn.com
Cost: Alc £28, set-price L/D £17. ☺ H/wine £12
Times: 12.15-2pm/7.15-9.30pm.
Closed L Sat, D Sun, all Mon, 1st wk Jan, 1 wk Oct
Additional: Bar food L; Sunday L; Children welcome; Vegetarian dishes on request
Style: Classic/Formal
Smoking: No smoking in dining room

TOWCESTER,

Vine House Restaurant

Mellow limestone building, dating from the 16th century, with immaculate gardens and a subtly lit and comfortably furnished interior. Julie Springett presides over the front of house assisted by an obliging team of young staff. Marcus Springett's cooking is broadly modern British, but French and Oriental influences are apparent. A sensible menu, with four dishes at each course, ensures quality and consistency. Starters on offer included poached asparagus with garlic and nettle purée dribbled with olive oil, and salmon fishcakes with a melt-in-the-mouth brown crust and a tangy tomato butter sauce. A main course of maize-fed chicken jambonette demonstrated impressive technical skill. Chicken thighs, with a great natural flavour, were filled with garlic, shallot and herb duxelle, wrapped in bacon and roasted. The dish was served with bread sauce, truffle sauce and home-made chips. For a luscious dessert try floating island meringue with poached strawberries.

100 High Street Paulerspury
NN12 7NA
Map 4: SP64
Tel: 01327 811267
Fax: 01327 811309
Chef: Marcus Springett
Owners: Marcus & Julie Springett
Cost: Set-price L /D£24.95. ☺
H/wine £11.95
Times: 12.30-1.45pm/D 7.30-10pm.
Closed L Sat-Wed, all Sun, 2 wks after Xmas
Additional: Children welcome; Vegetarian dishes not always available
Seats: 45. Private dining room 11
Style: Informal/Traditional
Smoking: No smoking in dining room

Directions: 2 miles S of Towcester, just off A5

NORTHUMBERLAND

BAMBURGH,

Victoria Hotel

A vibrant modern brasserie with conservatory roof, and similarly upbeat food. Smoked haddock fishcakes with sweet red pepper coulis was spot on, and lamb shank with petit pois and rosemary jus very tender. Crème brûlée was immaculate.

Front Street NE69 7BP
Map 12: NU13
Tel: 01668 214431
Fax: 01668 214404

Telephone for further details.

Directions: Turn of A1, N of Alnwick onto B1342, follow signs to Bamburgh. Hotel opposite village green

BELLINGHAM,

Riverdale Hall Hotel

The cosy restaurant of this Victorian country hotel offers simple, well constructed dishes that get the very best out of fresh ingredients. The fresh fish dishes regularly on offer are partculary tempting.

NE48 2JT
Map 12: NY88
Tel: 01434 220254
Fax: 01434 220457
E-mail:
iben@riverdalehall.demon.co.uk

Cost: Alc £17.50, set-price L £9.95/D £19.95. ☺ H/wine £8.90
Times: Noon-2.30pm/6.45-9.15pm
Additional: Bar food; Sunday L; Children welcome
Style: Informal/Country-house
Smoking: No-smoking area; No pipes & cigars
Accommodation: 20 en suite ★ ★

Directions: Turn off B6320, after bridge, hotel on L

BERWICK-UPON-TWEED,
Marshall Meadows Hotel

The main hotel restaurant in this stately Georgian mansion is strong on classical French and modern British cuisine, with the occasional local touch such as baked fillet of lamb in a Holy Island Mead Wine and honey mustard sauce.

TD15 1UT
Map 12: NT95
Tel: 01289 331133
Fax: 01289 331438
E-mail: stay@marshallmeadows.co.uk

Cost: Alc £22, set-price L £7.90/D £22. ☺ H/wine £8.90
Times: Noon-2pm/6.30-9.30pm
Additional: Bar food L; Sunday L; Children welcome
Style: Country-house
Smoking: No smoking in dining room
Civil licence: 180
Accommodation: 19 en suite ★ ★ ★

Directions: Just off A1 N of Berwick

BLANCHLAND,
Lord Crewe Arms Hotel

Flagstone floors and vaulted ceilings in a historic building. Tempting traditional dishes might include roast quail followed by red deer or fish of the day. Try the delicious plum and almond tart for dessert.

Nr Consett DH8 9SP
Map 12: NY95
Tel: 01434 675251
Fax: 01434 675337

E-mail: lord@crewearms.freeserve.co.uk

Telephone for further details

Directions: 10 miles South of Hexham on B6306

CHOLLERFORD,
Swallow George Hotel ❀❀

Large windows in this two-tiered restaurant permit the enjoyment of panoramic views over the garden, the countryside, and the River Tyne. Built where the old Roman road crosses the river, the hotel is strong on hospitality and comfort, and secure in the execution of fine classical cooking. The short set-price lunch and dinner menus are supplemented by an equally short *carte*. Lobster cooked to your liking and a variety of grills further extend the choice. Typical evening starters might be rillette of pea and ham with pickled beetroot, or duck liver parfait with toasted brioche. Moving on through the courses, the choice could include salmon retsina with a tomato and onion salad, pan-fried fillet of hake with asparagus, or pot-roasted baby chicken with a bacon and shallot sauce. Sample some of the classic desserts: vanilla crème brûlée with seasonal berries and a peanut cookie, raspberry cheesecake with a fresh raspberry coulis, or quenelle of vanilla Mascarpone with a strawberry salad. For a more sophisticated experience try warm salad of quail with truffle dressing from the *carte*, and turbot rossini.

Hexham NE46 4EW
Map 12: NY96
Tel: 01434 681611
Fax: 01434 681727
Chef: Paul Montgomery
Cost: Alc £35, set-price L £15/D £25.95. ☺ H/wine £12.50
Times: Noon-2pm/6.30-9.30pm
Additional: Bar food L; Sunday L; Children welcome
Seats: 80
Style: Country-house
Smoking: No smoking in dining room
Civil licence: 50
Accommodation: 47 en suite ★ ★ ★

Directions: From A6079 take B6318. 400 yds on opposite side of river

CORNHILL-ON-TWEED,
Tillmouth Park Hotel ❀

A magnificent mansion with wood-panelled library dining room overlooking floodlit parkland. Dishes change daily, from perhaps roasted loin of tuna, crisp caponata and tomato sauce, to trio of lamb cutlets, braised red cabbage, crisp polenta and red currant.

Additional: Sunday L (noon-2pm); Children welcome
Style: Classic/country house
Civil licence: 60
Accommodation: 14 en suite

Directions: On A693, 3 miles E of Cornhill-on-Tweed rdbt on A1(M)

TD12 4UU
Map 12: NT83
Tel: 01890 882255
Fax: 01890 882540
E-mail: reception@tillmouthpark.f9.co.uk
Cost: Alc £22.48, set-price L £7.50/D £26. ☺ H/wine £10.50
Times: D only, 7-8.45pm

HEXHAM,
De Vere Slaley Hall ❀

Fairways Brasserie is a striking room with interesting pictures and topiary trees. Dishes sampled include roasted cod steak with bacon and Welsh rarebit, and poached pear with Mascarpone brioche tart.

Additional: Sunday L (12.45-2pm); Children welcome
Style: Informal/modern
Civil licence: 250
Accommodation: 139 en suite ★ ★ ★ ★

Directions: From A69 take A68 towards Darlington, follow signs to Slaley Hall

Slaley NE47 0BY
Map 12: NY96
Tel: 01434 673350
Fax: 01434 673152
E-mail: slaley.hall@devere-hotels.com
Cost: Alc £25, set-price D £23.50. ☺ H/wine £12.95
Times: D only, 7-10pm

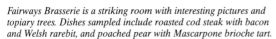

NOTTINGHAMSHIRE

LANGAR, Langar Hall ❀

NG13 9HG
Map 8: SK73
Tel: 01949 860559
Fax: 01949 861045
E-mail: langarhall-hotel@ndirect.co.uk
Cost: Alc £30, set-price L £10/D £17.50. ☺ H/wine £10.50
Times: Noon-3pm/7-9pm
Additional: Sunday L; Children welcome
Style: Country-house
Smoking: No smoking in dining room
Civil licence: 40
Accommodation: 10 en suite ★ ★

Wonderful country house in a parkland setting, with an abundance of antiques and memorabilia. The menu is English – rabbit and ham terrine, seared lemon sole – with a commendable wine list.

Directions: Off A46 and A52, in village centre (behind church)

NETHER LANGWITH,
Goff's Restaurant ❀

Langwith Millhouse Mansfield
NG20 9JF
Map 8: SK57
Tel: 01623 744538
Fax: 01623 747953
E-mail:
goodfood@goffs60.freeserve.co.uk
Cost: Set-price L £16.50/D £35.
H/wine £10.50
Times: Noon-3pm/7-midnight. Closed
L Sat, all Mon & Tue, 1 wk Jan, Bhs
Additional: Sunday L; Children
welcome
Style: Informal/Country-house
Smoking: No-smoking area

An 18th-century mill house in attractive grounds next to a former cotton mill. Seafood ramekin was followed by oriental-style duck breast fanned onto a bed of fresh noodles.

Directions: Telephone for directions

NOTTINGHAM,
Hart's Restaurant ❀❀❀

1 Standard Court Park Row
NG1 6GN
Map 8: SK53
Tel: 0115 9110666
Fax: 0115 9110611
Chef: Mark Gough
Owner: Tim Hart
Times: Noon-2pm/7-10.30pm
Additional: Sunday L; Children
welcome
Seats: Private dining room 14
Style: Modern
Smoking: No-smoking area; No pipes
& cigars; Air conditioning

Fashioned from the shell of an old hospital, Hart's Restaurant is light, bright and airy. Paintings on the wall are original modern works of geometric style, the floorboards are polished and the plain wooden tables are well spaced, allowing full appreciation of the chic, comfortable ambience. A good range of dishes on the *carte* is complemented by a small set-price option. On a recent visit the inspector opted for the freedom of the former and was very pleased with the result. The meal began with a delightful ciabatta roll served piping hot, the thin crispy outer shell contrasting well with the moist fluffy interior. Grilled baby squid with spiced tomatoes was ordered as a starter – sounds simple enough but when it arrived it was a lot more complex and interesting than expected. The first surprise was a well seasoned and nicely made mash flavoured with basil and a hint of garlic which worked well as a base for the gently grilled tender squid to sit on. A second surprise of two small chorizo sausages rendered the whole dish 'vibrant and funky'.

No more surprises in the main course of monkfish with a herb crust and saffron pasta, and the dessert of lemon tart – just careful, modern cooking of exceptional vitality and flavour. *Best Short Wine List (see pages 18-19).*

Directions: Follow signs for Castle and from Maid Marian Way take last L after Casino into Park Row. At top turn L into site of old General Hospital

NOTTINGHAM,

Merchants Restaurant ❀

Contemporary, relaxing restaurant. The brasserie-style cooking produces excellent breads – walnut, tomato – and an enjoyable tiger prawn linguini. Spinach tossed with caramelised red onions made a terrific side dish. Dessert – jam roly poly with custard.

Cost: *Alc* £22, set-price L £14.50/D £16.50. ☺ H/wine £9.95.
Times: Noon-2.30pm/6.30-10.30pm. Closed L Sat, D Sun, 25 Dec
Additional: Bar food L; Sunday L; Children welcome
Seats: 70. Private dining room 20
Style: Chic/Modern
Smoking: Air conditioning

29-31 High Pavement
The Lace Market NG1 1HE
Map 8: SK54
Tel: 0115 9589898
Fax: 0115 9414322
E-mail: admin@lacemarkethotel.co.uk
Chef: Dean Rogers
Owner: Lace Market Hotel Ltd

Directions: Follow town centre signs for Galleries of Justice. Entrance is opposite

NOTTINGHAM,

Sonny's ❀❀

Not so much minimalist as just simple in style, Sonny's is a predominantly white space with lots of artwork. The attractions are attentive and friendly service, a compact but interesting wine list, with about a dozen by the glass, and a menu as up-to-date as its surroundings. Tender venison carpaccio with fig chutney, smoked trout with horseradish rösti, pea and mint risotto, and cod wrapped in prosciutto with a tapenade dressing set the tone. Sirloin steak with Stilton butter sits alongside a modern take on fish and chips in the form of rare tuna steak with a pile of rocket and smoked chilli oil and a side order of the thinnest of pommes frites. Desserts tend to be rich, from treacle tart with clotted cream ice cream, to baked chocolate pudding with fudge sauce and custard, although there is also Colston Bassett Stilton with apple chutney and oatcakes.

Additional: Sunday L; Children welcome
Seats: 80
Style: Informal/minimalist
Smoking: No pipes & cigars; Air conditioning

3 Carlton Street Hockley
NG1 1NL
Map 8: SK54
Tel: 0115 9473041
Fax: 0115 9507776
Chef: David Hodgins
Owner: Rebecca Mascarenhas
Cost: *Alc* £25, set-price L £10. ☺
H/wine £8.95.
Times: Noon-2.30pm/7-11pm.
Closed Bhs

Directions: City centre, close to Market Square and Victoria Centre

OXFORDSHIRE

BANBURY, **Wroxton House Hotel** ❀

Converted from three 17th-century cottages, the restaurant here offers an appetising selection of dishes to suit most palates, including pan-fried pavé of venison, and seared duo of Welsh lamb cannon and cutlet, with winter fruit soup to end.

Smoking: No smoking in dining room; Jacket & tie preferred
Civil licence: 40 **Accommodation:** 32 en suite ★★★

Directions: From M40/J11 take A422 towards Stratford-upon-Avon. Hotel in 3 miles on A422

Wroxton St Mary OX15 6QB
Map 4: SP44
Tel: 01295 730777
Fax: 01295 730800
E-mail: wroxtonhse@aol.com
Cost: A/c £38, set-price L £12.95/D £26. ☺ H/wine £12
Times: Noon-2pm/7-9.30pm
Additional: Bar food; Sunday L; Children 12+
Style: Classic/Country-house

BICESTER,
Bignell Park Hotel ❀

Chesterton OX6 8UE
Map 04: SP52
Tel: 01869 241444/241192
Fax: 01869 241444

Telephone for further details

Directions: On A4095, Witney road

A dramatic galleried restaurant in a charming hotel, with fine artwork, beams and fireplace. The classy cooking produces the likes of goats' cheese ravioli and red pepper coulis, and excellent breast and confit leg of duck.

BLEWBURY, **Blewbury Inn** ❀❀

London Road OX11 9PD
Map 4: SU58
Tel: 01235 850496
Chef: Franck Pèigne
Owners: Franck & Kalpana Pèigne
Cost: A/c £20.25, set-price D £15 ‾ H/wine £10
Times: Noon-3pm/6-11pm. Closed D Sun, L Mon; D 25 Dec
Additional: Bar food L, Sunday L
Seats: 24
Smoking: No smoking in dining room
Style: Bistro-style/Country-house

Modest but appealing white-painted pub on the edge of Blewbury, a rambling village nestling beneath the Oxfordshire

Downs. Homely interior comprising two rooms, one a traditionally furnished bar (set for a 'modern' makeover), the other an intimate restaurant featuring an eclectic mix of furnishings and a relaxing atmosphere. Chef/patron, Franck Pèigne, offers a short list of seasonally-changing dishes, with a distinct Gallic flavour reflecting his Brittany origins, on the evening *carte*; lighter lunchtime food is simpler. The interesting, often adventurous, evening dishes make good use of fresh local ingredients. Follow a terrine of lobster and seafood, served on good leaves dressed in basil oil with smoked mussels and artichoke, or a summer vegetable soup infused with pesto, with sea bass on a spinach fondue with tempura king prawns and a cider and coriander butter, or a perfectly cooked shoulder of lamb with provençale vegetables and a rosemary and marjoram jus. Round off with a smooth white chocolate mousse, well presented with a pear poached in star anise and vanilla syrup.

Directions: On A417 between Wantage and Reading

BRITWELL SALOME,
The Goose NEW

A very handy lunch stop from the M40, and a brilliant dinner destination for some very good food in an easy going country-pub setting. Modern ideas range from chump of lamb with gratin of spinach and boulangère potatoes to an updated pork pie with apple and pear chutney.

Additional: Bar food L; Sunday L; Children welcome
Style: informal/modern
Smoking: No smoking in dining room

Directions: M40 J6 take B4009 to Watlington and on towards Benson. Pub on R, 1.5 miles

OX9 5LG
Map 4: SU69
Tel: 01491 612304
Fax: 01491 614822
E-mail:
barber@thegoose.freeserve.co.uk
Cost: *Alc* £27 (L only); set-price D
£20.25. ☺ H/wine £10.50
Times: Noon-3pm/7-11pm. Closed D
Sun, all Mon, 1st 2 wks Jan

BURFORD, The Bay Tree 🏵

12-14 Sheep Street OX18 4LW
Map 4: SP21
Tel: 01993 822791
Fax: 01993 823008

Telephone for further details

Historic house whose restaurant overlooks a walled garden. Typical dishes include twice-baked smoked goats' cheese soufflé and roasted fillet of beef, pork or lamb. Imaginative desserts might include praline and mint mousse with a pomegranate salsa.

Directions: Sheep St off main street in centre of Burford

BURFORD,
Cotswold Gateway Hotel ❀

OX18 4HX
Map 4: SP21
Tel: 01993 822695
Fax: 01993 823600
E-mail: cotswold-gateway@dial.pipex.com

Telephone for further details

Directions: On A40 at Burford, top of hill by roundabout

The varied menu features Portabella mushrooms with goats' cheese and tomatoes to start with, salmon in a dill and white wine sauce or beef forestière to follow, and finally chocolate truffle torte with a raspberry coulis.

BURFORD,
The Inn For All Seasons ❀

The Barringtons OX18 4TN
Map 4: SP21
Tel: 01451 844324
Fax: 01451 844375
E-mail: sharp@innforallseasons. com
Cost: *Alc* £17.50. ☺ H/wine £9.95
Times: 11.30-2.30pm/6.30-9.30pm
Additional: Bar Food; Sunday L; Children welcome
Style: Rustic/Traditional
Smoking: No pipes & cigars
Accommodation: 10 en suite ★ ★ ★

Directions: On A40 at The Barringtons, 3 miles from Burford & 17 miles from Cheltenham

A 16th-century coaching inn with log fires and stone walls. French-influenced fare includes roulade of free-range chicken, and pot-roasted shank of Cotswold lamb on a rich red wine sauce.

BURFORD,
Jonathan's at the Angel ❀

Lovely Cotswold cottage comprising a bar and two restaurant areas with beams, stripped floors and open fires. High praise for the fish soup, and caramelised pork belly with mustard mash.

Style: Informal/brasserie
Smoking: No smoking in dining room
Accommodation: 3 en suite

Directions: From A40, turn off at Burford rdbt, down hill 1st R into Swan Lane, 1st L to Pytts Lane, L at end into Witney Street

14 Witney Street OX18 4SN
Map 4: SP21
Tel: 01993 822714
Fax: 01993 822069
E-mail: jo@theangel-uk.com
Cost: *Alc* £18.50. ☺ H/wine £12.75
Times: Noon-2pm/7-9.30pm.
Closed L Tues & Weds, D Sun, all Mon, 20 Jan-9 Feb
Additional: Sunday L; Children 9+

BURFORD, **The Lamb Inn**

Lovely 15th-century inn, built of Cotswold stone, with flagstone floors, log fires and gleaming antiques. In fine weather pre-dinner drinks or light lunches can be taken in the pretty cottage garden to the rear. The restaurant is elegant and subtly understated, with crisp white linen and silver candlesticks, and service is professional and friendly. An imaginative range of British dishes with a French influence is offered from a daily dinner menu, priced for two or three courses. From a choice of seven starters, expect the likes of smoked chicken and Parma ham risotto with Mozzarella, or a Pithivier of smoked trout and horseradish with vermouth and cream. The five mains might range from fillet of sea bass with roasted baby fennel and red pepper cream, to roast partridge on cranberry and pear compote, juniper berry jus and game chips.

Sheep Street OX18 4LR
Map 4: SP21
Tel: 01993 823155
Fax: 01993 822228
Chef: Pascal Clavaud
Owners: Richard & Caroline De Wolf
Cost: Set-price D £25. ☺ H/wine £10
Times: D only, 7-9pm.
Closed 25 & 26 Dec
Additional: Bar food L; Sunday L
(12.30-1.45pm)
Seats: 50
Style: Classic/Traditional
Smoking: No smoking in dining room
Accommodation: 15 en suite ★ ★ ★

Directions: 1st L as you descend the High Street

CHALGROVE,
Red Lion Inn

Well-maintained traditional inn fronted by a small brook in the heart of the village. The menu is imaginative – dishes like seafood tagliatelle with garlic and white wine make this eatery popular with the locals.

OX44 7SS
Map 4: SU69
Tel: 01865 890625
Fax: 01865 890795
Cost: *Alc* £16.50, set-price L /D
£12.50. ☺ H/wine £9.50
Times: Noon-3pm/7-11.30pm.
Closed D Sun, 25 Dec
Additional: Bar food; Sunday L;
Children welcome
Style: Rustic/Traditional
Smoking: No smoking in dining room

Directions: From M40 J6 to Watlington, R onto B480 towards Stadhampton. 200yds fork R signed Cuxham. 3.5m turn L into Chalgrove. Inn in village centre.

CHINNOR,
Sir Charles Napier

Consistently good food, a great wine list with something for everyone, a peaceful setting amid seven acres of lovely gardens and meadows, and a relaxed and informal atmosphere are what seduce people at this pub-restaurant. If furniture is mismatched, that's the intention. Fish is a strong suit on the handwritten menus – bouillabaisse with saffron potatoes, crispy oriental salmon with stir-fried vegetables – and game crops up in season: perhaps roast partridge with celeriac purée and quince. If a rustic note is hit by such dishes as braised oxtail

Spriggs Alley OX9 4BX
Map 4: SP70
Tel: 01494 483011
Fax: 01494 485311
Chef: José Cau
Owner: Julie Griffiths
Cost: *Alc* £27.50, set-price L
£14.50/D £15.50. ☺ H/wine £12.50
Times: Noon-2.30pm (3.30pm Sun)/7-10pm. Closed D Sun, all Mon, 25 & 26 Dec

with a confit of potatoes and shallots, this is counterbalanced by the refinements of crab ravioli, or soufflé suissesse. Top-drawer produce is impeccably handled. Ribeye of beef, for instance, is 'perfectly cooked rare' and served on smooth cauliflower purée surrounded by sautéed cubes of swede, complemented by a deeply-flavoured red wine reduction. Bread-and-butter pudding has been declared 'most delicious', and a good crop of English cheeses are all in excellent condition.

Additional: Bar food L; Children 7+ at D
Seats: 75. Private room 40
Smoking: No-smoking area

Directions: M40 J6 follow signs to Chinnor. In Chinnor turn R at roundabout. Up hill to Spriggs Alley

CHIPPING NORTON,

Chavignol ❀❀❀

The beamed restaurant is on two floors, painted in sunny yellow and blue, with a jazzy-looking menu of Miro-like colours and bold shapes. If you've an hour to spare, drool over the wine list, which features super fine wines from all over the world, but there's also a good range at under £25. It is also difficult to exercise restraint when faced with whole oven-fresh loaves and Echiré butter. First course creamy skate and grain mustard mousse in a timbale layered with tomato fondue was a super combination, served with contrasting skate beignet and a tomato vinaigrette. Even more impressive, both in taste and presentation, was poached duck egg glazed with hollandaise on buttered spinach set in a globe artichoke with deep-fried herring roe, baby beetroots and beetroot and chive dressing. The relatively simpler concept of pan-fried duck topped with sautéed foie gras set on mushy pea with rösti potatoes and a light caramelised sherry vinegar sauce was also extremely well prepared. The assiette of desserts would easily serve three.

7 Horsefair OX7 5AL
Map 4: SP32
Tel/Fax: 01608 644490
Chef: Marcus F Ashenford
Owners: Mark & Donna Maguire
Cost: Alc £38, set-price L £25/D £48. H/wine £13
Times: 12.30-2pm/7-10pm. Closed Sun & Mon, 3 wks Jan
Additional: Children welcome
Seats: 28. Private dining room 10
Style: Chic/Rustic
Smoking: No smoking in dining room

Directions: On Banbury side of main Chipping Norton road

CLANFIELD,

Plough at Clanfield ❀❀

Characterful Elizabethan manor house where a professional yet unstuffy atmosphere prevails throughout. The decor is traditional with white and pink linens, well spaced tables and padded leather menus. The cooking is predominantly English and French and makes good use of seasonal, fresh ingredients. A lovely well-balanced flavour in a haddock, potato and chive soup made for a memorable start to a recent meal. Pigeon breast with wild mushrooms, bacon, couscous and pistachios followed and a nicely presented if white chocolate mousse with baby figs closed proceedings. An alternative meal might begin with seared scallops with a Keta caviar, followed by fillet of Aberdeen Angus beef and concluding with an iced red currant and Grand Marnier parfait. Good homemade chocolates accompany decent cafetière coffee for the postprandial come-down.

Bourton Road OX18 2RB
Map 4: SP20
Tel: 01367 810222
Fax: 01367 810596
E-mail: ploughatclanfield@hotmail.com
Chef: Rosemary Hodges
Owners: Mr & Mrs J C Hodges
Cost: Alc £32.50, set-price L £17.75/D £32.50
Times: 12.15-2pm/7-9.30pm. Closed 26 -29 Dec
Additional: Bar food L; Sunday L; Children 12+
Seats: 35. Private dining room 10
Style: Traditional/Country-house
Smoking: No smoking in dining room
Accommodation: 6 en suite ★ ★ ★

Directions: On junct of B4020 & A4095 between Faringdon & Witney

DEDDINGTON,
Dexters Restaurant ❀❀

Jamie Dexter Harrison has moved this restaurant across the square into larger premises. The ground floor is mainly given over to a bar where a huge piece of rough-hewn wood forms the bar top, contrasting with the vibrant blue and green acrylic table tops. The crisp A4 daily menu is in keeping with the modern interior. The *carte* is littered with fashionable dishes such as crispy duck salad with hoi sin and string vegetables, Thai fish cakes and chargrilled vegetables and goats' cheese tart. The cooking is more than competent and the duck salad was a real hit with tender pieces of duck. Two smallish fishcakes were full of flavour, with lots of white fish, and coriander successfully married to a chilli salsa and a light lime mayonnaise. The wild sea bass on a ratatouille sauce with basil oil and Modena vinegar was also well-balanced. For dessert, a chocolate parfait with apricots marinated in chardonnay. The concise wine list is reasonably priced.

Directions: Village centre, A4260 from Banbury; L at lights

Market Place OX15 0SE
Map 4: SP43
Tel: 01869 338813
Chef: Jamie Dexter Harrison
Owners: J D Harrison, R Blackburn
Cost: *Alc* £26.50, set-price L & D £15.50 & £19.50. ☺ H/wine £11.50
Times: Noon-2.15pm/7-9.15pm. Closed Sun & Mon
Additional: Bar food L
Seats: 60
Style: Informal/Modern
Smoking: No pipes & cigars

DORCHESTER-ON-THAMES,
George Hotel ❀

Beamed restaurant in a historic hotel. Fresh produce features and dishes are well presented – scallops with baby leeks on puy lentils, and lamb with borlotti beans and mint-scented jus.

Additional: Bar food; Sunday L; Children welcome
Style: Traditional/Country-house
Smoking: No smoking in dining room
Accommodation: 18 en suite ★ ★ ★

Directions: In town centre

High Street OX10 7HH
Map 4: SU59
Tel: 01865 340404
Fax: 01865 341620
Cost: *Alc* £29.50. ☺ H/wine £9.10
Times: Noon-2.15pm/7-9.30pm

DORCHESTER-ON-THAMES,
White Hart Hotel ❀

Charming historic inn in the village centre. A summer meal began with 'nicely tender' sautéed squid, followed by pan-fried salmon on a bed of vegetable spaghetti. Strawberry and peach crumble was well flavoured.

Additonal: Bar food; Sunday L; Children welcome
Style: Informal/Chic
Smoking: No smoking in the dining room
Accommodation: 19 en suite ★ ★

Directions: Just off A415/A4074

High Street OX10 7HN
Map 4: SU59
Tel: 01865 340074
Fax: 01865 341082
E-mail: whitehart.dorchester@virgin.net
Cost: *Alc* £20, set-price L £7.50. ☺ H/wine £9.95
Times: Noon-2.30pm/6.30-9.30pm

EYNSHAM,
Off the Square ❀❀

Behind a surprisingly deceptive exterior and concealed in a narrow side street is this really pretty restaurant. The flair and

Lombard Street OX8 1HT
Map 4: SP40
Tel: 01865 881888
Fax: 01865 883537

professionalism of Christian Butler in front of house ensures a smooth beginning to any meal, and the distinguished cooking along modern British lines leaves little to be desired. In these assured and very pleasant conditions a recent inspection lunch was reported to be 'a treat', the chicken liver and foie gras parfait starter having a softly subtle flavour and the accompanying fig chutney tasting quite delicious. The calves' liver main dish was perfectly seared, and placed on caramelised onion with excellent creamy mash and a Madeira jus. A dessert of Pavlova with freshly poached strawberries and raspberries served with crème de framboise coulis brought forth ecstatic comments which were not dulled by the espresso coffee. The short menus work very well, and some recommended dinner choices include seared foie gras lobster salad, followed by pan-fried halibut on a shellfish risotto with a velouté of oysters, or perhaps roasted veal sweetbreads wrapped in prosciutto with a cappuccino of mushrooms.

Directions: From Oxford take A40 towards Cheltenham. Follow signs for 'Eynsham village only', at T-junction , Lombard Street isstraight ahead

Chef: Philip Baker
Owner: Martin Richards
Cost: Set-price L £19.50/D £31. ☺
H/wine £15
Times: Noon-2.30pm/7-9.30pm.
Closed D Sun, all Mon, 1st 2 wks Jan
Additional: Sunday L; Children welcome
Seats: 35. Private dining room 12
Style: Chic/Formal
Smoking: No pipes & cigars

FARINGDON,
The Lamb at Buckland

Buckland SN7 8QN
Map 4: SU29

Tel: 01367 870484
Fax: 01367 870675
Cost: Alc £25. ☺ H/wine £9.95
Times: Noon-2pm/6.30-9.30pm.
Closed 25 & 26 Dec

Traditional country pub where simplicity, freshness and accuracy make for high quality cuisine. An extensive wine list ensures compatibility with dishes in the vein of lobster and shellfish fricassée, or roast grouse with all the traditional accompaniments.

Additional: Bar food; Sunday L; Children welcome
Style: Informal
Smoking: No smoking in dining room

Directions: Midway between Oxford & Swindon on A420, 4 miles E of Faringdon

---

FARINGDON,
Sudbury House Hotel **NEW**

London Street SN7 8AA
Map 4: SU29
Tel: 01367 241272
Fax: 01367 242346
E-mail: sundburyhouse@cix.co.uk

Impressive pillars and a grand piano are features of the restaurant. Vibrant vegetables accompanied accurately cooked fillet of salmon, followed by an excellent lemon meringue pie from the dessert trolley.

Directions: Off A420 signposted Folly Hill

Telephone for further details

GORING, # The Leatherne Bottel ❀❀

RG8 0HS
Map 4: SU68
Tel: 01491 872667
Fax: 01491 875308
E-mail: leathernebottel@aol.com
Chef: Julia Storey
Owner: Annie Bonnet
Cost: Alc £35, set-price D £19.50. ☺
H/wine £14.50
Times: Noon-2pm/7-9pm.
Closed D Sun, 25 Dec
Seats: 45

This idiosyncratic riverside restaurant can be found down a twisty country lane. There is plenty of seating on the terrace for outside dining, and the interior of this cottagey building has cosy rooms with modern art on the walls. A cheaper lunch menu has been introduced and a set-price evening menu Monday to Friday, which changes every month. Dishes range from the relatively straightforward to the more adventurous; from large flat mushrooms on black olive toast and blackened salmon, char-grilled with cucumber and yoghurt to cassoulet of flageolet beans and peas tossed with lemon balm and mint,

The Leatherne Bottel

Seats: 45
Style: Traditional
Smoking: No pipes

served with lambs' tongues flavoured with horseradish and ginger and roast suckling pig with coriander, galangal, chilli and lemon, sage and onion bhajis and sweet and sour sauce. Desserts are good and there is a well chosen predominantly French wine list.

Directions: M4 J12 or M40 J6, signed from B4009 Goring-Wallingford

GREAT MILTON, Le Manoir Aux Quat Saisons ❀❀❀❀❀

As ravishing as ever, with an organic kitchen garden to die for, but following a multi-million pound refurbishment, they've chucked out the chintz and gone for a lighter, more modern look. The cooking, however, under the impressive direction of new Head Chef, Gary Jones, does not rest on its laurels. Reading the *carte* provides the ultimate lesson in how stunning, high quality ingredients, cooked with respect, need little in the way of pretentious extras: roast suckling pig with marjoram-scented jus; steak of turbot poached in milk and cloves, spring vegetables and morel sauce. Details – imaginative canapés, the simplicity of an appetiser of softly marinated salmon with spring leaves and herb dressings, a lavish assembly of finely crafted petits fours – all speak of a kitchen under tight but inspired control. A starter of langoustine ravioli made from saffron infused pasta was served with its own bisque, simply an unadulterated nage of the crushed bones, the slightest hint of tomato and the refreshing background and depth of finely cut vegetables and seasonings. A dish of profound honesty that needed no technical sleight of hand. The challenge of our main course – pan-fried squid, red mullet, salt cod brandade and 'oscietra gold' caviar – was to harmoniously draw together the four contrasting main ingredients. Despite minor flaws, every forkful is a reminder that this kitchen truly lets the food do the talking. The French translation does not convey the true decadence that was a platter of chocolate, although in contrast to the earlier courses, the stunning techniques seemed to almost eclipse the ingredients. Battalions of skilled staff are on hand to provide highly professional and attentive service.

Directions: From M40 J7 follow A329 towards Wallingford. At 1 mile turn R, signposted Great Milton Manor

OX44 7PD
Map 4: SP60
Tel: 01844 278881
Fax: 01844 278847
E-mail: lemanoir@blanc.co.uk
Chef/Owner: Raymond Blanc
Cost: *Alc* £80, set-price L £32/D £79. H/wine £20
Times: 12.15-2.45pm/7.15-9.45pm
Additional: Sunday L; Children welcome
Seats: 120. Private dining room 55
Style: Modern/Country-house
Smoking: No smoking in dining room; Air conditioning
Civil licence: 55
Accommodation: 32 en suite ★ ★ ★ ★

AA Wine Shortlisted for Award-see page 18

HENLEY-ON-THAMES,
Red Lion Hotel 🏵🏵

As close as you can get to the Thames without wetting your feet, the front rooms of the 16th-century hotel offer fabulous views of the river, rowing clubs and famous regatta course. The cooking is confident and the kitchen is skilful and hardworking. Home-made vegetable tortellini were a delight to eat as a component in a main course of paupiettes of lemon sole with an accomplished fennel and chive cream sauce. Offal can be tricky, but our inspector happily polished off the first-course plate of lambs' kidneys, artichokes and cherry tomatoes in a filo basket. Apricot tart was much improved by a zingy, spiced fruit compote. The good-value set menu might include clear ham soup with pea fritters, followed by pork tenderloin with braised cabbage and sage butter sauce.

Hart Street RG9 2AR
Map 4: SU78
Tel: 01491 572161
Fax: 01491 410039
Chef: Stephen Fowler
Owners: The Miller family
Cost: *Alc* £26, set-price L & D £16.
☺ H/wine £12
Times: Noon-3pm/7-10.30pm
Additional: Bar food L; Sunday L; Children welcome
Seats: 35. Private dining rooms 8-80
Style: Traditional
Smoking: No pipes & cigars
Accommodation: 26 en suite ★ ★ ★

Directions: On the right when entering Henley by the bridge

HORTON-CUM-STUDLEY,
Studley Priory Hotel 🏵🏵

Nr Oxford OX33 1AZ
Map 4: SP51
Tel: 01865 351203
Fax: 01865 351613
E-mail: res@studley-priory.co.uk
Chef: Simon Grannage
Cost: *Alc* £40, set-price L £15/D £30.
H/wine £18
Times: 12.30-1.45pm/7.30-9.30pm
Additional: Bar Food L; Sunday L; Children welcome
Seats: 60. Private dining room 35
Style: Traditional/Country-house
Smoking: No smoking in dining room
Civil licence: 50
Accommodation: 18 en suite ★ ★ ★

An impressive Elizabethan manor house set in extensive grounds, offering an oasis of peace and tranquillity just six miles from the bustle of Oxford city centre. Originally a Benedictine nunnery, the building was extended following Henry VIII's dissolution of the monasteries. Today's elegant dining room, with its beamed ceiling, mullion windows and heavy drapes, overlooks the mature gardens. In contrast to the building's age, the menu offers diners imaginative and skilfully prepared modern English cuisine. Canapés are taken in the bar, while an *amuse-bouche* could feature a tempura of salmon on mixed leaves with chilli and lime dressing. One could open with English goats' cheese sausage – cheese wrapped in strips of steamed courgette and carrot – served with a tarte Tatin of cherry tomatoes and an asparagus cappuccino, perhaps move on to roasted turbot fillet resting on a crisp bacon and shallot rösti with well-balanced red wine and parsley butter sauce, and close with caramelised apple tart with custard ice and a pecan crumble crust. Coffee and petits fours complete the picture. Staff are predominantly French, friendly and professional.

Directions: At top of hill in the village

KINGHAM,

Mill House Hotel ☸

Chipping Norton
OX7 6UH
Map 4: SP22
Tel: 01608 658188
Fax: 01608 658492
E-mail: stay@millhouse-hotel.co.uk
Cost: Alc £27.75, set-price L
£13.95/D £22.75. ☺ H/wine £11.75
Times: Noon-2.30pm/7-9.30pm

Cotswold stone mill house, dating back to the Domesday Book of 1086, set in seven acres of gardens with its own trout stream. Dishes are carefully prepared from quality local produce.

Additional: Bar food; Sunday L; Children 5+
Style: Traditional/country-house
Smoking: No smoking in dining room; Jacket & tie preferred
Accommodation: 23 en suite ★★★

Directions: Clearly signed from B4450. On southern outskirts of Kingham village

MIDDLETON STONEY,

Jersey Arms Hotel ☸

Bicester OX6 8SE
Map 4: SP52
Tel: 01869 343234
Fax: 01869 343565
E-mail: jerseyarms@bestwestern.co.uk
Cost: Alc £21.60. ☺ H/wine £9.75
Times: Noon-2.15pm/6.30-9.30pm

Quiet, friendly hotel restaurant where historic beams and a village-inn atmosphere meet touch-of-the-Med terracotta and a cosmopolitan menu. Try duckling and Brie salad, or pan-seared salmon on peppers with a pesto dressing.

Additional: Bar food; Sunday L; Children welcome
Style: Informal
Smoking: No smoking in dining room
Accommodation: 20 en suite ★★

Directions: On B430, 3 miles from Bicester, 10 miles N of Oxford

MILTON COMMON,
The Oxford Belfry ❀

Benefiting from a recent major refurbishment the hotel restaurant is spacious and thoughtfully decorated. The dinner menu might include grilled fillet of red snapper served on a salad of baby corn, mussels and spring onions.

Additional: Bar food; Sunday L; Children welcome
Style: Classic/Country-house
Smoking: No smoking in dining room; Air conditioning
Civil licence: 400
Accommodation: 130 en suite ★★★★

Directions: From S: M40 J7. Top of slip road turn R, immediate L (50yds). From N: M40 J8a. Top of slip road turn 1st L after golf club. Take 1st R, hotel 1m on L

Nr Thame OX9 2JW
Map 4: SP60
Tel: 01844 279381
Fax: 01844 279624
E-mail: oxfordbelfry@marstonhotels.co.uk
Cost: Alc £30, set-price L £19.50/D £26. ☺ H/wine £13
Times: 12.30-2.30pm/7-9.30pm

OXFORD, **Bistro 20** ❀

Interesting upbeat brasserie feel enhanced by bold colours, friendly service and confident cooking. Try fillet of cod on spiced lentils, and a blasting cappuccino tiramisu with terrific flavour. Wonderful rye and olive breads come extra.

Directions: Telephone for directions

20 Magdalen Street OX1 3AE
Map 4: SP50
Tel: 01865 246555
Fax: 01865 204333

Telephone for further details

OXFORD,
Cotswold Lodge Hotel ❀

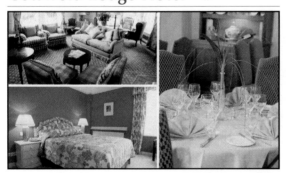

66a Banbury Road OX2 6JP
Map 4: SP50
Tel: 01865 512121
Fax: 01865 512490
Cost: Alc £35.50, set-price L £15.25/D £18.25. ☺ H/wine £14.95
Times: Noon-2.30pm/6.30-10pm

Elegant candlelit restaurant with a country house atmosphere, serving French and modern British cuisine – perhaps oak-smoked salmon, pan-fried guinea fowl with Pommery mustard sauce, and sticky toffee pudding.

Additional: Sunday L; Children 12+
Style: Informal/Country-house
Smoking: No pipes & cigars
Accommodation: 49 en suite ★★★

Directions: Take A4165 (Banbury Road) off A40 ring road, hotel 1.5m on left.

OXFORD, Fallowfields Country House Hotel ❀

Faringdon Road
Kingston Bagpuize
OX13 5BH
Map 4: SU49
Tel: 01865 820416
Fax: 01865 821275
Cost: *Alc* £31.50. H/wine £13.75
Times: 12.30-3pm/7-9.30pm.
Closed 25 & 26 Dec
Additional: Bar food; Sunday L;
Children 8+
Style: Classic/country-house
Smoking: No smoking in dining room
Civil licence: 100
Accommodation: 10 en suite ★ ★ ★

*Personally run, charming country house hotel offering a short menu
built around solid cooking skills. Marrow flower filled with scallop
and seafood mousse with dill cream sauce, and Gressingham duck
with potato and rosemary cake, roast beetroot and Marsala sauce
show the style.*

Directions: From A34 at Abingdon take A415 (Witney). At mini-
roundabout in Kingston Bagpuize turn L. Fallowfields is 1 mile
on L

OXFORD, Gee's Restaurant ❀❀ NEW

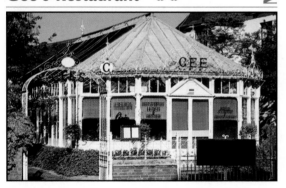

61 Banbury Road OX2 6PE
Map 4: SP50
Tel: 01865 553540
Fax: 01865 310308
E-mail: info@gees-restaurant.co.uk
Chef: Michael Wright
Owner: Jeremy Mogford
Cost: *Alc* £25, set-price L £9.50. ☺
H/wine £11
Times: Noon-2.30pm/6-11pm.
Closed 25 -26 Dec
Additional: Sunday L; Children
welcome
Seats: 75
Style: Informal/chic
Smoking: No smoking in dining room;
Air conditioning

Gee's was once a well-known greengrocer and florist and its
Victorian glass conservatory lends itself admirably to being a
restaurant. It has, in fact, been one for many years, but has
been given a new lease of life by Jeremy Mogford, owner of
the Old Parsonage Hotel a few minutes walk away. The
conservatory makes an airy, bright backdrop for some good
cooking, backed up by a short, buzzy wine list, and friendly
service. The menu covers a lot of ground, but has its heart in
the Mediterranean. A pair of inspectors worked their way
through rillettes of guinea fowl with beetroot jelly, and a
seafood risotto for starters, went on to a classic roast partridge
with roast carrots, red cabbage, fondant potatoes and Madeira
jus, as well as sea bass with mash and ratatouille, and finished

with a delicately set coffee pannacotta with brandied apricots, and a lovely pot-roast quince with clotted cream. But, having been stuck for choice, they tried an excellent passion fruit tart with blackcurrant sorbet for good measure; desserts are well recommended.

Directions: From ring road take Banbury Rd to city centre via Summertown. 1m on R after North Parade

OXFORD, Lemon Tree ❀❀

268 Woodstock Road OX2 7NW
Map 4: SP50
Tel/Fax: 01865 311936
Chef: Francois Nieto
Owner: Clinton Pugh
Cost: Alc £29. ☺ H/wine £9.95
Times: Noon-11pm. Closed Xmas & 1 Jan
Additional: Sunday L; Children welcome
Seats: 84
Style: Classic/Mediterranean
Civil licence: 150

Massive mirrors and glass openings in the roof create a feeling of space at the Lemon Tree, and small panes of blue glass send out cool beams of coloured light on sunny days – when people are more likely to be outside making the most of the garden. A black and white floor, ochre walls and twisted lights create a modern setting, and a globally inspired menu brings a touch of the modish to this stretch of the Woodstock Road. Mediterranean fish soup, and entrecôte of Aberdeen Angus with béarnaise sauce and chips are as mainstream as the kitchen gets, otherwise dealing in Mozzarella deep-fried in tempura with a salad of exotic fruits and chilli dressing, or a main course of roast lamb tournedos on a risotto of creamed tarragon and asparagus. Vegetarians get a good deal, from a mille-feuille of aubergine with goats' cheese and red pepper coulis to a 'harlequin' risotto with chargrilled asparagus and butternut squash in a passion fruit and mango sauce, while fish dishes might run to a starter of smoked salmon with coriander noodle salad and a main course of chargrilled loin of tuna fashionably coated in chermoula. A dab hand with pastry is responsible for puddings of lemon tart, or pineapple tarte Tatin, and there may also be poached pear glazed with Gorgonzola. France and Chile head up the punchy, international wine list.

Directions: From M40 J8 take A40 towards Oxford. At 3rd rdbt turn L into Woodstock Rd. Restaurant 0.75m on L

OXFORD, Liaison ❀

Well established, city centre Chinese restaurant, with some Thai and Vietnamese dishes. Main courses centre around roast duck, chicken or beef and there is an excellent range of dim sum.

Directions: Behind Westgate Centre & multi-storey car par

29 Castle Street OX1 1LJ
Map 4: SP50
Tel: 01865 242944

Telephone for further details

OXFORD, Old Bank Hotel

The restaurant, Quod, is located at the front of this impressive former bank. Cooking is Italian, offering the likes of risotto primavera, monkfish wrapped in bacon and a decent pannacotta.

Additional: Children welcome
Style: Bistro style/modern
Smoking: No-smoking area; Air conditioning
Accommodation: 43 en suite ★ ★ ★ ★

Directions: Approach city centre via Headington. Over Magdalen Bridge into High Street. Hotel 75yds on L

92-94 High Street OX1 4BN
Map 4: SP50
Tel: 01865 799599
Fax: 01865 799598
E-mail: quod@oldbank-hotel.co.uk
Cost: *Alc* £20, set-price L £8.75. ☺
H/wine £9.95
Times: 11am-11pm.
Closed 25 & 26 Dec

OXFORD, Le Petit Blanc ❀❀

71-72 Walton Street OX2 6AG
Map 4: SP50
Tel: 01865 510999
Fax: 01865 510700
Chef: Martin White
Owner: Raymond Blanc
Cost: *Alc* £25, set-price L & D £12.50
& £15. ☺ H/wine £9.95
Times: Noon-3pm (3.30pm Sat &
Sun)/6-11pm (10pm Sun).
Closed 25 Dec
Additional: Sunday L; Children
welcome
Seats: 150. Private dining room 20
Style: Informal/modern
Smoking: No-smoking area; Air-
conditioning

A simple menu, but dishes are well executed using top quality ingredients. The smart bright modern decor is courtesy of Terence Conran and the atmosphere is relaxed and continental. A selection of simple but delicious breads might lead into a perfectly timed goats' cheese soufflé set atop a rocket salad with tomato concasse and a hazelnut dressing. Smoked haddock would make an appropriate follow up, particularly a piece of fish of the quality enjoyed by the inspector, pan-fried as it was with a perfectly crisped skin and set on good buttery crushed new pots. A dessert of banana and caramel vacherin with layers of white and caramel meringue was decent though perhaps less than inspiring. All in all an excellent find in such an unassuming area of the city.

Directions: From centre of Oxford, N up St Giles, L down Little Clarendon St and R at end into Walton Street

OXFORD, The Randolph ❀

New Chef Michael Quinn now runs the kitchen at this well-known Oxford hotel. Expect kipper pâté, followed by Cumberland sausage with black pudding, mashed potato and onion gravy, and perhaps peach schnapps parfait with orange compote.

Smoking: No smoking in dining room
Accommodation: 119 en suite ★ ★ ★ ★

Directions: At corner of Beaumont St and Magdalen St, opposite Ashmolean Museum

Beaumont Street OX1 2LN
Map 4: SP50
Tel: 0870 400 8200
Fax: 01865 791678
E-mail: gm1170@forte-hotels.com
Cost: *Alc* £37-£45, set-price L/D £14-
£18. ☺ H/wine £12.50
Times: 12.30-2pm/7-10pm
Additional: Bar food; Sunday L;
Children welcome
Style: Classic/Traditional

OXFORD, Shillingford Bridge Hotel ✿

See Wallingford, Oxfordshire

STADHAMPTON, The Crazy Bear ✿✿

Bear Lane OX44 7UR
Map 4: SU69
Tel: 01865 890714
Fax: 01865 400481
Chef: Graham Belcher
Owner: Jason Hunt
Cost: Alc £25, set-price L/D £14.95.
☺ H/wine £ 11.95
Times: Noon-3.30pm/7-10pm.
Closed D Sun, all Mon
Additional: Bar food; Sunday L;
Children welcome
Seats: 50. Private dining room 35
Style: Chic
Smoking: No-smoking area; Air
conditioning
Accommodation: 13 en suite

Tucked away behind houses and a petrol station, you're only aware this 16th-century pub exists because of the signs. However, nothing quite prepares you for the flamboyance of the interior; a seven-foot stuffed bear and a zebra skin are amongst the wonderful curios. There are two dining options; a Thai brasserie downstairs and the fine dining restaurant up a half-flight of stairs whose sloping ceiling displays a sea of wine bottles. Tables are unclothed zinc and small, lighting is subdued (tricky to eat one's lobster Thermidor by). The bar offers draught champagne, perhaps to accompany Iranian caviar or Irish rock oysters. In the kitchen the commitment to fine food is a serious matter as illustrated by a tarte Tatin dessert with perfect caramelisation and good home-made vanilla ice cream – something of a highlight. Other dishes that caught the eye included a ravioli of lobster set on a ragout of butternut squash in a lobster bouillon, and an osso buco of monkfish topped with tiny crispy squid on a vegetable chiffonade with a confit of cherry tomato and sweet soy.

Directions: From London leave M40 J7, turn L onto A329, continue for 5 miles, L after petrol station and L again into Bear Lane

STEEPLE ASTON, The Holt Hotel ✿

Traditional-style hotel restaurant where friendly staff bring you well-produced, attractively served modern British cuisine. The roast rump of lamb with apple-scented potato cake might be followed by the delightful apple crumble with custard sauce.

OX6 3QQ
Map 4: SP42
Tel: 01869 340259
Fax: 01869 340865
E-mail: info@holthotel.co.uk
Cost: Set-price D £24. ☺
H/wine £10.95
Times: 12.30-2pm/7-9.30pm.
Closed L Sat
Additional: Bar food; Sunday L;
Children 5+
Style: Traditional/Country-house
Smoking: No smoking in dining room
Accommodation: 86 en suite ★ ★ ★

Directions: Follow A426 through Kidlington towards Deddington. Hotel on R at traffic lights.

STONOR,

Stonor Arms Hotel 🏵🏵

Nr Henley-on-Thames RG9 6HE
Map 4: SU78
Tel: 01491 638866
Fax: 01491 638863
E-mail: stonorarms.hotel@virgin.net
Chef: Steven Morris
Cost: *Alc* £30, set-price L £18.50. ☺
H/wine £11.50
Times: Noon-2pm/7-9.30pm
Additional: Bar food; Sunday L;
Children welcome
Seats: 50. Private dining room 26
Style: Informal
Smoking: No smoking in dining room
Civil licence: 50
Accommodation: 10 en suite ★★★

A peaceful country inn in the heart of the Oxfordshire
countryside with a popular restaurant. The traditional walled
gardens are delightful and can be enjoyed from the light and
summery conservatory area. Alternatively the cosy,
traditionally styled dining room area with its dark red walls
and beautiful paintings is ideal for times when the occasional
glimpse through ornate windows is reminder enough of the
wintry outdoors. But come rain or shine the modern British
cuisine is sure to make an impression. On a recent visit our
inspector enjoyed a starter of a single large raviolo filled with a
light smoked haddock mousse with a pleasant texture and a
clear flavour. Braised beef with cabbage and gratin
dauphinoise proved a successful centrepiece to the meal thanks
to the quality of the beef and a well-flavoured sauce.
A well-made pecan and praline parfait was a perfect
conclusion to an enjoyable meal.

Directions: In centre of village

THAME, Spread Eagle Hotel 🏵

Cornmarket OX9 2BW
Map 4: SP70
Map: 01844 213661
Fax: 01844 261380
E-mail: enquiries@
spreadeaglehotel.fsnet.co.uk
Cost: Set-price L /D £12.95. ☺
H/wine £10.75
Additional: Bar food; Sunday L;
Children welcome
Style: Classic/Traditional
Civil licence: 200
Accommodation: 33 en suite ★★★

*Coaching inn with a pine-panelled restaurant – Fothergill's –
dominated by a portrait of the famous innkeeper. Fothergill's Choice
includes seared tuna, and medallions of beef with rich red wine jus.*

Directions: M40 – J6 from S, J8 from N. Town centre on A418
(Oxford to Aylesbury road)

WALLINGFORD,
Shillingford Bridge Hotel ❀

Shillingford OX10 8LZ
Map 4: SU68
Tel: 01865 858567
Fax: 01865 858636
E-mail:
shillingford.bridge@forestdale.com

Stunning riverside views and traditional decor make a pleasing setting for high quality dining. Good quality sautéed chicken livers layered with black pudding and served with a simple red wine and shallot sauce began an enjoyable meal.

Cost: Alc £28, set-price L £15.95/D £18.95. ☺ H/wine £9
Times: 12.30-2pm/7.30-10pm. Closed L Sat
Additional: Bar food; Sunday L; Children welcome
Style: Country-house
Smoking: No smoking in dining room
Civil licence: 150
Accommodation: 42 en suite ★ ★ ★

Directions: From M4 J10 take A329, through Wallingford towards Thame. From M40 J6 take B4009, then R onto A4074 then L at Shillingford Brdbt towards Wallingford

WALLINGFORD,
Springs Hotel ❀❀

Wallingford Road
North Stoke OX10 6BE
Map 4: SU68
Tel: 01491 836687
Fax: 01491 836877
E-mail: info@thespringshotel.co.uk
Chef: Paul Franklin
Cost: Alc £37, set-price D £25. ☺
H/wine £13
Times: Noon-2pm/6.45-9.45pm
Additional: Sunday L; Children welcome
Seats: 80. Private dining room
Style: Classic/Country-house
Smoking: No smoking in dining room
Accommodation: 31 en suite ★ ★ ★

Springs is a Tudor-style country house hotel with a large-windowed restaurant overlooking a spring-fed lake with swans and ducks. The dinner menu is more adventurous than at lunch; foie gras and wild mushroom terrine came with baked goats' cheese on a crispy smoked bacon salad and toasted pine kernels; seared fillet of sea bass rested on a bed of buttered spinach that came with a rosemary butter sauce. As for the cooking, a duck terrine was slightly dry but a main course of fillets of rainbow trout was served with a really good bisque sauce. A brûlée for dessert had a 'lovely' consistency and came flecked with vanilla seeds. The wine list is sound, balanced and includes a reasonable choice of half bottles.

Directions: From A4130 to Wallingford take A4074 (Reading); over first roundabout, turn R on B4009 (Goring). Hotel 1 mile on R

WESTON-ON-THE-GREEN,
Weston Manor Hotel ❀❀

Bicester OX6 8QL
Map 4: SP51
Tel: 01869 350621
Fax: 01869 350901
E-mail: westonmanor@hotmail.com
Chef: Michael Keenlyside
Owner: Dudley Osborn
Cost: Alc £35, set-price L £24.50. ☺
H/wine £14.50
Times: Noon-2pm/7-9.45pm. Closed L Sat & Sun
Additional: Bar food; Children 6+
Seats: 70. Private dining room 40
Style: Country-house
Smoking: No smoking in dining room
Accommodation: 36 en suite ★ ★ ★

This splendid manor house has a wealth of history, and is particularly popular with the business community who make good use of the conference and banqueting facilities. The public rooms include an imposing foyer-lounge and the magnificent vaulted restaurant with minstrels' gallery and original panelling. The service is formal and mostly quiet, but the attentive staff do smile. The menu is produced, where possible, from local ingredients. Standards are high and dishes might include pithiviers of wild mushroom and spinach with a Madeira cream sauce, and a mousseline of turbot, served with smoked haddock and poached quail's egg and spinach sauce 'vin blanc' which was well-judged and 'a delight'. An assiette de canard – duck breast, confit of duck leg and a saucisse de foie gras – was served on a bed of red cabbage that had a good

Weston Manor Hotel

balance of sweet and sour. The predominantly French wine list is strong on the classics.

Directions: 2 mins from M40 J9 via A34 (Oxford) to Weston-on-the-Green; hotel in village centre

WOODSTOCK,

The Bear Hotel ❀❀

Park Street OX20 1SZ
Map 4: SP41
Tel: 0870 400 8202
Fax: 01993 813380
E-mail: heritagehotelswoodstock.bear@forte-hotels.com
Chef: Gary McGuinness
Cost: *Alc* D £30, set-price L £14.95.
☺ H/wine £15
Times: 12.30-2pm/7-10pm
Additional: Bar food; Sunday L; Children welcome
Seats: 50. Private dining room 20 & 30
Style: Traditional
Smoking: No smoking in dining room; Air conditioning
Accommodation: 44 en suite ★ ★ ★

Thirteenth-century former coaching inn offering modern creature comforts whilst retaining much of its historic character. Even if exposed stone walls, heavily beamed ceilings and log fires hold no attraction for you the quality classical French and modern British cuisine should win round the most hardened cynic. To start, perhaps, a medley of seafood with a white wine and basil sauce; or goats' cheese, artichoke and potato terrine with spicy tomato oil and mixed leaves for vegetarian diners. On a recent visit smoked haddock with poached eggs, spinach and hollandaise sauce won great approval but a tenderloin of lamb wrapped in Parma ham and puff pastry with sauce gribiche served to the next table looked equally tempting. Profiteroles with strawberry yoghurt syllabub and bitter chocolate sauce are not to be missed.

Directions: Town centre, facing the market square

WOODSTOCK,
Feathers Hotel 🏵🏵🏵

In the centre of Woodstock, the Feathers manages to combine high standards of service and professionalism with an easy-going and cheerful approach. Mark Treasure's cooking is polished and assured; a six-course tasting menu might be centred around honey-glazed breast of Gressingham duck with button onions, pommes Maxim and claret glaze. Although the *carte* is relatively short, each dish has many elements; roasted best end of lamb coated in a fine herb crumb and served with dauphinoise potatoes, shallots, and spinach, though perfectly timed and succulent, perhaps needed more depth of flavour, and a tranche of turbot, served on basil mash with an emulsion of tomatoes, black olives, garlic and olive oil, was a tad overcooked. The best dish sampled on the inspection visit was roasted foie gras on green split peas with fine Italian smoked bacon, a perfect marriage of textures and flavours finished with a well-balanced Madeira sauce and topped with parsnip crisps. Good puddings include raspberry sablé with vanilla ice cream or rich dark chocolate terrine with candied oranges and sorbet. Good bar food is served in the Whinchat Bar.

Directions: Town centre

Market Street OX20 1SX
Map 4: SP41
Tel: 01993 812291
Fax: 01993 813158
E-mail: enquiries@feathers.co.uk
Chef: Mark Treasure
Owner: Empire Ventures Ltd
Cost: *Alc* D only £40, set-price L £17.50 & £21/D £48. H/wine fr £11.75
Times: 12.30-2pm/7.30-9pm
Additional: Bar food L (D Mon-Fri only); Sunday L; Children welcome
Seats: 60
Style: Modern/Country-house
Smoking: No smoking in dining room; Air conditioning
Accommodation: 22 en suite ★★★

WOODSTOCK,
Kings Head Inn 🏵

Traditional 16th-century village inn with squishy sofas for pre-prandial drinks and open fires in season. Try roasted trio of tomatoes, or charred ceviche of scallops, then maybe English lamb cutlets with five peppers. Diablo di cioccolato speaks for itself.

E-mail: t.fay@kings-head.co.uk
Cost: *Alc* £17.50-£27.50. ☺ H/wine £10.95
Times: Noon-2pm/7-9pm. Closed D Sun
Additional: Sunday L; Children 12+ at D
Style: Rustic/Traditional
Smoking: No smoking in dining room
Accommodation: 3 en suite

Chapel Hill Wootton OX20 1DX
Map 4: SP41
Tel/Fax: 01993 811340

Directions: On A44 2 miles N of Woodstock turn R to Wootton. The Inn is located near church on Chapel Hill

RUTLAND

OAKHAM,
Barnsdale Lodge Hotel ❀

The Avenue
Rutland Water LE15 8AH
Map 8: SK80
Tel: 01572 724678
Fax: 01572 724961
E-mail:
barnsdale.lodge@bt.connect.com
Cost: *Alc* L £30. ☺ H/wine £10.95
Times: Noon-2.30pm/6.30-9.45pm
Additional: Bar food; Sunday L;
Children welcome
Style: Edwardian
Smoking: No-smoking area; No pipes
& cigars
Civil licence: 100
Accommodation: 45 en suite ★ ★ ★

The aroma of baking bread may greet you on arrival at this 17th-century farmhouse and fine, freshly cooked dishes such as jambonette of guinea fowl are served in the series of intimate Edwardian rooms that make up the stylish restaurant.

Directions: Telephone for directions

OAKHAM, Hambleton Hall ❀❀❀❀

Hambleton LE15 8TH
Map 8: SK80
Tel: 01572 756991
Fax: 01572 724721

Telephone for further details

Overlooking Rutland Water, Hambleton is the epitome of the small but perfect English country house hotel. One of the strengths of the cooking is in the quality and sourcing of ingredients. Aaron Patterson has built up a whole network of small, local producers to provide him with organic Dexter beef, Bresse chickens, hoggets and Gloucester Old Spot pork. The cooking is very French, very polished – and truly delicious. Outstanding dishes have included pan-fried foie gras on a sweet-sour marinated aubergine and a sweet tomato-pepper purée, as well as wonderfully tender poached langoustines with a pear and vanilla-flavoured bisque. Pig's trotters are braised until the rind becomes soft and caramelised though still intact, stuffed with a sweetbread farce and lightly textured chicken mousse, then served with a perfectly pitched jus flavoured with some morels and root vegetables. A number of savoury dishes have a surprisingly sweet edge; in fact, the least sweet of the

AA *Shortlisted for*
Wine Award-see page 18

dishes we sampled was the essentially simple but delightful pain perdu for dessert: brioche soaked in cream and eggs, pan-fried in butter then topped with caramelised pear and caramel ice-cream. The formal dining-room is well served by the highly attentive, skilled, largely French team. Wines are arranged by the country, region and price, in that order, and include a notable range of sweet wines. An additional number of bottles are open to order by the glass.

Directions: From A1 – A606 Oakham. After 8.4 miles take turning signed Hambleton/Egleton only. Hotel on R in main street of Hambleton village

OAKHAM, **Whipper-In Hotel**

A 17th-century coaching inn with oak beams and hunting prints. Dishes include smoked salmon with a sushi vegetable, Rutland sausage with puy lentils, and lemon scented crème brûlée.

Additional: Bar food; Sunday L; Children welcome
Style: Rustic/Traditional
Smoking: No smoking in dining room
Accommodation: 24 en suite ★★★

Directions: In the market place, town centre

The Market Place LE15 6DT
Map 8: SK80
Tel: 01572 756971
Fax: 01572 757759
E-mail: mairead@brook-hotels.demon.co.uk
Cost: *Alc* £22.50, set-price L £10.95/D £18.95. ☺ H/wine £9.95
Times: Noon-2.30pm/7-9.30pm

STRETTON, **Ram Jam Inn** ❀

Refurbished restaurant using plants and flowers to define different areas. Options include filled baps, a choice from the char-grill (steak and Rutland sausage), daily fresh fish and delicious afternoon teas.

Additional: Bar food; Sunday L; Children welcome
Style: Bistro-style
Smoking: No-smoking area
Accommodation: 7 en suite ★★

Directions: On N/bound carriageway of A1, 8 miles N of Stamford; S/bound exit Oakham B668, follow signs under bridge to inn.

Great North Road LE15 7QX
Map 8: SK91
Tel: 01780 410776
Fax: 01780 410361
E-mail: rji@rutnet.co.uk
Cost: *Alc* £15. ☺ H/wine £9.95
Times: Noon-10pm. Closed 25 Dec

UPPINGHAM, **Lake Isle Hotel** ❀❀

High Street East
LE15 9PZ
Map 4: SP89
Tel/Fax: 01572 822951
Chef: David Whitfield
Owners: David & Claire Whitfield
Cost: Set-price L £7.50 & £13.50/D £18.50 & £26.50. ☺ H/wine £9.75

The restaurant at this town-house hotel is a panelled room furnished with pine tables and chairs, a dresser and green blinds, with a log fire in the small adjacent bar. Service is as informal and cheerful as the surroundings, something that could also be said of a menu that follows a set-price format with around three choices at each course. Start with a soup – perhaps asparagus and tarragon – go on to an intermediate dish of a filo basket of smoked salmon, avocado and pears, and then a main course of pan-fried sea bream with marinated Mediterranean vegetables, followed by farmhouse cheeses with maltloaf. The kitchen goes in for some robust flavours. Chicken, chestnuts and pearl barley go into a broth floated with crisp sage dumplings, and scallops are paired with smoked haddock in a terrine enlivened by a dressing of tomato and balsamic vinegar. Game features in season: breast of guinea fowl with bacon and wild mushrooms, or breast of pheasant stuffed with a mousseline of shallots, wild mushrooms and pine kernels and a 'lively and spicy' red wine reduction of the cooking juices. The wine list runs to over 300 bins, with some noble producers and vintages, although a page giving the selection of the house should ease decision-making.

Times: 12.30-1.45pm/7-9.30pm. Closed L Mon
Additional: Sunday L; Children welcome
Seats: 40. Private dining room 10
Style: Rustic
Smoking: No smoking in dining room; Air conditioning
Accommodation: 12 en suite ★ ★

Directions: Town centre, on foot via Reeves Yard; via Queen Street by car

SHROPSHIRE

CHURCH STRETTON,
Stretton Hall Hotel

Brightly decorated restaurant in a 200-year-old country manor house. Crab and Gruyère tart with spinach soufflé and grain mustard typified the precision in combination and presentation of the excellent modern European cuisine.

Additional: Bar food; Sunday L; Children welcome; Vegetarian dishes not always available
Style: Classic
Smoking: No smoking in dining room
Accommodation: 12 en suite ★ ★ ★

Directions: Off A49 Ludlow to Shrewsbury road, in village of Stretton

All Stretton SY6 6HG
Map 7: SO49
Tel: 01694 723224
Fax: 01694 724365
E-mail: charlie@strettonhall.freeserve.co.uk
Cost: *Alc* £25, set-price D £16.50. ☺
H/wine £9.95
Times: Noon-2pm/7-9pm

CHURCH STRETTON, **The Studio** ❀❀

59 High Street SY6 6BY
Map 7: SO49
Tel: 01694 722672
Chef: Ed Van Doesburg
Owners: Ed & Jane Van Doesburg
Cost: *Alc* £19.95, set-price L £9.50 & £11.50. ☺ H/wine £8.95
Times: Noon-2pm/7-10pm. Closed Sun, Mon, Xmas, Bhs
Additional: Children welcome
Seats: 36
Style: Informal/eclectic
Smoking: No smoking in dining room

At one time a coaching inn, the Studio is a pleasant and airy space decorated in warm tones to create a relaxing atmosphere, with pictures and ornaments collected from Asia and Africa mingling with contemporary art. Simplicity is the kitchen's underlying principle, from tomato and basil soup to Dutch apple tart with whipped cream. Starters take in tarts too – figs with honey and goats' cheese, or pear and Stilton with rosemary – or perhaps prawn and dill croquettes with saffron mayonnaise, with main courses extending to fillet of local beef on mushroom purée with Madeira sauce, or rack of lamb roasted with cumin and served with roasted red peppers. Fish might be represented by chargrilled salmon in herb butter with creamed leeks, or smoked haddock fishcakes with chive sauce. Vegetables get the thumbs up in the form of soufflé potatoes, curried cabbage and cauliflower in red pepper sauce, and crème brûlée is a favourite dessert: 'excellent' raspberry or spiced pear, say.

Directions: From A49 into village. L at crossroads into High Street

CLEOBURY MORTIMER,

The Crown Inn   NEW

Hopton Wafers DY14 0NB
Map 7: SO67
Tel: 01299 270372
Fax: 01299 271127
E-mail: desk@crownathopton.co.uk
Cost: *Alc* L £17.50, set-price D £19.95. ☺ H/wine £9.95
Times: Noon-3.30pm/6.30-late. Closed L Mon, D Sun, D 25 Dec
Additional: Bar food; Sunday L; Children welcome
Style: Traditional
Smoking: No smoking in dining room
Accommodation: 7 en suite

Sixteenth-century inn with exposed beams and roaring fires. Imaginative dishes could include roast avocado with bacon, stilton and rosemary. Follow this with roast monkfish wrapped in bacon, chicken en croûte with garlic herb velouté, or loin of lamb.

Directions: M5/M42 J5 on to A433 to Great Witley, then B4202 to Cleobury Mortimer

CLEOBURY MORTIMER,

Redfern Hotel

Home-cured hams and cider casks hang from the beams in the Georgian restaurant, where English dishes such as braised shoulder of lamb and home-smoked rainbow trout fillets are served.

Additional: Bar food L; Sunday L; Children welcome
Style: Bistro-style/Informal
Smoking: No smoking in dining room
Accommodation: 11 en suite ★ ★ ★

DY14 8AA
Map 7: SO67
Tel: 01299 270395
Fax: 01299 271011
E-mail: jon@redfern-hotel.demon.co.uk
Cost: *Alc* £20, set-price L £5.55/ D £18.75. ☺ H/wine £7.50
Times: Noon-2pm/7.30-9.30pm

Directions: Midway on A4117 between Kidderminster and Ludlow. For Kidderminster leave at M5 J3

DORRINGTON,
Country Friends Restaurant

Country friends maybe, but not country cousins. The ancient building, full of old beams, antique furniture and an inglenook fireplace, is the well-established home of a restaurant offering sound modern British cooking. The menu, priced for two, three or four courses, offers half a dozen choices at each stage, beginning with the likes of tomato, red pepper and pesto soufflé or confit of duck, then breast of Trelough duck with oriental sauce or venison on celeriac purée with sloe gin sauce. Vegetarian choice might be ricotta and spinach gnocchi with sage and walnut pesto. From a list of desserts that included chocolate tart with pistachio ice cream and baked lemon cream, we enjoyed a beautiful queen of puddings. Freshly made coffee comes with home-made petits fours including chocolate truffled raisins. The good list of dessert wines is also worthy of exploration.

Shrewsbury SY5 7JD
Map 7: SJ40
Tel: 01743 718707
E-mail: whittaker@ countryfriends.demon.co.uk
Chef: Charles Whittaker
Owners: Charles & Pauline Whittaker
Cost: Set-price L/D £29.95. H/wine £12.50
Times: Noon-2pm/7-9pm. Closed Sun & Mon
Additional: Bar food L; Children welcome; Vegetarian dishes not always available
Seats: 35
Style: Country-house
Smoking: No smoking in dining room

Directions: On A49 in centre of village, 6 miles S of Shrewsbury

LUDLOW, The Cookhouse

Contemporary-style roadside inn retaining the look of the farmhouse it once was. It is an eatery for all occasions – the stylish café, which serves breakfast and lunch, transforming into an evening bistro. In addition, there's a restaurant offering an in-and-out lunch menu (for busy people who need to enjoy their meal within the hour) and an evening *carte*. At a recent inspection there were two starters including chicken liver parfait with a creamed grain mustard topping, light and simple, served with rocket and raddichio, drizzled with mustard oil dressing. Seared salmon with an accurately-made tomato butter sauce was one of the two main courses, set on a bed of spinach. From a choice of three desserts, the lemon tart had a zippy filling and excellent pastry, served with a sharp raspberry coulis.

Bromfield SY7 8LR
Map 7: SO57
Tel: 01584 856565
Fax: 01584 856661

Telephone for further details

Directions: 1 mile north of Ludlow on A49 to Shrewsbury

LUDLOW, The Courtyard ✿

A charming courtyard restaurant rich in greens and terracotta. Dark pine furniture is complemented by rustic ceramic touches such as attractive napkin rings and oil lamps. Discover devilled pork with stir-fry vegetables.
Additional: Bar food L; Children welcome
Style: Bistro-style/Informal
Smoking: No smoking in dining room; Air conditioning

Quality Square SY8 1AR
Map 7: SO57
Tel: 01584 878080
Cost: Alc £22. ☺ H/wine £9.80
Times: Noon-2pm/7-9pm. Closed Sun, D Mon-Wed, 25 & 26 Dec, 1 Jan, May Bh

Directions: Town centre, off Market Place

LUDLOW, Dinham Hall Hotel

The lovely old hotel, standing in an attractive garden directly opposite Ludlow Castle, dates back to 1792. Classic French cuisine adds a European dimension to this quintessential English market town: Beulon oysters; home-made terrine of

By The Castle SY8 1EJ
Map 7: SO57
Tel: 01584 876464
Fax: 01584 876019
Chef: Olivier Bossut
Owner: Pierre Mifsud

foie gras with truffled country bread and a glass of Coteau du Layon; cannon of rabbit with olive sauce on tomato confit. The cooking has undoubted style – gâteau of crab was well constructed and the intense saffron beurre blanc added a rich, overall flavour. A main course of seared sea bass on a bed of langoustine tortellini with carrot and tarragon beurre blanc was carefully cooked and full of flavour. The accompanying vegetables in a side dish, however, struck a more local note in their unseasonal plainness. Strawberry crème brûlée, from a choice of five desserts, was generous in size with a delicate, crisp topping.

Cost: *Alc* £28.50, set-price D £28.50. H/wine £11.50
Times: 12.30-2pm/7-9pm
Additional: Sunday L; Children 8+
Seats: 30. Private dining room 30. Jacket & tie preferred
Style: Classic/country-house
Smoking: No smoking in dining room.
Accommodation: 15 en suite ★ ★ ★

Directions: Town centre, off Market Place

LUDLOW, Hibiscus

17 Corve Street SY8 1DA
Map 7: SO57
Tel: 01584 872325

As we went to press, AA three-rosetted chef Claude Bosi (previously of Overton Grange, Ludlow) had taken over Oaks Restaurant (now Hibiscus) from Ken Adams. Check our website (www.theaa.com/hotels) for the latest details.

Telephone for further details

Directions: Town centre, bottom of hill below Feathers Hotel

LUDLOW, Merchant House

62 Lower Corve Street SY8 1DU
Map 7: SO57
Tel: 01584 875438
Fax: 01584 876927
Chef: Shaun Hill
Owners: Shaun & Anja Hill
Cost: Set-price L/D £29.50. H/wine £13.50
Times: 12.30-2pm (Fri-Sat only)/7-9pm. Closed all Sun & Mon, L Tue-Thu, 1 wk Xmas, 1 wk Spring
Additional: Vegetarian dishes by arrangement
Seats: 42
Style: Informal
Smoking: No smoking in dining room

Shaun Hill's solo style in the kitchen (backed up by Anja Hill front of house) dictates the tone for the whole operation. In the hands of someone as talented as Mr Hill, this is undoubtedly a good thing. The cooking is necessarily no-nonsense and concentrates on the essentials rather than the frivolous. Superbly-timed scallops, for instance, with a judiciously-spiced lentil and coriander sauce or similarly well-judged monkfish with mustard and cucumber are staples of the menu and typical of the style. Hill is adept at obtaining every nuance of flavour, as with a 'superbly moist' squab pigeon served with wild mushrooms and an intense jus and the crunchiest of spring greens. The short, daily set menu might also feature calves' sweetbreads with potato and olive cake, and wild duck with celeriac and morels. Desserts perhaps sum up the style best; apricot tart may sound pretty prosaic but in Shaun Hill's hands we are talking about 'the best fruit tart I've ever come across', in the words of one inspector. All in all, it's a very special place and, in so many ways, an example to others.

Directions: Town centre, next to Unicorn pub

LUDLOW, Mr Underhills

A bright and airy dining room with two walls of french windows overlooking the garden, river and weir, and the ideal place to enjoy the modern British cooking of Christopher Bradley. The atmosphere is relaxed, and dinner is from a no-choice set menu, likes and dislikes having been discussed in advance. Spring menus have begun with seared salmon with savoy cabbage, chorizo and peas, or warm salad of asparagus on a pancake of herb risotto, or maybe smoked haddock, salmon and cod fish cakes with a champagne chive beurre blanc. Main courses are equally focussed, loin of local wild venison with red wine, thyme and Paris brown mushrooms, for example, or breast of barbary duck with haricots blancs. The choice comes at dessert – 'at least 7' speciality cheeses, or maybe pears poached in lemongrass and vanilla with pistachio ice cream, Creole coffee parfait, or the inspector's favourite, lemon tart. The carefully compiled wine list features an interesting special selection with French country wines under £15.

Directions: From Castle Square: with Castle in front, turn immediately L, proceed round castle, turn R before bridge, restaurant on L

Dinham Weir SY8 1EH
Map 7: SO57
Tel: 01584 874431
Chef: Christopher Bradley
Owners: Christopher & Judy Bradley
Cost: Set-price L/D £25. ☺
H/wine £13
Times: L by arrangement only, D 7.30-8.30pm. Closed Tues
Additional: Children welcome; Vegetarian dishes by arrangement
Style: Modern/relaxed
Seats: 24
Smoking: No smoking in dining room
Accommodation: 6 en suite

LUDLOW,
Overton Grange Hotel ✿✿✿

Wayne Vicarage brings a touch of flair to the kitchen at this Edwardian mansion with lovely views across the Shropshire countryside. The concise menu, updated versions of French classics, is sensibly balanced and not overly elaborate. Apple and ginger give extra edge to seared scallops, beautifully fresh and bursting with flavour. Fresh sea bass is served roasted with bouillabaisse potatoes and fennel bouillon. The cooking also displays a strong vein of originality – roast Bresse pigeon with pink praline, or roast rack of veal with liquorice with a fresh pear and black pepper. A dessert assiette of rhubarb and crème vanille proved deliciously refreshing and enjoyable, though it would be difficult to pass up the whisky mille-feuille with whisky sauce or red wine soufflé with cinnamon ice cream. Good coffee, petits fours and homemade bread.

Directions: On B4361 off A49

Hereford Road SY8 4AD
Map 7: SO57
Tel: 01584 873500
Fax: 01584 873524
Chef: Wayne Vicarage
Owner: Grange Hotels Ltd
Cost: Alc £35, set-price L/D £22.50.
☺ H/wine £13
Times: 12.15-2pm/7.15-10pm.
Closed D Sun, L Mon, 2 wks Jan
Additional: Sunday L; Children welcome
Seats: 35. Private dining room 8-60
Style: Informal/Country-house
Smoking: No smoking in the dining room
Accommodation: 14 en suite ★ ★ ★

LUDLOW,

Roebuck Inn Restaurant

The restaurant at this traditional village inn, with its beams, open fires and panelled walls, is a light and airy room, with terracotta walls, colourful tablecloths, rattan chairs and palms. The menu is as vibrant and modern as the surroundings, taking in Moroccan lamb patties with spicy couscous, 'firm but creamy' wild mushroom risotto drizzled with truffle oil, and tenderloin of pork stuffed with Armagnac-soaked prunes, as well as more mainstream game casserole, fish pie and griddled calves' liver. Fish dishes and daily specials are chalked up on a blackboard, where an inspector chose 'a very good combination' of boned partridge with a parsnip and sage stuffing and quince sauce accompanied by 'perfectly cooked and colourful' vegetables. A wide choice of British and Irish cheeses comes with home-made walnut bread and oatcakes, or there might be 'lovely, crisp' lemon tartlet with a sharp, creamy filling and raspberry coulis. A good wine list and friendly staff complete the picture.

Directions: Just off A49, halfway btw Ludlow & Leominster

Brimfield SY8 4NE
Map 7: SO57
Tel: 01584 711230
Fax: 01584 711654
E-mail: dave@roebuckinn.demon.co.uk
Chefs: Jonnie Waters, David Willson-Lloyd
Owners: David & Susan Willson-Lloyd
Cost: Alc £25. ☺ H/wine £9.95
Times: Noon-2.30pm/7-9.30pm
Additional: Bar food; Sunday L; Children welcome
Seats: 46. Private dining room 16
Style: modern/chic
Smoking: No smoking in dining room
Accommodation: 3 en suite

MARKET DRAYTON,

Goldstone Hall

Rural Georgian manor with unusual walled garden and an agreeable atmosphere. The hotel restaurant is decked out with scant regard for the whims of contemporary fashion preferring simple, familiar country-house decor. The menu changes daily, is devotedly seasonal and makes good use of local produce. Unafraid of simplicity, a plate of mussels steamed open with wine and garlic might be found in the starter options, or for a more exotic starting point try spicy crab cakes with mango and paw paw salsa. Main courses range from beer battered goujons of salmon with ranch dressing to pasta noodles tossed in pesto, fresh Parmesan cheese and herbs. Again a focus on classic simplicity motivates the dessert options – vanilla cheesecake, chocolate truffle or a selection of English cheeses to name but three.

Directions: From A529, 4 miles S of Market Drayton, follow signs for Goldstone Hall Gardens

Goldstone TF9 2NA
Map 7: SJ63
Tel: 01630 661202
Fax: 01630 661585
E-mail: enquiries@goldstonehall.com
Chef: Carl Fitzgerald-Bloomer
Owners: John Cushing, Helen Ward
Cost: Alc £25, set-price L £14.95/D £15.80. ☺ H/wine £10.50
Times: Noon-2.30pm/7.30-10.30pm
Additional: Sunday L; Children welcome
Seats: 40. Private dining room 20
Style: Country-house/Formal
Smoking: No cigars & pipes
Civil licence: 100
Accommodation: 8 en suite ★★★

MARKET DRAYTON,
Rosehill Manor

Charming country house set in attractive gardens, parts of which date back to the 16th-century. The hotel restaurant offers such delicacies as sautéed lambs' kidneys with button onions in a rosemary and port sauce.

Smoking: No smoking in dining room
Civil licence: 90
Accommodation: 9 en suite ★★

Directions: From roundabout at Turnhill take A35/41 towards Newport, hotel on right

TF9 2JF
Map 7: SJ63
Tel: 01630 638532/637000
Fax: 01630 637008
Cost: Alc £24.50, set-price D £21. ☺
H/wine £10.50
Times: D only, 7-9.30pm.
Closed D Sun
Additional: Sunday L (noon-3pm);
Children welcome
Style: Country-house

MUCH WENLOCK, Raven Hotel ❀❀

Barrow Street TF13 6EN
Map 7: SO69
Tel: 01952 727251
Fax: 01952 728416
E-mail: enquiry@ravenhotel.com
Chefs: Kirk Heywood & Nick Jones
Cost: Alc £25, set-price L £15. ☺
H/wine £12
Times: Noon-2pm/7-9.15pm. Closed
25 Dec
Additional: Bar food L; Sunday L
Seats: 40. Jacket & tie preferred
Style: Semi-formal
Smoking: No smoking in dining room
Accommodation: 15 en suite ★★★

Directions: Town centre

Created from ancient almshouses adjacent to the original 17th-century coaching inn, the cosy restaurant combines the old and the new plus some interesting memorabilia relating to their unique historic connection to the modern day Olympic Games. In hot weather, tables are laid out in the delightful inner courtyard. The short modern menu is lively, the style refined but not over-ambitious, the execution consistent and the service attentive and friendly – in short, an excellent restaurant of its type. A terrine of pressed ham and fine herbs typically showed good contrast of flavours and textures, smartly complemented by a red onion and port marmalade. Main courses might include perfectly-cooked fillet of beef with potato rösti and madeira sauce, game pie, or salmon and sole parcel wrapped in Savoy cabbage and served with a cockle and lemon sauce. Pear poached in mulled wine with elderflower ice cream makes a perfect finish.

NORTON,
Hundred House Hotel ❀❀

Aromatic bunches of drying flowers and herbs hang in great profusion from the beams of this old hotel, and exposed mellow brickwork, quarry tiled floors, stained glass and dark wood panelling help to foster a medieval effect. Open log fires and cast iron pots further embellish the picture. In the kitchen the products of the large vegetable and herb garden go into the

Bridgenorth Road TF11 9EE
Map 7: SJ70
Tel: 01952 730353
Fax: 01952 730355
E-mail:
hphundredhouse@messages.co.uk
Chef: Stuart Phillips
Owners: Phillips Family

Hundred House Hotel

Cost: Alc fr £25. ☺ H/wine £12.50
Times: Noon-2.30pm/6-10pm
Additional: Bar food; Sunday L;
Children welcome
Seats: 60. Private dining room 35
Style: Traditional
Smoking: No-smoking area
Accommodation: 10 en suite ★★

making of some highly successful modern British cooking. A short list of restaurant specials expands the choice available from the *carte*: casserole of turbot and scallops in a lobster bisque, perhaps, or cassoulet of wild boar with pork sausage, cannellini beans and white wine. Otherwise try starters like buckwheat blinis topped with smoked salmon, pink peppercorn-cured salmon, and tiger prawns served with pickled cucumber and crème fraîche, and main dishes such as roast fillet of beef topped with chèvre, and served with pommes Anna and balsamic sauce, or pan-fried venison with individual suet pudding and a port and pepper reduction. Dessert might be apricot and almond flan.

Directions: Midway between Telford & Bridgenorth on A442. In centre of village

OSWESTRY, The Old Mill Inn ☸

Country inn housed in a converted watermill, where enjoyable dishes, like a chunky game terrine and beautifully presented salmon Norweige, can be taken in the bars or conservatory restaurant.

Additional: Bar food L; Sunday L; Children welcome
Style: Traditional/Country-house
Smoking: No-smoking area; Air conditioning

Directions: From A5 follow B4579 signed Trefonen & Llansillin; after Ashfield take 1st R towards Llansillin then 1st R again

Candy SY10 9AZ
Map 7: SJ22
Tel: 01691 657058
Fax: 01691 680918
E-mail: theoldmill.inn@virgin.net
Cost: Alc £12.35. ☺ H/wine £8.25
Times: Noon-2.30pm/6-9.30pm.
Closed Tue

OSWESTRY,
Pen-y-Dyffryn Country Hotel ☸☸

A charming old house dating back to the mid-19th century when it was built as a rectory. Five acres of attractive grounds set the scene and details such as the log fire in the attractively decorated restaurant create a complete picture of elegance and tranquillity. The kitchen lavishes care and attention on dishes such as grilled venison sausage served on a swede purée with roasted meat juices. Main course dishes might include poached fillet of Greenland cod coated with a creamy cheese and chive sauce, or pan-fried supreme of chicken glazed with English mustard and Welsh clover honey. This is an establishment with many praiseworthy attributes, not least the warm and friendly hospitality of proprietors Audrey and Miles Hunter.

Rhydcroesau SY10 7JD
Map 7: SJ22
Tel: 01691 653700
Fax: 01691 650066
E-mail: stay@peny.co.uk
Chef: David Morris
Owner: Miles & Audrey Hunter
Cost: Set-price D £20.50. ☺
H/wine £9.50

Directions: Leave A5 at Oswestry, follow signs to Llansilin. Hotel 3miles W on B5480

OSWESTRY, **Wynnstay Hotel**

Church Street SY11 2SZ.
Map 7: SJ22
Tel: 01691 655261
Fax: 01691 670606
Cost: Alc £23, set-price L £10.50/D
£16.95. ☺ H/wine £8.95
Times: Noon-2pm/7-9.30pm. Closed
D Sun
Additional: Bar food; Sunday L;
Children welcome
Style: classic/informal
Smoking: No smoking in dining room;
Air conditioning
Civil licence: 90
Accommodation: 29 en suite ★ ★ ★

*Hotel with a Georgian heart and a unique 200 year-old crown
bowling green. The restaurant offers Italian cooking that combines
trattoria favourites – pollo cacciatore – with the more modish
polenta with Dolcelatte and wild mushrooms.*

Directions: In centre of town, opposite church

SHIFNAL, **Park House Hotel**

Park Street TF11 9BA
Map 7: SJ70
Tel: 01952 460128
Fax: 01952 461658

Telephone for further details

The hotel has been developed and extended from two 17th-
century houses to create an attractive hotel with elegant
public rooms, including the dining room with its period-style
furnishings. A good choice of dishes is offered from the *carte*
or set-price four-course menu. Fresh home-made rolls were
served warm, and a delicately flavoured salmon and spinach
roulade was complemented by orange and basil salad with
red pepper coulis. An intermediate course of celery soup was
followed by braised shoulder of lamb, melt-in-the-mouth
tender, served with a robust red wine, root vegetable, Puy
lentil and wild mushroom broth. Lime crème brûlée, chosen
from a tempting selection of desserts, had a light, crisp crust
and an intense flavour of lime in the creamy mixture
beneath.

Directions: From M54 J4 take A464 through Shifnal; hotel is
200 yards after railway bridge

SHREWSBURY,
Albright Hussey Hotel

The gardens of this traditional country-house hotel are graced
by the presence of Australian black swans. In keeping with its
farmhouse origins the dining room boasts panels, beams and
napery galore. The cooking is modern British so expect the
likes of a buttery filo parcel stuffed full of crab and
accompanied by a dry, well-spiced mixed bean salsa on the
starters menu. For a main course you might enjoy pink cutlets
of Shropshire lamb around a tower of dauphinoise potatoes
with vegetables and a pleasant sweet jus. Banana delice with
caramelised apricot sauce and chocolate parfait was a good
example of accurate composition coupled with careful
presentation in a dessert menu that also might include hot rice
pudding croquettes with blackcurrant compote or chestnut

Ellesmere Road SY4 3AF
Map 7: SJ41
Tel: 01939 290571/290523
Fax: 01939 291143
Chef: David Burns
Owners: Franco, Vera & Paul
Subbiani
Cost: Alc £23.50-£30, set-price D fr
£19.95. ☺ H/wine £10.95
Times: Noon-2.15pm/7-10pm
Additional: Bar food; Sunday L;
Children 4+
Seats: 84. Private dining room 8-180
Style: Rustic/Country-house
Smoking: No smoking in dining room

Albright Hussey Hotel

Civil licence: 180
Accommodation: 14 en suite ★ ★

charlotte, heather honey and malt whisky ice cream. Ebullient Italian owners and friendly young staff make for a hospitable night out.

Directions: On A528, 2 miles from centre of Shrewsbury

SHREWSBURY,
Rowton Castle Hotel ❀ NEW

Halfway House SY5 9EP
Map 7: SJ41
Tel: 01743 884044
Fax: 01743 884949
E-mail: post@rowtoncastle.co.uk
Cost: Set-price L/D £23.95. ☺ H/wine £10.50
Times: Noon-2pm/7-9.30pm

Baronial grandeur softened by candlelit intimacy. Steeped in history and swathed in oak panelling the restaurant takes a modern approach to cuisine with dishes such as marinated lamb, mint and sun-dried tomato risotto.

Additional: Bar food; Sunday L; Children welcome
Style: Country-house
Smoking: No smoking in dining room
Civil licence: 110
Accommodation: 19 en suite ★ ★ ★

Directions: From Shrewsbury take A458 towards Welshpool. Hotel 4m on R

SHREWSBURY, Sol Restaurant ❀❀❀

82 Wyle Cop SY1 1UT
Map 7: SJ41
Tel: 01743 340560
Fax: 01743 340552
Chef: John Williams
Owners: John & Debbie Williams
Cost: Set-price L £19.50/D £27.50. H/wine £9.95
Times: 12.30-1.45pm/7-9.30pm. Closed Sun & Mon, 1 wk winter, 1 wk summer
Additional: Children 8+
Seats: 45. Private dining room 25
Style: Chic/Modern
Smoking: No smoking in dining room

However inclement the weather, a little sunshine is guaranteed at Sol. The optimistic yellows and oranges of the decor might have been inherited from the building's previous life as a tapas

bar, but it makes an appropriate upbeat setting for John Williams's punchy style of cooking. Some of the Mediterranean feel appears to have rubbed off on the kitchen too; a Spring inspection began with an appetiser of a demi-tasse of gazpacho that was a good indicator of the light but well-defined flavours to come. Produce is well chosen and the cooking sensitive, resulting in dishes such as a 'top-notch' ballotine of foie gras presented with a remarkably intense tomato and basil gelée, or saddle of Ludlow venison with caramelised baby onions, roasted squash and balsamic lentils. Fish, such as fillets of Cornish red mullet with saffron and basil fettucini and lobster jus, and John Dory and sea bass with summer greens are accurately cooked, with a lightness of touch to the saucing that ensures key flavours are not overwhelmed. Desserts tend to the classic, with elegantly presented versions of, for instance, passion fruit brûlée with raspberry sorbet.

Sol Restaurant

Directions: From A5 by-pass follow town centre signs, cross English Bridge & restaurant is at top of hill on L after Lion Hotel. Best to park at bottom and walk up.

TELFORD,
Valley Hotel ✤

Listed Georgian building at the World Heritage site, where honest cooking encompasses traditional steamed puddings and Mediterranean-influenced dishes like squid stuffed with couscous and char-grilled vegetables.

Additional: Bar food L; Sunday L; Childen welcome
Style: Traditional/Country-house
Smoking: No smoking in dining room
Civil licence: 200
Accommodation: 35 en suite ★ ★ ★

Directions: Follow signs to Ironbridge Gorge. At mini roundabout at bottom turn L, hotel 200yds on L

TF8 7DW
Map 7: SJ60
Tel: 01952 432247
Fax: 01952 432308
E-mail: valley.hotel@ironbridge.fsnet.co.uk
Cost: Alc £25, set-price L & D £21. ☺
H/wine £9.75
Times: Noon-2pm/7-9.30pm

WORFIELD,
Old Vicarage Hotel ✤✤✤

The inspector paid The Old Vicarage Hotel the rare compliment of saying that if she lived nearby, she would be

Bridgnorth
WV15 5JZ
Map 7: SO79
Tel: 01746 716497
Fax: 01746 716552
E-mail: admin@the-old-vicarage.demon.co.uk
Chef: Blaine Reed
Owners: Peter & Christine Iles
Cost: Set-price L £18.50/D £22-£36.
☺ H/wine £14.50
Times: Noon-1.45pm/7-9pm.
Closed L Sat
Additional: Sunday L; Children 8+
Seats: 42. Private dining room 14
Style: Traditional/Country-house
Smoking: No smoking in dining room
Accommodation: 14 en suite ★ ★ ★

happy to come here for all her meals. The strength of the cooking is in its consistency, high level of technical skills and committment to sourcing local produce. Hereford beef, Shropshire lamb and venison appear regularly on the menu, the latter, for instance, served with root vegetable dauphinoise, watercress salsa and Madeira jus. From a little further afield, Devon red mullet is given extra savoury depth with crispy Parma ham, wilted greens and oyster and dill velouté. A detailed, well annotated cheese list might include Shropshire Blue (actually made in Nottinghamshire) and Berkswell from the West Midlands. As well as deliciously wicked sounding desserts such as crème brûlée with passion fruit curd ice cream, traditionalists will enjoy the Old Vicarage spotted dick with vanilla custard and honeycomb ice cream. A choice of coffees is served with extremely good petits fours. Service at the subtly refurbished Edwardian house is courteous and professional throughout, and the extensive wine list has been chosen with care and intelligence.

Directions: From Wolverhampton take A454 Bridgnorth road; from M54 J4 take A442 towards Kidderminster.

Old Vicarage Hotel

SOMERSET

BATH,

Bath Priory 🌼🌼🌼

Several hours can easily drift away once ensconced in the comfort of one of the banquettes of the dining room overlooking the lovely gardens. Pristine, crisp linen clothes the tables and the service is as smooth as silk. Robert Clayton's Modern British menu is clearly conceived and well focused. Everything is there for a purpose, undisguised by superflous additions or frivolous garnishing. An inspection dinner started with a generously filled ravioli of smoked haddock with a finely judged lobster sauce. The notable success of the following 'steamed breast of guinea fowl with lime and its leg roasted in herbs, with red wine sauce' derived from the contrasting treatment of the parts, the one refined and delicate, the other big and robust, drawn together by a common identity and accurate saucing. Other typical dishes might include roast chicken and goats' cheese sausage with lemon dressing, and sautéed sea bass, tagliolini and cep sauce. Dessert duos include mulled poached pear with pear parfait, and praline crème brûlée with peach sorbet, although our crispy apple tart with rum and raisin ice cream was a missed textural opportunity. The wine list is surprisingly sensibly priced with a good choice of half-bottles.

Directions: At the top of Park Lane, on W side of Victoria Park, turn L into Weston Rd; 300 yds on L

Weston Road BA1 2XT
Map 3: ST76
Tel: 01225 331922
Fax: 01225 448276
Chef: Robert Clayton
Owner: Andrew Brownsword
Cost: Set-price L £22.50/D £39.
H/wine £14.50
Times: Noon-2pm/7-9.30pm
Additional: Sunday L; Children 3+
Seats: 40. Private dining room 18
Style: Country-house
Smoking: No smoking in dining room
Accommodation: 28 en suite ★ ★ ★ ★

BATH, Bath Spa Hotel ❀❀

Sydney Road BA2 6JF
Map 3: ST76
Tel: 0870 400 8222
Fax: 01225 444006
E-mail: heritagehotels-bath.bath-spa@forte-hotels.com
Cost: *Alc* £35. ☺ H/wine £19
Times: D only, 7-10pm
Additional: Sunday L (noon-2.30pm);
Children welcome
Seats: 80. Private dining room 40
Style: Traditional/Formal
Smoking: No smoking in dining room;
Air conditioning
Civil licence: 100
Accommodation: 98 en suite
★ ★ ★ ★ ★

The Vellore Restaurant is in what was the ballroom of this grand hotel, set in immaculately maintained grounds overlooking the city. Furnished in keeping with its period, with high moulded ceilings, it takes its name from the city in India where the original owner served with the British army. Given the grandeur of the surroundings, it comes as no surprise to see foie gras partnering chicken livers in a parfait with morels, or a main course of Brixham lobster and Dover sole Thermidor, and even caviar in a dressing with dill for tartare of salmon and smoked salmon. Beef fillet in a blue cheese crust with glazed shallots and thyme sauce, and poached halibut with chervil beurre blanc and asparagus might be reassuringly familiar, but there's a racier side to the menus too: Thai vegetable soup with coconut and coriander, for example, and a main course of Asian-style crispy duck with wok-fried vegetables, shiitaki mushrooms and a sticky sauce. Mascarpone mess with honeycomb and berries makes a healthier variation on the Eton variety, but there might also be clotted cream crème brûlée.

Directions: From A4 turn L onto A36 Warminster, R at mini roundabout and pass fire station, turn L into Sydney Place

BATH, Cliffe Hotel ❀

Regency country house set in terraced grounds overlooking the Avon valley. The recently re-decorated restaurant might offer hake chowder, roasted stuffed peppers and apple charlotte.

Smoking: No smoking in dining room
Civil licence: 50 **Accommodation:** 11 en suite ★ ★ ★

Directions: From A36 take B3108 (Bradford-on-Avon), turn R before rail bridge, to Limpley Stoke. Hotel on brow of hill

Crowe Hill Limpley Stoke BA3 6HY
Map 3: ST76
Tel: 01225 723226
Fax: 01225 723871
E-mail: cliffe.hotel@virgin.net
Cost: *Alc* £22.50. ☺ H/wine £12.50
Times: 12.30-2pm/7-9.30pm
Additional: Bar food; Sunday L;
Children welcome
Style: Traditional/country-house

BATH, Clos du Roy ❀❀

Semi-circular, first-floor restaurant with a theatrical, musical theme in refreshing yellows and whites. This upper-floor elevation provides splendid views and is ideal for pre- or post-theatre dining. A French/European approach produces uncomplicated masterpieces such as salmon mousse served with a mint cream sauce – a delightful combination. Main courses might include pan-fried fillet of plaice with capers and olives served with a black pepper butter, or vegetarian diners can enjoy casserole of mushroom, pimento and onion in a

1 Seven Dials Saw Close BA1 1EN
Map 3: ST76
Tel: 01225 444450
Fax: 01225 404044
Chef: Simon King
Owner: Philippe Roy
Cost: *Alc* £26.50, set-price L
£13.95/D £19.50. ☺ H/wine £9.95
Times: Noon-2.30pm/6-10.30pm
Additional: Sunday L; Children
welcome

Clos du Roy

Seats: 100
Style: Modern/Traditional
Smoking: No pipes & cigars

Directions: Next to Theatre Royal

creamed paprika sauce served with pilaff rice. Desserts range from iced nougat terrine served with apricot coulis, to orange and Drambuie bread and butter pudding served with sauce anglaise. The generally simple but high quality Menu du Jour is particularly good value.

BATH,

Combe Grove Manor Hotel ❀

The Georgian Restaurant has lovely views across Limpley Stoke Valley. Lively dishes include seared gilt-head bream fillet with spinach mash and roquette pesto, and breast of chicken with Provençal crust.

Smoking: No smoking in dining room
Civil licence: 50
Accommodation: 40 en suite ★ ★ ★ ★

Directions: A4 from Bristol to roundabout (Newton St Loe), 2nd exit for Combe Down (5 miles). At Combe Down continue for 1.5 miles, hotel entrance on R

Brassknocker Hill
Monkton Combe BA2 7HS
Map 3: ST76
Tel: 01225 834644
Fax: 01255 834961
E-mail: dawn.gibbs@combegrovemanor.com
Cost: Alc £30, set-price L £16/D £25.
☺
Times: D only, 7-9.30pm
Additional: Sunday L (noon-2.30pm); Children 7+
Style: Country-house/Formal

BATH, The Moody Goose ❀❀

7A Kingsmead Square BA1 2AB
Map 3: ST76
Tel/Fax: 01225 466688
Chef: Stephen Shore
Owners: Stephen & Victoria Shore
Cost: Alc £30, set-price L £10/D £20.
☺ H/wine £11
Times: Noon-3pm/6-11.30pm.
Closed Sun, 2 wks Jan, Bhs
Seats: 30. Private dining room 8
Style: Classic/formal
Smoking: No smoking in dining room

Directions: Telephone for directions

The restaurant is situated in an elegant Georgian terrace in the heart of Bath, and the mix of interior styling reflects the history of the building. The gold walls are offset with deep-blue furniture and original French watercolours from the

1920s; the eponymous goose stands proud in the centre of the restaurant, looking feisty enough to take on all-comers. Parfait of foie gras with red wine and sherry jelly works well as a starter, served with toasted brioche. Other modern British dishes might include trio of pork with spiced cranberries, chargrilled fillet of sea bass with tomato and vanilla dressing, and iced nougatine parfait with figs macerated in rum and white wine. A warm tranche of smoked salmon is given an interesting edge with horseradish mash and watercress vinaigrette. British farmhouse cheeses are served with home-made plum chutney, Bath Olivers and olive bread.

BATH, No. 5 Bistro ❁❁

A very popular bistro-style restaurant with a relaxed atmosphere and a modern menu including many fresh fish specials. A recent meal began with a nicely seared, full flavoured piece of tuna with a gently spiced coating. This was served with a simple mixed leaf salad and a delicate Thai dressing which brought together all the flavours admirably. Although the standard of composition of the fish main course was comparable to that of the starter, the dish was seriously let down by its presentation. This could however be written off as part of the relaxed charm of the establishment and in any case the sea bass in question was fresh and flavourful and accompanying vegetables were accurately cooked. A toffee mousse with lemon curd ice cream was an inventive and largely successful conclusion to the meal. Bring your own wine option on Monday and Tuesday evenings – no corkage charge.

Directions: 30 yds from Poultney Bridge towards Laura Place

5 Argyle Street BA2 4BA
Map 3: ST76
Tel: 01225 444499
Fax: 01225 318668
E-mail: charleshome@no-5-bistro.fsbusiness.co.uk
Chef: Stephen Smith
Owners: Stephen Smith, Charles Home
Cost: *Alc* £23. ☺ H/wine £9.95.
Times: Noon-2.30pm/6.30-10pm (11pm Sat). Closed Sun, L Mon, 1 wk Xmas
Additional: Children welcome
Seats: 35
Style: Bistro-style/Informal
Smoking: No smoking in dining room

BATH, The Olive Tree at The Queensberry Hotel ❁❁

Russel Street BA1 2QF
Map 3: ST76
Tel: 01225 447928
Fax: 01225 446065
E-mail: queensberry@dial.pipex.com
Chef: Mathew Prowse
Owners: Stephen & Penny Ross
Cost: *Alc* £30, set-price L £12.50 & £14.50/D £24. ☺ H/wine £11.50
Times: Noon-2pm/7-10pm. Closed L Sun, 4 days Xmas
Additional: Children welcome

A popular restaurant with a strong local following, The Olive Tree – with its dragged paintwork, tiled floor and antique rugs – still brings a touch of Tuscany to the Georgian hotel basement. The lively-sounding *carte* usually includes a fish ragout, made variously with lobster, tiger prawns and monkfish or perhaps sea bass, red mullet, mussels and prawns. Other typical main courses include Cornish hake fillet with stir-fried squid and chorizo with sweet chilli sauce, and roast loin of lamb with apricot and almond couscous, roast tomato and cumin dressing.

More vibrant flavouring defines Thai spiced crab cakes with mango and coriander salsa, and salad of crispy pancetta, slow-roasted tomatoes and parmesan with salsa verde. For pudding there may be iced espresso and hazelnut torte with coffee syrup, or lemon mousse with sablé biscuits and vanilla-poached raspberries. The wine list is short and punchy.

Seats: 60. Private dining room 30
Style: Informal/Modern
Smoking: No smoking in dining room; Air conditioning
Accommodation: 29 en suite ★ ★ ★

Directions: 100yds north of Assembly Rooms in Lower Lansdown

BATH, Restaurant Lettonie

35 Kelston Road BA1 3QH
Map 3: ST76
Tel: 01225 446676
Fax: 01225 447541
Chef: Martin Blunos
Owners: Siân & Martin Blunos
Cost: Set-price L £25/D £47.50. H/wine £29.95
Times: 12.30-2pm/7-9.30pm. Closed Sun & Mon, 2 wks Jan, 2 wks Aug
Additional: Children welcome; Vegetarian dishes by prior arrangement
Seats: 38. Private dining room 8
Style: Classic/Informal
Smoking: No smoking in dining room

Directions: 2 miles from Bath on A431 Bilton Road

The Georgian restaurant-with-rooms has fabulous views from the elegant restaurant although the pictures on the wall are of Latvian country scenes, courtesy of Martin Blunos's uncle in Riga. Other personal touches include photos to emphasise this is also his family home. The repertoire is interesting, combining Eastern European ethnic touches with French classics. Scrambled duck egg served in the shell topped with Sevruga caviar, accompanied by blinis and a glass of iced vodka is a signature dish that is worth the price of admission alone. The theme is reprised in the pre-dessert of an eggshell filled with vanilla cream, topped with mango purée and biscuit soldiers. However, it was the dessert that proved the stunner of our inspection meal – an ingenious assiette of nuts that included in the line-up hazelnut sponge tart, macadamia kulfi with gold leaf and an amaretto soufflé that was a 'little mouthful of heaven' served in an eggcup. This playful edge also appeared in a main course of lamb cutlets with a mini shepherd's pie with glazed onions, garlic and peppers served with a basil mint jus, but although beautifully prepared, the total added up to less than the quality of the parts. Some of the many rich dishes on offer might include pan-fried foie gras on cep risotto, and honey-glazed belly of pork with a truffle cream sauce; more delicate tastes are catered for with steamed fillet of brill with smoked haddock ravioli, parsley purée and a light Sauternes cream sauce. A serious wine list includes a good selection of half-bottles.

BATH, Royal Crescent Hotel – Pimpernels ❀❀❀

16 Royal Crescent BA1 2LS
Map 3: ST76
Tel: 01225 823333
Fax: 01225 339401
E-mail: reservations@royalcrescent.co.uk
Chef: Steven Blake
Owner: Cliveden Ltd
Cost: *Alc* fr £42, set-price L £15/D £32.
Additional: Bar food L; Sunday L; Children welcome
Seats: 70. Private dining room 90
Style: Chic/Modern
Smoking: No smoking in dining room; Air conditioning
Civil licence: 90
Accommodation: 45 en suite
★ ★ ★ ★ ★

The light and spacious room in the Dower House (previously known as the Brasserie & Bar), has lovely handprinted 18th-century French wallcoverings. Abundant freshly-cut floral

Directions: In city centre follow signs to Royal Crescent

displays are in harmony with the secret garden which lies beyond the French windows. The *carte* adopts a more modern British air with some dishes incorporating Eastern flavours. Rather strong-tasting brandade of cod served with pesto mash and red wine sauce, however, was innacurately described on the menu. Clever construction and combination of flavours made a dish of rabbit sausage with black pudding mash more memorable. Slow roasted pork with wilted cabbage and mange-tout was tender and succulent, with a hint of the orient about the jus; less successful was another main course of halibut wrapped in pancetta with red wine sauce. Desserts were also uneven – apple soufflé and chocolate fondant with coffee ice cream. In sum, some hits, some misses and not quite the sparkle that this masterpiece of fine Georgian architecture really deserves.

BATH, Woods Restaurant ✿

9-13 Alfred Steet BA1 2QX
Map 3: ST76
Tel: 01225 314812
Fax: 01225 443146

Telephone for further details

Directions: opposite the Assembly Rooms

Restaurant comprising three interconnecting dining rooms with an informal café-bar at one end. Dishes sampled include wonderfully fresh scallops, and seared chicken breast with aubergine and a cream-based sauce.

BECKINGTON, Woolpack Inn ✿

Bath BA3 6SP
Map 3: ST85
Tel: 01373 831244
Fax: 01373 831223

Telephone for further details

A charming coaching inn from the 16th century, with flagstones, beams and open fireplaces. Eat in the formal candle-lit restaurant or smart bar. Twice-cooked goats' cheese soufflé recommended.

Directions: Village centre. On A36 (Bath – Southampton) near junction with A361

BRUTON, Truffles ⊛⊛

Truffles has had a complete makeover: it is now open-plan over two floors, with a gallery overlooking the lower level and a decor of terracotta, cream and beech wood giving a light and airy feel. The kitchen's style remains the same, with modern, round-the-world influences applied to the classical repertoire. Duck rillettes with wild mushroom pâté come with black bean salsa; pigeon breasts are wrapped in Parma ham and served on a bed of apple and red cabbage spiced with chorizo. Sausages are a favoured starter: pheasant and apple with red wine and shallot sauce, or nicely-balanced salmon and crab on wilted spinach with a thin sauce of tomato and chervil – 'a good combination and well-executed'. Honey-glazed breast of duck, just pink, as requested, with a 'superbly crisp skin', made a good choice of main course for an inspector, who also enjoyed frozen espresso gâteau consisting of coffee and crème fraîche ice creams in meringue. Incidentals like canapés and petits fours are appreciated, and the wine list has a better-than-average choice of half-bottles.

Directions: Bruton centre, at start of one-way system, on L

95 High Street BA10 0AR
Map 3: ST63
Tel/Fax: 01749 812255
Chef: Martin Bottrill
Owners: Denise & Martin Bottrill
Cost: Alc £24.95, set-price D £13.95.
☺ H/wine £10.95
Times: D only, 7-10pm. Closed D Sun, all Mon
Additional: Sunday L (noon-2pm); Children 6+
Seats: 30. Private dining room 12
Style: chic/modern
Smoking: No pipes & cigars; Air conditioning

DULVERTON,
Ashwick House Hotel ⊛

South-facing restaurant with french windows opening onto a large terrace overlooking the gardens and Barle valley. Skilful cooking of quality ingredients is offered from a short four-course menu.

Additional: Sunday L (12.30-1.45pm); Children 8+; Vegetarian dishes not always available
Style: Country-house
Smoking: No smoking in dining room; Jacket & tie preferred
Accommodation: 6 en suite ★★
Credit cards: None

Directions: From M5 J27 follow signs to Dulverton, then take B3223 Lynton road and turn L after second cattle grid

TA22 9QD
Map 3: SS92
Tel/Fax: 01398 323868
E-mail: ashwickhouse@talk21.com
Cost: Set-price L £14.95/D £21. ☺
H/wine £9.50
Times: D only, 7.15-8.30pm.

EXFORD, Crown Hotel ⊛⊛

Originally a coaching inn, the hotel boasts a lovely terrace and water garden, with many unusual varieties of shrubs and

Park Street TA24 7PP
Map 3: SS83
Tel: 01643 831554
Fax: 01643 831665
E-mail: bradleyhotelsexmoor@easynet.co.uk
Chef: Matthew Gardner
Owners: Michael Bradley, John Atkin
Cost: Alc £27.50, D £20. ☺ H/wine £11.25
Times: D only, 7-9pm
Additional: Bar food; Sunday L (noon-2.30pm); Children welcome
Seats: 28. Private dining room 15
Style: Chic/Romantic
Smoking: No-smoking area
Accommodation: 17 en suite ★★★

Directions: Village centre facing the green

flowers. The dining room has soft green carpeting and well-spaced tables. Sporting prints decorate the walls. The menu is priced according to the number of courses taken, although some dishes, such as pan-fried red mullet niçoise-style, carry a supplement. Typical starters might include smoked chicken and crisp noodle salad with mango dressing or seared scallops with confit tomatoes, asparagus and a balsamic vinaigrette. Our inspector ate roasted duck on red cabbage with fondant potato, spiced pear puree and red wine jus; an alternative choice might have been loin of venison on spinach with shallot confit, cherry tomatoes, roasted potatoes and black olive jus gras. The wine list is serious and interesting, especially the house selection, with some nice wines available by the glass. Good bar food.

FROME,
Talbot Inn Restaurant &

Mells BA11 3PN
Map 3: ST74
Tel: 01373 812254
Fax: 01373 813599
E-mail: talbot.inn@lineone.net
Cost: Alc £23. ☺ H/wine £9.50
Times: Noon-2.30pm/7-11pm.
Closed 25 Dec
Additional: Bar food L; Sunday L;
Children welcome
Style: English/traditional
Accommodation: 8 rooms

Directions: From M5 J23 follow Wells
& Shepton Mallet signs towards
Frome. Before Frome turn L to Mells

Service is friendly and informal at this 15th-century coaching inn.
Warm salad of pan-seared scallops and tiger prawns might be
followed by guinea fowl with smoked bacon rösti, or fillet of pork
wrapped in puff pastry.

HINTON CHARTERHOUSE,
Homewood Park &&&

Bath BA3 6BB
Map 3: ST75
Tel: 01225 723731
Fax: 01225 723820
E-mail: res@homewoodpark.com
Chef: Andrew Hamer
Owner: A Moxon
Cost: Alc £45, set-price L £19.50.
H/wine £16
Times: Noon-1.30pm/7-9.30pm
Additional: Bar food; Sunday L;
Children welcome
Seats: 60. Private dining room 40
Style: Traditional/Country-house
Smoking: No smoking in dining room
Civil licence: 50
Accommodation: 19 en suite ★ ★ ★

Designed as a sampler of the *carte* dishes, the eight-course tasting dinner is really not to be missed. The inspector was particularly impressed with a terrine of duck leg confit and foie gras with a balsamic and Sauternes jelly, duck crackling and candied apple, altogether a pretty excellent dish. The menu changes according to the seasons – in winter, a well hung chump of West Country lamb may be served with kidney, parsley and winter vegetables, in spring with flageolet beans, spring cabbage and green beans. Sourcing of ingredients is another priority – wild, not farmed, sea bass, for example, to be served with saffron, wild mushrooms and roasted baby fennel. Dessert was described as 'stunning' – caramelised pear with a Poire William pannacotta. All three dining rooms are fresh, light and airy-looking and service is impeccably attentive.

Directions: 5 miles SE of Bath off A36, turning marked
Sharpstone

HOLFORD, Combe House Hotel

Seventeenth-century former tannery, where good use is made of fresh local produce. A summer meal included a generous portion of oven baked gammon and cumberland sauce. Austrian coffee cake with rum was 'super'.

Additional: Bar food L; Children welcome
Style: Country house
Smoking: No smoking in dining room
Accommodation: 19 en suite ★ ★

Directions: M5 J24 (A39 Bridgwater) towards Minehead. Turn L up lane between Holford Garage and Plough Inn

Bridgwater TA5 1RZ
Map 3: ST14
Tel: 01278 741382
Fax: 01278 741322
E-mail: enquiries@combehouse.co.uk
Cost: Set-price D £18.75. ☺
H/wine £7.95
Times: D only, fr 7.30pm

HUNSTRETE,
Hunstrete House Hotel

One of the glories of this fine 18th-century house is its old walled kitchen garden, both functional and aesthetically splendid, which provides organic, year-round produce for the kitchen, cut flowers for the house and enjoyment for visitors. Stewart Eddy makes the most of his good fortune with dishes such as roast squab pigeon with pancetta, wild mushrooms and a velouté of the first spring vegetables scented with Madeira or, from the vegetarian menu, a mixed salad of deep-fried vegetables with aged balsamic vinegar. Other typical dishes include sweet, succulent scallops with ravioli filled with the coral, dressed with herb oil, as well as Cornish sea bass with fondue of mussels, tomato and basil with a bouillabaisse sauce. An oriental thread runs through the menu: crab, ginger, nori seaweed, crispy oysters and pickled vegetables; nougatine parfait with exotic fruits, star anise syrup and pineapple sorbet; compote of black cherries with lemon parfait and lemongrass ice cream. The dining room is beautifully proportioned and has a timeless, aristocratic air enhanced by a slight sense of faded elegance.

Directions: On A368 – 8 miles from Bath

Pensford BS39 4NS
Map 3: ST66
Tel: 01761 490490
Fax: 01761 490732
E-mail: info@hunstretehouse.co.uk
Chef: Stewart Eddy
Cost: Set-price D £35. ☺
Seats: 50. Private dining room 14 & 30. Jacket & tie preferred
Style: Country-house
Smoking: No smoking in dining room
Civil licence: 50
Accommodation: 23 en suite ★ ★ ★

MINEHEAD, Periton Park Hotel

Middlecombe TA24 8SN
Map 3: SS94
Tel/Fax: 01643 706885
Cost: *Alc* £23.50, set-price D £23.50.
☺ H/wine £8.95
Times: D only, 7-9pm. Closed Jan
Additional: Children 12+
Style: Country-house
Smoking: No smoking in dining room
Accommodation: 8 en suite ★ ★

Directions: Off A39 signposted Porlock & Lynmouth. Hotel about 1 mile on L

The restaurant, in a former billiard room, offers an interesting carte and an extensive wine list. Local produce includes Gressingham duck, prime sirloin steak and Exmoor venison.

PORLOCK,
Andrew's on the Weir

An excellent new restaurant with a talented chef-patron and committed staff. Andrew Dixon has come into his own at this small but attractively furnished restaurant-with-rooms, overlooking Porlock Weir and the Channel beyond. The emphasis on local sourcing of high quality ingredients is demonstrated by the list of kitchen suppliers on the menu. Regional ingredients might include Exmoor spring lamb (loin en croûte, roast rump, kidneys, braised tongue and sweetbread ravioli) or poached Lynmouth Bay lobster with linguine, baby vegetables and lobster sauce. Recommended dishes include tartlet of crab and saffron with asparagus tips, beautifully cooked fresh fillet of pan-roasted cod with herb crust, rissolées potatoes and a jus of lentils. Meat cooking is notable judging by tender loin of local pork with a ravioli of confit belly pork, sauté black pudding and red wine sauce, as well as fillet of Devon beef with oxtail ravioli, savoy cabbage with bacon, roast salsify, horseradish hollandaise and red wine jus. Finish with one of the accomplished desserts such as grapefruit bavarois with orange granite and orange sauce. The straightforward wine list offers excellent value, although there is limited choice by the glass.

Porlock Weir TA24 8PB
Map 3: SS84
Tel: 01643 863300
Fax: 01643 863311
E-mail: aotw@fsbusiness.co.uk
Chef: Andrew Dixon
Owners: Andrew Dixon &
Sarah Baudains
Cost: Alc £32.50, set-price L £10.50
& £14/D £25. ☺ H/wine £10.25
Times: Noon-2pm/7-9pm. Closed D
Sun, all Mon, 2nd & 3rd wk Jan, 2nd
& 3rd wk Nov
Additional: Sunday L; Children 12+
Seats: 30. Private dining room 16
Style: Informal/Country-house
Smoking: No smoking in dining room
Accommodation: 5 en suite

Directions: From M5 J25 follow A358 towards Minehead, then A39 through Porlock & onto Porlock Weir, 1.5m

PORLOCK, The Oaks Hotel

Open fires in cooler weather, attractive furnishings that include some period pieces, a garden with views over the bay and Exmoor, and an enterprising wine list of quality: all added together, they make a visit to the Oaks enjoyable and relaxing. Dinner works around a set-price four course menu with a small choice at each course except the intermediate one of fish: this could be kedgeree, or 'excellent' monkfish with a surprisingly subtle lime and ginger sauce. Starters range from a soup – perhaps chicken and leek – to cheese and mushroom pancake, while main courses generally receive a classical treatment: breast of Gressingham duckling with orange sauce, fishcakes with lemon and dill mayonnaise, or slices of Exmoor venison, simply roasted pink, full of flavour, with a robust port sauce ('a delicious combination'). Hot chocolate soufflé is worth the wait, light and airy with a rich gooey centre, or go for something like home-made rum and raisin ice cream, or crème caramel.

TA24 8ES
Map 3: SS84
Tel: 01643 862265
Fax: 01643 863131
E-mail: oakshotel@aol.com
Chef: Anne Riley
Owners: Tim & Anne Riley
Cost: Set-price D £26. H/wine £9
Times: D only, 7-8.30pm. Closed
Nov-Mar
Additional: Vegetarian choice not
always available
Seats: 22
Style: Traditional/Country-house
Smoking: No smoking in dining room
Accommodation: 9 en suite ★ ★

Directions: At bottom of Dunstersteepe Road, on L, on entering Porlock from Minehead

SHAPWICK,
Shapwick House Hotel

Beamed restaurant offering an interesting menu of four starters and mains. Rustic leek and potato soup was followed by tender shank of lamb and a pleasing mandarin and white chocolate gâteau.

Monks Drive TA7 9NL
Map 3: ST43
Tel: 01458 210321
Fax: 01458 210729
E-mail: keith@shapwickhouse.free-
on-line.co.uk

Directions: From M5 J23 follow signs to Glastonbury. L onto A39. After 5 miles Hotel signed on L

Telephone for further details

SHEPTON MALLET,
Bowlish House

Bowlish BA4 5JD
Map 3: ST64
Tel: 01749 342022
Chef: Deirdre Forde
Owners: John & Deirdre Forde
Cost: *Alc* £24.95, set-price D
£24.95.☺ H/wine £10.95
Times: L by arrangement, D 7-
9.30pm. Closed Sun & Mon (ex by
arrangement), 1 wk winter/spring
Additional: Children welcome
Seats: 28-30. Private dining room 20
Style: Classic/country house
Smoking: No smoking in dining room

Directions: 0.25 mile from town
centre on A371 Wells road

A plant-filled conservatory and views over the garden beyond
might distract some non-serious diners from the main business
in hand here, but not for long. The Grade II listed Georgian
building on the edge of town attracts a wide ranging clientele
to dinner – lunch is not available. A four-course *carte* and a
short set menu show the range, and a meal opens on a
tantalising note with *amuse bouches*. From the latter menu
comes the choice of starters like baked Somerset goats' cheese
wrapped in ribbons of courgettes on a bed of aubergines and
mixed leaf salad. Other openers might be ham hock terrine
with lentil salad, or foie gras and chicken liver parfait with red
onion marmalade. Moving on to the main course, expect
perhaps roast fillet of monkfish with roasted garlic cloves and a
rich red wine sauce, or porcini, walnuts and chestnut parcels
with Madeira sauce. A well-described cheese list is offered as
an alternative or an addition to dessert, which might be sticky
toffee pudding and toffee sauce with vanilla ice cream, or
ginger stem meringue roulade.

SHEPTON MALLET,
Charlton House

Charlton Road
BA4 4PR
Map 3: ST64
Tel: 01749 342008
Fax: 01749 346362
E-mail: reservations-
charltonhouse@btinternet.com
Chef: Adam Fellows
Owners: Mr & Mrs Roger Saul
Cost: *Alc* £38.50, set-price L
£16.50/D £35. H/wine £14.50
Times: Noon-2pm/7.30-9.30pm
Additional: Bar meals L; Sunday L;
Children welcome
Seats: 84. Private dining room 26 &
36
Style: chic/country-house
Smoking: No smoking in dining
room
Civil licence: 70
Accommodation: 17 en suite ★ ★ ★

Just outside town in landscaped grounds, parts of the building
dating from the 16th century, Charlton House is owned by the
founders of Mulberry and features the company's fabrics,

furnishings, china and glass as well as a collection of antiques, paintings and curios. The restaurant, all polished floorboards and flounces and frills, is the domain of Adam Fellows, whose strength lies not only in his ability to fuse apparently incompatible elements, Scottish salmon with foie gras, a purée of Savoy cabbage, pancetta and mesclun salad, for instance, but in his impeccable sourcing of raw materials; meat comes from a local farmer who butchers and hangs it as requested, ducks are from the Quantocks, and so on. Something of a signature dish is steamed scallops, 'the best I've tasted' skilfully balanced by a filo parcel of lemon balm, coriander and apple dunked in a separate serving of light curry sauce. Equally fine treatment is brought to meat dishes: an assiette of duck consisting of 'lovely, succulent and fully flavoured' leg confit with a parfait of the liver, a spicy oriental 'soup' and duck ravioli, the last perhaps lacking the finesse of the other components. Desserts are well-handled too: lavender crème brûlée, or a 'stunner' of delicately spiced pear and almond tart in light and buttery pastry served with subtly-flavoured cinnamon ice cream and a small cup of mulled wine.

Directions: M4 J 17, follow A350 S. At Trowbridge join A361. Hotel is located 1 mile before Shepton Mallet on L

SHIPHAM,

Daneswood House Hotel

Cuck Hill Winscombe BS25 1RD
Map 3: ST45
Tel: 01934 843145
Fax: 01934 843824
E-mail: daneswoodhousehotel@
compuserve.com
Chefs: Heather Mathews,
Mrs E Hodges
Owners: Mr D & Mrs E Hodges
Cost: Set-price L £15.95/D £29.95. ☺
H/wine £10.50
Times: 12.30-2pm/7-9.30pm. Closed
L Sat, D Sun, 26 Dec-4 Jan
Additional: Sunday L; Children
welcome
Seats: 50. Private dining room 12
Style: Country house
Smoking: No smoking in dining room
Accommodation: 17 en suite ★ ★ ★

A charming Edwardian hotel in its own grounds with wonderful views across the Bristol Channel towards Wales. The popular restaurant is decorated in period style with William Morris colours and fine frescoes. Quality local ingredients handled in the modern British way appear on the daily set-price menus – very short at lunchtime and rather longer in the evening. Cream of artichoke soup and pot roast Mendip lamb followed by white and dark chocolate terrine with three fruit coulis would be a typical daytime choice. In the evening a meal might begin with wild rabbit and foie gras terrine with truffle-marinated wild mushrooms, or perhaps baked apple with melting goats' cheese, served with crisp potato rösti and a walnut salad. Butter-fried guinea fowl with an aubergine timbale, wild mushroom and artichoke Pithivier might follow, with competition from perhaps roasted Quantock duck breast, fondant potato, rosemary-braised red cabbage and a blackcurrant sauce. Lavender-scented crème brûlée is a fragrant-sounding dessert, or there might be blackcurrant poached pears with an almond pastry cream and fromage frais sorbet. A good selection of cheese, and ports and dessert wines by the glass.

Directions: From Bristol take A38 towards Bridgwater. Shipham on L. (Hotel on Chedder side of the village)

STON EASTON, Ston Easton Park 🌸🌸

A Palladian mansion set in extensive grounds with a river and man-made lake. The intimate dining room reflects the classical style of the house, and diners can enjoy views out across the parkland. The food is strictly modern British, and the alternatives are arranged over a rather pricey *carte* and an equally costly set menu. From the set dinner menu might come tortellini of langoustine and red mullet with bok choi, olive oil and tomato juice, or perhaps lemon verbena and cep mushroom risotto with Parmesan crisps. The listed main courses could include poached fillet of Cornish turbot with tender leeks and sorrel butter sauce, or braised pig's trotter stuffed with sweetbreads and chanterelles with a parsnip purée. Desserts come warm or cold, such as chocolate fondant with cherry fromage blanc sorbet in the former camp, and glazed lemon cream with caramel and cinnamon tuilles in the latter. A choice of coffees and petits fours is included in the price.

Bath BA3 4DF
Map 3: ST65
Tel: 01761 241631
Fax: 01761 241377
E-mail: stoneastonpark@stoneaston.co.uk
Chef: Les Rennie
Owners: Mr & Mrs P L Smedley
Cost: *Alc* £39.50, set-price L £16/D £39.50. H/wine £15.50
Times: Noon-2pm/7-9.30pm
Additional: Bar food; Sunday L; Children 7+
Seats: 40. Private dining room 30. jacket & tie preferred
Style: Classic/country house
Smoking: No smoking in dining room
Accommodation: 21 en suite ★ ★ ★ ★

Directions: On A37 from Bristol to Shepton Mallet, about 6 miles from Wells

TAUNTON, Brazz 🌸

Brazz is big and bold, with a dome resembling the night sky and a feature fish tank full of silver dollar fish. Food is equally stylish and fun to eat. There is also a branch of Brazz in Exeter – 10-12 Palace Gate, EX1 1JA Tel 01392 252 525

Castle Bow TA1 1NF
Map 3: ST22
Tel/Fax: 01823 252000
Cost: *Alc* £16. ☺ H/wine £9.50
Times: 11.30-3pm/6.30-10.30
Additional: Bar food L; Sunday L; Children welcome
Style: Chic/Modern
Smoking: Air conditioning

Directions: Follow signs to town centre, castle & museum

TAUNTON, Castle Hotel 🌸🌸🌸

The historic wisteria-clad hotel has launched the careers of several famous chefs. Richard Guest is the present incumbent and, under the direction of Kit Chapman, is continuing to offer the reinterpretive modern British cooking with which the Castle is associated. There are cosmopolitan dishes on the menu such as salad of gambas prawns with black radish, pink grapefruit and vanilla, but it is the refined, rural tradition which really captures the imagination. Spiced beef jelly is served with beetroot chutney, braised oxtail with cauliflower purée, and slow-cooked mutton with rosemary fondant potato, buttered greens and gravy. A terrine of head cheese (brawn), made with ham hock, beef shin and pig's cheek was moist and tender, though our inspector questioned the need for the floral

Castle Green TA1 1NF
Map 3: ST22
Tel: 01823 272671
Fax: 01823 336066
E-mail: reception@the-castle-hotel.com
Chef: Richard Guest
Owners: The Chapman Family
Cost: *Alc* £34. set-price L /D £24. ☺ H/wine £11.50
Times: 12.30-2pm/7-9.30pm
Additional: Sunday L; Children welcome
Seats: 60. Private dining room 80
Style: Classic/Formal

Castle Hotel

Smoking: No smoking in dining room
Accommodation: 44 en suite ★ ★ ★

garnish. Saddle of rabbit with a parfait of the liver and confit of leg was skilfully prepared and well flavoured, but a fillet of halibut with truffle mash and Muscat jus was not so good. An abberation from the rest of the meal, which ended with excellent puddings – hot chocolate and orange fondant with marmalade ice cream, and a highly enjoyable light melon and vanilla jelly.

Directions: Town centre follow directions for Castle & Museum

---

TAUNTON,
Meryan House Hotel ❀

Period dining room with beamed ceiling and inglenook fireplace. Starters include warm salad of smoked duck, choose from main courses such as chicken with a Parmesan crust or fillet of salmon with fresh asparagus.

Bishops Hull Road TA1 5EG
Map 3: ST22
Tel: 01823 337445
Fax: 01823 322355

Telephone for further details

Directions: From Taunton/A38 direction Wellington. Take 1st right into Bishops Hull Road, after crematorium.

TAUNTON,
Mount Somerset Hotel ❀

Classic Regency country house with an oak-panelled restaurant lit by crystal chandeliers. Local produce is a feature in dishes such as marinated saddle of venison with black cherry jus.

Henlade TA3 5NB
Map 3: ST22
Tel: 01823 442500
Fax: 01823 442900
Cost: *Alc* £32/set-price L £16.95/D £24.50 & £27.50. ☺ H/wine £12.50
Times: Noon-2pm/7-9.30pm
Additional: Sunday L; Children welcome
Style: Classic/country house
Smoking: No-smoking area
Accommodation: 11 en suite ★ ★ ★

Directions: 3miles SE of taunton. From M5 J25 take A358 (Chard), urn R in Henlade (Stoke St Mary), then L at T-junct, Hotel entrance 400yds on R

WELLINGTON, **Bindon House** ❀❀

Langford Budville TA21 0RU
Map 3: ST12
Tel: 01823 400070
Fax: 01823 400071
E-mail: bindonhouse@msn.com
Chef: Patrick Roberts
Owners: Lynn & Mark Jaffa
Cost: Alc £45, set-price L fr £12.95/
D £32.50. H/wine £12.50
Times: Noon-2.30pm/7.30-9.30pm
Additional: Sunday L; Children 10+
Seats: 35-50. Private dining room 29
Style: Traditional/Country-house
Smoking: No smoking in dining room
Civil licence: 50
Accommodation: 12 en suite ★★★

This Grade II-listed baroque country house is not too far from
the M5, but you'd never realise it. On a fine summer's night,
take a drink on the terrace and enjoy the exquisite country
setting. Inside, enjoy the stunning surroundings; the Duke of
Wellington provides the theme, with the bedrooms named
after his battles, and the restaurant called Wellesley. Beef
Wellington is inevitable on the classically-inclined menu, here
served with dauphinoise and a thyme sauce, and other main
courses might take in grilled Dover sole with hollandaise, roast
rack of lamb with roast potatoes, and chargrilled chicken
breast with turned vegetables and a port infusion. Crab (in a
tian with aubergine and peppers), foie gras, and scallops
(roasted and set on broccoli purée) are the sort of up-market
ingredients used for starters, with orange and Grand Marnier
soufflé with blood orange sorbet, or chocolate fondant with
pistachio ice cream among luxurious puddings.

Directions: From Wellington B3187 to Langville Budville,
through village & R towards Wiveliscombe, R at jct, past Bindon
Farm, R after 450yds

WELLS,
Ancient Gate House Hotel ❀

20 Sadler Street BA5 2RR
Map 3: ST54
Tel: 01749 672029
Fax: 01749 670319
Cost: Alc £18.50, set-price L £5.90/
D £14.90. ☺ H/wine £8.90
Times: Noon-2pm/7-10pm
Additional: Bar food L; Sunday L;
Children welcome
Style: Italian/Traditional
Smoking: No smoking in dining room
Accommodation: 9 rooms
(7 en suite) ★

Directions: The corner of Cathedral
Green and Sadler Street

*A 14th-century hotel situated on Cathedral Green overlooking the
west front of Wells Cathedral. The hotel's Rugantino Restaurant
offers a good choice of typically Italian dishes.*

WELLS, Market Place Hotel ❀

One Market Place BA5 2RW
Map 3: ST54
Tel: 01749 672616
Fax: 01749 679670
E-mail:
marketplace@heritagehotels.co.uk
Cost: *Alc* £21.50. ☺ H/wine £10.50
Times: 12.30-2pm/7-9.30pm. Closed
L Sun
Additional: Bar food; Children
welcome
Style: Informal/Modern
Smoking: No smoking in dining room
Accommodation: 38 en suite ★ ★ ★

Ancient building with a modern outlook, situated close to the cathedral. Expect the likes of rib-eye steak with bubble and squeak, and blood orange cheesecake with lemon and vodka syrup.

Directions: A39 – A371. In centre of town, down one-way system. Directly in front of Conduit in Market Square

WILLITON, Curdon Mill ❀

Vellow TA4 4LS
Map 3: ST04
Tel: 01984 656522
Fax: 01984 656197
E-mail: curdonmill@compuserve.com
Cost: Set-price l £14.50/D £19 & £24.
☺ H/wine £8.85
Times: Noon-2pm/7-9pm. Closed L
Mon, D Sun
Additional: Sunday L; Children 8+
Style: Traditional/country house
Smoking: No smoking in dining room
Civil licence: 96
Accommodation: 6 en suite ★ ★

Directions: From the A358, take
Vellow/Stogumber road. Hotel 1 mile
on L

Charming pink sandstone, former watermill enjoying marvellous views. Start with Cornish crab cakes or avocado mousse, perhaps, and move on to salmon en croûte, pork tenderloin stuffed with apricots and wild rice, or mushroom strudel.

WILLITON,
White House Hotel ❀❀❀

The weighty wine list, even after more than thirty years, still draws acclaim and keeps up to date with new varieties. Dick and Kay Smith's enthusiasm for good honest food and wine remains undiminished, and Mr Smith will think nothing of jumping into the car and setting off to Brixham for the catch of the day. Indeed, their whole day revolves around constructing the menu for the evening. A demi-tasse of soup, such as lobster bisque or beautifully crafted sorrel and potato, is followed by an entrée such as the ever-popular steamed Withycombe asparagus with hollandaise or soufflé suissesse. There is usually a choice of three main courses, lightly roasted,

Long Street TA4 4QW
Map 3: ST04
Tel: 01984 632306/632777
Chefs/Owners: Dick & Kay Smith
Cost: Set-price D £31.50. H/wine £14
Times: D only fr 7.30pm.
Closed Nov-mid May
Additional: Children 4+
Seats: 20-24
Style: Informal
Smoking: No smoking in dining room
Accommodation: 10 en suite ★ ★
Credit cards: None

White House Hotel

Directions: On A39 in the centre of village

boned-out loin of local spring lamb, perhaps, or a much-praised chargrilled breast of wood pigeon served rare and thinly sliced on hot beetroot. Fish is cooked with some imagination but additional elements are never allowed to detract from the focus and freshness of the main ingredient. Omelette soufflé au Grand Marnier and a summer fruit pannacotta show a kitchen that enjoys cooking both the classics and the contemporary. The dining room is idiosyncratically and engagingly relaxed in style with exposed stone work, original paintings, modern ceramics and mismatched tables and chairs.

WINCANTON,
Holbrook House Hotel

A classic French and modern British interpretation defines the food at this comfortable country house, and after that mouthful of an introduction there's nothing left to do but sample it! The cooking has been consistently recommended for the skill and imagination which produces starters such as pithivier of truffle, ratte potatoes, smoked bacon and mushrooms served on wilted spinach and celery diamonds, and boudin of chicken, foie gras and morels on a bed of braised Puy lentils and creamed leeks. The high standard continues into the main course, where the choice might be between noisette of veal with spring vegetables and truffle ravioli, and roast rack of spring lamb with minted pea purée, girolles mushrooms and rosemary fondant. Neither do the desserts disappoint, and chocolate and pistachio soufflé served with a bitter chocolate sauce, or iced liquorice parfait with honey-roast pears and honeycomb are sure to hit the spot.

Directions: From A303 at Wincanton, turn left on A371 towards Castle Cary and Shepton Mallet

Holbrook BA9 8BS
Map 03: ST72
Tel: 01963 32377
Fax: 01963 32681
E-mail:
holbrookhotel@compuserve.com
Chef: Mark Harrington
Owners: Mr & Mrs John McGihley
Cost: Alc £34, set-price L fr £11/D fr £29.50. H/wine £15
Times: 12.30-2pm/7.30-9.30pm
Additional: Bar food; Sunday L; Children welcome
Seats: 30. Private dining room 40
Style: Classic/Country-house
Smoking: No smoking in dining room
Civil licence: 80
Accommodation: 15 en suite ★★★

WINSFORD, Karslake House

This charming listed building began life as a malthouse in the 15th century. The kichen concentrates on simple, straightforward combinations of top quality, locally sourced produce. Highlight of a recent meal was wild mushroom risotto.

Directions: From A396, follow signs to Winsford and Exford. Enter Winsford, turn L at garage. On R past the Royal Oak Inn

Halse Lane TA24 7JE
Map 3: SS93
Tel/Fax: 01643 851242
Cost: Set-price D £30. H/wine £14
Times: D only, 7-9pm. Closed Feb
Additional: Children 12+; Vegetarian dishes not always available
Style: Taditional/country house
Accommodation: 6 en suite

WITHYPOOL,
Royal Oak Inn ✿

Exmoor TA24 7QP
Map 3: SS93
Tel: 01643 831506
Fax: 01643 831659

Telephone for further details

Carte *and set-price menus are offered, plus interesting bar meals, all featuring fresh local ingredients. Oven-baked chicken breast with leeks, bacon and Marsala sauce was followed by raspberry and Amaretto trifle.*

Directions: 7 miles N of Dulverton off B3223

WIVELISCOMBE,
Langley House Hotel ✿✿

Langley Marsh TA4 2UF
Map 3: ST02
Tel: 01984 623318
Fax: 01984 624573
E-mail: user@langley.in2home.co.uk
Chef: Peter Wilson
Owners: Peter & Anne Wilson
Cost: Set-price D £27.50 & £32.50. H/wine £12.50
Times: D only, 7.30-9pm
Additional: Children 7+
Seats: 18. Private dining room 20
Style: Informal/Country-house
Smoking: No smoking in dining room
Accommodation: 8 en suite ★ ★

Nestling in peaceful countryside at the foot of the Brendon Hills, parts of Langley House date back to the 16th century, although it is predominantly Georgian. The small but comfortable restaurant features an inglenook fireplace and painted beams. The four course dinner menu offers a choice only at the dessert stage, but dishes are invariably tempting and delicious. Sometimes wonderfully fresh fish is the starter and local cheese the third course; other times fish is the entrée, as with a piece of grilled sea bass with provençal herb crust on a bed of leeks with a beurre blanc that inspired our inspector to comment it would be difficult to imagine a more enjoyable piece of fish! Tender fillet of Somerset lamb, cut from the saddle, was enhanced but not overpowered by an onion and cassis purée. Icky sticky pudding with toffee sauce is always a favourite.

Directions: Off B3277 0.5 mile from Wiveliscombe on Langley Marsh Rd

YEOVIL,
Little Barwick House ✿✿✿

Barwick Village
BA22 9TD
Map 3: ST51
Tel: 01935 423902
Fax: 01935 420908
Chef: Timothy Ford
Owners: Emma & Timothy Ford
Cost: Alc £28.45, set-price L £19.95 & £25.95/D £28.45. ☺ H/wine £11.50

Tim Ford has moved from Summer Lodge to become chef-patron at the listed Georgian dower house set in three and a half acres of delightful wooded gardens. The restaurant is at the focus of Little Barwick House's operation and there is strong emphasis on sourcing fresh specialist West Country ingredients. The dining room has been completely revamped and looks very attractive in cream and blue with well-spaced tables, high ceilings, subtle candlight and high quality napery.

Little Barwick House

Times: Noon-2.30pm/7-9.30pm.
Closed Mon
Additional: Bar food L; Sunday L;
Children welcome
Seats: 40. Private dining room 20
Style: Chic/Country-house
Smoking: No smoking in dining room;
Air conditioning
Civil licence: 40
Accommodation: 6 en suite ★

The menu changes daily and the restaurant is open for both lunch and dinner. A recent meal included wild mushroom risotto, followed by pink-roasted Dorset lamb served on a purée of aubergine with a light rosemary jus, ending with a dessert of apple tarte Tatin and vanilla ice cream. Other dishes typical of the vibrant, unfussy style might include pressed terrine of local ham hock with butter beans and grain mustard dressing, and pan-fried sea bream with courgettes and pesto crushed potatoes. Traditional Sunday lunch includes a delicious pudding buffet. The wine list has been carefully chosen, with many quality wines in half and full bottles from exceptional value vin de pays and New World wines to realistically priced Cru-class Clarets and Burgundies.

Directions: Turn off A371 Yeovil/Dorchester opposite Red House pub, 0.25 mile on L

YEOVIL,
Yeovil Court Hotel ❀ ✿

West Coker Road BA20 2NE
Map 3: ST51
Tel: 01935 863746
Fax: 01935 863990
E-mail:
verne@yeovilcourt.freeserve.co.uk
Cost: A/c £16. ☺ H/wine £9.25
Times: Noon-1.45pm/7-9.45pm
Closed L Sat, D Sun
Additional: Bar food; Sunday L;
Children welcome
Style: informal/traditional
Smoking: No smoking in dining room
Accommodation: 30 en suite ★★★

Family-run hotel serving good country cooking. Home-made bread, and soups such as leek and potato, or caramelised pork fillet served with heaps of fresh vegetables, and lemon tart with strawberry coulis, show the range.

Directions: On A30 2.5 miles W of town centre

STAFFORDSHIRE

ACTON TRUSSELL,
Moat House ❀❀

Not to be confused with the more ubiquitous hotel chain, a
pleasant, spacious conservatory has been grafted onto the
canalside, 15th-century moated manor house. Meals begin with
a selection of five home-made breads plus an appetiser, and
there's no shortage of choice in the following courses. Dishes
occupy a comfortable middle ground between the fashionable
and the traditional, sometimes offering an interesting twist on
a familiar idea, as in potato and sorrel salad with pressed
smoked chicken terrine or a tranche of cod with polenta,
mange-tout, frisée and chorizo sausage. Seasonal, rustic
ingredients come to the fore in calves' liver on a swede and
parsnip tart with black pudding, pancetta and Madeira sauce,
but there are also plenty of dishes with the sunnier notes of the
Mediterranean. The cheese menu offers a good selection,
taken either as an extra course or instead of dessert – if you're
really sure you can forgo the toffee and date parfait with a rich
Baileys cream.

Directions: M6 J13 towards Stafford, 1st R to Acton Trussell;
Moat House by church.

Lower Penkridge Road ST17 0RJ
Map 7: SJ91
Tel: 01785 712217
Fax: 01785 715344
E-mail: info@moathouse.co.uk
Chef: Matthew Davies
Owners: The Lewis family
Cost: *Alc* £30, set-price L £20. ☺
H/wine £10.50
Times: Noon-2pm/7-9.30pm.
Closed 25 & 26 Dec, 1 Jan
Additional: Bar food; Sunday L;
Children welcome
Seats: 120. Private dining rooms 40 &
55
Style: Classic/traditional
Smoking: No smoking in dining room;
Air conditioning
Civil licence: 120
Accommodation: 32 en suite ★ ★ ★

LEEK,
Three Horseshoes Inn ❀

*Ivy clad farmhouse-style inn a stone's throw from the Peak District
national park. The restaurant serves a strong selection of homecooked dishes along the lines of chuck of beef braised in red wine.*

Cost: *Alc* £20. ☺ H/wine £ 10.50
Times: D only, 6.30-9pm. Closed D Sun, 26 Dec-2 Jan
Additional: Bar food; Sunday L (12.30-1.45pm); Children
welcome
Style: Informal/Rustic
Smoking: No smoking in dining room
Accommodation: 6 en suite ★ ★

Directions: Telephone for directions

Buxton Road Blackshaw Moor
ST13 8TW
Map 7: SJ95
Tel: 01538 300296
Fax: 01538 300320

STOKE-ON-TRENT, George Hotel

Georgian-style hotel restaurant in the centre of town. The menu takes a predominantly traditional approach with dishes along the lines of marinated fennel with smoked salmon trout, or noisettes of lamb infused with rosemary.

Additional: Bar food; Sunday L
Style: Informal/Traditional
Smoking: No pipes & cigars
Accommodation: 39 en suite ★★★

Directions: M6 J15 or 16 onto A500. Exit A53 towards Leek. Turn L onto A50 (Burslem)

Swan Square Burslem ST6 2AE
Map 7: SJ84
Tel: 01782 577544
Fax: 01782 837496
E-mail: georgestoke@btinternet.com
Cost: Alc £26, set-price L £10.95/D £16.95. ☺ H/wine £9.75
Times: Noon-2pm/7-9.30pm.
Closed 25 Dec

STOKE-ON-TRENT,
Haydon House Hotel

Skilfully-prepared dishes show the flair of Chef Nick Mason at this restored Victorian townhouse. Enjoy dishes like chicken with black pudding and raspberry coulis, and beef fillet with a rich port wine sauce. Desserts are also rewarding.

Additional: Bar food; Children welcome
Style: Country-house
Civil licence: 40
Accommodation: 23 en suite ★★★

Directions: From M6 junction 15 A500 to Stoke-on-Trent, turn onto A53 Hanley/Newcastle, at roundabout take 1st exit, go up hill, take 2nd left at top of hill

Haydon Street Basford ST4 6JD
Map:
Tel: 01782 711311
Fax: 01782 717470
E-mail: members@touristnetuk.com
Cost: Alc £20, set-price L £11.50/D £15.90. ☺ H/wine £8.95
Times: Noon-2pm/7-10pm.
Closed L Sat & Sun

WATERHOUSES, Old Beams
Restaurant with Rooms

Leek Road ST10 3HW
Map 7: SK05
Tel: 01538 308254
Fax: 01538 308157
Chef: Nigel Wallis
Owners: Nigel & Ann Wallis
Cost: Alc £38, set-price L £23. ☺ H/wine £15.95
Times: Noon-1.30pm/7-9.15pm.
Closed L Sat, D Sun, all Mon, Jan
Additional: Sunday L; Children welcome
Seats: 36. Private dining room 10
Style: Comfortable
Smoking: No-smoking area
Accommodation: 5 en suite ★★

Directions: On A523, Leek to Ashbourne Road

It's been over 20 years for the Wallis family at their distinctly Gallic restaurant with rooms – congratulations are definitely in order. 'There should be one of these in every town!' enthused one inspector, thoroughly impressed by the relaxed atmosphere and the sheer passion for food on display. The restaurant is divided into three distinct areas, including a conservatory dominated by a flamboyant mural. Nigel Wallis' cooking is perhaps more restrained, but there is obvious affection in dishes that are consistently rewarding and distinguished by their concentration on flavour. Thus some excellent sea bass comes with sweet scallops, Puy lentils and a light red wine sauce. Beautifully moist corn-fed chicken, served in sherry and cep sauce, with a wonderful array of top notch fungi on the side. The commitment to freshness and seasonality is apparent and the not-overlong menu features a daily changing fresh fish dish. Desserts tend towards the indulgent, with the likes of prune and Armagnac soufflé and a crunchy nougatine with caramelised bananas and confit of kumquats. A wine list of sensible length is well-chosen and marked-up with restraint.

SUFFOLK

ALDEBURGH, **Lighthouse** NEW

A bistro style restaurant in the heart of Aldeburgh. Approach is fresh and casual with a focus on simple modern British cuisine. Mains might include duck confit with plum chutney or local cod fillet roasted with a tapenade crust.

Additional: Sunday L; Children welcome
Style: Informal/Rustic
Smoking: No-smoking area; No pipes & cigars; Air conditioning

Directions: From A12, N of Woodbridge, take Aldeburgh turning. In Aldeburgh turn R into High St, Restaurant is on R

77 High Street IP15 5AU
Map 5: TM45
Tel/Fax: 01728 453377
Cost: *Alc* L £15, set-price D £15.75.
☺ H/wine £10.50
Times: Noon-2.30pm/6.30-10pm
(11pm for Aldeburgh Festival).
Closed 1 wk Oct, 2 wks Jan

ALDEBURGH, **Regatta Restaurant**

Bright bistro with nautical murals, pine floor and tables. The lively menu, with daily chalkboard for fresh fish, ranges through griddled squid, excellent fish and chips, and jam roly-poly.

Additional: Bar food L; Sunday L; Children welcome
Style: Bistro-style/Informal
Smoking: No-smoking area; Air conditioning

Directions: Town centre

171 High Street
IP15 5AN
Map 5: TM45
Tel: 01728 452011
Fax: 01728 453324
E-mail: regatta.restaurant@
aldeburgh.sagehost.co.uk
Cost: *Alc* £15. ☺ H/wine £9.50
Times: Noon-2pm/6-10pm.
Winter opening times may differ

ALDEBURGH,
Wentworth Hotel NEW

Sea views are part of the dining experience here. Not surprisingly fish features on the daily set menus, like roast black bream fillet, and pan-fried skate with lemon spiced rice. Calves' liver, poached chicken and roast loin of pork might also appear.

Additional: Bar food L; Sunday L; Children welcome
Style: Traditional/country-house
Smoking: No smoking in dining room
Accommodation: 37 en suite ★ ★ ★

Directions: From A12 take A1094 to Aldeburgh. In Aldeburgh straight on at mini-rdbt, turn L at x-roads into Wentworth Rd, Hotel on R

Wentworth Road IP15 5BD
Map 5: TM45
Tel: 01728 452312
Fax: 01728 454343
E-mail:
wentworth.hotel@anglianet.co.uk
Cost: Set-price L £12.50/D £13.50. ☺
H/wine £9
Times: Noon-2pm/7-9pm.
Closed 27 Dec-6 Jan

BECCLES,
Swan House

Small 16th-century coaching inn with oak beams and panelled walls. The Anglo-international menu might offer freshly made pasta, braised aromatic shank of lamb, or confit of chicken with honey glaze.

By the Tower NR34 9HE
Map 5: TM48
Tel: 01502 713474
Fax: 01502 716400
Cost: *Alc* £22, set-price L & D £14.50 & £17.90. ☺
H/wine £8.90
Times: Noon-2.15pm/6.45-9.30pm. Closed 26 Dec, 1 Jan
Additional: Sunday L
Style: Informal/Country-house **Smoking:** No pipes & cigars

Directions: Next to church tower in Market Place

BROME,
Cornwallis Country Hotel NEW

Original 16th-century dower house approached by a long leafy avenue and set in 21 acres of beautiful parkland with an ornamental lake. The restaurant overlooks the gardens with their fine topiary trees, and extends into the lounge and a vine-laden Victorian conservatory. The menu offers an interesting choice, priced for two, three or four courses. Starters range from goats' cheese brûlée to braised leg of chicken with sun-dried tomato, asparagus mousse and pickled samphire salad. To follow there might be blackened salmon with spinach rösti, spaghetti of vegetables and keta fish cream, or candied aubergine and basil polenta with Mozzarella, chive and tomato salsa. Finish with a lemon tart with a tuile basket of blackcurrant sorbet.

Directions: From A140 Ipswich to norwich road take B1077 to Eye, turn L into entrance after 20 mtrs

IP23 8AJ
Map 5: TM17
Tel: 01379 870326
Fax: 01379 870051
E-mail: info@thecornwallis.com
Chef: Kevin Booth
Owners: Beth & Jeffrey Ward
Cost: *Alc* £23, set-price L/D fr £20. ☺
H/wine £9.95
Times: 12.30-2.30pm/6.30-10pm
Additional: Bar food; Sunday L; Children welcome
Style: Traditional/country-house
Seats: 50; Private dining room 30
Smoking: No smoking in dining room
Civil licence: 100
Accommodation: 16 en suite ★★★

BURY ST EDMUNDS, Angel Hotel

The Abbeygate restaurant has chandeliers from a French monastery and overlooks one of the prettiest Georgian squares in England. Seasonal dishes include oyster gratin and marinated cushion of venison.

Angel Hill IP33 1LT
Map 5: TL86
Tel: 01284 753926
Fax: 01284 750092
E-mail: sales@theangel.co.uk
Cost: *Alc* £27.95, set-price L £17.65/D £25.15. H/wine £9.95
Times: 12.30-2pm/7.30-9.30pm. Closed L Sat
Additional: Bar food; Sunday L; Children welcome
Style: Classic/Chic
Smoking: No smoking in dining room
Accommodation: 66 en suite ★★★

Directions: Town centre, close to Tourist Information

BURY ST EDMUNDS,

42 Churchgate

42 Churchgate Street IP33 1RG
Map 9: TG04
Tel/Fax: 01284 764179
Chef: Nigel Snook
Owners: Nigel & Samantha Snook
Cost: Set-price L £11.95/D £20. ☺
H/wine £9.95
Times: Noon-2pm/6.30-9.30pm;
Closed Sun, Mon, 2 wks Jan, 2 wks
Aug
Additional: Bar food L;
Children welcome
Seats: 48
Style: Informal/modern
Smoking: No-smoking area;
No pipes

Modern, unfussy setting for this market-town newcomer whose owners previously ran Les Parisiens in Warminster, Wiltshire. The simple restaurant is divided into three small rooms, each decorated in pale lemon and burgundy, and offers a Mediterranean-inspired menu. At lunch this runs to a mix of snacky items such as crêpes and salads, along with more serious dishes such as supreme of guinea fowl, citrus fruit confit and white wine sauce. Dinner is more expensive. Our inspector was very happy with her lunch, especially a starter of potato gnocchi with pepper and basil sauce 'a lovely dish for cold weather'. A medley of fish, salmon ('good'), red mullet ('excellent') and cod came with a chive risotto that had a good, overall soupy consistency, and sugar and lemon crêpes were pronounced 'lovely'. There's a small wine list with some six offered by the glass (in two sizes).

Directions: 200 metres from the Abbey

BURY ST EDMUNDS,

Leaping Hare Restaurant

Stanton IP31 2DW
Map 5: TL86
Tel: 01359 250287
Fax: 01359 252372
Cost: Alc £22, set-price L £12.50. ☺
H/wine £9
Time: Noon-3.30pm/7-9.30pm.
Closed all Mon & Tue, D Wed,Thu &
Sun, 2 wks Xmas

Charming vineyard restaurant in a converted medieval barn. Sitting beneath the beautifully vaulted ceiling with its wealth of exposed beams, diners are treated to dishes such as pigeon terrine, spinach and riccota gnocchi and nettle and parmesan risotto.

Additional: Sunday L; Children welcome
Style: Informal/Rustic **Smoking:** No smoking in dining room

Directions: From Bury St Edmunds take A143 towards Diss
approx. 8m and follow brown tourist signs for Wyken Vineyards

BURY ST EDMUNDS,

Maison Bleue

30-31 Churchgate Street IP33 1RG
Map 5: TL86
Tel: 01284 760623
Fax: 01284 761611
Cost: Alc £24, set-price L £14.95/D
£18.95. ☺ H/wine £9.50

Bistro-style restaurant, with smart all-French staff, specialising in fish and shellfish. Recommendations include mushrooms and crayfish tails, chicken stuffed with Parma ham and mozzarella, and tart au citron.

Maison Bleue

Times: Noon-2.30pm/6.30-9.30pm(10pm Fri & Sat). Closed Sun, 3 wks Jan
Additional: Bar food L; Children welcome
Style: Classic/Modern
Smoking: No smoking in dining room

Directions: Town centre. Churchgate St is opposite cathedral

FRESSINGFIELD,
Fox & Goose Inn ❀❀

Built in 1509 as an eating place, this traditional building is still owned by the church, which is clearly visible across the adjoining graveyard. In contrast to the old world surroundings – beams, blazing fires, prints and memorabilia – the menu is modern brasserie in style. Dishes are as varied as chicken satay with warm peanut sauce, eggs Benedict, and grilled haloumi cheese with gremolata and pitta bread. Main courses include grilled lamb with a swede and carrot purée and roast shallots, and salmon, monkfish and tiger prawns with griddled Mediterranean vegetables. All the meat is free-range, and separate children's and vegetarian menus are available. The pudding menu ranges from chocolate crème brûlée to warm Bakewell tart.

Directions: A140 & B1118 (Stradbroke) L after 6 miles – in village centre by church

Nr Diss IP21 5PB
Map 5: TM27
Tel: 01379 586247
Fax: 01379 586688
E-mail: fox@foxgoose.freeserve.co.uk
Chef: Maxwell Dougal
Owners: Tim & Pauline O'Leary
Cost: Alc £22, set-price L £9.50 & £12.50/D £17.50. ☺ H/wine £13.50
Times: Noon-2pm/6-9pm.
Closed 25 & 26 Dec
Additional: Bar food; Sunday L; Children welcome
Seats: 40. Private dining room 20
Style: Rustic/Traditional
Smoking: No smoking in dining room

HINTLESHAM, Hintlesham Hall ❀❀❀

IP8 3NS
Map 5: TM04
Tel: 01473 652268
Fax: 01473 652463
E-mail: reservations@hintlesham-hall.co.uk
Chef: Allan Ford
Owner: David Allan
Cost: Alc £36. Set-price L £21/D £27. H/wine £12.95

Elegantly and luxuriously furnished and decorated public rooms are what you'd expect from the first appearance of the perfectly symmetrical proportions of the Georgian façade of this grand country-house hotel. Although men are expected to wear a jacket and tie at dinner, the atmosphere is anything but stuffy, with a friendly greeting from the porter and pleasant and attentive staff in the restaurant. The menu is quietly unintimidating, too, and full of interest, from Jerusalem artichoke soup glazed with herbs to fillet of Scottish beef crusted with girolles on a Marsala reduction. That Allan Ford moves with the times is shown in smoked eel and mussel chowder given a Thai touch with lime leaves and coriander, or an anchovy tempura, a light, crisp batter enclosing the fish, served on a salad of baby squid dressed with white wine and saffron. Quality ingredients are handled with skill – chargrilled calves' liver, on sprout mash with braised endive, is described as 'excellent quality and perfectly cooked' and combinations work well, as in a 'well-balanced' winter main course of pheasant stuffed with watercress and chestnuts on mulled wine sauce with a sweet potato galette. 'First-class' pastry shows up in desserts of perhaps sweet pumpkin tart with cinnamon ice cream, and there might also be something along the lines of Grand Marnier and candied kumquat soufflé. Canapés in the bar start the ball rolling – tiny scallop tartlets, perhaps, or tomato and chicken mille-feuille, and breads and petits fours are impressive.

Directions: 5 miles west of Ipswich on the A1071 Hadleigh road

Times: Noon-1.45pm/7-9.30pm. Closed L Sat
Additional: Sunday L; Children 10+
Seats: 100. Private rooms 16-80. Jacket & tie preferred
Style: country-house/formal
Smoking: No smoking in dining room
Civil licence: 80
Accommodation: 33 en suite ★ ★ ★ ★

AA *Shortlisted for* Wine Award-see page 18

IPSWICH, Il Punto ✤

NEW

Vibrant modern French/British cooking in the novel setting of an old passenger river boat. Lots of polished wood and elegant table settings overlooking estuary docks. The wide range includes a decent confit of duck, pork belly and zesty sausage.

Neptune Quay IP4 1AX
Map 5: TM14
Tel: 01473 289748

Telephone for further details.

Directions: Telephone for directions

IPSWICH, **Marlborough Hotel** ✤✤

A delightful hotel with a country-house atmosphere, located in a quiet residential area. Pre-prandial drinks are served in the contemporary bar, while food is eaten in Victorian surroundings in the restaurant, overlooking lovely gardens which are illuminated at night for the benefit of diners. The cooking is adventurous, and there is good use of locally-sourced and organically-farmed produce. An inspection meal began impressively with warm salad of rabbit and sage meatballs served with leaves and mustard sauce, and continued positively with Aldeburgh cod served with a lobster and king prawn risotto and a delicate ginger butter sauce. Elsewhere on the *carte* there might be Herdwick lamb fillet – a notably tasty breed of sheep – lightly roasted and served with lyonnaise potatoes and pesto, or breast of duck with crusted peppercorns

Henley Road IP1 3SP
Map 5: TM14
Tel: 01473 257677
Fax: 01473 226927
E-mail: reception@themarlborough.co.uk
Chef: Simon Barker
Owner: Robert Gough
Cost: *Alc* £37, set-price L £18/D £23.95. ☺ H/wine £9.95
Times: 12.30-2.30pm/7-9.30pm. Closed L Sat
Additional: Bar food; Sunday L; Children welcome
Seats: 40. Private dining room 26
Style: Modern/Comfortable

Marlborough Hotel

Smoking: No smoking in dining room
Civil licence: 70
Accommodation: 22 en suite ★ ★ ★

and honey on a cassis sauce. A sampled lemon tart with citrus cream did not quite make the grade, but chocolate coffee fudge petits fours made up for any slight disappointment. The concise wine list is well chosen and offers good value. Service from friendly young staff is another high point.

Directions: Take A1156 from A14, or A1214 from A12. Turn R at Henley Road/A1214 crossroads

IPSWICH, Scott's Brasserie ❀

An old maltings building houses this upmarket brasserie, where recent highlights of the Mediterranean-influenced carte *have included duck and orange terrine with red onion and mild chilli jam, Cromer crab cakes, and caramelised lemon tart.*

Style: Bistro-style/Informal
Smoking: No-smoking area; No pipes & cigars

Directions: Near Buttermarket shopping centre, close to Cox Lane and Foundation Street car parks

4a Orwell Place IP4 1BB
Map 5: TM14
Tel: 01473 230254
Fax: 01473 218851
Cost: Set-price L, £9.95/13.50, D £16.95/19.95. ☺ H/wine £9.95
Times: Noon-2.30pm/6.30-9.30pm. Closed L Sat, all Sun, Bhs
Additional: Children welcome

IXWORTH, Theobalds Restaurant ❀❀

68 High Street Nr Bury St Edmunds IP31 2HJ
Map 5: TL97
Tel/Fax: 01359 231707
E-mail: theorest@aol.uk
Chef: Simon Theobald
Owners: Simon & Geraldine Theobald

Theobalds is in a building that was erected in 1650 and looks it: a huge inglenook in the lounge, a proliferation of beams and upright timbers, and ladderback chairs at well-spaced tables blending in well. The seasonally changing menus may bring a taste of the Orient to rural Suffolk in the shape of scallops and king prawns stir-fried with spring onions, chilli, ginger and soy, although the kitchen's heart is generally closer to home, with starters ranging from twice-baked Cheddar soufflé, through crab and sweetcorn soup, to terrine of calves' tongue with red onion chutney. Main courses are normally matched with a well-made sauce, often alcoholic: rosemary and Madeira for herb-flecked fillet of lamb, mandarin and ginger for roast quail breast, and rich white port – described by an inspector as 'very good' – for escalope of salmon on wilted spinach. Vegetables get the thumbs up, and tarts are a favoured pudding, their pastry exemplary, as in caramelised apple and almond with vanilla ice cream, or lemon and lime with lemon sorbet. France is the backbone of the wine list, which is baldly arranged by colour in ascending price order, although a close reading may root out some other countries.

Cost: *Alc* £30, set-price L £19.
H/wine £14
Times: 12.15-1.30pm/7-9.15pm.
Closed L Sat, D Sun, all Mon, 2 wks Aug
Additional: Sunday L;
Children 8+ at D
Seats: 46.
Style: Smart/Comfortable
Smoking: No smoking in dining room

Directions: 7 miles from Bury St Edmunds on A143 Bury/Diss road

LAVENHAM, Angel Hotel ❀

Decent food served in a typical English inn setting – that's lots of exposed beams, whitewashed walls and plain wooden tables. Clientele tends to be a mix of locals and hotel residents who all think very highly of the food. Cheerful, relaxed service.

Market Place CO10 9QZ
Map 5: TL94
Tel: 01787 247388
Fax: 01787 248344
E-mail: angellav@aol.com
Cost: *Alc* £17. ☺ H/wine £7.95
Times: Noon-2.15pm/6.45-9.15pm.
Closed 25, 26 Dec
Additional: Bar food; Sunday L;
Children welcome
Style: informal/traditional
Smoking: No-smoking area; No pipes & cigars
Accommodation: 8 en suite ★ ★

Directions: Take A143 from Bury St Edmunds and turn onto A1141 after 4 miles; hotel is on Market Place, off High Street

LAVENHAM,
Great House Restaurant ❀

Quality French cuisine meets English rural idyll in this 15th-century country house restaurant and hotel. Grilled salmon, monkfish and red mullet with pink peppercorn sauce set high standards. Attractive courtyard available for the warmer months.

Market Place CO10 9QZ
Map 5: TL94
Tel: 01787 247431
Fax: 01789 248007
E-mail: info@greathouse.co.uk
Cost: *Alc* £29 (D only), set-price L £9.95 & £14.95/D £19.95. ☺ H/wine £11.50
Times: Noon-2.30pm/7-9.30pm.
Closed D Sun, all Mon, 3 wks Jan
Additional: Bar food L; Sunday L;
Children welcome
Style: Informal/country-house
Smoking: No smoking in dining room
Accommodation: 5 en suite

Directions: In Market Place (turn into Market Lane from High Street)

LONG MELFORD,

Chimneys Restaurant ⊛⊛

Hall Street CO10 9JR
Map 5: TL84
Tel: 01787 379806
Fax: 01787 312294
Chef: Wayne Messenger
Owners: Samuel & Zena Chalmers
Cost: H/wine £11.75
Times: Noon-2pm/7-9pm.
Closed Sun, Bhs
Additional: Children welcome
Seats: 45
Style: Classic/traditional

Chimneys occupies a 16th-century timbered building, with an interior in keeping: dark wooden beams, whitewashed walls with prints adding splashes of colour, and exposed brickwork around an inglenook. The menu is less traditional than might be expected in the surroundings. King prawns are given a zing with red onion and chilli, and sea bass is baked with lemon and ginger and served with fragrant coconut rice. Seasonality comes to the fore in some dishes, as in a casserole of guinea fowl, venison and pheasant with winter vegetables, while others have a heartiness to them: lamb shank is braised with beans and served on garlic mash, for instance. Fish might show up in fillet of Scottish salmon topped with pesto and cheese, and puddings might range from homely apple charlotte to passion fruit macaroon. Fudge comes with coffee, and the wine list features mainly French and New World bottles.

Directions: On main street of Long Melford village

LONG MELFORD,

Scutchers Restaurant ⊛

Westgate Street CO10 9DP
Map 5: TL84
Tel: 07000 728824
Fax: 07000 785443

Bright and busy bistro, decorated in blue and yellow with pine tables and chairs. Dishes from an interesting menu include warm smoked duck salad, and seared fillet of sea bass.

Cost: Alc £24.50. H/wine £9.50
Times: Noon-2pm/7-9.30pm. Closed Sun, Mon, 1st wk Jan
Additional: Children welcome
Style: Bistro-style/informal
Smoking: No pipes & cigars; Air conditioning

Directions: About a mile from Long Melford towards Clare

LOWESTOFT, **Ivy House Farm**

A beautiful converted 18th-century thatched barn makes a great setting to enjoy modern European cooking. Start perhaps with terrine of lemon sole, followed by grilled fillet of turbot with roasted fennel, or tagliatelli with roasted peppers.

Ivy Lane Beccles Road
Oulton Broad NR33 8HY
Map 5: TM59
Tel: 01502 501353
Fax: 01502 501539
E-mail: ivyhousefm@aol.com
Cost: *Alc* £25. ☺ H/wine £9.95
Times: Noon-1.45pm/7-9.30pm
Additional: Bar food; Sunday L;
Children welcome
Style: Informal/rustic
Smoking: No smoking in dining room
Accommodation: 19 en suite ★ ★ ★

Directions: From Lowestoft, follow
A146 (Norwich). Hotel approx
0.25 mile after junction with A1117
(Ipswich), over small railway bridge

MILDENHALL, **Riverside Hotel**

Imposing Georgian building with a comfortable, modern restaurant. Well-flavoured seared cod with wild mushrooms was followed by an unusual tarte Tatin, made from a small, sweet, whole cored apple, covered in pastry.

Style: Chic/country house
Smoking: No-smoking area; Jacket & tie preferred
Accommodation: 92 bedrooms en suite ★ ★ ★

Directions: From M11 J 9 take A11 for Norwich. At 'Fiveways' rdbt take A1101 into town. Left at mini-rdbt, hotel last on L before bridge

Mill Street IP28 7DP
Map 5: TL77
Tel: 01638 717274
Fax: 01638 715997
E-mail: cameronhotels@
riversidehotel.freeserve.co.uk
Cost: *Alc* £20, set-price L £12.50/
D £20.50. ☺ H/wine £12.75
Times: Noon-3pm/7-9.30pm.
Additional: Bar food; Sunday L;
Children welcom

NAYLAND, **White Hart Inn**

Following a recent refurbishment the 15th-century coaching inn has retained many of its original features, but has been given a new contemporary look with whitewashed walls, crisp white linen and the unusual feature of a glass door over the cellar. Guests are well looked after by attentive, friendly staff. The cooking is best described as modern farmhouse with

High Street Nr Colchester
CO6 4JF
Map 5: TL93
Tel: 01206 263382
Fax: 01206 263638
E-mail: nayhart@aol.com
Chef: Neil Bishop
Owner: Michel Roux
Cost: *Alc* £18.50. H/wine £11

French influences: grilled confit of rabbit legs with pan-fried Jerusalem artichoke and walnut butter; roast fillet of pork with caramelised shallots and apples and a light cider sauce. There were slip-ups, however, on our inspection visit – indistinct flavours in a duck and pheasant terrine, and disappointing roast cod that did not match the quality of the red wine sauce with which it was served. Seasonal fruit tart, however, was simply *comme il faut*. The wine list features a total of about 60 wines from around the world, thoughtfully selected to suit a range of palates and budgets.

Directions: Village centre, 6 miles N of Colchester on A134

Times: Noon-2pm/6.30-9.30pm.
Closed Mon, 26 Dec-4 Jan
Additional: Sunday L; Children welcome
Seats: 55. Private dining room 40
Style: Modern/traditional
Smoking: No pipes & cigars
Accommodation: 6 en suite

NEWMARKET, Bedford Lodge Hotel

New restaurant with limestone floors, arched windows and ornate woodwork, including a conservatory-style area. Halibut with white wine sauce and a choux ring with rich caramel sauce were enjoyable dishes.

Directions: From town centre follow A1303 towards Bury St Edmunds for 0.5m

Bury Road CB8 7BX
Map 5: TL66
Tel: 01638 663175
Fax: 01638 667391
E-mail: info@bedfordlodgehotel.co.uk

Telephone for further details

ORFORD,
The Crown & Castle NEW

Owners Ruth and David Watson are no strangers to the Restaurant Guide, having owned both Hintlesham Hall and the Fox & Goose at Fressingfield. They have now arrived at the Crown & Castle, where much use is made of local produce, Butley-Orford oysters and local free range chicken featured on the sensibly priced and straightforward menu at a summer inspection. The wine list is helpfully written and service is slick and polite.

Directions: Turn off B1084 in village

IP12 2LJ
Map 5: TM45
Tel: 01394 450205
Fax: 01394 450176
E-mail:
info@crownandcastlehotel.co.uk

Telephone for further details

POLSTEAD, The Cock Inn

Charming 17th-century village pub overlooking the green. Traditional dishes served at lunchtime are complemented by a more elaborate frequently-changing evening menu, typically featuring leek and mustard crumble or scallops with a bacon and watercress salad.

Directions: From Colchester take A134 towards Sudbury, then R to Stoke-by-Nayland. L at Angel Inn & follow signs for Polstead

CO6 5AL
Map 5: TM14
Tel/Fax: 01206 263150

Telephone for further details

SOUTHWOLD, The Blyth NEW

Seafood's the thing at this distinctive building – once the Station Hotel for the now-defunct Southwold railway. Spanish cod stew impressed, with chunks of fresh, pan-fried fillet and a stew of potato, pepper and spicy chorizo sausage.

Style: Informal/modern **Smoking:** No smoking in dining room
Accommodation: 13 en suite ★ ★

Directions: From A12 follow signs to Southwold, Hotel 4 miles

Station Road IP18 6AY
Map 5: TM57
Tel/Fax: 01502 722632
E-mail: pieravenue@bt21.com
Cost: *Alc* £22. ☺ H/wine £9.50
Times: Noon-2pm/7-9pm. Closed Mon, Tue
Additional: Bar food; Sunday L; Children welcome; Vegetarian dishes not always available

SOUTHWOLD, **The Crown**

Old posting inn where the high quality restaurant co-habits with both pub and wine bar. The food is unpretentious and of a very high quality. A succulent pork fillet was very enjoyable and the crème brûlée spot on.

Smoking: No smoking in dining room; Air conditioning
Accommodation: 12 rooms ★★

Directions: Take A1095 from A12; hotel at top of High Street

90 High Street IP18 6DP
Map 5: TM57
Tel: 01502 722275
Fax: 01502 727263
Cost: Alc £18.50, set-price L £25.50.
☺ H/wine £9.95
Times: 12.15-2pm/7-9.30pm
Additional: Bar food; Sunday L;
Children 5+
Style: Informal/Traditional

SOUTHWOLD, **Swan Hotel**

This 17th-century coaching inn plays host to an elegant hotel restaurant with a large selection of appetising and imaginative dishes on offer. Main courses such as breast of Aylesbury duck with lime marmalade are a strong attraction.

Style: Classic/Formal
Smoking: No smoking in dining room
Accommodation: 45 en suite ★★★

Directions: Take A1095 off A12; follow High Street into Market Place, hotel on L

Market Place IP18 6EG
Map 5: TM57
Tel: 01502 722186
Fax: 01502 724800
E-mail: swan.hotel@adnams.co.uk
Cost: Alc £30.50, set-price L £18/D
£25. ☺ H/wine £9.95
Times: Noon-1.45/7-9.30pm.
Closed for L until Etr
Additional: Bar food L; Sunday L;
Children 5+

STOWMARKET, **Tot Hill House** ❀

Georgian house with equine art and hand-painted horse-motif plates. Roast seabass with delicate truffle mash was followed by a stunning dessert of ginger shortbread and rhubarb mille-feuille.

IP14 3QH
Map 5: TM05
Tel/Fax: 01449 673375
Cost: Alc £27.95. ☺ H/wine £13.50
Times: Noon-1.30pm/7-9.30pm.
Closed L Sat, D Sun, all Mon & Tue,
2 wks Jan, 2 wks Aug/Sep
Additional: Sunday L; Children
welcome; Vegetarian main course by
request only
Style: Classic/Formal
Smoking: No smoking in dining room;
Jacket & tie preferred

Directions: On eastbound
carriageway of A14 midway between
Ipswich & Bury St Edmunds

SUDBURY, **Red Onion Bistro** ❀

Open, informal bistro with a modern trendy feel. No shortage of flavours what with authentic Greek lamb kebabs say, or chargrilled chicken breast. Or really give your taste buds something to write home about with a zingy lemon syllabub.

Additional: Children welcome
Style: Bistro-style/informal
Smoking: No-smoking area; no pipes & cigars

Directions: On A131 Chelmsford road out of Sudbury

57 Ballingdon Street CO10 6DA
Map 5: TL84
Tel: 01787 376777
Fax: 01787 883156
Cost: Alc £15, set-price L £8.75/D
£10.75. ☺ H/wine £7.75
Times: Noon-2pm/6.30-
9.30pm.Closed Sun

WESTLETON, The Westleton Crown

Friendly, attentive service and sound home cooking can be expected at this old coaching inn. Appealing menus offer vegetarian and seafood specialities, and our inspector made particular mention of the home made bread.

IP17 3AD
Map 5: TM46
Tel: 0800 328 6001
Fax: 01728 648239

Telephone for further details

Directions: Telephone for directions

WOODBRIDGE, Captain's Table

A relaxed yet sophisticated atmosphere runs throughout this 16th-century part-beamed cottage, where a patio area in the walled garden is called into use for al fresco eating in warm weather. Inside, natural wood tables and chairs and a pale yellow colour scheme are the backdrop for straightforward, even understated menus: Thai-style steamed mussels, rock oysters, chargrilled fillet steak with parsley butter and chips, and Cumberland sausages with mash and onion gravy. But the kitchen certainly comes up with the goods in terms of flavours. 'Mouthwatering' ham-hock terrine is bound in a rich jelly and complemented by a small mound of red onion relish, while slow-roasted duck leg, its skin crisp, flesh tender, comes with spot-on sweet and slightly sour red cabbage. The same approach is brought to desserts of bread-and-butter pudding or rich, lightly textured chocolate marquise.

3 Quay Street IP12 1BX
Map 5: TM24
Tel: 01394 383145
Fax: 01394 388508
Chef: Pascal Pommier
Owners: Jo & Pascal Pommier
Cost: Alc £17. ☺ H/wine £8.95
Times: Noon-2pm (3pm Sun)/6.30-9.30pm (10pm Fri, Sat) Closed D Sun
Additional: Sunday L; Children wel.
Seats: 50. Private dining room 24
Style: Bistro-style/informal
Smoking: No-smoking area

Directions: From A12, pass garden centre on L. Quay St is opposite station & theatre; restaurant 100 yds on L

WOODBRIDGE, Seckford Hall Hotel

Sophisticated, elegant hotel restaurant in an attractive Tudor manor house. Elizabeth I is reputed to have held court here and the roast fillet of cod and the chocolate truffle were certainly fit for royalty.

Style: Traditional/country-house
Smoking: No smoking in dining room; Air conditioning
Civil licence: 125 **Accommodation:** 32 en suite ★ ★ ★

Directions: Signposted on A12 (Woodbridge by-pass). Do not follow signs for town centre

IP13 6NU
Map 5: TM24
Tel: 01394 385678
Fax: 01394 380610
E-mail: reception@seckford.co.uk
Cost: Alc £27.50, set-price L £13.50.
H/wine £10.95
Times: 12.30-1.45pm/7.30-9.30pm.
Closed 25 Dec
Additional: Bar food L; Sunday L;
Children welcome

YAXLEY, Bull Auberge

Ipswich Road Nr Eye IP23 8BZ
Map 5: TM17
Tel/Fax: 01379 783604
E-mail: bullauberge@aol.com
Cost: Alc £16.25, set-price L £10. ☺
H/wine £9.50
Times: Noon-2pm/7-9pm
Additional: Bar food L; Children 5+
Smoking: No-smoking area

Directions: Adjacent to A140, Norwich to Ipswich road on junction with B1117 to Eye

Smart dining room in a 15th-century inn. Try seared calf's liver and kidney with potato rösti and raspberry vinegar sauce, or grilled monkfish wrapped in Parma ham and served with roasted vegetables. Finish with tarte au citron.

YOXFORD,

Satis House Hotel ✿

East meets west at this Georgian country house, with its pretty batik table linen. A wide choice of Malaysian dishes is offered, or a Malaysian banquet can be arranged to suit individual tastes.

Additional: Children 7+
Style: Country-house
Smoking: No smoking in dining room
Accommodation: 8 en suite ★ ★

Directions: On A12 just N of village

IP17 3EX
Map 5: TM36
Tel: 01728 668418
Fax: 01728 668640
E-mail: yblackmore@aol.com
Cost: *Alc* £25, set-price L £13.95/
D £19.75. ☺ H/wine £10.95
Times: D only. (L by arrangement)
Closed Sun & Mon

SURREY

BAGSHOT,

Pennyhill Park Hotel ✿✿✿

Stables, golf course and formal gardens surround the well-preserved, Victorian country house hotel, yet London is only 27 miles away, and Heathrow even closer. The cooking, perhaps as a result, takes an international tone with dishes ranging from marinated langoustines with caviar Chantilly and gazpacho sauce to roast cannon of lamb with swede fondant, honey and ginger coated vegetables, coriander and garlic jus. Ingredients are carefully chosen – roast breast of black-legged guinea fowl, for example, served with chive and Mascarpone risotto and white wine sauce. The cooking is big and bold, no timidity of flavouring here, with the likes of panache of seafood on beetroot and horseradish risotto with Zinfandel and star anise jus, or fillet of beef with celeriac purée, cep ravioli, stuffed pig's trotter and truffle sauce. Desserts are equally forceful. Baked coconut cream with poached exotic fruit salad, sitting in lemongrass and exotic fruit consommé or hot chocolate rum and raisin fondant make a strong final statement to a meal.

Directions: On A30 between Bagshot and Camberley

London Road GU19 5ET
Map 4: SU96
Tel: 01276 471774
Fax: 01276 475570
E-mail: pennyhillpark@msn.com
Chef: Karl Edmunds
Owners: Exclusive Hotels
Cost: *Alc* £50, set-price L £22.50/D £50. H/wine £20
Times: 12.30-2.30pm/7-10pm.
Closed L Sat, all Sun & Mon
Additional: Sunday L (private bookings only); Children 12+
Seats: 40. Private dining room 4-200. Jacket & tie preferred
Style: Country-house/Formal
Smoking: No smoking in dining room; Air conditioning
Civil licence: 120
Accommodation: 115 en suite ★ ★ ★ ★ ★

CHURT,
Pride of the Valley Hotel

Oak-panelled walls and high-backed chairs lend a baronial feel to this dining room, though the cooking is contemporary. Try the quail with truffle stuffing, and a tasty hot chocolate soufflé with a fabulous chocolate truffle ice cream.

Style: Country-house/formal
Smoking: No smoking in dining room
Accommodation: 16 rooms ★★

Directions: Telephone for directions

Jumps Road Farnham GU10 2LE
Map 4: SU84
Tel: 01428 605799
Fax: 01428 605875
E-mail: prideovalley@cs.com
Cost: *Alc* £25.50, set-price L £19.50.
☺ H/wine £10.95
Times: Noon-2.30pm/7-10pm.
Closed L Sat
Additional: Bar food; Sunday L;
Children welcome

CLAYGATE,
Le Petit Pierrot Restaurant

Small, personally run French restaurant, with a tented ceiling and Pierrot masks adorning the walls. Crème brûlée with prunes and Armagnac was the highlight of a recent meal.

Additional: Children 8+
Style: Chic/French **Smoking:** No pipes

Directions: Telephone for directions

4 The Parade KT10 0NU
Map 4: TQ16
Tel: 01372 465105
Fax: 01372 467642
Cost: Set-price L £12.25-£20.25/D
£23.50. ☺ H/wine £10.85
Times: 12.15-2.30pm/7.15-9.30pm.
Closed L Sat, all Sun, 1 wk Xmas,
2 wks in Summer, Bhs

EGHAM, Runnymede Hotel

Windsor Road TW20 0AG
Map 4: TQ07
Tel: 01784 436171
Fax: 01784 436340
E-mail:
leftbank@runnymedehotel.com
Chef: Laurence Curtis
Owner: Ralph Trustees Ltd
Cost: *Alc* £26.75, set-price L £17.95.
H/wine £13.95
Times: 12.15-3.30pm/7-11pm.
Closed L Sat, D Sun
Additional: Sunday L (12.15-3pm);
Children welcome
Seats: 150. Private dining room 350
Style: Modern/Minimalist
Smoking: No-smoking area; Air
conditioning

The modern minimalist interior design of the Left Bank Restaurant emphasises its enviable location on the banks of the Thames by the clever use of an aquatic theme that includes tanks full of brightly-coloured fish. A visible grill section allows guests to tune in on the sizzling live action as they dish up the griddled tiger prawns with coconut chilli sauce or chargrilled lamb cutlets with braised haricots and roasted vegetables. Fish and seafood dishes also include crab guacamole, lobster thermidor with salad and fries, and skate, capers and mash. An oriental note is added with dishes such as crispy barbecue duck salad and sesame crusted tuna with wok-fried soy greens.

Civil licence: 150 **Accommodation:** 180 en suite ★★★★

Directions: On A308 Windsor road from M25 J3

EWELL, C'est la Vie ❀

17 High Street KT17 1SB
Map 4: TQ26
Tel: 020 83942933
Fax: 020 83935549
Cost: Alc £20.25, set-price L £9.95/D
£16.95. ☺ H/wine £9.75
Times: Noon-3pm/7-midnight
Additional: Sunday L; Children 12+
Style: Rustic
Smoking: No-smoking area; Air
conditioning

Directions: Village 1 mile from
Epsom towards Kingston. Restaurant is
5 mins walk from rail station

*French music sets the mood at this popular local eatery, and the
French menus translate into dishes like roast quails with a garlic
confit and taragon sauce, and roast sea bass fillet with pan-fried
aubergine and red onion butter.*

FARNHAM, Bishop's Table Hotel ❀❀

27 West Street GU9 7DR
Map 4: SU84
Tel: 01252 710222
Fax: 01252 733494
E-mail: bishops.table@btinternet.com
Chef: Anton Hayter
Owner: Mr K Verjee
Cost: Alc £26, set-price D £22. ☺
H/wine £10.65
Times: 12.30-2pm/7-9.45pm.
Closed L Sat, 26 Dec-3 Jan
Additional: Sunday L
Seats: 55. Private dining room 20
Smoking: No smoking in dining room
Accommodation: 17 en suite ★★★

First impressions at the Bishop's Table, which was built in the
18th century, are of a warm and inviting atmosphere,
engendered by friendly, well-motivated staff and comfortable
surroundings. The restaurant is a smartly appointed room, with
upholstered dining chairs, drapes at the windows and well-set
tables. In here you can expect to find some classically inspired
dishes – medallions of beef fillet with sautéed foie gras and
creamed truffle sauce, for instance – alongside more robust-
sounding items, such as roast breast and braised leg of guinea
fowl with garlic confit and bean cassoulet. The kitchen is
equally at home with meat and fish, turning out starters of
wood pigeon on pickled vegetables with a port and balsamic
sauce, and mille-feuille of seafood encircled by queen scallops,
gazpacho dressing adding some pizzazz. That thought goes into
each dish is shown by an inspector's notable main course of
fillet of brill braised with leeks and wild mushrooms served
with a sauce of mussels and chervil. Puddings hit the spot too,
not least strawberry soufflé, light in texture but deeply
flavoured, with vanilla ice cream. The wine list is fairly
compact but still manages to offer reasonable choice.

Directions: In the centre of the town

GUILDFORD,

The Angel Posting House ❀❀

91 High Street GU1 3DP
Map 4: SU94
Tel: 01483 564555
Fax: 01483 533770
Chef: Jeremy O'Connor
Owner: Roger Brown
Cost: *Alc* £40, set-price L £14.50 &
£18.50/D £23.50. ☺
H/wine fr £10.50
Times: Noon-2pm/7-9.30pm
Additional: Children welcome
Seats: 24. Private dining rooms 8, 14,
70
Smoking: No smoking in dining room;
Air conditioning
Accommodation: 21 rooms ★★★

In the centre of Guildford's High Street, this timber-framed building dates back to 1300. The restaurant is in the oldest part of the hotel, below ground in a stone-vaulted undercroft which still has remains of the original spiral staircase. The restaurant menu is rather more contemporary, and amalgamates French and English cooking. New chef, Jeremy O'Connor, has refined the *carte*, and the roast pithivier of game with sautéed wood pigeon, wild mushrooms and Madeira sauce was a well-prepared and interesting dish with good flavour and tender meat, all lightly cooked. The same delicate touch had been applied to a supreme of Cornish turbot with champagne sauce which came on a bed of spinach and a selection of baby vegetables. Desserts fared well, particularly a soufflé glace of fresh seasonal fruits which had good flavour.

Directions: In town centre (one way street)

HASLEMERE,

Lythe Hill Hotel ❀❀ NEW

Petworth Road GU27 3BQ
Map 04: SU93
Tel: 01428 651251
Fax: 01428 644131
E-mail: lythe@lythehill.co.uk
Chef: Roger Clarke
Cost: *Alc* £42.50. ☺ H/wine £14.50
Times: D only, 7.15-9.15pm
Additional: Bar food L; Sunday L
(12.15-2.15pm); Children welcome
Seats: 60. Private dining room 16
Style: Traditional
Smoking: No pipes & cigars
Civil licence: 130
Accommodation: 41 en suite ★★★★

Low ceiling beams and dark panelled walls are all part of the dining experience at this beautifully restored 15th-century building. The black and white timbered Auberge de France Restaurant has been used as a courthouse in its time, but the concentration nowadays is on fine French cuisine, temptingly displayed on a well-chosen *carte*. Haddock timbale with parsley sauce and fresh asparagus was a well-flavoured recent appetiser, while terrine of guinea fowl and foie gras was a gamey starter served with a tasty pickled walnut and red onion chutney. Roast lamb with a sage and veal jus arrived mouth-wateringly tender and cooked to perfection. Other main choices might be fresh seafood on a bed of egg noodles with saffron sauce, or pan-fried fillet of beef with a casserole of wild mushrooms and roasted garlic. Honey-glazed figs on a vanilla sauce with ice cream might grace the dessert menu, along with perhaps chilled parfait of William pears and almonds, or crêpes Suzette, flamed at the table.

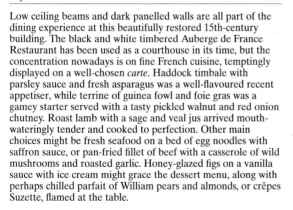

Directions: 1 mile E of Haslemere on B2131

HORLEY,
Langshott Manor ֎֎

Small wood framed Elizabethan manor house set in its own beautiful grounds. The hotel dining room is oak beamed and thoroughly in keeping with the country house setting, made all the more delightful by small touches such as an intriguing hot air balloon feature in the fireplace. On a recent visit the inspector enjoyed a starter of home smoked fillet of salmon with a black truffle vinaigrette. This was successfully accompanied by a salmon, potato and chive fishcake on a bed of cucumber salad, with a piece of smoked salmon with basil oil making up the delightful trio. A main course of a nicely fresh sea bass fillet on two rolls of crab canelloni proved well conceived and satisfying. A highly creditable banana Tatin with coconut ice cream rounded off an excellent meal.

Directions: From A23 Horley, take Ladbroke Road turning off Chequers Hotel roundabout, 0.75 mile on R

Langshott Lane RH6 9LN
Map 4: TQ24
Tel: 01293 786680
Fax: 01293 783905
E-mail: admin@langshottmanor.com
Chef: Stephen Toward
Owners: Peter & Deborah Hinchcliffe
Cost: *Alc* £35, set-price L £25/D £37.50. H/wine £17
Times: Noon-2.30pm/7-9.30pm
Seats: 42. Private dining room 22
Additional: Sunday L; Children welcome
Style: Classic/Country-house
Smoking: No smoking in dining room; Jacket & tie preferred
Civil licence: 40
Accommodation: 15 en suite ★ ★

KINGSTON-UPON-THAMES,
Ayudhya Thai ֎֎

14 Kingston Hill KT2 7NH
Map GtL: B2
Tel/Fax: 020 8549 5984/8546 5878
Chefs: Koy, Thanpho
Owner: Miss S Thanpho
Times: 11-3pm/6.30-11pm. Closed Mon
Additional: Bar food; Sunday L; Children 3+
Seats: 70
Smoking: No pipes & cigars

A well-established Thai restaurant with traditional teak panelling and carvings, and many patriotic visual references to the Thai royal family. The impressive range of quality Thai dishes owes as much to the use of first-class ingredients as to the skill of the cooking and the honesty of the flavours produced. Prawns stuffed with crabmeat, pork and spring onions, wrapped in a thin pancake and deep fried is just one of several delicious starters sampled in the past, while Kai Bai Toey, marinated chicken in screwpine leaves and wrapped was succulent and tender. Spicy mixed seafood was a successful main dish, including first-rate prawns, squid, crab claws and mussels all gently stirfried to give an excellent combination of seafood. Another was a flat noodle stirfry with beansprouts, spring onions, egg and crushed peanuts, served with a fragrant jasmine Thai rice. Fresh fruit such as lychees and rambutan make a preferable dessert to the traditional Thai selections available, especially for the uninitiated.

Directions: 0.5 mile from Kingston town centre on A308, and 2.5 miles from Robin Hood rdbt at junction of A3

KINGSTON-UPON-THAMES,

Frère Jacques

10-12 Riverside Walk off Bishops Hall
KT1 1QN
Map GtL: B2
Tel: 020 8546 1332
Fax: 020 8546 1956
E-mail: john@frerejacques.co.uk
Cost: A/c £20, set-price L £9.90/D
£17.50. ☺ H/wine £10.90
Times: Noon-11pm. Closed 25 Dec,
1 Jan
Additional: Bar food L; Sunday L;
Children welcome
Style: Bistro-style/French
Smoking: No-smoking area; Air
conditioning

*An affordable choice where Thames-side dining is concerned.
Expect staples such as French onion soup, moules marinière, and
steak with loads of frites. Predominantly French staff and music add
to the atmosphere. Daily specials add to the menu options.*

Directions: 50 metres S of the Kingston side of Kingston Bridge.
By the river

OCKLEY,

Bryce's Seafood Restaurant

*Taking great pride in offering freshly caught fish, the restaurant's
menu is accordingly varied in content but always consistent in its
thoughtful, skilled approach to preparation. Cajun spiced salmon
fillet on roasted peppers strongly recommended.*

RH5 5TH
Map 4: TQ14
Tel: 01306 627430
Fax: 01306 628274
Cost: A/c £25.50, set-price
L £21.50/D £24. ☺ H/wine £10.50

Times: Noon-2.30pm/7-9.30pm. Closed D Sun in Nov, Jan &
Feb, 25-26 Dec, 1 Jan
Additional: Bar food; Sunday L; Children welcome
Style: Informal/Traditional
Smoking: No smoking in dining room

Directions: 8 miles south of Dorking on A29

OTTERSHAW, **Foxhills** ⊛   **NEW**

*A manor house with high-ceilinged restaurant, serving modern
European food. Expect potato and celeriac cake with roquette, black
olives and feta cheese, perhaps followed by Moroccan spiced lamb
brochettes with saffron basmati and curry oil.*

KT16 0EL
Map 4: TQ06
Tel: 01932 872050
Fax: 01932 874762
E-mail: mhayton@ibm.net
Cost: A/c £25, set-price L £18/
D £22.50. ☺ H/wine £11.50

Times: Noon-3pm (Clubhouse, ex Sat)/D 7.30-10pm
Additional: Sunday L; Children welcome
Style: Traditional/country-house
Smoking: No pipes & cigars
Accommodation: 38 en suite ★ ★ ★ ★

Directions: A320 to Woking from M25. At 2nd rdbt take last
exit Chobham Road, turn right into Foxhills Road, follow unti T
junction, turn right into Stonehill Road

PEASLAKE,
Hurtwood Inn Hotel ❀

Walking Bottom GU5 9RR
Map 4: TQ04
Tel: 01306 730851
Fax: 01306 731390
E-mail: sales@
hurtwoodinnhotel.freeserve.co.uk
Cost: *Alc* £24, set-price D £17. ☺
H/wine £10.70
Times: D only, 7-9.30pm.
Closed D Sun.
Additional: Bar food; Sunday L (noon-2.30pm); Children welcome
Style: Classic/country-house
Smoking: No-smoking area
Accommodation: 17 en suite ★★★

Candles and lilies adorn the oak panelled restaurant in this delightful country hotel. An art deco feel sits well with the decadence of seared monkfish escalopes with lemon couscous and a caviar dressing.

Directions: Leave A25 at Gomshall, follow signs to Peaslake, approx. 2.5m, hotel in centre of village.

REDHILL,
Nutfield Priory ❀

Nutfield RH1 4EL
Map 4: TQ35
Tel: 01737 824400
Fax: 01737 823321
E-mail: nutpriory@aol.com
Chef: David Evans
Owners: Hand Picked Hotels
Cost: *Alc* £35, set-price L £16/D
£27.50. H/wine £12.95
Times: Noon-3pm/7-11pm.
Closed L Sat
Additional: Bar food L; Sunday L;
Children welcome
Seats: 60. Private dining room 6-100
Style: Country-house
Smoking: No smoking in dining room
Civil licence: 60
Accommodation: 60 en suite ★★★★

Built as an extravagant folly in 1872, the flights of fancy at Nutfield Priory are all architectural. The cooking is restrained and enjoyable, and a recent piña colada bavoir with passion fruit sorbet scored full marks. Best Corporate Wine list (see pages 18-19).

Directions: On A25 1 mile E of Redhill

REIGATE,
The Dining Room ❀❀

Although involved in quite a bit of TV work, Executive Chef Tony Tobin appears still to spend the majority of his time cooking at the modern-looking, first-floor restaurant. The menu reads well and there are some interesting and creative

59a High Street
RH2 9AE
Map 4: TQ25
Tel/Fax: 01737 226650
Chef: Tony Tobin
Owner: Elite Restaurants Ltd

combinations and a good use of spices. Seared sea scallops with crispy crab cakes and hot and sweet sauce made a first-rate starter, both colourful and full of flavour. North and South African influences were drawn upon for a main course of Sosatie lamb cutlet with apricot and lemon couscous. Global ideas also are evident in other dishes such as seared beef fillet with pickled spiced beetroots and wasabi potato pikelets, and grilled veal chop with buttered spinach and garam masala potatoes. Sunday lunch offers both grilled pork fillet with liquorice and ginger, and sirloin of beef 'served the way it should be'. The wine list is short but well-chosen. The set lunch menu is particulary good value.

Cost: *Alc* £35, set-price L £13.50/ D £16.95. ☺ H/wine £10.95
Times: Noon-2pm/7-10pm. Closed L Sat, D Sun, 1st 2 wks Aug
Additional: Sunday L; Children welcome
Seats: 50
Style: Modern
Smoking: No smoking in dining room; Air conditioning

Directions: First floor restaurant on Reigate High Street

RICHMOND-UPON-THAMES,
Richmond Gate Hotel ❀❀

Georgian country-house hotel with an elegant dining room styled with classical swags and tails, and where high standards of service complement the opulent ambience. The succinct menu and understated descriptions give little indication of the excellence of the dishes. The appetiser set the standard – a five bean and tomato terrine – the beans suspended in a delicate tomato aspic, shaped into a triangle, wrapped in thinly sliced carrot, and surrounded by dots of red chilli and green basil oil. Other highlights of the meal were the sea-fresh, dive-caught scallops featured in the starter, and the breathtaking presentation of the dessert, a warm chocolate fondant pudding topped with a wafer-thin slice of air-dried pineapple onto which was placed a small ball of banana Mascarpone, with a sugar spiral set around it, and a six-inch cylindrical tuille towering over the dish – more ironic than pretentious – and delicious to eat.

Richmond Hill TW10 6RP
Map GtL: B2
Tel: 020 8940 0061
Fax: 020 8332 0354
E-mail: richmondgate@corus.co.uk
Chef: Christopher Basten
Owners: Corus & Regal Hotels
Cost: Set-price L £19.75/D £29.50. ☺ H/wine £14.95
Times: 12.30-3pm/7-10pm. Closed L Sat, L Bhs
Additional: Bar food; Sunday L; Children welcome
Style: Classic/country-house
Seats: 30. Private dining room 70
Smoking: No smoking in dining room
Civil licence: 70
Accommodation: 68 en suite ★ ★ ★ ★

Directions: At top of Richmond Hill, opposite Star & Garter and just outside Richmond Park

RIPLEY,
Michels' Restaurant ❀❀❀

13 High Street GU23 6AQ
Map 4: TQ05
Tel: 01483 224777
Fax: 01483 222940
Chef: Erik Michel
Owners: Erik & Karen Michel
Cost: *Alc* £40, set-price L fr £18/D fr £23. H/wine fr £8
Times: 12.30-1.30pm/7.30-9pm. Closed L Sat, D Sun, all Mon, 2 wks Jan, 2 wks Aug
Additional: Sunday L; Children welcome
Seats: 45. Private dining room 12
Style: Country-house/Homely
Smoking: No pipes & cigars

Fresh flowers and collections of china ornaments decorate the dining-room of the Georgian-fronted Queen Anne building, along with paintings, many of which are by Erik Michel and his family. In fine weather guests can sit in the lovely walled garden. The cooking is stylish, bold and interesting, and rooted in French classicism: scallops are marinated in blood orange juice, extra virgin olive oil and lemon thyme and served with chicory salad; fillets of sea bass, salmon and monkfish are served with sauerkraut and a Riesling juniper cream sauce. Deluxe ingredients are sprinkled throughout the menu: foie gras is served with pot au feu of spring chicken ballentine with herbs and béarnaise sauce, whilst lobster and caviar top a poached duck egg with oyster served with lobster sauce flavoured with basil. Saddle of boned farmed rabbit is taken upmarket by a marinade of cream and white Port, then filled with its forcemeat before being roasted and served with mustard sauce, braised lettuce and pleurot mushrooms. Desserts include the welcome inclusion of real rum baba set on pastry cream and served with tropical fruit. Wines are nearly all French.

Directions: Take M25 J10 towards Guildford. First exit to Ripley just past lights on R

SHERE, Kinghams ❀❀

Gomshall Lane GU5 9HE
Map 4: TQ04
Tel: 01483 202168
E-mail: paul@kinghams-restaurant.co.uk
Chef/Owner: Paul Baker
Cost: Alc £27, set-price L £11.95/ D £13.95. ☺ H/wine £10.95
Times: Noon-2.30pm/7-9.30pm. Closed D Sun, all Mon, 25 Dec-4 Jan
Additional: Sunday L; Children welcome
Seats: 48. Private dining room 28
Style: Traditional
Smoking: No smoking in dining room

This 17th-century beamed cottage in a picturesque village near Guildford, with a cosy, warm feel to it, attracts customers from miles around. They come for the good-value, weekly-changing set-price menu and for an imaginative *carte* of broad appeal. Fish and seafood are given some unusual treatments among starters. Salmon, for instance, is marinated in tequila, sea salt and lime and served on a bed of shredded cucumber and chervil, while monkfish, cod and salmon go into a sausage of 'clear and precise flavours' plated with succulent, garlicky king prawns. The same ingenuity shines through meatier starters too, with roasted pigeon on walnut salad accompanied by red onion and apple tarte Tatin, with main-course fillet of lamb given the Wellington treatment with a mushroom and tarragon cream. Market-fresh fish is chalked up on a board, while an inspector was impressed by the accurate timing and quality of tender, pink, crisp-skinned duck breast with an apple and pear pancake. Desserts take in the likes of gooey chocolate pudding on vanilla sauce, or lemon and lime tart, and both the Old and New Worlds are represented on the fairly-priced wine list.

Directions: From Dorking follow A25; from Guildford follow A246 then A25

STOKE D'ABERNON,
Woodlands Park Hotel ❀

The Oak Room restaurant, furnished in keeping with the Victorian property, overlooks mature gardens. Dishes sampled included a light starter of seared scallops, and breast of corn-fed chicken with linguini.

Woodlands Lane Cobham KT11 3QB
Map 4: TQ15
Tel: 01372 843933
Fax: 01372 842704
E-mail: info@woodlandspark.co.uk
Cost: Alc £25.50, set-price L £18.75/D £26. ☺ H/wine £14.95
Times: D only, 7-9.45pm. Closed D Sun
Additional: Bar food; Sunday L (12.15-2.30pm); Children welcome
Style: Traditional/Country-house
Smoking: No smoking in dining room
Civil licence: 110
Accommodation: 59 en suite ★ ★ ★ ★

Directions: M25 J10, A3 towards London. Through Cobham centre & Stoke D'Abernon. L at garden centre into Woodlands lane. Hotel on 0.5m on L

TADWORTH, Gemini ❀

An innocuous red-brick building close to the town station plays host to some striking cuisine. Main courses might include marinated braised lamb shanks or a duo of sea bass and red mullet in crispy beer batter.

Additional: Sunday L; Children welcome at L, 12+ at D
Style: Informal/Traditional
Smoking: No smoking in dining room

Directions: M25 J8, on rdbt turn R to Sutton, on 3rd rdbt take 2nd exit to Tadworth. At traffic lights turn R, restaurant is on L

28 Station Approach KT20 5AH
Map 4: TQ25
Tel/Fax: 01737 812179
Cost: Alc £30, set-price L £15.50/D £27. ☺ H/wine £10.50
Times: Noon-2.30pm/7-9.30pm. Closed all Mon, L Sat, D Sun, 2wks Xmas & New Year

THAMES DITTON, Avant Garde ❀

A pleasant restaurant with dark green and cream decor, and a traditional cooking style. Recommended dishes include queen scallop cassoulet, and loin of lamb in a grain mustard sauce. Tasty raspberry brûlée to finish.

Directions: 5 mins from Hampton Court Palace

75 High Street KT7 0SF
Map GtL: B1
Tel/Fax: 020 8398 5540

Telephone for further details

WEYBRIDGE, Oatlands Park Hotel ❀

A grand parkland setting giving views of lush countryside. The elegant hotel restaurant offers three menus and seasonal offerings may include lusty soups and roasts, salmon on potato cake with parsley sauce and a plethora of desserts.

Smoking: No-smoking area
Civil licence: 200
Accommodation: 136 en suite ★ ★ ★ ★

Directions: Through town, up Monument Hill, L into Oatlands Drive. Hotel on L

146 Oatlands Drive KT13 9HB
Map 4: TQ06
Tel: 01932 847242
Fax: 01932 842252
E-mail: oatlandspark@btinternet.com
Cost: Alc £30, set-price L £21/D £26. H/wine £14.50
Times: 12.30- 2pm/7-9.30pm
Additional: Bar food; Sunday L; Children welcome
Style: Classic/Country-house

SUSSEX
EAST

ALFRISTON,
Moonraker's Restaurant ❀

High Street BN26 5TD
Map 5: TQ50
Tel: 01323 870472

A pretty cottage restaurant in the village centre, dating from the 16th century, and retaining a great deal of charm. The well-balanced menu offers interesting dishes, and desserts are a strength.

Telephone for further details

Directions: Signposted from A27 between Brighton & Eastbourne

BRIGHTON, Black Chapati ❀❀

12 Circus Parade New England Road BN1 4GW
Map 4: TQ30
Tel: 01273 699011
Chef: Stephen Funnell
Owners: Stephen Funnell, Lauren Alker
Cost: Alc £23. ☺ H/wine £10
Times: D only, 7-10pm (fr 6.30pm Sat). Closed Sun & Mon, 3 wks Xmas, 2 wks Jul
Additional: Children 6+
Seats: 32
Style: Informal/Modern
Smoking: No pipes & cigars

There is little evidence of the unleavened bread here and you could be easily confused when confronted with the menu. But should you be enticed by the likes of pan-fried glass noodles, Vietnamese pancakes with pickled beansprouts, grilled chicken with lemon grass and coconut, or steamed rice served with Malaysian pickles, then you will be pleasantly surprised. The restaurant is well away from the centre of the town and sea-front, and is to be found in a small parade of shops along the main London Road. The decor has moved on from the previous black and white minimalist scheme. The walls are now a soft yellow, and new funky wooden chairs have been introduced. The overall feel, however, is still spartan. But the point of this restaurant is the refined fusion cooking which can be truly excellent. The scallops were superb, the slow-braised belly of pork, flavoured with Chinese five spice and sauced with a reduction, delicious. Puddings include a creditable poached pear shortbread with butterscotch sauce. The wine list is short but well chosen and reasonably priced. Breton and Normandy cider and Pilsner Urquell are also available.

Directions: Directions are complex. Readers are advised to use a local map

BRIGHTON, La Marinade ❀

77 St George Road Kemp Town BN2 1EF
Map 4: TQ30
Tel/Fax: 01273 600992
E-mail: voila@globalnet.co.uk
Cost: Set-price L £15/D £21. ☺ H/wine £10.50
Times: Noon-2pm/7-10pm. Closed D Sun, all Mon, L Tue, 1 wk Winter, 1 wk Summer

A new look has altered the setting, but the food remains unchanged. Snails in garlic and parsley followed by leg of lamb Provençal style, or roast duck breast with orange sauce, and perhaps cinnamon crème brûlée to finish.

Additional: Sunday L; Children 3+
Style: Bistro-style/Chic
Smoking: No-smoking area; Air conditioning

Directions: From Palace Pier take direction of Marina, turn L at Royal Sussex Hospital sign, then first L

BRIGHTON, One Paston Place ❀❀❀

1 Paston Place BN2 1HA
Map 4: TQ30
Tel: 01273 606933
Fax: 01273 675686
Chef: Mark Emmerson
Owners: Mark & Nicole Emmerson
Cost: Set-price L £16.50 & £19.

Arguably the best restaurant in town, it is run with a passion by Mark and Nicole Emmerson. Just off the seafront and a stone's throw from the town centre, it's located in a smart, essentially suburban street. Initial impressions are positive – small, discreet, inviting – somehow you just know it's going to be good. A smart mural dominates the whole of one wall, the rest is pale yellow. An antique sideboard doubling as a dispensing bar adds a bit of weight to the room. The atmosphere is relaxed, confident, calm and refreshing. The hand-written menu is French in style with simple, enticing dishes that concentrate on essential ingredients and flavours. Chargrilled asparagus with violet artichokes and fresh morel sabayon was a boldly, confident dish, followed by a robust, gleamingly fresh fillet of sea bass, fresh peas and pancetta ragout with pommes boulangère. Other dishes typical of the vivid repertoire include corn-fed pigeon with salsify, thyme and potato galette, and confit of tuna, fennel salad, red wine and liquorice vinaigrette. Raspberry soufflé with raspberry ripple ice-cream was perfectly executed, and crammed with fresh raspberries, but equally enticing would be a bitter chocolate tarte with blood orange and saffron sorbet. The wine list is concise and carefully chosen.

H/wine £12-£14
Times: 12.30-1.45pm/7.30-9.45pm. Closed Sun, Mon, 1st 2 wks Jan & Aug
Additional: Children 7+; Vegetarian dishes by request at time of booking
Seats: 45
Style: Informal/Chic
Smoking: No pipes & cigars; Air conditioning

Directions: Just off the seafront about halfway between the Palace Pier and the Marina

BRIGHTON, Terre à Terre

71 East Street BN1 1HQ
Map 4: TQ30
Tel: 01273 729051
Fax: 01273 327561
Cost: Alc £21.40. ☺ H/wine £10.25
Times: Noon-5.30pm/6-10.30pm. Closed L Mon, 25-26 Dec, 1 Jan
Additional: Children welcome
Style: Informal/modern
Smoking: No-smoking area; No pipes & cigars; Air conditioning

Directions: Town centre near Cannon cinema, close to Palace Pier

Wittily styled, global vegetarian food in a contemporary setting. Dosy dunce dosas, scrumpy Camembert soufflé, and Chianti pomodoro bolla might follow an imaginative range of nibbles, salads or starters.

BRIGHTON, Whytes

Pale cream walls hung with some arty pictures, red banquette seating, and white napery make up the decor at this small restaurant not far from the sea. It might be on a bit of a backstreet, but a loyal following is large enough to ensure that the place can be busy. A punchy menu as unpretentious as the surroundings is part of the attraction, with simplicity a keynote: a starter of scallops and sage wrapped in bacon served on aubergine purée with coriander sauce is about as complicated as dishes get. Timing and seasoning are irreproachable, as in a perfectly-timed poached egg topping a starter of grilled provençale vegetables dribbled with basil oil, or a main course of braised lamb shank, of 'fabulous flavour', falling off the bone, served with crushed root vegetables and fondant potato. The fish dish of the day might be grilled halibut with king prawns, and a vegetarian option could be a strudel of spiced vegetables with herby couscous and a sweet tomato and oregano sauce. Warm chocolate fondant with raspberry sauce makes a rich end to a meal, or go for prune and Armagnac ice cream. The short wine list offers a decent choice.

33 Western Street BN1 2PG
Map 4: TQ30
Tel/Fax: 01273 776618
E-mail: janthony@lineone.net
Chef: Paul Gunn
Owner: John Anthony
Cost: Alc £25.50 ☺ H/wine £9.95
Times: D only, 7-10pm. Closed Sun, Mon, 26 Dec-5 Jan, 21 Feb-7 Mar
Additional: Children welcome
Seats: 40. Private dining room 18
Style: Informal/Modern
Smoking: No-smoking area; Air conditioning

Directions: On the Brighton-Hove border, Western St is off the seafront, 1st R after the Norfolk Resort Hotel

CROWBOROUGH,
Winston Manor Hotel ❀❀

Recently acquired by Chasley Hotels as their flagship property, resulting in some impressive improvements. The food is modern British. Canapés included a nice quiche Lorraine and vegetable samosas. The cooking is of a high standard and includes some stunning pastry work. Pan-fried scallops, served with an intense tomato fondue with a raw salsa of courgettes, peppers, and tomatoes were excellent, followed by a main course of confit and breast of duck on sweet garlic mash, which came with braised Puy lentils and a good 'really clean rich claret-based duck jus'. The puddings are first rate: three superbly-executed chocolate puddings: a white chocolate ganache mille-feuille, a stunning chocolate torte, and a Baileys chocolate assemblage.

Directions: Midway between Tunbridge Wells and Uckfield on A26

Beacon Road TN6 1AD
Map 5: TQ53
Tel: 01892 652772
Fax: 01892 665537
Chef: Andrew Owen
Cost: Alc £30, set-price D £21.50. ☺
H/wine £10.50
Times: D only, 7-9.30pm
Additional: Bar food; Sunday L; Children welcome
Seats: 30-50
Style: Traditional/Country-house
Smoking: No smoking in dining room
Civil licence: 45
Accommodation: 51 en suite ★ ★ ★

EASTBOURNE, **Grand Hotel** ❀❀

Major refurbishment has restored this already impressive hotel, which stands on the Western Promenade, to its former glory. The Mirabelle Restaurant boasts high ceilings, Zoffany wallpaper, sumptuous carpet and, from the best tables, views across the garden to the sea beyond. The menu can be perused and the meal ordered in the smart lounge bar, and canapés of salmon and lemon mayonnaise, Welsh rarebit and rillettes of duck with plum chutney set the taste buds tingling at a recent inspection dinner. A full-flavoured langoustine cappuccino lifted the meal to great heights which were sustained right to the end of the evening. Whole roast chicken with truffle and a truffle jus was carved at the table, the meat sweet and delicious and the vegetables, like steamed and deep-fried asparagus and crisp Parmentier potatoes, faultless. A 'wonderfully rich' chocolate fondant came with a white chocolate ice cream, and home-made fruit and walnut bread was served with an excellent cheeseboard. Good espresso and a huge choice of home-made petits fours rounded off this splendid meal, and the service throughout was polished and attentive.

Directions: At the western end of the seafront

King Edward's Parade BN21 4EQ
Map 5: TV69
Tel: 01323 435066
Fax: 01323 412233
Chef: Keith Mitchell, Marc Wilkinson
Owners: Elite Hotels Ltd
Cost: Set-price L £18/D £31. H/wine £12.95
Times: 12.30-2pm/7-10pm. Closed Sun, Mon, 1st 2 wks Jan
Additional: Children 7+
Seats: 50. Private dining rooms 6-200. Jacket and/or tie preferred
Style: Country-house/Formal
Smoking: No smoking in dining room; Air conditioning
Civil licence: 200
Accommodation: 152 en suite ★ ★ ★ ★ ★

FOREST ROW,
Ashdown Park Hotel ❀❀

An extended country house overlooking a lake and set in unrivalled grounds. Ashdown Park has some magnificent features such as a converted chapel with stained glass windows, working organ and wonderful acoustics for conferences. The hotel attracts well-heeled corporate and private guests, and serves ambitious classically-based food with a lightness of touch which invariably satisfies. Dinner might start with warm oyster and watercress tart with champagne sauce, or perhaps chicken liver parfait with toasted brioche and Earl Grey tea jelly. Fish is well represented among the main choices, such as roasted monkfish wrapped in pancetta with tomato fondue and crispy noodles,

Wych Cross
RH18 5JR
Map 5: TQ43
Tel: 01342 824988
Fax: 01342 820206
E-mail: reservations@ashdownpark.com
Chef: John McManus
Owners: Elite Hotels
Cost: Alc fr £40, set-price L £23/D £35. ☺ H/wine £13.50
Times: 12.30-2pm/7.30-9.30pm(7-10pm Sat)
Additional: Sunday L

Ashdown Park Hotel

Seats: 120. Private dining room 150.
Jacket and/or tie preferred
Style: Traditional/Country-house
Smoking: No smoking in dining room
Civil licence: 150
Accommodation: 107 en suite
★ ★ ★ ★

or there could be saddle of venison with crushed celeriac and roasted roots spiked with juniper. Tantalising-sounding desserts make decision making at this stage difficult, but clotted cream rice pudding drizzled with fudge sauce sounds like a winner, and so does chocolate and orange parfait with Armagnac Chantilly. Lunch is a shorter, slightly lighter version of dinner, and at both meals the friendly service in crisp coat tails suits the elegant, formal setting.

Directions: From A22 at Wych Cross take Hartfield turning, hotel is 0.75 mile on R

HASTINGS, Beauport Park Hotel

Battle Road TN38 8EA
Map 5: TQ80
Tel: 01424 851222
Fax: 01424 852465
E-mail: reservations@
beauportprkhotel.demon.co.uk

Elegant Georgian manor house set in 40 acres of gardens and parkland. Start with warm lobster salad with tiger prawns and smoked salmon, say, followed by a traditional steak Diane flambé or baked monkfish tail.

Directions: On A2100, 3 miles from both Hastings and Battle

Telephone for further details

HASTINGS, Röser's Restaurant ✿✿✿

64 Eversfield Place
TN37 6DB
Map 5: TQ80
Tel/Fax: 01424 712218
E-mail: gerald@rosers.co.uk
Chef: Gerald Röser
Owners: Mr & Mrs G Röser
Cost: *Alc* £37, set-price L £20.95/D
£23.95. ☺ H/wine £11.50

Do not judge by appearances. The washed-out façade on a washed-out promenade would be easy to walk straight past. Inside, the atmosphere is unpretentious, the decor is simple, the crockery deliberately unmatched Wedgwood, but you are in assured and serious hands. Gerald Röser keeps his concepts simple, but the French classicism is lifted by some more original notes as in the preserved lemons and broad beans with roast guinea fowl or the lime and coriander pickle with red mullet. Location allows him to take advantage of ingredients such as razorshells, gratinated with garlic butter and Parmesan, and best-end of Romney Marsh lamb which he marinates in olive oil, ginger, coriander and rosemary, served with couscous (for two). An autumnal first course salad of pigeon sat on a well-dressed mound of lettuce and sliver of luscious foie gras; sea bass was meaty and fresh, the skin crisp and scented with truffles, served with salsify, puréed potatoes, carrot and spinach. Apple mille-feuille with layers of lightly poached Granny Smith apples and Calvados-flavoured crème patissière with butterscotch sauce vies for attention with its chocolate mousse, made with fine French chocolate and served with coffee cream sauce. Impressive wine list – and excellent Illy espresso.

Times: Noon-2pm/7-10pm. Closed L Sat, all Sun & Mon,1st 2 wks Jan, 2nd 2 wks Jun
Additional: Children welcome
Seats: 30. Private dining room 30
Style: Traditional
Smoking: No pipes & cigars

Directions: On the seafront, opposite Hastings pier

HERSTMONCEUX,
Sundial Restaurant ❀❀

It may not win awards for innovation, but the classical-based cooking at this long-serving, auberge-style restaurant is consistently of a high standard and it remains popular with its loyal local following. The emphasis is French – moist and succulent 'navarin d'agneau au porto'; 'le loup de mer Grenobloise'; 'les écrevisses à la fleur d'herbes de Provence' – but given the origins of the chef/patron, some Italian influences inevitably appear in dishes such as 'l'osso bucco alla Romana and 'les orecchiette alla matriciana', semolina pasta with a tangy red pepper sauce. The lamb came with a lovely creamy risotto which prompted the comment: 'You can take the Italian out of Italy, but you can't keep the Italian out of the cooking.' The menu changes regularly, but retains old favourites such as sole meunière and pepper steak. Wines are almost exclusively French, with a very good claret section, although the selection of Italian wines, almost all from small growers, would repay exploration.

Hailsham BN27 4LA
Map 5: TQ61
Tel: 01323 832217
Fax: 01323 832909
Chef: Giuseppe Bertoli
Owners: Giuseppe & Laure Bertoli
Cost: *Alc* £35, set-price L £22/D £30
Times: Noon-2pm/7-9.30pm. Closed D Sun, all Mon, 25 Dec-20 Jan, 9 Aug-1st wk Sept
Additional: Sunday L; Children welcome
Seats: 50. Private dining room 22
Style: Classic/Country-house
Smoking: No smoking in dining room

Directions: In centre of village, on A271

HOVE, Quentin's ❀❀

Quentin's is as down to earth as its setting on Hove's main shopping street. It's a fairly compact space with a stripped wooden floor, scrubbed pine tables and schoolroom-type chairs, and terracotta walls hung with foodie prints. The monthly-changing menu is unpretentious too, and the kitchen shows a keen awareness of how to transform good-quality raw materials into interesting combinations of flavours and textures. Quail is used in cannelloni with wild mushroom sauce, and confit of duck comes with marinated vegetables and sesame-roasted peanuts, with the range of starters extended perhaps by first-rate scallops simply pan-fried, laid on a bed of interesting leaves and topped with a light soufflé of the corals. Locally-landed fish kicks off the selection of main courses, with meat dishes running to perhaps pork fillet roasted with honey and cloves with Calvados sauce plated with hotpot potatoes. Saucing skills come to the fore in a good seasonal dish of braised oxtail with fondant potatoes and chunks of roasted carrot, cabbage and parsnip. Apple pie with lavender ice cream is something of a signature dish, or there might be a chocolatey dessert like gâteau with autumn fruits. Service is relaxed and friendly, and the wine list offers a reasonable choice at sensible prices.

42 Western Road BN3 1JD
Map 4: TQ20
Tel/Fax: 01273 822734
Chef: Quentin Fitch
Owners: Candy & Quentin Fitch
Cost: Set-price L & D £19.95. ☺ H/wine £9.95
Times: Noon-2pm/7-9.30pm. Closed L Sat, all Sun & Mon, last wk Dec, last 2 wks Aug
Additional: Children welcome
Seats: 28. Private dining room 20
Style: Bistro-style/rustic
Smoking: Air conditioning

Directions: On the south side of Western Road between Brunswick Square and Palmeira Square

JEVINGTON,
Hungry Monk Restaurant ⊛

Polegate nr Eastbourne
BN26 5QF
Map 4: TQ50
Tel/Fax: 01323 482178
Cost: Set-price L/D £26. H/wine £10
Times: D only, 6.45-9.30pm.
Closed Bhs ex Good Fri
Additional: Sunday L (noon-2pm);
Children 4+ in main dining room
Style: Informal
Smoking: No smoking in dining room;
Air conditioning; Jacket & tie
preferred

Antiques, beams and log fires characterise this 14th-century flint cottage, once a monastic retreat. French country cooking merges with English on a varied set-price menu.

Directions: Follow A22 towards Eastbourne. Turn R on to B2105. The restaurant is between Polegate and Friston

LEWES, The Shelleys ⊛⊛

High Street BN7 1XS
Map 5: TQ41
Tel: 01273 472361
Fax: 01273 483152
Chef: Robert Pierce
Owners: Grace Hotels
Cost: Alc £28.50, set-price L
£18.50/D £28.50. H/wine £13.50
Times: Noon-2.15pm/7-9.15pm
Additional: Bar food L; Sunday L;
Children welcome
Seats: 30. Private dining room 40
Style: Classic/Country-house
Smoking: No smoking in dining room
Civil licence: 50
Accommodation: 19 en suite ★ ★ ★

Not a new pop group but the former family home of the Romantic poet. The 16th-century inn features a high-ceilinged restaurant furnished in classical style which contrasts light pastel walls and curtains with dark Chippendale-style chairs, and overlooks a lovely garden. A good choice of dishes from a well-conceived menu might include South Coast bouillabaisse with rouille and herbe croûtes, and best end of lamb set on caramelised boulangère potatoes finished with a thyme sauce. Chargrilled breast of duck gets a modern twist with vanilla flavouring and a mango salsa. Dishes are seasonal – a Spring menu also offered pan-fried scallops on saffron pasta cake with gazpacho sauce, and roast guinea fowl set on a bed of Savoy cabbage with wild mushroom sauce. Coconut tart with passion fruit Mascarpone and coconut sorbet was appreciated for its lightness and strength of flavour. The wine list is sensibly laid out, clearly annotated and very reasonably priced.

Directions: Town centre

NEWICK,

Newick Park Country Estate

BN8 4SB
Map 5: TQ42
Tel: 01825 723633
Fax: 01825 723969
E-mail: bookings@newickparkco.uk
Chef: Timothy Neal
Owners: Michael & Virginia Childs
Cost: *Alc* £40, set-price L £19.50/D £32.50. H/wine £9.75
Times: Noon-3pm/7-9.30pm
Additional: Sunday L; Children 1+
Seats: Private dining rooms 6-60. Jacket & tie preferred
Style: Classic/country-house
Smoking: No smoking in dining room.
Civil licence: 80
Accommodation: 16 en suite ★ ★ ★

The essence of country-house eating. The large estate, surrounding the listed Georgian house, includes a walled garden and beautiful parkland. The elegant dining room gleams with polished silver and glassware, and the linen is crisp and starched. The cuisine is classically based with a few modern twists and although the menu reads well and the sophisticated cooking aims high, the less fiddly dishes are probably the best bet. Hot-smoked saddle of venison was perfectly timed and matched with the richest of buttery cabbage and an unctuous cassis jus, but a warm tartlet of Cornish crab and ginger with lime crème fraîche and caviar and a pear tarte Tatin were less successful in delivering the promised flavours. Vegetarian choice includes local goats' cheese, tomato and basil risotto with sun-dried tomato dressing. British farmhouse cheeses are served with walnut bread, and fresh coffee or herbal teas with home-made petits fours.

Directions: From Newick on A272 between Haywards Heath/Uckfield, turn S on Church Road, at end of road turn L. Hotel 0.25 mile on R

RYE, Landgate Bistro

Popular bistro in a lovely narrow street. Salmon and salt cod fishcakes might be followed by cod with ginger and spring onion or pigeon breasts with red wine sauce. Gooseberry and elderflower fool features among the desserts.

5-6 Landgate TN31 7LH
Map 5: TQ92
Tel: 01797 222829

Telephone for further details

Directions: From the High Street head towards Landgate. The bistro is in a row of shops on the left

RYE, Mermaid Inn ✿

Although uncompromising in its retention of a warm historic atmosphere a traditional approach to cooking is complemented by occasional contemporary touches ensuring the best of both worlds. Carte options include grilled supreme of duckling.

Additional: Bar food; Sunday L; Children welcome
Style: Traditional/Tudor
Smoking: No smoking in dining room; Jacket & tie preferred
Accommodation: 31 en suite ★ ★ ★

Mermaid Street TN31 7EU
Map 5: TQ92
Tel: 01797 223065
Fax: 01797 225069
E-mail: mermaidinnrye@btclick.com
Cost: *Alc* fr £32, set-price L £16/D £32. H/wine £12.95
Times: Noon-2.15pm/7-9.30pm

Directions: Town centre. Car park through archway

UCKFIELD, Buxted Park

A Victorian conservatory in the hotel's orangery forms the centrepiece of the restaurant. The cuisine can show considerable flair and dedication, as in a well-judged piquant monkfish escabeche.

Additional: Bar food; Sunday L; Children welcome
Style: Chic/Modern
Smoking: No smoking in dining room
Civil licence: 80
Accommodation: 44 en suite ★ ★ ★ ★

Directions: Turn off A22 Uckfield bypass (London-Eastbourne road), then take A272 to Buxted. Cross set of traffic lights, entrance to hotel is 1 mile on R

Buxted TN22 4AY
Map 5: TQ42
Tel: 01825 732711
Fax: 01825 732770
Cost: Set-price L £14.95/D £25. H/wine £12.50
Times: Noon-3pm/7-midnight (last orders 9.45pm)

UCKFIELD, Horsted Place

One of Britain's finest examples of Gothic revivalist architecture, Horsted Place is surrounded by its own estate which includes a golf club. Inside there are many fine architectural features and a typical country house style dining room – formal but not too stuffy. The Pugin Restaurant provides a *carte*, and vegetarian and set-price menus at lunchtimes. The cuisine is described as modern European, which includes dishes such as fillet of beef with shallot and coriander pancake on pak choi with a celery and pesto dressing. A chicken confit and foie gras terrine was well constructed, and came drizzled with a coriander pesto and some rocket leaves dressed with a hazelnut, apple and cider vinegar dressing. A main course of seared diver-caught scallops was served on crushed potato and thyme with braised tomato sauce. Desserts are ambitious, but there are simpler options. The wine list is noteworthy and covers some eleven different countries.

Directions: Two miles South of Uckfield on A26

Little Horsted TN22 5TS
Map 5: TQ42
Tel: 01825 750581
Fax: 01825 750459
E-mail: hotel@horstedplace.co.uk
Chef: Allan Garth
Cost: *Alc* £36, set-price L £14.95/D £32. ☺ H/wine £17.50
Times: Noon-2pm/7-9.30pm
Additional: Sunday L; Children 7+
Seats: 40. Private dining rooms up to 24; Jacket & tie preferred
Style: Country-house
Smoking: No smoking in dining room
Civil licence: 100
Accommodation: 20 en suite ★ ★ ★

WILMINGTON, Crossways Hotel ❀❀

A warm and friendly country-house hotel with a relaxed style and a popular local following. The elegant restaurant with its tasteful furnishings and attractive decor is the main focus of attention, where the well-balanced cooking meets with hearty approval. A recent inspection meal generated praise right from the word go, when tasty nibbles, fresh rolls and a choice of salted or garlic butter set the taste buds off. Light seafood pancakes filled with salmon and smoked haddock in a cream sauce was a welcome starter, and devilled duck – a roast breast of Gressingham duck with a light ginger and lemongrass sauce – was tender and full of flavour. Dessert in the shape of white chocolate mousse served with fresh raspberries and strawberries and an excellent raspberry coulis was another good choice. The short monthly menu always offers a dish made from the day's catch, along with the likes of guinea fowl with wild mushrooms and Madeira sauce, or fillet of beef stuffed with fried garlic and served with Stilton sauce. A good blend of fresh filtered coffee and home-made petits fours round things off pleasantly.

Directions: A27, 2 miles W of Polegate

Nr Polegate BN26 5SG
Map 4: TQ50
Tel: 01323 482455
Fax: 01323 487811
E-mail: crossways@fastnet.co.uk
Chefs: Juliet Anderson & David Stott
Owners: David Stott & Clive James
Cost: Set-price D £28.95. H/wine £11.95
Times: D only, 7.30-8.30pm. Closed Sun, Mon, Jan
Additional: Children 12+; Vegetarian dishes not always available
Seats: 22
Style: Modern/Country-house
Smoking: No smoking in dining room
Accommodation: 7 en suite

SUSSEX
WEST

AMBERLEY,
Amberley Castle 🌸🌸

Arundel BN18 9ND
Map 4: TQ01
Tel: 01798 831992
Fax: 01798 831998
E-mail: info@amberleycastle.co.uk
Chef: Billy Butcher
Owners: Martin & Joy Cummings
Cost: Set-price L £12.50/D £35.
H/wine £17
Times: 12.30-2pm/7-9.30pm
Additional: Sunday L; Children 12+
Seats: 38. Private dining room 48.
Jacket & tie preferred
Style: Country-house
Smoking: No smoking in dining room
Civil licence: 48
Accommodation: 20 en suite ★ ★ ★

The castle is 900 years old and so historic and glorious that all
that seems missing from the dining hall are reeds on the floor,
pewter goblets of mead and a few scavenging dogs sniffing for
crumbs. Still, the modern environment is as luxurious as it is
inspiring, a gilded, soaring ceiling that shows to best advantage
the bold Norman architecture and restored artwork. The menu
provides an interesting mix of classical and modern British
cooking with a dash of spice: mille-feuille of scallops with a
wasabi purée; seared salmon with truffled risotto, poached egg,
champagne sauce; roast loin of lamb, aubergine caviar, tomato
crisps, basil and baby fennel; orange crème brûlée, caramelised
orange crisp, lemon sorbet and lime tuile. The styling of dishes
is often stunning, but sometimes the actual food seems to lack
clarity and harmony. A slight simplification, a touch more
attention to consistency and this could be cooking that's a real
match for its setting.

Directions: Off B2139 between Amberley and Houghton

ARDINGLY,
Avins Bridge Restaurant 🌸

Relax in front of a log fire in this endearingly simple restaurant in a
converted Victorian station hotel. First class beef Wellington and a
perfectly executed raspberry crème brûlée demonstrated a
commitment to quality ingredients and clarity of flavour.

Additional: Children 6+
Style: Bistro-style/informal
Smoking: No-smoking area
Accommodation: 3 en suite

College Road
RH17 6SH
Map 4: TQ32
Tel: 01444 892393
E-mail:
enquiries@theavinsbridge.co.uk
Cost: Alc £25. ☺ H/wine £10
Times: Noon-2pm/7-9.30pm.
Closed Sun & Mon, 24 Dec-14 Jan

Directions: From A23 take Crawley/East Grinstead exit. At 2nd
rndbt take 3rd exit for Ardingly. Go through village and turn R
for Ardingly College, restaurant in 1 mile

ARUNDEL,

Arundel Swan Hotel

Formality blends with comfort at this smart restaurant where carte and set menu vie for attention. Options include crab and lime mousse, navarin of seafood, and Cajun tuna steak, and puds like tarte Normande or chocolate marquise.

Additional: Bar Food; Sunday L; Children welcome
Style: Classic/Chic
Smoking: No smoking in dining room; Air conditioning
Accommodation: 15 en suite ★★★

Directions: Town centre

27-29 High Street BN18 9AG
Map 4: TQ00
Tel: 01903 882314
Fax: 01903 883759
E-mail: info@swan-hotel.co.uk
Cost: *Alc* £25, set-price L & D
£14.95. ☺ H/wine £8.95
Times: Noon-2.30pm/6.30-9.30pm

ARUNDEL,

Burpham Country House

Old Down Burpham BN18 9RJ
Map 4: TQ00
Tel: 01903 882160
Fax: 01903 884627
Cost: Set-price D £19 & £23.50. ☺
H/wine £10.80
Times: D only, 7.30-9pm. Closed
Mon, 1 wk Nov, 1-14 Jan
Additional: Children 10+
Style: Traditional/country-house
Smoking: No smoking in dining room.
Jacket & tie preferred
Accommodation: 10 en suite ★★★

A Swiss influence can be detected in both the menu and wine list. Enjoy the likes of Zurcher Geschetzeltes (a buttery veal dish) alongside local fish with leek sauce.

Directions: 3 miles NE of Arundel, off A27

ARUNDEL,

Norfolk Arms Hotel

A very high ceiling and well-spaced tables lend a roomy atmosphere to this smallish dining room. Good choice of traditional English dishes like seared pheasant breast on fennel mash and port jus, and oven-baked salmon with dill beurre blanc.

Cost: Set-price D £17.85. ☺ H/wine £8.95
Times: Noon-2pm(Sat & Sun only)/7-9.30pm
Additional: Bar food L; Sunday L; Children welcome
Style: Classic/Formal
Smoking: No smoking in dining room
Civil licence: 60
Accommodation: 34 en suite ★★★

Directions: In Arundel High St

High Street BN18 9AD
Map 4: TQ00
Tel: 01903 882101
Fax: 01903 884375

BOSHAM,
Millstream Hotel ❀

Bosham Lane PO18 8HL
Map 4: SU80
Tel: 01243 573234
Fax: 01243 573459
E-mail: info@millstream-hotel.co.uk

Telephone for further details

Well appointed restaurant in a village hotel, where options might include home-smoked salmon, followed by fillet of venison, pigeon breast and roast stuffed quail on an apricot and brandy coulis.

Directions: Take A259 exit for Chichester rdbt and in village follow signs for Quay

BRACKLESHAM,
Cliffords Cottage Restaurant ❀❀

Bracklesham Lane PO20 8JA
Map 4: SZ89
Tel: 01243 670250
Chef: Tony Shanahan
Owners: Tony & Brenda Shanahan
Cost: *Alc* £24, set-price D £19.50. ☺
H/wine £9.25
Times: D only, 7-9pm. Closed D Sun-Tue, 1st 2 wks Nov, 1st wk Feb
Additional: Sunday L (12.30-1.30pm);
Children 5+
Seats: 28. Jacket & tie preferred
Style: Traditional
Smoking: No smoking in dining room;
Air conditioning

A charming thatched roof cottage with a low-beam ceiling and cream painted walls. The atmosphere is warm and friendly thanks in large part to the relaxed and attentive service of Mrs Shanahan and her staff. On a recent warm May evening a seafood starter proved a well prepared dish with a good mix of Dover sole, scallops and fresh prawns served with a flavoursome Noilly Prat and saffron sauce. The stakes were nicely raised then with mignons de boeuf forestière – quality meat in tender fillets served with a well made Madeira and forest mushroom sauce. The resolution was a calming iced Grand Marnier and strawberry parfait with mango purée washed down with a good blend of filtered coffee and chocolate mints. The wine list is well balanced, reasonably priced and includes a selection of new world wines.

Directions: From A27 at Chichester take A286 to Birdham, turn L onto B2198 to Bracklesham

BURPHAM, George & Dragon ❀

Arundel BN18 9RR
Map 4: TQ00
Tel: 01903 883131
Cost: ☺ H/wine £11.50
Times: D only, 7-9.30pm.
Closed D Sun, 25 Dec

Once a public house, now a relaxing restaurant with decent service. Interesting dishes include home-made langoustine ravioli and truffle sauce, and roast rump of lamb with tomato and rosemary infusion. Some puddings made to order.

Additional: Bar food; Sunday L (noon-2pm); Children 10+
Style: Classic
Smoking: No pipes & cigars; Air conditioning

Directions: 2.5 miles up no-through road signposted Burpham off A27, 1 mile E of Arundel

CHICHESTER, **Comme Ça** ❀❀

An autumn visit on a fine day made the virginia creeper-clad building absolutely glow in the bright sunshine; inside it is equally welcoming with stencilled walls, masses of dried flowers and deep yellow and green cloths. It's all very French *rustique*, a mood underlined by the French chefs, owners and waiters. The Norman origins of Michel Navet are evident in moules à la normande, but other French regions are drawn on for dishes such as baked farm Munster cheese in filo pastry with sauce vierge, or a melting compote of wild rabbit braised with prunes and Armagnac sauce. There's even a touch of French neo-colonialism with red mullet Vietnamese-style topped with stem ginger, straw mushrooms and roasted sesame seeds. Sunday lunch is always popular, with a special value menu and a children's menu supplementing the *carte*.

Directions: On A286 near Festival Theatre

67 Broyle Road PO19 4BD
Map 4: SU80
Tel: 01243 788724
Fax: 01243 530052
Chefs: Michel Navet,
Olivier Vennetier
Owners: Michel Navet,
Jane Owen-Navet
Cost: *Alc* £32, set-price L £17.95. ☺
H/wine £9.95
Times: 11.30am-2pm/6-10pm.
Closed D Sun, all Mon, Bhs
Additional: Bar food L; Sunday L;
Children welcome
Seats: 100. Private dining room 40/20
Style: Rustic
Smoking: No smoking in dining room

CHICHESTER, **Croucher's Bottom Country Hotel** ❀

A traditional country hotel-style restaurant that is doing good business due to some very sound cooking. This takes in foie gras parfait with fig chutney, confit of duck leg with tiny roast potatoes, lardons and shallots, and chocolate tart.

Smoking: No-smoking area
Accommodation: 16 en suite ★ ★ ★

Directions: From A27 S of Chichester take A286 to The Witterings. Hotel 2m on L.

Birdham Road PO20 7EH
Map 4: SU80
Tel: 01243 784995
Fax: 01243 539797
E-mail:
crouchers_bottom@btconnect.com.
Cost: *Alc* £23.50. ☺ H/wine £11.95
Times: D only, 7-9pm
Additional: Children 12+
Style: Country-house

CHICHESTER, **Hallidays** ❀

A charming thatched building with low-beamed ceilings and bright decorations. The strong wine list complements classic cooking like toasted scallops with lentils and ginger, and peppered beef fillet with parsnip. Home-made bread is a highlight.

Additional: Sunday L; Children welcome
Style: Classic/Traditional
Smoking: No-smoking area; No pipes & cigars

Directions: Telephone for directions

Funtingdon PO18 9LF
Map 4: SU80
Tel: 01243 575331
Cost: *Alc* £28, set-price L £10.50. ☺
H/wine £9.75
Times: 12.30-1.30pm/7-9.30pm.
Closed L Sat, D Sun, all Mon, 2 wks
Mar, 1 wk Sep

CHICHESTER, **The Ship Hotel** ❀

With one foot in its bona fide nautical heritage and the other in the world of modern British cuisine, a stimulating dining experience is guaranteed. Dishes such as pumpkin soup with cinnamon or smoked haddock with truffle oil abound.

Style: Classic/Traditional
Smoking: No smoking in dining room
Accommodation: 36 en suite ★ ★ ★

Directions: From the inner ring road at large Northgate roundabout turn L into North St; hotel on L

North Street PO19 1NH
Map 4: SU80
Tel: 01243 778000
Fax: 01243 788000
Cost: *Alc* £25, set-price L £16.95/D £19.95. ☺ H/wine £9.90
Times: Noon-2pm/7.15 (5.45 in summer)-9.30pm
Additional: Bar food; Sunday L;
Children welcome

CHILGROVE, White Horse Inn

Chichester PO18 9HX
Map 4: SU81
Tel: 01243 539219
Fax: 01243 535301
E-mail: thehappycaterer@FSB.co.uk
Cost: *Alc* £15, set-price L £15/D £20.
☺ H/wine £12.50
Times: Noon-2pm/7-10pm.
Closed D Sun, all Mon
Additional: Bar food; Sunday L;
Children welcome
Style: Traditional/Country-house
Smoking: No smoking in dining room;
Air conditioning

Well-known inn with huge but user-friendly wine list and French menu with translations. Medallions of pork with a blackcurrant sauce, and chargrilled rib-eye steak with béarnaise, demonstrate the flavour, along with trademark chef's specials.

Directions: On the B2141 between Chichester and Petersfield

CLIMPING,
Baliffscourt Hotel

Littlehampton BN17 5RW
Map 4: SU90
Tel: 01903 723511
Fax: 01903 723107
E-mail: bailiffscourt@hshotels.co.uk
Chef: Paul Bellingham
Owners: Mr & Mrs S Goodman
Cost: *Alc* £45, set-price L £15.95/D
£35. H/wine £15.25
Times: Noon-2.15pm/7-10pm
Additional: Bar food L; Sunday L;
Children 12+
Seats: 45. Private dining room 24
Style: Traditional/Country-house
Smoking: No smoking in dining room
Civil licence: 60
Accommodation: 31 en suite ★★★

An unusual building constructed last century from medieval materials and antique architectural salvage. The restaurant boasts a beamed, vaulted ceiling, tapestry adorned walls and a magnificent medieval fireplace. A varied choice of menus should suit all occasions and, in each case, the cooking is refined, modern and classy. A meal from the top-of-the-range set-price menu might open with terrine of confit rabbit with pease pudding and a sherry dressing, followed by pan-fried fillet of beef with oxtail dumplings and a rich red wine sauce. Alternative main courses might include ravioli of Jerusalem artichoke with asparagus dressed with a truffle oil infused cream. Desserts include warm rice pudding infused with lemongrass with a lime syrup, and dark chocolate marquise with a white chocolate ice cream.

Directions: W of Littlehampton off the A259, signposted Bailiffscourt

COPTHORNE,
Copthorne London Gatwick ❀❀

Copthorne Way RH10 3PG
Map 5: TQ33
Tel: 01342 348800
Fax: 01342 348833
E-mail: coplgw@mill-cop.com
Chef: Richard Duckworth
Owner: Millennium & Copthorne
Hotels
Cost: *Alc* £25, set-price L £18.95/D
£23.95. ☺ H/wine £14.50
Times: 12.30-2pm/7-10pm.
Closed L Sat, all Sun, Bhs
Additional: Bar food; Children welcome
Seats: 50. Private dining room 10
Style: Rustic/Country-house
Smoking: Air conditioning
Civil licence: 120
Accommodation: 227 en suite ★ ★ ★ ★

A 16th-century farmhouse lies incongruously at the centre of
this sprawling airport hotel, and despite the proximity of
Gatwick there is still a sense of seclusion inside the 100 acres
of wooded and landscaped gardens. A further retreat from the
hectic outside world can be found in the formal restaurant,
where exposed beams, crisp linen and soft chairs provide a
harmonious setting for the modern cooking. The food is well
displayed on a set-price Menu of the Week, where starters like
fish terrine or white onion soup might be followed by pan-fried
saddle of venison with root vegetables, rösti and red wine
sauce, or nage of seafood – salmon, red fish, mussels and
prawns in a highly scented aniseed liquor. From the *carte*
choose from delicacies such as blue cheese and cauliflower
soufflé, or sautéed Dutch calves' liver with Black Forest ham,
herb mash, red onion compote and red wine gravy. Starters are
similarly sophisticated, with seasonal berries and fruits with a
Riesling water ice, or prawns, roasted vegetables and mango
with white wine jelly and lemon and coriander salsa.

Directions: From M23 J10 follow
A264 signed East Grinstead; take 3rd
exit off 1st roundabout

COPTHORNE,
The Old House Restaurant ❀❀ 𝗡𝗘𝗪

Effingham Road RH10 3JB
Map 5: TQ33
Tel: 01342 712222
Fax: 01342 716493
Owners: Mr C & Mrs M Dorman
Cost: *Alc* L £30, set-price L £16/D
£29. H/wine £10.75
Times: 12.15-4pm/7-midnight. Closed
D Sun, L Sat, Spring Bh 1 wk
Additional: Sunday L; Children
welcome at L, 10+ at D
Seats: 80. Private dining room 30
Style: Informal/Country-house
Smoking: No-smoking area; No pipes
& cigars; Air conditioning

Directions: Telephone for directions

Full of character and charm the restaurant offers a wealth of
old beams, inglenook fireplaces and cosy alcoves. Tables are
suitably placed for intimate candlelit dinners and the elegant

fittings are complemented by a friendly atmosphere. The seasonal menu might include a starter of slices of avocado with marinated peppered fresh salmon and new potatoes, served on a tossed leaf salad with a wholegrain mustard dressing. This might be agreeably followed by a pan-fried fillet of Scottish beef topped with a confit of buttered leeks and glazed Stilton cheese, served with a Madeira sauce. Original desserts make for a memorable conclusion to the meal – a meringue swan filled with a light milk chocolate and brandy mousse floating on a red cherry sauce, or perhaps 'Tipsy Parson' – whisky, rum, egg whites and cream whisked, chilled and served with tuille nut biscuits.

CUCKFIELD, Ockenden Manor

Ockenden Lane RH17 5LD
Map 4: TQ32
Tel: 01444 416111
Fax: 01444 415549

Telephone for further details

Directions: Village Centre, off main street

A 16th-century property in the centre of the village overlooking the South Downs. The lavishly furnished dining room, with oil paintings, candelabras and ornate oak panelling provides the setting for a dignified dining experience, with friendly staff happy to deliver good service. Two menus make good use of seasonal produce and fresh herbs from the hotel's garden, and a tasting menu is also available with samples from across the kitchen's output. A starter of potted salmon with seared langoustine was followed by very fresh grilled cod with a cassoulet of white beans, bursting with flavour. Summer truffle cut thinly and sprinkled around the plate added a touch of luxury. The wine list is extensive and a range of first growth Burgundies catches the eye.

EAST GRINSTEAD,
Gravetye Manor Hotel ❀❀❀

Dating from 1598 and enlarged over the centuries, in grounds that include a massive kitchen garden providing super-fresh fruit and vegetables, Gravetye has been a shining example of the country-house style since it was established in the late 1950s. A set-price lunch and dinner menu, with two choices per course, runs alongside a longer, more ambitious *carte*, all assembled with thought. Given the surroundings, it's no surprise to see pan-fried foie gras (with tortellini, baby spinach and cep cappuccino), or caviar partnering fillet of sea bass with crab risotto. Even simple-sounding dishes belie the workmanship that goes into them: a starter of tomato mousse, for example, is delicately flavoured, faultlessly textured, with a

RH19 4LJ
Map 5: TQ33
Tel: 01342 810567
Fax: 01342 810080
E-mail: gravetye@relaischateaux.fr
Chef: Mark Raffan
Owners: The Herbert Family
Cost: Alc £52,
set-price L £32/D £40
Times: 12.30-2pm/7-9.30pm.
Closed D 25 Dec (non-residents)
Additional: Sunday L; Children welcome

Gravetye Manor Hotel

Seats: 50. Private dining room 18.
Jacket & tie preferred
Style: Classic/country-house
Smoking: No smoking in dining room
Accommodation: 18 en suite ★ ★ ★

Directions: From M23 J10 take A264
towards East Grinstead. After 2 miles
take B2028 (signposted Haywards
Heath/Brighton)

savoury jelly on top, surrounded by marinated tomatoes, baby
fennel and artichokes, all gleaming with tapenade dressing and
looking too pretty to eat. A main course of steak pudding with
a rich red wine sauce, sautéed kidneys and potato purée might
be just what the doctor ordered on a cold winter's night, and
the kitchen never loses its grasp of what makes dishes work
successfully. Fillets of Dover sole (perfectly timed, as is
everything else), for instance, are accompanied by a ragout of
mussels, langoustines, tomato and basil 'of excellent flavour'
and a good foil for the fish. 'Petits fours could have kept me
quiet without a pud', wrote an inspector who nevertheless
tucked into a tart, its pastry 'superbly thin and crisp', filled
with Armagnac-saturated prunes in a Mascarpone filling,
topped with 'delicious' Armagnac ice cream. Afternoon tea
and breakfast both get high marks, prices include service, and
the wine list is a well-chosen, global collection that makes good
reading for aficionados.

AA Wine Shortlisted for Award-see page 18

FINDON, Findon Manor Hotel 🏵🏵

High Street Nr Worthing BN14 0TA
Map 4: TQ10
Tel: 01903 872733
Fax: 01903 877473
E-mail: findon@dircon.co.uk
Chef: Stanley Ball
Owners: Mike & Jan Parker-Hare
Cost: Set-price L £17.95/D £21. ☺
H/wine £11.50
Times: Noon-2pm/7-9pm
Additional: Bar food; Sunday L
Seats: 40 Private dining room 30;
Jacket & tie preferred

Findon Manor is a former rectory situated in the centre of the
village. A beamed lounge doubles as a reception and a cosy
bar (which offers a good range of bar food and is popular with
the locals). The oak-floored restaurant overlooks the hotel's
garden and is painted a soft green. Freshly-made rolls had
good flavour and were an excellent start to the meal. A lobster
bisque with crayfish quenelles was full of flavour and carefully
seasoned. The soup came garnished with shards of asparagus
and samphire, but the quenelles were not actually a mousse,
but rather chopped meat bound with crème fraîche and herbs.

From the seven main courses the fillet of lamb with red wine sauce and crushed potatoes was delicious and perfectly cooked. Other offerings included venison and chestnut roulade and the one fish option was red snapper and chargrilled fennel. The puddings include a hot lemon and hazelnut sponge, and kahlua ice cream. The wine list is predominantly French with a smattering of New World wines.

Directions: 500 metres off A24 in Findon village, 3 miles N of Worthing.

Style: Classic/Country-house
Smoking: No smoking in dining room
Civil licence: 50
Accommodation: 11 en suite ★ ★ ★

GOODWOOD, **Marriott Goodwood Park Hotel** ❀❀

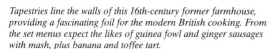

As its name suggests, this former coaching inn, dating from the late 18th century, is part of the Goodwood Estate along with the famous racecourse. Smartly-appointed rooms and excellent leisure facilities, apart from the location, are attractions, while a long, high-ceilinged, comfortable dining-room done out in rich fabrics. From the grill menu come beef sirloin with béarnaise sauce, and tuna steak with hollandaise, while a more novel approach shows up among other fish dishes, from a starter of home-cured salmon lasagne, served cold with olive oil and pink peppercorn dressing, to home-smoked cod with a caper and tomato dressing and truffle oil mash. Meats tend to receive more traditional treatments – rillettes of duck with cucumber pickle, say, or seared calves' liver with sage gravy – while an inspector was impressed by the delicate flavour of a starter of a warm tartlet of Stilton and spring onions, and by a main-course roulade of salmon and sole – 'deliciously fresh and accurately cooked' – with vegetable spaghetti. Successful pairings at dessert stage have included 'delicious' almond-scented pannacotta with lime compote, and unusual sweet basil syrup with chocolate mousse. Breads are said to be 'excellent', and the wine list is typical of the surroundings.

Chichester PO18 0QB
Map 4: SU80
Tel: 01243 775537
Fax: 01243 520120
Chef: Phillip Edwards
Cost: Set-price L £15/D £19. ☺ H/wine £11.95
Times: Noon-2pm/7-9.30pm (10pm Sat, Sun). Closed L Sat
Additional: Sunday L; Children welcome
Seats: 100. Private dining room 120
Style: Classic/country-house
Smoking: No smoking in dining room
Civil licence: 120
Accommodation: 94 en suite ★ ★ ★ ★

Directions: 3 miles NE of Chichester. From Portsmouth E along A27, staying S of Chichester. Signposted within area

HORSHAM, **Random Hall Hotel** ❀

Tapestries line the walls of this 16th-century former farmhouse, providing a fascinating foil for the modern British cooking. From the set menus expect the likes of guinea fowl and ginger sausages with mash, plus banana and toffee tart.

Style: Traditional/Formal
Smoking: No smoking in dining room; Jacket & tie preferred
Accommodation: 15 en suite ★ ★ ★

Directions: 4 miles W of Horsham, 15 miles SW of Gatwick Airport

Stane Street Slinfold RH13 7QX
Map 4: TQ13
Tel: 01403 790558
Fax: 01403 791046
Cost: Set-price L £16.50/D £24. ☺ H/wine £11
Times: Noon-2pm/7-10pm.
Closed 28 Dec-10 Jan
Additional: Bar Food; Sunday L; Children 6+

LICKFOLD, **Lickfold Inn** ❀

Wooden beams, a black iron stove and uneven floors are features of this colourful, stylish restaurant. Seared scallops, chargrilled tuna with mango and chilli salsa, and steamed snapper wrapped in banana leaves are typical choices.

Directions: NE of Midhurst, Lickfold signed from A286

Nr Petworth GU28 9EY
Map 4: SU92
Tel: 01798 861285
Fax: 01798 861342

Telephone for further details

LOWER BEEDING,
South Lodge Hotel 🏵🏵🏵

Brighton Road Horsham RH13 6PS
Map 4: TQ22
Tel: 01403 891711
Fax: 01403 891766
E-mail: inquiries@
southlodgehotel.dial.iql.co.uk
Chef: Lewis Hamblet
Owner: Mr G Pecorelli
Cost: Alc £48, set-price L £18.50/D
£35. H/wine £16.50
Times: Noon-2pm/7-10pm
Additional: Sunday L; Children 8+ (no
restriction at Sun L)
Seats: 40. Private dining room 12/14.
Jacket & tie preferred
Style: Classic/Country-house
Smoking: No smoking in dining room
Civil licence: 80
Accommodation: 41 en suite ★ ★ ★

The camellia on the wall outside the restaurant is actually older than the Victorian house itself. Once home to the noted botanist Frederick Ducane Godman, the outside wall of the Tudor dwelling, against which the shrub was growing, was incorporated into the new house when it was rebuilt. Inside there is classical oak panelling and old Islamic porcelain and pottery collected by Godman. There is a touch of the collector, also, about the menu with its inclusion of elements and influences from around the globe. Loin of South Downs lamb is served with falafel and light tarragon jus; poached tamarillo adds an unexpectedly exotic note to pan-fried loin of venison with rich game jus. An unusual vegetarian starter is velouté of sweet potatoes with pickled ginger. Ingredients are carefully chosen – line-caught sea bass, with saffron and dill cream sauce, for example – and some unusual techniques are explored in dishes such as ballotine of black-leg chicken filled with shallots marinated in fortified wines and sliced onto thyme risotto. Excellent cheese menu. The place in the area for afternoon tea.

Directions: At junction of A279 (Horsham) and A281, turn onto the Cowfold/Brighton road. Hotel is 0.5 mile on R

MIDHURST, Angel Hotel 🏵🏵

North Street GU29 9DN
Map 4: SU82
Tel: 01730 812421
Fax: 01730 815928
E-mail: angel@hshotels.co.uk

'The Angel has changed hands (now under the same ownership as the nearby Spread Eagle) and no longer has two

restaurants, just a high quality brasserie situated at the front of the hotel', reports our inspector. This new brasserie has a warm, fairly refined feel, with tables sufficiently well spaced to give both comfort and relative privacy, and offers a short menu of uncomplicated modern dishes. First-rate seared scallops with clam chowder, breast of guinea fowl with roasted shallots and red wine dressing, and apple tart with rosemary ice cream and caramel sauce made up our test dinner, prepared by a team that was just settling in. Excellent breads and sound petits fours are a plus. The wine list is relatively compact, but offers a good selection by the glass.

Directions: Town centre, junction of A286 and A272

Chef: Simon Malin
Owners: Mr & Mrs Goodman
Cost: Alc £27, set-price L £9.75. H/wine £11.60
Times: Noon-2.30pm/6.30-10pm
Additional: Sunday L; Children welcome
Seats: 50. Private dining room 50
Style: bistro-style/informal
Smoking: No-smoking area; No pipes & cigars
Civil licence: 35
Accommodation: 28 en suite ★ ★ ★

MIDHURST,
Southdowns Country Hotel 醱醱

Trotton GU31 5JN
Map 4: SU82
Tel: 01730 821521
Fax: 01730 821790
E-mail: reception@southhotel.freeserve.co.uk
Chef: Darren Lunn
Owners: Richard Lion, Dominic Vedovato
Cost: Alc £30, set-price L £14.95/D £25. ☺ H/wine £10.95
Times: Noon-2pm/7-10pm
Additional: Bar food; Sunday L; Children 10+
Seats: 60. Private dining room 18; Jacket & tie preferred
Style: Traditional/Country-house
Smoking: No smoking in dining room; Air conditioning
Civil licence: 100
Accommodation: 20 en suite ★ ★ ★

Idyllic location hidden away down a country lane belies the actual proximity of civilisation in the form of Midhurst and Petersfield. The spacious Country Restaurant is the main focus for the hotel's culinary exertions and the menu testifies to a love of bold flavours and quality ingredients. Strips of confit of pheasant are combined with a mushroom and croûton salad with a balsamic and walnut dressing to produce a fresh, succulent starter. Main courses might include roasted plaice with a Mediterranean garnish and a niçoise sauce, or perhaps grilled prime fillet steak served with grilled tomatoes, field mushrooms and a traditional béarnaise sauce. Vegetarian diners are well catered for with the likes of porcini roast garlic and oyster mushroom risotto and Italian caponata of aubergine on offer. Dark and white chocolate fondant and lemongrass and rosemary crème brûlée are amongst the many high quality desserts.

Directions: 1 mile off A272 Petersfield Road

MIDHURST, Spread Eagle Hotel 醱醱

Take a seat next to the inglenook fireplace under the ancient beams of this luxuriously historic establishment and you may be keeping company with the likes of Shakespeare, Dickens and Elizabeth I (or so it is claimed.) Despite the abundance of historic charm the hotel is not embarrassed to offer the most modern of facilities and, likewise, the restaurant cuisine

South Street
GU29 9NH
Map 4: SU82
Tel: 01730 816911
Fax: 01730 815668
E-mail: spreadeagle@hshotels.com
Chef: Steve Crane
Owners: Mr & Mrs Goodman

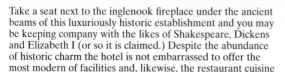

does not stoop to conquer. Modern British is the approach and a set-price menu might offer starters along the lines of asparagus soup with truffle oil, or grilled scallops with a warm artichoke mousse and a chive velouté. A main course of roast rump of lamb with garlic potatoes, provençal vegetables and rosemary oil might be just the thing for a cold winter's night, whilst pan fried fillet of sea bass with a tomato minestrone and basil ravioli might be one lighter option for a summer lunch.

Directions: Town centre, corner of South and West Streets.

ROWHOOK, Chequers Inn ❀

A 15th-century inn, full of character with beamed ceilings and wooden floors. Quality ingredients and a sure hand in the kitchen showed in a vibrant blanquette of monkfish and mussels with herb couscous and parsnip crisps.

Directions: Telephone for directions

STORRINGTON, Fleur de Sel ❀❀

There is little remaining at this smart restaurant to evoke the private boys' school it once housed. The original timber beams and large inglenook fireplace are nowadays complemented by a stylish blue and lemon colour scheme, while outdoors there's a courtyard garden complete with pond and fountain which makes the ideal place for enjoying aperitifs. The cooking is

Spread Eagle Hotel

Cost: *Alc* £45, set-price L £10/D £35. H/wine £12.95
Times: 12.30-2pm/7-9.30pm
Additional: Bar food L; Sunday L; Children welcome
Seats: 60. Private dining room 25
Style: Traditional
Smoking: No smoking in dining room
Civil licence: 80
Accommodation: 39 en suite ★ ★ ★

Nr Horsham RH12 3PY
Map 4: TQ13
Tel/Fax: 01403 790480

Telephone for further details

Manleys Hill
RH20 4BT
Map 4: TQ01
Tel: 01903 742331
Fax: 01903 740649
Chef: Michel Perraud
Owners: Michel & Bernadette Perraud
Cost: *Alc* £33-£50, set-price L £16.50/D £20.50. ☺ H/wine £12.50

deeply rooted in the classical French style, and a French team provides service with a friendly, attentive manner. The short-choice set menu offers the likes of terrine of sole with tomato and basil butter sauce, followed by a trio of fish and baby vegetables with an aniseed cream sauce, and perhaps pear mousse cake with red fruit and peach sauces. The lengthier *carte* might feature pan-fried escalope of foie gras with grape sauce, then fillet of brill filled with salmon soufflé and served with cider cream sauce. Desserts provide the expected sublime finish in the form of warm chocolate soufflé with pistachio ice cream, or almond macaroon with prune and Armagnac ice cream. A mainly French wine list has a few token New World offerings.

Directions: On A283, off A24, just E of Storrington

Times: Noon-2pm/7-10pm. Closed L Sat, D Sun, all Mon, 2 wks Jan
Additional: Sunday L; Children 10+; Vegetarian dishes by request
Seats: 50. Private dining room 20
Style: Classic/Chic
Smoking: No pipes & cigars

STORRINGTON, Old Forge

6 Church Street RH20 4LA
Map 4: TQ01
Tel: 01903 743402
Fax: 01903 742540
E-mail: enquiry@oldforge.co.uk
Chef: Clive Roberts
Owners: Mr & Mrs N C Roberts
Cost: *Alc* £28, set-price L £8.50/D £24. ☺ H/wine £12
Times: 12.30-1.30pm/7.15-9pm. Closed L Sat, D Sun, all Mon & Tue, 2 wks Spring, 2 wks Autumn
Additional: Sunday L; Children welcome
Seats: 34. Private dining room 10
Style: Traditional/Beamed
Smoking: No-smoking area; No pipes & cigars

Three small cosy rooms with white-painted walls and low beamed ceilings. A cricketing theme to the decor is a cheerful influence and not at all overbearing. A meal from the set menu might open with Jerusalem artichoke soup topped with herb cream, follow with roast beef and Yorkshire pudding, and close with bitter chocolate terrine with orange and ginger. *Carte* alternatives may include char-grilled vegetable and wholemeal pancake gâteau with a basil and tomato vinaigrette, Dover sole with fennel and a smoked salmon sauce, and cinnamon figs with honey lemon cream. The wine list offers a good selection of new world wines in addition to the usual range of continental favourites. A substantial choice of dessert wines, including Elysium 1997 Black Muscat, California, offers an additional point of interest.

Directions: On a side street in the village centre

TURNERS HILL,
Alexander House ❀❀❀

East Street
RH10 4QD
Map 4: TQ33
Tel: 01342 714914
Fax: 01342 717328
E-mail: info@alexanderhouse.co.uk
Chef: Neil Wiggins
Owner: I.H.G

Neil Wiggins has hit his stride and is cooking on top form. His style of cooking is pared-down but confident and assured and the silly little mistakes which held things back in the past have been eliminated. A single Rye Bay scallop, nicely caramelised outside and just cooked within, was a true appetiser, presented on a tiny salad with some herbs and good olive oil. A super

Alexander House

Cost: *Alc* £45, set-price L £24/D £32. H/wine £15.25
Times: Noon-2pm/7-9.30pm
Additional: Bar food; Sunday L
Seats: 60. Private dining room 6-50; Jacket & tie preferred
Style: Country-house
Smoking: No smoking in dining room
Civil licence: 60
Accommodation: 15 en suite ★ ★ ★

pheasant sausage managed to avoid the common fault of dryness, and was bursting with flavour; the accompanying bed of earthy cep risotto and Madiera jus was absolutely spot-on. Marvelously fresh roast cod with baby leeks, salsify and red wine jus was all the more impressive for its simplicity of approach. A small crème brûlée made a fashionable pre-dessert, but the main dessert sampled, apple tarte Tatin perhaps could have done with a bit more caramelising.

Directions: On B2110 between Turners Hill and East Grinstead, 6m M23 J10

WORTHING,
Ardington Hotel ❀

Steyne Gardens BN11 3DZ
Map 4: TQ10
Tel: 01903 230451
Fax: 01903 526526
Cost: *Alc* £25, set-price D £19.50. ☺ H/wine £11.75
Times: D only, 7-8.45pm. Closed 24 Dec-5 Jan
Additional: Bar meals L; Sunday L; Children welcome
Style: Classic
Accommodation: 45 en suite ★ ★ ★

Competent cooking skills marry well with quality produce to produce a range of highly enjoyable dishes. Sample wild mushroom gateau with thyme cream sauce, and baked fillet of Nile perch in a tomato, basil, olive and caper sauce.

Directions: Town centre

WORTHING,
Findon Manor Hotel ❀❀

See Findon, West Sussex

TYNE & WEAR

GATESHEAD, Eslington Villa Hotel

Edwardian building, set in two acres of beautiful grounds. The restaurant has well spaced tables adorned with lilies in tall vases. risotto of smoked cheese and chives and tarragon chicken show the style.

Smoking: No smoking in dining room
Accommodation: 18 en suite ★ ★

Directions: Off A1(M) along Teme Valley, turn R at Eastern Avenue, then L into Station Road

8 Station Road Low Fell NE9 6DR
Map 12: NZ26
Tel: 0191 4876017
Fax: 0191 4200667
Cost: Alc £23, set-price L £10.95. ☺
H/wine £11.50
Times: Noon-2pm/7-9.45pm. Closed
L Sat, D Sun, 25 & 26 Dec, 1 Jan, Bhs
Additional: Sunday L; Children
welcome
Style: Chic

NEWCASTLE UPON TYNE, Cafe 21

Comfortable café restaurant with a blackboard menu offering an eclectic selection of modern dishes – duck confit, braised butter beans and endive rubs shoulders with seared scallops, oven dried tomatoes, gremolata and olive oil. Attentive service.

Style: Bistro-style
Smoking: No-smoking area; No pipes & cigars

Directions: From A696, follow signs for Darras Hall, L at mini-roundabout, 200yds to restaurant

35 The Broadway Darras Hall
Ponteland NE20 9PW
Map 12: NZ26
Tel/Fax: 01661 820357
Cost: Alc £25, set-price L £13/early D
£10.50 & £13.50. ☺ H/wine £10.50
Times: Noon-2pm/5.30-10.30pm.
Closed L Mon-Fri, all Sun, Bhs
Additional: Children welcome

NEWCASTLE UPON TYNE,
The Fisherman's Lodge ❀❀

This popular restaurant on the outskirts of Newcastle attracts customers from the city centre, even at lunch times. Although only minutes away from the outer suburb of Jesmond, its picturesque location, a steep valley and nearby stream makes a marked contrast to the urban sprawl. Fish is the main focus, and accounts for at least half the dishes on the menu. Good canapés, fresh bread and both plain and herbed butters precede the meal. A duck liver pâté was served with onion marmalade, and the fresh roasted cod fillet, wonderfully fresh, was perfectly cooked. An iced apple parfait was 'very good'. Home-made almond tuile sheets separated the smooth flavoursome parfait and proved an 'excellent contrast'. The mainly French wine list does include several New World wines, including some from Canada, and a sheet of 'Wines of the Month'.

Directions: 2.5 miles from city centre, off A1058 (Tynemouth) road at Benton Bank, middle of Jesmond Dene Park

Jesmond Dene Jesmond NE7 7BQ
Map 12: NZ26
Tel: 0191 2813281
Fax: 0191 2816410
Chefs: Stephen Jobson, Paul Amer
Owner: Tom Maxfield
Cost: Alc £40, set-price L £19.50/D
£34.50. H/wine £13.50
Times: Noon-2pm/7-11pm.
Closed L Sat, all Sun, Bhs
Additional: Children welcome
Seats: 70. Private dining rooms 14 &
36
Style: Classic/Country-house
Smoking: No smoking in dining room

NEWCASTLE UPON TYNE,
The Magpie Room ❀❀

A football stadium seems an unlikely setting for a serious restaurant, but the Magpie is within Newcastle United's home ground, with views over the pitch in one direction and the city

St James Park
NE1 4ST
Map 12: NZ26
Tel: 0191 2018439
Chef: Ian Lowrey

The Magpie Room

Owners: Second Stand Ltd/Newcastle Utd
Cost: *Alc* £25, set-price L £13/D £18.
☺ H/wine £12.95
Times: Noon-2.30pm/7-10.30pm.
Closed L Sat, D Sun, all Mon
Additional: Sunday L; Children welcome
Seats: 80 (Match day 140). Jacket & tie preferred
Style: Modern/Formal
Smoking: Air conditioning
Civil licence: 120

centre in the other (plans in the air to relocate the restaurant may result in the loss of the city view). Although closed to the public on match days, tours of the stadium are on offer on Sundays, when it's a popular place for family lunch. Smoked haddock risotto with a poached egg and lemon hollandaise, then Thai-style belly-pork with crab ravioli are the sort of ideas the kitchen deals in successfully, with gutsier items running to terrine of ham hock, potato and parsley with a dressing of yellow split peas, and beef fillet with big chips and tomato horseradish. Fish and shellfish are well handled, as in a tasty starter of crab in paper-thin ravioli with sweetcorn sauce, and fresh, moist and flaky pan-fried cod with a creamy sauce of plump mussels, al dente asparagus and parsley. Poire William and almond crumble with rice pudding ice cream was a successful pudding at inspection, and there may also be pineapple tarte Tatin with coconut ice cream, or lime tart. Club supporters can do their bit by going for Newcastle United's own-label wines, including champagne, on the well-chosen wine list.

Directions: From the south, follow Gateshead A1 signs, then A692 over Redheugh Bridge, Blenheim St & then L on Bath Lane

NEWCASTLE UPON TYNE,

Malmaison Hotel ✵

Quayside NE1 3DX
Map 12: NZ26
Tel: 0191 2455000
Fax: 0191 2454545
Cost: *Alc* £25, set-price L £10/D £12.
☺ H/wine £13.95
Times: Noon-2.30pm/6-11pm
Additional: Sunday L; Children welcome
Style: Informal/chic
Smoking: Air conditioning
Accommodation: 116 en suite ★★★

Chic French brasserie at the Malmaison Hotel on the redeveloped quayside. From an attractive menu the roasted cod with garlic shrimps was wonderfully fresh, served with a robust wine jus.

Directions: Telephone for directions

NEWCASTLE UPON TYNE,

Taylor's Wharf

As we went to press we heard about a change of direction for this restaurant in line with a new name: 'Big Mussel'. Previously renowned for its emphasis on seafood, mussel dishes will now make up around a third of the menu, with half kilo pots for starters and kilo pots as a main course, accompanied by fries, bread and dips. Other dishes may include Waterzooi (traditional Belgian fish casserole), and monkfish steak wrapped in Ardennes ham, with green peppercorn, tomato and cucumber dressing. Desserts such as Belgian apple pie and Belgian ice creams, and a selection of Belgian bottled and draft beers, continue the theme.

Directions: From N side of Tyne Bridge, turn L into Mosley Street, L into Dean Street and L again into The Side

15 The Side NE1 3JE
Map 12: NZ26
Tel: 0191 2321057
Fax: 0191 2320496

Telephone for further details

NEWCASTLE UPON TYNE,

Treacle Moon

NEW

Byronic themed restaurant with softly rich decor and highly praised cooking. Try the artistic red pepper and celeriac mille feuille with stilton sauce, then superbly-fresh scallops with crab and fennel risotto. Leave space for warm orange polenta cake.

Additional: Children welcome **Style:** Chic/Modern
Smoking: No-smoking area; No pipes & cigars; Air conditioning

Directions: Telephone for directions

5-7 The Side NE1 3JE
Map 12: NZ26
Tel: 0191 2325537
Fax: 0191 2211745
Cost: *Alc* £35, set-price L £12.95. ☺
H/wine £12.75
Times: Noon-2pm/6-10.30pm.
Closed L Sat, all Sun, Bhs

NEWCASTLE UPON TYNE,

21 Queen Street

Terence Laybourne is on the move in the near future, although relocation plans remain uncertain at the time of writing. We can say with confidence, however, that wherever he cooks will be a place worth visiting. The menu has evolved to suit the needs of a younger, more trendy clientele, but there is no compromise in terms of good quality ingredients and there is the confidence not to complicate unnecessarily by over-elaborate techniques. Staff look more atuned to a brasserie-style operation but are attentive and have an impressive knowledge of the dishes on offer. Amongst first courses such as thin tomato tart with pistou and a friture of garden herbs, and smoked salmon roulade with cream cheese and caviar, a dish of roasted sea scallops with black bean vinaigrette stood out for its quality, succulence and perfect timing. Local Northumbrian lamb, as tasty and tender as you can get, was another star turn accompanied by pearl barley, fried new potatoes and roasted plum tomatoes with a wonderfully concentrated flavour. Butter roast, corn-fed chicken gets a faux-rustic treatment with braised cabbage, country bacon and foie gras sauce, and the wheel has turned full circle for retro classics such as braised fillets of sole with lobster truffle and sauce Mornay. There's even a touch of tongue-in-cheek 70s glitz in the Piña Colada sauce that accompanies a pineapple and coconut mille-feuille.

21 Queen Street Quayside
NE1 3UG
Map 12: NZ26
Tel: 0191 2220755
Fax: 0191 2210761
Chef: Terence Laybourne
Owners: Terence & Susan Laybourne
Cost: *Alc* £36, set-price L £14.50 & £17.50/D £20.50 & £25. ☺ H/wine £12.50
Times: Noon-2pm/7-10.30pm.
Closed L Sat, all Sun, Bhs
Additional: Children welcome; Vegetarian dishes by request
Seats: 70
Style: Modern/Minimalist
Smoking: No pipes

Directions: Queen Street runs parallel to and just behind Newcastle Quay – almost under the Tyne Bridge on N side of the river

NEWCASTLE UPON TYNE,

Vermont Hotel

A striking listed building in a dramatic central location next to the castle keep and the Tyne bridge. A number of dining options are offered but this award applies to the Blue Room, a sedate and reasonably formal restaurant serving ambitious cuisine with professional, attentive service. On a recent visit a good selection of breads and canapés opened the evening positively. A dish of local goats' cheese roasted in sesame on a herb salad with chilli and tomato oil dressing and a dollop of horseradish ice cream proved to be lively and well constructed, although perhaps a bit too busy. A loin of lamb in a brioche paste with lavender proved a very worthy main course but was somewhat overshadowed by a rival dish of John Dory with spiced crumb and a grapefruit butter sauce – superb quality fish with a sharp, slightly bitter sauce.

Directions: City centre, by the Castle and swing bridge

Castle Garth NE1 1RQ
Map 12: NZ26
Tel: 0191 2331010
Fax: 0191 2331234
E-mail: info@vermont-hotel.co.uk
Chef: Thierry Billot
Owners: Lincoln Group
Cost: Alc £35.95. ☺
Times: D only, 6.30-10.45pm. Closed Sun & Mon, 1st 2 wks Aug, 1st 2 wks Jan
Additional: Bar food; Children welcome
Seats: 80. Private dining room 20
Style: Classic
Smoking: No-smoking area
Accommodation: 101 en suite
★ ★ ★ ★

SUNDERLAND, Brasserie 21

A light and spacious converted warehouse right on the quayside. Daily specials augment the contemporary menu, with its grilled calves' liver with apples, onions and bacon, and slow-cooked ham knuckle with braised beans and parsley mash.

Cost: Alc £20, set-price L £12.50 & £14.50. ☺ H/wine £10
Times: Noon-2pm/5.30-10.30pm. Closed Sun & Mon, Bhs
Style: Bistro-style/Modern
Smoking: No pipes & cigars

Directions: Telephone for directions

Wylam Wharf Low Street SR1 2AD
Map 12: NZ35
Tel: 0191 5676594
Fax: 0191 5103994

SUNDERLAND, Swallow Hotel ✿

Classically-styled sea front restaurant. Interesting starters like chicken, mango and coconut salad with herb oil. Main courses range from seared medallion of salmon to pan-fried pork loin, with perhaps lemon and mint tartlet for dessert.

Directions: On A184 (Boldon): at roundabout after Boldon turn L, then 1st R to Seaburn. L at next roundabout, follow road to coast. Turn R; hotel is 100mtrs on R

Queen's Parade Seaburn SR6 8DB
Map 12: NZ35
Tel: 0191 5292041
Fax: 0191 5294227
E-mail: info@swallowhotels.com

Telephone for further details

WARWICKSHIRE

ABBOT'S SALFORD,

Salford Hall Hotel ✿✿

Salford Hall Hotel is a 15th-century manor house that has been restored with care and attention to detail. Among the many marvellous features is the wonderful oak panelling in the restaurant. Home-made canapés precede dinner, and there is a choice of wholemeal or white rolls. Modern British in style, the kitchen is probably trying just a touch too hard: home-cured gravad lax is topped with a pan-seared scallop, a braised blade of Aberdeenshire beef is accompanied by, amongst other things, crisp pancetta; a fillet of Brixham sea bass is served on a leek and smoked haddock risotto. There is no question about the excellence of the produce, but one has to question the way the ingredients are combined. When the kitchen applies itself to getting the simplest dishes right, it succeeds.

Evesham WR11 5UT
Map 4: SP05
Tel: 01386 871300
Fax: 01386 871301
E-mail: reception@salfordhall.co.uk
Chef: Rob Bean
Cost: Set-price L £15.95/D £25. H/wine £12.25
Times: Noon-2pm/7-10pm. Closed L Sat, Xmas
Additional: Bar food L; Sunday L; Children 2+
Seats: 50. Private dining room 50
Style: Country-house
Smoking: No smoking in dining room

Civil licence: 50 **Accommodation:** 34 en suite ★★★

Directions: On A439 8 miles W of Stratford-upon-Avon

ALDERMINSTER,

Ettington Park Hotel ✿✿

Stratford-upon-Avon
CV37 8BU
Map 4: SP24
Tel: 01789 450123
Fax: 01789 450472
Chef: Chris Hudson
Owners: Arcadian Hotels
Cost: Alc £30.50, set-price L £15/D £30.50. H/wine £17.50
Times: Noon-2pm/6-9.30pm
Additional: Bar food; Sunday L; Children welcome
Seats: 40. Private dining room 100; Jacket & tie preferred
Style: Classic/Country-house
Smoking: No smoking in dining room
Accommodation: 48 en suite ★★★★

The panelled Oak Room restaurant of the Victorian Gothic mansion is particularly stylish and features a fine rococco ceiling and view across the garden to the family chapel. The style of cooking is eclectic and modern with a touch of brasserie about it. Starters might include deep-fried 'Crottin' goats' cheese in filo pastry with black olive tapenade, tomato and green herb dressing or shiitaki, oyster and wild mushroom risotto with Parmesan tuile and cep sauce. It's not easy to make Scotch fillet steak sound interesting – so the concept of serving it with spiced chutney, sweet potato rösti, sugarsnap peas and star anise jus is intriguing. Desserts might include iced apricot parfait with apricot coulis or dark and white chocolate truffle cake with coffee bean sauce. Farmhouse cheese is served from the trolley with home-baked breads.

Directions: 5 miles S of Stratford

ATHERSTONE,

Chapel House Hotel ❀❀

Friar's Gate CV9 1EY
Map 4: SP39
Tel: 01827 718949
Fax: 01827 717702
Chef: Adam Bennett
Owner: David Arnold
Cost: *Alc* £30. ☺ H/wine £9.95
Times: D only, 7-9.30pm.
Closed D Sun, Xmas, Bhs
Additional: Sunday L; Children 10+
Seats: 50. Private dining room 14
Style: Classic/Country-house
Smoking: No smoking in dining room
Accommodation: 14 en suite ★★

Hospitable hotel nestling beside the church and partly enclosed by a high brick wall. The dining room is carefully decorated in Georgian period style and overlooks the well-tended mature gardens. The cooking encompasses French, British and Mediterranean styles. Starter options might, for example, include terrine of pheasant and foie gras with Calvados, steamed Shetland mussels with Thai spices and coconut milk or smoked chicken broth with cannellini beans and parsley. Main course dishes such as roast loin of venison with parsnip purée, wild cranberries and a five spice jus are supplemented by a 'catch of the day' and daily special option. Desserts such as glazed egg-custard tart with nutmeg ice cream are difficult to resist, but if you can't make your mind up or you're just feeling adventurous there is always the 'wait and see' option.

Directions: Town centre

KENILWORTH,

Restaurant Bosquet ❀❀

97a Warwick Road
CV8 1HP
Map 4: SP27
Tel: 01926 852463
Chef: Bernard Lignier
Owners: B J & J Lignier
Cost: Set-price L & D £25.
H/wine £12.50
Times: Noon-1.15pm/7-9.15pm.
Closed L Sat, all Sun & Mon, 1 wk
Xmas, 3 wks Aug

A traditional 'front room' style French restaurant with friendly and attentive service from Mme Lignier, la patronne. M. Lignier cooks in classic style: foie gras is usually accompanied with a lively sauce or chutney, perhaps ginger and rhubarb or spice and fig. Other fruity pairings include mandarins with roast partridge or saddle of venison, or lime, pineapple and banana in a lightly-curried sauce with loin of veal. Saucing plays its essential part – truffle sauce with a sausage of veal sweetbreads with apple and grapes, red wine and shallot for a fillet of Scottish beef. The choice of fish dishes depends on market availability. Desserts might include an eggy and creamy crème brûlée on a shallow dish. Freshly-made filter coffee is strong but not bitter and comes with home-made petits fours.

Additional: Children welcome; Vegetarian dishes not always available
Seats: 26 **Style:** Classic/Traditional
Smoking: No pipes & cigars

Directions: In main street of Kenilworth

KENILWORTH, Simpsons

Warwick Road CV8 1HL
Map 4: SP27
Tel: 01926 864567
Fax: 01926 864510

Telephone for further details

A double-fronted restaurant at one end of Warwick Road, buzzing at lunchtime with well-dressed customers. The interior – green and dark wood hung with striking paintings and prints – is very French in feel and Andreas Antona is a classically trained chef, so it is no surprise to see foie gras ravioli, Sauternes sauce and nage on the menu. You might also find honey-glazed kleftico, crushed potatoes, and olive and caper sauce, in homage to Antona's roots, and modern influences too with, lemon oil, aged balsamic and beetroot vinaigrette. The best dish sampled was a fresh-tasting, punchy red mullet and tomato tart with parsley sauce and tapenade dressing. Braised shin of beef served with the foie gras ravioli, roast vegetables, celeriac purée and port wine sauce was bold, strongly flavoured and not for the faint-hearted.

Directions: In main street

ROYAL LEAMINGTON SPA,
Lansdowne Hotel ❀

87 Clarendon Street CV32 4PF
Map 4: SP36
Tel: 01926 450505
Fax: 01926 421313
Cost: Set-price D fr £18.95. ☺
H/wine £8.95
Times: D only 7-8.30pm. Closed
D Sun (ex residents), 25-26 Dec

Regency town house with a newly decorated restaurant. Sound technical skills, quality produce and seasonality are key to the success of the dishes. The shortbread served with coffee is 'heavenly'.

Additional: Children 5+
Style: Traditional town house
Smoking: No smoking in dining room; Jacket & tie preferred
Accommodation: 14 en suite ★

Directions: Town centre, crossroads of Warwick Street and Clarendon Street

ROYAL LEAMINGTON SPA,
Leamington Hotel and Bistro ❀

64 Upper Holly Walk CV32 4JL
Map 4: SP36
Tel: 01926 883777
Fax: 01926 330467
Cost: Alc £16. ☺ H/wine £9.75
Times: Noon-1.45pm/7-9.45pm

Stylishly appointed bistro in a Victorian dining room where period features and picture adorned walls create a sophisticated though casual atmosphere. Starters might include open ravioli with wild mushrooms followed perhaps by palliarde of chicken.

Additional: Sunday L; Children welcome
Style: Bistro-style **Smoking:** No pipes & cigars
Civil licence: 65
Accommodation: 30 en suite ★ ★ ★

Directions: Along Newbold Terrace, turn L at lights. Hotel on right-hand corner of Willes Road & Upper Holly Walk

ROYAL LEAMINGTON SPA,
Mallory Court Hotel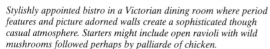

Harbury Lane Bishop's Tachbrook
CV33 9QB
Map 4: SP36
Tel: 01926 330214
Fax: 01926 451714
E-mail: reception@mallory.co.uk

Set in ten acres of beautifully landscaped grounds, this country house has an impressive panelled dining room offering an extensive menu. A starter of a ravioli of goats' cheese with red pepper coulis was a whole cheese grilled with a sheet of pasta

Mallory Court Hotel

Chef: Allan Holland
Owners: Allan Holland, Jeremy Mort
Cost: Alc £55, set-price L £25/D £37.50
Times: Noon-3pm/7-10pm
Additional: Bar food L; Sunday L; Children 9+
Seats: 50. Private dining room 15
Style: Country-house
Smoking: No smoking in dining room
Accommodation: 18 en suite ★ ★ ★

on top. The cheese was a little under-cooked and still crumbly, but the sauce was very good. Perhaps a better choice would have been grilled squid salad with Seville orange dressing or mosaic of rabbit with cabbage and ceps. There are classic luxury dishes on the menu such as roulade of smoked salmon, fillet of turbot in Champagne, Chateaubriand with béarnaise sauce and hot mandarin Napoleon soufflé. Tournedos Rossini had fine foie gras and a rich, shiny sauce – 'lovely beefy flavour, good consistency'. Other main courses include roast monkfish with red wine sauce and fillet of venison with chocolate sauce. A glazed lemon tart had a lemony, well-textured filling and was served with a ball of blackcurrant sorbet. Dinner concludes with very good cafetière coffee with home made petits fours.

Directions: From M40 J13 (northbound) take A452 (signed Leamington Spa), next L into Oakley Wood Rd (B4087). R into Harbury Ln. Hotel on R. From M40 J14/A452 into Mallory Rd, then B4087

STRATFORD-UPON-AVON,

Billesley Manor Hotel ✿✿

Billesley Alcester
B49 6NF
Map 4: SP25
Tel: 01789 279955
Fax: 01789 764145
E-mail: enquiries@billesleymanor.co.uk
Chef: Adrian Kirikmaa
Owner: Haydin Fentum

A topiary garden of chess pieces is part of the 11 acres of parkland around this 16th-century manor, and although a sense of history permeates the place, with fine panelling, a stag's head above the fireplace in the great hall, and exposed stone, there's also the chance of swimming, croquet and tennis. The dining room has the air of a gentleman's club, with oils dotting the dark wooden panels and olive-green button-back leather chairs at elegantly set tables. While beef fillet with foie gras and truffle in Madeira sauce sounds as luxuriously traditional as the surroundings, the kitchen also works in a more modish frame of mind, turning out codling with braised lentils and chorizo, or pink rump of lamb in light tapenade accompanied by roasted cherry tomatoes and saffron potatoes. That saucing is a strength is confirmed by a butter-based sauce with the slightest hint of a kick of sweet chilli served with tender pan-fried medallions of monkfish and asparagus, with perhaps terrine of duck, smoked chicken and tarragon among other starters. The same consideration goes into puddings: for example, 'devilishly smooth and very light' chocolate tart hinting of ginger, its pastry thin and crisp, surrounded by diced pears in vanilla syrup. House wines from Australia head up the long wine list.

Cost: *Alc* £32, set-price L £15/D £22.50. ☺ H/wine £14.50
Times: Noon-2.30pm/7-10.30pm. Closed L Sat
Additional: Bar food L; Sunday L; Children 6+
Seats: 42. Private dining room 17
Style: Chic/Modern
Smoking: No smoking in dining room
Civil licence: 74
Accommodation: 41 en suite ★ ★ ★ ★

Directions: On A46, 3 miles west of Stratford-upon-Avon

STRATFORD-UPON-AVON,
The Boathouse

Swan's Nest Lane CV37 7LS
Map 4: SP25
Tel/Fax: 01789 297733
Chef: Sean Brebner
Owner: W Meredith-Owen
Cost: *Alc* £30, set-price L £10.95. ☺ H/wine £11.95
Times: Noon-2pm/6-11pm. Closed L Sat, Mon & Tue, all Sun, Xmas
Additional: Bar food L; Children welcome
Seats: 90
Style: Bistro-style/Chic

A restaurant above a working boathouse at the water's edge must have a boating theme, and indeed this does: bare floorboards and a lot of rope incorporated into the decor, with simply appointed wooden-topped tables in cast-iron stands. The air of a bistro might hang about the place, but the menus range near and far, from East (Thai-spiced chicken spring roll with peanut and coriander salad) to West (tomato tarte Tatin with spinach and ricotta lasagne). A starter of boudin of foie gras and chicken, light of texture, rich of flavour, with bean purée and pancetta, and main-course roast saddle of rabbit with grain mustard and thyme sauce with sweet potato might take their inspiration from across the Channel, but a fusion of cultures is evident in such dishes as seared Szechuan-style tuna with lobster and saffron mash on shellfish emulsion. Whatever, the kitchen handles everything with skill, as in 'a lovely cut' of really fresh and meaty roast halibut in a herb crust well-partnered by sun-dried tomato risotto, or a perfect example of classic crème brûlée. Wines from Languedoc-Roussillon, imported direct, are the house speciality.

Directions: From town centre, cross river by Clopton Bridge toward Oxford and Banbury, then double back around roundabout 50 yards on, then 1st L

STRATFORD-UPON-AVON, Desports ❀❀

13-14 Meer Street
CV37 6QB
Map 4: SP25
Tel/Fax: 01789 269304
E-mail: bookings@desports.co.uk
Chef: Paul Desport
Owners: Julie & Paul Desport
Cost: *Alc* £29, set-price L £14. ☺
H/wine £10.50
Times: Noon-2pm/6-11pm. Closed
Sun & Mon, Jan
Additional: Children welcome
Seats: 50
Style: Informal
Smoking: No-smoking area; No pipes
& cigars

Directions: In town centre between
Market Place and Shakespeare Centre

A vivid use of spices in a menu full of imaginative ideas makes for some exciting eating. Roast sea bass comes with fennel seed mash, tomato and vanilla oil, and bitter chocolate tart is served with cardamom ice cream. Beetroot risotto with chives and shaved Parmesan balanced the sweetness of the root vegetable with a generous drizzle of lemon oil. A main course combined crispy duck breast au poivre with sesame noodles and duck spring roll with shoots and greens. Fine cheeses are supplied by Paxton and Whitfield. On the first floor of an Elizabethan building, the vibrant yellow walls contrast well with the traditional black beams under the fine vaulted ceiling. The contemporary look is enhanced by twisted iron light fittings and cobalt blue napkins. The atmosphere is relaxed and every diner is warmly greeted.

STRATFORD-UPON-AVON,
Grosvenor Hotel ❀

Try interesting modern dishes at the Garden Room restaurant. Medallions of monkfish with tiger prawns as a starter, main course of plaice and salmon gâteau or breast of pheasant, and perhaps mango cheesecake for dessert.

Directions: Telephone for directions

Warwick Road CV37 6YT
Map 4: SP25
Tel: 01789 269213
Fax: 01789 266087

Telephone for further details

STRATFORD-UPON-AVON,
Lambs of Sheep Street ❀

An early 16th-century building retaining original timber beams and historic character. The restaurant is contrastingly modern in culinary approach; crisp duck pieces in a balsamic style sauce or an inventive baked monkfish dish for example.

Times: Noon-2pm/5-10.30pm. Closed 25 & 26 Dec
Additional: Children welcome
Style: Bistro-style/Informal
Smoking: No pipes & cigars

Directions: From Stratford town centre, head towards 'Waterside' and 'Royal Shakespeare Theatre'. Sheep Street is 1st R on Waterside

12 Sheep Street CV37 6EF
Map 4: SP25
Tel/Fax: 01789 292554
E-mail: lambs@ukgateway.net
Cost: *Alc* £18.80, set-price L/D
£12.50. ☺ H/wine £8.95

STRATFORD-UPON-AVON,

The Shakespeare ❀

Charming 18th-century hotel restaurant with a profusion of exposed beams, creaking staircases and open fires. Cuisine is predominantly classical with unusual twists such as an impeccable broad bean capuccion with bacon and tomato shreds.

Chapel Street CV37 6ER
Map 4: SP25
Tel: 0870 400 8182
Fax: 01789 415411
Cost: *Alc* £25, set-price L £16.95/
D £25. H/wine £27.50
Times: D only, 6-10pm
Additional: Bar food L; Sunday L
(12.30-3pm); Children welcome
Style: Classic/Traditional
Smoking: No smoking in dining room
Civil licence: 48
Accommodation: 74 rooms ★ ★ ★ ★

Directions: Follow signs to town centre. Round one-way system up Bridge Street. At roundabout turn L. Hotel is 200yds on L

STRATFORD-UPON-AVON,

Welcombe Hotel ❀❀

Stunning views across a formal Italian garden and landscaped parkland to the countryside beyond can create a bit of a distraction for diners at this impressive hotel-restaurant. Part of the grounds were once owned by Shakespeare, but the building is firmly Victorian, the Jacobean touches to the architecture purely imitation. Interesting menus offer the genuine article, however, with accomplished cooking resulting in some fine dishes which received an enthusiastic 'thumbs up' at an inspection meal. Perfectly-timed pan-fried sea scallops and langoustine with toasted pine kernel risotto got this meal off to a racing start, chased by a rich and enjoyable chicken breast with foie gras sausage, truffle risotto, braised herb chicken leg and an Alsace wine sauce. A salad of green bean and shallot provided a nice combination of 'crunch and bite', while a fairly average mango tarte Tatin was elevated to divine heights by a heavenly pink grapefruit and yoghurt ice cream. Nautical-style waiters in white drill jackets with monogrammed breast pockets keep things moving in the light and airy dining room.

Warwick Road CV37 0NR
Map 4: SP25
Tel: 01789 295252
Fax: 01789 414666
E-mail: sales@welcombe.co.uk
Chef: Ben Davies
Owner: Yamara UK Ltd
Cost: *Alc* £45.50, set-price L
£21.50/D £39.50. H/wine £18
Times: 12.30-2pm/7-9.30pm
Additional: Bar food; Sunday L;
Children 10+
Seats: 60. Private dining room
20-100. Jacket & tie preferred
Style: Country-house/Formal
Smoking: No smoking in dining room
Civil licence: 50
Accommodation: 64 en suite ★ ★ ★ ★

Directions: On A439 1 mile from town centre

WARWICK,
Ardencote Manor Hotel ❀

Lye Green Road Claverdon
CV35 8LS
Map 4: SP16
Tel: 01926 843111
Fax: 01926 842646
E-mail: hotel@ardencote.com
Cost: Set-price D £24.95. ☺
H/wine £10.95
Times: D only, 7-9pm.
Additional: Sunday L (12.30-2pm)
Style: Traditional/Country-house
Smoking: No smoking in dining room;
Jacket & tie preferred
Civil licence: 120
Accommodation: 18 en suite ★★★

The imaginative modern menu in The Oak Room is one of several eating options. Terrine of pheasant, venison and pigeon might be followed by baked fillet of halibut with smoked mussel sauce, and amaretto cheesecake.

Directions: From A4189 in Claverdon follow signs for Shrewley. Hotel 0.5m on R

WISHAW,
The De Vere Belfry ❀❀

Sutton Coldfield B76 9PR
Map 7: SP19
Tel: 01675 470301
Fax: 01675 470178
Chef: Eric Bruce
Cost: *Alc* £30, set-price L £11.50/D
£29.95. H/wine £14.95
Times: 12.30-2.30pm/7.30-10.30pm.
Closed D Sun, some Bhs
Additional: Sunday L; Children 14+
Seats: 70. Jacket & tie preferred
Style: Rustic/Country-house
Smoking: No smoking in dining room
Civil licence: 70
Accommodation: 324 en suite
★★★★

Extensive leisure facilities are close at hand to help burn off calories acquired at the cosmopolitan French hotel-restaurant. A choice of menus ensures that all tastes and time schedules are catered for. For example the 'Lunch Menu Express' is offered for 'those who don't have time to linger' – speedy service whilst retaining quality in dishes such as deep fried lemon sole fillets with tomato sauce and caper mayonnaise, or Cumberland sausage lyonnaise on garlic mash. A meal taken from the *carte* option might take you on a journey through clam chowder marbled with cassoulet of seafood, fillet of venison with millefeuille of pear and pistachio, ending in crème caramel with oranges in cognac.

Directions: At junction of A446 & A4091, 1 mile NW of M42 J9

WEST MIDLANDS

BALSALL COMMON, **Haigs Hotel** ❀❀

Kenilworth Road CV7 7EL
Map 7: SP27
Tel: 01676 533004
Fax: 01676 535132
Chef: Paul Hartup
Owners: Alan & Hester Harris
Cost: Alc £29, set-price D £22.95. ☺
H/wine £10.25
Times: D only, 7.30-9.30pm.
Closed D Sun
Additional: Sunday L (12.30-2pm);
Children welcome
Seats: 60. Private dining room 28
Style: Formal
Smoking: No smoking in dining room
Accommodation: 23 en suite ★★

A small privately-run hotel with an attractive floral-themed restaurant. Airy, bright and comfortable decor complements friendly and attentive service and British cooking of great technique and vitality. A warm smoked venison salad with a raspberry vinaigrette and baked sausage of guinea fowl on a bed of fresh egg noodles were the stand-out dishes in the varied starter options from the *carte*. To follow perhaps roasted half of wild duck with a black pudding mousse, or cannon of Warwickshire lamb. A refined blackberry crème brûlée and a luxuriant dark chocolate terrine with vanilla sauce typify the dessert options. The set dinner menu follows similar lines with a typical meal opening with slices of oak-smoked Scottish salmon followed by grilled sirloin steak with a brandy and peppercorn sauce and closing in a fresh fruit salad. The wine list is unpretentious whilst covering most areas.

Directions: On A452, 4 miles N of NEC/Airport, on L before village centre

BALSALL COMMON,
Nailcote Hall ❀❀

Elizabethan manor house with heavy timbers and open fires. The traditional Oak Room restaurant provides an attractive setting for formal dining, with beams, an inglenook, and super Walter Dendy Sadler engravings on the walls. The alternative place to eat is the Mediterranean-style Rick's Bar, where the bistro atmosphere is accentuated by a regular programme of live music. The Oak Room *carte* offers half a dozen starters and main courses, plus a choice of dishes from the grill – fillet steak, Dover sole and lamb cutlets. Kick off with roast quail with salsify and herb salad, or seared scallops wrapped in pancetta with a sweet carrot and coriander sauce. To follow, perhaps twice-cooked blade of beef with caraway cabbage, Guinness and ceps jus, or saffron-marinated cod with Camembert, spinach, lardons and cider.

Directions: On B4101 (Balsall/Coventry), 10 mins from NEC/Birmingham Airport

Nailcote Lane Berkswell CV7 7DE
Map 7: SP27
Tel: 024 76446174
Fax: 024 76470720
E-mail: info@nailcotehall.co.uk
Chef: Wayne Thompson
Owner: Rick Cressman
Cost: Set-price L £21.50/D £32.50.
H/wine £13.50
Times: Closed L Sat, D Sun
Additional: Sunday L; Children
welcome
Seats: 45
Style: Classic/Country-house
Smoking: No smoking in dining room
Civil licence: 120
Accommodation: 38 en suite ★★★★

BARSTON, **The Malt Shovel**

Stylish dining in the converted barn restaurant, or go casual in the country pub-style bar/bistro. Either way, pick from an exciting menu including slow-braised lamb shank, or fresh fish from the specials board.

Barston Lane B92 0JP
Map 4: SP27
Tel/Fax: 01675 443223
Cost: Alc £25. ☺ H/wine £9.95
Times: Noon-3pm/6.30-10pm.
Closed D Sun, 25 & 26 evening

Additional: Bar food; Sunday L; Children 10+
Style: Informal/Rustic
Smoking: No-smoking area; No pipes & cigars; Air conditioning

Directions: From M42 J5 take turn towards Knowle. 1st L on Jacobean Lane, R at T-junction (Hampton Lane). Sharp L into Barston Lane. Restaurant 0.5m.

BIRMINGHAM, **Bank**

Bank, a branch of the popular London restaurant, is housed in an imposing contemporary building; once inside you are hit by the size and scale of the operation. The interior is bright and vibrant almost to the point of shocking; diners can view the kitchen through a glass wall and there's a long, stool-lined bar, lipstick red tub chairs and banquette seating. The cooking is self-described as 'liberated French with a twist on the classics', but the menu has also been freed from all constraint of length and the brasserie choice is vast. Terrine of foie gras with fig compote and brioche was a well-executed standard, followed by impeccably-cooked, plump, seared scallops with garlic mash. Equally satisfying was a contrasting main course of moist and flavoursome glazed belly of pork with chinese cabbage. Fish cakes, lobster and chips, lamb cutlets with olives, peppers and sun-dried tomatoes are amongst the choice of main courses. An apple and yoghurt crunch Martini tasted better than it sounded, attractively served in a cocktail glass. Bitter chocolate tart has also been praised.

4 Brindley Place B1 2JB
Map 7: SP08
Tel: 0121 633 7001
Fax: 0121 633 4465
Chefs: Idris Caldora &
David Colcombe
Owners: BGR plc & Ann Tonks
Cost: Alc £18, set-price L £12.50. ☺
H/wine £9.90
Times: Noon-3pm(Sat brunch fr
11am, Sun 11-5.30pm)/5.30-11pm.
Closed D Sun
Additional: Bar food; Sunday Brunch;
Children welcome
Seats: 250. Private dining room 100
Style: Modern
Smoking: No-smoking area; Air
conditioning

Directions: Brindley Place is just off Broad St (A456)

BIRMINGHAM,
Birmingham Marriott

12 Hagley Road Five Ways
B16 8SJ
Map 7: SP08
Tel: 0121 4521144
Fax: 0121 4563442
Chef: Ian Mansfield

The Elgar theme is reflected in the striking trompe-l'oeil, handpainted murals of the Malvern Hills. The setting for Ian Mansfield's cooking is one of simple elegance. The style is intelligent, accurate and consistent and there is little chance of leaving disappointed. Not that the cooking is in any way dull. The combinations may be largely classic, with modern influences such as the use of spicing (cannelloni of crab and Swiss chard with cardamom jus; gratin of rhubarb and strawberries, ginger and saffron ice cream), but there is a dexterity in the kitchen that marks it out from many of its peers. Take a starter of plump and sweet roast scallops with crispy chorizo and a silky pea purée that was an absolute delight in its simplicity. Similarly, roast squab pigeon arrived with the meat judged to perfection, allied to slightly too tart choucroute of celeriac with a restrained liquorice sauce. Desserts are from a similarly precise mould, with a towering warm croustade of pineapple being a masterpiece of architecture but, more importantly, with a well-judged companion of coconut ice cream.

Cost: *Alc* £38, set-price L £21.50/D £29.50. H/wine £16.50
Times: 12.30-2.30pm/7-10.30pm. Closed L Sat
Additional: Sunday L; Children welcome
Seats: 70. Private dining room 20
Style: Classic
Smoking: Air conditioning
Accommodation: 98 en suite
★ ★ ★ ★ ★

Directions: City end of A546, at the Five Ways roundabout.

BIRMINGHAM, Langtry's at The Birmingham Marriott

Clever use of subdued lighting and an abundance of plants in a green colour scheme create an ambience of quiet, cool tranquillity. The effect is enhanced by the use of wicker furniture and well-spaced tables, and in this relaxed setting the accomplished British cooking comes with an unexpected but welcome punch. Home-made brown and bacon bread made a promising start to an inspection meal, while the warm prawn and salmon cake with a herb tartare thrilled the palate with its exciting flavours and good seasoning. The meal continued on an upward tilt with succulent guinea fowl and 'brilliant' gratin dauphinoise, served with an intense jus and tender young beans, a hint of sage and a julienne of bacon. There was praise, too, for the classic and well-executed warm chocolate sponge with a wicked chocolate malt ice cream, and the espresso and rich but light truffles were faultless. Elsewhere on this recommended *carte* expect dishes like casserole of rabbit chasseur with tomatoes and tarragon, and roast cod with creamed leeks, butter beans and smoked salmon.

12 Hagley Road Five Ways B16 8SJ
Map 07: SP08
Tel: 0121 4521144
Fax: 0121 4563442
Chef: Ian Mansfield
Cost: *Alc* £25. ☺ H/wine £13.50
Times: 11.30-2.30pm/6-10pm. Closed Sun
Additional: Bar food L; Children welcome
Seats: 50
Style: Bistro-style/Traditional
Smoking: No-smoking area; Air conditioning
Accommodation: 98 en suite
★ ★ ★ ★ ★

Directions: Telephone for directions

BIRMINGHAM, Chung Ying Garden ✿

Set in the old Thorp Street army barracks, this luxurious Chinese restaurant offers an enormous choice of around 400 different dishes. The cuisine is predominantly Cantonese, and there are many variations on familiar themes.

17 Thorp Street B5 4AT
Map 7: SP08
Tel: 0121 6666622
Fax: 0121 6225860
E-mail: chungying@aol.com
Cost: *Alc* £17, set-price L/D fr £14. ☺ H/wine £9.50
Times: Noon-midnight (11pm Sun). Closed Xmas
Additional: Sunday L; Children welcome
Style: Luxurious
Smoking: Air conditioning

Directions: City centre, off Hurst Street, nr Hippodrome Theatre and shopping centre, just off A38

BIRMINGHAM,

Copthorne Birmingham

Goldsmiths Restaurant generates immediate interest with dishes such as haggis-stuffed quail with rhubarb confit, and loin of venison with bubble and squeak, wild mushrooms and red wine sauce.

Additional: Children welcome
Style: Classic/traditional
Smoking: No-smoking area; Air conditioning
Accommodation: 212 en suite ★ ★ ★ ★

Directions: City centre

Paradise Circus B3 3HJ
Map 7: SP08
Tel: 0121 2002727
Fax: 0121 2001197
E-mail: sales.birmingham@mill-cop.com
Cost: Alc £26.95, set-price D £23.95 & £26.95. ☺ H/wine £10.95
Times: D only, 7-10.30pm.
Closed Sun, 25 Dec

BIRMINGHAM

Directory ֎֎ NEW

Housed in a former Telephone Exchange (one of the few Grade I buildings in Birmingham) this restaurant has been open since the middle of 1999. The interior is modern but the design according to its owners is not 'achingly trendy.' There are both carte and set-price menus and there is an emphasis on fish and crustacea. An appetiser of gravad lax and small crab fish cake with a sweet dill pickle was strong on flavour and was followed by wonderful home-made breads. A starter of ravioli of crab and Savoy cabbage with roast salisfy, saffron velouté and lobster oil comprised a single raviolo filled with a light blend of crab and cabbage. The best dish was the pan-fried chicken breast with lobster interspersed between chicken slices. The chicken was moist, nicely seasoned and well-balanced in flavour. The dish was served with a lasagne – a light lobster mousse layered between sheets of spinach pasta which came in a tower shape. Desserts included banana tarte Tatin. The menus and wine lists are as slick as the staff uniforms – smart grey suits. The wine list includes the usual suspects in both old and new world wines.

Directions: From M6 J6 take A38 to city centre, over flyover, join filter road from L with Thistle Hotel on L take 1st L at rndbt, R at next rndbt (Colmore Row) 2nd R (Newhall St) 1st R (Edmund St)

103 Edmund Street B3 2HZ
Map 7: SP08
Tel: 0121 2362620
Fax: 0121 2364994
E-mail: directoryrestaurant@bigthyme.co.uk
Chefs: Jonathan Bishop, Dean Mace
Owners: N A Wilson, A J Wilson, G M Ingram
Cost: Alc £28.50, set-price L /D £17.50. ☺ H/wine £10.50
Times: Noon-2.30pm/6-11pm.
Closed L Sat, all Sun, Bhs
Additional: Bar food; Children welcome
Seats: 80. Private dining room 25
Style: Modern/Minimalist
Smoking: No-smoking area; No pipes; Air conditioning

BIRMINGHAM, **Leftbank**

A converted 19th-century banking hall now boasting polished wooden floorboards and walls lined with oil paintings. Dishes such as roast cod with mozzarella and spinach salad, or roast barbary duck well worth investing in.

79 Broad Street B15 1AH
Map 7: SP08
Tel: 0121 6434464
Fax: 0121 6435793
Cost: Set-price L £14 & £16/D £24.50 & £29.30. ☺ H/wine £9.90

Times: Noon-3pm/7-midnight.
Closed L Sat, all Sun, 25 Dec-2 Jan, Bhs
Additional: Children welcome
Style: Classic/Modern
Smoking: No pipes & cigars; Air conditioning

Directions: From M6 J6 follow signs for city centre, Restaurant in centre, next to Novotel Hotel

BIRMINGHAM,
Le Petit Blanc

A new Petit Blanc restaurant in the heart of Birmingham, smartly designed, long in shape and contemporary in style. Laid-back young staff provide friendly and attentive service. The large menu offers a variety of options – a small fixed menu, a Blanc Vite selection of quick dishes, and the main *carte*. The latter is quite extensive and features a number of French regional dishes such as braised pig's cheek, herb pancakes, and fish soup. Deep-fried crab cake with green onion risotto and chilli oil dressing was an uncomplicated and well executed starter. The main course of liver was sautéed pink as requested, topped with crisp bacon, set on seasoned spinach and served with a piquant jus. From a good choice of desserts, a bitter chocolate feuillantine came with a rich hazelnut sauce, garnished with vanilla ice cream.

9 Brindley Place B1 2HS
Map 7: SP08
Tel: 0121 633 7333
Fax: 0121 633 7444

Telephone for further details

Directions: Telephone for directions

BIRMINGHAM,
Restaurant Gilmore

A converted precious metal rolling mill at the end of a narrow alley might sound like an unprepossessing setting, but dismiss such doubts at once! This quality eatery is packed with character and atmosphere, and the seating is comfortable. Its relative proximity to Birmingham's excellent fish and meat markets mean that quality produce is always on tap, and the proof of this can be found in the eating. Chef Paul Gilmore offers a balanced set menu with four well-priced supplements which show off his culinary imagination and skill. Sweet cured Scottish salmon in dill and lime juice might head the starter choices, along with baked field mushrooms on toast with pecorino cheese and mild chilli. The pace hots up with the likes of pan-fried loin of pork and spiced apple couscous with grain mustard sauce, or maybe breast of Deben duckling and honey-roasted parsnip mash with cracked black peppercorn sauce. Desserts are unlikely to disappoint, such as chocolate mousse with candied orange cream, or bread-and-butter pudding with sauce Anglaise.

27 Warstone Lane
B18 6JQ
Map 7: SP08
Tel: 0121 2333655
Fax: 01543 415511
Chef: Paul Gilmore
Owners: Paul & Dee Gilmore
Cost: Set-price L £13.50 & £17/ D £24. ☺ H/wine £12.50
Times: 12.30-2pm/7.30-9.30pm.
Closed L Sat, all Sun & Mon, 1 wk Xmas, 1 wk Etr, 2 wks Aug
Additional: Children welcome
Seats: 36
Style: Chic
Smoking: No-smoking area; Air conditioning

Directions: In 'Jewellery Quarter' 1 mile N of city centre

BIRMINGHAM, **Shimla Pinks**

214 Broad Street B15 1AY
Map 7: SP08
Tel: 0121 6330366
Fax: 0121 6433325
Cost: *Alc* £14.95, set-price L £6.95/
D £12.95. ☺ H/wine £10.50
Times: Noon-3pm/6-11pm. Closed
L Sat & Sun
Additional: Children welcome
Style: Chic/Modern
Smoking: Air conditioning

Directions: In city centre, opposite
Novotel and near the ICC

This trendy Indian restaurant is set in the centre of Birmingham, and is usually packed in the evenings. Wide range of traditional dishes served with style, including chicken Nentara, Rogan Josh and Tikka Masala.

COVENTRY,
Brooklands Grange Hotel

Behind the Jacobean façade Brooklands Grange is a modern and comfortable business hotel. The Victorian restaurant room is richly decorated and plays host to a fine variety of modern British cuisine with international influences. A meal from the set-price menu might find you savouring deep-fried camembert with prune, apple and shallot confit as a fitting precursor to award winning pork sausages braised in cider with apples and juniper on onion mash. Indulge in deep-fried banana with vanilla ice cream for dessert. Alternatively the 'Light Meals and Bar Food' menu offers such delights as plain grilled fillet steak with mushrooms, tomatoes and chips; pan-fried fish cakes with sweet chilli sauce; or aubergine and red pepper toasts with feta and olive salad and balsamic vinegar for vegetarian diners.

Directions: Leave A5 at Oswestry, follow signs to Llansilin through town. Hotel is 3 miles W of Oswestry on B4580 Llansilin Road.

Holyhead Road CV5 8HX
Map 4: SP37
Tel: 024 7660 1601
Fax: 024 7660 1277
E-mail: brooklands-grange@virgin.net
Chef: Gina Kemp
Cost: *Alc* £30, set-price L/D £16. ☺
H/wine £10.95
Times: Noon-2pm/7-10pm. Closed
L Sat & Bhs
Additional: Children welcome
Seats: 25
Style: Country-house
Smoking: No smoking in dining room
Accommodation: 10 en suite ★★★

COVENTRY, **Hylands Hotel**

Modern hotel, convenient for both the railway station and the city centre, with an attractive outlook over the nearby park. Restaurant 153 is contemporary in style and has attracted a restaurant design award for its London brasserie look. The high standards of service provided are commensurate with the quality of the cooking. An extensive choice ranges through smoked duck faggot with mushy peas and Madeira sauce, and calves' liver pan-fried with young cabbage leaves and creamed Stilton with a light sherry sauce. The menu also boasts an award-winning dish: fillet of cod encrusted with red pesto, oven roasted with a goats' cheese and chilli macaroni and served with asparagus cappuccino. The summer dessert menu included summer pudding, triple chocolate cheesecake and lemon meringue crème brûlée.

Directions: Five minutes walk from Coventry railway station

Warwick Road CV3 6AU
Map 4: SP37
Tel: 024 7650 1600
Fax: 024 7650 1027
Chef: Darion Smethurst
Owners: The Allied SAINIF Group
Cost: *Alc* £20, set-price L £12.75/D
£15.75. ☺ H/wine £11.95
Times: Noon-2pm/7-10pm. Closed
L Sat, 26-31 Dec, Bhs
Additional: Sunday L; Children
welcome
Style: Chic/modern
Seats: 80
Smoking: No Smoking; Air
conditioning
Accommodation: 61 en suite ★★★

HOCKLEY HEATH,
Nuthurst Grange Hotel ❀❀

Nuthurst Grange Lane Solihull
B94 5NL
Map 7: SP17
Tel: 01564 783972
Fax: 01564 783919
E-mail: info@nuthurst-grange.co.uk
Chef/Owner: David L Randolph
Cost: *Alc* L fr £20, set-price D fr
£29.50. H/wine £13.90
Times: Noon-2pm/6-9.30pm.
Closed L Sat
Additional: Sunday L; Children
welcome
Seats: 60. Private dining room 90
Style: Country-house
Smoking: No smoking in dining room
Civil licence: 90
Accommodation: 15 en suite ★ ★ ★

Modern British cuisine with light French and Mediterranean influences. The hotel enjoys a secluded location hiding amongst its own landscaped gardens and woodlands and the dining room is elegantly furnished and decorated. The inspector began a recent meal with an appetiser of scallop mousse with a dill sauce. Although harbouring slight reservations about the basic concept he found it light in texture with an under-stated flavour. This was followed by a starter of potted guinea fowl with Parmesan crisps and an apple, red onion and sultana chutney, leading into a lamb main. A cut of best end of Cornish lamb was lovely and pink and was set off nicely by a delightful mini moussaka and a basil and tomato mousse. For dessert a bitter lemon tart demonstrated a well judged balance of bitterness and sweetness.

Directions: Off A34000, 0.5m S of Hockley Heath, turning at sign into Nuthurst Grange Lane.

MERIDEN, Manor Hotel ❀❀

Main Road CV7 7NH
Map 4: SP28
Tel: 01676 522735
Fax: 01676 522186
Chef: Peter Griffiths
Cost: *Alc* £27, set-price L & D
£19.95. ☺ H/wine £12.95
Times: Noon-2pm/7-9.45pm. Closed
L Sat, 27-30 Dec
Additional: Bar food; Sunday L;
Children welcome
Seats: 150. Private dining room 8-220
Style: Modern/formal
Smoking: No smoking in dining room;
Air conditioning
Accommodation: 114 en suite ★ ★ ★

Directions: From M42 J6 take A45
towards Coventry. 0.5m after fly-over,
turn R across dual carriageway onto
B4104. Over mini-roundabout. Hotel
on L

The Georgian manor is a popular hotel within easy reach of the National Exhibition Centre and the motorway network. The restaurant offers good value, too, with a kitchen that does not go in for undue complication – what you order is what you get. At a winter test meal, double-baked goats' cheese soufflé came with wilted rocket and spicy diced vegetables provençale.

The main course was a splendid fricassée of monkfish, salmon and red mullet with a good saffron and plum tomato risotto, plus separate vegetables of Savoy cabbage with smoked bacon, mélange of fine green beans, sweetcorn and baton carrots, new potatoes as well as dauphinoise. White chocolate and pistachio brûlée let the side down a little, overrich and dense in texture, but strong coffee and good petits fours redressed the balance.

MERIDEN,
Marriot Forest of Arden Hotel

Attractive split-level restaurant; starters such as chicken liver salad with sherry vinegar and madeira sauce, followed by red snapper with salsa, or venison faggots with onion gravy. Try the chocolate and orange brûlée for dessert.

Maxstoke Lane CV7 7HR
Map 4: SP28
Tel: 01676 522335
Fax: 01676 523711

Telephone for further details

Directions: From M42 J6, take A45 (Coventry) after Stonebridge island, then left (Shepherds Lane), 1.5 miles on left

SUTTON COLDFIELD, New Hall

Walmley Road B76 1QX
Map 7: SP19
Tel: 0121 3782442
Fax: 0121 3784637
Chef: Simon Brough
Owner: Thistle Hotels
Cost: *Alc* £41.75, set-price D £28.50.
☺ H/wine £15.95
Times: Noon-2pm/7-9.30pm. Closed L Sat
Additional: Bar food L; Children 8+
Seats: 60. Private dining room 60.
Jacket & tie preferred
Style: Country-house
Smoking: No smoking in dining room
Civil licence: 60
Accommodation: 60 en suite ★ ★ ★ ★

New Hall is said to be the oldest manor house in England, dating back to the 12th century, surrounded by a lily-filled moat and set in twenty acres of private gardens and open parkland. The whole setting is glorious. The stonework, windows and ceilings are liberally sprinkled with coats of arms, emblems and inscriptions, each a testament to the families that have owned the place. The ambience of the restaurant, and indeed the style of the menu, also have much in common with the country house approach. The staff are smart, professional and pleased to offer advice without being too formal. A set-price menu and a seasonal *carte* are offered. The general style of the menu is English: cream of cauliflower soup, salmon fishcakes and wild poached salmon. A pressed ham hock terrine with toasted foie gras was particularly successful, with the hot and cold contrasting well and a roast sea bass was another 'exciting' success. The fish was served with a vibrant warm tomato and caper dressing, an impressive marriage of flavours. Desserts include trifles, tarts and a selection of British and French cheeses. The wine list is serious with many delights to be found.

Directions: On B4148 E of Sutton Coldfield, close to M6 & M42

WALSALL,

The Fairlawns at Aldridge

178 Little Aston Road Aldridge
WS9 0NU
Map 7: SP09
Tel: 01922 455122
Fax: 01922 743210
E-mail: welcome@fairlawns.co.uk
Chef: Mark Bradley
Owners: John & Tammy Pette
Cost: *Alc* £30, set-price L £17.50/D
£24.50. ☺ H/wine £11.50
Times: Noon-2pm/7-9.30pm.
Closed L Sat, most Bhs
Additional: Bar Food L; Sunday L;
Children welcome
Seats: 70. Private dining room 8-90
Style: Informal/traditional
Smoking: Air conditioning
Civil licence: 100
Accommodation: 50 en suite ★ ★ ★

Light pastel shades and soft lighting create a pleasant
background to this charming hotel restaurant, and a welcoming
atmosphere in which to enjoy some sound modern British
cooking. There is plenty of choice: a *carte* is supplemented by a
seasonal speciality blackboard, while the set-price menus are
bolstered by a separate vegetarian menu. From the former, an
'award-winning' black pudding is grilled and served on a crispy
potato cake with a rich claret reduction, or rillettes of pork and
roasted peppers come cold with spiced bean salad; three home-
made soups are also on offer. Platter of Cornish lamb might
follow, chargrilled with a mini hotpot and a home-made faggot,
or expect prime fillet of steak, ribeye of Scotch beef, or
medallions of fillet steak. Vegetarians might select roasted red
pimentos stuffed with quorn, or chestnut and orange rissole on
a cream of mushroom sauce with sweetened braised red
cabbage. For dessert, try poached prunes with Calvados ice
cream, baked banana cheesecake served with hot toffee sauce,
or the ubiquitous bread-and-butter pudding.

Directions: Outskirts of Aldridge, 400 yards from crossroads of
A452 (Chester Road) & A454 (Little Aston Road)

WIGHT, ISLE OF

GODSHILL,

Cask and Taverners Inn ❀

High Street PO38 3HZ
Map 4: SZ58
Tel: 01983 840707
Cost: *Alc* £25.75, set-price L
£10.25/D £15.95. ☺ H/wine £7.90
Times: Noon-2.30pm/7-9.30pm

Simple well prepared food in a separate cottage-style restaurant area.
A starter of smooth liver parfait accompanied by an onion
marmalade might lead into a roast rack of lamb sliced onto a
rosemary sauce.

Additional: Bar food; Sunday L; Children welcome
Style: Classic/Rustic
Smoking: No smoking in dining room

Directions: From Shanklin take A3020 3 miles into Godshill

RYDE,
Biskra Beach Hotel

Stylish dining venue with sea views to boot. Scrubbed pine tables and minimalist decor set the scene for unusual soups, contemporary pasta dishes such as tortellini of chorizo and skilfully cooked duck with red cabbage and game faggots.

Additional: Bar food; Sunday L; Children welcome
Style: Informal/Minimalist
Smoking: No pipes & cigars
Civil licence: 100
Accommodation: 14 en suite ★★

Directions: W from the Esplanade to rdbt & into St Thomas's St. Hotel on R

17 St Thomas's Street PO33 2DL
Map 4: SZ59
Tel: 01983 567913
Fax: 01983 616976
E-mail: info@biskra-hotel.com
Cost: Alc £25. ☺ H/wine £9
Times: Noon-2pm/7-11pm

SEAVIEW,
Priory Bay Hotel ✸

Exquisite decor and surroundings ensure a sumptuous dining experience in this high-class country house hotel restaurant. Enjoy confit of leg of duck with cocoa beans and Chorizo with charlotte of white chocolate for dessert.

Additional: Bar food L; Sunday L; Children welcome
Style: Country-house/Formal
Civil licence: 40
Accommodation: 18 en suite ★★★

Directions: On B3330 to Nettlestone, 0.5m from St Helens

Priory Drive PO34 5BU
Map 4: SZ69
Tel: 01983 613146
Fax: 01983 616539
E-mail: enquiries@priorybay.co.uk
Cost: Alc £30, set-price D £24. ☺
H/wine £12
Times: Noon-2pm/7.30-9.30pm

SEAVIEW,
Seaview Hotel & Restaurant ✸✸

High Street PO34 5EX
Map 4: SZ69
Tel: 01983 612711
Fax: 01983 613729
E-mail: reception@seaviewhotel.co.uk
Chef: Charles Bartlett
Owners: Nick & Nicky Hayward
Cost: Alc fr £22. ☺ H/wine £9.10
Times: Noon-2pm/7.30-9.30pm.
Closed D Sun ex Bhs, 3 days Xmas

Set in an unassuming Victorian seaside resort, this aptly named hotel draws the crowds with its character and great location overlooking the Solent. The nautical theme of its bars is echoed in the choice of two dining rooms: The Sunshine Room has a contemporary edge with its clean lines, blue and white decor and collection of model ships, while the Front Restaurant is more formal and traditional with white linen, ticking clocks and water colours. The same menu is served in both but smoking is permitted in the Sunshine Room. Starters have a brasserie feel, are delivered with style and could include fried chicken livers, bacon, spinach and mushrooms in a puff pastry tart with a béarnaise sauce, or home-made blinis with smoked salmon and horseradish cream. Main courses might feature smoked haddock on a bed of spinach mash with a hollandaise sauce, or perhaps breast of chicken on a bed of roasted vegetables with a lemon thyme sauce. Vying for dessert selection could be poached meringue with crunchy praline and crème anglaise alongside steamed treacle pudding with fresh cream.

Directions: Take B3330 from Ryde to Seaview, L into Puckpool Hill & follow signs for Hotel

Additional: Sunday L; Children 5+ at D
Seats: 30 & 50
Style: Modern/Traditional
Smoking: 1 no-smoking dining room; No pipes & cigars; Air conditioning
Accommodation: 16 en suite ★ ★ ★

VENTNOR,
The Royal Hotel ❀❀

Attempts have been made to modernise this Victorian Hotel but a delightful old fashioned atmosphere remains. The deep yellow walls, windows framed by elaborate drapes and the blue carpet combine to make the formal dining room quite striking. The cooking is mainly French, but risottos and pasta appear alongside such English classics as Bakewell tart on the menus. An asparagus soup was a little disappointing, but in a main dish red snapper and aubergine caviar complemented each other perfectly. Other main courses include best end of lamb with pommes Dauphinoise and a rosemary scented jus and fresh Ventnor Lobster Thermidor. Wines are recommended with each menu, along with The Directors selection from around the world. Prices are reasonable and care has been taken with compiling this list.

Directions: On A3055 coastal road

Belgrave Road PO38 1JJ
Map 4: SZ57
Tel: 01983 852186
Fax: 01983 855395
E-mail: royalhotel@zetnet.co.uk
Chef: Alan Staley
Owner: William Bailey
Cost: Set-price L £15/D £25. H/wine £10.50
Times: D only, 7-9.15pm. Closed 2 wks Jan
Additional: Bar food L; Sunday L (12.30-2pm); Children welcome
Seats: 100. Private dining room 40. Jacket & tie preferred
Style: Classic/Traditional
Smoking: No smoking in dining room
Accommodation: 55 en suite ★ ★ ★ ★

YARMOUTH,
George Hotel ❀❀❀

Travellers of a gastronomic bent might like to know that the ferry from Lymington drops them a short walk away from the George, in a great location twixt castle and quay in this picturesque yachting village. The brasserie, with its Solent views, has a *carte* that deals in pheasant sausage with red cabbage, corned-beef hash or roast skate on red wine sauce, and date and walnut tart, while the restaurant is a more serious-looking room done out in maroon and green. The menu here is a set-price affair with a handful of choices at each course, with starters and main courses fairly divided between meat and fish: pan-fried veal sweetbreads with lentils and a cabbage and truffle sauce might be followed by tournedos of sea bass with vegetable cannelloni and tomato confit. The kitchen takes some ambitious combinations and brings them off with aplomb. Witness a starter of crab tortellini with white onion purée, or another of a salad of roast quail and veal tongue, layers of tender meat interspersed with potato galette finished off with a poached egg, or a main course of 'pinpoint-accurate' loin of lamb with an inventive and successful beetroot fondant. Other dishes may be more traditional, as in

Quay Street PO41 0PE
Map 4: SZ38
Tel: 01983 760331
Fax: 01983 760425
E-mail: res@thegeorge.co.uk
Chef: Kevin Mangeolles
Owners: Jeremy & Amy Willcock, John Illsley
Cost: Set-price D £42.50. H/wine £12.50
Times: D only (restaurant) 7-10pm. Closed Sun, Mon
Additional: Children 8+
Seats: 35. Private dining room 20
Style: Classic/traditional
Smoking: Air conditioning
Civil licence: 60
Accommodation: 17 en suite ★ ★ ★

roast breast of pigeon with dauphinoise potatoes and truffle sauce, while innovative puddings take in chocolate fondant with 'terrific' coconut ice cream, saffron parfait with poached clementines, and chestnut mousse with a matching sorbet. Staff are knowledgeable, enthusiastic, but easy-going, and the user-friendly wine list is fairly priced and packed with character.

Directions: Ferry from Lymington. Hotel visible from ferry between castle and pier

WILTSHIRE

ALDBOURNE, Raffles Restaurant

A small village in something of a time warp houses this converted cottage just off the central green. While James Hannan comes up with the goods in the kitchen, Mary presides over the dining room with a friendly presence which goes down well with the local community. A very well-priced set lunch menu typically offers starters like avocado with tomato and Mozzarella cheese salsa, and smoked duck breast with apple sauce, while the main course might bring grilled fillet of sea bream with lime butter sauce, or breast of pigeon with ginger wine sauce. The *carte* is enriched with specials such as cannon of lamb with herb and mustard crust and red wine sauce, or fillet steak with brandy cream and mushroom sauce. Otherwise expect such starters as quenelles of crab with smoked salmon and salad, or sautéed chicken livers on blinis with port wine sauce, going on perhaps to salmon fishcakes with spinach and sorrel sauce, or pan-fried escalope of veal with sage and Marsala wine. Wines from around the world are sold by the bottle or the glass.

The Green SN8 2BW
Map 4: SU27
Tel: 01672 540700
Fax: 01672 540038
Chef: James Hannan
Owners: James & Mary Hannan
Cost: *Alc* £15, set-price L £10.50. ☺
Times: 12.30-2pm/7-10pm.
Closed L Sat & Tue, D Sun, all Mon, 26-31 Dec, 1st 2 wks Sep
Additional: Sunday L ; Children welcome
Seats: 36
Smoking: No smoking in dining room

Directions: On B4192 between M4 J14 &15

BRADFORD-ON-AVON,
Georgian Lodge

A popular venue in the centre of this wonderful riverside town. Within an old and charming Georgian property, the restaurant has been stylishly refurbished along clean modern lines. Split levels give even more character, a brasserie feel downstairs, plush and traditional surroundings upstairs. Fresh flowers and bright summery decor are enhanced by clever lighting. Slick professional service is not too formal or intrusive and excellent guidance is provided by the restaurant manager. An exciting and extensive menu offers something for every palate, tempting canapés and beautiful crusty bread set the standard, our inspector enjoyed succulent chicken breast cooked to perfection, accompanied by a tasty pea risotto. Other main courses included choices of salmon, turbot and duck breast. Desserts ranged from Tiramisu Parfait to a simple but well executed lemon tart.

25 Bridge Street BA15 1BY
Map 3: ST86
Tel/Fax: 01225 862268

Telephone for further details

Directions: Town Centre, off Silver Street, S of River Avon

BRADFORD-ON-AVON,
Woolley Grange ❀❀

Woolley Green BA15 1TX
Map 3: ST86
Tel: 01225 864705
Fax: 01225 864059
E-mail: woolley@luxury-hotel.demon.co.uk
Chef: Philip Rimmer
Owners: Nigel & Heather Chapman
Cost: Set-price L £15.50/D £34.50. ☺
H/wine £10.50
Times: Noon-2pm/7.30-9.30pm
Additional: Bar food; Sunday L;
Children welcome
Seats: 60. Private dining room 22
Style: Country-house
Smoking: No smoking in dining room
Accommodation: 23 en suite ★ ★ ★

This splendid 17th-century Jacobean manor house, set in beautiful countryside, offers memorable modern British cuisine and a special welcome to children. White linen tablecloths, fresh flowers and well-spaced tables all feature in the comfortable, formal dining room. Highlights from a recent dinner included home-made breads; 'the Roquefort and tarragon, one of the best breads I've tasted', enthused one inspector. Attaining equal praise was a light and airy banana soufflé dessert, with rich, full-flavoured hot butterscotch sauce and caramel ice cream; this really hit the spot. A starter of warm leek and Roquefort tart with rocket salad and rosemary oil was also well presented and offered an enjoyable combination of flavours and texture. A main-course medallions of organic Hazlebury pork, with accurate chestnut risotto and truffle sauce was thought marginally less noteworthy, and came with a side plate of crispy crackling and spinach. Good choice of coffee; cafetière, cappuccino and espresso with petits fours, which include coconut macaroon, white chocolate covered nuts and choux cream bun. Well-rounded wine list with a good selection of half bottles.

Directions: On B105 at Woolley Green, 1 mile NE of Bradford, 20 mins from M4 J17

CASTLE COMBE, **Castle Inn** ❀

Chippenham SN14 7HN
Map 3: ST87
Tel: 01249 783030
Fax: 01249 782315
E-mail: res@castle-inn.co.uk
Cost: Alc £18. ☺ H/wine £11.95
Times: Noon-2pm/7-9.30pm.
Closed 25 Dec (ex residents)
Additional: Bar food; Sunday L;
Children 4+
Style: Informal/rustic
Smoking: No smoking in dining room
Accommodation: 11 en suite ★ ★ ★

Directions: In village centre, M4 J17

Set in an 'Area of Outstanding Natural Beauty' this 12th-century inn is quite in keeping with its surroundings. The glass-topped conservatory restaurant offers high quality English cuisine such as baked lamb leg steak with rosemary, chilli and red onion.

CASTLE COMBE,
Manor House Hotel ❀❀❀

Chippenham SN14 7HR
Map 3: ST87
Tel: 01249 782206
Fax: 01249 782159
E-mail: enquiries@manor-house.co.uk
Chef: Mark Taylor
Cost: A/c £43, set-price L £16.95 &
£18.95/D £35. ☺ H/wine £18.95
Times: Noon-3.30pm/7-9pm(9.30pm
Sat & Sun)
Additional: Bar food; Sunday L;
Children welcome
Seats: 75. Private dining rooms 12-30;
Jacket & tie preferred
Style: Classic/Country-house
Smoking: No smoking in dining room
Civil licence: 100
Accommodation: 45 en suite ★ ★ ★ ★

Directions: Off B4039 near centre of
village, R immediately after the bridge

Set in 26 acres, with a romantic Italian garden, the 14th-
century country house has an elegant, lofty, beamed restaurant
that overlooks the peaceful grounds and river stocked with
wild brown trout. The latter, however, is absent from the
classic menu – perhaps Mark Taylor is not as proficient with a
rod as he is preparing terrine of chicken, sweetbreads and
truffle with sauce gribiche, or smoked fillet of beef with port
wine, lentils and puréed parsnip. Fish does appear, in Cornish
red mullet soup or fillet of sea bass with spiced ratatouille and
basil butter. There are some engaging ideas – Trelough duck,
for example, is given character with vanilla, red wine, sour
cherries and fondant potato. Simpler lunch dishes might
include watercress and pear soup, and pan-fried turbot with
broccoli purée and caper butter. Amongst the selection of
traditional English grand hotel dishes, there is Chateaubriand
for two, game in season and crêpes Suzette flamed at the table.
The British cheese menu is exceptionally well put together and
annotated. The heavyweight wine list, too, is clearly described
and includes a good selection of half-bottles.

COLERNE, **Luckham Park** ❀❀

Chippenham SN14 8AZ
Map 3: ST87
Tel: 01225 742777
Fax: 01225 743536
E-mail:
reservations@lucknampark.co.uk
Chef: Robin Zavou

The restaurant at Lucknam Park, an impressive Palladian
mansion surrounded by 500 acres of parkland, is an elegant
bow-fronted room, with a hand-painted ceiling and crystal
chandeliers. The carte runs in tandem with a set-price menu,

although those choosing the latter can swap dishes from the main menu for a supplement. With a few exceptions, dishes lean on the great French traditions, from terrine of foie gras parfait with caramelised pears and Sauternes jelly, to bouillabaisse-style sautéed bream. Périgord truffles go into a ravioli with quail's egg and beans for a salad of roasted quail, and another starter might be nage of langoustines and scallops in a light Champagne and oyster sauce. Workmanship and good judgement are evident. Witness an inspector's main course of roast loin of lamb, pink and sweetly flavoured, topped with courgette mousse spiked with sweetbreads ('delicate, deft and delectable') served on top of squares of courgette, carrot, asparagus and fondant potato with an accomplished thyme-flavoured jus. Pastry is well-reported, from a mille-feuille of foie gras to a dessert of a 'shatter-on-touch' basket holding white chocolate ice cream served alongside chocolate soufflé. Some noble names crop up on the wine list, but prices soon soar.

Cost: Alc £64, set-price D £40. H/wine £17.50
Times: D only, 7.30-9.30pm (7-10pm Fri & Sat)
Additional: Bar food (in leisure spa); Sunday L (12.30-2.30pm); Children 12+
Seats: 80. Private room 30. Jacket & tie preferred
Style: Classic/Country-house
Smoking: No smoking in dining room
Civil licence: 60
Accommodation: 41 en suite ★ ★ ★ ★

Directions: From M4 J17 take A350 to Chippenham, then A420 towards Bristol for 3m. At Ford turn L towards Colerne. After 3m turn R at crossroads. Hotel 0.25m on R

FORD, White Hart Inn ❀

Chippenham SN14 8RP
Map 3: ST87
Tel: 01249·782213
Fax: 01249 783075

Telephone for further details

Directions: M4 J17 or 18, 10 minutes drive on A420 Colerne road

Idyllically-placed 15th-century coaching inn with intimate, candle-lit restaurant. Interesting, well-presented dishes might include vegetable tempura with sweet chilli jam, and grilled John Dory fillet with seared scallops on creamy mashed potatoes. Service is easy and friendly.

HINDON, The Grosvenor Arms ❀❀

There's a touch of theatre about the informal dining room where guests can watch the chefs at work in the glass-fronted, open-plan kitchen. The modern British menu includes staples such as smoked chicken Caesar salad with aïoli, carpaccio of beef with rocket and mustard dressing and loin of pork with sage and onion risotto and baked black pudding. As well as a top-class, well-annotated cheese menu, there are desserts such as caramelised rice pudding with sour cherry sauce or parfait of hazelnut and praline with cinnamon and elderflower syrup.

High Street Nr Salisbury SP3 6DJ
Map 3: ST93
Tel: 01747 820696
Fax: 01747 820869
Chef: Chris Lee
Owners: Martin Tarr & Paul Toogood
Cost: Alc £25. ☺ H/wine £10.75
Times: Noon-2.30pm/7-9.30pm
Additional: Bar food; Sunday L; Children 5+
Seats: 42. Private dining room 20
Style: Bistro-style/Informal

Smoking: No smoking in dining room
Accommodation: 10 en suite ★ ★

Directions: 1 mile from both A350 & A303

HINDON, **Lamb at Hindon Hotel** ❀

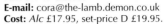

Salisbury SP3 6DP
Map 3: ST93
Tel: 01747 820573
Fax: 01747 820605
E-mail: cora@the-lamb.demon.co.uk
Cost: Alc £17.95, set-price D £19.95.
☺ H/wine £9.50
Times: Noon-1.45pm/7-9.30pm
Additional: Bar food; Sunday L;
Children welcome
Style: Traditional/Country-house
Smoking: No smoking in dining room
Accommodation: 14 en suite ★ ★

Sophisticated bar meals plus a more formal restaurant menu lift this cosy, stone-built free house above the norm. Dinner might include seared monkfish with lobster sauce, or sautéed kidneys with Guinness.

Directions: In village centre, 1 mile off A303 & A350

INGLESHAM,
Inglesham Forge Restaurant ❀❀

Fish dominates the starter menu at this converted 16th-century forge, but meat takes pride of place among the main choices, particularly fillet steak in a variety of guises. Tortellini 'à la Forge', and Parma ham with a fan of seasonal melon are conspicuous non-seafood first courses, along with soup of the day which may or may not have an oceanic flavour. For fish lovers the choice is wide: assorted seafood gratinée, with mussels and scampi served hot with herb and garlic butter, or seafood Breton in a traditional white wine sauce, sprinkled with Parmesan cheese and grilled. Pan-fried Mediterranean sardines, and sizzling baked scampi in garlic butter add to the fishy options. Beef stroganoff, tournedos Forge, fillet steak royale and chargrilled fillet steak head the main list, but it's not all beef. Breast of duck with morello cherries, wild guinea fowl marinated and cooked in a red wine sauce, and rack of lamb with a thyme and red wine sauce create a pleasing diversity.

Swindon SN6 7QY
Map 4: SU29
Tel/Fax: 01367 252298
Chef: Manuel Gomez
Owners: Manuel & Jacqueline Gomez
Cost: Alc £24. ☺ H/wine £10.75
Times: Noon-2pm/7-10pm.
Closed L Sat & Mon, all Sun
Additional: Children welcome
Seats: 30
Style: Classic/Rustic
Smoking: No pipes & cigars

Directions: In hamlet just off A361 midway between Highworth and Lechlade

LITTLE BEDWYN,
The Harrow Inn ❀❀

Roger and Sue Jones took over this country pub towards the end of 1998 and have quickly gained a loyal following. It was AA *Seafood Pub of the Year* last year and has collected some favourable reviews. The crockery is a striking blue and yellow and the food is equally vibrant to the eye and to the palate. Fish features strongly, and you might expect to see, in season, lobster, clams, Brixham crab, Scottish langoustine and Dorset cockles. Tuna is fresh cut, sea bass and salmon wild, and wet fish from day boats only. There were olives on the table, soon

Nr Marlborough SN8 3JP
Map 4: SU26
Tel/Fax: 01672 870871
E-mail: dining@harrowinn.co.uk
Chef: Roger Jones
Owners: Roger & Sue Jones
Cost: Alc £30. ☺ H/wine £13
Times: Noon-2pm/7-9.30pm.
Closed D Sun, all Mon, 4 wks Xmas,
4 wks Aug
Additional: Bar food L; Sunday L

The Harrow Inn

Seats: 32
Style: Rustic/Minimalist
Smoking: No smoking in dining room;
Air conditioning

joined by a wonton, scallop and dipping sauce, cooked to perfection and full of exciting flavours. A starter of wild mushroom risotto was followed by pan-fried John Dory, again well timed, served with grilled scallops and asparagus set on a crisp pat of rösti. Lemon and ginger terrine was very chilled but delivered all the promised flavours.

Directions: Take Marlborough Road from Hungerford, after 2 miles Little Bedwyn signposted

MALMESBURY,
The Horse & Groom

A rustic bar with log fires and a wooden floor is complemented by a more formal dining room in which such delights as gingered chicken stir fry and West Country butterbean casserole may be sampled.

Additional: Bar food; Sunday L; Children welcome
Style: Rustic/Traditional
Smoking: No-smoking area
Accommodation: 3 rooms

Directions: M4 J17, take 2nd roundabout exit, B4040 (Cricklade). 2 miles to Charlton, pub on L

The Street Charlton SN16 9DL
Map 4: ST98
Tel: 01666 823904
Fax: 01666 823390
Cost: *Alc* £21. ☺ H/wine £ 7.75
Times: Noon-3pm/7-11pm.
Closed 25 & 26 Dec, 1 Jan

MALMESBURY,
Knoll House Hotel ❀❀

The small country hotel has a Mediterranean heart with its bright, upbeat restaurant picking up style points through a wood floor, white muslin curtains and striking modern art. The menu is brasserie style and though strong on modern Med buzz words – chorizo, Mozzarella, and saffron oil – there is a well-explored theme of updated English dishes running through the repertoire. A meal taken in the depths of winter proved the point. It opened with soundly-made, well-balanced goats' cheese and basil ravioli with a tomato salsa, went on to a robust smoked haddock rarebit with hollandaise sauce, and finished with a good, rich chocolate cappuccino cup. The wine list travels around the world.

Directions: From M4 J17 take A429 (Cirencester); turn onto B4042 (Swindon); hotel is 500yds on L

Swindon Road SN16 9LU
Map 3: ST98
Tel: 01666 823114
Fax: 01666 823897
E-mail:
knollhotel@malmesbury64.co.uk
Chef: Alan Johnson
Cost: *Alc* £25. ☺ H/wine £9.75
Times: Noon-1.45pm/7-9pm.
Closed 27-30 Dec
Additional: Bar food; Sunday L;
Children welcome
Seats: 30. Private dining room 30
Style: bistro-style/modern
Smoking: No smoking in dining room
Accommodation: 22 en suite ★ ★ ★

MALMESBURY,

Mayfield House Hotel ❀

A welcoming beamed bar is the starting point for a meal at this well-run hotel. Expect goats' cheese on garlic croûte with red onion marmalade and yellow pepper salsa, roast cod with herb crust on ratatouille, and raspberry parfait.

Crudwell SN16 9EW
Map 3: ST98
Tel: 01666 577409
Fax: 01666 577977
E-mail: mayfield@callnetuk.com

Cost: Set-price D £17.95. ☺ H/wine £8.75
Times: D only, 6.30-8.45pm
Additional: Bar food L; Sunday L (noon-1.45pm); Children welcome
Style: Country-house
Smoking: No smoking in dining room
Accommodation: 24 en suite ★ ★

Directions: 10 minutes from M4 J17. On A429 between Malmesbury and Cirencester, in village centre

MALMESBURY,

Old Bell Hotel ❀❀

Abbey Row SN16 0AG
Map 3: ST98
Tel: 01666 822344
Fax: 01666 825145
Chef: Michael Benjamin
Owners: Nigel Chapman, Nicholas Dickinson
Cost: Alc £26, set-price L £15/D £19.75. ☺ H/wine £15
Times: 12.30-2.30pm/7-9.30pm.
Additional: Bar food; Sunday L;
Seats: 60. Private dining rooms 24
Style: Classic/Traditional
Smoking: No smoking in dining room
Civil licence: 50
Accommodation: 31 en suite ★ ★ ★

The Abbott of Malmesbury founded this hostelry in 1220, and a sense of antiquity pervades the building, with its stone walls, log fires, paintings and traditional furnishings. The restaurant, in an Edwardian extension, is an attractive room, all candlelight and gleaming cutlery and glasses on large, white-clad tables. If the surroundings seem old-fashioned, the set-price menus are anything but. White crabmeat goes into a salad starter with pink grapefruit and avocado cream and a dressing of carrot and ginger, and free-range chicken is made into a bourride along with garlic mayonnaise and accompanied by wild mushrooms and saffron potatoes. Combinations are generally successful – braised calves' kidneys with a terrine of potatoes, onions and bacon and Marsala sauce, say, or a main course of slow-roasted pork cutlet with braised cabbage, caramelised onions and smoked bacon while others pile on the flavours and can confuse the taste buds a little. Finish with something traditional, like peach melba, or stick your neck out and go for vanilla pannacotta with a poached mandarin and red wine sauce. The wine list is a globetrotting collection of quality with France outweighing other regions.

Directions: In centre of town

MARLBOROUGH, Ivy House Hotel

High Street SN8 1HJ
Map 4: SU16
Tel: 01672 515333
Fax: 01672 515338
E-mail: ivyhouse@btconnect.com
Cost: Alc £28, set-price L 12.95. ☺
H/wine £9
Additional: Bar food; Sunday L;
Children welcome
Style: Classic/Country-house
Smoking: No smoking in dining room
Accommodation: 30 en suite ★ ★ ★

*Clear flavours and balanced combinations distinguish the food at
this Palladian-style restaurant. Highly recommended dishes include
smoked haddock and spinach tartlet, roast Gressingham duck with
cardamom-scented risotto, and a yummy banana Tatin with coconut
ice-cream.*

Directions: Town centre in main street

MELKSHAM, Shaw Country Hotel

Bath Road Shaw SN12 8EF
Map 3: ST96
Tel: 01225 702836
Fax: 01225 790275
E-mail:
shawcountryhotel@ukbusiness.com
Cost: Alc £19.50, set-price L/D
£13.50. ☺ H/wine £8.95

*A welcoming country house hotel dating back to the 16th century in
which the Mulberry Restaurant offers rustic charm alongside classic
and often more adventurous cuisine such as a successful Cajun
salmon with chilled cucumber.*

Times: Noon-1.30pm/7-9.15pm. Closed D Sun, 26-28 Dec, 1 Jan
Additional: Bar food, Sunday L; Children welcome
Style: Rustic/country house
Smoking: No smoking in dining room
Accommodation: 13 en suite ★ ★

Directions: 1 mile NW of Melksham on A365, from M4 J17
or J18

NOMANSLAND, Les Mirabelles

Forest Edge Road Nr Salisbury
SP5 2BN
Map 4: SU22
Tel/Fax: 01794 390205

Telephone for further details

*Good quality ingredients speak for themselves in dishes like fresh
scallop and crab tart with a cream and chive sauce, and tender lamb
fillet stuffed with kidneys and herbs. This popular arched restaurant
is friendly and relaxed.*

Directions: A36 (Salisbury – Southampton); turn R into New
Road (signposted Nomansland); straight ahead at crossroads and
over cattle grid. Within a mile restaurant on R by church

PURTON,
The Pear Tree at Purton ❀❀

Church End SN5 9ED
Map 4: SU08
Tel: 01793 772100
Fax: 01793 772369
E-mail: dine@peartreepurton.co.uk
Chef: Alan Postill

A charming Cotswold-stone hotel transformed from the local
vicarage into an elegant country retreat. The conservatory
restaurant overlooks delightful gardens and provides the
perfect setting for Alan Postill's modern British repertoire,

The Pear Tree at Purton

Owners: Francis & Anne Young
Cost: Set-price L £17.50/D £29.50.
H/wine £11.50
Times: Noon-2.30pm/7-9.30pm.
Closed L Sat, 26-30 Dec
Additional: Sunday L; Children
welcome
Seats: 50. Private dining rooms 50 &
20
Smoking: No pipes & cigars
Civil licence: 50
Accommodation: 18 en suite ★ ★ ★

which embraces interesting combinations and quality
ingredients. Canapés of cheese tartlet and salmon terrine
wrapped in spinach provide a sound prelude, while home-made
bread rolls afford fine accompaniment. Starters could include
pan-fried collop of monkfish with minted pea purée and butter
sauce, or perhaps a terrine of local hare with winter chutney
and juniper sauce; a pre-main-course filo tartlet of chicken and
tarragon mousseline with a purée of button mushrooms proved
noteworthy on a spring menu. Main courses vying for selection
could be breast of guinea fowl with a bacon, foie gras and
thyme farce and sweet Muscat sauce, against roasted cod steak
with tomato and saffron risotto and crispy leek. From the
desserts list, warm prune and Armagnac tart, orange salad and
lime syllabub catches the eye. Sound tea comes with competent
petits fours, and attentive, friendly service is delivered by a
young team.

Directions: From M4 J16 follow signs to Purton. Turn right at
Spa shop, hotel 0.25 mile on right

REDLYNCH,
Langley Wood Restaurant ❀

Salisbury SP5 2PB
Map 4: SU22
Tel: 01794 390348
E-mail: langleywood@lineone.net
Cost: Alc £25. ☺ H/wine £9.75
Times: 12.30-2pm/7-10pm. Closed
L Sat, D Sun, all Mon & Tue
Additional: Sunday L; Children
welcome
Style: Informal/traditional
Smoking: No smoking in dining room

*Hidden away in its own extensive grounds, a small country house
restaurant in which diners are treated to dishes such as fresh salmon
with sun dried tomato tapenade or guinea-fowl with couscous and
cumin.*

Directions: In village, between Downton (on A338 Salisbury to
Bournemouth) & Landford (A36 Salisbury)

ROWDE, George & Dragon ❀❀

High Street SN10 2PN
Map 3: ST96
Tel: 01380 723053
Fax: 01380 724738
E-mail: gd-rowde@lineone.net
Chef: Tim Withers
Owners: Tim & Helen Withers
Cost: *Alc* £25, set-price L £8.50 &
£10. ☺ H/wine £9.50
Times: Noon-2pm/7-10pm. Closed
Sun & Mon, 25 Dec, 1 Jan
Additional: Bar food; Children
welcome
Seats: 35
Style: Informal/Traditional
Smoking: No smoking in dining room

Village pub, dating from 1675, providing a relaxed setting for some cosmopolitan cooking, with a beamed ceiling, simple tables and a mixture of chairs. The menu centres round fish and shellfish, including starters of River Exe oysters, or scallop mousseline with spiced lentil sauce. A blackboard menu of fresh market fish from Cornwall ranges from roast hake with aïoli and peppers, through Thai fish curry and grilled turbot hollandaise, to whole grilled lobster with garlic or herb butter. Non-fish options could be medallions of venison with wild mushroom sauce or pan-fried calves' liver with orange and onion confit. Round your meal off with a choice from the pudding menu, perhaps prune and Armagnac tart or rhubarb and honey saffron custard.

Directions: On A342 Devizes-Chippenham road

SALISBURY,
Howard's House Hotel ❀❀❀

Teffont Evias SP3 5RJ
Map 4: SU12
Tel: 01722 716392
Fax: 01722 716820
E-mail: paul.firmin@virgin.net
Chefs: Paul Firmin, Boyd McIntosh
Owner: Paul Firmin
Cost: *Alc* £29.20, set-price D £19.95.
☺ H/wine £9.95
Times: D only, 7.30-9.30pm. Closed
Xmas
Additional: Sunday L (12.30-2pm);
Children welcome
Seats: 30
Style: Informal/country-house
Smoking: No smoking in dining room
Accommodation: 9 en suite ★ ★

The hotel is set in lovely gardens in one of the more beautiful Wiltshire villages. It offers a stylish restaurant, fairly simple, with huge flower arrangements by the door, white-clothed tables, good cutlery, plain glassware – in some ways the cooking reflects this simple, straightforward look. However, proprietor Paul Firmin, with head chef Boyd McIntosh, follow exacting standards to prepare classic dishes such as terrine of local pheasant and Gressingham duck with red onion marmalade and dressed leaves, and smoked fillet of Scottish beef, rosemary and garlic galette, sautéed parsnips and a Madeira jus. Our own test meal was impressive. It opened with a crisp confit of Gressingham duck served with macerated oranges, Puy lentils and a balsamic dressing ('the textures and flavours were super'). Our main course was an accomplished home-smoked fillet of salmon with steamed leeks and a saffron sauce that delivered all the promised flavours. A rich chocolate pie ('the lightest and crispest of pastries with the richest chocolate filling, such quality in the chocolate') was balanced by a very delicate white peach ice cream and an intense orange coulis. The excellent fixed-price menu offers tremendous value for cooking of this quality and could bring asparagus and winter vegetable soup, seared calves' liver with red onion marmalade, potato galette and a Madeira jus, and white chocolate and orange crème brûlée.

Directions: A36/A30 from Salisbury, turn onto B3089, 5 miles W of Wilton, 9 miles W of Salisbury

SALISBURY, **Milford Hall Hotel**

The Alderman Wort restaurant offers light lunch, set price and carte menus. Dishes include lime and crab cheesecake starter, roast salmon with chorizo and basil or roast confit of duck main course, and steamed chocolate fondant dessert.

Directions: At junction of Castle St, A30 ring rd & A345 (Amesbury), less than 0.5 miles from Market Square

206 Castle Street SP1 3TE
Map 4: SU12
Tel: 01722 417411
Fax: 01722 419444
E-mail: milfordhallhotel@cs.com

Telephone for further details

SWINDON, **Blunsdon House Hotel**

The Ridge Restaurant offers the more formal eating choice at this friendly family-run hotel, with plenty of freshly-prepared dishes. Expect seared lobster and sea scallops in Thai spices, or beef fillet on a truffle Madeira sauce.

Smoking: No-smoking area; Air conditioning; Jacket & tie preferred
Civil licence: 200 **Accommodation:** 120 en suite ★ ★ ★ ★

Directions: 3 miles N of town centre. From A419 take turning signposted Broad Blunsdon, then first L

Blunsdon SN2 4AD
Map 4: SU18
Tel: 01793 721701
Fax: 01793 721056
E-mail: info@blunsdonhouse.co.uk
Cost: Set-price D £21.50. ☺ H/wine £10.25
Times: D only 7.15-midnight
Additional: Bar food; Sunday L; Children welcome
Style: Classic/Formal

SWINDON,
Chiseldon House Hotel

Traditional-style country-house hotel located just outside Swindon, and popular for weddings and conferences. The beautiful Orangery Restaurant is the setting for some modern English cooking. On this occasion, in January, dinner was selected from a restricted menu. The starter, a tomato and Mozzarella tart, had a triangular base of puff pastry, well cooked and served with a fresh pesto dressing. This was followed by grilled trout, again accurately timed, and presented with thyme butter, new potatoes and salad. The dessert comprised a creamy mixed berry cheesecake with a tartly contrasting coulis.

New Road Chiseldon SN4 0NE
Map 4: SU18
Tel: 01793 741010
Fax: 01793 741059

Telephone for further details

Directions: Easily accessible from M4 J15 & 16, on B4006. Short distance from Swindon town centre

WARMINSTER, **Angel Inn** NEW

Upton Scudamore BA12 0AG
Map 3: ST84
Tel: 01985 213225
Tel: 01985 218182
Cost: Alc £21. ☺ H/wine £9.75
Times: Noon-3pm/7-11pm. Closed 25 Dec
Additional: Bar food L; Sunday L; Children welcome
Style: Informal/Rustic
Smoking: No-smoking area
Accommodation: 5 en suite

Directions: From either A36 or A350 follow signs for Upton Scudamore. Inn in village centre

Restaurant with rooms, recently completely refurbished, with rustic wooden floors, open fires and a garden for summer dining. Modern British dishes are prepared from quality fresh ingredients.

WARMINSTER,
Bishopstrow House ❀❀

Set in 27 acres of rolling countryside, with a private river frontage, Bishopstrow House was built in 1817 of Bath stone, now largely covered in creeper. The interior is as elegant as the façade suggests, with antique furniture, paintings on the walls, log fires and fresh flowers everywhere. The menu ranges far and wide in its search for ideas, taking in carpaccio of yellow-fin tuna with soy mustard dressing, Thai-style fishcakes with sweet chilli sauce, and seared scallops with squid-ink risotto. Some dishes, for example grilled breast of chicken in tarragon sauce with grilled asparagus and colcannon, are picked out as low in cholesterol and low in fat, perhaps for those using the hotel's extensive leisure and health facilities, while others have a rustic edge: confit of Quantock duck with leeks, braised Puy lentils and pancetta, or rabbit pot-au-feu with mushrooms and bacon. Crispy apple sorbet might be the only healthy option among desserts, flanked as it may be by sticky toffee pudding with butterscotch sauce, and melting chocolate sponge with cappuccino ice cream.

BA12 9HH
Map 3: ST84
Tel: 01985 212312
Fax: 01985 216769
E-mail: enquiries@bishopstrow.co.uk
Chef: Chris Suter
Owners: Simon Lowe,
Andrew Leeman, Howard Malin
Cost: Alc £35. ☺ H/wine £13.50
Times: Noon-2.30pm/7.30-9.30pm
Additional: Bar food; Sunday L;
Children welcome
Seats: 65
Style: Classic/country-house
Smoking: No smoking in dining room
Civil licence: 65
Accommodation: 32 en suite ★★★★

Directions: From Warminster take
B3414 (Salisbury). Hotel is signposted

WHITLEY, The Pear Tree ❀ NEW

Top Lane SN12 8QX
Map 3: ST86
Tel: 01225 709131
Fax: 01225 702276
Cost: Alc £23.50, set-price L £11.95.
☺ H/wine £9.95
Times: Noon-2pm/6.30-9.30pm(10pm
Fri & Sat). Closed 25 & 26 Dec, 1 Jan
Additional: Bar food; Sunday L;
Children welcome
Style: Informal/Rustic
Smoking: No smoking in dining room

Directions: Telephone for directions

The old skittle alley belonging to this rural Cotswold pub makes a splendid eating place, with its pitchfork curtain poles and garden tool collage. Popular dishes include broccoli and cheddar soup, and duck confit on sautéed oyster mushrooms.

WORCESTERSHIRE

ABBERLEY, The Elms ❀❀

Gilbert White, a pupil of Sir Christopher Wren, built the house in 1710 and the drive was originally planted with elm trees, which have since been replaced by majestic limes. It is a Grade II listed building, a hotel since 1946, set in 10 acres of grounds overlooking the Teme Valley and the Malverns. There is a French influence to the *carte*, which offers a comprehensive choice of seasonal dishes from good quality produce.

WR6 6AT
Map 3: SO76
Tel: 01299 896666
Fax: 01299 896804
E-mail: elmshotel@ukonline.co.uk
Chef: Martyn Pearn
Owners: Mr & mrs R Vaughan
Cost: Alc £38.50, set-price L £20/D
£38.50. H/wine £14.50

Start, perhaps, with seared red mullet fillet with a fine ratatouille tomato vinaigrette and tempura of herbs, followed by marinated, roasted rack of Cotswold lamb with confit garlic and rosemary jus. Speciality desserts include tarte Tatin with caramel sauce and vanilla ice cream, and hot passion fruit soufflé with its own sorbet.

Directions: 15 minutes from M5 J5. 10 miles from Worcester

Times: 12.30-2pm/7.30-9.30pm
Additional: Bar food L; Sunday L:
Children 3+
Seats: 40. Private dining room 20:
Jacket & tie preferred
Style: Classic/country house
Smoking: No smoking in dining room
Civil licence: 60
Accommodation: 21 en suite ★ ★ ★

BROADWAY,
Collin House Hotel ❀

Collin Lane WR12 7PB
Map 4: SP03
Tel: 01386 858354
Fax: 01386 858697
E-mail: collin.house@virgin.net
Cost: Alc £20-£28, set-price L
£12.50. ☺ H/wine £10.50
Times: Noon-2pm/7-9pm. Closed
24-28 Dec
Additional: Bar Food (ex Sat D);
Sunday L; Children 10+
Style: Traditional/Country-house
Smoking: No smoking in dining room
Accommodation: 6 en suite ★ ★

Listed 17th-century building with a beamed, candlelit restaurant. Traditional-style dishes include grilled fillet of beef with sauce béarnaise and lemon syllabub served with an almond tuile.

Directions: 1m NW of Broadway. Hotel is signposted from roundabout on A44

BROADWAY,
Dormy House Hotel ❀

Willersey Hill WR12 7LF
Map 4: SP03
Tel: 01386 852711
Fax: 01386 858636
E-mail:
reservations@dormyhouse.co.uk
Cost: Alc £40, set-price D £31.50.
H/wine £12.75
Times: 12.30-2pm/7-9.30pm (9pm
Sun). Closed L Sat, 24-27 Dec
Additional: Bar food; Sunday L;
Children welcome (except at D)
Smoking: No-smoking area; Air
conditioning. Jacket & tie preferred
Accommodation: 48 en suite ★ ★ ★

Once a 17th-century farmhouse, this hotel sits high above Broadway. The menus might offer roast supreme of corn-fed chicken with tiger prawns or sautéed scallops on spinach noodles. To finish with flair try crêpes flambé with marinated oranges and coffee Mascarpone.

Directions: Take Saintbury turn, off A44, L at staggered crossroads

BROADWAY,

Lygon Arms ❀❀

In the heart of Broadway, the Lygon is everyone's dream of the perfect coaching inn. Original stone walls, antique furniture, flowers and log fires abound; in the Great Hall, you dine under a high barrel-vaulted ceiling, surrounded by stags' heads, coats of arms, tapestries, armour and rich furnishings. Service is crisp, professional and friendly. The French and British cooking commands the attention with its interesting use of classical garnishing – artichokes Barigole with goats' cheese and red onion charlotte, for example, or cabbage and foie gras pithivier with roasted squab pigeon in Madeira sauce. A risotto of wild mushrooms with sautéed foie gras and baby asparagus was a little subdued in flavour though well executed. An excellent hot, melt-in-the-mouth watercress mousseline featured in a dish which also involved Cornish turbot, with fresh, hand-made noodles and a drizzle of red pepper pesto. Classic grill dishes are also available, and a separate vegetarian menu offers a super choice. For dessert, our inspector plumped for a very impressive exotic fruit tart with lime bavarois and blackberry coulis speared with what looked like a large icicle.

High Street WR12 7DU
Map 4: SP03
Tel: 01386 852255
Fax: 01386 858611
E-mail: info@the-lygon-arms.co.uk
Chef: Graeme Nesbitt
Cost: Set-price L £22.50 (Sun £25)/D £39.50. H/wine £15.50
Times: Noon-2pm/7.30-9.15pm (10pm Fri & Sat)
Additional: Bar food L; Sunday L; Children 8+ at D
Seats: 90. Private dining room 70; Jacket & tie preferred

Style: Traditional/Country-house
Smoking: No smoking in dining room
Civil licence: 80
Accommodation: 65 en suite ★ ★ ★ ★

Directions: In the centre of the High Street

BROMSGROVE.

Grafton Manor Restaurant ❀❀

Grafton Manor is a delight, set in acres of grounds, which include a lake and a private chapel. The interior style of the restaurant is an eclectic mixture, an 18th-century dining room, with Queen Anne-style chairs and William Morris wallpaper. The menu is imaginatively put together, influenced by predominantly European and Indian cooking. Breads include one made with sun-dried tomato and another Goan variety made with cumin, fenugreek and mustard seed. A first course of vine tomato, Mozzarella and basil tart with grilled sardines and black olive tapenade had a thin and crispy puff pastry, filled with a sweet onion confit and sliced tomatoes. 'Beautiful' fillets of sardines were placed on top with the tapenade placed on top of all of them. The menu does include straightforward Indian dishes, such as lamb cooked with yoghurt and roasted spices with curried swede purée and lemon rice, and Bombay prawns. Somehow all of this works together. A lemon posset with Amaretti biscuits, a cross between a mousse and a set cream, was delicious, and the wine list is well-judged and intelligent.

Grafton Lane B61 7HA
Map 7: SO97
Tel: 01527 579007
Fax: 01527 575221
Chefs: Simon Morris, William Henderson
Owners: The Morris Family
Cost: Set-price L £20.50/D £27.85 & £32.75. H/wine £9.80
Times: 12.30-1.30pm/7-9.30pm. Closed L Sat, Bhs
Additional: Sunday L; Children welcome
Seats: 60. Private dining room 60

Style: Country-house
Smoking: No smoking in dining room
Civil licence: 80

Directions: Off the B4091, 1.5 miles S of Bromsgrove

BROMSGROVE,
Pine Lodge Hotel ❀

A touch of the Mediterranean in the beautiful Worcestershire countryside at the Parador restaurant, with options like loin of tuna with roasted tomatoes and tarragon dressing.

Directions: On A448 Kidderminster road 1 mile W of Bromsgrove centre

Kidderminster Road B61 9AB
Map 7: SO97
Tel: 01527 576600
Fax: 01527 878981
E-mail: enquiries@pine-lodge-hotel.co.uk
Cost: Alc £30, set-price L £16/D £19.50. ☺ H/wine £11.50
Times: Noon-2.30pm/7-10pm.
Closed L Sat
Additional: Bar food; Sunday L; Children welcome
Style: Modern/Mediterranean
Smoking: No smoking in dining room; Air conditioning
Civil licence: 200
Accommodation: 114 en suite
★ ★ ★ ★

CHADDESLEY CORBETT,
Brockencote Hall ❀❀❀

Seventy acres of landscaped parkland surround the hall, with a large lake reflecting the fine proportions of the buildings themselves. The country-house style is reinforced by the interior design and by professional and friendly staff who generate a cosseting atmosphere. Dinner can take on the feeling of an elegant house party, with the charming Petitjeans seemingly ever-present. Menus are rooted in the best French traditions, and to them Didier Philipot adds his own contemporary dash. Pan-fried Périgord foie gras ('brilliantly accurate') comes with a globe of Cumbrian air-dried ham filled with Puy lentils, and frogs' legs with Hereford snails, a potato and garlic pancake and parsley cream. Fish and shellfish have been high points, from a starter of caramelised scallops with oysters and chicory in lettuce butter, to a main course of roasted Devon turbot with 'excellent' Guérande butter, shallots and thyme and a jus judiciously infused with vanilla.

Kidderminster DY10 4PY
Map 7: SO87
Tel: 01562 777876
Fax: 01562 777872
E-mail: info@brockencotehall.com
Chef: Didier Philipot
Owners: Alison & Joseph Petitjean
Cost: Alc £47.40, set-price L £22.50/D £27.50. ☺ H/wine £12.80
Times: Noon-1.30pm/7-9.30pm.
Closed L Sat
Additional: Sunday L; Children welcome
Seats: 60. Private dining room 32
Style: Traditional/Country-house
Smoking: No smoking in dining room
Accommodation: 17 en suite ★ ★ ★

Directions: On A448, just outside village, btw Kidderminster & Bromsgrove (M5 J5, M42 J1)

Spot-on timing never wavers, as in roast rack of lamb crowned with sweetbreads served with cheesy crushed potatoes. A dessert of water-melon essence with candied ginger cream is an example of the kitchen's enterprise, offered alongside seamless interpretations of the familiar: spicy baked apple with toffee and pimento ice cream, or 'excellent' bitter chocolate tart with pistachio ice cream. A page of house selections opens the exclusively French wine list.

EVESHAM,

The Evesham Hotel ✿

A well-deserved reputation for food comes from seasonal dishes like pheasant breast stuffed with black pudding, garlic and wild mushrooms, and monkfish with a pine-nut crust on a tomato and red pepper sauce. Friendly family-centred hotel.

Additional: Sunday L; Children welcome
Style: Regency
Smoking: No smoking in the dining room
Accommodation: 40 en suite ★ ★ ★

Directions: Coopers Lane is off road alongside River Avon

Coopers Lane, off Waterside
WR11 6DA
Map 4: SP04
Tel: 01386 765566
Fax: 01386 765443
E-mail: evesham.hotel@virgin.net
Cost: *Alc* £21. ☺ H/wine £10.50
Times: 12.30-2pm/7-9.30pm.
Closed 25 & 26 Dec

EVESHAM,

The Mill at Harvington ✿✿

Anchor Lane Harvington
WR11 5NR
Map 4: SP04
Tel/Fax: 01386 870688
Chefs: Jane Greenhalgh,
Bill Downing, John Hunter
Owners: Simon & Jane Greenhalgh
Cost: Set-price L £13.95/D £ 24. ☺
H/wine £10.25
Times: Noon-1.45pm/7-8.45pm
Additional: Bar food; Sunday L;
Children welcome
Seats: 58. Private dining room 16
Style: Classic/Traditional
Smoking: No smoking in dining room
Accommodation: 21 en suite ★ ★

Handsome Georgian buildings at this former mill have been converted to create a small hotel in lovely rural surroundings fronting the River Avon. The setting will have particular appeal to birdwatchers, who may be able to spot herons, kingfishers and partridges. Attractive public rooms include a lounge with fine views, a conservatory bar and an elegant restaurant. The three-course dinner menu is priced according to the choice of main course, ranging from salmon in pastry (butter, currants and finely chopped stem ginger sandwiched between two fillets of salmon, wrapped in pastry and baked) to prime Scottish fillet steak with Maitre d'Hotel butter. These could be preceded by king prawns with Thai sauce, or a salad of warm duck.

Directions: Turn S off B439, opposite Harvington village, down Anchor Lane

EVESHAM,

Riverside Hotel ❀❀

Standing in three acres of gardens sloping down to the River Avon, this family owned and run hotel offers a relaxed style of service by dedicated staff. The pleasant and comfortable lounge enjoys views over the river, as does the elegant restaurant. The fixed price menus are printed daily on A4 sheets in bold modern graphics. The style of cooking has settled down to what could be described as modern British, although the kitchen is keen on using Asian spices, and European influences are apparent. Locally-grown baby leeks are wrapped in Parma ham, their own Riverside fishcakes come with a remoulade, and English lambs' sweetbreads come with a 'well judged' tarragon sauce. Main courses follow the same idiom: roast rack of lamb with home-made jelly and chargrilled prime ribeye steak with shoestring fries and béarnaise sauce are typical. Desserts include hot Dutch apple pancake and hot baked bananas with rum and glazed cream.

Directions: 2 miles from town centre on B4510 (Offenham). At end of narrow lane marked 'The Parks'

The Parks Offenham Road WR11 5JP
Map 4: SP04
Tel: 01386 446200
Fax: 01386 40021
E-mail: riversidehotel@
theparksoffenham.freeserve.co.uk
Chef: Rosemary Willmott
Owners: Vincent & Rosemary
Willmott
Cost: Set-price L £17.95/D £28.95.
H/wine £11.95
Times: 12.30-2pm/7.30-9pm.
Closed D Sun, all Mon, Xmas, 1st 2
wks Jan (ex wk/ends)
Additional: Bar food L; Sunday L;
Children welcome
Seats: 48
Style: Country-house
Smoking: No smoking in dining room
Accommodation: 7 en suite ★★

EVESHAM,

Wood Norton Hall ❀❀

Wood Norton WR11 4YB
Map 4: SP04
Tel: 01386 420007
Fax: 01386 420679
Chef: Steve Waites
Owners: BBC
Cost: Alc £32.50, set-price L £19.50.
H/wine £14.50
Times: 12.30-2pm/7-10pm.
Closed L Sat
Additional: Bar food; Sunday L;
Children welcome
Seats: 60. Private dining room 36
Style: Traditional/Country-house
Smoking: No smoking in dining room
Civil licence: 70
Accommodation: 45 en suite ★★★★

Impressive Victorian property set amid a 170-acre estate just northwest of Evesham. At the start of World War II it was purchased by the BBC and became the largest broadcasting centre in Europe. Since then it has been a training centre for the Corporation and today provides excellent business, conference and function facilities. The hall retains many original features, including carved oak panelling and ornate fireplaces, not least in the magnificent Le Duc's Restaurant. The menu choice includes a set-price luncheon, a six-course menu gourmand (Friday and Saturday only), a vegetarian selection, and the *carte*, which offers five starters and main courses. A typical choice might be chicken and duck liver parfait with caramelised button onions and truffle vinaigrette, followed by fillet of sea bass with sautéed potatoes, scallops, lemongrass and chilli butter.

Directions: 2 miles NW of Evesham on A4538. Hotel is 0.5 mile on R

MALVERN, Colwall Park Hotel ❀❀

Walwyn Road Colwall WR13 6QG
Map 3: SO74
Tel: 01684 540206
Fax: 01684 540847
E-mail:
colwallparkhotel@hotmail.com
Chef: Matthew Weaver
Owners: Clive & Heather Sturman
Cost: Alc £35, set-price L £15.50/D
£22.50. ☺ H/wine £12
Times: 12.30-2pm/7.30-9pm
Additional: Bar food; Sunday L;
Children welcome
Seats: 40. Private dining room 10
Style: classic/Edwardian
Smoking: No smoking in dining room
Accommodation: 23 en suite ★ ★ ★

Built in 1903 as part of Colwall Racecourse, the hotel now stands alone in its own grounds following the closure of the course after the Second World War. The restaurant has been refurbished in shades of burgundy and pink, and the fabric designs reflect its Edwardian origins; with comfortable upholstered dining chairs, quality napery and panelling, the room exudes a feeling of well-being and ease. Dishes are well-thought-out, with each component adding dimension: a starter of lasagne of roasted mackerel, for instance, is a 'rich and well-cooked' fillet of fish layered between thin sheets of pasta in an 'intense' tomato sauce balanced by a lightly-herbed vinaigrette. Similarly, a main course of basil-crusted John Dory is accompanied by a saffron, mussel cream and chive mash, whilst a bed of slightly crisp cabbage acts as a 'calming influence' to the Puy lentils, lardons of bacon and 'rich, powerful' sauce served with a 'tender, accurately cooked' roast pheasant breast. Puddings range from an unusual iced bread-and-butter pudding to classic crêpes Suzette.

Directions: On B4218 between Ledbury and Malvern

MALVERN,
Cottage in the Wood ❀❀

Holywell Road
Malvern Wells WR14 4LG
Map 3: SO74
Tel: 01684 575859
Fax: 01684 560662

An elegant late Georgian dower house with an attractive restaurant hung with Indian and Mogul paintings. Views from the restaurant are stunning, looking across 30 miles of the Severn Valley to the Cotswold Hills on the horizon. The hotel has been run by the Pattin family for 13 years, with a daughter on reception, dad behind the bar and a son in the kitchen. The food is modern English with influences from around the globe. Options might include tiger prawns with ginger and coriander on a bed of couscous with chilli jam, or rib of Orkney beef on a bed of roots with oxtail and aged vinegar. Puddings range from kirsch and cherry parfait with crème fraîche sorbet, to baked apple with sultanas and mincemeat served with cinnamon ice cream.

E-mail: proprietor@cottageinthewood.co.uk
Chef: Dominic Pattin
Owners: The Pattin Family
Cost: *Alc* £30, set-price L £10.95 & £13.95. H/wine £13.50
Times: 12.30-2pm/7-9pm
Additional: Sunday L; Children welcome
Seats: 45
Style: Country-house
Smoking: No smoking in dining room; Air conditioning
Accommodation: 20 en suite ★ ★ ★

AA Wine Shortlisted for Award-see page 18

Directions: 3 miles S of Great Malvern off A449. 300yds N of B4209 turning on opposite side of road

MALVERN,

Croque-en-Bouche
Restaurant 🏵🏵🏵

Marion and Robin Jones have found a simple but successful formula for this splendid restaurant in a converted Victorian bakery. They open Thursday to Saturday for dinner only, with Robin out front and Marion cooking. Bookings are carefully staggered and the cooking perfectly timed. There is a cosy bar where guests can enjoy a pre-dinner drink and the intimate restaurant, adorned with stylish flower arrangements, has just six tables. The menu is quite simple but offers up to six courses and provides excellent value for money. Wine is also an important element, as Robin also runs a wine merchant's business. The list is huge, the prices fair and a good selection is available by the glass. Robin is clearly knowledgeable and happy to help with guests' wine selection. The talented couple are also keen gardeners and grow their own produce for the restaurant. Marion describes her cooking as European with oriental influence, and this is bore out by choices from a recent menu, which included leg of Welsh mountain lamb in a Bordelaise style, marinated in parsley and olive oil, roasted with braised garlic and spinach and served with a claret and thyme gravy. In contrast, breast of Hereford duck was roasted with a hoisin glaze and accompanied by oriental greens, including mizuna Tokyo Belle, tatsoi and jade greens from the garden, with an orange and coriander sauce.

221 Wells Road WR14 4HF
Map 3: SO74
Tel: 01684 565612
Fax: 0870 7066282
E-mail: mail@croque-en-bouche.co.uk
Chef: Marion Jones
Owners: Marion & Robin Jones
Cost: Set-price D £26.50 & £40.50. H/wine £12
Times: D only, 7-9.30pm. Closed Sun-Wed, Xmas-New Year, 1 wk May, 1 wk Sep
Additional: Children welcome
Seats: 22. Private dining room 6
Style: Modern
Smoking: No smoking in dining room

Directions: 2 miles S of Gt Malvern on A449

MALVERN,
Foley Arms Hotel ❀

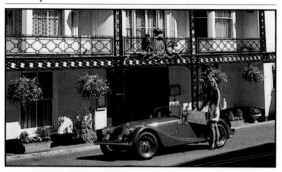

14 Worcester Road WR14 4QS
Map 3: SO74
Tel: 01684 573397
Fax: 01684 569665
E-mail:
reservations@foleyarmshotel.com
Cost: Set-price L £8.50/D £19.50. ☺
H/wine £9.20
Times: Noon-2.15pm/7-9.30pm.
Closed L Sat
Additional: Bar food; Sunday L;
Children welcome
Style: Traditional/country-house
Accommodation: 30 en suite ★ ★ ★

The oldest hotel in Malvern offers modern British cooking in a restaurant filled with antique furniture and dressers full of china. The likes of crab cakes flavoured with dill and ginger, and fillet of lamb with herb mash are served in a friendly, informal way.

Directions: Telephone for directions

MALVERN,
Holdfast Cottage ❀❀

Little Malvern WR13 6NA
Map 3: SO74
Tel: 01684 310288
Fax: 01684 311117
E-mail: holdcothot@aol.com
Chef: Jane Knowles
Owners: Stephen & Jane Knowles
Cost: Alc £24. ☺ H/wine £10.50
Times: D only, 7.30-8.45pm. Closed
D Sun, Xmas, 1st 2 wks Jan
Additional: Children welcome
Seats: 24. Private dining room 14
Style: Country-house
Smoking: No smoking in dining room
Accommodation: 8 en suite ★ ★

Attractive hotel developed from a 17th-century cottage, in a country setting surrounded by orchards and farmland with wonderful views of the Malvern Hills. The restaurant with its soft green decor provides a relaxing setting overlooking a wisteria-laden terrace and an acre of gardens. Antique oak tables are set with silver cutlery, fresh flowers and candles. The set-price, four-course dinner menu offers a good choice of imaginative dishes, perhaps home-smoked trout and prawn salad with lemon mayonnaise, followed by Thai-grilled chicken breast with coriander, coconut and lime, or a vegetarian option such as roast peppers stuffed with mushroom ratatouille topped with pine nuts and Parmesan.

Directions: On A4104 midway between Welland and Little Malvern

OMBERSLEY,
The Venture In Restaurant ⌘⌘

Main Road WR9 0EW
Map 3: SO86
Tel/Fax: 01905 620552
Chef/Owner: Toby William Fletcher
Cost: Set-price L £13.95 & £16.95/D
£25.95. H/wine £9.95
Times: Noon-2pm/7-9.45pm. Closed
D Sun, all Mon, 2wks winter &
summer, 26 Dec, Bhs
Additional: Sunday L; Children 8+
at D
Seats: 32
Smoking: No-smoking area; No pipes
& cigars

Directions: From Worcester N
towards Kidderminster – A449
(approx 5 miles). Turn L at Ombersley
turning – 0.75m on R

The recent refurbishment of this attractive property on the high street of a picturesque village has only added to the charm and antique character of the restaurant. The exposed beams have been stripped back to their original state and the plain, cream coloured walls reflect the glow of an open fire. The culinary approach is modern and British, although traditional and international influences are not entirely shunned. A starter of crispy duck confit was excellently cooked, and this coupled with a well-judged accompaniment of sage and garlic flavoured soft polenta and a powerful, rich and intense duck jus made for an impressive opening to the meal. Early promise was fully realised in the main of fresh, accurately cooked and seasoned roast cod with pan-fried scallops and a hint of truffle oil. An excellent coconut tart served with exotic fruit sorbet made up for a slightly restrictive dessert menu.

PERSHORE, Epicurean ⌘⌘⌘

Such is the demand on Pat McDonald's time from his TV and consultancy work, that his restaurant is only open two nights a week – Thursday and Friday, but at least you are assured that the chef is actually in the kitchen. The result is an exceptional no-choice, set menu for which you have to book weeks in advance. It is served in a tiny, modern setting of wood floors, deep blue and white decor and bar area with squishy sofas. Memorable dishes have included fresh garden pea soup with lobster and basil ravioli; pressed terrine of pork knuckle and foie gras; roast squab pigeon with broad beans, tomato and morels with a jus of summer truffles; cheese with a warm almond and poire William tartlet. An excellent idea is the matching of wines by the glass with the menu or you can order from a very wide-ranging list.

76 High Street WR10 1DU
Map 3: SO94
Tel: 01386 555576
Fax: 01386 555572
E-mail:
epicurean.restaurant@lineone.net
Chef/Owner: Patrick McDonald
Cost: Set-price D £30. H/wine £12.50
Times: Thu & Fri D only from 7pm
Seats: 24
Style: Chic/Modern
Smoking: No pipes & cigars
Credit cards: None

Directions: On High Street

STOURPORT-ON-SEVERN,
Menzies Stourport Manor ⌘⌘

The former home of Prime Minister Sir Stanley Baldwin, considerably extended, is now a modern hotel with good corporate facilities set in 24 acres of grounds on the eastern edge of the town. Set-price lunch, set-price dinner and *carte*

Hartlebury Road DY13 9LT
Map 7: SO87
Tel: 01299 289955
Fax: 01299 878520
E-mail: info@menzies-hotels.co.uk
Chef: John Trueman

menus are offered and a French influence is apparent in the cooking. For example, a starter of duck leg confit was finished in the oven with wholegrain mustard and brioche crumb and set on a bed of orange segments and lambs' tongue salad. A main course of grilled fillet of red mullet was served with a twist of squid ink pasta, roast pepper sauce and a medley of Mediterranean vegetables. Desserts range from iced blueberry parfait to spotted dick with custard.

Civil licence: 400 **Accommodation:** 68 en suite ★ ★ ★ ★

Directions: Off B4193

Cost: *Alc* £26, set-price L £10.95/D £19.95. h H/wine £11.50
Times: 12.30-2pm/7-9.30pm
Additional: Bar food; Sunday L; Children welcome
Seats: 100. Private dining room 25-300
Style: Modern/Country-house
Smoking: No smoking in dining room; Air conditioning

UPTON UPON SEVERN,
White Lion Hotel

Dating back to 1510 this delightful hotel restaurant offers top quality cuisine. Thai red curry and salmon croquettes were light and well flavoured, and medallions of beef fillet were tender and perfectly cooked.

Style: Old world **Smoking:** No smoking in dining room
Accommodation: 10 en suite ★ ★ ★

Directions: From A422 take A38 towards Tewkesbury. After 8pm take B4104 for 1 mile, after bridge turn L to hotel

21 High Street WR8 0HJ
Map 3: SO84
Tel: 01684 592551
Fax: 01684 593333
Cost: H/wine £12.55
Times: Noon-2pm/7-9pm.
Closed 26 Dec, 1 Jan
Additional: Bar food; Sunday L; Children welcome

WORCESTER, **Brown's Restaurant**

Converted corn mill in an idyllic setting on the banks of the River Severn, yet only a short walk from the city centre. Furnishings are smart and understated set against painted brick walls relieved by mirrors, prints and portraits, and picture windows take in the river view. Set-price menus at both lunch and dinner provide a reasonable choice, supplemented by daily specials, and the wine list is mainly French. Starters might include whole grilled baby squid with herb salsa, followed by sauté of calves' liver with pancetta and mash, or the fresh fish dish of the day. To finish there is a choice of three puddings or cheese – perhaps hot citrus surprise, or Pavlova with cream and berries.

Smoking: No-smoking area; No cigars & pipes

Directions: City centre, along river bank, car park opposite

The Old Cornmill South Quay WR1 2JJ
Map 3: SO85
Tel: 01905 26263
Fax: 01905 25768
Chefs: W R Tansley & L Jones
Owners: W R & P M Tansley
Cost: Set-price L £18.50/D £35.50. H/wine £11.95
Times: 12.30-1.45pm/7.30-9.30pm.
Closed L Sat, D Sun, all Mon, 24-31 Dec
Additional: Children 8+
Seats: 110
Style: Modern

WORCESTER,
Glass House Restaurant

The setting of a 16th-century ex-grammar school coupled with polished floorboards and stained glass windows creates a classic but modern atmosphere. Expect honest, high quality cuisine such as roasted tomato risotto.

Style: Classic/Modern
Smoking: No-smoking area; Air conditioning

Directions: Off north end of High St, next to St Swithuns church

Church Street WR1 2RH
Map 3: SO85
Tel: 01905 611120
Fax: 01905 616616
Cost: *Alc* £23, set-price L £8.95. ☺ H/wine £9.50
Times: Noon-2pm/7-10pm.
Closed Sun & Mon, 1-14 Jan
Additional: Children welcome

YORKSHIRE EAST RIDING

BEVERLEY,

The Manor House

Northlands Walkington HU17 8RT
Map 8: TA03
Tel: 01482 881645
Fax: 01482 866501
E-mail: derek@the-manor-house-hotel.fsbusiness.co.uk
Chef: Derek Baugh
Owners: Derek & Lee Baugh
Cost: Alc £30, set-price D £18.50. ☺
H/wine £11.95
Times: D only, 7-9.15pm.
Closed Sun, Bhs
Additional: Children 12+
Seats: 50. Private dining room 24
Style: Country-house
Smoking: No pipes and cigars
Accommodation: 7 en suite ★★

Built in the late 19th century, the Manor is a small country house hotel in three acres of grounds. The conservatory dining room has an outlook on the terrace and lawns, and an Eastern influence can be detected behind some of the starters – mussel soup with korma-scented lentils, for instance, or duck and leek confit with grape chutney and a Thai-style dipping sauce – while seared scallops are fashionably partnered with dry-cured ham, and the vibrant flavours in a crisp tart of roasted tomatoes and goats' cheese topped with pesto brings a hint of the Mediterranean to the north. Main courses are from more familiar territory: roast guinea fowl, given a novel twist with apple bubble-and-squeak and tarragon and bramble sauce, or seared calves' liver with lambs' kidneys ('perfectly cooked') and colcannon. A fish of the day comes with sautéed Mediterranean vegetables, lobster Thermidor may also be a possibility, and something like bread-and-butter pudding with blackberry coulis will round things off nicely.

Directions: 4 miles SW off B1230

BEVERLEY,

Tickton Grange Hotel

Tickton HU17 9SH
Map 8: TA03
Tel: 01964 543666
Fax: 01964 542556
E-mail: maggy@tickton-grange.demon.co.uk
Cost: Alc £33, set-price L £15.95/ D £25. H/wine £11.75
Times: Noon-2pm/7-9.30pm

A charming country house, well known for its 'Tickton Truffle', a chocolate delicacy. Typical dishes could include field mushroom and thyme ragout wrapped in chestnut pancakes, or chicken breast in lemon and coriander yoghurt.

Additional: Bar food L; Sunday L; Children welcome
Style: Classic/Country-house
Smoking: No smoking in dining room
Civil licence: 60
Accommodation: 17 en suite ★★★

Directions: From Beverley take A1035 towards Bridlington. Hotel on L, after 3 miles, just past village of Tickton

WILLERBY,
Willerby Manor Hotel

Tones of umber and soft burgundies frame picturesque views across the formal gardens of this historic building. The hotel restaurant offers smart, attentive and professional service, and cuisine along the lines of roasted pheasant or chargrilled red mullet.

Additional: Bar food; Sunday L (12.30-2.30); Children welcome
Style: Classic
Smoking: No-smoking area; no pipes & cigars; Air conditioning
Civil licence: 300
Accommodation: 51 en suite ★★★

Directions: Off A1105 W of Hull, just off main street in Willerby

Well Lane HU10 6ER
Map 8: TA03
Tel: 01482 652616
Fax: 01482 653901
E-mail: info@willerbymanor.co.uk
Cost: Set-price D £16.75. ☺ H/wine £8.50
Times: D only, 7-9.30pm. Closed D Sun, Bhs

YORKSHIRE NORTH

ALDWARK, **Aldwark Hotel** NEW

A 19th-century manor house with a brasserie in addition to the elegant restaurant. The latter is a high-ceilinged room with a chandelier and open fire, where imaginative and skilfully prepared dishes are provided in a more formal atmosphere. There was a good range of warm home-made rolls on the table – white, walnut, tomato, and basil. A starter of tortellini of salmon and herbs was carefully made and full of flavour, set on a bed of trompettes with beetroot leaves adding a pleasing pepperiness. Fillet of venison, cooked nicely pink and tender, was served with a parsnip purée and a richly flavoured but well balanced morel sauce. To finish, the pear Tatin had perfect pastry and beautifully caramelised pears and came with a decent vanilla ice cream.

Directions: from A1, A59 towards Green Hammerton, then B6265 towards Little Ouseburn, follow signs Aldwark bridge/Manor. A19 through Linton on Ouse to Aldwark

York YO61 1UF
Map 8: SE46
Tel: 01347 838146
Fax: 01347 838867
E-mail:
reception@aldwarkmanor.co.uk

Telephone for further details

APPLETON-LE-MOORS,
Appleton Hall Hotel 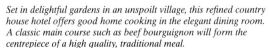 NEW

Set in delightful gardens in an unspoilt village, this refined country house hotel offers good home cooking in the elegant dining room. A classic main course such as beef bourguignon will form the centrepiece of a high quality, traditional meal.

Style: Country-house
Smoking: No smoking in dining room
Accommodation: 9 en suite ★★

Directions: Village 2 miles N of A170, 1 mile E of Kirbymoorside, 5m W of Pickering

York YO62 6TF
Map 8: SE78
Tel: 01751 417227
Fax: 01751 417540
Cost: Set-price D £25. H/wine £12.50
Times: D only, 6.30-9.15pm

ARNCLIFFE,
Amerdale House Hotel 🏵🏵

There are fine views of the unspoilt dales and fells from each bedroom of this delightful old manor house, as well as from the welcoming, comfortably furnished drawing room and dining room. Local Dales lamb and other meats feature on the daily-changing, four-course menu together with fresh fish from Aberdeen and regional cheeses. Fruit, vegetables and herbs from the garden are supplemented, whenever possible, with local produce. After salmon kedgeree or a smoked chicken and Waldorf salad with mixed leaves, main course choice might be between roast tenderloin of pork on caramelised apple with grain mustard sauce or fillet of cod baked under a couscous crust with roasted peppers and baby leeks. Desserts also chart an even course between the modern, the classic and the comforting – raspberry and mango set in passion fruit jelly; floating islands with berries; steamed syrup sponge with custard sauce.

Directions: On edge of village

Littondale Skipton BD23 5QE
Map 7: SD97
Tel: 01756 770250
Fax: 01756 770266
Chefs: Nigel Crapper,
Anthony Chamley
Owners: Paula & Nigel Crapper
Cost: Set-price £30. H/wine £12.95
Times: D only, 7.30-8.30pm.
Closed mid Nov-mid Mar
Additional: Children 8+; Vegetarian dishes not always available
Seats: 22
Style: Country-house
Smoking: No smoking in dining room
Accommodation: 11 en suite ★ ★

ASENBY,
Crab & Lobster Restaurant 🏵🏵

Crab Manor is a Georgian house set in beautiful grounds. The purity of the exterior and grounds give no hint of the riot of ephemera inside the dining room, which is covered in bric-à-brac and antiques. Pots, pans, parasols and puppets hang from the ceilings and ledges, while windows sills and sideboards are covered with fishing pots, old tin signs and mock crabs. The menu is less cluttered, and the primary influences are French and Italian, although some Asian touches have crept in. A Thai fishcake was well-shaped and had a good spicy flavour, a bouillabaisse soup was correctly served with aïoli and rouille croûte, while grilled salmon was 'full of flavour' and served on a black pudding risotto. Fillet of beef came with mushroom polenta and a poached turbot with a spinach, almond and cauliflower purée. The rice pudding with caramel topping was thick and creamy and the meal was finished with excellent coffee.

Directions: Leave A1 for A19 at Dishforth, just N of Boroughbridge & Ripon, take A19 towards Teeside, 1st L

Dishforth Road YO7 3QL
Map 8: SE37
Tel: 01845 577286
Fax: 01845 577109
E-mail:
reservations@crabandlobster.co.uk
Chef: Steven Dean
Owners: David & Jackie Barnard
Cost: Alc £30, set-price L £14.50/D £22.50. ☺ H/wine £11
Times: 11.30am-3pm/6.30-11pm
Additional: Bar food; Sunday L; Children 12+
Seats: 36 & 70. Private dining rooms 12 & 24
Style: Chic/Rustic
Smoking: No smoking in dining room; Air conditioning
Civil licence: 50

BOROUGHBRIDGE,
The Dining Room 🏵

An attractive, bow-fronted building in the main town square houses a modern, freshly decorated restaurant with neutral-toned furnishings and walls hung with contemporary art. Main courses might include seared salmon marinated in lime and coriander.

Additional: Sunday L; Children welcome
Style: Modern/Minimalist

Directions: A1(M)/Boroughbridge junction. Follow signs into town centre, opposite the fountain in St James square

20 St James Square YO51 9AR
Map 8: SE36
Tel: 01423 326426
Cost: Alc £25. ☺ H/wine £8.95
Times: Noon-1.30pm/6-10pm.
Closed L Sat, D Sun, all Mon & Tue

BUCKDEN **The Buck Inn Hotel** 🏵🏵

The Buck is a traditional Georgian coaching inn which has retained lots of its olde worlde charm and character. This two-storey inn faces south-west and looks across the village green towards the old deer park. Its white stone walls are decorated with old armour, horse brasses and paintings by local artists. Menus are a medley of European dishes, from a Greek feta cheese salad and seared smoked salmon to a ham and foie gras terrine, which was excellent, 'good chunks of ham, less of foie gras, but a superb parsley jelly'. There are five main choices on the set-price menu, including perhaps sautéed medallions of pork with sauerkraut and sauce au poivre, or a fillet steak with Parmesan mash, whole grain mustard sauce and caramelised shallots. Fish dishes include a wonderfully fresh roasted sea bass, placed on a rather heavy olive oil mash. A coffee pannacotta had a lovely balance and a good rich coffee flavour. The wine list is interesting, and includes many wines by the glass, halves and a fine wine list.

Directions: In centre of village

Near Skipton BD23 5JA
Map 7: SD97
Tel: 01756 760228
Fax: 01756 760227
E-mail: thebuckinn@buckden.yorks.net
Chef: William Mallinson
Owners: Roy & Marjorie Hayton
Cost: *Alc* £23.95. ☺
Times: D only, 6.30-9.30pm
Additional: Bar food; Sunday L; Children 5+
Seats: 40
Style: Classic/Traditional
Smoking: No smoking in dining room
Accommodation: 14 en suite ★★

BURNSALL, **Red Lion Hotel** 🏵

A charming Dales inn beside the River Wharf. Meat from local farms features on the seasonal menus, notably rack of spring lamb roasted with garlic and herb butter, and loin of pork with shallots and apple sauce.

Directions: On B6160 between Bolton Abbey (A59) & Grassington

By the Bridge BD23 6BU
Map 7: SE06
Tel: 01756 720204
Fax: 01756 720292
E-mail: redlion@daelnet.co.uk
Cost: *Alc* £29, set-price D £25. ☺
H/wine £11.50
Times: D only, 7-9.30pm
Additional: Bar food; Sunday L (noon-3pm); Children welcome
Style: Traditional
Smoking: No smoking in dining room
Civil licence: 50
Accommodation: 11 en suite ★★

CARLTON, **Foresters Arms**

The setting of a 16th-century inn hosts an ambitious pub restaurant that competes with the best in its seafood dishes. Vegetarians and carnivores also well catered for and a super cheese menu is a real bonus.

Cost: *Alc* £30. H/wine £9.80
Times: Noon-2pm/7-9.30pm. Closed D Sun, L Tue, all Mon, Jan
Additional: Bar food L; Sunday L; Children welcome
Style: Classic/Informal
Smoking: No-smoking area

Directions: Off A684, 5 miles S of Leyburn

Carlton-in-Coverdale
DL8 4BB
Map 7: SE19
Tel: 01969 640272

CRATHORNE,

Crathorne Hall Hotel ❀❀

TS15 0AR
Map 8: NZ40
Tel: 01642 700398
Fax: 01642 700814
Cost: *Alc* £30, set-price D £27.50. ☺
H/wine £14.50
Times: Noon-2.30pm/7-10pm

Regal dining room in a delightful country-house setting. The coat of arms, log fire and oil paintings set the mood for high class cuisine such as oven baked guinea fowl with woodland mushrooms in a light mustard cream.

Additional: Bar food; Sunday L; Children 5+
Style: Classic/Country-house
Smoking: No smoking in dining room
Civil licence: 140
Accommodation: 37 en suite ★★★★

Directions: From A19, take junction signposted Crathorne and follow the signs. Hotel entrance is to the L on way into village

EASINGTON, **Grinkle Park Hotel** ❀

Nineteenth century country house hotel set in thirty-five acres of beautiful parkland. The deep pinks of the restaurant establish a warm atmosphere suitable for the indulgence of smoked wild boar and pan-fried ostrich steak.

Additional: Bar food; Sunday L; Children welcome
Style: Country-house **Smoking:** No pipes & cigars
Accommodation: 20 en suite ★★★

Directions: 9 miles from Guisborough, signed off A171 Guisborough-Whitby road

Saltburn-by-the-Sea TS13 4UB
Map 8: NZ71
Tel: 01287 640515
Fax: 01287 641278
E-mail: grinkle.parkhotel@bass.com
Cost: *Alc* £28, set-price L £13.25/D £19.95. ☺ H/wine £9.75
Times: 12.15-1.45pm/7.15-9pm

ESCRICK,

The Parsonage Hotel ❀❀

Parsons in the early 19th century must have led the life of Riley, judging by the size and style of this country-house hotel. Well-tended grounds, relaxing lounges, a spacious conservatory and a traditional and elegant restaurant are all part of the appeal. If dishes sound complicated – sautéed pigeon with brioche fingers, apple and vanilla chutney and white bean casserole, followed by fillet of beef with a foie gras omelette, Parmentier potatoes, morels and Madeira sauce – the kitchen manages to pull things together. Fish is handled well, from a

York Road YO19 6LF
Map 8: SE64
Tel: 01904 728111
Fax: 01904 728151
Chef: Kenny Noble
Cost: Set-price L £14/D £24.50. ☺ H/wine £10.95
Times: Noon-2pm/7-9.30pm
Additional: Bar food L; Sunday L; Children welcome
Seats: 32. Private dining room 20

starter of seared scallops with a mini-black pudding and parsley mash, to 'superb' sea bass with a well-matched creamy coriander sauce, crab ravioli and spring onion potatoes. Vegetarians are treated with respect, and puddings might take in a well-made, tangy orange and passion fruit tart. The wine list is fairly evenly split between France and the New World, although other countries get a peep in and there are six house wines.

Directions: From York head S on A19, Parsonage on R, 4 miles out of town in Escrick village

Style: Traditional/Country-house
Smoking: No smoking in dining room
Civil licence: 50
Accommodation: 21 en suite ★ ★ ★

HACKNESS, Hackness Grange Country House ✺

North Yorkshire National Park
Scarborough YO13 0JW
Map 8: SE99
Tel: 01723 882345
Fax: 01723 882391
E-mail: hacknessgrange@
englishrosehotels.co.uk
Cost: Alc £27.50, set-price L
£12.50/D £25. H/wine £12.95
Times: Noon-2pm/7-9.30pm
Additional: Bar food L; Sunday L;
Children welcome
Style: Classic/country-house
Smoking: No smoking in dining room
Accommodation: 33 en suite ★ ★ ★

Restaurant overlooking parkland and a lake full of ducks, serving modern British dishes such as roast cod on a tian of pease pudding, or shank of lamb in garlic and rosemary.

Directions: A64 to Scarborough, then A171 towards Whitby. Follow signs to Hackness/Forge Valley National Park. Hotel through Hackness on L

HARROGATE, The Boar's Head Hotel ✺✺

Ripley Castle Estate HG3 3AY
Map 8: SE35
Tel: 01423 771888
Fax: 01423 771509
E-mail: boarshead@ripleycastle.co.uk

The Boar's Head is so named because Thomas Ingilby saved King Edward III from a wounded boar and thus received his

knighthood. The Ingilbys have lived at Ripley for over 600 years and own both the castle and the hotel. The latter is an original coaching inn in a Grade I listed village overlooking the cobbled market square. The hotel's furniture and paintings come from Ripley Castle and the dining room is richly decorated in baronial blues and reds. Service is provided by professional French waiting staff, and the wine list is long and global. The three-course dinner menu is priced according to the choice of main course, perhaps roast salmon supreme topped with a soft poached egg, mini fishcake and fennel hollandaise, or glazed duck breast with hot and cold couscous and mango compote. A five-course *menu gourmand* is also available.

Directions:

Chef: Steve Chesnut
Owners: Sir Thomas & Lady Ingilby
Cost: Alc £19, set-price L £11.95/D £25. ☺ H/wine £12
Times: Noon-2.30pm/6.30-10pm
Additional: Bar food; Sunday L; Children welcome
Seats: 40. Private dining room 40
Style: Classic/Chic
Smoking: No smoking in dining room; Air conditioning
Accommodation: 30 en suite ★ ★ ★

HARROGATE The Courtyard

A bright, fresh restaurant in the heart of the town, surrounded by antique shops. A starter of 'sweet and juicy' scallops was followed by local best end of lamb – 'super flavour' – and lemon brûlée.

Additional: Children welcome
Style: Chic/modern
Smoking: No smoking in dining room

Directions: Telephone for directions

1 Montpellier Mews HG1 2TG
Map 8: SE35
Tel/Fax: 01423 530708
Cost: Alc £25, set-price L £12.95. ☺ H/wine £9.50
Times: Noon-2.30pm/6-10pm.
Closed Sun

HARROGATE, Dusty Miller ❀❀

The Dusty Miller was built in the early 1800s as a pub, and fresh flowers, polished wood and a roaring fire in the bar provide an inviting glow. The restaurant is cosy and traditional in style, furnished with antiques. The quality of the ingredients shines through the dishes and the presentation is immaculate. Starters among a choice of seven from the *carte* were a plate of hors d'oeuvres, a good fish soup, and a salad of Whitby crab. Mains range through baked turbot with pesto mash, supreme of pheasant with orange and champagne, and rack of Nidderdale lamb. There is also a short set-price daily menu, with one or two options at each course – maybe Thai crab fishcakes and chargrilled lemon chicken.

Directions: Situated on B6165, 10 miles from Harrogate

Low-Laithe Summerbridge
HG3 4BU
Map 8: SE35
Tel: 01423 780837
Chef: Brian Dennison
Owners: Brian & Elizabeth Dennison
Cost: Alc £33, set-price D £24. ☺ H/wine 11.90
Times: D only, 7-11pm.
Closed Sun, Mon, 2 wks mid Aug
Additional: Children 9+
Seats: 28. Private dining room 14
Style: Traditional/Formal

HARROGATE,
Harrogate Brasserie Hotel ❀

Much attention has been paid here to creating the right ambience. Deep colours, stripped wood, dramatic lighting and regular live jazz create an intimate, romantic feel. Modern British cuisine including an excellent seafood platter.

Style: Informal/Rustic
Smoking: No-smoking area; No pipes & cigars
Accommodation: 14 rooms ★ ★

Directions: In town centre, 500 mtrs from railway station, behind theatre

28-30 Cheltenham Parade
HG1 1DB
Map 8: SE35
Tel: 01423 505041
Fax: 01423 722300
E-mail:
harrogate.brasserie@zoom.co.uk
Cost: Alc £19.50, set-price D £12.50. ☺ H/wine £8.95
Times: D only, 6-10pm.
Closed Bh Mons
Additional: Children 4+

HARROGATE, Olivers 24 ❀❀

24 Kings Road HG1 5JW
Map 8: SE35
Tel: 01423 568600
Fax: 01423 531838
E-mail
restaurant@olivers24.demon.co.uk
Chef: Dean Sowden
Owners: James & Sandy Greetham
Cost: Alc £25. ☺ H/wine £8.95
Times: Closed Sun, L Mon, Xmas
Additional: Bar food; Children
welcome
Style: Modern
Smoking: No pipes & cigars; Air
conditioning

Directions: Telephone for directions

A breath of fresh air has swept into Harrogate with this highly-regarded restaurant, and it has drawn in customers from York and Leeds eager to share the experience. Dean Sowden's cooking speaks for itself, and past inspection meals have resulted in fulsome praise for his technique and for the imagination of his creations. A list of robust-sounding dishes masks the lightest of touches: mini casserole of Toulouse sausage, white beans, tomato and spring vegetables as a starter perhaps, or fusilli pasta with smoked chicken and pancetta, and a creamy thyme and garlic sauce. Friday night here is lobster night, and with some advance warning the restaurant will cook your crustacean just the way you like it. The dessert list maintains the buzz and allure found elsewhere on the menu: caramelised lime tart with orange syrup and lemon Chantilly cream sits alongside warm chocolate fondant with black cherry compote and white chocolate ice cream.

HARROGATE,
Rudding Park House ❀❀

Follifoot HG3 1JH
Map 8: SE35
Tel: 01423 871350
Fax: 01423 872286
E-mail: sales@rudding-park.co.uk
Chef: Jason Wardill
Owner: Simon Mackaness
Cost: Alc D £24.50, set-price L
£11.50/D £24.50. ☺ H/wine £13
Times: 12.30-2.30pm/7-9.30pm
Additional: Bar food; Sunday L;
Children welcome
Seats: 90. Private dining rooms 6-250
Style: Chic/Modern
Smoking: No pipes & cigars; Air
conditioning
Civil licence: 200
Accommodation: 50 en suite ★ ★ ★ ★

Directions: 3 miles S of Harrogate,
just off the A658 linking the A61 from
Leeds to the A59 York road

Impressive hotel on a 230-acre estate, built in the same style as the adjacent Rudding House, which is used for conferences and functions. The Clocktower bar and brasserie is strikingly decorated, with stripped floors and maroon walls in the bar, and green walls, tartan curtains and red and green chairs in the restaurant. It provides an appropriate setting for contemporary cooking with some Asian influences. The extensive menu, priced for two or three courses, encompasses an excellent chicken liver parfait, and hot, seared spicy tiger prawns with tomato noodles, lime and ginger sauce. Among the mains are roast pheasant with truffled wood mushrooms, roast shallots and game sauce, and a selection of seafood braised in a sweet red Thai curry served with steamed Persian rice.

HARROGATE, **Studley Hotel** ✿

Swan Road HG1 2SE
Map 8: SE35
Tel: 01423 560425
Fax: 01423 530967

Telephone for further details.

Directions: Adjacent to the Valley Gardens on Swan Road

Exceedingly good value food, such as spinach and wild mushrooms in a pastry case, topped with poached egg and cream, and roulade of chicken, ham, chicken mousseline and spinach in a tomato and tarragon sauce.

HARROGATE, **The White House** ✿✿

10 Park Parade HG1 5AH
Map 8: SE35
Tel: 01423 501388
Fax: 01423 527973
E-mail: info@whitehouse-hotel.demon.co.uk
Chef/Owner: Jennie Forster
Cost: *Alc* £25. ☺ H/wine £12.50
Times: 12.30-2pm(bookings only)/7-9pm. Closed D Sun
Additional: Sunday L (bookings only); Children welcome
Seats: 30. Private dining room 50
Style: Classic/Bistro-style
Smoking: No smoking in dining room
Civil licence: 50
Accommodation: 10 en suite ★ ★ ★

Inspired by a Venetian villa, the White House was built in 1836 and retains many original features, including fine cornicing in the elegant dining room. The food is rather more modern in style, and the menu urges guests on to full indulgence with bons mots from infamous wits, such as 'too much of a good thing can be wonderful' (Mae West) which introduces the dessert selection. The *carte* offers a choice of five dishes at each of three courses, all simple and direct. Typical options are ink fish risotto with baby squid and prawns, Cajun chicken with rocket and lime, and bread-and-butter pudding with Grand Marnier. The alternative to pudding is cheese and oatcakes, and tea or coffee is served 'with goodies'.

Directions: Opposite Christchurch, parallel with A59 close to Wetherby/Skipton junction

HAWES, Simonstone Hall Hotel

Fine hospitality and quality British cooking make this smart Georgian hunting lodge a great place to stay. A winter meal kicked off with ceviche of salmon, swiftly followed by a subtle yet dynamic courgette and smoked bacon soup. Desserts are cosmopolitan.

Additional: Bar food; Sunday L (noon – 2pm); Children welcome
Style: Traditional/Country-house
Smoking: No smoking in dining room
Civil licence: 45
Accommodation: 18 en suite ★ ★

Directions: 1.5m N of Hawes on road signed to Muker & Buttertubs

Simonstone DL8 3LY
Map 7: SD88
Tel: 01969 667255
Fax: 01969 667741
E-mail:
hotel@simonstonehall.demon.co.uk
Cost: *Alc* £22.50, set-price L
£12.95/D £15.95. ☺ H/wine £8.95
Times: D only 6.30-9pm.

HELMSLEY, The Black Swan

An attractive dining room in the Elizabethan section of this historic and well-respected hotel. The cuisine is largely traditional with dishes such as roast sirloin of beef and grilled Dover sole executed with artful aplomb.

Additional: Bar food L; Sunday L; Children welcome
Style: Traditional/Country-house
Smoking: No smoking in dining room
Accommodation: 45 rooms ★ ★ ★

Directions: Take A170 from Scarborough or Thirsk; Black Swan is in centre of village, at top end of Market Place

Market Place YO62 5BJ
Map 8: SE68
Tel: 0870 400 8112
Fax: 01439 770174
Cost: *Alc* £35, set-price L £14/D
£26.50. H/wine £14
Times: Noon-2pm(Sun 12.30pm)/7-9pm

HELMSLEY,
Feversham Arms Hotel

Rich, opulent colours and mahogany and velvet fittings establish archetypal elegance. An unusual rustic Spanish 'soup' provoked great enthusiasm from our inspector. Crisp duck on a tangy marmalade sauce was of a similarly high quality.

Additional: Bar food; Sunday L; Children 7+
Style: Traditional
Smoking: No smoking in dining room
Accommodation: 18 en suite ★ ★ ★

Directions: 125 mtrs N of Market Place

1 High Street YO62 5AG
Map 8: SE68
Tel: 01439 770766
Fax: 01439 770346
E-mail: reception@feversham-helmsley.fsnet.co.uk
Cost: *Alc* £20, set-price L £15/D £20.
☺ H/wine £10
Times: Noon-2pm/7-10pm

HELMSLEY, The Star Inn

Located in a peaceful village on a back road, this attractive low-beamed thatched house a real find. Well-tended gardens are ideal for alfresco dining, and there is a separate bar and a 'coffee loft' upstairs where guests can have coffee and cigars on chaise longues and comfy sofas, while admiring the trompe l'oeil painting. Andrew Pern cooks, while wife Jacquie is responsible for front of house, and both seem to go from strength to strength.The daily written menus are more extensive at lunch-times and more ambitious in the evenings. Ballantine of salmon with smoked salmon salad with sour dressing proved light and full flavoured, and a 'Yorkshire

Harome YO6 5JE
Map 8: SE68
Tel: 01439 770397
Chef: Andrew Pern
Owners: Andrew & Jacquie Pern
Cost: *Alc* £25. ☺ H/wine £11
Times: 11.30-2pm/6.30-9.30pm .
Closed D Sun, all Mon, 1 wk Nov,
25 Dec, 2 wks Jan
Additional: Bar food; Sunday L (noon-6pm); Children welcome
Seats: 36. Private dining room 10
Style: Informal/Chic

The Star Inn

Smoking: No smoking in dining room

portion' of rack of lamb impressed, full of rosemary and served with a mini shepherds pie. Six desserts are offered, a seventh as a mini portion and a selection of British cheeses. The ginger parkin was 'excellent', as was the coffee.

Directions: From Helmsley take A170 towards Kirkbymoorside, after 1.5m turn R towards Harome. After 1.5m Inn is 1st building on R

HETTON, Angel Inn ❀❀

The lovely 500-year-old Dales pub is all oak beams, log fires and charming nooks and crannies. The restaurant adds a more elegant note with stylish napery and furnishings, but meals are also served in the bar-brasserie. One of the house specials, not to be missed, is Little Moneybags, filo pastry filled with seafood such as sweet scallops, lobster and salmon served with lobster sauce. Healthy local appetites are well catered for with slow-cooked, full-flavoured confit of lamb shoulder with roasted root vegetables, or braised salted beef with zamponi and horseradish dumplings. A Mediterranean dimension comes with Provençal fish soup, homemade bresaola and platters of roasted Tuscan vegetables with pesto. Although it was October, we finished our inspection meal with a well-made, tangy summer pudding sporting a lovely dollop of clotted cream. Dessert wines include a stunning Yarden Muscat from Israel. *Best Pub Restaurant Wine List (see pages 18-19)*.

Directions: In village centre, B6265 (Rylestone) from Skipton by-pass

Skipton BD23 6LT
Map 7: SD95
Tel: 01756 730263
Fax: 01756 730363
E-mail: info@angelhetton.co.uk
Chefs: John Topham, Bruce Elsworth
Owners: Denis Watkins, John Topham, Julie Watkins
Cost: *Alc* £25, set-price L £19/D £20.
☺ H/wine £10.50
Times: D only, 6-10pm.
Closed D Sun, 2 wks Jan
Additional: Bar food; Sunday L (noon-2pm); Children welcome
Seats: 56
Style: Rustic
Smoking: No-smoking area;
No pipes & cigars

HOVINGHAM,
Worsley Arms Hotel

High Street YO62 4LA
Map 8: SE67
Tel: 01653 628234
E-mail: worsleyarms@aol.com
Cost: Set-price D £25. H/wine £11
Times: D only, 7-10.30pm.
Additional: Bar food; Sunday L (noon-3pm); Children welcome
Style: Classic/Traditional
Smoking: No smoking in dining room
Civil licence: 90
Accommodation: 18 en suite ★ ★ ★

Directions: On B1257

Elegant restaurant, recently refurbished, offering a well balanced menu of interesting dishes, including pan-seared duck breast with honey glazed vegetables, and a well made lemon tart.

KNARESBOROUGH,
Dower House Hotel

Several adventurous dishes feature on the interesting menus at this intimate, candlelit restaurant. Roast loin of pork with fruit compote and a light sherry cream should please, followed by chocolate and malt tart on a coffee bean stock.

Additional: Bar food; Sunday L; Children welcome
Style: Bistro-style/Informal
Smoking: No smoking in dining room
Accommodation: 31 en suite ★ ★ ★

Directions: At Harrogate end of Knaresborough High Street

Bond End HG5 9AL
Map 8: SE35
Tel: 01423 863302
Fax: 01423 867665
E-mail:
enquiries@bwdowerhouse.co.uk
Cost: Alc £15-£23, set-price L £5.50-£10.90. ☺ H/wine £9.95
Times: Noon-2pm/ 7-9.30pm

KNARESBOROUGH,
General Tarleton Inn ❀❀

This former 14th-century coaching inn has been sympathetically restored, extended and adapted. The bars are beamed in olde worlde style, and do a brisk business serving excellent bar meals. The restaurant, which is only open in the evening, is formal, and characterised by its fine stone walls. Starters may include 'Little Money Bags' – seafood in a crisp pastry bag with lobster sauce; or terrine of ham shank and foie gras, or black pudding with smoked haddock and Yorkshire rarebit. Main dishes include braised lamb shank forestière cooked in its own juices – 'the lamb was excellent' – and served with lardons, onions and mushrooms. The influences here are mainly English and French: fillet of halibut with a soft herb crust and roast breast of Goosnargh duckling. Desserts include a delicious sticky toffee pudding. The wine list is imaginative and brilliantly complements the food.

Directions: A1M/Boroughbridge Junction. Follow A6065 (Knaresborough) for 3 miles to Ferrensby

Boroughbridge Road Ferrensby
HG5 0QB
Map 8: SE35
Tel: 01423 340284
Fax: 01423 340288
E-mail: gti@generaltarleton.co.uk
Chef: John Topham
Owners: Denis & Juliet Watkins, John Topham
Cost: Set-price D £25. ☺
H/wine £9.95
Times: D only, 7-9.30pm.
Closed D Sun
Additional: Bar food; Sunday L (Noon-2pm); Children welcome
Seats: 60. Private dining room 35
Style: Informal/Modern
Smoking: No smoking in dining room
Accommodation: 14 en suite ★ ★ ★

MALTON,

Burythorpe House Hotel ✸

Set price and carte menus offer a wide choice. Fish dish highlights include fillet of turbot en croûte with red onion salsa and grilled whole dover sole served off the bone with lemon garnish.

Telephone for further details

Directions: Edge of Burythorpe village, 4 miles S of Malton

Burythorpe YO17 9LB
Map 8: SE77
Tel: 01653 658200
Fax: 01653 658204
E-mail:
reception@burythorpehousehotel.com

MARKINGTON, Hob Green Hotel ✸

Good local produce and quality cooking are winners at this peaceful hotel. A Friday fish menu offers lots of choice, and from the daily menus expect wood pigeon with mango and rum sauce, or baked Barnsley chop.

Additional: Bar Food L; Sunday L; Children welcome
Style: Traditional/Country-house
Smoking: No pipes & cigars
Accommodation: 12 en suite ★ ★ ★

Directions: One mile W of village off A61

Harrogate HG3 3PJ
Map 8: SE26
Tel: 01423 770031
Fax: 01423 771589
Cost: Alc D £35, set- price L
£13.95/D £23.50. ☺ H/wine £10.95
Times: Noon-1.30pm/7-9.30pm

MIDDLEHAM, Waterford House ✸✸

Waterford House is an attractive period house situated just off the square in this Yorkshire village. Waterford is a small hotel, which probably could be described more accurately as a restaurant with rooms. The owners, Brian and Everyl Madell, are responsible for the cellar and kitchen respectively. The menus rely heavily on seasonal produce, and there is a choice between a smallish carte and the 'Waterford House Menu Bon Vivant'. Savouries arrive before the meal and then, by way of an introduction, an appealing green salad is served. Several classic dishes are offered on all the menus such as rack of Yorkshire lamb, sliced into cutlets, and tournedos Rossini which was an excellent fillet cooked to order. The tournedos was tender, flavoursome, and served on a garlic croûton paté, with wild mushrooms and a beautiful red wine and Madeira sauce. The dessert was the highlight of the meal, however, raspberry crème brulée with a perfect texture. The wine list is the preserve of Mr Madell and he guides customers skilfully through the list.

Kirkgate
DL8 4PG
Map 7: SE18
Tel: 01969 622090
Fax: 01969 624020
Chef: Everyl M Madell
Owners: Everyl & Brian Madell
Cost: Alc £25, set-price L £19.50/
D £22.50. ☺ H/wine £10
Times: Noon-2.30pm(reservations
only)/7-9.30pm
Additional: Sunday L; Children
welcome
Seats: 20
Style: Country-house
Smoking: No smoking in dining room
Civil licence: 24
Accommodation: 5 en suite ★

Directions: Just off Market Square

MIDDLEHAM,

White Swan Hotel ⊛⊛

Refurbishment and first-class interior design have brought real style to this old coaching inn on Middleham's market square, although the original beams and flagged floors remain, and open fires are lit in winter. Eating in the bar is a possibility, but foodies pile into the restaurant for the up-to-the-minute menu that runs from merguez sausage with roast vegetables and red pepper dressing to chicken breast topped with crisp pancetta with wild mushroom sauce and tarragon and cream potatoes. An oriental influence is brought to some dishes – tempura of scallops with chilli chutney, commendably crisp batter enclosing soft seafood, and smoked chicken fishcakes with spicy tomato salsa – while the Mediterranean shines out of others: chunky fish soup, or pistou salad. Sauces show good judgement and skill: thyme and juniper with duck breast, a drizzle of a rich, deep red wine sauce with grilled fillet of sea bass with roasted vegetables, and a sharp berry coulis cutting the richness of chocolate mousse. Staff are friendly but unobtrusive and are happy to recommend wines from the extensive list.

Market Place DL8 4PE
Map 7: SE18
Tel: 01969 622093
Fax: 01969 624551
E-mail: whiteswan@easynet.co.uk
Chef: Andy Morris
Owners: Christine & Richard Wager
Cost: Alc £20. ☺ H/wine £8
Times: Noon-2pm/6.30-9pm
Additional: Bar food; Sunday L; Children welcome
Seats: 50. Private dining room 20
Style: Traditional
Smoking: No-smoking area
Accommodation: 11 en suite ★★

Directions: Exit A1 at Leeming Bar, take A684 to Leyburn, then take A6108 to Ripon, 1.5m to Middleham

MIDDLESBROUGH,

The Purple Onion ⊛⊛

French brasserie Les Halles-style with a dash of San Francisco, where gold mirrors, ornate brass ceiling fans, palms and other exotica set the scene for a fun and funky venue. Naturally purple onion soup is an appetiser on the evening menu, served bistro-style topped with a Swiss-cheese croûton. A house speciality is *cioppino di mare*, a San Francisco fish stew, including half a lobster, mussels, tiger prawns, squid, salmon, halibut, sole, crab and clams in a tasty tomato and chilli broth. There's a daily fresh fish board, vegetarian options and an entrées list with chargrilled steaks, pan-fried chicken, and oven-baked rump of lamb with bubble-and-squeak.

80 Corporation Road TS1 2RF
Map 8: NZ41
Tel: 01642 222250
Fax: 01642 248088
E-mail: purpleonion@ndirect.co.uk
Chefs: Graeme Benn, Tony Chapman, Bruno McCoy
Owners: John McCoy & Bruno McCoy
Cost: Alc £12. ☺ H/wine £10.95
Times: Noon-3pm/5.30-late. Closed D Sun, 25 & 26 Dec, 1 Jan
Additional: Bar food L; Sunday L; Children welcome
Seats: 80. Private dining room 26
Style: Bistro-style/Informal
Smoking: No-smoking area; Air conditioning
Civil licence: 60

Directions: Exit A66 at Hospitality Inn near Riverside Football Stadium. Restaurant centrally located nr Law Courts/Odeon Cinema

NORTHALLERTON,

The Golden Lion

Attractive period hotel where a new kitchen team is striving to achieve regional excellence by providing post-classical dishes served with cosmopolitan bravado. Real signs of talent were evident in a stunningly simple calves' liver and bacon main course.

High Street Dl7 8PP
Map 9: SE39
Tel: 01609 777411
Fax: 01609 773250

Cost: Alc £25.50, set-price L fr £3.95/D £11.95. ☺
H/wine £8.95
Times: Noon-2.30pm/7-9.30pm
Additional: Bar food; Sunday L; Children welcome
Style: Classic/Traditional
Smoking: No smoking in dining room
Civil licence: 90
Accommodation : 25 en suite ★ ★

Directions: From A684 take A167 through built-up area, take 3rd exit on rdbt to town centre. At 3rd rdbt turn L into High St

PICKERING,

Fox and Hounds
Country Inn ❀

Chef's specials like braised beef joint with rich flageolet bean and onion sauce, and chargrilled lamb steak with mash potato and mint gravy, supplement a lengthy carte at this traditional country inn. Tangy vegetables served separately.

Main Street Sinnington York
YO62 6SQ
Map 8: SE78
Tel: 01751 431577 ????? see stat
Fax: 01751 432791 ????

E-mail: foxhoundsinn@easynet.com uk
Cost: Alc £19.50. ☺ H/wine £10.50
Times: Noon-2.30pm/6.30-9pm
Additional: Bar food; Sunday L; Children welcome
Style: Classic/Traditional
Smoking: No smoking in dining room
Accommodation: 10 en suite ★ ★

Directions: In centre of Sinnington, 300 yards off A170 between Pickering and Helmsley

PICKERING,

White Swan ❀

Sixteenth century coaching inn re-born as a luxurious, relaxing hotel and restaurant. Extensive menu including seared pigeon and pea tart or crisp suckling pig with caramelised onion mash and black pudding.

Market Place YO18 7AA
Map 8: SE78
Tel: 01751 472288
Fax: 01751 475554

E-mail: welcome@white-swan.co.uk
Cost: Alc £22. ☺ H/wine £11.95
Times: Noon-3pm/7-9.30pm
Additional: Bar food; Sunday L; Children 3+
Smoking: No smoking in dining room
Accommodation: 12 en suite ★ ★

Directions: Between the church and steam railway station

RAMSGILL,
Yorke Arms ❀❀

Pateley Bridge HG3 5RL
Map 7: SE17
Tel: 01423 755243
Fax: 01423 755330
E-mail: enquiries@yorke-arms.co.uk
Owners: Gerald & Frances Atkins
Cost: *Alc* £24. ☺ H/wine £11.50
Times: Noon-2pm/7-9pm.
Closed D Sun (ex residents)
Additional: Bar food L; Sunday L;
Children welcome
Seats: 60. Private dining room 10
Style: Traditional country inn
Smoking: No smoking in dining room
Accommodation: 13 en suite ★ ★

Originally used for making cheese for a monastery, the Yorke
Arms takes its name from the family who established a
shooting lodge here in the 18th century. A sense of history still
pervades the creeper-clad building in a lovely location in
Nidderdale. A large 17th-century oak dresser decorated with
pewter dominates one end of the main restaurant, with its
Windsor chairs, wooden tables and polished floorboards. The
menu adds a modish twist to the traditional, so Yorkshire
hotpot (local lamb with ham hock) comes with parsley and
mushroom risotto, and beetroot relish accompanies salmon
cake. A test meal brought 'well-made', light scallop ravioli
topped with asparagus, and an 'excellent' calves' liver, 'cooked
just right', with black pudding and sweet potato mash. A
seasonal fruit tart, plum with Cassis sorbet, say, or 'lovely,
tangy' apricot dribbled with dark chocolate, are likely
puddings, alongside a savoury like Welsh rarebit with capers.
The wine list runs to around 70 bins.

Directions: Take B6265 from Ripon. Turn R in Pateley Bridge
for Ramsgill

ROSEDALE ABBEY,
Milburn Arms Hotel ❀❀

Pickering YO18 8RA
Map 8: SE79

Welcoming hotel, parts of which date back to the 16th century,
set in the centre of the village in a fold of the North Yorkshire
Moors. Diners have a choice between the bistro for informal
meals and the fine-dining Priory Restaurant. The latter is a
split-level room hung with two large wine-related tapestries.
The *carte* offers a choice of half a dozen starters, including
gravad lax of Scottish salmon with deep-fried tempura mussels,
and confit of rabbit and olive wrapped in filo pastry with a
lemon and thyme jus. Mains range from baked cod fillet with a
butter herb crust on a lobster and crayfish bisque, to marinated
topside of venison on julienne of savoy cabbage and parsnip,
with a gin and lemongrass reduction.

Tel/Fax: 01751 417312
E-mail: info@milburnarms.com
Chef: Stephen Turner
Owners: Terry & Joan Bentley
Cost: *Alc* £27. ☺ H/wine £8.95
Times: D only, 7-11pm.
Closed 25 Dec
Additional: Bar food; Sunday L (noon-
2.30pm); Children 8+ in restaurant
Seats: 60
Style: Country-house
Smoking: No smoking in dining room

Civil licence: 50
Accommodation: 11 en suite ★ ★

Directions: In village centre, 3 miles W of A170 at Pickering

SCARBOROUGH,
Wrea Head Country Hotel

Professional and friendly service in an oak-panelled restaurant with view of wooded and landscaped gardens. An extensive wine list ensures the right match for dishes such as grilled breast of chicken on sweet honey couscous.

Scalby YO13 0PB
Map 8: TA08
Tel: 01723 378211
Fax: 01723 355935
E-mail: wreahead@englishrosehotels.co.uk
Cost: Alc £35, set-price L £12.50/D £25. H/wine £13.50
Times: Noon-2pm/7-9.15pm
Additional: Bar food; Sunday L; Children welcome
Style: Traditional/Country-house
Smoking: No smoking in dining room
Civil licence: 40
Accommodation: 20 en suite ★ ★ ★

Directions: Take A171 N from Scarborough, past Scalby village until hotel is signposted

SELBY, **Restaurant Martel** **NEW**

This new restaurant is housed in a magnificent Georgian hall previously used as a hunting lodge. The decor is in keeping with the building, with an element of modernism which is meant to reflect the style of the food. The walls are painted a lemon colour and hung with interesting pictures and military silks. The chef has previously worked with Marco Pierre White whose influence is there to be seen in the menus. In conjunction with the *carte*, there is also a lunch menu. The kitchen provides excellent brown and white bread rolls. A starter of ravioli of crab with stirfry vegetables on sweet and sour sauce lacked flavour but the pasta was very light. A main course of duck breast, cooked pink, faired much better. This dish had a deep rich flavour and the duck had a lovely crisp skin. Fresh and vibrant young vegetables were well chosen to match the dish and the port sauce was wonderful. The superb puddings included a crème brûlée with raspberries. The wine list is predominantly French but also covers several alternatives from the New World as well as Spain, Italy and Germany. This is a safe list and to its credit includes many half-bottles.

Gateforth Hall Gateforth YO8 9LJ
Map 8: SE63
Tel: 01757 228225
Fax: 01757 228189
E-mail: martel@uk.packardbell.org
Chef: Martel Smith
Owners: Martel & Zoe Smith
Cost: Alc £30, set-price L £14.50 & £17. ☺ H/wine £ 12.75
Times: Noon-2pm/7-10pm.
Closed L Sat, D Sun, all Mon
Additional: Children welcome
Seats: 43
Style: Modern/Country-house
Smoking: No-smoking area

Directions: From A1 take A63 signed Selby. Through Monk Fryston, turn R at garage & L at bottom of road. Approx 2m follow sign for restaurant on L

SKIPTON,
Coniston Hall Lodge **NEW**

The Bistro is housed in a 17th-century barn with flagstone floors and stone walls. Seared scallops with cucumber beurre blanc made a delightful start to a satisfying meal.

Additional: Bar food; Sunday L; Children welcome
Style: Bistro-style
Smoking: No smoking in dining room
Civil licence: 40
Accommodation: 40 en suite ★ ★ ★

Directions: On A65, 5m NW of Skipton

Coniston Cold BD23 4EB
Map 7: SD95
Tel: 01756 748080
Fax: 01756 749487
E-mail: conistonhall@clara.net
Cost: Alc £22.50, set-price £14.95. ☺ H/wine £9.95
Times: 11.30-5pm/6-10pm

SKIPTON, Devonshire Arms 🏵️🏵️

Fine country house hotel, owned by the Duke and Duchess of Devonshire, and set by the River Wharf in the heart of the Yorkshire Dales. The Burlington Restaurant is traditional in design and furnished with antiques from Chatsworth House, while the brasserie provides a less formal alternative. Local produce, some grown in the hotel's own gardens, is a feature of both menus. Dishes from a spring menu in the Burlington included assiette of rabbit (pie, liver and fillet), Mansergh Hall lamb with Anna potatoes, Puy lentils and tomato jus, and nougatine parfait, passion fruit sorbet and raspberry coulis. New chef Steve Williams will be making his mark in the coming months and the menus will see some changes.

Civil Licence: 120
Accommodation: 41 en suite ★ ★ ★

Directions: On B6160 to Bolton Abbey, 250 yards N of A59 roundabout junction

Bolton Abbey BD23 6AJ
Map 7: SD95
Tel: 01756 710441
Fax: 01756 710564
Chef: Steve Williams
Owners: The Duke & Duchess of Devonshire
Cost: Set-price D £42. H/wine £14.50
Times: D only, 7-10pm
Additional: Sunday L (noon-4pm); Children welcome
Seats: 80. Private dining room 4-90. Jacket & tie preferred
Style: Country-house/Formal
Smoking: No smoking in dining room

SKIPTON,

Hanover International Hotel 🏵️

Watery themes in the decor mirror the delightful views over the adjacent canal to the countryside beyond. The daily changing set-price menu might include chicken breast in a wild mushroom sauce, grilled trout or vegetable stir fry.

Additional: Bar food; Children welcome
Style: Chic/Modern
Smoking: No smoking in dining room
Civil licence: 200
Accommodation: 75 en suite ★ ★ ★

Directions: From M62 J26 onto M606, follow signs for A650 (Keighley), then A629 (Skipton). Hotel 1 mile S of town centre

Keighley Road BD23 2TA
Map 7: SD95
Tel: 01756 700100
Fax: 01756 700107
Cost: Set-price D £15.95. ☺
H/wine £9.95
Times: D only fr 7pm. Closed 25 & 26 Dec

STADDLE BRIDGE,

McCoys (Tontine Inn) 🏵️🏵️

Restored with considerable faith back in 1979, and in the intervening 21 years, the investment has been amply rewarded. The restaurant is a comfortable mismatch of colours, and menus are elegantly hand-written. It has, in common with such restaurants as the River Café in London and Rick Stein's in Padstow, a confidence in its daily menu – making a choice difficult. The food is presented with confidence, and though the place may not have quite the subtlety of those other establishments, the food is correctly served. Grilled English muffins, smoked salmon and scrambled eggs are served with crisp pancetta and chive beurre blanc which was a 'delightful blend of robust flavours'. The eggs were creamy, fluffy, light and 'superbly' seasoned. A charcoal-grilled chicken breast with guacamole, chilli oil and tomato salad was astutely judged. The style and standards are extremely good, and service is comfortably informal.

Directions: At the junction of A19 & A172, Stokesley road

Northallerton DL6 3JB
Map 8: SE49
Tel: 01609 882671
Fax: 01609 882660
Chef: Marcus Bennett
Owners: Tom McCoy, Eugene McCoy
Cost: Alc £28. H/wine £12.75
Times: Bistro noon-2pm/7-10pm /Restaurant D only Fri & Sat. Closed 25 & 26 Dec, 1 Jan
Additional: Bar food; Sunday L; Children welcome
Seats: 26 (Bistro 70). Private dining rooms 14 & 30
Style: Eclectic
Smoking: Air conditioning

SUTTON ON THE FOREST,
Rose & Crown

A pretty converted inn, set in the heart of this charming village. Enter the restaurant and there is a small, wooden-floored bar with terracotta walls and a Mediterranean feel, and move through to the bright sunny dining room with pale yellow walls that continues the theme. The short menu (four choices at each course) is supplemented by specials from the blackboard – maybe pan-fried scallops with sweet chilli dressing or fillet of turbot with mussels. A recent inspection meal took in chicken and duck terrine with a balsamic reduction -a 'good dense terrine', wrapped in a fine jacket of Parma ham. A main course of roasted monkfish on saffron risotto with king prawns and asparagus was a thick chunk of fish with a crispy golden top, pan-fried in butter, and the risotto was creamy and well made.

Main Street YO61 1DP
Map 8: SE56
Tel: 01347 811333
Fax: 01347 811444

Telephone for further details

Directions: Telephone for directions

TADCASTER,
Hazlewood Castle

The castle is on a grand scale and Restaurant 1086 is a fascinating room with decent music, goldfish, comfy chairs, and interesting frescos (clouds above and unfinished plaster to the sides). The Big Idea menu provides superb value, and is available 12 noon-2pm, 6-6.45pm Tuesday to Friday and all evening Monday. The Hazlegrill Kitchen menu offers no nonsense fare – smoked salmon, sirloin steak and steamed syrup sponge. The main menu fields an excellent choice of interesting dishes: a creamy Yorkshire risotto of braised fennel and lamb shank; roast fillet of sea bass with mussel, saffron and tomato broth and, the highlight, prune and custard tart with apple and cider sorbet. The wine list is fun, and there is a wine table where guests are encouraged to choose their wine from the label.

Paradise Lane Hazlewood LE24 9NJ
Map 8: SE44
Tel: 01937 535353
Fax: 01937 530630
E-mail: info@hazlewood-castle.co.uk
Chefs: John Benson-Smith & Matthew Benson-Smith
Cost: *Alc* £29.50, set-price L £17.50/D £29.50 & £35. ☺
H/wine £14.95
Times: Noon-2pm/6-9.30pm.
Closed D Sun, L Mon & Sat
Additional: Sunday L; Children welcome
Seats: 80

Style: Rustic/Modern
Smoking: No smoking in dining room;
Air conditioning
Accommodation: 21 rooms ★ ★ ★

Directions: Signed from A64, W of Tadcaster

WEST WITTON,
Wensleydale Heifer Inn

Traditional inn dating from 1631 offering country cooking served at candlelit tables; perhaps sea bass with olive crust and basil purée, or fillet of beef with braised oxtail.

Additional: Bar food; Sunday L; Children welcome
Style: Rustic/Traditional
Accommodation: 14 en suite ★ ★

Wensleydale DL8 4LS
Map 8: SE08
Tel: 01969 622322
Fax: 01969 624183
E-mail: heifer@daelnet.co.uk
Cost: *Alc* £26.25, set-price D £19.50 & £24.50. ☺ H/wine £9.95
Times: Noon-2pm/7-9pm

Directions: From Leyburn take A684 towards Hawes. 4 miles to West witton, inn on R

YARM, Judges Hotel 🏵🏵

Kirklevington TS15 9LW
Map 8: NZ41
Tel: 01642 789000
Fax: 01642 782878

Telephone for further details

A former judge's lodgings, this country mansion is set amid beautiful gardens and parkland. Much thought and care is evident in the presentation of the food. Three home made and 'fresh from the oven' canapés were delivered to the lounge, of which a Stilton choux pastry was the highlight. The starter chosen in the restaurant was also a winner, a fine combination of roasted smoked haddock on a crisp potato and parsnip rösti with slightly garlicky spinach and a soft poached egg. The main course was another good match, breast of tender duck on a pool of plum sauce, accompanied by bacon lardons, mixed greens and pommes cocotte. Dessert was a simple but effective banana soufflé with a light chocolate sauce. Attention to detail extended to home-made petits fours served with coffee.

Directions: From A69 take A67 towards Kirklevington, hotel 1.5 miles on left.

YORK,
Ambassador Hotel 🏵

123 The Mount YO24 1DU
Map 8: SE65
Tel: 01904 641316
Fax: 01904 640259
E-mail: stay@ambassadorhotel.co.uk
Cost: Set-price D £19.50. ☺
H/wine £10.50
Times: D only, 6.30pm-11.30pm.
Closed 25 Dec
Additional: Bar food L;
Children welcome
Style: Classic/Informal
Smoking: No smoking in dining room
Civil licence: 50
Accommodation: 25 en suite ★ ★ ★

Spacious hotel restaurant with large round candlelit tables, warm colours and a grand piano. Cuisine is primarily English although some international influenced dishes are offered. Try leg of duck stuffed with Cumberland sausage.

Directions: 5 minutes walk from city centre, near junction of A1036 and A59

YORK, Dean Court Hotel ✿

Duncombe Place YO1 7EF
Map 8: SE65
Tel: 01904 625082
Fax: 01904 620305
E-mail: info@deancourt-york.co.uk
Cost: Alc £30, set-price L £14.50/D
£25. ☺ H/wine £11.75
Times: 12.30-2pm/7-9.30pm
Additional: Bar food; Sunday L;
Children 6+ at D
Style: Classic/Informal
Smoking: No smoking in dining room
Civil licence: 50
Accommodation: 39 en suite ★ ★ ★

Spacious and airy traditional hotel dining room with wonderful views towards York Minster. Seasonal ingredients are a strong feature and fresh fish dishes such as seared collops of monkfish are a particular attraction.

Directions: City centre, directly opposite York Minster

YORK, Grange Hotel ✿✿

1 Clifton YO30 6AA
Map 8: SE65
Tel: 01904 644744
Fax: 01904 612453
E-mail: info@grangehotel.co.uk
Chef: David Bates
Owner: Jeremy Cassel
Cost: Alc £30, set-price L £14/D £25.
H/wine £10
Times: Noon-2pm/7-10pm. Closed L
Sat, L Sun
Additional: Children welcome
Seats: 35. Private dining room 60
Style: Classic
Smoking: No smoking in dining room
Civil licence: 60
Accommodation: 30 en suite ★ ★ ★

Just a few minutes' walk from the centre, this Regency town-house hotel has two eating options apart from the restaurant: a seafood bar and a basement brasserie. The Ivy Restaurant is made up of two rooms, one small and square with a trompe l'oeil marquee, its 'sides' pulled open to reveal a racecourse, and the other more clubby, with deep-red walls hung with prints. The kitchen gives a modern spin to classics, so duck foie gras and rabbit terrine turns up with pickled walnuts, while main-course loin of lamb is topped with a mint soufflé and sauced with a light tomato and mint gravy. An inspector started with plump, sweet roasted scallops with herb risotto and went on to a main course of roast partridge, the meat nicely moist, with super-smooth parsnip purée with Bayonne ham and a well-balanced sauce of port and pepper. Fish-eaters might have the chance of fillet of turbot in a red wine sauce with roasted leeks, and chocoholics could go for dark chocolate tart with espresso and Mascarpone cream, with apple and blackberry charlotte – a good example of its kind – among fruitier puddings.

Directions: 400yds to N of city walls on A19

YORK,
Knavesmire Manor Hotel ❀

302 Tadcaster Road
YO24 1HE
Map 8: SE65
Tel: 01904 702941
Fax: 01904 706274
E-mail: knavesmire@easynet.co.uk
Cost: Alc £18, set-price D £14.50. ☺
H/wine £9.50
Times: D only, 6.30-9.30pm.

Knavesmire Manor is the former home of the Rowntree family, overlooking York racecourse, and the Brasserie, decorated in Edwardian style, provides the perfect setting for some lively food.

Additional: Sunday L (noon-2pm); Children welcome
Style: Classic/country-house
Smoking: No smoking in dining room
Civil licence: 50
Accommodation: 21 en suite ★ ★

Directions: A64 to York, then A1036 York-Bishopthorpe leads on to Tadcaster Rd. Hotel on left overlooking racecourse

YORK, Melton's ❀❀

7 Scarcroft Road YO23 1ND
Map 8: SE65
Tel: 01904 634341
Fax: 01904 635115
Chefs: Michael Hjort &
Adam Holliday
Owners: Michael & Lucy Hjort
Cost: Alc £25, set-price L £15.50/D
£20. ☺ H/wine £12
Times: Noon-2pm/5.30-10pm.
Closed L Mon, D Sun; 3 wks Xmas,
1 wk end Aug
Additional: Sunday L; Children
welcome
Seats: 30. Private dining room 16
Style: Individual
Smoking: No-smoking area; Air
conditioning

The Hjorts have given themselves tenth birthday presents: a wooden floor instead of carpet, banquette seating under the murals and pictures, more mirrors, tablecloths, even air-conditioning. Customer-friendliness extends to an appealing set-price lunch and a cut-price early-evening menu that deals in the likes of salt-cod salad with eggs and olives, and roast fillet of gurnard under a mustard and herb crust. The eclectic *carte* holds much of interest, too, from mackerel escabèche with coriander and ginger, to daube of beef with citrus persillade, or oriental bream with stir-fried vegetables. An inspector enjoyed a starter of prawn and gravad lax feuilleté and went on to devilled chicken of deep and bold flavours served with 'excellent' saffron risotto, then concluded with a 'winner' of 'the lightest of light' passion fruit tart. A good wine list and prices that include mineral water, coffee and service all add to the comfort factor.

Directions: From centre head south across Skeldergate Bridge, restaurant opposite Bishopthorpe Road car park

YORK, Middlethorpe Hall ❀❀❀

Bishopthorpe Road
Middlethorpe YO23 2GB
Map 8: SE65
Tel: 01904 641241
Fax: 01904 620176
E-mail: info@middlethorpe.com

Only a mile and a half from the centre, overlooking the racecourse, this large, beautifully-proportioned country house, built in 1699, is in 20 acres of attractive gardens and parkland. Furnished and decorated in keeping with its age, the hall is

Middlethorpe Hall

Chef: Martin Barker
Owner: Historic House Hotels
Cost: Set-price L £21.50/D £37.50.
H/wine £13.90
Times: 12.30-1.45pm/7-9.45pm.
Closed L 25 Dec (ex residents)
Additional: Sunday L; Children 8+
Seats: 60. Private dining room 14-50.
Jacket & tie preferred
Style: Traditional/country-house
Smoking: No smoking in dining room
Accommodation: 30 en suite ★ ★ ★

sumptuously and elegantly comfortable, with deep sofas, antiques and oil paintings throughout. The restaurant, divided into three rooms, is oak-panelled, with big shuttered windows overlooking the gardens, and if it seems formal (gentlemen are required to wear jacket and tie) the staff are friendly and enthusiastic. Martin Barker's Menu of the Month, taking in such luxuries as lobster and truffles, runs alongside a set-price dinner menu generous in its choice, with a separate section for vegetarians. 'Traditional English' is the self-declared style, and indeed ingredients have good pedigrees, but a more global influence is behind most of the kitchen's output: mussels go into a minestrone with pistou, and roast duck is flavoured with five spice and partnered by wild rice. Precision never falters, from the earthy, aromatic flavours of cep risotto with thyme and garlic oil – 'absolutely heavenly' – to roast sea bass in a light, well-balanced red wine sauce on wilted spinach, with Parmentier potatoes and roasted vegetables adding another dimension of texture. Puddings are no less successful, represented by lemon tart, 'first-class' passion fruit sorbet, and Grand Marnier soufflé. Canapés, appetisers – perhaps lightly textured seafood mousse – and breads have all been singled out, and the wine list is what you'd expect in the surroundings.

Directions: 1.5 miles S of York, next to the racecourse

YORK, Mount Royale ❀

The Mount YO24 1GU
Map 8: SE65
Tel: 01904 628856
Fax: 01904 611171
E-mail:
reservations@mountroyale.co.uk

The elegant restaurant overlooks the garden. The menu might offer chicken liver parfait with tomato and apple chutney, and fillet of halibut with king prawn, saffron and Champagne sauce.

Telephone for further details

Directions: W on A1036, towards racecourse

YORK, York Pavilion Hotel ❀❀

45 Main Street Fulford YO10 4PJ
Map 8: SE65
Tel: 01904 622099
Fax: 01904 626939
E-mail: anna@yorkpavilionhotel.co.uk
Chef: David Spencer
Owners: Andrew Cossins &
Irene Cossins
Cost: Alc £25, set-price L £14.95/D
£23. ☺ H/wine £11.95

Tourists and traffic can make York hard-going sometimes, so it's always a relief to have a little oasis of comfort and calm to retreat to. The attractive Georgian hotel is situated in its own gardens and grounds to the south of the city with a brasserie-style restaurant that features a regularly-changing menu with many daily specials. The cooking is stylish and confident – mackerel, lime and ginger fishcake on thai coconut noodles came in for a 'super' accolade. Juicy, full-flavoured rack of

York Pavilion Hotel

Times: Noon-2pm/6.30-9.30pm
Additional: Sunday L; Children welcome
Seats: 80. Private dining rooms 8-30
Style: Bistro-style/Brasserie
Smoking: No-smoking area
Civil licence: 130
Accommodation: 57 en suite ★ ★ ★

Directions: From York city centre head S on A19 (Selby), hotel 2 miles on L

lamb was imaginatively presented on a hotpot of potatoes with a rich rosemary jus. Other choices might include spinach and ricotta tart with marinated mushrooms and tarragon salad or roast fillet of salmon with horseradish mash, wilted rocket, red wine and beurre blanc. An intriguing twist on an old-fashioned homely technique is a pheasant and chestnut steamed suet pudding with parsnip mash and crispy grilled pancetta.

YORKSHIRE SOUTH

CHAPELTOWN, Greenhead House

84 Burncross Road Sheffield S35 1SF
Map 8: SK39
Tel/Fax: 0114 2469004
Cost: Alc £30. H/wine £12.50
Times: Noon-1pm/7-9pm. Closed L Wed & Sat, all Sun-Tue, Xmas-New Year, 2 wks Etr, last 2 wks Aug

With its own walled garden, Greenhead House has a country feel in an otherwise built-up area. An inspection meal took in pheasant and pork terrine, salmon and squid with olive oil and lemon sauce, and chocolate and chestnut macaroons.

Additional: Children 7+
Style: Country-house
Smoking: No smoking in dining room

Directions: M1 J35 follow signs to Chapeltown, straight across 2 roundabouts onto Burncross Rd. Restaurant is on R, 200mtrs

ROTHERHAM, Swallow Hotel ⊛

West Bawtry Road S60 4NA
Map 8: SK49
Tel: 01709 830630
Fax: 01709 830549
Cost: Set-price L £10.75/D £19.75. H/wine £12.50
Times: Noon-2pm/6.30-9.45pm. Closed L Sat

Open plan restaurant with an informal, modern feel. Culinary approach is modern British, for example an enjoyable venison and mushroom sausage. However signs of Mediterranean influence are evident in chargrilled shark steak with a piquant cream sauce.

Additional: Bar food L; Sunday L; Children welcome
Style: Informal/Modern
Smoking: No smoking in dining room; Air conditioning
Accommodation: 100 en suite ★ ★ ★

Directions: From the M1 J37 follow signs for Rotherham on A630. Proceed to end of dual carriageway, L at rdbt. Hotel on R

SHEFFIELD, Charnwood Hotel

10 Sharrow Lane S11 8AA
Map 8: SK38
Tel: 0114 258 9411
Fax: 0114 255 5107
E-mail:
king@charnwood.force9.co.uk
Cost: Alc £23.50, set-price D £15.25.
☺ H/wine £9.95
Times: D only, 6.30-10.30pm.
Closed Sun, Bhs
Additional: Bar food; Children
welcome
Style: Traditional/Parisienne
Smoking: No pipes & cigars
Civil licence: 90
Accommodation: 22 en suite ★★★

*Leo's brasserie makes an informal setting for some modern cooking
that takes in a very good hot and cold hors d'oeuvre plate –
including a smoked haddock with Welsh rarebit, and a goat's cheese
brûlée – and a good pecan pie soufflé.*

Directions: M1 J33 & A621. 1.5 miles SW of city centre, off
London Road

SHEFFIELD,
Milano Restaurant

Stone-built Grade II listed former police station – also a park-
keeper's lodge in its time – the interior of which has been
dramatically transformed to create a vibrantly decorated
restaurant, comprising two dining areas, a large foyer and bar
area. To the rear is a south-facing terrace where tapas are
served in the summer. The name Milano is a bit of a red
herring – it is not an Italian restaurant. The food takes its
influences from around the globe – king prawns cooked in
coconut milk with lime and chilli; roast Old Spot chop with
cumin potatoes, hummus and dates; and leg of Goosenargh
chicken with aubergine and Moroccan spices. Puddings range
from lemon tart with iced meringue parfait to spotted dick
with butterscotch sauce.

Directions: Telephone for directions

Archer Road Millhouses
S8 0LA
Map 8: SK38:
Tel: 0114 2353080
Fax: 0114 2353010
Chefs: Jason Fretwell, Nick Long
Owners: Mr G Bohan, Mr P Brady,
Mr M Mori
Cost: Alc £26, set-price D £10.95 &
£12.95. ☺ H/wine £9.75
Times: D only 6-10pm. Closed Sun
Additional: Children 12+
Seats: 66. Private dining room 28
Style: Chic/Minimalist
Smoking: No-smoking area; No pipes
& cigars; Air conditioning

SHEFFIELD,
Mosborough Hall Hotel

*16th-century manor house convenient for both the M1 and the city
centre. Our test meal produced a good piece of smoked haddock on
a perfect Parmesan risotto, Barbary duck with a shallot confit and
Baileys brûlée.*

Additional: Bar food; Sunday L; Children welcome
Style: Traditional/country-house
Smoking: No-smoking area
Civil licence: 80
Accommodation: 23 en suite ★★★

Directions: Hotel on A616, 5 miles from M1 J30

High Street Mosborough S20 5EA
Map 8: SK38
Tel: 0114 2484353
Fax: 0114 2477042
Cost: Alc £26, set-price L £11.95/
D £16.95. ☺ H/wine £10
Times: Noon-2pm/7.30-10pm.
Closed L Sat, D Sun, Bhs

SHEFFIELD, Rafters Restaurant

The colour scheme is new – terracotta and lemon – but the cooking remains reliable and accomplished. Try slow roast cod with salsa verdi, or roast chicken with mushy peas, mustard mash and black pudding.

Smoking: No pipes & cigars
Credit cards: American Express only

Directions: Telephone for directions

220 Oakbrook Road
Nethergreen S11 7ED
Map 8: SK38
Tel/Fax: 0114 2304819
Cost: Set-price D £23.95. ☺
H/wine £9.50
Times: D only, 7-10pm.
Closed Sun, Tue, 1st 2 wks Aug
Additional: Children 5+
Style: Classic/Modern

SHEFFIELD,
Smith's of Sheffield

After five years, during which time it has gained a loyal following, Smith's is due for a change, and by the time this guide is published it should have a larger bar area and a spanking new decor. The menu will remain the same, however, to everyone's relief, as it cuts and weaves its way between the East (as in a starter of wonton of rich confit of Gressingham duck with slices of the breast accompanied by bamboo shoots, sweet chilli jam and wasabi-infused crème fraîche), the Med (provençale fish soup) and home base (for haddock deep-fried in beer batter with mushy peas and chips, or sausages and mash with black pudding). The sourcing of materials is taken seriously, resulting in such flavourful main courses as traditionally reared pork roasted in Parma ham served with a ragout of lentils and pancetta, and grilled fillet of Aberdeen Angus with duxelle and a jus of shallots, thyme and red wine. This quality is also noted in the fish, as in well-timed roast sea bass with a mixture of sautéed wild mushrooms. Flexibility shows a user-friendly approach, with some dishes available as both starters and mains – fishcakes, say, Caesar and Greek salads, or spaghetti with rocket, red pesto and Parmesan – and a good-value set-price menu running alongside the *carte* on weeknights. Finish with something traditional like rhubarb and apple crumble, served here in a tartlet, with smooth rhubarb coulis, vanilla sauce and vanilla ice cream. The wine list, arranged by style, is a well-assembled collection from around the world, with a decent number sold by the glass.

34 Sandygate Road
S10 5RY
Map 8: SK38
Tel: 0114 266 6096
Chef: Richard Smith
Owners: Richard & Victoria Smith & Sallie Tetchner
Cost: *Alc* £25, set-price D £17.50. ☺
H/wine £9.50
Times: D only, 6.30-10pm. Closed Sun, Mon
Additional: Children welcome
Seats: 60. Private dining room 20
Style: Bistro-style/Informal
Smoking: No smoking in dining room

Directions: From Sheffield centre take A57; at Crosspool turn R onto Sandygate Road. 100yds on R

YORKSHIRE WEST

BRADFORD, Apperley Manor

Spacious restaurant overlooking the gardens, where a fine opener of spicy salmon and cod fish cakes was followed by top quality rack of lamb set on a well made rösti.

Accommodation: Bar food; Sunday L; Children welcome
Style: Classic/Traditional   **Smoking:** No-smoking area
Accommodation: 13 en suite ★ ★ ★

Directions: On A658 Bradford to Harrogate road

Apperley Lane
Apperley Bridge BD10 0PQ
Map 7: SE13
Tel: 0113 2505626
Fax: 0113 2500075
E-mail: janette@apperley-manor.co.uk
Cost: *Alc* £20, set-price L £10.95/D £14.95. ☺ H/wine £9.45
Times: Noon-2pm/6.30-9.30pm.
Closed Mon & Tue

DEWSBURY,
Healds Hall Hotel ❀

Leeds Road Liversedge
WF15 6JA
Map 8: SE22
Tel: 01924 409112
Fax: 01924 401895
Cost: Alc £25, set-price L £9.50 &
£12/D £18.50. ☺ H/wine £8.25
Times: Noon-2.30pm/6.30-9.30pm.
Closed L Sat, D Sun (ex residents), Bh
Mon
Additional: Bar food L; Sunday L;
Children welcome
Style: Chic/Formal
Smoking: No smoking in dining room;
Air conditioning
Accommodation: 24 en suite ★★

An attractive 18th-century listed building in the heart of West Yorkshire. A strong local following testifies to the consistent quality of the modern British cuisine, which might include grilled fillet of hake on a bed of fennel.

Directions: On A62
Leeds/Huddersfield road near M1 J40
and M62 J26-27 (turn right at Swan
pub)

HALIFAX,
Holdsworth House Hotel ❀❀

Holdsworth HX2 9TG
Map 7: SE02
Tel: 01422 240024
Fax: 01422 245174
E-mail: info@holdsworthhouse.co.uk
Chef: Neal Birtwell
Owners: Gail Moss, Kim Pearson
Cost: Alc £25, set-price L £10. ☺
H/wine £10.95
Times: Noon-1.45pm/7-9.30pm.
Closed L Sat & Sun, Xmas
Additional: Bar food; Children welcome
Seats: 45. Private dining room 130
Style: Classic/Country-house
Smoking: No smoking in dining room
Civil licence: 120
Accommodation: 40 en suite ★★★

Built in 1633, Holdsworth is a splendid example of a yeoman's hall. Attractive gardens and a pretty courtyard outside, and a profusion of panelling, mullioned windows, open fires and antiques within. Dinner can extend to four courses, and the menu shows a kitchen working in the modern idiom, which translates into such starters as bruschetta with wild mushrooms, rocket and Pecorino dressed with olive oil, Thai-spiced prawns with lime, and potted beef with roasted red onion confit. Prime cuts and fine materials turn up among main courses: grilled Dover sole, tournedos Rossini, or chargrilled ribeye steak with pepper sauce for traditionalists, or perhaps a seasonal dish of pheasant poached in cider with winter vegetables. Fish is well handled, as in fillet of turbot with 'great' olive mash, plum tomatoes and basil, a combination of 'light, fresh and thoroughly enjoyable' flavours, while pudding may be the highlight of a meal: perhaps 'superb' mandarin and ginger soufflé with marmalade ice cream. The wine list, arranged by grape variety, holds much of interest.

Directions: From Halifax take A629
(Keighley), 2 miles turn R at garage to
Holmfield, hotel 1.5 miles on R

HAWORTH,
Weavers Restaurant

Follow the cobbled streets up to the Brontë Parsonage Museum and discover the rural cluttered charm of this delightful bar and restaurant. Traditional honest fare such as steak and kidney pudding sits alongside occasional hints of culinary modernity.

Additional: Bar food D; Children welcome
Style: Informal
Smoking: No smoking in dining room; Air conditioning
Accommodation: 3 en suite

Directions: From A629 take B6142 to Haworth centre, by Brontë Museum car park

15 West Lane BD22 8DU
Map 7: SE03
Tel: 01535 643822
Fax: 01535 644832
E-mail: colinandjane@aol.com
Cost: Alc £22.50, set-price D £13.50.
☺ H/wine £9.95
Times: D only, 6.30-9.30pm.
Closed Sun & Mon, 1 wk after Xmas,
1 wk Jun

HUDDERSFIELD,
The Lodge Hotel

Interesting food in an art-nouveau setting. Seasonal menus run to seafood in a Champagne and seaweed broth, and pavé of lemon sole and wild salmon with Parmesan crust on lobster bisque. Several dessert wines by the glass.

Additional: Bar food L; Children 5+
Style: Classic/Country-house
Smoking: No smoking in dining room
Accommodation: 12 en suite ★ ★

Directions: M62 J24 (Huddersfield), L at 1st lights (Birkby Road) then A629, R after Nuffield Hospital (Birkby Lodge Road), 100 yds on L

48 Birkby Lodge Road Birkby
HD2 2BG
Map 7: SE11
Tel: 01484 431001
Fax: 01484 421590
Cost: Set-price L £10.95-£14.95/D
£23.95. ☺ H/wine £10.95
Times: Noon-2pm/7.30-9.45pm.
Closed L Sat, D Sun, Bh Mons

HUDDERSFIELD, The Weavers Shed Restaurant

The Weaver's Shed was originally a cloth-finishing mill adjoined to the mill owner's residence. Now, it is a welcoming country restaurant-with-rooms with a style of cooking that shows both modern and classic influences, paralleling the blend of styles in the ensuite bedrooms. It is one of the few restaurants in the North to have its own kitchen garden, a one-acre plot that includes an orchard and extensive herb and vegetable gardens. The cooking emphasises clean, natural flavours and seasonal ingredients, simply prepared and presented: cream of celeriac soup; twice-baked Hawes Wensleydale soufflé; confit leg of Lunesdale duckling with 'hotpot' vegetables, french beans and duck essence. Market fish of the day is grilled, steamed or pan-seared with crushed new potaotes, lemon and parsley butter. Vegetarians benefit from the garden freshness with roast squash in sautéed flatcap, field and wild mushrooms with buttered jus of roast vegetables and cardamom. The sticky toffee pudding is as good as you'll find anywhere.

Directions: Telephone for directions

Acre Mill's Knowl Road
Golcar HD7 4AN
Map 7: SE03
Tel: 01484 654284
Fax: 01484 650980
E-mail: info@weavers-shed.demon.co.uk
Chefs: Ian McGunnigle, Robert Jones, Stephen Jackson, Cath Sill
Owners: Mr & Mrs Stephen Jackson
Cost: Alc £22, set-price L £13.95. ☺
H/wine £12.95
Times: Noon-2pm/7-10pm.
Closed Sat L, all Sun & Mon, 25 Dec, 31 Dec, 1 Jan
Additional: Children welcome
Seats: 65. Private dining room 32
Style: Country-house
Smoking: No pipes & cigars
Accommodation: 5 en suite

ILKLEY, Box Tree Restaurant ❀❀❀

Ilkley isn't the most obvious place to find this typically French town restaurant. There's a timeless quality to the warm and rich decor in shades of red, flamboyant ornaments and plethora of plates and paintings that adorn the walls, although some elements – crockery that's seen better days, dog-eared menus – seem a little frayed around the edges. The modern French and English cuisine is straightforward and makes use of quality ingredients. The most technically challenging dish sampled at a recent inspection was turbot stuffed with langoustines with langoustine sauce, but the more understated simplicity of confit of duck leg with ceps sauce ultimately proved the more successful. A terrine of duck foie gras, mi-cuit and set in its own fat, French farmhouse-style, also showed a kitchen that works best when it keeps to its natural idiom. Bavarois of artichoke with crab was also well-made, and tarte Tatin is paired with spiced bread ice cream. A choice of coffees, all ground to order, is a nice touch. The extensive wine list, with an outstanding range of clarets, has bargains for those who know their wines.

Directions: On A65, on the Skipton side of Ilkley near the church

35-37 Church Street
LS29 9DR
Map 7: SE14
Tel: 01943 608484
Fax: 01943 607186
E-mail: info@theboxtree.co.uk
Chef: Thierry Le-Prêtre-Granet
Cost: Alc £32.50, set-price L & D £19.50. ☺ H/wine £14
Times: 12.30-2.30pm/7-9.30pm. Closed D Sun, all Mon, Xmas-New Year, last 2 wks Jan
Additional: Sunday L; Children welcome
Seats: 50. Private dining room 16
Style: Classic/Traditional
Smoking: No smoking in dining room

ILKLEY,
Rombalds Hotel ❀❀

An elegant Georgian townhouse situated on the edge of Ilkley Moor; the restaurant, decorated in Wedgwood Blue, has high ceilings, alcoves and attractive cornices. Canapés are served in the bar and an appetiser to tickle the taste buds at the table. The modern European menu ranges through starters such as potato cake of feta cheese and apricot with tomato salsa vinaigrette, and a warm salad of chicken livers and chorizo sausage with rocket and balsamic dressing. Follow with lemon sole paupiettes, pheasant cassoulet with herb and lemon dumplings, or a vegetarian puff pastry case crammed with oyster mushrooms in a rosemary cream. Save room for a triple chocolate torte, or plum, orange and almond tart with sauce anglaise.

Directions: From A65 lights in town, turn up Brook Street, cross The Grove to Wells Road and hotel is 600 yds on L

11 West View Wells Road LS29 9JG
Map 7: SE14
Tel: 01943 603201
Fax: 01943 816586
E-mail: reception@rombalds.demon.co.uk
Chef: Andrew Davey
Owners: Colin & Joanna Clarkson
Cost: Alc £24.50, set-price L £9.95/ D £12.95. ☺ H/wine £9.75
Times: Noon-2pm/6.30-9pm
Additional: Bar food; Sunday L; Children welcome
Seats: 34. Private dining rooms 20 & 50
Style: Country-house
Smoking: No smoking in dining room
Civil licence: 70
Accommodation: 15 en suite ★★★

LEEDS,

Brasserie Forty Four 🕸🕸

44 The Calls LS2 7EW
Map 8: SE23
Tel: 0113 2343232
Fax: 0113 2343332
Chef: Jeff Baker
Owner: Michael Gill
Cost: *Alc* £22, set-price L/D £9.75 &
£12.95. ☺ H/wine £10.50
Times: Noon-2pm/6-10.30pm (11pm
Fri, Sat). Closed L Sat, all Sun, Bhs
Additional: Children welcome
Seats: 110. Private dining room 45
Style: Informal/Modern
Smoking: No pipes & cigars; Air
conditioning

Located in the restored Liverpool-Leeds Canal area known as
The Calls, the popular brasserie, housed in a former grainstore,
has colourful and comfy chairs, black wooden floors and white
painted block walls adorned with glass-encased cookery books.
The cooking style is appropriately youthful and cosmopolitan,
and our meal started well with a Roquefort and sweet onion tart,
but an overseasoned potted rabbit and foie gras terrine proved a
weak link. Good marks, however, for retro veal meatballs
Italienne with saffron risotto, and for charred yellowfin tuna on a
white bean purée with a coulis of Spanish peppers. Lively flavour
combinations add a vibrant edge to desserts such as a deliciously
light coconut crème caramel served with ripe, sweet pineapple
and a Malibu and orange coulis. As well as lunchtime specials
and evening early bird menus, there's a one-course light lunch
for a fiver. You can't beat that.

Directions: From Crown Point Bridge, L past Church, L into
High Court Road. On the river

LEEDS, Fourth Floor Café at Harvey Nichols 🕸

107/111 Briggate LS1 6AZ
Map 8: SE23
Tel: 0113 2048000
Fax: 0113 2048080
Cost: *Alc* £26, set-price L £16/D £18.
☺ H/wine £12.25
Times: Noon-3pm/6(7pm Sat)-
10.30pm. Closed Sun, D Mon-Wed,
25 & 26 Dec, 1 Jan
Additional: Children welcome
Style: Chic/Modern
Smoking: No-smoking area; Air
conditioning

Directions: In Harvey Nichols
department store

*All the style and sophistication you would expect from such a setting
both in decor and in cuisine. The* carte *menu might include falafel
cake with aubergine, chilli jam and a tomato and coriander dressing.*

LEEDS,
Haley's Hotel 🏵🏵

Shire Oak Road Headingley
LS6 2DE
Map 8: SE23
Tel: 0113 2784446
Fax: 0113 2753342
E-mail: sales@haleys.co.uk
Chef: Jon Vennell
Owner: John Appleyard
Cost: *Alc* £28.90, set-price L
£13.95/D £25. ☺ H/wine £12.25
Times: D only, 7.15-9.45 pm. Closed
D Sun, 26-30 Dec
Additional: Sunday L (12.15-2pm);
Children welcome
Seats: 52.
Private dining rooms 12 & 22

Named after a master stonemason, who was prominent in Leeds at the turn of the last century, Haley's Hotel consists of two elegant Victorian houses set in a quiet tree-lined cul-de-sac. The hotel is renowned for its proximity to Headingley Cricket Ground, but is also only two miles from Leeds city centre. While the style of the menus does not quite reflect Yorkshire's famously straightforward approach, the set-price menus remain the simplest: cream of broccoli soup, chicken liver parfait, pan-fried salmon and grilled sirloin of beef. The *carte* is more adventurous and most of the dishes here have an imaginative twist to them: a tartare of tuna is served with dressed beetroot, olive oil and sherry vinaigrette with garlic croûtons and a pan-fried fillet of beef with a mille feuille of asparagus and a tomato and red wine sauce. The desserts include the usual vogueish suspects such as lemon tart and tarte Tatin.

Style: Traditional/Country-house
Smoking: No smoking in dining room; Air conditioning
Civil licence: 52
Accommodation: 29 en suite ★★★

Directions: On A660 (Leeds/Otley) in Headingley between Lloyds and HSBC banks

LEEDS,
Leeds Marriott Hotel 🏵

A former jeweller's, still with the shop counter and many clocks in cases. An extensive menu encompasses grills, pasta dishes, and the likes of braised lamb shank with mint dumplings.

Additional: Bar food; Sunday L; Children welcome
Style: Bistro-style/informal
Smoking: No-smoking area; Air conditioning
Civil licence: 350
Accommodation: 244 en suite ★★★★

4 Trevelyan Square Boar Lane
LS1 6ET
Map 8: SE23
Tel: 0113 2366366
Fax: 0113 2442317
Cost: *Alc* fr £18.50. ☺
H/wine £12.75
Times: 12-30-2.30pm/6.30-11pm

Directions: From M1 or M62, follow signs to city centre, turn into Sovereign Street, L at lights, R into NCP car par, adjacent to Hotel

LEEDS,
Oulton Hall Hotel

Rothwell Lane Oulton LS26 8HN
Map 8: SE23
Tel: 0113 282 1000
Fax: 0113 282 8066
E-mail: oulton.hall@devere-hotels.com

The Brontë Restaurant pays decorative homage to the literary sisters.
Modern British dishes include pan-fried sea bass on fine beans and
asparagus with ginger butter, and a good caramel bavarois.

Cost: *Alc* £30, set-price L £15. ☺ H/wine £12.95
Times: 12.30-2.30pm/7-10pm.
Closed L Sat
Additional: Sunday L; Children welcome
Style: Classic
Smoking: No smoking in dining room. Jacket preferred
Accommodation: 152 en suite ★ ★ ★ ★ ★

Directions: M62 J30, follow signs to Rothwell

LEEDS,
Pool Court at 42 ❁❁❁

44 The Calls
LS2 7EW
Map 8: SE23
Tel: 0113 2444242
Fax: 0113 2343332
E-mail: poolcourt@aol.com
Chef: Jeff Baker
Owner: Michael Gill
Cost: Set-price L £14.50 & £19/D
£29.50 & £39. H/wine fr £13.95

Although it adjoins the hotel '42 The Calls', the restaurant is
independently operated, but shares the same cool,
sophisticated style. The decor is deep blue and white, with
gleaming chrome, pale blonde surfaces and pewter
decorative ice buckets. Long, heavy blue cloths dress the
tables with a crisp white linen overlay. The cooking is
balanced and considered; a starter of boudin blanc,

composed of corn-fed chicken and truffles, had pronounced flavours and a light, fluffy texture, accompanied by a parsley and celeriac remoulade. A superb cut of fresh turbot was meaty and succulent, given extra emphasis by the wrapping of Parma ham. Served with pressed spinach, sweet ripe vine tomatoes and tender roasted globe artichokes, it was 'a delight' to eat. The pace dropped slightly with a mango 'tarte au fine' which lacked fruity flavour although this was compensated by the happy combination of an intense passion fruit ice and sweet basil-scented sauce anglaise. Details are all good from the olives served with the aperitifs to the luxurious Belgian chocolate truffles that come with the coffee.

Directions: From M1 follow A61 (Harrogate) into city centre, cross River Aire via Crown Point Bridge. 2nd L at roundabout on to Maude St and you arrive at The Calls

Times: Noon-2pm/7-10pm (10.30pm Fri & Sat). Closed L Sat, all Sun, Bhs
Additional: Children welcome (ex babies)
Seats: 38
Style: Classic/Minimalist
Smoking: No smoking in dining room

LEEDS,

Rascasse

Canal Wharf Water Lane
LS11 5PS
Map 8: SE23
Tel: 0113 2446611
Fax: 0113 2440736
Chef: John Lyons
Owner: Nigel Jolliffe
Cost: Alc £31, set-price L & early D £13.50 & £17. ☺ H/wine £12
Times: Noon-2pm/6.30-10pm. Closed L Sat, all Sun, 1 wk after Xmas, Bh Mons
Additional: Children welcome
Seats: 100
Style: Chic/Modern
Smoking: No pipes; Air conditioning

Built in 1815 as a granary warehouse, Rascasse (named after one of the essential ingredients of bouillabaisse) is a large, split-level space with a spiral staircase leading up to the bar, wooden floors, mainly round tables, comfortable upholstered dining chairs and stainless-steel and glass screens. 'Trendy yet elegant' is how one diner described it. France is the restaurant's main inspiration. Mediterranean fish soup redolent of anise, Roquefort and walnut salad, and a generous portion of fondant of foie gras, ham hock and truffled haricots blancs ('good texture and flavour') have all appeared among starters. Grilled calves' liver and pancetta with sauce diable, pommes purée and braised cos lettuce made a noteworthy main. Fish is accurately timed, as in baked fillet of sea bass with beurre noisette, confit tomatoes, noodles and spring onions. Puddings wave the *drapeau tricolore* in the shape of soufflés (orange and Grand Marnier, or apricot), lemon tart and crème brûlée, while the wine list is surprisingly catholic, with around ten bottles sold by the glass.

Directions: 0.5 mile from M621 J3; follow signs to City Centre, turn L Water Lane, then R on Canal Wharf. On Canal Basin. 4 min walk from railway station

LEEDS,

Shear's Yard ❀

The Calls LS2 7EY
Map 8: SE23
Tel: 0113 2444144
Fax: 0113 2448102
E-mail: shearsyard@ydg.co.uk
Cost: *Alc* £22, set-price L /D £12.95.
☺ H/wine £11.95
Times: Noon-2.30pm/6-10.30pm.
Closed Sun, Bh Mon, 1 wk Xmas/New
Year

A converted riverside chandlery retaining many original features. A continental feel runs through both menus with dishes such as ravioli of goats' cheese and spinach and risotto of scallops setting a high standard.

Additional: Bar food; Children welcome
Style: Bistro-style/Informal
Smoking: No-smoking area; Air conditioning
Civil licence: 90

Directions: From Motorway follow signs for Leeds City Centre/loop road. Restaurant is at junction 15 of loop road

RIPPONDEN,

Over The Bridge Restaurant ❀

Millfold HX6 4DJ
Map 8: SE23
Tel: 01422 823722
Fax: 01422 824810
Cost: *Alc* £24.50. ☺
Times: D only, 7.30-9.30pm.
Closed Sun, Mon, Bhs
Additional: Children welcome
Style: Classic/Chic
Smoking: No pipes & cigars

The bridge in question links the Old Bridge Inn – a 14th-century monastic building – to this, its sister establishment, set in similarly picturesque converted weavers' cottages. A splendid venue for excellent food such as glazed duck breast.

Directions: M62 J22(E)/J24(W), A58 from Halifax, in village centre by church

WENTBRIDGE,
Wentbridge House Hotel ❀

WF8 3JJ
Map 8: SE41
Tel: 01977 620444
Fax: 01977 620148
E-mail: wentbridgehouse@
wentbridge.fsbusiness.co.uk
Cost: *Alc* £30, set-price L £14.50/D
£23. ☺ H/wine £12.50
Times: 12.15-2.30pm.
Closed D 25 Dec
Additional: Bar food L; Sunday L;
Children welcome
Style: Classic/Country-house
Smoking: No pipes
Civil licence: 70
Accommodation: 18 en suite ★★★

Traditional and classical cooking is the mainstay of this delightful wood-panelled restaurant. From a wide choice try medallions of venison with creamed celeriac and beetroot jus, or poached turbot with a cappuccino of lobster bisque and chervil oil.

Directions: 0.5 mile off the A1, 4 miles S of M62/A1 interchange

WETHERBY, **Wood Hall Hotel** ❀❀

Trip Lane
Linton LS22 4JA
Map 8: SE44
Tel: 01937 587271
Fax: 01937 584353

Telephone for further details

Stately Georgian residence set in 100 acres of parkland on a rise overlooking the River Wharfe. Public rooms are impressive, including the oak-panelled bar and elegant dining room. The menu reads well and offers a good range of imaginative dishes, like a starter of crispy duck confit with pickled baby vegetable salad and balsamic vinaigrette. Main courses encompass grilled sea bass with potato, tomato and spicy onion salad, and baked guinea fowl supreme with streaky bacon, dauphinoise potatoes and sage jus. Finish with a classic lemon tart with citrus sorbet.

Directions: In town, take turning opposite Windmill pub signed Wood Hall and Linton

CHANNEL ISLANDS
GUERNSEY

CATEL, Cobo Bay Hotel 🥕🥕

Popular family-run hotel overlooking Cobo Bay on the glorious west coast of Guernsey. The hotel has a loyal following with guests enjoying the spectacular sunsets from their balconies, and settling down to delicious modern European cooking in the candlelit dining room. Fresh seafood is one of the highlights on the interesting menu here. A salad of fresh hand-picked Guernsey spider crab and avocado pear whets the appetite, with its accompaniments of baby leeks, wilted leaf spinach and orange and Dijon mustard dressing. A fitting choice of main dishes includes seared Guernsey scallops with a twist – wrapped in panchetta, with spring onion, beetroot and cherry tomato salsa, balsamic reduction and sweet potato crisps, or perhaps roast fillet of fresh local sea bass, complemented by aubergine and sweet pepper caviar, spicy chorizo oil and roasted baby fennel. Guernsey fare also appears on the dessert menu with an inspired cinnamon pavlova infused with Guernsey cream liqueur and white chocolate, dark chocolate sauce and griottines.

Cobo GY5 7HB
Map: 16
Tel: 01481 257102
Fax: 01481 254542
E-mail: info@cobobay.guernsey.net

Telephone for further details

Directions: From St Peter Port, at roundabout go up hill to Cobo seafront, turn R

CATEL, La Grand Mare Hotel 🥕🥕

The Coast Road
Vazon Bay GY5 7LL
Map: 16
Tel: 01481 256576
Fax: 01481 256532
Chef: Fergus Mackay
Owners: Simon & Christopher Vermeulen
Cost: *Alc* £25, set-price L £12.50/D £17.95. ☺ H/wine £8
Additional: Bar food L; Sunday L; Children welcome
Seats: 80. Private dining room 30
Smoking: No-smoking area

Directions: 15 min from both St Peter Port and the airport. Hotel is opposite Vazon Bay

A hotel, golf and country club set right across the road from the beach. In this splendid location the hotel offers a wide range of sports and leisure activities, and no excuse needed either to be active or lazy. Inevitably much of the guest attention focuses on the restaurant, where classical French cooking takes the island's freshest ingredients – including fish and seafood – and gives them the gentlest of modern British handling. The result is shown on the impressive *carte*, where the choice includes some house specialities, including the hotel's famous crêpes Suzette, as well as a vegetarian menu, and a separate list of fish dishes. A typical dinner might begin with pressed game terrine with a quenelle of red onion marmalade and salad garnish, move on to pan-fried veal fillet filled with a tomato confit and a black olive and lime sauce, or perhaps fillet of Guernsey brill baked in foil with julienne of fennel and Mouton Cadet blanc, and finish up with a shortbread teardrop filled with cream and forest berries.

PERELLE, L'Atlantique Hotel

Perelle Bay St Saviours GY7 9NA
Map: 16
Tel: 01481 264056
Fax: 01481 263800
Chef: Richard Torode
Owner: Patrick Lindley
Cost: Alc £25, set-price L £11.95/D £17.50. ☺
Times: D only, 6.30-9.30pm. Closed Jan-Mar
Additional: Bar food; Sunday L (noon-2pm); Children welcome
Seats: 50
Style: Modern/Relaxed
Smoking: No-smoking area; No pipes & cigars; Air conditioning
Accommodation: 21 en suite ★★★

Sunset-spotting is a favoured pastime at this relaxed and modern hotel restaurant offering an excellent vantage point over the bay. Cuisine is a mixture of classic and modern. First courses might include a seared fillet of tuna which, on inspection, proved to be accurately peppered and served with a well judged bitter leaf salad an a thick clam and tomato broth. The main course demonstrated the great advantage this establishment has in its access to truly excellent local produce – a really excellent piece of sea bass well cooked with nicely caramelised fennel and new potatoes. Service is very traditional – both in its ritualised approach and in its attentive professionalism.

Directions: On west coast road overlooking Perelle Bay

ST MARTIN, La Barbarie Hotel

Saints Road Saints Bay GY4 6ES
Map: 16
Tel: 01481 235217
Fax: 01481 235208
E-mail: barbarie@guernsey.net
Cost: Alc £22.50, set-price D £14.95. ☺ H/wine £8.75
Times: Noon-2pm/6.15-9.30pm

Comfortable cottage-style hotel restaurant with cheerful service and an extensive, good value carte. Local fish dishes are top of the bill: salmon, crab and coriander cakes or seared seven spice sea bass to name but two.

Additional: Bar food L; Sunday L; Children welcome
Style: Informal/traditional
Smoking: No-smoking area
Accommodation: 33 en suite ★★★

Directions: At traffic lights in St Martin take road to Saints Bay – hotel is on R at end of Saints Road

ST MARTIN, Idlerocks Hotel ✸

Jerbourg Point GY4 6BJ
Map: 16
Tel: 01481 237711
Fax: 01481 235592
Cost: Alc £25, set-price D £14.50. ☺ H/wine £9.90
Times: Noon-2pm/6.30-9pm

The hilltop, seaside location of this informal and sophisticated hotel is quite breathtaking. The restaurant cuisine is comparable in its freshness and simplicity. Try fillet of salmon with Cajun seasoning, or grilled Mediterranean prawns.

Additional: Bar food L; Sunday L; Children welcome
Style: Informal/Traditional
Smoking: No smoking in dining room
Accommodation: 28 en suite ★★★

Directions: 5 mins drive from St Peter Port on main road

ST MARTIN,

St Margaret's Lodge ❀

Hotel restaurant overlooking the garden. An imaginative selection of dishes is offered, including good local seafood.

Telephone for further details

Directions: Out of airport, turn L. Follow road for 1 mile. Hotel on L

Forest Road GY4 6UE
Map: 16
Tel: 01481 235757
Fax: 01481 237594
E-mail: smlhotels@gtonline.net

ST PETER PORT,

The Absolute End ❀

An attractive fisherman's cottage situated on the 'absolute end' of the pier. Unsurprisingly seafood is the main focus and dishes such as local skate in black butter and capers sauce are a real treat.

Directions: Less than 1 mile from town centre, going N on seafront road to St Sampson

Longstore GY1 2BG
Map: 16
Tel: 01481 723822
Fax: 01481 729129
Cost: *Alc* £27.50, set-price L £12. ☺
H/wine £8.90
Times: Noon-2pm/7-10pm.
Closed Sun, Jan
Additional: Children 2+
Style: Classic/Traditional
Smoking: No-smoking area; No pipes & cigars; Air conditioning
Civil licence: 50

ST PETER PORT,

Battens ❀❀

An elegant, comfortable, spacious restaurant and cheerful modern brasserie with superb harbour views to the outer islands. Mediterranean influences are apparent with dishes like fillet of sea bass with aubergine caviar and roasted cherry tomato vinaigrette, or seared scallops with mizuna salad, sauce nero and watercress dressing. A more straightforward approach comes across in other dishes such as ham, parsley and potato terrine with toasted home-made bread and sultana chutney, followed by pan-fried breast of chicken served with a sweetcorn risotto and red wine sauce. The wine list is reasonably priced and offers a good selection of wines by the glass.

Directions: In the centre of St Peter Port

1 Fountain Street GY1 1DA
Map: 16
Tel: 01481 729939
Fax: 01481 729938

Telephone for further details

ST PETER PORT, Da Nello's

46 La Pollet GY1 1WF
Map: 16
Tel: 01481 721552
Fax: 01481 724235
Cost: *Alc* £20, set-price L £9.50/D
£15.95. ☺ H/wine £8.50
Times: Noon-2pm/6.30-10.30pm.
Closed Jan
Additional: Sunday L; Children
welcome
Style: Modern/Italian
Smoking: No-smoking area; Air
conditioning

*Impressively-refurbished eatery boasting a varied menu that
specialises in some excellent fish dishes -Scottish salmon or
Guernsey sea scallops. The menu offers alternatives such as chicken
breast with bresaola.*

Directions: In town centre, 100yds from North Beach
car park

ST PETER PORT, La Frégate

Les Cotils GY1 1UT
Map: 16
Tel: 01481 724624
Fax: 01481 720443
E-mail: lafregate@guernsey.net
Chef: Neil Maginnis
Owner: G.S.H Ltd
Cost: *Alc* £25, set-price L £14.50/D
£20. H/wine £9.50
Times: 12.30-1.45pm/7-9.45pm
Additional: Children 10+
Seats: 70. Private dining room 25.
Jacket & tie preferred
Style: Classic/Modern
Smoking: No pipes & cigars; Air
conditioning
Accommodation: 13 en suite ★ ★ ★

Spring 2000 brought a total refurbishment to the dining room
and bar of this 18th-century manor with panoramic views of
the harbour, and the terrace is now called into service for
alfresco dining in summer. Fish and shellfish figure
prominently, from half a lobster with mayonnaise, or home-
smoked coquilles St Jacques, to main courses of the catch of
the day (perhaps turbot or Dover sole, with a choice of
hollandaise or lobster butter), or sea bass with duxelle in a
parsley crust. The largely mainstream style can be pushed out
to accommodate scallops with spicy cabbage and beansprouts
and a soy dressing, or pot-au-feu de fruits de mer scented with
saffron and lemongrass, while meat eaters could choose from
steak tartare, strips of beef fillet stir-fried with ginger, garlic
and black beans, or rack of lamb carved at the table.
Pannacotta with raspberry compote, or crêpes Suzette bring
things to a satisfying conclusion, and the Eurocentric wine list
also has a page of New World bottles.

Directions: Town centre, above St Julian's Avenue

ST PETER PORT,

Merchant House Restaurant

The restaurant is centrally located in an 18th-century townhouse, which retains many original features. A nice variation on a theme was Thai-style moules marinière, followed by classic brill meunière.

38 High Street GY1 2JU
Map: 16
Tel: 01481 728019
Fax: 01481 725875

Cost: Alc £22, set-price L £10/D £12.50. ☺ H/wine £9.50
Times: Noon-1.45pm/6.45-9.30pm. Closed Sun
Additional: Children 6+
Style: Classic/Elegant
Smoking: No smoking in one dining room; No pipes & cigars

Directions: Telephone for directions

ST PETER PORT,

Le Nautique Restaurant ❀

Quay Steps GY1 2LE
Map: 16
Tel: 01481 721714
Fax: 01481 721786
Cost: Alc £25, set-price L £14.50/D £20. ☺ H/wine £8.30
Times: Noon-2pm/6.30-9.45pm. Closed L Sat, all Sun
Style: Classic/Traditional
Smoking: No pipes & cigars

An idyllic sea-side setting adds a real sense of romance to this converted stone warehouse with an attractively understated dining room. A beautifully translucent fillet of cod nicely balanced with a light mustard sauce typified the quality cuisine.

Directions: Sea front opposite Harbour and Victoria Marina

ST PETER PORT,

Old Government House Hotel ❀

Peruse the two menus whilst enjoying striking views of the town and harbour through large restaurant windows in this historic hotel. Complement the sea view with scallops on polenta, or try rack of lamb with thyme jus.

PO Box 47 Ann's Place
GY1 4AZ
Map: 16
Tel: 01481 724921
Fax: 01481 724429
E-mail: ogh@guernsey.net

Cost: Alc £23, set-price D £18.75. ☺ H/wine £9
Times: D only 7-9.45pm.
Additional: Sunday L (noon-2pm); Children welcome
Style: Classic/Traditional
Smoking: No-smoking area
Accommodation: 68 en suite ★ ★ ★ ★

Directions: Telephone for directions

ST PETER PORT,
St Pierre Park Hotel ❀❀

Rohais GY1 1FD
Map: 16
Tel: 01481 728282
Fax: 01481 712041
E-mail: stppark@itl.net
Chef: John Hitchen
Owner: Ann Street Brewery

Classic formal dining option in a spacious purpose-built hotel. A selection from the set menu might result in baked avocado and goats' cheese in filo, followed by local mushroom soup with sherry, leading into pan-fried breast of duck with a lentil and redcurrant jus, and concluding in caramelised lemon tarte with kumquat compote and crème fraîche. Alternatives from the *carte* include a good range of fresh fish dishes such as fillet of sea bass with a tomato and broad bean ragout and shellfish broth, or whole Dover sole with garlic spinach and a light lemon and veal reduction.

Cost: *Alc* £30, set-price L £14.50/D £21.50. ☺ H/wine £12.50
Times: Noon-2pm/7-10pm. Closed L Sat, D Sun
Additional: Sunday L; Children welcome
Seats: 70. Jacket & tie preferred
Style: Classic
Smoking: No-smoking area; Air conditioning
Accommodation: 135 en suite ★ ★ ★ ★

Directions: 1 mile from town centre on route to west coast

HERM

HERM,
White House Hotel ❀ NEW

Sit in the conservatory and look out to sea while you enjoy the formal country house surroundings and your menu of seared cutlet of salmon, or fricassée of oyster mushrooms with snipped chives and shallots.

Additional: Bar food L; Sunday L; Children 10+
Style: Country-house/Formal
Smoking: No smoking in dining room; Air conditioning; Jacket & tie preferred
Accommodation: 39 en suite ★ ★

GY1 3HR
Tel: 01481 722159
Fax: 01481 710066
E-mail: hotel@herm-island.com
Cost: Set-price D £18.80. ☺
H/wine £9
Times: 12.30-1.30pm/7-9pm.
Closed Oct-Etr

JERSEY

GOREY,

Jersey Pottery Restaurant ❀❀

Gorey Village JE3 9EP
Map: 16
Tel: 01534 851119
Fax: 01534 856403
E-mail: jsypot@itl.net
Chef: Tony Dorris
Owners: The Jones Family
Cost: L only, *Alc* £18. H/wine £11.50
Additional: Bar food L; Sunday L;
Children welcome
Seats: 250
Style: Informal
Smoking: No-smoking area

With grapevines overhead and a bounty of shellfish on the table, shear decadence awaits you. The conservatory-style surroundings afford plenty of natural light, and an abundance greenery and decorative pottery adds to Arcadian atmosphere. With dishes such as a pre-starter of squid, cockles and olives; a starter of melon with crab and prawns; and a main of whole Jersey lobster salad with prawns, this place is a true heaven for shellfish addicts. However if, like our inspector, a week or so in Jersey has more than sated your appetite in that direction you may be pleased to know that dishes such as roast sirloin of Scottish beef; and chicken, crispy bacon, avocado and rocket salad are all prepared with equal devotion and flair.

Directions: In Gorey village, well signposted from main coast road.

GOREY, **Suma's** ❀❀

Gorey Hill St Martins JE3 6ET
Map: 16
Tel: 01534 853291
Fax: 01534 851913
Chef: Shaun Rankin
Owners: Malcom Lewis &
Susan Duffy
Cost: *Alc* £28.50, set-price L £14.50.
☺ H/wine £8.75
Times: Noon-3pm/6.30-10pm.
Closed D Sun, 20 Dec-20 Jan
Additional: Sunday L; Children
welcome
Seats: 45
Style: Informal/Modern
Smoking: Air conditioning

Directions: Take A3 E from St Helier to Gorey. Restaurant is 100yds before harbour on L

Full length windows offer views of the harbour, boats and all things nautical. Inside, the restaurant is as much in touch with mainland metropolitan chic as it is with its idyllic surroundings – flashy maple bar and modern fittings cohabiting with whitewashed walls. The small but clearly hard working team offer service seven days and nights a week plus breakfast at weekends. The dinner menu is extensive with starters such as grilled Jersey scallops with braised oxtail and chestnut salad; and wild mushroom and bok parcel with white bean purée and a kaffir lime curry emulsion. Mains such as woodland mushrooms with crisp shallots and tarragon, and half Jersey lobster and crab salad with plum tomatoes and basil find favour with movers and shakers, yachties and tourists alike – particularly when the champagne is flowing (served by the glass.)

GOREY, **The Village Bistro** ❀❀

Gorey Village
JE3
Map: 16
Tel: 01534 853429
Chef: David Cameron

This small, intimate restaurant really delivers in flavours and service. An old church building in the middle of the village is the setting. The decor follows a sun, moon and stars theme with

The Village Bistro

Owners: David Cameron & Sandra Daziel
Cost: Alc £26.50, set-price L £13.50.
☺ H/wine £7.50
Times: Noon-2pm/7-10pm. Closed L Tue-Thu, all Mon, 2 wks Oct (half term), 2 wks Feb (half term)
Additional: Sunday L; Children welcome
Seats: 40
Style: Bistro-style/Informal
Smoking: No pipes & cigars

Directions: Village centre

blues and yellows achieving a bistro feel whilst maintaining a good measure of rustic informality. An inspector's choice of starters produced a paté with the texture and lightness of a mousse, 'quennelled' onto crisp croutons and sitting on top of a thin julienne of French beans tossed in a walnut vinaigrette. A main of steamed fillet of brill in a shellfish cream offered fish of unquestionable quality; a well flavoured cream; and a dish of perfectly cooked vegetables with strong, distinctive flavours fully retained. Desserts include chocolate fondant with pistachio ice cream, and panecotta with shortbread and local strawberries served with a strawberry coulis.

ROZEL, Château La Chaire

JE3 6AJ
Map: 16
Tel: 01534 863354
Fax: 01534 865137
E-mail: res@chateau-la-chaire.co.uk
Chef: Simon Walker
Owners: Hatton Hotels
Cost: Alc £27.50, set-price L £14.95.
☺ H/wine £10.25
Times: Noon-2pm/7-9.45pm
Additional: Bar food L; Sunday L; Children welcome
Seats: 60. Private dining room 20. Jacket & tie at D

High up over Rozel Bay, Château La Chaire has a fabulous position on the side of a wooded valley, surrounded by five acres of terraced gardens. Built as a gentleman's residence in 1843, the Château retains much of the discreet atmosphere of a private country house. In the oak-panelled dining room with conservatory extension, guests can choose from a daily-changing menu. Our inspector enjoyed a successful pan-fried breast of chicken with roast vegetables and champ – and the brown bread is particularly moreish.

Style: Classic country house
Smoking: No-smoking area; No pipes & cigars
Accommodation: 14 en suite ★ ★ ★

Directions: From St Helier NE towards Five Oaks, Maufant, then St Martin's Church & Rozel; 1st L in village, hotel 100m

ST AUBIN, Somerville Hotel

Commanding spectacular views of St Aubin's Bay, this friendly hotel attracts a strong leisure following. Expect grilled salmon with bok choi, and Thai chicken patties with coconut and coriander, plus a highly recommended lime tart with coconut ice cream.

Additional: Bar food L; Sunday L; Children welcome
Style: Classic/informal
Smoking: No smoking in dining room
Accommodation: 59 en suite ★★★

Directions: From village follow harbour, then take Mont du Boulevard

Mont du Boulevard JE3 8AD
Map: 16
Tel: 01534 741226
Fax: 01534 746621
E-mail: somerville@dolanhotels.com
Cost: Set-price L £9.95/ D £15. ☺
H/wine £11.50
Times: 12.30-2pm/7-9pm

ST BRELADE, The Atlantic Hotel ❀❀

A new entrance to the hotel dining room leads to an area of dark plum-coloured carpets, potted palms and softly curved pelmets which frame excellent views of the gardens and sea beyond. At inspection a skinless chicken 'winglet' dipped in curry batter made a super opening to the meal. The high quality of ingredients in the official starter of crab and scallops was made somewhat redundant by an excess of hollandaise sauce, but a main dish of John Dory with olives and spinach afforded one of the best fishes the inspector had tasted in a while and the accompaniment was simple but effective. A coconut and lemon soufflé proved to be a dessert of technical excellence and great depth of flavour. The wine list is extensive and the sommelier knowledgeable and helpful.

Directions: From St Brelade take the road to Petit Port, turn into Rue de Sergente and R again, signed to hotel

Mont de la Pulente JE3 8HE
Map: 16
Tel: 01534 744101
Fax: 01534 744102
E-mail: atlantic@itl.net
Chef: Ken Healy
Owners: Patrick Burke & family
Cost: Alc £35, set-price L £16.50/D £25. ☺ H/wine £10.50
Times: fr12.45pm/fr 7.30pm.
Closed Jan-Feb
Additional: Bar food; Sunday L; Children welcome
Seats: 80. Private dining room 24. Jacket & tie preferred
Style: Classic/Formal
Smoking: No pipes & cigars
Accommodation: 50 en suite ★★★★

ST BRELADE, Hotel la Place ❀❀

Atmospheric medieval style restaurant in a rural 17th-century farmhouse complex. The whole set up bristles with care and enthusiasm – from the readable, loving descriptions in the wine list to the formal but caring service style. A recent inspection began with a pre-starter of marinated salmon carefully presented on thin slices of cucumber. This was followed by a really quite rich dish of three large fresh scallops surrounded by mousse filled tortellini and a small tomato salad. The main course featured a nicely trimmed loin of lamb with a tasty

Route du Coin La Haule JE3 8BT
Map: 16
Tel: 01534 744261
Fax: 01534 745164

Telephone for further details.

Hotel la Place

stuffing of mushroom farce and a strong red wine jus. A dessert of apricot and almond strudel was perhaps a slight disappointment with pastry dominating. However a selection of petits fours, including brandy snap with cream filling and chocolate truffle rolled in toasted coconut managed to placate the inspector's sweet tooth in a most agreeable fashion.

Directions: Before St Aubin turn up La Haule Hill by La Haule Manor Hotel, then L at sign towards red houses, Hotel 400yds on R

ST BRELADE, Hotel l'Horizon ⚜⚜

St Brelade's Bay JE3 8EF
Map: 16
Tel: 01534 43101
Fax: 01534 46269
Chef: Paul Wells
Owner: Arcadian Hotels
Cost: *Alc* £28.50, set-price L £19.50/D £25. ☺ H/wine £12.50
Times: 12.30-2.30pm/7.30-10pm
Additional: Bar food L; Sunday L; Children welcome
Seats: 40. Private dining room 24. Jacket & tie preferred
Style: Classic/Modern
Smoking: No-smoking area; Air conditioning
Accommodation: 107 en suite
★★★★

One of the most popular hotels on the island, with a choice of three eating options, the most serious of which is the art deco style Grill. Formal but friendly service and views over St Brelade's Bay create an ideal venue for sampling modern British cuisine along the lines of chorizo and herb sausage on mash with veal gravy, tortellini of langoustine with scallop and chive or fillet of veal wrapped in pancetta with wasabi and leek mash. Desserts might include poached nectarines with nectarine sorbet and raspberry purée, three chocolate assiette or rice pudding with plum sauce. The set-price option offers a choice of three starters followed by a choice of soup or sorbet before proceeding to a choice from four mains and three puddings and ending with coffee and excellent petits fours such as dark chocolate truffles.

Directions: Overlooking St Brelade's Bay

ST BRELADE,

Sea Crest Hotel

The bay can not only be seen but heard from this welcoming hotel situated on the picturesque bay of Petit Port. Diners travel from all over the island to eat a stylish selection of dishes, although the *carte* still features old-time favourites such as Steak Diane and crêpes Suzette. More sophisticated preparations such as ballotine of chicken and quail with celeriac remoulade and mushroom vinaigrette, and grilled fillet of skate and a salad of wilted greens, grilled polenta and ginger and soy dressing are perhaps more typical of the kitchen's refined and contemporary outlook. Local seafood is always superb: Jersey scallops are grilled and served with a gazpacho sauce, but crab and lobster is always hard to beat, especially when simply served with cucumber salad, marinated new potatoes and herb mayonnaise.

Directions: From Red Houses follow Route Orange, A13 to Hotel, on R at bottom of dip

Le Route du Petit Port JE3 8HH
Map: 16
Tel: 01534 746353
Fax: 01534 747316
E-mail: seacrest@super.net.uk
Chef: Hector McDonald
Owners: Julian & Martha Bernstein
Cost: *Alc* £30, set-price L £14.25/ D £19.50. ☺ H/wine £10.50
Times: 12.30-2pm/7.30-9.45pm. Closed Mon, mid Feb-mid Mar
Additional: Bar food L; Sunday L; Children welcome
Style: Classic/chic
Seats: 60
Smoking: Air conditioning
Accommodation: 7 en suite ★★★

ST CLEMENT,

Green Island Restaurant

JE2 6LS
Map: 16
Tel: 01534 857787
Fax: 01534 619309
E-mail: AMW@psilink.co.uk
Cost: *Alc* £18.50, set-price L £14.50. ☺ H/wine £9.50
Times: Noon-2.30pm/7-9.30pm. Closed D Sun, all Mon, Xmas & New Year, 2 wks Nov, 2 wks Feb
Additional: Children welcome
Style: Bistro-style/Rustic

Delightful beachside restaurant with terrace overlooking the sea. A sauté of squid and chorizo with 'mopping up' sauce and crusty bread was the highlight of this year's inspection.

Directions: Telephone for directions

ST HELIER,

Grand Hotel

The 'Victoria' restaurant at the Grand Hotel takes its name from a statue of said illustrious Queen standing in the foreground of a view that extends out towards St Aubin. A relaxing, understated ambience is achieved through pleasant light decor, comfortable seating and background live piano. The modern French cuisine includes starters such as duck leg on blackened pineapple with oriental salad and plum sauce, as selected by an inspector on a recent visit. A mixed grill of seafood formed the main course and the inspector was particularly impressed with the quality of the sauce – a beurre

The Esplanade JE4 8WD
Map: 16
Tel: 01534 722301
Fax: 01534 737815
E-mail: grand.jersey@devere-hotel.com
Chef: Lee Carroll
Owners: De Vere Hotels
Cost: *Alc* £30, set-price L £15.50/D £23.50. ☺ H/wine £11
Times: 12.30-2.15pm/7-10pm. Closed L Sat, D Sun, Bhs

Grand Hotel

Additional: Bar food; Sunday L;
Children welcome
Seats: 140. Private dining room 22.
Jacket & tie preferred
Style: Modern/Formal
Smoking: No-smoking area; Air
conditioning
Accommodation: 114 en suite
★ ★ ★ ★

blanc made with rich butter and lemon and run through with
chive, chervil and tomato pieces. However the highlight of the
meal came with a dessert of bitter chocolate tart and citrus
anglais in which the quality of the chocolate really shone
through.

Directions: On outskirts of town, overlooking Victoria Park

ST SAVIOUR,

Longueville Manor 🏵🏵🏵

JE2 7WF
Map: 16
Tel: 01534 725501
Fax: 01534 731613
E-mail: longman@itl.net
Chef: Andrew Baird
Owners: Malcom Lewis & Sue Dufty
Cost: *Alc* £43, set-price L £20/D £42.
H/wine £9.75
Times: 12.30-2pm/7-9.30pm
Additional: Bar food L; Sunday L;
Children welcome
Seats: 45. Private dining room 16
Style: Country-house/formal
Smoking: No-smoking area
Accommodation: 32 en suite ★ ★ ★ ★

Acres of well-tended grounds contribute to the country-house
feel at the manor, which dates from the 13th century. Comfort
and style are paramount here, with an interior notable for lots
of heavy panelling, rich colours, fresh flowers and antiques.
The oak-panelled dining room is non-smoking, while the other
is lighter and more contemporary in feel. The kitchen makes
great use of fresh local produce, particularly seafood, from
Jersey crab (in lasagne with spring onions and ginger) and
scallops (wrapped in bacon, with a salad of French beans and
globe artichoke) to main-course ragout of lobster, langoustines,
crab and scallops scented with lemongrass. Some dishes have a
rustic ring to them, as in warm salad of roast pork cheek with
glazed apples and crackling, or pot-roast chicken with crisp
pancetta and mash, while others are classically inspired: grilled
fillet of Aberdeen Angus and foie gras, wild mushrooms and
truffle jus, for instance. Foie gras may also turn up as a starter,
as it did at inspection ('delicious, smooth texture, good
flavour') with orange marmalade and toasted brioche, along

with a well-presented salad of smoked salmon, grapefruit and
avocado. Puddings take in a terrine of white and dark
chocolate of intense flavour, apple and sultana pudding, and
banana crème brûlée with rum and raisin ice cream.

Directions: From St Helier take A3 to Gorey, hotel 0.75m on L

SARK

LITTLE SARK,

La Sablonnerie

GY9 0SD
Map: 16
Tel: 01481 832061
Fax: 01481 832408
Chef: Colin Day
Owner: Elizabeth Perrée
Cost: *Alc* £20.80, set-price L
£24.50/D £27.50. ☺ H/wine £7.80
Times: Noon-2.30pm/7-9.30pm.
Closed mid Oct-Etr
Additional: Bar food; Sunday L;
Children welcome
Seats: 39. Private dining room 12
Style: Chic/French
Smoking: No-smoking area;
No pipes & cigars

Beautiful, remote and peaceful: thus are summed up the
charms of this converted 16th-century farmhouse which offers
a discreet and restful break for the discerning traveller. Since
there is no motor traffic on Sark apart from tractors, guests
must either walk or cycle the few miles from the ferry, or ride
in one of the hotel's own horse-drawn carriages. The trip is
worth any amount of effort, as the immaculate Sablonnerie
offers an old-fashioned welcome that makes it difficult to
leave. Dinner in the candle-lit restaurant begins with canapés
in the bar, where the five-course menu can be perused. Starters
might include terrine of monkfish and salmon with roasted
yellow pepper dressing, followed by best end of lamb filled
with a purée of veal and tarragon leaves served on a gâteau of
spinach with a light garlic sauce. Soup and a water ice offer the
chance to pause between these two courses, before rushing on
to warm chocolate tart with vanilla and dark rum sauce, or
almond mousse with poached pears and caramel sauce. A
selection of cheeses, plus coffee and petits fours, completes the
picture.

Directions: On southern part of island

MAN, ISLE OF

CASTLETOWN,

The Chablis Cellar

Overlooking Castletown harbour, this beautifully furnished restaurant comprises three separate dining rooms, all elegantly styled with period decor. Fresh flowers and crisp linen reflect the attention to detail pursued by friendly and professional waiting staff. Typical starters include seared king scallops on a bed of baked leeks surrounded by a caramelised soy sauce. Main courses might range from veal with a pink peppercorn and cream reduction, or pan-fried sea bass fillet, crowned with roasted vegetables and a warm olive butter. Adventurous desserts might feature exotic fruits with lime syrup.

21 Bank Street IM9 1AT
Map 6: SC26
Tel: 01624 823527

Telephone for further details

Directions: Approach Castletown, bridge over harbour, 3 storey building on left. Small car park.

DOUGLAS,

Waterfront Restaurant ⊛

First floor restaurant in an old stone building overlooking Douglas harbour. The carte *and set-price menus provide a good choice of seafood, grills and vegetarian dishes, and feature good home-made sausages.*

North Quay IM1 4LE
Map 6: SC37
Tel: 01624 673222
Fax: 01624 673145
E-mail: jean@fabfood.enterprise-plc.com

Directions: Telephone for directions

Telephone for further details

PORT ERIN,

Bradda Glen Café Bar & Restaurant ⊛

Take a window seat and admire Port Erin beach and soak up the pleasant atmosphere of the traditional restaurant. The pan-fried king scallops with tian of pepperonata can be recommended, bursting with flavour.

IM9 6PJ
Map 6: SC16
Tel: 01624 833166
Cost: Alc £18. ☺ H/wine £8.95
Times: Noon-2.30pm/7-9pm.
Closed Mon

Additional: Bar food; Sunday L
Style: Informal/Chic
Smoking: No smoking in dining room

Directions: Follow signs from Promenade, then past hotels, entrance 450yds beyond

SCOTLAND
ABERDEEN CITY

ABERDEEN, **Ardoe House**

Built in 1878 for a soap manufacturer, Ardoe House has been much extended and altered over the years and now has a conference and a leisure centre. Many original features remain, however, including the oak-panelled front hall and staircase and the oak fireplace in the dining room. The well-balanced menus offer a generous choice (vegetarians are looked after well here), and some interesting combinations result in flavoursome dishes, from the simplicity of a salad of Parma ham, tomatoes and Parmesan with garlicky tapenade, to a gutsy main course of breast of chicken stuffed with wild mushrooms and foie gras served with a truffle and Madeira jus. Fruity accompaniments are not uncommon – a warm plum and orange compote for confit of duck leg, a citrus salad for a terrine of smoked salmon and monkfish with a caper dressing among the starters, and an apricot and apple compote with blueberry marmalade for roast loin of Highland venison. Traditionalists could play safe with grilled fillet or sirloin of Aberdeen Angus, and puddings do the trick with clootie dumpling with Drambuie custard, or lemon tart with peach ice cream.

Directions: 3 miles from Aberdeen on B9077, on L

South Deeside Road Blairs AB12 5YP
Map 15: NJ90
Tel: 01224 860600
Fax: 01224 861283
E-mail: info@ardoe.macdonald-hotels.co.uk
Chef: Ivor Clark
Owner: Macdonald Hotels plc
Cost: Alc £35, set-price D £29.50. ☺
H/wine £15.50
Times: Noon-2pm/6.30-9.45pm
Additional: Bar food; Sunday L; Children welcome
Seats: 80. Private dining room 2-500. No jeans at D
Style: Traditional/Country-house
Smoking: No smoking in dining room
Accommodation: 110 en suite
★★★★

ABERDEEN,
Maryculter House Hotel

The Priory Restaurant at this historic country house hotel has stone walls, open fires and wrought iron ceiling lights. The menu features quality Scottish produce, including Deeside game and salmon.

Additional: Bar food; Children 4+
Style: Rustic/country-house
Smoking: No smoking in dining room
Civil licence: 180
Accommodation: 23 en suite ★★★

Directions: 8 miles west of Aberdeen off A93 or B9077

South Deeside Road AB12 5GB
Map 15: NJ90
Tel: 01224 732124
Fax: 01224 733510
E-mail: maryculter.house.hotel@dial.pipex.com
Cost: Alc £22.50. ☺ H/wine £14.25
Times: D only, 7-9.30pm. Closed Sun

ABERDEEN, **Norwood Hall** ✿

An elegant and refined hotel restaurant with a beautifully ornate carved wood ceiling. A fine dining experience with a sense of occasion without being in any way stuffy. Chicken breast stuffed with pheasant and leek mousseline recommended.

Additional: Bar food; Sunday L; Children welcome
Style: Country-house
Smoking: No smoking in dining room
Civil licence: 65
Accommodation: 21 en suite ★★★

Directions: Off A92, at 1st roundabout, turn L & continue to hotel sign

Garthdee Road Cults AB15 9FX
Map 15: NJ90
Tel: 01224 868951
Fax: 01224 869868
E-mail: info@norwood-hall.co.uk
Cost: Alc £25. H/wine £11.75
Times: Noon-2pm/7-9.30pm

ABERDEEN, **Simpsons Hotel** ❀

59 Queens Road AB15 4YP
Map 15: NJ90
Tel: 01224 327777
Fax: 01224 327700
E-mail: address@simpsonshotel.com
Cost: *Alc* £25. ☺ H/wine £9.95
Times: Noon-2pm/6.30-9.45pm.
Closed 26 Dec, 1 Jan
Additional: Bar food L; Sunday L;
Children welcome
Style: Chic/modern
Smoking: No-smoking area; Air
conditioning
Accommodation: 37 en suite ★ ★ ★

*Split-level brasserie with Moroccan pillars supporting a colonnade
of arches. Smoked haddock and leek fritters were followed by rack
of lamb with lime salsa, and a rich chocolate mousse.*

Directions: Telephone for directions

ABERDEENSHIRE

ABOYNE,
White Cottage Restaurant ❀❀

An archetypal roadside cottage restaurant with all the
expected ingredients, including a rural setting, and a garden
with duck pond. Inside it is low-ceilinged with beams and
wooden pillars, and a bright, cheerful feel. The daily-changing
set-price dinner menu and lighter, more flexible lunch choices
concentrate on fish and Scottish beef, and both have met with
approval. Little pan-fried rösti sea-cakes made from halibut
and scallops and served with sauce gazpacho were soft yet
crispy, almost oriental in style. Fillet of beef stroganoff on rice
was surprisingly light and harmonious, with lemon substituting
for paprika, while a topping of crème fraîche was an
inspiration, allowing for cream to be added according to taste.
A sweet and tart apple and Worcesterberry pie came with a
good crème anglaise. Chef/patron Laurie Mill's modern
Scottish cooking also shows itself in dishes like bourride – a
fish stew of mussels, rock turbot and cod with garlic aïoli,
and flash-fried loin of lamb with creamed watercress and
rosemary jus.

Craigwell AB34 5BP
Map 15: NO59
Tel/Fax: 013398 86265
Chef: Laurie Mill
Owners: Laurie & Josephine Mill
Cost: *Alc* £18.35, set-price D £29.50.
☺ H/wine £12.80
Times: 11.30am-2.45pm/6.30-
9.15pm. Closed Sun, Mon, 25-29
Dec, 1 wk Jul, 1 w/end Aug, 1 wk
Autumn
Additional: Bar food; Children
welcome
Seats: 36. Private dining room 24.
Jacket & tie preferred
Style: Rustic/Country-house
Smoking: No-smoking area; No pipes
& cigars

Directions: On A93 between Aboyne and Kincardine O'Neil

BALLATER,
Balgonie House Hotel ❀❀

Built in the Arts and Crafts style in 1898, and set in four acres
of grounds. The simply-designed dining room has lovely views
over the gardens towards the hills of Glen Muick. Dinner
follows a set format with a short choice at each course except

Braemar Place
AB35 5NQ
Map 15: NO39
Tel/Fax: 013397 55482
Chef: John Finnie
Owners: John & Priscilla Finnie

the second, which is a fish dish: perhaps smoked haddock and cod fishcake with tapenade, or gratin of crab with sherry sauce. Fine local produce is used, from a starter of breast of guinea fowl in a bramble and raspberry dressing, to main courses of roast partridge with cranberry compote and game jus, or fillet of Aberdeen Angus on a croûte with mushroom duxelle finished with a rich Burgundy jus. A main-course option is always fish: salmon from the Dee, or cod fillet under a herb crust bordered with pesto. Puddings range from the fruity – gooseberry and apple pancakes, say – to traditional warm chocolate sponge topped with toffee sauce and served with custard.

Directions: On outskirts of Ballater, signposted off A93 (Ballater-Perth)

Cost: Set-price L £18.50/D £30. H/wine £16
Times: 12.30-2pm (reservations only)/7-9pm. Closed 5 Jan-10 Feb
Additional: Sunday L; Children welcome; Vegetarian dishes not always available
Seats: 30
Style: Country-house
Smoking: No smoking in dining room
Accommodation: 9 en suite ★ ★

BALLATER,

Darroch Learg Hotel ❀❀❀

Darroch Learg, build of granite in the 1880s, is in four acres of wooded grounds to the west of town and has a superb outlook over the Dee Valley to the mountains beyond. The conservatory restaurant is an elegant, light and airy room, with blue and beige Nina Campbell wallpaper, table lamps on the smartly set dining tables, and fresh flowers. This is the setting for a well-assembled dinner menu with some interesting and successful combinations: a potato and lime salad and mustard dressing for a starter of seared calves' liver, fried squid in ink sauce with a main course of grilled fillet of sea bass with avocado salsa. Scotland provides most of the raw materials: Shetland trout, smoked on the premises, is complemented by a free-range poached egg and chive hollandaise, saddle of local lamb is accompanied by girolles and rosemary cream. Dishes are well-conceived and hang together: crisp rösti-like potato supports a ragout of 'delicious' wild mushrooms and braised shin of beef – 'what flavour!' – served with fillet of Aberdeen Angus, cooked exactly as requested, and exceptionally light and smooth celeriac purée, a Madeira sauce proving ideal for the mixture of flavours. Puddings end on an upbeat note in the form of crème brûlée, given a lift with toffeed apple and apple sorbet, or 'superb' zesty-flavoured lemon tart with a puddle of contrastingly sweet raspberry coulis. Extras like breads and petits fours are first-rate, and helpful tasting notes remove any intimidation from the long wine list; eight bottles are served by the glass.

Braemar Road AB35 5UX
Map 15: NO39
Tel: 013397 55443
Fax: 013397 55252
E-mail: nigel@darroch-learg.demon.co.uk
Chef: David Mutter
Owners: Franks Family
Cost: Set-price L £19.50/D £34. H/wine £15
Times: 12.30-2pm/7-9pm. Closed Xmas, Jan (ex New Year)
Additional: Bar food L; Sunday L; Children welcome
Seats: 48
Style: Country-house
Smoking: No smoking in dining room
Accommodation: 18 en suite ★ ★ ★

Directions: On A93 at the W end of village

BALLATER,

Glen Lui Hotel

Situated in a quiet corner of the village with views out towards Lochnagar, this bright airy hotel restaurant is understandably popular. Dishes such as an excellent North Sea sole significantly add to the appeal.

Cost: Alc £20. ☺ H/wine £9.20
Times: Noon-2pm/6-9pm.
Additional: Sunday L; Children welcome
Style: Informal/Country-house
Smoking: No smoking in dining room
Accommodation: 19 en suite

Directions: Off A93 in the village of Ballater

AB35 5RP
Map 15: NO39
Tel: 013397 55402
Fax: 013397 55545
E-mail: infos@glen-lui-hotel.co.uk

BALLATER,

Green Inn ❀❀

'No supplements' is the praiseworthy statement at the top of the menu at the Green Inn, so guests know where they are even if they start with foie gras parfait with a purée of haricot beans studded with truffle and Gewürztraminer sorbet. Careful sourcing means that game and venison are from local forests and moors, eggs and chickens are free-range, and a green policy means that only male lobsters are cooked in the kitchen. All this translates into vibrantly flavoured dishes tasting of their ingredients, from partridge and lentil soup, through rich shellfish risotto (lobster, crab, mussels, cockles and langoustine) with Parmesan shavings and a slice of truffle, to roast loin of venison with a gravy of the pan juices hinting of chocolate. An Eastern influence is seen occasionally – a ginger and soy dressing for breast of duck on home-made black pudding with crushed apples, for instance – but cheeses are resolutely Scottish, and puddings might include Valrhona chocolate terrine with Agen prunes soaked in malt whisky, of which a number are sold as after-dinner drinks alongside home-made liqueurs.

Directions: On A93 in centre of Ballater on the Green

9 Victoria Road
AB35 5QQ
Map 15: NO39
Tel/Fax: 013397 55701
Chef: Mr J J Purves
Owners: Mr & Mrs J J Purves
Cost: Alc £29.50
Times: D only, 7-9pm. Closed Sun & Mon (Mar-Oct), 2 wks Oct
Additional: Children welcome
Seats: 30
Style: Modern/Scottish
Smoking: No pipes & cigars; Air conditioning
Accommodation: 3 en suite.

BANCHORY,

Banchory Lodge Hotel ❀ NEW

Adventurous cooking using prime ingredients, with tables overlooking the River Dee. Recently enjoyed dishes included smoked salmon and prawn roulade, and breast of duck on a bed of wild mushrooms. Watch out for superb orange and cointreau mousse.

Cost: Alc £25. ☺ H/wine £10.95
Additional: Bar food L; Sunday L; Children welcome
Style: Traditional/country house
Smoking: No-smoking area
Accommodation: 22 en suite ★ ★ ★

Directions: Off A93 13m W of Aberdeen

AB31 5HS
Map 15: No39
Tel: 01330 822625
Fax: 01330 825019
E-mail: banchorylodgeht@btconnect.com

BANCHORY,

Raemoir House Hotel ✤✤

AB31 4ED
Map 15: NO69
Tel: 01330 824884
Fax: 01330 822171
E-mail: raemoirhse@aol.com
Chef: John Barber
Owners: Roy & Lesley Bishop-Milnes
Cost: Set-price D £24 & £27.50. ☺
H/wine £13.60
Times: Noon-2pm/7-9pm
Additional: Bar food L; Sunday L;
Children welcome
Seats: 40. Private dining room 15
Style: Country-house
Smoking: No smoking in dining room
Accommodation: 21 en suite ★★★

A new chef arrived at the hotel this past Christmas and the style of the cuisine has shifted from modern Scottish cooking to modern British. The menus still list local produce, including West Coast scallops and Ayrshire bacon, but there is a large sprinkling of risottos, polenta, pesto, etc. The dining room has been relocated to the beautiful oval room, the walls of which are covered with Victorian tapestries. There is a real fire and the tables are lit by candles in the evening – all very refined and elegant. Separate set-price menus are offered at lunch and dinner. The latter is more ambitious and you can sample the three-course menu which includes dishes such as home-made gravad lax with West Coast scallops and basil and garlic dressing, fillet of beef, celeriac mousseline, courgette and celeriac brunoise and Meaux mustard reduction followed by a duet of Highland whisky cranachans in tuile and gingersnap baskets. Coffee and petits fours are included.

Directions: A93 to Banchory then A980, hotel at crossroads after 2.5 miles

BANCHORY, Tor-na-Coille Hotel ✤

AB31 4AB
Map 15: NO69
Tel: 01330 822242
Fax: 01330 824012
E-mail: tornacoille@btinternet.com
Cost: Set-price D £26.50. ☺
H/wine £13.95
Times: D only, 7-9.30pm.
Closed 24-29 Dec
Additional: Sunday L(noon-2pm);
Children welcome
Style: Traditional/Country-house
Smoking: No smoking in dining room
Civil licence: 100
Accommodation: 22 en suite ★★★

Directions: From Aberdeen take A93
(18 miles)

Victorian mansion retaining much of its original charm. The menu, priced for two and three courses, features Taste of Scotland specialities including an intensely flavoured cullen skink risotto with seared scallops.

INVERURIE,

Thainstone House Hotel ❀❀

AB51 5NT
Map 15: NJ72
Tel: 01467 621643
Fax: 01467 625084

Telephone for further details

Directions: 2 miles from Inverurie on the A96 Aberdeen road

A distinctive Scottish mansion with classical dimensions which provides an appropriate setting for gourmet cooking based on quality local produce. The combination of the elegant 19th-century surroundings and the innovative modern food served in Simpson's Restaurant is what distinguishes this place. Technical skill and flair are very evident in dishes like a smooth parfait of chicken livers and foie gras served on a slice of tomato and olive bread with a sweet chutney and crisp lettuce leaves. An impressive main dish recently sampled was mille-feuille of salmon layered with tasty slices of aubergine, with a vibrant thyme jus, and some delicious vegetables which formed an integral part of the plate: turned carrots, green beans in bacon wraps, spinach and fondant potato. But the highlight was undoubtedly the pudding: poached pear with cinnamon ice cream and a superb claret syrup decorated with red and black berries nearly took the breath away.

NEWBURGH, Udny Arms Hotel ❀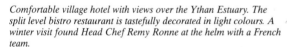

Main Street Ellon AB41 6BL
Map 15: NJ92
Tel: 01358 789444
Fax: 01358 789012
E-mail: enquiry@udny.demon.co.uk

Comfortable village hotel with views over the Ythan Estuary. The split level bistro restaurant is tastefully decorated in light colours. A winter visit found Head Chef Remy Ronne at the helm with a French team.

Telephone for further details

Directions: Village centre – A92 Aberdeen/Peterhead, turn right to Newburgh

PETERHEAD, Waterside Inn ❀

Fraserburgh Road AB42 1BN
Map 15: NK14
Tel: 01779 4711 21
Fax: 01779 470670
Cost: *Alc* £30, set-price L £15/D £21.
☺ H/wine £13.50
Times: 12.30-2pm/7-9.45pm

A sophisticated comfortable restaurant with attractive views over the river. The decor is unpretentious and traditional – an eminently suitable setting for carefully prepared Scottish and European style fare including fresh fish and local game.

Additional: Bar Food; Sunday L; Children welcome
Style: Classic/Traditional
Smoking: No smoking in dining room
Civil licence: 250 **Accommodation:** 109 en suite ★ ★ ★ ★

Directions: Follow A90 (A952) to roundabout on outskirts of Peterhead; turn L for Fraserburgh

ANGUS

AUCHTERHOUSE,
Old Mansion House Hotel

'A most elegant room with splendid features' is how the inspector described the dining room at this country-house hotel. An ornate plaster ceiling and an enormous stone fireplace, red velvet drapes, and white-clothed tables all add to the atmosphere. The confident cooking style is modern with French influences, and the daily-changing set-price menu is supported by the Taste of Scotland *carte*. A summer meal began with tasty canapés, served in the library bar, including a small tartlet with salmon and cream cheese, and a cherry tomato stuffed with wild boar paté. A well executed starter of Orkney crabmeat salad on finely diced fresh beetroot was accompanied by lightly seared Loch Fyne scallops. This was followed by soup – cream of leek and potato with smoked haddock adding an extra dimension. Roast loin of Perthshire lamb was cooked pink, and had a 'good clear flavour', vegetables were also well flavoured, and raspberry crème brûlée was made with local fruit.

DD3 0QN
Map 11: NO33
Tel: 01382 320366
Fax: 01382 320400
E-mail: oldmansionhouse@ netscapeonline.co.uk
Chef: Timothy Cribben
Owners: Jannick & Maxine Bertschy
Cost: Alc £28, set-price L £18.50/D £28. ☺ H/wine £12.50
Times: Noon-2pm/6-9pm
Additional: Bar Food; Sunday L; Children welcome
Style: Country-house/Formal
Seats: 50. Private dining room 25
Smoking: No smoking in dining room
Accommodation: 8 en suite ★★★

Directions: From Dundee take A923 (Coupar Angus road), then B954 for 2 miles. Hotel on L

CARNOUSTIE, 11 Park Avenue

Service is cheerful and attentive, and commitment and enthusiasm show clearly in the cooking, balancing simple but effective main courses such as venison with red wine and crème de cassis, with imaginative starters and desserts.

11 Park Avenue DD7 7JA
Map 12: NO53
Tel/Fax: 01241 853336
E-mail: cparkavenue@aol.com
Cost: Alc £25. ☺ H/wine £10.95
Times: D only, 7-10pm. (L by arrangement only) Closed Sun, Mon, 1st 2 wks Jan

Additional: Children welcome **Style:** Classic/Modern
Smoking: No-smoking area; No pipes & cigars

Directions: From Dundee take A92 N (Arbroath). After 10-12 miles turn R to Carnoustie; at crossroads L, then R at mini-roundabout. Restaurant on L

INVERKEILOR,
Gordon's Restaurant

Small restaurant in a building originally constructed in the 1800s. Stained-glass windows in sandstone walls and an open fire under beamed ceilings give a rustic feel in contrast to the up-to-date, modern Scottish cuisine on offer. First course options might include white crab and ginger pavé with crushed avocado, chive blinis with a coriander, orange and vanilla dressing. This might be followed by stuffed fillet of salmon with Finnan haddock and mustard rarebit, or breast of Guinea fowl with a roasted walnut and ceps mousseline. The high standard of inventiveness and quality is maintained in the dessert options with banana malt and toffee torte accompanied with a candy crunch and trio of banana, and hot vanilla soufflé with poached figs and balsamic and Marscapone ice cream typifying the approach. Extensive Scottish farmhouse cheese board including Pentland, Howgate Blue, St Andrews and Tobermory cheddar.

Main Street by Arbroath DD11 5RN
Map 15: NO64
Tel/Fax: 01241 830364
Chef: Gordon Watson
Owners: Gordon & Maria Watson
Cost: Alc £27.50, set-price L £16. ☺ H/wine £9.80
Times: Noon-1.45pm/7-9pm. Closed D Sun, L Sat & Tue, all Mon, last 3 wks Jan, 2 wks Sep/Oct
Additional: Sunday L; Children welcome
Seats: 24
Style: Classic/Rustic
Smoking: No-smoking area

Directions: Just off A92 (Arbroath to Montrose), follow Inverkeilor signs

ARGYLL & BUTE

ARDBEG, **Ardmory House Hotel** ✦

Ardmory Road Isle of Bute PA20 0PG
Map 10: NS06
Tel: 01700 502346
Fax: 01700 505596
Cost: Alc £40, set-price L £12.50/
D £18.50. ☺ H/wine £9.40
Times: (L by arrangement only)
D only, 7- 9pm

Standing on a hillside overlooking the bay, this welcoming hotel restaurant offers traditional Scottish fayre with some international influence. Try breast of duck pan-fried in a raspberry, orange and port sauce.

Additional: Bar food; Sunday L (noon-2.30pm)
Smoking: No smoking in dining room
Accommodation: 5 en suite ★ ★

Directions: N from Rothesay on A844. 1m turn L up Ardmory road. 300 metres on left

ARDUAINE,
Loch Melfort Hotel ✦✦

Oban PA34 4XG
Map 10: NM71
Tel: 01852 200233
Fax: 01852 200214
E-mail: lmhotel@aol.com
Chef: Philip Lewis
Owners: Philip & Rosalind Lewis
Cost: Set-price D £30. H/wine £12.50
Times: D only, 7.30-9pm
Additional: Bar food; Children welcome
Seats: 70. Private dining room 18
Style: Modern/Scottish
Smoking: No smoking in dining room
Accommodation: 26 en suite ★ ★ ★

Loch Melfort Hotel is in a splendid position, next to the National Trust for Scotland's gardens and with wonderful views over Asknish Bay. Big windows in the restaurant give diners the chance to enjoy the broad expanse of water, and the sea provides much of the produce on the menu. Simplicity is a keynote too – Luing langoustines are served with mayonnaise as a starter, and main-course escalope of Craignish salmon is baked with champagne and accompanied by hollandaise – while more complicated treatments might extend the range to take in lightly grilled codling, 'moist and tender', with roasted garlic and cardamom sauce with a portion of crunchy vegetables, or pan-seared fillet of red snapper with salsa verde and lime-roasted tomatoes. Elsewhere there may be a terrine to start – perhaps one of foie gras, or game with Cumberland sauce – and Scotland's finest produce is used in main courses of chargrilled Aberdeen Angus with parsley butter, or saddle of Morayshire lamb roasted with garlic and rosemary and served with a bullace and caper gravy. Something like dark chocolate torte hinting of rum will bring things to a happy conclusion, and the wine list has a fair showing of halves, with house wines sold by the glass, carafe or bottle.

Directions: From Oban, 20 miles S on the A816; from Lochgilphead, 19 miles N on A816

BRIDGE OF ORCHY,
Bridge of Orchy Hotel ✿✿

PA36 4AD
Map 10: NN23
Tel: 01838 400208
Fax: 01838 400313
E-mail: bridgeoforchy@onyxnet.co.uk

Telephone for further details.

Directions: On A82, 6 miles N of
Tyndrum on main Glasgow – Skye
road

With a revamped *carte* and an augmented kitchen staff this busy
roadside hotel restaurant goes from strength to strength. A
recent meal began with a 'surprise' of a delicious fresh
langoustine served at the table in the elegant and comfortable
dining room. The meal proper opened with 'a selection of
Scottish seafood poached in light fish and tomato stock' –
otherwise known as fish soup. Such a grand description is
forgivable in this context for the soup was really quite delicious
– combining the good fresh flavours of prawns, scallops, crab,
white fish and salmon. The main course featured a prime fillet of
Scottish beef, cooked to such perfection that the flavour shone
through, and mingled tantalisingly with the red wine and pickled
walnut sauce. To finish, a really tangy citrus tart, lovely and
fresh with a good zesty flavour and a drizzle of chocolate sauce.

CLACHAN-SEIL,
Willowburn Hotel ✿✿

By Oban PA34 4TJ
Map 10: NM71
Tel: 01852 300276
Fax: 01852 300597
E-mail: willowburn.hotel@virgin.net
Chef: Chris Mitchell
Owners: Chris Mitchell, Jan Wolfe
Cost: Set-price D £25. H/wine £10.50
Times: D only, 7- 8.30pm.
Closed Jan-Feb
Additional: Children welcome
Seats: 24
Style: Informal
Smoking: No smoking in dining room
Accommodation: 7 en suite ★ ★

Directions: 11 miles S of Oban via
A816 and B844 (Easdale) over
Atlantic Bridge

The restaurant overlooks the hotel grounds with the lawn
stretching down to the shore of Clachan Sound. The dining
room is decorated with a collection of pictures and models of
birds native to Scotland. The four-course set-price menu
changes daily and is based completely on fresh produce, much
of which is sourced locally. Tasty canapés are presented before
the meal, and included a small pastry case with a flavourful

salmon mousse and strips of pepper. A starter of baked
mushroom stuffed with crab, though plain, was much liked.
The Cullen skink was light, creamy and the smoked fish flavour
came through strongly. Delicious diver-caught scallops were
served with a creamy tomato and basil sauce and accompanied
by tomato and courgette, sliced and layered, and a triangle of
quiche which included blue cheese, broccoli and mushrooms –
'quite excellent'. The meal was finished with a Muscat brûlée
which was the 'highlight – lovely texture and flavour to the
filling which was liberally laced with grapes'. The service is
friendly and relaxed.

DERVAIG,
Druimard Hotel ✿✿

Visitors appreciate the charm and character of this country-
house hotel as well as its stunning views over Glen Bellart.
Drinks can be taken in the conservatory before dinner in the
restaurant, with its fine table settings. The menu is a set five
courses with no choice until pudding, when a decision has to be
made about, say, passionfruit chiffon, chocolate pecan tartlet
with chocolate sorbet, or amaretti and peach trifle. The meal
might start with duck and pork terrine with Cumberland sauce,
or goats' cheese fondant with potato wafers and beetroot, with
a sorbet or soup – perhaps creamy smoked haddock – to
follow. The main course might be meat – pan-fried duck breast
with blackberry and apple sauce or fish – baked fillet of halibut
with tarragon sauce on stir-fried cabbage with smoked bacon.
Scottish cheeses with oatcakes round things off before
cafetière coffee with petits fours.

Directions: From Craignure ferry turn R to Tobermory. Go
through Salen, turn L at Aros, signposted Dervaig, hotel on
right-hand side before village

Isle of Mull PA75 6QW
Map 13: NM45
Tel: 01688 400291/400345
Fax: 01688 400345
Chef: Wendy Hubbard
Owners: Mr & Mrs H R Hubbard
Cost: Set-price D £28.50. H/wine
£9.50
Times: D only 6.30-8.30pm.
Closed Nov-Mar
Additional: Bar food L (residents
only); Children welcome
Seats: 28
Style: Classic/country-house
Smoking: No smoking in dining room
Accommodation: 5 en suite ★★

DUNOON, Chatters ✿

*Informal restaurant in a converted town cottage, serving coffees, teas
and good home baking. There's a serious approach at dinner, with a
menu featuring Loch Fyne shellfish and local venison.*

Additional: Bar food; Children welcome
Style: Bistro-style/Informal

Directions: Telephone for directions

58 John Street PA23 8BJ
Map 10: NS17
Tel/Fax: 01369 706402
E-mail: chatters@bun.com
Cost: Alc £27. ☺ H/wine £11
Times: Noon-3pm/6-10pm.
Closed Sun -Tue, part Feb & Mar

DUNOON, Enmore Hotel ✿

*Georgian residence offering sea views and an intimate dining room
with candles, silver and fine china. Local produce features in dishes
of lamb noisettes with rosemary jus, and pan-fried salmon escalope.*

Style: Informal/Country-house
Smoking: No smoking in dining room
Accommodation: 10 en suite ★★

Directions: From Glasgow M8/A8 (Greenock) & ferry, or via
Loch Lomond, A815 to Dunoon. Hotel on promenade btw 2
ferry terminals, 1 mile N of Dunoon

Marine Parade Kirn PA23 8HH
Map 10: NS17
Tel: 01369 702230
Fax: 01369 702148
E-mail: enmorehotel@btinternet.com
Cost: Alc £23, L £15 (reservations
only)/D £25. ☺ H/wine £12.50
Times: Noon-3pm/7-9pm.
Closed Xmas-Feb
Additional: Bar food; Sunday L;
Children welcome

ERISKA,

Isle of Eriska ❀❀❀

Few other hotels can claim the distinction of being situated on a private island. Owned by the Buchanan-Smith family for over a quarter of a century, the Victorian mansion house is approached by a small bridge. In the best Scottish country house tradition, they boast 'a good table': fish and shellfish is superb; langoustines fill a ravioli set in a broth of local oysters, squat lobsters and Sevruga caviar, or else there may be poached home-smoked cod topped with rarebit and mustard crust on a herb and broom-bud salad. In spring, best end of new season's lamb is carved at the table from the trolley and served with caraway jelly and its own roasting gravy. Ingredients, especially vegetables, sparkle with imagination much produce is wild or organically grown. Gâteau of artichokes and St George's mushrooms, salsify confit and thyme jus with breast of farm-reared Scottish guinea fowl, for example, or celeriac purée, baby carrots and turnips in a crispy pastry tart to accompany sea bass stuffed with marinated tomato and peppers. As well as desserts such as honey soufflé with nougatine sauce, the set dinner includes a savoury and selection of British farm cheeses.

Directions: On a private island with vehicular access to mainland

Ledaig by Oban PA37 1SD
Map 10: NM94
Tel: 01631 720371
Fax: 01631 720531
E-mail: office@eriska-hotel.co.uk
Chef: Robert MacPherson
Owners: The Buchanan-Smith Family
Cost: Set-price D £37.50.
H/wine £8.80
Times: D only, 8-9pm. Closed Jan
Additional: Bar food L (residents only); Children welcome
Seats: 40. Jacket & tie preferred
Style: Traditional/Country-house
Smoking: No smoking in dining room
Accommodation: 17 en suite ★★★★

KILCHRENAN,

Taychreggan Hotel ❀❀

Built as a drovers' inn around a cobbled courtyard 350 years ago, Taychreggan is in an enviable position on the shore of Loch Awe and set against a backdrop of trees and hills. Walking, bird-watching and fishing are all part of the appeal, with comfortable lounges, a bar with a tempting choice of malts, and an elegant restaurant with views over the water for people who like their creature comforts. The daily changing menu, backed up by an impressive wine list, runs to five courses, with two or three choices at each course, and shows classical influences brought to bear on good-quality local ingredients. Canapés in the bar start things off nicely, and a typical meal could begin with slices of pan-fried pigeon breast, cooked rare, on braised red cabbage with a redcurrant jus followed by a soup – spicy sweet potato and honey, say. A meat main course might be roast breast of guinea fowl on a bed of garlic mash served with a sweet red wine sauce and baby vegetables. Dessert might bring rum baba with fruit salad, followed by a selection of Scottish cheese.

Directions: One mile before Taynuilt, turn L onto B845 and follow signs to loch side

Taynuilt PA35 1HQ
Map 10: NN02
Tel: 01866 833211/833366
Fax: 01866 833244
E-mail: taychreggan@btinternet.com
Chef: Jerome Prodandu
Owner: Annie Paul
Cost: Set-price D £28. H/wine £10.95
Times: D only, 7.30-9pm
Additional: Bar food L; Children 14+
Seats: 45
Style: French/minimalist
Smoking: No smoking in dining room
Accommodation: 19 en suite ★★★

KILLIECHRONAN,

Killiechronan House ❀

Advanced booking is strongly recommended for any wishing to try out this popular country-house hotel restaurant. Dishes such as marinated chicken breast in garlic and lime will ensure that your forethought is rewarded.

Isle of Mull
PA72 6JU
Map 10: NM53
Tel: 01680 300403
Fax: 01680 300463
E-mail: me@managedestates.co.uk

Killiechronan House

Cost: Set-price D £25.90.
H/wine £11.15
Times: D only, 7-8.30pm
Additional: Children 8+
Style: Country-house
Smoking: No smoking in dining room
Accommodation: 6 en suite ★ ★

Directions: Leaving ferry turn R to Tobermory (A849), in Salen (12 miles) turn L to B8035, after 2 miles turn R to Ulva ferry (B8073). Killiechronan on R

KILMARTIN,
Cairn Restaurant

Built as a grocer and draper's emporium in 1840, this restaurant serves refreshingly unpretentious food in a friendly atmosphere. The style is bistro and the menu offers tried and tested favourites.

Additional: Bar food; Sunday L; Children 10+ at D
Style: Informal/Rustic

Directions: On A816 Lochgilphead-Oban road

Lochgilphead PA31 8RQ
Map 10: NR89
Tel: 01546 510254
Fax: 01546 510221
E-mail: marion.thomson@virgin.net
Cost: ☺ H/wine £9.50
Times: Noon-3pm(Mar-Oct)/6.30-9pm. Closed Tue

LOCHGILPHEAD,
Cairnbaan Hotel

NEW

A wonderfully relaxing canal-side hotel, serving traditional Scottish dishes made from quality local ingredients. A decent langoustine bisque, and lightly pan-fried scallops show the scope, with raspberry and passionfruit tart, and strong fresh coffee.

Directions: From Lochgilphead on A816 2 miles. Hotel situated off B841

Crinan Canal Cairnbaan PA31 8SJ
Map 10: NR88
Tel: 01546 603668
Fax: 01546 606045
E-mail: cairnbaanhotel@virgin.net

Telephone for further details

OBAN,
Dungallan House Hotel

Let your imagination drift across the sea to neighbouring islands while enjoying the restaurant's fresh seafood. If grilled or deep-fried fillets of sole do not appeal, there are some tasty alternatives like grilled sirloin steak.

Additional: Bar Food L; Sunday L; Children welcome; Vegetarian dishes by prior arrangement
Smoking: No smoking in dining room
Accommodation: 13 (11 en suite) ★ ★

Directions: From Argyll Square in Oban follow signs for Gallanach. Approx 0.5 miles from Square

Gallanach Road PA34 4PD
Map 10: NM82
Tel: 01631 563799
Fax: 01631 566711
E-mail: welcome@dungallanhotel-oban.co.uk
Cost: Set-price L £10-£20/D £25. ☺
H/wine £9.95
Times: 12.30-2pm (boking required)/
7.30-8.30pm. Closed Nov-Feb
Style: Classic/Country-house

OBAN, **Manor House Hotel**

Gallanach Road PA34 4LS
Map 10: NM82
Tel: 01631 562087
Fax: 01631 563053
E-mail: me@managedestates.co.uk
Cost: *Alc* 24.95.Set-price L £13.95/
D £24.95.H/wine £12.10
Times: Noon-2pm/6.45-9pm.
Additional: Bar food L; Children 12+
Seats: 30
Smoking: No smoking in dining room
Accommodation: 11 en suite ★ ★
Civil licence: 20

Directions: 300 metres past Oban
ferry terminal

Former Georgian dower house with great views over Oban Bay.
Local scallops, Isle of Mull venison, and wild mushrooms may
feature on the short, daily changing dinner menu, alongside fillet of
hake with squat lobster tails, capers and lemon.

OBAN,
Waterfront Restaurant

NEW

Railway Pier PA34 4LW
Map 10: NM82
Tel: 01631 563110

Telephone for further details

Directions: Telephone for dirtections

The philosophy of this speciality seafood restaurant is neatly
summed up on a sign below the kitchen which reads 'From the
pier to the pan – as fast as we can'. The freshness of the
produce is not in any doubt, as the straightforward cooking
methods aptly demonstrate. The building is an old fisherman's
mission opposite the fishing fleet, utilitarian on the outside and
deliberately simple inside, with blue and white painted walls,
and black and white floor tiles. A short printed menu and large
blackboard show that other tastes are catered for along with
the expected fish and seafood. A delicious lobster and crab
bisque opened a May inspection meal, while fresh langoustines
served in the shell with garlic butter all but melted in the
mouth. There was no faulting the crème brûlée, either, and
coffee was strong and fresh. This restaurant has quickly built
up a sound local reputation, and is increasingly popular with
tourists. The friendly staff are informally attentive.

OBAN, **Willowburn Hotel** ❁❁

See Clachan-Seil, Argyll & Bute

PORT APPIN, **Airds Hotel** ❁❁❁

The challenge here is to concentrate on the food without being
distracted by the stunning view – and, oh, what a view – of the
loch and mountains. Residents pre-book their dinner from
their rooms, but chance diners can order on arrival. The menu
structure is quite simple, with a choice of three starters, a soup
course, three main courses and a wider selection of desserts.
High quality, regional, fresh ingredients are used with
intelligence and restraint and dishes keep hold of an innate
sense of simplicity. On our visit, seared langoustines and red
mullet with aubergine caviar and herb salad was followed by
an uncharacteristically heavy and contrived roasted pepper

Appin PA38 4DF
Map 14: NM94
Tel: 01631 730236
Fax: 01631 730535
E-mail: airds@airds-hotel.com
Chefs: Graeme Allen &
Steve McCallum
Owners: The Allen Family
Cost: Set-price D £40. H/wine £11.50
Times: D only, 7.30-8.30pm.
Closed 6-26 Jan
Additional: Children welcome;
Vegetarian dishes not always available

soup that struck the only false note of an otherwise very fine meal. Roast chicken breast with morel sauce, fondant potato and confit of roasted shallots with lardons was a dish of considerably more refinement, full of delicate, even flavour. There are some truly imaginative ideas here, tempered by understanding of flavour balance – cod on a bed of creamed white beans with baby squid, parsley, lemon and olive oil; breast of guinea fowl and the leg roasted in a mild curry sauce. Raspberry and Drambuie ice cream, and poached pear shortcake with caramel and lime sauce are amongst the alternatives to the selection of farmhouse cheeses.

Directions: Leave A828 at Appin, hotel is 2.5 miles between Ballachulish and Cannel

Seats: 36
Style: Country-house
Smoking: No smoking in dining room
Accommodation: 12 en suite ★ ★ ★

STRACHUR, Creggans Inn

Established roadside inn noted for charm, character and outstanding views over Loch Fyne. Good bar menu with local oysters, mussels, and steaks, and a more formal dining room strong on fish.

Additional: Bar food; Children welcome
Style: country-house/minimalist
Smoking: No smoking in dining room
Civil licence: 100
Accommodation: 17 en suite ★ ★ ★

Directions: From Glasgow A82, along Loch Lomond, then W on A83 (through Arrochar/Rest and be Thankful) onto A815 to Strachur. Or by car ferry from Gourock to Dunoon onto A815 to Strachur

PA27 8BX
Map 10: NN00
Tel: 01369 860247
Fax: 01369 860637
E-mail: info@creggans-inn.co.uk
Cost: Alc £25, set-price D £25. ☺
H/wine £13.
Times: D only, 7-9pm

TARBERT, Columba Hotel

Intimate hotel restaurant located in a conservation area by Loch Fyne. Service is attentive and friendly. Menu is based on quality raw ingredients nicely balanced with local fish and game: try the baked sea bass.

Additional: Bar food; Children welcome
Style: Traditional **Smoking:** No smoking in dining room
Accommodation: 10 en suite ★ ★

Directions: On A83 into Tarbert, L & around harbour, follow road for 0.5m. Hotel on R

East Pier Road PA29 6UF
Map 10: NR86
Tel/Fax: 01880 820808
E-mail: columbahotel@fsbdial.co.uk
Cost: Set-price D £20.50. ☺
H/wine £10.95
Times: Noon-2pm/7-9pm.
Closed L Sun, D Thu-Sun, 26 Dec

TIGHNABRUAICH, Royal Hotel

Located right on the water's edge of the Kyles of Bute, this 150-year-old hotel – a landmark for yachtsmen – specialises in fish straight from the nets. Simplicity is the keyword, and cannon of lamb blini with creamed celeriac is typical.

Additional: Bar Food; Children welcome
Style: Classic
Smoking: No smoking in dining room
Accommodation: 11 en suite ★ ★

Directions: From Strachur, on A886, turn R onto A8003 to Tighnabruaich. Hotel on R at bottom of hill

Shore Road PA21 2BE
Map 10: NR97
Tel: 01700 811239
Fax: 01700 811300
E-mail: royalhotel@btinternet.com
Cost: Set-price D £26.50.
H/wine £12.95
Times: D only 7-9pm

TOBERMORY,

Highland Cottage

A charming cottage-style hotel built within an idyllic conservation area. The regularly changing menu might include braised leg of Glengorm lamb with a rosemary and red wine jus or pan-fried lemon sole with capers.

Additional: Children welcome
Style: Informal/Traditional
Smoking: No smoking in dining room
Accommodation: 6 en suite ★★

Directions: Opposite fire station. From Main Street proceed up Back Brae, turn L at top by White House and below Arts Centre. Follow road round to R, L at next junc

Breadalbane Street Isle of Mull PA75 6PD
Map 13: NM55
Tel: 01688 302030
Fax: 01688 302727
E-mail: davidandjo@highland cottage.co.uk
Cost: *Alc* £30, set-price D £21.50. ☺
H/wine £11
Times: D only, 7-9pm.
Closed mid Oct-mid Nov, Xmas, parts of Jan & Feb

AYRSHIRE, EAST

DARVEL,

Scoretulloch House ❀❀

Grand dining room and more informal brasserie in an attractive 500-year-old building with fabulous gardens. A meal at the restaurant might start with a well flavoured beetroot soup, followed by a slice of stuffed bacon chop, and end with a good quality pannacotta with a raspberry coulis. The brasserie takes a more straightforward approach offering simple dishes from focused ingredients with seafood a particular strong point. An extensive wine list with a focus on Australian wines and an exclusively Scottish cheeseboard are on offer in both venues.

Directions: Take M 74 J8 for A71. Hotel clearly signed 1 mile S of A71 (Strathaven-Kilmarnock), just E of Darvel

KA17 0LR
Map 11: NS53
Tel: 01560 323331
Fax: 01560 323441
E-mail: mail@scoretulloch.com

Telephone for further details.

FENWICK,

Fenwick Hotel

Seafood and game feature strongly at the Fenwick, and their speciality, lobster, is highly regarded. Best end of lamb with wild mushrooms, Armagnac and prune stuffing also went down well.

Additional: Bar food; Sunday L; Children welcome
Style: Informal
Smoking: No-smoking area
Civil licence: 100
Accommodation: 31 en suite ★★★

Directions: Telephone for directions

KA3 6AU
Map 11: NS44
Tel: 01560 600478
Fax: 01560 600334
Cost: ☺ H/wine £10
Times: Noon-3pm/6-9.30pm

AYRSHIRE, NORTH

BRODICK,

Auchrannie Hotel

Isle of Arran KA27 8BZ
Map 10: NS03
Tel: 01770 302234
Fax: 01770 302812
E-mail: info@auchrannie.co.uk
Chef: Andrew Yuill
Owner: Linda & Iain Johnstone
Cost: *Alc* £21.50, set-price D £24. ☺
H/wine £11.95
Times: D only, 7-10pm
Additional: Children welcome
Seats: 52
Style: Country-house/Formal
Smoking: No smoking in dining room
Accommodation: 28 en suite ★★★

The hotel building was formerly the home of the dowager duchess of Hamilton, widow of the 12th Duke of Hamilton and Earl of Arran. The Garden Restaurant is divided into a traditional dining area in the original mansion and a light and airy conservatory extension. The daily-changing menu is priced for two, three and four courses. Starters range from salad of Arran smoked salmon to terrine of Highland game, wrapped in Parma ham and served with home-made cranberry compote and spiced mandarins. Main courses encompass fillet of local beef on a wild thyme roost with vegetables and oyster mushrooms, and monkfish and salmon ravioli in a saffron and tapenade sauce topped with deep-fried leeks.

Directions: From ferry terminal turn R and follow coast road through Brodick village, then take second L past golf club

BRODICK,

Kilmichael Hotel

A friendly haven of elegance and comfortable luxury in a house believed to be the oldest house on the island. Set menu options might include rack of Scottish lamb served on red cabbage.

Additional: Children 12+
Style: Traditional/Country-house
Smoking: No smoking in dining room
Accommodation: 8 en suite ★★

Glen Cloy Isle of Arran KA27 8BY
Map 10: NS03
Tel: 01770 302219
Fax: 01770 302068
E-mail: antbutty@aol.com
Cost: Set-price D £25.50.
H/wine £11.85
Times: D only 7-8.30pm.
Closed Tue & Wed, Nov-Mar

Directions: Turn R on leaving ferry terminal, through Brodick & L at golf club. Continue past church & onto private drive

DALRY, Braidwoods

The converted miller's cottage is at the end of a lane heading nowhere, but who would wish to go further when there is cooking of such a standard to enjoy? The two small rooms

Drumastle Mill Cottage
KA24 4LN
Map 10: NS24
Tel: 01294 833544
Fax: 01294 833553

feature open beams and exposed stone and the pale blue walls are hung with interesting modern artwork. The menu is short and straightforward, nothing over-elaborate about either the descriptions or the style of cooking. There is more sophistication, however, to Keith Braidwood's cooking than at first meets the eye, even more impressive when you realise he is virtually alone in the kitchen. A sample meal started with a smooth, rich and satisfying foie gras and chicken liver parfait served with toasted sultana brioche and gooseberry and sultana chutney adding an edge, followed by an intermediate course of a warm tart of courgette, tomato and goats' cheese sprinkled with toasted pine kernels and served with a roasted pepper coulis, just the job for a hot summer's evening. Turbot, as fresh as the proverbial daisy, was roasted and served with seared sweet scallops plus a pea and asparagus risotto that could have made an excellent lunch on its own. There is usually at least one chocolate dessert, perhaps a warm dark chocolate and maple tart with a rocher of cinnamon ice cream. British cheeses are from the excellent Iain Mellis.

Chef: Keith Braidwood
Owners: Keith & Nicola Braidwood
Cost: Set-price L £17 (£20 Sun)/D £27.50. H/wine £12.95
Times: Noon-1.45pm/7-9pm. Closed D Sun, L Tue, all Mon, 1st 3 wks Jan, 2 wks Sep
Additional: Sunday L; Children welcome
Seats: 24
Style: Contemporary/cottage
Smoking: No smoking in dining room

Directions: 1 mile from Dalry on the Saltcoats Road

KILWINNING, Montgreenan Mansion House Hotel

Elegant dining room in an imposing 19th-century parkland mansion. The menu changes daily but might include roast monkfish on a bed of braised fennel with lobster and herb bisque, or chicken supreme stuffed with woodland mushrooms.

Montgreenan Estate KA13 7QZ
Map 10: NS34
Tel: 01294 557733
Fax: 01294 850397
Cost: *Alc* £24, set-price L £13.95/D £25.80. ☺ H/wine £12.95
Times: 12.30-2pm/7-9.30pm

Additional: Bar food; Sunday L; Children welcome
Style: Country-house
Smoking: No smoking in dining room
Civil licence: 110
Accommodation: 21 en suite ★ ★ ★

Directions: 4 miles N of Irvine, & 19 miles (20 minutes) S of Glasgow on A736

LOCHRANZA,
Harold's Restaurant ⊛

Part of the visitor centre of the Isle of Arran distillery. Morning coffee, light lunches, and afternoon teas during the day, but a good modern menu and a more stylish approach at dinner. Try chowder of west coast seafood, or a rosemary infused, garlicky rack of Ayrshire lamb.

Isle of Arran Distillery KA27 8HJ
Map 10: NR95
Tel: 01770 830264
Fax: 01770 830364
Cost: *Alc* £25. ☺ H/wine £9.50.
Times: Noon-3pm. D 7-9.30pm. Closed D Mon & Sun, Jan-Apr

Additional: Bar food; Sunday L; Children welcome
Style: modern/bistro-style
Smoking: No-smoking area; Air conditioning

Directions: Telephone for directions

AYRSHIRE, SOUTH

AYR, Fairfield House Hotel

A stylish Victorian mansion boasting unrestricted views over the Firth of Clyde. The hotel restaurant offers a carefully-honed menu with main courses such as marinated Highland Venison with roast shallots, cherry and juniper berry reduction.

Style: Country-house/Formal
Smoking: No smoking in dining room
Accommodation: 45 en suite ★★★★

Directions: Town centre, down Miller Rd to T junction with traffic lights, filter L, immediately R into Fairfield Rd

12 Fairfield Road
KA7 2AR
Map 10: NS32
Tel: 01292 267461
Fax: 01292 261456
E-mail:
reservations@fairfieldhotel.co.uk
Cost: *Alc* £26. ☺ H/wine £10.95
Times: D only, 7-9pm
Additional: Bar food; Sunday L;
Children welcome

AYR, Fouters Bistro ❀❀

A plain decor of blue, white and terracotta, enhanced by some stencil work, creates a warm, inviting backdrop at this vaulted cellar restaurant with a flagstone floor. Attentive but casual service, a wine list that offers four bottles from Switzerland, and fine produce handled with honesty and without undue fuss are all part of the appeal. Shetland salmon goes into a fishcake (to accompany pan-seared West Coast scallops in an orange and cardamom sauce as a main course) or might turn up as a starter, seared and served with a Noilly Prat sauce ('simply delicious', noted an inspector). Mussels are given the classic treatment, and tender medallions of Carrick venison arrive on red cabbage braised with apple in a juniper-infused game sauce. Pot-roast shank of local lamb, falling off the bone, is full of flavour, with a gravy of the cooking juices, red wine and tarragon, plated on top of Arran mustard mash, while chargrilled steaks are something of a speciality. Puddings are from the school of iced tiramisu parfait and lemon tart.

2A Academy Street KA7 1HS
Map 10: NS32
Tel: 01292 261391
Fax: 01292 619323
E-mail: quality-food@fouters.co.uk
Chefs: Laurie Black, Laurent Cabede
Owners: Laurie & Fran Black
Cost: *Alc* £21.50, set-price D £15. ☺
H/wine £9.95
Times: Noon-2pm/5.30-10pm.
Closed Sun, 25-27 Dec, 1-3 Jan
Additional: Children welcome
Seats: 38. Private dining room 14
Style: Bistro-style/Informal
Smoking: No-smoking area; No pipes;
Air conditioning

Directions: Town centre, opposite
Town Hall, down Cobblestone Lane

GIRVAN, Wildings

A great atmosphere is created by effervescent service at this family-run restaurant. Roast cod had a lovely natural flavour, followed by crêpes filled with caramelised pears served with home-made ice cream.

Directions: Just off A77 at N end of village

Montgomerie Street KA26 9HE
Map 10: NX19
Tel: 01465 713481

Telephone for further details

MAYBOLE, Ladyburn ❀

Sip an aperitif and admire the hilly landscape from the attractive natural garden of this charming and welcoming country house before sitting down to a carefully cooked three-course dinner. Appealing traditional and French cookery awaits you.

Style: Country-house
Smoking: No smoking in dining room; Jacket & tie preferred
Civil licence: 30
Accommodation: 5 en suite ★★

Directions: Telephone for directions

KA19 7SG
Tel: 01655 740585
Fax: 01655 740580
E-mail:
jhdh@ladyburn.freeserve.co.uk
Cost: Set-price L, fr £15/D fr £30.
H/wine £12
Times: 12.30-1.30pm/7.30-8.15pm.
Closed L Mon, Tue & Sun

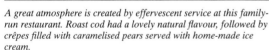

TROON, Highgrove Hotel ❀❀

Loans Road KA10 7HL
Map 10: NS33
Tel: 01292 312511
Fax: 01292 318228

Telephone for further details.

More a restaurant with accommodation than a hotel, so diners benefit from this intensity of focus. A light modern touch was evident throughout a recent visit which began with three tasty and tender chicken fillets combined with a Caesar salad and shaved fresh parmesan. A main of fillet of beef on a pâté croûton with wild oyster mushrooms was a generous and well crafted dish and a raspberry bread-and-butter pudding with sauce anglaise proved a very satisfying end to a most pleasant meal. All of this took place in the attractive split-level restaurant which offers very fine views over the Firth of Clyde and a formal yet relaxing atmosphere.

Directions: A77 from Ayr (Glasgow), L at Prestwick Airport, first R to Old Irvine. First L to Loans, R at mini rdbt to Highgrove

TROON, Lochgreen House ❀❀❀

Monktonhill Road Southwood
KA10 7EN
Map 10: NS33
Tel: 01292 313343
Fax: 01292 318661
Chef: Andrew Costley
Owners: Bill & Cath Costley
Cost: Set-price D £29.95.
H/wine £12.50
Times: Noon-2pm/7-9pm
Additional: Sunday L;
Children welcome
Smoking: No smoking in dining room;
Air conditioning; Jacket & tie preferred
Accommodation: 15 en suite ★ ★ ★

The newly built restaurant is unique in design and the high ceilings, oak beams and tapestried walls have a baronial air, just right for a celebratory dinner after a round or two on the adjacent fairways of Royal Troon Golf Course. Wines are now stored library style up to the ceiling, complete with sliding library ladders. Three large chandeliers add a sense of opulence. Proprietor Bill Costley was for many years a member, coach and gold medal winner with the Scottish Culinary Team, so not surprisingly there is a distinct Scottish influence in the menus. A folksy ingredient, however, such as ham hough, is gentrified into a super smart, textbook terrine with lentils and fine herbs served with celeriac remoulade and sauce gribiche. Fish cookery is emphasised, from the simplicity of steamed fillet of halibut with fresh saffron, vine tomatoes and sauce Bouillabaisse to the exoticism of seared tuna loin with ginger, coriander pomme purée and red wine sauce flavoured with Chinese spices, or the originality of salmon and lobster gratin with rice pilaf served in a large oval dish. Desserts have a welcome lightness of touch – passionfruit delice with passionfruit sorbet was both colourful and refreshing.

Directions: Off A77 (Prestwick Airport) onto B749, SE of Troon

TROON, Marine Hotel ❀

Crosbie Road KA10 6HE
Map 10: NS33
Tel: 01292 314 444
Fax: 01292 316 922
E-mail: marine@paramount-hotels.co.uk

Telephone for further details

Elegant split-level restaurant overlooking the fairway. An enjoyable lunch comprised smooth chicken liver paté, crispy duck confit, and poached pear with toffee sauce and a basket of honey ice cream.

Directions: Take A77 from Glasgow, (following signs for Prestwick Airport) and turn onto B789

TROON, Piersland House Hotel ❀❀

Craigend Road KA10 6HD
Map 10: NS33
Tel: 01292 314747
Fax: 01292 315613
Chef: John Rae
Owner: Aristo Hotels
Cost: Alc £20, set-price L £9.95. ☺
H/wine £10.50

Good quality ingredients, hearty portions and interesting flavour combinations account for the popularity of this hotel restaurant with business travellers, tourists and locals alike. Not that there's much wrong with the venue. In fact the mock-Tudor manor house is rather magnificent, as befits the one time residence of the whisky producing Walker family, and the

Piersland House Hotel

Times: Noon-2.30pm/6.45-9.30pm
Additional: Bar food; Sunday L;
Children welcome
Seats: 42. Private dining room 94
Style: Modern/Country-house
Smoking: No smoking in dining room
Civil licence: 73
Accommodation: 28 en suite ★★★

dining room is suitably elegant. But it is the food that takes centre stage here with starters such as crisp fried confit of duck with onion marmalade and a juniper and thyme sauce; and mains such as roast loin of venison with a thyme flavoured scone, creamed lentils and a good meaty jus impressing visually as well as in terms of flavour. An extensive bar menu is also available for a more informal but still high quality dining experience.

Directions: Opposite Royal Troon Golf Club

TURNBERRY, Malin Court ❀❀

KA26 9PB
Map 10: NS20
Tel: 01655 331457
Fax: 01655 331072
E-mail: info@malincourt.co.uk
Chef: Andrea Beach
Cost: Set-price D £22. ☺
H/wine £11.95
Times: 12.30-2pm/7.30-9pm
Additional: Sunday L;
Children welcome
Seats: 80
Style: Informal/Modern
Accommodation: 18 en suite ★★★

Recently refurbished in pastel shades, Cotters Restaurant has beautiful views over the Firth of Clyde and the Turnberry Golf Course looking towards the Isle of Arran. Dinner might start with warm salad of pigeon, smoked bacon and mushroom finished with balsamic vinegar, or smoked haddock pâté with crusty bread and curry mayonnaise. There is a choice of either soup, such as white onion with herb croutons, or sorbet, followed by main courses such as breast of chicken stuffed with haggis, shallots and tarragon, or pan-fried red snapper with citrus fruits on a bed of spinach. Vegetarian dishes include baked fennel and goats' cheese gratin. Coconut and Drambuie mousse coated with crisp white chocolate is amongst the choice of desserts. The menu is priced according to the number of courses taken, including the option of a single course only.

Directions: On A719 one mile from A77 on N side of village

TURNBERRY, Turnberry Hotel

KA26 9LT
Map 10: NS20
Tel: 01655 331000
Fax: 01655 331706
Chef: D S Cameron
Owner: Starwood Hotels & Resorts
Cost: *Alc* £50, set-price D £49.
H/wine £20.50
Times: D only, 7.30-9.30pm
Additional: Sunday L (1-2.30pm);
Children welcome
Style: Classic/country-house
Seats: 180. Private dining room 16
Accommodation: 132 en suite
★ ★ ★ ★ ★

The world-famous hotel enjoys tremendous views over to the Isle of Arran, the Mull of Kintyre and Ailsa Craig, as well as the adjoining golf courses. The main restaurant offers dining in the Grand Style – you couldn't call it dull, but it is sometimes a little lacking in sparkle. Desserts of chocolate crème brûlée and a cream Kahlua were the best part of the meal; also good was a lentil and smoked bacon soup served with a swirl of cream. Less impressive, however, was a rather dry confit of duck with salad and overcooked medallions of Buccleuch beef. Straightforward vegetables – mini sweetcorn, cauliflower and mange-tout – were served on the side. Filter coffee and neatly presented petits fours to finish.

Directions: On A77. Turn R at Turnberry village, hotel is 0.5 mile on R opposite golf courses

DUMFRIES & GALLOWAY

CASTLE DOUGLAS,
Plumed Horse Restaurant

Main Street
DG7 3AU
Map 11: NX76
Tel: 01556 670333
Fax: 01556 670302
E-mail: plumed.horse@virgin.net
Chef: Tony Borthwick
Owners: Tony Borthwick,
Charles Kirkbride
Cost: *Alc* £23.45-£30.90, set-price L
£11.95-£14.50/ D £29.50 (midweek
only). ☺ H/wine £9.99
Times: 12.30-1.30pm/7-9pm. Closed
L Sat, all Mon, 1 wk Jan, 1 wk Sep
Additional: Sunday L; Children
welcome; Vegetarian dishes not
always available
Seats: 30. Private dining room 20
Style: Classic/Chic
Smoking: No smoking in dining room;
Air conditioning

A warm yellow colour scheme complemented by a rich blue carpet creates a lush atmosphere for fine dining. Prices are very reasonable given the extremely high quality of ingredients, the artfulness of the composition and the accuracy and skill of the realisation throughout the wide ranging menu. Sunday lunch is a big crowd-puller with a three course meal following the lines of smoked salmon with sour cream; followed by roast loin of pork with traditional vegetables, Yorkshire pudding and a sherry sauce; and ending with bread-and-butter pudding. The evening *carte* offers a broad range of starters from sautéed scallops with smoked salmon broth and Beluga caviar to salad of home marinated goats' cheese pearls with a fresh herb and olive oil dressing. The main course menu is similarly extensive and includes vegetarian options such as charlotte of spiced aubergine with a panaché of green summer vegetables and a pesto dressing.

Directions: Take A75 to Castle Douglas then on A713 towards Ayr, 3 miles from Castle Douglas

GATEHOUSE-OF-FLEET,
Cally Palace Hotel ❀

Spacious restaurant in a country house with an attractive view of five hundred acres of parkland and forest. Modern British cuisine is served, such as broccoli and Stilton soup or roast fillet of beef, for example.

Additional: Bar food L; Sunday L; Children welcome
Style: Country-house
Smoking: No smoking in dining room; Air conditioning; Jacket & tie preferred
Accommodation: 56 en suite ★★★★

Directions: From A74(m) take A75, through Dumfries towards Newton Stewart

DG7 2DL
Map 11: NX55
Tel: 01557 814341
Fax: 01557 814522
E-mail: cally@cphotel.demon.co.uk
Cost: Set-price D £26. H/wine £12
Times: 12.30-1.30pm/6.45-9pm.
Closed Jan

KIRKCUDBRIGHT,
Selkirk Arms Hotel ❀❀

Originally a hostelry frequented by Burns, the Selkirk Arms, on the High Street of this pretty harbour town, is now a smart hotel. Dinner in the attractive restaurant, which looks out on the leafy garden, is from a set-price menu with a good balance of choices. Fresh, locally-sourced produce is the backbone of the operation, with sirloin or fillet steak from Galloway cattle given traditional treatments, and salmon is seared and served on tomato pasta with cardamom beurre blanc. Searing might also be applied to a starter of scallops on a saffron fish cream, deep-fried sweet potato and tomato crisps giving good contrast, or there might be wood pigeon salad dressed with hazelnuts and toasted pine kernels. A compote of cinnamon-spiced apple and black pudding gives an added dimension to tender, pink saddle of venison with a well-made, delicately-flavoured honey sauce, and the kitchen shows a deft touch in handling bold flavours, with wild mushroom and oxtail risotto accompanying chicken breast in a Madeira and tarragon sauce. Desserts return to safer waters, with crêpes Suzette or a nicely light strawberry bread-and-butter pudding. Breads are 'moreish', particularly the salmon and lemon, and the number of wines sold by the glass is limited on an otherwise decent list.

Directions: 5 miles S of A75 junction with A711

Old High Street DG6 4JG
Map 11: NX65
Tel: 01557 330402
Fax: 01557 331639
E-mail:
reception@selkirkarmshotel.co.uk
Chef: Ian Barron
Owners: EJ & SJ Morris
Cost: *Alc* £22. ☺ H/wine £7.95
Times: D only, 7-9.30pm.
Closed Xmas
Additional: Bar food; Sunday L;
Children welcome
Seats: 60. Private dining room 22
Style: Informal/traditional
Smoking: No smoking in dining room
Civil Licence: 100
Accommodation: 16 en suite ★★★

LOCKERBIE, Dryfesdale Hotel ❀

A cosy hotel restaurant with views over the Moffat hills and a warm welcoming atmosphere. Local produce features heavily on the menu, including a mature Lockerbie cheese in a masterful twice-baked cheese soufflé on wilted leeks.

Additional: Bar food; Sunday L; Children welcome
Style: Traditional/Country-house
Smoking: No smoking in dining room
Civil licence: 60
Accommodation: 15 en suite ★★★

Directions: M74 J17 to Lockerbie

DG11 2SF
Map 11: NY18
Tel: 01576 202427
Fax: 01576 204187
E-mail:
reception@dryfesdalehotel.co.uk
Cost: £25, set-price L £10.95/
D £19.95. ☺ H/wine £13.50
Times: Noon-2pm/6.30-9pm.

MOFFAT,

Beechwood Hotel

Harthope Place DG10 9RS
Map 11: NT00
Tel: 01683 220210
Fax: 01683 220889
Cost: Set-price L £15/D £25.
H/wine £11
Times: Noon-2pm/7-8.45pm.
Closed L Mon-Thu, 2 Jan-18 Feb
Additional: Sunday L; Children
welcome
Style: Classic/country-house
Smoking: No smoking in dining room
Accommodation: 7 en suite ★ ★

If you're looking for fine Scottish cuisine this elegant hotel restaurant is definitely worth a visit. Locally produced ingredients are at the heart of the many dishes, including terrine of chicken and haggis, and seared loin of venison.

Directions: At N end of High Street turn R into Harthope Place (hotel signed)

MOFFAT,

Well View Hotel

Ballplay Road DG10 9JU
Map 11: NT00
Tel: 01683 220184
Fax: 01683 220088
E-mail: info@wellview.co.uk
Chef: Janet Schuckardt
Owners: Janet & John Schuckardt
Cost: Set-price L £14/D £28.
H/wine £12
Times: 12.30-1.30pm/7-9pm.
Closed L Sat
Additional: Sunday L; Children 5+;
Vegetarian dishes not always
available
Seats: 20. Private dining room 6.
Jacket & tie preferred
Style: Country-house
Smoking: No smoking in dining room
Accommodation: 6 en suite ★

Directions: From Moffat take A708
(Selkirk); turn left after fire station in
Ballplay Road, 300yds to hotel.

A restful and refined small Victorian hotel, named after one of the several sulphurous wells which led to Moffat's growth as a Victorian spa town. The set dinner starts with a canapé then soup, perhaps cream of tomato and harissa with warm homemade soda bread. The fish course might be seared fillet of cod on a bed of spring cabbage and pancetta with tarragon dressing. A pause for a sorbet, then onto the main course – you'd be in luck if it was the medallions of Annandale lamb with spicy fruit couscous and Madeira and redcurrant jus. After cheese and a pudding such as coconut meringue ice cream cake with exotic fruits, there's coffee and sweetmeats in the lounge. All meat is served pink and vegetables crisp, but the menu encourages diners to express any preference for extra cooking. The nightly menu also suggests a selection of wines chosen from the excellent cellar to complement the meal.

NEWTON STEWART,
Creebridge House Hotel

DG8 6NP
Map 10: NX46
Tel: 01671 402121
Fax: 01671 403258
E-mail: info@creebridge.co.uk
Cost: *Alc* £25, set-price D £19.95. ☺
H/wine £12.95
Times: D only
Additional: Bar food, Sunday L;
Children welcome
Style: Traditional/Country-house
Smoking: No smoking in dining room
Civil licence: 50
Accommodation: 19 en suite ★ ★

Country-house restaurant overlooking gardens and woodland;
celebrated Galloway lamb dishes are offered alongside Solway
salmon, roast venison, and fettuccine with asparagus, walnuts and
roast garlic.

Directions: Telephone for directions

NEWTON STEWART,
Kirroughtree House ❀❀❀

Minnigaff DG8 6AN
Map 10: NX46
Tel: 01671 402141
Fax: 01671 402425
E-mail: kirroughtree@n-
stewart.demon.co.uk
Chef: Ian Bennett
Owner: McMillan Hotels Ltd
Cost: Set-price L £13.50/D £30.
H/wine £13.75
Times: Noon-1.30pm/7-9pm. Closed
3 Jan-mid Feb
Additional: Sunday L
Seats: 45. Jacket & tie preferred
Style: Country-house
Smoking: No smoking in dining room
Accommodation: 17 en suite ★ ★ ★

Try and come when the rhododendrons are in bloom, filling
the beautifully landscaped gardens with colour. The house has
a classic country-house style, but is saved from stiffness by
caring and friendly local staff. The Scottish-French cuisine,
however, has more aspiration and is a showcase for the
kitchen's undoubted battery of confident technical skills.
Typically, Ian Bennett might offer an appetiser of cappuccino
of garden peas with white truffle oil, followed by tartare of
Scottish salmon with cucumber, gazpacho sauce and caviar,
then breast of Gressingham duck glazed with honey and
crushed peppercorns, potato pancake, Savoy cabbage, glazed
pearl onions and cassis sauce. Desserts might feature a choice
of pear and blueberry sablé with kirsch sabayon and melba
sauce or mille-feuille of chocolate with macerated raspberries
and mint anglaise. Good petits fours, including a delicious, tiny
lemon tart.

Directions: From A75 turn left into
A712 (New Galloway), hotel entrance
300yds on left

PORTPATRICK, **Fernhill Hotel**

A choice of two restaurants both offering stunning views and featuring fresh lobster from the in-house holding facility. Other dishes might include pan-fried escalopes of pork fillet in a cider sauce.

Additional: Bar food L; Sunday L; Children welcome
Style: Informal/Traditional
Smoking: No-smoking area
Accommodation: 23 en suite ★ ★ ★

Directions: A77 from Stranraer. R before war memorial. Hotel 1st L

DG9 8TD
Map 10: NW95
Tel: 01776 810220
Fax: 01776 810596
E-mail:
fernhill@portpatrick.demon.co.uk
Cost: Alc £25.50, set-price D £22.50.
☺ H/wine £9.35
Times: Noon-2pm/6.30-9.30pm

PORTPATRICK,
Knockinaam Lodge ❀❀❀

Stranraer DG9 9AD
Map 10: NW95
Tel: 01776 810471
Fax: 01776 810435
Chef: Tony Pierce
Owners: Michael Bricker, Pauline Ashworth
Cost: Set-price L £29/D £38. H/wine £12
Times: Noon-2.30pm/7.30-11pm
Additional: Bar food L; Sunday L; Children 12+
Seats: 32. Private dining room 6-8
Style: Country-house
Smoking: No smoking in dining room
Civil licence: 40
Accommodation: 10 en suite ★ ★

The lodge is in an idyllic position for those wanting to get away from it all, and late sunsets during summer give guests the chance to enjoy the sea views over dinner. Inside, a warm, country-house atmosphere prevails, with efficient, friendly staff ensuring that things run like clockwork. Dinner is a set four courses, the only choice a toss-up between a pudding or a selection of British and French cheeses. The kitchen uses the finest ingredients Scotland has to offer, from lobster, made into a sausage as a first course and served with dill butter, to Highland roe-deer, given the Wellington treatment as a main course and sauced with a Madeira and vanilla jus. Meals can start with pan-fried fillet of turbot with sauce vierge, or a stunning-looking roulade of foie gras within spinach surrounded by rabbit confit and then Parma ham. Steamed asparagus with truffled hollandaise and Parmesan, or a 'superb' piece of sea bass dotted with sauce nero and chive oil might come next, with a crescendo reached at main course: breast of Gressingham duck with a spring onion and raspberry reduction and vegetable couscous, or faultlessly roasted noisette of Aberdeen Angus topped with a flawless chicken and artichoke mousse with a truffle and port reduction and pommes Anna. Perfectly timed soufflés are worth the short wait: Calvados with Granny Smith sorbet, say, or Sambucca with moreish white chocolate ice cream. Canapés have 'plenty of zing', breads and petits fours are impressive, and the massive wine list shows quality throughout, with some fine clarets and around twenty house wines.

Directions: A77 or A75 follow Portpatrick. 2 miles W of Lochans watch for Colfin Smokehouse & hotel signs and follow

North West Castle Hotel

*A meal here is a real occasion, with a pianist playing during dinner.
A traditional-style menu includes chef's woodland game terrine, and
roast sirloin of prime Scotch beef.*

Style: Classic/Traditional
Smoking: No smoking in dining room; Jacket & tie preferred
Civil licence: 180 **Accommodation:** 73 en suite ★ ★ ★ ★

Directions: Town Centre

DG9 8EH
Map 10: NX06
Tel: 01776 704413
Fax: 01776 702646
E-mail: nwc@mcmhotel.demon.co.uk
Cost: Set-price L £9.50/D £21. ☺
H/wine £9.50
Times: Noon-2pm/7-9.30pm
Additional: Bar Food L; Sunday L;
Children welcome; Vegetarian dishes
by request only

DUNBARTONSHIRE, WEST

BALLOCH,
Cameron House Hotel ❀❀❀

A 14th-century stone keep formed the centrepiece for this
impressive baronial-style mansion, completed in the 18th
century, in a glorious position on the shore of Loch Lomond
amid 100 acres of grounds. The refined ambience of the
Georgian Room, where a pianist plays at the grand piano, is
where the kitchen displays its energies to best effect. Canapés
– lamb compote on sweet sultanas and finely diced pear – and
good breads show a seriousness of intent, a feeling not
dispelled by a glance at the menu. Combinations have been
thought through and work well, as in smoked ham and tomato
consommé with basil dumplings and soft white beans, or a
main course of quail baked with pigeon accompanied by
cumin-scented sea kale and forestière sauce. Upmarket
materials crop up all over the place, not just for their own
sakes, but to integrate with other ingredients. Foie gras goes
into a terrine with smoked ham in a light sherry and shallot
dressing, for instance, making a successful starter
complemented by a 'delicious' toasted brioche, while lobster is
casseroled with Mull scallops and served with ink tortellini and
keta caviar cream, and grilled fillet of beef is set on a smoked
bacon and potato pancake and edged with truffle jus. An
essence of wine and beetroot 'worked a lot better than
anticipated' for an inspector who enjoyed the colour and taste
sensations of it with fresh, moist turbot on pesto mash and

Loch Lomond G83 8QZ
Map 10: NS38
Tel: 01389 755565
Fax: 01389 759522
E-mail:
devere.cameron@airtime.co.uk
Chef: Peter Fleming
Owner: De Vere Hotels
Cost: Alc £47, set-price D £41.50
Times: D only, 7-10pm
Seats: 42. Private dining room 40;
Jacket & tie preferred
Style: Traditional/Formal
Smoking: No smoking in dining room;
Air conditioning
Accommodation: 96 en suite
★ ★ ★ ★ ★

Directions: M8/A82 to Dumbarton:
take road to Luss, hotel signed 1 mile
past Balloch on R

roast fennel. Puddings are approached with verve too: bitter chocolate ravioli with a sweet saffron cream, or lavender-infused crème brûlée on warm berry coulis garnished with red berries and a light redcurrant jelly, all decorated by spirals of spun sugar. Service, from a uniformed team, is correct, professional and attentive, and the extensive wine list features fine vintages as well as a good range by the glass.

CLYDEBANK, Beardmore Hotel

Beardmore Street G81 4SA
Map 11: NS56
Tel: 0141 951 6000
Fax: 0141 951 6018
E-mail: beardmore.hotel@hci.co.uk
Chef: Derek Donaldson
Cost: Alc £25. ☺ H/wine £13
Times: D only, 7-10pm. Closed Xmas
Additional: Sunday L; Children 12+
Style: Chic
Smoking: No smoking in dining room; Air conditioning
Accommodation: 168 en suite
★ ★ ★ ★

Directions: M8 J19, follow signs for Clydeside Expressway to Glasgow Rd, then Dumbarton Rd (A814), then signs for Clydebank Business Park. Hotel on L within HCI International Medical Centre complex

The Citrus restaurant thankfully lacks the stuffy formality normally associated with this level of hotel, modern or otherwise. Closed at lunchtime, the dinner menu is short and changed frequently, with about half a dozen choices at each course. The kitchen does a good job – seared bass with diced potato salad flavoured with truffle oil and sherry dressing was quite delicious; roast Highland venison with a forestière garnish impressed with its succulent, full-flavoured wild meat and neatly prepared winter vegetables. There's a nice local touch in the malt whisky jus with breast of pigeon and mushroom ravioli. Only one main fish dish, though, on the sample menu – panfried halibut, smoked salmon, lime and ginger butter. Dark chocolate truffle with caramelised pecans was all it should be – rich, smooth and decadent.

DUNDEE CITY

DUNDEE, Sandford Hotel

Late Victorian hotel with a popular restaurant that enjoys a great deal of local support as well as the usual business-leisure-golfer mix. Decent modern cooking with a French accent: game terrine and red onion marmalade, or Angus beef and marinated pigeon breast with rösti.

Additional: Bar food; Sunday L; Children welcome
Style: Traditional/country-house
Smoking: No smoking in dining room
Civil licence: 60
Accommodation: 16 en suite ★ ★ ★

Directions: 4 miles south of Tay Bridge at jctn of A92 and B946

Newport Hill Wormit DD6 8RG
Map 11: NO43
Tel: 01382 541802
Fax: 01382 542136
E-mail:
sandford.hotel@btinternet.com
Cost: Set-price L/D £22.75. ☺
H/wine £11
Times: Noon-2.30pm/7-9.30pm

EDINBURGH, CITY OF

EDINBURGH, Atrium 🏵🏵🏵

10 Cambridge Street EH1 2ED
Map 11: NT27
Tel: 0131 228 8882
Fax: 0131 228 8808
Chef: Neil Forbes
Owners: Andrew & Lisa Radford
Cost: Alc £27 & £32, set-price L £14
& £18/D £25. H/wine £12
Times: Noon-2.30pm/6.30-10pm.
Closed L Sat, all Sun, 25 Dec-2 Jan
Additional: Children welcome
Style: Rustic
Smoking: Air conditioning

Directions: From Princes Street, turn
into Lothian Road, 2nd L and 1st R,
by the Traverse Theatre.

Some things don't change at Atrium. The tables are still made of railway sleepers and the lighting is still so dim that staff may have to find a patch of light before they can describe the breads. The cooking style remains the same too, despite a change of chef, who seamlessly continues the tradition of bringing a hint of the Mediterranean to the Auld Reekie. In tandem with the *carte* is a good-value set-price menu producing perhaps wild mushroom and tarragon pasta, maize-fed chicken breast in Madeira sauce, then chocolate marquise with orange sorbet. Otherwise, expect escabèche of sea bass, followed by pan-fried pigeon breast served in its own juices with lentils and bacon. Warm Thai-style chicken salad with coriander oil may break out of the mould, but more mainstream to the operation is a rustic dish of saddle of wild rabbit, juicy and tender, with truffled cannellini beans and red wine sauce. First-class produce is put to good use: fillet of Buccleuch beef with wild mushroom ravioli, or 'sweet and tender' saddle of lamb, cooked pink, with niçoise vegetables that included 'superb' black olives and 'delectable' pulpy garlic cloves. A fish main course might be roast fillet of salmon with creamy mussel sauce, wilted spinach and mash, and puddings end on a high: warm chocolate pudding with a matching sauce, or prune and Armagnac tart, a good example of fine pastry-work, of deep flavour surrounded by its own sauce. Those daunted by the long wine list could hit the quick selection page, the sommelier's suggestions, or stick to the 20-odd served by the glass.

EDINBURGH,
Balmoral Hotel, Hadrian's

Brasserie-style restaurant with its own identity as the hotel's second eaterie (see entry over page). Expect wild mushroom and chicken boudin and tender grilled calves' liver with smoked bacon and olive oil mash.

Directions: Hotel at east end of Princes Street; hotel is next to Waverley Station

1 Princes Street EH2 2EQ
Map 11: NT27
Tel: 0131 5576727
Fax: 0131 5578740

Telephone for further details

EDINBURGH,

Balmoral Hotel, Number One ✿✿

1 Princes Street
EH2 2EQ
Map 11: NT27
Tel: 0131 5576727/5562414
Fax: 0131 5578740
Chef: Jeff Bland
Owner: RF Hotels Ltd
Cost: *Alc* £40, set-price L £20/D £36.
☺ H/wine fr £16
Times: Noon-2pm/7-10pm (10.30pm
Fri & Sat). Closed L Sat & Sun
Additional: Sunday L
Seats: 50. Private dining room 30
Style: Modern/Minimalist
Smoking: No-smoking area; Air
conditioning
Accommodation: 186 en suite
★ ★ ★ ★ ★

A hushed haven of excellence tucked away from the rough and
tumble of Princes Street. The oriental-style lacquered walls
and many baby trees lend this restaurant a Far-Eastern feel,
but the cooking is British. The wide-ranging *carte* might
include several luxury items brought together in an
uncomplicated way using well-honed skills. Recently enjoyed
flashed langoustines were cooked to perfection, being tender,
sweet and slightly charcoaly from the grill, and they did not
need the accompanying diced pepper garnish or tomato coulis
which, though delicious, were superfluous. Praise was lavished
on a delicate dish of oxtail with foie gras, Puy lentils and a red
wine reduction, which was served on quickly sautéed savoy
cabbage. A warm rice pudding with nutmeg ice cream also
stood up well to the test, and a 'deeply-satisfying' espresso
came with a delectable selection of petits fours.

Directions: Hotel at east end of Princes Street; hotel is next to
Waverley Station

EDINBURGH,

Bonars Restaurant ✿

56 St Mary's Street EH1 1SX
Map 11: NT27
Tel: 0131 556 5888
Fax: 0131 556 2588
E-mail: bonars@lineone.net

*Simplicity and freshness are the keynotes here. A recent lunch
displayed super value for money, pairing game pasta with roasted
artichokes to start, followed by well-fried salmon on a creamed
langoustine sauce.*

Telephone for details

Directions: Near John Knox House

CLOSED

EDINBURGH,

The Bonham ✿

35 Drumsheugh Gardens
EH3 7RN
Map 11: NT27
Tel: 0131 6239319
E-mail: restaurant@thebonham.com

*Georgian town house hotel with a striking brasserie-style restaurant
serving exquisitely presented dishes, notable for their colour, texture
and innovative ingredients.*

The Bonham

Cost: *Alc* D £25, set-price L £15. ☺
H/wine £15
Times: Noon-2.30pm/6.30-10pm
(9.30pm Sun). Closed 3-7 Jan
Additional: Sunday L
Style: Informal/Modern
Smoking: No-smoking area; No pipes
& cigars
Accommodation: 48 en suite ★ ★ ★ ★

Directions: Located close to west end of Princes Street

EDINBURGH,
Le Café St Honore ❀

*Atmospheric dining at an authentic French-style café down a back
lane in the city centre; buzzing at lunchtime and candlelit at night
with soft jazz playing in the background.*

Times: Noon-2.15pm/7-10pm(Apres-Cinq 5-7pm). Closed L Sat,
all Sun (ex for Edinburgh Festival), 1 wk Oct, 3 days Xmas, 3
days New Year
Additional: Children welcome
Style: Bistro-style
Smoking: No-smoking area

34 NW Thistle Street Lane
EH2 1EA
Map 11: NT27
Tel: 0131 2262211
Fax: 0131 6247905
Cost: *Alc* £16-£24.50, set-price L
£13.50 & £18/D £23.50-£30.50. ☺
H/wine £9.75

Directions: City centre

EDINBURGH,
Channings Restaurant ❀❀

South Learmonth Gardens
EH4 1EZ
Map 11: NT27
Tel/Fax: 0131 3152225/6
E-mail:
restaurant@channings.co.uk
Chef: Richard Glennie
Owner: Peter J Taylor
Cost: Set-price L £15/D £23.50. ☺
H/wine £15

Channings has recently undergone a major refurbishment
programme. The lower ground floor restaurant is richly
decorated and retains superb Edwardian features. By contrast,
the bar and conservatory restaurant are light and bright with
clean contemporary lines. The menu is modern Scottish with
European influences. Expect the likes of hot smoked salmon
topped with avocado salsa, poached langoustine and gazpacho

dressing, or tasty new season lamb on sardalaise potato, with a Savoy cabbage parcel of shredded shank, cabbage and carrot. Apple assiette is an innovative dessert, with a crisp filo finger, a dauphinoise-style cake of sliced apple, a brûlée and a fresh-tasting sorbet.

Civil licence: 50
Accommodation: 46 en suite ★★★★

Directions: From Princes St follow signs to Forth Bridge (A90), cross Dean Bridge and take 4th R into South Learmonth Ave. Follow road to R at bottom of hill

Times: Noon-2pm/6.30-9.30pm(10pm Fri & Sat). Closed L Sun, 23-27 Dec (ex for Xmas L); 7 Jan
Additional: Bar food
Seats: 80. Private dining room 20
Style: Informal/Traditional
Smoking: No smoking in dining room

EDINBURGH,

Duck's at Le Marché Noir ✿

Fresh linen and candlelit tables set the scene for modern British dishes – perhaps roast venison on butternut squash with port and lentil sauce, and seared king scallops with spiced couscous.

Additional: Children welcome;
Vegetarian dishes not always available
Style: Classic
Smoking: No-smoking area

Directions: Follow the 'Mound' across Princes Street, George Street, Queen Street to bottom of Dundas Street

2/4 Eyre Place EH3 5EP
Map 11: NT27
Tel: 0131 5581608
Fax: 0131 5560798
E-mail: bookings@ducks.co.uk
Cost: *Alc* L £15/D £25. ☺
H/wine £9.50
Times: Noon-2.30pm/6-10.30pm.
Closed L Sat & Sun, 25, 26 Dec

EDINBURGH,

George Inter-Continental ✿

Former banking hall now established as Carvers restaurant which, alongside the long established Le Chambertin, provides a good range of cuisine for hotel guests and public alike. Traditional meals alongside such novelties as ostrich haggis.

Additional: Bar food; Sunday L (Carvers only);
Children 12+ ex for Carvers
Style: Classic/Formal (Informal/Traditional – Carvers)
Smoking: No-smoking area; Air conditioning
Civil licence: 100
Accommodation: 195 en suite ★★★★

Directions: At E end of George St, nr St Andrew's Square

19-21 George Street EH2 2PB
Map 11: NT27
Tel: 0131 2251251
Fax: 0131 2265644
E-mail: edinburgh@interconti.com
Cost: *Alc* £29,(£25 Carvers), set-price (L/D £18.50 Carvers)/ L £13/D £28.
☺ H/wine £13
Times: 12.30-2pm(noon-2.30pm Carvers)/7(6.30pm Carvers)-10pm.
Le Chambertin closed – L Sat, all Sun & Mon, Xmas/New Year

EDINBURGH, Haldanes ❀❀

39a Albany Street EH1 3QY
Map 11: NT27
Tel: 0131 5568407
Fax: 0131 5562662
E-mail: gkelso1547@aol.com
Chef: George Kelso
Owners: George & Michelle Kelso
Cost: Set-price L £12-£15/D £25.50.
☺ H/wine £12.75
Times: Noon-1.30pm/6-11pm.
Closed L Sat, Sun & Mon,
25 & 26 Dec
Additional: Children welcome
Seats: 50. Private dining rooms 14
& 20
Style: Traditional/Country-house
Smoking: No smoking in dining room

If the lower-ground floor of a Georgian building housing a hotel sounds gloomy and forbidding, think again. Haldanes is light and spacious, intimate and elegant, with an open fire in the lounge and a small courtyard at the back. A short selection of house specialities, inspired mainly by Scottish traditions, are found on the menu: oak-smoked salmon with lemon and capers, followed by a number of ways with steaks. The same indigenous materials are used to advantage in other dishes too, as in saddle of venison with wild mushrooms in a rich red wine sauce, or roast breast of maize-fed guinea fowl with creamed leeks and bacon. An exotic element may creep in here and there – a spicy chilli dressing for moist, nicely flavoured crab cakes topped with deep-fried leeks, for instance – although more mainstream to the operation is something like lamb shank braised with chunky mushrooms, shallots and diced red peppers served with garlicky creamed broad beans. Desserts end on an upbeat note in the form of 'excellent' iced honey and praline parfait on mango coulis with roasted strawberries, or dark chocolate terrine with marinated black cherries. Four house wines, from South Africa and France, are sold by both glass and bottle.

Directions: Telephone for directions

EDINBURGH,
Holyrood Hotel ❀❀   NEW

Newly-built hotel next door to the new Scottish parliament. Split-level Flints restaurant is an impressive and superbly comfortable room, smart and exciting with leather armchairs described as 'the best restaurant chairs I have ever sat in.' The food is stylish – confit of wild duck with sweetbreads, baby beets, garlic croûtons, shallots and a pepper leaf salad tossed with balsamic and grapeseed oil was prepared at the table and served in a deep bowl. A seared fillet of turbot, surrounded with mussels, clams and root vegetable bouillabaisse, was deliciously fresh but also a little overcooked. Other dishes included smoked haddock and spring onion risotto topped with poached egg; seared salmon with chermoula crust, spiced couscous and saffron essence; Amaretto cheesecake with rich chocolate sauce.

Civil licence: 200
Accommodation: 157 en suite ★★★★

Directions: Edinburgh city centre near the Royal Mile

Holyrood Road EH8 6AE
Map 11: NT27
Tel: 0131 5504500
Fax: 0131 5504545
E-mail:
gm@holyrood-macdonald.co.uk
Chef: Jo Queen
Cost: Alc £35, set-price L £12/D £25.
H/wine £13.50
Times: 12-2pm (12.30-2.30pm
Sat/Sun), 5-9.30pm
Additional: Sunday L; Children
welcome
Style: Bistro style/modern
Seats: 78. Private dining room 6 -150
Smoking: No smoking in dining room;
Air conditioning

EDINBURGH, Iggs ❀❀

15 Jeffrey Street EH1 1DR
Map 11: NT27
Tel: 0131 5578184
Fax: 0131 6523774
Chef: Andy McQueen
Owner: Iggy Campos
Cost: Alc £30, set-price L £12.50.
H/wine £11
Times: Noon-3.30pm/6-10.30pm.
Closed Sun
Additional: Children welcome
Seats: 50
Style: Chic/Spanish
Smoking: No-smoking area;
Air conditioning

Large mirrors, clever use of lighting, mustard-coloured walls and reproduction antique seating all create an elegant setting at Iggs, named after the owner. Despite dishes of perhaps Thai fishcakes on a plum and tomato galette with Asian pesto, the kitchen generally works around the classic repertoire, adding its own character as it does so. Bouillabaisse, a simple salad of Serrano ham with winter leaves and shavings of Manchego, or duck leg confit on a compote of tomatoes and grain mustard may be as complicated as starters get, resulting in clear, vibrant flavours. Main courses, too, show an admirable respect for treating good-quality ingredients with simplicity: supreme of halibut on fennel fondue with lobster sauce, or pink loin of lamb with pear and potato gratin, wild mushrooms and a juniper berry jus. Cheeses are Spanish and come with quince paste, and desserts might include traditional steamed orange sponge with Grand Marnier cream, or plum tart with bread ice cream.

Directions: At the heart of Edinburgh's Old Town, just off the Royal Mile

EDINBURGH, Malmaison ❀

One Tower Place Leith EH6 7DB
Map 11: NT27
Tel: 0131 4685000
Fax: 0131 4685002

Telephone for further details

Former seaman's mission at Leith with a cosy wood-panelled brasserie. Dishes sampled were a meaty ham hock and lentil terrine, roast cod with garlic shrimps, and an excellent crème brûlée.

Directions: From the city centre follow Leith Docklands, through 3 sets of lights and L into Tower Street

EDINBURGH, The Marque

If The Marque's vivid yellow walls bring to mind the sunshine of Provence, that is clearly the intention in a restaurant whose menu brings more than a hint of the Mediterranean to the city. Plum tomato and salsa soup with rouille, pan-roast salmon with aïoli and Parmesan and bouillabaisse broth, plus corn-fed chicken with Parma ham, lentil salsa, wild mushrooms and spinach are typical. Ingredients are impeccable, from wood pigeon (as a starter with spring onion and bacon mash and baked beans), to Buccleuch beef (as a main course with garlic confit crumble, black pudding, parsley mash and a cassoulet of pancetta and Toulouse sausage), and seasonal fruits (as in apple and blackberry crumble with honey ice cream).

Directions: Telephone for directions

19-21 Causewayside EH9 1QF
Map 11: NT27
Tel: 0131 4666660
Fax: 0131 4666661
Chefs: Glyn Stevens & John Rutter
Owners: Lara Kearney, John Rutter, Glyn Stevens
Cost: Alc £23, set-price L/D £12.50 (pre/post theatre). ☺ H/wine £11.95
Times: 11.45-2pm (12.30-2pm Sat/Sun)/5.45-10pm (11pm Fri/Sat). Closed Mon, 25-27 Dec, 1-3 Jan
Additional: Children welcome
Seats: 50. Private dining room 6
Smoking: No smoking in dining room

EDINBURGH, Marriott Dalmahoy

Although the main building was constructed in 1720 to William Adam's design, conversions and extensions over the years mean that this is now a large hotel, with a leisure centre, a choice of two golf courses and tennis courts. Set in extensive parkland, the hotel has views over the Pentland Hills and to Edinburgh Castle. The restaurant, which takes its name from the hills, is an elegant Regency-style room, with some tables overlooking the 18th green of the east course. Ravioli of pigeon and wild mushrooms with chasseur sauce, followed by shank of lamb braised with lentils and root vegetables in red wine, or grilled calves' liver with mash and shallots soaked in red wine sound reassuring enough, but the kitchen generally takes an imaginative approach to the fine ingredients it has at its disposal. A grape and walnut salad is topped with a rarebit of Dunsyre Blue and beer, and main courses have included some successful pairings: fillet of beef stuffed with smoked salmon, squares of tuna and salmon wrapped in Parma ham served on caramelised endive with a bacon vinaigrette, and pavé of cod topped with chicken livers and nuts, then wrapped in bok choi and set on a purée of flageolet beans. Pear Belle Hélène, or apple tarte Tatin may sound positively prosaic but are no less appreciated.

Directions: On A71, 3 miles from Calder roundabout, opposite Ratho turn off

Kirknewton EH27 8EB
Map 11: NT27
Tel: 0131 3331845
Fax: 0131 3331433
Chef: Alan Mathews
Cost: Alc £25-£35, set-price £16/D £22.50. ☺ H/wine £12.75
Times: 12.30-2pm/7-10pm. Closed L Sun
Additional: Bar food; Sunday L; Children welcome
Seats: 150. Private dining room 14-40
Style: Classic/Formal
Smoking: No smoking in dining room
Accommodation: 215 en suite
★ ★ ★ ★

EDINBURGH, Martin's Restaurant

A quiet side street in the centre is the setting for Martin's, its off-white walls hung with original artwork and some prints, and an otherwise predominantly green decor. The kitchen takes a safe and sound approach to some dishes – lambs' liver pan-fried with bacon, grilled fillet of cod with new potatoes – but never falters in its understanding of what will work well together. A starter of grilled hake on cod brandade with a herb jus has been a good combination of flavours and light textures, and the constituents of a main course of confit of duck leg in red wine sauce with dauphinoise potatoes, roasted celeriac and black pudding are brought together to make a pleasing whole. The range might be extended by the likes of roasted pigeon breast wrapped in Parma ham with vanilla sauce, or beetroot tagliatelle with chickpeas and a lime dressing, while desserts

70 Rose Street North Lane EH2 3DX
Map 11: NT27
Tel: 0131 2253106
Fax: 0131 2203403
Chef: David Romanis
Owners: Martin & Gay Irons
Cost: Alc £32, set-price L £12.50 D £25. H/wine £12.60
Times: Noon-2pm/7-10pm. Closed L Sat, all Sun & Mon, approx 4 wks from Dec 24, 1 wk May/Jun, 1 wk Oct
Additional: Children 8+
Seats: 30. Private dining rooms 8-18
Style: Minimalist/Formal
Smoking: No smoking in dining room

could run from coconut and cardamom rice pudding with spicy mango coulis and plum jam, to a skilfully prepared and presented trio of chocolate – sorbet, mousse and brownie. The wine list has been assembled with care and offers some good producers at fair prices.

Directions: North Lane is off Rose Street which runs parallel to and behind Princes Street

EDINBURGH,
Norton House Hotel ❀❀

Despite its secluded location amid 55 acres of parkland, this extended Victorian mansion is conveniently located for the city, the airport and the motorway network. The Gathering, located in the grounds, is a popular rendezvous for an informal meal, but for fine dining, earning our two-rosette award, choose the Conservatory Restaurant. Service is attentive and friendly, and the set-price dinner menu offers a range of some eight dishes at each of three courses. These might include a trio of Scottish salmon with a lemon and dill dressing, followed perhaps by escalope of beef with ginger spring onions, sesame oil and lemon grass-scented rice. Finish with a whisky and chocolate truffle or a platter of Scottish farmhouse cheeses.

Ingliston EH28 8LX
Map 11: NT27
Tel: 0131 3331275
Fax: 0131 3335305

Telephone for further details

Directions: M8 J2, off A8, 0.5 mile past Edinburgh Airport

EDINBURGH, **Restaurant**
Martin Wishart ❀❀ NEW

A decoratively minimalist restaurant; plain off-white walls with large contemporary paintings, stone floor with the tables covered in white linen, tableware and smart glasses. The Waterfront, a fashionable part of the Leith docklands, can be glimpsed through black venetian blinds. A short and impressive daily-changing menu might list escabèche of red mullet, foie gras and asparagus 'Tourte', a gratin of sea bass with a soft herb crust, and a roasted saddle of French farmed rabbit served with a carrot and cardamom purée and braised Belgian endive wrapped in Vantreche bacon. The fillet of roast sea bass with paysanne of celeriac, salsify, turnip, pommes Parisiennes, served with an oyster beignet and champagne velouté was notable for the fish which was beautifully fresh. The wine list will please both fans of New and Old World wines; good vintages and super wines by the glass.

54 The Shore Leith EH6 6RA
Map 11: NT27
Tel: 0131 553 3557
Fax: 0131 467 7091
Chef/Owner: Martin Wishart
Cost: *Alc* £30, set-price L £12.50 & £14.50/D £45. H/wine £11
Times: Noon-2.30pm/7-10pm. Closed L Sat, all Sun & Mon, Xmas, 1 Jan, Bhs
Additional: Children welcome; Vegetarian dishes not always available
Seats: 30
Style: Modern/Minimalist
Smoking: No smoking in dining room

Directions: Telephone for directions

EDINBURGH,

Rhodes & Co ❀❀

3-15 Rose Street EH2 2YJ
Map 11: NT27
Tel: 0131 220 9190

Telephone for further details

Directions: Telephone for directions

Gary Rhodes comes to Edinburgh. The stylish brasserie and bar has been designed by David Collins and takes a suggestion of 1950's style to inform an overall atmosphere of smart modernity. The room is spacious with large wall tiles, round pillars, a parquet floor and leather clad chrome tubular chairs. The cooking is modern British although some older dishes make a welcome reappearance – smoked haddock topped with Welsh rarebit, poached eggs benedict and cauliflower and macaroni cheese for example. On a recent visit, the inspector went for a starter of deep fried mackerel fillets, which won approval for a light crispy coat, effective seasoning and the distinctiveness of the mackerel. Salt and pepper duck breast with spicy plums was a main dish of delicious flavour, and a light and moist sticky pudding demonstrated great finesse. A selection of speciality teas is an interesting alternative to after-dinner coffee.

EDINBURGH,

Sheraton Grand Hotel ❀❀❀

1 Festival Square EH3 9SR
Map 11: NT27
Tel: 0131 2216423
Fax: 0131 2296254
Chef: Nicolas Laurent
Cost: *Alc* £30 & £35, set-price L £27.50/D £29. H/wine £16
Times: Noon-2.30pm/7-10.30pm. Closed L Sat, all Sun, 1st wk Jan
Seats: 50. Private dining room 20. Jacket & tie preferred
Style: Classic/Traditional
Smoking: No-smoking area; Air conditioning
Accommodation: 261 en suite
★ ★ ★ ★ ★

Directions: Off Lothian Road

A strikingly modern building, with a central staircase leading from the marble lobby to the popular bar, the Terrace restaurant, with views over the Usher Hall, for burgers, steaks and perhaps grilled tuna with coriander and shallot butter, and the cosseting environment of the Grill Room. This deals with the luxury end of the market, taking Scotland's best produce and giving it a novel touch, from a nage of salmon and lobster with a star anise infusion, to partridge with a shallot and sage sausage, endive and creamed potato and celeriac. Chargrilled squid is partnered with tender langoustines in a starter, but the kitchen handles humbler ingredients equally well, as in pan-fried sweetbreads in a hazelnut jus with beetroot and mesclun salad. Seared swordfish in a spicy coconut and coriander sauce with linguine and pak choi makes a flavour-packed main course, and simple treatments are effective too: slices of pink roast lamb with a fine truffled stock-based jus, chopped black olives and sliced courgette, for instance. Attractive presentation is a strong point, not least among puddings of perhaps Black Forest chocolate fondant. France is the backbone of the wine list, where prices match the surroundings.

EDINBURGH, 36

at The Howard Hotel
36 Great King Street EH3 6QH
Map 11: NT27
Tel: 0131 556 3636
Fax: 0131 556 3663
E-mail: 36@thehoward.com
Chef: Malcolm Warham
Owner: Peter J Taylor
Cost: Alc D £29, set-price L £15. ☺
H/wine £12
Times: D only. Closed 24-27 Dec
(ex L 25 Dec), 3, 4 & 7 Jan
Additional: Sunday L (noon-2pm)
Seats: 55. Private dining room 18
Style: Modern/Minimalist
Smoking: No smoking in dining room
Accommodation: 15 en suite ★ ★ ★ ★

36 is situated alongside the Howard, and connected by an internal staircase to the basement. In contrast to the elaborate and ornate style of the hotel, 36 is modern, with plain white walls, decorated by abstracts on canvas and lit by tiny spotlights which cast pools of indigo and magenta light. The *carte* is short and the descriptions succinct. A cannelloni of smoked haddock and sole with a tomato and tarragon salsa was 'imaginative and successful'. The pan fried beef fillet with braised oxtail ravioli, turnip sauerkraut and roasted shallots was full of flavour; first class beef, tender and juicily succulent. Desserts are ambitious and include an apple and cider soup with poached apple and apple fritters. In keeping with the style of the menu, the wine list is short and includes the usual suspects.

Directions: Turn off Princes St into Frederick St for 0.5 mile and turn R into Great King St. Past traffic lights, hotel on L

EDINBURGH, Tower Restaurant ❀

Smart brasserie-style restaurant offering fantastic views from the fifth floor of the Museum of Scotland. Seafood, steaks and salads feature, alongside dishes such as loin of lamb with minted couscous.

Additional: Sunday L; Children welcome
Style: Chic/Modern
Smoking: No smoking in dining room

Directions: Level 5 of Museum of Scotland

Museum of Scotland Chambers Street
EH1 1JF
Map 11: NT27
Tel: 0131 2253003
Fax: 0130 2474220
Cost: Alc £15-£30, set-price L £12/
D £10.95. ☺ H/wine £12
Times: Noon-11pm.
Closed 25 & 26 Dec

EDINBURGH, The Vintners Room ❀

Relaxed and stylish with cooking to match. Predominantly coastal, with good use made of fresh fish and shellfish. A recent lunch included roast cod with langoustine jus and seared scallops with saffron and mussels.

Additional: Children welcome **Seats:** 50
Style: Informal/Traditional
Smoking: No-smoking area

Directions: At end of Leith Walk; L into Great Junction Street, R into Henderson Street. Restaurant is in old warehouse on R

The Vaults 87 Giles Street
Leith EH6 6BZ
Map 11: NT27
Tel: 0131 554 6767
Fax: 0131 467 7130
E-mail:
vintners@thevintnersrooms.demon.co.uk
Cost: Alc £29, set-price L £11.50 &
£15. ☺ H/wine £12
Times: Noon-3.30pm/7-midnight.
Closed Sun, 2 wks from Xmas

EDINBURGH, Winter Glen ❀❀

3A1 Dundas Street EH3 6QG
Map 11: NT27
Tel: 0131 4777060
Fax: 0131 6247087
Chef: Graham Winter
Owners: Graham Winter & Blair Glen
Cost: Alc £25, set-price D £23 & £26.
☺ H/wine £12.50
Times: Noon-2pm/6.30-10pm.
Closed Sun, 25 Dec, 1st wk Jan
Additional: Children 10+
Seats: 60. Private dining room 24
Style: Rustic/Traditional
Smoking: No pipes & cigars

Rich drapes and elegant tables give an country house ambience to this basement restaurant. Cooking is contemporary Scottish and 'its good to see a city restaurant committed to quality at lunch time' remarked the inspector. Spiced crabcake with cumin, coriander and scallions on a citrus lime caramel to start, which came as two lightly battered, golf ball sized cakes with 'souffle-light' filling and good, accurate flavours. A main course of griddled halibut steak, marinated in olive oil and coriander, accompanied by a chilli, butter bean and tomato cassolet was fresh and perfectly cooked, the fish flaking nicely. For dessert, iced lime and coconut parfait was 'smooth and not too icy'.

Directions: Telephone for directions

EDINBURGH,
Witchery by the Castle ❀❀

Castle Hill EH2 1NE
Map 11: NT27
Tel: 0131 2255613
Fax: 0131 2204392
E-mail: mail@thewitchery.com
Chef: Douglas Roberts
Owner: James Thomson
Cost: Alc fr £27, set-price L/D
£9.95(pre & post theatre supper). ☺
H/wine £13.95
Times: Noon-4pm/5.30-11.30pm.
Closed 25 Dec

The Witchery, approached via a close leading from the Royal Mile, is actually a pair of rooms: the Secret Garden, with stone walls and doors opening on to an urn-filled terrace, where guests can dine in summer, and the Witchery itself, with heraldic painted ceilings and ancient panelling. If the rich, dark and jewel-like interior has been described as 'Gothic', the menus by and large are contemporary interpretations of reassuringly familiar dishes. Simple starters of Loch Fyne oysters, shellfish bisque given a twist with grilled red mullet, or whisky-cured salmon with capers and lime may jostle for attention alongside steak tartare with a quail's egg, and home-smoked Barbary duck with beetroot sorbet. Venison Wellington is given a sauce of figs and chocolate, lamb shank is braised with cassoulet, sea bass (perfectly timed) steamed and accompanied by crisp bacon and vanilla oil, and king scallops seared and served with smoked haddock brandade and sage butter. Ginger crème brûlée, or pineapple tarte Tatin with coconut ice cream are what to expect for pudding, and a dozen wines by the glass should simplify choice if a list approaching 1,000 bottles seems a bit daunting.

Directions: At the entrance to Edinburgh Castle at the very top of the Royal Mile

Additional: Sunday L
Seats: 120
Style: Classic/Chic
Smoking: Air conditioning

AA Wine Shortlisted for *Award-see* page 18

FALKIRK

FALKIRK,

Park Lodge Hotel NEW

Popular corporate and banqueting hotel offering a fine dining experience, or something more simple according to taste. Recently sampled dishes include chicken liver pate with herb salad, and sweet cured bacon steaks, all from quality Scottish ingredients.

Directions: From M8 take A803 to Falkirk, Hotel 1mile beyond Mariner Leisure Centre. From M9, A803 through Falkirk, follow signs Dollar Park

Camelon Road FK1 5RY
Map 11: NS88
Tel: 01324 628331
Fax: 01324 611593
E-mail: park@queensferry-hotels.co.uk

Telephone for further details.

GRANGEMOUTH,

Grange Manor Hotel

Modern treatment of traditional dishes produces some interesting flavour combinations at the Grange Manor, such as roast lamb with mushroom and apricot mousse, celeriac purée and caramelised fruits.

Directions: M9 J6 200mtrs on right, M9 J5 then A905 for 2 miles

Glensburgh FK3 8XJ
Map 11: NS98
Tel: 01324 474836
Fax: 01324 665861
E-mail: info@grangemanor.co.uk
Cost: Alc £30, set-price L £9.95/
D £22.75 & £24.75.
☺ H/wine £10.95
Times: Noon-2pm/7-9pm.
Closed all Sun, L Sat
Additional: Bar food;
Children welcome
Style: Classic/country-house
Smoking: No-smoking area
Accommodation: 37 en suite ★★★

POLMONT,

Inchyra Grange ❀

Grange Road FK2 0YB
Map 11: NS97
Tel: 01324 711911
Fax: 01324 716134

Seared scallops with Parma ham and ratatouille make an interesting starter, typical main courses include pan-fried crab cakes or seared noisettes of lamb. Chocolate flan with pistachio ice cream and chocolate sauce might feature for dessert.

E-mail: info@inchyra.macdonald-hotels.co.uk

Telephone for further details

Directions: M9 J4 or 5. In Polmont, nr BP social club

FIFE

ANSTRUTHER,

Cellar Restaurant ❀❀❀

24 East Green KY10 3AA
Map 12: NO50
Tel: 01333 310378
Fax: 01333 312544

Telephone for further details

Peter Jukes continues to keep his customers happy at his stone-walled, candlelit seafood restaurant, as he has been doing for well on 20 years. He sources from the best suppliers – as an inspector noted, 'he has a halibut man, a scallops man', and so on – so the raw materials are top-notch, and generally straightforward treatments are characterised by good judgement and accurate timing: fillet of cod in a pesto crust is roasted and served with basil mash, for instance, while halibut might be grilled and accompanied by greens, pine nuts and bacon with a pot of hollandaise. Lighter meals are served at lunchtime – seared tuna with cracked pepper, coriander leaves and a niçoise dressing, for example – while appetisers of salmon quiche or smoked haddock vol au vents in the evening are a foretaste of the serious business to follow. An omelette filled with creamy Finnan haddock has been a light and effective starter, and 'yummy', rich crayfish bisque, hinting of brandy, with cream and Gruyère and chunks of shellfish, remains as popular as ever. Expect to be asked how you would like your salmon cooked, as if it were steak, but leave it to the kitchen and it will be spot on, perhaps spiced and pan-blackened to give it a crisp coating but flaking at the touch of a fork, accompanied by sun-dried tomato couscous and crème fraîche to counter the deep flavour of the fish and spices. Those who must could choose spinach and nutmeg soup, then fillet of local beef with green peppercorn sauce, and puddings are as familiar as prune and Armagnac parfait, or crème brûlée. Sensibly priced whites hold sway on the wine list, which also features some classy vintages.

Directions: Behind the Scottish Fisheries Museum

CUPAR, Eden House Hotel

2 Pitscottie Road KY15 4HF
Map 11: NO31
Tel: 01334 652510
Fax: 01334 652277
E-mail: lv@eden.u-net.com
Cost: Alc £25, set-price L & D £20.
☺ H/wine £10.50
Times: Noon-2pm/6.30-9pm.
Closed L Sun, 25 Dec, 1 Jan
Additional: Bar Food; Children welcome
Style: Classic/Traditional
Smoking: No smoking in dining room
Accommodation: 11 en suite ★ ★

Directions: Turn R after railway bridge in Cupar. Hotel is 100yds to R

Intimate conservatory restaurant in a small family-run hotel overlooking Haugh Park. The cooking is uncomplicated and shows dedication to natural flavours, for example roasted rack of lamb with an almond and redcurrant sauce.

CUPAR,
Ostlers Close Restaurant

Bonnygate KY15 4BU
Map 11: NO31
Tel: 01334 655574
Fax: 01334 654036
Chef: James Graham
Owners: James & Amanda Graham
Cost: Alc L £19, D £30.
H/wine £11.50
Times: 12.15-2pm/7-9.30pm.
Closed L Wed & Thu, all Sun & Mon, 2 wks May
Additional: Children 6+ at D; Vegetarian dishes on request
Seats: 28

Directions: In small lane off main street (A91) of Cupar

The restaurant comprises three interconnecting cottagey rooms, tucked away down a side alley. Amanda Graham is a natural at running the front of house (and she makes the puddings). In the kitchen, her husband James issues a hand-written daily menu, simply constructed and carefully sourced so as to extract every last vestige of natural flavour from the top-class ingredients. Organic vegetables and herbs are grown specially for the restaurant, supplemented by produce from the garden. Dishes might feature St George's mushrooms picked that same morning by James, or Shetland lamb two ways – roasted saddle and braised casserole with 'clapshot'. The cooking tends to the robust and makes good use of game and offal. Individual ravioli of oxtail are served with crispy pigs' trotters and oxtail gravy; pot-roast breasts of wood pigeon with red cabbage and roasted celeriac. When roasted roe venison is on the menu, diners might also be offered the kidneys and some liver to go with it. Rösti-style haddock fishcakes with superb Mull scallops and herby mayonnaise was a nice twist on the standard offering, lightened by the use of grated potato. The wine list is extensive and reasonably priced.

DUNFERMLINE,
Keavil House Hotel

A 16th-century country house with a conservatory restaurant overlooking extensive gardens. Carefully prepared Taste of Scotland specialities are prepared from fresh local produce.

Additional: Bar food L; Sunday L; Children welcome
Style: Informal/modern
Smoking: No smoking in dining room
Civil licence: 100
Accommodation: 47 en suite ★★★

Directions: M90 J3, 7 miles from Forth Road Bridge, take A985, turning R after bridge. From Dunfermline, 2 miles W on A994

Crossford KY12 8QW
Map 11: NT08
Tel: 01383 736258
Fax: 01383 621600
E-mail: keavil@queensferry-hotels.co.uk
Cost: Alc £25.70, set-price L £5.99-£9.99/D £19.95. ☺ H/wine £9.95
Times: Noon-2pm/7-9pm

GLENROTHES, The Restaurant
at Rescobie

This delightful small hotel has been completely refurbished and seems to have taken on a new lease of life. It stands in well-tended gardens with the feel of a country house on the edge of the town, and the elegant dining room has kept its original 1930s character. There is no bar, but drinks are willingly served in the lounge. Delicious salmon, on a warm potato salad with a light mustard dressing was offered as an appetizer – most of the dishes are simple, with an emphasis on balance and freshness; a first course of smoked haddock and saffron risotto came topped with fresh leaves and a poached egg. Breast of pigeon, cooked pink and with a lovely flavour, came with a ravioli of smooth chicken mousse, laced with mushroom and thyme jus. Desserts are beautifully presented, the passion fruit parfait came topped with a home-made marshmallow and surrounded by a passion fruit jus with just a hint of lemon. The wine list comes annotated with the two owners' recommendations.

Directions: From A92 at Glenrothes take A911 to Leslie; at end of Leslie High St, straight ahead & 1st L

6 Valley Drive Leslie
KY6 3BQ
Map 11: NO20
Tel: 01592 749555
Fax: 01592 620231
E-mail: rescobiehotel@compuserve.com
Chef: Scott Dougall
Owners: Andrew & Fabienne Davidson
Cost: Set-price D £17.95 & £22.95. ☺ H/wine £9.90
Times: D only, 7-9pm. Closed Sun & Mon, 25, 26, 31 Dec, 1 & 2 Jan
Additional: Children 12+
Seats: 12 & 20. Private dining room 20
Style: Chic/Country-house
Smoking: No smoking in dining
Accommodation: 10 rooms ★★

KIRKCALDY,
Dunnikier House Hotel

The elegant surroundings of this 18th-century country house hotel set the scene for sophisticated, modern cuisine. Enjoy fillets of sea bass on a bed of sauteed courgettes. To follow perhaps a rosewater brûlée.

Additional: Bar food; Sunday L; Children welcome
Style: Traditional/country-house
Smoking: No smoking in dining room
Civil Licence: 40
Accommodation: 14 en suite ★★★

Directions: turn off A92 at Kirkcaldy West, take 3rd exit at roundabout signed 'Hospital/Crematorium', then 1st L past school

Dunnikier Park FY1 3LP
Map 12: NT29
Tel: 01592 268393
Fax: 01592 642340
E-mail: recp@dunnikier-house-hotel.co.uk
Cost: Alc £22.50, set-price L £15.75/D £20. ☺ H/wine £9
Times: Noon-2pm/6-9pm.

LUNDIN LINKS,
Old Manor Hotel ❀❀

Leven Road KY8 6AJ
Map 12: NO40
Tel: 01333 320368
Fax: 01333 320911
E-mail:
enquiries@oldmanorhotel.co.uk
Chef: Alan Brunt
Owners: Alistair, George &
Michael Clark
Cost: *Alc* £27.50, set-price D £26.50.
H/wine £10.95
Times: D only, 7-11pm. Closed 1 Jan
Additional: Sunday L
Seats: 36. Private dining room 12-60
Style: classic/country-house
Smoking: No smoking in dining room
Civil licence: 100
Accommodation: 23 en suite ★★★

Lovely views over Lundin Golf Course and Largo Bay are to be had from this country-house hotel on the edge of the village. The public areas invite relaxation, the Coachman's Bistro offers a popular, informal eating option, and fine dining takes place in the Aithernie Restaurant, an elegantly decorated room furnished with a mixture of mahogany and oak, and oil paintings, all lit by candlelight and table lamps. Scottish seafood has a strong presence on the set-price menus, from the successful flavour combinations of a cake of Largo Bay crab and spring onions with warm mango salsa, to a main course of lightly seared Montrose king scallops with saffron cream. Soups are commended – blue cheese and leek – and meatier offerings might run from game terrine to roast breast of guinea fowl stuffed with pigeon mousse on cranberry sauce. To finish, there might be white chocolate and Amaretto mousse with dark chocolate sauce. The comprehensive wine list has a good selection of half-bottles.

Directions: On A915 Leven-St Andrews road in the village

MARKINCH,
Balbirnie House ❀❀

Balbirnie Park KY7 6NE
Map 11: NO20
Tel: 01592 610066
Fax: 01592 610529

A stylish new conservatory restaurant in a lovingly restored luxury hotel. The new venue makes the most of views onto the

wonderful gardens, featuring woods and a burn running through, and the decor is bright and cheerful with light pastel shades dominating. Imaginative and more traditional cooking along the lines of mushroom risotto with a powerful truffle oil, or perfectly cooked fillet of beef with a béarnaise sauce and game chips. Classic desserts such as apple tart make for a satisfying conclusion to the meal. The wine list is fairly extensive and offers a well sourced and reasonably priced range. Service is professional and attentive.

Directions: M90 J3, follow signs for Glenrothes and Bay Bridge, R onto B9130 to Markinch and Balbirnie Park

Telephone for further details.

PEAT INN,

The Peat Inn ⊛⊛

Cupar KY15 5LH
Map 12: NO40
Tel: 01334 840206
Fax: 01334 840530
Chef: David Wilson
Owners: David & Patricia Wilson

One of the original restaurants-with-rooms, The Peat Inn has served for nearly thirty years as a culinary beacon to the discerning gourmet traveller. Enter through the humble porch into the open, beamed lounge where there seems to be a perpetually burning log fire, and instantly sink with gratitude into a deep sofa, surrounded by enough historical and culinary bijouterie to open a mini-museum. The restaurant is chintzy and has beautiful antique furniture; uniquely, the candlesticks are made from cannibalised knives and forks. Meat dishes are one of the kitchen's strengths – fillet of beef in Madeira sauce with roast shallots and potato cake was superb in terms of simplicity, balance and sheer quality of ingredients. Other great classic French dishes include cassoulet of lamb, pork and duck with flageolet beans, and whole local lobster in herb broth with fresh pasta. The six-course tasting menu is a good way to sample some of the house specialities in slightly smaller portions. The extensive wine list includes both renowned vintages and a reasonable choice of New World labels.

Cost: Alc £34, set-price L £19.50/D £28. ☺ H/wine £15
Times: up to 1pm/7-9.30pm.
Closed Sun, Mon, 25 Dec, 1 Jan
Additional: Children welcome
Seats: 48. Private dining rooms 12 & 24
Smoking: No smoking in dining room
Accommodation: 8 en suite ★ ★

Directions: At junction of B940/B941, 6 miles SW of St Andrews

AA Wine Shortlisted for Award-see page 18

ST ANDREWS,
Inn at Lathones

A country inn that has benefited from some sympathetic renovation over the last few years, the result being a restaurant full of character and charm. The main dining room is quite intimate with a beamed ceiling, white panelled walls and an impressive stone fireplace as focal point. Alternatively the four hundred-year-old stable block houses a similarly attractive bar/grill area, and offers the added bonus of 'The Grey Lady' – the resident ghost and her horse, though the inspector could not confirm this particular feature. He was however able to confirm the high quality of cuisine and service on offer with dishes such as Aubergine tian (a lovely light aubergine mousse set on top of very thin slices of courgettes, lightly studded with red peppers and encased in aubergine leaves).

Directions: 5m S of St Andrews on A915. Inn 0.5m before Largoward on left, just after hidden dip

Largoward KY9 1JE
Map:
Tel: 01334 840494
Fax: 01334 840694
E-mail: lathones@theinn.co.uk

Telephone for further details.

ST ANDREWS, **Old Course Hotel**

The Old Course, which has stunning sea views, takes its name from the adjacent golf links – in fact, it's next to the 17th hole. The Sands Brasserie takes a Pacific rim approach to cooking, with such dishes as yellow fin tuna with tropical fruit salsa, or Asian pesto scallops, while the fourth-floor Road Hole Grill gives a modern spin to the classics, using the finest Scottish produce.

Additional: Sunday L (Sands);Children welcome
Style: Bistro-style/classic
Smoking: No-smoking area; No pipes and cigars;
Civil licence: 100
Accommodation: 146 en suite ★★★★★

Directions: Situated close to A91 on the outskirts of the city

KY16 9SP
Map 12: NO51
Tel: 01334 474371
Fax: 01334 477668
E-mail: info@oldcoursehotel.co.uk
Cost: *Alc* £41.50, (Sands £20)
set-price D £38.50. H/wine £16.50
(Sands £13)
Times: 10am-6pm (noon-10pm
Sands)/7-10pm. Closed Xmas week
(restaurant)

ST ANDREWS, **Parkland Hotel**

Main courses might include loin of venison with braised red cabbage and mild pink peppercorn sauce, or seared trout fillet with shallots, oyster mushrooms and crispy parma ham. Try passion fruit flan with fruit coulis for dessert.

Cost: A/c £25 H/wine £13.95
Times: 12-2.00pm/7-9.00pm Open 7 days all year
Accommodation: 6 rooms ★★

Directions: West of town centre, opposite Kinburn Park

Kinburn Castle Double Dykes Rd
KY16 9DS
Map 12: NO51
Tel: 01334 473620
Fax: 01334 460850
E-mail: parklands@aol.com

ST ANDREWS,
Rufflets Country House

Smart country house hotel set in stunning grounds. The comfortably appointed Garden Restaurant overlooks a formal terrace with superb topiary and colourful flowerbeds. A daily changing set-price menu is offered at dinner together with a good range of keenly priced wines. A starter of smoked

Strathkinness Low Road KY16 9TX
Map 12: NO51
Tel: 01334 472594
Fax: 01334 478703
E-mail: reservations@rufflets.co.uk
Chef: William Thomson
Owner: Ann Russell

Rufflets Country House

Cost: Set-price L £18/D £32.
H/wine £14
Times: D only, 7-9pm
Additional: Bar food; Sunday L
(12.30-2pm); Children welcome
Seats: 80. Private dining room 20
Style: Traditional/Country-house
Smoking: No smoking in dining room

haddock risotto was topped with a perfectly judged poached egg and chive butter sauce. This was followed by wonderfully rich braised oxtail set on bed of oyster mushrooms and served with mashed potato, roasted root vegetables and reduced braising juices. A well made crème brûlée completed the meal, accompanied by a lightly caramelised banana.

Civil licence: 30 **Accommodation:** 22 en suite ★ ★ ★

Directions: On B939 1.5 miles W of St Andrews

ST ANDREWS, Rusacks Hotel ❀❀

Pilmour Links KY16 9JQ
Map 12: NO51
Tel: 0870 400 8128
Fax: 01334 477896
Chef: Derek Anderson
Owner: Forte Heritage Hotels
Cost: Alc £31.90, set-price L £9.50.
☺ H/wine £13.50
Times: 12.30-2pm/7-9.30pm
Additional: Bar Food L; Sunday L;
Children welcome
Seats: 66. Private dining room 50
Style: Informal/Scottish
Smoking: No smoking in dining room
Civil licence: 80
Accommodation: 68 en suite ★ ★ ★ ★

A superb split level restaurant enjoying stunning views over the first and 18th tees and out to sea. Features such as huge art deco picture windows, wooden floors, leather chairs and crisp white linen create a lively contemporary feel. Cuisine is definitely well above par with starters such as Dunsyre blue cheese soufflé with a light garlic and chive dressing leading convincingly into main dishes such as seared fillet of turbot with a black olive jus. Fish also makes a strong showing with grilled fillet of sea bass served with a lemon grass risotto and a seafood bisque demonstrating a real flair for sensitive but inventive composition. Desserts such as dark chocolate truffle cake flavoured with MacAllan whisky and served with an apricot coulis and After-Eight ice cream provide the perfect excuse to delay any golf related exercise that little while longer.

Directions: From M90 J8 take A91 to St Andrews. Hotel on L on entering the town

ST ANDREWS,

St Andrews Golf Hotel ❀❀

40 The Scores KY16 9AS
Map 12: NO51
Tel: 01334 472611
Fax: 01334 472188
Chef: Colin Masson
Owners: The Hughes Family
Cost: Alc £30. ☺ H/wine £12
Times: D only, 7-9.30pm.
Closed 26 Dec
Additional: Sunday L (12.30-2pm);
Children welcome
Seats: 60. Private dining room 18
Style: Traditional
Smoking: No smoking in dining room
Accommodation: 22 en suite ★ ★ ★

This town house hotel, comprising two large Victorian houses, overlooks the bay and many of the rooms enjoy lovely views of the coastline and nearby links golf course. The hotel restaurant has a good local trade in addition to residents who come mainly for the golf. Canapés included a light rosemary scone with Parma ham and Mascarpone and an 'excellent' little salmon cake with crème fraîche and lumpfish roe. A pressed terrine of feather game was meaty and nicely served with warmed wild mushrooms, and followed by loin of Perthshire lamb, wrapped in cabbage and Parma ham, cooked pink, beautifully tender and delicately flavoured. Lemon tart came with a notable vanilla ice cream. The wine list is clearly a passion of the proprietor and there is a good selection of halves and interesting wines by the glass.

Directions: Enter town on A91, cross both mini-roundabouts, turn L at Golf Place and first R into The Scores. Hotel 200 yards on R

ST ANDREWS, **West Port** ❀❀❀ **NEW**

170-172 South Street KY16 9EG
Map 12: NO51
Tel: 01334 473186
Fax: 01334 479732
Chef: Alan Mathieson
Owners: Robin & Beverley Waterbury
Cost: Alc £27.50, set-price L £8.95.
☺ H/wine £10.50
Times: Noon-2pm (2.30pm Sat & Sun), 6.30-9.45pm. Closed Mon
Additional: Bar food L; Sunday L; Children welcome
Style: Chic/minimalist
Seats: 78
Smoking: No smoking in dining room; Air conditioning

At long last Scotland's major golf resort has joined the 'big league' with its exciting new restaurant. The atmosphere and decor are decidedly modern, with simplicity and a relaxed, informal style the keynote. The plain white walls, sturdy wood floor, contemporary tables, uncovered but with crisp white linen napkins, and the friendly staff in an informal 'uniform' of white and beige, are the perfect foil for the dishes of the talented new chef, Alan Mathieson. He has a broad-based clientele with students from nearby St Andrew's University as well locals and visitors – all enthusiastic about the restaurant. The style of cooking is difficult to categorise but Alan Mathieson's dishes are innovative and reflect global influences. Delicious home-made bread rolls came with olive oil and the starter of confit of duck on the bone, just a bit more than rare but with outstanding flavour, was most impressive. This was accompanied by a dressed hazelnut salad and a delightful roulade of foie gras on a crisp, golden pomme rösti drizzled with thyme jus. The main course was very well balanced with a wonderfully fresh sea bream, lightly pan fried and presented on a fondant potato topped with a sauté salsify, accompanied by trompette mushrooms and a white bean and truffle sauce.

To finish, an attractively presented mille-feuille, offering a good bittersweet combination, had been created from crisp cinnamon pastry triangles layered with delicate pieces of fresh strawberries and rhubarb. All the dishes well deserved their accolade of three rosettes.

Directions: Adjacent to West Port Archway, within walls of old town. 100mtrs W of Blackfriars Abbey

ST MONANS,
The Seafood Restaurant

16 West End KY10 2BX
Map 12: NO50
Tel/Fax: 01333 730327
Chef: Craig Millar
Owners: The Butler Family
Cost: *Alc* £24, set-price L £14 & £18.
☺ H/wine £10
Times: Noon-3pm/7-11pm. Closed Mon, Dec-Jan
Additional: Bar food L; Sunday L; Children welcome (ex for D)
Seats: 36
Style: Informal/Modern
Smoking: No smoking in dining room

The restaurant has wonderful sea views over the old fishing harbour and the Firth of Forth, with a traditional bar in a 400-year-old converted fisherman's cottage, a 36-seater harbour-side terrace for summer dining, and a lounge area with a fire and aquaria. A feature of the restaurant itself is an 800-year-old freshwater well. Kick off with pan-seared hand-dived scallops with crisp lardons and honey mustard dressing, perhaps with an intermediate course of smoked haddock and potato soup. Main courses range from grilled fillet of cod, with crisp fried Black Forest ham and spicy Thai coconut sauce, to one non-fishy option such as roast lamb steak with butter beans and haricots verts. Finish with a classic crème brûlée or a daily selection of mature cheeses.

Directions: Take A959 from St Andrews to Anstruther, then head west on A917 through Pittenweem. In St Monans go down to harbour then R.

GLASGOW, CITY OF

GLASGOW, Amber Regent

A Chinese restaurant in elegant surroundings serving excellent value lunches and dinners Cantonese style. House specialities include aromatic crispy dishes such as lamb, chicken or duck, and dim sum are great starters. Chow mein and chicken satay equally enjoyable.

Directions: Telephone for directions

50 West Regent Street G2 2QZ
Map 11: NS56
Tel: 0141 331 1655

Telephone for further details.

GLASGOW,
Devonshire Hotel of Glasgow ❀

Intimate hotel restaurant (just four tables), ten minutes from the city centre. Begin perhaps with a rustic velouté of wild mushrooms; main courses are substantial, as are desserts – pear and cinnamon tart was pronounced 'delicious'.

Additional: Bar food L; Children welcome
Style: Informal/Modern
Smoking: No smoking in dining room
Civil licence: 50
Accommodation: 14 en suite ★ ★ ★

Directions: On Great Western Road turn L at lights towards Hyndland, 200 yards turn R and R again

5 Devonshire Gardens
G12 0UX
Map 11: NS56
Tel: 0141 3397878
Fax: 0141 3393980
E-mail: devonshire@aol.com
Cost: *Alc* £30. ☺ H/wine £12.50
Times: 12.30-2.30pm/7-10pm.
Closed L Sun

GLASGOW, **Eurasia** ❀❀ NEW

Ferrier Richardson is a well-known chef restaurateur in Glasgow, and his latest venture has been given the thumbs up both by the business community's movers and shakers, and our own inspector. The philosophy is simple: the best Scottish produce aligned with Asian herbs and spices in a warm and welcoming environment where the service is special. This successful formula can be enjoyed in a very open restaurant with formally-set tables and the kitchen visible through a glass partition. The setting is the former headquarters of an insurance company, an ultra-modern building, right in the city centre. Lunch kicked off with a smooth chicken liver terrine, spiced apple and shallot pickle, before going on to pan-roasted fillet of beef, with potato confit, roast vegetables and a red wine sauce. The meat was a terrific advertisement for Scottish beef, and freshly chopped coriander added a delightful perfume to the sauce. Vanilla seed ice cream and a dribble of toffee sauce were the perfect accompaniment for praline nut tart, and strong espresso came with a wafer-thin shortbread.

150 St Vincent Street G2 5NE
Map 11: NS56
Tel: 0141 2041150
Fax: 0141 2041140
Chef/Owner: Ferrier Richardson
Cost: *Alc* £33.45, set-price L £16.95. H/wine £14.95
Times: Noon-2.30pm/7-11pm.
Closed L Sat, all Sun, Bhs
Additional: Children welcome
Seats: 140. Private dining room 40
Style: Classic/Modern
Smoking: Air conditioning

Directions: From George Square, up St Vincent St, past Hope St, Restaurant on L

GLASGOW, **Gamba** ❀

Bright basement restaurant with clean, simple lines, smart, attentive service adds to the appeal. A global approach is given to top-notch fruits of the sea: terrine of trout with rocket and Thai jelly, or a main course of roast sea bream with chilli oil, red peppers and sweet soya

225a West George Street G2 2ND
Map 11: NS56
Tel: 0141 572 0899
Fax: 0141 572 0896
E-mail: atomkins@btconnect.com
Chef: Derek Marshall
Owners: Alan Tomkins,
Derek Marshall
Cost: *Alc* £26, set-price L £11.95. ☺ H/wine £12.95
Times: Noon-2.30pm/5-10.30pm.
Closed Sun, 1-2 Jan, Bh Mon
Additional: Children 14+
Seats: 66
Style: Classic/informal
Smoking: No pipes and cigars;
Air conditioning

Directions: Nr Blythswood Square

GLASGOW,
Glasgow Moat House

Congress Road G3 8QT
Map 11: NS56
Tel: 0141 3069988
Fax: 0141 2212022
Cost: Alc £25. ☺ H/wine £12.85
Times: D only, 7-10.30pm.
Closed Sun
Additional: Bar food; Sunday L;
Children welcome
Style: Informal/Traditional
Smoking: Air conditioning
Accommodation: 283 en suite
★★★★

*An elegant and comfortable interior and a fine outlook over the
river complement the caring, innovative approach to food. A moist
and flavoursome Guinea fowl in a well-judged tarragon essence met
with strong approval.*

Directions: Adjacent to Scottish Exhibition & Conference
Centre, follow signs

GLASGOW,
Killermont Polo Club

*Polo is an eccentric but convincing choice of theme for this high
quality Punjab restaurant offering innovative Dum Pukht cuisine in
a sophisticated manor house setting. Koh-E-Avadh Lamb Gosht, for
example, was packed with flavour and most enjoyable.*

2002 Maryhill Road
Maryhill Park G20 0AB
Map 11: NS56
Tel: 0141 946 5412
Fax: 0141 946 0812

Cost: Alc £20, set-price L £5.95. ☺ H/wine £10.95
Times: Noon-2pm/5-11pm. Closed L Sun, Xmas & New Year
Style: Classic/Country-house

Directions: Telephone for directions

GLASGOW,
Lux   NEW

*The upstairs, upmarket option of two dynamic restaurants co-
habiting in the old railway station. Carefully composed modern
Scottish cuisine (such as a delightful crostini of Orkney scallops)
makes this an excellent addition to the Glasgow restaurant scene.*

1051 Great Western Road
G66 4NA
Map 11: NS56
Tel: 0141 576 7576
Fax: 0141 576 0162

Cost: Set-price D £25. ☺ H/wine £16
Times: D only 6-10.30pm. Closed D Mon & Sun,
25 & 26 Dec, 1 Jan
Additional: Children 5+
Style: Modern/Minimalist
Smoking: No-smoking area; Air conditioning

Directions: Telephone for directions

GLASGOW, **Malmaison**

278 West George Street G2 4LL
Map 11: NS56
Tel: 0141 5721001
Fax: 0141 5721002
E-mail: glasgow@malmaison.com
Cost: *Alc* £26, set-price L £9/D £12.
☺ H/wine £13.95
Times: Noon-2.30pm/6-11pm.
Closed L Sat
Additional: Sunday L;
Children welcome
Style: classic/French
Smoking: Air conditioning
Accommodation: 72 en suite ★★★

*Popular French-style brasserie in the crypt of what was once
St Giles' Cathedral. Dishes sampled include a good fishcake on
wilted spinach with lemon butter sauce.*

Directions: From George Square take Vincent Street to Pitt
Street – hotel is on corner of this and West George Street

GLASGOW, **Nairns** ✿✿

13 Woodside Crescent
G3 7UP
Map 11: NS56
Tel: 0141 3530707
Fax: 0141 3311684
E-mail: info@nairns.co.uk
Chef: Derek Blair
Owners: Nick & Topher Nairn
Cost: Set-price L £13.50 & £17/
D £27.50. H/wine £14.50
Times: Noon-1.45pm/6-9.45pm.
Closed Sun, 25 & 26 Dec, 1 & 2 Jan
Additional: Children welcome
Seats: 100
Style: Chic/Contemporary
Smoking: No pipes & cigars;
Air conditioning

This fashionable restaurant is housed in a converted Georgian
townhouse in one of the imposing crescents in the centre of
Glasgow. The restaurant is split between two floors, both
serving the same menu. The ground floor features a notable
ebony fireplace, a massive bowl of twisted willow and steel
lamps, while the basement, which has kept its flagstone floor,
has walls hung with contemporary photographs. The set-price
menu is brief, as are the descriptions, and consists of four
starters, mains courses and desserts. Prawn cocktail, butter
bean soup, breast of duck, ginger and sweet potato mash,
aromatic jus and baked potato tart are typical. Tender confit of
duck leg was served with red peppers on mixed leaves with a
light sweet and sour dressing. Pan-seared cod, an excellent
piece of fish, was served on crushed new potatoes and wilted
spinach, topped with a poached egg and hollandaise. The
desserts include well made parfaits, tarts and home-made ice
creams.

Directions: Telephone for directions

GLASGOW,
No Sixteen ❀

16 Byres Road G11 5JY
Map 11: NS56
Tel: 0141 339 2544
Fax: 0141 576 1505

Pleasant, unpretentious, a little cramped, but with a great buzz. Make sure you book and enjoy the kitchen's keep-it-simple cooking. From a daily changing menu we chose Thai fishcakes, and meaty lamb shank coated in grain mustard; there's home-baked bread too.

Cost: Alc £18. ☺ H/wine £11
Times: Noon-2.30pm/6-10pm. Closed L Sun-Fri, D Sun. 1st 2 wks Jan
Additional: Children welcome
Style: informal/bistro-style
Smoking: No pipes & cigars

Directions: Two minutes walk from Kelvinhall tube station; at bottom of Byres Road

GLASGOW, One Devonshire Gardens Hotel ❀❀❀

1 Devonshire Gardens G12 0UX
Map 11: NS56
Tel: 0141 3392001
Fax: 0141 3371663
E-mail:
onedevonshire@btconnect.com
Chef: Andrew Fairlie
Owner: Residence International
Cost: Alc £40, set-price L £21 & £27.50. H/wine £19
Times: Noon-2pm/7.15-10pm. Closed L Sat
Additional: Sunday L; Children welcome
Seats: 40. Private dining rooms 11 & 32
Style: Classic/Modern
Smoking: No smoking in dining room
Accommodation: 27 en suite ★ ★ ★

The menu is well constructed – Andrew Fairlie really knows how to whet the taste buds with dishes such as roast breast of milk-fed squab with braised cabbage, truffled gnocchi and a Port sauce. The style is Scottish-French and some of the best dishes sampled this year include home-smoked lobster with lime and herb butter, pure essence and melting texture, as well as velvety, melt-in-the mouth braised shin of veal complete with marrow bone and gutsy red wine jus. As well as a choice of hot desserts – top-class hot chocolate pudding with chocolate Amaretti ice-cream or spiced soufflé with rum, raisins and mulled wine – there is a dessert trolley, cheeses or sorbets and ices. The set lunch menu extracts dishes from the main *carte*, which makes two courses – foie gras parfait with spiced pear and apple and toasted brioche, followed by roast wing of skate with buttered spinach and fondant potatoes, for example – good value indeed. The dining room of the highly individual terraced townhouse hotel features high ceilings, oak panelling and striped walls hung with Picasso prints. Attentive service and skilled advice from the extremely helpful sommelier.

Directions: On Great Western Road turn L at lights towards Hyndland, 200 yards turn R and R again

GLASGOW, La Parmigiana

447 Great Western Road
G12 8HH
Map 11: NS56
Tel: 0141 334 0686
Fax: 0141 332 3533
Cost: *Alc* £25, set-price L £9.50/
D £11.50. ☺ H/wine £10.95
Times: Noon-2.30pm/6-11pm. Closed
Sun, 25 & 26 Dec, 1 & 2 Jan, Etr Mon
Additional: Childern welcome
Style: Classic/Informal
Smoking: No pipes & cigars;
Air conditioning

Directions: Close to Kelvinbridge
underground station

An atmospheric, long established West End restaurant, now focussing on continental, cosmopolitan-style dishes. Chargrilled scallops with olive oil and fresh lemon juice demonstrated a flair for delicate, modest simplicity as did a rustic carpaccio of beef.

GLASGOW, Rococo NEW

One of Glasgow's newer upmarket restaurants situated close to Sauchiehall Street, and attracting business clients at lunchtime. The decor is fresh, with its designer furniture, polished Italian limestone flooring and comfortable leather chairs. In this opulent setting the expectations for the food are high, and a sample lunch taken recently found that anticipation was more than rewarded. Parfait of duck livers with a spiced fruit chutney was smooth and full flavoured with a deliciously lingering taste of garlic. 'A picture on a plate' was how lemon sole with crab mousse and saffron essence was described, the lightly-cooked sole and firm mousse filling surrounded by a neat arrangement of vegetables. Bitter chocolate and praline tart with spiced pear marmalade brought the meal to a satisfactory conclusion. Unsurprisingly, the wine list is one of the best in Glasgow.

202 West George Street G2 2NR
Map 11: NS56
Tel: 0141 221 5004

Telephone for further details (phone for limited details)

Directions: Telephone for directions

GLASGOW, 78 St Vincent Street NEW

A former bank with high ceilings and blond wood parquet floor. Sound modern cooking without fripperies produces baked guinea fowl sausage on a parsnip purée with parsley cream, and medallions of marinated pork loin. Geared towards speedy lunches.

Style: Classic/Bistro-style
Smoking: No-smoking area

Directions: Telephone for directions

78 St Vincent Street G2 5UB
Map 11: NS56
Tel: 0141 248 7676
Fax: 0141 248 4663
E-mail: frontdesk@78stvincent.com
Cost: Set-price L £13.95/D £24.50. ☺
H/wine £12.95
Times: Noon-2pm/5-10.30.
Closed 25 Dec, 1Jan
Additional: Sunday L;
Children welcome

GLASGOW, Sherbrooke Castle Hotel NEW

The Sherbrooke Castle is an impressive, turreted red-sandstone building, within its own grounds, in Pollokshields, a residential area to the south of the city centre. The restaurant, named

11 Sherbrooke Avenue Pollokshields
G41 4PG
Map 11: NS56
Tel: 0141 427 4227
Fax: 0141 427 5685

Morrison's after the gentleman who built the house as his own home in 1896, is a part-panelled room with striking red decor, a stained-glass window and a carved oak fireplace where an open fire may burn in winter. The set-price menu, although short, is full of interest, taking in things like spicy lentil and coriander soup and a vegetarian main course of polenta and ricotta gâteau with wild mushrooms and a herb salad. Meatier starters may run to a warm salad of black pudding, new potatoes and a poached egg, or beef carpaccio with beetroot and mustard dressing, with main courses of roast breast of pheasant with chestnut and rosemary jus and a risotto of pearl barley, as well as classic tournedos Rossini. Sea bream goes into lasagne along with aubergine purée and a tasty dressing of ratatouille, while salmon is rolled with sole and sauced with orange and cardamom. Artful presentation comes to the fore in desserts, as in a single, large lemon tart, 'lovely and tangy', with good, light pastry, and an unusual Mascarpone and basil ice cream, decorated with a blob of cream studded with sliced strawberries and redcurrants.

E-mail: mail@sherbrooke.co.uk
Chef: Peter Cook
Owner: George McCulloch
Cost: Alc £26, set-price L £26. ☺
H/wine £11.50
Times: 12.30-2.15pm/6.30-9.45pm
Additional: Bar food; Sunday L;
Children welcome
Seats: 40. Private dining room 18
Style: Traditional/country-house
Smoking: No smoking in dining room;
Air conditioning
Accommodation: 25 en suite ★ ★ ★

Directions: From city centre take M8 west to J23. Turn L into Dumbreck Rd, then 2nd L into Nithsdale Rd. Hotel 700m on R

GLASGOW, **Shish Mahal** ❀

Park Road G4 9JF
Map 11: NS56
Tel: 0141 334 7899
Fax: 0141 572 0800
E-mail: asif786@email.com
Cost: Alc £15, set-price L £5.25 & £6.50. ☺ H/wine £8.95
Times: Noon-2pm/5-11.30pm.
Closed L Sun
Additional: Children 5+
Style: Classic/chic/modern
Smoking: No-smoking area

Directions: Exit M8 at Charing Cross junction and proceed down Woodlands Drive

A strong commitment to traditional style and quality coupled with attentive service accounts for the long standing popularity of this family-run restaurant. Artfully marinated Tandoori chicken tikka and a sweet gulab jamon made a particular impact.

GLASGOW, **Stravaigin** ❀❀

'Think global, eat local' is the motto of this off-beat basement restaurant where the tables are closely set and the chairs not the most comfortable on the planet. To call the style fusion food is an understatement, with items on the menu like 'Vietnamese-style marinated quail on candy smoked aubergine concasse with nuoc mam gung dressed herb salad'. And that's just for starters. But despite the descriptions, dishes seem to please, showing a kitchen that's in control. Starters could include seared lambs' kidneys in Marsala with pumpkin ravioli and pesto, and there might be main courses of pan-fried breast of Borders pheasant on crushed sweet potato with a reduction of roast garlic and Sauvignon and a light chilli relish, or Szechuan-marinated roast Barbary duck on roast onions and fondant potato with a fricassée of pumpkin, star anise and flageolet beans. Invention is just as strong at pudding stage, with not just one but a duo of crème brûlées: vanilla with a caramelised crust, and ginger with a rich 'Belgian' lid. It might come as a relief to know that cheeses, served with good old quince jelly and bannocks, are indigenous.

30 Gibson Street G12 8NX
Map 11: NS56
Tel: 0141 3342665
Fax: 0141 3344099
Chef/Owner: Colin Clydesdale
Cost: Set-price L/D £23.95.
H/wine £11.25
Times: Noon-2.30pm/5-11pm.
Closed L Sun-Thu, 25 & 26 Dec,
1 & 2 Jan
Additional: Bar food L;
Children welcome
Seats: 76
Style: Informal/Off beat
Smoking: No pipes & cigars;
Air conditioning

Directions: Next to Glasgow University. 200 yds from Kelvinbridge underground.

GLASGOW, Ubiquitous Chip ❀❀

Ronnie Clydesdale still reigns supreme at 'The Chip', which has been going since 1971, and has thus become something of a Glasgow landmark. A restaurant of many parts, it's situated in trendy Ashton Lane on the edge of Glasgow University campus. The main dining area is a lofty courtyard (with lots of live greenery, cobbled floor and pine tables); the inner sanctum, normally reserved for evenings, is more formal. Upstairs there is another brasserie-styled eating area offering food at more modest prices. Velouté of free-range chicken and truffle oil, braised lettuce and mushroom duxelle, opened one of the best meals we've had here in the last few years. It was neatly backed up by a robust winter dish of wild Dumfriesshire rabbit braised with cinammon, and served with a tomato-olive mash and battered onion rings; apple and ice cream pie was a neat twist on a great classic. It's good to note that the menu is currently showing lots of innovation, and that there's a good buzz to the place. *Best German Wine List (see page 18).*

12 Ashton Lane G12 8SJ
Map 11: NS56
Tel: 0141 3345007
Chef/owner: Ronnie Clydesdale
Owner: Ronnie Clydesdale
Times: Noon-2.30pm/5.30-11pm.
Closed 1 & 2 Jan
Additional: Children welcome

Directions: Telephone for directions

HIGHLAND

ARISAIG, Arisaig House ❀❀❀

Gardens of beech woods and an arboretum are a principal feature of Arisaig, with a number of paths, including one leading down to the sea. Inside, light and a sense of refinement fill the rooms, from the inner hall, with its carved oak staircase, the vaulted drawing room, where a log fire burns in cooler weather, to the part-panelled dining room. Bread is baked daily, game is cooked in season and the majority of ingredients are sourced locally. Lunch offers two choices at each course – perhaps based around grilled sea bass with tuna confit, or pan-fried fillet of beef in a wild garlic crust with red wine sauce – and dinner around four except at the second, which is something salady, a sorbet or soup: perhaps 'delicious' cream of onion with port. Simple-sounding treatments belie the skill and labour that the kitchen puts into dishes: home-cured gravad lax, thinly sliced and almost melting in the mouth, with a contrasting emulsion of Arran grain mustard sauce, or roast jambonette of quail with creamed celeriac in truffle sauce. Precise timing and well-judged sauces are a feature of main courses, as in breast of Barbary duck with bitter orange sauce

Beasdale PH39 4NR
Map 13: NM68
Tel: 01687 450622
Fax: 01687 450626
Chef: Duncan Gibson
Owners: Ruth, John &
Andrew Smither, Alison Wilkinson
Cost: Set-price D £39.50.
H/wine £14.50
Times: 12.30-2pm/7.30-8.30pm.
Closed Nov-Etr
Additional: Bar food L; Children 10+
Seats: 32. Jacket & tie preferred
Style: Classic/Country-house
Smoking: No smoking in dining room
Civil licence: 32
Accommodation: 12 en suite ★ ★ ★

Directions: On A830 Fort William to Mallaig road, 3 miles east of Arisaig village

served with sweet potato purée, or fillet of halibut topped with finely shredded leeks smeared with truffle oil, surrounded by quenelle-shaped potatoes, an assertive oyster sauce bringing the whole dish together. Portion sizes are just right, meals are well-paced, and, as usual, a wait is inevitable if you want a sweet soufflé (Bailey's and chocolate chip, say), although you could always go for something cold: smooth and rich lemon tart with 'super' crème fraîche ice cream, for instance.

BREAKISH,
Rendezvous Restaurant

A small former roadside schoolhouse serving seafood dishes and unusual daily specials. A generous bowl of princess scallops and mussels steamed in white wine, garlic and herbs received high praise, as did grilled monkfish with prawn and brandy sauce.

Additional: Sunday L (12.30-2pm); Children welcome; Vegetarian choice not always available
Style: Informal/country

Directions: Just N of Skye Bridge

Old School House
Isle of Skye IV42 8PY
Map 13: NG62
Tel: 01471 822001
Fax: 01471 822986
Cost: *Alc* £20. ☺ H/wine £8.95
Times: D only, 6-9.30pm. Closed Tue, October school holidays

BOAT OF GARTEN, Boat Hotel

PH24 3BH
Map 14: NH91
Tel: 01479 831258
Fax: 01479 831414
E-mail: holidays@boathotel.co.uk
Chef: Peter Woods
Owners: Ian & Shona Tatchell
Cost: *Alc* £32, set-price D £27.50. H/wine £12
Times: D only, 7.30-9.30pm. Closed Jan
Additional: Bar food; Sunday L; Children welcome
Seats: 40. Private dining room 50
Style: Modern
Smoking: No smoking in dining room
Civil licence: 70
Accommodation: 32 en suite ★★★

Directions: Turn off A9 N of Aviemore onto A95. Follow signs to Boat of Garten

New owners took over the Boat only in autumn 1999, so changes are in the air. Expect to find within this traditional Victorian building a well-stocked bar, a spacious, comfortable sitting room, and a restaurant decorated in contemporary style, with strong colours and original artwork. The best of Scotland's produce finds its way on to the daily-changing, set-price menus and a confident touch translates it into some interesting, successful dishes. That old favourite of prawn and avocado salad is lifted by a citrus beurre blanc and topped with filo, while breast of Grampian chicken is stuffed with herb mousseline, finished with a velouté of grain mustard and chorizo and flash-roasted. Another mousseline, of chicken and scallops in champagne sauce, made a 'quite delicious' starter at inspection, while a light seafood nage gave another dimension to moist and tender butter-grilled turbot with langoustines. Some main courses attract a supplement – best end of Scottish lamb in a mint and peppercorn crust, or a duo of grouse and wild duck breasts on chanterelles with lardons and Puy lentils – and a modern spin is given to traditional desserts: banana and date bread-and-butter pudding with chocolate and banana sauces ('really quite wicked'), or a compote of fruit on caramelised rice pudding. The short wine list has a decent choice of halves, with house wines sold by the bottle and carafe.

BRORA, Royal Marine Hotel

Country house designed by the renowned Scottish architect Sir Robert Lorimer. The elegant dining room is the setting for specialities such as whisky cured salmon, and pan-seared fillet of venison.

Additional: Bar food; Sunday L; Children welcome
Style: Traditional/Country-house
Smoking: No smoking in dining room
Accommodation: 22 en suite ★ ★ ★

Directions: Turn off A9 in village toward beach and golf course

Golf Road KW9 6QS
Map 14: NC90
Tel: 01408 621252
Fax: 01408 621181
E-mail: highlandescape@btinternet.com
Cost: Alc £24. ☺ H/wine £10
Times: L all day/6.30-9pm

COLBOST,
Three Chimneys Restaurant ❀❀❀

It's worth coming to this 100-year-old traditional crofter's cottage for the sea views alone, nestled as it is on the shore of Loch Dunvegan in a remote corner of Skye. But the cooking is the attraction, of course, and sounds of contentment can be heard within the surroundings of bare stone walls, low ceilings and candlelight. The emphasis is on local, and therefore seasonal, produce, with a modern slant given to traditional ideas, as in 'restrained' chilli and lime couscous with saffron cream for a brochette, 'using the freshest seafood', of monkfish, scallops and prawns, or smoked ham and haddie in a starter of twice-baked soufflé 'absolutely bursting with flavours'. If the produce of the sea is the kitchen's muse – from 'a real stunner' of lobster bisque, through langoustines served simply with 'beautifully dressed' organically grown leaves and herbs, to perfectly timed halibut fillet with red pepper sauce – meat eaters will not be disappointed by well-timed fillet of beef on a potato and sage cake with a mushroom and Madeira sauce, and puddings receive praise too: coffee meringue with dark chocolate sauce, or 'superb' apple and frangipane tart with cinnamon ice cream. Half a dozen wines by the glass head up the long and helpfully annotated wine list.

Dunvegan Isle of Skye IV55 8ZT
Map 13: NG24
Tel: 01470 511258
Fax: 01470 511358
E-mail: eatandstay@threechimneys.co.uk
Chef: Shirley Spear
Owners: Eddie & Shirley Spear
Cost: Alc £40, set-price L £18/ D £34.
Times: 12.30-2.30pm(check winter opening)/6.30-9.30pm.
Closed L Sun, 3 wks Jan
Additional: Children welcome
Seats: 30. Private dining room 21
Style: Chic/Rustic
Smoking: No smoking in dining room
Accommodation: 6 en suite ★ ★

Directions: From Dungevan take B884 to Glendale. Restaurant is at Colbost 4.5 miles from main road

CONTIN, Coul House Hotel

By Strathpeffer IV14 9EY
Map 14: NH45
Tel: 01997 421487
Fax: 01997 421945
Cost: *Alc* £24.50, set-price D £19.50
& £29.50. ☺
Times: Noon-2pm/7-9pm
Additional: Bar food; Sunday L;
Children welcome
Style: Traditional/Country-house
Smoking: No smoking in dining room
Accommodation: 20 en suite ★★★

Coul House dates from 1821 and the restaurant, with its ornate ceiling and mountain views, is the original Mackenzie dining room. Taste of Scotland dishes include seafood, steaks and salmon.

Directions: A9 and A385 to Contin. 0.5m up private drive on R

DINGWALL, Kinkell House

Delicious home-baked bread and delightful views across the valley set the scene for the short, carefully chosen menu, which might feature collops of monkfish with wilted spinach, noilly prat and sorrel sauce. Interesting wine list.

Additional: Sunday L; Children welcome
Style: Country-house
Smoking: No smoking in dining room
Civil licence: 50 **Accommodation:** 9 en suite ★★

Directions: On B9169 10 miles N of Inverness, 1 mile from A9 & A835

Easter Kinkell
Conon Bridge
IV7 8HY
Map 14: NH55
Tel: 01349 861270
Fax: 01349 865902
E-mail: kinkell@aol.com
Cost: *Alc* D £24.50, set-price
L £12.95. ☺ H/wine £10
Times: 12.30-2.30pm/7-9pm.
Closed L Sat

DORNOCH,
2 Quail Restaurant NEW

Castle Street IV25 3SN
Map 14: NH78
Tel: 01862 811811
E-mail: enquiries@2quail.co.uk
Chef: Michael Carr
Owners: Kerensa & Michael Carr
Cost: Set-price D £27.50.
H/wine £12.50
Times: D only, 7.30-9.30pm.
Closed Sun, Mon, 2 wks Feb/Mar
Additional: Children welcome
Seats: 16. Private dining room 8-10
Smoking: No-smoking area;
No pipes & cigars
Accommodation: 2 en suite

A 100-year-old Sutherland-stone house on the main street of this charming coastal town is the setting for two intimate, cosy dining rooms decorated in warm, relaxing tones, with fireplaces and masses of books. The kitchen gives an international slant to fine materials sourced virtually over the threshold, so langoustines are potted and served with a truffle oil salad, a thick cut of salmon is seared and well matched by guacamole and hollandaise, and goose and apple go into a filo parcel. Saucing is a strong point with main courses. Sage-infused gravy makes a good foil for roast breast of Gressingham duck, just pink, with an apple and parsnip tarte Tatin, and thyme and sherry are combined in a jus for medallions of roast venison. A vegetarian main course is always available, and fish might appear as roasted salmon with provençale vegetables. The same thought about what makes a happy marriage of flavours extends to puddings: a dark chocolate tart, its pastry good and light, with coconut ice cream has been pronounced 'delicious', and there might be classic raspberry crème brûlée too. The wine list runs to over 50 bins, some good-quality producers among them, with a decent choice of half-bottles.

Directions: 200yds past war memorial on L side of main street

DULNAIN BRIDGE,
Muckrach Lodge Hotel

Victorian shooting lodge with a conservatory restaurant overlooking landscaped gardens. Exquisite orange and Drambuie parfait followed roasted breast of duck with onion flan and an earthy butter bean casserole.

Telephone for further details

Directions: On A938, 0.5 mile form Dulnain Bridge

PH26 3LY
Map 14: NH92
Tel: 01479 851257
Fax: 01479 851325
E-mail: muckrach.lodge@sol.co.uk

DUNDONNELL,
Dundonnell Hotel 🏵🏵

Little Loch Broom
Nr Ullapool IV23 2QS
Map 14: NH08
Tel: 01854 633204
Fax: 01854 633366
E-mail: selbie@dundonnellhotel.co.uk
Chef: Isabel Bellshaw
Owners: Selbie & Flora Florence
Cost: Alc fr £20, set-price D £27.50.
☺ H/wine £9.75
Times: D only, 7-8.30pm.
Closed Jan/ Feb
Additional: Bar food;
Children welcome
Seats: 70
Style: Informal
Smoking: No smoking in dining room
Accommodation: 28 en suite ★★★

Sheltering under the An Teallach mountain range, with lovely views down Little Loch Broom, this roadside hotel is a welcoming and hospitable place. Eating in the bistro-style surroundings of the bar, or the spacious dining room, which, under its coffered ceiling, offers a daily-changing set-price menu with around a handful of choices per course, with the second a toss-up between an interesting soup – perhaps gazpacho with crab and coriander – and a sorbet. Fine local ingredients are used, from steamed mussels with saffron butter sauce, to baked loin of lamb, perhaps stuffed with mushrooms and thyme then wrapped in filo, or fillet of Aberdeen Angus, roasted and sliced on rösti with a Madeira jus. A starter of roast scallops with cauliflower purée and a well-conceived raisin and caper vinaigrette could be followed by a full-bodied main course of pan-fried breast of guinea fowl with a confit of the leg in red wine sauce, or grilled haddock fillet brushed with a langoustine and garlic butter. Vegetables might take in stir-fried cabbage, sautéed mushrooms and fondant potatoes, with puddings along the lines of orange brûlée cheesecake with Cointreau sauce, or home-made whisky and marmalade ice cream. The wine list gives a decent variety of styles, and the house wine is particularly good value.

Directions: On A832 Ullapool/Gairloch road, 14 miles from Braemore junction

Dundonnell Hotel

FORT WILLIAM,
Inverlochy Castle Hotel ❁❁❁

Torlundy PH33 6SN
Map 14: NN17
Tel: 01397 702177
Fax: 01397 702953
E-mail: info@inverlochy.co.uk
Chef: Simon Haigh
Cost: Set-price L fr £23/D £50.
H/wine £18
Times: 12.30-1.45pm/7-9.15pm.
Closed 7 Jan-12 Feb
Additional: Sunday L;
Children welcome
Seats: 34. Private dining room 15.
Jacket & tie preferred
Style: Country-house/Formal
Smoking: No smoking in dining room
Civil licence: 50
Accommodation: 17 en suite ★ ★ ★ ★

The main dining room (one of three, all decorated with period furniture presented as gifts by the King of Norway) of the world-famous hotel has achingly beautiful loch and mountain views. Service is slick and well versed in catering for a high-powered, international clientele who expect nothing but the best. The cuisine is modern British in style, and makes full use of fine local ingredients including scallops from the Isle of Skye, hand-picked wild mushrooms and local game. Simon Haigh ensures standards are maintained, rightly understanding the need to keep things sophisticated but still essentially straightforward. A light chicken boudin was served with duck confit and a slab of almost crisp, caramelised toasted foie gras, with apple pearls in a sauce that was just a swirl of Calvados, pan juices and apple juice. Saucing was also somewhat elemental in a main course of fresh, meaty turbot poached with oysters and topped with black caviar. Excellent petits fours include fudge. Extensive wine list.

Directions: 3 miles N of Fort William on A82, just past the Golf Club

FORT WILLIAM, Moorings Hotel

Banavie PH33 7LY
Map 14: NN17
Tel: 01397 772797
Fax: 01397 772441
Cost: Set-price D £26. ☺
H/wine £9.95
Times: D only, 7-9.30pm
Additional: Bar food;
Children welcome
Style: Rustic
Smoking: No smoking in dining room;
Air conditioning
Accommodation: 21 en suite ★ ★ ★

Directions: From A82 take A830 W 1
mile. 1st R over Caledonian Canal on
B8004

*Sitting alongside 'Neptune's Staircase' on the Caledonian Canal with
views of Ben Nevis and surrounding mountains the hotel certainly
doesn't want for location. The restaurant serves good European
cuisine and boasts an extensive wine list.*

FORT WILLIAM,
No 4 Cameron Square

4 Cameron Square PH33 6AJ
Map 14: NN17
Tel: 01397 704222
Fax: 01397 704448

Telephone for further details

Directions: Just off pedestrianised
High Street next to Tourist
Information Office

*Intimate restaurant with a small cocktail bar and bright conservatory
extension. There is a good-value business lunch, and a dinner menu
of interesting dishes prepared from carefully sourced produce.*

GLENFINNAN, The Prince's House ✸

*A friendly atmosphere and honest cooking make eating here a
pleasure. Loch Linnhe mussels, medallions of wild venison or fillet
of Loch Lochy trout show the strength of local produce. For dessert,
try spiced Lambrusco jelly*

Additional: Bar food; Children 8+
Style: Traditional
Smoking: No smoking in dining room
Civil licence: 30
Accommodation: 9 en suite ★ ★

Directions: Take A830 NW of Fort William, continue for
approx 15 miles

by Fort William PH37 4LT
Map 14: NM98
Tel: 01397 722246
Fax: 01397 722307
E-mail:
princeshouse@glenfinnan.co.uk
Cost: Set-price D £27. ☺ H/wine £10
Times: D only, 7-9pm. Closed Sun,
Xmas, New Year, Jan, Feb

GRANTOWN-ON-SPEY,
Culdearn House

Woodlands Terrace PH26 3JU
Map 14: NJ02
Tel: 01479 872106
Fax: 01479 873641
E-mail: culdearn@globalnet.co.uk
Cost: *Alc* £25, set-price D £25. ☺
H/wine £11.95
Times: D only, 6.45-9pm (booking essential for non-residents).
Closed 1 Nov-14 Mar

Charming small hotel restaurant, serving straightforward dishes based on quality ingredients. Loin of Moray lamb comes pan-fried with rosemary and red wine jus, while Tulchan pheasant is served with apple and cider sauce. Booking essential.

Additional: Children 10+; Vegetarian dishes by request only
Style: Country house **Smoking:** No smoking in dining room
Accommodation: 9 en suite

Directions: From SW on A95 turn at 30mph sign

HALKIRK, Ulbster Arms Hotel

Bridge Street KW12 6XY
Tel: 01847 831641
Fax: 01847 831206
Cost: Set-price D £21.50. ☺
H/wine £9
Times: Noon-1.45pm/7-8.45pm
Additional: Bar food; Sunday L;
Children welcome

Popular sporting hotel serving a formal four-course dinner. Options might include a salad of smoked salmon and home-made gravad lax, and loin of Caithness lamb served with ratatouille and aubergine gâteau.

Style: Country-house
Smoking: No smoking in dining room
Accommodation: 10 en suite ★ ★

Directions: Halkirk off A9, 3m N of Spittal

INVERMORISTON,
Glenmoriston Arms Hotel

IV3 6YA
Tel: 01320 351206
Fax: 01320 351308
E-mail: scott@lochness-glenmoriston.co.uk
Cost: Set-price D £25. ☺
H/wine £9.85
Times: Noon-2pm/7-9pm.
Closed Jan-Feb

Antique guns and paintings of Highland scenes adorn the beamed restaurant, where the menu might feature warm cheese brûlée with spiced aubergine and leek, Scottish lamb with vanilla, thyme and mushroom jus, or pheasant with apples and Calvados.

Additional: Bar food; Children 8+
Style: Traditional/Country-house
Smoking: No smoking in dining room
Accommodation: 8 en suite ★ ★

Directions: At the junction of A82/A877

INVERNESS,
Bunchrew House Hotel

Bunchrew IV3 8TA
Map 14: NH64
Tel: 01463 234917
Fax: 01463 710620
E-mail: welcome@bunchrew-inverness.co.uk
Cost: *Alc* £29.50, set-price L £19.50/D £26.50. H/wine £12.50
Times: 12.30-1.45pm/7-8.45pm

Relax in the quiet elegance of this fine 17th-century country mansion whose restaurant looks out across the shores of Beauly Firth. Main courses might include roast saddle of venison with a juniper and rosemary sauce.

Additional: Bar food L; Sunday L; Children welcome
Style: Classic/Country-house
Smoking: No smoking in dining room
Civil licence: 90
Accommodation: 11 en suite ★ ★ ★

Directions: 2.5 miles from Inverness on A862 towards Beauly

INVERNESS,
Culloden House Hotel ❀❀

Bonnie Prince Charlie left for the battle of Culloden from the grounds of this fine Adam-style Georgian mansion. The dining room is decorated with fine ornate plaster-work and filled with antique furnishings, and chef Michael Simpson prepares a fine daily-changing four-course menu in addition to his Tastes of Scotland menu. A selection of freshly-baked rolls are offered with balls of butter. Starters from the latter menu were a delight. The West Coast kiln-smoked salmon with dill butter and a light salad had a lovely flavour, the cream of smoked haddock soup with chives was akin to a light Cullen skink. The fillet of beef stuffed with foie gras was sensational and 'the tenderest I can recall' This was served with dauphinoise potatoes and snap peas and carrots bound with a strip of leek. An individual tartlet with toffee and banana with vanilla ice cream was served in silver pots. The wine list is comprehensive and well-laid out.

Civil licence: 45
Accommodation: 28 en suite ★ ★ ★ ★

Directions: From Inverness take A96 (Airport road), R at sign 'Culloden'. After 1.2 miles L at dovecote after 2 sets of traffic lights

Culloden IV2 7BZ
Map 14: NH64
Tel: 01463 790461
Fax: 01463 792181
E-mail: user@cullodenhouse.co.uk
Chef: Michael Simpson
Cost: A/c L £25, set-price D £35.
H/wine £13.85
Times: 12.30-2pm/7-8.45pm
Additional: Sunday L; Children 12+
Seats: 60. Private dining room 24;
Jacket & tie preferred
Style: Country-house
Smoking: No smoking in dining room

INVERNESS, Glenmoriston
Town House Hotel ❀❀

Situated on the north bank of the River Ness, overlooking the Cathedral and Eden Court Theatre, this popular hotel has had a major facelift and emerges all the better for it. The split-level dining room, decorated in calming shades of blues and creams, has fresh white linen, fine place settings and an interesting display of fine Italian wines on a specially designed wrought iron stand. As might be expected from Italian ownership, the style of cooking is distinctly Mediterranean: Ligurian fish soup; breast of pheasant with wild mushroom polenta, glazed shallots and bacon rashers; chocolate and Amaretto torte. Creamy smoked salmon risotto with deep fried squid and marinated leeks made a stylish first course, followed by an equally accomplished loin of lamb with pesto crust and cannellini beans. And bravo to a kitchen confident enough to serve fresh, young spinach leaves – uncooked.

Accommodation: 15 en suite ★ ★ ★

Directions: 5 mins from town centre, on river opposite the theatre

20 Ness Bank IV2 4SF
Map 14: NH64
Tel: 01463 223777
Fax: 01463 712378
E-mail: glenmoriston@cali.co.uk
Chef: Steven Devlin
Owner: Adrian Pieraccini
Cost: A/c £30, set-price D £24.95.
H/wine £12.50
Times: Noon-2pm/6.30-9.30pm
Additional: Sunday L;
Children welcome
Seats: 50. Private dining room 15
Style: Modern/Formal
Smoking: No pipes & cigars

INVERNESS,
The Riverhouse ❀

As the name suggests riverside views await diners at this stylish formal restaurant. An open plan design allows a ringside spectator's seat for the preparation of dishes such as pan seared calf's liver and West Coast scallops.

1 Greig Street
IV3 5PT
Map 14: NH64
Tel: 01463 222033
Cost: A/c £24.95, set-price D £24.95.
☺ H/wine £11

The Riverhouse

Times: 12.15-2.15pm/6.30-9.30pm.
Closed L Sun, Mon (ex 1 Jun-30 Sep)
& Wed , 2 wks Nov, 2 wks Jan
Additional: Children 5+
Style: Classic/formal
Smoking: No smoking in dining room

Directions: Overlooking the river on corner of Huntly Street and Greig Street

ISLE ORNSAY, Duisdale Hotel NEW

The enthusiastic new owners have hugely improved the old hunting lodge in the Sleat peninsula. In the dining room, overlooking the dovecote and herb garden, there is a pretty collection of blue and white china and a log-burning carved fireplace decorated with Delft tiles. Dinner is a civilised affair, with a daily-changing, set-price five-course menu. The innovative modern Scottish cooking emphasises fresh local fish and game. Lovely, fresh salmon fishcakes with a tasty dill sauce, coated with ground almonds and studded with spring onions, had not a jot of potato filler. Soup of the day might be pumpkin and oregano soup or prawn chowder, served with delicious home-baked bread. A succulent and crispy main course of seared slices of duck breast with sugar-coated leg of duck was set off by a citrus and claret sauce. Follow local cheese and home-made oatcakes with honeycomb parfait with raspberries from the garden. Super breakfasts.

Directions: 7m north of Armadale ferry, and 12m south of Skye Bridge on A851

Sleat Isle of Skye IV43 8QW
Map 13: NG71
Tel: 01471 833202
Fax: 01471 833404
E-mail:
marie@duisdalehotel.demon.co.uk
Chef/Owner: Marie Campbell
Cost: Set-price D £29. H/wine £8.50
Times: D only 7.30-9pm.
Closed Nov-Mar
Additional: Children 4+
Seats: 40
Style: Traditional/Country-house
Smoking: No smoking in dining room
Accommodation: 17 en suite ★ ★ ★

ISLE ORNSAY, Hotel Eilean Iarmain

Forming the nucleus of a restored fishing and crofting community this 19th-century island inn provides traditional values of hospitality from the friendly Gaelic-speaking staff. Restaurant meals might include locally fished trout oven baked with toasted almonds.

Sleat Isle of Skye IV43 8QR
Map 13: NG71
Tel: 01471 833332
Fax: 01471 833275
Cost: Set-price L £16.50/D £31. ☺
H/wine £12
Times: Noon-2pm(pre-booked
only)/7.30-9pm
Additional: Bar food; Sunday L;
Children welcome
Style: Traditional/Country-house
Smoking: No smoking in dining room
Accommodation: 16 en suite ★ ★

Directions: Overlooking harbour – cross bridge at Kyle of Lochalsh then take A850 and A851, then down to harbour front

ISLE ORNSAY, **Kinloch Lodge**

Isle of Skye IV43 8QY
Map 13: NG71
Tel: 01471 833214
Fax: 01471 833277
E-mail: kinloch@dial.pipex.com
Chefs: Claire Macdonald & Peter Macpherson
Owners: Lord & Lady Macdonald
Cost: Set-price D £37. H/wine £7
Times: D only at 8pm. Closed Xmas
Additional: Children 8+
Seats: 30
Style: Country-house
Smoking: No smoking in dining room
Accommodation: 14 en suite ★★

Lord Macdonald, with his wife, chef and cookery writer Claire, has been running his ancestral home as a hotel for nearly 30 years. The substantial, white-painted house is in a lovely position, just yards above a sea loch, and the interior is furnished and decorated in comfortable country-house style. Guests help themselves to pre-dinner drinks from trays in the drawing room before taking their places at polished tables in the portrait-hung, silverware-laden dining room. Dinner is a set five courses, with a choice of starter and main course, one of which is always fish or shellfish. Meals are notable for the quality and freshness of the raw materials used, and the style is generally straightforward: scallop soufflé, or a salad of quails' eggs, avocado and crispy bacon to start, followed by roast saddle of Highland venison with a sauce of port, ginger and green peppercorns, or fillet of sea bass on a bed of sautéed cucumber with a spicy red pepper, chilli and coriander salsa. In between comes a soup perhaps leek and mushroom and puddings of, say, rich chocolate and almond cake, or vanilla bavarois with a fruit compote, are served before cheese. Meals are well-paced, service is friendly, and the wine list is an enterprising global selection.

Directions: 1 mile off main road, 6 miles S of Broadford on A851, 10 miles N of Armadale

KENTALLEN, **Holly Tree Hotel**

The hotel is an Edwardian former railway station with a Rennie Mackintosh theme throughout. The restaurant, which has huge windows overlooking the loch, specialises in local seafood and game.

Additional: Sunday L; Children welcome
Smoking: No smoking in dining room
Accommodation: 10 en suite ★★

Directions: 3m S of Ballachulish on A828

Kentallen Pier PA38 4BY
Map 14: NN05
Tel: 01631 740292
Fax: 01631 740345
Cost: *Alc* £25, set-price L £6. ☺ H/wine £12.50
Times: Noon-2pm/7-9.30pm

KINGUSSIE, **The Cross**

Tony Hadley treats the subtly sophisticated restaurant, a former tweed mill, as a stage set for his singular passion, wine. He stocks over 400 wines and is liable, during the course of a

Tweed Mill Brae Ardbroilach Road PH21 1TC
Map 14: NH70
Tel: 01540 661166
Fax: 01540 661080

meal, to produce a plethora of books and bottles to educate the guests as he takes them on a tour of the vineyards of the world. His hospitality is superb and generous, and guests who come here are likely to feel like dinner guests at a swish house party. The impression is enhanced by the nightly changing, five-course menu sympathetically cooked by Ruth Hadley and Becca Henderson, with no choice until the main course. Our inspection dinner started with textbook seared scallops with asparagus salad – simple, sweet, light and perfect. A contrast to the disappointing courgette, onion, mint and goats' cheese soup. Salmon cakes with sweetcorn salsa, and the main course, excellent Gressingham duckling with honey and soy sauce brought the meal back on track before we finished with a freshly made pear and butterscotch tart with caramel ice.

Directions: Town centre, 300m uphill from lights along Ardroilach Road & turn left onto Tweed Mill Brae

E-mail: fabulousfood@thecross.co.uk
Chefs: Ruth Hadley,
Becca Henderson
Owners: Tony & Ruth Hadley
Cost: Set-price D £37.50.
Times: D only, 7-9pm. Closed Tue,
1 Dec-28 Feb
Additional: Children 8+; Vegetarian dishes by prior arrangement
Seats: 28
Style: Rustic/Modern
Smoking: No smoking in dining room
Accommodation: 9 en suite ★ ★

KINGUSSIE,
Osprey Hotel ❀

Small stone-built hotel in the Spey Valley; typical dishes served in the cosy dining room are venison and apple patties, and poached fillet of salmon with citrus sauce.

Additional: Children 10+; Vegetarian choice not always available
Style: Informal/Traditional
Smoking: No smoking in dining room
Accommodation: 8 en suite ★ ★

Directions: South end of High Street off A9

Ruthven Road PH21 1EN
Map 14: NH70
Tel/Fax: 01540 661510
E-mail:
aileen@ospreyhotel.freeserve.co.uk
Cost: Set-price D £23. ☺ H/wine £9
Times: D only, 7.30-8.30pm

KINGUSSIE,
The Scot House Hotel ❀

Wholesome Scottish fare on a choice of menus, start with melon and local raspberries for example, then noisettes of Highland lamb or Salmon Strathspey with a light cheese and dill sauce, topped off with Ecclefechan flan.

Telephone for further details

Directions: South end of main village street

Newtonmore Road PH21 1HE
Map 14: NH70
Tel: 01540 661351
Fax: 01540 661111
E-mail: shh@sirocco.globalnet.co.uk

LOCHINVER,
Inver Lodge ❀ NEW

A backdrop of unspoilt wilderness and mountains, and a modern hotel which capitalises on the views. Six courses might include wild mushroom and truffle risotto, roast pepper soup, and poached turbot with baby fennel and onion bouillon.

Telephone for further details.

Directions: A835 to Lochinver, through village, L at village hall, follow private road for 0.5 mile

IV27 4LU
Map 14: NC02
Tel: 01571 844496
Fax: 01571 844395
E-mail: stay@inverlodge.com

MUIR OF ORD,
The Dower House

A relaxing and informal atmosphere pervades this small hotel on the edge of the village in four acres of lovely gardens. Aperitifs and nibbles are served by the log fire in the cosy sitting room, with dinner at 8 o'clock among the polished wood of the traditionally furnished dining room; Mena Aitchison takes wine orders from a comprehensive, well-chosen list. Robyn Aitchison's style is commendably straightforward, allowing the freshness of ingredients to shine through, and he shows a good sense of balance in his no-choice dinner menus (although farmhouse cheeses can be taken instead of pudding). Produce is well-sourced, too, with a kitchen garden supplying vegetables and herbs. Fillet of cod with courgette, lemon and capers might precede a main course of whole partridge with lentils, Savoy cabbage and wild mushrooms. Alternatively, cheese and tomato tart might be followed by halibut in a fennel crust. Desserts have included tarte Tatin, bread-and-butter pudding and exceptionally light pear soufflé drizzled with bitter dark chocolate sauce.

Directions: From Muir of Ord take A862 (Dingwall) 1 mile, L at double bend

Highfield IV6 7XN
Map 14: NH55
Tel/Fax: 01463 870090
E-mail: eat@thedowerhouse.co.uk
Chef: Robyn Aitchison
Owners: Mr & Mrs RG Aitchison
Cost: Set-price D £30. H/wine £15
Times: L by arrangement/7.30-9.30pm. Closed Xmas
Additional: Children 6+
Seats: 26
Style: Informal/country-house
Smoking: No smoking in dining room
Accommodation: 5 en suite ★

NAIRN, The Boath House

The lovingly-restored Georgian country mansion comes complete with small lake stocked with both brown and rainbow trout. The comfortable public rooms, warmed by roaring open fires, double as gallery space for exhibitions of contemporary Highland art. The daily-changing set menu makes good use of home-grown, local and regional ingredients, organic wherever possible. Meat is excellent, as befits members of the Scotch Beef Club; our Inspector particularly enjoyed a juicy, full-flavoured, roasted rump of rose veal on a bed of garlicky mash, with asparagus, fine beans and a light Madiera and thyme jus. Other typical dishes might include fillet of cod and 'Isle of Skye' scallops served with fresh pasta and vermouth velouté, and smoked ham hock terrine with gribiche sauce. A very, very rich chocolate truffle cake was moderated by an excellent pumpkin sorbet with just a hint of spice to offset the sweetness of the cake.

Directions: 2m E of Nairn on A96 (Inverness to Aberdeen road)

Auldearn IV12 5TE
Map 14: NH85
Tel: 01667 454896
Fax: 01667 455469
E-mail: wendy@boath-house.demon.co.uk
Chef: Charles Lockley
Owners: Don & Wendy Matheson
Cost: Set-price L £19.95/D £29.50. H/wine £9.50
Times: 12-30-2pm/7-9pm. Closed L Wed, all Mon & Tue
Additional: Sunday L; Children welcome
Seats: 24. Private dining room 8
Style: Country-house
Smoking: No smoking in dining room
Civil licence: 30
Accommodation: 7 en suite ★ ★ ★

NAIRN, Golf View Hotel ✤

Seabank Road IV 12 4HD
Map 14: NH85
Tel: 01667 452301
Fax: 01667 455267
Cost: Set-price D £24.75. ☺
Times: Noon-2pm/7-9.15pm
Additional: Bar food; Sunday L;
Children welcome
Style: Traditional/Country-house
Smoking: No smoking in dining room
Accommodation: 48 en suite ★ ★ ★ ★

The wood-panelled dining room offers a short but carefully balanced menu alongside daily specials. Try home-made turnip and saffron soup with cumin cream, or Brie cheese 'strudel' with roast parsnip and apple compote.

Directions: 15 miles SE of Inverness, 7 miles from airport on A96. In Nairn turn L at Parish church and continue to end of Seabank Road

NAIRN, Newton Hotel ✤

Inverness Road IV12 4RX
Map 14: NH85
Tel: 01667 453144
Fax: 01667 454026
E-mail: newton@morton-hotels.com
Cost: Set-price D £23.50. ☺
Times: Noon-2pm/7-9.15pm
Additional: Bar food; Sunday L;
Children welcome
Smoking: No smoking in dining room
Accommodation: 57 en suite ★ ★ ★ ★

Two menus offering a taste of the Highlands and daily changing specials ensure a good range of options in this country house hotel restaurant. Collop of grilled salmon with a scallop mousse was well textured and flavoursome.

Directions: West of the town centre

ONICH, Allt-nan-Ros Hotel ✤✤

Just a stone's throw from the edge of Loch Linnhe, this white-painted Victorian hotel offers genuine Highland hospitality and beautiful views. In the formal dining room, with its quiet, attentive service, the set-price dinner menu competes for attention with the breathtaking views across the loch to the rugged hills beyond. Though not extensive, Mark Walker's four-course menu offers much interest, giving modern yet sympathetic treatment to quality Scottish ingredients. Freshly made canapés of chicken satay and gravad lax on a croûton led

PH33 6RY
Map 14: NN06
Tel: 01855 821210
Fax: 01855 821462
E-mail: allt-nan-ros@zetnet.co.uk
Chef: Mark Walker
Owners: James & Fiona MacLeod
Cost: Set-price L £12.50 & £14.95/
D £28. H/wine £11.50
Times: 12.30-1.45pm/7-8.30pm.
Closed Xmas

Allt-nan-Ros Hotel

Additional: Bar food L; Sunday L; Children welcome
Seats: 50
Style: Traditional/Country-house
Smoking: No smoking in dining room
Accommodation: 20 en suite ★★★

Directions: On the shores of Loch Linnhe, 10 miles S of Fort William on A82

the way on a spring visit. Seared monkfish tail with lemon risotto, asparagus spears and a chervil butter sauce proved a well-balanced choice to start, followed by a robust, roasted wild leek soup with white truffle oil and crème fraîche. Next came a main dish of loin of local venison with savoy cabbage, red pepper chutney and a rosemary and port wine jus, before an equally rich dessert offering of chocolate pudding with warm hazelnut cream sauce. Good house wine by the glass, with cafetière coffee and petits fours to finish in the lounge.

ONICH, Onich Hotel ✿ NEW

nr Fort William PH33 6RY
Map 14: NN06
Tel: 01855 821214
Fax: 01855 821484
Cost: Set-price D £23. ☺
H/wine £11.75
Times: D only, 7-9pm
Additional: Children welcome
Style: Traditional
Smoking: No smoking in dining room
Accommodation: 25 en suite ★★★

Directions: Beside A82, 2m N of Ballachulish Bridge

Wild mushroom soup, roast pheasant and a decadent chocolate marquise made a satisfying meal at this hotel restaurant, which offers superb views over Loch Linnhe and the mountains of Glencoe.

PLOCKTON, Haven Hotel ✿ NEW

Innes Street IV52 8TW
Map:
Tel: 01599 544223/544334
Fax: 01599 544467
Cost: Set-price D £27. ☺
H/wine £6.95
Times: Noon-2pm (prior arrangement only)/7-8.30pm. Closed 20 Dec-1st Feb

Set beside the harbour in this pretty conservation village, the Haven Hotel's attractive restaurant might feature feuille of smoked sea trout and brill on a bed of leeks topped with parsnip shavings and a lemon and parsley sauce.

Additional: Children 7+
Style: Classic/Formal
Smoking: No smoking in dining room
Accommodation: 15 en suite ★★

Directions: Turn off A87 just before Kyle of Lochalsh; after Balmacara look for sign to Plockton

POOLEWE, Pool House Hotel

Enchanting waterside setting where otters may be glimpsed at sunset. The cuisine is equally seductive with the natural ability of chef John Moir showing through in roast medallions of venison with haggis and venison gravy.

Additional: Bar food; Children 14+; Vegetarian dishes available by arrangement
Style: Classic/Country-house
Smoking: No smoking in dining room
Accommodation: 10 en suite ★ ★ ★

IV22 2LD
Map 14: NG88
Tel: 01445 781272
Fax: 01445 781403
E-mail: poolhouse@inverewe.co.uk
Cost: Set-price D £35.50.
H/wine £12.50
Times: D only, 7-8.45pm. Closed Jan & Feb, (Bookings only Nov-Dec)

Directions: 6 miles N of Gairloch on A832. Located in the village

PORTREE, Bosville Hotel

Bosville Terrace Isle of Skye
IV51 9DG
Map 13: NG44
Tel: 01478 612846
Fax: 01478 613434
E-mail: bosville@macleodhotels.co.uk
Times: 11.30am-10pm
Additional: Bar food; Sunday L; Children welcome
Style: Chic/traditional
Smoking: No smoking in dining room
Accommodation: 15 en suite ★ ★

Restaurant themed around a ship's chandlery, with seafood as a speciality, using the finest local ingredients – langoustine tails in thermidor sauce, and king scallops with green garlic butter.

Directions: In centre of Portree

PORTREE, Cuillin Hills Hotel

Isle of Skye IV51 9QU
Map 13: NG44
Tel: 01478 612003
Fax: 01478 613092
E-mail:
office@cuillinhills.demon.co.uk
Cost: Alc £26, set-price L £8.95/ D £26. ☺ H/wine £10.95
Times: D only, 6.30-9pm
Additional: Bar food; Sunday L (12.30-2pm); Children welcome
Smoking: No smoking in dining room
Style: Traditional/country-house
Accommodation: 30 en suite ★ ★ ★

Spectacularly located hotel with a split-level restaurant overlooking Portree Bay towards the Cuillin mountains. The French influenced dishes are based on quality Scottish produce.

Directions: Signed to right 0.25 miles from Portree on A855 north

PORTREE,

Rosedale Hotel ❀

Harbour front hotel with dramatic views over the rugged coastline. The menu relies on Scottish style and fresh local ingredients to produce tantalising dishes such as the enormous seafood platter – simply prepared, uncomplicated, honest and enjoyable.

Additional: Children welcome
Style: Traditional
Smoking: No smoking in dining room
Accommodation: 23 en suite ★ ★

Directions: Centrally located on waterfront in Portree

Isle of Skye IV51 9DB
Map 13: NG44
Tel: 01478 613131
Fax: 01478 612531
Cost: Set-price D £18. ☺
H/wine £10.95
Times: D only, 7-11pm.
Closed 1 Nov-30 Apr

SHIELDAIG,

Tigh an Eilean Hotel ❀

The hotel is under new ownership but the kitchen continues to offer dishes based on quality ingredients, including local seafood. The comfortable dining room overlooks the bay towards Shieldaig Island.

Cost: Set-price D £26.25. H/wine £9.45
Times: D only, 7-8.30pm. Closed Nov-Mar
Additional: Bar food; Children welcome ??? see stat
Style: Chic
Smoking: No smoking in dining room
Accommodation: 11 en suite ★

Directions: In centre of Shieldaig, at water's edge

Strathcarron IV54 8XN
Map 14: NG85
Tel: 01520 755251
Fax: 01520 755321
E-mail:
tighaneileanhotel@shieldaig.fsnet.co.uk

SPEAN BRIDGE,

Old Pines Restaurant with Rooms ❀❀

Set in the Great Glen, with fine views of the surrounding mountains, the Scandinavian-style log cabin with stone extensions has inviting lounges, heated by wood stoves, crammed full of family photos, books and magazines. The no-choice set menu is served at 8pm and the top-of-the-range, genuine cooking features local produce plus items smoked on the premises. Portions are generous – Mallaig fish soup with garlic mayonnaise was almost a meal in itself. An intermediate course is usually soup, perhaps fennel and leek or a palate-refreshing walnut and cheese salad dressed with raspberry vinegar and walnut oil. A lime juice marinade added extra zip to a juicy breast of free-range chicken, as did spiced red cabbage with chargrilled home-smoked salmon. Fruity meringues make a regular appearance, for example, hazelnut with raspberries, raspberry ice-cream and raspberry sauce. Local cheeses are served in good condition. Selected glasses from the interesting, ever-growing and reasonably-priced wine list are paired with several of the courses.

By Fort William
PH34 4EG

Map 14: NN28
Tel: 01397 712324
Fax: 01397 712433
E-mail: billandsukie@oldpines.co.uk
Chef: Sukie Barber
Owners: Bill & Sukie Barber
Cost: Set-price D £24.50 & £30. ☺
H/wine £10.50
Times: L served all day, D from 8pm.
(closed D Sun ex residents Apr-Sep)
2 wks in winter
Additional: Children welcome (no babies & small children at D)
Seats: 30
Style: Informal/Country-house
Smoking: No smoking in dining room
Civil licence: 30 indoor/150 marquee
Accommodation: 8 en suite

Directions: A82, 1 mile N of Spean Bridge take B8004 next to Commando Memorial towards Gairlochy. 300yds on R

SPEAN BRIDGE,
Old Station Restaurant

Warm up by a coal fire and take your choice from the attractive menu offered by this old restored station building, including bean and vegetable chilli with tortilla chips. The service is very friendly.

Additional: Bar food; Children welcome
Style: Informal/Traditional
Smoking: No-smoking area

Directions: Approximately 10 miles N of Fort William, in centre of village (follow signs for BR station)

Station Road PH34 4EP
Map 14: NN28
Tel: 01397 712535
Cost: Alc £20. ☺ H/wine fr £11
Times: 11-5.30pm/6-9pm. Closed all Mon, D Sun & Tue-Thu, end Oct-Etr

---

STRONTIAN,
Kilcamb Lodge Hotel ❀❀

At one time a barracks and a hunting lodge, this small hotel is in an incomparable spot, set in 28 acres of lawns and woodland facing a half-mile private beach on Loch Sunart. The restaurant, with its softly-toned decor and plain wooden furniture, has the same views, and there's also much to admire on the plates. Vegetables and herbs are grown organically using seaweed as fertiliser, free-range eggs come from the chickens outside, and the kitchen buys the best that Scotland has to offer, from Aberdeen Angus to Atlantic cod. Dinner follows a set format with three or four choices per course except the second, which is soup – perhaps smooth, light and creamy cauliflower dribbled with coriander purée. A meal might start with confit of duck leg with mushroom risotto, or a simple but effective salad of seared Shetland scallops with pancetta garnished with rocket pesto. Roast loin of venison, 'deliciously tender and full-flavoured', in juniper jus might be partnered by goats' cheese gnocchi on braised red cabbage to make a fine main course, or perhaps seared peppered salmon with pimento couscous and basil sauce. Puddings don't let the side down either, from cranachan to glazed lemon tart with raspberry sorbet, while the wine list is a well-balanced assembly with a fair number sold by the glass.

Directions: Take the Corran ferry off A82. Follow A861 to Strontian. First L over bridge in centre of village

Acharacle PH36 4HY
Map 14: NM86
Tel: 01967 402257
Fax: 01967 402041
E-mail: kilcamblodge@aol.com
Chef: Neil Mellis
Owners: Peter & Anne Blakeway
Cost: Set-price D £29.50. ☺
H/wine £9.75
Times: Noon-2pm/D at 7.30pm
Additional: Bar food L; Children 8+
Seats: 26
Style: Classic/Country-house
Smoking: No smoking in dining room
Accommodation: 11 en suite ★★

TAIN, Glenmorangie House ❀ **NEW**

A small country house restaurant with a very sociable dining arrangement and a limited but high quality set menu. The menu is responsive to local availability: a salad of langoustines with whisky-cured smoked salmon was a last-minute bonus.

Additional: Sunday L; Children 12+
Style: Classic/Country-house
Smoking: No smoking in dining room
Accommodation: 9 en suite ★★

Directions: N on A9 turn R onto B9175 (just before Tain) & follow signs for hotel

Cadboll Fearn IV20 1XP
Map 14: NH78
Tel: 01862 871671
Fax: 01862 871625
E-mail: relax@glenmorangieplc.co.uk
Cost: Set-price L £20/D £38.50. ☺
H/wine £15
Times: Noon-2.30pm/fr 7.30pm

TAIN,
Mansfield House Hotel ✿✿

Scotsburn Road IV19 1PR
Map 14: NH78
Tel: 01862 892052
Fax: 01862 892260
E-mail: mansfield@cali.co.uk
Chef: David Lauritson
Owners: Norman, Norma &
David Lauritson
Cost: *Alc* £25. ☺ H/wine £14
Times: Noon-2pm/7-9pm
Additional: Sunday L; Children 8+
(after 8pm)
Seats: 28. Private dining room 20
Style: Traditional/Country-house
Smoking: No smoking in dining room
Civil licence: 45
Accommodation: 18 en suite ★ ★ ★

An impressive mansion house, built in the 1870s and substantially extended in 1902, Mansfield House retains many original features, including pine panelling and ornate plaster ceilings, making it the ideal showcase for the owners' collection of fine porcelain. At dinner, canapés are fresh, and there is a good selection of home-made breads. The kitchen uses fine local produce in imaginative ways: seared langoustine with pickled vegetables, dill and parmesan biscuit, collop of pork seasoned with Thai spices and served on pak choi with a Strathdon sauce, timbale of citrus risotto with calamari rings and a smoked salmon rose. The consommé of chicken and sun-dried tomatoes with garden chives had good flavours and the marinated duck was moist and tender. It came seared, on crisp leaves with its own crackling. Desserts are elaborate, and the hot chocolate pudding served with a mocha crème Anglaise was served in an individual pastry tartlet. Coffee and petits fours are good and the service pleasant and friendly.

Directions: From S on A9, ignore 1st turning to Tain and after 0.5m turn R at sign for police station

TONGUE, # Ben Loyal Hotel ✿

IV27 4XE
Map 14: NC55
Tel: 01847 611216
Fax: 01847 611212
E-mail:
thebenloyalhotel@btinternet.com
Cost: Set-price D £22.50. ☺
H/wine £9
Times: Noon-2.15pm/7-8.30pm.
Closed 25 & 26 Dec, 1 Jan
Additional: Bar food; Sunday L;
Children welcome
Style: Informal/Rustic
Smoking: No smoking in dining room
Accommodation: 11 en suite ★ ★

A friendly and informal hotel with lovely views. The five-course dinner menu may include fillet of sea bass with crisp ginger, olive oil and balsamic vinegar. Leave space for the delicious steamed sponge puddings!

Directions: The hotel stands in the centre of this village at the junction of A836/A838

TORRIDON,

Loch Torridon Hotel ⊛⊛

Achnasheen IV22 2EY
Map 14: NG95
Tel: 01445 791242
Fax: 01445 791296
E-mail:
enquiries@lochtorridonhotel.com
Chef: Neil Dowson
Owners: David & Geraldine Gregory
Cost: Set-price D £38. H/wine £15
Times: Noon-2pm/7.15-8.45pm
Additional: Bar food L; Children 10+
Seats: 40. Private dining room 15
Style: Country-house
Smoking: No smoking in dining room
Civil licence: 40
Accommodation: 20 en suite ★ ★ ★

Directions: From Inverness, follow
signs to Ullapool (A835).
At Garve take A832 to Kinlochewe;
take A896 to Torridon. Don't turn off
to Torridon village – hotel is one mile
on L

Set in one of the most impressive parts of the Scottish
Highlands on the shores of Loch Torridon, the house dates
from 1887 and was once the grand shooting lodge of the first
earl of Lovelace. It has been carefully restored to its original
Victorian splendour, with ornate ceilings, huge log fires and
sumptuous furnishings, and a great range of malt whiskies is
offered in the wood-panelled bar. The set-price dinner menu
lists three options at each of three courses. Tartare of West
Coast scallops with langoustines and oyster vinaigrette is a
typical starter, followed by marinated venison with celeriac
fondant, braised fig and red wine sauce. Finish with Scottish
cheeses and oatcakes, or poached garden rhubarb with vanilla
parfait, passion fruit sorbet and jus fraises.

ULLAPOOL,

Altnaharrie Inn ⊛⊛⊛⊛⊛

IV26 2SS
Map 14: NH19
Tel: 01854 633230
Chef: Gunn Eriksen
Owners: Fred Brown, Gunn Eriksen
Cost: Set-price D £75. H/wine fr £11
Times: D at 8pm.
Additional: Children 8+; Advance
notice required for vegetarian dishes
Seats: 16
Style: Country-house/Waterside
Smoking: No smoking in dining room
Accommodation: 8 en suite

Directions: Telephone from Ullapool
for instructions on ferry

The ultimate in destination restaurants, the journey to get here
makes this more of a gastronomic pilgrimage! Both hotel and
food are stunning in every respect. The boat trip across the sea
loch alone could inspire poets. Everything at Altnaharrie has
been chosen according to William Morris's principles of home
decorating: have nothing in your homes that you do not know
to be useful or believe to be beautiful, although the aesthetic is
more in terms of a Scandinavian, even Japanese refinement,

and Gunn's tapestries and ceramics acquire more significance through the lack of clutter elsewhere. Dinner is served at 8pm, with diners congregating in the drawing room for drinks beforehand. The atmosphere can be hushed in the white-walled dining room, as Fred brings the sweetest of langoustine tails and bowls of home-made mayonnaise, but it is a hush born out of expectation. Lobster could not be more succulent, characteristically served with two sauces, creamy champagne and one made of lobster coral. It typifies the brilliance of a cook whose technical skills are self-evident but who knows when to stop cooking and let the ingredients shine through. A morel soup (elixir would be a better term) filled the room with earthy aroma, before roast fillet of calf with Burgundy red wine sauce, enoki mushrooms and trompettes de mort, a truffley ragout of artichokes and a copper pan of truffled mash with parmesan 'the most amazing potatoes I have ever eaten'). Choice comes at pudding stage, from a range that might include cloudberry ice cream with raspberries and slices of warm pineapple. The fine selection of cheeses is kept in top condition, and the wine list is an enthusiast's delight.

WHITEBRIDGE,
Knockie Lodge Hotel ✿✿

IV2 6UP
Map 14: NH41
Tel: 01456 486276
Fax: 01456 486389
E-mail: info@knockielodge.co.uk
Chef: Mark Dexter
Owner: Nicholas Bean
Cost: Set-price D £37.50
Times: D only, 8 for 8.30pm.
Closed mid Oct-1 May
Additional: Bar food L; Children 10+;
Vegetarian dishes by arrangement
Seats: 30. Private dining room 10
Style: Country-house
Smoking: No smoking in dining room
Accommodation: 10 en suite ★★

Built as a shooting lodge over 200 years ago by the chief of Clan Fraser, Knockie Lodge enjoys a peaceful yet dramatic setting overlooking Loch nan Lann. The hotel is favoured by walkers and those who enjoy the highland scenery and, as a result of all this outdoor activity the restaurant is busier in the evenings. The menu is a set four courses with no choice except at dessert, and is supported by a very interesting wine list. Dinner is leisurely, with canapés and aperitifs in the lounge till about 8.15/8.30. The canapés were lovely; crispy battered onion rings, king prawns and fruit on a skewer and spicy sausage with barbecue-type sauce. The meal started with ravioli of ricotta cheese with a local farm egg. Knockie Lodge steamed fillet of Scottish salmon topped with pesto served on a warm salad of tomato and basil was 'delicious'. Roast breast of peppered duck served with a crispy spring roll, glazed bay vegetables and a port sauce was another elaborately-presented creation. Desserts are good and included tarte Tatin served with a subtly flavoured home-made ice cream.

Directions: On B862, 8 miles north of Fort Augustus

LANARKSHIRE, NORTH

CUMBERNAULD,
Westerwood Hotel

Spacious and elegant first floor dining room serving innovative dishes – begin with chargrilled asparagus with Parmesan and a balsamic dressing, perhaps, followed by chicken with foie gras stuffing, served on buttered noodles.

1 St Andrews Drive
Westerwood G68 0EW
Map 11: NS77
Tel: 01236 457171
Fax: 01236 738478
E-mail:
westerwoodhotels@btinternet.com
Cost: Alc £23, set-price L £9.95/
D £20. ☺ H/wine £11.35
Times: Noon-2pm/7-10pm.
Closed L Sat
Additional: Bar food; Sunday L;
Children welcome
Style: Classic/Formal
Smoking: No smoking in dining room;
Air conditioning
Accommodation: 49 en suite ★★★★

Directions: Take exit from A80 signposted Ward Park. At mini roundabout take 1st L, at 2nd roundabout turn R, leads into St Andrew's Drive

LANARKSHIRE, SOUTH

BIGGAR, Shieldhill Castle

In the midst of soothingly tranquil scenery, Shieldhill, a fortified manor house, has 800 years of history behind it, its 'new' wing added in 1820. The oak-panelled lounge leads into Chancellor's, a room of high carved ceilings and views towards Tinto Hill. The kitchen's output is well represented by a starter of fresh and well flavoured haddock fishcakes with balsamic vinaigrette and a salad of seasonal leaves, followed by 'very tender' seared beef fillet on rösti with wild mushrooms and truffle jus. Materials are well-sourced, with lamb and game from the estate appearing in several guises on the menu. An inspection meal concluded with a well executed dessert of layers of shortbread, chantilly cream and seasonal berries, perfect on a summer afternoon. The wine list has some fine clarets and Burgundies, with plenty of New World choice, and a page of house selections keeps its feet firmly on the ground.

Quothquan ML12 6NA
Map 11: NT03
Tel: 01899 220035
Fax: 01899 221092
E-mail: enquires@shieldhill.co.uk
Chef: Ashley Gallant
Owners: Mr & Mrs R Lamb
Cost: Alc £32, set-price L/D £17.50.
☺ H/wine fr £12.95
Times: Noon-2pm/7-10pm
Additional: Bar food; Sunday L;
Children welcome
Seats: Private dining rooms 25 & 25
Style: Classic
Smoking: No smoking in dining room
Civil licence: 200
Accommodation: 16 en suite ★★★

Directions: Off B7016 (Carnwath), turn L, 2 miles from centre of Biggar

BIGGAR,
Toftcombs Country House

Peebles Road ML12 6QX
Map 11: NT03
Tel: 01899 220142
Fax: 01899 221771
E-mail: toftcombs@aol.com
Cost: *Alc* £20. ☺ H/wine £9.80
Times: Noon-2.30pm/6-9pm.
Closed Mon & Tue Jan-Mar
Additional: Bar food; Sunday L;
Children welcome
Style: Traditional/Country-house
Smoking: No smoking in dining room
Accommodation: 4 en suite

Beautifully restored baronial mansion offering modern Scottish cooking, with dishes such as millionaire's pie (salmon and prawns in a cream sauce), beef Stroganoff, and spicy East Indian chicken.

Directions: On A702 N of Biggar

EAST KILBRIDE,
Crutherland Hotel ❀

Elegant restaurant in a renovated mansion house. Stylish dishes might include tuna loin with Parmesan shavings and citrus dressing, or seared Goosnagh duck breast with salsify, creamed leek and truffle on red cabbage.

Strathaven Road G75 0QZ
Map 11: NT03
Tel: 01355 577000
Fax: 01355 220855
E-mail: info@crutherland.macdonald-hotels.co.uk

Cost: *Alc* £35, set-price D £30. ☺ H/wine £15.50
Times: Noon-2pm/7-10pm. Closed L Sat
Additional: Bar food L; Sunday L; Children welcome
Style: Traditional
Smoking: No smoking in dining room; Air conditioning
Accommodation: 76 en suite ★ ★ ★ ★

Directions: From E Kilbride take A726 towards Strathaven. 1.5 miles, & beyond Torrance roundabout, hotel on L

ROSEBANK,
Popinjay Hotel ❀

Tudor-style hotel with grounds extending to the banks of the River Clyde. New blood has revitalised the kitchen, with terrine of confit meats, roasted breast of guinea fowl, and a tangy lemon tart getting the thumbs up.

Lanark Road ML8 5QB
Map 11: NS84
Tel: 01555 860441
Fax: 01555 860204
E-mail: sales@popinjayhotel.co.uk

Cost: *Alc* £27.50, set-price L £9.95/D £17.50. ☺ H/wine £9.95
Times: Noon-2.30pm/6.30-10.30pm
Additional: Bar food; Sunday L; Children welcome
Style: traditional
Smoking: No-smoking area; Air conditioning
Accommodation: 45 en suite ★ ★ ★

Directions: On A72 between Hamilton & Lanark

LOTHIAN, EAST

DIRLETON,
The Open Arms Hotel ❀

The intimate fine dining restaurant of this long-established hotel presents a regularly changing four-course fixed-price menu, which has a contemporary approach to the best of Scottish produce.

Cost: Set-price L £17.95/D £29.50. H/wine £10.95
Times: Noon-2.30pm/7-9.30pm
Additional: Sunday L; Children welcome
Seats: 35
Style: Classic/Country-house
Smoking: No smoking in dining room; Air Conditioning
Accommodation: 10 en suite ★ ★ ★

Directions: From A1 (S) take A198 to North Berwick, then follow signs for Dirleton – 2 miles W. From Edinburgh take A6137 leading to A198.

EH39 5EG
Map 12: NT58
Tel: 01620 850241
Fax: 01620 850570
E-mail: openarms@clara.co.uk
Chef: John Kay
Owners: Tom & Emma Hill

GULLANE,
Greywalls Hotel ❀❀

Designed by Lutyens, this crescent-shaped house was built in 1901 as a holiday home overlooking Muirfield Golf Course and the Firth of Forth. Gertrude Jekyll is responsible for the gardens, and the country-house style of the interior extends to a panelled library with a log fire and a grand piano. Menus follow a set-price format, with three choices at each course at lunch, four at dinner, when the second of four courses is either a salad or a 'wee bowl' of well-flavoured soup, perhaps sweet potato and wild garlic. Top-notch ingredients are used to good effect, from peat-smoked Shetland salmon with focaccia, to a main course of peppered fillet of Aberdeen Angus with caramelised shallots and garlic, while foie gras may make a luxurious partner for applewood-smoked halibut or, more traditionally, go into a terrine with duck as a starter. Fruity accompaniments often give bright, zestful flavours to the main component of a dish – spicy mango salsa with langoustine salad, say, Seville marmalade sauce with breast of Barbary duck, or passionfruit and lime sauce with sliced breast of guinea fowl. Puddings get nods of approval – pannacotta, perhaps, or rich chocolate torte with a toasted coconut sauce – and the wine list is a masterly compilation of styles and prices, from pedigree clarets to Canada.

Directions: From Edinburgh take A1 to North Berwick slip road, then follow A198 along coast to far end of Gullane – Greywalls is up last road on L

Muirfield EH31 2EG
Map 12: NT48
Tel: 01620 842144
Fax: 01620 842241
E-mail: hotel@greywalls.co.uk
Chef: Simon Burns
Owners: Giles & Ros Weaver
Cost: Set-price L £20/D £37.50. H/wine £12.50
Times: 12.30-2pm/7.30-9pm. Closed Nov-Mar
Additional: Bar food L; Sunday L; Children welcome; Vegetarian choice not always available
Seats: 40. Private dining room 20. Jacket & tie preferred
Style: Traditional/Country-house
Smoking: No smoking in dining room
Accommodation: 23 en suite ★ ★ ★

GULLANE,

La Potinière ❀❀❀

2000 marks David and Hilary Brown's quarter-century at La Potinière. Not only have they stayed the course, but the cooking remains as good as ever. It is, however, the sort of place one loves or loathes and it is not without its idiosyncracies. David serves single-handedly and the pace is leisurely but patience is a virtue, so relax, chat and let the world go by. Consider, in particular, the wines; David's cellar features an abundance of classic wines from the best names and shippers, and he enjoys discussing and advising; some regulars telephone to learn the menu, then ask him to match it with wines. Hilary's food is a triumph of simplicity over contemporary complexity and she can still show the new kids on the block a thing or two about real cooking. There are no gimmicks, what you see is what you get and everything has a part to play. Potage St Germain was a beautiful balance of pea and mint flavours, followed by salmon pan-fried to perfection with a delectable crisped skin and a luscious sauce vierge, then an impeccable 'filet de lièvre au chou rouge' with a touch of redcurrant in the sauce. An Aladdin's cave of ingredients made for a real salad experience, rightly a course on its own. A thin slice of Brie in tip-top condiditon is simply accompanied by a wedge of apple, then a pannacotta of definitive silky-smoothness. The oohs and aahs heard all around the pretty, country restaurant told their own story. Here's to the next 25 years.

Directions: Village centre

Main Street
EH31 2AA
Map 12: NT48
Tel/Fax: 01620 843214
Chef: Hilary Brown
Owners: David & Hilary Brown
Cost: Set-price L £23.50/D £35.
H/wine £13.75
Times: L at 1pm/D at 8pm. Closed
L Mon-Wed, Fri & Sat, D Sun-Thu,
1 wk Jun, Oct
Additional: Sunday L;
Children welcome; Vegetarian dishes
with prior notice
Seats: 26
Style: Rustic/French
Smoking: No smoking in dining room
Credit cards: None

LOTHIAN, WEST

LINLITHGOW,

Champany Inn ❀❀

Traditional decor, polished oak tables and gleaming copper plates. First and foremost this is a steak restaurant, renowned for the quality of its Aberdeen Angus beef, all hung and prepared in house and cut to order. Lobster, salmon and cod also appear on the menu, along with two poultry dishes. The style of the restaurant is formal and it is noticeably busier in the evenings. Breads are home-made, and the nine starters are mainly fish/seafood along with three soups, Cullen skink comes with succulent pieces of haddock. Lamb chops feature on the menu and are an excellent choice when the new season's lamb has arrived. The beef comes with a selection of mustards, including the house honey and whisky one. The wine list is a tome – 25 listed Champagnes, and wines from all over the world but particular attention should be paid to the South Africans.

Directions: 2 miles NE of Linlithgow at junction of A904 & A803

EH49 7LU
Map 11: NS97
Tel: 01506 834532
Fax: 01506 834302
E-mail: info@champany.com
Chefs: Clive Davidson, David Gibson, Kevin Hope
Owners: Clive & Anne Davidson
Cost: *Alc* £35-£45, set-price
L £16.75. H/wine £14.50
Times: 12.30-3pm/7-midnight.
Closed L Sat, all Sun, 25 & 26 Dec
Additional: Bar food; Sunday L;
Children 8+
Seats: 50. Private dining room 30
Style: Rustic/Country-house

LINLITHGOW,
Livingston's Restaurant ❀❀

52 High Street
EH49 7AE
Map 11: NS97
Tel: 01506 846565
Chef: Julian Wright
Owners: Mr & Mrs R N Livingston
Cost: Set-price L £15.99/D £27.50. ☺
H/wine £11.75
Times: Noon-2.30pm/6-9pm. Closed
Sun & Mon, 1st 2wks Jan, 1 wk Jun,
1 wk Oct
Additional: Children 8+
Seats: 40
Style: French/Traditional
Smoking: No-smoking area; Air
conditioning

At one time a stable, Livingston's is reached via an arch off Linlithgow's main street. The dining area is on two levels, the lower one a conservatory, and candles flicker on the wooden tables in the evening. If fillet of Aberdeen Angus with a creamy whisky sauce sounds like a paean to Scotland, the menus also take a broadly European thrust. A warm salad of smoked chicken and chorizo with pine nuts makes a fine starter, to be followed by something like fillet of sea bass with spicy couscous and a red pepper 'soup', or pan-fried sirloin steak with a red onion tarte Tatin. Good judgement is evident in a smoked salmon fishcake, and a stuffing of local black pudding with apple for chicken breast, and in puddings of banana bread-and-butter pudding, served warm with iced banana, and caramelised pineapple with a matching sorbet. Service is attentive and pleasant, and house wines from South Africa open the globally sourced wine list.

Directions: Opposite Post Office

UPHALL,
Houston House Hotel ❀❀

Broxburn EH52 6JS
Map 11: NT07
Tel: 01506 853831
Fax: 01506 854220
E-mail:
info@houstoun.macdonaldhotels.co.uk
Chef: David Veal
Owner: Macdonald Hotels
Cost: Alc £27.45, set-price L £18.50.
☺ H/wine £14.50
Times: Noon-2pm/7-9.30pm.
Closed L Sat
Additional: Bar food L; Sunday L;
Children welcome
Style: Traditional/Country-house
Smoking: No smoking in dining room;
Jacket & tie preferred (Sat D only)
Accommodation: 72 en suite ★★★★

A tastefully extended 17th-century house with a country club boasting its own Italian bistro, Houston House is surrounded by acres of gardens and grounds. While you could opt for fillet steak with classic béarnaise sauce and chips, the kitchen works around the contemporary European themes of a terrine of smoked chicken, rabbit and pancetta with apple and thyme chutney and truffle oil, followed by the likes of crispy duck confit with garlic and rosemary mash and bourguignonne garnish, or steamed cod with saffron potatoes, sautéed fennel and wild mushrooms. Decisive flavours are handled well enough to result in well-balanced dishes: witness a starter of pan-fried pigeon with barley risotto and a mango and chilli salsa, or a main course of roasted red snapper with ginger and black olive mash and a 'broth' of baby vegetables. Puddings can be busy – iced lemon parfait in a tuile parcel with a red berry and yogurt sauce, or a crisp pastry tartlet of light chocolate mousse surrounded by an orange marmalade sauce. A couple of pages of 'recommendations of the house' aid choosing a bottle of wine from the long list.

Directions: At junction between A89
and A899

MORAY

ARCHIESTOWN,
Archiestown Hotel ֍֍

Archiestown is a small village close to the Speyside Way, the Whisky Trail and, most important for fisherfolk, that finest of salmon rivers. The bistro at the hotel – small, Victorian, on the village square – is a veritable Aladdin's cave of memorabilia along the lines of fishing, whisky and wartime, while the wood-burner ensures that guests are cosy while pondering the menu; there is also a garden for outdoor dining in summer. Simply prepared, freshly cooked food, based around seasonal local ingredients, is the attraction here. Crab salad, tagliatelle with Parma ham and asparagus, or a soup – perhaps tomato and orange – to start, and then sugar-baked ham with Madeira sauce, sole in a creamy grape sauce, or devilled kidneys. Flavours can be robust, and portions generous, but those who can manage dessert could go for fruit salad, treacle pudding, or chocolate and Cointreau slice.

Directions: Turn off A95 onto B9102 at Craigellachie

Aberlour AB38 7QL
Map 15: NJ24
Tel: 01340 810218
Fax: 01340 810239
Chef: Judith Bulger
Owners: Judith & Michael Bulger
Cost: Alc £22.50. ☺ H/wine £12
Times: Noon-2pm/6.30-9pm.
Closed Oct-9 Feb
Additional: Bar food; Sunday L;
Children welcome
Seats: 25. Private dining room 15
Style: Bistro-style/Rustic
Smoking: No-smoking area
Accommodation: 8 rooms ★★

CRAIGELLACHIE,
Craigellachie Hotel ֍֍

AB38 9SR
Map 15: NJ24
Tel: 01340 881204
Fax: 01340 881253
E-mail: info@craigellachie.com
Chef: Anthony Allcott
Cost: Set-price L £16.95/D £28.
H/wine £12.95
Times: Noon-2pm/6-10pm
Additional: Bar food L; Sunday L;
Children welcome
Seats: 30. Private dining rooms 8-40
Style: Informal/Rustic
Smoking: No smoking in dining room
Civil licence: 40
Accommodation: 26 en suite ★★★

Situated in the heart of Speyside, this impressive Victorian hotel extends its warm welcome to a cosmopolitan clientele. The small Quaiche Bar is famed for its impressive hoard of some 300 single malt whiskies (priced from £2.50 to £100 per dram), 'with a selection like that, who needs food', quipped one inspector. The restaurant is spread across three small dining rooms, but it's the Ben Aigan Room where the main action is seen, with its tartan table covers, fishing memorabilia and traditional ambience. The daily changing fixed-price menu offers innovative, contemporary dishes based on quality ingredients from Scotland's abundant larder. This delivers on the plate as home smoked galantine of quail and pigeon with Parma ham and fresh mango, or perhaps a rich casserole of Loch Fyne langoustine and mussels with tarragon and

courgettes. Steamed tower of local seafood on a lobster and crab gratin, or roasted best end of Duffus venison on a cake of red cabbage and apple with a port and raspberry glaze could follow. Finish with warm caramel and apple crêpes and iced cinnamon parfait.

Directions: In the village centre

DRYBRIDGE,

Old Monastery Restaurant

Buckie AB56 5JB
Map 15: NJ46
Tel: 01542 832660
Fax: 01542 839437

New owners, but the chef of six-years standing remains the same at this long-established country restaurant that has been carved out of a Benedictine church and cloisters. The informal atmosphere of the Cloisters Bar remains the setting for the good-value lunch operation, with the more formal chapel restaurant coming into use for dinner. Lots of modern ideas punctuate the short *carte* with the likes of fresh crab gratinéed in a velouté sauce, and pan-fried duck breast served with lime and chilli lentils summing up the repertoire well. Our inspector thoroughly endorsed a test meal that opened with chicken boudin delicately laced with fines herbes and served with apple sauce. Grilled fillet of salmon was simply presented with a potato and parsley sauce, and therein lay its success – flavours were natural and honest. Finally, a contrasting dark and white chocolate parfait served with prunes and Armagnac was pronounced 'quite delicious'.

E-mail: buchanan@oldmonasteryrestaurant.freeserve.co.uk
Chefs: Keith Mitchell, Calum Buchanan, Susan Innes
Owners: Calum & Valerie Buchanan
Cost: Alc £29.50, set-price L £12.95. H/wine £10.75
Times: Noon-2pm/6.45-9pm. Closed Sun D, all Mon, 3 wks Jan
Additional: Sunday L; Children 8+ at D
Seats: 42
Style: Chic/idiosyncratic
Smoking: No smoking in dining room

Directions: Leave A98 at Buckie junction onto Drybridge Road, continue for 2.5m (don't turn into Drybridge village). Restaurant on L at top of hill

ELGIN,

Mansion House Hotel

The Haugh IV30 1AW
Map 15: NJ26
Tel: 01343 548811
Fax: 01343 547916
E-mail: reception@mhelgin.co.uk
Cost: Alc £27, set-price L £15.50/D
£27. ☺ H/wine £11
Times: Noon-2pm/7- 9pm

An elegant, formal setting for enjoyable dishes such as chicken liver parfait with home-made chutney and oatcakes, and roast rack of lamb with black pudding and red wine sauce.

Additional: Bar food; Sunday L; Children welcome
Style: Country-house
Smoking: No smoking in dining room
Civil licence: 180
Accommodation: 23 en suite ★ ★ ★

Directions: In Elgin turn off A96 into Haugh Road; hotel at end of road by river

FORRES, Knockomie Hotel ❀

Grantown Road IV36 2SG
Map 14: NJ05
Tel: 01309 673146
Fax: 01309 673290
E-mail: stay@knockomie.co.uk
Cost: *Alc* £28, set-price D £28.50.
H/wine £11.95
Times: D only 7-10pm
Additional: Bar food; Sunday L;
Children welcome
Style: Modern/Country-house
Smoking: No smoking in dining room
Accommodation: 15 en suite ★ ★ ★

*Charming country house hotel restaurant where an elegant and
formal dining environment is well matched by grand and lavish
cuisine. Adventurous approach to flavour evident in seared scallops
on sesame flavoured pak choy leaves with basil couscous.*

Directions: On A940 1 mile S of Forres

ORKNEY

ST MARGARET'S HOPE,
Creel Restaurant ❀❀

The Creel, on the seafront of a village on South Ronaldsay, the
most southerly of the Orkney Islands, might not seem the most
accessible destination in the realm, but 'full tonight with an
appreciative clientele' noted an inspector on a June visit.
'Wonderfully fresh seafood, lamb and beef' from the islands
are the magnet, together with locally grown vegetables and
herbs, and a kitchen that knows what to do without
unnecessarily messing about with flavours. Bresaola
(marinated in Orkney beer, smoked over oak chips and served
with rhubarb chutney) is a house speciality, and a rebellion is
likely to ensue if Orcadian fish stew – the fish cooked
separately before being added to a 'beautifully perfumed'
tomato and basil sauce – were removed from main courses.
Otherwise expect parton bree (crab soup), or brandade of salt
cod with lemon mayonnaise, followed by grilled fillet steak
with a marmalade of onions, ginger and chillies, or spankingly
fresh halibut with savoury brown lentils. Finish perhaps with
home-baked butter shortbread filled with local strawberries
and fresh cream with vanilla sauce. The wine list, short as it is,
gives no cause for complaint.

Front Road KW17 2SL
Map 16: ND49
Tel: 01856 831311
E-mail: alan@thecreel.freeserve.co.uk
Chef: Alan Craigie
Owners: Alan and Joyce Craigie
Cost: *Alc* £27.50. ☺ H/wine £9.60
Times: D only, 7-9pm.
Closed Jan, Feb
Additional: Children welcome
Seats: 34
Style: Informal/Traditional
Smoking: No smoking in dining room

Directions: 13 miles S of Kirkwall on A961, on seafront in
village

PERTH & KINROSS

ABERFELDY,
Guinach House Hotel ⚜⚜

'By the Birks' Urlar Road PH15 2ET
Map 14: NN84
Tel: 01887 820251
Fax: 01887 829607
Chef: Albert Mackay
Owners: Mr & Mrs A Mackay
Cost: Set-price D £25. ☺
H/wine £9.95
Times: D only, 7-9.30pm.
Closed 4 days Xmas
Additional: Children welcome;
Vegetarian menu by arrangement
Seats: 22
Style: Country-house
Smoking: No smoking in dining room
Accommodation: 7 en suite ★★

The small restaurant is the focal point of this family-run hotel on the southern edge of town (and non-residents are strongly advised to book). Dinner is of four courses from a well-balanced menu with reasonable choice, and the kitchen makes the most of good-quality, fresh ingredients, from ceps (with herbs and cream for a sauce for spaghetti), through locally cured ham (with sun-dried tomatoes in a brandy-based sauce for veal), to humble brambles (in a liqueur cream with florentines). Starters might run from chopped pheasant salad with apples and celery, to perfectly cooked medallions of monkfish fried in a 'delicious' light batter served with sweet-and-sour sauce. Soup comes next – kidney hinting of port, or cream of vegetable – before the main business: roast saddle of local lamb stuffed with apricots and thyme accompanied by a potato galette sandwiched between two pieces of black pudding with a stock-based jus, or poached fillet of haddock with tomato, chives and prawns topped with a hard-boiled egg. Game appears in season – Glen Lyon venison on a juniper and wine sauce, for instance – and puddings are a strong point, from poached pear fanned on a brandy and ginger syrup, to white chocolate and Amaretto mousse.

Directions: From Aberfeldy: A826 (Crieff) hotel is on R

AUCHTERARDER,
Auchterarder House ⚜⚜

An imposing manor house standing in 17 acres of wooded grounds and landscaped gardens. Silk-lined walls and oak panelling set the tone in the ornate restaurant, with its formal, spacious settings and softly-lit candles in the evening. The small menu oozes quality and luxury, and in the words of a smitten inspector, 'the palate should be prepared for a powerful symphony rather than a delicate string quartet'. A recent meal began with superb nibbles, breads and *amuse-bouches*, before moving on to an exquisite ballotine of foie gras on candied apple with port anise and potato vermicelli.

PH3 1DZ
Map 11: NN91
Tel: 01764 663646
Fax: 01764 662939
E-mail:
auchterarder@wrensgroup.com
Chef: William Deans
Owner: Rebecca Fraser
Cost: Set-price L £14.50 & £16.50/
D £39.50. H/wine £15
Times: Noon-2pm/7-9.30pm
Additional: Sunday L; Children 12+

When cut into, the soft liver flowed over the apple in fondant style, demonstrating expert poise and bold flavours. Breast of Gressingham duck on a rhubarb and vanilla compote was powerful in texture and flavour, and truffle and vanilla chocolate chip pudding with preserved fruits and a spicy red wine sauce was a triumph. Service is slick, attentive and professional, but beware of the persuasive charms of the sommelier who may coax a more costly choice than anticipated.

Seats: 36. Private dining rooms 16 & 30. Jacket & tie preferred
Style: Classic/Country-house
Smoking: No smoking in dining room
Civil licence: 65
Accommodation: 15 en suite ★★★

Directions: 1.5 miles N of Auchterarder on B8062

AUCHTERARDER, Cairn Lodge

With Gleneagles on the doorstep and Carnoustie and St Andrews within easy reach, this welcoming small hotel in landscaped grounds is something of a golfer's paradise. Recently extended, its public areas include a comfortable sitting room, a large bar with an impressive range of malts, and the elegant Capercaillie restaurant. The sensibly-short, monthly-changing menu shows what a kitchen can do with the best of Scottish produce. Game crops up in season, perhaps as a broth with beetroot chips, or as a terrine of pheasant, venison and chicken, with red onion marmalade, and in main-course roast pheasant carved on to boulangère potatoes accompanied by wild mushrooms. Otherwise, there might be chargrilled medallions of beef on a bed of pesto mash surrounded by pink peppercorn sauce, while fish might be given a classical treatment: mussels grilled in garlic butter, followed by West Coast prawns in Thermidor sauce. Puddings are of the pecan pie and chocolate cheesecake variety, with a selection of ripe cheeses and home-made walnut bread as an alternative.

Orchil Road PH3 1LX
Map 11: NN91
Tel: 01764 662634
Fax: 01764 664866
E-mail: email@cairnlodge.co.uk
Chef: M. Riva
Owners: Mr & Mrs Donald
Cost: Set-price D £29.50.
H/wine £13.50
Times: Noon-2.30pm/6-9.30pm
Additional: Bar food; Sunday L; Children welcome
Seats: 50. Private dining room 35
Style: Country-house
Smoking: No smoking in dining room
Accommodation: 11 en suite ★★

Directions: From A9 take A824 (Auchterader). Hotel at S end of town, on road to Gleneagles

AUCHTERARDER, Duchally Country Estate   NEW

PH3 1PN
Map 11: NN91
Tel: 01764 663071
Fax: 01764 662464
Chef: Stephen McGuire
Owner: Mike Barker
Cost: Set-price D £28.50.
H/wine £11.90
Times: Noon-2.30pm/7-9.30pm
Additional: Bar food; Sunday L; Children welcome

Under enthusiastic new ownership, a major refurbishment programme has recently been completed at this welcoming Victorian mansion house. Standing in extensive natural wooded grounds the hotel restaurant is a stylish and welcoming venue to sample dishes from a daily changing menu. Dishes are based on quality ingredients and the modern style of cooking allows natural flavours to shine through. Amongst the starters you may find terrine of confit duck leg and foie gras presented on a honey and sultana brioche – a well composed dish with the duck contrasting nicely with the fois gras. On a recent visit this starter was followed by a lightly pan-fried saddle of lamb topped with a basil mousse, and by a dessert of mousse of crème fraîche with a hint of vanilla served with a syrup of summer fruits. All in all a very civilised fine dining experience

Directions: S from Auchterarder onto A9 towards Glasgow for 0.5m. Turn onto A823, bearing L towards Dunfermline. 0.5m turn L at Duchally sign

Seats: 36
Style: Country-house
Smoking: No smoking in dining room
Accommodation: 13 rooms ★★★

AUCHTERARDER,
Gleneagles Hotel ❀❀

Surrounded by its legendary golf course, Gleneagles is renowned world-wide as a top international resort hotel. Set in beautiful grounds it offers a wealth of recreational pursuits, including an equestrian centre, shooting school, leisure club and health spa. While the bar captures the atmosphere of an ocean liner and the drawing room serves its famous afternoon teas, the elegant fine dining Strathearn Restaurant is the place for dinner. Here tailed and dinner-suited waiting staff deliver professional service to the accompaniment of a pianist. Smoked Scottish salmon with lemon, carved at the table, or fillet of Angus beef flambé, carved from the trolley, are popular, time-honoured choices from a traditional menu with a few modern influences. Less conventional diners might choose lemon-crusted sea trout on a celeriac remoulade with shredded crisp sugar snaps, follow with roasted saddle of rabbit, savoy cabbage, spring chanterelle and truffle oil, and perhaps finish with a milk chocolate and raspberry tart, hazelnut praline and orange ice cream. Wide choice of petits fours and agreeable coffee to close.

Directions: Just off A9, well signposted

PH3 1NF
Map 11: NN91
Tel: 01764 662231
Fax: 01764 662134
E-mail: resort.sales@gleneagles.com
Chef: Andy Hamer
Cost: *Alc* £55, set-price L £27/ D £42.50. H/wine £18.50
Times: D only, 7-10.30pm
Additional: Sunday L (12.30-2.30pm); Children welcome
Seats: 240. Private dining rooms
Style: Classic/Formal
Smoking: No-smoking area
Accommodation: 222 en suite
★★★★★

BLAIR ATHOLL, The Loft ❀❀

The Loft was exactly that – a hayloft, to be precise. Now it's a warmly decorated space with stone walls and wooden floors. The menu – a sensibly short compilation of a handful of choices at each course – shows a kitchen picking the best of Scotland's larder and working around some modern ideas.

River Tilt Park
PH18 5TE
Map 14: NN86
Tel: 01796 481377
Fax: 01796 481511
Chef: Paul Higgins
Owner: Mrs P M Richardson
Cost: *Alc* £22.50. ☺ H/wine £9.50
Times: Noon-2.30pm/6-9pm. Closed Mon & Tue fr Jan-Mar
Additional: Bar food; Sunday L; Children welcome (in the conservatory)
Style: Rustic/French
Smoking: No smoking in dining room; Air conditioning

Shetland and smoked salmon are made into a fishcake and served with chilli jam, and breast of wood pigeon goes into a salad with oyster mushrooms and pine nuts. Among main courses, seared medallions of Aberdeen Angus are set on a white pudding croûton, partnered with a spinach and potato cake and sauced with red wine jus, and fillet of cod is simply seared and accompanied by a citrus and herb butter sauce and mustard mash. Vegetarian dishes are well thought out, from a salad of goats' cheese, plum tomatoes and basil with a hazelnut and pepper dressing, to a main course of leek and Puy lentil lasagne with rosemary and pesto and a sharp red pepper coulis. Banana and toffee cheesecake may round things off nicely, and the wine list is a mixed bag of fairly priced bottles with a page of fine wine – at a price.

Directions: Off A9, 6 miles north of Pitlochry. In the village turn sharp L at Tilt Hotel.

The Loft

BLAIRGOWRIE,
Altamount House Hotel ❀❀

A small but elegant hotel restaurant with views over attractive gardens. White walls with an ornate plastered ceiling, a marble fireplace and a varnished wooden floor with large red rug all contribute to a civilised but unstuffy atmosphere. Chef Robert Ramsay is now well established and is approaching modern Scottish cuisine with increasing confidence and flair. A sign of this is the introduction of the chef's recommended set menu – three courses with no choice at any stage, though those of a less trusting nature can make their own selection from a short but innovative *carte*. A recent meal opened with an excellent dish of lightly seared Shetland scallops presented on a bed of lightly creamed leeks and diced bacon with a light chilli cream. High standards were maintained with a main of chargrilled prime Scottish fillet of beef which proved moist and tender with a lovely honest flavour.

Directions: On entering town from A93 take 1st R into Golf Course Rd. Continue for 1.5 miles then L at T junction. Hotel 1 mile on L

Coupar Angus Road PH10 6JN
Map 15: NO14
Tel: 01250 873512
Fax: 01250 876200
E-mail: althotel@netcomuk.co.uk
Chef: Robert Ramsay
Owners: Robert & Sally Glashan
Cost: *Alc* £31, set-price D £22.50. ☺
H/wine £10.50
Times: Noon-2pm/6.30-9pm.
Closed 1st 2 wks Jan
Additional: Bar food; Sunday L;
Children 7+
Seats: 22. Private dining room 20 &
130
Style: Informal/Country-house
Smoking: No smoking in dining room
Civil licence: 100
Accommodation: 7 en suite ★★

BLAIRGOWRIE,
Kinloch House Hotel ❀❀❀

An ivy-hung early-Victorian mansion, Kinloch House is set amid its own grounds and has views to Loch Maree and the Sidlaw Hills. Oak panelling, antiques and open fires set the scene inside, the richly wallpapered dining room hung with oil paintings. The Scottish menu takes in such items as Highland salmon marinated in whisky and herbs with poached prawns, and roast loin of roe-deer with rosemary, port and redcurrant sauce, but the materials for the main menu are equally impressively sourced: meats are supplied locally and hung in-house, fish and game are all wild, vegetables are organically grown, and even pasta and sausages are made on the premises. All this translates into a memorable dining experience from the four-course menu, supplemented by a page of alternatives. Lightly seared scallops on a risotto of bacon, mushrooms and herbs in a light butter sauce made a 'delicious', distinctly

PH10 6SG
Map 15: NO14
Tel: 01250 884237
Fax: 01250 884333
E-mail: info@kinlochhouse.com
Chef: Bill McNicoll
Owners: The Shentall Family
Cost: Set-price D £33.50.
H/wine £14.95
Times: 12.30-2pm/7-9.15pm.
Closed 18-29 Dec
Additional: Bar food L; Sunday L;
Children 7+
Seats: 55. Private dining room 16-20.
Jacket & tie preferred
Style: Classic/Country-house
Smoking: No smoking in dining room

Kinloch House Hotel

Accommodation: 20 en suite ★ ★ ★

Directions: Three miles W of
Blairgowrie on A923

flavoured starter at inspection, and the same adjective was
applied to an intermediate course of sole fillet stuffed with
mildly spiced crab topped with cheese soufflé drizzled with
chive sauce. Equally, a terrine of sweetbreads and chicken
might be followed by avocado mousse spiked with spicy tomato
sauce. Loin of Perthshire lamb in a rosemary-flavoured
reduction of the cooking juices makes a main course of
'wonderfully honest flavour', the meat rolled in rosemary, garlic
and thyme and presented on mashed potato with a mould of
courgette purée, with perhaps fillet of sea bass stuffed with its
own mousse in a light tarragon sauce also appearing. Aberdeen
Angus steaks and Scottish prawns are specialities, and puddings
could extend to a scooped-out blood orange filled with soufflé
with Grand Marnier sorbet; a savoury like devilled kidneys
might be an alternative. Dinner here has a sense of occasion
without being stuffy, thanks to the service, and the wine list is
noteworthy both in terms of quality and extent.

COUPAR ANGUS,
Moorfield House Hotel

Peacefully tucked away in its own grounds, Moorfield House is
a welcoming and relaxing sort of a place. Eating in the roomy
bar is a possibility, but the smartly decorated restaurant,
actually a pair of adjoining rooms linked by an arch, is the
place to head for. Dinner runs to four courses, with around
three choices at each course except the second, which is either
soup – strongly flavoured tomato with pesto, perhaps – or a
sorbet, sometimes something unusual like carrot and ginger.
Starters range from classic lobster bisque to a rustic terrine of
pork, veal and mushrooms with apple chutney, with
somewhere between them perhaps tender pan-fried scallops on
a herb pancake with coral sauce. Main-course components are
brought together to make some successful dishes too: seared
salmon and monkfish on horseradish mash with a stew of
fennel and leeks, say, or chicken and asparagus roulade on a
ragout of new potatoes, baby onions and beans. Puddings get
the thumbs up in the form of rich dark chocolate tart, with
good light pastry, served with mango sauce and cardamom ice
cream, or vanilla pannacotta with peppered strawberries.
Europe has the edge on the New World on the short wine list,
with France dominating.

Directions: On A923 halfway between Coupar Angus and
Blairgowrie

Myreriggs Road By Blairgowrie
PH13 9HS
Map 11: NO23
Tel: 01828 627303
Fax: 01828 627339
Chefs: Angela Tannahill,
Paul Bjormark
Owners: Jayne & Paul Bjormark
Cost: Set-price L £14.50/D £27.50.
H/wine £9.95
Times: Noon-2pm (booking
essential)/7-9.30pm.
Closed last wk Dec
Additional: Bar food; Sunday L;
Children welcome
Seats: 34
Style: French/Traditional
Smoking: No-smoking area;
No pipes & cigars
Accommodation: 12 en suite ★ ★ ★

CRIEFF, Crieff Hydro

Lively informal brasserie in a popular hotel. Extensive wine list goes hand in hand with high quality cuisine such as marinated wild salmon poached in white wine with a green lip mussel. Gluten-free menu also available.

Additional: Bar food L; Sunday L; Children welcome
Style: Modern/Formal
Smoking: No smoking in dining room; Air conditioning; Jacket & tie preferred
Accommodation: 200 en suite ★ ★ ★

Directions:

Ferntower Road PH7 3LQ
Map 11: NN82
Tel: 01764 655555
Fax: 01764 653087
Cost: *Alc* £19, set-price L £12.50/ D £19. ☺ H/wine £12
Times: 10.30am-10pm

DUNKELD, Atholl Arms Hotel

Listed building, c1790, with a traditionally styled dining room overlooking the River Tay. Options include steaks, crispy duck confit, and seared fresh fillet of salmon with creamy citrus sauce.

Additional: Bar Food; Sunday L; Children 8+
Style: Country-house
Smoking: No smoking in dining room
Accommodation: 12 en suite ★ ★

Directions: A9 & A923 (Blairgowrie) to Dunkeld, 1st building on R

Bridgehead PH8 0AQ
Map 11: NO04
Tel/Fax: 01350 727219
E-mail: cdarbishire@aol.com
Cost: *Alc* £15. ☺ H/wine £8.95
Times: Noon-2.30pm/6-9.30pm.
Closed Jan-20 Mar

DUNKELD, Kinnaird ❀❀❀

Kinnaird, simply Kinnaird. That's a measure of the grandeur of this splendid 9000 acre estate and fine Edwardian mansion. It may be grand, but the welcome is a warm one and the house has several inviting sitting rooms and a snooker room warmed by open fires. The restaurant is decorated with exquisite hand-painted Italian frescos and has magnificent views over the Tay Valley. The cooking is as smart as the setting. A black truffle risotto made a memorable first course, full of flavour and aroma from the real thing, not faked from oils. The freshness of a really fine piece of turbot was brought out by steaming, an under-used technique; when served with amazingly full-flavoured, plump little cockles and tagliatelle with locally-smoked butter it becomes a dish of considerable distinction. The style of cooking is rooted in the French classical tradition; other main courses might include roast milk-fed squab pigeon on celeriac purée with small cabbage parcels and truffle bouillon, and breast of duck with choucroute, caramelised apple, fondant poatoes and spiced duck jus. Desserts include hot date soufflé with chocolate sorbet, and nougat glace with poached pears and caramel sauce. A big (in both length and importance) wine list has big prices to match.

Seats: 35. Private dining room 15. Jacket & tie preferred
Style: Country-house
Smoking: No smoking in dining room
Accommodation: 9 en suite ★ ★ ★

Directions: From A9 north take B898 Dalguise/Kinnaird/Balnaguard road for approx 4.5 miles. Hotel main gates on R

Kinnaird Estate PH8 0LB
Map 11: NO04
Tel: 01796 482440
Fax: 01796 482289
E-mail:
enquiry@kinnairdestate.demon.co.uk
Chef: Trevor Brooks
Owner: Mrs Constance Ward
Cost: Set-price L £30/D £45. H/wine £18
Times: Noon-1.30pm/7-9.30pm.
Closed Mon-Wed in Jan & Feb
Additional: Sunday L

AA Wine Award-see page 18
Shortlisted for

KILLIECRANKIE,
Killiecrankie Hotel ❀❀

The restaurant at this small, welcoming hotel, set in its own grounds near the Pass of Killiecrankie, has a decor of warm peach offset by soft turquoise, its dining chairs covered in a tartan fabric of rust and turquoise. Dinner, from a set-price four-course menu of sensibly restricted choice, shows a kitchen working in the modern Scottish style, which translates into such dishes as a smoked salmon parcel of marinated Shetland mussels, prawns and anchovies with chive vinaigrette, and pan-fried fillet of venison with pistachio and ginger compote, garlic mash and a rich port jus. Simple treatments let flavours speak for themselves: fillet of halibut is lightly grilled and served on well-timed spinach risotto (described as 'delicious') alongside gently-seared Shetland scallops dressed with pesto, and breast of Gressingham duck is roasted with pickled cherries and served with a piquant sauce. Puddings along the lines of orange crème brûlée, or dark chocolate mousse drizzled with red fruit coulis on a light chocolate sponge base precede a plate of Scottish and Irish cheeses. Service is smart and hospitable, and the wine list runs to around fifty bins, plus a page of halves, with a house selection of eight bottles.

Directions: From A9 take B8079 for Killiecrankie, hotel on R just past village signpost

Pitlochry PH16 5LG
Map 14: NN96
Tel: 01796 473220
Fax: 01796 472451
E-mail: enquiries@killiecrankiehotel.co.uk
Chef: Mark Easton
Owners: Colin & Carole Anderson
Cost: Set-price D £32.50. H/wine £13
Times: D only, 7-8.30pm. Closed Jan, Mon & Tue in Dec, Feb & Mar
Additional: Children 5+
Seats: 34
Style: Classic/Informal
Smoking: No smoking in dining room
Accommodation: 10 en suite ★★

KINCLAVEN,
Ballathie House Hotel ❀❀

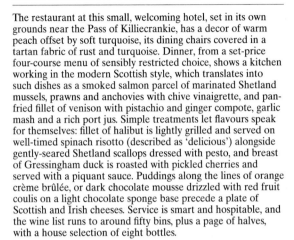

Stanley PH1 4QN
Map 11: NO13
Tel: 01250 883268
Fax: 01250 883396
E-mail: email@ballathiehousehotel.com
Chef: Kevin MacGillivray
Cost: Set-price L £18.50/D £35. H/wine £11.75
Times: 12.30-2pm/7-9pm
Additional: Bar food L; Sunday L; Children welcome
Seats: 70. Private dining room 32. Jacket and tie preferred
Style: Country-house
Smoking: No smoking in dining room
Civil licence: 60
Accommodation: 43 en suite ★★★

In the heart of the countryside overlooking the Tay, this splendid mansion combines the grandeur of a former age with modern comforts. The restaurant, with its ornate ceiling, marble fireplace, fresh flowers and candles on white-clothed tables, has a view over the gardens to the river. Canapés, perhaps a tartlet of home-smoked salmon, are served in the bar before dinner. Quality Scottish materials and prime cuts – from fillet of Aberdeen Angus (with brandy and pepper sauce) to Isle of Skye langoustines (as a main course with creamy tomato and coriander risotto) – form the basis of the menus. Flourishes like quails' eggs turn up here and there: hard-boiled with light, smooth, rich chicken and goose liver pâté on a salad of chicory and orange segments, soft-boiled in game consommé. The list of main courses might kick off with loin of

venison roasted with rosemary and juniper, served on creamed Savoy cabbage, smoked bacon and pine nuts, with the range extended by something like grilled scallops on a cake of polenta, chilli and Parmesan with aubergine purée.
Attractively presented crème brûlée makes a good end to a meal. The extensive wine list has a decent selection of house wines and half- bottles.

Directions: Off A93 at Beech Hedges, follow signs for Kinclaven, approx 2 miles

KINNESSWOOD,

Lomond Country Inn ⚜

Refreshingly unpretentious, small country hotel overlooking Loch Leven, offering honest Scottish fare based on fresh ingredients. Enjoy Cullen skink, west coast mussels, baked chicken breast stuffed with haggis, and Scottish cheeses.

Additional: Bar food; Sunday L; Children welcome
Style: informal/traditional **Smoking:** No smoking in dining room
Accommodation: 12 en suite ★ ★

Directions: On A911, 10 mins from M90/J5 (Glenrothes) or J7 (Milnathort)

KY13 9HN
Map 11: NO10
Tel: 01592 840253
Fax: 01592 840693
E-mail: the.lomond@dial.pipex.com
Cost: *Alc* £18.50, set-price L £10/ D £12.50. ☺ H/wine £8.50
Times: Noon-2.30pm /6-10pm

KINROSS,

Croft Bank House ⚜⚜

Two menus run side by side at this Victorian restaurant-with-rooms. The one in the Backroom Brasserie, supplemented by blackboard specials, runs to a warm salad of pigeon breast with a bramble and port dressing, or smoked salmon and prawns in a parcel with dill mayonnaise, followed by beef and mushroom pie, or venison sausages with mash. A more complicated approach is taken in the more formal dining room: a terrine of salmon, sole and monkfish with a citrus dressing and crème fraîche, say, then breast of local pheasant stuffed with apricots and sage in a gamey red wine sauce. An inspector started with smooth chicken liver parfait garnished with quails' eggs and cherry tomatoes dressed with a 'delicious' sauce of port, orange and redcurrants, then had thinly cut slices of breast of woodland pigeon, cooked pink, on mash with a richly flavoured game jus. Ingredients are well-sourced – wild salmon from Shetland, for instance – prime cuts of meat are used, vegetables are seasonal, and dinner could close with a classic raspberry crème brûlée.

Directions: Just off M90 J6 towards Kinross

KY13 8TG
Map 11: NO10
Tel/Fax: 01577 863819
Chef: Bill Kerr
Owners: Bill & Diane Kerr
Cost: *Alc* £24. ☺ H/wine £10.95
Times: Noon-2pm/6.30-9pm. Closed D Sun, all Mon, 1st 2 wks Sep
Additional: Sunday L; Children 3+
Seats: 24. Private dining room 24
Style: Bistro-style
Smoking: No smoking in dining room
Accommodation: 3 en suite

PERTH,

Huntingtower Hotel ⚜

Two stylish dining options available but it's the formal Oak Room that gets our vote. The wide ranging menu successfully blends the modern with the classical. Desserts a particular strong point, tarte Tatin for example.

Crieff Road Almondbank PH1 3JT
Map 11: NO12
Tel: 01738 583771
Fax: 01738 583777
E-mail:
reception.huntingtower@talk21.com

Huntingtower Hotel

Cost: *Alc* £20, set-price L £9.95. ☺
H/wine £10.50
Times: Noon-2.30pm/6.30-9.30pm
Additional: Bar food L; Sunday L;
Children welcome
Style: Modern/Country-house
Smoking: No smoking in dining room
Civil licence: 100
Accommodation: 34 en suite ★ ★ ★

Directions: 5 mins from Perth, on A85 Crieff/Crianlarich Road.
Just off A9

PERTH, Kinfauns Castle 🥕🥕

Grand and distinctive, Kinfauns Castle dates back to 1822 and
is set in grounds overlooking the Tay. Sweeping staircases,
stately gallery, ornate ceilings, marble fireplaces and Far
Eastern artefacts set the scene. The oak-panelled dining room
is housed in the castle's old library, with its immense windows
and ceiling displaying the coat of arms of the original owners.
The menu is short but balanced and appealing, while the
lengthy wine list includes some fine vintages with prices to
match, and a notable selection of Pétrus. After canapés, a
spring menu started with a filo flan of courgettes, tomato and
warm feta cheese with pine nuts and a tangy pesto. A panaché
of fish – sea bass, monkfish, salmon and turbot – on a saffron
risotto with baby vegetables and a crayfish and chive beurre
fondue provided the main course, while a chocolate fondant
with teardrops of white and dark chocolate sauce proved a
highlight. Good flavoured soup, perhaps cream of celery and
stilton or cream of asparagus, follows starters, while filter
coffee and petits fours round things off.

Kinfauns PH2 7JZ
Map 11: NO12
Tel: 01738 620777
Fax: 01738 620778
E-mail: email@kinfaunscastle.co.uk
Chef: Jeremy Brazelle
Owner: James A Smith
Cost: Set price L £18.50/D £32. ☺
H/wine £14
Times: Noon-1.30pm/7-8.30pm.
Closed 4-26 Jan
Additional: Bar food L; Sunday L;
Children 12+
Seats: 48. Private dining room 12;
Jacket & tie preferred
Style: Classic/Country-house
Smoking: No smoking in dining room
Civil licence: 50
Accommodation: 16 en suite ★ ★ ★

Directions: Two miles beyond Perth on A90 Dundee road; turn
L at sign for Kinfauns Castle

PERTH, Let's Eat 🥕🥕

Based on the sure-fire formula of serving quality ingredients,
carefully prepared and simply presented, this restaurant
provides a level of consistency few can beat. Drinks are served
in the small lounge area, and the interior decoration is
refreshingly traditional – no ostentatious swags, no pared to
the bone minimalism – just almost neutral comfort suitable for
all occasions. Seasonal produce works well with fresh seafood
and other local fare: West Coast mussels, Dunkeld smoked
salmon, and prime Scotch fillet steak all feature. Dishes
sampled were a wild mushroom risotto with truffle oil cream
and Parmesan shavings; pan-roasted fillet of cod with home-
made chips, pea purée and aïoli; and a very enjoyable soft
chocolate brownie with vanilla ice cream.

Let's Eat Again is little sister to Let's Eat, closer to the city
centre and convenient for business people and shoppers. (33
George Street PH1 5LA, tel: 01738 633771.) The informal
menu features quality ingredients from Scotland's larder.

77-79 Kinnoull Street PH1 5EZ
Map 11: NO12
Tel: 01738 643377
Fax: 01738 621464
Chef: Tony Heath
Owners: Tony Heath, Shona Drysdale
Times: Noon-2pm/6.30-9.45pm.
Closed Sun & Mon, 2 wks Jan,
2 wks Jul
Additional: Children welcome
Seats: 65
Style: Bistro-style/Informal
Smoking: No smoking in dining room

Directions: On corner of Kinnoull
Street and Atholl Street, close to
North Inch

PERTH,
Murrayshall Hotel ❀❀

New Scone PH2 7PH
Map 11: NO12
Tel: 01738 551171
Fax: 01738 552595
Chef: Clive Lamb
Owner: Old Scone Ltd
Cost: Alc £23.95, set-price D £23.95.
☺ H/wine £12.50
Times: D only, 7-9.45pm
Additional: Sunday L (noon-2.30pm);
Children welcome
Seats: 55. Private dining room 40.
Jacket & tie preferred
Style: Traditional/Country-house
Smoking: No smoking in dining room;
Air conditioning
Accommodation: 41 en suite ★★★

Golf may be big at Murrayshall, with its two courses, but it has
plenty of other things going for it: acres of parkland, lovely
views, a welcoming log fire in the bar on cooler evenings, and a
comfortably kitted-out restaurant. Pan-fried Oban scallops
encased by fillets of Dover sole with endive meunière, and
collops of Highland venison encrusted in caraway seeds show
what the kitchen can do with top-quality indigenous produce,
while its framework of ideas encompasses chilli jam, enhancing
a terrine of Gressingham duck layered with spinach and lentils,
and lime butter sauce with seared fillet of red mullet on oven-
dried tomatoes with a polenta scone. Meat is cooked pink and
vegetables are crisp, warns the menu, and indeed medallions of
pan-fried beef in balsamic jus arrive rare and succulent
alongside a crescent-shaped plate of crunchy vegetables.
Puddings maintain the equilibrium, from strawberry soufflé
with its own sorbet to light, smooth, subtly-flavoured coffee
charlotte. France and the New World are the focal points of
the wine list, where there are over a dozen half-bottles.

Directions: From Perth A94 (Coupar Angus) turn R signed
Murrayshall before New Scone

PERTH,
The Seafood Restaurant ❀❀

168 South Street PH2 8NY
Map 11: NO12
Tel: 01738 449777
Fax: 01738 629893
E-mail: fish@kerachers.co.uk
Chef: Kevin McElhinney
Owner: Peter Keracher
Cost: Alc £14, set-price L £6.90/
D £10.90. ☺ H/wine £10.90
Times: Noon-2pm/6-10pm.
Closed Sun, Mon
Additional: Bar food;
Children welcome
Seats: 40
Style: Classic/modern
Smoking: No-smoking area

There have been changes since last year: the façade has gone
from green to blue; the former retail fish counter has vanished;
the ground floor area is now the wine bar/bistro; and a new
chef has arrived. The menu format in the contemporary-styled
upstairs restaurant is, however, as before – a good-value set-
price menu plus a small *carte* and blackboard specials. Fresh
seafood remains the house speciality – hand-dived scallops
with crispy leeks and tomato and basil sauce, marinated
Orkney herring in dill and shallot sauce, and fresh haddock
stuffed with smoked and peppered mackerel served with roast
pepper sauce. For non-fish lovers there's always fillet of
Scottish beef with a rich port and shallot jus, on the menu 'By
Popular Demand!'

Directions: Town centre, at corner of Scott Street and South
Street

PITLOCHRY, Green Park Hotel

Attractive dining room overlooking gardens to Loch Faskally. A daily-changing menu of traditional dishes such as pan-fried chicken with black pudding or roast lamb with rosemary mousse and roast garlic jus, and poached pear with mustard cream.

Directions: Off A9 at Pitlochry, follow signs

Clunie Bridge Road PH16 5JY
Map 14: NN95
Tel: 01796 473248
Fax: 01796 473520
E-mail: bookings@thegreenpark.co.uk

Telephone for further details

PITLOCHRY,
Knockendarroch House Hotel

Comfortable tourist hotel. Roast breast of guinea fowl is offered, filled with a lemon-scented mousseline, wrapped in bacon and finished with sherry sauce. Almond crème caramel and orange salad might be offered for dessert.

Directions: On entering town from perth, 1st R (East Moulin Road) after railway bridge, then 2nd L, last Hotel on L

Higher Oakfield PH16 5HT
Map 14: NN95
Tel: 01796 473473
Fax: 01796 474068
E-mail: info@knockendarroch.co.uk

Telephone for further details.

PITLOCHRY, Pine Trees Hotel

Converted Victorian mansion house set peacefully in 14 acres of mature gardens. The hotel has recently undergone a dramatic refurbishment and the upgrade extends in full measure to the restaurant. The decor is elegant and the setting tranquil with views over the lawn and borders. A new chef has introduced an innovative *carte* and a daily changing set-price menu that is stuffed with interesting, quality dishes. A starter of terrine of duck leg confit and foie gras offered an excellent combination of flavours which was given further depth by an interesting plum chutney stuffed into shallots. To follow, roasted rack of Perthshire lamb comes highly recommended – cooked to perfection with a tarragon jus and excellent vegetable accompaniments. To finish perhaps try an interesting and unusual dessert in the form of a warm Bramley apple soup laced with brambles and accompanied with home made vanilla ice cream.

Strathview Terrace PH16 5QR
Map 14: NN95
Tel: 01796 472121
Fax: 01796 472460

Telephone for further details.

Directions: Signed at N end of town

ST FILLANS, Four Seasons Hotel

A fine lochside setting with glorious views over Loch Earn to the snow-capped mountains beyond awaits diners at this

Loch Earn Crieff PH6 2NF
Map 11: NN62
Tel: 01764 685333
Fax: 01764 685444
E-mail:
info@thefourseasonshotel.co.uk
Chef: Jonathan Brown
Owner: Andrew Low
Cost: Set-price D £23.95. ☺
Times: For L telephone for times;
D 7-9.30pm
Additional: Bar food; Sunday L;
Children welcome
Seats: 60. Private dining room 20
Style: Informal
Smoking: No pipes & cigars
Accommodation: 12 en suite ★ ★ ★

welcoming hotel. The Meall Reamhar restaurant affords a relaxed ambience and takes full advantage of the spectacular setting with most tables overlooking the loch, while on warm days the terrace offers an alfresco option. The kitchen serves a contemporary Scottish repertoire of imaginative dishes exploiting the best local produce. For instance, Orkney scallops with a garlic and basil dressing and braised couscous, or perhaps a nage of rope-grown Loch Fyne mussels with a saffron and tomato sauce and star anis to start. Main courses that catch the eye include grilled fillet of East Coast halibut served on a bed of asparagus and a citron dressing, or pan-fried fillet of free-range pork with a dariole of haggis, caramelised apple and a whisky cream. Desserts show their style in a Kirsch cream with compote of summer berries and pear and ginger tart with crème chantilly.

Directions: From Perth take A85 W, through Crieff & Comrie. Hotel at west end of village

SPITTAL OF GLENSHEE,
Dalmunzie House Hotel

Turreted country house where the magnificent setting within 6500 acre estate contributes to a general atmosphere of grandeur and luxury. Local meats and fresh seasonal vegetables make for a good quality, traditional menu.

Style: Traditional/Country-house
Smoking: No smoking in dining room; Jacket & tie preferred
Accommodation: 16 en suite ★ ★

Directions: Turn off A93 at Spittal of Glenshee, hotel 200yds on L

Blairgowrie PH10 7QG
Map 15: NO17
Tel/Fax: 01250 885224
E-mail: dalmunzie@aol.com
Cost: Set-price D £25. ☺
H/wine £9.50
Times: 12.30-5.30pm/7.30-8.30pm.
Closed 1-28 Dec
Additional: Bar food L;
Children welcome

RENFREWSHIRE

LANGBANK, Gleddoch House

As befits what was once the home of a shipping magnate, Gleddoch House has magnificent views over the Clyde as well as over its 360-acre estate (where there are a number of sporty things to do, from off-road adventure-driving to horse-riding). Canapés with drinks in the bar set the mouth watering before diners move on to the spacious and rather formal dining room. From the classical repertoire come halibut bonne femme, steak au poivre and lobster Thermidor, but the kitchen generally brings its own ingenuity to bear on dishes. Grape and sloe-gin syrup accompanies a terrine of chicken, duck and goose livers with pistachios and a glug of Armagnac, and main-course grilled fillet of salmon comes on a sabayon of Cullen skink. An inspector found a golden-brown filo parcel of haggis, neeps and tatties 'different and enjoyable', and was impressed by the top-quality meat and the saucing skills evident in tournedos of beef topped with wild mushrooms and spinach duxelle all glazed with correctly-made béarnaise and served with a duo of sauces: Arran mustard and Madeira. Six house wines kick off the wine list, which is strongest on France.

PA14 6YE
Map 10: NS37
Tel: 01475 540711
Fax: 01475 540201
E-mail:
gleddochhouse@ukonline.co.uk
Chef: Brian Graham
Cost: Alc £35, set-price L £20/D £35.
☺ H/wine £12.50
Times: 12.30-2pm/7.30-9.30pm
Additional: Sunday L;
Children welcome
Seats: 120. Private dining room 40
Style: Traditional/Country-house
Accommodation: 38 en suite ★ ★ ★ ★

Directions: From Glasgow take M8 (Greenock) then B789 Houston/ Langbank exit. Follow signs to hotel

SCOTTISH BORDERS

GATTONSIDE,
Hoebridge Inn Restaurant ✱

Nineteenth-century building with exposed beams and whitewashed stone walls which provide a certain Spanish flavour. Friendly and relaxed. Try crispy skinned barbary duck sliced onto a soy and ginger glaze with sweet and sour wun-tuns.

Additional: Children 6+
Style: Rustic
Smoking: No-smoking area; No pipes & cigars

Directions: Take B6360 from either A7 or A68. Restaurant in village centre

Nr Melrose TD6 9LZ
Map 12: NT53
Tel: 01896 823082
E-mail: hoebridge@easynet.co.uk
Cost: *Alc* £20. ☺ H/wine £9.25
Times: D only, 6.30-9pm. Closed Mon, Sun & from Oct-Mar, all Feb

JEDBURGH,
Jedforest Hotel ✱✱

Camptown TD8 6PJ
Map 12: NT62
Tel: 01835 840222
Fax: 01835 840226
E-mail: mail@jedforesthotel.freeserve.co.uk
Chef: John Fortune
Owners: Mr & Mrs S Ferguson
Cost: *Alc* £28. ☺ H/wine £10
Times: Noon-2pm/7-9pm
Additional: Sunday L
Seats: 40
Style: Country-house
Smoking: No smoking in dining room
Accommodation: 8 en suite ★★★

New owners have totally refurbished this charming country-house hotel. The elegant lounge has views over the landscaped gardens and the hotel's own 35 acres of river valley, and the restaurant remains an attractive and stylish room. The kitchen sticks largely to time-honoured favourites, with occasional dashes into pastures new: smoked fish roulade dressed with lime, coriander and yogurt, say, followed by apricot-glazed roast breast of guinea fowl stuffed with pine nuts. Otherwise, smoked haddock and potato soup, or distinctly-flavoured game terrine with poacher's pickle are what to expect among starters. Scotland's produce is well-sourced in main courses of Aberdeen Angus fillet with a potato pancake, wild mushrooms and port-infused gravy, loin of venison with redcurrant and game jus, and well-timed tournedos of salmon in tomato coulis with fennel, french beans and new potatoes. Finish with perhaps chocolate bread-and-butter pudding with custard, or fly the flag with Drambuie-flavoured crème brûlée and oatmeal cream. The wine list is a good balance of the Old and New Worlds, with a decent showing of half-bottles and good house wines by the glass.

Directions: Just off A68, 3 miles south of Jedburgh

KELSO,

The Roxburghe Hotel ✸✸

Heiton TD5 8JZ
Map 12: NT73
Tel: 01573 450331
Fax: 01573 450611
E-mail: hotel@roxburghe.net
Chef: Keith Short
Owners: The Duke &
Duchess of Roxburghe
Cost: *Alc* £32.50, set-price L
£14.50/D £25. ☺ H/wine £15
Times: 12.30-2pm/7.30-9.45pm.
Closed Xmas
Additional: Bar food; Sunday L;
Children welcome
Seats: 35. Private dining room 16
Style: Country house
Smoking: No smoking in dining room
Civil licence: 50
Accommodation: 22 en suite ★ ★ ★

Sporting guests predominate (those who enjoy shooting, fishing and golf) amongst the mix of business visitors and tourists. Owned by the Duke of Roxburghe, the impressive Jacobean mansion enjoys a peaceful location amidst acres of parkland close to the River Teviot. The menu features local ingredients wherever possible and herbs from their own garden; perhaps crispy chives with leek and poached egg tart with hazelnut butter sauce, or rocket and Parmesan salad and coriander vinaigrette with seared smoked salmon. Straight-to-the-point dishes might include roasted halibut with leaf spinach and creamy mash, or tournedos of Scotch beef with a mustard pepper crust. The good luncheon menu might feature traditional haggis, neeps and tatties along with braised ox tongue and gherkins and a selection of Scottish cheese.

Directions: On A698, 3 miles S of Kelso in Heiton village

MELROSE,

Burt's Hotel ✸✸

The Square
TD6 9PN
Map 12: NT53
Tel: 01896 822285
Fax: 01896 822870
E-mail: burtshotel@aol.com
Chef: Gary Moore
Owners: The Henderson Family

A smart, elegant and popular restaurant which has a long-established clientele. Located in the centre of Melrose, the restaurant has the feel of a gentleman's club to it. The room is elegant: the walls are covered with green striped paper hung with hunting and fishing prints. The menu is billed as 'A Taste of Scotland' and the kitchen does use local produce where possible and the establishment is a member of the Scotch Beef Club. Some dishes are perhaps a little overcomplicated – a layered smoked haddock, aubergine and ratatouille glazed with brie and crowned with an avocado salsa, for example, but the meats – border lamb chops, sirloin and fillet steaks – are tremendous. The desserts are ambitious – iced banana parfait with compote of fruit comes in a spun sugar basket with a mango filling. Burt's has a good wine list with comprehensive coverage of both old and new worlds with an excellent range of halves.

Directions: Centre of Melrose

Cost: Set-price L £20.75/D £27.75. ☺ H/wine £11.65
Times: Noon-2pm/7-9pm.
Additional: Bar food; Sunday L; Children 10+
Seats: 50. Private dining room 20
Style: Country-house
Smoking: No smoking in dining room
Accommodation: 20 en suite ★ ★

PEEBLES,
Castle Venlaw Hotel ❀

Edinburgh Road EH45 8QG
Map 11: NT24
Tel: 01721 720384
Fax: 01721 724066
E-mail: stay@venlaw.co.uk

A splendid turreted mansion set high above town. Choose two or three courses from the weekly-changing menu, such as pan-fried peppered pheasant with parsnip purée, or baked fillet of brill with turmeric and puy lentil sauce.

Cost: Set-price D £23. ☺ H/wine £10
Times: Noon-2.15pm/7-8.30pm
Additional: Bar Food; Sunday L; Children welcome
Style: Traditional/Country House
Smoking: No smoking in dining room
Accommodation: 13 en suite ★ ★ ★

Directions: Off A703 Peebles/Edinburgh road, 0.75 mile from Peebles

PEEBLES,
Cringletie House Hotel ❀

EH45 8PL
Map 11: NT24
Tel: 01721 730233
Fax: 01721 730244
E-mail: enquiries@cringletie.com
Cost: H/wine £14.50
Times: Noon-2pm/7-9pm
Additional: Sunday L;
Children welcome
Style: Classic/Country-house
Smoking: No smoking in dining room
Accommodation: 14 en suite ★ ★ ★

Opulent dining room of a fine baronial country house with a beautiful walled garden which supplies much of the kitchen's produce. The traditional menus make excellent use of local produce to create dishes such as smoked haddock and coriander fishcake.

Directions: 2.5 miles N of Peebles on A703

SWINTON, **Wheatsheaf Restaurant with Rooms** ❀❀

Main Street TD11 3JJ
Map 12: NT84
Tel: 01890 860257
Fax: 01890 860688
Chef: Alan Reid
Owners: Alan & Julie Reid
Cost: Alc £26. ☺ H/wine £10.45
Times: Noon-2.15pm/6-9.30pm.
Closed D Sun (in winter), all Mon,
1st 2 wks Jan
Additional: Bar food; Sunday L;
Children welcome
Seats: 26. Private dining room 18
Style: rustic
Smoking: No smoking in dining room
Accommodation: 7 en suite

Directions: B6461 – half-way
between Kelso and Berwick-upon-
Tweed; A6112 – half-way between
Duns and Coldstream.

The Wheatsheaf manages successfully to be all things to all men, a combination of country inn, restaurant and hotel. The main dining area has a pitch pine ceiling, cane chairs and tables, stone walls and intimate lighting, all giving a casual but traditional feel, and there is a cottage-style lounge with an open fire and a mixture of sofas and easy chairs. A seasonal menu is augmented by a blackboard that lists daily-changing specials, giving an extensive range of dishes. Some leave you in no doubt as to the country you are in. Clapshot and black pudding accompany pink slices of wood pigeon on a red wine and grain mustard sauce, and tender and succulent roast fillet of Highland venison comes on spicy red cabbage with an exemplary sauce of juniper berries and Cassis. Spot-on timing shows up in fish dishes too, as in a starter of rarely-encountered sturgeon fillet on spicy tomato sauce, and main-course seared fillet of wild salmon on sautéed pak choy with a lemon butter sauce. Parfaits are a favoured dessert – iced Drambuie with raspberry coulis, or a duo of orange and chocolate with warm chocolate sauce. Exemplary crème brûlée might be flavoured with lemon and nutmeg one day, chocolate and Tia Maria the next. Service is relaxed and friendly, and the global wine list has some good vintages and a decent range of half-bottles.

SHETLAND

LERWICK, **Shetland Hotel** ❀

Modern hotel opposite the main ferry terminal. The bistro is a popular choice, but the formal dining room rewards with local crab-claws sautéed in Shetland butter and a large, meaty helping of roast rack of lamb glazed with herbs.

Additional: Bar food; Sunday L; Children welcome
Style: Classic/formal **Smoking:** No smoking in dining room
Accommodation: 65 en suite ★ ★ ★

Directions: Opposite ferry terminal, on main road N from town centre

Holmsgarth Road ZE1 0PW
Map 16: HU44
Tel: 01595 695515
Fax: 01595 695828
E-mail:
reception@shetlandhotel.co.uk
Cost: Set-price D £23.50. ☺
H/wine £9.50
Times: Noon-2pm/7-9.30pm.

STIRLING

BALQUHIDDER,

Monachyle Mhor ❁❁

Lochearnhead FK19 8PQ
Map 11: NN52
Tel: 01877 384622
Fax: 01877 384305
E-mail:
monachylemhorhotel@balquhidder.
freeserve.co.uk
Chef: Tom Lewis
Owners: Jean, Rob & Tom Lewis
Cost: L only Alc £20, set-price L
£17.50/D £29 & £31. H/wine £10
Times: Noon-2pm/7-8.45pm
Additional: Bar food L; Sunday L;
Children 8+
Seats: 40. Private dining room 12
Style: Chic/Modern
Smoking: No smoking in dining room
Accommodation: 10 en suite ★ ★

Guests return time and time again to this secluded bolt-hole in the heart of the picturesque Braes of Balquhidder where the Lewis family provide a truly warm welcome and delicious food. The innovative set-price menu changes daily and includes game from the estate, fresh fish and prime Scottish beef. A new organic garden provides unusual vegetables and herbs. At times the cooking fuses regional ingredients with foreign techniques, or exotic ingredients with classic techniques or sometimes both in one dish, for example seared West coast scallops on steamed bok choy with an Italian parsley and wasabi hollandaise topped with crispy leeks. Other times, there's just a hint of a twist, perhaps pan-fried entrecote of Monachyle venison with confit of sweet potato and a juniper and coriander game stock with warm pickled pear. No-nonsense puddings include warm bread-and-butter pudding with whisky and raisin custard.

Directions: On A84, 11 miles N of Callander turn R at Kingshouse Hotel. Monachyle Mhor 6 miles.

BRIDGE OF ALLAN,

Royal Hotel ❁

Hotel restaurant refurbished in classic style. An interesting starter of charred salmon with orange couscous was followed by tender rack of lamb with an aromatic crust.

Cost: Alc £27, set-price D £22.50. ☺ H/wine £11.75
Times: Noon-2pm/7-9.30pm
Additional: Bar food L; Sunday L; Children welcome
Style: Classic/traditional
Smoking: No smoking in dining room
Civil Licence: 80
Accommodation: 32 en suite ★ ★ ★

Directions: Telephone for directions

Henderson Street FK9 4HG
Map 11: NS79
Tel: 01786 832284
Fax: 01786 834377
E-mail: stay@royal-stirling.co.uk

CALLANDER,

Roman Camp Hotel ❀❀❀

FK17 8BG
Map 11: NN60
Tel: 01877 330003
Fax: 01877 331533
E-mail: mail@roman-camp-hotel.co.uk
Chef: Ian McNaught
Owners: Eric & Marion Brown
Cost: *Alc* £48, set-price L £19.50/D £36. H/wine £15
Times: Noon-2pm/7-9pm
Additional: Sunday L; Children welcome
Seats: 65. Private dining room 40
Style: Country-house/Formal
Smoking: No smoking in dining room; Air conditioning
Civil licence: 80
Accommodation: 14 en suite ★★★

Directions: Turn L into driveway at east end of Callander main street

A long, low pink building in 20 acres of gardens, Roman Camp was built in the early 17th century. Rooms have been given the country-house treatment, with an elegant drawing room overlooking the River Teith, a library with a secret chapel hidden behind the panelled walls, and an oval dining room hung with 1930s tapestries. Well-spaced tables, upholstered chairs and clever use of lighting mean that meals here are lingered over. The *carte* features such main courses as pan-fried calves' liver with garlic confit and lime jus, or chicken breast with black pudding and prosciutto with a Calvados and tarragon sauce, but the set-price, four-course tasting menu is popular at dinner. While it involves no choice, this is a balanced selection of dishes. A complimentary pre-starter of perhaps artichoke and foie gras parfait with a swirl of red pepper sauce may start the ball rolling before three pieces of 'lovely, pink and tender' breast of grouse on a potato scone finished with wild mushrooms. Next comes an interesting soup, like creamed asparagus with coriander oil, or white bean and ham cappuccino topped with thinly sliced truffle. Dishes are not only well thought-out and properly executed but look attractive too, as in a main course of lightly baked sea trout presented on scallop ravioli in turn sitting on a bed of spinach accompanied by langoustine velouté, the whole dish topped with a 'spaghetti' of crisp vegetables. Good planning means that if the starter on the market-led menus is fish – minestrone of monkfish and scallops, say – then the main course will be meat: beef fillet with pesto and red pepper risotto, for instance. A pre-dessert of something like refreshing bramble jelly comes before puddings of 'beautifully presented' dark chocolate, hazelnut and coconut pavé with praline ice cream, or passionfruit and mango soup with basil ice cream. The wine list, unusually, is listed alphabetically by country, with a section of fine clarets for those wanting to push the boat out.

DUNBLANE,

Cromlix House Hotel ❀❀

Kinbuck Nr Dunblane FK15 9JT
Map 11: NN70
Tel: 01786 822125
Fax: 01786 825450
E-mail: reservations@cromlixhouse.com

An imposing Edwardian country house of great individuality and character set amidst neatly tended gardens at the heart of an imposing three thousand acre estate. Two elegant dining rooms, resplendent in white linen, gleaming silver and candle-

Cromlix House Hotel

Chef: Paul Devonshire
Owners: David & Ailsa Assenti
Cost: Set-price L £20 & £27/D £42.
H/wine £16
Times: 12.30-1.30pm (Mon-Fri Oct-
Mar, reservations only) /7-8.30pm.
Closed 1st 3 wks Jan
Additional: Sunday L;
Children welcome
Seats: 42. Private dining rooms 12,
25 & 42
Style: Classic/Country-house
Smoking: No smoking in dining room
Accommodation: 14 en suite ★ ★ ★

lit tables, provide the backdrop to some innovative modern
cooking. The short daily-changing *carte*, which makes the most
of Scotland's quality larder, offers just two choices at each turn
as well as a vegetarian option, yet still calls for some difficult
decisions. A spring dinner followed canapés with a pavé of
salmon accompanied by a smoked haddock risotto, poached
egg and caviar sauce – 'possibly one flavour too many', noted
our inspector. However, a pre-main course cream of Jerusalem
artichoke soup showed the kitchen's true style, as did a well-
balanced main course of roasted best end of lamb, fine
ratatouille, salsa verde, sweetbreads and a nicely restrained
thyme jus. To finish, a good chocolate fondant and stem ginger
ice cream. Cafetière coffee with a varied selection of well-
made petits fours along with professional, knowledgeable and
friendly service complete the picture.

Directions: From A9 take B8033 (Kinbuck), through village, 2nd
L after small bridge

PORT OF MENTEITH,
Lake of Menteith Hotel ❀❀

Stirling
FK8 3RA
Map 11: NN50
Tel: 01877 385258
Fax: 01877 385671
Chef: Stewart Taylor
Owners: Graeme &
Ros McConnachie
Cost: Set-price L £15/D £29.50. ☺
H/wine £11

On the edge of the only lake in Scotland, this charming hotel
has lovely views over the water to the Isle of Inchmahome and
the hills beyond, and guests can enjoy the outlook from both
the inviting sitting room and the conservatory-style restaurant.
The kitchen takes a catholic approach to the fine ingredients it
uses, producing salmon boudin flavoured with dill, served with
a red pepper coulis and crispy leeks, then peppered fillet of

halibut on a bed of soy and tarragon-scented risotto with a shallot and saffron dressing. Wild mushrooms might turn up as a starter, filled with courgette and tomato fondue, then baked and drizzled with pesto, in an intermediary soup, or sautéed as a partner for pan-fried sirloin of Aberdeen Angus with caramelised shallots. Ways with fruit make successful puddings, from slices of poached pear sandwiched between biscuits layered with whipped cream and dribbled with strawberry coulis, to a prune compote topping for vanilla and nutmeg rice pudding.

Directions: On A873 in Port of Monteith

Times: Noon-2pm/7-8.30pm.
Closed 1st 2 wks Jan
Additional: Sunday L; Children 6+
Seats: 32
Style: Traditional/Country-house
Smoking: No smoking in dining room;
Air conditioning
Accommodation: 16 en suite ★ ★

STIRLING,

River House Restaurant 🏵

Family-friendly restaurant, part of a strikingly constructed conference complex with loch and castle views. Coffee, lunches and more adventurous evening fare are served, including delicious steamed Orkney salmon.

Cost: Alc £18, set-price L £6.95. ☺ H/wine £8.95
Times: Noon-3pm/6-10pm. Closed 25 Dec, 1 Jan
Additional: Sunday L; Children welcome
Style: Bistro-style/informal
Smoking: No smoking in dining room

Directions: 3 mins from J10 of M9. Follow signs for Stirling ring road and Castle Business Park

Castle Business Park
Craigforth FK9 4TW
Map 11: NS79
Tel: 01786 465577
Fax: 01786 462255

STIRLING,

Stirling Highland 🏵🏵

A bar named the Headmaster's Study and a restaurant called Scholars are giveaways that this impressive hotel was at one time a high school. Nowadays, it's popular with both business people and with visitors to this historical town. The traditional style of the restaurant, with its part-panelled walls, wood-effect wallpaper, crisp white linen and quality table settings, suggests a kitchen equally steeped in tradition, but in fact the menus take some wider twists and turns. Parma ham goes into a roulade with garlicky soft cheese, another starter of fresh and smoked salmon with avocado is dressed with lime and dill, and

Spittal Street FK8 1DU
Map 11: NS79
Tel: 01786 272727
Fax: 01786 272829
E-mail: stirling@paramount-hotels.co.uk
Chef: Ian Hamilton
Owners: Paramount Hotels
Cost: Alc £30, set-price L £9.50/
D £22.50. ☺ H/wine £13.50
Times: Noon-2.30pm/7-9.30pm.
Closed L Sat
Additional: Sunday L;
Children welcome
Seats: 80. Private dining rooms
10-100
Style: Traditional/formal
Smoking: No smoking in dining room;
Air conditioning
Civil Licence: 100
Accommodation: 94 en suite ★ ★ ★ ★

ribeye steak is glazed with Brie and then pan-fried. Quality ingredients are well-handled – breast of wood pigeon has been tender and moist, and cannon of Ayrshire lamb, cooked pink, has been full of flavour – and combinations work well: the former with a tower of black pudding and apple, the latter in a crisp rosemary crust with a 'delicious' claret jus. Salmon from the Tay might be topped with herbs and accompanied by Noilly Prat sauce, or plaited with sole and plated on tomato coulis. Puddings have included zesty lemon posset with lime sablé biscuits, and caramelised bananas with vanilla ice cream, and the wine list offers a choice from around the world.

Directions: In the road leading to Stirling Castle – follow Castle signs

STRATHBLANE,
Country Club Hotel 🏵

Classically presented dining room with an interesting menu: roulade of guinea fowl with balsamic beetroot dressing, and a platter of three fishes with samphire and a white wine and mussel sauce.

Directions: From Glasgow, follow A81 through Strathblane, turn L after leaving village

Milngarvie Road G63 9EH
Map 11: NS56
Tel: 01360 770491
Fax: 01360 770345

Telephone for further details

STRATHYRE,
Creagan House 🏵🏵

Just north of the village, Creagan is a restored 17th-century farmhouse with access to forest walks. The restaurant is a spacious, baronial-style affair with a massive fireplace at one end, large tables and high-backed dining chairs. The wine list is an interesting mixture of classics and lesser-known estates, all personally chosen. Hostess Cherry Gunn is in charge of front-of-house, and the menu bears the stamp of her husband's personality too, with dishes as varied as cumin-seared monkfish on a bed of greens with coconut squat lobsters and an olive oil sauce, or Bishop Kennedy cheese fried in macadamia nut couscous served with red grape coulis. Fennel, tomato and mushroom soup has been described as 'flawless', and another starter might be pink breast of pigeon with pears and hazelnuts in Madeira sauce. Tender and well-flavoured collop of venison might be sauced with bramble, port and orange and accompanied by a selection of locally grown, interesting vegetables, with another main course perhaps fillet of cod roasted on provençale vegetables with a sauce of red pepper, vodka and black olives. Finish with Scottish cheeses, or something indulgent like chocolate and hazelnut mousse cake.

Directions: 0.25 miles N of village off A84

Callander FK18 8ND
Map 11: NN51

Tel: 01877 384638
Fax: 01877 384319
Chef: Gordon Gunn
Owners: Gordon & Cherry Gunn
Cost: Set-price D £22.50. ☺
H/wine £9.45
Times: D only, 7.30-8.30pm.
Closed Feb, 1 wk Oct
Additional: Children 10+; Vegetarian dishes by prior arrangement
Seats: 15(functions 35). Private dining room 6; Jacket & tie preferred
Style: Baronial dining hall
Smoking: No smoking in dining room
Civil licence: 35
Accommodation: 5 en suite ★

WALES
ANGLESEY, ISLE OF

BEAUMARIS,
Ye Olde Bulls Head Inn 🏵🏵

Castle Street LL58 8AP
Map 6: SH67
Tel: 01248 810329
Fax: 01248 811294
E-mail: info@bullsheadinn.co.uk
Chef: Ernst van Halderen
Owners: Keith Rothwell &
David Robertson
Cost: *Alc* £28.95, set-price D fr £25.
H/wine £13.75
Times: D only, 7-9.30pm.
Closed Sun, 25 & 26 Dec, 1 Jan
Seats: 45. Private dining room 15.
Jacket & tie preferred
Style: Chic/Minimalist
Smoking: No smoking in dining room
Accommodation: 15 en suite ★ ★

The old coaching inn atmosphere has gone from this restaurant, sympathetically replaced with a contemporary feel that comes from subdued lighting and minimalist furniture. Modern British cooking is on the menu, and the broad choice might cover starters such as beef carpaccio with marinated local wild mushrooms and basil oil, or rilette of salmon with dill and lime crème fraîche. The emphasis on local ingredients continues into the main course, where pan-fried fillet of cod with pancetta, butterbeans and a herb oil might rub shoulders with saddle of rabbit with leek fritter, cider and black pudding sauce, or maybe fillet of Welsh beef with a goats' cheese glaze, red onion confit and Conwy mustard sauce. A vivid imagination has produced the dessert menu: expect Welsh honey parfait with fresh summer berries and poppy seed meringue, or roasted pecan and fig tart with a rosemary ice cream.

Directions: Town centre, main street

BRIDGEND

BRIDGEND, Coed-y-Mwstwr Hotel 🏵

The restaurant, with its impressive domed ceiling, is the ideal setting for enjoyable dishes such as succulent seared tuna with tabouleh salsa and roasted pepper coulis, followed perhaps by a 'refreshingly tart' apple and sultana crumble.

Style: Classic/Country-house
Smoking: No-smoking area; No pipes & cigars
Civil licence: 120
Accommodation: 23 en suite ★ ★ ★

Directions: M4 J35, A473 (Bridgend) into Coychurch, R at petrol station and up hill for 1 mile

Coychurch CF35 6AF
Map 3: SS97
Tel: 01656 860621
Fax: 01656 863122
Cost: *Alc* £19.50, set-price D £24.
H/wine £10.95
Times: Noon-2pm/7-10pm
Additional: Bar food; Sunday L;
Children welcome

BRIDGEND,
The Great House ❀

Leicester's is a modern yet comfortable restaurant set in a restored 15th-century listed building. Menu may include roasted goose breast with red cabbage, broccoli and carrots, Black beef fillet, or potato and vegetable rarebit.

Cost: Alc £27.50, set-price L £11.95. ☺ H/wine £10.75
Times: Noon-2pm/6.45-9.30pm. Closed D Sun, 4 days Xmas
Additional: Bar food L; Sunday L; Children welcome
Style: Modern/Country-house
Smoking: No smoking in dining room; Air conditioning
Accommodation: 16 en suite ★ ★ ★

Directions: M4 J35, A473 then A48 signed Porthcawl and Laleston

Laleston CF32 0HP
Map 3: SS97
Tel: 01656 657644
Fax: 01656 668892
E-mail: greathse1@aol.com

CARDIFF

CARDIFF, La Brasserie, Champers, Le Monde ❀

A wine bar, a brasserie and a Spanish Bodega, all in the same building and all owned by Benigno Martinez. Not far from the station, these three operations are characterised by their busy informal atmosphere and Spanish cooking.

Cost: Alc £20-£25, set-price L £5.95 & £6.95. ☺ H/wine £9.45
Times: Noon-2.30pm/7-12.15am. Closed Sun (ex for D Champers), 25 & 26 Dec
Additional: Bar food (Tapas in Champers); Children welcome
Style: Bistro-style/Rustic
Smoking: Air conditioning (ex Champers)

Directions: Telephone for directions

60 St Mary Street Cardiff CF1 1FE
Map 3: ST17
Tel: 029 2037 2164/ (Champers 0037 3363)/(Le Monde 2038 7376)
Fax: 029 2066 8092
E-mail: chefuk@globalnet.co.uk

CARDIFF,
Cardiff Bay Hotel ❀

A sophisticated hotel restaurant located on the boundary between the city centre and Cardiff's waterfornt development. Culinary highlights include a good ham terrine and an apple mille-feuille with excellent cinnamon risotto.

Additional: Bar food; Sunday L; Children welcome
Style: Classic/Traditional
Smoking: No smoking in dining room; Air conditioning
Civil licence: 200
Accommodation: 156 en suite ★ ★ ★ ★

Directions: From A48M follow 'Docks & Cardiff E'. L at rdbt, R fork onto flyover. At 3rd rdbt take 2nd exit (Ocean Way-Atlantic Wharf). L at rdbt (Penarth). Over next rdbt, under flyover, L at 1st lights; hotel on R

Schooner Way
Atlantic Wharf
CF10 4RT
Map 3: ST17
Tel: 029 2047 5000
Fax: 029 2048 1491
E-mail: sales.cbh@awhotels.com
Cost: Alc £19.50, set-price L £10.95.
☺ H/wine £10.50
Times: Noon-2pm/7-10pm.
Closed L Sat, Bhs L

CARDIFF,

Le Cassoulet ❀❀

5 Romilly Crescent Canton CF1 9NP
Map 3: ST17
Tel: 029 2022 1905/2039 5347
Fax: 029 2022 1905
E-mail: lecassoulet@ukonline.co.uk
Chefs: Yvonnick Le Roy,
Gilbert Viader
Owners: Mr & Mrs G Viader
Cost: Alc £30, set-price L £18. ☺
H/wine £11.50
Times: Noon-2pm/7-10pm. Closed
Sun, Mon, 2 wks Xmas, 3 wks Aug
Additional: Children welcome
Seats: 40
Style: Chic/French
Smoking: No pipes & cigars

Popular French restaurant with pretty stencilled walls and
stained glass windows. The French proprietor imports key
items on the menu directly from France, including foie gras
from the south-west, and unpasteurised cheese from
Fromagerie Xavier in Toulouse, his home town. These are also
available for customers to buy and take home. The south-
western influence is evident throughout the menu, with dishes
such as cassoulet Toulousain, a haricot bean stew with neck
end of pork, confit of duck and Toulouse sausage served in an
earthenware dish, or corn-fed chicken breast roasted with
thyme and accompanied by foie gras braised in a light straw-
flavoured stock with a vegetable garnish.

Directions: From M4 follow B4267 Canton, Restaurant is next
to Post Office

CARDIFF,

Chikako's Japanese Restaurant ❀

10-11 Mill Lane CF1 1FL
Map 3: ST17
Tel: 029 20665279
Fax: 029 20665279

*Japanese outpost in city centre offering graceful service and
authentic cuisine. Typical dishes include byoza, misoshiru, tempura,
teppanyaki and green tea ice-cream, with Japanese plum wine to
finish with.*

Telephone for further details

Directions: Opposite Marriott Hotel in Mill Lane café quarter

CARDIFF,

Copthorne Cardiff-Caerdydd ❀

Copthorne Way
Culverhouse Cross CF5 6DH
Map 3: ST17
Tel: 02920 599100
Fax: 02920 599080

*Restaurant with stunning lake views serving dishes based on quality
ingredients – Welsh Black beef fillet with wild mushrooms, and pan-
fried red mullet on a pear and celery compote with saffron jus.*

Telephone for further details

Directions: M4 J33 take A4232 (Culverhouse Cross), 4th exit at
rdbt (A48). 1st left

CARDIFF,

Le Gallois ❀❀

6-8 Romilly Crescent CF11 9NR
Map 3: ST17
Tel: 02920 341264
Fax: 02920 237911
E-mail: le.gallois@virgin.net
Chef: Padrig Jones
Owners: Graham & Anne Jones
Cost: Set-price L £11.95/D £27.
H/wine £9.50
Times: Noon-2.30pm/6.30-10.30pm.
Closed Sun, Mon, Xmas, New Year,
3 wks Aug
Additional: Children welcome
Seats: 50
Style: modern/minimalist
Smoking: No-smoking area;
No pipes & cigars; Air conditioning

Padrig Jones' restaurant is a real find. It's small, but on a split level which gives a more spacious feel, and it has quickly established a sound reputation through an uncompromising emphasis on quality – lunch in particular offers cracking value for money. A pair of inspectors explored the short, modern menu. Starters of poached duck egg wrapped in Parma ham with sauce Choron, and smoked haddock with herb crumb, tomato and basil salad and chive dressing were both well-timed and delivered every expected flavour. Malaysian laksa with steamed plaice was an accomplished soup-like dish with well-balanced flavours from an infusion of chilli and coconut and texture added by some noodles and crisp cabbage. Its counterpart was a splendid confit of rabbit, served with a bubble-and-squeak cake and ratatouille. Good desserts came in the shape of a mango and pear tart with pineapple sorbet and a simple confit of plums with rice pudding. The wine list is a fair size with coverage around the world, plus some local wines; all carry fair mark-ups. Booking is strongly advised.

Directions: Telephone for directions

CARDIFF,

Gilby's Restaurant ❀

Old Port Road
Culverhouse Cross CF5 6DN
Map 3: ST17
Tel: 029 2067 0800
Fax: 029 2059 4437
E-mail: www.gilbysrestaurant.co.uk

An eighteenth-century barn conversion with open plan kitchen and the potential for alfresco dining on the cobblestone patio. Excellent fresh fish selection a major attraction alongside meat dishes such as pork Milanese.

Cost: ☺ H/wine £10.95
Times: Noon-2.30pm/6-10.30pm. Closed D Sun, all Mon, 10 days Xmas & New Year, Bhs
Additional: Sunday L; Children 7+
Style: Chic/Rustic
Smoking: No smoking in dining room

Directions: From M4 J33 follow signs for Airport/Cardiff West. Take A4050 Barry/Airport road and R at 1st mini roundabout.

CARDIFF,

Manor Parc Country Hotel ❀

Thornhill Road Thornhill
CF4 5UA
Map 3: ST17
Tel: 029 2069 3723
Fax: 029 2061 4624

Classical surroundings and a striking lantern ceiling in this hotel restaurant, where the menu has an Italian feel with dishes such as loin of veal with white wine, mushrooms and cream, or pancakes with spinach and Parmesan.

Cost: *Alc* fr £26, set-price L fr £16. ☺ H/wine £11
Times: Noon-2pm/7-10pm. Closed D Sun, 24-30 Dec
Additional: Sunday L
Style: Country-house
Smoking: No-smoking area
Civil licence: 80
Accommodation: 12 en suite ★★★

Directions: N of Cardiff on A469

CARDIFF,

Metropolis Restaurant & Bar ❀

60 Charles Street CF1 4EG
Map 3: ST17
Tel: 029 2034 4300
Fax: 029 2066 6602

Fresh and stylish restaurant offering simple modern dishes like pan-fried salmon cutlets with a coriander, caper and lime dressing served with couscous, if the wide range of light bar snacks fail to satisfy your hunger.

Cost: *Alc* £20, set-price L £7.95. ☺ H/wine £10.95
Times: Noon-3pm/6-11pm. Closed Sun, 25 & 26 Dec, 1 Jan, Bhs
Additional: Bar Food L
Style: Chic/Modern
Smoking: Air conditioning

Directions: In city centre, off Queen Street

CARDIFF,

New House Hotel ❀❀

Thornhill CF4 5UA
Map 3: ST17
Tel: 029 2052 0280
Fax: 029 2052 0324
Chef: Ian Black
Cost: *Alc* £30, set-price L £12.50/
D £19.95. H/wine £10.95
Times: Noon-2pm/7-9.45pm.
Closed 26 Dec, 1 Jan
Additional: Bar food; Sunday L;
Children 8+
Seats: 35. Private dining room 40
Style: Classic/Country-house
Smoking: No-smoking area
Civil licence: 200
Accommodation: 36 en suite ★★★

Perched on the Cardiff side of Caerphilly mountain with stunning views over the city and beyond. This converted and extended Georgian residence enjoys a country house feel although it's just a few minutes' drive out of the capital. The Regency-style dining room offers classic comfort, and plenty of time to peruse the seasonal *carte* and set-price menus which chef Ian Black has carefully compiled. From the former you might choose parfait of chicken livers on artichoke with fennel seed brioche and honey and mustard dressed leaves; or perhaps pot-steamed mussels with lemongrass in a Thai curry foam. The same influences can be seen in main choices such as Boursin chicken roasted with avocado, soft polenta and vegetable crisps, or rarebit of lobster and asparagus tips with warm tabouleh. The East is clearly present in hoi sin duck with Szechuan noodles and sugar-snap peas, while roasted haddock with prosciutto ham under a parsley and oat crumble, with creamed leeks and sauté potatoes has a modern British feel.

Directions: Take A469 to the north of city. Entrance on L shortly after crossing the M4 flyover

CARDIFF,

St Davids Hotel ❀❀❀

A seven-story atrium towers above the lobby of this imaginatively designed hotel, and although the restaurant is surprisingly small it is ultra-modern in design with impressive views that give the illusion of being on board a large yacht. Waiters in white 'Spencer' jackets continue the nautical theme. Much attention to design detail has been paid, down to the last narrow frosted vase with its exotic single bloom; more care, however, needs to be taken with the standard of food served. Too many little slips and oversights marred our inspection meal, each trivial perhaps but cumulatively unimpressive. The basics are in place, though, and the menu steers a steady course between the safe waters of dishes such as grilled scallops with tomato and basil dressing and the riskier depths of a duo of guinea fowl with lentilles du Puy, bacon and red wine reduction. Welsh produce is much in evidence – Penclawdd cockles in a chive broth with medallions of monkfish; fillet of salt marsh lamb with provençale couscous, rosemary scented jus; ribeye of Black beef in Bercy sauce, roasted vegetables and parsley mash. The set lunch menu might comprise risotto of squid ink, roast squid and herb oil, followed by fillet of lamb, aubergine caviar, roasted shallots and tarragon and warm chocolate fondant.

Havannah Street CF10 6SD
Map 3: ST17
Tel: 029 2045 4045
Fax: 029 2048 7075
E-mail: reservations@fivestar-htl-wales.com
Chef: Martin Green
Owner: R F Hotels
Cost: A/c £33, set-lunch £14.50/ D £25. ☺ H/wine £15
Times: 12.30-2.30pm/6.30-10.30pm
Additonal: Bar food; Sunday L; Children welcome
Seats: 120. Private dining room 40
Style: Chic/Minimalist
Smoking: No smoking in dining room; Air conditioning
Civil licence: 270
Accommodation: 136 en suite
★ ★ ★ ★ ★

Directions: From M4 J33 take A432 9 miles to Cardiff Bay. At rdbt over Queens Tunnel take 1st L, then immediate R

CARDIFF,

Woods Brasserie ❀

Modern brasserie in a listed building, exuding lively bustle and enthusiasm. Expect punchy dishes along the lines of squash risotto, Caesar salad and rump of Welsh salt-marsh lamb. Puddings might include caramelised rice pudding with Armagnac prunes.

Additional: Children welcome
Style: Modern/minimalist
Smoking: Air conditioning

Pilotage Building
Stuart Street CF10 5BW
Map 3: ST17
Tel: 029 2049 2400
Fax: 029 2048 1998
Cost: A/c £25 ☺ . H/w £11
Times: Noon-2pm/7-10pm.
Closed Sun & Mon, 1 wk spring, 1 wk autumn, 25-26 Dec, 31st Dec, Bh Mon

Directions: From M4 J33, take A4232 towards Cardiff Bay for approx 8m. Take turning signposted Techniquest Museum. Restaurant 500yds on R

CREIGIAU,

Caesars Arms ❀

Admirable, simple cuisine. Starter of wild mushroom risotto might be followed by sea bass baked in rock salt or fillet of Welsh mountain Black beef. Fresh summer fruits are picked twice daily from an adjoining farm.

Cardiff Road CF15 9NN
Map 3: ST08
Tel: 029 20890486
Fax: 029 20892176

Telephone for further details

Directions: From M4 J34 take A411 (Cardiff). Turn L at Creigiau

CARMARTHENSHIRE

BRECHFA,
Tŷ Mawr Country Hotel

SA32 7RA
Map 2: SN53
Tel: 01267 202332
Fax: 01267 202437
E-mail:
tymawr@tymawrcountryhotel.co.uk
Cost: Set-price D £23. ☺
H/wine £9.50
Times: 12.30-2pm/7.30-9pm.
Closed L Sat

Despite the exposed stone walls and large feature fireplace, recent refurbishment of the restaurant has given it an almost art deco ambience. Varied and enthusiastic cooking produces dishes such as a melt-in-the-mouth shank of Welsh lamb.

Additional: Bar food; Sunday L; Children welcome
Style: Chic/Elegant **Smoking:** No smoking in dining room
Accommodation: 5 rooms, 4 en suite ★★

Directions: Off B4310, village centre

CARMARTHEN, Falcon Hotel

Lammas Street SA31 3AP
Tel: 01267 234959
Fax: 01267 221277
E-mail:
reception@falconcarmarthen.co.uk

Telephone for further details

Attractive town centre restaurant. Try a starter of pan-fried cockles and spring onions in white wine au gratin, followed by grilled fillet of Towy salmon, and perhaps a simple baked hot chocolate pudding for dessert.

Directions: In town centre, opposite monument

CARMARTHEN,
Four Seasons Restaurant

Nantgaredig SA32 7NY
Map 2: SN42
Tel: 01267 290238
Fax: 01267 290808
E-mail: jen4seas@aol.com
Cost: Set-price D £25. ☺ H/wine £10
Times: (L by arrangement only)
D only, 7.30-9.30pm. Closed Sun &
Mon, Xmas
Additional: Children 5+

Pretty restaurant in a converted farm building, with a conservatory front and adjoining terrace with outdoor seating. Well-constructed dishes make use of quality local ingredients: Carmarthen ham with fresh fruits to start, or Brechfa smoked salmon with chicory, followed by fillet of Welsh Black beef.

Style: Informal/Country-house
Smoking: No smoking in dining room

Directions: From A40 turn onto B4310 at Nantgaredig; L up hill, 0.25 mile on R

LAUGHARNE, Cors Restaurant ✿✿

Newbridge Road SA33 4SH
Map 2: SN31
Tel: 01994 427219
Credit cards: None

Telephone for further details

Chef patron Nick Priestland is an artist, and some of his bold abstract paintings adorn the walls of the former vicarage – now a strikingly decorated restaurant with rooms. The menu has an Italian/Mediterranean bias, well chosen to match the ebullient interiors and flamboyant garden. Dishes are presented in primary colours with similarly vibrant flavours. Such bold simplicity depends on quality ingredients and the best local bounty is used to good effect in dishes such as hot seared smoked salmon with sweet mustard sauce, rack of salt marsh lamb with rosemary crust, and pan-fried fillets of sea bass with a red wine jus.

Directions: From Carmarthen follow A40, turn L at St Clears and 4m to Laugharne

LLANDEILO,

Cawdor Arms Hotel ❀❀

Built as a coaching inn at the end of the 18th century, the Cawdor Arms is a welcoming place, with an open fire, leather chairs, flower arrangements and portraits hanging on the walls. Brechfa trout, Carmarthenshire lamb and Welsh Black beef are just some of the fine local produce the kitchen calls on, turning them into contemporary dishes along the lines of charred breast and confit of St David's duckling with a salad of Puy lentils, parsnip purée and tapenade, or steamed tranche of Towy salmon with fennel risotto and cockles sautéed with bacon. A tartlet is normally among starters – perhaps spring onion, Parma ham and Parmesan with pesto, or spicy onion with a carrot and coriander dressing – alongside something like brandade of Gower cod. Something fruity tends to round things off – glazed raspberry tart with passion fruit Mascarpone cream, say, or plum crumble with vanilla ice cream – with perhaps chocolate or cappuccino parfait also on offer.

Additional: Bar food L; Sunday L; Children welcome
Seats: 60. Private dining rooms 22
Style: Classic/Traditional
Smoking: No smoking in dining room
Accommodation: 17 en suite ★★★

Directions: Large Georgian building in town centre, at junction of A40 and A483

Rhosmaen Street SA19 6EN
Map 3: SN62
Tel: 01558 823500
Fax: 01558 822399
E-mail: cawdor.arms@btinternet.com
Chef: Rod Peterson
Owners: John, Sylvia & Jane Silver
Cost: Alc £23.50, set-price L £14.95/D £23.50. ☺ H/wine £9.90
Times: Noon-2pm/7.30-9.30pm

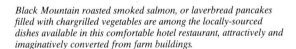

CEREDIGION

ABERPORTH,

Penbontbren Farm Hotel ❀

Black Mountain roasted smoked salmon, or laverbread pancakes filled with chargrilled vegetables are among the locally-sourced dishes available in this comfortable hotel restaurant, attractively and imaginatively converted from farm buildings.

Cost: ☺ H/wine £9.80
Times: D only, 7-8.30pm. Closed Xmas
Additional: Children welcome
Style: Traditional
Smoking: No smoking in dining room
Accommodation: 10 en suite ★★

Directions: E from Cardigan on A487 to Tanygroes. 1 mile after Tanygroes take 2nd R signposted Penbontbren

Glynarthen Cardigan SA44 6PE
Map 2: SN25
Tel: 01239 810248
Fax: 01239 811129

ABERYSTWYTH,
Belle Vue Royal Hotel ❀

A pleasing sea view restaurant in a 19th-century family-owned promenade hotel. The menu exercises a classic traditional remit to great aplomb in dishes such as rack of herb-crusted lamb with a sauce niçoise.

Marine Terrace
SY23 2BA
Map 6: SN58
Tel: 01970 617558
Fax: 01970 612190
E-mail: reception@
bellevueroyalhotel.fsnet.co.uk
Cost: *Alc* £23. ☺ H/wine £10
Times: 12.30-1.45pm/6.30-9.15pm.
Closed D 25 Dec
Additional: Bar food L; Sunday L;
Children welcome
Style: Modern/Traditional
Smoking: No pipes & cigars;
Air conditioning
Accommodation: 37 en suite ★ ★ ★

Directions: Overlooking Cardigan
Bay

ABERYSTWYTH, Conrah Hotel ❀❀

Ffosrhydygaled Chancery
SY23 4DF
Map 6: SN58
Tel: 01970 617941
Fax: 01970 624546
E-mail: hotel@conrah.freeserve.co.uk
Chef: Stephen Michael West
Owners: Mr & Mrs F J Heading
Cost: Set-price L £19/D £27. ☺
H/wine fr £11
Times: Noon-2pm/7-9pm.
Closed Xmas
Additional: Bar food L; Sunday L;
Children 5+; Vegetarian dishes not
always available
Seats: 50. Private dining room 60.
Jacket & tie preferred
Style: Country-house/Formal
Smoking: No smoking in dining room
Civil licence: 50
Accommodation: 17 en suite ★ ★ ★

Edwardian and Victorian influences can be seen in the architecture of this mellow country house hotel, and the restaurant reflects both period styles. Glorious views over the gardens and the Welsh mountains can be enjoyed from this airy room, where classic Welsh and modern international cooking styles come together successfully. Choose to eat two, three or four courses from the daily set-price menu, or a shorter choice at lunch time. Perhaps begin with home-smoked duck breast with fruit chutney, or deep-fried fritters of laverbread, cockles and capsicum with sesame seed dressing. The quality of the mainly local produce is seen in main dishes like honey-roast rack of Welsh lamb with oranges, pine nuts, black-eye beans and Grand Marnier sauce; or chargrilled Welsh Black beef sirloin steak with horseradish, leek and shallots and a pickled walnut and red wine sauce. A satisfying dessert of syrup sponge with butterscotch sauce and clotted cream might complete the picture, with dessert wines served by the glass.

Directions: On A487, 3 miles S of Aberystwyth

ABERYSTWYTH, Nanteos

Rhydyfelin SY23 4LU
Map 6: SN58
Tel: 01970 624363
Fax: 01970 626332
E-mail: book@nanteosmansion.co.uk

Telephone for further details

Substantial Georgian house specialising in weddings and small conferences. Set menu using good local produce, typical dishes might include melon with fruit coulis, Welsh lamb or smoked salmon, and baby pavlovas with seasonal berries.

Directions: B4340 to Trawscoed S of Aberystwyth. Nanteos signposted on L

EGLWYSFACH, Ynyshir Hall

Machynlleth SY20 8TA
Map 6: SN69
Tel: 01654 781209
Fax: 01654 781366
E-mail: info@ynyshir-hall.co.uk
Chef: Chris Colmer
Owners: Rob & Joan Reen

Dating from the 16th century, Ynyshir Hall is in a peaceful spot amid 14 acres of landscaped grounds. The interior is decorated in vibrant colours, the restaurant in a strong blue, further enlivened by owner Rob Reen's paintings hanging on the walls. If menu descriptions make dishes sound complicated – roast halibut with linguine, crushed avocado, shiitaki mushrooms, baby calamari and truffle oil, for instance – the kitchen shows a keen eye for presentation. Flavours are clear and complementary too, and top-quality ingredients are handled with accuracy, as in a main course of steamed sea bass with lobster ravioli and fennel velouté and a warm salad of mange-tout and pine nuts. Pastry is a strong point, the 'lightest, thinnest' encasing a potent cheese filling, some potato added for texture, offset by 'wonderful, intense' tomato and red pepper chutney. Desserts show the same invention and presentational skills: Horlicks ice cream and apple crisps accompany apple confit and apple rice pudding, for example, and lime and ginger crème brûlée, in a copper pot, comes with Muscat jelly and orange sorbet. Superlatives are heaped on the

AA Wine Shortlisted for Award-see page 18

extras, from 'super' breads and canapés, a 'simple, brilliant green' pre-starter of parsley soup concealing an oyster, and 'very moreish' petits fours. *Best Presented Wine List (see pages 18-19).*

Style: Country-house. **Smoking:** No smoking in dining room
Accommodation: 10 en suite ★ ★ ★

Directions: On A487, 6 miles from Machynlleth

Cost: Set-price L £22/D £36.
Times: 12.30-1.30pm/7-8.30pm.
Closed Jan
Additional: Bar food L; Sunday L; Children 9+
Seats: 30. Private dining room 16. Jacket & tie preferred

GWBERT-ON-SEA, **Cliff Hotel** ✤ NEW

SA43 1PP
Map 2: SN15
Tel: 01239 613241
Fax: 01239 615391

Telephone for further details

Directions: Telephone for directions

Privately owned hotel on the cliff top. An impressive meal began with lobster cappuccino served with a light dumpling, followed by tournedos of beef topped with flash-fried foie gras.

CONWY

ABERGELE, **Kinmel Arms** ✣✣

St George LL22 9BP
Map 6: SH97
Tel/Fax: 01745 832207
Chef/owner: Gary Edwards
Cost: *Alc.* £13.95, set-price L/D £13.95
Times: Noon-2pm/7-9pm. Closed D 25 Dec
Seats: 40

17th-century former coaching inn with an informal atmosphere on the edge of the historic Kinmel Estate. The short *carte* might offer sea bass with saffron sauce, Kinmel venison with local elderberry sauce, roast monkfish with Moroccan spices or pan-fried skate wings with caper butter.

Directions: A55 towards Conwy; L signed 'St George'; L at top of hill, inn on L

BETWS-Y-COED,
Tan-y-Foel Hotel ❀❀❀

Capel Garmon LL26 0RE
Map 6: SH75
Tel: 01690 710507
Fax: 01690 710681
E-mail: tanyfoel@wiss.co.uk
Chef: Janet Pitman
Owners: Mr PK & Mrs JC Pitman
Cost: *Alc* £30. H/wine £11
Times: D only, 7.30-8.30pm,
(booking essential)
Additional: Children 7+; vegetarian
dishes by arrangement
Seats: 16
Style: Modern
Smoking: No smoking establishment
Accommodation: 7 en suite ★ ★

Any chef who can make boring old rainbow trout palatable deserves our accolade. Janet Pitman rose superbly to the challenge with an intriguing and unusual main course of rainbow trout with black treacle, chilli and sesame seed vinaigrette. Her lively, vibrant cooking lights up the verdant, colour washed dining-room cosily warmed by a wood-burning stove. The bright and bold modern design is a welcome contrast to the archetypal country-house setting, a 16th-century stone house perched on a wooded hillside. Pitman uses local and organic ingredients wherever possible to produce a short, daily-changing menu that is full of robust flavours and skilfully-executed dishes frequently displaying a touch of the Orient. As a starter, there may be a choice of crisp crumb, lemon and parmesan-coated fillet of trout set on shredded mange-tout drizzled with nero sauce or a warm salad of asparagus and deep-fried Parma ham laced with tarragon mustard vinaigrette. Welsh venison is served with bubble-and-squeak potato, buttered carrots and Shrewsbury sauce. The high standard was maintained in our dessert of crêpes with chopped nuts set on a rich chocolate sauce with a creamy mocha ice cream.

Directions: A5 onto A470; 2 miles N towards Llanrwst, then turning for Capel Garmon. Hotel on L before village

COLWYN BAY,
Café Niçoise ❀

124 Abergele Road LL29 7PS
Map 6: SH87
Tel: 01492 531555

Simple, friendly restaurant with wooden floors and terracotta walls. Roast monkfish with herb risotto and red wine and garlic jus was a good combination, with firm fish and tender rice.

Cost: H/wine £7.95
Times: Noon-2pm/7-10pm. Closed Sun, L Mon & Tue, 1 wk Jan, 1 wk Jun
Additional: Children 7+ at D
Style: Bistro-style/modern
Smoking: No-smoking area

Directions: From A55 take Old Colwyn exit, L at slip road, R at mini-roundabout, R towards Bay; restaurant is on L

CONWY, The Old Rectory ❀❀❀

Llanrwst Road Llansanffraid Glan
Conwy LL28 5LF
Map 6: SH77
Tel: 01492 580611
Fax: 01492 584555
E-mail:
info@oldrectorycountryhouse.co.uk
Chef: Wendy Vaughan
Owners: M & W Vaughan
Cost: Set-price D £29.90.
H/wine £14.90
Times: D only at 7.30 for 8pm.
Closed 20 Dec-1 Feb
Additional: Children 5+
Style: Traditional/Country-house
Smoking: No smoking in dining room
Accommodation: 6 en suite ★ ★

This is a house that is full of charm. Delightful terraced
gardens overlook the Conwy Estuary and Snowdonia beyond,
and the intimate public rooms are complemented by the
classical design of the interior. Dinner is served house-party
style, which can make for a lengthy evening, but the food more
than compensates with cooking that is based on carefully
chosen ingredients put together in simple, skilful and
immediately appealing combinations. Spiced monkfish, of
excellent quality and cooked to perfection, may be served with
creamy vanilla risotto and well-flavoured red wine sauce. The
main course regularly features locally reared Welsh Black beef
and mountain lamb, succulent and full of flavour. Imaginative
accompaniments might include olive potatoes, sweet potato
and butternut squash wrapped in leek, and a spinach parcel of
minced lamb and Puy lentils. There is a choice of two puddings,
such as luscious lemon and raspberry crème brûlée, or home-
made ice cream and sorbet, Welsh and Celtic farm cheeses or a
grilled goats' cheese savoury. Excellent home-made bread rolls,
good unsalted butter, freshly brewed coffee and hand-made
chocolates all add to the enjoyment of the meal. The welcome
and service are second to none.

Directions: On A470, 0.5 mile S of
junction with A55

LLANDUDNO,

Bodysgallen Hall Hotel ❀❀❀

LL30 1RS
Map 6: SH78
Tel: 01492 584466
Fax: 01492 582519
E-mail: info@bodysgallen.com
Chef: David Thompson
Owner: Historic House Hotels
Cost: Set-price L £17.50/D £33.90.
H/wine £12.75
Times: 12.30pm-1.45pm/7.30-9.30pm
Additional: Bar food L; Sunday L;
Children 8+
Seats: 60. Private dining room 40.
Jacket & tie preferred
Style: Country-house
Smoking: No smoking in dining room;
Air conditioning
Accommodation: 35 en suite ★ ★ ★

David Thompson is a talented and keen competiton chef which
shows in the excellent visual presentation of his dishes. The

menu is lengthy and ambitious, and dining at the beautifully restored 17th-century house, with its superb gardens, is always a pleasure. Thompson has the advantage of having his own kitchen and herb garden, plus a fine array of regional ingredients such as Welsh lamb and Welsh Black beef, local Conwy pork, cockles and mussels. Dinner might begin with pan-fried fillet of salmon with scallop ravioli, poached quail egg and lemongrass risotto or a terrine of foie gras, confit of ham and dates with toasted walnut brioche. Main courses typically include sliced loin of venison with herb polenta and beetroot dressing, and fillet of red mullet with pan-fried scallops, coriander noodles and a vanilla nage. Vegetables are chosen to accompany each dish, and grilled fillet steak or plainly grilled fish are available upon request. Baked apple tarte Tatin with a light caramel sauce and Calvados parfait is recommended.

Directions: From A55 take A470 (Llandudno). Hotel 1 mile on R

Bodysgallen Hall Hotel

LLANDUDNO, Empire Hotel ❀

Church Walks LL30 2HE
Map 6: SH78
Tel: 01492 860555
Fax: 01492 860791
E-mail: emphotel@aol.com
Cost: *Alc* £25, set-price L £15/D £25. H/wine £13.75
Times: D only, 6.45-9.30pm. Closed 10 days Xmas
Additional: Bar food; Sunday L (12.30-2pm); Children welcome
Style: Classic/traditional
Smoking: No-smoking area; No pipes & cigars; Air conditioning
Accommodation: 58 en suite ★★★

Leading Llandudno hotel, traditionally run, with a classically elegant restaurant. The daily menu might offer fresh Conwy mussels, or chargrilled prime Welsh beef fillet steak.

Directions: From A55 take A470 to Llandudno. Proceed along the main street (Mostyn Street/Upper Mostyn Street). Hotel at end and facing town

LLANDUDNO,
Imperial Hotel ❀

With a commitment to local and market fresh produce and a focus on traditional hospitality values this hotel restaurant has much to recommend it. The menu is accordingly extensive, offering such delights as loin of forest venison in a juniper berry crumb.

Additional: Bar food L; Sunday L; Childern welcome
Style: Traditional
Smoking: No smoking in dining room
Civil licence: 150
Accommodation: 100 en suite ★★★

Directions: On The Promenade

The Promenade LL30 1AP
Map 6: SH78
Tel: 01492 877466
Fax: 01492 878043
E-mail: imphotel@btinternet.com
Cost: Set-price L £12/D20. ☺
H/wine £10
Times: 12.30-2pm/6.30-9.30pm

LLANDUDNO, Martins Restaurant with Rooms ❀❀

11 Mostyn Avenue Craig Y Don
LL30 1YS
Map 6: SH78
Tel: 01492 870070
Fax: 01492 876661
E-mail:
martins@walesuk4.freeserve.co.uk
Chef: Martin James
Owners: Martin James & Jan Williams
Cost: *Alc* £25, set-price L £14.95/
D £17.95. ☺ H/wine £11.50
Times: Noon-2pm/6-late.
Closed Sun & Mon
Seats: 30. Jacket & tie preferred
Style: Classic/Country-house
Smoking: No smoking in dining room
Accommodation: 4 en suite

Once the home of the Archdruid of Wales, this mid-terrace Edwardian villa is now a well-appointed restaurant-with-rooms. There's a small bar in the corner, the wine list runs to only two pages but has much of interest, and the short menu goes straight to the point: sliced pigeon breast salad with lardons, smoked salmon with a quenelle of smoked trout, followed by roast duckling with blackcurrant and Cassis sauce, or baked monkfish with a sauce of prawns, white wine, tomato and herbs. A starter of warm smoked cod terrine with tomato mayonnaise and a potato and chive salad impressed with its lightness and flavours, and successful main courses have included sautéed local plaice with nut butter, and best end of Welsh lamb with onion marmalade and a smooth red wine jus. The generous choice of desserts runs from something like light, fresh-tasting lemon tart with vanilla ice cream to baked rice pudding tartlet topped with glazed bananas and banana mousse.

Directions: Telephone for details

LLANDUDNO, St Tudno Hotel ❀❀❀

Promenade LL30 2LP
Map 6: SH78
Tel: 01492 874411
Fax: 01492 860407
E-mail: studnohotel@btinternet.com
Chef: David Harding
Owners: Martin & Janette Bland
Cost: *Alc* £28, set-price L £16.95. ☺
H/wine £10.50
Times: 12.30-2pm/7-9.30pm
Additional: Bar food L; Sunday L;
Children 8+
Seats: 60
Style: Chic/Formal
Smoking: No smoking in dining room;
Air conditioning
Accommodation: 20 en suite ★ ★

The Garden Room Restaurant at this Victorian seafront hotel is a bright, summery room, with a decor of greens and yellows, plants and flowers, and large windows giving plenty of light. A seasonal menu runs alongside a daily-changing *carte,* so choice is generous, and the kitchen makes exemplary use of local produce, from a hotpot of Conwy mussels with parsley and garlic cream, to main courses of fillet of Welsh Black beef with pommes Anna, and grilled fillet of turbot with prawns and parsley butter. Luxuries might pop up in the shape of foie gras parfait, or sevruga caviar accompanying smoked salmon, and assemblies are well-judged with technical skills evident throughout. Take a starter of perfectly cooked, juicy scallops in puff pastry with a 'true-tasting' basil and Champagne sauce, considered 'delicious', or pink breast of Trelough duck with a crisp and succulent confit of the leg on apple rösti, all bound together by a Calvados jus. Sunday lunch is a traditionalist's dream of roast beef with all the trimmings, or roast leg of Welsh lamb with mint sauce and redcurrant jelly, and cheeses are Welsh farmhouse. Puddings run the gamut from lemon meringue pie to exotic passion fruit tart with coconut ice cream, while the extensive wine list shows a discerning eye and has a good choice by the glass. *Winner of the AA Wine Award for Wales (see page XX)*.

Directions: Town centre, on Promenade opposite the pier entrance

St Tudno Hotel

TREFRIW, Princes Arms Hotel

Mouthwatering dishes include roast duck breast on braised cabbage with juniper berries, served with a wild mushroom sauce, or salmon steak poached and set on leeks braised in white wine with a Welsh rarebit topping.

Telephone for further details

Directions: At far end of village on L

LL27 0JP
Map 6: SH76
Tel: 01492 640592
Fax: 01492 640559
E-mail: princes.arms@easynet.co.uk

DENBEIGHSHIRE

LLANDEGLA, Bodidris Hall ✿✿

An impressive manor house, surrounded by ornamental gardens and mature woodlands, the classic interior still retains original oak beams and inglenook fireplaces. The cooking shows considerable flair and style, and has the confidence to break out of the traditional country-house repertoire: there may be best end of Welsh lamb and Welsh Black beef tournedos on the menu, but there is also mahi mahi cooked with an olive crust, wilted greens and oriental sauce, and tian of prawn and avocado in Caesar dressing with gazpacho sauce. Enthusiasm shows through in dishes such as seared sea scallops with chive butter sauce and fresh mussels, and guinea fowl supreme with sweet potato purée, smoked bacon, Madeira sauce and deep-fried herbs. Cafetière coffee comes with hand-made chocolates.

Directions: Llandegla is on A525 (Wrexham-Ruthin). In village (from Wrexham direction) turn R onto A5104. Hotel is signed 1 mile on L

Wrexham LL11 3AL
Map 7: SJ25
Tel: 01978 790434
Fax: 01978 790335
E-mail: bodidrishall@micro-plus-web.net
Chef: Kevin Steel
Owner: W J Farden
Cost: Set-price L £17.50/D £35. H/wine £11
Times: Noon-2pm/7-9pm
Additional: Bar food L; Sunday L; Children 14+
Seats: Private dining room 24; Jacket & tie preferred
Style: Traditional/Country-house
Smoking: No smoking in dining room
Civil licence: 65
Accommodation: 9 en suite ★ ★ ★

LLANDRILLO,
Tyddyn Llan Hotel ❀❀

Corwen LL21 0ST
Map 6: SJ03
Tel: 01490 440264
Fax: 01490 440414
E-mail:
tyddynllanhotel@compuserve.com
Chef: Sean Ballington
Owners: Peter & Bridget Kindred
Cost: Set-price D £25 & £27. ☺
H/wine £14
Times: 12.30-2pm/7-9pm.
Closed L Mon, 2 wks Jan
Additional: Bar food L; Sunday L;
Children welcome
Seats: 65. Private dining room 45
Style: Classic/Country-house
Smoking: No smoking in dining room
Civil licence: 35
Accommodation: 10 en suite ★ ★

A Georgian country house in a green and pleasant setting
(good for walking, fishing and riding). The restaurant is an
elegant panelled room, windows opening on to the verandah
and garden, with well-spaced tables and fine linen and
tableware. Galantines and terrines are favoured starters, the
former represented by roast quail stuffed with foie gras
mousse, the latter by guinea fowl confit layered with foie gras
and wild mushrooms in a cabbage lining with a walnut and dill
vinaigrette drizzled around the plate. Thai-seasoned tuna with
sesame-dressed leaves and tomato chutney makes a simple but
enjoyable main course, or perhaps honey-roast duck breast
with a confit of the leg with braised red cabbage and chestnuts
on an orange and ginger jus, say, or seared fillets of sea bass
and red mullet on a potato and celeriac tian with wild
mushroom ravioli. Glazed lemon tart with lime parfait makes a
bright and refreshing pudding, with perhaps an assiette of
chocolate, including fudge and mousse, for seekers of
indulgence.

Directions: Take B4401 from Corwen to Llandrillo. Restaurant
on R leaving village

LLANGOLLEN,
Bryn Howel Hotel ❀

LL20 7UW
Map 7: SJ24
Tel: 01978 860331
Fax: 01978 860119

Restaurant overlooking well-tended gardens with a backdrop of
breathtaking mountains – an ideal setting for a feast, or for smoked
breast of pheasant placed on plum couscous with chervil or charred
cannon of Welsh lamb.

E-mail: hotel@brynhowel.demon.co.uk
Cost: Alc £27.50. H/wine £13.90
Times: Noon-2pm/7-10pm. Closed L Sat
Additional: Bar food L; Sunday L; Children welcome
Style: Classic/Country-house
Smoking: No smoking in dining room
Civil licence: 300
Accommodation: 36 en suite ★ ★ ★

Directions: Two miles east of Llangollen on A539

RUTHIN,
Ye Olde Anchor ❀

Rhos Street LL15 1DX
Map 6: SJ15
Tel: 01824 702813
Fax: 01824 703050

Telephone for further details

Popular old world dining room with oak beams and wooden tables.
Friendly service and a useful wine list. Menu specialising in steaks
and chicken with a separate fish selection and some specials.

Directions: In Ruthin at junction of A525 & A494

FLINTSHIRE

EWLOE,
De Vere St Davids Park ❀

St Davids Park CH5 3YB
Map 7: SJ36
Tel: 01244 520800
Fax: 01244 520930
Cost: *Alc* £35, set-price L £13.95 &
£19.50 /D £19.50. ☺ H/wine £12.95
Times: Noon-2.30pm/7-10pm
Additional: Sunday L;
Children welcome
Style: Informal/traditional
Smoking: No smoking in dining room;
Air conditioning
Civil licence: 100
Accommodation: 145 en suite
★ ★ ★ ★

Fountain Restaurant in this elegant hotel makes a feature of classic
flavours and the freshest possible ingredients. The Gourmet Menu
might include ballotine of guinea fowl and wild mushroom or
poached fillet of salmon with a light fish nage

Directions: A494 Queensferry to Mold for 4 miles, then B5127
towards Buckley.

HAWARDEN,

The Brasserie ✾

68 The Highway CH5 3DH
Map 7: SJ36
Tel: 01244 536353
Fax: 01244 520888
Cost: *Alc* £21, Set-price L £12.50. ☺
H/wine £9.95
Times: Noon-2pm/6.45-9.15pm.
Closed L Sat
Additional: Sunday L; Children
welcome
Style: Modern/Minimalist
Smoking: No pipes & cigars

*A super little restaurant with fresh, minimalist orange and blue
décor. The food is light and modern with starters such as baked
goats' cheese croûtes and mains including seared fillet of cod on
creamed potatoes.*

Directions: From M56 take A55, through Queensferry, take road
signed Ewloe & Buckley. Turn L, restaurant 1m on R

NORTHOP,

Soughton Hall Hotel ✾✾

CH7 6AB
Map 7: SJ26
Tel: 01352 840811
Fax: 01352 840382
Chef: Paul Wright
Owners: John &
Rosemary Rodenhurst

Former Bishop's Palace, built in 1714 and set in 150 acres of
parkland and beautifully furnished with antiques, tapestries
and baroque marble fireplaces. The atmosphere is welcoming
and unstuffy, and there are two eating options, Stables, in the
old stable block, is a lively, informal setting for dishes like
tagliatelle of confit of duck with chargrilled vegetables and
honey and seseme seed dressing, or breast of chicken stuffed
with spiced sausage and cheese served with a gateau of
Provençal vegetables. For more formal fine dining, modern
British cooking is served in the Reubens Restaurant, with its
candelabra, high ceilings and crystal.

Cost: *Alc* £25. ☺ H/wine 11.95
Times: Noon-3pm(all day Sat)/7-11.30pm
Additional: Bar food(ex for D Fri & Sat); Sunday L; Children 6+
Seats: 120. Private dining room 45
Style: Rustic
Smoking: No smoking in dining room
Civil licence: 60
Accommodation: 14 en suite ★★★

Directions: Off A5119, 1 mile S of Northop

GWYNEDD

ABERDYFI, Penhelig Arms Hotel

LL35 0LT
Map 6: SN69
Tel: 01654 767215
Fax: 01654 767690
E-mail: penheligarms@saqnet.co.uk
Cost: Set-price D £21. ☺ H/wine £10
Times: Noon-2pm/7-9.30pm.
Closed 25 & 26 Dec
Additional: Bar food; Sunday L;
Children welcome
Style: Informal/Modern
Smoking: No smoking in dining room
Accommodation: 10 en suite ★ ★

*All change here, with new decor and lighting creating a
contemporary feel compatible with the 18th-century property.
The set-price menu offers a good choice of modern British dishes.*

Directions: From Machynlleth take A439 coastal route (9 miles)

ABERDYFI,
Plas Penhelig Hotel

*Traditional country house hotel with a beamed ceiling and open fire
in the restaurant. Expect the likes of baked fillet of halibut with
lovage sauce, and coffee meringue ice box pudding.*

LL35 0NA
Map 6: SN69
Tel: 01654 767676
Fax: 01654 767783

Telephone for further details

Directions: From Machynlleth take A493 coastal route (9 miles)

ABERSOCH, Neigwl Hotel ❀

*Privately owned and personally run, this traditional hotel restaurant
commands splendid views over Cardigan bay. The dinner menu
might include fillet of breast of duck served with a ginger and orange
sauce.*

Additional: Children welcome
Style: Traditional/Formal
Accommodation: 9 en suite ★ ★

Lon Sarn Bach Pwllheli
LL53 7DY
Map 6: SH32
Tel: 01758 712363
Fax: 01758 712544
E-mail: neigwl.hotel@which.net
Cost: Set-price D £19.50-£24.50. ☺
H/wine £9
Times: D only, 7-9pm. Closed Jan

Directions: 400 yards through village centre on the L

ABERSOCH, Porth Tocyn Hotel

Overlooking Cardigan bay and the mountains of Snowdonia
the visual feast is equal to the culinary. The dining room
windows are obligingly panoramic whilst the decor sensibly
avoids competing with the view, preferring instead light
simplicity and unpretentious adornment. The cuisine is,
however, far from retiring. The starter menu boasts such
delicacies as quail Balantine stuffed with thyme and apricot
farce over a liquorice sauce with parsnip purée. The main

Bwlch Tocyn Pwllheli LL53 7BU
Map 6: SH32
Tel: 01758 713303
Fax: 01758 713538
E-mail: porthtocyn.hotel@virgin.net
Chefs: Guy Lamble,
Louise Fletcher-Brewer
Owners: The Fletcher-Brewer Family
Cost: Set-price D £23.50 & £30. ☺
H/wine £11

Porth Tocyn Hotel

Times: 12.15-2pm/7.30-9.30pm.
Closed mid Nov-wk before Easter
Additional: Bar food L; Sunday L;
Children 7+ at D
Seats: 50. Jacket and tie preferred
Style: Country-house
Smoking: No smoking in dining room
Accommodation: 17 en suite ★★★

Directions: 2.5 miles beyond village
of Abersoch, through hamlets of Sarn
Bach and Bwlch Tocyn. Follow signs
marked 'Gwesty/Hotel' and 'Remote
Hotel' from Sarn Bach onwards.

course options might include an inventive vegetarian dish of
baked pancake gâteau layered with mushrooms, spinach, beef
tomatoes and brie with a basil beurre blanc. Fish dishes are
well represented with roast salmon and poached delice of
turbot, and meat dishes might include pan fried loin of
venison. Any thoughts of view-gazing are quite forgotten by
the time the luxurious strawberry Queen-of-Puddings arrives.
An extensive wine list completes an experience of sensual
indulgence.

ABERSOCH, White House Hotel ❀

*A bright, spacious restaurant with views of Cardigan Bay, offering
an interesting choice – flash-fried king prawns in tarragon cream
sauce followed by best end of roast Welsh lamb with redcurrant jus.
Finish with Eton Mess or sticky toffee pudding.*

Pwllheli
LL53 7AG
Map 6: SH32
Tel: 01758 713427
Fax: 01758 713512
E-mail:
whitehousehotel@btinternet.com
Cost: *Alc* £25, set-price D £22.50. ☺
H/wine £12
Times: D only, 7-9.30pm.
Closed Xmas wk, 1-21 Feb
Additional: Sunday L (noon-2pm);
Children welcome
Style: Classic/Traditional
Smoking: No smoking in dining room
Accommodation: 13 en suite ★★★

Directions: Hotel on A499
Pwllheli/Abersoch Road, on R (from
Pwllheli)

BALA, Palé Hall ❀❀

This Victorian mansion cannot fail to impress, and the interior
is no disappointment either, with a vaulted hall, elegant
lounges and a high-ceilinged dining room. Tried and tested
gravad lax with dill mayonnaise, or leek and goats' cheese
parcels might be among starters, with cream of onion soup
given a zing with blue cheese pasta, and a duet of melons
marinated in cinnamon, cardamom and honey served with
spicy pear sorbet. Main courses might run from Wellington-
style fillet of local beef, or loin of Welsh lamb in rosemary
sauce with honey-roasted parsnips, to more adventurous
treatments: a star anise-scented sauce for breast of Barbary

Palé Estate Llandderfel LL23 7PS
Map 6: SH93
Tel: 01678 530285
Fax: 01678 530220
E-mail: palehall@fsbdial.co.uk
Chef: Phillip Nahed
Owner: Saul Nahed
Cost: Set-price L £15.95/D £23.95. ☺
H/wine £10.95
Times: Noon-2pm/7-8.30pm
Additional: Sunday L
Seats: 40. Private dining room 20.
Jacket & tie preferred

Palé Hall

Style: Country-house
Smoking: No smoking in dining room
Civil licence: 40
Accommodation: 17 en suite ★★★

duck with pears glazed in red wine, and a pool of saffron cream sauce for bacon-wrapped, garlic-stuffed fillet of monkfish with spicy couscous. Puddings straddle poached pears with vanilla meringue and raspberry coulis, and rich tiramisu or chocolate cappuccino mousse, while the wine list is notable for a Welsh white and a handful from the Lebanon as well as European and New World bottles.

Directions: Just off B4401, 4 miles from Llandrillo

BARMOUTH,
Ty'r Graig Castle Hotel ❀

An unusual late-Victorian country house hotel with stunning views of Cardigan Bay. Try fillet of wood smoked trout to begin, followed perhaps by medallions of Welsh Black beef fillet.

Additional: Sunday L (12.30-2pm); Children welcome
Style: Classic/Country-house
Smoking: No smoking in dining room
Accommodation: 12 en suite ★★

Llanaber Road LL42 1YN
Map 6: SH61
Tel: 01341 280470
Fax: 01341 281260
E-mail: tyrgraig.castle@btinternet.com
Cost: Alc £20. ☺ H/wine £7.80
Times: 12.30-2pm/7-9pm.
Closed D Sun, Jan

Directions: On coast road 0.75 miles towards Harlech

BONTDDU, Bontddu Hall Hotel ❀❀

Superbly located overlooking the beautiful Mawddach Estuary, this 19th-century house was once the country retreat of the

Dolgellau LL40 2UF
Map 6: SH61
Tel: 01341 430661
Fax: 01341 430284
E-mail:
reservations@bontdduhall.fsnet.co.uk
Chef: David Murphy
Owners: Margaretta & Michael Ball
Cost: Alc £15, set-price D £25. ☺
H/wine £14
Times: Noon-2pm/7-9.30pm.
Closed Nov-Mar
Additional: Bar food; Sunday L;
Children 2+
Seats: 60. Private room 20. Jacket and tie preferred
Style: Country-house
Smoking: No smoking in dining room
Civil licence: 150
Accommodation: 20 en suite ★★★

Lord Mayor of Birmingham. Thankfully you don't need a grand title or an elected public position nowadays in order to enjoy the fine views from the restaurant, or indeed the traditional British cooking with classical French overtones for which Bontddu Hall is renowned. Chef David Murphy's daily-changing dinner menu offers a formal choice, and there's a lighter brasserie-style lunch menu. From the former the options might cover chicken liver parfait with an apple and pear chutney, and smoked salmon and spinach roulade with a herb mayonnaise. For the main course, loin of Meironnydd mountain lamb on a herb mash with a redcurrant and rosemary sauce might sit alongside tower of pork medallions with honeyed apples and melted Stilton on an orange port wine jus. There's a wide choice of home-made ice creams and sorbets for dessert, or for those who must have their puddings hot, a classic bread-and-butter pudding with an English custard. Cheese can be taken as an extra course for a supplement.

Directions: From A470 1 mile N Dolgellau take A496 to Barmouth, then 4 miles to Bontddu. Hotel on R on entering village

CAERNARFON,
Seiont Manor Hotel 🏵

The tranquillity of the Welsh countryside envelopes the converted barn buildings of this professionally run hotel and restaurant. A la carte options might include strips of chicken flavoured with Thai spices, lemongrass and lime.

Civil licence: 100
Accommodation: 28 en suite ★ ★ ★

Directions: From Bangor follow signs for Caernarfon. Leave Caernarfon on A4086. The hotel is 3 miles on L

Llanrug LL55 2AQ
Map 6: SH46
Tel: 01286 673366
Fax: 01286 872840
Cost: *Alc* £30, set-price L £13.50/ D £23.50. ☺ H/wine £10
Times: 12.30-2pm/7-10pm
Additional: Bar food; Sunday L; Children welcome
Style: Traditional/Country-house
Smoking: No smoking in dining room

CAERNARFON,
T'yn Rhos Country Hotel 🏵🏵

Developed from the original farmstead, the bright airy restaurant enjoys views over the garden and rolling countryside. There is a gravitas to the cuisine despite the relaxed, informal atmosphere of the place and the set menu and *carte* options give full reign to head chef Carys Davies' culinary prowess. On a recent visit the set menu offered a starter of home cured gravad lax of salmon with a rosette of guacamole, and a main of braised beef cooked in Guinness on

Llanddeiniolen LL55 3AE
Map 6: SH56
Tel: 01248 670489
Fax: 01248 670079
E-mail: enquiries@tynrhos.co.uk
Chefs: Carys Davies, Ian Cashen
Owners: D N & L Kettle
Cost: Set-price L £12.95/D £19.50. ☺ H/wine £9.95
Times: Noon-2pm/7-9pm. Closed D Sun, 23-30 Dec
Additional: Children 6+
Seats: 35. Private dining room 15
Style: Informal/Traditional
Smoking: No smoking in dining room
Accommodation: 14 en suite ★ ★

bubble and squeak coated with a vegetable broth. Desserts may be selected from the *carte*, which might include pear clafoutis tart. The wine list is very extensive and includes useful notes for the non-expert.

Directions: In hamlet of Seion between B4366 & B4547

DOLGELLAU, Dolserau Hall Hotel

The restaurant is in a Victorian conservatory with magnificent views across the Wnion Valley. Traditional British dishes include honey roast ham, poached salmon, and roast seasoned duckling.

Additional: Children 6+
Style: Traditional/Country-house
Smoking: No smoking in dining room
Accommodation: 15 en suite ★ ★ ★

Directions: Situated 1.5 miles from Dolgellau on lane between A470 to Dinas Mawddwy and A494 to Bala

LL40 2AG
Map 6: SH71
Tel: 01341 422522
Fax: 01341 422400
E-mail: aa@dolserau.co.uk
Cost: Set-price D £21.95. ☺
H/wine £8.75
Times: D only, 7-8.30pm.
Closed Nov-mid Feb

DOLGELLAU, Penmaenuchaf Hall ❀❀

Penmaenpool LL40 1YB
Map 6: SH71
Tel: 01341 422129
Fax: 01341 422787
E-mail: eat@penhall.co.uk
Chef: Laurence Rissel
Owners: Mark Watson,
Lorraine Fielding
Cost: *Alc* £35, set-price L £17.50/
D £29.50. H/wine £11
Times: Noon-2pm/7-9.30pm
Additional: Sunday L; Children 6+
Seats: 50. Private dining room 20
Style: Country-house
Smoking: No smoking in dining room
Civil licence: 50
Accommodation: 14 en suite ★ ★ ★

Built in 1860 for a Bolton cotton magnate, whose crest is still above the main entrance, Penmaenuchaf is a substantial country house amid 20 acres of terraced gardens and woodlands with lovely views of the Mawddach Estuary and mountains. An air of comfortable luxury hangs about the place, with its elegantly decorated and smartly furnished rooms. The panelled dining rooms are a showcase for some of Wales's best produce: crab from Cardigan Bay, St David's duckling, Welsh Black beef and venison from the west coast; herbs and vegetables come from the kitchen garden too. But the style is far from limited, with crab going into a cake with polenta and accompanied by a Parmesan tuile and chive beurre blanc for a starter, and a main course, for example, of roast rack of mountain lamb with a rosemary and port jus, dauphinoise potatoes, roast garlic and celeriac purée. Vegetarians are well looked after, and apart from Welsh farmhouse cheeses the pudding list takes in apple and rhubarb charlotte with prune and honey custard as well as dark chocolate fondant with white chocolate sauce.

Directions: From A470, take A493 (Tywyn/Fairbourne), entrance 1.5 miles on L by sign for Penmaenpool

DOLGELLAU,
Plas Dolmelynllyn ❀

Mahogany panelled dining room in a 16th-century manor house. An Arcadian mountainside setting complements the sumptuous dining options such as beef braised in stout with tangerines and a parsnip and watercress mash.

Additional: Bar food L; Children 8+
Style: Traditional/Country-house
Smoking: No smoking in dining room
Accommodation: 10 en suite ★ ★ ★

Directions: Village centre on A470, 4 miles N of Dolgellau

Ganllwyd LL40 2HP
Map 6: SH71
Tel: 01341 440273
Fax: 01341 440640
E-mail: info@dolly-hotel.co.uk
Cost: Set-price D £24.50. ☺
H/wine £10.25
Times: D only, 7-8.30pm.
Closed 1 Nov-Feb 28

HARLECH,
Castle Cottage ❀

Cosy cottage style restaurant with low beamed ceilings and a genuine sense of antiquity. The choice is not particularly expansive but it changes every week, is always carefully prepared and features local produce whenever possible.

Additional: Children welcome
Style: Traditional/Country-house
Smoking: No smoking in dining room
Accommodation: 6 rooms (4 en suite)

Directions: Just off High Street (B4573) 100yds from Harlech Castle

Pen Llech LL46 2YL
Map 6: SH53
Tel/Fax: 01766 780479
Cost: Set-price D £23. ☺
H/wine £10.50
Times: D only, 7-9.30pm.
Closed 3 wks Feb

LLANBERIS,
Y Bistro ❀

Regularly changing menu, in Welsh with English translations, featuring local produce. Quail stuffed with prunes and apricots and garnished with pigeon breast followed a prawn risotto with dressed leaves.

Additional: Children welcome
Smoking: No smoking in dining room; Jacket & tie preferred

Directions: In the centre of the village at the foot of Mount Snowdon by Lake Padarn

43-45 Stryd Fawr (High Street)
LL55 4EU
Map 6: SH56
Tel/Fax: 01286 871278
E-mail: ybistro@fsbdial.co.uk
Cost: Set-price D £23. ☺
H/wine £9.50
Times: D only, 7-midnight.
Closed Sun ex Bhs

PORTMEIRION,
Hotel Portmeirion ❀❀

Nestling under the wooded slopes of the famous village, the Portmeirion has a fine view over the sandy Traeth Bach estuary. Menus are in Welsh, with English translations, although, apart from ingredients, the style seems closer to the Italianate surroundings than to the heart of Wales. A light laverbread pesto gives a Welsh twist to a warm salad of goats' cheese and asparagus, while other starters show a fondness for

Penrhyndeudraeth
LL48 6ET
Map 6: SH53
Tel: 01766 770000
Fax: 01766 771331
E-mail: hotel@portmeirion-wales.com
Chefs: Billy Taylor, Colin Pritchard
Additional: Sunday L; Children welcome

Hotel Portmeirion

Seats: 100. Private dining room 30
Style: Classic, country-house
Smoking: No smoking in dining room
Civil licence: 100
Accommodation: 40 en suite ★ ★ ★

matching fruit and meat: mango with smoked chicken and Parma ham in a mustard seed dressing, say, or green figs in a tian of smoked duck with avocado and cherry tomatoes. Fine local supplies show to good effect in main courses of perhaps baked salmon dressed with pesto and tomatoes on a bed of provençale vegetables, and fillet of Pen Llyn beef with a casserole of pulses and smoked bacon. Fruit surfaces again at pudding stage, among them plum and almond tart, or sponge steeped in strawberry syrup with Chantilly cream, strawberries and raspberry coulis, although chocoholics might find soft chocolate torte more to their liking. A Welsh white pops up among the house wines on the long, well-chosen wine list, which has a useful page of bottles at less than £15.

Directions: Off A487 at Minffordd

PWLLHELI,

Plas Bodegroes ❀❀❀

An impressive avenue of mature beech trees frames the colourful gardens. Inside the fine Georgian house, a small but comfortable drawing room leads into a surprisingly light and airy contemporary style dining room with polished light wood flooring, all-white napery and porcelain, pale green painted walls and woodwork. Clean and uncluttered, the look avoids being clinical by the clever, subtle use of halogen lighting and interesting local artwork. The menu brackets starters and main courses by price, and features much local produce. To start with, there may be a top-rate ballotine of guinea fowl studded with pistachios and prunes or a warm salad of monkfish, Carmarthen ham and mushrooms. Chris Chown has some imaginative ideas – pigeon, foie gras and almond pastilla brings a touch of North Africa to North Wales. He also has the confidence in the quality of his ingredients to present dishes with admirable simplicity – whole local brill grilled with sea salt and lemon butter, or shoulder of lamb braised with pea and mint purée. Baked monkfish in a softish, salty herb crust with smoked prawn sauce, however, lacked distinction. Desserts might include cinnamon biscuit of rhubarb and apple with elderflower custard. The wine list is extensive and well put together, with plenty of halves.

Directions: On A497, 2 miles NW of Pwllheli

Nefyn Road LL53 5TH
Map 6: SH33
Tel: 01758 612363
Fax: 01758 701247
E-mail: gunna@bodegroes.co.uk
Chef: Chris Chown
Owners: Chris & Gunna Chown
Cost: Alc £26. H/wine £12
Times: D only, 7-9pm. Closed Mon, Dec-Feb
Additional: Sunday L (noon-2pm); Children welcome; Vegetarian dishes not always available
Seats: 40. Private dining room 16
Style: Modern/Welsh
Smoking: No smoking in dining room
Accommodation: 10 en suite ★ ★

TALSARNAU,

Hotel Maes Y Neuadd

The light and airy dining room overlooks the gardens to the mountains and sea beyond. The dinner menu is lengthy, in terms of courses rather than choices (dinner is priced per number of courses taken), and uses local produce wherever possible. There is excellent local lamb (lowland, mountain or salt marsh according to season), Welsh Black beef and seafood, some caught especially for the hotel by a local fisherman. Sushi canapés are made from salmon smoked locally. A tuna tartare with pickled cucumber made a storming start to our inspection dinner, followed by a teacup of mushroom consommé topped with a cheese soufflé. Cockle and laverbread stew in a rich broth was a fine combination, although the cockles were a touch gritty. Trio of mountain lamb, in this case noisettes, smoked kidney and sausage was also impressive. Vegetables that complement each of the three main courses come from the hotel's own walled kitchen gardens, currently awaiting organic certification (the gardeners are properly credited on the menu). The Grande Finale lives up to its name with Welsh cheeses plus a dessert such as chocolate and satsuma mille-feuille plus glazed seasonal fruits, plus home-made ice creams and sorbets. The wine list impresses in range and quality, with a fair selection of halves and daily recommendations to match the daily changing menu.

Civil licence: 65 **Accommodation:** 16 en suite ★ ★

Directions: Off B4573 between Talsarnau & Harlech (sign on corner of unclassified road)

Harlech LL47 6YA
Map 6: SH63
Tel: 01766 780200
Fax: 01766 780211
E-mail: maes@neuadd.com
Chef: Peter Jackson
Owners: Mr & Mrs Slatter,
Mr & Mrs Jackson
Cost: Set-price L £9.50-£13.75/
D £27-£34. H/wine £9.85
Times: Noon-1.45pm/7-9pm
Additional: Bar food L; Sunday L;
Children 8+ at D
Seats: 50. Private dining room 12
Style: Country-house
Smoking: No smoking in dining room

AA Wine Award-see page 18
Shortlisted for

MONMOUTHSHIRE

ABERGAVENNY,

Llansantffraed Court Hotel

Llanvihangel Gobion NP7 9BA
Map 3: SO21
Tel: 01873 840678
Fax: 01873 840674
E-mail: reception@llch.co.uk

Telephone for further details

Directions: From Abergavenny take B4598 signposted Usk towards Raglan. After 3.5 miles, white gates on L are hotel entrance.

Impressive red brick mansion with a small lake and fountain in the grounds. Starters might include mille-feuille of red mullet and tiger prawns with warm basil oil. Highlights among the main courses are seared monkfish and Gower Peninsula scallops served in a mussel and saffron broth, or roast saddle of rabbit with pistachio stuffing and parsnip mash. Desserts might include glazed lemon tart with gin and tonic sorbet or chilled soufflé flavoured with cointreau.

ABERGAVENNY,

Llanwenarth Arms Hotel ❀

With the Usk Valley in the background and the River Usk in the fore, the food must share the billing with a visual feast – fortunately our succulent steak and kidney pie was easily up to the task.

Smoking: No pipes & cigars; Air conditioning
Accommodation: 18 en suite ★★

Directions: On A40 midway between Abergavenny and Crickhowell

Brecon Road NP8 1EP
Map 3: SO21
Tel: 01873 810550
Fax: 01873 811880
Cost: Alc £20. ☺ H/wine £6
Times: Noon-2pm/7-11pm
Additional: Bar food; Sunday L;
Children welcome
Style: Informal/Rustic

ABERGAVENNY,

Walnut Tree Inn ❀❀❀

The Walnut Tree remains a gastronomic landmark. Franco Taruschio's Italian-Welsh cooking is dynamic, inventive and inspirational; the fact he manages to handle a menu that is as extensive as it is without falter makes the place even more awesome. The seasons are properly celebrated – a main course of roast cod with potato rösti, caponata and pine nuts was an appropriate taste of pure summer flavours. There is splendid home-made pasta in the form, perhaps, of ever-popular lasagne Bolognese or vincisgrassi Maceratese, an 18th-century recipe for pasta with porcini mushrooms, truffles and Parma ham. Pure Italian dishes include bresaola cured to Taruschio's own recipe, brodetto Adriatico and potato gnocchi with pesto and broad beans, but many dishes simply marry local produce with Mediterranean style: abbacchio (young Welsh lamb) with roast potatoes; roast monkfish, scallops, prawns and laverbread sauce; salmon with barba di frati and rhubarb sauce. Desserts include a lovely range of home-made ice-creams in flavours such as praline and Gianduia, as well as old favourites such as rum baba with strawberries and crème Chantilly and chocolate brandy loaf with coffee bean sauce. Weather permitting, food is also served alfresco.

Llandewi Skirrid NP7 8AW
Map 3: SO31
Tel: 01873 852797
Chef: Franco Taruschio
Owners: Franco & Ann Taruschio
Times: Noon-3pm/ 7-10.15pm.
Closed Sun, Mon,1 wk Xmas, 2 wks
Feb (please telephone to check times)
Additional: Bar food;
Children welcome
Seats: 42
Style: Informal
Credit cards: None

Directions: Three miles NE of Abergavenny on B4521

CHEPSTOW,

Marriot St Pierre Hotel ❀

The Orangery is a circular restaurant attached to a 14th-century manor house. Expect the likes of smoked haddock mousseline, and loin of pork with apples, chestnuts, roasted shallots and thyme.

Style: Bistro-style/Traditional
Smoking: No smoking in dining room; Air conditioning
Accommodation: 148 en suite ★★★★

Directions: From M48 J2 follow A466 towards Chepstow. Take 3rd exit at 1st roundabout, and at next take A48 signposted to Caerwent. Hotel 2 miles on L

St Pierre Park NP6 6YA
Map 3: ST59
Tel: 01291 625261
Fax: 01291 629975
Cost: Alc £25. ☺ H/wine £10.95
Times: D only
Additional: Sunday L;
Children welcome

CHEPSTOW,

Wye Knot Restaurant ❀❀

The Back NP6 5HH
Map 3: ST59
Tel: 01291 622929
Chef: Kevin Brookes
Owners: Kevin Brookes &
Lisa Mansfield
Cost: *Alc* £30, set-price L £12.95/
D £14.95. ☺ H/wine £10.95
Times: 12.30-2pm/7-10pm.
Closed L Sat, D Sun, all Mon
Additional: Sunday L;
Children welcome
Seats: 35
Style: Informal/Traditional
Smoking: No smoking in dining room

A simple little restaurant utterly devoid of fancy – or fanciful – touches and not overpriced considering the quality of the food. It is not easy to find, being rather tucked away, but the local foodies have discovered it and its reputation is growing. Speciality breads are baked on the premises every day, and might include tarragon and seed mustard, sun-dried tomato and pesto, olive and onion or granary with walnuts and sultana. Leave room for the likes of Thai crab cakes with sautéed sea scallops on a sweet chilli sauce, or maybe a half crayfish thermidor. The main choices could include pork tenderloin served on a creamy mash, black pudding and smoked bacon with honey and wholegrain mustard sauce, or perhaps fillet of Welsh lamb wrapped in Parma ham with a chicken, tomato, black olive, basil and pepper mousseline. The regularly-changing blackboard menus list half a dozen or so puddings: prune and apple sticky pudding with Armagnac ice cream, or warm chocolate tart studded with sun-dried cherries, served with Amaretto and pistachio ice cream and cherry sauce.

Directions: From M4 take M48, then onto Chepstow, following signs for Chepstow Castle & Riverbank

TINTERN,

Parva Farmhouse Hotel ❀

Chepstow NP16 6SQ
Map 3: SO50
Tel: 01291 689411
Fax: 01291 689557

A 17th-century former farmhouse with a beamed restaurant and 14-foot inglenook fireplace. A varied choice at dinner might include baked salmon in a light vermouth sauce, or Burgundy beef pie.

Cost: Set-price D £19.50. ☺ H/wine £9.50
Times: D only, 7-8.30pm
Additional: Children welcome
Style: Informal/Traditional
Smoking: No smoking in dining room
Accommodation: 9 en suite ★ ★

Directions: North end of Tintern on A466 alongside the Wye, 0.75 mile from the Abbey

TINTERN, Royal George Hotel ✸

Delightful hotel restaurant with an intimate cottagey feel created by oak beams that date from the sixteenth century. Roast rack of Welsh lamb and steamed fillet of monkfish are both typical offerings of the varied menu.

Style: Chic/Country-house **Smoking:** No smoking in dining room
Accommodation: 16 en suite ★ ★

Directions: On A466 between Chepstow & Monmouth, 10 minutes drive from M4 J22

Chepstow NP16 6ST
Map 3: SO50
Tel: 01291 689205
Fax: 01291 689448
E-mail: royalgeorgetintern@hotmail.com
Cost: Alc £16.70, set-price L £9.75/ D £22. ☺ H/wine £9
Times: Noon-2pm/7-9.30pm
Additional: Bar food; Sunday L; Children welcome

USK, Bush House of Usk ✸

A bistro atmosphere is pleasantly achieved through red and green decor, Lautrec prints and terracotta pots in this intimate little restaurant. Look out for the individual steak and ale pie and 'simply delicious' Thai fish cakes.

Additional: Sunday L; Children welcome
Style: Bistro-style/Informal
Smoking: No-smoking area; No pipes & cigars

Directions: Follow the Usk exit from A449. Restaurant in centre of town

15 Bridge Street NP5 1BQ
Map 3: SO30
Tel: 01291 672929
Fax: 01291 671215
Cost: Alc £22, set-price D £12.95. ☺ H/wine £9.95
Times: Noon-2pm/7-9pm.
Closed D Sun, L Mon & Tue,
1 or 2 wks end Jan

USK, Three Salmons Hotel ✸

Ostlers is the restaurant in this former coaching inn. Choose from parfait of duck livers, rosette of Welsh lamb, tartlet of roasted leeks, cannelloni of spinach and wild mushrooms, perhaps ending with warm pear Tatin for dessert.

Directions: M4 J24, A449 N, first L A472 to Usk. Hotel in centre of village

Bridge Street NP15 1RY
Map 3: SO30
Tel: 01291 672133
Fax: 01291 673979
E-mail: restaurant@threesalmons.com
www.worldwide.co.uk/3salmons/

Telephone for further details

WHITEBROOK,
Crown at Whitebrook ✸✸

The mock Tudor of the building sits comfortably with the French-influenced but essentially modern British cookery at this friendly restaurant. The hotel cuisine makes excellent use of quality local ingredients in a seasonal set-price menu, and the food is complemented by a well-chosen wine list. A recently enjoyed starter was a well-made and tasty tart of fresh wild mushrooms, Parmesan and mixed leaves, and this was followed by fillet of pork with a herb stuffing and mustard sauce, a tender and evenly flavoured dish. Pear poached in a red wine syrup and served with a vanilla crème fraîche was a subtle but tasty dessert. At lunchtime a short menu offers light snacks such as moules marinière, and salmon and leek fish cake with a mussel and cream sauce, while heartier set-price choices might be roast rack of lamb with a thyme crust, or chargrilled fillet of beef with a mustard sauce. Dinner offers similar dishes, plus perhaps roast loin of rabbit, or oven-baked pork tenderloins.

Directions: Turn W off A66 immediately S of bigsweir Bridge (5m from Monmouth), 2m on unclassified road

Monmouth NP25 4TX
Map 3: SO50
Tel: 01600 860254
Fax: 01600 860607
E-mail: crown@whitebrook.demon.co.uk
Chef: Mark Turton
Owners: Angela & Elizabeth Barbara
Cost: Set-price L £15.95/D £27.95. H/wine £9.95
Times: Noon-2pm/7-9pm. Closed L Mon, 1st 2 wks Jan, 1st 2 wks Aug
Additional: Sunday L; Children 8+
Seats: 32. Private dining room 12
Style: Rustic/Country-house
Smoking: No smoking in dining room
Accommodation: 12 en suite ★ ★

NEWPORT

NEWPORT, Celtic Manor Resort

In terms of scale and facilities, this golfing and conference hotel has few peers. Executive dining takes place at Owens, situated in a boldly stylish conservatory decorated with unique pieces of Celtic artwork. The cooking could be described as Celtic fusion. Welsh ingredients are commendably to the fore – New Quay mackerel served on vegetable noodles with soy and sesame dressing; Cardigan Bay lobster in a salad with mango, sugar snaps, chicory, quail eggs and basil dressing; flame-grilled wood pigeon from Monmouthshire on mushy peas, thyme-scented potato scone, foie gras and natural jus with pearl barley. 'Pastai Meithior' is a pie made from shank of young Welsh mountain lamb with vegetables and fresh herbs. Abergavenny red summer pudding with Snowdonia elderflower sorbet makes a flag-waving finale.

Directions: On A48 just off M4 J24 towards Newport

Coldra Woods NP18 1HQ
Map 3: ST38
Tel: 01633 413000
Fax: 01633 412910
E-mail: postbox@celtic-manor.com
Chef: Peter Fuchs
Cost: *Alc* £35, set-price D £27.50. ☺
H/wine £11.75
Times: D only, fr 7pm.
Closed D Sun & Mon
Additional: Children welcome
Seats: 54
Style: Chic/Modern
Smoking: No-smoking area; No pipes & cigars; Air conditioning
Civil licence: 800
Accommodation: 400 en suite
★ ★ ★ ★ ★

NEWPORT, Junction 28

Relaxed stylish brasserie in convenient location serving modern British cuisine. Try following the Thai red monkfish curry and fine noodles with deep-fried choux pastry with hot fudge, toasted almonds and vanilla ice cream.

Smoking: Air conditioning

Directions: M4 J28, follow signs Risca Brymawr, then L in 0.5m signed Caerphilly. R at mini-roundabout, then 1st L beyond St Basil's church.

Station Approach Bassaleg NP1 9LD
Map 3: ST38
Tel: 01633 891891
Fax: 01633 895978
Cost: *Alc* £25, set-price L £6.95-£11.95/D £11.95.☺ H/wine £9.95
Times: Noon-2pm(4pm Sun)/5.30-9.30pm. Closed D Sun, last wk Jul-1st wk Aug
Additional: Sunday L; Children welcome

PEMBROKESHIRE

FISHGUARD,
Tregynon Country Restaurant

Gwaun Valley SA65 9TU
Map 2: SM93
Tel: 01239 820531
Fax: 01239 820808
E-mail: tregynon@online-holidays.net
Cost: *Alc* £23.50, set-price D £23.50.
H/wine £11.45
Times: D only 7.30-8.30pm (prior bookings only)(Days open may vary)
Additional: Children 8+
Style: Traditional/Country-house
Smoking: No smoking in dining room

Directions: Take B4313 towards Fishguard. Take 1st R and 1st R again and follow signs

A warm welcome and accomplished cuisine such as home-smoked gammon await at this charming 16th-century farmhouse hotel and restaurant, hidden away in the beautiful Gwaun Valley.

HAVERFORDWEST,
Wolfscastle Country Hotel ✤

Wolf's Castle SA62 5LZ
Map 2: SM92
Tel: 01437 741225/741688
Fax: 01437 741383
E-mail: andy741225@aol.com
Cost: *Alc* £19.75. ☺ H/wine £7.25
Times: Noon-2pm/6.45-9pm.
Closed D Sun, 24-26 Dec
Additional: Bar food; Sunday L;
Children welcome
Style: Traditional/Country-house
Smoking: No smoking in dining room
Civil licence: 60
Accommodation: 20 en suite ★ ★

Charmingly set in a stone-built Victorian vicarage, this tastefully decorated restaurant makes a big feature of local produce and unpretentious, careful composition. A braised shoulder of lamb with an apricot stuffing was particularly flavoursome.

Directions: From Haverfordwest take A40 towards Fishguard. Hotel in centre of Wolf's Castle

PEMBROKE, Court Hotel ✤

Lamphey SA71 5NT
Map 2: SM90
Tel: 01646 672273
Fax: 01646 672480
E-mail:
enquiries@lampheycourt.co.uk
Cost: *Alc* £20. ☺ H/wine £9.95
Times: 12.30-1.45pm/7-9.30pm
Additional: Bar food; Sunday L;
Children welcome
Style: Country-house
Smoking: No smoking in dining room;
Air conditioning
Accommodation: 37 en suite ★ ★ ★

Directions: Hotel signed in Lamphey

The formal Georgian restaurant or the light and airy conservatory are both ideal settings for classic cuisine along the lines of noisettes of Welsh lamb set on a bed of sautéed leeks with a Dijon mustard sauce.

PEMBROKE, Left Bank ✤ NEW

The name of this French-influenced restaurant is a reference to the building's previous incarnation as a high street bank. The decor is modish and metropolitan and matched by bright, punchy cooking such as mussel and saffron stew with herb dumplings.

Additional: Children welcome
Style: Informal/Modern **Smoking:** No-smoking area

Directions: Telephone for directions

63 Main Street SA71 4DA
Map 2: SM90
Tel: 01646 622333
Cost: *Alc* £28, set-price D £19.50 & £24.50. H/wine £8.90
Times: Noon-2.30pm/7-9.30pm.
Closed Sun, Mon, 2-3 wks after Xmas

ST DAVID'S, Morgan's Brasserie

In a side street close to the magnificent cathedral, Morgan's provides a relaxed environment, with colourful artwork suspended from exposed stone walls, wooden-backed chairs and clothed tables. The menu runs to duck confit with Cumberland sauce, followed by local fillet steak in red wine sauce, but fish and shellfish, as fresh as they get and accurately cooked, are the mainstays. Moules marinière, the sauce so good 'you had to go at it with a spoon', or a simple crab salad with avocado dressing might start things going. Laverbread and cockle sauce brings a proudly Welsh approach to fillet of sea bass, and there might also be paupiettes of lemon sole stuffed with prawns served on crab sauce, or pan-seared scallops on bouillabaisse sauce. Cheeses are Welsh, and puddings trot the globe in the shape of Celtic crunch ice cream, berry crème brûlée, and Dom Pedro (ice cream blended with Tia Maria and whisky).

Directions: 60yds off Cross Square

20 Nun Street SA62 6NT
Map 2: SM72
Tel/Fax: 01437 720508
E-mail: ceri@morgbras.freeserve.co.uk
Chef: Ceri Morgan
Owners: Mr Ceri &
Mrs Elaine Morgan
Cost: *Alc* £23. ☺ H/wine £10.50
Times: D only, 7-9pm. Closed Sun,
Jan-Feb, (check opening times out of season)
Additional: Children welcome
Seats: 32
Style: Classic/Informal
Smoking: No smoking in dining room

ST DAVID'S, St Non's Hotel ❀

Spacious restaurant offering a carte *of modern dishes, perhaps scallops and tiger tail prawns with black bean sauce on a bed of egg noodles, and Welsh lamb cutlets with redcurrant sauce.*

Additional: Bar food; Children 1+
Style: Bistro-style/Informal
Smoking: No smoking in dining room
Accommodation: 20 en suite ★★

Directions: Close to Cathedral and St Non's Retreat

Catherine Street SA62 6RJ
Map 2: SM72
Tel: 01437 720239
Fax: 01437 721839
E-mail: st.nons@enterprise.net
Cost: *Alc* £18, set-price L fr £3.95. ☺
H/wine £10.50
Times: Noon-2pm/7-9pm.
Closed Nov & Dec

ST DAVID'S,
Warpool Court Hotel

Originally a 19th-century cathedral choir school, Warpool Court's commanding location above St Bride's Bay, fine views, and peace and tranquillity offer contemporary visitors much to sing about. The original house interior boasts thousands of hand-painted antique tiles, while the spacious dining room overlooks the attractive lawned gardens toward the ocean. The modish menu, based around fresh ingredients, innovative combinations and presentation, also draws on the fruits of the sea. This rolls out as smoked haddock and leek tart glazed with Welsh rarebit, or perhaps monkfish mousse on a mussel and saffron sauce with deep-fried leek to start. On a spring menu our inspector chose roast salmon set on a Parmesan and truffle oil risotto with glazed vegetables and followed by a vanilla crème brûlée served with warm shortbread biscuits. Meat dishes might include best end of lamb with wild mushrooms, rosemary braised potato and carrot cake, while a kumquat mousse with poached kumquats in syrup offer a light finish. Service was judged friendly, attentive and professional, while the wine list is well conceived with some excellent growers and vintages.

Directions: From Cross Square, left by Midland Bank into Goat St, at fork follow hotel signs.

SA62 6BN
Map 2: SM72
Tel: 01437 720300
Fax: 01437 720676
E-mail: warpool@enterprise.net
Chef: John Daniels
Owner: Peter Trier
Cost: Set-price L £19.50/D £37. ☺
H/wine £12.50
Times: Noon-2pm/7-9.15pm.
Closed Jan
Additional: Bar food; Sunday L;
Children 1+
Seats: 50
Style: Traditional/Country-house
Smoking: No smoking in dining room
Civil licence: 100
Accommodation: 25 en suite ★★★

TENBY,
Panorama Hotel ❀

The Esplanade SA70 7DU
Map 2: SN10
Tel/Fax: 01834 844976
E-mail:
robin@panoramahotel.force9.co.uk
Cost: *Alc* £25, set-price D £19.95. ☺
H/wine £9.25
Times: D only, 7-9pm

Personally run hotel that's been carved out of a Victorian terrace overlooking South Beach and Caldy Island. The strong level of commitment extends to the food – one of the main strengths here. Fish features, but there's also Welsh lamb and beef.

Additional: Sunday L (noon-2pm); Children 5+
Style: Classic/traditional
Smoking: No smoking in dining room
Accommodation: 7 en suite ★ ★

Directions: From A478 follow South Beach & town centre signs, sharp L at mini-rnbt, under railway and up Greenhill Rd. Go along South Pde to Esplanade.

TENBY, Penally Abbey Hotel ❀

SA70 7PY
Map 2: SN10
Tel: 01834 843033
Fax: 01834 844714
E-mail: penally.abbey@btinternet.com
Cost: *Alc* £28, set-price L £18/D £28.
H/wine £12.95
Times: 12.30-2.30pm/7.30-9.30pm

No shortage of charm and character here, with Gothic windows framing views over wooded gardens (complete with ruined chapel) out towards the sea. Large greenlip mussels proved an ideal introduction to an excellent Welsh lamb fillet.

Additional: Sunday L; Children 7+
Style: Country-house
Smoking: No smoking in dining room
Civil licence: 45
Accommodation: 12 en suite ★ ★ ★

Directions: From Tenby take A4139 to Penally

POWYS

BRECON, The Best Western Castle of Brecon ❀

Castle Square LD3 9DB
Map 3: SO02
Tel: 01874 624611
Fax: 01874 623737
E-mail: hotel@breconcastle.co.uk
Cost: *Alc* £20, set-price L £10/
D £22.90 . ☺ H/wine £8.40
Times: D only, 7-9pm. Closed Xmas.

Early 19th-century coaching inn offering impressive Usk Valley views and historical ruins (Brecon Castle). The large restaurant brings homely, robust fare such as own-made tomato soup, and peppered local beef.

Additional: Sunday L (noon-2pm); Children welcome
Style: Classic/rustic
Smoking: No smoking in dining room
Civil licence: 40
Accommodation: 42 en suite ★ ★

Directions: Follow signs to town centre. Turn opposite Boars Head towards Cradog Golf Club, turn right after 200yds in Castle Square

BUILTH WELLS,
Caer Beris Manor Hotel ❁

LD2 3NP
Map 3: SO05
Tel: 01982 552601
Fax: 01982 552586
E-mail:
caerberismanor@btinternet.com
Cost: Set-price D £25. ☺
H/wine £9.95
Times: Noon-2.30pm/7.30-9.30pm

Former home of Lord Swansea set in 27 acres, with a panelled 16th-century restaurant. Greenland prawns, seared fillet of Welsh Black beef, and apple pie made a fine meal.

Additional: Bar food; Sunday L; Children welcome
Style: Country-house
Smoking: No smoking in dining room
Civil licence: 100
Accommodation: 23 en suite ★ ★ ★

Directions: Off A483 on W side of town

CRICKHOWELL, Bear Hotel ❁❁

NP8 1BW
Map 3: SO21
Tel: 01873 810408
Fax: 01873 811696
E-mail: bearhotel@aol.com
Chef: Denver Dodwell
Owners: Judy Hindmarsh &
Stephen Hindmarsh
Cost: *Alc* £25. ☺ H/wine £8.95
Times: (L by request), D only, 7-midnight. Closed Sun, 25 Dec
Additional: Bar food; Children 6+
Seats: 70. Private dining room 60
Style: Bistro-style/Informal
Accommodation: 35 en suite ★ ★ ★

A charming restaurant, or rather two as the dining operation is divided: one room is heavily beamed with stone walls and flagged floor, while the other is candle-lit, romantic and intimate. The same quality produce and skilled cooking goes into the food served in both, however, and modern trends are followed to very good effect. Potted duck scented with orange and thyme and served with a pear and date chutney and toasted brioche is a typical starter, or you might try fresh tuna loin rolled in soy, mustard and herbs and thinly sliced with a little Japanese dressing. The *carte* continues with the likes of lightly roasted loin of Welsh lamb sliced onto ratatouille, served with a little faggot of liver, kidney and mushroom and a madeira jus, or perhaps loin of locally farmed venison, roasted pink and sliced onto roast parsnips and chestnut risotto with sautéed spinach and a cranberry sauce. The desserts show the same concentration of ingredients: vanilla cream of bread-and-butter pudding with bananas and rum is one such winner.

Directions: Town centre off A40

CRICKHOWELL, Gliffaes Hotel ❁❁

NP8 1RH
Map 3: SO21
Tel: 01874 730371
Fax: 01874 730463
E-mail: calls@gliffaeshotel.com
Chef: Justin Howe

Built in Italianate style as a private residence in 1884, Gliffaes stands in 33 acres of gardens and parkland. Oak panelling, open fires and comfortable, period furnishings all help define the country-house character of the place, and the panelled

restaurant opens on to a terrace 150 feet above the Usk (salmon and trout fishing are possible). Game and fish feature well on the menus: loin of local venison with chestnut purée, say, and seared fillet of cod with champ and a tarragon beurre blanc. One inspector was impressed by a starter of 'beautifully fresh' seared scallops with cauliflower cream as well as by melt-in-the-mouth tournedos Rossini, 'a very good example of this classical dish'. Classics surface again at pudding stage in the shape of pear Belle Hélène and tiramisu, or there might be 'delicious' orange-poached pear with 'excellent' home-made pistachio ice cream alongside a good crop of farmhouse cheeses.

Directions: 1 mile off A40, 2.5 miles W of Crickhowell

CRICKHOWELL, **Manor Hotel**

An elevated position above the town ensures excellent views of the achingly beautiful landscape. The dining room is tasteful and low key, the cooking light and modern. Savour seared salmon on vegetable couscous.

Additional: Bar food; Sunday L; Children welcome
Style: Informal/Country-house
Smoking: No smoking in dining room
Civil licence: 200
Accommodation: 22 en suite ★ ★ ★

Directions: 0.5 mile W of Crickhowell on A40 Brecon rd

CRICKHOWELL,
Nantyffin Cider Mill Inn

Once a drovers' inn and a fully working cider mill this listed building now uses the historic atmosphere to good effect, preserving many original features. Balsamic chicken casserole illustrates the modern European approach to cuisine.

Additional: Bar food; Sunday L; Children welcome
Style: Bistro-style/Rustic
Smoking: No smoking in dining room

Directions: 1 mile west of Crickhowell on A40 at junction with A479

Gliffaes Hotel

Owners: Nicholas & Peta Brabner/James & Susie Suter
Cost: *Alc* £35, set-price D £23.50. ☺
H/wine £12
Times: D only, 7.30-9.15pm
Additional: Bar food L; Sunday L (noon-2.30pm); Children welcome
Seats: 70. Private dining room 30. Jacket and tie preferred
Style: Traditional/country-house
Smoking: No smoking in dining room
Civil licence: 40
Accommodation: 22 en suite ★ ★ ★

Brecon Road NP8 1SE
Map 3: SO21
Tel: 01873 810212
Fax: 01873 811938
Cost: Set-price L £15.95/D £19.95. ☺
H/wine £9
Times: Noon-2pm/7-9.30pm

Brecon Road NP8 1SG
Map 3: SO21
Tel/Fax: 01873 810775
E-mail: nantyffin@aol.com
Cost: *Alc* £19. ☺ H/wine £12.95
Times: Noon-3pm/6.30-10pm.
Closed Mon, 1 wk Nov, 1 wk Jan

KNIGHTON,

Milebrook House Hotel

Milebrook LD7 1LT
Map 7: SO27
Tel: 01547 528632
Fax: 01547 520509
E-mail: hotel@milebrook.kc3ltd.co.uk
Cost: *Alc* £19.50, set-price L £11.95/
D £19.50. ☺ H/wine £10.80
Times: Noon-2.30pm/7-10.30pm.
Closed L Mon
Additional: Bar food L; Sunday L;
Children 8+
Style: country-house
Smoking: No smoking in dining room
Accommodation: 10 en suite ★★

18th-century house with a well-deserved reputation for good food and accommodation. Expect cream of winter vegetable soup, loin of lamb wrapped in bacon with lots of fresh vegetables, and crème brûlée.

Directions: 2 miles E of Knighton on A4113 (Ludlow)

LLANFYLLIN, **Seeds**

A cosy cottage-style olde worlde restaurant with plenty of charm and character enhanced by exposed beams and stone flagged floors. Modern British cuisine including roast barbary duck breast with orange and cointreau sauce.

Additional: Bar food L; Sunday L; Children welcome
Style: Informal/Rustic   **Smoking:** No smoking in dining room

5 Penybryn Cottage
High Street SY22 5AP
Map 7: SJ11
Tel: 01691 648604
Cost: *Alc* L only, £14.85,
set-price D £19.50. ☺ H/wine £9.95
Times: 11am-2.15pm/7-9pm.
Closed Mon, 2 wks Jan

Directions: Village centre, on A490, 13 miles from Welshpool

LLANGAMMARCH WELLS,

Lake Country House Hotel ⚜⚜

Great afternoon teas are served in the lounge in front of a log fire but luckily the Victorian country-house hotel comes complete with golf course, lake, river and wooded grounds in which to walk off indulgent excess. The elegant, formal dining room is spacious and serves stylish food, carefully prepared and home-produced from the breads to the sweetmeats. Interesting soups – celeriac and saffron, for example – kick off the set four-course menu, followed by entrées such as home-cured gravad-lax with a Dijon mustard and dill dressing. Choose between four main courses such as breast of free-range chicken with a trompette mushroom mousse, broad beans and peas, and a haunch of Welsh venison on braised red cabbage with cocotte potatoes and poached figs on a juniper sauce. We sampled an excellent, luscious, vanilla-flavoured pannacotta with poached fruits. Owners and staff are amongst the most hospitable and friendly you'll find.

LD4 4BS
Map 3: SN94
Tel: 01591 620202
Fax: 01591 620457
E-mail: lakehotel@ndirect.co.uk
Chef: Sean Cullingford
Owners: Jean-Pierre & Jan Mifsud
Cost: Set-price L £17.50/D £30.
H/wine £11.50
Times: 12.30-3.30pm/7.30-9pm
Additional: Bar food L; Sunday L;
Children 8+ at D
Seats: 40. Private dining room 20 &
36. Jacket & tie preferred
Style: Country-house
Smoking: No smoking in dining room
Civil licence: 70
Accommodation: 19 en suite ★★★

Directions: A483 from Garth, turn L for Llangammarch Wells & follow signs to hotel

LLANWDDYN,

Lake Vyrnwy Hotel ❀❀

Lake Vyrnwy SY10 0LY
Map 6: SJ01
Tel: 01691 870692
Fax: 01691 870259
E-mail: res@lakevyrnwy.com
Chef: David Richards
Owner: Market Glen Ltd
Cost: *Alc* £35, set-price L £15.95/
D £27.50. ☺ H/wine £12.75
Times: 12.30-2.15pm/7-9.15pm
Additional: Bar food; Sunday L;
Children welcome
Seats: 80. Private dining rooms
30-125. No jeans or trainers
Style: Classic/country-house
Smoking: No smoking in dining room.
Civil licence: 125
Accommodation: 35 en suite ★ ★ ★

A wonderful country hotel set in 26,000 acres of mature woodland, popular with tourists, huntin', shootin' and fishin' folk and, yes, quad bikers. The restaurant/conservatory overlooks the lake, and the set menu uses local produce plus herbs and vegetables from the garden when available. Spicy Cornish crabcakes are served with a young asparagus dressing; main courses might feature breast of honey-roasted duck forestière with Madeira jus or baked cannon of Welsh lamb wrapped in spinach and basil mousse. Crème brûlées ring the changes with variations such as vanilla or Baileys for flavouring, and the kitchen shows its skill in baking with the accompanying shortbread or crisp Florentine biscuits. A selection of British regional cheeses are served with black pepper bread and chutney. The Tavern Bar offers traditional, homemade pies, puddings and stews. Friendly staff.

Directions: Follow Tourist signs on A495/B4393, 200yds past dam at Lake Vyrnwy

LLANWYFYD WELLS,

Carlton House Hotel ❀❀❀

Take full advantage of the fact this is a restaurant-with-rooms because Mary Ann Gilchrist's breakfast scrambled eggs are 'the best on the planet'! Her talents, luckily, are much wider than this alone; she is a great chef with enviable technical ability and she brings a keen intelligence to her cooking. There is a strong emphasis on seasonal produce coupled with the freshest of local produce. From two nightly-changing, no-choice menus, our inspector sampled the Chef's Menu which includes, for a supplement, a pre-selected choice of wines. Spiced Finnan haddock risotto cake with wholegrain mustard sauce and curry oil, was followed by roast cannon of Welsh lamb with crushed Jersey Royals, leek fondue, asparagus and sauce Paloise (mint-flavoured Hollandaise). This was lamb as it is meant to be, tender, flavoursome and, well, simply sublime. There was only one way to follow this – with a warm chocolate fondant with home-made caramel ice cream. To add to the gastronomic experience, both Mary Ann and her husband Alan create a warm and inviting atmosphere and are committed to satisfying everyone's needs and expectations.

Dolycoed Road LD5 4RA
Map 3: SN84
Tel: 01591 610248
Fax: 01591 610242
Chef: Mary Ann Gilchrist
Owners: Alan & Mary Ann Gilchrist
Cost: Set-price D £24 & £32. ☺
H/wine £9.95
Times: D only 7-8.30pm.
Closed Sun, 10-28 Dec
Seats: 14
Style: Traditional
Smoking: No smoking in dining room
Accommodation: 7 rooms (5 en suite)
★ ★

Directions: In the town centre

The dining room is south-facing, comfortable and cosy with wood panelling and new high-backed chairs. There are some wonderful paintings plus antiques, plants and various *objets*. An intelligent wine list complements the exciting food.

LLYSWEN, Griffin Inn

A delightful establishment unashamed of making the most of its traditional charm. Local ingredients feature including a wide range of justly popular winter game dishes based on grouse, partridge, pheasant and venison amongst others.

Style: Traditional **Smoking:** No smoking in dining room
Accommodation: 7 en suite ★ ★

Directions: On A470 in village

Brecon LD3 0UR
Map 3: SO13
Tel: 01874 754241
Fax: 01874 754592
E-mail: info@griffin-inn.freeserve.co.uk
Cost: *Alc* £20. ☺ H/wine £9.95
Times: D only, 7-9pm.
Closed D Sun, 25 & 26 Dec
Additional: Bar food; Sunday L (at 1pm); Children welcome

LLYSWEN, Llangoed Hall

Brecon LD3 0YP
Map 3: SO13
Tel: 01874 754525
Fax: 01874 754545
E-mail: llangoed-hall-co-wales-uk@compuserve.com
Chef: Daniel James
Owner: Sir Bernard Ashley
Cost: *Alc* £40, set-price L £24.50/ D £35. H/wine £18.50
Times: Noon-2pm/7-9.30pm
Additional: Sunday L
Seats: 50. Private dining room 50. Jacket & tie preferred

Set in 17 acres of grounds overlooking the meandering River Wye, this imposing Edwardian country house was remodelled by Clough Williams-Ellis (of Portmeirion fame) and transformed by Bernard Ashley into today's splendid hotel. Inside, wood-burning open fires, antiques and works of art, and Laura Ashley fabrics and furnishings temper grandeur with comfort. In the kitchen, Daniel James matches the opulent surroundings with some accomplished, imaginative and interesting dishes constructed from quality seasonal local produce. Typical offerings could see a ragout of seafood in a cucumber soup or risotto of wild mushrooms and Parmesan with a basil dressing to start. A braised leek, crab and herb ravioli with fennel and oyster cream could accompany a main course fillet of turbot, while a breast of duck could team up with savoy cabbage and an olive sauce. For dessert, try a banana parfait with hazelnut tuille and caramel sauce. Olives and nuts in the lounge with aperitifs, an *amuse-bouche –* perhaps hot vichyssoise – to open, and decent cafetière coffee and petits fours – fruit jelly, meringue and brownie – to close.

Style: Country-house/Formal
Smoking: No smoking in dining room
Civil licence: 50 **Accommodation:** 23 en suite ★ ★ ★ ★

Directions: On A470, 2 miles from Llyswen heading towards Builth Wells

AA Wine Award-see page 18
Shortlisted for

MONTGOMERY, **Dragon Hotel** ✿

Charming 17th-century coaching inn, with beams salvaged from the ruins of the castle nearby. Try salad of grilled swordfish, or wild boar parfait to start, with game casserole or braised guinea fowl to follow.

Additional: Bar food; Sunday L
Style: Classic/Traditional
Smoking: No-smoking area; No pipes & cigars
Accommodation: 20 en suite ★ ★

Directions: Behind the Town Hall

SY15 6PA
Map 7: SO29
Tel: 01686 668359
Fax: 01686 668287
E-mail: reception@dragonhotel.com
Cost: *Alc* £25, set-price L/D £18.50.
☺ H/wine £8.95
Times: Noon-2pm (bookings only)/
7-9pm

NANT-DDU,
Nant Ddu Lodge Hotel ✿

It's a 19th-century hunting lodge, but the Med dictates the look of the restaurant and lends its style heavily to the food. Thus, there could be brochette of monkfish and king prawns with basil pesto, and fillet of herb-crusted turbot with caramelised shallots and wild mushroom sauce.

Additional: Bar food; Sunday L; Children welcome
Style: Bistro-style/informal
Smoking: No smoking in dining room
Accommodation: 22 en suite ★ ★ ★

Directions: 6 miles N of Merthyr Tydfil, and 12 miles S of Brecon on A470

Cwm Taf Nant Ddu
CF48 2HY
Map 3: SO12
Tel: 01685 379111
Fax: 01685 377088
E-mail: enquiries@nant-ddu-lodge.co.uk
Cost: *Alc* £20. ☺ H/wine £8.95
Times: Noon-3pm/6.30-11pm

THREE COCKS,
Three Cocks Hotel ✿✿

15th-century former coaching inn offering largely Belgian cuisine in a relaxing olde worlde atmosphere. Settle in the elegantly panelled dining room in expectation of smoked ham from the Ardennes with onions pickled in honey, or frogs' legs in garlic butter for starters. Mains might include loin of Welsh lamb on ratatouille, breast of duck with honey and xeres sauce, or fricassée of Cornish lobster on a bed of noodles. Desserts such as hazelnut nougatine are a strong temptation but the rugged countryside of the Brecon Beacons is close at hand should you feel the need to walk off any over-indulgence.

Accommodation: 7 rooms (6 en suite) ★ ★

Directions: On A438 in the village of Three Cocks, 4 miles from Hay-on-Wye, 11 miles from Brecon.

Brecon LD3 0SL
Map 3: SO13
Tel: 01497 847215
Fax: 01497 847339
Chefs: Thomas Winstone & Richard Hughes
Owners: Mr & Mrs M Winstone
Cost: *Alc* £30, set-price L/D £27. ☺
H/wine £8.75
Times: Noon-1.45pm/7-9pm.
Closed Tue
Additional: Bar food; Sunday L;
Children welcome
Seats: 30
Style: Rustic/Belgian
Smoking: No pipes & cigars

WELSHPOOL, **Golfa Hall Hotel** ✿

Originally a farmhouse, this fine modern hotel is on the Powys Castle estate. Dishes of Welsh lamb and salmon steak are supplemented by exotic specialities from the Japanese chef.

Directions: On A458 (Dolgellau), 1.5 miles W of Welshpool on R

Llanfair Road SY21 9AF
Map 7: SJ20
Tel: 01938 553399
Fax: 01938 554777

Telephone for further details

RHONDDA CYNON TAFF

MISKIN, Miskin Manor Hotel

Manor house surrounded by 20 acres of grounds, with a panelled restaurant and restful decor. Elaborate dishes from a diverse menu feature local produce.

Style: Rustic/country-house
Smoking: No smoking in dining room
Civil licence: 200 **Accommodation:** 46 en suite ★★★★

Directions: 8 miles W of Cardiff. M4 J34, follow hotel signs

Groes Faen Pontyclun CF72 8ND
Map 3: ST08
Tel: 01443 224204
Fax: 01443 237606
E-mail: info@miskin-manor.co.uk
Cost: *Alc* £30. ☺ H/wine £10.50
Times: Noon-2pm (Sun 3pm)/7-10pm
(Sun 8.45pm). Closed L Sat
Additional; Bar food L; Sunday L;
Children welcome

SWANSEA

REYNOLDSTON, Fairyhill

Remotely set on the Gower Peninsula, an Area of Outstanding Natural Beauty, Fairyhill has been described as 'a gem of a country house'. It's an 18th-century building within its own grounds that include flower gardens, a trout stream and a lake as well as sections set aside for herbs and vegetables. The restaurant, a series of rooms that range from the traditional to the modern and minimalist, is a showcase of the best of Welsh produce. Crisp-fried Penclawdd cockles 'a bit like posh whitebait in texture and presentation' served in the bar are a reminder of the treasures to be found on the nearby coast, and main courses on the menu take in seared loin of Brecon venison (with sage tagliatelle, confit tomatoes and pesto) and breast of Pembrokeshire duck (cooked rare and served with apple and tarragon and a cider sauce). An inspector kicked off with a 'superb' tiny shepherd's pie and an *amuse-bouche* of laverbread and crème fraîche roulade with tomato and basil sauce ('just a morsel, but beautifully made') before moving on to a tartlet of Welsh goats' cheese with leeks and sage and butter sauce. The main course was loin of Welsh lamb en croûte ('a Welsh version of beef Wellington') in a claret jus with 'wonderful' pea and mint purée and a good accompaniment of tiny new potatoes and root vegetables. Apple and Llanboidy rarebit with spicy apple chutney made a memorable conclusion to the meal, although the sweeter-of-tooth could go for something like white and dark chocolate terrine with mocha sauce. Wines are an enthusiasm here, but those daunted by the tome of a list could choose one of the recommendations of the day printed on the menu.

Directions: Just outside Reynoldston, off the A4118 from Swansea

SA3 1BS
Map 2: SS48
Tel: 01792 390139
Fax: 01792 391358
E-mail: postbox@fairyhill.net
Chefs: Paul Davies, Adrian Coulthard
Owners: Paul Davies, Andrew Hetherington, Jane & Peter Camm
Cost: Set-price L £17.50/D £32.
H/wine £12.50
Times: 12.30-1.30pm/7.30-9pm.
Additional: Sunday L; Children 8+
Seats: 60. Private dining room 40
Style: modern/country-house
Smoking: No smoking in dining room
Accommodation: 8 en suite ★★

AA Shortlisted for *Wine* Award-see page 18

SWANSEA,
Dermott's Restaurant NEW

If it were not for the distinctive blue sign in lights outside, it would be easy to pass by this admirable little restaurant. Dermott Slade, with the help of his family, has worked his socks off and created a local restaurant from absolute scratch

219 High Street
SA1 1NN
Map 3: SS69
Tel/Fax: 01792 459050
Chef: Dermott Slade
Owners: Dermott & Wendy Slade

that any city would be proud of. Clean and modern in design, it has a beech floor, blue ceiling recess, blue check table coths and sepia prints of Old Swansea. His Dorchester training shows in dishes such as 'pan-roasted wild pigeon breasts with pan-fried bubble-and-squeak and caramelized carrots with cabbage and white truffle sauce', but his culinary influences are wide ranging and you are also likely to find New World dishes such as 'baked shoulder of hake topped with crab and ginger crust on lemongrass scented potatoes with tomato and pimento butter sauce'.

Directions: M4 J45 onto A4118 to city centre, to Railway Station. With station on L, 150mtrs along High Street

Cost: Set-price D £23.50. ☺
H/wine £10.95
Times: D only, 7.30pm-late.
Closed Sun & Mon, 25 Dec-10 Jan,
2 wks Aug
Additional: Children welcome
Style: Informal/Modern
Seats: 40
Smoking: No-smoking area

SWANSEA, Windsor Lodge

Elegant Georgian house in a quiet residential area near the town centre. The relaxed and welcoming atmosphere is ideal for enjoying dishes such as deep fried skate with Tempura batter and Thai mayonnaise.

Mount Pleasant SA1 6EG
Map 3: SS69
Tel: 01792 642158
Fax: 01792 648996
Cost: Set-price D £22.50. ☺
H/wine £8.95
Times: 12.30-2.30pm(by arrangement)/7.30-midnight.
Closed D Sun, 25 & 26 Dec
Additional: Bar food; Children welcome
Style: Chic/Country-house
Smoking: No smoking in dining room
Accommodation: 19 en suite ★ ★

Directions: Town centre, L at station, R immediately after 2nd set of lights

VALE OF GLAMORGAN

BARRY, Egerton Grey Hotel

Nineteenth-century rectory of particular architectural merit offering modern cuisine in an elegant mahogany panelled dining room. Amongst the main courses might be found roast breast of Gressingham duck with a redcurrant and port wine jus.

Porthkerry CF62 3BZ
Map 3: ST16
Tel: 01446 711666
Fax: 01446 711690
E-mail: info@egertongrey.co.uk
Cost: *Alc* £25, set-price L/D £13.50.
☺ H/wine £10.50
Times: Noon-2pm/7-10pm
Additional: Bar food L; Sunday L; Children welcome
Style: Country-house
Smoking: No smoking in dining room; Jacket & tie preferred
Civil licence: 45
Accommodation: 10 en suite ★ ★ ★

Directions: M4 J33, follow signs for Airport then Porthkerry, & L at hotel sign by thatched cottage

WREXHAM

LLANARMON DYFFRYN CEIRIOG,
West Arms Hotel ❀

Llangollen LL20 7LD
Map 7: SJ13
Tel: 01691 600665
Fax: 01691 600622
E-mail: gowestarms@aol.com
Cost: Set-price D £21.90. ☺
H/wine £10.90
Times: D only, 7-9pm.

Former farmhouse dating from the 16th century, with inglenook fireplaces, beams and slate-flagged floors. Marinated breast of wild mallard was an enjoyable choice from the short set-price menu.

Additional: Bar food; Sunday L (noon-2pm); Children welcome
Style: Country-house
Smoking: No smoking in dining room
Civil licence: 70
Accommodation: 15 en suite ★★

Directions: Exit A483 (A5) at Chirk and follow signs for Ceiriog Valley (B4500) – 11 miles

ROSSETT, Rossett Hall Hotel ❀

Chester Road LL12 0DE
Map 7: SJ35
Tel: 01244 571000
Fax: 01244 571505
E-mail:
reservations@rossetthallhotel.co.uk

Telephone for further details

Elegant Georgian mansion in mature grounds. Fish starters include fresh smoked haddock tartlet with pesto and swordfish with a roasted sweet pepper salsa. Daily changing fresh sweets include bread-and-butter pudding and fruit salad.

Directions: M56, take M53 to Wrexham – becomes A55. Take A483 Chester/Wrexham exit to Tossett (B5445). Hotel in centre of village

WREXHAM, Cross Lanes Hotel ❀

Cross Lanes Bangor Road
Marchwiel LL13 0TF
Map 7: SJ35
Tel: 01978 780555
Fax: 01978 780568
E-mail:
guestservices@crosslanes.co.uk
Cost: Alc £21. ☺ H/wine £9.65
Times: Noon-3pm/7-10pm.
Closed D 25 & 26 Dec
Additional: Bar food; Sunday L;
Children welcome

Brasserie option in a late-19th-century country house hotel standing in six acres of beautiful grounds. The style is traditional with period furnishings and bric-à-brac. Goujons of Scotch Beef rolled in paprika proved a tender and flavoursome dish.

Style: Bistro-style/Rustic
Smoking: No-smoking area
Civil licence: 140
Accommodation: 16 en suite ★★★

Directions: On A525, Wrexham to Whitchurch road, between Marchwiel and Bangor-on-Dee

NORTHERN IRELAND
ANTRIM

BALLYMENA,

Galgorm Manor

BT42 1EA
Map 1: D5
Tel: 028 2588 1001
Fax: 028 2588 0080

Telephone for further details

A 19th-century mansion house on an 85-acre estate beside the River Maine. In the elegant restaurant the scene is set for a very fine dining experience, courtesy of chef Jean Yves Annino and his talented crew. The cooking is innovative and well rounded, and at a recent meal a selection of decent home-made breads and rolls served with fresh butter proved a good omen. Mille-feuille of scallops in a saffron sauce was delightful, while confit of half duck with orange and ginger was so tender and juicy that a knife was barely required. A plateful of vegetables included piped potatoes, roast potatoes, cauliflower, broccoli, haricots beans bound with bacon, and a herby tomato. The chef's imagination and creativity showed itself in the beignets of chocolate fondant with pear purée. The wine list has many fine bottles.

Directions: 1 mile outside Ballymena, on A42 between Galgorm and Cullybackey

CARNLOUGH,

Londonderry Arms

NEW

20 Harbour Road BT44 0EU
Map 1: D6
Tel: 028 2888 5255
Fax: 028 2888 5263

A charming coastal hotel serving food cooked with honesty and simplicity. From the daily-changing menu expect asparagus with ham and Parmesan, and grilled turbot with saffron sauce and spinach. Try lemon tart with fresh raspberries and Mascarpone.

Telephone for further details.

Directions: 14 miles N or Larne on coast road

PORTRUSH,

Ramore Restaurant

The Harbour BT56 8DF
Map 1: C6
Tel: 01265 824313
Fax: 01265 823194
Owners: George & Jane McAlpin
Cost: *Alc* £20. H/wine £8.95
Times: D only, 6-10pm.
Closed Sun & Mon
Additional: Bar food;
Children welcome
Seats: 75
Smoking: No smoking in dining room;
Air conditioning

Recently revamped modern minimalist restaurant. The dining area is split level and decked out with a sophisticated sparsity of colours – black and white decor with a grey floor but with carefully placed splashes of colour from vibrant cushions. The atmosphere is completed by background modern jazz and friendly, professional staff. Although the cuisine is equally modern regular flashes of classicism ensure that real substance lies behind inventive concept. Take for example a simple but satisfying starter of hot and spicy Dublin Bay prawn cocktail, or a tantalising main of fillet of lamb with Asian ratatouille, aïoli and rustic coriander pesto. Desserts might include baked peaches in Marsala wine and Marscarpone.

Directions: On the harbour

BELFAST

BELFAST,
Cayenne ❀

The old Roscoff has been completely revamped with a new name, decor (with striking phone book montage) and simpler cuisine, though chef/owner Paul Rankin is still very much in charge.

Cost: *Alc* £20, set-price L £14.50. ☺
Times: Noon-2.30pm/6-11.15pm. Closed L Sat, all Sun
Additional: Children welcome
Smoking: No-smoking area; Air conditioning

Directions: At top of Belfast's 'Golden Mile', Shaftesbury Square area

7 Lesley House Shaftesbury Square
BT2 7DB
Map 1: D5
Tel: 028 9033 1532
Fax: 028 9031 2093

BELFAST,
Deanes ❀❀❀

Right in the centre of the city, the Baroque-style brasserie on the ground floor bustles with noise and vibrancy. Upstairs, in the restaurant, the look is more formal and chic with crisp linen, comfortable high-backed chairs and a row of mirrors along one wall. Michael Deane rarely misses a service or a trick – cooking, adding the final touches and keeping a careful eye on every diner's progress. His travels to other parts of Britain and to the Far East are reflected in a menu which might include dishes as diverse as hotpot of monkfish, shiitaki and lemongrass, and roast venison, pommes Anna, foie gras, chocolate and shiitaki. Salmon appears in various guises: as a carpaccio with sticky rice, cucumber and soya, or crisped with spiced risotto, bok choy and chilli. Clonakilty black pudding is given a proud, upmarket pairing with roast squab, foie gras, asparagus and potato. Deane has an admirably light touch with ballotines, perhaps chicken with chorizo risotto or chicken and lobster with mushroom and potato salad. Cannon of lamb is the preferred cut for its tenderness and sweetness, presented in tower form with ratatouille, couscous, crispy leeks and curry oil or with whipped and fried parsnips, confit garlic and shallot. Desserts include an assiette of caramel, and warm chocolate tart with white chocolate ice cream.

Directions: Telephone for directions

38-40 Howard Street BT1 6PD
Map 1: D5
Tel: 02890 331134
Fax: 02890 560001
Chef: Michael Deane
Owners: Michael Deane,
Brian & Lynda Smyth
Cost: Set-price D £36.50. H/wine £16
Times: D only 7-9.30pm.
Closed Sun & Mon, Xmas , New Year,
Etr, 2 wks Jul
Seats: 40
Style: Chic/Formal
Smoking: No pipes & cigars;
Air conditioning

BELFAST,
Malone Lodge Hotel ❀

Revitalised city centre hotel offering formal dining in the comfortable Green Door restaurant. Recommended dishes include wild mushroom risotto with Parmesan crackling and neatly presented rack of lamb.

Directions: At Hospital rdbt exit towards Bouchar Road. L at 1st rdbt, R at lights, 1st L into Eglantine Avenue

60 Eglantine Avenue BT9 6DY
Map 1: D5
Tel: 028 9038 8000
Fax: 028 9038 8088
E-mail: info@malonelodgehotel.com

Telephone for further details

DOWN

BANGOR,
Clandeboye Lodge Hotel

Elegant restaurant serving bold modern cooking. Local seafood and game feature, maybe timbale of scallop, lobster and red crab with seared foie gras, and venison with damson jelly and juniper.

Directions: Leave A2 at newtownards sign, 1st junction L, 300yds

10 Estate Road Clandboye BT19 1UR
Map 1: D5
Tel: 028 91852500
Fax: 028 91852772
E-mail: info@clandeboyelodge.com

Telephone for further details

BANGOR, Shanks

The Conran-designed building still impresses with its use of light wood and the collection of Hockney prints around the walls. Robbie Millar brings a sense of European style and flair to the menu and sources his ingredients carefully. Fashion is present in dishes such as sliced breast of duck with mushroom and Parmesan crostini, truffle aïoli and balsamic jam, or seared tuna with spiced aubergine chutney and light coconut cream, but concepts are well executed and there are also some original ideas – monkfish 'hot-pot' of white beans, Toulouse sausage, tomato, peppers and saffron, for example – as well as comfortably familiar ones given an upmarket twist. Classic seared foie gras on toasted brioche with poached grapes and Sauternes was meltingly rich, but a more complex main course of skate tempura with spiced coriander creamed noodles, cucumber and Ponzu sauce had too many conflicting components. Desserts have a vivid quality: gratin of pink grapefruit with local honey ice cream; cinnamon glazed vanilla rice pudding with roasted fresh figs; chocolate truffle mousse with Mascarpone cream and 'superb' pistachio custard. *Best Northern Ireland Wine List (see pages 18-19).*

Directions: From A2 (Belfast-Bangor), turn R onto Ballysallagh Road 1 mile before Bangor, 1st L after 0.5 mile (Crawfordburn Road) to Blackwood Golf Centre. Shanks is in the grounds

The Blackwood
Crawfordsburn Road
BT19 1GB
Map 1: D5
Tel: 02891 853313
Fax: 02891 852493
Chef: Robbie Millar
Owners: Robbie & Shirley Millar
Cost: Set-price L £18.95/D £32.50.
H/wine £12.50
Times: 12.30-2.30pm/7-10pm.
Closed L Sat, all Sun & Mon,
25 & 26 Dec, Etr Tue
Additional: Children welcome
Seats: 70. Private dining room 30
Style: Chic/Modern
Smoking: No-smoking area; No pipes & cigars; Air conditioning

HOLYWOOD, Rayanne House

An elegant Victorian country house and restaurant much frequented by the smart set of Belfast and its environs. Candle-lit dining in a beautiful setting is part of the attraction, but the food itself is the real magnet. The dinner choices are presented on a set-price menu, with starters like fresh dessert pear with stilton on a spicy port sauce, and crispy duck and beansprout salad with sweet and sour sauce. A sorbet made from the likes of peach and passionfruit refreshes the palate before the appearance of such dishes as oven-baked rack of lamb with walnut and herb stuffing on a rosemary and redcurrant sauce, or grilled Cajun-spiced fillet of salmon with green beans and red pepper purée. Desserts have been lavished with praise, and might include hot caramelised lemon torte, or blackcurrant and port trifle. Staff offer a friendly, informal service supervised by owner Ann McClelland. There's a good wine list with plenty of New World wines at reasonable prices.

60 Desmesne Road BT18 9EX
Map 1: D5
Tel: 028 9042 5859
Fax: 028 9042 3364

Telephone for further details.

Directions: From A2 take Belfast Road into Holywood; immediate R into Jacksons Road leading to Desmesne Road

PORTAFERRY,

The Narrows ⚘⚘

NEW

8 Shore Road BT22 1JY
Map 1: D5
Tel: 028 42728148
Fax: 028 42728105
E-mail: info@narrows.co.uk
Chef: Danny Millar
Owners: Will & James Brown
Cost: *Alc* £24. ☺ H/wine £11.95
Times: Noon-2.30pm/6-9.30pm
Additional: Sunday L; Children welcome
Seats: 50. Private dining room 45
Style: Informal/Rustic
Smoking: No smoking in dining room
Accommodation: 13 en suite

The Narrows has won a number of awards for architectural excellence, with its combination of the old and new created from natural and reclaimed materials. Its setting on the shorefront overlooking Strangford Loch is dazzling enough, so there is no need for pretension inside. Simple pine tables and floor produce a bistro atmosphere, and the menu is casually written-up on a blackboard. The food is another matter. Portaferry mussels with garlic and smoked ham was an exciting recent starter, the mussels plump and delicious, and the other ingredients rich without being overpowering. Seared scallops with truffle mash and buttered leeks was a perfectly executed dish, served with butter and chive sauce. Another winner was the chocolate tart with coconut ice cream. The seafood comes straight out of the loch itself, but there is also meat on the menu: corn-fed chicken with spring vegetable risotto perhaps, and spring lamb with basil mash and red pepper jus. A global selection of wine is reasonably priced.

Directions: From Belfast follow A20 to Portaferry. The Narrows is the yellow building on the shore

PORTAFERRY,

Portaferry Hotel ⚘

10 The Strand BT22 1PE
Map 1: D5
Tel: 028 42728231
Fax: 028 42728999
E-mail: portferryhotel@iol.ie

Telephone for further details

Smart hotel restaurant with views over Strangford Lough. A good choice of dishes might include confit of duck with stir-fried vegetables, and cod with herb crust, grain mustard sauce and tagliatelli.

Directions: Opposite Strangford Lough ferry terminal

LONDONDERRY

LIMAVADY,

The Lime Tree ❀

60 Catherine Street BT49 9DB
Map 1: C5
Tel: 028 77764300

Informal restaurant with cheerful decor and friendly service. Dishes sampled from an interesting menu were seafood tagliatelli, pork fillet satay, and choux bun with banana, ice cream and caramel sauce.

Cost: *Alc* £17.24, set-price L £6.95(£12.95 Sun)/
D £12.95(ex Sat). ☺ H/wine £9.25
Times: Noon-2pm/6-9.30pm(8.30pm Sun).
Closed Mon & Tue, 1 wk Feb/Mar, 12th Jul, 1wk Nov
Additional: Sunday L; Children welcome
Style: Informal/Rustic

Directions: Entering Limavady from the Derry side, the restaurant is on the right side on a small slip road

LONDONDERRY,

Beech Hill Hotel ❀

32 Ardmore Road BT47 3QP
Map 1: C5
Tel: 02871 349279
Fax: 02871 345366
E-mail: info@beech-hill.com

Hotel restaurant housed in 18th-century listed building. After sampling the cuisine, stir-fried fillet of beef, black bean sauce and soy noodles for example, take a few minutes to admire the surrounding 32 acres of grounds.

Cost: *Alc* fr £35, set-price L £16.95/D £25.95.
H/wine £12.95
Times: Noon-2.30pm/6-9.45pm. Closed 24 & 25 Dec
Additional: Bar food; Sunday L; Children welcome
Style: Traditional/Country-house
Smoking: No-smoking area; No pipes & cigars
Accommodation: 27 en suite ★ ★ ★

Directions: A6 Londonderry to Belfast road, turn off at Faughan Bridge. 1 mile further to Ardmore Chapel. Hotel entrance is opposite.

REPUBLIC OF IRELAND

The Republic of Ireland hotel-restaurants listed below have built their reputations on the quality of their food; all have earned our coveted Rosette award. The information has been supplied by AA Hotel Services, Dublin.

Please note that the area codes given apply only within the Republic. If dialling from outside you should check the telephone directory. Area codes for numbers in Britain and Northern Ireland cannot be used directly from the Republic.

CO CARLOW

Ballykealey Country House and Restaurant ❀ ★★★

Ballon 050 359288

Dolmen Hotel ❀ ★★★

Kilkenny Road, Carlow 050 342002

CO CAVAN

Kilmore Hotel ❀ ★★★

Dublin Road, Cavan 049 4332288

The Park Hotel ❀ ★★

Virginia Park, Virginia 049 8547235

CO CLARE

Gregans Castle ❀❀ ★★★

Ballyvaughan 065 7077 005

Temple Gate Hotel ❀ ★★★

The Square, Ennis 065 6823300

Sheedy's Restaurant & Hotel ❀❀ ★★

Lisdoonvarna 065 7074026

Dromoland Castle Hotel ❀❀ ★★★★★

Newmarket-on-Fergus 061 368144

CO CORK

Bay View Hotel ❀❀ ★★★

Ballycotton 021 646746

Sea View Hotel ❀❀ ★★★

Ballylickey 027 50073

Casey's of Baltimore Hotel ❀ ★★★

Baltimore 028 20197

The Lodge & Spa at Inchydoney Island ❀❀ ★★★★

Clonakilty 023 33143

Arbutus Lodge Hotel ❀ ★★★

Middle Glanmire Road, Montenotte, Cork 021 501237

Hayfield Manor ❀ ★★★★

Perrott Avenue, College Road, Cork 021 315600

Quality Hotel & Suites ❀❀ ★★★

Cork 021 275858

Rochestown Park Hotel ❀ ★★★★

Rochestown Road, Douglas, Cork 021 892233

Courtmacsherry ❀ ★★

Courtmacsherry 023 46198

Castlehyde Hotel ❀ ★★★

Castlehyde, Fermoy 025 31865

Garryvoe Hotel ❀ ★★

Garryvoe 021 646718

Inishannon House Hotel ❀❀ ★★★

Inishannon 021 775121

Trident Hotel ❀ ★★★

Worlds End, Kinsale 021 4772301

Castle Hotel ❀ ★★

Main Street, Macroom 026 41074

Longueville House Hotel ❀❀❀ ★★★

Mallow 022 47156

Midleton Park ❀❀ ★★★

Midleton 021 631767

Eldon Hotel ❀ ★★

Bridge Street, Skibbereen 028 22000

Devonshire Arms Hotel and Restaurant ❀ ★★

Pearse Square, Youghal 024 92827

CO DONEGAL

Kee's Hotel ❀❀ ★★★

Stranorlar, Ballybofey 074 31018

Ostan Gweedore ❀❀ ★★★

Bunbeg 075 31177

Harvey's Point Country Hotel ❀❀❀ ★★★

Lough Eske, Donegal 073 22208

Fort Royal Hotel ❀❀ ★★★

Fort Royal, Rathmullan 074 58100

Sand House Hotel ❀❀ ★★★

Rossnowlagh 072 51777

CO DUBLIN

Bewley's Hotel Ballsbridge ❀ ★★★

Merrion Road, Ballsbridge, Dublin 01 6681111

Buswells Hotel ❀ ★★★

23-27 Molesworth Street, Dublin 01 6146500

Clarion Stephen's Hall All-Suite Hotel ❀❀ ★★★

The Earlsfort Centre, Lower Leeson Street, Dublin 01 6381111

Conrad International Dublin ❀❀ ★★★★

Earlsfort Terrace, Dublin 01 6765555

Herbert Park Hotel ❀ ★★★★

Ballsbridge, Dublin 01 6672200

Longfield's Hotel ❀ ★★★

Fitzwilliam Street, Dublin 01 6761367

Marine Hotel ❀❀ ★★★

Sutton Cross, Dublin 01 8390000

Red Cow Morans Hotel ❀ ★★★★

Red Cow Complex, Naas Road,
Dublin 01 4593650

Shelbourne Meridien Hotel ❀ ★★★★

St Stephen's Green, Dublin 01 6766471

The Clarence ❀❀❀ ★★★★

6-8 Wellington Quay, Dublin 01 4070800

The Fitzwilliam Hotel ❀❀ ★★★★

St Stephen's Green, Dublin 01 4787000

The Hibernian Hotel ❀❀❀ ★★★

Eastmoreland Place, Ballsbridge,
Dublin 01 6687666

The Merrion Hotel ❀❀❀❀ ★★★★★

Upper Merrion Street, Dublin 01 6030600

The Plaza Hotel ❀❀ ★★★★

Belgard Road, Tallaght, Dublin 01 4624200

The Schoolhouse Hotel ❀❀ ★★★

2-8 Northumberland Road, Dublin 01 6675014

Portmarnock Hotel and Golf Links ❀❀ ★★★★

Strand Road, Portmarnock 01 8460611

CO GALWAY

Ballynahinch Castle ❀❀ ★★★★

Ballynahinch 095 31006

Cashel House Hotel ❀❀ ★★★

Cashel 095 31001

Zetland Country House Hotel ❀❀ ★★★

Cashel Bay, Cashel 095 31111

Abbeyglen Castle Hotel ❀❀ ★★★

Sky Road, Clifden 095 21201

Alcock & Brown Hotel ❀ ★★★

Clifden 095 21206

Ardagh Hotel & Restaurant ❀❀ ★★★

Ballyconneely Road, Clifden 095 21384

Rock Glen Country House Hotel ❀❀ ★★★

Clifden 095 21035

Glenlo Abbey Hotel ❀❀ ★★★★

Bushypark, Galway 091 526666

Westward House Hotel ❀❀ ★★★★

Dangan, Upper Newcastle, Galway 091 521442

Galway Bay Golf & Country Club Hotel ❀❀ ★★★

Oranmore 091 790500

Ross Lake House Hotel ❀ ★★★

Rosscahill, Oughterard 091 550109

Lough Inagh Lodge Hotel ❀❀ ★★★

Inagh Valley, Recess 095 34706

Eldons Hotel ❀ ★★

Roundstone 095 35933

CO KERRY

The White Sands Hotel ❀ ★★★

Ballheige 066 7133 102

Dingle Skellig Hotel ❀ ★★★

Dingle 066 51144

Dromquinna Manor ❀ ★★★

Blackwater Bridge, Kenmare 064 41657

Park Hotel Kenmare ❀❀❀ ★★★★

Kenmare 064 41200

Sheen Falls Lodge ❀❀ ★★★★

Kenmare 064 41600

Aghadoe Heights Hotel ❀❀❀ ★★★★

Killarney 064 31766

Arbutus Hotel ❀ ★★

College Street, Killarney 064 31037

Cahernane Hotel ❀❀ ★★★

Muckross Road, Killarney 064 31895

Killarney Park Hotel ❀ ★★★★

Kenmare Place, Killarney 064 35555

Muckross Park Hotel Ltd ❀ ★★★★

Muckross Village, Killarney 064 31938

Great Southern Hotel ❀ ★★★★

Parknasilla 064 45122

Butler Arms Hotel ❀❀ ★★★

Waterville 066 9474144

CO KILDARE

Leixlip House Hotel ❀❀ ★★★

Captains Hill, Leixlip 01 6242268

Moyglare Manor ❀❀ ★★★

Moyglare, Maynooth 01 6286351

Keadeen Hotel ⊛⊛ ★★★

Newbridge 045 431666

Barberstown Castle ⊛⊛ ★★★

Straffan 01 6288157

The Kildare Hotel & Country Club ⊛⊛⊛ ★★★★★

Straffan 01 6017200

CO KILKENNY

Mount Juliet Hotel ⊛⊛ ★★★★

Thomastown 056 73000

CO LIMERICK

Dunraven Arms Hotel ⊛⊛⊛ ★★★

Adare 061 396633

Castle Oaks House Hotel ⊛ ★★★

Castleconnell 061 377666

Castletroy Park Hotel ⊛⊛ ★★★★

Dublin Road, Limerick 061 335566

Limerick Inn Hotel ⊛ ★★★

Ennis Road, Limerick 061 326666

CO MAYO

Cill Aodain Hotel ⊛ ★★

Main Street, Kiltimagh 094 81761

Belmont Hotel ⊛ ★★★

Knock 094 88122

Ardmore Country House Hotel ⊛ ★★★

The Quay, Westport 098 25994

Knockranny House Hotel ⊛ ★★★★

Westport 098 28600

The Olde Railway Hotel ⊛ ★★

The Mall, Westport 098 25166

CO MONAGHAN

Nuremore Hotel ⊛⊛ ★★★★

Carrickmacross 042 9661438

CO SLIGO

Markree Castle ⊛⊛ ★★★

Collooney 071 67800

Silver Swan Hotel ⊛ ★★

Sligo 071 43231

CO TIPPERARY

Cahir House Hotel ⊛ ★★★

The Square, Cahir 052 42727

Nenagh Abbey Court Hotel ❀ ★★★

Dublin Road, Nenagh 067 41111

Grant's Hotel ❀❀ ★★★

Castle Street, Roscrea 050 523300

CO WATERFORD

Waterford Castle Hotel ❀❀ ★★★★

The Isla, Waterford 051 878203

CO WESTMEATH

Hodson Bay Hotel ❀❀ ★★★

Hodson Bay, Athlone 090 292444

Prince Of Wales Hotel ❀ ★★★

Athlone 090 272626

CO WEXFORD

Dunbrody Country House & Restaurant ❀❀ ★★★

Arthurstown 051 389600

Courtown Hotel ❀ ★★

Courtown Harbour 055 25210

Marlfield House Hotel ❀❀ ★★★

Gorey 055 21124

Clarion Brandon House Hotel and Leisure ❀ ★★★

Wexford Road, New Ross 051 421703

Kelly's Resort Hotel ❀❀ ★★★★

Rosslare 053 32114

Danby Lodge Hotel ❀ ★★

Killinick, Rosslare Harbour 053 58191

Ferrycarrig Hotel ❀❀ ★★★★

Ferrycarrig, Wexford 053 20999

Talbot Hotel Conference & Leisure Centre ❀ ★★★

Trinity Street, Wexford 053 22566

Whitford House Hotel ❀ ★★★

New Line Road, Wexford 053 43444

CO WICKLOW

Brooklodge at MacCreddin ❀❀ ★★★★

Macreddin Village, Macreddin 040 236444

Hunter's Hotel ❀ ★★★

Rathnew 040 440106

Tinakilly Country House & Restaurant ❀❀ ★★★

Rathnew 040 469274

Woodenbridge Hotel ❀ ★★★

Woodenbridge 040 235146

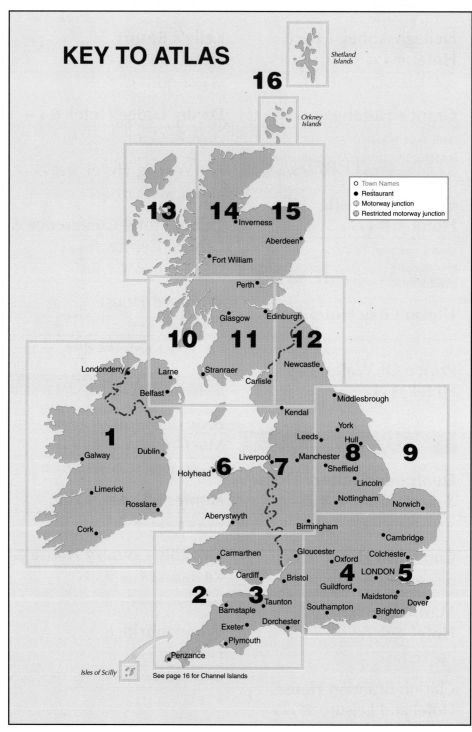

KEY TO ATLAS

Shetland Islands

16

Orkney Islands

○	Town Names
●	Restaurant
⓪	Motorway junction
⓪	Restricted motorway junction

13

14 ● Inverness **15**

● Aberdeen

● Fort William

● Perth

Glasgow ● ● Edinburgh

10 **11** **12**

Londonderry ● Larne ● ● Newcastle
● Stranraer

Belfast ● Carlisle ●

1 ● Middlesbrough

● Kendal

● York

Leeds ● ● Hull

Galway ● Dublin ● Liverpool ● **7** Manchester ● **8** **9**

6 ● Sheffield

Holyhead ● ● Lincoln

Limerick ● Nottingham ●

Rosslare ● Norwich ●

Aberystwyth ●

Cork ● ● Cambridge

Birmingham ●

Gloucester ● Colchester ●

Carmarthen ● ● Oxford

2 **3** Cardiff ● ● Bristol **4** LONDON **5**

Taunton ● Guildford ● Maidstone ●

Barnstaple ● Southampton ● ● Brighton ● Dover

Exeter ● Dorchester ●

Plymouth ●

Isles of Scilly Penzance ● See page 16 for Channel Islands

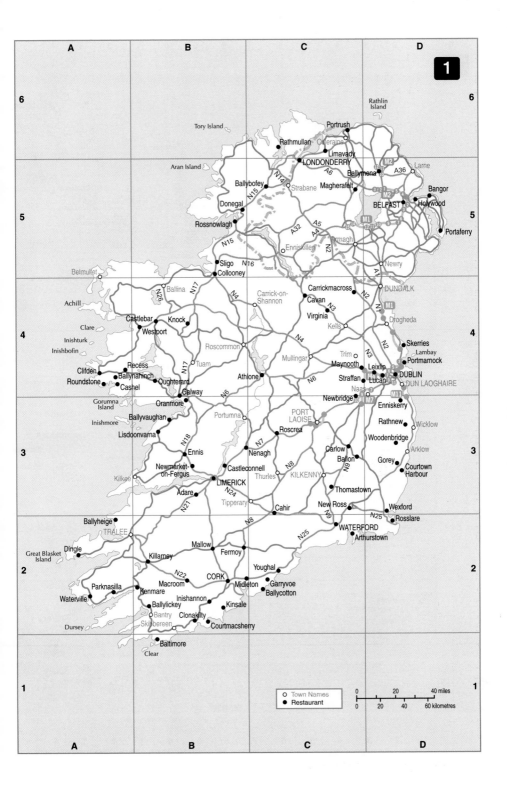

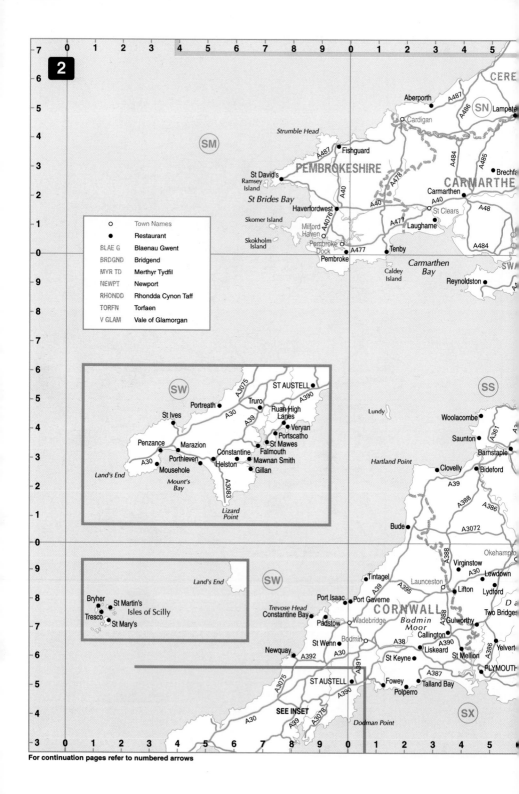

2

○	Town Names
●	Restaurant
BLAE G	Blaenau Gwent
BRDGND	Bridgend
MYR TD	Merthyr Tydfil
NEWPT	Newport
RHONDD	Rhondda Cynon Taff
TORFN	Torfaen
V GLAM	Vale of Glamorgan

CERE

SN Lampete

Aberporth   A487   A486

Cardigan

Strumble Head

Fishguard   A487

PEMBROKESHIRE

St David's
Ramsey Island

A487   A40

St Brides Bay

Haverfordwest   A4076

Skomer Island

Milford Haven   A4076

Skokholm Island

Pembroke Dock

Pembroke   A477   Tenby

Caldey Island

Carmarthen Bay

Brechfa

A484   A485

CARMARTHE

Carmarthen   A40   A48

St Clears   A40

A477   Laugharne

A484

SWA

Reynoldston

SM

SW

ST AUSTELL

A3075

Truro   A390

Portreath   A30

St Ives

Ruan High Lanes

A39   Veryan

Penzance   Marazion   Portscatho
St Mawes
Constantine   Falmouth
Porthleven   Helston   Mawnan Smith
Mousehole   Gillan

A30

Land's End

Mount's Bay   A3083

Lizard Point

Lundy

SS

Woolacombe

Saunton   A361

Barnstaple

Hartland Point   Clovelly   Bideford

A39

SW

Land's End

Bryher   St Martin's   Isles of Scilly
Tresco
St Mary's

Trevose Head
Constantine Bay   Padstow

Port Isaac   Port Gaverne

Tintagel   Launceston   A395

Bude   A3072

Virginstow
Okehampto
A30   Lewdown
Lifton   Lydford
Two Bridges
D a

CORNWALL

Wadebridge

Bodmin Moor

A38   Gulworthy

St Wenn   Bodmin   A30   Callington   A390
Newquay   A392   Liskeard   St Mellion   Yelvert
St Keyne   A386
PLYMOUTH

A3075

ST AUSTELL   A390

A38   Fowey   A387   Talland Bay
Polperro

SX

SEE INSET

A30   A99   A3078

Dodman Point

A391

A388

A386

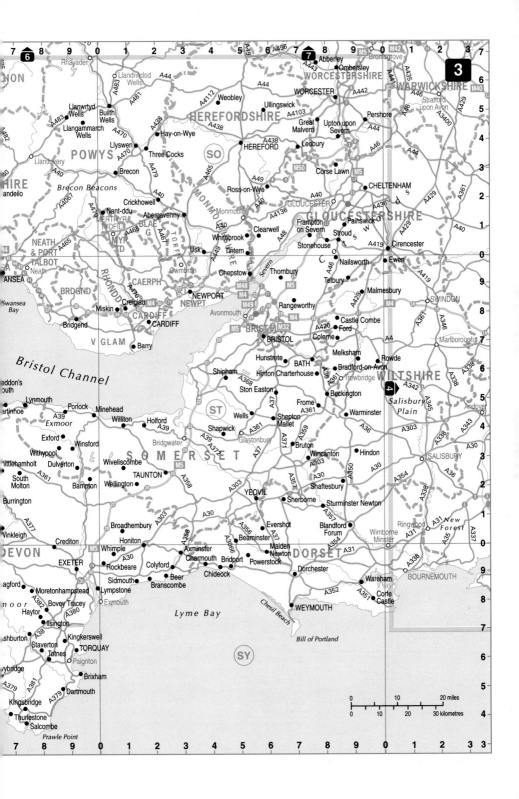

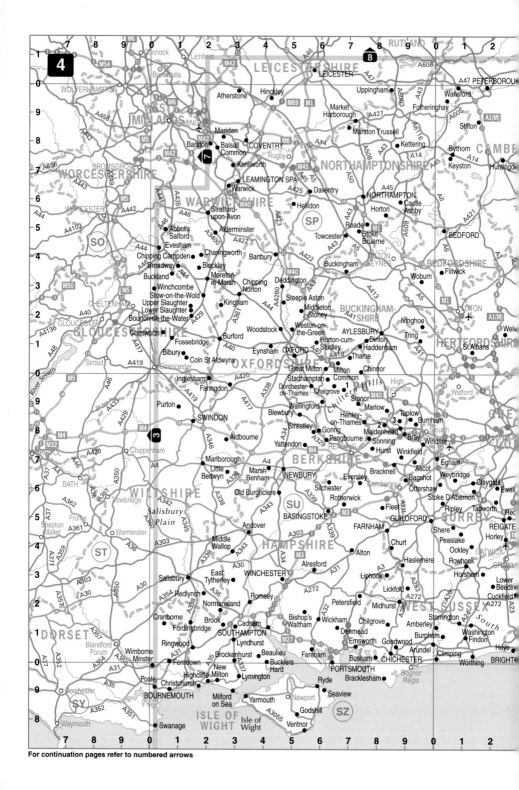

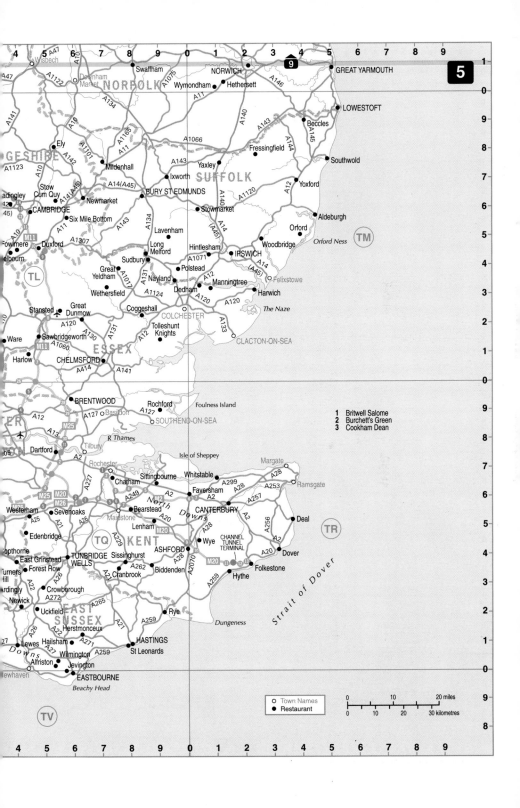

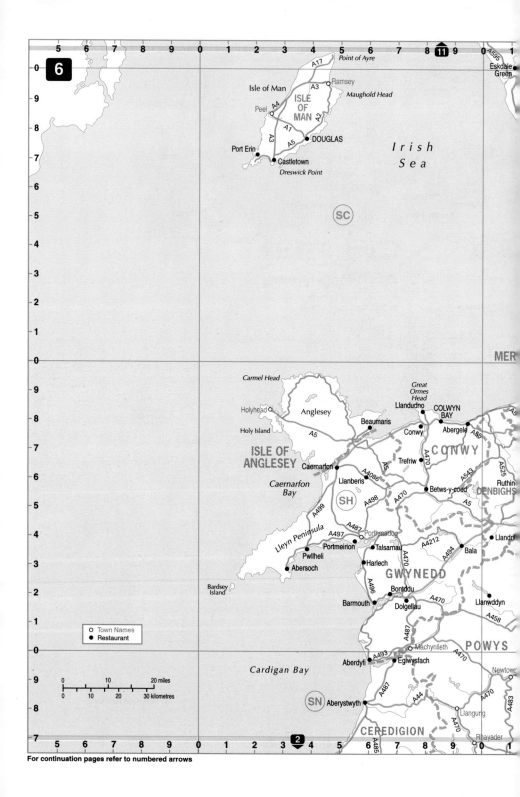

6

5 6 7 8 9 0 1 2 3 4 5 6 7 8 **11** 9 0 A595 1

A17 Point of Ayre

Eskdale Green

Ramsey
A3
Maughold Head

Isle of Man

ISLE OF MAN

A4
Peel

A2

A1
A5
DOUGLAS

Port Erin
A3
A5
Castletown
Dreswick Point

Irish Sea

SC

MER

Carmel Head

Great Ormes Head

Holyhead
Anglesey
A5
Llandudno
COLWYN BAY
A55

Beaumaris
Conwy
Abergele

Holy Island

ISLE OF ANGLESEY

Trefriw
A470
CONWY
A543
A525

Caernarfon
A5

Caernarfon Bay

Llanberis
A4086
Betws-y-coed
Ruthin
DENBIGHS

SH

A498
A470
A5

A499

A487
Porthmadog
AA212

Lleyn Peninsula

A497
Portmeirion
Talsarnau
A494
Bala
Llandri

Pwllheli

A496
Harlech

Abersoch

GWYNEDD

Bardsey Island

Bontddu
A470
Llanwddyn

Barmouth
Dolgellau
A458

A487
A470

Machynlleth
POWYS

Aberdyfi
A493
Eglwysfach
A470
Newtow

Cardigan Bay

A487
A44
A470
A483

SN
Aberystwyth

Llangurig

A470

CEREDIGION
A485
Rhayader

○ Town Names
● Restaurant

0   10   20 miles
0 10 20 30 kilometres

5 6 7 8 9 0 1 2 3 **2** 4 5 6 7 8 9 0 1

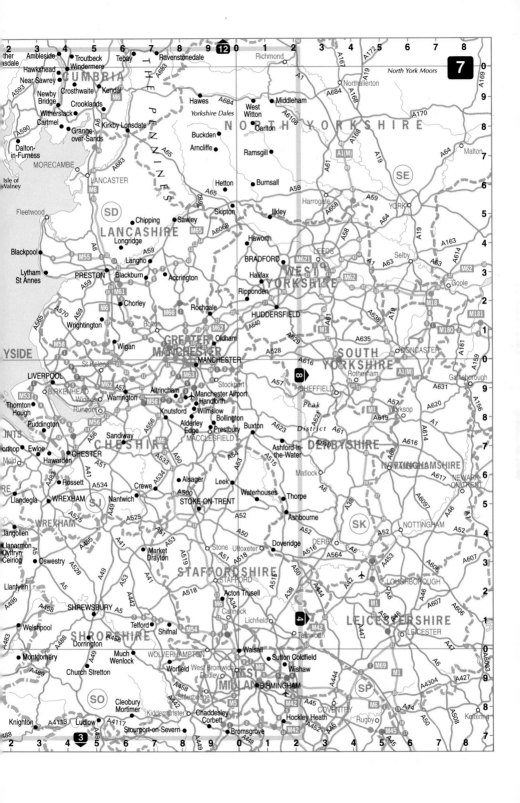

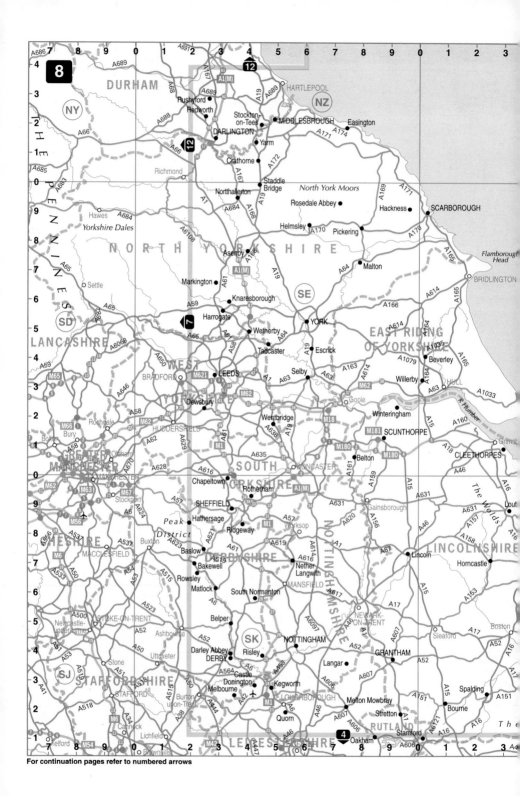

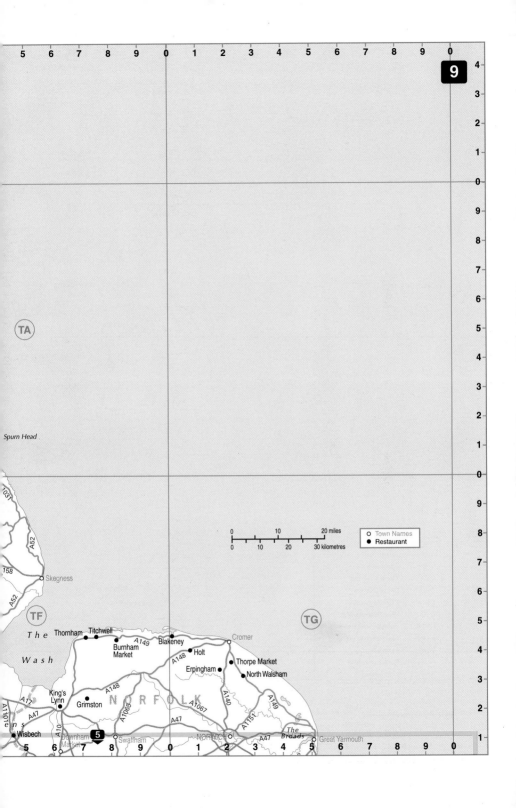

9

5 6 7 8 9 0 1 2 3 4 5 6 7 8 9 0

4
3
2
1
0

9
8
7
6

TA

5
4
3
2

Spurn Head

1
0

9

| | 0 | 10 | 20 miles | ○ Town Names |
| 0 | 10 | 20 | 30 kilometres | ● Restaurant |

8
7

158

○ Skegness

6
5

TF

TG

The Thornham Titchwell

A149 Blakeney

Cromer ○

4

Wash

Burnham
Market

Holt
A148

Thorpe Market

3

Erpingham

North Walsham

King's
Lynn

A148

N O R F O L K

A140

A149

2

● Wisbech

Grimston

A1065

A47

A1067

A1151

*The
Broads*

Great Yarmouth ○

1

Downham
Market

5

○ Swaffham

NORWICH ○

A47

5 6 7 8 9 0 1 2 3 4 5 6 7 8 9 0

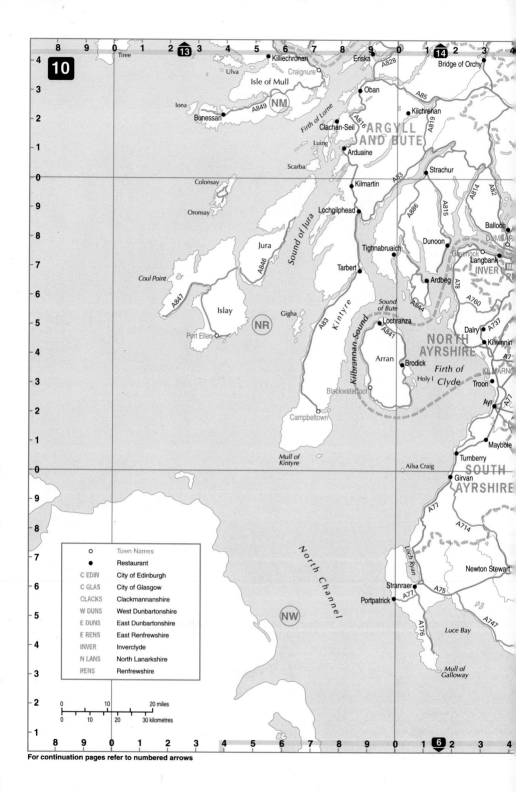

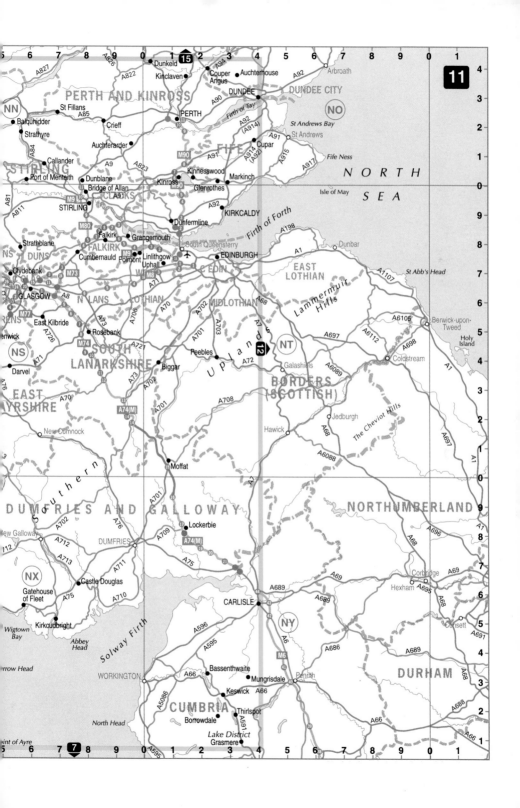

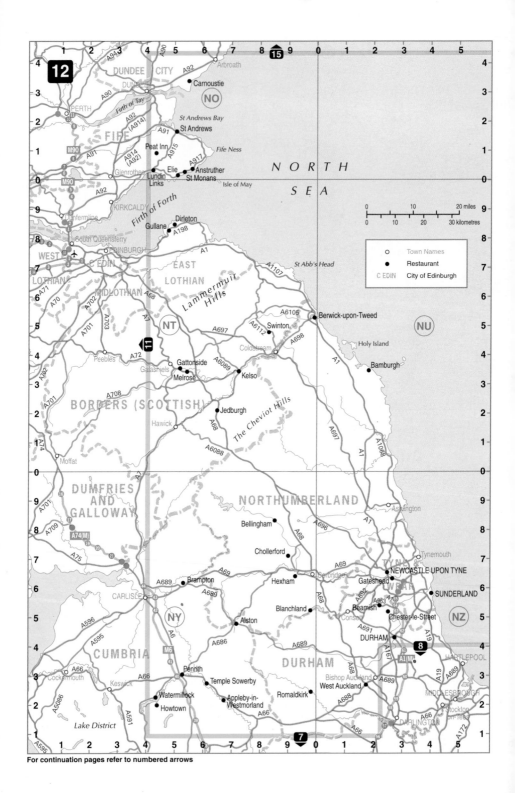

For continuation pages refer to numbered arrows

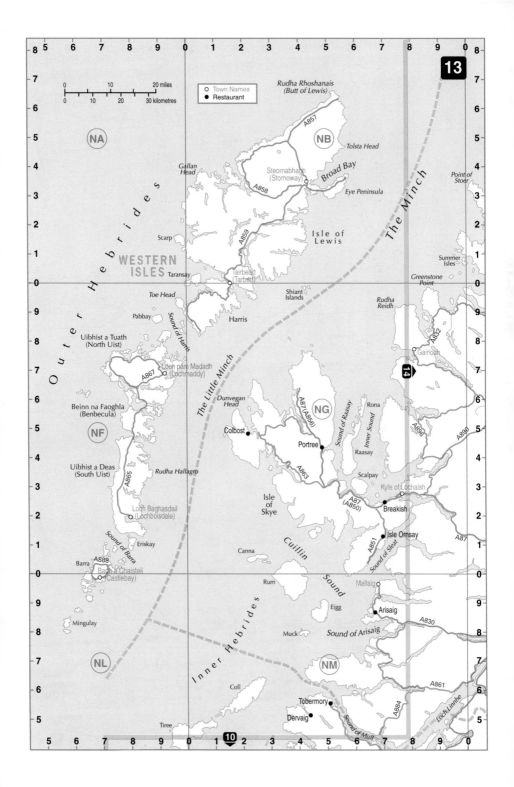

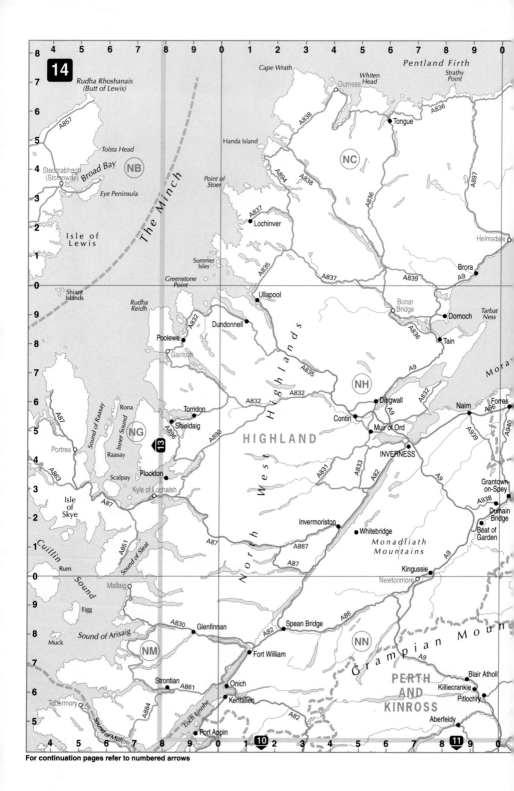

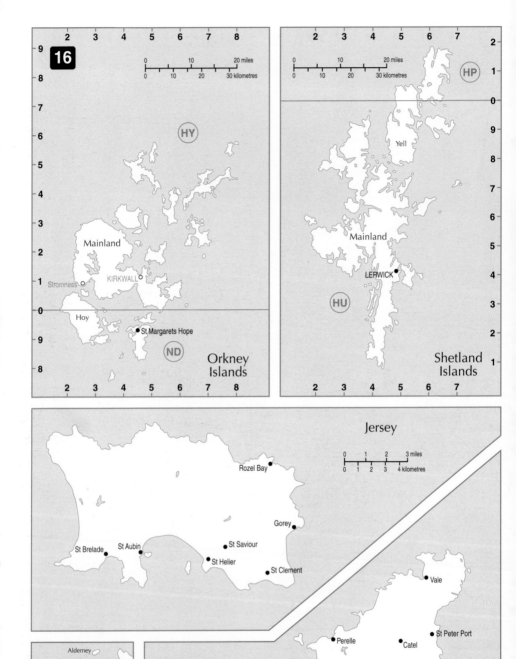

16

2	3	4	5	6	7	8

0   10   20 miles
0   10   20   30 kilometres

9
8
7
6   HY
5
4
3
2   Mainland
1   Stromness ○   KIRKWALL ○
0
Hoy
9   ● St Margarets Hope
ND
8

Orkney Islands

2	3	4	5	6	7	8

2	3	4	5	6	7

0   10   20 miles
0   10   20   30 kilometres

2
1   HP
0
9   Yell
8
7
6
5   Mainland
4   LERWICK ●
3
HU
2
1

Shetland Islands

2	3	4	5	6	7

Jersey

0   1   2   3 miles
0   1   2   3   4 kilometres

Rozel Bay ●

Gorey ●

St Brelade ●   St Aubin ●   ● St Saviour
● St Helier
● St Clement

Alderney ◦

● Herm
Guernsey ◦ ● Sark

Jersey ◦

Guernsey

0   1   2   3 miles
0   1   2   3   4 kilometres

● Vale

Perelle ●   ● Catel   St Peter Port ●

St Martin ●

Greater London

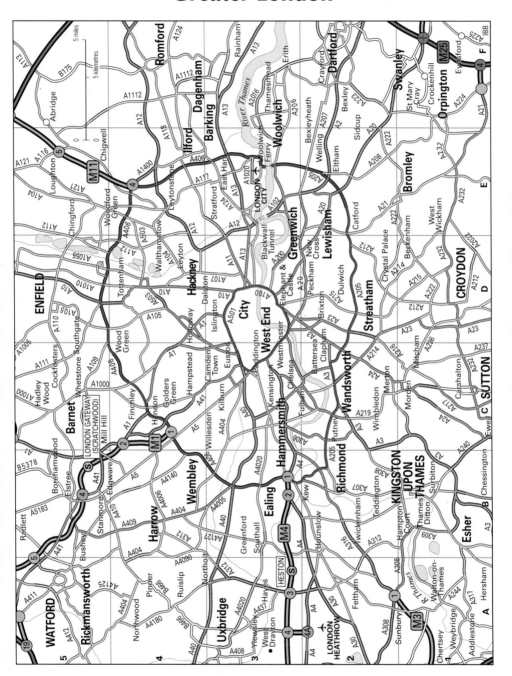

Central London

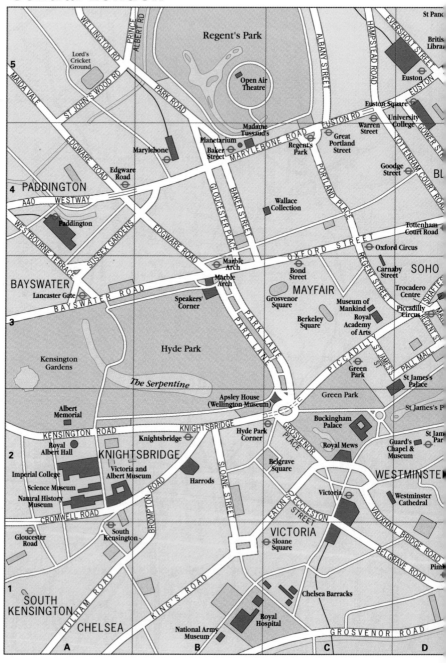

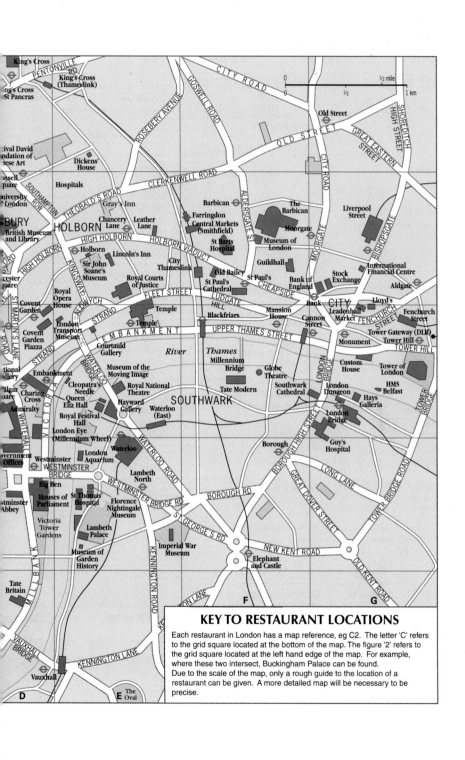

King's Cross
PENTONVILLE RD
King's Cross (Thameslink)
ng's Cross
St Pancras
CITY ROAD
0   ½ mile
0   ½   1 km
Old Street
GOSWELL ROAD
ROSEBERY AVENUE
SHOREDITCH HIGH STREET
GREAT EASTERN STREET
OLD STREET
ival David
ndation of
ese Art
Dickens'
House
CLERKENWELL ROAD
CITY ROAD
ssell
quare
Hospitals
niversity
London
THEOBALD'S ROAD
Gray's Inn
Barbican
The Barbican
Liverpool Street
BURY
British Museum
and Library
HOLBORN
Chancery
Lane
Leather
Lane
Farringdon
Central Markets
(Smithfield)
ALDERSGATE ST
Moorgate
MOORGATE
BISHOPSGATE
SOUTHAMPTON ROW
HIGH HOLBORN
St Barts
Hospital
Museum of
London
HIGH HOLBORN
Holborn
HOLBORN VIADUCT
City
Thameslink
Guildhall
International
Financial Centre
ORD
Sir John
Soane's
Museum
Lincoln's Inn
Old Bailey
Bank of
England
Stock
Exchange
Aldgate
cester
quare
KINGSWAY
Royal Courts
of Justice
St Paul's
Cathedral
St Paul's
CHEAPSIDE
Bank
Royal
Opera
House
FLEET STREET
LUDGATE HILL
Bank
CITY
Lloyd's
St MARTIN'S LANE
Covent
Garden
ALDWYCH
STRAND
Temple
Blackfriars
Mansion
House
Cannon
Street
Leadenhall
Market
FENCHURCH STREET
Fenchurch
Street
tional
llery
London
Transport
Museum
Covent
Garden
Piazza
STRAND
Temple
EMBANKMENT
UPPER THAMES STREET
Monument
Tower Gateway (DLR)
Tower Hill
TOWER HILL
Courtauld
Gallery
River Thames
Millennium
Bridge
Custom
House
Tower of
London
algar
uare
Embankment
WATERLOO BRIDGE
Museum of the
Moving Image
Globe
Theatre
LONDON BRIDGE
HMS
Belfast
Charing
Cross
Admiralty
Cleopatra's
Needle
Queen
Eliz Hall
Royal National
Theatre
Tate Modern
Southwark
Cathedral
London
Dungeon
Hays
Galleria
WHITEHALL
Royal Festival
Hall
Hayward
Gallery
Waterloo
(East)
SOUTHWARK
London
Bridge
TOWER BRIDGE
London Eye
(Millennium Wheel)
Waterloo
London
Bridge
vernment
Offices
Westminster
London
Aquarium
WATERLOO ROAD
Borough
Guy's
Hospital
WESTMINSTER
BRIDGE
Lambeth
North
BOROUGH HIGH STREET
LONG LANE
Big Ben
WESTMINSTER BRIDGE RD
BOROUGH RD
TOWER BRIDGE ROAD
OLD KENT ROAD
Houses of
Parliament
St Thomas'
Hospital
Florence
Nightingale
Museum
ST GEORGE'S RD
GREAT DOVER STREET
tminster
Abbey
Victoria
Tower
Gardens
Lambeth
Palace
NEW KENT ROAD
Museum of
Garden
History
KENNINGTON ROAD
Imperial War
Museum
Elephant
and Castle
F
G
Tate
Britain
MILLBANK
ON LANE
VAUXHALL
BRIDGE
KENNINGTON LANE
Vauxhall
D
E The Oval

KEY TO RESTAURANT LOCATIONS

Each restaurant in London has a map reference, eg C2. The letter 'C' refers to the grid square located at the bottom of the map. The figure '2' refers to the grid square located at the left hand edge of the map. For example, where these two intersect, Buckingham Palace can be found.

Due to the scale of the map, only a rough guide to the location of a restaurant can be given. A more detailed map will be necessary to be precise.

London Postcode Index

Index

S

Y

Z

Please send this form to:
  Editor, The Restaurant Guide,
  Lifestyle Guides,
  The Automobile Association,
  Fanum House,
  Basingstoke RG21 4EA

Readers'
Report form

Readers' Report Form

Please use this form to recommend any restaurant you have visited which is not already in our guide. Recommendations, and/or any adverse comments will be carefully considered, and passed on to our Hotel & Restaurant inspectors, but the AA cannot guarantee to act on them nor to enter into correspondence about them. Complaints are best brought to the attention of the management of the restaurant at the time, so that they can be dealt with promptly and, it is hoped, to the satisfaction of both parties.

Date:

Your name (block capitals)

Your address (block capitals)

....

....

....

....

Name & Address of Restaurant

....

....

....

Comments

....

....

....

....

....

....

....

(please attach a separate sheet if necessary)   PTO

Readers' Report Form

About The Restaurant Guide   YES   NO

Have you bought this guide before?   ☐   ☐

Have you bought any other restaurant guides recently? If yes, which ones?

....

....

What do you find most useful about this guide?

....

....

....

....

....

....

....

....

Is there any other information you would like to see added to this guide?

....

....

....

....

....

....

....

....

....